The Routledge Handbook of Critical Discourse Studies

The Routledge Handbook of Critical Discourse Studies provides a state-of-the-art overview of the important and rapidly developing field of Critical Discourse Studies (CDS). Forty-one chapters from leading international scholars cover the central theories, concepts, contexts and applications of CDS and how they have developed, encompassing:

- approaches
- analytical methods
- interdisciplinarity
- social divisions and power
- domains and media.

Including methodologies to assist those undertaking their own critical research of discourse, this *Handbook* is key reading for all those engaged in the study and research of Critical Discourse Analysis within English Language and Linguistics, Communication, Media Studies and related areas.

John Flowerdew is Emeritus Professor at City University of Hong Kong and a visiting professor at Lancaster University. He has authored and co-authored several books including: *Advances in Discourse Studies* (with V.K. Bhatia and R. Jones, 2008), *Critical Discourse Analysis in Historiography* (2012), *Discourse in English Language Education* (2013) and *Discourse in Context*, (2014). He serves on the editorial boards of a range of international journals, including *Critical Discourse Studies, Journal of Pragmatics, Journal of Language and Politics* and *Journal of English for Specific Purposes*.

John E. Richardson is a Reader in Critical Discourse Studies at Loughborough University. He is Editor of the international journal *Critical Discourse Studies* and has authored or edited several books including: *Analysing Media Discourses* (2011), *Analysing Fascist Discourse* (2013), *Advances in Critical Discourse Studies* (with M. Krzyżanowski, D. Machin and R. Wodak, 2014) and *British Fascism: A Discourse-Historic Analysis* (2017).

Routledge Handbooks in Applied Linguistics

Routledge Handbooks in Applied Linguistics provide comprehensive overviews of the key topics in applied linguistics. All entries for the handbooks are specially commissioned and written by leading scholars in the field. Clear, accessible and carefully edited *Routledge Handbooks in Applied Linguistics* are the ideal resource for both advanced undergraduates and postgraduate students.

THE ROUTLEDGE HANDBOOK OF SECOND LANGUAGE ACQUISITION
Edited by Susan Gass and Alison Mackey

THE ROUTLEDGE HANDBOOK OF LANGUAGE AND INTERCULTURAL COMMUNICATION
Edited by Jane Jackson

THE ROUTLEDGE HANDBOOK OF LANGUAGE TESTING
Edited by Glenn Fulcher and Fred Davidson

THE ROUTLEDGE HANDBOOK OF MULTILINGUALISM
Edited by Marilyn Martin-Jones, Adrian Blackledge and Angela Creese

THE ROUTLEDGE HANDBOOK OF TRANSLATION STUDIES
Edited by Carmen Millán-Varela and Francesca Bartrina

THE ROUTLEDGE HANDBOOK OF LANGUAGE AND HEALTH COMMUNICATION
Edited by Heidi E. Hamilton and Wen-ying Sylvia Chou

THE ROUTLEDGE HANDBOOK OF LANGUAGE AND PROFESSIONAL COMMUNICATION
Edited by Stephen Bremner and Vijay Bhatia

The Routledge Handbook of Critical Discourse Studies

Edited by John Flowerdew and John E. Richardson

Routledge
Taylor & Francis Group

LONDON AND NEW YORK

First published 2018
by Routledge
2 Park Square, Milton Park, Abingdon, Oxon OX14 4RN

and by Routledge
711 Third Avenue, New York, NY 10017

Routledge is an imprint of the Taylor & Francis Group, an informa business

British Library Cataloguing-in-Publication Data
A catalogue record for this book is available from the British Library

Library of Congress Cataloging-in-Publication Data
A catalog record for this book has been requested

ISBN: 978-1-138-82640-3 (hbk)
ISBN: 978-1-315-73934-2 (ebk)

Typeset in Bembo
by Apex CoVantage, LLC

Contents

List of figures   ix
List of tables   xi
List of contributors   xii
Acknowledgements   xviii

Introduction   1
John Flowerdew and John E. Richardson

PART I
Approaches   **11**

1 CDA as dialectical reasoning   13
   Norman Fairclough

2 Socio-cognitive discourse studies   26
   Teun A. van Dijk

3 The Discourse-Historical Approach   44
   Martin Reisigl

4 Multi-modal critical discourse analysis   60
   Per Ledin and David Machin

5 Cognitive Linguistic critical discourse studies   77
   Christopher Hart

6 Spatial cognition   92
   Piotr Cap

7 Corpus-based approaches   106
   Nicholas Close Subtirelu and Paul Baker

Contents

8 Cultural approach to CDA (CCDA): from theory to practice   120
   Dalia Gavriely-Nuri

9 Positive discourse analysis   133
   Tom Bartlett

PART II
Analytical methods   **149**

10 Systemic functional linguistics   151
    Meriel Bloor and Thomas Bloor

11 Critical discourse studies and context   165
    John Flowerdew

12 Ethnography and critical discourse studies   179
    Michał Krzyżanowski

13 Pragmatics and critical discourse studies   195
    Alexandra Polyzou

14 Metaphor   215
    Carl Jon Way Ng

15 Rhetoric and argumentation   228
    Manfred Kienpointner

16 Deliberative discourse   242
    Isabela Fairclough

PART III
Interdisciplinarity   **257**

17 Critical discourse studies and social theory   259
    Bernhard Forchtner

18 Discourse-Theoretical Analysis (DTA)   272
    Nico Carpentier

19 Critical discourse analysis and media studies   285
    Sean Phelan

20 Critical discourse analysis and history   298
    Mariana Achugar

21 Critical discourse analysis and politics   312
    Laura Filardo-Llamas and Michael S. Boyd

22 Critical discourse studies in/of applied contexts   328
    Crispin Thurlow

PART IV
Social divisions and power   **343**

23 Class and class warfare   345
    David Block

24 Race/ethnicity   359
    Susana Martínez Guillem

25 Feminist critical discourse analysis   372
    Michelle M. Lazar

26 Sexuality in critical discourse studies   388
    Heiko Motschenbacher

27 Discourses about nationalism   403
    Ruth Wodak

28 Neoliberalism, globalization and critical discourse studies   421
    Christian W. Chun

29 The discursive construction of terrorism and violence   434
    Aditi Bhatia

30 Fascist discourse   447
    John E. Richardson

PART V
Domains and media   **463**

31 Critical discourse analysis and educational discourses   465
    Rebecca Rogers

Contents

32 Legal discourse   480
    Jothie Rajah

33 Critical discourse analysis and ecology   497
    Arran Stibbe

34 Journalism and critical discourse studies   510
    Darren Kelsey

35 Textbooks   525
    Felicitas Macgilchrist

36 Critical discourse studies and branding   540
    Alon Lischinsky

37 The critical analysis of musical discourse   553
    Theo van Leeuwen

38 The power of semiotic software: a critical multimodal perspective   566
    Emilia Djonov and Theo van Leeuwen

39 Social media critical discourse studies (SM–CDS)   582
    Majid KhosraviNik

40 Critical discourse analysis of reality television   597
    Göran Eriksson

41 Critical discourse analysis and film   612
    John A. Bateman

Index   626

Figures

4.1	Page with visual coordination from promotional university brochure	66
4.2	Vision for research in Vision 2016 with a typical emphasis on space	69
4.3	The goal and strategies for research	70
4.4	English translation of the goal and strategies for research	71
5.1	EMERGE/ESCAPE schema	83
5.2(a)	LINE schema	84
5.2(b)	EXPAND schema	84
5.3(a)	FREE MOTION schema	85
5.3(b)	IMPEDED MOTION schema	85
5.4(a)	One-sided volitional ACTION schema	86
5.4(b)	Two-sided volitional ACTION schema	86
5.5	Caused ACTION schema	87
6.1	Dimensions of deixis	93
6.2	Events located on spatial, temporal and modal axes	95
7.1	Overview of the methodology used in the fiscal cliff study	110
7.2	Time frame of fiscal cliff negotiations for corpus collection	112
7.3	Concordance lines for *hikes* in FOX corpus	115
7.4	Concordance lines for *revenue* in CNN corpus	117
12.1	'Regular' meeting of a unit at the European Commission (2009)	186
12.2	'Nexus of Practice' of the European Convention	187
12.3	Communication channels in the European Convention	188
14.1	SMU Annual Report	223
16.1	Proposal for the structure of practical reasoning in deliberative activity types	245
16.2	'Framing' decisions: the argumentative function of metaphors, analogies and definitions	249
21.1	Sample of possible political genres	317
21.2	Cartoon distributed by the DUP at the 2003 Assembly elections	317
21.3	Shifting uses of Obama's first person plural pronoun	321
22.1	The linguistic work of copywriters	335
22.2	The linguistic work of copywriters	335
22.3	The linguistic work of copywriters	336
27.1	Jobbik election poster 2010, translated: "Put an end to parasitism. You can also vote Jobbik!"	411
27.2	Body-politics and the "nation"	413
27.3	The Hungarian Arrow Cross	414
27.4	Topos of history	416

Figures

35.1   Previous textbook page: 'Sozialstaat und Ungleichheit' ('Welfare state
        and inequality')   533
35.2   New textbook page: 'Gesellschaft im Wandel' ('Changing society')   533
38.1   Layout templates in PowerPoint 2003   575
38.2   Layout templates in PowerPoint 2007   576
38.3   A slide from a cultural studies lecture   577
38.4   Slides from a cultural studies lecture on skin and touch with
        content-relevant theme design   578
39.1   Orthographic communication of stance in discourse
        of Persian nationalism   590
39.2   Visual representation of Iranian Persian national(ist) identity   591
40.1   Original episode aired April 15, 2013 by © Kanal 5, produced by *Bada Bing*   604
40.2   Original episode aired April 2, 2012 by © Kanal 5, produced by *Bada Bing*   607
40.3   Original episode aired April 22, 2013 by © Kanal 5, produced by *Bada Bing*   609
41.1   Screenshots contrasting two over-the-shoulder views of Richard Nixon
        taken from corresponding points of the interview   621

Tables

3.1	Discursive Strategies in the DHA	52
4.1	The activity plan included in the document Operational Plan	73
5.1	Typology of construal operations, cognitive systems and discursive strategies	81
6.1	Spatial proximization framework and its key lexico-grammatical items	99
7.1	Top 10 keywords in FOX News corpus	113
7.2	Top 10 keywords in CNN corpus	114
7.3	Top 10 collocates of *hikes* in COCA	116
11.1	Hymes's speaking mnemonic	167
12.1	C.2. Discourse-historical analysis – example: meta-discourses on practice and agency in the European Convention	189
16.1	Critical questions for the evaluation of practical proposals	246
21.1	Keywords OCSC vs. CORPS	322
21.2	Keywords comment corpus vs. Open ANC	322
23.1	Classes, survey results, example occupations and descriptions	348
31.1	Socio-political area and orientation toward inquiry	468
31.2	Critical Discourse Analysis of inter-racial allies	473
35.1	Transformations from previous to new textbook	534
35.2	Hierarchies of 'operators', the processes for formulating textbook tasks	535
36.1	Top lexical items by frequency	548
38.1	Layout template labels and categories in PowerPoint 2003	575

Contributors

Mariana Achugar is a Guggenheim fellow. She works as Associate Professor at the Department of Modern Languages, Carnegie Mellon University, Pittsburgh, USA. Her work focuses on understanding the dynamic nature of semiotic work as part of historical processes in case studies of key social problems/issues (e.g., contested recent pasts, gender differences, educational access, discrimination, etc.).

Paul Baker is Professor of English Language at Lancaster University. His research interests include corpus approaches to discourse analysis, with a focus on language, gender and sexuality, media representation and health. He has published 14 books including *Using Corpora in Discourse Analysis* (2006) and *Sexed Texts* (2008).

Tom Bartlett is Reader in Language and Communication at Cardiff University. His research interests are in Systemic Functional Linguistics and applications of discourse analysis, particularly in relation to participatory governance. His key publication in this area is *Hybrid Voices and Collaborative Change* (2012).

John A. Bateman is Professor of Applicable Linguistics in the English and Linguistics Departments of Bremen University. His research areas include functional linguistic approaches to multi-modal document design, the semiotics of film, computational dialogue systems, ontology and discourse structure. He has been investigating the relation between language and other semiotic systems for many years, publishing widely in all these areas.

Aditi Bhatia is Associate Professor in the Department of English at The Hong Kong Polytechnic University. Her research interests include discourse analysis, with particular reference to the study of political, media and other public discourses. Her most recent monograph is *Discursive Illusions in Public Discourse: Theory and Practice* (2015).

David Block is ICREA Research Professor in Sociolinguistics at the University of Lleida (Spain). He has published on a variety of language in society topics and is currently examining issues around class, social movements, multiculturalism, bi/multilingualism and identity, drawing on scholarship in political economy, sociology, anthropology and geography.

Meriel Bloor is Fellow of the Centre for Applied Linguistics, University of Warwick, and formerly lectured in linguistics and discourse analysis. Her publications centre on specialist registers and ESP, and she is currently researching medical communication. She is co-author with Thomas Bloor of *The Practice of Critical Discourse Analysis* (2007).

Thomas Bloor retired after a career in linguistics and language education. He worked at Aston University for 21 years and has since been a Fellow. His main research interests have focused on discourse analysis and grammar, especially SFL. He is co-author with Meriel Bloor of *The Functional Analysis of English* (2013).

Michael S. Boyd teaches English language and discourse studies at Roma Tre University and UNINT in Rome, Italy. His main research interests include CDA, new media, legal linguistics and interpreting studies. His publications can be found in various collections about Political Discourse as well as *CADAAD Journal, Journal of Pragmatics* and *International Journal of Law, Language and Discourse*.

Piotr Cap is Professor of Linguistics at the University of Łódź, Poland. His interests are in pragmatics, critical discourse studies, political linguistics and genre theory. His recent books include: *Proximization: The Pragmatics of Symbolic Distance Crossing* (2013) and *The Language of Fear: Communicating Threat in Public Discourse* (2016).

Nico Carpentier is Professor at the Department of Informatics and Media of Uppsala University. In addition, he holds two part-time positions, those of Associate Professor at the Communication Studies Department of the Vrije Universiteit Brussel (VUB – Free University of Brussels) and Docent at Charles University in Prague.

Christian W. Chun is Assistant Professor of Culture, Identity and Language Learning in the Applied Linguistics Department at the University of Massachusetts Boston. His book, *The Discourses of Capitalism: Everyday Economists and the Production of Common Sense,* was published in 2017.

Emilia Djonov is a lecturer in early childhood at Macquarie University, Australia. Her research in (critical) multi-modal analysis, social semiotics and multiliteracies has been published in journals such as *Visual Communication, Social Semiotics* and *Text & Talk*. She has co-edited the volume *Critical Multimodal Studies of Popular Discourse* (2014, with Sumin Zhao).

Göran Eriksson is a professor of Media and Communication Studies at Örebro University, Sweden. His research interests include the relationship between journalism and politics and the development of reality television. His works have been published in journals such as *Critical Discourse Studies, Journal of Language and Politics* and *Media, Culture and Society*.

Isabela Fairclough is Senior Lecturer at the University of Central Lancashire. Her publications focus on the critical analysis of political discourse from the perspective of argumentation theory and include the monograph *Political Discourse Analysis* (2012, with Norman Fairclough). She has been developing a new framework for the analysis and evaluation of deliberative practice and is currently investigating the impact of institutional contexts on rational decision-making, in relation to the debate on shale gas exploration (fracking) in the UK.

Norman Fairclough is Emeritus Professor at Lancaster University. He has published many papers and books on CDA, including *Language and Power, Discourse and Social Change, Critical Discourse Analysis, Analysing Discourse, Discourse in Late Modernity* (with Lilie Chouliaraki) and *Political Discourse Analysis* (with Isabela Fairclough).

Contributors

Laura Filardo-Llamas lectures in English at the University of Valladolid, Spain. Her main research area is discourse analysis and conflict resolution, applied particularly to ethno-nationalist conflicts and domestic violence. Some of her publications can be found in *Ethnopolitics, Peace and Conflict Studies, CADAAD Journal* and *Critical Discourse Studies.*

John Flowerdew is Emeritus Professor in the Department of English, City University of Hong Kong, and visiting professor in the Department of English Language and Linguistics, University of Lancaster. His research interests focus on political and academic discourse. In political discourse, developing a theory of critical discourse analysis in historiography, he has published two books and a series of papers on Hong Kong's transition from British to Chinese sovereignty under the slogan of 'one country, two systems'.

Bernhard Forchtner is a Lecturer at the School of Media, Communication and Sociology, University of Leicester. He has published in the field of memory studies, at the interface of sociological theory and critical discourse analysis, and on prejudice and discrimination. He is currently editing (together with Ruth Wodak) *The Routledge Handbook on Language and Politics.*

Dalia Gavriely-Nuri is a research fellow at *The Truman Research Institute for the Advancement of Peace* at The Hebrew University of Jerusalem, and an Associate Professor at Hadassah Academic College, Jerusalem. She specialises in the cultural and discursive aspects of peace and war, national security and the Arab–Israel conflict. Her last books: *Israeli Peace Discourse* (2015), *The Normalization of War in Israeli Discourse* (2013).

Susana Martínez Guillem is Assistant Professor in the Department of Communication & Journalism at the University of New Mexico, USA. Her research interests are in cultural studies, critical discourse studies, migration, anti-racism and social inequality. Her work has appeared in, among others, *Discourse & Society, Critical Discourse Studies* and *European Journal of Cultural Studies.*

Christopher Hart is a Senior Lecturer in Linguistics at Lancaster University. He is author of *Critical Discourse Analysis and Cognitive Science: New Perspectives on Immigration Discourse* (2010) and *Discourse, Grammar and Ideology: Functional and Cognitive Perspectives* (2014).

Darren Kelsey is Senior Lecturer and Head of Media, Culture, Heritage at Newcastle University. His research interests focus on media, discourse, mythology and ideology. Darren has published research on: war and terrorism, riots and the 'sick society', bankers and the financial crisis, populism and Nigel Farage, digital media and surveillance.

Majid KhosraviNik is a Lecturer in Media and (Digital) Discourse Studies at Newcastle University, UK. He works at the intersection of discourse and identity politics within the general guidelines of Critical Discourse Studies. He has concentrated on theory and application of CDS on digital spaces within the last five years. Among his publications are the monograph *Discourse, Identity and Legitimacy* (2015) and the co-edited book *Right-Wing Populism in Europe* (2013).

Manfred Kienpointner is a Professor of General Linguistics at the University of Innsbruck, Austria. His key research interests are within the study of rhetoric and argumentation.

Moreover, he has contributed to the fields of contrastive linguistics and (im)politeness research. His key publications include *Alltaglogik* (1992); 'Varieties of Rudeness' (1997, in: *Functions of Language* 4.2., 251–287); and *Latein-Deutsch kontrastiv* (2010).

Michał Krzyżanowski is Chair in Communication and Media at the University of Liverpool, UK. He works on public discourse in the context of social, political and institutional change. He is Editor-in-Chief of the *Journal of Language and Politics* and coeditor of book series *Bloomsbury Advances in Critical Discourse Studies*.

Michelle M. Lazar is Associate Professor in the Department of English Language and Literature at the National University of Singapore. She actively researches in CDA in the areas of feminist praxis, sexuality, politics and multi-modality. She is the founding editor of two Routledge book series: *Critical Studies in Discourse and Language* and *Gender & Sexuality*.

Per Ledin is Professor in Swedish at Södertörn University, Sweden. He has published widely in different areas of discourse studies, including writing development, multi-modality and critical linguistics. His recent publications include papers on the assessment of writing tests, the semiotics of lists and tables and the language of New Public Management.

Alon Lischinsky is Senior Lecturer in Communication and Discourse at Oxford Brookes University. His scholarly interests focus on corporate reporting and branding as discursive activities, including questions of sustainability and Corporate Social Responsibility reporting, environmentally-themed public relations and advertising, and greenwash. He is currently working on an introductory volume to corpus linguistic applications in scholarly and professional settings (with Sylvia Jaworska and Rachelle Vessey).

Felicitas Macgilchrist is Department Head at the Georg Eckert Institute of International Textbook Studies, and Professor of Media Research at the University of Göttingen, Germany. Current research draws on discourse analysis, ethnography and generative critique. Publications include *Journalism and the Political* (2014) and *Diskursforschung: Ein interdisziplinäres Handbuch* (*Discourse Studies: An Interdisciplinary Handbook,* Transcript).

David Machin is Professor in the department of Media and Communication, Örebro University, Sweden. His interests lie in multi-modality, critical discourse studies and visual design. His books include *The Language of War Monuments* (2013) and *Visual Journalism* (2015). His current research is in the multi-modal communication of administration in institutions.

Heiko Motschenbacher is a Senior Lecturer in English Linguistics at the University of Siegen and co-editor of the *Journal of Language and Sexuality*. His research interests include language, gender and sexuality, critical discourse studies, sociolinguistics, applied linguistics, language and Europeanisation and English as a lingua franca. His recent book publications include: *Gender Across Languages*, Volume IV (with Marlis Hellinger; 2015) and *Language, Normativity and Europeanisation* (2016).

Carl Jon Way Ng is Assistant Professor in the Department of English at City University of Hong Kong. His research interests lie broadly in multi-modal approaches to the analysis of corporate and political discourses, particularly in advanced Asian capitalist societies like Singapore and Hong Kong.

Sean Phelan is Senior Lecturer at the School of Communication, Journalism and Marketing, Massey University, New Zealand. He teaches and researches in critical communication and media studies. He is the author of *Neoliberalism, Media and the Political* (2014) and co-editor of *Discourse Theory and Critical Media Politics* (2011).

Alexandra Polyzou is a Senior Lecturer in Language, Communication and Applied Linguistics at Canterbury Christ Church University, UK. Her research interests include cognitive aspects of critical discourse analysis, and intersectional analyses of gender, sexuality, class and national identities. She is currently working on hetero-normative discourses in sexual health media discourse.

Jothie Rajah is Research Professor at the American Bar Foundation, Chicago. She received her LLB and BA (Honours in English) from the National University of Singapore. Her PhD was awarded by Melbourne Law School, Australia. Her current project studies post-9/11 discourses on law.

Martin Reisigl has a PhD in Applied Linguistics and is currently Substitute Professor for German Studies at the TU Dortmund University and Assistant Professor for Sociolinguistics at the University of Bern. His research interests include discourse studies, sociolinguistics, pragmatics, text linguistics, politolinguistics, rhetoric, argumentation analysis and semiotics.

John E. Richardson is a Reader in Critical Discourse Studies, Department of Social Sciences, Loughborough University. His research interests include structured social inequalities, British fascism, argumentation and multi-modal commemoration. His most recent book is *British Fascism: A Discourse-Historic Analysis* (2017, ibidem Verlag). He is Editor of the international journal *Critical Discourse Studies* and co-editor of Bloomsbury book series *Advances in Critical Discourse Studies*.

Rebecca Rogers is a Professor of Literacy Education and Critical Discourse Studies in the College of Education at the University of Missouri-St. Louis. Her research examines networks of practice that promote and sustain educational equity. She is currently serving as the President of the Literacy Research Association. She is a Board member of Educators for Social Justice. Her research has been published in many books and journals.

Arran Stibbe is a reader in Ecological Linguistics at the University of Gloucestershire, UK, and author of *Ecolinguistics: Language, Ecology and the Stories We Live By* (2015) and *Animals Erased: Discourse, Ecology and Reconnection with Nature* (2012). He teaches a range of courses including ecolinguistics, ecocriticism and communication for leadership.

Nicholas Close Subtirelu is Assistant Teaching Professor in Applied Linguistics at Georgetown University. He examines ideologies pertaining to racial and linguistic diversity in discourse around politics and education. Recent work has been published in *Journal of Sociolinguistics* and *Language in Society* and on his blog Linguistic Pulse (www.linguisticpulse.com).

Crispin Thurlow is Professor of Language and Communication in the Department of English at the University of Bern, Switzerland. He is on the editorial board of *Critical Discourse Studies* and *Discourse, Context & Media*. More information about his work can be found at: www.crispinthurlow.net.

Teun A. van Dijk had a personal chair of Discourse Studies at the University of Amsterdam until 2004, and has been Professor of Discourse Studies at Pompeu Fabra University, Barcelona since 1999. He has mainly contributed to the following domains of research: generative poetics, text grammar, the cognitive psychology of discourse processing, racism and discourse, news analysis, discourse and power, ideology, context and knowledge. He is one of the founders of Critical Discourse Studies and founder of six international journals, of which he still edits *Discourse & Society, Discourse Studies, Discourse & Communication* and *Discurso & Sociedad* (www.dissoc.org). Teun A. van Dijk holds three honorary doctorates.

Theo van Leeuwen is Professor of Language and Communication at the University of Southern Denmark. He has published widely on critical discourse analysis, multi-modality and social semiotics. His books include *Reading Images* and *Multimodal Discourse* (both with Gunther Kress), *Introducing Social Semiotics, Speech, Music, Sound* and *Discourse and Practice*. He is a founding editor of the journal *Visual Communication*.

Ruth Wodak is Emerita Distinguished Professor of Discourse Studies at Lancaster University, UK, and affiliated to the University of Vienna. Besides various other prizes, she was awarded the Wittgenstein Prize for Elite Researchers in 1996 and an Honorary Doctorate from University of Örebro in Sweden in 2010. Widely published in the areas of identity politics, racism and discrimination, as well as organisational discourses, her most recent monograph is *The Politics of Fear: What Right-Wing Populist Discourses Mean* (2015).

Acknowledgements

Every effort has been made to contact copyright holders. Please advise the publisher of any errors or omissions, and these will be corrected in subsequent editions.

Introduction

John Flowerdew and John E. Richardson

Critical Discourse Studies (CDS) is an inter-disciplinary approach to language in use, which aims to advance our understanding of how discourse figures in social processes, social structures and social change. CDS draws heavily on social theories and seeks to develop a critically contextualised approach to linguistics which identifies issues of ideology, power and inequality as central to our field of studies. The scope of critical discourse studies is not limited to linguistic studies, nor to work that is primarily empirical or analytical. However, like other approaches to discourse analysis, CDS is wedded to the principle of examining real-world examples of language in use, with the text as our main unit of analysis. CDS practitioners are united in seeing language as a form of social practice and that its proper focus is in its contexts of use (Fairclough 1989; Fairclough, Mulderrig and Wodak 2011; Wodak and Meyer 2016a). According to Fairclough (1989: 2), "using language is the commonest form of social behaviour". In its view of language as social action, CDS is inspired by the work of Austin (1962) and Wittgenstein (1965), with their emphasis on language as always doing something. It is impossible to examine language in use – what people do with language and how this 'doing' is linked to wider inter-personal, institutional, socio-cultural and material contexts – if the tokens of discourse analysed are concocted by the writers. CDS is problem-driven (as opposed to theory-driven) and aims to uncover hidden features of language use and debunk their claims to authority. It aims to make the implicit explicit in language use. As Jaworski and Coupland (2015: 5) put it, "[CDS] is a forensic activity, with a libertarian political slant". CDS is practised in a wide range of fields, apart from language studies, such as anthropology, business studies, geography, health studies, media studies, psychology and tourism studies. In this sense it is a very inter-disciplinary enterprise.

CDS developed historically out of *Critical Linguistics* (CL), an approach to language study developed at the University of East Anglia, UK. CL sought to emphasise the role of ideology and power relations in the practice of language use and the persuasive power of syntactic forms, such as the passive and nominalised forms (Fowler et al. 1979; Kress 1989). In this way it tried to reveal instances of misrepresentation and/or discrimination in public discourse through a process of "defamiliarization and conscious-raising" (Fowler 2009: 273; see also Filardo-Llamas and Boyd, this volume). While CDS is rapidly becoming the favoured acronym, Critical Discourse Studies (CDS) was previously referred to as Critical Discourse

Analysis (CDA) and, in fact, the initial pre-publication title for this volume used this term. While we prevaricated for some time over whether to update the title, our minds were made up with the change of title of the third edition of Wodak and Meyer's (2016a) influential *Methods of Critical Discourse Studies* from the title of the first two editions, which was *Methods of Critical Discourse Analysis*. As van Dijk (2009: 62) has observed, the rationale for this change of designation resides in the fact that CDA was increasingly not restricted to applied analysis, but also included philosophical, theoretical, methodological and practical developments. This, indeed, is reflected in many of the chapters in this volume (although the case studies included as a part of nearly all of the chapters focus on analysis); hence our decision to update the title.

CDS seeks to relate theories of language to theories of society. We study society through discourse, and contextualise (and understand) discourse through an analysis of its historical, socio-political and cultural foundations. Discourse and language are seen in a dialectical relationship, with social structures affecting discourse and discourse affecting social structure. In the former process, while individuals may exercise discursive agency, this is done within the constraints imposed by social conventions, ideologies and power relations. In the latter process, rather than merely representing social reality, discourse(s) actually (re)create social worlds and relations; for example, doctors and patients interact in certain predictable ways. At the same time, discourse is seen as an essential component in the creation of knowledge and meaning.

CDS is not a method of discourse studies, but a group of varying approaches each with distinctive, but also overlapping methods (Wodak and Meyer 2016b). Approaches presented in the third edition of Wodak and Meyer's (2016a) *Methods of Critical Discourse Studies* include the Discourse-Historical Approach, associated with Ruth Wodak and colleagues; the socio-cognitive approach of Teun van Dijk; Norman Fairclough's dialectical-relational approach; Siegfried Jäger and Florentine Maier's Foucauldian approach; and Theo van Leeuwen's social practice approach, all of which are represented in one way or another in this volume. However, these are just some approaches and, again, many others are represented in this volume.

These approaches draw on various linguistic theories – in particular systemic functional linguistics, pragmatics and, increasingly, cognitive linguistics – and non-linguistic theories, such as theories of (social) cognition and (critical) social theories, e.g., those of Bourdieu, Castells, Foucault, Giddens, Gramsci, Habermas, Harvey and Marx. In terms of methods employed, these include traditional qualitative textual analysis, discourse-pragmatic analysis and corpus-assisted methods, but also ethnographic methods such as interviews, focus groups and participant observation.

The data analysed in CDS can be political discourse of various genres (inter alia policy documents, press releases, speeches and party election materials) mass-media texts (including newspapers, television and film), historical and official documents, various types of internet data, and ethnographic data collected by means of observation, interviews and focus groups. The size of a data set may range from the very local – a single written text or conversation – to the more global – corpora of hundreds or even thousands of texts. Such data may be drawn from anywhere in the world, although there has historically been a (perhaps unfortunate) emphasis on Europe, at the expense of other continents (which we have tried to partially redress in selecting our authors for this volume).

The term *discourse* may be used to refer to language use in general. In this sense it is a non-count noun. In CDS, the term *discourse* may also be used to refer to a specific set of meanings expressed through particular forms and uses which give expression to particular institutions or social groups (Kress 1989). In this sense it may be used as a count noun and we can talk of discourses – neoliberal discourse, racist discourse, fascist discourse, sexist discourse, anti-immigration discourse, etc. – each of these discourses being recognisable in terms of the ideologies they convey and the linguistic and other semiotic structures through which they are expressed. According to this notion of discourse, it may be realised by all semiotic systems, not just language, including visual and aural (multi-modal) systems of signs, and indeed recent approaches to CDS have increasingly been focusing on multi-modal aspects of discourse, e.g., Machin and Mayr (2012).

Discourses are underpinned by ideologies, which are sets of beliefs and values belonging to particular social groups. Ideology affects both how we relate to people in our social world and the discourse(s) with which we engage. Ideology is more than individual ideas formed through experience: ideology and its signs develop "through the process of social interaction, [and are] defined by the social purview of the given time period and the given social group" (Vološinov 1973 [1929]: 21). An ideology may be disseminated to promote the interests of specific social groups. It may involve an *us* versus *them* situation, positive *in-group* and negative *out-group* representations. van Dijk (1998: 44) characterises this in terms of an *ideological square,* as follows:

- emphasise positive things about Us
- emphasise negative things about Them
- De-emphasise negative things about Us
- De-emphasise positive things about Them

Gee (1990: 6) suggests that ideology under Marx

> is an "upside-down" version of reality. Things are not really the way the elite and power-ful believe them to be: rather, their beliefs invert reality to make it appear the way they would like it to be, the way it "needs" to be if their power is to be enhanced and sustained.

Certain cruder interpretations of Marx's position suggest that such ideological work is one-way traffic: that the economic relations of society simply *create* false ideas which are held often contrary to people's true interests. Such interpretations fail for two reasons. First, they fail to realise how ideology does "not just reflect 'reality' but partially help[s] to create, to constitute it" (Gee 1990: 8); second, Marx's point about ideology relates not to issues of "logical or empirical falsity but of the superficial or misleading way in which truth is asserted" (McLellan 1986: 18). Ideology, then, "is not just any system of ideas of beliefs but ways of thinking in which historically transient exploitative forms of social organisation are represented as eternal, natural, inevitable or 'rational'" (Jones 2001: 227).

Such discourses have been the focus of much CDS research. For example, Wodak et al.'s (2009 [1999]) influential study analysing the relationships between the discursive construction of national sameness and difference, which leads to political and social exclusion of specific out-groups in contemporary Austria (Reisigl this volume); or Flowerdew's (2013) study of the (discursive) conflict between Great Britain and China over the return of sovereignty over Hong Kong; or Achugar's (2008) monograph on the discursive manifestations of the conflict over how to remember and interpret the actions of the military during the 1973–1985 dic-tatorship in Uruguay. Ideologies can come to be accepted as part of common sense through a process of *legitimation* (Hodge and Kress 1993; van Leeuwen 2008), that is to say, a set of beliefs and values becomes accepted by virtue of the fact that society accepts the authority of those disseminating them.

Another important dimension of social practice and social relations is that of power. Fol-lowing Foucault (1982), power is seen by CDS practitioners as ubiquitous in society, and elites may maintain control through their exercise of power. Gramsci's (1971) theory of hegemony explains how power may be exercised not just through physical coercion, but covertly, through ideology and discourse. According to Gramsci, the ruling class, the bourgeoisie, has created a hegemonic culture, which has disseminated its own beliefs, values and norms in such a way that their power and authority have come to be taken as common sense and accepted by all members of society. Hegemony is "a condition in which the governed accept or acquiesce in authority without the need for the application of force. Although force was always latent in the background, hegemony meant leadership rather than domination" (Cox 2004: 311). With the successful institution of hegemony, the subordinate classes consent to the leadership of the ruling class and the dominance of their institutions and values. In short, this equates with consenting to unequal class relations. When successful, the ruling class can implant its values with the minimum of force since the ruled acquiesce to the power and political legitimacy of the rulers. In the words of Gramsci:

> The "normal" exercise of hegemony [. . .] is characterised by the combination of force and consensus which vary in their balance with each other, without force exceeding consensus too much. Thus it tries to achieve that force should appear to be supported by the agreement of the majority, expressed by the so-called organs of public opinion – newspapers and associations.
>
> *(Quaderni del Carcere, 1638, cited in Joll 1977: 99)*

Thus, a hegemonic ruling class is one that gains support for itself from other classes. The less powerful (the working-class and others), unwittingly, identify with the values promoted by the bourgeoisie and accept the *status quo* rather than rebelling. This relationship from the discursive perspective is referred to by Fairclough as *discursive hegemony* (2003: 218). Discursive power may be exercised in three ways, according to Holzscheiter (2005, cited in Wodak 2014a: 306): *in discourse,* where social actors struggle over the interpretation of meaning; *over discourse,* where social actors are included or excluded from a given discourse; and *of discourse,* where discourse conventions exercise power over social actors (although individuals might exercise agency and themselves influence and contribute towards changing such conventions). In essence, hegemony is maintained by the ruling class *teaching* the value of their authority to the general public, particularly their central claim to political legitimacy. Education therefore lies at the heart of hegemony – indeed, Gramsci argues "[e]very relationship of hegemony is necessarily a pedagogic relationship" (1971: 350).

Identity, which is a further important concept in CDS, refers to the way individuals and groups see themselves in relation to others. Identity is a fluid construct, as it is subject to change over time and space. Furthermore, identity may be multiple; we may refer to an individual or group's *identities*. Identity is manifested through one's social practice, an important part of which, as already mentioned, is discursive practice. Identity may also be projected onto others through discourse (Kress 1989). For instance, a commercial company may project a particular identity onto its employees, for example, an airline cabin crew as sexually alluring. Such identities may or may not be accepted by their recipients (Chiapello and Fairclough 2002: 195).

Another feature uniting practitioners of CDS is that of critique. The common goal is to challenge inequitable distribution of power in society through the analysis of discourses which demonstrate such discursive inequities through an analysis of their texts (Reisigl 2008). In this way, specific problems of communication may be resolved, resulting in improved communication. Following Hegel, however, criticism is not simply a negative judgement, but has a positive emancipatory function. CDA thus has a specific agenda in bringing about social change, or at least supporting struggle against inequality (van Dijk 2001). Wodak and Meyer (2016b: 65), identify three forms of critique that were developed as part of the DHA: "discourse immanent critique", aimed at identifying internal contradictions, inconsistencies or dilemmas within a practice; "socio-diagnostic critique", which draws on social theory and contextual knowledge in order to point out the "manipulative character" of some discursive practices; and "prognostic critique", which uses the insights gained through immanent and socio-diagnostic critique in order to "contribute to the improvement of communication". Critique needs to be based upon sound ethical values, such as democracy, honesty, integrity, transparency, accountability, objectivity, respect for others, lawfulness and loyalty to others. These are Western values, given that most CDS work has been conducted in Western countries, although there has been a recent movement towards more multi-cultural approaches (Gavriely-Nuri this volume; Shi-xu 2004, 2014; Zhang et al. 2011).

A number of contributions in this volume, including those of Macgilchrist, Rogers and Bartlett, allude to the emancipatory role that CDA can play by means of critique. Macgilchrist (this volume), for example, argues that "While the majority orients to dominant modes of representation, which maintain socio-political hierarchies, an increasing number of studies are orienting to fissures and ruptures in the discourse, asking where the dominant is disrupted, and what this means for the shaping of future socio-political orders". Rogers (this volume) refers to this as a "reconstructive agenda", while Bartlett (this volume), following Martin (2004), refers to such an approach as *Positive Discourse Analysis* (PDA). Some have argued, however, that there is a danger with such an approach of allowing CDS to be appropriated for the purposes of propaganda (e.g., Flowerdew 2008: 207).

Important in the analysis of discourses is the role of context (Flowerdew, this volume). As Fairclough notes, texts are embedded in their context of production, distribution and reception in the social, economic and cultural world. Discourse analysis, according to this view, involves:

> analysing the relationship between texts, processes, and social conditions, both the immediate conditions of the situational context and the more remote conditions of institutions and social structures.
>
> *(Fairclough 1989: 26)*

Fairclough (1992: 73) identifies three integrated levels of discourse in analysis, involving analysis of text, analysis of discourse practices (production, distribution and consumption), and analysis of social practices, where the micro-level of the text is constrained by the meso-level of discourse practices, which is in turn constrained by the macro-level of social practice, or social conditions, involving the role of power. This might suggest a one-way model, but the relationships are interactive, involving a continual shunting between the micro-analysis of texts, the macro-analysis of social structures and formations and power relations and the mediating role of discursive practices and discourse processes (Richardson 2007). Wodak (2014b, this volume) identifies four levels of contextual analysis:

- the immediate co-text
- the other texts and discourses that the text draws upon
- the conditions of text production, distribution and reception
- the wider socio-political formation

Wodak also emphasises the importance of intertextuality and recontextualisation, where an element of one text is incorporated into another. Because this inevitably involves the creation of a new meaning to the recontextualised element, it becomes amenable to manipulation. A third proponent of the CDA approach to discourse analysis, who has a rather different approach to context as compared to Fairclough and Wodak and other practitioners, is Teun van Dijk. van Dijk (2008) offers a socio-cognitive view of context, which grants prominence to the mental processes involved in how we relate to people in our social world. For van Dijk, these mental models represent the mediating link between text and context, between text and social structure:

> It is theoretically essential to understand that there is no other way to relate macro-level notions such as group dominance and equality with microlevel notions of text, talk, meaning and understanding. Indeed, the crucial notion of reproduction needed to explain how discourse plays a role in the reproduction of dominance, presupposes an account that relates discourse structures to social cognitions and social cognitions to social structures.
>
> *(van Dijk 1993: 280)*

A mental models approach is also adopted by Hart (2013, 2014, this volume), among others, although Hart goes further and introduces theoretical insights from cognitive linguistics. Because cognitive linguistics sees language as an integral part of cognition in general, it seeks to identify direct relations between patterns of language and patterns of thought. Perhaps the best-known example of this approach is Lakoff and Johnson's (1980) conceptual metaphor theory, which has been taken up by some discourse analysts (e.g., Charteris-Black 2004; Ng this volume), who have sought to identify ideological patterns underlying conceptual metaphors in discourse. Hart's (2013, 2014, this volume) contribution broadens this approach away from conceptual metaphor to consider grammatical patterning and its relation to ideology, an essential component of context.

A number of CDS practitioners have emphasised the historical dimension of any analysis (see Achugar this volume, for a more in-depth review). As Achugar (this volume), notes:

> When making meaning, we give continuity to our experience beyond an instance connecting past, present and future. In every instance our actions make history impacting others, but at the same time we are affected by the actions of others with whom we coexist and who have come before.

The first CDS practitioner to emphasise the importance of history whom we can mention is Norman Fairclough, who, in his *Discourse and Social Change* (Fairclough 1992), argued that any approach to discourse and social change should be "a method for historical analysis" (9). At the level of text, this can be shown through demonstrating how intertextual relations highlight changes in social structure. Another CDS practitioner employing a historical approach is Wodak, with her Discourse-Historical Approach (DHA) (see Reisigl this volume, for a detailed treatment), which emphasises that the historical context should always be analysed and integrated into the interpretation of discourses and texts (e.g., Wodak and Meyer 2016b). DHA studies have shown how intertextuality and recontextualization function in discourse. As Reisigl (this volume) notes, in today's world we are challenged by a range of political, economic and ecological changes at all levels of nations and societies. A historical approach to discourse is well equipped to study such changes (also Achugar 2008; Flowerdew 2013).

CDS is not without its detractors. It has been critiqued for bias in its selection and interpretation of texts (Blommaert 2005), for being too deterministic (Hammersley 1997) and for ignoring lay interpretations in favour of its own (Jones and Collins 2006; Stubbs 1994). Of course, as in any field, there is good and less good work. What CDS scholars can do to alleviate these problems is to explain clearly and in detail what the data consists of and how it was collected; to analyse the relevant context of the texts under analysis in detail; to be upfront about their individual position vis a vis the data; to be self-reflective at every stage of the research process; to engage in multi-perspectival studies involving triangulation of data; and to consider multiple perspectives when it comes to interpretation, making sure to separate out interpretation from analysis. These are just some of the measures that can be adopted to ensure good quality work. CDS is fundamentally a qualitative approach to research and not best suited to quantitative methods, although it can be combined with such methods. Furthermore, recent developments in corpus-assisted discourse analysis have shown how a quantitative dimension can be introduced to support the qualitative analysis (see Anthony and Baker 2015; Baker this volume).

The volume in outline

The aim of this *Handbook* is to provide an accessible, authoritative and comprehensive introduction to Critical Discourse Studies (CDS), covering the main theories, concepts, contexts and applications of this important and rapidly developing field of study. In more detail, across 41 original chapters, this book will:

- Provide a clear and accessible state-of-the-art overview of the field for advanced undergraduate and graduate students
- Identify and give clear descriptions and examples of central concepts and theories in CDS
- Cover the main fields and genres where CDS has been applied
- Not only summarise the contours of a subject or sub-field (its concerns, development and principle works) in each chapter, but also present the authors' contributions to that sub-field through a worked example
- Emphasise the *critical* dimension of work in a particular area – that is, the chapters present and discuss what is *critical* about CDS research on (for example) pragmatics or gender
- Provide methodologies to help students, teachers and researchers to conduct their own critical research of discourse
- Reflect the international character of critical discourse research by bringing together a range of the very best scholarship in CDA/CDS from around the world

The first section of the *Handbook* presents **Approaches** to CDS. It is vital to remember that neither Critical Discourse Studies nor the earlier Critical Discourse Analysis (CDA) are *methods;* it is insufficient to state that you are going to offer a 'critical discourse analysis' of a topic or problem without detailing which approach to critical analysis you are working within. Section 1 covers the current predominant approaches to CDS, from the more established theoretical-analytic positions of the Dialectical-Relational Approach (N. Fairclough), the Socio-cognitive Approach (van Dijk), the Discourse-Historical Approach (Reisigl) and Multi-modal CDA (Ledin and Machin), through to newer approaches stressing the role of cognition (Hart, Cap), culture (Gavriely) and corpora (Subtirelu and Baker) in exploring the roles that discourse plays in social and political processes. The section ends with Positive

Discourse Analysis (Bartlett) which, despite its distractors, we feel is an approach that offers a contribution in focusing on discourses and texts that offer hope and solutions rather than emphasising problems and negative forces, as is often the case in mainstream CDS.

Section 2 presents a range of **Analytic Methods** frequently applied, and so closely associated with, CDS. The early work of CL demonstrated the utility of Systemic Functional Linguistics to the critical analysis of discourse, and the theoretical principles and analytic techniques of SFL are still frequently applied in CDA to examine the ways that semantic networks carry meaning potential in social and cultural contexts (Bloor and Bloor). CDA involves the critical analysis of text in context, and two chapters in this section (Flowerdew and Krzyżanowski) discuss ways in which we can take issues of context and contextualization seriously, and so build these into our analysis. Developing and enriching this understanding, we have two chapters that further explore the relations between meaning and context, examining pragmatics (Polyzou) and metaphor (Ng). Finally for this section, two chapters examine discourse advanced in contexts of disagreement, and the various contributions of the rhetorical (Kienpointner) and deliberative traditions of argumentation (I. Fairclough) in making sense of such discourse.

A key feature of work in CDS, both in particular studies and across the field as a whole, is its **Inter-disciplinarity**. CDS continues to be enriched by authors drawing on the work of scholars in various cognate fields – whether these are the insights of scholars in media studies (Phelan), who provide context and analytic insight into the institutional/discursive practices of media organisations, or those of political studies in providing corresponding clarity on political processes (Filardo-Llamas and Boyd). The chapter by Forchtner discusses the ways that CDS draws, variously and sometimes contradictorily, from a miscellany of social theory, and that being both more aware and systematic in the ways that we utilise the insights of social theory would be beneficial. Other disciplinary synergies are currently embryonic, but their further development could offer rich rewards for both theoretical/analytic (Carpentier) and applied (Thurlow) research.

Section 4 concerns **Social Divisions and Power**. Here, authors examine continued structured social inequalities on the basis of class (Block), gender (Lazar), race and ethnicity (Martínez Guillem) and sexuality (Motschenbacher), and the ways that inequity and discrimination relate to discourse. The nation state holds great significance in both constituted/constituting social identities and in power relations (Wodak), which are, perhaps increasingly, contested and overlaid with transnational discourses of globalisation and neoliberalism (Chun). Neoliberalism is an aggressive ideological project, in that it subverts democratic governance and seeks to impose a form of marketised citizenship on the general populace. However other ideologies have a more direct and material relationship with political violence, and so this section ends by examining what CDS can offer to the analysis of terrorism (Bhatia) and fascism (Richardson).

The final section of the *Handbook* examines various **Domains and Media,** demonstrating the ways that the theoretical principles and analytic techniques of CDS have been applied in many different fields in the social and human sciences, whether in education (Rogers), law (Rajah), ecological studies (Stibbe) or business (Lischinsky). Valuable critical analysis has been published examining various mass media, their complex (often ideological) messages and the ways that these discourses are produced and consumed. Key, in this regard, is research analysing journalism (Kelsey), textbooks (Macgilchrist) and television (Eriksson). In more recent years, CDS has broadened out beyond these traditional media to embrace other semiotic systems, such as computer software (Djonov and van Leeuwen), film (Bateman), music (van

Leeuwen) and the interactive producer/consumer affordances of 'web 2.0' (KhosraviNik). Discourse is now approached as a multi-modal semiotic phenomenon, not a purely linguistic one, as the chapters in this final section demonstrate.

In commissioning and editing this *Handbook,* we wanted to publish state-of-the-art chapters that demonstrated what a critical approach can bring to our analysis and understanding of both discourse and society. We specifically wanted to reflect the diverse range of research being written across the world. We hope that the published chapters go some way to achieving this. One regret is that there is not parity in the ratio of male to female authors. The original draft contents of the book *were* equal; however, with some authors pulling out, others replaced, the final contents became unfortunately skewed towards male authors.

References

Achugar, M. (2008). *What we remember: The construction of memory in military discourse,* DAPSAC Series. Amsterdam: Benjamins.

Anthony, L. and Baker, P. (2015). ProtAnt: A tool for analysing the protoypicality of texts. *International Journal of Corpus Linguistics* 20(3): 273–292.

Austin, J. L. (1962). *How to do things with words.* Cambridge, MA: Harvard University Press.

Blommaert, J. (2005). *Discourse: A critical introduction.* Cambridge: Cambridge University Press.

Charteris-Black, J. (2004). *Corpus approaches to critical metaphor analysis.* Hampshire: Palgrave Macmillan.

Chiapello, E. and Fairclough, N. (2002). Understanding the new management ideology: A transdisciplinary contribution from critical discourse analysis and new sociology of capitalism. *Discourse & Society* 13(2): 185–208.

Cox, R. W. (2004). Beyond empire and terror: critical reflections on the political economy of world order. *New Political Economy* 9(3): 307–323.

Fairclough, N. (1989). *Language and power.* New York: Longman.

Fairclough, N. (1992). *Discourse and social change.* Cambridge: Polity.

Fairclough, N. (2003). *Analysing discourse: Textual analysis for social research.* London: Routledge.

Fairclough, N., Mulderrig, J. and Wodak, R. (2011). Critical discourse analysis. In T. A. van Dijk (ed.), *Discourse studies: A multidisciplinary introduction,* 357–378. London: Sage.

Flowerdew, J. (2008). Critical discourse analysis and strategies for resistance. In V. K. Bhatia, J. Flowerdew and R. Jones (eds.), *Advances in discourse analysis,* 195–210. London: Routledge.

Flowerdew, J. (2013). *Discourse in English language education.* London: Routledge.

Foucault, M. (1982). The subject and power. In H. Dreyfus and P. Rabinow (eds.), *Michel Foucault: Beyond structuralism and hermeneutics.* Chicago: University of Chicago Press.

Fowler, R. (2009). Notes on critical linguistics. In J. E. Joseph (ed.), *Language and politics: major themes in English studies,* Vol. 4. London: Routledge.

Fowler, R., Hodge, B., Kress, G. and Trew, T. (1979). *Language and control.* London: Routledge & Kegan Paul.

Gee, J. P. (1990). *Social linguistics and literacies: ideology in discourses.* London: The Falmer Press.

Gramsci, A. (1971). *Selections from the prison notebooks.* Q. Hoare and G.N. Smith (trans.). London: Lawrence and Wishart.

Hammersley, M. (1997). On the foundations of critical discourse analysis. *Language and Communication* 17: 237–248.

Hart, C. (2013). Constructing contexts through grammar: Cognitive models and conceptualisation in British Newspaper reports of political protests. In J. Flowerdew (ed.), *Discourse and contexts,* 159–184. London: Continuum.

Hart, C. (2014). *Discourse, grammar and ideology: Functional and cognitive perspectives.* London: Bloomsbury.

Hodge, R. and Kress, G. (1993). *Language as Ideology,* 2nd edn. London: Routledge.

Holzscheiter, A. (2004). *Power of discourse and power in discourse: An investigation of transformation and exclusion in the global discourse of childhood.* PhD thesis, Free University of Berlin, Berlin.

Jaworski, A. and Coupland, N. (2015). Introduction. In A. Jaworski and N. Coupland (eds.), *The discourse reader,* 3rd edn, 1–35. Abingdon: Routledge.

Joll, J. (1977). *Gramsci.* London: Fontana.

Jones, P. E. (2001). Cognitive linguistics and Marxist approach to ideology. In R. Dirven, B. Hawkins and E. Sandikcioglu (eds.), *Language and ideology. Volume 1: Theoretical cognitive approaches*, 227–251. Amsterdam: Benjamins.

Jones, P. E. and Collins, C. (2006). Political analysis versus critical discourse analysis in the treatment of ideology: Some implications for the study of communication. *Atlantic Journal of Communication*, 14(1–2): 28–50.

Kress, G. (1989). *Linguistic processes in sociocultural practice*, 2nd edn. Oxford: Oxford University Press.

Lakoff, G. and Johnson, M. (1980). *Metaphors we live by*. London: University of Chicago Press.

Machin, D. and Mayr, A. (2012). *How to do critical discourse analysis: A multimodal approach*. Los Angeles: Sage.

McLellan, D. (1986). *Ideology*. Minneapolis, MN: University of Minnesota Press.

Martin, J. R. (2004). Positive discourse analysis: Power, solidarity and change. *Revista Canaria de Estdios Ingleses* 49: 179–200.

Reisigl, M. (2008). Analyzing political rhetoric. In R. Wodak and M. Krzyżanowski (eds.), *Qualitative discourse analysis in the social sciences*, 96–120. London: Palgrave.

Richardson, J. E. (2007). *Analysing newspapers: An approach from critical discourse analysis*. Houndmills: Palgrave Macmillan.

Shi-xu. (2004). *A cultural approach to discourse*. London: Palgrave Macmillan.

Shi-xu. (2014). *Chinese discourse studies*. London: Palgrave Macmillan.

Stubbs, M. (1994). Grammar, text and ideology: Computer-assisted methods in the linguistics of representation. *Applied Linguistics* 15(2): 201–223.

van Dijk, T. A. (1993). Principles of critical discourse analysis. *Discourse & Society*, 4(2): 249–283.

van Dijk, T. A. (1998). *Ideology: A multidisciplinary approach*. London: Sage.

van Dijk, T. A. (2001). Critical discourse analysis. In D. Tannen, D. Schiffrin and H. Hamilton (eds.), *Handbook of discourse analysis*, 352–371. Oxford: Blackwell.

van Dijk, T. A. (2008). *Discourse and power*. London: Palgrave Macmillan.

van Dijk, T. A. (2009). Critical discourse studies: A sociocognitive approach. In R. Wodak and M. Michael (eds.), *Methods of critical discourse analysis*, 2nd edn, 62–86. London: Sage.

van Leeuwen, T. (2008). *Discourse and practice: New tools for CDA*. Oxford: Oxford University Press.

Vološinov. (1973 [1929]) *Marxism and the philosophy of language*. L. Matejka and I. R. Titunik (trans.). Cambridge, MA: Harvard University Press.

Wittgenstein, L. (1965). *Philosophical investigations*. New York: The Macmillan Company.

Wodak, R. (2014a) Critical discourse analysis. In C. Leung and B.V. Street (eds.), *The Routledge companion to English studies*, 302–316. London and New York: Routledge.

Wodak, R. (2014b) Discourse and politics. In J. Flowerdew (ed.), *Discourse in context*, 321–346. London: Bloomsbury.

Wodak, R. and Meyer, M. (eds.) (2016a). *Methods of critical discourse analysis*. London: Sage.

Wodak, R. and Meyer, M. (2016b). Methods of critical discourse analysis: history, agenda, theory and methodology. In R. Wodak and M. Meyer (eds.), *Methods of critical discourse analysis*, 3rd edn, 1–33. London: Sage.

Wodak, R., de Cillia, R., Reisigl, M. and Liebhart, K. (1999/2009). *The discursive construction of national identity*, 1st and 2nd edn. Edinburgh: Edinburgh University Press.

Zhang, H., Chilton, P., He, Y. and Jing, W. (2011). Critique across cultures: Some questions for CDA. *Critical Discourse Studies* 8(2): 95–107.

Part I
Approaches

1

CDA as dialectical reasoning

Norman Fairclough

Introduction

In this chapter I summarise how my approach to CDA has changed over 30 years, and then present the most recent version of it: CDA as 'dialectical reasoning'. This emphasises the relationship between critique, explanation and action. I discuss how this view of CDA might support political action to change social life for the better, referring to the 'Kilburn Manifesto' for transcending neoliberalism. The focus upon dialectical reasoning and political action differentiates this chapter from one in an earlier *Routledge Handbook* (Fairclough 2012).

CDA is a form of *critical* social analysis. Critical social analysis shows how forms of social life can damage people unnecessarily, but also how they can be changed. CDA's contribution is elucidating how discourse is related to other social elements (power, ideologies, institutions, etc.) and offering critique of discourse as a way into wider critique of social reality. But the objective is not just critique, it is change 'for the better'. Academic critique alone cannot change reality, but it can contribute to political action for change by increasing understanding of existing reality and its problems and possibilities. Better understanding requires better explanations. CDA offers better explanatory understanding of relations between discourse and other components of social life.

CDA combines *critique* of discourse and *explanation* of how discourse figures in existing social reality as a basis for *action* to change reality. This in summary form is what I mean by 'dialectical reasoning': a way of reasoning from critique of discourse to what should be done to change existing reality, by way of explanation of relations between discourse and other components of reality. For example: critique of the discourse of modern universities, and explanation of how it figures within the 'marketisation' of universities, as a basis for action to change them. If universities represent students as 'consumers' (creating a problematic or 'false' analogy between the two), and this can be explained as part of a strategy to privatise universities, there is arguably something amiss which should be changed (Fairclough 1993). This relation between critique, explanation and (political) action is the essence of CDA. Though CDA is not itself action, it is a step towards it, identifying and sometimes advocating lines of action. We cannot move from critique towards action except via explanation: without explanatory understanding of social reality, including causal and dialectical relations (I explain 'dialectical relations' below) between discourse and other elements of social life, we cannot know what needs to be changed, what can be changed, and how. Explanation is of particular importance in this approach to CDA, and other key features of the approach depend upon it. The focus is not just on power *in* discourse but also power *behind* discourse, not just on critique of manipulation but also critique of ideology, not just on particular aspects of existing social reality (e.g., representations of migrants in the press) but also its capitalist character and how that impacts upon all its aspects (Fairclough 1989, 2014).

Social reality is mediated by ideas and discourse: there are social entities (people, events, practices, institutions), and there are beliefs/ideas about and representations of them, and analysis needs to encompass both and the relations between them. These relations are both cognitive and causal: both matters of representation-and-interpretation and matters of cause-and-effect, both epistemological relations which are open to critique, and ontological relations which require explanation (Bhaskar 1989: 101–102). Discourse is meaningful, but also a cause of and an effect of other social (and material) elements. One consequence is that objects of critical social analysis are simultaneously material and semiotic (discoursal), and analysis needs to focus upon (dialectical) relations between the two (Jessop 2004). A second consequence is that critical social analysis is 'transdisciplinary', it brings together disciplines whose concerns are material facets of social realities, and semiotic/discoursal facets. CDA itself does not provide analyses of capitalism, neoliberalism, politics, media, etc., which it needs for explanation, but collaborates with other disciplines and theories, such as media or organisation studies, or 'cultural political economy' (Jessop 2004, Fairclough 2010: 453–526), or 'critical realism' (Fairclough, Jessop and Sayer 2004).

A third consequence is that critical social analysis and CDA are both normative and explanatory critique: critique on the basis of norms or values, and critique on the basis of causal and dialectical relations. CDA begins with *normative critique* of discourse (simply 'critique' above), assessing it against norms (e.g., speak the truth, speak sincerely, speak justly), then moves via explanation of normatively problematic discourse to *explanatory critique* of features of social reality which lead to such discourse, and towards *action* – features of reality which have such effects need changing. Some forms of CDA are largely normative, but this is not enough to change reality: normative critique of people's language and practices as, for example, racist needs to be combined with explanatory critique of aspects of social reality as producing such racism and needing to be changed.

An approach to CDA

There have been three main versions of my approach, which has changed over time largely in response to social changes. The first, oriented to the post-World War 2 social settlement, centred upon critique of ideological discourse as part of a concern with the reproduction of the existing social order (Fairclough 1989). The second, corresponding to the shift to neoliberalism from the 1970s, centred upon critique of discourse as part of social change, especially part of attempts to impose 'top-down' neoliberal restructuring (Fairclough 1992). The third, corresponding to the 2007+ financial and economic crisis, centres upon critique of deliberative discourse as part of a wider concern with struggles over strategies to overcome the crisis (Fairclough and Fairclough 2012). The emphasis shifts between versions, but in a cumulative way that incorporates earlier concerns into new syntheses. For example, critique of ideology remains important throughout. Fairclough (2014) gives a detailed account of these changes and a critical comparison with other approaches.

Fairclough (1989), the main formulation of the first version, is a radical view of CDA. It emphasises power *behind* discourse as well as *in* discourse – how people with power shape the 'order of discourse' and the social order, as well as controlling specific interactions like interviews. It correspondingly emphasises ideology rather than just persuasion and manipulation. It views discourse as a stake in, as well as a site of, social struggle including class struggle. It aims to raise consciousness of how language contributes to the domination of some people by others, as a step towards social emancipation. The 2007+ crisis indicates a continuing need for radical change. As the huge gap between rich and poor has continued to increase even during the crisis, it would seem that only a struggle for fundamental social and political changes can reverse this and other damaging tendencies. If CDA wants to contribute, it needs to be radical.

The core of the first version is critique of ideology. Let's take an example. Current debates about overcoming the crisis are often about return to economic 'growth', and it is generally just taken for granted that 'growth' is necessary, though this is not true for all economies. It is *capitalist* economies that require continuous growth, because that is the nature of 'capital', and failure to grow adequately is regarded as a crisis. Moreover it is not just growth that is necessary, so also is the discursive assumption that it is: the need for growth must be beyond question, mere common sense. Yet the real reason why growth is necessary for capitalism is difficult to legitimise in societies which claim to be democratic – why should those who already have more than enough always require more? Where reasons *are* given, they tend to be 'rationalisations', spurious 'reasons' that are nevertheless more persuasive. Sometimes these take a proverbial form: 'a rising tide raises all boats'. 'Trickle-down' economics claims that entrepreneurs should be richly rewarded for producing growth because it benefits us all, but this is arguably a rationalisation, as this is not really why businesses are driven to continuously increase their turnover and profits (Fairclough and Fairclough 2012). A focus on ideology goes with a focus on explanation (as defined in Fairclough and Fairclough 2012: 134): ideology critique is a form of explanatory critique which explains why features of discourse which are open to normative critique are nevertheless necessary for maintaining the social order. It also goes with a focus on critique of power behind discourse and of capitalism. Approaches to CDA which lack these focuses may talk about ideologies, but they cannot do ideology critique.

The second version of my approach (Fairclough 1992) focused upon critique of discourse as a part of top-down social change in the implementation of neoliberal capitalism. An example is the 'marketisation' of universities as part of a general push to restructure public services on a market model. This was partly a discursive process: marketising universities meant making their discourse more like that of private corporations, and wider changes in structure, management and practices first appeared in new representations of the nature and activities of universities. This included ideological change in common sense assumptions, e.g., students are consumers, universities are businesses in competition.

Such changes in discourse included changes in *discourses* (ways of representing reality), *genres* (ways of interacting discursively) and *styles* (ways of being, identities, in their discourse aspect), all of which are different in the 'market university'. These were evident in a variety of spoken and written *texts* (e.g., policy documents, publicity materials for recruiting students, management meetings). Over time the *order of discourse* changed – the configuration of discourses, genres and styles which defines the discursive character and potential of universities – as part of a general shift in their structure, management and practices. There were changes in *intertextuality* and more specifically *interdiscursivity*: different discourses, different genres and different styles came to be combined in new ways, producing hybrid articulations of academic and market discourse (Fairclough 1993). All versions of this approach to CDA are 'textually-oriented' (Fairclough 1992): discourse analysis includes detailed analysis of texts, both linguistic (grammatical, semantic, pragmatic, genre) analysis and interdiscursive analysis of hybrid articulations. Dynamically and historically, such hybrid combinations result from the *recontextualization* of market discourse in universities, shifting discourse (discourses, genres, styles) from one context to another. Discourse can contingently (subject to circumstances and conditions) be *operationalised: enacted* in ways of (inter)acting, *inculcated* in ways of being, *materialised* in, e.g., the forms of buildings. It is because changes in discourse can mutate and generalise into wider social changes in these ways that they are such a significant part of social change. This is a matter of the *dialectical relations* between discourse and other social elements, which I return to below. Operationalisation can be intra-semiotic: discourses can be enacted as genres or inculcated as styles. All the italicised terms in this paragraph are concepts and categories in this second version (Fairclough 2012).

The third version focuses upon critique of political debate as an element of struggles over strategies to overcome the 2007+ crisis. The focus is upon deliberation (practical argumentation) about what should be done because that is the primary genre of political discourse, requiring an 'argumentative turn' that incorporates argumentation theory into CDA. Concerns in earlier versions (e.g., ideology) do not disappear; they are now addressed in terms of arguments and their elements (premises, conclusions). Action (genre) is seen as the primary aspect of discourse, and representation and identity (discourses, styles) are addressed as aspects of actions rather than in isolation. Critical social analysis needs the focus upon practical argumentation to go beyond just claiming *that* discourse may have constructive effects on social reality, to showing *how* it can do so: discourses provide reasons for/against acting in certain ways. Discourses may have constructive effects where practical arguments which include these reasons stand up to critical evaluation and lead to decisions, which lead to action, and to transformative effects on reality (Fairclough and Fairclough 2012).

CDA as dialectical reasoning

CDA is analysis of discourse, but it is also itself a form of discourse. In Fairclough (2013) I suggested that it is a form of practical argumentation: argumentation from a set of premises to a claim about what should be done. According to Fairclough and Fairclough (2012), the premises in practical argumentation are: a Circumstantial premise which represents an existing state of affairs, a Goal premise which specifies an alternative state of affairs as goal on the basis of a Value premise (the values and concerns one is arguing from) and a Means-Goal premise which claims that the advocated line of action in the conclusion (or Claim) of the argument is a means of achieving the goal. The values and goals in CDA follow from its critical aims, including for instance the value of social justice and the goal of a just society. Practical argumentation moves from problems to solutions: the Circumstantial premise doesn't just represent an existing state of affairs, it 'problematises' (Fairclough 2013) it, diagnoses what the problem is, what needs changing, while the Goal premise and the Claim advocate a solution, what change to aim for (the goal) and what action to take to achieve it (the Claim).

CDA is more specifically 'dialectical reasoning', a form of practical argumentation which gives prominence to the connection between critique, explanation and action. We can characterise it as four steps:

1   Normative critique of discourse.
2   Explanation of normatively criticised discourse in terms of features of the existing state of affairs (existing social reality).
3   Explanatory critique of the existing state of affairs.
4   Advocating action to change the existing state of affairs 'for the better'.

It can be used for critical analysis of political discourse, e.g., political debates, whose main argument type is practical argumentation. So CDA is a form of practical argumentation which critically analyses, and is in a sense in dialogue with, practical argumentation in politics.

The focus of such critical analysis is upon discourse as a part of political activity types, such as political problem-solving, seeking political solutions to problems like the funding of education. In the *Nicomachean Ethics,* Aristotle characterises politics as action in pursuit of the highest good, based upon decisions, which arise out of deliberation (Fairclough and Fairclough 2012). So change in reality (achieving the 'highest good') requires action, action requires decision, decision requires deliberation. We can link this to Levinson's idea of 'activity types' (1992: 71) and his question "in what ways do the structural properties of an activity constrain (especially the functions of) the verbal contributions that can be made towards it?". We can broaden this question to ask how 'verbal contributions' (e.g., debates or other forms of deliberation) affect the activity they are a part of, as well as how they are affected by being part of the structure of that activity. The Aristotelian sequence deliberation-decision-action-change is instantiated for instance in political problem-solving, and the deliberation in this case includes parliamentary debate, which we should analyse as a step in the sequence and in relation to the other steps (decision, action, change).

Dialectical reasoning extends earlier accounts of dialectical relations between discourse and other social elements (Fairclough 2010) and of the 'constructive' effects of discourses on the wider social reality. It also offers a distinctive approach to 'problematisation' of existing states of affairs, which involves steps 1–3 above and is based upon CDA's theory of discourse, including the claim above that relations between discourse and social entities are both cognitive and causal. On the basis of this theory, CDA sees normative critique of discourse as a 'point of entry' into explanatory social critique, and problematisation, of existing social reality. This is a contribution of CDA to critical social analysis with august precursors: Aristotle advocated starting from *phainomena* and *endoxa,* generally accepted beliefs and opinions, what people say; and Marx began his critique of political economy with a critique of the discourse of the political economists (Fairclough and Graham 2002).

The problematisation of the existing state of affairs begins with normative critique of its discourse, then moves to explanation of what features of the existing state of affairs bring about normatively criticised features of discourse, and what effects such features can have on the state of affairs. This identifies dialectical relations between discourse and other social elements: for instance, representation of students as consumers can be internalised in their beliefs and behaviour. The next step is explanatory critique of the existing state of affairs: for example, marketisation of universities can be criticised because of what it leads to (its consequences) and 'false analogies' it rests on (as assumptions) such as that between students and consumers. Explanatory critique identifies the problem in ('problematises') the existing state of affairs, in this case the marketisation of universities. This provides a normative view of problematisation: in political deliberation, problematisation is often open to critique for lacking this explanatory basis. Because identification of the problem is linked to advocacy of a solution, problematisation links the existing state of affairs represented in the Circumstantial premise to the goal (Goal premise) and advocated action to achieve it (Claim) which constitute the advocated solution. How the existing state of affairs is problematised limits the range of possible solutions (goals and actions).

The movement from problematisation to advocated solution is itself characterised by dialectical relations between discourse and non-discursive social elements. The problem (marketisation of universities) is a problem of structures and practices, not just of discourse, yet any solution would be discursive: an 'imagined' state of affairs (goal) which the 'imagined' action (in the Claim) would be a means of achieving, to replace the problematised state of affairs (Fairclough and Fairclough 2012). But this means that, as well as being steps in political problem-solving, action and change are imagined in deliberation, and *how* they are imagined affects what range of actions and changes are possible: only actions which are imagined can be decided upon and taken, limiting the possibilities for change. In terms of dialectical relations, imagined actions may be realised (operationalised) in real actions, and thereby imagined change may be realised in real change. So the discourse (deliberation) is affected by its position in political problem-solving, but it also affects the range of possibilities in the subsequent steps of decision, action and change, constraining it further or enabling it to be widened, through dialectical relations both within the deliberation and between the deliberation and the other steps.

Through an understanding of 'dialectic', we can comprehend the relation between a form of deliberation and the way it affects and is affected by other steps in an activity type (e.g., parliamentary debate in political problem-solving). Dialectic is one of three interconnected facets of argumentation recognised since classical times: logic, dialectic and rhetoric. Dialectic is the dialogical aspect of argumentation, including the critical questioning of arguments in dialogue. Dialectical deliberation is a way of arriving at and settling on 'imaginaries' for possible alternatives to problematised states of affairs (goals in Goal premises) and for actions (means) to achieve them, in a critical dialogical process. Such advocated solutions emerge from evaluating different arguments and reasons, weighing them against each other, retaining what is good and discarding what is bad. This is an epistemological process of determining the right thing to do, the right way to change the existing state of affairs, and the right way to achieve that.

Bhaskar (1993: 3) suggests a general notion of dialectic which dialectical deliberation is an instance of: "any process of conceptual or social conflict, interconnection and change, in which the generation, interpenetration and clash of oppositions, leading to their transcendence in a fuller or more adequate mode of thought or form of life, plays a key role". Dialectical deliberation is a discursive (more specifically, argumentative) process, but the dialectic is not purely discursive. It includes dialectical relations between discourse and other elements of states of affairs in which discourse is operationalised, including decision, action and change as steps in an activity type. So there is a 'relational' dialectic as well as the epistemological (and purely discursive) dialectic. But through the relational dialectic, deliberation as a step in an activity type also contributes to an 'ontological' dialectic in which a clash between the existing state of affairs and imagined alternatives can lead to a more adequate state of affairs. And it contributes to a 'practical' dialectic, in which a clash between existing ways of acting and imagined alternatives can lead to better ways of acting. Dialectical deliberation is a learning (epistemological) process in which learning about better reasons and arguments is at the same time learning about better states of affairs and better actions which might achieve them.

CDA can be seen as dialogue with the political argumentation which it critiques, a sort of deliberation that is however one-sided because those whose argumentation is challenged don't usually take part. But CDA also aims to contribute to deliberation in political action to change the existing state of affairs 'for the better'. CDA is not itself politics, but its critique and analysis can support politics, as critical social analysis in general aims to do. Through dialogue with existing practical arguments, CDA formulates its own practical arguments in support of action to achieve goals which offer solutions to the problems it diagnoses (its own problematisations of existing states of affairs). CDA does not always explicitly advocate solutions, sometimes it is just 'negative' critique of existing states of affairs, but possible solutions are usually implicit. Arguably CDA should explicitly link diagnosis of problems to identification of solutions, 'negative' to 'positive' critique (see Bartlett in this volume).

Practical argumentation can be critically questioned in three main ways (Fairclough and Fairclough 2012). A practical conclusion (Claim) can be questioned on the grounds that the consequences of the advocated action would undermine essential goals; premises can be questioned in terms of truth or 'rational acceptability'; the argument itself can be questioned on the grounds that the conclusion (Claim) does not follow from the premises. The critical questioning of Claims and of Circumstantial and Goal premises, like the problematisation of the existing state of affairs discussed above, requires explanation. It is only on the basis of explanatory analysis of the existing state of affairs that we can determine what consequences are likely to follow from what actions, whether the problematisation of the state of affairs is adequately supported by explanation, and whether the imagined state of affairs (goal) is achievable in the existing state of affairs. Consequently, the critique of Claims and Circumstantial and Goal premises is explanatory critique, as well as normative critique.

My emphasis on explanation is not new, it has been a feature of my approach from the beginning (Fairclough 1989), but the integration of critique, explanation and action enabled by the turn to argumentation is new. The argumentative turn also has other advantages. It is a response to criticism that CDA merely seeks to justify conclusions and solutions which accord with practitioners' political 'biases'. By being explicit about its own argumentation, CDA makes it clear that its objectives are critical, explanatory and transformative but not justificatory, and also how its argumentation can be critically questioned and challenged, and be open to retrospective evaluation in the light of subsequent events. An example in my work was a paper on marketisation of universities published 22 years ago (Fairclough 1993), whose analysis (problematisation) of the state of affairs in universities in terms of relations between marketisation and changes in discourse, and whose suggested solutions, appear to have been broadly vindicated by events. CDA could provide the process of public deliberation with a systematic critique of proposals and alternatives. Deliberation in public decision-making has a number of stages (see the 8-stage model in Chapter 6 of Fairclough and Fairclough 2012), and CDA could be included at the stage where proposals (e.g., by government) are critically tested, and, if found deficient, assessed against alternatives. Where available alternatives are themselves deficient, CDA can produce its own alternatives and arguments in support of them.

The argumentative turn also helps to avoid a confusion about how CDA should be evaluated, which can arise from quantitative tendencies in the current popularity of corpus linguistics. Numbers may have a very minor supporting role, but the quality of CDA is a matter of how well its argumentation and the critique and analysis incorporated within it stand up to critical questioning and to the turn of events. It may also provide a yardstick against which work which is claimed to be CDA can be measured. For example, much work in CDA focuses upon the contrast between positive self-representation and negative other-representation, the 'us' and 'them' distinction, sometimes focusing narrowly on, for instance, the pronoun 'we'. Such issues of representation are important, but we need to establish their importance by integrating our analysis of them into critical and explanatory analysis of the social and discursive activity in which they assume importance, as CDA analysts often do, but not always.

The Kilburn Manifesto: a case study

The Kilburn Manifesto (KM) is a political manifesto for transcending neoliberalism (Hall, Massey and Rustin 2015). Why use a manifesto to illustrate CDA as dialectical reasoning? Because CDA's concern is not just with criticising existing reality but also with political action to change it, and manifestos are part of political action. KM has arisen from a body of analysis and debate centred recently around the journal *Soundings,* but extending back to the 1970s crisis and emergence of neoliberalism, and including earlier manifestos. Stuart Hall's Gramscian political approach in Cultural Studies, which I drew upon in Fairclough (1989), has been particularly influential. Can CDA, as well as learning from it, help to take further KM's view of neoliberalism and the political struggle against it? Can there be a 'give-and-take' between the critical analysis of CDA and the politics of such political groups? I refer to parts of the KM by chapter number, apart from the introductory Framing Statement.

Discourse in KM

Hall, Massey and Rustin (Framing Statement: 8) begin by stating that

> mainstream political debate does not recognise the depth of the crisis, nor the consequent need for radical rethinking. . . . We therefore offer this analysis as a contribution to the debate, in the hope that it will help people on the left think more about how we can shift the parameters of the debate, from one concerning small palliative and restorative measures, to one which opens the way for moving towards a new political era and new understandings of what constitutes the good society.

Discourse ('debate') is at the heart of KM, and the central idea is that a social 'settlement' like neoliberalism (or a part of it such as marketised universities) has its particular 'parameters' or 'terms of debate' which must be changed in changing the settlement. Changing the terms of debate can produce a form of debate which 'opens the way' to transcending neoliberalism. CDA can use this idea, but it can also help to take it further.

Discourse figures in two main ways in KM, as 'debate' (a form of deliberation) and as 'vocabularies' (i.e., 'discourses' in the sense of particular ways of representing aspects of reality). On the one hand there is debate, the forms of argument that feature within it, and the 'terms of debate', including what can/cannot be politically debated and how this changes as social settlements change, e.g., from social democracy to neoliberalism. On the other hand, there are the vocabularies which are predominantly used to describe people and things, worldviews and the theories which underlie them, the various social (political, cultural) effects they have, and again how they change as socioeconomic settlements change. There is a separate chapter on vocabularies (Chapter 1). They are 'enacted' in practices (e.g., the 'freedom of choice' ascribed to individuals is enacted in the 'mandatory exercise' of 'free choice' in, for instance, choosing your doctor), and both of them 'embody and enforce the ideology of neoliberalism', affirming that one is 'above all a consumer, functioning in a market'. Such vocabularies affect our identities, our relationships and our world contribute to forming ideologies and 'common sense', and contribute to placing us in a 'political straitjacket' by limiting the options we have. So 'discourse matters'. In the changes of vocabulary associated with neoliberalism, people are enjoined to be ('interpellated as') 'consumers', be they students, patients, passengers or whatever. The 'so-called truth underpinning this change in descriptions' is that 'individual interests are the only reality that matters' and these are 'purely monetary', and the 'theoretical justification' which lies behind this is 'the idea of a world of independent agents whose choices, made for their own advantage, paradoxically benefit all' (Chapter 1: 9–11).

The connection between debate and vocabularies is suggested in: "Neoliberal ideas set the parameters – provide the 'taken-for-granteds' – of public discussion, media debate and popular calculation" (Framing Statement: 17). This actually connects debate with neoliberal 'ideas' rather than vocabularies, but since ideas appear in the discursive form of vocabularies (discourses), we may take it that it is the latter that 'set the parameters' of debate, which amounts to providing the 'taken-for-granteds', the assumptions. The assumptions in debate depend on, and vary with, the discourse (vocabulary).

Changing the terms of debate

How can CDA as dialectical reasoning add to and help develop KM's discourse-oriented analysis of neoliberalism and its view of political struggle to transcend it? What are 'terms of debate', and what is involved in changing them, from the perspective of this version of CDA, and how is it that a form of debate with the right terms, produced by changing the terms of debate, could 'open the way' to transcending neoliberalism, as the Manifesto suggests? What does 'open the way' mean?

The terms of a particular debate, such as the political debate in Britain about how to overcome the 2007+ crisis, depend upon which discourses are included or favoured, as opposed to excluded or disfavoured. For example, was a revolutionary political discourse included in this debate, and if so was it a favoured discourse or a disfavoured and marginal one? I would say that it was a marginal presence. The selection (inclusion/exclusion) of discourses determines what we can take to be other aspects of the terms of debate, including what is assumed or taken for granted. For example, the necessity of restoring economic growth in the aftermath of the crisis was an assumption associated with the most prominent economic discourses, both neoliberal and Keynesian. Other aspects of the terms of debate which are discourse-dependent include: how existing states of affairs can be problematised, and therefore what range of solutions (goals and actions) are available; what range of reasons for or against actions are available, and what counts as 'reasonable'; what range of explanations are available, and what counts as 'explanatory'. Changing the terms of debate is basically changing the range of discourses which are included and favoured, but doing so also changes these other aspects.

In terms of the 'educative' aspect of politics (see below), problematisation makes a particularly clear connection for political activists between changing the terms of debate and opening up possibilities for action and change, because how states of affairs are problematised affects the solutions (action and change) that are available. Hall, Massey and Rustin (Framing Statement: 21) state that the purpose of KM is to develop "a political project which transcends the limitations of conventional thinking as to what is 'reasonable' to propose or do". But although KM is much concerned with explanation, it does not explicitly connect explanation to critique and action, nor to debate, whereas these connections are crucial in CDA as dialectical reasoning. The selection (inclusion/exclusion, favouring/disfavouring) of discourses delimits the range of both reasons and explanations and therefore what counts as 'reasonable' and 'explanatory', and these are important aspects of the terms of debate. For example, both neoliberal and Keynesian economic discourses provide reasons in favour of actions which promote economic growth, and arguments along these lines count as reasonable in the perspective of these discourses (though not in the perspective of Green economic discourses). And for many political-economic discourses, explanation in terms of structures is an essential condition for debate to count as explanatory. Changing the terms of debate with respect to explanation can mean adding it where it is absent, or improving it where it is present. Highlighting 'reasons' and 'causes', and as I suggest below 'motives', might give a useful focus to the 'educative' political aims of KM.

How is it, from the perspective of CDA as dialectical reasoning, that a form of debate produced by changing the terms of debate could 'open the way' to radical change, including the transcendence of neoliberalism? It is partly because changing the possibilities for problematising the existing state of affairs also changes the range of possible solutions, and the alternative states of affairs and action to achieve them that can be imagined and advocated, potentially including radical change. It is also to do with dialectical relations between discourse and other social elements. Such dialectical relations are identified through explanation of how aspects of the existing state of affairs lead to normatively problematic discourse, and how the latter affects the former.

Debate (a form of deliberation) needs to be analysed as part of the sequence deliberation-decision-action-change associated with activity types such as political problem-solving, as I argued earlier. Action and change are steps in the sequence, but they are also imagined in debate, and how they are imagined affects the range of actions and changes that are possible. In terms of dialectical relations, imagined actions may be realised ('operationalised') in real actions, and thereby imagined change may be realised in real change. Changing the discourses means changing the possibilities for imagined action and change, which means also changing the possibilities for real action and change. I also suggested how the 'epistemological' dialectic of debate connects with a 'relational' dialectic (dialectical relations between discourse and other social elements) and thereby 'ontological' and 'practical' dialectics. In this perspective, debate is seen as a necessary part of action to bring about change, the terms of debate as affecting (constraining/enabling) the possibilities for action and change, and changing the terms of debate as changing those possibilities, either further constraining them, or enabling them to be opened up and extended. But what can these CDA ideas contribute to the political aims of KM? They can perhaps help people grasp how existing discourse can block social change, how changing the 'terms of debate' can open it up, and so how important it is to critique and challenge the terms of debate.

The 'educative' function of politics

Hall and O'Shea (KM Chapter 3: 22) formulate a strategy for left politics and a view of its 'educative' character:

> The left and the Labour Party must take the struggle over common sense seriously. Politics, as Gramsci insisted, is always "educative". We must acknowledge the insecurities which underlie common sense's confusions and contradictions, and harness the intensity and anger. . . . Labour must use every policy issue as an opportunity, not only to examine the pragmatics, but to highlight the underlying principle, slowly building an alternative consensus of "popular philosophy". It must harness to this the already strongly existing sense of unfairness and injustice. In other words, it must engage in a two-way learning process, leading to what Gramsci called "an organic cohesion in which feeling-passion becomes understanding".

Let us rework this in terms of CDA as dialectical reasoning. The fourth sentence ("Labour must. . . ") advocates a way of arguing and deliberating in political debate: in its argumentation over policies, the left should argue about goals and values ("highlight the underlying principle") as well as means to achieve goals ("examine the pragmatics"). It should debate not only with other political positions and arguments but also with "common sense" argumentation. It should "engage in a two-way learning process" which both transforms the "confusions and contradictions" of common sense and "harness[es]" its "feeling-passion", seeking to convert it into "understanding" and to achieve an "organic cohesion" between the two, thereby taking "struggle over common sense seriously" and seeking to shift common sense towards a new consensus. Although they do not formulate it in this way, what Hall and O'Shea are advocating is a shift in the terms of debate, which is at the same time a shift in common sense. The left needs to draw upon common sense to do it: to draw upon the "passion" and "sense of unfairness and injustice" to shift values, but also to convert them into "understanding" by formulating goals and actions which resonate with them. In so doing, the left is also seeking to form political constituencies and political subjects, which do not exist "ready-made. . . they have to actively be constructed" (Chapter 11, 197), as well as political agents to bring about change.

This takes us in the direction of an issue which I do not have space to properly address here: how rhetoric and deliberation are combined in political deliberation. It suggests that while rhetoric is, as generally recognised, to do with persuading people, it is not just a matter of accommodating to or playing upon what they already feel, believe and take for granted. In politics it is, or ought to be, engaging critically and constructively with people's common sense feelings and beliefs in working up practical arguments and policies which they can become the subjects of and agents for. Rhetoric can have a positive and constructive role in political deliberation.

Drawing upon the "feeling-passion" of common sense, e.g., people not just believing and claiming that something is unfair but feeling and being moved by the unfairness, is drawing upon values (in Value premises) and how people evaluate things on the basis of them. But 'values' as we note in Fairclough and Fairclough (2012) is too narrow, 'concerns' would be more comprehensive. People argue from *motives* which animate and drive them, including their passions (which may include greed and gross self-interest); they argue from their emotions and feelings, not just from values arrived at through reasoning; an agent needs to 'care' about the realisation of a value to turn it into a motive for action. There is a difference between acting on the basis of reasons and arguments (and analysis and evidence) and acting on the basis of feelings and passions, but they are not simply alternatives: people argue and deliberate (i.e., evaluate and respond to others' arguments) on the basis of affective concerns, motives, which shape their interpretation of circumstances (and how they 'problematise' them) and the goals and actions which they advocate. This dialectical view of argument as merging reasons and motives, as well as causes, resonates with the Gramscian perspective which informs KM.

But shouldn't the left's attempt to shift the terms of debate also include a shift towards dialectical reasoning? Dialectical reasoning is a powerful political as well as analytic tool which can be of service to would-be political agents (anyone seeking to change reality for the better – politicians, party members, political activists, active citizens), as well as to critical social analysts as I suggested earlier. It starts from critique of discourse, i.e., from things which are largely discernible though not always discerned – problematic features of discourse and arguments. It then seeks to explain such features in terms of less discernible (partly 'underlying') features of existing reality, thereby extending critique beyond discourse to the wider social reality, and identifying what aspects of reality need changing, what change is possible, and how it might be achieved, as a basis for a practical conclusion about what action to take. Critique of discourse (debate) is an effective wedge to open up the wider social reality to analysis/ critique and thereby action/change because the discourse is a part of the wider reality, a step towards action and change which imagines and prefigures them as well as representing and explaining the existing reality. This is not a novel view. As I said earlier, Marx's critical method, drawing upon Aristotle, takes critique of discourse as its point of departure. Moreover, seeing and critiquing argumentation not in isolation but as the beginning of action is the basis for interpreting its dialectical character in a materialist rather than idealist way.

Politicians and political activists are used to deliberating and debating, and identifying and engaging with the arguments of others, but what Hall and O'Shea are proposing is an art of political debate which is not easy to achieve and requires learning, in formal education or practical politics or ideally a combination of the two. So too does dialectical reasoning. Part of what is involved here is changes in schooling (language education) similar to the 'critical language awareness' advocated within CDA as a part of 'education for democracy' in the 1990s (Fairclough 2010), as part of the educational conditions for making radical social change an option.

Gramsci (1995: 297–303) argues that dialectic is a "new way of thinking, a new philosophy", but also "a new technique" which he calls "the technique of thought", which will "provide people with criteria" to "carry out checks and make judgements" and "correct distortions in common sense ways of thinking". It is "as important to teach this technique as it is to teach reading and writing". Dialectical reasoning provides a technique of thought and a way of arguing and deliberating which can identify, explain, critique and open the way to changing the terms of debate, itself as part of a way of acting to change existing reality. It is I think consistent with the Gramscian perspective of KM, and it can be learned and taught and transmitted through left politics in a form which meshes with Hall and O'Shea's view of the struggle over common sense. It is perhaps a way for CDA to contribute to political action to change existing reality for the better.

What would people need to know about dialectical reasoning? These are essential elements.

1   How to recognise an argument. Arguments are often partly implicit, and need to be reconstructed from texts, i.e., formulated in an explicit way.
2   How to identify what type of argument it is.
3   How to identify the premises and conclusion of an argument, including which discourses are drawn upon and what reasons are given.
4   How to evaluate (critically question) a practical argument: its Claim, in terms of its likely consequences; its premises, including values, goals and the representation/ problematisation of circumstances; and the inference from premises to conclusion.
5   How to identify an explanation and its constituent parts (*explanans* and *explanandum*), and how to evaluate it.
6   How to identify reasons, motives and causes, and the connections between them.
7   How to evaluate and critique argumentation as the first step in the sequence: deliberation-decision-action-change.
8   How to develop counter-arguments.
9   How to identify the 'terms of debate' and their limitations, how to approach changing the terms of debate.

Conclusion

I have envisaged people in CDA opening a dialogue with those involved in political action. Often the same person does both, so the dialogue might be in part between different sides of oneself. Working in a transdisciplinary way with colleagues in Sociology or Politics departments can also be seen as opening a dialogue, but the dialogue with politics seems less transient and more a matter of what we do anyway. The perspective of political action should be consistently brought into what we do, and we need more reflection on the connections and the differences between analytical (critical-explanatory) concerns and political concerns. CDA and politics are different but connected, and it is important to insist upon both the connection and the difference to avoid confusion. In terms of the Aristotelian sequence, CDA contributes to deliberation (as does politics), but decision and action are not part of CDA but of political action. However, CDA as dialectical reasoning shows how deliberation enables and constrains decision, action and change, and how they can be opened up by changing the terms of debate.

Acknowledgements

I am grateful for comments on a draft of this chapter by the late Doreen Massey, and my thanks to Isabela Fairclough for discussion of ideas in the chapter and comments on several drafts.

Further reading

Fairclough, N. (2014). Introduction. In *Language and power,* 3rd edn, 1–50. London: Routledge.
This Introduction explains the relationship between the latest version of my approach to CDA, which I am using in this paper, and earlier versions, compares my approach to CDA with three other approaches, and responds to some criticisms of my approach.
Fairclough, N. and Fairclough, I. (2016). Textual analysis. In M. Bevir and R.A.W. Rhodes (eds.), *Routledge handbook of interpretive political science*, 186–198. London: Routledge.
This chapter sets out an approach to analysing political discourse, with a focus upon textual analysis. It gives a view of what analysing texts involves, and of what is distinctive in political texts. It reviews some other approaches to political text analysis, and presents our own with a focus upon analysis of argumentation. It claims that discourse-based interpretive political analysis must include explicit textual analysis – though it often does not.

References

Bhaskar, R. (1989). *Reclaiming reality*. London: Routledge.
Bhaskar, R. (1993). *Dialectic: The pulse of freedom*. London: Verso.
Fairclough, I. and Fairclough, N. (2012). *Political discourse analysis*. London: Routledge.
Fairclough, N. (1989). *Language and power*. London: Longman.
Fairclough, N. (1992). *Discourse and social change*. Cambridge: Polity Press.
Fairclough, N. (1993). Critical discourse analysis and the marketization of public discourse: The universities. *Discourse and Society* 4(2): 133–168.
Fairclough, N. (2010). *Critical discourse analysis,* 2nd edn. London: Longman.
Fairclough, N. (2012). Critical discourse analysis. In J. Gee and M. Handford (eds.), *The Routledge handbook of discourse analysis,* 9–20. London: Routledge.
Fairclough, N. (2013). Critical discourse analysis and critical policy studies. *Critical Policy Studies* 7(2): 177–197.
Fairclough, N. (2014). Introduction. In *Language and power,* 3rd edn, 1–50. London: Routledge.
Fairclough, N. and Graham, P. (2002). Marx as critical discourse analyst: The genesis of a critical method and its relevance to the critique of global capital. *Estudios de Sociolinguistica* 3(1): 185–229. Reprinted in Fairclough (2010), 301–346.
Fairclough, N., Jessop, B. and Sayer, A. (2004). Critical realism and semiosis. In J. Joseph and J. Roberts (eds.), *Realism, discourse and deconstruction,* 23–42. London: Routledge.
Gramsci, A. (1995). *Further selections from the prison notebooks*. London: Lawrence and Wishart.
Hall, S., Massey, D. and Rustin, M. (2015). *After neoliberalism? The Kilburn Manifesto*. London: Lawrence and Wishart.
Jessop, B. (2004). Critical semiotic analysis and cultural political economy. *Critical Discourse Studies* 1(2): 159–174.
Levinson, S. (1992). Activity types and language. In P. Drew and J. Heritage (eds.), *Talk at work: interaction in institutional settings,* 66–100. Cambridge: Cambridge University Press.

2

Socio-cognitive discourse studies

Teun A. van Dijk

Introduction

In the summer of 2014, on July 28, half a million British readers of the *Daily Telegraph* were served the usual 'view' of their newspaper on immigration:

Coalition deserves credit for progress on tackling unchecked immigration

David Cameron's Government is finally taking steps to stop abuses of immigration system that were ignored by his predecessors

Voters consistently tell opinion pollsters that immigration is among their biggest concerns – so it is incumbent upon our political leaders to address the issue. The last government patently failed to do so, presiding over the greatest inflow of foreign nationals in this country's history while doing nothing to plan for their arrival.

Until 1997, most voters believed that successive governments, by and large, had operated sensible immigration controls. However, Labour's decision to open the jobs market – not least to workers from the old Warsaw Pact bloc – saw the system weakened to the point of collapse. Putting it back together, and reviving public confidence in the UK's ability to control its own borders, has been a tall order.

In his article on the page opposite, David Cameron argues that the Coalition has begun this process, by clamping down on abuses and making sure we take in the right people who will benefit the country. He also announces new measures to tackle the "pull" that an easily accessible benefits system exerts: instead of unemployed EU workers being able to claim Jobseekers' Allowance or child benefit for six months, that will be reduced to a maximum of three. Recruitment agencies will also be required to advertise jobs in the UK and not just exclusively abroad.

By itself, this will not be enough to fix the problem – the Government is hampered by EU rules and, as Mr Cameron says, the failures of a welfare and education system that has produced too few qualified workers. Ministers still look unlikely to reach their target of reducing net immigration to "tens of thousands" before the next election. But they certainly deserve much credit for their sustained efforts to get to grips with a problem their predecessors simply ignored.

A *systematic discourse analysis* of this editorial will attend to many of the typical features of this media genre, such as its characteristic overall organisation, its (political) topics or the argumentative or rhetorical strategies employed to persuasively present this 'view' to the readers. As with many newspaper genres, this editorial also has a headline, in this case summarising the newspaper's opinion as defended in the editorial, printed on top and in bold characters. In the online newspaper version, the article is accompanied by a picture of UKIP leader Nigel Farage (not reproduced here) under the headline. More generally, as is the case for all coherent text and talk, the editorial has the usual local syntactic and semantic structures that define its grammaticality and meaningfulness as a discourse. Among many aspects of discourse semantics, the expression "*stop abuses*" in the headline presupposes that there *were* such abuses of the immigration system under the previous (Labour) government. Among many more properties of editorials, such a discourse analysis would pay attention to the way such a 'view' is formulated as an opinion or appraisal, by such lexical expressions as "*deserves credit*" in the very headline. The other chapters in this *Handbook* detail these kinds of systematic and explicit discourse analysis (see also Bhatia, Flowerdew and Jones 2008; Blommaert 2004; Tannen, Hamilton and Schiffrin 2015; Titscher et al. 2000; van Dijk 2011; Wooffitt 2005).

Critical Discourse Studies (CDS) typically goes beyond such a classical study of the structural properties of text or talk, and relates these discourse structures to social structures. It may begin to identify the author(s) of the text as editors of a newspaper as a powerful media organisation, able to influence the opinions of hundreds of thousands of readers. More specifically, such a critical analysis will remind of the well-known fact that the *Telegraph* is a conservative newspaper, and may be expected to support a conservative government. That analysing such a broader sociopolitical context of this editorial is relevant for discourse analysis, and not an irrelevant fact of 'background', may be shown by relating the opinion of the editorial with broader policies of the media organisation, as well as those of the ruling Conservative Party. In other words, such a study of the sociopolitical context of this editorial is carried out in order to be able to explain *why* the text has the appraisal structure it displays.

CDS not only engages in social and political analyses of the context of text and talk, but more specifically takes an explicit stand (also a 'view') on the abuse of power a large media organisation may have by manipulating the attitudes of readers on immigration. It explains that and how the symbolic elites of politics and the mass media are able to control public discourse and attitudes and thus may contribute to the reproduction of racism and xenophobia in the country (see Fairclough 1995; Hart 2011, 2015; Hart and Cap 2014; Hart and Lukes 2007; Jäger and Link 1993; Toolan 2002; van Dijk 2008b; van Leeuwen 2008; Weiss and Wodak 2003; Wodak and Meyer 2015).

Socio-cognitive discourse studies

In the structural and critical discourse studies mentioned above and explained in detail in most of the chapters of this *Handbook,* there is still a crucial dimension missing: the **socio-cognitive** dimension. Socio-cognitive Discourse Studies (SCDS) more broadly relates discourse structures to social structures via a complex socio-cognitive interface.

As in Cognitive Linguistics, SCDS critically describes the cognitive aspects of the use of some concepts or metaphors (e.g., as expressed in *inflow of foreign nationals*) (see, e.g., Croft and Cruse

2004; Evans and Green 2006; Hart 2015; Hart and Lukes 2007; Lakoff 1987, 2002). But more broadly, SCDS deals with the ongoing communicative Common Ground and the shared social knowledge as well as the attitudes and ideologies of language users as current participants of the communicative situation and as members of social groups and communities (see references below).

As we shall see in more detail below, a socio-cognitive approach not only makes explicit the fundamental role of mental representations, but also shows that many structures of discourse itself can only (completely) be described in terms of various cognitive notions, especially those of information, beliefs or knowledge of participants. Among many other discourse structures, this is the case for phonological stress, syntactic word order, topic and focus, the structures of propositions, local coherence relations between propositions, pronouns and co-reference, global meanings or topics of discourse, indexical expressions, evidentials, terms of appraisal, metaphors, frames, implications, presuppositions and argumentations.

SCDS does so in terms of explicit psychological theories of mental representations, such as individual mental models of journalists or other language users, and the ways these models *mediate* between shared social cognition (knowledge, attitudes, ideologies), societal structures and actual text and talk. Thus, whereas most CDS studies describe and explain discourse in terms of its social and political contexts, SCDS goes one crucial step further and includes a *cognitive interface* between discourse and society. It claims that there is no direct link between such different structures as those of discourse and society, and that social or political structures can only affect text and talk through the *minds* of language users. This is possible because social members represent both social structures as well as discourse structures in their minds, and thus are able to relate these mentally before expressing them in actual text and talk.

A socio-cognitive approach to discourse is a particular application of a more general theory or philosophy of *social constructionism,* which holds that social and political 'reality' are constructions of social members (Burr 2003; Parker 1998).

Different from some other forms of social constructionism, such as Discursive Psychology (see Potter and Wetherell 1987), this approach not only holds that such 'constructions' are mental representations, implemented by the brain, but also that these mental processes and representations should be taken seriously and analysed in detail, for instance in terms of contemporary advances in the cognitive sciences.

It has often been recalled in contemporary discourse studies that Discourse Analysis (DA) is not a *method* of analysis, but an area or discipline of study, using many different qualitative and quantitative methods. Similarly, it has repeatedly been stated that CDA is not a method either but a critical attitude while doing DA, also using many methods, for instance by focusing on discursive forms of power abuse, as was signalled above for the *Telegraph.*

The same should be affirmed for SCDS. Socio-cognitive Discourse Studies is not a method either, but may use many different methods. It is a multidisciplinary type of CDS relating discourse structures with social structures through a cognitive interface. The cognitive component of this type of multidisciplinary discourse study may be methodologically as diverse as its analysis of discourse or social structures. Hence, instead of speaking of socio-cognitive discourse analysis, we prefer to speak of *Socio-cognitive Discourse Studies* (SCDS) – as we have done above – admitting many different theories, analytical or ethnographic methods, experimental procedures, and practical applications, carried out within a critical perspective.

The cognitive interface

Since the characteristic property of SCDS is its emphasis on the cognitive interface between discursive and social structures, this chapter selectively focuses on this component, also because basic notions of cognition and social psychology are less known in the study of discourse. Yet, a section of a single chapter obviously cannot possibly provide a fully fledged introduction to all relevant psychological notions involved, and hence only presents a very brief account of those concepts we need for Socio-cognitive Discourse Studies.

Although each aspect of socio-cognitive theory would require lengthy explanation, we summarise the theory in terms of its major notions, as follows (for details, see, e.g., Graesser, Gernsbacher and Goldman 2003; van Dijk and Kintsch 1983; van Oostendorp and Zwaan 1994):

Mind, memory and discourse processing

a   **Cognitive processes**, such as thinking, perceiving, knowing, believing, understanding, interpreting, planning, hoping, feeling, etc., take place in the **mind** or **memory** of individual **social actors as members** of social groups and communities.

b   These cognitive processes in memory are implemented in (various regions of) the **brain**, (as yet only partly) made explicit in neuropsychology, further ignored in this chapter. Yet relevant to know about the relation between discourse and the brain is that brain lesions, e.g., caused by accidents, illness or deterioration (e.g., Alzheimer's) may cause aphasia or other linguistic and discursive **disorders**.

c   Cognitive processes in memory operate on specific cognitive structures usually called (mental) **representations**, e.g., by forming, changing, storing, or (de)activating them. Thus, thoughts, knowledge, beliefs, interpretations, plans, attitudes or ideologies are different kinds of mental representation.

d   Cognitive processes and representations cause and **control all human action and interaction** and hence also all language use and discourse. We partly describe and explain discourse in terms of these 'underlying' properties of the mind.

e   Generally, a distinction is made between **Short Term Memory (STM)** and **Long Term Memory (LTM).** Because of its specific functions, STM is also called **Working Memory (WM),** where 'online' processes of attention, understanding or the production of action take place, often in fractions of seconds and with the limited information stored in the memory buffer(s) of WM. LTM stores the results of these processes, for instance in the form of knowledge or beliefs, which may be activated and used again by WM for future operations, for instance when we remember something or when we need that 'information' for perception, action or discourse.

f   **Discourse production and comprehension** are very complex cognitive processes executed ongoingly ('online') and *in parallel* by specific operations in Working Memory, for instance for the processing of sounds, images, phonemes, morphemes, lexical items, syntactic structures, local and global meanings, overall patterns of text or talk (superstructures) and structures and strategies of interaction. At present we only have very limited insight into the details of these processes of WM and their (limited) memory resources or timing, especially for the higher levels of discourse.

g   One of the (many) problems to be resolved of these many complex parallel processes involved in the production and understanding of discourse is how they are **controlled** and **coordinated** in fractions of a second and with apparently limited memory resources. Just a summary of all processes involved would fill pages of description (or computer program code) – ranging from phonemes, graphemes or image parts on the 'lower' levels to producing or understanding overall meanings, topics, conversational interaction or narrative or persuasive strategies at the 'higher' levels of parallel processing. For complex discourse, part of this **Control System** probably consists of overall **semantic macro-structures** ('topics') that control the production and comprehension of local sentence meanings (propositions).

h   The processes of language use and discourse activate and apply specific **linguistic and discursive knowledge systems** of units, rules and strategies in LTM, such as those of grammar, the lexicon, local and global semantics, pragmatics, conversation and other forms of interaction.

i   Whereas many of the concepts and processes of memory and discourse processing mentioned above are (partly) made explicit in **psycholinguistics,** the **cognitive psychology of discourse** specifically also focuses on the description and explanation of **'higher' level processing** of discourse. Such higher level processes may involve the establishment of local coherence between meanings (propositions) of sentences and its expression in various types of cohesion or co-reference (e.g., pronouns), the overall coherence of topics and their expression in headlines, titles or summaries, the schematic overall organisation (superstructures) of stories, argumentation, news or other genres, or the complex local and global coordination of speech acts and conversational interaction.

Personal cognition: mental models

j   Whereas traditionally the semantics of language and discourse was limited to the description of local or global meanings, for instance in terms of propositions, cognitive psychology has shown that such meanings are based on underlying **mental models**.

k   Mental models are *subjective* representations of events or situations in **Episodic or Autobiographical Memory** (EM), the personal part of LTM where we store our ongoing and past personal experiences. If we observe, participate in, or read or hear about an event, we ongoingly construe a mental model of that event.

l   Since we observe, participate or talk about events many thousands of times in our lives, mental models have a **standard schematic structure** of a limited number of categories that allow very fast processing, probably developed during human evolution, such as Setting (Place, Time), Participants (and their Identities, Roles and Relationships), Event or Action (and its Intention or Purpose). Such a schema allows us to 'analyse' and understand a situation or event in fractions of seconds and then take appropriate action, as is also the case in conversation.

m   **Producing a meaningful discourse** about an event, such as a story or news article, involves the (partial) expression of a mental model of that event. Similarly, **understanding such a discourse** consists in the construction or updating of a mental model of the event.

n   Mental models are **individual, personal, subjective and multi-modal**. They not only subjectively represent a situation or an event, but also opinions and emotions, and partly in terms of vision, sounds, gestures, motor movements, etc., as processed by different parts of the brain. Hence traditional notions such as (possibly different) speaker or hearer meaning of the 'same' discourse, are accounted for by the different personal mental models of the participant language users.

o   The **direct communicative intention** of much discourse is the transmission of the mental model of speakers/writers. Hearers/readers, however, construe their own, possibly (quite) different 'interpretation' of such discourse in terms of their own mental model. The little we later **remember** of a discourse are fragments (usually only the higher level macrostructure representing main topics) of our mental model of a discourse, and not of what was actually said or meant by the speaker or writer.

p   Language users not only construe mental models of the events or situations they talk, write, read or hear *about,* but also of the very communicative situation *in which* they ongoingly participate. These mental models are called **context models,** or simply **contexts** (van Dijk 2008a, 2009). They make sure that discourses (and their speech acts and interactions) are **appropriate** in the current communicative situation. This is a specific form of **adaptation,** as is the case for all human interaction (more or less well) adapted to the social situation or the natural or physical environment. Whereas mental models representing what discourse is about (refers to) may be called **semantic models,** context models may also be called **pragmatic models**.

q   Context models are specific instances of our **ongoing experiences** in which we represent (and hence understand) the social situation in which we are currently involved and active (or that define our **plans** for future action). These more general **models of experience** are probably shaped by evolutionary processes of adaptation: humans can only survive when they are able to (more or less) appropriately but efficiently analyse, understand and act upon current social situations or natural environments. In our everyday lives, much of this modelling has been automatised and only partly conscious, as is the case for the actions we perform in them.

r   As is the case for all mental models, also context models consist of a **schematic structure,** such as Setting, Participants and Action, but then are specified for communicative actions, speech acts or conversational interaction, and Participants with communicative identities, roles and relations. The information of these context categories must be **relevant** for ongoing discourse. There are many *socially* relevant aspects of interaction (such as the appearance or clothes of participants) which are however not (always) *communicatively* relevant as part of the pragmatics discourse, and hence do not systematically influence its appropriateness (as is the case for current time and place, the identities of speakers or their relations, intentions or purposes).

s   Producing discourse, thus, not only consists in forming or activating a semantic model of an event we want to speak or write about, but *before that* of planning, construing and **dynamically adapting** a context model: where, when, with whom, as what, how, and with what purpose we are right now or soon talking or writing. In other words, pragmatic models control the communicative expression of semantic models: Indeed, it depends on the communicative situation *what* we talk about with whom, and especially also *how* we (should) do so. Thus, apart from speech acts and appropriateness in general, context models control the **discourse genre** and **style** of discourse.

Social cognition: knowledge, attitudes and ideologies

t   Social members not only produce or understand discourse as individual persons, with their own personal history, autobiographical experiences, knowledge, opinions and emotions, but also as **social actors and as members** of groups, communities, organisations or institutions (Augoustinos, Walker and Donaghue 2006; Fiske and Taylor 2007; Hamilton 2005).

u   As is the case for their **knowledge of language and discourse,** shared with other members of linguistic and discursive communities, social actors also share **sociocultural knowledge of the world** with other members of various epistemic communities, as well as **attitudes, ideologies, norms and values** with other members of various kinds of social groups. These forms of **social cognition** are generally located in what is traditionally called **Semantic Memory,** part of LTM, but perhaps better called **Social Memory**.

v   The **acquisition and application of world knowledge** is crucial for all cognitive processes of perception, understanding, action, interaction, language use, communication and discourse.

w   In **discourse understanding** such knowledge is activated and applied in the understanding of words, sentence meanings and overall discourse meanings, and in the **construction of personal mental models**. And vice versa, the understanding of discourse and the formation of mental models of specific events may be generalised and abstracted from in the **acquisition or modification of generic knowledge** of the world. Knowledge is presupposed, expressed, conveyed, corrected, etc. in many ways in nearly all structures at all levels in discourse, such as *stress* distribution or word order to organise *topic* (known) and *focus* (new or more salient) information in sentences, the expression of knowledge sources in *evidentials,* the use of *presuppositions* and *implications* or the *rights* of participants to tell about new events in *conversation.*

x   As yet we have only fragmentary insight into the location(s) of socioculturally shared knowledge in the brain and in their **structures or organisations in memory,** e.g., in terms of *hierarchical relations between concepts* (e.g., a car is a vehicle), or as *frames, stereotypes* or more dynamic *scripts* or *scenarios.* It has also been proposed that, like mental models of concrete events, such generic knowledge is *multi-modal,* e.g., involving vision, sound, smell, sensorimotor and emotional information (e.g., what we know or have experienced about cars).

y   Generally ignored in linguistics and cognitive psychology, but extensively dealt with in the social sciences (which in turn usually ignore a cognitive approach), social actors may also act and communicate as **members of social movements or ideological groups,** and share **attitudes** about fundamental social issues, such as immigration, abortion or terrorism (Eagly and Chaiken 1993). Although extensively studied in social psychology, the detailed cognitive structures of these attitudes are at present unknown. As is the case for generic knowledge, also socially shared attitudes may be applied and specified in the personal opinions of the mental models of group members – and finally (partly) expressed in discourse.

z   Finally, these social attitudes may themselves be organised by more fundamental underlying ('positive' or 'negative') **ideologies**, such as socialism, feminism, neoliberalism, racism and anti-racism, militarism and pacifism, and so on. Although also the cognitive location and organisation of ideologies is at present unknown, they probably feature **fundamental categories** defining social groups, such as the identity, actions, goals, norms and values and resources of a group, as well as their (often polarised) relations with other groups (allies or enemies). This **polarisation** between *Us* (*ingroup*) and *Them* (*outgroup*) may also appear in the specific social attitudes, and then in the mental models and the discourses expressing such models (van Dijk 1998).

This brief summary of the socio-cognitive processes and representations involved in language use and discourse ignores many details, as well as details at present unknown in psychology. Yet, the theoretical framework does show not only how cognition is involved in (the processing of) actual talk or text, but also why it is needed in the very *description and analysis* of many discourse structures:

(i)   **Stress, intonation and word order** of sentences depend on what *information* is currently known, focused on, new or unexpected, and as currently shared an dynamically changed as *Common Ground* among participants.

(ii)   **Meanings** of words, sentences or sequences of sentences are produced on the basis of the grammar and other linguistic and discursive knowledge of language users, and on the basis of the shared generic, sociocultural knowledge of members of a epistemic communities.

(iii) **Coherence** relations between sentences or turns of conversation may be partly expressed by linguistic or discursive forms of cohesion (e.g., by pronouns or definite articles), but are based on and defined by relations between participants or events in underlying *mental models* of language users.

(iv)   **Opinion and emotion words**, as well as volume or intonation, are expressions of personal opinions and emotions represented in (multi-modal) *mental models*.

(v)   **Global topics or themes** (or frames, etc.) as semantic macrostructures are planned and interpreted as the macrostructures of underlying *mental models,* and control the sequential online production or interpretation of the local meanings of sentences.

(vi)   **Deictic or indexical expressions** refer to or presuppose information in the schematic categories of the *context model:* Time/Place/Perspective, Participant (Identities, Roles and Relations), current social or communicative action, as well as the Intentions and current Knowledge (Common Ground) of the participants.

(vii) **Speech acts** are produced on the basis of appropriateness conditions defined in terms of the properties of *context models* (such as the knowledge, wishes, intentions or power of the participants) – as is the case for expressions of **politeness**.

(viii) **Evidentials,** whether as specific morphemes in some languages, or as more explicit expressions in many languages (e.g., *I saw, heard, read, etc. that. . .; She said that. . .*), are expressions of how knowledge expressed in discourse was acquired, for instance in terms of current or old experience or context models (for detail, see e.g., Aikhenvald 2004).

(ix)   **The conventional, schematic, canonical structures (superstructures)** of various discourse genres are planned and understood as expressions of shared cultural knowledge of the schematic organisation of such discourse genres, as is the case for **narrative** or **argumentation,** or the conventional organisation of **news reports** or **scientific articles**.

(x)   **Metaphors** are based on the multi-modal structure of mental *models of experience.* Thus large numbers of refugees or immigrants may be (negatively and manipulatively) described as WAVES because of the anxiety of the experience of drowning in huge waves – as well as on the basis of general, *sociocultural knowledge* of waves – as we shall see in more detail below in the analysis of the editorial of the *Telegraph*.

(xi)   **Ideological polarisation** at all levels of discourse, emphasising the Good properties of Us (ingroup) and Bad properties of Them (outgroup), express underlying attitudes (e.g., on immigration or abortion) and ideologies (e.g., of racism or sexism), via particular, personal mental models of specific events, for instance as polarised topics, lexicon, metaphors, images, etc.

Although also this list is far from complete, it may have become obvious that many properties of words, sentences and discourses cannot be accounted for without at least partial description of properties of underlying mental representations, such as models, knowledge and other forms of social cognition – besides the socioculturally shared knowledge of grammar and discourse genres – of individual language users on the one hand, and of social groups or communities on the other hand.

The fundamental role of knowledge

At several points above we have mentioned the role of knowledge in the account of discourse structure. Although many details of the cognitive representation (and neuropsychological processes) of knowledge are still unknown, it must be stressed that the core of the socio-cognitive account of discourse consists of the personal and socially shared knowledge of language users as social actors and members of epistemic communities (for details, see van Dijk 2014).

We have seen that all our everyday experiences, and hence our personal knowledge of events, are stored as subjective, multi-modal **mental models**. These mental models control topic and comment, local coherence as well as the contents of stories, among many other discourse structures.

However, such mental models, as well as the ways these are (partly) expressed in discourse, are in turn based on **socioculturally shared generic or historical knowledge,** organised in many different (and as yet only partly understood) ways in memory.

In *didactic (expository, etc.) discourse,* such discourse structures may also be expressed directly, for instance in explanations, definitions, textbooks, etc. Hence, not all discourse is based on mental models.

Generic knowledge, thus, may be directly *acquired* by didactic discourse, or by generalisation and abstraction from mental models of personal experience or as expressed in stories or news reports. For instance, most of what we know about terrorism in general is derived from specific mental models of news reports in the media. And, vice versa, once acquired, such generic knowledge is again *applied* or *instantiated* in the formation of new mental models construed in the understanding of new stories.

Context models, subjectively representing the relevant aspects of ongoing communicative situations, crucially have a *Knowledge Device.* This device at each moment 'calculates' what knowledge recipients (probably) have: **Common Ground** (see also Clark 1996). Such a device is able to operate (although we cannot look in the minds of recipients) because it is based on (i) shared sociocultural knowledge between participants as members of the same Epistemic Community, (ii) knowledge derived from previous encounters, conversations or emails (mental models and context models), e.g., among family members, friends or acquaintances, (iii) information derived from mutual observation and participation in the same communicative situation (as defined by the current state of the dynamic context model, (iv) information derived from what has been said or written before in the same discourse (i.e., the mental model construed thus far).

Complex, efficient strategies allow language users to efficiently process all these knowledge sources and at each point of a conversation infer, more or less correctly, what the recipients already know. It is this the information of the Epistemic Device that ongoingly controls the production of the discourse structures we have mentioned above: phonological stress (new or salient information tends to have more stress than known information), word order (in English often known information comes first), topic and comment, definite articles, implications and presuppositions, etc. The general **epistemic and pragmatic strategy** of discourse is that knowledge that is supposed to be known by the recipients tends to remain implicit, less prominent or presupposed.

These general epistemic strategies apply for all discourse genres, but some discourse genres will tend to be more explicit than others. Hence, in conversations among family members or friends who know each other well, discourse obviously will tend to be much more implicit than conversations among strangers, or news reports in the press.

Besides these many epistemic strategies, text and talk may further be controlled by various **social rules, norms and values.** We may not tell what we know to anyone in any situation. Thus, speakers who have personal experiences of an event usually have more *right* or *priority* to tell a story than others who don't have such an experience (as an epistemic source) (Stivers, Mondada and Steensig 2011). In some situations, such as exams or interrogations, we *must* tell what we know. Doctors sometimes do not tell all they know about the health conditions of patients. The Official Secrets Act in the UK, and similar laws in many countries, also limit what (secret) knowledge may not be divulged. Newspapers receive vast amounts of information, but only publish a fragment of such information. Thus, we read much more about terrorism or migration in the newspaper than about 'our' racism or sexism.

In other words, the *management of knowledge* in discourse is a vast and complex problem, dealt with in various forms of **Epistemic Discourse Studies,** which describes and explains what knowledge is made explicit, detailed, emphasised, implied, presupposed, suggested, hidden, manipulated in and by discourse.

The *Telegraph* editorial and its cognitive basis

With the theoretical framework presented above, many of the structures of the editorial of the *Telegraph* can now be accounted for in socio-cognitive (and later in more sociopolitical) terms. Again, we give a summary of examples, because a complete description would need dozens, if not hundreds of pages:

Media discourse

The editorial is a specific genre of media discourse, and as such planned and executed on the basis of the generic knowledge and the specific (ongoing) *context model* of the journalist who during writing knows current *time* (day, hour) and *place* (UK) in order to be able to write on *current* affairs and within a *deadline,* and in her or his professional *role* as journalist or editor, and *employee* of a media organisation, and for *readers* of that organisation, with the *intention* to inform or influence them, and on the basis of shared (Common Ground) *knowledge* about immigration in the UK (for details on media discourse, see, e.g., Bell 1991; Richardson 2007; van Dijk 1988a,b).

Editorial

More specifically, the journalist of the editorial presupposes specific political knowledge, and formulates a personal or institutional *opinion,* based on underlying conservative *attitudes* on immigration and general conservative *ideologies* against foreigners, on the one hand, and against Labour, on the other hand. These underlying context models, event models – and their specification in terms of opinions – control the evaluative (appraisal) expressions in the editorial. On the other hand, editorials are a *persuasive, argumentative genre,* and hence the *discursive knowledge* of the journalist of that genre controls the argumentative structures of the editorial (see also Le 2010).

Let us now focus on some of the more specific structures of the editorial:

(1) Coalition deserves credit for progress on tackling unchecked immigration

> **David Cameron's Government is finally taking steps to stop abuses of immigration system that were ignored by his predecessors**

This compound **Headline** summarises the (i) overall meaning (semantic macrostructure) of the editorial, as represented in the current mental model of the journalist about the event (the tackling of immigration by the coalition government of the UK), and (ii) the overall positive opinion (as expressed by **positive appraisal terms** *deserves credit, progress, tackling, finally*) of the journalist or newspaper as represented in their event model. Indeed, another newspaper or other readers might express the 'same' event in another mental model, with another opinion, and expressed in another editorial or discourse. The **metaphors** *tackling* and *taking steps* express the positive aspects of the mental model representing positive government actions and policies in terms of challenge and as forward movement. The (positive) mental model of the journalist is a specification of the (i) positive attitude shared by the journalist about the current government and (ii) the negative attitude about immigration, both based on a conservative ideology. **Presuppositions** as expressed by *unchecked, abuses, ignored by predecessors,* express a negative opinion about (previous) Labour governments in the event model, as well as immigration, both based again on underlying polarised attitudes and ideologies between Us/Ingroup (Conservatives, English) and Them/Outgroups (Labour, Immigrants). Similarly, the **temporal adverb** *finally* presupposes the information in the mental model of the journalist that this government action comes after a long time (of ignorance of former governments) and also implies a positive evaluation of the current government. Although the previous governments are not explicitly mentioned, their identity is **implied,** and hence part of the mental models of both journalist (and readers, based on their general political knowledge) that these previous governments were Labour governments.

(2)   Voters consistently tell opinion pollsters that immigration is among their biggest concerns – so it is incumbent upon our political leaders to address the issue.

As is the case for all discourse, and hence also for this editorial, but not requiring further analysis here, the production and comprehension of this editorial and this paragraph presupposes vast amounts of socioculturally shared knowledge, e.g., about politics and policies (voters, polls, leaders, government) and about immigration. This paragraph more specifically is based on a **mental model** of the journalist about (negative) past and (positive) current immigration policy. The model also features an **opinion** in the form of a recommendation (*address the issue of immigration*), as is typical of the genre of editorials (and known and expected by the readers). This recommendation is based on a more general political **norm** (*incumbent*), expressed here in the form of an argumentation: if voters are concerned about an issue, political leaders should address it. Such a norm may be part of underlying **attitudes** about elections (*voters, polls*) and policies (*address the issue*) and a more general democratic **ideology,** featuring the will of the people. At the same time, this sentence may be read as expressing a **populist ideology,** featuring attitudes about the determining influence of polls on government policy. Since it is known that the *Telegraph* does not exactly favour such people power for all issues, but does so for the issue of immigration, the application of a populist ideology here specifically controls a mental model featuring a *negative opinion* about immigration – as all readers will understand it in their mental models, although the editorial itself doesn't say so in this first sentence. Hence, discourses are like icebergs, of which much implied information is present in the underlying mental models of the participants but not in the 'surface' of discourse itself. Such a negative opinion is consistent with conservative attitudes and ideologies, and since (on the basis of information of the context model) the *Telegraph* is a conservative newspaper, readers will be able to derive an implication in their mental model even when the editorial is not explicit.

(3) The last government patently failed to do so, presiding over the greatest inflow of foreign nationals in this country's history while doing nothing to plan for their arrival.

We have seen above that ideologies tend to be polarised between positive US (ingroup) and negative THEM (outgroup). This sentence, expressing a mental model about the policies of the past (Labour) government patently does so in a (very) negative description of Labour governments – again without mentioning Labour explicitly, but only indirectly referring to the "last government". Again, such an interpretation requires readers to activate their political-historical knowledge to make this inference. The negative description of the previous Labour government not only expresses a negative opinion in the mental model of the (journalist of) the *Telegraph,* applying a more general negative attitude about Labour, itself specifying a Conservative ideology, but it does so with rhetorical emphasis with the use of specific lexical items: *patently, greatest inflow (. . .) in history, doing nothing.* Indeed, underlying ideological polarisation precisely shows in emphasising the negative properties of THEM.

As we have seen above, the **metaphor** expressed as *the greatest inflow* is the standard one for the description of the arrival of many immigrants, namely immigration represented as a vast and menacing FLOOD in which we all may drown, in this case rhetorically enhanced by a **historical comparison** (*greatest of history*). These are precisely the – very concrete – (multimodal) mental models conservative media and political discourse use to oppose immigration, because they create fear among the population and thus are able to **manipulate** both the population (voters) as well as government policies.

(4) Until 1997, most voters believed that successive governments, by and large, had operated sensible immigration controls. However, Labour's decision to open the jobs market – not least to workers from the old Warsaw Pact bloc – saw the system weakened to the point of collapse. Putting it back together, and reviving public confidence in the UK's ability to control its own borders, has been a tall order.

As is often the case for editorials, this paragraph **reminds** the readers of a previous government and (immigration) policies, by activating an old mental model many readers may no longer remember. Again we find the ideologically polarised negative (*weakened, collapse,* etc.) opinion about Labour policies, as opposed to *sensible* policies (of Conservative governments).

Although the underlying (conservative) political ideology primarily is used to discredit Labour and to support the current Conservative government, this paragraph as well as the whole editorial is specifically focused on the issue of immigration, and more specifically on *controls* of immigration. This implies that immigration must be limited (against the *opening* of the job market by Labour), a normative mental model, applying a negative attitude about immigration and immigrants, itself based on a conservative ideology.

The **metaphor** of *opening* the job market, and hence the country, represents these as a BUILDING, as is also the case for the *system* which is metaphorically described as being at the point of *collapse*. As is the case for the WAVE and FLOOD metaphors for immigration (fear to drown), the COLLAPSE metaphor construes concrete mental models with emotions of fear (to be crushed by immigrants). The sequence of expressions controlled by mental models applying populist ideologies here features *public confidence,* and the metaphor expressed as *reviving* (presupposing that such confidence was nearly dead).

(5) In his article on the page opposite, David Cameron argues that the Coalition has begun this process, by clamping down on abuses and making sure we take in the right people who will benefit the country. He also announces new measures to tackle the "pull" that an easily accessible benefits system exerts: instead of unemployed EU workers being able to claim Jobseekers' Allowance or child benefit for six months, that will be reduced to a maximum of three. Recruitment agencies will also be required to advertise jobs in the UK and not just exclusively abroad.

After the rhetorically emphasised expression of the underlying negative mental models of earlier Labour immigration policies, the ideological polarisation in this paragraph predictably emphasises the positive policies of the current Conservative government. Interestingly, and quite uniquely, the paragraph deictically (*opposite page*) – and hence expressing the context model of both journalist and readers – refers to an article in the same newspaper by Conservative Leader David Cameron himself, summarised and supported in the editorial. In other words, the **ideological alignment** of the *Telegraph* with the Conservative government could not be more explicit – at least on the issue of immigration policy.

As before, the ideological polarisation not only is represented and expressed between Conservative and Labour, but also between Conservative/Us/We English as ingroup and Them/immigrants as outgroup, e.g., by emphasising negative actions of THEM: *abuses.* Government action **metaphorically** represented and expressed as *clamping down* in such a case implies a positive **value**, because it is an energetic way to counter something negative (abuses).

The underlying immigration attitude of the *Telegraph* is then made explicit by **presupposing** that a positive immigration policy only admits the *right* people, defined as people who *benefit* the country. Again, the explicit positive appraisal terms express underlying values that **polarise** the **attitude** on immigration between *right* and *wrong* immigrants, and policies that *benefit* or *harm* the country.

The rest of the paragraph summarises the new Conservative immigration policy (as set out by Cameron), and – as elsewhere in the editorial – features several interesting **implications** and **presuppositions**. For instance, the expression *the "pull" of easily accessible benefits* presupposes that there are or were such easily accessible benefits, and that such benefits do exercise such "pull" – presuppositions which at the same time apply that the ease of getting benefits is bad – a normal specification of a negative value in a conservative attitude about benefits, itself dominated by a conservative ideology. The rest of the policy also implies limitation (*allowances*) from six to three months, as a specification of the general conservative value of attitudes about immigration: Reduction.

(6) By itself, this will not be enough to fix the problem – the Government is hampered by EU rules and, as Mr Cameron says, the failures of a welfare and education system that has produced too few qualified workers. Ministers still look unlikely to reach their target of reducing net immigration to "tens of thousands" before the next election. But they certainly deserve much credit for their sustained efforts to get to grips with a problem their predecessors simply ignored.

The final paragraph of the editorial again expresses an opinion, as part of the *Telegraph's* model of the current situation in the UK, **presupposing** that there is a problem and that this problem must be fixed. But in this case, the problem is not attributed to Labour, but to EU rules, consistent with the Telegraph's negative attitude about the EU. Interesting is the observation on the (alleged) failures of the welfare and education system in the UK, because it is not explicitly attributed to Labour, as could be expected in the negative ideological logic of the editorial. But continuing the expressions of the general attitude on immigration, the newspaper seems to agree with the aim of a significant reduction of immigration. Finally, the **ideological polarisation** between Conservative and Labour is again specified by the positive attitude about the current government with the explicit evaluation expressed as *deserve much credit, sustained efforts* and *get to grips,* and the negative attitude about Labour by repeating the evaluation that it *ignored* the problem of immigration – again presupposing that indeed there is a problem.

Conclusions of the socio-cognitive analysis

In this brief socio-cognitive analysis of some of the discursive structures of this editorial in the *Telegraph,* we have been able to observe how these structures are controlled by underlying models, knowledge, attitudes and ideologies. Global and local semantic coherence is controlled by a mental model representing policies of the current government about immigration, itself based on general, sociocultural knowledge about politics, policies, voters and governments, on the one hand, and on immigration on the other hand. Indeed, such a coherence could not be explained merely in terms of the meaning of words, but requires description and explanation in terms of underlying mental representations.

Secondly, consistent with its general genre properties (as applied in the context model controlling its appropriate production and comprehension), the editorial also formulates opinions and recommendations, and these are expressed on the basis of current opinions of the mental model of the current policies about immigration. This model is itself controlled by underlying conservative attitudes and ideologies, polarising between Good Conservatives and Bad Labour, on the one hand, and between Good UK and Bad immigration (and even between good and bad immigrants), on the other. The lexical appraisal system and its coherence are thus based on the opinions in the mental model. These opinions are applications in the current situation of more general underlying *norms* (such as those of populist democracy) and *values* (about good and bad government in general, and about immigration policies in particular). The rhetorical enhancement of these appraisals finally express the nature of ideological ingroup-outgroup polarisation in discourse, namely by enhancing Our good things and Their bad things.

Many of the semantic properties of the editorial also need a more explicit socio-cognitive analysis, as is the case for the *implications* and the *presuppositions* in the article – as defined by their presence in the mental model but not as expressed in the text. The same is true for the usual metaphors, e.g., about immigration and government actions against it, namely in terms of a threatening FLOOD in which we may all drown, if not for the energetic policies of the Conservative governments.

This kind of socio-cognitive analysis shows first of all that a mere discourse analysis of topics, themes, local meanings, lexical items or appraisals only yields very incomplete insights into the meanings and functions of the editorial. Crucial is to show and explain not only how it is produced or understood, but to specify the more detailed layers of cognitive control of the current mental model of the journalist, and how this mental model is itself controlled by socially shared attitudes about immigration, the Conservatives and Labour, and how these attitudes themselves are fundamentally controlled by underlying conservative ideologies. Obviously, these attitudes and ideologies not only are relevant to describe and explain the current editorial but more generally the opinions (part of models of specific events and situations) as expressed in other editorials.

Obviously, the socio-cognitive analysis as presented is merely a more informal version of a more sophisticated analysis, which would require a detailed description of the underlying mental models, attitudes and ideologies, and their structures, and how exactly these structures directly or indirectly control discourse structures.

Although editorials are mainly about opinions, the analysis should finally not ignore the fundamental fact that all discourse, as is also the case here, is based on vast amounts of underlying knowledge, as explained above. In this case the knowledge about past and current immigration and immigration policies, as specified in the model, and more broadly on socio-culturally shared knowledge about immigration, the UK, governments, policies and so on – which all control the semantic coherence of the editorial.

Brief sociopolitical analysis

As we have seen above, Critical Discourse Studies generally relate discourse structures to social and political structures, and specifically to forms of power abuse. The specific claim of a socio-cognitive approach is that such relations are mediated by the kind of socio-cognitive analysis we have presented above.

Indeed, it would be a superficial shortcut to interpret the editorial only in terms of the *Telegraph* as a media organisation, or of the profession of journalists, or their readers. Such a sociological analysis would allow us to make explicit the processes and interactions of news gathering, the internal organisation and power structure of the newspaper as an organisation, the relations between newspapers and governments, as well as the role of newspapers in the lives of citizens, among many other topics.

Some of these social structures impinge on structures of discourse, such as the role of editorials as public discourse manifesting a relation between newspaper and government, as exemplified in the context model of writing editorials.

A more sociopolitical analysis also would make explicit the conditions of access (of politicians) to the news media, as is the case for David Cameron's article to which the editorial refers. And finally, the most obvious sociopolitical aspect explaining the alignment of the *Telegraph* as a newspaper with the current (2014) government would be in terms of the political power structure in the UK, and the relations between media and politics.

Yet, much of such a sociopolitical analysis of the media in general, and of the *Telegraph* and the Conservative government, in particular, in less macrostructural terms, would precisely involve a detailed analysis of public media discourse at the micro-level, namely *how* exactly the newspaper supports the government. We have seen that such a critical analysis is fundamentally incomplete without a socio-cognitive analysis, for instance in terms of mental models, attitudes and ideologies.

If the *Telegraph* aligns itself with the Conservative government, this is not only through discourse, but more fundamentally by the attitudes and ideologies expressed in a coherent corpus of discourses, of editorials as well as of news articles. Such underlying representations control all aspects of the production of these discourses, and at the same time explain how the readers will read and understand the discourses, and construe their own mental models, partly also based on the same underlying attitudes and ideologies.

It is at this crucial point where the *critical* analysis of discourse becomes relevant. That a conservative newspaper supports a Conservative government is hardly surprising, even if we need to show, in detail, how this is done discursively and cognitively. The same is true for its critical stance about Labour.

But in this case, the editorial is hardly politically innocent, because it also deals with immigration. True, assuming that conservative organisations often oppose immigration, or are in favour of strict immigration controls, as shown in this editorial, may be expected. But the crucial point is that such public discourses may and do influence millions of readers, and that such readers (as the very editorial makes explicit) also may be voters. Merely reading the newspaper, or even understanding the meaning of its discourses, is part of the general properties of media and communication. But by the explicit and persuasive expression of underlying attitudes and ideologies against immigration, it is more than likely that readers will form or reinforce their own negative attitudes on immigration.

More specifically, the newspaper not only conveys attitudes against immigration (e.g., on the basis of the job market), but more specifically against immigrants as 'abusing the system'. This is not an attitude most British readers can form on the basis of personal experiences (personal mental models), but an attitude they primarily acquire through the public discourse of (conservative) governments and media. And that kind of negative attitude, together with other ones about immigrants, is based on more fundamental xenophobic and racist ideologies.

In other words, the editorial not only formulates a conservative opinion on immigration policies, and thus not only aligns itself with the Conservative government, but **manipulates** its readers in the formation of xenophobic and racist attitudes and ideologies (see also Le Cheminant and Parrish 2010).

Much research on the reproduction of prejudice, discrimination and racism has shown that such attitudes and ideologies may result in many forms of everyday discrimination against immigrants. Indeed, if the *Telegraph* explicitly advocates to keep ('wrong') immigrants outside of the country, and collectively accuses immigrants of (welfare) abuses, then it is hardly surprising that its readers will want to keep immigrants out of their neighbourhood, street, pub or family (for details about racism and the press, see, e.g., Campbell 2010; Downing and Husband 2005; Jäger and Link 1993; Richardson 2004; van Dijk 1987, 1991, 1993).

How and why this happens, and why a newspaper may have such ideological and manipulative power is (partly) shown by the kind of socio-cognitive discourse analysis we have presented above. Of course, such an analysis needs to be expanded with a more general – and very complex – analysis of how (what kind of) newspaper readers acquire their knowledge, opinions, attitudes and ideologies, and what the role is of the newspaper and the other media in this form of epistemic and ideological acquisition.

Obviously, we also know that media discourse is not automatically accepted by all the recipients, and that some recipients may resist or reject its opinions, attitudes and ideologies. Yet, on the issue of immigration, where many people have only indirect acquaintance of immigrants, and where the persuasive messages are not inconsistent with the daily experiences or the interests of the readers, such ideological influence may be pervasive – as research on general attitudes and prejudices on immigrants show.

These attitudes are not innate, but learned. And since not based on everyday experiences, such acquisition is by public discourse (or conversations with friends or family members in turn based on such discourse). Newspapers and television play a fundamental role in this kind of ideological manipulation by the symbolic elites.

Further reading

van Dijk, T. A. (1998). *Ideology: A multidisciplinary approach*. London: Sage.
This is the first of the series of books offering a multidisciplinary account of the relations between discourse and cognition, in this case of ideology as the fundamental mental representation shared

by members of (ideological) groups. It shows how ideologies control social attitudes and personal mental models, which in turn control polarised ideological discourse (Us vs. Them).

van Dijk, T. A. (2008). *Context and discourse. A sociocognitve approach*. Cambridge: Cambridge University Press.

This is the first monograph of two about the relations between discourse and the communicative situation defined as mental context models, which control how discourse is adapted to the relevant properties of the communicative situation, defining its appropriateness. Also in this monograph the notion of context is analyzed in terms of cognitive and social psychology, sociology, anthropology and linguistics (including a critique of the notion of context as used in Systematic Linguistics). This theory of context also serves as the basis of pragmatics.

van Dijk, T. A. (2014). *Discourse and knowledge: A sociocognitive approach*. Cambridge: Cambridge University Press.

Although there are thousands of books about both discourse and knowledge as fundamental notions of the humanities and social sciences, this is the first book systematically relating these notions, again in a multidisciplinary perspective, and reviewing a large amount of literature in epistemology, psychology, sociology, anthropology and linguistics. It offers the basis for a new, epistemic analysis of text and talk.

References

Aikhenvald, A. Y. (2004). *Evidentiality*. Oxford, New York: Oxford University Press.

Augoustinos, N., Walker, I. and Donaghue, N. (2006). *Social cognition: an integrated introduction*, 2nd edn. London: Sage.

Bell, A. (1991). *The language of news media*. Oxford, Cambridge: Blackwell.

Bhatia, V. K., Flowerdew, J. and Jones, R. H. (eds.) (2008). *Advances in discourse studies*. London, New York: Routledge.

Blommaert, J. (2004). *Discourse: a critical introduction*. Cambridge, New York: Cambridge University Press.

Burr, V. (2003). *Social constructionism*. London, New York: Routledge.

Campbell, C. P. (ed.) (2010). *Race and news: Critical perspectives*. New York: Routledge.

Clark, H. H. (1996). *Using language*. Cambridge: Cambridge University Press.

Croft, W. and Cruse, D. A. (2004). *Cognitive linguistics*. Cambridge: Cambridge University Press.

Downing, J. and Husband, C. (2005). *Representing race: racisms, ethnicities and media*. London, Thousand Oaks, CA: Sage.

Eagleton, T. (1991). *Ideology: an introduction*. London: Verso Eds.

Eagly, A. H. and Chaiken, S. (1993). *The psychology of attitudes*. Fort Worth, TX: Harcourt Brace Jovanovich.

Evans, V. and Green, M. (2006). *Cognitive linguistics: an introduction*. Edinburgh: Edinburgh University Press.

Fairclough, N. (1995). *Critical discourse analysis: The critical study of language*. London, New York: Longman.

Fiske, S. T. and Taylor, S. E. (2007). *Social cognition: from brain to culture*, 3rd edn. New York, England: Mcgraw-Hill Book Company.

Goldman, A. I. (1999). *Knowledge in a social world*. Oxford, New York: Clarendon Press, Oxford University Press.

Graesser, A. C., Gernsbacher, M. A. and Goldman, S. R. (eds.) (2003). *Handbook of discourse processes*. Mahwah, NJ: Erlbaum.

Hamilton, D. L. (ed.) (2005). *Social cognition*. New York: Psychology Press.

Hart, C. (ed.) (2011). *Critical discourse studies in context and cognition*. Amsterdam, Philadelphia: Benjamins.

Hart, C. (2015). *Critical discourse analysis and cognitive science: new perspectives on immigration discourse*. Basingstoke: Palgrave Macmillan.

Hart, C. and Cap, P. (eds.) (2014). *Contemporary critical discourse studies*. London: Bloomsbury.

Hart, C. and Lukes, D. (eds.) (2007). *Cognitive linguistics in critical discourse analysis: application and theory*. Newcastle: Cambridge Scholars Pub.

Jäger, S. and Link, J. (1993). *Die vierte Gewalt: Rassismus und die Medien* (The fourth power: racism and the media). Duisburg: DISS.

Kintsch, W. (1998). *Comprehension: a paradigm for cognition*. Cambridge: Cambridge University Press.

Lakoff, G. (1987). *Women, fire and dangerous things: what categories reveal about the mind*. Chicago: University of Chicago Press.

Lakoff, G. (2002). *Moral politics. How liberals and conservatives think.* Chicago: University of Chicago Press.

Le, E. (2010). *Editorials and the power of media. Interweaving of socio-cultural identities.* Philadelphia: Benjamins.

Le Cheminant, W. and Parrish, J. M. (2010). *Manipulating democracy: Democratic theory, political psychology, and mass media.* Abingdon, New York: Routledge.

Parker, I. (ed.) (1998). *Social constructionism, discourse, and realism.* London, Thousand Oaks, CA: Sage.

Potter, J. and Wetherell, M. (1987). *Discourse and social psychology: Beyond attitudes and behaviour.* London: Sage.

Richardson, J. E. (2004). *(Mis)representing Islam. The racism and rhetoric of British broadsheet newspapers.* Amsterdam, Philadelphia: Benjamins.

Richardson, J. E. (2007). *Analysing newspapers: An approach from critical discourse analysis.* New York: Palgrave Macmillan.

Stivers, T., Mondada, L. and Steensig, J. (eds.) (2011). *The morality of knowledge in conversation.* Cambridge, New York: Cambridge University Press.

Tannen, D., Hamilton, H. E. and Schiffrin, D. (eds.) (2015). *The handbook of discourse analysis.* Malden: John Wiley & Sons, Inc.

Titscher, S., Meyer, M., Wodak, R. and Vetter, E. (2000). *Methods of text and discourse analysis.* London, Thousand Oaks, CA: Sage.

Toolan, M. J. (ed.) (2002). *Critical discourse analysis: Critical concepts in linguistics.* New York: Routledge.

van Dijk, T. A. (1984). *Prejudice in discourse. An analysis of ethnic prejudice in cognition and conversation.* Amsterdam, Philadelphia: Benjamins.

van Dijk, T. A. (1987). *Communicating racism: Ethnic prejudice in thought and talk.* Newbury Park: Sage.

van Dijk, T. A. (1988a). *News analysis: Case studies of international and national news in the press.* Hillsdale, NJ: Erlbaum.

van Dijk, T. A. (1988b). *News as discourse.* Hillsdale, NJ: Erlbaum.

van Dijk, T. A. (1991). *Racism and the press.* London: Routledge.

van Dijk, T. A. (1993). *Elite discourse and racism.* Newbury Park: Sage.

van Dijk, T. A. (1998). *Ideology: A multidisciplinary approach.* London, England: Sage.

van Dijk, T. A. (ed.) (2007). *Discourse studies. 5 vols. Sage benchmarks in discourse studies.* London: Sage.

van Dijk, T. A. (2008a). *Discourse and context. A sociocognitive approach.* Cambridge, New York: Cambridge University Press.

van Dijk, T. A. (2008b). *Discourse and power.* Basingstoke, England, New York: Palgrave Macmillan.

van Dijk, T. A. (2009). *Society and discourse: How social contexts influence text and talk.* Cambridge, New York: Cambridge University Press.

van Dijk, T. A. (2014). *Discourse and knowledge: A sociocognitive approach.* New York: Cambridge University Press.

van Dijk, T. A. and Kintsch, W. (1983). *Strategies of discourse comprehension.* New York Toronto: Academic Press.

van Leeuwen, T. J. (2008). *Discourse and practice. New tools for critical discourse analysis.* Oxford, New York: Oxford University Press.

van Oostendorp, H. and Zwaan, R. A. (eds.) (1994). *Naturalistic text comprehension. Advances in Discourse Processing,* Vol. LIII. Norwood, NJ: Ablex.

Weiss, G. and Wodak, R. (eds.) (2003). *Critical discourse analysis: Theory and interdisciplinarity.* New York: Palgrave Macmillan.

Wodak, R. and Meyer, M. (eds.) (2015). *Methods of critical discourse analysis,* 3rd edn. London, Thousand Oaks: Sage.

Wooffitt, R. (2005). *Conversation analysis and discourse analysis: A comparative and critical introduction.* London, Thousand Oaks, CA: Sage.

3

The Discourse-Historical Approach

Martin Reisigl

1. Introduction

This chapter introduces the Discourse-Historical Approach (DHA), which has developed over the last 30 years as a main version of Critical Discourse Studies – first in Vienna, then also in Lancaster, Loughborough, Bern, Örebro and elsewhere. Section 2 starts with the history of the approach. Section 3 continues with a general description of the theoretical and methodological framework of the DHA. It explains basic characteristics and research interests and sketches the influences of sociolinguistics, pragmatics and text linguistics on the one hand, and of Critical Theory, history, argumentation theory and *politolinguistics* on the other hand. This section is divided into four subsections: the first covers central features and claims of the DHA and compares them with other discourse-analytical approaches, including approaches to Critical Discourse Studies; the following subsections explain the crucial concepts of critique, discourse and context. In section 4, the chapter outlines heuristic steps of a research practice designed for this specific approach, and remarks on future challenges conclude the chapter in section 5.

2. The history of the Discourse-Historical Approach

In English-speaking countries, the label "Discourse-Historical Approach" and its acronym "DHA" stand for one of the most prominent critical approaches to the study of discourse. The label stresses the strong historical research interest of the approach, and this designation has to be taken as a synecdochic self-description that names a part – a very important one – for the whole. Not all analyses carried out within the theoretical and methodical framework of the DHA show a clear historical orientation. The range of interests transcends the historical alignment by far. Throughout the past three decades, the exponents of the approach have continuously elaborated their theory, methodology and methods, again and again stimulated by new topics of research, by valuable comments and critique of the scientific peer group, and by many inspiring insights in various social sciences. A short history, segmented into four stages, helps to illustrate the multiplicity of relevant subjects and interests.[1]

Phase 1 – Viennese Critical Discourse Analysis *ante litteram* (1987–1993): The study for which the DHA was developed reconstructed the constitution of anti-Semitic stereotypes, as they emerged in (semi)public discourses in the 1986 Austrian presidential campaign of Kurt Waldheim. The former UN general secretary had kept secret his National Socialist engagement (Wodak et al. 1990; Heer et al. 2008). Four features of the DHA crystallised from this project: its interdisciplinary and especially historical alignment; teamwork; triangulation of data, theories, as well as methods; and the attempt to practically apply the findings. The pioneering discourse-analytical research combined sociolinguistics and studies on narration, stylistics, rhetoric and argumentation with historical and sociological research when analysing linguistic manifestations of anti-Semitic prejudice in their historical context. The data included both oral and written genres: historical expert reports, national as well as international newspapers, statements of politicians, daily news broadcasts and TV news, interviews, TV discussions, hearings, documentaries and a vigil commemorating Austrian resistance (see also Reisigl and Wodak 2001: 91–143). An exhibition about the issue was prepared in order to satisfy the aims of practical critique and public enlightenment.

A further research project focussed on the discourse about the Austrian Year of commemoration in 1988, the year in which the 50th anniversary of Austria's integration into the Third Reich in 1938 was commemorated. The study, entitled "Languages of the Past" (Wodak et al. 1994), analysed (1) media debates about the expert report published by an international commission of historians on Waldheim's Nazi past in February 1988; (2) the political commemoration of the Austrian *Anschluss* in March 1938; (3) the unveiling of a "memorial against war and fascism" by the sculptor Alfred Hrdlicka, as well as the controversial discussions that preceded it; (4) the premiere of the play *Heldenplatz* by Thomas Bernhard, which deals with Austrian anti-Semitism and its terrorising long-term impact on surviving Jewish victims; and (5) the commemoration of the 50th anniversary of the *November pogrom* (9 November 1938). The empirical data included a range of media genres as well as statements and speeches of Austrian politicians. The linguists and historians examined the conflicting representations of the Austrian history and related controversial claims, such as the claim of "Austria as the first victim of the Nazi politics of dictatorship and territorial expansionism".

In the second half of the 1980s, additional DHA research was published, examining doctor-patient communication, the comprehensibility of laws and news broadcasts and guidelines for non-sexist language use in administrative texts (see Wodak 1996; Lalouschek, Menz and Wodak 1990; Lutz and Wodak 1987; Kargl et al. 1997). This research shows a critical and practical engagement for the improvement of communication in various social institutions, but does not specifically focus on the historical dimension of discourses.

Phase 2 – The DHA becomes institutionalised in Vienna (1993–1997): In the 1990s, the Discourse-Historical Approach was increasingly acknowledged as one of the main approaches to Critical Discourse Analysis. It was further developed in a number of studies, for example, a study on racist discrimination against migrants from Romania and a study on the discourse about the nation and national identity in Austria (Matouschek, Wodak and Januschek 1995; Wodak et al. 1998, 2009 [1999]). The latter book is the most influential of all DHA studies thus far; first published in 1999, an extended second edition was published in 2009. The study analyses the relationships between the discursive construction of national sameness and difference, which leads to political and social exclusion of specific out-groups. This study focussed on political speeches, focus groups, interviews, political campaigns and the press as empirical data. The empirical data refer to political and media events relating to 1995, particularly to political commemoration, in Austria. It offers a general theoretical and methodical framework that can be applied for the analysis of the discursive construction of national identities in various contexts and national states.[2] From 1994 to 1996, a sociological as well as discourse-analytical project also dealt with the "language of diplomacy", a by-product of which was the comparative study on "methods of text analysis" (Titscher et al. 1998).

Phase 3 – The Research Centre "Discourse, Politics, Identity (DPI)" (1997–2003): The third phase comprises the years of the Research Centre "Discourse, Politics, Identity" in Vienna. Ruth Wodak founded the centre with her Wittgenstein Prize awarded in 1996. The prize allowed her to fund research projects analysing a wide range of subjects, and to support a large research team of postgraduate and postdoctoral colleagues. The topics and social issues investigated between 1997 and 2003 were:

1 overt and covert forms of racism in political discourses in national parliaments of six EU member states, especially in debates on asylum and migration (Wodak and van Dijk 2000);
2 internal communication in organisations of the European Union and discourses on un/employment in EU committees, especially in European Commission agencies and expert committees (Muntigl, Weiss and Wodak 2000);
3 the discursive construction of European identities in German, British and French speeches of politicians (e.g., Wodak and Weiss 2005);
4 the Austrian discourse on the enlargement of the European Union (Galasinska and Krzyżanowski 2008);
5 controversial debates on the issue of "permanent Austrian neutrality", which was legally institutionalised in October 1945 (Bischof, Pelinka and Wodak 2001; Kovács and Wodak 2003);
6 the controversial discourse on the role of the German Wehrmacht during World War II and on the two exhibitions about the "Crimes of the Wehrmacht", organised by the Institute for Social Research in Hamburg (Heer et al. 2003, 2008).

The six research projects were united by an interest in the relationships between discourse, politics/policy and identity, as well as by a focus on transnational and global phenomena. Thus, the emphasis increasingly shifted from the Austrian to the European level, and this transnational focus was maintained and elaborated in the fourth phase.

Phase 4 – The further internationalisation of the DHA (2004–present): Two research projects mark the transition from the third to the fourth phase: The first analysed the print-mediated discourse on the Constitution of the European Union (Oberhuber et al. 2005; Krzyżanowski and Oberhuber 2007; Krzyżanowski 2010), and the second focussed on discourses of integration, discrimination and migration in the European Union (Krzyżanowski and Wodak 2008). In 2004, when Lancaster University offered a personal chair to Ruth Wodak, Lancaster became a second centre of the DHA. In the following decade, the DHA was also established at the universities of Loughborough, Bern and Örebro.[3]

In Vienna, former research interests remain relevant, e.g., doctor-patient interaction, feminist critical discourse analysis, and political commemoration. Among other things, the Viennese researchers pay attention to representations and narrations of pain and illness experience (Menz et al. 2010) and to questions of comprehension and interpreting in intercultural interactions between doctors and patients with limited proficiency in the first language of the doctors (Reisigl 2011b; Menz 2013). Furthermore, they analysed the commemorative rhetoric in 2005, a multiple year of Austrian commemoration (de Cillia and Wodak 2009), and the commemorative rhetoric in 2015, another salient year of political commemoration in Austria. By taking into consideration the period 1995–2015, in a still ongoing research project, they extended the first ground-breaking research on the discursive construction of national identity to a comparative long-term study on political commemoration. In addition, the importance of metatheoretical and methodological reflections on discourse studies grew during the last decade – both in Vienna and Lancaster (e.g., Wodak and Krzyżanowski 2008).

From 2004 onwards, Wodak's team in Lancaster continued research on identity politics, migration and discrimination, as well as on the relationships between discourse and politics.[4] The research projects carried out at Lancaster University concentrated, among other topics, on discourses about refugees and asylum seekers in the British press from 1996–2006 (e.g., Delanty, Wodak and Jones 2011 [2008]), on the discursive construction of the Scots language (Unger 2013), on (multilingual) language policies in the European Union (e.g., Krzyżanowski and Wodak 2010; Unger, Krzyżanowski and Wodak 2015) as well as on media ethics and the development of a media-related European public sphere from the 1950s until 2004 (Triandafyllidou, Wodak and Krzyżanowski 2009). Furthermore, Ruth Wodak and her research team continued to investigate the daily routines of professional politicians and mass-mediated representations of politicians' everyday life in TV series (Muntigl, Weiss and Wodak 2000; Wodak 2011 [2009]). This practice-based research, interested in the internal perspectives of discourse participants, exemplifies the trend of incorporating ethnographic methodology in the DHA. The ethnographic research on everyday practices in political institutions is also a crucial topic for Michal Krzyżanowski (2011, also this volume).

Among the many research areas which have recently earned critical attention by discourse-historical analysts are right-wing populism and fascist discourses in Europe, as well as discourses on environment and climate change. Various case studies embracing different genres, including genres with a strong emphasis on visual communication such as political posters, leaflets, comics, documentaries, etc., have been carried out with respect to these research fields during the last years. Among the studies on right-wing populism are Reisigl (2007b), (2012a), (2014a); Richardson and Wodak (2009); Wodak, KhosraviNik and Mral (2013); Januschek and Reisigl (2014); Wodak and Forchtner (2014); and Wodak (2015). Wodak (2015) compares European populists with members of the "tea-party" with respect to rhetoric (including argumentation) and performance. She traces back how various persuasive images and posters have been recontextualised and glocalised across populist parties in Europe. Wodak (2015), as well as Reisigl (2012a, 2014a), look at the close relationship between the "logics of media" and the "logics of populism". Multimedia discourses of European (particularly British, but also Austrian, Italian, etc.) fascism in the 20th century and especially in the British post-war period are analysed with respect to their multi-modal realisations in text and talk, visual communication and music in Wodak and Richardson (2013) and Copsey and Richardson (2015). A systematic comparison between fascist and right-wing populist rhetoric is to be found in Reisigl (2012b). Various facets of discourses on environment and climate change are subjects of investigation in Reisigl and Wodak (2009, 2016), Sedlaczek (2012, 2014), Forchtner (2015) and Krzyżanowski (2015).

This condensed historical overview shows that the Discourse-Historical Approach is a flexible and productive variety of CDS that always opts for a problem-oriented perspective. Such a perspective demonstrates a clear preference for interdisciplinary research, since the selected discourse-related social problems are multidimensional. Despite its interdisciplinary character, however, the Discourse-Historical Approach has strong roots in linguistics.

3. General characteristics and research interests of the Discourse-Historical Approach

The Discourse-Historical Approach does not just look at the historical dimension of discourses, but is – more extensively – concerned with the following areas of discourse studies:

- discourse and discrimination (e.g., racism, ethnicism, nationalism, xenophobia, islamophobia, sexism);
- language barriers in various social institutions (such as hospitals, court rooms, authorities, academic language, media);
- discourse and politics/policy/polity (e.g., politics of the past/political commemoration, nation-building, European Union, migration, asylum, multilingualism, language policy, populism);
- discourse and identity (e.g., national and supranational/European identity, linguistic identity);
- discourse and history (e.g., National Socialism, fascism, commemoration, history of discourse studies);
- discourse in the media (both classical print media and new social media);
- organisational communication (e.g., in institutions of the European Union);
- discourse and ecology (climate change).

The Discourse-Historical Approach considers discourse analysis not just to be a method of language analysis, but a multidimensional project incorporating theory, methods, methodology and empirically based research practices that yield concrete social applications. The sociolinguistic background is informed by the work of Basil Bernstein and Aaron Cicourel as well as by interactional and ethnographic sociolinguistics relying on Erving Goffman's sociology of everyday life. Pragmatic influences relevant for the Discourse-Historical Approach are speech act theory, cognitive pragmatics, *Gesprächsanalyse* (as the unorthodox German and Austrian version of conversation analysis), and Functional Pragmatics (coined by Ehlich, Rehbein, Redder, Hoffmann, etc.). The textlinguistic and text semiotic framework is strongly influenced by Wolfgang Dressler. Sometimes, Systemic Functional Linguistics (SLF) turns out to be a helpful linguistic toolbox for the DHA. The interest in rhetoric is strongly developed, particularly with respect to tropes, genre theory (e.g., regarding political speeches), and persuasion (including argumentation). The philosophical semiotics of Charles Sanders Peirce forms a basis both for a sign-related and an epistemological foundation of the DHA. As a consequence, the Discourse-Historical Approach embraces a weak realism or moderate constructivism as its epistemological starting point. Two further philosophical points of reference are Ludwig Wittgenstein with his "Philosophical Investigations", and Critical Theory, particularly the models of communicative action, discourse ethics and deliberative democracy proposed by Jürgen Habermas. In addition, Pierre Bourdieu's critical sociological thinking is of importance, especially his concepts of *field* and *habitus* (see also Forchtner, this volume). As far as the historical dimension is concerned, the conceptual history proposed by Reinhart Koselleck and Hayden White's metahistorical approach are partly integrated into the analytical framework. The theories, methods, models and principles of argumentation advanced by Stephen Toulmin, Jürgen Habermas, Josef Kopperschmidt, Manfred Kienpointner, Martin Wengeler and the proponents of Pragma-Dialectics (i.e., Frans van Eemeren, Rob Grootendorst, Francisca Snoeck Henkemans, Peter Houtlosser) serve as a basis for argumentation analysis (Reisigl 2014b).

If political communication becomes the central object of research, German *politolinguists* (e.g., Burkhardt, Hermanns, Klein, Niehr, Wengeler) represent a vital source of theoretical and methodical inspiration. However, the commitment to an allegedly "engaged neutrality" (Burkhardt 1996) is refused, because critical discourse analysts call into question the idea of a neutral and value-free science. In this sense, the project of a *critical politolinguistics* is pursued within the DHA framework (Reisigl 2008).

3.1 Positioning the approach within the field of discourse studies

Locating the Discourse-Historical Approach within the broad field of discourse studies, we can observe that it takes its place within the area of Critical Discourse Studies. This means that the proponents of the approach are politically engaged and often application-oriented. They make practical claims of emancipation and criticise discursively constituted power abuse, injustice and social discrimination, and they make epistemic claims of revelation or enlightenment. Similar to other critical discourse analysts, they put emphasis on the practice-related quality of discourses, the context dependence of discourses, and the constructed as well as constructive character of discourses. Like their CDA fellows, they prefer to focus on problem-related "authentic" data and to employ multiple methods of analysis. They share with other CDA scholars that they reject a purely formalist and context-abstract view on language. They pay attention to multi-modal macro- as well as micro-phenomena, to intertextual and interdiscursive relationships, as well as to social, historical, political, economic, psychological and other factors relating to the verbal and non-verbal phenomena of communication.

Despite all these commonalities, there are a series of distinctive features. First, the DHA puts weight on historical subjects and on the historical anchoring, change and echo of specific discourses more than other CDA approaches. Second, in extensive research projects it follows the principle of triangulation more systematically than other CDA approaches do. Third, team research usually plays a greater role. Fourth, the practical application of the analytical insights, i.e., practical critique, is occasionally a more important objective. For instance, DHA activists may put forward guidelines on non-discriminatory language use. Fifth, the concept of rhetoric is more comprehensive than the one suggested by other CDA protagonists (e.g., Fairclough and van Dijk), and it is not pejorative. In the DHA, "rhetoric" includes argumentation as a central area. Sixth, the argumentation analysis is more important than in other CDA approaches, except for the approach propagated by Isabela and Norman Fairclough, and it is more concerned with the analysis of the content of argumentation schemes.[5] Seventh, the semiotic perspective is more clearly connected with the wide-ranging model of Charles Sanders Peirce, whereas the social-semiotic approach of Theo van Leeuwen and Gunther Kress stands in the tradition of Saussure and its followers (Fairclough's work includes a reference to Peirce's concept of "semiosis" too, but Fairclough does not align himself with Peircean philosophy). Eighth, in contrast to the mono-perspectival concept of discourse propagated by Fairclough and van Leeuwen (i.e., a discourse relates to one perspective on social reality), the DHA opts for a multiperspectival concept of discourse (i.e., a discourse including various perspectives on social reality). Ninth, reference to Functional Pragmatics is a distinguishing feature of the Discourse-Historical Approach. Tenth, the reference to poststructuralist theories is less pronounced than in other CDA approaches (e.g., the Duisburg Group), whereas Habermas and Critical Theory play a more significant role. Despite these distinctions, DHA protagonists are repeatedly establishing seminal cooperations with proponents of the other CDA approaches.

3.2 *The concept of critique*

The term "critical discourse analysis" was introduced in the 1980s in order to mark a difference from an allegedly descriptive discourse analysis. What Fairclough, van Dijk and others had in mind when they stood up for "Critical Discourse Analysis" initially was particularly the political meaning of social critique. Political critique means to judge the status quo, e.g., a specific discourse or (dis)order of discourse, against the background of an alternative (ideal) state and preferred values, norms, standards or criteria with respect to shortcomings or contradictions.

At least three theoretical sources are relevant for the understanding of "critique", as it prevails in the Discourse-Historical Approach: (1) Critical Theory of the first generation (Adorno, Horkheimer, Benjamin) inspires the DHA where it comes to criticising oppressive, discriminatory and exploitative ideologies, power abuse as well as the culture industry. Here, ideologies are suspected of justifying particular interests and social inequalities under the guise of common public interests. (2) The relationship to Foucault can be characterised as a relationship of strong interest with various reservations. Foucault's understanding of critique as an attitude and "the art of not being governed in this specific way and at this specific price" (Foucault 1990: 12) is taken up. This critique challenges the naturalisation of social relationships. (3) Further central points of reference are the later Critical Theory of Jürgen Habermas, his discourse ethics and his theory of deliberative democracy (see Forchtner 2010, 2011).

The four validity claims originally distinguished by Habermas serve as criteria for a differentiated concept of critique in the DHA: (theoretical) truth, (expressive) truthfulness, normative rightness and comprehensibilty. The validity claim of comprehensibility forms the basic claim for every communication. Particularly, the question of comprehensibilty is in the centre of research on language barriers in various social institutions (e.g., in doctor-patient interactions in hospitals; see Wodak, Menz and Lalouschek 1989). The question of truthfulness becomes especially crucial in studies on political or rhetorical manipulation and in studies of lying. However, the suspicion that a discourse participant could be lying involves not just the validity claim of truthfulness, but also the validity claim of truth. A person who tells a lie infringes both claims simultaneously. The two validity claims of (theoretical) truth and normative rightness are central in almost all discourse-historical studies. Truth will often be at stake in political discourses about the past, in discourses about national identities (e.g., referring to national stereotypes) and in discourses about the causes and consequences of climate change. Questions of normative rightness are salient in political discourses justifying or criticising human actions in the past, in deliberative discourses evolving around the question of what should be done or shouldn't be done, in discourses involving discrimination, in discourse on climate change, etc.

The Discourse-Historical Approach proposes a science that includes critique in all of its stages, i.e., in the context of discovery, of justification and of application. Three forms of critique distinguished in the Discourse-Historical Approach are the *text* or *discourse immanent critique, the socio-diagnostic critique* and *the prospective critique* (see Reisigl and Wodak 2001: 32–35).

1   *Text* or *discourse immanent critique* is primarily knowledge-related. It assesses conflicts, contradictions and inconsistencies in text-internal or discourse-internal structures, for example with respect to cohesion, presuppositions, argumentation and turn-taking structures. This form of critique relies – among other things – on rhetorical, textlinguistic, pragmatic, politico-linguistic and argumentation theoretical norms or criteria. With respect to the argumentation-related norms, the DHA draws on the ten pragma-dialectical rules

for constructive arguing, i.e., the freedom of arguing, the obligation to give reasons, the correct reference to the previous discourse by the antagonist, the obligation to matter-of-factness, the correct reference to implicit premises, the acceptance of shared starting points, the use of plausible schemes of argumentation, logical validity, the acceptance of the discussion's results and the clarity of expression and correct interpretation (see van Eemeren and Grootendorst 1992; van Eemeren, Garssen and Meuffels 2009).

2   *Socio-diagnostic critique* is both epistemic and deontic. It aims at exposing manipulation in and by discourse, at revealing ethically problematic aspects of discursive practices. This form of critique focusses on discrepancies between discursive and other social practices and functions as a form of social control. It relies on social, historical and political background knowledge. This critique includes the critique of ideology, the critique of the ethos of social actors, pragmatic critique, political critique and "social critique" (relating, for instance, to social recognition).

3   *Prospective critique* is strongly application-oriented. It is practical, aimed at reducing dysfunctional communication and language barriers, at improving communication within public institutions by elaborating proposals and guidelines on the basis of careful fieldwork. The philosophical model of deliberative democracy can serve as a normative point of reference for this form of critique. If the model is systematically linked to argumentation theory, it can serve as a valuable theoretical and methodical criterion that allows for the possibility to assess and organise important areas of public political decision-making. Such a model should keep loyalty to at least three things:

(i)   to principles of rationality, e.g., the pragma-dialectical rules of sound argumentation;
(ii)   to principles of justice (a) with respect to equality of political (basic democratic) and human rights, (b) with respect to distribution, (c) with respect to compensation and (d) with respect to performance; and
(iii) to the awareness of suffering and to the empathy as well as solidarity with victims of discrimination and disadvantaged fellow human beings.

3.3 The concept of discourse

At least ten features characterise the concept of discourse, as it is proposed by the Discourse-Historical Approach:

1   Discourse is a socially constituted as well as constitutive semiotic practice. In order to grasp the practical character of discourses, functionally oriented pragmatics is central. In order to understand the semiotic character, Peircean semiotics and social semiotics are highly relevant.

2   With respect to its socially constitutive character, discourse represents, creates, reproduces and changes social reality.

3   With respect to its semiotic and pragmatic character, a discourse is a communicative and interactional macro-unit that transcends the unit of a single text or conversation.

4   A discourse is composed of specific groups of actual texts, conversations, interactions and other semiotic events as well as action units. These concrete semiotic units are *tokens*, i.e., singular signs (in Peirce's terms, *sinsigns*). They serve specific purposes in social contexts, and are produced by somebody, distributed by somebody and received by somebody.

5   These actual discursive units relate to specific genres and other semiotic action patterns, i.e., to *types* (in Peirce's terms, *legisigns*).

6   The discursive units belonging to a specific discourse are intertextually linked by a macro-topic that diversifies into various discourse topics, subtopics, content-related argumentation schemes (topoi), etc.

7   Discourses are situated within (political, economic, etc.) fields of action. The discursive units are functionally connected within these fields of action. Fields of action form the frames of discourses.

8   Within these functional frames, discourses become parts of dispositifs and contribute to the constitution of social order. Dispositifs are goal-oriented complexes or networks of discourse, knowledge, power and subject constitution. As parts of dispositifs, discourses help to organise, (re)produce and transform social relationships (including power relations) and social positions, institutions, knowledge and ideologies, identities and subjects, etc.

9   Discourses develop around social problems. The problems become starting points of argumentation. Argumentation is both a verbal (partly also visual) and cognitive pattern of problem-solving (see Kopperschmidt 2000: 32, 45, 59f.; Reisigl 2014b: 70). These patterns surround claims of truth and/or claims of normative rightness. The claims are dealt with from different perspectives. Thus, a discourse involves multiple perspectives.

10   Discourse undergoes historical change relating to social change. Historical change deserves special attention in the DHA.

In order to approach various discursive features and strategies, discourse-historical analyses systematically go through five simple questions:

These questions are analytically answered by qualitative research on a variety of data (genres), and partly also by corpus-based quantitative research. The discourse-analytical categories are

Table 3.1 Discursive Strategies in the DHA

Questions to approach discursive features	Discursive strategies	Purpose
How are persons, objects, phenomena, events, processes and actions named and referred to linguistically in the discourse in question?	**nomination**	discursive construction of social actors; discursive construction of objects, phenomena, events; discursive construction of processes and actions
What characteristics or qualities are attributed to social actors, objects, phenomena, events, processes and actions mentioned in the discourse?	**predication**	discursive characterization of social actors, objects, phenomena, events processes and actions (e.g., positively or negatively)
What arguments are employed in discourse?	**argumentation**	persuading addressees of the validity of specific claims of truth and normative rightness
From what perspective are these nominations, attributions, arguments expressed?	**perspectivisation**	positioning the speaker's or writer's point of view and expressing involvement or distance
Are the respective utterances articulated overtly, are they intensified or mitigated?	**mitigation and intensification**	modifying the illocutionary force of utterances in respect to their epistemic or deontic status

not completely fixed, but have, at least partially, to be modified, adapted and newly developed for each research object. There is no space to elaborate on the particular discourse-analytical categories and their specific analytical application in the DHA. Thus, I just want to selectively refer the readers to Reisigl and Wodak (2001: 31–90); Reisigl and Wodak (2009, 2016); Wodak et al. (2009 [1999]: 30–47) for more information and details.

3.4 The concept of context

Context is a key notion of Critical Discourse Studies (CDS). It has become a defining moment of discourse, because (critical) discourse analysts frequently conceive of discourse as "text in context". CDS pay special attention to the social, political, historical and cognitive context.

Context can be broken down into a macro-, meso- and micro-dimension. The Discourse-Historical Approach distinguishes among four dimensions of "context":

1   The immediate, language internal co-text and co-discourse regards thematic and syntactic coherences, lexical solidarities, collocations, connotations, implications, presuppositions and local interactive processes.
2   The intertextual and interdiscursive relationship between utterances, texts, genres and discourses (e.g., with respect to discourse representation, allusions, evocations) is a further contextual research dimension.
3   Social factors and institutional frames of a specific context of situation include: degree of formality, place, time, occasion, addressees, interactive and political roles, political and ideological orientation, gender, age, profession, level of education, ethnic, regional, national, religious identities, etc.
4   On a meso- and macro-level, the broader sociopolitical and historical context is integrated into the analysis. At this point, fields of action and the history of the discursive event as well as of discourse topics are looked at.

The Discourse-Historical Approach pays special attention to the fourth dimension, the historical context. Three ways of doing a discourse-historical analysis can be distinguished:

1   A discourse fragment or utterance is taken as a starting point, and its prehistory is reconstructed by relating the present to the past. To give an example: At the first glance, an utterance such as "We take care of your Carinthia" produced by three Austrian politicians of the right-wing populist party BZÖ in a regional election campaign in 2009 may seem to be "harmless". The seemingly "innocent" character gets lost if a discourse-historical analysis – interested in *recontextualisation* – a crucial concept for the analysis of the historical dimension of discourses – detects that the sentence "Take care of my Carinthia" has both been uttered in 1991 by Jörg Haider and in 1945 by Friedrich Rainer, the National Socialist Gauleiter of Carinthia, when he had to resign at the end of World War II (Reisigl 2013: 82–84).
2   A diachronic series or sequence of thematically or/and functionally connected discourse fragments or utterances is taken as a starting point, and their historical interrelationships are reconstructed within a specific period. This way, specific discourse elements can be related to each within a particular period of the past, e.g., a period of some months, years, decades, etc.

3   A third way consists in the critical analysis of how different social actors, e.g., politicians in contrast to historians, talk, write, sing, etc. about the past, and in the comparison of the different semiotic representations with respect to claims of truth, normative rightness and truthfulness.

The three ways can be combined, for instance, if a comparative long-term study is carried out on political commemoration in Austria in the years 1995, 2005 and 2015.

When analysing the historical dimension of discourses, we are faced with two challenges:

1   Time-relatedness of the internal perspective and the perspective of discourse analysts: In order to do justice to the historical situatedness of discourses, discourse analysts should try to understand the perspectives of the historical discourse participants. On the other hand, every discourse-historical analysis is itself time-related, connected to the perspective of a present. This tension can adequately be dealt with, if we keep in mind that our discourse-historical analysis is not just an analysis of the past, but also of the present.

2   Discrepancies between asserted and lived continuities or discontinuities: On the one hand, a discourse-historical analysis has sometimes to focus on the discrepancy between the assertion of a continuity and factual discontinuities in the area of the *res gestae*. Such a discrepancy can be detected in national rhetorics, where historical breaks are tropologically done away by temporal synecdoches for reasons of positive national self-presentation. To give an example: In some Austrian commemorative speeches from 2008, there is talk of a 90-year-existence of the Austrian Republic, although this republic did not exist between 1934 and 1945 (see Reisigl 2009). On the other hand, a discourse-historical analysis may focus on the discrepancy between the assertion of a discontinuity and the factual continuity until present times. Here, we may think of the echo of fascism and National Socialism after 1945, or of the proximity of right-wing populism and right-wing extremism.

4. Research practice

Of course, the research practice varies from research project to research project, depending on a series of pragmatic reasons (e.g., resources of time, money and researchers) and on the claim that good science should always be open to unexpected findings that get researchers to modify their research plan. A simplified and idealised sequence of eight stages and steps in research practice is explained in Reisigl (2008: 101–117) and Reisigl and Wodak (2009: 96–120 and 2016: 34–56). This sequence can be summarised as follows:

1   activation and consultation of preceding theoretical knowledge, i.e., recollection, reading and discussion of previous research;

2   systematic collection of data and context information with respect to discourses and discursive events, social fields as well as actors, semiotic media, genres, texts, conversations, linguistic action patterns, etc.;

3   selection and preparation of data for the specific analyses, i.e., selection and downsizing of data according to transparent criteria, transcription of tape recordings, etc.;

4   specification of research question and formulation of assumptions on the basis of a literature review and a first skimming of the data;

5   qualitative pilot analysis that allows testing categories and assumptions as well as the further specification of assumptions (this stage includes a linguistic macro-, meso- and micro-analysis as well as a context analysis);

6   detailed case studies of a whole range of data, primarily qualitatively, but in part also quantitatively;

7   formulation of critique on the basis of the interpretation of the findings: the relevant context knowledge is taken into account when the text- or discourse-internal, socio-diagnostic as well as prospective dimensions of critique are referred to;

8   application of analytical findings, where it is possible.

Usually, the different stages and steps are realised recursively. They have to be adjusted to each specific discourse-historical research.

5. Conclusion

Change is a basic historical category. At present, we are confronted with a series of far-reaching social, political, economic and ecological changes. These changes occur at local, regional, national, supranational and global levels. Discourse is highly relevant for all of these changes. Thus, the Discourse-Historical Approach finds a vast field of research activity also in the coming years. New topics relating to new problems and known topics relating to the aggravation of already existing social problems urgently require the critical attention of DHA proponents. Changing discourses on migration and asylum, discourses on changing national and supranational identities, discourses on climate change, discourses on new media, and – not least – discourses on the various political pasts are only a selection of subjects that will remain important research objects. In order to do justice to its empirical objects, the DHA will have to look at new relationships between discourse and discrimination, and it will have to advance its theoretical and methodological development, also with respect to the question of what it means to analyse the historical dimension of discourses. Within this context, the DHA will have to pay attention to the interdiscursive links of the discourse on asylum and refugees and the discourse on climate change, just to mention two imperative challenges. Discourse and discrimination and language barriers in crucial social institutions will also remain two important objects of research and practical critique. The respective research belongs to the core area of the DHA, though the historical dimension of discourses is not at the centre of this research. The success of prospective criticisms strongly depends on the question whether the interdisciplinary cooperation among linguistics, historical research, sociology, political science, philosophy and climatology can further be improved, in order to lead to an even more integrative DHA framework.

Notes

1 For the history of the approach, see also Reisigl (2011a: 462–473).

2 The politics of identity and exclusion was further investigated in a series of case studies on Austria and led to research on supranational identities (see Reisigl 2007a; de Cillia and Wodak 2009).

3 Quite soon after the publication of "Discourse and Discrimination" (Reisigl and Wodak 2001), John E. Richardson also started to become involved in discourse-historical research (Richardson 2004).

4 Veronika Koller moved to Lancaster in 2004 as well, independently of Wodak. Synergetic cooperations developed soon. Koller combines the socio-cognitive approach of CDS and metaphor analysis with the Discourse-Historical Approach (e.g., Koller 2008, 2009).

5 The focus on content-related topoi has partly been misunderstood. For a clarification, see Reisigl (2014b).

Further reading

Wodak, R., de Cillia, R., Reisigl, M. and Liebhart, K. (2009). *The discursive construction of national identity*, 2nd rev. and ext. edn. Edinburgh: Edinburgh University Press.

Martin Reisigl

The authors study general and specific discursive strategies and linguistic devices employed to construct national identities. The book pays particular attention to Austria, but many theoretical, methodical and empirical findings are also relevant for various other cases of discursive nation building.

Reisigl, M. and Wodak, R. (2001). *Discourse and discrimination: Rhetorics of racism and antisemitism.* London: Routledge.

This is a study of how racism, antisemitism and ethnicism are (re)produced and reflected in discourse. The authors first survey five established discourse-analytical approaches before providing their own model of the Discourse-Historical Approach and three case studies (on right-wing populist "xenophobia", on everyday antisemitism and on bureaucratic racism).

Reisigl, M. (2008). Analyzing political rhetoric. In R. Wodak and M. Krzyżanowski (eds.), *Qualitative discourse analysis in the social sciences,* 96–120. London: Palgrave.

The chapter introduces the politolinguistic analysis of political communication from a DHA perspective. It explains how political communication can be studied with respect to its rhetorical and argumentative structure. Eight steps of a specific research practice are spelled out in a qualitative pilot analysis of a right-wing populist discourse fragment.

Reisigl, M. and Wodak, R. (2016). The discourse-historical approach. In R. Wodak and M. Meyer (eds.), *Methods of critical discourse analysis,* 3rd rev. edn, 23–61. London, Thousand Oaks, CA, New Delhi: Sage.

The chapter offers an overview of the basic characteristics of the Discourse-Historical Approach. It explains key concepts such as critique, ideology, power, discourse, genre, text, context, recontextualisation, intertextuality and interdiscursivity. Further, it explicates important principles and analytical tools of this critical approach to discourse. Finally, the pilot analysis of online news reporting on climate change illustrates the research practice of the DHA.

References

Bischof, G., Pelinka, A. and Wodak, R. (eds.) (2001). *Neutrality in Austria: Contemporary Austrian studies.* New Brunswick, London: Transaction Publishers.

Burkhardt, A. (1996). Politolinguistik: Versuch einer Ortsbestimmung. In J. Klein and H. Diekmannshenke (eds.), *Sprachstrategien und Dialogblockaden,* 75–100. Berlin, New York: de Gruyter.

Cillia, R. de and Wodak, R. (eds.) (2009). *Gedenken im "Gedankenjahr": Zur diskursiven Konstruktion österreichischer Identitäten im Jubiläumsjahr.* Innsbruck: Studienverlag.

Copsey, N. and Richardson, J. E. (eds.) (2015). *Cultures of post-war British fascism.* London, New York: Routledge.

Delanty, G., Wodak, R. and Jones, P. (eds.) (2008/2011). *Identity, belonging and migration.* Liverpool: Liverpool University Press.

Forchtner, B. (2010). Jürgen Habermas and the critical study of language. *CADAAD – Critical Approaches to Discourse Analysis across Disciplines* 4(1): 18–37.

Forchtner, B. (2011). Critique, the discourse-historical approach and the Frankfurt School. *Critical Discourse Studies* 8(1): 1–14.

Forchtner, B. (2015). Extrem rechte Parteien im Klimawandel: Ein (kurzer) Blick auf die Schweiz, Österreich und Deutschland. In G. Heinrich and K-D. Kaiser (eds.), *Naturschutz und Rechtsradikalismus,* 128–135. Berlin: Bundesamt für Naturschutz.

Foucault, M. (1990). *Was Ist Kritik?* Berlin: Merve.

Galasinska, A. and Krzyżanowski, M. (eds.) (2008). *Discourse and transformation in central and eastern Europe.* Basingstoke: Palgrave Macmillan.

Heer, H., Manoschek, W., Pollak, A. and Wodak, R. (eds.) (2003). *Wie Geschichte gemacht wird. Zur Konstruktion von Erinnerungen an Wehrmacht und Zweiten Weltkrieg.* Vienna: Czernin.

Heer, H., Manoschek, W., Pollak, A. and Wodak, R. (eds.) (2008). *The discursive construction of history: Remembering the Wehrmacht's war of annihilation.* Basingstoke: Palgrave Macmillan.

Januschek, F. and Reisigl, M. (eds.) (2014). *Osnabrücker Beiträge zur Sprachtheorie 86: Populismus in der digitalen Mediendemokratie.* Duisburg: Universitätsverlag Rhein-Ruhr.

Kargl, M., Wetschanow, K., Wodak, R. and Perle, N. (1997). *Kreatives Formulieren: Anleitungen zu geschlechtergerechtem Sprachgebrauch.* Vienna: Bundesministerium für Frauenangelegenheiten und Verbraucherschutz.

Koller, V. (2008). *Lesbian discourses: Images of a community.* London, New York: Routledge.

Koller, V. (2009). Analysing collective identity in discourse: social actors and contexts. In *SEMEN* 27. http://semen.revues.org/8877

Kopperschmidt, J. (2000). *Argumentationstheorie zur Einführung*. Hamburg: Junius.

Kovács, A. and Wodak, R. (eds.) (2003). *NATO, neutrality and national identity: The case of Austria and Hungary*. Vienna: Böhlau.

Krzyżanowski, M. (2010). *The discursive construction of European identities: A multi-level approach to discourse and identity in the transforming European Union*. Frankfurt am Main: Lang.

Krzyżanowski, M. (2011). Ethnography and critical discourse analysis: Towards a problem-oriented research dialogue. *Critical Discourse Studies* 8(4): 231–238.

Krzyżanowski, M. (2015). International leadership re-/constructed? On the ambivalence and heterogeneity of identity discourses in European Union's policy on climate change. *Journal of Language and Politics* 14(1): 110–133.

Krzyżanowski, M. and Oberhuber, F. (2007). *(Un) doing Europe: Discourses and practices of negotiating the EU constitution*. Brussels: Lang.

Krzyżanowski, M. and Wodak, R. (2008). *The politics of exclusion: Debating migration in Austria*. New Brunswick: Transaction Publishers.

Krzyżanowski, M. and Wodak, R. (2010). Hegemonic multilingualism in/of the EU institutions: An inside-outside perspective on European language policies and practices. In C. Hülmbauer, E. Vetter and H. Böhringer (eds.), *Mehrsprachigkeit aus der Perspektive zweier EU-Projekte: Dylan meets Linee*, 115–133. Frankfurt am Main: Lang.

Lalouschek, J., Menz, F. and Wodak, R. (1990). *"Alltag in der Ambulanz": Gespräche zwischen Ärzten, Schwestern und Patienten*. Tübingen: Narr.

Lutz, B. and Wodak, R. (1987). *Information für Informierte: Linguistische Studien zu Verständlichkeit und Verstehen von Hörfunknachrichten*. Vienna: Verlag der Österreichischen Akademie der Wissenschaften.

Matouschek, B., Wodak, R. and Januschek, F. (1995). *Notwendige Maßnahmen gegen Fremde? Genese und Formen von rassistischen Diskursen der Differenz*. Vienna: Passagen.

Menz, F. (ed.) (2013). *Migration und medizinische Kommunikation: Linguistische Verfahren der PatientInnenbeteiligung und Verständnissicherung in ärztlichen Gespräche mit MigrantInnen*. Göttingen: Vandenhoeck & Ruprecht unipress.

Menz, F., Lalouschek, J., Sator, M. and Wetschanow, K. (2010). *Sprechen über Schmerzen: Linguistische, kulturelle und semiotische Analysen*. Essen/Duisburg: Universitätsverlag Rhein-Ruhr.

Muntigl, P., Weiss, G. and Wodak, R. (2000). *European Union discourses on un/employment: An interdisciplinary approach to employment policy-making and organizational change*. Amsterdam: Benjamins.

Oberhuber, F., Bärenreuter, C., Krzyżanowski, M., Schönbauer, H. and Wodak, R. (2005). Debating the European constitution: On representations of Europe/the EU in the press. *Journal of Language and Politics* 4(2): 227–271.

Reisigl, M. (2007a). *Nationale Rhetorik in Fest- und Gedenkreden: Eine diskursanalytische Studie zum "österreichischen Millennium" in den Jahren 1946 und 1996*. Tübingen: Stauffenburg.

Reisigl, M. (2007b). The dynamics of right-wing populist argumentation in Austria. In F.H. van Eemeren, J.A. Blair, C.A. Willard and B. Garssen (eds.), *Proceedings of the sixth conference of the international society for the study of argumentation*, 1127–1134. Amsterdam: Sic Sat 2007/International Center for the Study of Argumentation.

Reisigl, M. (2008). Analyzing political rhetoric. In R. Wodak and M. Krzyżanowski (eds.), *Qualitative discourse analysis in the social sciences*, 96–120. London: Palgrave.

Reisigl, M. (2009). Spoken silence – bridging breaks: The discursive construction of historical continuities and turning points in Austrian commemorative speeches by employing rhetorical tropes. In R. Wodak and G. Auer Borea (eds.), *Justice and memory: Confronting traumatic pasts: An international comparison*, 213–240. Vienna: Passagen.

Reisigl, M. (2011a). Grundzüge der Wiener Kritischen Diskursanalyse. In R. Keller, A. Hirseland, W. Schneider and W. Viehöver (eds.), *Handbuch Sozialwissenschaftliche Diskursanalyse. Volume 1: Theorien und Methoden*, 3rd edn, 459–497. Wiesbaden: VS Verlag für Sozialwissenschaften.

Reisigl, M. (2011b). Schwierige Verständigung. Interkulturelle Gespräche auf der Kopfschmerzambulanz. In P. Holzer, M. Kienpointner, J. Pröll and U. Ratheiser (eds.), *An den Grenzen der Sprache: Kommunikation von Un-Sagbarem im Kulturkontakt*, 101–127. Innsbruck: iup.

Reisigl, M. (2012a). Zur kommunikativen Dimension des Rechtspopulismus. In Sir Peter Ustinov Institut, A. Pelinka and B. Haller (eds.), *Populismus – Herausforderung oder Gefahr für die Demokratie?*, 141–162. Vienna: Braumüller.

Martin Reisigl

Reisigl, M. (2012b): Rechtspopulistische und faschistische Rhetorik – Ein Vergleich. In *Totalitarismus und Demokratie / Totalitarianism and Democracy. Zeitschrift für internationale Diktatur- und Freiheitsforschung / An International Journal for the Study of Dictatorship and Liberty*. 9/2/2012: Populismus und Faschismus/ Populism and Fascism. Göttingen: Vandenhoeck & Ruprecht: 303–323.

Reisigl, M. (2013). Critical discourse analysis. In R. Bayley, R. Cameron and C. Lucas (eds.), *The Oxford handbook of sociolinguistics*, 67–90. Oxford: Oxford University Press.

Reisigl, M. (2014a). Österreichischer Rechtspopulismus im Zeitalter von Mediendemokratie und medialer Erlebnisgesellschaft. In F. Januschek and N. Reisigl (eds.), *Osnabrücker Beiträge zur Sprachtheorie 86: Populismus in der digitalen Mediendemokratie*, 71–99. Duisburg: Universitätsverlag Rhein-Ruhr.

Reisigl, M.(2014b). Argumentation analysis and the discourse-historical approach: A methodological framework. In C. Hart and P. Cap (eds.), *Contemporary critical discourse studies*, 67–96. London: Bloomsbury.

Reisigl, M. and Wodak, R. (2001). *Discourse and discrimination: Rhetorics of racism and antisemitism*. London: Routledge.

Reisigl, M. and Wodak, R. (2009). The discourse-historical approach. In R. Wodak and M. Meyer (eds.), *Methods of critical discourse analysis*, 2nd edn, 87–121. London, Thousand Oaks, CA, New Delhi: Sage.

Reisigl, M. and Wodak, R. (2016). The discourse-historical approach. In R. Wodak and M. Meyer (eds.), *Methods of critical discourse studies*, 3rd edn, 23–61. London, Thousand Oaks, CA, New Delhi: Sage.

Richardson, J. E. (2004). *(Mis)representing Islam: The racism and rhetoric of British broadsheet newspapers*. Amsterdam: Benjamins.

Richardson, J. E. and Wodak, R. (2009). The impact of visual racism: Visual arguments in political leaflets of Austrian and British far-right parties. *Controversia* 6(2): 45–77.

Sedlaczek, A. (2012). *Die visuelle Repräsentation des Klimawandels in Dokumentarfilmen: Eine multimodale kritische Diskursanalyse*. MA Thesis, Vienna.

Sedlaczek, A. (2014). Multimodale Repräsentation von Klimawandel und Klimaschutz. *Wiener Linguistische Gazette*. 78A: 14–33.

Titscher, S., Wodak, R., Meyer, M. and Vetter, E. (1998). *Methoden der Textanalyse*. Opladen: Westdeutscher Verlag.

Triandafyllidou, A., Wodak, R. and Krzyżanowski, M. (eds.) (2009). *The European public sphere and the media: Europe in crisis*. New York: Palgrave.

Unger, J. W. (2013). *The discursive construction of Scots language: Education, politics and everyday life*. Amsterdam: Benjamins.

Unger, J. W., Krzyżanowski, M. and Wodak, R. (eds.) (2015). *Multilingual encounters in Europe's institutional spaces*. London: Bloomsbury Academic.

Van Eemeren, F. H., Garssen, B. and Meuffels, B. (2009). *Fallacies and judgments of reasonableness: Empirical research concerning the pragma-dialectical discussion rules*. Dordrecht: Springer.

Van Eemeren, F. H. and Grootendorst, R. (1992). *Argumentation, communication, and fallacies: A pragma-dialectical perspective*. Hillsdale, NJ: Erlbaum.

Wodak, R. (1996). *Disorders of discourse*. London/New York: Longman.

Wodak, R. (2009/2011). *The discourse of politics in action: Politics as usual*. New York: Palgrave.

Wodak, R. (2015). *The politics of fear: What right-wing discourses mean*. London: Sage.

Wodak, R., de Cillia, R., Reisigl, M. and Liebhart, K. (1999/2009). *The discursive construction of national identity*, 1st and 2nd edn. Edinburgh: Edinburgh University Press.

Wodak, R., de Cillia, R., Reisigl, M., Liebhart, K., Hofstätter, K. and Kargl, M. (1998). *Zur diskursiven Konstruktion nationaler Identität*. Frankfurt am Main: Suhrkamp.

Wodak, R. and Forchtner, B. (2014). Embattled Vienna 1683/2010: Right-wing populism, collective memory and the fictionalisation of politics. *Visual Communication* 13(2): 231–255.

Wodak, R., KhosraviNik, M. and Mral, B. (eds.) (2013). *Right-wing populism in Europe: Politics and discourse*. London/New York: Bloomsbury.

Wodak, R. and Krzyżanowski, M. (eds.) (2008). *Qualitative discourse analysis in the social sciences*. London: Palgrave.

Wodak, R., Menz, F. and Lalouschek, J. (1989). *Sprachbarrieren: Die Verständigungskrise der Gesellschaft*. Wien: Edition Atelier.

Wodak, R., Menz, F., Mitten, R. and Stern, F. (1994). *Die Sprachen der Vergangenheiten: öffentliches Gedenken in österreichischen und deutschen Medien*. Frankfurt am Main: Suhrkamp.

58

Wodak, R., Pelikan, J., Nowak, P., Gruber, H., de Cillia, R. and Mitten, R. (1990). *"Wir sind alle unschuldige Täter!" Diskurshistorische Studien zum Nachkriegsantisemitismus*. Frankfurt am Main: Suhrkamp.

Wodak, R. and Richardson, J. E. (eds.) (2013). *Analysing fascist discourse: European fascism in talk and text*. London: Routledge.

Wodak, R. and Weiss, G. (2005). Analyzing European Union discourses: Theories and applications. In R. Wodak and P. Chilton (eds.), *A new agenda in (critical) discourse analysis*, 121–135. Amsterdam: Benjamins.

Wodak, R. and van Dijk, T. A. (eds.) (2000). *Racism at the top: Parliamentary discourses on ethnic issues in six European states*. Klagenfurt-Celovec: Drava.

4

Multi-modal critical discourse analysis

Per Ledin and David Machin

Introduction

Multi-modality is becoming more common in CDA as scholars begin to introduce visual, sound and material design alongside their analyses of texts. But doing Multi-modal CDA (MCDA) is a field essentially still in its infancy. A few book titles have started to appear where multi-modality has been specifically formulated alongside CDA, such as Mayr and Machin (2012); Machin and Mayr (2012); Djonov and Zhao (2014); Abousnnouga and Machin (2013); and a journal special edition Machin (2013). But there is a need to develop and establish clear, robust concepts that can be used as part of CDA with its emphasis on digging out the discourses buried in texts to reveal the kinds of power relations and ideologies that they represent.

In fact, multi-modality, since emerging from linguistics in the late 1990s, still remains, in itself, rather fragmented. While ground-breaking work has been done, there is a need for consolidation and greater reflective work on concepts and how they are to be used for specific purposes. There is also an increasing sense that clearer links need to be made with existing fields of research into the visual, the sonic and the material, into whose longer traditions of investigation multi-modality is now entering. In this context it is important for CDA to identify which of an array of competing concepts are most suitable for its own needs. This is the purpose of this chapter.

In this chapter we show that MCDA needs to depart from a fundamentally social question: What semiotic resources are drawn upon in communication, or discourse, in order to carry out ideological work? And the *social* here as a point of departure is highly important in order to distinguish this approach from other kinds of multi-modal work which have a very different starting point. The chapter begins by looking at the origins of multi-modality and the different paths it has taken. It then deals with criticisms that have been raised against these paths. These two steps are important to indicate the necessity for a *social* approach. This allows us to show what might be the most productive ways to proceed for CDA. In the next part of the chapter, we then show exactly how this approach would work by carrying out an analysis of a set of university performance management documents which contain writing, photography, layout, tables, bulleted lists and numbers. In these documents semiotic resources are combined and organised in a way that re-contextualises (van Leeuwen and Wodak 1999) the social practices of research and teaching so that the management discourse can take control of them. This is necessary in order that these social practices can be transformed and presented as things that can be counted and measured, where outputs can be increased. We show how this cannot be fully understood through language analysis alone. And, most importantly, we show how the different kinds of semiotic resources are deployed to do very different things – because each has very specific affordances, which can be deployed for the purposes of re-contextualisation. These different kinds of semiotic resources should not be conceived as independent modes as they always operate, and indeed evolved, in relationship to others. A *social* point of departure here focusses specifically on how the different semiotic resources are deployed, in combinations, in this process of the re-contextualisation of social practices for ideological purposes.

Origins of multi-modality

A handful of very different books have been credited as founding the field of multi-modality. Two of these are Kress and van Leeuwen's *Reading Images* (1996) and O'Toole's *The Language of Displayed Art* (1994). The hugely different nature of these books characterises much of the variation that is now found in writing presented as multi-modality.

The two books were greatly influenced by the work of Michael Halliday (1978), where emphasis was on the social use of language. This differed from other theories of language. There was emphasis on how language should be understood as being shaped through its cultural, historical and social uses. There was also a shift away from the idea of a more rigid, or formal, grammar, to one of a system of semantic choices, or alternatives. Halliday's Systemic Functional Linguistics (SFL) sees language as an overall system of choices made up of layers of smaller subsystems which build into the whole. An important endeavour in SFL is to model these systems and subsystems called 'systemic networks'. These networks are seen as being based on three metafunctions underlying semiosis. Semiotic modes (connected systems of resources) are simultaneously used to say something about the world (the ideational metafunction), to signal our relationships (the interpersonal metafunction) and marshal these into a structured whole (the textual metafunction) (Halliday and Hasan 1985) (see Bloor and Bloor, this volume).

Reading Images and *The Language of Displayed Art* extended the social interpretation of language and its meanings to different aspects of visual communication. *Reading Images* draws on Hallidayan concepts but is also highly interdisciplinary, using semiotics and visual psychology. The book was influenced by the systemic part of Halliday's work and the drive to identify the systems of choices underlying communication. But it was also driven by the social part. Here analysis of all instances of communication tells us something about the contexts where they were produced, about social relations, about ideology and the kinds of motivated ideas that are being shared. This aspect of their work was also influenced by the work of the Marxist linguist Voloshinov (1973), which stresses that language must never be studied in abstract or in an unhistorical manner. The meaning of words is part of a struggle over the definition of reality where the powerful in society will seek control over this process. Signs are never fixed but have affordances which are always realised in communicative interactions, which will carry traces of the power relations underlying them. We show that this latter point is key for the way that multi-modality can be best tied to CDA.

The Language of Displayed Art is different in that it is more influenced by the systemic part of Halliday's work, with less emphasis on power. This book is oriented to show how concepts and forms of analysis used in linguistic-based systemic functional linguistics can be used to describe and model the systems that underlie works of art and sculpture.

These books have both been highly influential in linguistics, and *Reading Images* has been widely read and referenced beyond. Since the publications of these books, several strands of multi-modality have emerged. *Reading Images* has itself inspired a more critically oriented and interdisciplinary strand of multi-modality which has taken a more social rather than systemic approach. Here emphasis is more on the affordances of semiotic resources than on the system itself (Bezemer and Kress 2010; van Leeuwen 2005; Jewitt 2008; Kress 2010; Abousnnouga and Machin 2013; Djonov and van Leeuwen 2011). Like *Reading Images,* these works study uses of semiotic resources to make situated meaning and the ideologies and values that these carry, with an attempt to place these in the institutional contexts and interests that they serve.

While *Reading Images* has had a wider interest across academic disciplines, much of the work published as 'multi-modality', particularly from linguists, is more closely related to O'Toole's work. This work is often presented as 'social semiotic', but appears more driven by the systemic part of Halliday. Here excellent work has been produced (e.g., Martinec and Salway 2005; O'Halloran 2008; Caldwell 2014; Bateman 2008) which seek to provide insights into the systems that underlie different modes of communication. Such works produce systems networks of the found patterns, or show how different modes fulfil Halliday's communicative metafunctions. For example, O'Halloran (2008) shows how mathematics can be understood as multisemiotic discourse involving language, visual images and symbolism.

Another strand of multi-modality is the cognitive approach, inspired mainly by the work of Forceville (1996). This approach studies how visual metaphors, in film, advertising and cartoons, for example, as with metaphors in language (Charteris-Black 2014), can be used to shape perceptions of particular phenomenon. This approach has been taken on by some critical discourse analysts, for example, to show some visual metaphorical patters in the representation of immigrants (Catalano and Waugh 2013).

A further strand of multi-modality is Interactional Analysis, developed mainly through the innovative work of Scollon and Scollon (2004) and Norris (2004, 2011). This strand of multi-modality is a form of ethnographic work that draws attention to the way that meaning making is done through a highly subtle interplay of different semiotic resources such as language, gesture and posture, and in relation to context, proximity and rich cues in the environment. Looking at the subtleties of the specific multi-modal ensembles can reveal how different meanings are communicated at different levels, for example identity cues in social interactions (Norris 2011).

In sum, multi-modality shifts away from an emphasis on language as a site of meaning making, taking the traditions of the fine-grained analysis of linguistics to look at the use, and nature of, other semiotic resources. This has the potential to produce predictive models of the building blocks of different forms of communication, of graphic design, gesture, space, art, etc., and in turn create a more powerful tool for analysis of the actual use of resources in context.

Criticisms of multi-modality

There have been criticisms made of multi-modality, and these are highly useful for our purposes in this chapter, since they provide clear leads as to how we should proceed with multi-modal CDA. To begin with, it has been argued that across different published work in multi-modality there is a lack of consistency in how terms are used, where authors tend to come up with their own unique meanings (Forceville 2010). This has led to an expansion of new terminology which remains largely isolated and untested rather than developing and refining clear, defendable concepts. One reason for this expansion of untested concepts, Forceville (2010) argues, is that multi-modality takes on wide-raging topics rather than more localised studies around one thing, or one genre. The pattern has been to encompass more and more things rather than to try to focus carefully to produce detailed and highly defendable concepts and principles around one object of study.

One characteristic of this lack of testing of theories is that the analysis that takes place could be characterised as *post hoc* (Machin 2009). In this case it is not clear if what is found from the analysis is simply a product of the given analytical framework, of the labelling of semiotic phenomena. Reynolds (2012) expressed concern that multi-modal analysis may suffer from producing lots of descriptive concepts but fall short on showing how these actually produce clear insights. Providing new concepts and labelling phenomena endlessly is not the same as actually doing analysis and showing the payoff (Antaki et al. 2003).

Aligned with such criticisms, it has been argued that multi-modality must avoid the 'tunnel vision' (Forceville 2010; Machin 2013) of seeing all research matters through one single theory of language. There lies a danger in overlooking robust, tried and tested forms of analysis that already exist in other academic fields. It is fruitful and good scholarly practice to engage with these fields which can offer guiding principles into which the finer kinds of analysis multi-modality can be organised, such as in film studies and media studies. Also, to engage with practitioners and take an ethnographic approach might be fruitful in order to explore the actual use of semiotic resources.

In our steps to better understand how to proceed with a multi-modal CDA, we can learn from the drive to label and apply concepts from SFL to other kinds of semiotic resources. There has been an ongoing discussion of the systemic approach of the Hallidayan tradition, where the question has been asked as to whether it is fruitful to treat all different modes in the same way (van Leeuwen 1999). SFL tends to use texts and other semiotic materials in order to establish 'the grammar', the underlying systemic resources, departing from the assumption that the semiotic behaviour of sign-makers is guided by more or less the same conventions, regardless of the contexts and semiotic modes involved. This drive for a universal theory for meaning making can make the systemic side of semiosis the actual object of analysis in itself.

Kress (2010: 104) argues that: "A multimodal social-semiotic approach assumes that all modes of representation are, in principle, of equal significance in representation and communication, as all modes have potential for meaning, though differently with different modes". However, we would suggest that, while it may be one thing to argue that more elaborated semiotic resources, such as typography or layout, for example, have potential for meaning, it is another thing to argue that resources/modes are of equal significance. The drive to use concepts from SFL, to isolate underlying systems with the assumption that all modes are the same, can mean that there is a danger that we lose focus on the affordances that different kinds of semiotic resources carry, and therefore why they are deployed in contexts for specific ideological purposes. Not all kinds of semiotic resources are suitable to be described by the three metafunctions. Semiosis may be built on three principled metafunctions in the case of language, as Halliday (1978) shows, but it is not necessarily true for all kinds of semiotic resources, as the example of layout shows. Layout evolved to fulfil the affordance of the textual function. Therefore it can carry out ideological work through positioning and the creating of relationships between elements. There will of course be a kind of ideational and interpersonal consequences or qualities involved in layout but it does not realise them in itself. It is not the case that layout relies on the three metafunctions carrying out equal semiotic work. It is problematic too, to think of the photograph through these terms. For photographic theorists such as Barthes (1977) and Tagg (1988) the affordance of the photograph is that it claims to represent unmediated reality and conceals the means of its production. We will say more about the consequences for this observation in the analysis section of this paper. But here we emphasise the need to foreground the idea of affordances: what can a semiotic resource be used to do? As Bateman (2013) argues it is always possible to simply take a set of categories such as the metafunctions to look at an object, but this may be the very kind of imposing of concepts for which multi-modality has been criticised.

We also believe that it is fruitful to view different kinds of semiotic resources as existing in a way that is always tightly interwoven. Semiotic resources are co-articulated in communication and evolved in this multi- or inter-semiotic way. Breaking this into isolated modes risks compromising this idea. Semiotic resources must be conceived in the first place of as interdependent. They have affordances, possibilities and limitations and have inherent dependencies on each other. For example, writing materialises two-dimensionally in space and must get some spatial arrangement and given letter-forms or typography.

That modes exist in the independent way was recognised by Halliday (1975). When observing his son learning language, he saw that the evolving textual metafunction was in many ways realised outside grammar, or was paralinguistic. So we become coherent in speech with prosody, body language, posture, etc. – which all also carry important interpersonal functions. But in SFL this observation has never fully been taken up where the main task is about describing the systems of grammar (Halliday 2004).

Finally, and crucially for multi-modal CDA, an approach to modes which focuses on the systemic part of communication can serve to downplay the situated semiosis unfolding in time and space. Simply this risks a sociological or contextual blindness, since utterances are viewed as resulting from grammatical systems and therefore become detached from the interests of real people (Berge 2012; Holmberg 2012).

Multi-modality and the re-contextualisation of social practice

We now carry out an analysis of a sample of management steering documents that deploy different kinds of semiotic resources in order to represent the social practices that take place in a university in a way that serves their own interests. Put simply, the complexities and interrelated processes of teaching, research, staffing, and wider economic and social shifts must be represented in a way that allows it to appear that it is a simple matter of measuring them and then increasing outputs. One highly productive way to view this process is through the notion of the 're-contextualisation of social practice' (van Leeuwen and Wodak 1999). This is useful as it draws particular attention to the sequences of activity, or 'scripts' that can be understood as the 'doing' of discourses. Here discourse can be thought of as representing knowledge of what goes on in a particular social practice, ideas about why it is the way it is, who is involved and what kinds of values they hold. Discourses tell us why these scripts are reasonable ways of acting in the world.

van Leeuwen and Wodak (1999) argue that social practices can be re-contextualised in language through substitutions, additions, deletions and re-ordering of the sequences that comprise events. A social practice can be thought of as including the following kinds of elements: participants, ideas, values and attitudes; activities; social relations; objects and instruments; time and setting and causality. Analysis, therefore, looks for the ways that these elements of a social practice, as they take place in a university, for example, have been re-contextualised in a document. What kinds of obvious causality and identities have been deleted or substituted, for example, and what has been added? This attention to re-contextualisation helps to focus a critical socially driven multi-modal analysis where we reveal the ideologies buried in the use of different kinds of semiotic resources.

The re-contextualisation of work practice in a university

We now move on to our illustration of doing multi-modal CDA using a sample of performance management documents from one Swedish university. In CDA there has been much interest in the way that neoliberal management discourses are now coming to dominate the running of public institutions (Fairclough 1993; Mautner 2014). It has been shown that linguistically and visually, on websites and brochures, there has been a shift to represent universities in a way that is more akin to private companies oriented to competiveness, customer relations and self-promotion, than to institutions creating an educated citizenship (Teo 2007; Zhang O'Halloran 2013). The documents we analyse here can be seen as part of this process.

From the viewpoint of the university management, such processes allow the university to become better value for money, to provide a better service to the public and also provide clear accountability (Hall 2012). But critics of this management strategy suggest rather that in such cases public institutions cease to be operated along priorities based on the experiences of professional employees – on their knowledge of research processes and pedagogy – but on criteria that comes from a more generic management language, which may have little relation to the former criteria (Power 1997). Employees become de-professionalised and energies are increasingly diverted away from former core activities to showing that targets are being met (Power 1997).

The examples we select for analysis in this section here are partly a shift to these managerial principles in one university in Sweden. This took the form of shifts in organisational structure and involved the introduction of a new system of interrelated documents in which practices of teaching and research were re-contextualised to suit management needs. There was a new university promotional brochure and a new vision statement document. A further document was created to lay out the strategies that would allow the vision to be fulfilled, and in other documents staff were to describe activities they were carrying out in order to meet targets that were created in order to actualise the strategies. We analyse samples from each of these documents, which all deploy and combine semiotic modes in different ways, relying on their specific affordances and interrelationships to communicate and legitimise a neoliberal management discourse.

Photographs and layout

Our first example is from a promotional brochure, comprised of 16 glossy pages of A4 size and representing the university in a design built on boxes and framing. This creates spaces which can be filled with photographs of students, modernist spaces in the university, verbal success stories from professors and deans, and charts displaying how numbers rise for publications, students, employees, rankings, etc.

In Figure 4.1 we find a typical page from the brochure. We see the layout which uses a system of boxes of different sizes. Floch (2001) shows how on the one hand we should be mindful of the kinds of representations we find, so here of persons, places and objects and kinds of connotations they communicate, but on the other hand we should also pay attention to the way they are presented in design. Design refers to the general template in which different semiotic modes are deployed, to how discourses are given materiality and communicated (Kress and van Leeuwen 2001), and is, in our data, materialised in different layouts relying on the semiotic principle of coordination. We deal with representation in the images first.

In this case, we are dealing with the mode of photography. A major affordance of photography is that it relies on what Peirce (1984) calls iconic signs. Whereas language is based on

Figure 4.1 Page with visual coordination from promotional university brochure

abstract symbols, iconic signs depict actual things in the world, or resemblances to these things. For Barthes (1977) a photograph has no code. It can be a connotative message, but this is at the level of production and reception and not at the level of the message itself. The affordance of the photograph is that it claims to represent unmediated reality. For Tagg (1988) this is the ideological trick of the photograph. It produces an all-seeing spectator yet removes the means of its production. In these photographs, therefore, we can see specific buildings, interiors and persons in the photos in a way that could not be directly depicted by language (Tagg 1988).

What is also important is that these photographs can communicate other symbolic and ideological meanings, where the denotation or descriptive power helps to naturalise them (Barthes 1977). In this case, while these images depict airy, communal spaces of different kinds, space in itself is a key signifier. Across these documents we find large communal-type spaces, with lots of glass and staircases, rather than smaller private spaces. There are no collectives or large groups of students; people are on their own or engaged in personal communication. We never find confined or densely crowded spaces or clutter. Throughout our corpus, as we will show, 'space' tends to take on metaphorical meanings (Lakoff and Johnson 1980) and stand for the 'luxury of space', the 'power over space', 'room to breathe', 'freedom'.

Another connotation in these images is a sense of dynamism and energy. Camera angles and cropping are used to create more exciting angles. A dynamism is also created in the layout, in which the size of the photos varies, with the young woman to the right being the largest one and interpersonally fore-grounded. The woman is represented in an open space, quite close to us, leaning forward and concentrating on a book. Language could in principle also have been used (it is in other parts of the brochure) to give her a name and a voice, so that she could tell us what is going on, but often photos in our corpus work through metonymy. This means that the individuality of the person or object depicted is not of interest in itself. In this case the woman represents a generic student. By the same token, research is met-onymically represented by test tubes in close distance, one of them being lifted by fingers, suggesting 'engagement in science', and by a close shot of two old books with patina in the right bottom corner, a metonymy possibly interpreted as 'the humanities', or 'study'. Across our sample, research is represented largely through hands using scientific equipment or point-ing to diagrams which appear from science. Research is depicted with immediacy due to the affordances of photography, but it is not easily comprehensible.

An important metaphorical meaning in these images is 'on the move'. Stairs are recurrent in our corpus, as found in the top-right photo, and suggest movement, speed and lightness. The bottom-left photo of a wavy railing has little sense without being interpreted metaphori-cally. In fact, in the graphic profile of the university engraved wavy lines are recurrent and used on all publications, including the template for PowerPoint presentations. This dynamism aligns with the core values of neoliberalism: ready for change, improving performance, being successful.

Moving on to the mode of layout, and including graphics, we find a semiotic principle which connotes a sense of boxing in the world and representing it as a framed set of compo-nents. We can think about this particular arrangement of photographs as a kind of conceptual representation that is part 'classificational' and part 'analytical' (Kress and van Leeuwen 1996). In classificational structures elements are represented through a kind of taxonomy, overt or covert, which usually suggest some kind of hierarchy, but which certainly suggests kinds of relations or commonality. Analytical processes in contrast set up part-whole relationships sug-gesting a fit between them. In both cases these kinds of structures can be used ideologically to suggest that such links, such taxonomies are natural and logical. Elements and identities which are very different in order, even with clashing interests, or which have specific places in causal chains, can be fused together or presented as parts of whole.

In terms of the re-contextualisation of social practice, we begin to see the substitution of complex processes such as research by a limited iconography and the deletion of actual participants (teachers and larger student numbers) and social relations. Additions are accom-plished by design and iconography to connote dynamism, the freedom of space and the logic of categorization.

Combining photographs with writing

Performance management must be made operational; it must represent what teachers and researchers do in a way that can be measured and monitored. A chain of documents was cre-ated along with the promotional brochure in order to do this, starting from a vision document called *Vision 2016,* published in 2011. This document introduced a new steering system at the university and was part of a rebrand that began in 2008 with the arrival of a new management and senior administration. At the time there was increasing pressure by the government to introduce more cost efficiency into universities and that they should demonstrate how they are serving the market needs of society. The document is a 20-page prestige brochure in colour, produced in cooperation with an advertising agency and given to all staff. It comprises statements from the Vice Chancellor and the management, combined with success stories from established professors, who are interviewed. Pages contain small amounts of text and photos, which follow the patterns of connotation, boxing and coordination that we observed in the promotional document. There is once again an emphasis on space in the layout as can be seen in Figure 4.2, in this case realised by empty white space on the page. The affordances of layout bring photographs and writing into blocks and arrange them so that they take on new meanings as a multi-modal ensemble.

Figure 4.2 states a vision for research (*forskning*). Here science is used to symbolise all research in the university, which is metonymically evoked through the easily recognisable iconography of the test tube and the gloved hand. Again cropping gives a dynamic character to the page. The sense of being 'on the move' reappears in the non-symmetrical layout, which separates visual and verbal components and arranges them almost like a staircase, rising up to the right.

In this case we want to look at the discourses communicated in writing. Here it is the goal for research:

> Our goal is to conduct free and creative research that meets different needs, and where we seek to go beyond traditional boundaries. We are a university that attracts eminent scholars and seeks partnerships that develop the quality of our research.

The symbolic values of the layout and photographs are echoed in verbal expressions like "free and creative", "seek to go beyond traditional boundaries", "develop the quality". Both visually and verbally we find the generic empty management-speak discussed by Chiapello and Fairclough (2002).

Characteristic of all of the documents in our corpus, it is not clear who is the agent of activities, who specifically will meet the goals. This ambiguity starts in the vision document itself. To begin with, the use of "we" is broad. For example:

> Our goal is to conduct free and creative research...

In this case the possessive form "our" could include everyone at the university. And possibly also in this case:

> We are a university that attracts eminent scholars...

"Our" and "we" are metonymically made synonymous with the university. But there is a constant ambivalence in the reference of these first person pronouns. The staff could be included in the "we" that attracts eminent scholars. The interpretation of "our" is more ambiguous – an employee could interpret it as management speaking from above or feel part of a vision of creativity. In CDA it has been shown that pronouns are one of the best grammatical categories for the expression and manipulation of social relations, status and power (van Dijk 1998: 203). The ambiguous "we" in the university documents has this effect of sometimes inviting staff as agents, but often clearly as objects, as having the participant role

FORSKNING

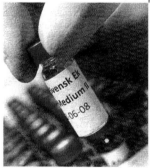

Vi har som mål att bedriva fri och kreativ forskning, som möter olika behov, och där vi eftersträvar ett gränsöverskridande angreppssätt. Vi är ett universitet som attraherar framstående forskare och söker samarbeten som utvecklar kvaliteten i forskningen."

Figure 4.2   Vision for research in Vision 2016 with a typical emphasis on space

of beneficiary or goal. In this way the management discourse can subtly involve everyone, so that it does not actually become a question of obeying. This must be understood as being part of the ensemble where there is a visual over-determination of space ('room to breathe', 'luxury', etc.), which creates a sense of something technical and simultaneously something creative and dynamic, free of clutter and divorced from the practical realities of everyday life. To resist the will of the "we" of the university is to be against these discourses communicated by photographs and layout.

The actual agents of the processes laid out in the vision statements are omitted through the use of nominalisations, here the recurring "research" but also the participle "boundary crossing". These nominalisations help to conceal other important micro details such as what is meant by "conduct free and creative research". Nominalisations delete agents, temporality and causalities, so that we don't get to know *what* needs to be developed *when* and by *whom*. Importantly at this point researchers are not an explicit part of the language. We see that the affordances of writing allow for de-contextualisation, so that the social practices of research, with all sorts of different priorities in different subject areas, can be re-contextualised and presented in a one-size-fits-all way and monitored by this powerful "we".

Language, lists and bullet points

In order to make the vision operational, the document *Vision, mål och strategier för Örebro universitet* ("Vision, goals and strategies for Orebro University") was produced in 2012. The high status of the document is signalled by its design. Unlike other university documents that are A4, this is produced in A5 with only 8 pages to provide, we were told by the senior administrators involved in its design, a practical, consultable reference for practice in the university. The design has many features of a promotional brochure and, once again, uses dynamic symbolic images and a highly spacious layout. The cover carries engraved fine, wavy light-blue lines, connoting a sense of 'on the move'. Images contain motion blurring which also suggests movement.

As seen in Figure 4.4, which provides the English translation, the goal for research from the vision is now attached to strategies and sits on its own page in large font surrounded by large borders. The design is built on the semiotic principle of coordination, and this time units of writing rather than the photographs become the boxed units in a bulleted list.

MÅL 2.
FORSKNING

Vi har som mål att bedriva fri och kreativ forskning, som mÖter olika behov, och där vi efterstravar ett gräns- Överskridande angreppssätt. Vi är ett universitet som attraherar framstående forskare och sÖker samarbeten som utvecklar kvaliteten i forskningen.

STRATEGIER

Vi ska . . .

2.1 kvalitetsprÖva våra forskningsresultat genom Ökad internationell vetenskaplig publicering.
2.2 utveckla våra internationella forskningssamarbeten.

2.3 stimulera aktiviteter fÖr att kraftigt Öka våra externa forskningsmedel.

2.4 uppmarksämma forskningsaktiviteter, forskningsresultat och konstnärligt utvecklingsarbete som bidrar till att upp-fylla universitetets Övergripande mål.

Figure 4.3   The goal and strategies for research

Research is the second of the four goals or targets of the university; we give a translation:

GOAL 2.

RESEARCH

Our goal is to conduct free and creative research that meets different needs, and where we seek a transnational approach. We are a university that attracts eminent scholars and looks for partnerships that develop the quality of the research.

STRATEGIES

We will. . .

2.1 test out the quality of our research in established international scholarly publishing.

2.2 develop our international research collaborations.

2.3 stimulate activities to significantly increase our external research funding.

2.4 pay attention to research activities, research results and developmental work in Applied Arts that contribute to the fulfilment of the university's main goals.

Figure 4.4   English translation of the goal and strategies for research

This document is comprised of bullet points throughout. The spacing used enhances the sense of dealing with discrete units. Presented in this form with numbers (2.1, 2.2, 2.3, 2.4) it is realised through abstract, or scientific, modality. Abstract or scientific modality claims to represent the bare technical details of a thing or process (Kress and van Leeuwen 1996) rather than the naturalistic details. It could be the difference between an actual photograph of a human heart, for example, and a labelled diagram to be used by medical students. Abstract modality brings a sense of logic, of data and of precision.

In the language of the strategies, the shifting, over-determined use of "we" is also found:

We will pay attention to research activities that contribute to the fulfilment of the university's main goals.

We will develop our international research collaboration.

Again the first sentence is more a concern for management, whereas the second seems to include actual researchers. As we have seen, the institutional "we" in the documents is sometimes acting upon the staff, i.e., part a management practice, sometimes involved in the actual work, i.e., part of the practices of teaching and research.

In the listed strategies we find extensive omission of social actors, through the recurring use of nominalisations such as "research", "collaboration" and "publishing". In the university

71

many staff operate on full-time, rolling, teaching contracts. What is not clear in this case is who is to be involved in these processes. Who will "increase external research funding"? Such things become ideas which are found in documents and discussed in meetings but which are never tied to concrete processes nor persons.

Nominalisations have a very specific use in this text. Halliday (1978) describes nominalisations as a shift from encoding as 'process' to encoding as 'product'. Such productisation allows for modifications. For example, things like "research" can then be placed in long compounds, sometimes in heavy nominal groups, such as "research-collaborations", "research-activities", "research-result", "research-funding", "development-work". In this way, different processes, like "research" and "activities" are brought together in a way that captures more or less anything done in research.

Compounds are also linguistically coordinated as discrete units – for example in strategy 2.4: "research activities, research results and developmental work in Applied Arts". What has happened here is that complex issues (such as research and teaching, different kinds of research carried out in humanities, science and Arts) become fused together by coordination. Details of differences, complexities and conflicting interests that might seem key to doing research and teaching from the point of view of academic employees are suppressed.

Multi-modally here the fragmentation and coordination of processes at the linguistic level are represented through connotations of technical modality working as part of the ensembles created by layout with boxing, space, the optimistic dynamic images which present the attributes of the university. Dense complex sentences are presented as discrete and logical units which themselves sit in luxurious space with room to breathe. The university is 'on the move', and these technical bullet points are the key. Once again, this is achieved in a fundamentally multi-modal way. Re-contextualisation here is done through extensive deletion of agency and causal relations in language and through additions of the meanings of precision, of separation and logic, through the layout.

Writing and (false) tables

From the lists of strategies a more detailed document was generated called *The Operational Plan* comprised of 32 pages containing different tables and instructions. Table 4.1 shows one of these tables called an 'activity plan'. This is the document where all course directors have to show how they are meeting one specific selection of targets. We can see in Table 4.1 that this is presented as a table where the administrators list target areas in the left-hand column. The activity, who is responsible and the completion date are to be filled in.

This is, we argue, a 'false' use of a table. Tables have evolved as a semiotic and multi-modal tool to have a very specific set of affordances. Here the connotations of these affordances are deployed for the purposes of re-contextualisation. This is important such tables dominate the steering documents and are extremely useful tools for creating a sense of agency and process where, in fact, as we have seen in the previous examples, details of these have been lost. What the affordances of these tables do is two things: they allow the very different, complex and often falsely isolated things placed in columns to appear of the same order. They also create a sense that there are indeed sequences of causality and identifiable agents.

To fill out this form a course director will list an activity that shows what they will do by a specific date to fulfil each target: increase quantity of publications, have well-trained teachers or create links between teaching and labour markets. In fact the actual processes and persons required to address all of these issues are complex, usually overlap and are based in structural issues regarding things like staff time, teaching loads, the fact that over half university staff have

Table 4.1 The activity plan included in the document Operational Plan

Target areas in Örebro university strategy	Activity	Who is responsible	Completed by
Priority target areas			
UKÄ's quality assessment			
External resources			
Attractiveness			
• *Increase the number of first-hand student applications*			
• *Increase the number of qualified applicants for teaching positions*			
Other target areas			
Education			
Establishment on the labour market			
Number of teachers with PhD/merited in applied Arts			
Particularly qualified teachers			
Arriving and departing students			
Research			
Field normalised citation index			
Level of publications, Norwegian model			
Number of applications approved			
Total volume of research			

temporary contracts, and that central government in Sweden controls student numbers. But there is no room for this on the table, and those required to complete the table may have no expertise or experience to allow them to do so. In fact what gets written in the activity column is mostly "seminars", "meetings" and "workshops". These events will be very unlikely to be able to address actual structural issues, but they allow staff to show that individual strategies are being followed.

In terms of the work of Kress and van Leeuwen (1996) and Ledin (2015), tables can be thought of as conceptual processes that are spatially structured. This means that elements are set into relation with one another not by narrative where clear causality, agents and outcomes are stated but by the use of graphical and spatial features. Conceptual processes suggest hierarchies of order and relations between elements through spatial arrangement. The use of the activity table serves just such a purpose.

Tables, when used properly, are powerful because their main affordance is to make detailed and systematic comparisons possible. First, the affordances of a table suggest that columns each contain an individual paradigm, in other words, things of the same order. The idea is that looking down the column all elements, whether written in language or numbers, are of one particular. So in one column we could have types of cars and in columns to the right numbers which show how much petrol each consumes, or how fast they go. In the activity table this is not the case, and columns do not contain actual paradigms. The targets in column one are each of a very different order. For example, "Field normalised citation index" is a complex and contested method for measuring research, and it is not clear what individual members of staff, many working as full-time teachers and others with little publishing experience, can do to address this. "Increase the number of first-hand student applications" is also highly complex, and it is hard to imagine what individual staff can do about this. But importantly it is a very different kind of thing to research. The affordances of the column, however, help to make these targets appear as being of the same paradigm. Clearly the table here, with its technical modality and classificatory structure, allows the management, as with the use of bullet points, to connote breaking things down into interrelated components and systematised processes, where they are not in fact so.

The second affordance of the table is that rows set up a syntagmatic relationship between the columns. In other words the boxes across a row are logically or sequentially related. For example, if in column 1 we find the name of a brand of car, we expect the following columns to provide information about that car. We can use the concept of 'given' and 'new' (Kress and van Leeuwen 1996) to bring out the syntagmatic affordances of the table.

The concept 'given and new' can be used to characterise what is represented as given established knowledge and information in a text or image, and what is represented as the new, or the contestable, the possible. We can think of the targets in the left column as the given. For example, we need to increase publications, or we need to have more applicants. These are represented therefore as taken for granted and established, rather than themselves being contestable. Here such targets are presented as technical information for practical purposes through the modality of the table. The columns to the right are then the new and, across the rows in this table, provide a sequence of the identified solution to the target being met, the agent and the time scale. And even though the thematic or given paradigm may be contradictory this is suppressed by placing it within the syntagm.

The process of re-contextualisation here is one of a process of substitution where the table presents a causal sequence of getting things done. This replacing those which comprise the actual social practices that take place in the university as regards teaching, research and student recruitment. The deployment of the table, like the bullet points, adds a sense that this is a systematic and rigorous process, when of course all actual details have been suppressed.

Conclusion

Overall this analysis finds many of the characteristics of management language found by other critical scholars: market-oriented buzzwords, such as 'dynamic', 'creative', 'quality', promotional genres which background the civic role of education to address a student as consumer, offering them a kind of pleasant experience. But this detailed multi-modal analysis, with a focus on the role of the affordances of different kinds of semiotic resources, has allowed us to show something else as regards the way this management discourse is realised. We have pointed to the co-articulation of semiotic resources to allow the complexities of processes in a university to be re-contextualised, breaking them down into product-ised elements, some of which can be seen visually in images, yet all presented as a technical process, where in each case output must increase. Processes and agents are absent and present in different ways in different semiotic ensembles, yet the sum allows a complete fragmentation of what goes on in a university in a way that favours the management discourse over that of the professional employees.

What we have also begun to show is that MDCA departs from the social question: what semiotic resources are drawn upon in this communication of discourse in order to carry out ideological work? In our case study, we have described how the modes of photography, writing and layout, with their different affordances, are deployed and combined as elaborated semiotic resources in the management discourse. We see this kind of affordance-driven approach as best aligned with the core aims of CDA, to draw out buried ideologies and reveal power relations. It avoids the risks run by more system-driven multi-modal approaches which might lose the way these different modes work simply by treating them all in the same way as language and assuming that all fulfil the three metafunctions in identical fashion.

We also believe that this analysis has helped to show the potential for understanding communication and ideology by dealing in detail with focused and isolated studies rather than by expanding the field of analysis across all forms of communication. This appears to be the best way forward to help create more robust tools and concepts. And we hope it also points to the need to draw on expertise from other fields of study, such as semiotics where there already exists a wealth of strong theory and descriptive tools. And finally we show how tools from multi-modality have a place in this, where they do indeed help us draw attention to the finer details of texts and other objects of analysis, in ways that other theories of the visual do not. But this must be done from a social rather than systemic perspective; it must show how and why different modes are deployed, and there simply must be clear analytical payoff.

Further reading

Machin, D., and Mayr, A. (2012). *How to do critical discourse analysis: A multimodal introduction*. London: Sage.

This book presents an introduction to carrying out critical analysis of the language, images and design of media and documents. Chapters offer different tools for analysis showing how these can be used to dig out buried ideologies.

Roderick, I. (2016). The politics of office design: Translating neoliberalism into furnishing. *Journal of Language and Politics* 15(3): 274–287.

This paper shows how we can carry out a multi-modal critical discourse analysis of office design. The author shows how the affordances of semiotic resources, such as framing and space, can be used to indicate how space is to be used, how fixed or flexible work roles are and what kinds of social relations are required. The analysis draws out the features of a more neoliberal kind of office space.

Ledin, P., and Machin, D. (2016). The evolution of performance management discourse in corporate strategy diagrams for public institutions. *Discourse, Context and Media* 13(B): 122–131.

This paper provides a model for analysing the affordances of flow charts and diagrams, for revealing the way that these can conceal the ideological interests of their makers. These are then applied to examples to show how the strategic diagrams of public institutions have changed over roughly a decade as they have sought to represent workplace practices for market principles. The paper shows how these have moved further into abstraction as performance management discourses have become more naturalised.

References

Abousnnouga, G. and Machin, D. (2013). *The language of war monuments*. London: Bloomsbury.

Antaki, C., Billig, M., Edwards, D. and Potter, J. (2003). Discourse analysis means doing analysis: A critique of six analytic shortcomings. *Discourse Analysis Online* 1: 1–22.

Bal, M. (1991). *Reading Rembrandt: Beyond the word-image opposition*. Cambridge: Cambridge University Press.

Barthes, R. (1977). *Image, music, text*. London: Fontana.

Bateman, J. (2008). *Multimodality and genre*. Basingstoke, New York: Palgrave: Macmillan.

Bateman, J. (2013). Review of the *Language of colour: An introduction* (2009) by Theo van Leeuwen, London: Routledge. *Linguistics and the Human Sciences* 9(1). https://journals.equinoxpub.com/index.php/LHS/article/view/20898/0

Berge, K. L. (2012). Om forsjellene mellom systemisk-funksjonell lingvistikk og tekstvitenksap. In S. Matre, R. Solheim and D. K. Sjøhelle (eds.), *Teorier om tekst i møte med skolens lese- og skrivepraksiser*, 72–90. Oslo: Universitetsforlaget.

Bezemer, J. and Kress, G. (2010). Changing text: A social semiotic analysis of textbooks. *Designs for Learning* 3(1–2): 10–29.

Caldwell, D. (2014). The interpersonal voice: Applying appraisal to the rap and sung voice. *Social Semiotics* 24(1): 40–55.

Charteris-Black, J. (2014). *Analysing political speeches: Rhetoric, discourse and metaphor*. Basingstoke: Palgrave Macmillan.

Chiapello, E. and Fairclough, N. (2002). Understanding the new management ideology: A transdisciplinary contribution from critical discourse analysis and the new sociology of capitalism. *Discourse & Society* 13(2): 185–208.

Djonov, E. and van Leeuwen, T. (2011). The semiotics of texture: From haptic to visual. *Visual Communication* 10(4): 541–564.

Djonov, E. and Zhao, S. (eds.) (2014). *Critical multimodal studies of popular discourse*. New York: Routledge.

Fairclough, N. (1993). Critical discourse analysis and the marketization of public discourse: The Universities. *Discourse & Society* 4(2): 133–168.

Floch, J-M. (2001). *Visual identities*. London: Continuum.

Forceville, C. (1996). *Pictorial metaphor in advertising*. London: Routledge.

Forceville, C. (2007). Review of Anthony Baldry and Paul J. Thibault, multimodal transcription and text analysis (Equinox 2006). *Journal of Pragmatics* 39: 1235–1238.

Forceville, C. (2010). Review of *The Routledge handbook of multimodal analysis,* Carey Jewitt (ed.), Routledge, London, 2009. *Journal of Pragmatics* 42: 2604–2608.

Hall, P. (2012). *Managementbyråkrati – organisationspolitisk makt i svensk offentlig förvaltning*. Malmö: Liber.

Halliday, M.A.K. (1975). *Learning how to mean: Explorations in the development of language*. London: Edward Arnold.

Halliday, M.A.K. (1978). *Language as social semiotic: The social interpretation of language and meaning*. London: Edward Arnold.

Halliday, M.A.K. (2004). *An introduction to functional grammar,* 3rd edn. London: Arnold.

Halliday, M.A.K. and Hasan, R. (1985). *Language, context, and text: Aspects of language in a social-semiotic perspective*. Oxford: Oxford University Press.

Holmberg, P. (2012). Kontext som aktivitet, situationstyp och praktik: En kritisk analys av kontextbegreppet i systemisk-funktionell teori. *Språk och stil* 22(1): 67–86.

Jewitt, C. (2008). Multimodality and literacy in school classrooms. *Review of Research in Education* 32: 241–267.

Kress, G. (2010). *Multimodality: A social semiotic approach to contemporary communication*. London: Routledge.

Kress, G. and van Leeuwen, T. (1996). *Reading images: The grammar of visual design*. London: Routledge.

Kress, G. and van Leeuwen, T. (2001). *Multimodal discourse: The modes and media of contemporary communication*. London: Arnold.

Lakoff, G. and Johnson, M. (1980). *Metaphors we live by*. Chicago: University of Chicago Press.

Ledin, P. (2015). Listans och tabellens semiotik. *Sakprosa* 7(1): 1–25. www.journals.uio.no/index.php/sakprosa/article/view/947

Machin, D. (2009). Multimodality and theories of the visual. In C. Jewitt (ed.), *The Routledge handbook of multimodal analysis,* 181–190. London: Routledge.

Machin, D. (2013). What is multimodal critical discourse studies? *Critical Discourse Studies* 10(4): 347–355.

Machin, D. and Mayr, A. (2012). *How to do critical discourse analysis*. London: Sage.

Mayr, A. and Machin, D. (2012). *The language of crime and deviance*. London: Bloomsbury.

Norris, S. (2004). *Analyzing multimodal interaction: A methodological framework*. London: Routledge.

Norris, S. (2011). *Identity in (inter)action: Introducing multimodal (inter)action analysis*. Berlin, Boston, MA: de Gruyter Mouton.

O'Halloran, K. L. (2008). Systemic functional multimodal discourse analysis (SF-MDA): Constructing ideational meaning using language and visual imagery. *Visual Communication* 7(4): 443–475.

Peirce, C. S. (1984). *Writings of Charles S. Peirce: A chronological edition. Vol. 2, 1867–1871*. Bloomington, IN: Indiana University Press.

Power, M. (1997). *The audit society: Rituals of verification*. Milton Keynes: Open University Press.

Reynolds, E. (2012). Review of Sigrid Norris, identity in (inter)action: Introducing multimodal (inter) action analysis. *De Gruyter Discourse Studies* 14(6): 805–817.

Scollon, R. and Scollon, S. W. (2004). *Nexus analysis*. London: Routledge.

Tagg, J. (1988). *The burden of representation: Essays on photographies and histories*. Basingstoke: Macmillan.

Teo, P. (2007). The marketization of higher education: A comparative case-study of two in Singapore. *CADAAD Journal* 1(1). http://cadaad.net/2007_volume_1_issue_1/12–18

van Dijk, T. A. (1998). *Ideology: A multidisciplinary approach*. London: Sage.

van Leeuwen, T. (1999). *Speech, music, sound*. Basingstoke: Macmillan.

van Leeuwen, T. (2005). *Introducing social semiotics*. London: Routledge.

Voloshinov, V. (1973). *Marxism and the philosophy of language*. Seminar Press, in liaison with the Harvard University Press and the Academic Press Inc. Cambridge: Harvard University Press.

Zhang, J. and O'Halloran, K. (2013). Toward a global knowledge enterprise: University websites as portals to the ongoing marketization of higher education. *Critical Discourse Studies* 10(4): 468–485.

5

Cognitive Linguistic critical discourse studies

Christopher Hart

1. Introduction

One of the more recent developments on the Critical Discourse Studies (CDS) landscape lies in critical applications of Cognitive Linguistics (e.g., Chilton 2004; Koller 2004; Hart 2010, 2011a, 2014a; Hart and Lukeš 2007). Cognitive Linguistic CDS (CL-CDS) is characterised by a shift in focus to the interpretation-stage of analysis (O'Halloran 2003; Hart 2010). That is, CL-CDS addresses the cognitive-semiotic processes involved in understanding discourse and the fundamental role that these processes play in the construction of knowledge and the legitimation of action. Cognitive Linguistic approaches to CDS thus typically present detailed semantic analyses of language usages. In particular, CL-CDS emphasises the conceptual nature of meaning construction and is concerned with modelling the conceptual structures and processes which, invoked by text in the course of discourse, constitute an ideologised understanding of the situations and events being described. Cognitive Linguistics itself is not a specific theory but a paradigm within linguistics comprised of several related theories. Accordingly, Cognitive Linguistics makes available to CDS a set of alternative 'tools' as different theories may be operationalised as methodologies in critical analyses of discourse. Theories in Cognitive Linguistics, however, share a common set of assumptions about the nature of language. These assumptions are naturally shared by Cognitive Linguistic studies in CDS and thus provide the common thread and theoretical backdrop that defines a more general Cognitive Linguistic school of CDS (cf. Hart 2011b, 2015). In this chapter, then, I begin, in Section 2, by introducing the Cognitive Linguistic perspective, reviewing the common aims and commitments of Cognitive Linguistic approaches to CDS. In Section 3, I introduce some of the methods employed in Cognitive Linguistic approaches. And finally in Section 4, I provide an example analysis using data sourced from three analyses newspaper articles reporting on the 2014 Million Mask March in London.

2. Cognitive Linguistic approaches to CDS: aims and commitments

Like most schools or approaches within CDS, Cognitive Linguistic approaches are not restricted to the application of a single analytical framework. Rather, what demarcates and characterises Cognitive Linguistic approaches is a particular theoretical perspective on language and a particular emphasis or orientation in doing critical discourse research. Cognitive Linguistic approaches, for example, subscribe to a view of language in which meaning is seen as conceptual in nature (Lakoff and Johnson 1980, 1999; Langacker 2008; Talmy 2000). Language usages are seen as prompts for the co-construction of meaning jointly performed through a range of conceptual processes or 'construal operations' (Croft and Cruse 2004). Principle aims of Cognitive Linguistic approaches are then (i) to model the conceptual structures invoked by language; and (ii) to disclose the ideological qualities and legitimating potentials which conceptual structures, invoked by particular language usages in contexts of social and political communication, may carry. In so doing, Cognitive Linguistic approaches are oriented to what Fairclough terms "interpretation-stage analysis", which involves "more psychological and cognitive concerns" (Fairclough 1995: 59) with how readers construct meaning (see Hart 2010; O'Halloran 2003). That is, Cognitive Linguistic approaches are concerned primarily with cognitive processes of semiosis.[1] This emphasis is based on the assumption that the processes of meaning construction which give power to texts to enact ideology and mobilise social action are necessarily "taking place in the minds of (interacting) individuals" (Chilton 2005a: 23).[2] Cognitive Linguistic approaches to CDS may also be seen as motivated by critical reactions to other strands of CDS (cf. Hart 2014a). As Jeffries (2010: 128) puts it:

> While sub-disciplines of linguistics like Critical Discourse Analysis have long asserted the truth of a Whorfian-style effect of culturally dominant texts, they have also been criticised for making too much of this in the absence of hard evidence of the process by which such hegemonic power is wielded and the objection that readers are not so vulnerable to ideological manipulation as the statements may suggest. However, the use of cognitive theories. . . as an "explanatory" device could help us to understand the mechanisms by which some such ideological influence may indeed operate.

To address the ideological and legitimating functions of language and conceptualisation, various frameworks in Cognitive Linguistics are drawn upon, including Force-Dynamics (Talmy 1988, 2000), Cognitive Grammar (Langacker 1987, 1991, 2002, 2008), Conceptual Metaphor Theory (Lakoff and Johnson 1980, 1999), Mental Spaces Theory (Fauconnier 1994, 1997), Conceptual Blending Theory (Fauconnier and Turner 2002), Text World Theory (Werth 1999) and Discourse Space Theory (Chilton 2004).[3] These frameworks, although addressing different aspects of meaning construction, all share a common view of language. It is this view which defines Cognitive Linguistics and thus Cognitive Linguistic approaches to CDS. It can be summarised under three major theses:

- **Symbolic thesis:** language is seen as a system of 'symbolic assemblies' (Langacker 1991, 2002) in which both words and grammatical constructions are paired with abstract knowledge structures that are conceptual in nature.
- **Experientialist thesis:** the knowledge structures with which linguistic units are paired are not innate or specific to the language system but are more general knowledge structures derived from experience, including (i) experiences we have as members of a particular culture or society and (ii) universal experiences we have as a consequence of the kind of bodies we have and our interactions with or observations of the physical environment.[4]
- **Encyclopaedic thesis:** Although paired immediately with a particular conceptual structure, linguistic meaning is not 'closed'. Words and constructions afford access to their

conceptual counterparts which, in turn, afford access to further conceptual structure within the same area of experience. Meaning in language, in other words, is open-ended.

From these epistemological commitments, a number of significant corollaries follow. For example, it follows from the symbolic thesis that grammar and lexicon are not distinct components of the language system. Words and constructions both carry semantic content which is distinguished only by its degree of abstractness. Grammatical constructions are not assembled ad hoc according to generative principles but are stored as discrete conventionalised units in the same way as words. Lexical and grammatical units may therefore be described as existing on the same continuum. Similarly, no distinction is made between literal and figurative language. Metaphorical expressions are principally no different from words or grammatical constructions in so far as they index abstract knowledge structures in the form of conceptual metaphors (Lakoff and Johnson 1980).

It follows from the experientialist thesis that language itself is not an autonomous cognitive faculty. The cognitive processes involved in language are not unique to language but are manifestations of more general cognitive processes found to function in other non-linguistic domains of cognition, including memory, perception and action. Space, in particular, represents a fundamental area of embodied experience. Spatial cognition therefore plays a key role in structuring concepts and conceptualisation and is naturally exploited in political discourse (Chilton 2004; Hart 2014a; see also Cap, this volume). Evans and Green (2006: 27) thus describe a *cognitive commitment* in Cognitive Linguistics as the "commitment to providing a characterisation of general principles of language which accord with what is known about the mind and brain from other disciplines". The conceptual processes maintained in Cognitive Linguistics to provide meaning to language therefore often have parallels in mental processes observed in other areas of cognitive experience. It further follows that meaning is 'situated', bound to one's own position in the cultural and physical context of interpretation.

It follows from all three theses that alternate language usages are functional in effecting *construal,* which refers to "our manifest ability to conceive and portray the same situation in alternate ways" (Langacker 2013: 43). Meaning is achieved in discourse as textual elements invoke the conceptual structures and processes they conventionally index in order to construct an (inter)subjective mental representation which constitutes a shared understanding of the referential situation. Since language provides multiple means of describing the same situation, however, competing language usages invite alternative conceptualisations. Crucially, then, it is in the particular construal of a situation that ideology and (de)legitimation are enacted. Conceptualisations invoked in discourse constitute only one potential, perspectivised, understanding of reality. The particular construal encoded defines reality in a way which accords with wider systems of knowledge and value (discourses) and acts heuristically to direct and delimit inference and action. It is then the aim of Cognitive Linguistic approaches to CDS to critically examine the conceptual structures and processes which are constitutive of meaning in discourse to disclose the particular patterns of belief and value they support.

3. Cognitive Linguistic approaches to CDS: methodological frameworks

Cognitive Linguistic approaches to CDS exploit the multitude of frameworks which Cognitive Linguistics makes available to address the conceptual structures and processes through which we make meaning. However, three programmes in particular currently stand out as being the most developed and widely applied:

- Image schema analysis
- Metaphor analysis
- Discourse world analysis

In **image schema analysis**, scholars address the way that situations and events are structured by image schemas. Image schemas are abstract holistic knowledge structures which emerge pre-linguistically from repeated patterns of embodied experience (Johnson 1987; Mandler 2004). They arise in basic domains like ACTION, FORCE, SPACE and MOTION encoding relational information pertaining, for example, to topology, sequence and causation. Image schemas form the foundations of the conceptual system and provide 'folk theories' of the way the world works. They later "work their way up into our system of meaning" (Johnson 1987: 42) to become paired with lexical and grammatical units inside the system of symbolic assemblies which makes up language. In discourse, they are invoked by their reflexes in text to constitute our most basic understanding of the event being described, defining its type and internal structure. Their selection in discourse thus serves an ideological function in categorising and organising reality as well as in directing inference. Different schemas, further, define different semantic roles within the event-structure, thus attributing particular qualities to the actors involved. There is also then an ideological dimension in assigning social actors to the different roles specified within the schema (Wolf and Polzenhagen 2003: 265). The ideological functions of image schemas have been studied in a range of discursive contexts (e.g., Chilton 1996; Hart 2011, 2013a,b; Nuñez Perucha 2011; Oakley 2005). In many of these cases, the image schemas involved have served as source domains in conceptual metaphors.

Metaphor analysis is perhaps the earliest and most recognised application of Cognitive Linguistics in CDS (see Ng, this volume, for a general overview). Several edited collections have been specifically dedicated to analysing metaphor from a broadly critical Cognitive Linguistic perspective (e.g., Dirven, Frank and Putz 2003; Musolff and Zinken 2009). From this perspective, metaphorical expressions in discourse are seen as linguistic reflexes of, or prompts for, conceptual structures and processes. Metaphors are not seen as mere tropes, then, but rather, the conceptual structures and processes involved in metaphor shape our thoughts and actions. Conceptual metaphors are therefore an important starting point in the cognitive study of ideology (Koller 2014). Findings from critical metaphor analysis show that a relatively finite number of familiar knowledge frames including JOURNEY, BUILDING, WAR, WATER, ILLNESS, WEATHER, GAMES and GAMBLING, as well as orientational and topological image schemas like UP–DOWN, NEAR–FAR and CONTAINER, are recruited to provide metaphorical understandings of a wide range of social and political phenomena (Charteris-Black 2004, 2006; Chilton 1996; Koller 2004; Musolff 2003, 2004). Metaphor analysis, it should be noted, is not restricted to the linguistic modality but has been usefully applied to the visual modality also (e.g., Bounegru and Forceville 2011; El Rafaie 2003; Forceville and Urios-Aparisi 2009). Here, scholars have shown that many of the conceptual metaphors evidenced by patterns of linguistic discourse find expression in visual discourse too.

Discourse world analysis (e.g., Chilton 2004; Filardo-Llamas 2013; Filardo-Llamas, Hart and Kaal 2016; Kaal 2012) aims to account for processes of meaning construction in discourse beyond the sentence. *Discourse worlds* are conceptual structures which represent the 'ontologies' defined in or presupposed by the text (Chilton 2004; Gavins 2007). They emerge as texts are interpreted contextually against a backdrop of broader systems of knowledge and value, encoded in frames and conceptual metaphors etc., which constitute common ground. According to Discourse Space Theory (Chilton 2004), discourse worlds are constructed inside a three-dimensional, deictically defined, mental or *discourse space*. Discourse worlds are constructed as elements – people, places, actions, events and propositions, inter alia – explicitly or implicitly referenced in the text get positioned at locations along three axes – space, time and evaluation – relative to a deictic centre, which represents a point of view in socio-political, temporal and evaluative 'space'. The basic organising principle of discourse worlds is thus (metaphorical) distance. Discourse worlds are important structures in the cognitive study of ideology since they represent the worldview espoused by the text which readers are asked to assume. In an important development of Discourse Space Theory, Cap (2006, 2008, 2011, 2013, 2015) outlines a model of proximisation. Within this framework, proximisation is defined as a conceptual contraction of the space between elements initially located at distal points along the socio-spatial, temporal or modal axes and the deictic centre representing the conceptualiser's 'situatedness' in social, physical, temporal, epistemic and axiological space (see Hart 2014a for a revised typology of proximisation operations). Proximisation is a powerful rhetorical strategy in interventionist discourses because it construes evolving actions or situations as personally consequential. It has been shown to operate in a range of interventionist discourses (Cap 2006; Hart 2010, 2014a; Filardo-Llamas 2013).

In some of my own work (Hart 2014a), I have tried to bring these three strands together inside a single integrated framework.[5] This framework, presented in Table 5.1, organises construal operations in relation to the more general cognitive systems on which they rely and a taxonomy of ideological discursive strategies which they potentially realise. Four strategies are identified. *Structural configuration* concerns the conceptualisation of basic event-structure and is realised through a construal operation of schematisation – the superimposition of an image schema. It relies on a more general cognitive ability to analyse complex scenes in terms of gestalt structures. *Framing* concerns the way actors and actions are attributed more specific qualities as alternative categories and frames are accessed, sometimes via metaphorical mappings, in their construal. It relies on a general cognitive capacity for comparison. *Identification* concerns which facets of a scene are selected for conceptualisation and the relative degree of salience with which elements of the scene are represented. Selection and salience effects are achieved through various construal operations referred to by Langacker (2002) as 'focal adjustments'. It can be argued, however, that the focal adjustments involved are ultimately a function of shifts in point of view (Hart 2015) and thus also relate to positioning strategies. Positioning is a broad strategy which concerns where we situate ourselves within the conceptualisation

Table 5.1 Typology of construal operations, cognitive systems and discursive strategies

System Strategy		Gestalt	Comparison	Attention	Perspective
Structural Configuration		Schematisation			
Framing	Construal operations		Categorisation Metaphor		
Identification				Focus Granularity Viewing frame	
Positioning					Point of view Deixis

and where other actors and actions are located relative to this position. It thus incorporates distancing and proximisation strategies and can be spatial, temporal, social, epistemic and axiological. It may pertain to grammatical constructions effected through a given viewing arrangement in a mental space or to larger stretches of text effected through the construction of a discourse world inside a discourse space. Positioning strategies are realised conceptually in point-of-view shifts and deictic organisation. They rely on a more general cognitive capacity for perspective-taking.

In the following section, I provide an example analysis applying aspects of CL-CDS. I focus specifically on image schema analysis in the context of discourse on political protests.

4. Example analysis: the Million Mask March 2014

In this section, I show how CL-CDS can be applied to reveal ideological and legitimating qualities of alternative conceptualisations of violence in press reports of political protests. Media reactions to political protests are important since it is the media who have the power to "characterise the events of the day and the social structure of society in a particular way" (Santa Ana 2002: 51). CL-CDS has previously been applied in studies of the 2009 G20 and 2010 Student Fee protests (Hart 2013a, b, 2014a, b). In this chapter, I take data from five online news reports of the 2014 Million Mask March. The Million Mask March consists of multiple protests staged in different cities around the world. However, London is usually one of the most widely attended. The protests, which take place on the 5th of November each year, are characterised by participants wearing Guy Fawkes masks. They are organised by a global activist network known as Anonymous and are intended to protest against austerity, infringements of civil rights and liberty, war crimes and corruption.[6] The data below is taken from online media reports of the London protest. Articles were published on the day of the event in the *Guardian*, the *Telegraph*, the *Independent*, the *Mail* and the *Express*.[7] The data is intended to illustrate, through qualitative analysis, some of the conceptual parameters along which ideology may be enacted. No quantitative comparisons are made. However, I hope it will be clear how this approach could be applied in large-scale quantitative, corpus-assisted, analyses.

An important finding in media studies of political protests is that they are treated as a spectacle, with a focus on violence, and without any serious discussion of the causes behind them (Murdock 1973). One way in which this is achieved conceptually is through headlines like

(1)   *Chaos breaks out* in London as Russell Brand joins thousands of masked Guy Fawkes protesters in dramatic Bonfire Night demonstration (*Mail*, 5.11.2014)

The italicised portion in (1) instantiates a conventionalised construction [Sbj BREAK *out*] whose Subject 'elaboration site' (Langacker 2008) is, according to FrameNet,[8] restricted to "fighting or other undesirable things". The construction is thus a fitting and frequent feature of discourse on political protests. Ideologically, however, the construction does a number of things. Firstly, the Subject elaboration site has as its specification abstract nouns or nominalisations likes 'chaos', 'trouble' and 'violence' which, through a process of **reification,** reduce complex interactions and relations to THINGS which have some kind of ontological existence (Radden and Dirven 2007: 78).[9] This process thus occludes attention to internal event-structure, including who did what to whom. It may therefore be said to realise an identification strategy as the actors involved, as well as the interactions between them, are glossed over. The construction as a whole, moreover, is paired with a concept [SUDDEN OCCURRENCE]. This meaning is likely derived from, or motivated by, the more literal, prototypical sense of 'break out' in the concept

[EMERGE/ESCAPE], which is structured by the image schema in Figure 5.1.[10] In Figure 5.1, a 'trajector' (TR) is seen to appear from having previously been invisible contained within a bounded 'landmark' (LM). The extent to which the construction in (1) will invoke the schema associated with the prototypical sense is the subject of debate (see Evans 2009). The important point for our purposes is that the construction, by virtue of its invocation of the [SUDDEN OCCURRENCE] concept, presents the 'chaos' as having come into ontological existence *suddenly* and *spontaneously* without causation and thus ignores the background to the situation.

When event-structure is spelled out, a crucial ideological dimension concerns the experiential realm to which the event in question is construed as belonging, as well as, within the event-structure, which actors are cast in which roles. Throughout a text, social actors can be seen to participate in different kinds of events, in different ways. This contributes to the construction of a worldview in which social actors behave in certain, more or less desirable, ways. Perhaps the most fundamental distinction here, in the context of political protests, concerns whether actors are construed as participating more often in physical or speech events. Within these categories are further distinctions. For example, in the realm of speech events are processes like CHANT, DEMAND, SHOUT, GOAD, THREATEN, WARN, CAUTION, etc., all of which can function to (de)legitimate the actors involved in different ways. Activating protesters more often in speech act events like CHANT and DEMAND compared to physical events, for example, politicises and therefore legitimises the protest by highlighting the message they are presenting. By contrast, activating protesters in physical events serves to depoliticise the protest by focussing on the spectacle rather than the message.

In the physical realm, events can be divided into those pertaining to basic experiential domains like ACTION, FORCE, MOTION and EXISTENCE IN SPACE.[11] There are then further divisions within each of these domains. There is thus ideological significance as to (i) which domains different actors are seen to participate in; (ii) within those domains, which particular event-types they are seen to participate in; and (iii) within particular event-types, which roles they are cast in.

For example, actors might be more often activated in events belonging to the domains of FORCE, MOTION or EXISTENCE IN SPACE compared to ACTION. Consider the contrast between (2) and (3). The event in (2) construes the police as active in an event pertaining to EXISTENCE IN SPACE. By contrast, the event in (3), in which it is protesters who are activated, belongs to the domain of ACTION. Such a structural configuration strategy serves to legitimate the police by presenting them as active in largely peaceful or peace-keeping events and to delegitimate protesters by presenting them as active in largely violent, criminal events[12].

(2) [Riot police ₜᵣ] [lined ₑₓᵢₛₜₑₙ𝒸ₑ ᵢₙ ₛₚₐ𝒸ₑ] [streets ₗₘ] as protesters donned sinister Guy Fawkes masks. (*Mail*, 5.11.2014)

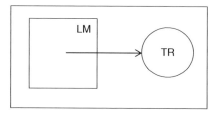

Figure 5.1 EMERGE/ESCAPE schema

(3) [The masked demonstrators – some as young as 14 – _AGENT_] also [kicked and dragged over _ACTION_] [security railings _PATIENT_]. (*Mail*, 5.11.2014)

Within each domain, actors may be activated in alternative event-types, encoding more subtle ideological differences. For example, when actors are activated in events pertaining to EXISTENCE IN SPACE, this may be in relation to SHAPE or EXTENT. In (2), the police are construed as forming a particular one-dimensional shape. The schema invoked is that of a LINE as in Figure 5.2(a). In (4), by contrast, protesters are activated in an event relating to EXTENT and construed as an expanding mass as in Figure 5.2(b). The image of an expanding mass invoked by examples like (4) may serve to create a sense of looming threat. This structural configuration strategy is often accompanied by a strategy of aggregation in social actor representation (van Leeuwen 1996) whereby large specified numbers of actors are presented as amassing.

(4) [Thousands _TR_] [gather _EXISTENCE IN SPACE_] for anti-capitalist protest in London (*Independent*, 5.11.2014)

The sense of threat created in (4) is realised in event-construals relating to ACTION and MOTION like (5) and (6) respectively.

(5) Arrests made after thousands of anti-capitalist protesters [storm _ACTION_] streets of London. (*Express*, 5.11.2014)
(6) Russell Brand and Vivienne Westwood joined thousands of masked anti-capitalist demonstrators who [descended on _MOTION_] Westminster for a Bonfire Night protests (*Mail*, 5.11.2014)

In (6), the construction [Sbj DESCEND *on* Obj] encodes a MOTION event. The MOTION event, however, is one involving concepts [DOWNWARD VERTICAL MOTION + SURFACE COVERAGE] so that the TR, 'thousands of masked anti-capitalist demonstrators', is construed as enveloping the

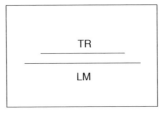

Figure 5.2(a)   LINE schema

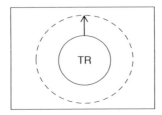

Figure 5.2(b)   EXPAND schema

LM, Westminster. This sense of enveloping may be rhetorically effective in creating a feeling of claustrophobia. This is in contrast to horizontal motion as in (7):

(7) Million Mask March draws thousands in London on global day of protest. (*Guardian*, 5.11.2015).

A further distinction in relation to horizontal motion concerns whether the event is one of FREE MOTION as in (8) or IMPEDED MOTION as in (9). The construal invoked in (8) is one of canonical unhindered motion based on the SOURCE-PATH-GOAL schema. In (9), however, the schematisation invoked by the construction [Sbj VERB$_{MOTION}$ *through* Obj] involves a conceptualisation of impeded motion. The Object e-site specifies an OBSTACLE on the path which, as in (9), may be affected in the realisation of the motion.[13] The alternative schemas invoked by (8) and (9) are modelled in Figure 5.3(a) and (b) respectively. In Figure 5.3(a), the LM is the GOAL of the motion – 'locations including Buckingham Palace and the BBC's central London studios'. In Figure 5.3(b), the LM is an OBSTACLE on the path of motion – 'rush-hour traffic'. The stepped arrow represents the effect of the event on the LM. The construal invoked by (9) thus serves to delegitimate the protest by highlighting its disruptive effects.

(8) [Thousands$_{TR}$], many wearing the Guy Fawkes masks which become a symbol of Anonymous. . . later [made their way $_{MOTION: FREE}$] . . . [towards $_{PATH}$] [other locations including Buckingham Palace and the BBC's central London studios$_{LM:GOAL}$]. (*Guardian*, 5.11.2014)

(9) [Hundreds of anti-establishment masked protesters$_{TR}$] [marched $_{MOTION: IMPEDED}$] [through $_{PATH}$] [rush-hour traffic $_{LM: OBSTACLE}$] in central London, bringing Whitehall to a standstill. (*Telegraph*, 5.11.2014)

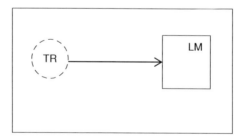

Figure 5.3(a)   FREE MOTION schema

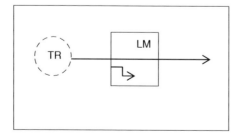

Figure 5.3(b)   IMPEDED MOTION schema

The final schemas that I will discuss in this chapter are those relating to the domain of ACTION.[14] Many ACTION schemas can be identified. Action-events may be volitional or non-volitional (i.e., caused). They may be directed or non-directed. Directed actions may be one-sided (asymmetrical) or two-sided (reciprocal). One-sided directed actions may be directed at ENTITIES or OBJECTS. They may also be mediated, i.e., enacted via an INSTRUMENT, or unmediated. Thus, in (3), protesters are activated in a volitional one-sided unmediated object-directed action-event. Construing events in terms of alternative action schemas has potential ideological and (de)legitimating effects. By way of example, consider the contrast between (10)–(12):

(10) During the march, [protesters AGENT] . . . [threw firecrackers ACTION: ONE-SIDED] at [police PATIENT] who were guarding the Victoria Memorial (*Mail*, 5.11.2014)

(11) [Officers in riot gear AGENT[1]] at a number of points later drew batons and [clashed with ACTION: TWO-SIDED] [members of the crowd AGENT[2]] (*Guardian*, 5.11.2014)

(12) [Officers AGENT] were [forced to CAUSATION] [draw their batons ACTION: REACTION] [as [missiles, plastic cones and road signs were launched along the mall EVENT] CIRCUMSTANCE]. (*Mail*, 5.11.2014)

The transitive construction in (10) construes the event, in which it is protesters who are activated, as a volitional, one-sided, entity-directed action-event. The event is volitional in the sense that it is brought about of the AGENT's own accord. It is entity-directed in the sense that the PATIENT in the action is an animate ENTITY rather than an inanimate OBJECT. It is one-sided in the sense that the transfer of energy between participants is uni-directional, from an AGENT to a PATIENT.[15] The schema invoked is modelled in Figure 5.4(a). In (11), by contrast, the reciprocal verb invokes a construal of the event as a volitional, two-sided, entity-directed action-event. The schema associated with reciprocal constructions such as [Sbj CLASH *with* Obj] is modelled in Figure 5.4(b). Crucially, in a two-sided action-event the transfer of energy between participants is bi-directional. That is, both participants are equally activated in the event-structure. Ideologically, therefore, while (10) serves to apportion responsibility for the

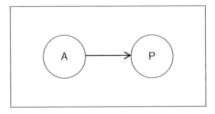

Figure 5.4(a)   One-sided volitional ACTION schema

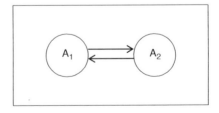

Figure 5.4(b)   Two-sided volitional ACTION schema

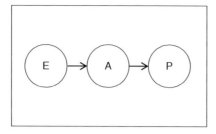

Figure 5.5 Caused ACTION schema

violence that occurred to only one participant, the protesters, (11) serves to attribute blame to both participants who thus share responsibility.

The construction in (12) is an expression of caused action. The agent in the process is no longer presented as the 'initiator' but as acting in response to a preceding circumstantial event. The action, in other words, is construed as a *reaction*. In reality, of course, every action is a reaction. While this is not recognised in examples such as (10), it is taken into account in examples such as (12). Conceptually, construing an event as reactive involves an expansion in the distribution of attention, directed by the coverage of the clause, so that it extends over a greater portion of event-structure (Langacker 2008; Talmy 2000).[16] This is modelled in Figure 5.5. In the schema, the interaction that constitutes the circumstantial event, with its own internal structure, is collapsed, for the sake of simplicity, into a single causal element (E).

Ideologically, construing an event as reactive as in (12) mitigates the action involved, presenting it as provoked, last resort, and in the interests of restoring order. By contrast, the narrower range of attention in volitional action-event-construals such as (10) presents the action as an unprovoked instance of gratuitous violence. Examples like (10) and (12) on the one hand, then, and (11) on the other, can be related to wider, ideologically opposed, discourses of political protest. While examples like (10) and (12) support discourses in which protests are demonised as a form of deviance and police behaviour is seen as above suspicion, examples like (11) at least recognise the role of the police in the violence that occurred and raise critical questions concerning their behaviour. Examples like (11) may thus be said to support a more liberal discourse on state-citizen relations.

5. Conclusion

In this chapter, I have introduced methods of CDS sourced from Cognitive Linguistics. Three approaches in particular have been identified: image schema analysis, metaphor analysis and discourse world analysis. I have outlined a particular view of meaning in language and discourse which is characteristic of these approaches. Namely, that meaning making in discourse is achieved as words and grammatical constructions invoke conceptual structures and processes which they conventionally index in order to impose a particular construal on the situation under consideration. In relating conceptual structures and processes to the more general cognitive systems on which they rely as well as the discursive strategies which they potentially realise, I have outlined a more general Cognitive Linguistic framework for CDS which takes in a range of methods to address a variety of conceptual phenomena through which ideology and legitimation may be enacted. In the final section of the chapter, I have conducted an image schema analysis of discourse on political protests to show how the selection of alternative grammatical constructions can lead to competing conceptualisations of the same target situation whose properties, in that context of use, may be ideologically load-bearing. In doing so, I hope to have demonstrated the way at least one aspect of CL–CDS may be applied.

Notes

1 This is not to deny the complex social, historical and other contextual factors necessarily involved in the discursive construction of knowledge, which are described in detail in other approaches to CDS. It is only to highlight and address the cognitive processes which are equally necessarily at play.
2 In this sense, CL–CDS has much in common with Teun van Dijk's 'socio-cognitive approach' (1998, 2008, 2014). CL approaches and the socio-cognitive approach, however, should not be conflated (cf. Wodak 2006). While the two share a general focus on cognition, they are epistemologically and methodologically quite different (see van Dijk, this volume, for an outline of the socio-cognitive approach). In many respects, of all the approaches within CDS, Cognitive Linguistic approaches have most in common with and can be seen as emerging from Critical Linguistics (Fowler et al. 1979; Fowler 1991; Hodge and Kress 1993). Like Critical Linguistics, the focus of CL–CDS is on linguistic structure rather than thematic content (see Hart and Cap 2014 for a 'map' of contemporary approaches to CDS). In marked contrast to Critical Linguistics, however, CL–CDS is explicitly concerned with the conceptual reflexes of lexicogrammatical structures. Moreover, epistemologically and methodologically, while Critical Linguistics orients to Systemic Functional Grammar, CL–CDS orients to Cognitive Linguistics (ibid.).
3 For useful overviews of Cognitive Linguistics see: Dąbrowska and Divjak (2015); Croft and Cruse (2004); Evans and Green (2006); Littlemore and Taylor (2014).
4 In this second claim, Cognitive Linguistics subscribes to the embodiment principle in Cognitive Science more broadly (Gibbs 2005; Pecher and Zwaan 2010; Shapiro 2010).
5 This is not in any way an attempt to subordinate specific Cognitive Linguistic approaches. It is merely to locate them with respect to a wider research context. It must also be recognised that not all scholars working with Cognitive Linguistic frameworks in CDS would necessarily place their work within the broader Cognitive Linguistic approach that I advocate.
6 www.facebook.com/events/485894658146587/, Accessed March 5, 2015
7 Articles available at:
www.dailymail.co.uk/news/article-2822591/Chaos-breaks-London-Russell-Brand-joins-thousands-masked-Guy-Fawkes-protesters-dramatic-Bonfire-Night-demonstration.html
www.express.co.uk/news/uk/531957/Anonymous-Million-Mask-March-Guy-Fawkes-Trafalgar-Square-Parliament-Square
www.theguardian.com/uk-news/2014/nov/05/million-mask-march-london-russell-brand-anonymous
www.telegraph.co.uk/news/uknews/law-and-order/11211981/Masked-protestors-fire-fireworks-at-the-Houses-of-Parliament.html
www.independent.co.uk/news/uk/home-news/million-masks-march-2014-thousands-gather-for-anticapitalist-protest-in-london-9842407.html Accessed March 5, 2015
8 https://framenet.icsi.berkeley.edu/
9 Reification may be a function of shifts in point of view and mode of viewing (Langacker 2008; see also Hart 2015).
10 Image schemas are subject to further construal as the structure of the event is necessarily conceived from one spatial point of view or another. Thus, every structural configuration strategy is accompanied by a spatial positioning strategy, giving rise to further ideological potentials. To discuss this, however, is beyond the scope of the current chapter (see Hart 2015 for extensive discussion).
11 In Cognitive Linguistics the notion 'event' is understood to cover both events and states (Radden and Dirven 2007: 270).
12 Where actions are not coded in the following examples it is because they do not relate to a particular contrast being highlighted.
13 This is contrast to the construction [Sbj VERB$_{\text{MOTION}}$ *along* Obj]. See Lee (1998) on the semantics of *through*.
14 On FORCE schemas in discourse on political protests see Hart (2013b, 2014a).

15 It is also mediated in the sense that the energy transfer is enacted through an 'energy transmitter' in the form of an INSTRUMENT. However, for present purposes we do not need to include this in the analysis.

16 In Hart (2015) it is argued that this extended range of attention is a function of construing the event from a maximally distal point of view which allows a wider angled scope over the situation.

Further reading

Hart, C. (2011). Force-interactive patterns in immigration discourse: A Cognitive Linguistic approach to CDA. *Discourse & Society* 22(3): 269–286.

Hart, C. (2013). Event-construal in press reports of violence in political protests: A Cognitive Linguistic approach to CDA. *Journal of Language and Politics* 12(3): 400–423.

These two papers analyse the ideological functions of image schemas in media discourses on immigration and political protests respectively.

Charteris-Black, J. (2004). *Corpus approaches to critical metaphor analysis.* Basingstoke: Palgrave.

This book analyses the ideological and rhetorical dimensions of metaphor from a cognitive perspective. It applies the tools developed to analyse a range of data, including British and American political speeches, financial reporting and religious texts.

Chilton, P. (2004). *Analysing political discourse: Theory and practice.* London: Routledge.

This book is the first to outline Discourse Space Theory. Chapters four, eight and nine are directly concerned with Discourse Space Theory. The books applies this model to international political discourses aimed as justifying military action.

References

Bounegru, L. and Forceville, C. (2011). Metaphors in editorial cartoons representing the global financial crisis. *Visual Communication* 10(2): 209–229.

Cap, P. (2006). *Legitimization in political discourse.* Newcastle: Cambridge Scholars Publishing.

Cap, P. (2008). Towards a proximisation model of the analysis of legitimization in political discourse. *Journal of Pragmatics* 40(1): 17–41.

Cap, P. (2010). Proximizing objects, proximizing values: Towards an axiological contribution to the discourse of legitimization. In U. Okulska and P. Cap (eds.), *Perspectives in politics and discourse,* 119–142. Amsterdam: Benjamins.

Cap, P. (2011). Axiological proximisation. In C. Hart (ed.), *Critical discourse studies in context and cognition,* 81–96. Amsterdam: Benjamins.

Cap, P. (2013). *Proximization: The pragmatics of symbolic distance crossing.* Amsterdam: Benjamins.

Cap, P. (2015). Crossing symbolic distances in political discourse space: Evaluative rhetoric within the proximisation framework. *Critical Discourse Studies* 12(3): 313–329.

Charteris-Black, J. (2004). *Corpus approaches to critical metaphor analysis.* Basingstoke: Palgrave Macmillan.

Charteris-Black, J. (2006). Britain as a container: Immigration metaphors in the 2005 election campaign. *Discourse & Society* 17(6): 563–582.

Chilton, P. (1996). *Security metaphors: Cold war discourse from containment to common house.* New York: Peter Lang.

Chilton, P. (2004). *Analysing political discourse: Theory and practice.* London: Routledge.

Chilton, P. (2005a). Missing links in mainstream CDS: Modules, blends and the critical instinct. In R. Wodak and P. Chilton (eds.), *A new research agenda in (critical) discourse analysis: Theory, methodology and interdisciplinarity,* 19–52. Amsterdam: Benjamins.

Chilton, P. (2005b). Manipulation, memes and metaphors: The case of *Mein Kampf.* In L. de Saussure and P. Schulz (eds.), *Manipulation and ideologies in the twentieth century,* 15–44. Amsterdam.

Croft, W. and Cruse, D. A. (2004). *Cognitive linguistics.* Cambridge: Cambridge University Press.

Dąbrowska, E. and Divjak, D. (eds.) (2015). *Handbook of cognitive linguistics.* Berlin: De Gruyter.

Dirven, R., Frank, R. and Putz, M. (eds.) (2003). *Cognitive models in language and thought: Ideology, metaphors and meanings.* Berlin: Mouton de Gruyter.

El Refaie, E. (2001). Metaphors we discriminate by: Naturalized themes in Austrian newspaper articles about asylum seekers. *Journal of Sociolinguistics* 5(3): 352–371.

El Refaie, E. (2003). Understanding visual metaphor: The example of newspaper cartoons. *Visual Communication* 2(1): 75–96.

Evans, V. (2009). *How words mean: Lexical concepts, cognitive models and meaning construction*. Oxford: Oxford University Press.

Evans, V. and Green, M. (2006). *Cognitive linguistics: An introduction*. Edinburgh: Edinburgh University Press.

Fairclough, N. (1995). *Media discourse*. London: Edward Arnold.

Fauconnier, G. (1994). *Mental spaces: Aspects of meaning construction in natural language*. Cambridge: Cambridge University Press.

Fauconnier, G. (1997). *Mappings in thought and language*. Cambridge: Cambridge University Press.

Fauconnier, G. and Turner, M. (2002). *The way we think: Conceptual blending and the mind's hidden complexities*. New York: Basic Books.

Filardo-Llamas, L. (2013). "Committed to the ideals of 1916": The language of paramilitary groups: The case of the Irish Republican Army. *Critical Discourse Studies* 10(1): 1–17.

Filardo-Llamas, L. (2015). Re-contextualising political discourse: An analysis of shifting spaces in songs used as a political tool. *Critical Discourse Studies* 12(3): 279–296.

Filardo-Llamas, L., Hart, C. and Kaal, B. (2016). *Space, time and evaluation in ideological discourse*. London: Routledge.

Fillmore, C. (1982). Frame semantics. In Linguistics Society of Korea (ed.), *Linguistics in the morning calm*, 111–137. Seoul: Hanshin Publishing Co.1.

Forceville, C. and Urios-Aparisi, E. (eds.) (2009). *Multimodal metaphor*. Berlin: Walter de Gruyter.

Fowler, R. (1991). *Language in the news: Discourse and ideology in the press*. London: Routledge.

Fowler, R., Hodge, R., Kress, G. and Trew, T. (1979). *Language and control*. London: Routledge and Kegan Paul.

Gavins, J. (2007). *Text world theory: An introduction*. Edinburgh: Edinburgh University Press.

Gibbs, R. (2005). *Embodiment and cognitive science*. Cambridge: Cambridge University Press.

Hart, C. (2008). Critical discourse analysis and metaphor: Toward a theoretical framework. *Critical Discourse Studies* 5(2): 91–106.

Hart, C. (2010). *Critical discourse and cognitive science: New perspectives on immigration discourse*. Basingstoke: Palgrave.

Hart, C. (2011a). Force-interactive patterns in immigration discourse: A Cognitive Linguistic approach to CDS. *Discourse & Society* 22(3): 269–286.

Hart, C. (ed.) (2011b). *Critical discourse studies in context and cognition*. Amsterdam: Benjamins.

Hart, C. (2013). Constructing contexts through grammar: Cognitive models and conceptualisation in British Newspaper reports of political protests. In J. Flowerdew (ed.), *Discourse and contexts*, 159–184. London: Continuum.

Hart, C. (2014a). *Discourse, grammar and ideology: Functional and cognitive perspectives*. London: Bloomsbury.

Hart, C. (2014b). Construal operations in online press reports of political protests. In C. Hart and P. Cap (eds.), *Contemporary critical discourse studies*, 167–188. London: Bloomsbury.

Hart, C. (2015). Viewpoint in linguistic discourse: Space and evaluation in news reports of political protests. *Critical Discourse Studies* 12(3): 238–260.

Hart, C. and Cap, P. (2014). Introduction. In C. Hart and P. Cap (eds.), *Contemporary critical discourse studies*, 1–16. London: Bloomsbury.

Hart, C. and Lukeš, D. (eds.) (2007). *Cognitive linguistics in critical discourse analysis: Application and theory*. Newcastle: Cambridge Scholars Publishing.

Hodge, R. and Kress, G. (1993). *Language as ideology*, 2nd edn. London: Routledge.

Jeffries, L. (2010). *Opposition in discourse: The construction of oppositional meaning*. London: Continuum.

Johnson, M. (1987). *The body in the mind: The bodily basis of meaning, imagination, and reason*. Chicago: University of Chicago Press.

Kaal, B. (2012). Worldviews: Spatial ground for political reasoning in Dutch election manifestos. *CADAAD* 6(1): 1–22.

Koller, V. (2004). *Metaphor and gender in business media discourse: A critical cognitive study*. Basingstoke: Palgrave.

Koller, V. (2014). Cognitive linguistics and ideology. In J. Littlemore and J. Taylor (eds.), *The Bloomsbury companion to cognitive linguistics*, 234–252. London: Bloomsbury.

Lakoff, G. and Johnson, M. (1980). *Metaphors we live by*. Chicago: University of Chicago Press.

Lakoff, G. and Johnson, M. (1999). *Philosophy in the flesh: The embodied mind and its challenge to western thought*. New York: Basic Book.

Langacker, R. W. (1987). *Foundations of cognitive grammar, vol. I: Theoretical prerequisites*. Stanford, CA: Stanford University Press.

Langacker, R. W. (1991). *Foundations of cognitive grammar, vol. II: Descriptive application*. Stanford, CA: Stanford University Press.

Langacker, R. W. (2002). *Concept, image, and symbol: The cognitive basis of grammar*, 2nd edn. Berlin: Mouton de Gruyter.

Langacker, R. W. (2008). *Cognitive grammar: A basic introduction*. Oxford: Oxford University Press.

Langacker, R. W. (2009). *Investigations in cognitive grammar*. Berlin: Mouton de Gruyter.

Langacker, R. W. (2013). *Essentials of cognitive grammar*. Oxford: Oxford University Press.

Lee, D. (1998). A tour through *through*. *Journal of English Linguistics* 26(4): 333–351.

Littlemore, J. and Taylor, J. R. (eds.) (2014). *Bloomsbury companion to cognitive linguistics*. London: Bloomsbury.

Mandler, J. M. (2004). *The foundations of mind: Origins of conceptual thought*. Oxford: Oxford University Press.

Marín Arrese, J. (2011). Effective vs. epistemic stance and subjectivity in political discourse: Legitimising strategies and mystification of responsibility. In C. Hart (ed.), *Critical discourse studies in context and cognition*, 193–224. Amsterdam: Benjamins.

Musolff, A. (2003). Ideological functions of metaphor: The conceptual metaphors of health and illness in public discourse. In R. Dirven, R. M. Frank and M. Pütz (eds.), *Cognitive models in language and thought: Ideology, metaphors and meanings*, 327–352. Berlin: Mouton de Gruyter.

Musolff, A. (2004). *Metaphor and political discourse: Analogical reasoning in debates about Europe*. Basingstoke: Palgrave.

Musolff, A. and Zinken, J. (eds.) (2009). *Metaphor and discourse*. Basingstoke: Palgrave.

Nuñez-Perucha, B. (2011). Critical discourse analysis and cognitive linguistics as tools for ideological research: A diachronic analysis of feminism. In C. Hart (ed.), *Critical discourse studies in context and cognition*, 97–118. Amsterdam: Benjamins.

Oakley, T. (2005). Force dynamic dimensions of rhetorical effect. In B. Hampe (ed.), *From perception to meaning: Image schemas in cognitive linguistics*, 443–475. Berlin: Mouton De Gruyter.

O'Halloran, K. (2003). *Critical discourse analysis and language cognition*. Edinburgh: Edinburgh University Press.

Pecher, D. and Zwaan, R. A. (eds.) (2010). *Grounding cognition: The role of perception and action in memory, language and thinking*. Cambridge: Cambridge University Press.

Radden, G. and Dirven, R. (2007). *Cognitive English grammar*. Amsterdam: Benjamins.

Reisigl, M. and Wodak, R. (2001). *Discourse and discrimination: Rhetorics of racism and anti-Semitism*. London: Routledge.

Santa Ana, O. (2002). *Brown tide rising: Metaphors of Latinos in contemporary American public discourse*. Austin, TX: University of Texas Press.

Shaprio, L. (2010). *Embodied cognition*. London: Routledge.

Stockwell, P. (1999). Towards a critical cognitive linguistics. In A. Combrink and I. Bierman (eds.), *Discourses of war and conflict*, 510–528. Potchefstroom: Ptochefstroom University Press.

Talmy, L. (1988). Force dynamics in language and cognition. *Cognitive Science* 12: 49–100.

Talmy, L. (2000). *Toward a cognitive semantics*. Cambridge, MA: MIT Press.

van Dijk, T. A. (1998). *Ideology: A multidisciplinary approach*. London: Sage.

van Dijk, T. A. (2008). *Discourse and context: A sociocognitive approach*. Cambridge: Cambridge University Press.

van Dijk, T. A. (2014). Discourse-cognition-society: Current state and prospects of the socio-cognitive approach to discourse. In C. Hart and P. Cap (eds.), *Contemporary critical discourse studies*, 121–146. London: Bloomsbury.

van Leeuwen, T. (1996). The representation of social actors. In C. R. Caldas-Coulthard and M. Coulthard (eds.), *Texts and practices: Readings in critical discourse analysis*, 32–70. London: Routledge.

Werth, P. (1999). *Text worlds: Representing conceptual space in discourse*. Harlow: Longman.

Wodak, R. (2006). Mediation between discourse and society: Assessing cognitive approaches in CDS. *Discourse Studies* 8(1): 179–190.

Wolf, H. G. and Polzenhagen, F. (2003). Conceptual metaphor as ideological stylistic means: An exemplary analysis. In R. Dirven, R. Frank and M. Putz (eds.), *Cognitive models in language and thought: Ideology, metaphors and meanings*, 247–276. Berlin: Mouton de Gruyter.

6

Spatial cognition

Piotr Cap

1. Introduction: Critical Discourse Analysis and cognitive linguistics

A significant part of today's CDA reveals a cognitive element, drawing on work on spatial-temporal cognition and conceptualization (Talmy 2000; Fauconnier and Turner 2002; Levinson 2003; Evans and Chilton 2010; among many others) in various interdisciplinary studies of ideologically motivated construals of meaning within different discourse domains (e.g., Cienki, Kaal and Maks 2010; Hart 2010; Dunmire 2011; Kaal 2012; Filardo-Llamas 2010, 2013). As shown in Hart's chapter (this volume), the cognitive-linguistic (CL) approach to CDA offers a disciplined theoretical perspective on the conceptual import of linguistic choices identified as potentially ideological. It thus affords a new and promising lens on persuasive, manipulative and coercive properties of discourse, worldview and conceptualization which have hitherto been beyond the radar of CDA (see also overviews in Hart 2014; Hart and Cap 2014; Filardo-Llamas, Hart and Kaal 2015).

As expressed by Levinson, the cognitive-linguistic approach to discourse presupposes the fundamental role of spatial cognition in relativization and subjective representation of processes and attitudes that involve a deictic point of view to 'anchor' ideas (2003). Werth (1999) and Gavins (2007) adopt a similar stance in explaining 'deictic coherence' in terms of 'text-' and 'discourse worlds'. They argue that all language use, and therefore also discourse, involves the (re-)construction of a mental space which functions as a cohesive conceptual frame for the representation of geographically and culturally bounded (social) realities (see also Searle 2010). These assumptions have been operationalized in models that link thought patterns in the mind to their linguistic and discursive representations, revealing ideological meanings. They have made a particularly rich contribution to theories of the basic, 'center-periphery' conceptual arrangement of the Discourse Space (DS) (Chilton 2004, 2005) and recently also to theories of the dynamic re-arrangement of the Space involving a strategic, context-bound deployment of lexico-grammatical choices (Cap 2013).

The present chapter is structured in two main parts. In the first part (Section 2), I describe contributions of the cognitive-linguistic research to the account of the core deictic architecture of the Discourse Space. I particularly acknowledge the role of that research in elucidating the DS center–periphery arrangement underpinning ideological and value-based positions in discourse. At the same time I argue that the best-known, 'formative' models such as Chilton's or Levinson's, have not exploited the potential that CL reveals with regard to the critical description of all complexities of the Space. While delivering a much-needed focus on *how people establish* representations and ideologically charged worldviews, they have nonetheless failed to explain *how people are made to establish* a worldview, in the service of speaker's pragmatic goals. I work on this issue in the second part of the chapter (Section 3), providing answers from Proximization Theory and its applications in the urgent discourses of anti-terrorism and anti-migration (Cap 2013, 2017). Having assessed the explanatory power of proximization in the account of the spatially grounded legitimization and coercion strategies, the chapter closes (Section 4) by defining new domains to be explored from an integrated critical-cognitive-pragmatic research perspective.

2. Formative models: *representing* worldviews in discourse space

The most comprehensive of the established CL models of discourse and (critical) discourse study seems to be Chilton's (2004, 2005) Discourse Space Theory (DST), though we must not brush aside several other approaches, such as Levinson's (2003), Werth's (1999) and Gavins's (2007).

In Chilton (2004: 57) a central claim is made that in processing any discourse people 'position' other entities in their 'world' (Werth 1999; Gavins 2007) by 'positioning' these entities in relation to themselves along three axes in three dimensions, 'spatial', 'temporal' and 'modal'. This arrangement presupposes the primacy of the spatial dimension as the remaining dimensions involve conceptualizations in spatial terms. Time is conceptualized in terms of motion through space ('the time to act has arrived'), and modality is conceptualized in terms of distance ('remotely possible') or (deontic modality) as a metaphoric extension of the binary opposition between the close of the remote (see below). The origin of the three dimensions is at the deictic center, which includes the symbolic Self, i.e., *I*, *we*, etc. All other entities and processes exist relative to ontological spaces defined by their coordinates on the space (*s*), time (*t*) and modality (*m*) axes (Figure 6.1). This makes it possible, Chilton argues, to conceptualize the ongoing kaleidoscope of ontological configurations activated by text.

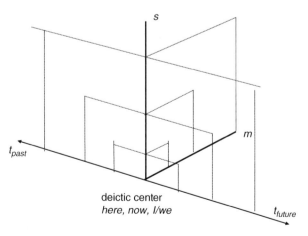

Figure 6.1 Dimensions of deixis
Source: adapted from (Chilton 2004: 58)

Figure 6.1 represents the basic interface of cognition and language shared by most of the CL models trying to account for the construal of discourse. At the heart of the account is the concept of deixis and, what follows, deictic markers. The spatial markers, such as *I/we* and *they*, 'located' on the *s* axis are the core of the linguistic representation, which is usually a representation in terms of binary oppositions extending into all three dimensions. Typically, entities and processes construed as 'close' in the spatio-temporal dimension are assigned positive values within the deontic modal dimension, while those construed as 'distant' are at the same time (or as a result) assigned negative values. In models other than Chilton's, the central status of the spatial deixis is reflected at theoretical and terminological levels, where 'US-good/THEM-bad' is more of a conceptual than solely linguistic dichotomy (cf. Text World Theory in Werth [1999], Gavins [2007] and Kaal [2012]).

How do models such as DST work for CDA? In his study of the discourse of the Kosovo war, Chilton (2004: 142) analyzes the following text, an excerpt from President Clinton's TV address to the American nation on March 24, 1999:[12]

(25) Ending this tragedy is a moral imperative. (26) It is also important to America's national interest. (27) Take a look at this map. (28) Kosovo is a small place, but it sits on a major fault line between Europe, Asia and the Middle East, at the meeting place of Islam and both the Western and Orthodox branches of Christianity. (29) To the south are our allies, Greece and Turkey; to the north, our new democratic allies in Central Europe. (30) And all around Kosovo there are other small countries, struggling with their own economic and political challenges – countries that could be overwhelmed by a large, new wave of refugees from Kosovo. (31) All the ingredients for a major war are there: ancient grievances, struggling democracies, and in the center of it all a dictator in Serbia who has done nothing since the Cold War ended but start new wars and pour gasoline on the flames of ethnic and religious division. (32) Sarajevo, the capital of neighboring Bosnia, is where World War I began. (33) World War II and the Holocaust engulfed this region. (34) In both wars Europe was slow to recognize the dangers, and the United States waited even longer to enter the conflicts. (35) Just imagine if leaders back then had acted wisely and early enough, how many lives could have been saved, how many Americans would not have had to die. (36) We learned some of the same lessons in Bosnia just a few years ago. (37) The world did not act early enough to stop that war, either.

Chilton's DST analysis can be summarized as follows. At the intersection point (the origin) of the three axes (see Figure 6.2 below; numbers refer to the sentences or [30'–31'] sentence parts responsible for a particular conceptual operation) is 'this map' (President Clinton is seen pointing to a visual aid). The map itself does not represent an objective reality; its task is to launch a reality space to be specified by the verbal commentary. A presupposition obtains: addressees must, in order to interpret the unfolding text as coherent, infer that (27) and the following sentences are intended to motivate (26) (that national interests are at stake) and (25) (that action is a moral imperative). On that presupposition, sentences (28), (29) and (30) can be regarded as setting up a 'map representation' space. This construal involves a conventional pragmatic function, by which cartographic images are taken to represent objective reality spaces (Fauconnier and Turner 2002). 'This map' in the studio (or 'in' the viewer's area) represents a conceptual space that is mutually understood as remote (viz. 'there' in [31]), but which the map presented 'here' and 'now' makes conceptually close. In the process of defining the map's conceptual projection space the use of 'could' ([30'] in 'countries that could be overwhelmed by a large new wave of refugees from Kosovo'), prompts the viewer/addressee

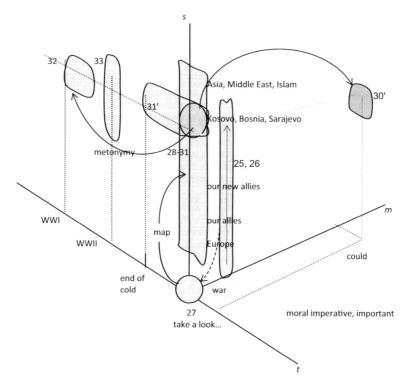

Figure 6.2 Events located on spatial, temporal and modal axes
Source: adapted from (Chilton 2004: 144)

to launch a space at the possibility point of *m* and in the near future zone of *t*. This is *not* part of the televised map picture; it is part of the conceptual 'picture' produced by the discourse, which conflates the apparently remote Kosovo space and the viewer/addressee space. The resulting proximity of the Kosovo space and its negatively charged entities (as opposed to the positively charged entities [President Clinton, his audience, allies in Europe] in the deictic center) allows transition to (31), which expresses a generalized likelihood of a major military conflict and thus threat to American interests. In (31), the positioning of the (31') embedded clause (' . . . who has done nothing since the Cold War but start new wars and pour gasoline on the flames of ethnic and religious divisions') as syntactic and intonational focus furthers this likelihood by a metaphoric phrase: the 'flames of divisions' (refugees fleeing from Kosovo) will cause a major 'fire' in the region as they 'meet' with (more) 'gasoline'.

On the *t* axis, the geopolitical and historical space is extended 'backwards', metonymically, by reference to the spatial location 'Sarajevo' (32). Kosovo is linked to Sarajevo, and Sarajevo is linked metonymically to World War I, and World War I to World War II and the Holocaust. The links can be considered metonymic since the relation between Kosovo, Sarajevo and WWI is one of conceptual 'contiguity' in a geopolitical frame which holds events progressing from the remote past toward the present. 'Sarajevo' is used to evoke the whole WWI frame, and 'this region' (33) is used in the same metonymic fashion to evoke the WWII and the Holocaust frames. These discursively linked frames constitute the groundwork for two sets of generalizations: (31) relating to the geographical space conceptualized 'around' Kosovo, and (34) – (35) relating to a flashback historical space conceptualized in connection with Sarajevo. These generalizations are used in turn to wrap up the entire representation ([36] – [37]) and justify its initial point (25), that is a moral imperative to act.

Altogether, Chilton's DST provides CDA with excellent insights in the representation of entities in political discourse space. First, it recognizes the fundamental role of distance from the 'Self' entities (in the deictic center) in conceptualizing other entities and events in political/public discourse. Obvious as this may seem, it is a vital prerequisite for any further inquiry in linguistic ways of construing distant objects and happenings as close to the deictic center. Second, it acknowledges that the distance is *relative* and that it is *symbolically* represented through discourse. This in turn makes possible further explorations in how the symbolic representations can be evoked strategically, for pragmatic effects. Third, the DST model shows that 'distance' involves a number of mutually interactive dimensions, which make mental representations of entities and events arise from a combined activation of different cognitive domains such as spatial, temporal and modal.

There are at the same time some obviously unattended issues, in both DST and other approaches grounded in the classical conception of deixis, deictic dimensions, and notably, deictic markers. As for DST, it can be described as a theory of general and relatively 'fixed' conceptual organization of entities in political discourse space. Its aim is to demonstrate how people's mental representations are positioned with respect to three cognitive dimensions; it is clearly *not* to show how *people are made to establish representations* that would suit the accomplishment of the discourse goals pursued by political speaker. The reason is that DST does not offer a systematic account of *quantifiable* lexico-grammatical items responsible for locating entities and events at different (measurable) distances from the deictic center determining the intensity of pragmatic powers of these entities/events. While it recognizes ideological, legitimizing, coercive, etc. discourse roles of certain words and expressions, it arbitrarily assigns them a static position on one of the three axes, in fixed distance to/from the deictic center (cf. Figure 6.2). Consequently, conceptual shifts from the DS periphery to the center are hardly accounted for; there is little systematic way to determine which *linguistic* items, in what numbers, and within which dimension, are the most effective in forcing a worldview upon the addressee. This 'deficit' follows from DST's conventional arrangement of the Discourse Space which indexes entities and events by primarily nominal phrases and pronouns. At the same time, the role (as well as typology) of verbal forms, a core element in the conceptual shifts, is underappreciated as these do not belong to the standard arsenal of deictic expressions.

The above problem echoes Verhagen's (2007: 49) scepticism concerning 'a substantial amount of arbitrariness' behind any classificatory systems in CL of language forms (especially deixis) reflecting different conceptualizations. Werth (1999), Gavins (2007) and especially Levinson (2003) demonstrate similar awareness. In his theory of spatio-temporal frames of reference, Levinson (2003) challenges the traditional Buehlerian view of deixis, on which deictic markers are considered merely a technical necessity for the possible interpretability of a language, rather than an instrument of strategic communication involving persuasion, legitimization and social coercion. Contesting the conception of deixis as a finite repository of 'deictic expressions', he argues for a much broader approach to deictic markers. This new approach involves bigger lexico-grammatical phrases and discourse stretches within which the 'conventional' deictic items (such as pronominals) combine with atypical indexical items (such as complex verb phrases) as the speaker constructs elaborate discourse forms to meet the changing contextual conditions. Levinson's (2003) perspective on the verbal element of the Discourse Space is productive as it helps understand how both an entity and (crucially) its *movement* become indexed and symbolically represented to establish the target vision construed by the speaker. This in turn opens up vistas for analysis of expressions such as 'they have set their course to confront us and our civilization',[3] which force conceptual shifts from the periphery of the Space to the center, in the service of constructing an ideologically charged worldview (entailing a specific act, e.g., a preventive action). Unfortunately, neither Levinson nor for instance Gavins (in many ways following up on Levinson in her 2007 work) attempt a formal lexico-grammatical typology of the extended deictic territory they argue for.

3. New developments: proximization theory and the *forcing* of worldviews

Chilton's (2004, 2005) DST and Levinson's (2003) spatio-temporal frames can be considered the most important reference models for several later works trying to revise and redefine the original account of conceptual shifts toward deictic center in strictly linguistic (lexical and grammatical terms). Aiming to determine specific linguistic items construing the shifts in the service of forcing worldviews, most of these works employ the concept of 'proximization'.

In its broadest sense, proximization is a discursive strategy of presenting physically and temporally distant events and states of affairs (including 'distant' adversarial ideologies) as increasingly and negatively consequential to the speaker and her addressee. Projecting the distant entities as gradually encroaching upon the speaker-addressee territory (both physical and ideological), the speaker seeks legitimization of actions and/or policies she proposes to neutralize the growing impact of the negative, 'foreign', 'alien', 'antagonistic', entities.

The term 'proximization' was first proposed by Cap to analyze coercion patterns in the US anti-terrorist rhetoric following 9/11 (Cap 2006, 2008, 2010). Since then it has been used within different discourse domains, though most commonly in studies of *state political discourses*: crisis construction and war rhetoric (Chovanec 2010), anti-migration discourse (e.g., Hart 2010), political party representation (Cienki, Kaal and Maks 2010), construction of national memory (Filardo-Llamas 2010) and design of foreign policy documents (Dunmire 2011). Findings from these studies have been integrated in Proximization Theory (PT) put forward by Cap (2013). The theory follows the original concept of proximization, which is defined as a forced construal operation meant to evoke closeness of the external threat, to solicit legitimization of preventive measures. The threat comes from DS-peripheral entities, referred to as ODCs ('outside-deictic-center'), which are conceptualized to be crossing the Space to invade the IDC ('inside-deictic-center') entities, the speaker and her addressee. The threat possesses a spatio-temporal as well as ideological nature, which means proximization can be considered in three aspects. 'Spatial proximization' is a forced construal of the DS-peripheral entities encroaching *physically* upon the DS central entities (speaker, addressee). Analogously to Chilton's DST, the spatial aspect of proximization is primary as the remaining aspects/strategies involve conceptualizations in spatial terms. 'Temporal proximization' is a forced construal of the envisaged conflict as not only imminent, but also momentous, historic and thus needing immediate response and unique preventive measures. Spatial and temporal proximization involve fear appeals (becoming particularly strong in reactionary political projects) and typically use analogies to conflate the growing threat with an actual disastrous occurrence in the past, to endorse the current scenario. Lastly, 'axiological proximization' involves construal of a gathering ideological clash between the 'home values' of the DS central entities (IDCs) and the alien and antagonistic (ODC) values. Importantly, the ODC values are construed to reveal potential to materialize (that is, prompt a physical impact) within the IDC, the speaker's and the addressee's, home territory.

Proximization Theory holds that all the three aspects or strategies of proximization contribute to the *continual narrowing of the symbolic distance* between the entities/values in the Discourse Space and their negative impact[1] on the speaker and her addressee. This does not mean, however, that all the three strategies are linguistically present (to the same degree) throughout each stretch of the unfolding discourse. While any use of proximization principally subsumes all of its strategies, spatial, temporal and axiological, the degree of their actual representation is continually motivated by their effectiveness in the evolving context. Extralinguistic contextual developments may thus cause the speaker to limit the use of one strategy and compensate it by an increased use of another, in the interest of the continuity of legitimization.

Compared to approaches such as Chilton's or Levinson's, Proximization Theory makes a new contribution at two levels, (i) cognitive-pragmatic and (ii) linguistic, or more precisely, lexico-grammatical. At the (i) cognitive-pragmatic conceptual level, the Spatial-Temporal-Axiological (STA) model of proximization revisits the ontological status and pragmatic function of deixis and deictic markers. As has been said, on classical views deixis is primarily a technical necessity for the possible interpretability of communication in the first place. Within the proximization approach deixis goes beyond its 'primary' status of a formal tool for the coding of elements of context to make all communication possible. It becomes, eventually, an instrument (or a component thereof) for legitimization, persuasion and social coercion. On the proximization view, the concept of deixis is not *reduced* to a finite set of 'deictic expressions', but rather *expanded* to cover bigger lexico-grammatical phrases and discourse expressions which the 'conventional' deictic markers (e.g., pronominals) get part of as the speaker constructs complex discourse forms to meet the changing contextual conditions. As a result, the 'component' deictic markers partake in forced conceptual shifts. An example of the proximization approach to deixis and deictic expressions is Cap's (2013: 109) spatial proximization framework (Table 6.1), which not only reflects the very constituents and the mechanism of proximization in the Discourse Space, but also plays a key role in abstracting the relevant (i.e., 'spatial') lexico-grammatical items. It thus allows a quantitative analysis yielding the intensity of spatial proximization (and thus the intensity with which a given worldview is forced) in a discourse timeframe.

The six categories depicted in the left-hand column of Table 6.1 are a stable element of the spatial proximization framework. The key items provided in the right-hand column depend on the actual discourse under investigation. In Table 6.1, they come from the domain of anti-terrorist rhetoric, which has been widely analyzed within the proximization paradigm. Table 6.1 includes the most frequent of the spatial proximization items in the 2001–2010 corpus of the US presidential addresses on the US anti-terrorist policies and actions.[5] Quantifiable items appear in square brackets and include combinations of words separated by slashes with the head word. For example, the item ['free people/nations/countries/societies/world'] includes the following combinations, all of which contribute to the general count of the first category: 'free people', 'free nations', 'free countries', 'free societies', 'free world'. The italicized phrases indicate parts that allow synonymous phrases to fill in the item and thus increase its count. For example, the item ['destroy *an IDC*'] in category 4 subsumes several quantifiable variations, such as 'destroy America', 'destroy our land' or 'destroy the free and democratic world'.[6]

The framework and its 6 categories capture not only the initial arrangement of the DS (categories 1, 2), but also (and crucially) the shift leading to the ODC-IDC clash (3, 4) and the (anticipated) effects of the clash (5, 6). The third category, central to the design of the framework, sets 'traditional' deictic expressions such as personal pronouns to work *pragmatically* together with the other elements of the superordinate VP. As a result, the VP acquires a

Table 6.1 Spatial proximization framework and its key lexico-grammatical items

Category	Key items
1. (Noun phrases [NPs] construed as elements of the deictic center of the DS [IDCs])	['USA', 'United States', 'America']; ['American people', 'Americans', 'our people/nation/country/society']; ['free people/nations/countries/societies/world']; ['democratic people/nations/countries/societies/ world']
2. (Noun phrases [NPs] construed as elements outside the deictic center of the DS [ODCs])	['Iraq', 'Saddam Hussein', 'Saddam', 'Hussein']; ['Iraqi regime/dictatorship']; ['terrorists']; ['terrorist organizations/networks', 'Al-Qaeda']; ['extremists/ radicals']; ['foreign regimes/dictatorships']
3. (Verb phrases [VPs] of motion and directionality construed as markers of movement of ODCs towards the deictic center)	['are determined/intend to seek/acquire WMD']; ['might/may/could/can use WMD against *an IDC*']; ['expand/grow *in military capacity that could be directed against an IDC*']; ['move/are moving/ head/are heading/have set their course toward confrontation *with an IDC*']
4. (Verb phrases [VPs] of action construed as markers of impact of ODCs upon IDCs)	['destroy *an IDC*']; ['set aflame/burn down *an IDC or IDC values*']
5. (Noun phrases [NPs] denoting abstract concepts construed as anticipations of impact of ODCs upon IDCs)	['threat']; ['danger']
6. (Noun phrases [NPs] denoting abstract concepts construed as effects of impact of ODCs upon IDCs)	['catastrophe']; ['tragedy']

Source: adapted from (Cap 2013: 109)

deictic status, in the sense that on top of conventionally denoting static DS entities (marked by pronominals), it also helps index a more challenging element of context, their movement, which establishes the target perspective construed by the speaker. Recall Bush's words, "they [terrorists] have set their course to confront us and our civilization" (footnote 3). The person deixis ('they') combines with the verb phrase that follows into a complex deictic structure marking *both* the antagonistic entity and its movement toward home entities in the deictic center.

Emerging from the spatial proximization framework (as well as the temporal and axiological frameworks [Cap 2013]) is the (ii) lexico-grammatical contribution of the STA model. The model makes it possible to extract *quantifiable* linguistic evidence of the use of different proximization strategies within a specific timeframe. The STA model can thus also account quantitatively for – as will be shown in 3.1 – the cases where one proximization strategy is dropped in favor of another one, for contextual reasons.

3.1 A case study of proximization in (state) political discourse

As has been mentioned, the main application of Proximization Theory so far has been to critical studies of state political discourse seeking legitimization of interventionist preventive measures against an external threat. In this section I give an example of this application, discussing instances of the US discourse of the war-on-terror. Specifically, I outline what proximization strategies were used to legitimize the US government's decision to go to war in Iraq (March 2003), and what adjustments in the use of the strategies were made later (from November 2003) as a result of contextual changes which took place in the meantime.

3.1.1 Initiating legitimization through proximization

Below I look at parts of G.W. Bush's speech at the American Enterprise Institute, which was delivered on February 26, 2003.[7] The speech took place only three weeks before the first US and coalition troops entered Iraq on March 19, and has often been considered (Silberstein 2004) a manifesto of the Iraq war. The goal of the speech was to list direct reasons for the intervention, while also locating it in the global context of the war on terror declared by G.W. Bush on the night of the 9/11 attacks. The realization of this goal involved a strategic use of various lexico-grammatical forms reflecting different proximization strategies.

Providing his rationale for war, President Bush had to confront the kind of public reluctance faced by many of his White House predecessors: how to legitimize the US involvement in military action in a far-away place, among a far-away people, of whom the American people knew little (Bacevich 2010). The AEI speech is remarkable in its consistent continuity of attempts to overcome this reluctance. It amply applies spatio-temporal and axiological proximization strategies, which are performed in diligently designed pragmatic patterns drawing from more general conceptual premises for legitimization:

> On a September morning, threats that had gathered for years, in secret and far away, led to murder in our country on a massive scale. . . . Our country is a battlefield in the first war of the 21st century. . . . We learned a lesson: the dangers of our time must be confronted actively and forcefully, before we see them again in our skies and our cities. . . . The world has a clear interest in the spread of democratic values, because stable and free nations do not breed the ideologies of murder. . . . Saddam Hussein and his weapons of mass destruction are a direct threat to our people and to all free people. . . . My job is to protect the American people. . . . We've tried diplomacy for 12 years. It hasn't worked. Today the goal is to remove the Iraqi regime and to rid Iraq of weapons of mass destruction. . . . The liberation of millions is the fulfillment of America's founding promise. The objectives we've set in this war are worthy of America, worthy of all the acts of heroism and generosity that have come before.

In a nutshell, the AEI speech states that there are WMD[8] in Iraq and that, given historical context and experience, ideological characteristics of the adversary as opposed to American values and national legacy, and Bush's obligations as standing US president, there is a case for legitimate military intervention. This complex picture involves historical flashbacks, as well as descriptions of the current situation, which both engage proximization strategies. These strategies operate at two interrelated levels, which can be described as 'diachronic' and 'synchronic'. At the diachronic level, Bush evokes ideological representations of the remote past, which are 'proximized' to underline the continuity and steadfastness of purpose, thus linking with and sanctioning current actions as acts of faithfulness to long-accepted principles and values. An example is the final part: "The liberation is. . . promise. The objectives. . . have come before". It launches a temporal analogy 'axis' which links a past reference point (the founding of America) with the present point, creating a common conceptual space for both the proximized historical 'acts of heroism' and the current and/or prospective acts construed as their natural 'follow-ups'. This kind of legitimization, performed by mostly temporal and axiological proximization (the originally past values become the 'here and now' premises for action),[9] draws, in many ways, upon the socio-psychological predispositions of the US addressee (Dunmire 2011). On the pragmatic-lexical plane, the job of establishing the link and thus winning credibility is performed by assertoric sequences, which fall within the addressee's 'latitude of acceptance' (Jowett and O'Donnell 1992).[10] The assertions there demonstrate different degrees of acceptability, from being indisputably acceptable ('My job is [. . .]'; 'The liberation of millions [. . .]'), to being acceptable due to credibility developed progressively within a 'fact-belief series' ('We've tried diplomacy for 12 years [FACT] [. . .] he's armed [BELIEF]'), but none of them is inconsistent with the key predispositions of the addressee.

At the synchronic level, historical flashbacks are not completely abandoned, but they involve proximization of *near* history, and the main legitimization premise is not (continuing) ideological commitments, but the *direct physical threats* looming over the country ('a battle-field', in President Bush's words). As the threats require a swift and strong preemptive response, the 'default' proximization strategy operating at the synchronic level is spatial proximization, often featuring a temporal element. Its task is to raise fears of imminence of the threat, which might be 'external' and 'distant' apparently, but in fact able to materialize anytime. The lexico-grammatical carriers of the spatial proximization include such items and phrases as 'secret and far away', 'all free people', 'stable and free nations', 'Saddam Hussein and his weapons of mass destruction', etc., which force dichotomous, 'good against evil' representations of the IDCs (America, Western [free, democratic] world) and the ODCs (Saddam Hussein, Iraqi regime, terrorists), located at a relative distance from each other. This geographical and geopoliti-cal distance is symbolically construed as shrinking, as, on the one hand, the ODC entities cross the DS towards its deictic center and, on the other, the center (IDC) entities declare a reaction. The ODC shift is enacted by forced inference and metaphorization. The inference involves an analogy to 9/11 ('On a September morning [. . .]'), whereby the event stage is construed as facing another physical impact, whose ('current') consequences are scrupulously described ('before we see them [flames] again in our skies and our cities'). This fear appeal is strengthened by the FIRE metaphor, which contributes the imminence and the speed of the external impact (Hart 2010).

While all spatial proximization in the text draws upon the presumed WMD presence in Iraq – and its potential availability to terrorists for acts far more destructive than the 9/11 attacks – Bush does not disregard the possibility of having to resort to an alternative rationale for war in the future. Consequently, the speech contains 'supporting' ideological premises, however tied to the principal premise. An example is the use of axiological proximization in 'The world has a clear interest in the spread of democratic values, because stable and free nations do not breed the ideologies of murder'. This ideological argument is not synonymous with Bush's proximization of remote history we have seen before, as its current line subsumes acts of the adversary rather than his/America's own acts. As such it involves a more 'typi-cal' axiological proximization, where the initially ideological conflict turns, over time, into a physical clash. Notably, in its ideological-physical duality it forces a spectrum of speculations over whether the current threat is 'still' ideological or 'already' physical. Since any result of these speculations can be effectively cancelled in a prospective discourse, the example quoted ('The world. . .') shows how proximization can interrelate, at the pragmalinguistic level, with the mechanism of implicature (Grice 1975).

3.1.2 Maintaining legitimization through adjustments in proximization strategies

Political legitimization pursued in temporally extensive contexts – such as the timeframe of the Iraq war – often involves redefinition of the initial legitimization premises and coercion patterns, and proximization is very well suited to enact these redefinitions in discourse. This promises a vast applicability of Proximization Theory as a truly dynamic cognitive-pragmatic model in CDA. The legitimization obtained in the AEI speech and, mainly, how the unfolding geopolitical context has put it to test is an illuminating case in point. Recall that although Bush has made the 'WMD factor' the central premise for the Iraq war, he has left half-open an 'emergency door' to be able to reach for an alternative rationale. Come November 2003 (a mere eight months into the Iraq war), and Bush's pro-war rhetoric adopts (or rather has to adopt) such an emergency alternative rationale, as it becomes evident that there have never been weapons of mass destruction in Iraq, at least not in the ready-to-use product sense. The change of Bush's stance is a swift change from strong fear appeals (forced before then by spatial proximization of the 'direct threat') to a more subtle ideological argument for legitimization, involving predominantly axiological proximization. The following quote from G.W. Bush's Whitehall Palace address of November 19 is a good illustration:

> By advancing freedom in the greater Middle East, we help end a cycle of dictatorship and radicalism that brings millions of people to misery and brings danger to our own people. By struggling for justice in Iraq, Burma, in Sudan, and in Zimbabwe, we give hope to suffering people and improve the chances for stability and progress. Had we failed to act, the dictator's programs for weapons of mass destruction would continue to this day. Had we failed to act, Iraq's torture chambers would still be filled with victims, terrified and innocent. . . . For all who love freedom and peace, the world without Saddam Hussein's regime is a better and safer place.

The now dominant axiological proximization involves a dense concentration of ideological and value-oriented lexical items (e.g., 'freedom', 'justice', 'stability', 'progress', 'peace' vs. 'dictatorship', 'radicalism') as well as of items/phrases indicating the human dimension of the conflict ('misery', 'suffering people', 'terrified victims' vs. 'the world' [being] 'a better and safer place'). All of these lexico-grammatical forms serve to build, as in the case of the AEI address, dichotomous representations of the DS 'home' and 'peripheral/adversarial' entities (IDCs vs. ODCs), and the representation of impact upon the DS 'home' entities. In contrast to the AEI speech, however, all the entities (both IDCs and ODCs) are construed in abstract, rather than physical, 'tangible' terms, as respective lexical items are not explicitly but only inferentially attributed to concrete parties/groups. For example, compare phrases such as 'all free people', 'stable and free nations', [terrorist] 'flames of hatred', etc., in the AEI address, with the single-word abstract items of general reference such as 'dictatorship' and 'radicalism', in the Whitehall speech. Apparently, proximization in the Whitehall speech is essentially a proximization of antagonistic values, and not so much of physical entities as embodiments of these values. The consequences for maintaining the legitimization stance which began with the AEI address are enormous.

First, there is no longer a commitment to a material threat posed by a physical entity. Second, the relief of this commitment does not completely disqualify the original WMD premise, as the antagonistic 'peripheral' values retain a capacity to materialize within the DS deictic center (viz. ' . . . a cycle of *dictatorship and radicalism* that brings millions of people to misery and *brings danger to our own people*', reiterating 'The world has a clear interest in the spread of democratic values, because *stable and free nations do not breed the ideologies of murder*' from the AEI speech). Third, as the nature of ideological principles is such that they are (considered) global or broadly shared, the socio-ideological argument helps extend the spectrum of the US (military) engagement ('Burma', 'Sudan', 'Zimbabwe'), which in turn forces the construal of failure to detect WMD in Iraq as merely an unlucky incident amongst other (successful) operations, and not as something that could potentially ruin the US credibility.

Add to these general factors the power of legitimization ploys in specific pragmalinguistic constructs ('programs for weapons of mass destruction',[11] the enumeration of the 'new' foreign fields of engagement [viz. 'Burma', etc., above], the always effective appeals for solidarity in compassion [viz. 'terrified victims' in 'torture chambers']) and there are reasons to conclude that the autumn 2003 change to essentially axiological discourse (subsuming axiological proximization) has helped a lot towards saving credibility and thus maintaining legitimization of not only the Iraq war, but the later anti-terrorist campaigns as well. The flexible interplay and the discursive switches between spatial and axiological proximization (both aided by temporal projections) in the early stages of the US anti-terrorist policy rhetoric have indeed made a major contribution.

4. Conclusion

Proximization Theory (PT) is where spatial cognition and CDA meet in a conspicuous way. While drawing on the essentially cognitive-linguistic approach to discourse (viz. Section 2), PT provides the CL representation of Discourse Space with a dynamic element reflecting the speaker's awareness of the constantly evolving context. In its account of discourse dynamics, PT focuses on the strategic, ideological and goal-oriented essence of construals of the near and the remote. Most importantly, it focuses on how the imagining of the closeness and remoteness can be manipulated in the public sphere and bound up with fear, security and conflict. Proximization Theory is thus a critically minded revision of the classical models of Discourse Space such as Chilton's DST or Levinson's spatio-temporal frames of reference. It is also a truly *linguistic* revision, in terms of linking specific construals to stable and recurrent sets of lexico-grammatical items.

The landscape of discourses where proximization could help CDA in its descriptive commitments and practices seems enormous. The domains addressed in CDA in the last 30 years have been racism, xenophobia, national identity, gender identity and inequality, media discourse, discourses of national vs. international politics, and many more. This list, by no means exhaustive, gives a sense of the spectrum of discourses where proximization seems applicable. Since the central commitments of CDA include exploring the many ways in which ideologies and identities are reflected, (re)-enacted, negotiated, modified, reproduced, etc., in discourse, any 'doing' of CDA must involve, first of all, studying the original positioning of the different ideologies and identities, and, in the majority of cases, studying also the 'target positioning', that is the *change* the analyst claims is taking place through the speaker's *use* of discourse. Doing CDA means thus handling issues of the conceptual arrangement of the Discourse Space (DS), and most notably, the core issue of the DS *symbolic re-arrangement*. As such, any CDA practice may need the apparatus of proximization to account for both the original and the target setup of the DS. Crucial for such an account is the proven capacity of the STA model to pinpoint specific, quantifiable lexico-grammatical choices responsible for strategic enactment of conceptual shifts. Anti-terrorist discourse clearly holds a lot of lexical material deployed, legitimization-wise, to force such strategic shifts. Among other domains, the most analytically relevant seem those whose discourses force the distinction between different ideologies and/or identities in a particularly clear-cut and appealing manner – to construe opposition between 'better' and 'worse' ideologies/identities. This is evidently the case with the discourses of xenophobia, racism, nationalism or social exclusion, all of which presuppose a rigid in-group vs. out-group distinction, arguing for a 'growing' threat from the out-group. It seems also the case with many national discourses, where similar opposition is construed between 'central-national' and 'peripheral-international' interests – the ongoing debate over the future of the Eurozone is a case in point.

Notes

1 The day the NATO intervention in Kosovo began.
2 I have saved the original numbering of the sentences (25–37).
3 G.W. Bush on Al-Qaeda terrorists allegedly harbored in Iraq (17 March 2003).
4 For the best legitimization of response, the speaker tends to project ODC actions as maximally consequential (i.e., threatening) to the IDC entities.
5 The corpus contains 402 texts (601,856 words) of *speeches and remarks,* downloaded from the White House website www.whitehouse.gov in January 2011. It includes only the texts matching at least two of the three issue tags: *defense, foreign policy, homeland security.*
6 See Cap (2013: 108–109) for details. See also the two other frameworks, temporal (: 116) and axiological (: 122), which we do not have space to discuss here.
7 The parts are quoted according to the chronology of the speech.
8 Weapons of mass destruction.
9 This is a secondary variant of axiological proximization. As will be shown, axiological proximization mostly involves the adversary (ODC); antagonistic values are 'dormant' triggers for a possible ODC impact.
10 Jowett and O'Donnell (1992) posit that the best credibility and thus legitimization effects can be expected if the speaker produces her message in line with the psychological, social, political, cultural, etc., predispositions of the addressee. However, since a full compliance is almost never possible, it is essential that a novel message is at least tentatively or partly acceptable; then, its acceptability and the speaker's credibility tend to increase over time.
11 The nominal phrase '[Iraq's] programs for WMD' is essentially an implicature able to legitimize, in response to contextual needs, any of the following inferences: 'Iraq possesses WMD', 'Iraq is developing WMD', 'Iraq intends to develop WMD', 'Iraq intended to develop WMD', and more. The phrase was among G.W. Bush's rhetorical favorites in later stages of the Iraq war, when the original premises for war were called into question.

Further reading

Chilton, Paul. (2005). Discourse space theory: Geometry, brain and shifting viewpoints. *Annual Review of Cognitive Linguistics* 3: 78–116. This article is a manifesto of Discourse Space Theory, arguing that the processes involved in making sense of language are anchored in human visual experience. It develops a model of (political) discourse analysis based on spatio-temporal conceptualizations and simple geometric principles.

Hart, Christopher. (2014). *Discourse, grammar and ideology: Functional and cognitive perspectives.* London: Bloomsbury. This book discusses the individual utility and the interconnectedness of three grammatical frameworks in CDA – functional grammar, multi-modal grammar and cognitive grammar. It offers ways of understanding the ideological effects of grammatical choices in texts drawn from the cognitive domains of space, time and value.

Cap, Piotr. (2017). *The language of fear: Communicating threat in public discourse.* Basingstoke: Palgrave. This book investigates linguistic strategies of threat construction and fear generation in contemporary public communication. It describes the ways in which the perception of closeness and remoteness can be manipulated in the public sphere and bound up with fear, security and conflict.

References

Bacevich, A. (2010). *Washington rules: America's path to permanent war.* New York: Metropolitan Books.

Cap, P. (2006). *Legitimization in political discourse: A cross-disciplinary perspective on the modern US war rhetoric.* Newcastle: Cambridge Scholars Press.

Cap, P. (2008). Towards the proximization model of the analysis of legitimization in political discourse. *Journal of Pragmatics* 40: 17–41.

Cap, P. (2010). Axiological aspects of proximization. *Journal of Pragmatics* 42: 392–407.

Cap, P. (2013). *Proximization: The pragmatics of symbolic distance crossing.* Amsterdam: Benjamins.

Cap, P. (2017). *The language of fear: Communicating threat in public discourse.* Basingstoke: Palgrave.

Chilton, P. (2004). *Analysing political discourse: Theory and practice.* London: Routledge.

Chilton, P. (2005). Discourse space theory: Geometry, brain and shifting viewpoints. *Annual Review of Cognitive Linguistics* 3: 78–116.

Chilton, P. (2010). From mind to grammar: Coordinate systems, prepositions, constructions. In Vyvyan Evans and Paul Chilton (eds.), *Language, cognition and space: The state of the art and new directions,* 640–671. London: Equinox.

Chilton, P. (2014). *Language, space and mind.* Cambridge: Cambridge University Press.

Chovanec, J. (2010). Legitimation through differentiation: Discursive construction of Jacques *Le Worm* Chirac as an opponent to military action. In Urszula Okulska and Piotr Cap (eds.), *Perspectives in politics and discourse,* 61–82. Amsterdam: Benjamins.

Cienki, A., Kaal, B. and Maks, I. (2010). Mapping world view in political texts using discourse space theory: Metaphor as an analytical tool. Paper presented at *RAAM 8 Conference,* Vrije Universiteit Amsterdam.

Dunmire, P. (2011). *Projecting the future through political discourse: The case of the bush doctrine.* Amsterdam: Benjamins.

Evans, V. and Chilton, P. (eds.) (2010). *Language, cognition and space: The state of the art and new directions.* London: Equinox.

Fauconnier, G. and Turner, M. (2002). *The way we think: Conceptual blending and the mind's hidden complexities.* New York: Basic Books.

Filardo-Llamas, L. (2010). Discourse worlds in Northern Ireland: The legitimisation of the 1998 agreement. In Katy Hayward and Catherine O'Donnell (eds.), *Political discourse and conflict resolution: Debating peace in Northern Ireland,* 62–76. London: Routledge.

Filardo-Llamas, L. (2013). Committed to the ideals of 1916: The language of paramilitary groups: The case of the Irish Republican Army. *Critical Discourse Studies* 10(1): 1–17.

Filardo-Llamas, L., Hart, Christopher and Kaal, Bertie (eds.). (2015). *Time, space and evaluation in ideological discourse.* Special issue of *Critical Discourse Studies* 12(3):

Gavins, J. (2007). *Text world theory: An introduction.* Edinburgh: Edinburgh University Press.

Grice, P. (1975). Logic and conversation. In Peter Cole and Jerry L. Morgan (eds.), *Syntax and semantics 3: Speech acts,* 41–58. New York: Academic Press.

Hart, C. (2010). *Critical discourse analysis and cognitive science: New perspectives on immigration discourse.* Basingstoke: Palgrave Macmillan.

Hart, C. (2014). *Discourse, grammar and ideology: Functional and cognitive perspectives.* London: Bloomsbury.

Hart, C. and Cap, P (eds.) (2014). *Contemporary critical discourse studies.* London: Bloomsbury.

Jowett, G. S. and O'Donnell, V. (1992). *Propaganda and persuasion.* Newbury Park: Sage.

Kaal, B. (2012). Worldviews: The spatial ground of political reasoning in Dutch election manifestos. *CADAAD* 6(1): 1–22.

Levinson, S. C. (2003). *Space in language and cognition: Explorations in cognitive diversity.* Cambridge: Cambridge University Press.

Silberstein, S. (2004). *War of words.* London: Routledge.

Talmy, L. (2000). *Toward a cognitive semantics.* Cambridge, MA: MIT Press.

Verhagen, A. (2007). Construal and perspectivization. In Dirk Geeraerts and Hubert Cuyckens (eds.), *The Oxford handbook of cognitive linguistics,* 48–81. Oxford: Oxford University Press.

Werth, P. (1999). *Text worlds: Representing conceptual space in discourse.* Harlow: Longman.

7

Corpus-based approaches

Nicholas Close Subtirelu and Paul Baker

Introduction

Corpus Linguistics is a relatively new field which was made possible as a result of the wider availability and use of personal computers in the last quarter of the twentieth century. The field's rationale is that we can better understand language production if we use computer software to identify linguistic patterns that occur across large sets of texts that have been collected in order to be representative of a particular language variety. As an example of how corpora are sampled in order to be balanced, the first corpus, the Brown Corpus which comprised 1 million words of written American English published in 1961, contained 500 samples of writing, each of about 2,000 words taken from 15 genres which included news, fiction, academic writing and government documentation.

Corpora are thus comprised of numerous text files which require the conversion of traditionally published works from paper into electronic form, while spoken language must be recorded and then transcribed. Existing electronic data (such as webpages) are often easier to collect although such texts may need to be 'cleaned', e.g., menus may need to be removed to avoid lexical repetitions.

While many corpora simply contain representations of the original text, it is also common to 'mark-up' a corpus by inserting 'tags' (or codes) into it. For example, header tags can be used to provide information about each file such as author, date of publication, genre, etc., while orthographic tags can indicate features that may have been stripped out of the original text during the encoding process such as use of bold print, headings, paragraph breaks or accented characters. Additional tags can be inserted to indicate the grammatical or semantic category of each word so that distinctions can be made between, e.g., uses of the word *round* as a noun, verb, adjective, adverb or preposition.

Theoretically, a corpus could be read from start to finish, or a set of files could be chosen (perhaps randomly) for more detailed analysis. However, that is not usually how corpus linguists conduct their research. Instead, the corpus is examined with the help of computer software which is able to quickly and accurately carry out complex calculations on the linguistic data, for example, helping analysts to identify words that are frequent (word lists), appear more frequently than would be expected (keywords) or occur near each other more often than expected (collocates). Corpus software can also present and sort information from the corpus in ways which make it easier for human analysts to make interpretations based on scanning multiple occurrences of the same word or phrase (concordances).

Early research in Corpus Linguistics tended to be based around analysis of lexical and grammatical patterns, particularly being useful in the creation of dictionaries and grammars, while multilingual corpora were helpful for translation. It was not until the 1990s that a small number of researchers began to see the value in applying corpus approaches to answer questions related to discourse and ideology. The following section covers the development of the field and is followed by a short illustrative study which uses some of the most well-known techniques in corpus linguistics to compare news media constructions around the 'fiscal cliff' negotiations that took place in the US in 2012–2013.

The development of a 'useful synergy'

The 1990s saw the first suggestions that corpus techniques could be used in order to carry out Critical Discourse Analysis (CDA). For example, Caldas Coulthard (1993, 1995) examined the representation of men and women speaking in a news-as-narrative discourse, using basic frequency information to note that terms referring to males were much more frequent than those referring to women. Additionally, men tended to be quoted more and were described more often as belonging to public institutions. On the other hand, women were more likely to be described in terms of their relationship to others (e.g., *wife, mother*). A key early paper was Louw's (1993) chapter on the concept of semantic prosody or a 'consistent aura of meaning with which a form is imbued by its collocates' (1993: 157). Examining a 37 million word corpus, Louw showed that certain words or phrases tended to be mainly used in positive or negative contexts, e.g., *bent on* has a negative prosody. The presence of such words or phrases in individual texts could thus indicate an author's (perhaps unconscious) stance towards a topic.

To our knowledge, the first paper which explicitly linked critical discourse studies with corpus approaches was Hardt-Mautner (1995) who makes the pertinent point

> Because critical discourse analysis is best suited to deal with small corpora the question of representativeness obviously looms large. There may be a temptation *to proclaim* features as typical rather than build up the notion of "typicality" on the basis of frequency. The hidden danger is that the reason why the texts concerned were singled out for analysis in the first place was precisely that they were not typical, but in fact quite unusual instances which aroused the analyst's attention.
>
> *(1995: 3)*

Analysis of frequencies, collocates and concordances grew in popularity during the late 1990s and 2000s as ways of identifying discourses or representations of particular identity groups or concepts, particularly in political contexts. The former work includes Krishnamurthy's (1996) work on the contexts of identity words like *tribal, ethnic* and *racial* and Hunston's study (1999) of the representation of deaf people while the latter is typified by Piper's (2000) research on the concept *lifelong learning* and Flowerdew's (1997) analysis of speeches by the last British governor of Hong Kong.

Another technique used by corpus analysts of discourse (and one which we apply in our illustrative study below), is the elicitation of *keywords,* a concept which has gradually changed over time. For example, Stubbs (1996) followed Williams (1976) in viewing a keyword as a word that has significance in a particular discourse and tells us about the values of a society (such as *employment* or *family*). Such words were identified through introspective or qualitative means but could then be subjected to analyses of concordance lines and collocates, for example, by interrogating them within a reference corpus. Teubert (2001) used a more statistically informed way of identifying some keywords by looking at the collocates of qualitatively chosen keywords in order to uncover new ones. However, the growing popularity of Scott's WordSmith Tools (1996) introduced a fully statistical approach to the identification of keywords which were redefined as words that occur statistically saliently (via log likelihood or chi-square tests) in one corpus (or text) when compared against another (reference) corpus (or text).

Keywords have been used as a springboard for related forms of analysis, including 'concordance keywords' (Marchi 2010, Taylor 2010), where a sub-corpus is created using concordance lines derived from particular search words and then keywords are elicited from that corpus (as a way of focussing in on the immediate lexical context around a word of interest). Baker (2005) also describes how annotated corpora can be used to find key semantic or grammatical categories – groups of words which may not be key alone but their combined frequencies are more common in one corpus when compared against another.

In the 2000s, a group led by Alan Partington conceptualised Corpus-Assisted Discourse Studies (CADS) which built and analysed corpora to analyse how discourse participants achieve (often political) goals via language or how participants differ in their use of language. A main aim of CADS is to discover non-obvious meaning and identify questions and puzzles that would otherwise have not been considered (Partington, Duguid and Taylor 2013: 1–24). Other key texts by this group include Partington (2003) and Partington, Flowerdew and Haarman (2004) while a special issue of *Corpora* journal (Partington 2010) covers a diachronic strand of CADS research which focusses on how discourse changes over time. Typically, CADS makes use of frequency and keyword lists as well as qualitative analyses of concordances although it differs from traditional CDA in that the critical aspect of analysis is often de-emphasised (Partington, Duguid and Taylor 2013: 339) and/or topics may be examined where researchers do not have strong preconceptions or beliefs about the existence of author bias or discourses which accentuate social problems. The analysis may be more exploratory, allowing such findings to emerge (or not).

Occurring concurrently, collaboration by Paul Baker, Ruth Wodak, Tony McEnery and others aimed to develop techniques which enabled Reisigl and Wodak's (2001) Discourse-Historical Approach (DHA) to be incorporated into corpus analyses of discourse. A project analysing the representation of immigration in the British press, from a critical perspective, attempted to outline how this 'useful methodological synergy' could be operationalised, resulting in a recursive multi-stage model which moved between different types of qualitative and quantitative analysis, bringing in social and historical context to explain findings and form new hypotheses (Baker et al. 2008). A follow-up project (see Baker, Gabrielatos and McEnery 2013) examined the representation of Muslims and Islam in the British press, positioning traditional corpus analyses of keywords and collocates alongside consideration of British press guidelines, changing audience figures and demographics, attitude surveys and the effect of relevant events like 9.11 and 7.7.

The availability of a new generation of corpus analysis tools has helped to spur on further (critical) discourse excursions with corpora. Alongside WordSmith, Laurence Anthony's freeware AntConc (Anthony 2011) has offered a robust and simple to use standalone tool which enables users to easily carry out analysis of their own corpora. Web-based tools have also made corpora accessible to much wider numbers of researchers. For example, a set of large reference corpora created by Mark Davies include the Corpus of Contemporary American English and the Corpus of Historical American English and are free to use online via an interface which allows collocates, frequencies and concordances among other techniques. Another web-based interface, Sketch Engine (Kilgarriff et al. 2014), also comes with preloaded reference corpora but allows users to upload their own corpora too. Sketch Engine affords an innovative form of collocational analysis called Word Sketches which groups collocates into grammatical sets. For example, it is possible to quickly identify how verb collocates of a word like *man* position males as mainly either the subject (*conquer, jump, mastermind*) or object (*accuse, bewitch, flatter*) of certain processes.

New tools have the potential to enable more sophisticated forms of analysis – see for example Baker and McEnery's (2015) use of the tool GraphColl which can create instant collocational networks to give a visual representation of relationships between a wide set of collocates and help to show the complex and shared relationships between numerous concepts.

As the last two paragraphs indicate, the field (or combination of fields) is still in development, and recent work has attempted to experiment with methods in order to test their validity, for example, by asking multiple researchers to independently analyse the same corpus (Marchi and Taylor 2009). The extent to which corpus approaches reduce subjectivity (or whether this is desirable or possible) is still open to debate. It may be that rather than reducing subjectivity in the analytic project as a whole, the incorporation of corpus approaches into critical discourse studies reduces the reliance on analysts' interpretations and judgements only in certain ways.

On the one hand, corpus approaches can provide more precise estimates of the frequency of textual features as well as a more transparent methodological description of how such estimates are arrived at than would be the case for fully qualitative research relying on only a small number of texts. For example, while an analysis of a single text might conclude that Muslims are often referred to as *extremists* in the press on the basis of the analyst's informed but subjective impressions of the text and other similar texts, corpus approaches enable us to estimate the frequency of this labelling within a particular sample of texts and provide a methodological justification for generalisations about such labelling in the press as a whole.

On the other hand, the tools and insights of corpus analysis offer very little with regards to other, perhaps more central, issues of subjectivity. Specifically, analysts' positions on whether or not the trends observed in frequency data are worthy of attention or socially problematic still depend heavily on analysts' theoretical or ideological commitments. Although the identification of social problems is crucial for CDA, it is not the intention of this chapter to address this issue directly.

Instead, the following section gives an illustrative example of how corpus linguistics can be integrated into CDA both for the purposes of gaining news insights into discourse that may have otherwise gone unnoticed as well as addressing the issues of representativeness and generalisation that we previously mentioned. Following Tognini-Bonelli (2001), we distinguish between corpus-based and corpus-driven approaches to the study of language. The corpus-based approach sees a corpus as a testing-ground for claims or theories about language derived through other means. In contrast, the corpus-driven approach attempts to minimise prior assumptions about the texts or language and instead to describe the corpus as comprehensively as possible without privileging preconceived ideas. Principled incorporation of either or both of these approaches into CDA can help support analysts' arguments about texts and discourses.

A case study: the 'fiscal cliff' negotiations

We illustrate the incorporation of both corpus-based and corpus-driven approaches into a small-scale study that examined US media's framing of a controversial federal budget negotiation involving disagreement between members of the two major political parties in the US. Specifically, this small-scale study attempted to determine how different media venues portrayed the events that constituted what has been called the 'fiscal cliff negotiations' of late 2012 and early 2013. A basic outline of the methodology is provided in Figure 7.1, and we discuss Steps 3 through 6 in greater detail below. Before describing our analysis further, however, we provide a brief background to the topic.

Step 1: Research topic and questions

- A general research question was put forward before background research and corpus collection.
- The question was refined after Steps 2 and 3.
- The final version was 'How did FOX's and CNN's coverage of the fiscal cliff negotiations differ?'

Step 2: Background research

- Varying accounts of the fiscal cliff negotiations were read, including some texts that ultimately became part of the corpus.
- Research was undertaken into media venues and news consumption in the United States.

Step 3: Corpus collection

- Informed by Step 2, a framework for data collection which attended to texts' time of publication, venue and genre was established.
- Texts were collected, 'cleaned' and divided into two corpora based on whether they were published by CNN or FOX.

Step 4: Corpus-driven analysis – keywords extraction

- Keywords were extracted from both corpora.

Step 5: Qualitative analysis

- We closely examined the usage of the keywords identified in Step 4 in context.
- We formed interpretations and generalisations about how these keywords were used in the corpora.

Step 6: Corpus-based analysis – collocation analysis

- When possible, we sought evidence for generalisations made in Step 5 by turning to corpus data, most often through the use of collocation analysis.

Figure 7.1 Overview of the methodology used in the fiscal cliff study

The fiscal cliff negotiations: background

In this section, we provide a summary of the fiscal cliff negotiations as we came to understand them during Step 2 of our research, which involved reading varying accounts of the fiscal cliff negotiations.

The *fiscal cliff* was a popular term referring to the undesirable effects expected to incur as a result of budgetary laws scheduled to take effect or expire in January 2013. These effects included increases in income tax rates and decreases in government spending. Income tax rates in the US were scheduled to rise in January 2013 because temporary reductions in tax rates, originally enacted during the administration of George W. Bush, were scheduled to expire. In addition, discretionary spending for various government agencies was scheduled to be reduced.

In general, Republicans (the more conservative of the two major political parties in the US) favoured keeping tax rates lower and reducing government spending. In contrast, Democrats (the other, more progressive, major political party in the US) generally favoured increasing tax rates on higher incomes and were opposed to reducing funding for government agencies.

At the time, control of the federal government was divided. The Democrats had a majority in the Senate (one of the two houses of Congress) and controlled the Presidency. The Republicans controlled the House of Representatives (the other house of Congress). Due to this divide, the two parties attempted to negotiate a compromise that would minimise the economic impact of the fiscal cliff.

President Barack Obama (a Democrat) and Representative John Boehner (a Republican and then Speaker of the House of Representatives) were the major negotiators and exchanged offers and counter-offers several times. Ultimately, a compromise was reached, which delayed decreases in government spending and made more modest increases in income taxes than were originally scheduled. In particular, the Bush-era income tax rates were extended for everyone making under \$400,000 per year. Bush-era tax rates were allowed to expire for all those making more than this amount, and these high-earning individuals saw their federal income tax rates rise from 35% to 39.6%.

Although seemingly a dry budgetary matter, we believe the issue is of potential interest in CDA as it reveals how something as ostensibly straightforward as how money will be appropriated and levied in the government can be differently understood and reported by those with different ideologies and interests.

Corpus collection and representativeness

After deciding on a general research topic and carrying out background research, the first step necessary for corpus-driven CDA is to define the criteria for determining what texts will be included in the corpus (Step 3 in Figure 7.1). Since the goal is ultimately to make grounded generalisations about some discourse, genre or text-producer, it is important that the corpus is representative of what the analyst intends to generalise about.

There are numerous considerations to make when determining which texts to include (see Biber 1993 for an overview of representativeness in corpus construction). Ultimately, arriving at decisions about what criteria should be used will require the analyst to closely investigate the various available texts and to carefully consider the dimensions upon which they might differ, such as date of publication, venue and genre.

In using date of publication as a criterion for text selection, it was necessary to have an understanding of the major events that constituted the fiscal cliff negotiations. The background

Date	Event
29 November 2012	Obama's initial offer
3 December 2012	Boehner's counter-offer 1
12 December 2012	Obama's counter-offer 1
15 December 2012	Boehner's counter-offer 2
17 December 2012	Obama's counter-offer 2
18 December 2012	Boehner introduces alternative offer, 'Plan B', to appeal to conservative members of Congress
1 January 2013	Congress passes American Taxpayer Relief Act
2 January 2013	Obama signs American Taxpayer Relief Act

Figure 7.2 Time frame of fiscal cliff negotiations for corpus collection

Relevant articles published on each of these dates or the day after were included in the creation of our corpora

research we undertook and summarised in the previous section informed our selection process. We determined that the major events that constituted the fiscal cliff negotiations were the offers and counter-offers exchanged between Obama and Boehner as well as the ultimate legislative resolution of the issue. This suggested a set of time periods from which to collect articles, which are outlined in Figure 7.2. We assumed that reporting would take place on the same day of or on the next day after these events.

Since we are interested in the way different media venues framed the event, we also used venue as a criterion in text selection. We selected two comparable venues: FOX News and CNN. They are comparable in the sense that both are large media conglomerates and have sizable presences both in cable television and online. In a Pew Research Center (2012) survey released shortly before the start of these events, the most popular specific venues (not news aggregators such as Google News) respondents named were CNN (14%) and FOX (9%). The same report indicates that the two contrast in terms of audience demographics. In particular, approximately 20% of Republicans name FOX News as their preferred online news source (compared to 9% of the general population). This reflects the widely held perception that FOX News is a conservative venue. In contrast, CNN has been accused of having a liberal or progressive bias particularly by conservative commentators (e.g., Kincaid 2005). Thus, the two provide an interesting contrast for examining how different media outlets presented the fiscal cliff negotiations.

Finally, we also used genre as a criterion in text selection. Large outlets such as FOX and CNN produce extremely large amounts of content from a variety of different perspectives. One important difference in genre involves those articles with explicit editorial content, opinion articles and those that are presented as mere reporting. Because we are interested in the subtleties of media framing in supposedly 'objective' news reports, we chose to exclude articles explicitly presented as opinion pieces and focus instead on articles in each venue's Politics section that were not explicitly opinionated.

Following these criteria, we collected articles mentioning the fiscal cliff negotiations from the Politics sections of each of the two media outlets' websites published during the different time frames we identified above (on the same dates as those listed in Figure 7.2 or the day after). This resulted in two corpora of similar size. The CNN corpus was 16,742 words, and the FOX corpus was 17,616 words. However, the two corpora had differing numbers of articles, with CNN consisting of 17 articles, and FOX consisting of 27 articles.

Corpus-driven analysis: extracting keywords

Satisfied that these two corpora were representative of the way these two venues reported on the fiscal cliff negotiations, we proceeded with our corpus-driven analysis. We used a common corpus technique known as keywords analysis to identify important quantitative trends in the corpora. Keywords are words that have a significantly higher frequency of occurrence in one corpus than in another comparison corpus. They, therefore, point to lexical differences between two corpora, which can be further analysed using CDA.

Three measures are important in selecting keywords to focus on in CDA to assure that these words are particularly characteristic of one corpus (and not of the other) and also widespread within that corpus (and not simply an idiosyncrasy of very few texts). The first and most important measure is keyness, which refers to the degree to which a word is more common in one corpus than in a comparison or reference corpus. The second measure is normed frequency, which refers to the number of times a word occurs within some standard number of words, often per 1,000 words. Normed frequency is preferred to raw frequency because the latter can be misleading in cases where two corpora have different overall word counts. Normed frequency is an important complement to keyness in CDA studies, because lower frequency words with high keyness may not be as relevant for analysis as more frequent words with lower keyness scores. The third measure is contextual diversity, which refers to the degree to which a word is spread across different texts in the corpus. It is often measured as the percentage of texts containing a word. Contextual diversity is particularly important to pay attention to in small corpora like ours, where a word may appear numerous times in a single text, giving the word a high keyness and normed frequency resulting from idiosyncratic usage in only a small number of texts.

To perform our keywords analysis, we limited the analysis to only those words that appeared at least once per thousand words (normed frequency) and in at least 20% of all texts (contextual diversity) in one of the two corpora. Then, we ranked the remaining words in each corpus according to their keyness scores. We identified the ten highest ranked words in these lists, excluding words like *fox,* which reflect transparently research-irrelevant features of the texts. These are presented in Tables 7.1 and 7.2.

Table 7.1 Top 10 keywords in FOX News corpus

		FOX			CNN	
	%diff[a]	norm freq[b]	CD[c]		norm freq[b]	CD[c]
final	945.42	1.25	33.33%		0.12	11.76%
hikes	565.27	1.59	48.15%		0.24	23.53%
crisis	489.24	1.76	51.85%		0.30	11.76%
only	220.76	1.53	48.15%		0.48	41.18%
making	193.76	1.93	55.56%		0.66	41.18%
raising	161.36	1.25	40.74%		0.48	29.41%
than	156.60	3.07	66.67%		1.19	64.71%
lawmakers	147.10	1.48	48.15%		0.60	41.18%
still	141.92	1.59	55.56%		0.66	41.18%
about	114.87	2.95	70.37%		1.37	64.71%

a. Percentage difference between normed frequencies in the FOX and CNN corpora
b. Normed frequency or frequency per 1,000 words
c. Contextual diversity or percentage of texts containing the word

Table 7.2 Top 10 keywords in CNN corpus

		CNN		FOX	
	%diff[a]	norm freq[b]	CD[c]	norm freq[b]	CD[c]
wealthiest	399.80	1.13	47.06%	0.23	11.11%
source	373.49	1.08	35.29%	0.23	11.11%
wealthy	347.19	1.02	47.06%	0.23	14.81%
reduction	299.84	1.13	52.94%	0.28	18.52%
big	278.79	1.08	29.41%	0.28	18.52%
higher	215.66	2.33	58.82%	0.74	29.63%
proposal	206.89	2.09	47.06%	0.68	25.93%
cliff	172.12	4.48	100.00%	1.65	51.85%
revenue	163.05	2.39	58.82%	0.91	33.33%
latest	155.54	1.02	23.53%	0.40	14.81%

a. Percentage difference between normed frequencies in the FOX and CNN corpora
b. Normed frequency or frequency per 1,000 words
c. Contextual diversity or percentage of texts containing the word

The results of the keywords analysis offer the analyst an entry point into the data rather than a readily interpretable set of findings. In particular, analysts can ask questions such as "Why was *cliff* used relatively more frequently by CNN than by FOX?" Seeking answers to such questions allows the analyst to generate findings that can be argued to be generalisable across numerous texts in the corpus and to represent frequent and distinctive (and, thus, presumably important) aspects of each corpus's contents.

Closer analysis using qualitative and corpus-based approaches

A closer, qualitative analysis of keyword usage can be undertaken drawing on any of the various approaches to critical discourse studies. However, we wish to highlight here how observations from qualitative approaches to CDA can be supported through corpus-based analysis. In particular, we have used the keywords we extracted to examine how FOX and CNN represented and evaluated changes to income tax rates. We combine qualitative analysis with insights from corpus data to provide more evidence for some of our generalisations.

We begin by examining *hikes* in the FOX corpus. We present the concordance lines for *hikes* in Figure 7.3, which show that it refers generally to an increase in *tax*. This observation is itself already revealing because it suggests FOX's coverage tended to represent tax rates as simply increasing. This representation is itself disputed, however, as many other actors represented the change not as an increase but as a return to prior rates after the end of temporary tax cuts. This perspective is exemplified by a quotation from then White House Press Secretary Jay Carney from an article in the CNN corpus ("Fiscal cliff talks still hung up on taxes", 13 December 2012): ". . . the president will not sign an extension of the Bush tax cuts for the wealthiest".

However, in addition to specifying an increase, we argue that the word *hikes* has a negative connotation, or, in Louw's terms, a negative semantic prosody, which further suggests a tendency for FOX writers to present the tax code changes as undesirable. We believe a corpus-based analysis is particularly insightful for providing evidence of this semantic prosody.

While our corpora are too small and specialised to provide generalisations about the general usage of a word, other corpora are designed to do just that, for example, the previously

#			
1	as Obama warns of middle class tax	hikes	
2	as the president demands tax	hikes	that many Republicans adamantly oppose.
3	to avert the series of year-end tax	hikes	and spending cuts. But Obama's campaign
4	on debt. But there will be federal tax	hikes	in 2013. That's because the legislation
5	last week to make his case for tax	hikes	on top earners, and has also turned to
6	are likely to continue pushing for tax	hikes	as part of those debates, while
7	Obama will use the money from tax	hikes	primarily to increase government spending
8	bill late Tuesday night that halts tax	hikes	for millions of Americans, lawmakers
9	gave up by getting $620 billion in tax	hikes	and a net of only $15 billion in spending
10	the bill includes $620 billion in tax	hikes	and $15 billion in spending cuts. As on
11	contained roughly $620 billion in tax	hikes	, and just a fraction of that in spending
12	In total, more than $600 billion in tax	hikes	and spending cuts were set to take effect
13	it was unbalanced, locking in tax	hikes	in the near-term in exchange for fuzzy
14	call for $1.6 trillion in tax	hikes	– four times the value of his proposed
15	spending on top of $1.6 trillion in tax	hikes	over the next decade. House Speaker John
16	Tuesday to a bill halting massive tax	hikes	and delaying a risky round of spending
17	ObamaCare tax	hikes	
18	reach a deal, a $500 billion mix of tax	hikes	and austere cutbacks on federal spending
19	Boehner 'Plan B' with threat of tax	hikes	looming
20	to avert the double-whammy of tax	hikes	and spending cuts could send the country
21	meet amid hard bargaining over tax	hikes	, debt ceiling
22	Many voiced frustration that tax	hikes	would only affect those making above
23	once Obama signs it, is that tax	hikes	that technically kicked in Jan. 1 for
24	and Marco Rubio, R-Fla. The tax	hikes	, combined with the spending cuts, could
25	on House Republicans if the tax	hikes	were not averted. "This is the House's
26	action, which technically triggered tax	hikes	. Without a resolution soon, taxes would

Figure 7.3 Concordance lines for *hikes* in FOX corpus (sorted to the left)

mentioned Corpus of Contemporary American English (COCA, which can be freely accessed online at corpus.byu.edu/coca/). At the time of writing, COCA contained 450 million words from various publications and media venues in the US. COCA's large and balanced sample of texts makes it possible to make generalisations about the use of particular words, phrases or other linguistic structures by US English speakers.

We can gain insight into the connotations of *hikes* by examining the words that co-occur with it in COCA. This type of analysis relies on another corpus technique known as collocation analysis. Collocation analysis attempts to determine the frequency of co-occurrence of two words, the tendency of one word to occur in the vicinity of a target word, specified in terms of a number of words to the left and to the right of the target. Candidate collocates of a particular target are compared by taking the number of occurrences in which the candidate term occurs inside the specified window around the target and dividing it by the total number of occurrences of the candidate term in the corpus as a whole. From this percentage, the COCA online interface calculates a Mutual Information (MI) score. Collocates are then ranked according to their MI score, which shows the strength of association between two words.

We have extracted collocates of *hikes* from COCA. Since part of speech can be specified in COCA, in order to ensure that we were finding other nouns that modify the noun *hikes*, we included only nouns as collocates and searched within two words to the left of *hikes*. In addition, we specified that each collocate must occur at least ten times within the specified span. Finally, we eliminated collocates that pertained to the sense of *hikes* referring to walks in nature. The resulting collocates, ranked by MI score, are presented in Table 7.3.

Table 7.3 demonstrates that the collocates of *hikes* tend to involve increases that are expected to be undesirable for most readers like *tuition, tax, price, fare* and *fee hikes*. Even in cases where we might expect readers to view the increase positively, like *wage hikes* or *pay hikes,* the increase is often represented as negative by text producers, for example, by referring to increases in salary demanded by public workers or organised labour. Thus, we argue that FOX's choice of *hikes* presents increases in tax rates as undesirable by drawing on the word's negative semantic prosody.

FOX's representation of scheduled or proposed changes to tax code as undesirable to the reader is made further apparent when we compare it to CNN's representation of these same changes. In particular, we argue that CNN represented these changes as more purposeful and less universal than FOX did, thereby presenting them as more desirable to the reader. CNN's more frequent use of the keyword *revenue* (see Table 7.2) represented changes to income tax structure in the United States as fulfilling a necessary or desirable purpose, raising money for the government. For example, one article ("Obama, Boehner move closer on taxes, spending cuts", 19 December 2012) mentioned that "Obama and Democrats argue that increased revenue, including higher tax rates on the wealthy, must be part of broader deficit reduction to prevent the middle class from getting hit too hard". We also present concordance lines for the use of *revenue* in the CNN corpus in Figure 7.4.

In addition, CNN's representation of the impending changes differed from FOX's in that CNN represented the higher tax rates as affecting a much smaller population than FOX. This is highlighted by the fact that both *wealthy* and *wealthiest* were keywords in the CNN corpus. Thus, rather than universal *tax hikes,* CNN made frequent reference to Democrats' proposals for increased tax rates for the upper class. For example, one article in the CNN corpus ("Obama warns of 'Scrooge' Christmas without tax-cut extension", 30 November 2012) reported that "House Minority Leader Nancy Pelosi said the election and polls show public support for extending the 'middle class' tax cut while raising rates for the wealthiest".

Table 7.3 Top 10 collocates of *hikes* in COCA

	relevant[a]	all[b]	%[c]	MI[d]
interest-rate	18	198	9.09%	13.43
tuition	37	4526	0.82%	9.95
tax	228	67433	0.34%	8.68
rate	143	58835	0.24%	8.20
price	136	62606	0.22%	8.04
fee	19	10340	0.18%	7.80
fare	10	5548	0.18%	7.77
wage	14	7994	0.18%	7.73
interest	41	76099	0.05%	6.03
pay	17	91573	0.02%	4.49

a. Instances of the collocate occurring within two words to the left of *hikes*
b. All instances of *hikes* in COCA
c. Percentage of occurrences of the collocate occurring within two words to the left of *hikes*
d. Mutual Information score

#			
1	offer a 1–1 ratio of spending cuts and	revenue	that Boehner would consider balanced.
2	a 1–1 ratio of spending cuts and	revenue	. Obama's proposal includes $130 billion
3	reform of the tax system would be "	revenue	neutral", meaning the changes would
4	that is so necessary" between	revenue	and cost-cutting, said Carney, who
5	difficult to later reduce government	revenue	by lowering them again. Obama and
6	sources said Obama lowered his	revenue	demand from $1.6 trillion to $1.4
7	it includes $1.2 trillion in	revenue	increases and $1.22 trillion in spending
8	latest offer includes $1.2 trillion in	revenue	increases on individual income and $1.2
9	proposal that includes $1.3 trillion in	revenue	for only $930 billion in spending cuts
10	calls for $1.6 trillion in increased	revenue	, some of it the result of higher tax
11	said the $1.6 trillion in increased	revenue	was higher than previously discussed.
12	and Democrats argue that increased	revenue	, including higher tax rates on the
13	wants to lock in the increased	revenue	from higher tax rates on top income
14	and loopholes to raise more	revenue	, but Obama also demands an end to the
15	now", Fallons said. "The more	revenue	we raise upfront through a tax rate
16	plan calls for $12 billion in new	revenue	and another $12 billion in spending cut
17	including an unspecified amount of	revenue	raised by eliminating tax deductions an
18	would put a trillion dollars worth of	revenue	on the table if he were willing to put
19	Boehner's "offer was insufficient on	revenue	and rates and had a bunch of stuff we
20	they would eliminate to raise	revenue	. It was implausible for Republicans to
21	magically achieve significant	revenue	on the order that we need for that
22	commitment to include significant	revenue	in any agreement. "The American people
23	spending cuts and additional tax	revenue	, but not higher tax rates. That would
24	to consider other ways to boost tax	revenue	as part of a broader deal that would in
25	2026 – The year that all federal tax	revenue	could potentially go to supporting
26	included both large increases in tax	revenue	and major cuts in government spending.
27	have offered to increase tax	revenue	by eliminating some deductions and loop
28	previously offered to increase tax	revenue	by eliminating unspecified deductions a
29	plan would increase tax	revenue	by almost $1 trillion over 10 years, a
30	a balance between increased tax	revenue	and spending cuts promised by the
31	generally oppose increasing tax	revenue	. They are particularly opposed to
32	increase or decrease of overall tax	revenue	, Carney said. Conservatives trying to
33	$1.2 trillion, putting the total	revenue	figure of the president's latest
34	in the future going to come up with	revenue	," Reid said. "They are going to come up

Figure 7.4 Concordance lines for *revenue* in CNN corpus (sorted to the left)

Discussion

We argue that FOX's coverage of the fiscal cliff negotiations presented impending or proposed changes to income tax structure in the US as undesirable to the reader (1) by framing them as increases over a normalised Bush-era system of taxation, (2) by representing these increases using the negatively evaluative word *hikes*, (3) by refraining from discussing any purpose or necessity of increased taxation, and (4) by making few distinctions between the effects of proposed changes on different income levels or social classes. In contrast, CNN's coverage of the fiscal cliff negotiations presented proposed changes to the tax structure as more legitimate or desirable to the reader (1) by specifying a purpose for them, generating revenue, and (2) by presenting the changes as impacting upon the upper class.

These venues' coverage of the fiscal cliff negotiations highlights how ostensibly 'objective' news reporting can subtly reflect the ideological positions or political-economic interests of those that produce or finance that reporting. The use of techniques from corpus linguistics such as keyword or collocation analysis are particularly helpful in supporting generalisations about discourse, both in the form of how words or phrases might be used generally as well as how characteristic of a set of texts a particular usage of a word or phrase is.

We end this chapter by noting that while we believe that Fowler's argument that "[c]ritical interpretation requires historical knowledge and sensitivity, which can be possessed by human beings but not by machines" (Fowler 1991: 68) still holds true, we hope that our analysis has demonstrated how machines can aid human beings to make more credible interpretations based on salient linguistic patterns in large amounts of data that may otherwise have been overlooked.

Further reading

Baker, P. (2013). *Using corpora to analyse gender*. London: Bloomsbury.
This book focusses on the application of corpus methods to examine gendered discourses and sex differences/similarities, covering a range of corpora including personal adverts, news articles and student-lecturer interactions.
Baker, Paul, Gabrielatos, Costas and McEnery, Tony. (2013). *Discourse analysis and media attitudes: The representation of Islam in the British press*. Cambridge: Cambridge University Press.
This book is a comprehensive study of the representation of Muslims and Islam in British newspapers, taking a critical discourse studies perspective. It shows how keywords, collocates and concordances can be used to direct analysts to close readings of salient and typical articles.
Mautner, Gerlinde. (2007). Mining large corpora for social information: The case of *elderly*. *Language in Society* 36: 51–72.
This article describes how large reference corpora can be used for critical analyses, focussing on the representation of elderly people.
Partington, Alan, Duiguid, Alison and Taylor, Charlotte. (2013). *Patterns and meanings in discourse: Theory and practice in corpus-assisted discourse studies (CADS)*. Amsterdam: Benjamins.
This book is a wide-ranging introduction to the combination of corpus approaches to discourse studies, using case studies to explore metaphor, evaluation, diachronic change, author style and impoliteness.
Subtirelu, Nic. (2015). "She does have an accent but . . .": Race and language ideology in students' evaluations of mathematics instructors on RateMyProfessors.com. *Language in Society* 44(1): 35–62.
This article is one example of how corpus linguistics can provide assistance in critical analyses of internet discourse.

References

Anthony, L. (2011). *AntConc (version 3.2.2) [computer software]*. Tokyo, Japan: Waseda University. www.antlab.sci.waseda.ac.jp/
Baker, P. (2005). *Public discourses of gay men*. London: Routledge.
Baker, P., Gabrielatos, C., KhosraviNik, M., Krzyżanowski, M., McEnery, T. and Wodak, R. (2008). A useful methodological synergy? Combining critical discourse analysis and corpus linguistics to examine discourses of refugees and asylum seekers in the UK press. *Discourse & Society* 19(3): 273–305.
Baker, P., Gabrielatos, C. and McEnery, T. (2013). *Discourse analysis and media attitudes: The representation of Islam in the British press*. Cambridge: Cambridge University Press.
Baker, P. and McEnery, T. (2015). Who benefits when discourse gets democratised? Analysing a Twitter corpus around the British benefits street debate. In Paul Baker and Tony McEnery (eds.), *Corpora and discourse studies: Integrating discourse and corpora*, 244–265. Basingstoke: Palgrave Macmillan.
Biber, D. (1993). Representativeness in corpus design. *Literary and Linguistic Computing* 8(4): 243–257.
Caldas-Coulthard, C. R. (1993). From discourse analysis to critical discourse analysis: The differential re-presentation of women and men speaking in written news. In John M. Sinclair, Michael Hoey and Gwyneth Fox (eds.), *Techniques of description*, 196–208. London: Routledge.
Caldas-Coulthard, C. R. (1995). Man in the news: The misrepresentation of women speaking in news-as-narrative-discourse. In S. Mills (ed.), *Language and gender: Interdisciplinary perspectives*, 226–239. Harlow: Longman.

Flowerdew, J. (1997). The discourse of colonial withdrawal: A case study in the creation of mythic discourse. *Discourse and Society* 8: 453–477.

Fowler, R. (1991). *Language in the news: Discourse and ideology in the press*. London and New York: Routledge.

Hardt-Mautner, G. (1995). 'Only connect': Critical discourse analysis and Corpus linguistics. *UCREL Technical Paper 6,* Lancaster University.

Hunston, S. (1999). Corpus evidence for disadvantage: issues in critical interpretation. Paper read at the *BAAL/CUP seminar 'Investigating discourse practices through corpus research: methods, findings and applications',* University of Reading, May 1999.

Kilgarriff, A., et al. (2014). The Sketch engine: Ten years on. *Lexicography* 1(1): 7–36.

Kincaid, C. (2005, August 29). CNN and the liberal propaganda machine. *Media Monitor.* www.aim.org/media-monitor/cnn-and-the-liberal-propaganda-machine/

Krishnamurthy, R. (1996). Ethnic, racial and tribal: The language of racism? In C.R. Cadlas-Coulthard and M. Coulthard (eds.), *Texts and practices: Readings in critical discourse analysis,* 129–149. London: Routledge.

Louw, B. (1993). Irony in the text or insincerity in the writer? In Mona Baker, Gill Francis and Elena Tognini-Bonelli (eds.), *Text and technology: In honour of John Sinclair,* 157–176. Philadelphia, Amsterdam: Benjamins.

Marchi, A. (2010). 'The moral in the story': A diachronic investigation of lexicalised morality in the UK press. *Corpora* 5(2): 161–190.

Marchi, A. and Taylor, C. (2009). 'If on a winter night two researchers': A challenge to assumptions of soundness of interpretation. *Critical Approaches to Discourse Analysis across Disciplines* 3(1): 1–20.

Partington, A. (2003). *The linguistics of political argument: The spin-doctor and the wolf-pack at the White House.* London and New York: Routledge.

Partington, A. (ed.) (2010). *Corpora special issue: Modern diachronic corpus-assisted studies.* Edinburgh: Edinburgh University Press.

Partington, A., Duguid, A. and Taylor, C. (2013). *Patterns and meanings in discourse: Theory and practice in corpus-assisted discourse studies (CADS).* Amsterdam: Benjamins.

Partington, A., Morley, J. and Haarman, L. (eds.) (2004). *Corpora and discourse.* Bern: Peter Lang.

Pew Research Center. (2012). Trends in news consumption: 1991–2012. www.people-press.org/2012/09/27/in-changing-news-landscape-even-television-is-vulnerable/

Piper, A. (2000). Lifelong learning, human capital, and the soundbite. *Text* 20: 109–146.

Reisigl, M. and Wodak, R. (2001). *Discourse and discrimination: Rhetorics of racism and antisemitism.* London: Routledge.

Scott, M. (1996). *WordSmith tools.* Oxford: Oxford University Press.

Stubbs, M. (1996). *Text and corpus analysis: Computer-assisted studies of language and culture.* Oxford: Blackwell.

Taylor, C. (2010). Science in the news: A diachronic perspective. *Corpora* 5(2): 221–250.

Teubert, W. (2001). A province of a federal superstate, ruled by an unelected bureaucracy: Keywords of the Euro-sceptic discourse in Britain. In A. Musolff, C. Good, P. Points and R. Wittlinger (eds.), *Attitudes towards Europe: Language in the unification process,* 45–88. Aldershot: Ashgate.

Tognini-Bonelli, E. (2001). *Corpus linguistics at work.* Amsterdam: Benjamins.

Williams, R. (1976). *Keywords,* 2nd edn. London: Fontana.

8

Cultural approach to CDA (CCDA)

From theory to practice

Dalia Gavriely-Nuri

Introduction

This chapter focuses on the connection between culture and discourse, an area of CDA that has been under-emphasized in research so far. The chapter presents the Cultural Approach to Critical Discourse Analysis (CCDA). CCDA is presented not only as merely a theoretical framework, but as a practical tool that can be used for decoding the cultural 'cargo' implied in the discourse.

Using the Israeli peace/war discourse as a case study, the chapter also introduces the 'Normalization Narrative' and the 'Estrangement Narrative.' As will be demonstrated, these narratives are an efficient tool in the cultural construction of social objects. As such, they form part of Critical Narrative Analysis (CNA), which is an important yet little used tool of CDA.

This chapter focuses on the Cultural Approach to Critical Discourse Analysis (CCDA) which aims at exposing and examining the ways in which cultural codes are embedded in discourse, and contribute to the reproduction of abuses of power (Gavriely-Nuri 2013, 2015). The connection between culture and discourse is relatively underdeveloped in a wide range of CDA studies – perhaps because of the complexity and ambiguity surrounding the concept of 'culture,' or perhaps simply because most CDA researchers come from the field of linguistics rather than that of Cultural Studies.

The chapter deepens the understanding of CCDA as a branch of CDA, and seeks to provide the critical scholar with a practical toolbox for discourse/culture analysis. In the analytic sections, the chapter will demonstrate how the two mega-narratives, the Normalization Narrative and the Estrangement Narrative, served for the cultural construction of 'war' and 'peace' in Israeli discourse by assisting in the 'normalization' of war and the 'estrangement' of peace.

The chapter has both theoretical and empirical goals. First, to illustrate how CCDA deepens understanding of the interdisciplinary aspects of CDA and of the interconnection between culture, cultural codes, narratives, and CDA; and second, to provide scholars with practical tools for the application of CCDA, focusing in particular on Critical Narrative Analysis (CNA) and 'Normalization strategies' vs. 'Estrangement strategies.'

The chapter will begin by contextualizing CCDA within the field of CDA and review relevant cultural works that emphasize the Culture/Discourse connection. Then, it will describe some basic CCDA theoretical and methodological principles. Next, two basic mechanisms for cultural construction will be introduced: narratives of Normalization and narratives of Estrangement. These mechanisms will exemplify and demonstrate how CCDA works in practice.

CCDA as a branch of CDA

Typically, CDA aims to shed light on the ways through which discourse helps to sustain social and political inequalities, abuses of power, and domination patterns (cf. Chilton 2004; Fairclough 1995). Hence, one of the core theoretical and empirical questions in CDA is: "how the human mind can be tricked, deceived or manipulated through the use of language" (Chilton 2005: 41). On the other hand, van Dijk argues that CDA researchers should be interested not only in *describing* some interesting properties of political rhetoric, but also in *explaining* them. "In order to explain them, we need to relate them to such socio-cognitive representations as attitudes, norms, values and ideologies" (van Dijk 2007: 62). As we shall see, the combination of these two statements can act as a point of departure for understanding the approach of CCDA.

Within the plethora of approaches to CDA, the Discourse-Historical Approach (DHA), which was developed by Ruth Wodak and collaborators (de Cillia, Reisigl and Wodak 1999; Wodak 2009 [1998]),

> takes into account the intertextual and interdiscursive relationships between utterances, texts, genres and discourses, as well as extra-linguistic social/sociological variables, the history and "archaeology" of an organization, institutional frames of a specific context of situation and processes of text production, text-reception and text consumption.
>
> *(Baker et al. 2008: 279–280)*

In a similar manner to DHA, the current chapter aims to emphasize another dimension of CDA, the cultural dimension, in order to lend more weight to CDA as a multidisciplinary approach.

Although many critical scholars have analyzed specific national cultures (e.g., de Leonardis 2008, Achugar 2007), the theoretical research on culture as a key element in the construction of discourse only truly began to develop in the last two decades (cf. Carpentier and Spinoy 2008; Kövecses 2006).

Current cultural debate concerning the relation between CDA and culture should aim to respond to these questions and challenges. Indeed, culture is an integral part of CDA, but it isn't being made explicit or problematized. As Shi-xu (2007) claimed:

> since discourse is saturated with culture and cultural contestation in particular, we should refrain from reproducing dominant and repressive language as far as possible and try instead to use a culturally pluralistic, inclusive, critical, and egalitarian form of academic discourse.
>
> *(Shi-xu 2007: 10)*

CCDA, as an interdisciplinary approach, will house under one umbrella concepts such as 'cultural memory,' 'cultural narratives,' 'cultural representations' and 'cultural discourse analysis' (Carbaugh 2007), as well as 'the cultural turn' (Fairclough 2003), 'textual culture' (Benwell 2005), 'cultural scripts' (Wierzbicka 1998), and many others.

Of special relevance to our discussion is Anna Wierzbicka's 'cultural script approach' (1998). Wierzbicka argues that ways of speaking characteristically of a given speech-community constitute a manifestation of a tacit system of 'cultural rules,' or, as she calls them, 'cultural scripts.' She demonstrates how the 'cultural scripts' approach offers an efficient tool for studying change and variation, as well as continuity, in social attitudes and cultural values. She applied her approach to German, Japanese, Chinese, Polish, (White) Anglo-American, Black American, and Anglo-Australian cultural norms. She argues that rather than perpetuating stereotypes based on prejudice and lack of understanding, 'cultural scripts' help outsiders grasp the 'cultural logic' underlying unfamiliar ways of speaking (Wierzbicka 1998).

In an issue of *Journal of Multicultural Discourses,* Scollo covered culturally inclusive approaches to discourse analysis and communication that critique Western-biased theories and methods, and concluded: "It is hoped that the essay will invite future extended discussions of culturally-inclusive approaches to discourse analysis in the journal."

Another valuable contribution to the field was made by Pardo (2010) who advanced our understanding of cross-cultural discourse with her introduction of Latin American discourse studies. Pardo seeks to reflect on "the influence of westernisation and academic colonialism on Latin American discourse studies." She offers a new paradigm for Latin American discourse studies involving dialogue with the Western tradition.

A relevant critique of CDA was raised by Shi-xu (2014) in his book *Chinese Discourse Studies.* This critique is expressed in the following paragraph:

> The cultural overgeneralization of the discipline of CDA is manifest in a number of ways. To start with, CDA practitioners usually portray themselves as if they were truth knowers and moral judges with regard to human communication, consciously or inadvertently; there in hardly ever questioning and reflection on their own cultural identities, interests and ideologies, or on the cultural origins, limitations and biases of their knowledge, perception and morality.
>
> *(p. 3)*

Shi-xu (2005, 2014) offered a new paradigm, 'Cultural Discourse Studies' (CDS), concerned with "the cultural diversity, dynamic and divisiveness of human discourses that have hitherto been suppressed, obscured or explained away in the mainstream" (2014: 24). The new paradigm "strives as its mission and objectives to highlight, deconstruct and neutralize ethnocentrism in current discourse and communication scholarship." Ultimately, "CDS aims to contribute to human cultural coexistence, peace and prosperity" (2014: 24).

In this chapter, I introduce CCDA as a way to enrich the ongoing discussion concerning the connection between culture and discourse in general, and between culture/discourse and critical analysis in particular. I do this not simply by focusing on the specific national culture of Israel, but mainly by referring to culture as a dominant discursive mechanism for the construction of social objects in general, as Shi-xu put it:

> What is urgently needed now, and a long time ahead, is the (re)construction and expansion of diverse cultural approaches at different levels of abstraction and from divergent cultural traditions. What requires more and quick efforts, too, is to work out to what extent and in what specific ways Asian, African, Latin American paradigms, for example, are interrelated and how synergy can be created. In the process, dialogue and comparison will be essential as a method and source of innovation and enrichment.
>
> *(Shi-xu 2014: 365, also see: Shi-xu 2005)*

I will also offer a practical toolbox that to my view is easy to use and can help critical discourse analysts who wish to adopt CCDA. I believe that my stance as an Israeli researcher gives me a hybrid perspective that combines both elements of the East and the West in thinking on the general issue of the encounter between culture and discourse.

CCDA: general principles

CCDA focuses on the cultural aspects of any given 'text': verbal and non-verbal alike. This approach is guided by the following principles:

- No text is independent of its cultural contexts.
- Rather than the deconstruction of linguistic structures, CCDA shall aim to uncover the cultural and cross-cultural codes embedded in discourse.
- CCDA employs tools and methodologies taken from the discipline of Cultural Studies, such as the heuristic of decoding cultural codes.
- Cross-cultural or multi-cultural perspectives facilitate the identification of unique elements of specific cultural codes and thus contribute to the process of decoding them.
- Decoding cultural codes demands not only intimate familiarity with a community's language, culture and history, but also special awareness of the idea that "social and historical creation... [is] treated as a natural event or as the inevitable outcome of natural characteristics" (Thompson 1990: 66).
- CCDA demonstrates that as far as the rhetoric of power is concerned, there is no difference between small and large cultural communities.
- CCDA seeks to expose the 'global dictionary' of power and manipulation. It does so, for example, by focusing on specific metaphors and idioms such as 'axis of evil' or 'preemptive strike.'
- CCDA analyses verbal and non-verbal practices (e.g., visual practices as well as cultural sites) alike, because it does not focus on the study of linguistic structures as such. That said, in this specific article I will focus mostly on verbal practices.
- CCDA analyses factual and fictional discourses alike. This is based on the assumption that a fictional short story has the same ability as a political speech to act as a repository for cultural codes and assist the continuation of power abuses.

Let us now delve in a little more detail into these general principles.

Cultural codes and discursive strategies

A clear definition of the concepts of 'discursive strategies' and 'cultural codes' is essential for understanding CCDA in practice. CCDA aims to expose the specific discursive strategies that enable the exclusion or the symbolic annihilation of social objects. 'Strategy' is "the process by which ends are related to means, intentions to capabilities, objectives to resources" (Gaddis 2005 [1982]: VIII). Considering that a strategy is a combination of goals and means (Fairclough 2009 [2001]: 174), CCDA is interested in discursive 'means' (e.g., metaphors, narratives, frames) that promote specific 'goals' (i.e., political agenda or specific policy). In this chapter, I will focus on Narratives (e.g., discursive means) and on two major Discursive Strategies that I have identified in the complicated process of discursive-cultural construction: 'Normalization' and 'Estrangement.'

I introduced the key CCDA concept of the 'Cultural code' in detail in former studies (Gavriely-Nuri 2015, 2014, 2010a,b), and will now briefly outline its basic principles: Cultural codes are compact packages of shared values, norms, ethos, and social beliefs. These 'packages' of meaning can appear, as, inter alia, historical events which the members of the community are very familiar with, geographical sites, or national heroes (or heroines) to which the community members ascribe a special added value. Understanding a cultural code's 'added value' is equivalent to decoding it. Cultural codes are constantly repeated in various contexts and combinations and thus come to both construct and reflect the community's 'common sense.'

Critical Narrative Analysis (CNA)

In comparison with metaphors, narratives have received little attention in CDA research (cf. Musolff 2010). Maybe this is because 'narratives' have been taken for granted and viewed as a too trivial and simple form. Yet, I argue that narratives should be given much more serious attention in CDA analysis. I see narrative as one of the most important tools in the construction of the social identity of either a group or a person. Narrative is a key in the creation of the sense of social or national affinity. The construction of narrative is an important step not only in the process of social construction of identity, but also in creating the imagined community.

Critical Narrative Analysis (CNA) is relatively popular in sociological and psychological research, in methodology and practice alike. For example, Frost (2009) has focused on narrative analysis in the interpretation of interviews; and Emerson and Frosh (2009) wrote a step-by-step analysis of the narratives of a sexually abusive young man. Narrative analysis and critical narrative analysis can be found even in business research (cf. Costa and Ferreira 2012). Nevertheless, the phrase 'critical narrative analysis' cannot be found in the CDA journals *Discourse & Society* or *Critical Discourse Studies*.

Souto-Manning (2014) has used the hybrid concept of CNA in her own research and proposed that "CNA unites CDA and narrative analysis in a mutually beneficial partnership that addresses both theoretical and methodological dilemmas in discourse analysis." Montesano, Montessori, and Morales Lopez (2015) define narrative as a powerful tool to depict a desired world or to envision alternatives to the status quo of any particular organisation, community, economic, or political system. They expressed this idea in the following words:

> narrative helps to rearticulate the status quo from an undesired version to a desired version, in which identities and concepts acquire new positions and new mutual relations. Narrative is a powerful tool in creating a new community and gaining its support or enthusiasm for a certain cause.
>
> *(207)*

These insights are also very relevant for understanding my own view of CNA.

I suggest that, in order to combine CDA and Narrative Analysis, it would be best to ignore the literary and psychological definitions of narrative, and instead to formulate a definition that is specific to critical research. As I see it, 'collective narrative' is a narrative that forms part of a group's identity. It is a story in a social and cultural context. It can also be defined as a story motivated by political interests and the wish to represent the consequences arising from such events in a way that reflects and serves political interests.

Two 'mega' narratives for cultural construction

I argue that, in general, cultural construction of social objects (such as a social group, a social phenomenon, or a social event) defines the social objects in one of two ways: either as a 'normal' object which forms part of normal life and normal society; or as a 'strange' object which does not form part of 'normal' life and normal society. Two mega-narratives are derived from this distinction, namely, one that 'normalizes' social objects and another that 'estranges' them.

The rest of the chapter will be dedicated to looking in more detail into some of these *normalizing* devices, especially narratives, and juxtaposing them against *estranging* devices. I will focus on the case study of what can be called 'Israeli discourse'; and more specifically on the cultural construction of the concepts of 'war' and 'peace.'

Case study: the cultural construction of war and peace in Israeli discourse

The concept of 'War-Normalizing Narrative' is in fact a set of strategies that aim to blur war's anomalous character by creating the misconception that war is a 'natural' or 'normal' event for a given society. On the other hand, the 'Peace-Estrangement Narrative' is a set of strategies intended for creating doubt as to the positive connotation usually associated with the concept of peace. For example, war can be depicted as an opportunity to demonstrate courage and brotherhood, while the actual condition of peace may be described as inherently dangerous, and peace initiatives may be represented as deceptive. 'War-Normalizing' strategies and 'Peace-Estrangement' strategies appear in various verbal and non-verbal contexts: these include political speeches, op-eds, literature, films, caricatures, and even national ceremonies.

Strategies of normalization

Three main strategies have been identified within the mega strategy of normalization: *euphemization, naturalization,* and *justification.* Let us first understand what these strategies generally aim to achieve:

- Euphemization – aims to color the social object in positive tones, in terms of its appearance, character, or valuation;
- Naturalization – aims to represent the social object as a force or event independent of human agency, or as an inevitable outcome of the laws of nature;
- Justification – aims to depict the social object as just, rational, worthy of support.

I will now exemplify these strategies as they are expressed in regard to a specific concept, in a specific place, and during a specific time: the object will be 'war,' the place will be Israel, and the time will be the years between 1967 and 1973.

The years between 1967 and 1973 were especially turbulent years in Israel. Israel was involved in three wars (the Six-Day War 1967, the War of Attrition 1969–1970, and the Yom Kippur War 1973) and was the target of hundreds of terror acts. As a result, the strategy of *normalizing* war was intensively activated by Israeli leaders in order to encourage fighters and civilians. Israeli leaders therefore aimed to construct war as being simply a part of normal life.

Euphemization and naturalization of war do not refer to a direct glorification of the idea of war, but the more subtle glorification of the fighters and civilians caught up in it. A common narrative from the Israeli discourse is the portrayal of a special kind of fighter: the hero against his own will. Usually this is the civilian who lives close to the border, and finds himself, or herself, on the front line. Thus, for example, in her speech to present the National Unity government in 1970, Prime Minister Golda Meir stated:

> Our fortifications and posts have withstood enemy bombings. The residents near the borders in the east and in the north have born the brunt of the battle with the utmost courage, and continue to do so [. . .] no man deserted his place, and the children in the border settlements have adjusted to the bomb shelters as to a natural way of life.[1]

Meir's narrative activates two war normalizing strategies: euphemization and naturalization.

War normalization echoes not only in politicians' discourses. As extraordinary as it sounds, during this period, war was sometimes viewed as a desirable and helpful time-out, a refuge from the grinding routine, 'war as adventure.' Sometimes, it could supply a solution to situations that seemed inescapable before the eruption of the war. For the fighter, the war presents one supreme goal: to survive. In light of this goal, problems of daily life seem less significant and feelings of a dead end and lack of meaning may fade. In *By God Mother, I Hate the War* (1968), a widely popular book written by Yigal Lev after the Six-Day War, we find the following narrative:

> Rami wanted the war. He had just finished his compulsory military duty, and since then he had been wandering, out of work. Rami said, maybe to himself, maybe to me: "You won't believe this, but I'm dying for a war to break out [. . .] I'm sick of everything. The food, the bed, the entertainment, I need something to shake me forwards. [. . .] I need the war, because I can't decide for myself."

I will complete this section with a narrative of war *justification*. Consider for example the narrative 'surgical strikes.' This narrative was quite common in the Israeli discourse surrounding the Second Lebanon War (2006).[2] It basically implies that like any good physician, Israel's military performs only precise and well-planned attacks or bombings on South Lebanon, causing minimal peripheral damage. This narrative was extensively used not only for winning the Israeli public's hearts and minds, but also for responding to international criticism directed against Israel's massive destruction of civilian property and infrastructure in Southern Lebanon. The narrative of a 'surgical strike' is thus an example of normalizing war by justification. In this context, we could also mention the well-known narrative (and metaphor) of 'smoking-gun' (conclusive evidence of nuclear weaponry in Iraq) that was used by the Bush administration in order to justify the US invasion of Iraq in 2003.

Strategies of estrangement

An unprecedented number of peace initiatives for Israel and its neighbors were continually obstructed by the UN and the United States in this period. Most researchers believe that Israel had a great opportunity to achieve peace from a very strong position following its 1967 victory. Yet, Israeli governments rejected at least ten such initiatives proposed by different countries and the United Nations. The Foreign Minister during those years, Abba Eban, sums up Israel's view of its role in these initiatives:

> We did not spare any effort, or course of action, or methods to promote dialogue with neighboring countries [. . .]. When this period's history would be summed up, I am

certain that international public opinion will be impressed by the number and diversity of Israel's peace initiatives.

(Knesset Records, February 18, 1969)

The failure of such initiatives and the consequent continuation of the occupation of the territories began to evoke criticism at both national and international levels. Israeli leaders were therefore not only confronted with political challenges, but also with rhetorical ones: the need to bridge Israel's traditional self-image as a peace-seeking nation and its new image as a victorious nation pursuing an uncompromising security policy. The Peace-Estrangement discourse was an efficient tool in this context.

Strategies of abstraction

Strategies of Abstraction are one of the most powerful strategies in the Israeli Peace-Estrangement discourse. The following strategies are included in this category:

*   Strategies of Distancing – A description that locates the targeted object in a distant conceptual realm. The description can be geographical, literal, conceptual, or metaphorical. The common narratives 'peace is a dream' and 'peace in heaven' are examples of distancing strategy.
*   Strategies of Impersonalization – An explanation of the relevant social object (e.g., peace) which removes the human factor and focuses on abstract organizational structures (i.e., movements, states).

In the following section I will illustrate how these strategies are exercised in reality regarding the construction of the concepts 'peace.' I will present some of the narratives of what can be described as the Israeli 'peace problem,' during the year between 1967 and 1973.

Like the normalization of war, the estrangement of peace or the construction of the 'peace problem' in this period can be found in the discourse of Israeli politicians, civilians, and even textbooks. The 'peace problem' refers, in this context, to the narrative of 'peace is dangerous.' This is an extremely popular strategy, since its use depicts the speaker as rational and cautious, while it presents those who support peace as reckless and irresponsible. Such rhetoric improves the speaker's image, portraying the speaker as a sophisticated politician who acts as Israel's responsible protector and helps it defend itself from committing the 'tragic mistake' of making peace with its enemies.

One example of this narrative is found in a statement made in 1970, by Knesset member Yoram Aridor in response to a conciliatory offer made by Gamal Abdel Nasser, who was Egypt's president at the time. Aridor warned his fellow Israeli citizens with the following words: "We mustn't test the sweetness of a poison, only because the wrapper claims it's a candy" (July 30, 1970).

To complete the picture, let us now briefly focus on peace estrangement in the context of Israeli school textbooks.

Strategies of estrangement in school textbooks

The conflict as a mechanical process

Mechanical strategies taken from the world of physical forces comprise aspects of peace-estrangement strategies. The use of mechanical analogies and physical metaphors abstracts the human aspect from human activities. In this way such strategies help evade the question of pointing the finger of blame, or responsibility, towards specific individuals. The following are some examples of this strategy in action, (all of the examples are quotes taken from Israeli textbooks):

- The penetration of the great powers to the vacuum created in the new states in Asia and Africa (Inbar 2000: 172).
- The escalation of the tensions between Jewish and Arab people in the 1920s and 1930s (Avieli-Tabibian 2009: 41).
- New centers of power began to rise around the world (Inbar 2000: 176).
- At the end of the 1920s, a new wave of violent acts against Jewish people erupted (Avieli-Tabibian 2009: 43).
- All this increased the friction between Jewish and Arab people (Avieli-Tabibian 2009: 43).
- The leaders of the Arab nations used the hatred towards Israel as a way to consolidate their people (Naveh 1999: 158).

These strategies use terms from the semantic field of mechanics, electricity, and physics, such as 'vacuum' and 'tension.' In the second example we find the following metaphor: "The escalation of the tensions between Jewish and Arab people" which makes reference to electrical fields rather than to relationships between groups of people. The metaphor seems to depict Jews and Arabs as two physical 'objects' that are influenced by the same electrical source, and implies that someone, somewhere, simply pushed a button and escalated the tension between them. A more important point is that this strategy also makes the tension between Arabs and Jews seem unavoidable: since it is not human will, but 'forces' that were responsible for this escalation.

Strategies of impersonalization

Historical accounts found in textbooks are abound with the use of *impersonalization* and of the passive voice, which blur the notion of human responsibility. The following are two illustrative examples of this strategy:

- On the Syrian border there were many fire exchanges (Naveh 2009: 158).
- During the 1990s, the political process was renewed (Avieli-Tabibian 2009: 204).

A related discursive strategy is that of *personifying* the state by using body metaphors (Musolff 2004, 2010). For example:

- Europe was embroiled in a net of treaties and agreements which tied its hands and every small spark could have ignited the fire of war (Inbar 2004: 82).
- [In the sixties] security problems on [Israel's] eastern and northern borders intensified (Avieli-Tabibian 2009: 180).

In some respects, the two strategies, that of impersonalization and that of personification, seem to be in opposition with one another. Yet, from the perspective of peace discourse analysis, they are similar in that they both lead to the blurring of the human factor in explanations of peace and war.

Hyper-causality strategies

The use of causality to explain historical events is another common link in the chain of peace abstraction. In my view, school textbooks' analytical-causal representations of peace (and war) are often too complex for high-school pupils, especially when they involve economical, psychological, political, and cultural factors. In other cases, narratives of causal explanations oversimplify the historical events described in the textbook. These two distinct processes lead to a single result: peace and war are made to appear as unavoidable results of deterministic processes, rather than the consequence of human choices and actions. The following is an example of such an explanation, found in an Israeli high-school textbook:

> Draw in your notebooks a timeline of the years 1930–1939 and mark the steps that pulled the world towards war. Explain how each of the steps undermined peace.
>
> *(Naveh 1999: 99)*

The last quotation emphasizes the importance of causality: the pupils get the impression that historical events happen step by step, according to rational and linear order.

In the above sections I have demonstrated several specific strategies that were used in Israeli discourse in order to normalize war and estrange peace: Euphemization, Naturalization, and Justification are *strategies of Normalization;* Abstraction (including Distancing and Impersonalization), as well as strategies of Mechanization and Hyper-causality are strategies of estrangement.

Conclusions and open questions

This chapter has looked in great detail at CCDA as a branch of CDA. It has sought to provide the critical scholar with a practical toolbox for the analysis of discourse/culture based on narrative analysis. The chapter focuses on two mega-narratives: normalization and estrangement. The analytic sections have demonstrated several specific strategies that that were used in Israeli political discourse as well as school textbooks in order to normalize war and estrange peace.

I argue that the mega-narratives presented here play an important role in the discursive-cultural construction of many 'social objects.' A complete narrative can be activated for the normalization of the traditional family structure during a certain period, or for the estrangement and undermining of social objects that represent an alternative for it.

These two mega-narratives also take part in the activation of cultural codes, another core concept of CCDA that was briefly discussed in this chapter. I will dedicate the rest of this chapter to introducing several open questions concerning cultural codes, which deserve future research:

• What is the process of cultural codes' creation?
• Who are the social agents that create cultural codes?
• What are the 'raw materials' comprising these codes?

No less interesting is the question of the 'politics' behind the construction of cultural codes:

• What are the specific political circumstances under which a specific cultural code was created?

Another interesting question that deserves future research is the question of 'recycling' cultural codes and narratives. Let me briefly introduce this idea.

129

Culture, cultural codes, and cultural narratives usually adopt an economical logic: preferring the adaptation of existing paradigms to the invention of new ones. In other words, rather than reinventing the wheel, the construction of culture and its components tends to follow existing cognitive frames. Following this logic, culture 'imports' (that is, re-uses or re-contextualizes) and then assimilates existing cognitive frames from the international imagined cultural market alike, while preserving and reproducing common existing motives from the local culture.

For example, the narrative of 'axis of evil,' coined by George W. Bush in 2003 in order to help define a clear enemy, was later recycled by the Israeli Prime Minister, Ehud Olmert, during the Second Lebanon War (2006). This was, of course, a re-contextualization of the well-known concept of the 'axis nations' in the Second World War, which related to the bitter memory of the Nazis and their allies.

Cultural codes and cultural narratives are a kind of a mannequin that can be dressed-up by national history-tailors according to the current societal needs and interests. For this reason, cultural codes and narratives are, in fact, immortal (much like literary motifs): they can drown in one place or society for a period and then emerge somewhere else, many years later, in a continuous intercultural process.

Notes

1 The Prime Minister's Office *Government yearbook*, 1970.
2 This strategy also features in US/UK discourse – it was big in 1998 to justify the 'Desert Fox' bombing of Iraq. I wish to thank John Richardson for this comment.

Further reading

Podeh, E. (2015). *Chances for peace: Missed opportunities in the Arab-Israeli conflict*. Austin, TX: University of Texas Press.
This book uses extensive sources in English, Hebrew, and Arabic to introduce various narratives on 90 years of attempted negotiations in the Arab-Israeli conflict.
Hyatt, J. and Simons, H. (1999). Cultural codes – who holds the key? The concept and conduct of evaluation in Central and Eastern Europe. *Evaluation* 5(1): 23–41.
The authors define Cultural Codes as symbols and systems of meaning that are relevant to members of a particular culture (or subculture). These codes can be utilized to facilitate communication within the 'inside group' and also to obscure the meaning to 'outside groups'.
Zhang, H., Chilton, P., He, Y. and Jing, W. (2011). Critique across cultures: some questions for CDA. *Critical Discourse Studies* 8(2): 95–107.
The authors focus on the meanings of the English word 'critical' and the Chinese words used to translate it, to address the question: Is the concept and practice of critique culturally relative or a human universal?

References

Achugar, M. (2007). Between remembering and forgetting: Uruguayan military discourse about human rights (1976–2004). *Discourse and Society* 18: 521–547.
Baker, P., Gabrielatos, C., KhosraviNik, M., Krzyżanowski, M., McEnery, T. and Wodak, R. (2008). A useful methodological synergy? Combining critical discourse analysis and corpus linguistics to examine discourses of refugees and asylum seekers in the UK press. *Discourse and Society* 19(3): 273–306.
Benwell, B. (2005). Lucky this is anonymous – Ethnographies of reception in men's magazines: A 'textual culture' approach. *Discourse and Society* 16(2): 147–172.
Carbaugh, D. (2007). Cultural discourse analysis: Communication practices and intercultural encounters. *Journal of Intercultural Communication Research* 36(3): 167–183.
Carpentier, N. and Spinoy, E. (eds.) (2008). *Discourse theory and cultural analysis – media, arts and literature*. New York: Hampton Press.

Chilton, P. (2004). *Analysing political discourse: Theory and practice.* London: Routledge.

Chilton, P. (2005). Missing links in mainstream CDA: Modules, blends and the critical instinct. In Ruth Wodak and Paul Chilton (eds.), *A new agenda in (critical) discourse analysis-theory, methodology and inter-disciplinary,* 19–51. Amsterdam, Philadelphia: Benjamins.

Costa, E. and Ferreira, J. (2012, July 11). A reference model perspective for conventional business narrative analysis: An essay on an entrepreneurial narrative. *African Journal of Business Management* 6(27): 8199–8219.

de Cillia, R., Reisigl, M. and Wodak, R. (1999). The discursive construction of national identities. *Discourse and Society* 10: 149–173.

De Leonardis, F. (2008). War as a medicine: The medical metaphor in contemporary Italian political language. *Social Semiotics* 18(1): 33–45.

Emerson, P. and Frosh, S. (2009). *Critical narrative analysis in psychology: A guide to practice.* Basingstoke: Palgrave Macmillan.

Fairclough, F. (2003). 'Political correctness': The politics of culture and language. *Discourse and Society* 14(1): 17–28.

Fairclough, N. (1995). *Critical discourse analysis.* London: Longman.

Fairclough, N. (2009/2001). A dialectical-relational approach to critical discourse analysis in social research. In Ruth Wodak and Michael Meyer (eds.), *Methods of critical discourse analysis,* 162–186. London: Sage.

Frost, N. (2009, February). 'Do you know what I mean?': The use of a pluralistic narrative analysis approach in the interpretation of an interview. *Qualitative Research* 9: 9–29.

Gaddis, J. L. (1982/2005). Grand strategy in the second term. *Foreign Affairs* 84: 2–15.

Gavriely-Nuri, D. (2010a). The idiosyncratic language of Israeli 'peace' – a Cultural Approach to Critical Discourse Analysis (CCDA). *Discourse and Society* 21(5): 1–21.

Gavriely-Nuri, D. (2010b). If both opponents 'extend hands in peace' – why don't they meet? – mythic metaphors and cultural codes in the Israeli peace discourse. *Journal of Language and Politics* 9(3): 449–468.

Gavriely-Nuri, D. (2013). *The normalization of war in the Israeli discourse.* Lanham, MD: Lexington Books, Rowman & Littlefield Education.

Gavriely-Nuri, D. (2015). *Israeli peace discourse: A cultural approach to CDA.* London, Amsterdam: Benjamins.

Kövecses, Z. (2006). *Language, mind and culture: A practical introduction.* Oxford: Oxford University Press.

Montesano Montessori, N. and Morales Lopez, E. (2015). Multimodal narrative as an instrument for social change: Reinventing democracy in Spain – the case of 15 M. *CADAAD* 7(2): 200–221.

Musolff, A. (2010). *Metaphor, nation and the Holocaust: The concept of the body politic.* New York: Routledge.

Pardo, L. (2010). Latin-American discourse studies: State of the art and new perspectives. *Journal of Multicultural Discourses* 5(3): 183–192.

Scollo, M. (2011). Cultural approaches to discourse analysis: A theoretical and methodological conversation with special focus on Donal Carbaugh's cultural discourse theory. *Journal of Multicultural Discourses* 6(1): 1–32.

Shi-xu. (2005). *A cultural approach to discourse.* Basingstoke: Palgrave Macmillan.

Shi-xu. (2007). Discourse studies and cultural politics: An introduction. In Shi-xu (ed.), *Discourse as culture struggle.* Hong Kong: Hong Kong University Press.

Shi-xu. (2014). *Chinese discourse studies.* London: Palgrave.

Souto-Manning, M. (2014). Critical narrative analysis: The interplay of critical discourse and narrative analyses. *International Journal of Qualitative Studies in Education* 27(2): 159–180.

Thompson, J. B. (1990). *Ideology and modern culture.* Stanford, CA: Stanford University Press.

van Dijk, T. A. (2007). War rhetoric of a little ally: Political implicatures and Aznar's legitimatization of the war in Iraq. In Hong Kong (ed.), *The soft power of war,* 61–84. Amsterdam: Benjamins.

Wierzbicka, A. (1998). German 'cultural scripts': Public sings as a key to social attitudes and cultural values. *Discourse and Society* 9(2): 241–282.

Wodak, R., de Cillia, R., Reisigl, M, and Liebhart, K. (2009/1998). *The discursive construction of national identity.* Edinburgh: Edinburgh University.

School textbooks:

Avieli-Tabibian, K. (2001). *The era of terror and hope 1870–1970.* Tel Aviv: Matah.

Avieli-Tabibian, K. (2008). *Journeys through time – nationalism in Israel and other nations, from its beginnings to 1920.* Tel Aviv: Matah.

Avieli–Tabibian, K. (2009). *Journeys through time – from peace to war and the holocaust*. Tel Aviv: Matah.

Bar Hillel, M. and Inbar, S. (2008). *Building a state in the Middle East*. Petah Tikva: Lilach.

Domka, E. (1998). *The world and the Jewish people in recent generations. Part 1, 1870–1920*. Jerusalem: Zalman Shazar Centre.

Inbar, S. (2000). *Revival and nation in Israel and the nations in modern times. 1945–1970*. Petach Tikva: Lilach.

Inbar, S. (2002). *Revolution and transition in Israel and the nations in modern times. 1939–1970*. Petach Tikva: Lilach.

Inbar, S. (2004). *Revolution and transition, a view of 1870–1920*. Petach Tikva: Lilach.

Naveh, E. (1999). *The 20th century on the verge of the future*. Tel Aviv.

Naveh, E., Neomi, V. and Shahar, D. (2008). *Nationalism in Israel and other nations – building a state in the middle east*. Tel Aviv: Reches Educational Project.

Naveh, E., Neomi, V. and Shahar, D. (2009). *Totalitarism and Holocaust*. Tel Aviv: Reches Educational Project.

9

Positive discourse analysis[1]

Tom Bartlett

Introduction

Back in 2005, the 32nd International Systemic Functional Linguistics Congress was sub-titled *Discourses of Hope: Peace, Reconciliation, Learning and Change,* and the organisers invited participants

> to think more politically about the various applications of their work, in terms of what they are trying to achieve, and to encourage a reorientation in critical thinking to what we might call Positive Discourse Analysis (PDA) – work which considers how people make the world a better place and designs interventions based on such considerations.[2]

Four years later there was a coda on PDA in Alba-Juez's (2009) overview of Critical Discourse Analysis, and PDA seemed to be about to take off. I personally jumped on the bandwagon by including the term in the subtitle of my 2012 monograph (Bartlett 2012). However, at the time of writing this chapter, PDA has no Wikipedia entry, only seven followers on academia. edu, and a Google search brings up very few publications that include the term, while Jim Martin, who first coined the term, has informed me that PDA as such is no longer a focus of his work. This state of affairs led me to consider whether my choice of subtitle had been a case of backing the wrong horse, perhaps even a dead one. However, at a 2014 event in Amsterdam to celebrate 20 years of Critical Discourse Analysis, the term came up surprisingly frequently in discussion. There were signs of life in the old horse yet!

One possible reason for the ambivalent status is that "positive" orientations to discourse analysis take many forms and work which falls within this category often does not use the label directly: engaged discourse analysis, applied discourse analysis, Public Consultative Discourse Analysis, and interventionist CDA are all related terms used by authors, while others argue that *all* Critical Discourse Analysis is positive inasmuch as critique is a necessary step in promoting change for the better. In this chapter, therefore, rather than provide an overview of the huge body of work that potentially fits any of these or similar glosses of "positive", I will discuss the origins of the term PDA itself, provide an outline of work that self-identifies as such, including a brief overview of my own case study in Guyana (Bartlett 2012), and suggest some underlying (though not always shared) principles in considering how the term might operate as a point of reference within critical discourse in general.

Origins and orientations

The term Positive Discourse Analysis first appears in Martin (2004, reprinted as Martin 2012a), though Martin (2012b: 3) cites the origins of this article as a 1999 meeting in Birmingham of the "core CDA group". In Martin's (2012b: 3) words, the paper

> argues the case for a more interventionist stance in ideologically oriented discourse analysis – one focusing not simply on deconstructing language in the service of power but focusing in addition on analysis of and participation in sites of successful social change.

Martin draws his inspiration from Kress's (1996: 15–16) critique of the perceived CDA focus on uncovering "inequitable, dehumanising and deleterious states of affairs" and his call for a move from "deconstructive activity to productive activity". Kress (2000: 160–161) expands on this notion through the key concept of "Design" which, rather than focusing on "the present through the means of past production" of others, "sets aside past agendas, and treats them and their products as resources in setting an agenda of future aims, and in assembling means and resources for implementing that". Martin broadly follows Kress in arguing that "deconstructive **and** constructive activity are both required" (2012a: 282, emphasis in original), but stresses the point that Design needs to be based on studies of "how people get together and make room for themselves in the word in ways that redistribute power without necessarily struggling against it". This is an idea he reemphasises in the paragraph in which the term PDA first appears (Martin 2012a: 283):

> [W]hen we come to design better futures we simply don't have enough information to move forward. Deconstruction is helpful, but not enough on its own – at least that is my experience in educational linguistics where a lot of guess-work had to go into designing possible worlds in the absence of helpful accounts of inspiring initiatives undertaken by others. The lack of positive discourse analysis (PDA) cripples our understanding of how change happens, for the better, across a range of sites. . . .

A similar call to positive arms comes from Luke (2002: 98) who argues for

> CDA to move beyond a focus on ideology critique and to document "other" forms of text and discourse – subaltern, diasporic, emancipatory, local, minority, call them what we may – that may mark the productive use of power in the face of economic and cultural globalization.

Luke goes on to argue (2002: 105) that CDA "must be able to demonstrate what 'should be' as well as what is problematic with text and discourse in the world" and that without identifying and documenting "preferred modes of emancipatory discourse" and "analytically deconstruct[ing. . .] positive and productive configurations of power/knowledge in discourse", CDA "risks becoming entrenched in a neo-Althussarian [sic] paradigm operating under the assumption that all media are forms of centrally controlled interpellation, and further assuming that the general populace are victims and objects of this ideological interpellation".

Luke's position raises a number of questions with regard to celebrating the positive. Firstly, to what extent does "analytically deconstruct[ing. . .] positive and productive configurations of power/knowledge in discourse" consider text-external features of the context, beyond simply providing an ideological backdrop? And relatedly, does the analysis of "positive and productive" texts, without a consideration of whether and how they are taken up by their audiences, similarly assume that the general populace are objects, if not victims, of ideological interpellation? Under what conditions are these positive discourses favourably and productively received by the minority groups they are supposed to be re-enfranchising? Moreover, is getting an oppressed minority on board a sufficient objective without also considering the extent to which alternative discourses have the potential to alter the status quo? As Kress (2000: 155) states, "[a]n adequate theory of semiosis will be founded on a recognition of the 'interested action' of socially located, culturally and historically formed individuals, as the remakers, the transformers, and the reshapers of the representational resource systems available to them". Bearing in mind that both the majority and the minoritised, those in power and those in opposition, are interested parties in the production and dissemination of discourse, this suggests that there is a need to consider the conditions of possibility under which alternative discourses may be produced, taken up and legitimated. Kress (2000: 156) continues:

> The remaking of resources is an effect both of the demands of particular occasions and of the social and cultural characteristics of the individual maker of signs. . . . Semiotic change is thus shaped and guided by the characteristics of broad social factors, which are individually inflected and shaped by the action of the individual in interaction with social others.

Kress raises a further point here in suggesting that, rather than appearing *ex vacuo,* counter-discourses are remade from the existing semiotic resources of the social groups involved, a point elaborated on by Cope and Kalantzis writing in the same volume (2000: 294):

> . . . the Design notion, on the other hand, starts with a very different set of assumptions about meaning and ends with a very different notion of culture. Instead of focus on stability and regularity, the focus is on change and transformation. Individuals have at their disposal a complex range of representational resources, never simply of one culture but of the many cultures of their lived experience; the many layers of their identity and the many dimensions of their being. The breadth, complexity and richness of the available meaning-making resources is such that representation is never simply a matter of reproduction. Rather, it is a matter of transformation: of construing meaning in a way which always adds something to the range of available representational resources.

In the following sections, I will provide a brief overview of selected papers from authors who explicitly identify with the term PDA. In doing so, and in the terms of the discussion so far, I consider the extent to which they not only complement critiques of hegemonic discourse with the analysis of more progressive, or "positive", texts, but also whether and how any suggestions are made for the design of counter-discourses beyond an implicit call for replication and in terms of the transformation of existing resources. Along the way I will consider additional features of the "P" in PDA that arise from specific research orientations, and in the conclusion I bring these together to suggest what PDA might contribute to wider CDA, not as a subdiscipline but as an orientation or, given CDA's own status as an orientation rather than a methodology (e.g., Wodak and Meyer 2009: 31), as a meta-orientation.

Jim Martin, SFL and appraisal

Volume 6 of the Collected Works of J.R. Martin (Wang Zhenhua 2012a) is entitled CDA/PDA, yet, despite being published 13 years after Martin first presented his paper in Birmingham, the term PDA only appears twice in the index: once for the eponymous paper based on that presentation and once for a short comment piece (Martin 2012c). The reason for this apparent evaporation of interest in the concept of PDA is very possibly that the "positive" orientation to text analysis is apparent in Martin's earlier work and continues as a substrate as his later work begins to focus on the more specific topic of restorative justice and, in particular, Youth Justice Conferencing in Australia. In this section I will take the 2004 article as a point of reference for a retrospective and then prospective gaze.

Taking up the mantle of celebrating "positive" texts, Martin's 2004 PDA article is centred around a textual analysis of a national enquiry into the separation of Aboriginal and Torres Strait Islander children from their families entitled *Bringing them Home* (1997). On the third anniversary of the report's release a quarter of a million people marched over Sydney Harbour Bridge demanding an official government apology (Martin 2012b: 287), a response Martin attributes to the use of indigenous voices in the report and an alignment of feelings between the victims and the wider Australian audience. Drawing on the analytical resources of Appraisal, a branch of Systemic Functional Linguistics largely developed by Martin and White (2005), Martin then provides a linguistic analysis of affect, solidarity and (re)alignment as they are construed in the text of the enquiry itself, in similar published testimonies, and in a folk song celebrating the legal restoration of Gurundji lands after a prolonged struggle. The analysis of popular culture as a source of positive discourse hearkens back to an earlier paper of Martin's (2012e, first published in 2002) in which he analyses, alongside secondary school texts, a children's storybook, an excerpt from the film *Educating Rita* and a rap interlude condemning IRA bombings as delivered by U2's Bono during a live performance of *Sunday Bloody Sunday*. In that paper Martin is presenting his "close reading" of texts based on SFL as "a tool for Critical Discourse Analysis", and a similar approach, clearly orienting towards PDA, is taken in later work such as his 2006 paper which "raises the important issue of how activists mobilise to give peace a chance, using the discourses of popular culture, where the power to influence masses of people resides" (Martin 2012d: 299). In this paper Martin revisits U2's *Sunday Bloody Sunday* and adds an analysis of an anti-imperialist *War Prayer* by Mark Twain and Raymond Briggs's graphic satirisation of the Falklands War *The Tin Pot General and the Old Iron Woman*. There is thus a continuity to Martin's work as he embraces CDA and PDA as part of the development of the Appraisal framework. There is also a continuing limitation in that Martin remains resolutely textual, so falling foul of the same constraints Luke (2002: 102) had identified in much CDA:

> My point is that a linguistic analysis and text analytical metalanguage, no matter how comprehensive, cannot "do" CDA in and of itself. It requires the overlay of a social theoretic discourse for explaining and explicating the social contexts, concomitants, contingencies and consequences of any given text or discourse.

According to Blommaert (2005: 34–35), CDA is guilty of linguistic bias in examining available texts without considering the absence of alternatives and failing to account adequately for either the social factors behind the production of these texts or the social consequences of their production. The same criticism is valid for Martin's PDA: with the exception of *Bringing Them Home*, there is little background provided to contextualise the texts as social acts and still less evidence for the wider uptake of their positive messages. Returning to the founding principles of PDA, while we may see heartening texts worth celebrating, we see little to help us understand "how change happens" let alone suggestions for strategic Design across different social contexts:

Martin's more recent work on restorative justice and Youth Justice Conferencing, while not appearing under the tag of PDA and focusing more on continuing injustices rather than battles won, perhaps comes closer to overcoming a textual bias in establishing principles for interventionist design. In a series of often collaborative papers (see Wang 2012b), Martin considers the different ways in which young offenders present themselves and their reactions to their offences. Drawing extensively on Maton's *Legitimation Code Theory* (2014), Martin analyses and contrasts participation that meet with the expectations of the Youth Justice system with that which does not and, at least implicitly, relates these to the socialisation patterns of the different individuals involved. While there seems to be no explicit recommendations for Design in these papers, their production in collaboration with groups from both sides of the justice divide is perhaps suggestive of plausible alternatives, though pointing more to a gradual and organic co-development than to direct intervention.

PDA and ecolinguistics

In 2001 Fill and Mühlhäusler published *The Ecolinguistics Reader,* an edited volume of writings linking ecology and language in three distinct ways: ecology as metaphor, language and environment, and critical ecolinguistics. In an article that draws direct comparisons between critical ecolinguistics and PDA, Stibbe (2014; see also this volume) provides an overview of work in this category, the essence of which he (2014: 117) defines as

> questioning the stories that underpin our current unsustainable civilisation, exposing those stories that are clearly not working, that are leading to ecological destruction and social injustice, and finding new stories that work better in the conditions of the world that we face.

Stibbe (2014: 118) goes on to elaborate that

> the "linguistics" side of ecolinguistics holds out the promise of detailed analysis of the linguistic mechanisms by which worldviews are constructed, reproduced, spread and resisted, while the "eco" side promises a sophisticated ecological framework to consider the role of those worldviews in preserving or undermining the conditions that support life.

As demonstrated in the dual focus of these quotations, Stibbe (2014: 124) agrees with Wodak (in Kendall 2007: 17) that the term *critical* does not imply "being negative" and that "proposing alternatives is also part of being critical". For example, ecolinguistics challenges "the pervasive code that sees unlimited economic growth as both a possible and a desirable goal for human societies" (Stibbe 2014: 118) while the more "positive" aspects aim to

> seek out and promote discourses which could potentially help protect and preserve the conditions that support life. . . through raising awareness of the role of language in ecological destruction or protection, informing policy, informing educational development or providing ideas that can be drawn on in redesigning existing texts or producing new texts in the future.

> *(Stibbe 2014: 119)*

In making explicit the link with PDA, Stibbe (2014: 124) suggests that both (his approach to) ecolinguistics and PDA are distinct from CDA not so much in their mode of analysis but in terms of their practical application: the raising of critical awareness of hidden ideologies in the case of CDA and, for PDA/ecolinguistics, the promotion of positive texts. Or, more specifically, an analysis and promotion of the "specific clustering of linguistic features that convey the worldview" of positive texts – for example, texts which "express scientific knowledge but without devaluing other species" or which resist "imposed metaphors from the West" and "reassert the traditional metaphors of local cultures" (Stibbe 2014: 124). There still appears to be a distinction between the promotion of existing texts and the design of new discourses here, however, for while Stibbe echoes Martin's (2012a: 282) call for a "yin/yang perspective", just as with much of Martin's work, it remains unclear how to make the constructive work effective beyond the promotion of texts or discursive features positively evaluated by the analyst. In both cases, then, it could be claimed that the focus on positive discourses advocated by Martin has pushed ahead while little progress has been made with respect to converting such analysis into Design or consideration of the specific social conditions affecting the uptake of both dominant and alternative discourses. As a consequence, text-based PDA suffers as much as CDA from the pitfalls of assuming a "hypodermic approach" to the transmission of ideology (O'Halloran's 2003). In response, Macgilchrist (2007) and Bartlett (2012) have attempted in different ways to embrace the problems of "variable, idiosyncratic uptake of text and discourse by audience" (Luke 2002: 101): Macgilchrist in terms of newspaper editorial policy and the cognitive uptake of counter-discourses by entrenched readerships, and myself through an ethnographic grounding of the texts analysed in both the local and wider contexts in which they were produced. These two approachs are covered in the following sections.

Macgilchrist: uptake and design

Macgilchrist (2007: 74) captures well the element of design that is missing in many PDA studies when she states from the outset that her paper "investigates strategies for propelling marginal discourses into the mainstream news media". The article builds on the idea that, although there is "a tendency for various news media to cover an issue or event in a very similar way", and that such repeated coverage sets up easily accessible frames of interpretation, nonetheless articles contesting these "predominant frames" are occasionally published and that, from a PDA perspective, such instances "could yield fruitful insights for those wishing to counter what they see as questionable dominant messages". Macgilchrist then considers five counter-discursive strategies and their potential for uptake:

(i)   *logical inversion:* a straight counter to the stated facts. Macgilchrist (2007: 77) concludes, following the analytical consensus, that "simply countering a dominant frame with logical arguments does not work. . . . The arguments are simply ignored or disbelieved";

(ii) *parody:* a mocking questioning of presupposed knowledge which Macgilchrist (2007: 78) considers a form of logical inversion with a similarly limited scope for uptake;

(iii) *complexification:* a two-sided account in which aspects of a story that do not fit the dominant frame are not filtered. Despite the degree of counter-discourse this strategy entails, Macgilchrist (2007: 80) argues, echoing O'Halloran's (2003) concept of the casual reader, that it is also limited in its uptake as "complexity takes time and column inches" while "very few casual readers get beyond the headlines and first paragraphs" which "tend to be written by (non-specialist) editors rather than the journalists themselves" and which draw the story into the predominant frames.

The last two strategies involve *reframing*, defined as "shifting an issue away from its conventional 'location' within one set of shared assumptions and reconstruing it within a different set of knowledges" so as to assign it a new interpretation in its new context (Macgilchrist 2007: 80):

(iv) *partial reframing*: in which a mainstream frame may be temporarily countered through the use of alternative frames (e.g., the depiction of a meddling EU rather than a despotic Putin) but which ultimately does not question the mainstream view that frames the article as a whole (e.g., the notion of a geopolitical power move by Russia) (Macgilchrist 2007: 80–81);

(v) *radical reframing:* "not only dialogue with other frames [. . . as in partial reframing] but also an inversion of the mainstream view of the issue" (Macgilchrist 2007: 81).

After an analysis of examples of radical reframing, the uptake of which is demonstrated by their acceptance for publication within the mainstream media, Macgilchrist (2007: 83–89) goes on to suggest four levels of explanation for the success of this strategy: lexicogrammar, and the specifics of the language used; the political economy of publication and the acceptance of counter-hegemonic articles provided they articulate at least one dominant frame; the cognitive linguistic concept of "blending" and the creation of credible narratives drawing on marginalised discourses; and the appropriate "curiosity gap" (Macgilchrist 2007: 88) between the paper's normal assumptions and the novel representation construed. This is

> based on the assumption that individuals seek moderate levels of uncertainty. . . if the article is too far from the reader's current knowledge of the world, it will be ignored; if the article tells readers what they already know, it will be deemed uninteresting.

Macgilchrist (2007: 89) concludes that radical reframing would appear to be the most effective way for having marginal discourses reproduced in dominant media but acknowledges that further research is necessary "to investigate. . . whether radical reframing is a more general phenomenon, applicable to other news media topics or indeed to other forms of social interaction". Coming from a very different angle and within a very different context, my own work on the contestation of discourses of development in Guyana came to very similar conclusions.

Bartlett: assimilation, accommodation and cultural capital

In Bartlett (2012) I present a longitudinal case study of discourse between the largely Makushi Amerindian population of the North Rupununi in Guyana and the Iwokrama International Rainforest Conservation and Development Programme (generally referred to just as 'Iwokrama'). This latter organisation was set up to study biodiversity in the Iwokrama Rainforest but had expanded its remit to include the sustainable social development of the thirteen indigenous communities living in and at the edge of the rainforest. These communities were brought together every second month for a two-day meeting of the North Rupununi District Development Board (NRDDB), which involved discussion between the communities and Iwokrama, the Government of Guyana and various NGOs and international organisations.

I initially approached my fieldwork with a strong CDA conviction that the economic, social and political advantages of the outside groups would translate into the symbolic capital of discourse (Bourdieu 1991) with the result that these groups would exert hegemonic control over the meetings, with my role being to raise the awareness of the community representatives to this imbalance and work with them in an attempt to level the playing field. However, I soon came to realise that something rather different was going on and that the local communities were making a very good job of this without my "expert" help, and my thesis gradually mutated into an exploration of the various locally contingent factors that may have explained the success of the communities in this particular context and which might be translated, in essence if not in exact form, to similar contexts elsewhere.

In interpreting the key texts analysed and the growing control of the local communities of the proceedings of the NRDDB, it was necessary to situate these texts and those producing them as acts and actors within a very specific sociocultural juncture. I therefore provided a background analysis of the conditions of possibility for the existing situation in terms of: the history of indigenous rights in Guyana, the postwar trajectory of international development discourses and practices, the history of interaction between local communities and development workers in the Rupununi, and the social organisation and discourse practices of the local communities. This analysis allowed me to provide meat to the bones of my textual analysis and prompted the following conclusions with regard to the success of local discourse practices within this specific sociocultural context:

- the "hegemonic" group in this case, Iwokrama, was a relatively willing collaborator in the communities sharing control over proceedings of the NRDDB, one result of which was that the meetings of the NRDDB displayed what Hasan (1996: 46–47) refers to as a low "convergent coding", i.e., the relative authority of Iwokrama and other outsiders was not simultaneously encoded by a range of semiotic codes. Of importance here was also the fact that the building in which later meetings took place had been constructed by the local communities specifically for this purpose, so that they had a sense of ownership over this space as a *place*;
- the individual statuses of specific community members legitimated their contributions in various ways. In the most striking case, Uncle Henry, a community elder who had also worked with outside groups in setting up the NRDDB, had both local and "imported" prestige as well as access to the appropriate codes for each (cf. Cope and Kalantzis, above), which allowed him to hybridise the institutionalised ways of speaking of the outside groups with the more locally contextualised and authority-laden voice of the local community. This often involved "translating" outside discourses into locally amenable terms – a move that allowed Uncle Henry to "smuggle into" dominant discourse frames the worldview, social structures and rhetorical teaching traditions of the local community.

In a similar way to Macgilchrist's analysis, therefore, my research suggested that the legitimation of marginalised voices was a function of their assimilation to and accommodation of the prevalent patterns of the dominant group, but went beyond this to suggest that certain voices were only legitimately available to specific participants. Revisiting these conclusions in writing this chapter, I see that they come very close to the potential for a more positive CDA as set out by Luke (2002: 106–107):

. . . the affirmative character of discourse can take many forms. The purview of CDA could include the documentation of:

1   minority discourses, diasporic voices, texts, and statements that are 'written out' and over by dominant institutions;

2   emergent discourses of hybrid identity generated by learners [or other marginal groups] counter to dominant pedagogic [and other] discourses;

3   idiosyncratic local uptakes. . . where human subjects take centrally broadcast or dominant texts and discourses and reinterpret, recycle and revoice them in particular ways that serve their local political interests; and

4   those micropolitical strategies of interruption, resistance, and counter-discourse undertaken by speakers in face-to-face institutional and interpersonal settings.

Beyond this, my work attempted to show not only a general movement in discourse practice, but also to provide a sociocultural explanation for this change in relating the ways of speaking of the various speakers to their sociocultural and institutional identities and in relating the discourse practices in general to the specific sociopolitical context, providing the local genealogies of discourse practices suggested by Benwell and Stokoe (2006: 41). However, this is where my research came to an end, without continuing to suggest how these findings might form the basis of future Design. Nonetheless, the suggestion is that basing the analysis of current discourse events on the sociocultural and linguistic conditions of possibility within a specific local context brings into focus, if not specific strategic interventions, then a potential space – Vygotsky's (1978: 86) Zone of Proximal Development (ZPD), where a range of possibilities can be discussed in conjunction with the participants themselves. Working with the individuals and groups involved is a further desirable element of positive discourse analysis and, while I critique development organisations for not fully involving local communities in their analyses and decision-making, my own analytical work suffers not only from failing to promote future developments but also from having being produced largely in isolation from the groups involved.

PDA in education and social activism

As stated above, the interpretation of what the positive in PDA means in practice remains something of an open question, and in relation to education, the term could be used to cover various progressive strands such as the Reading to Learn programme, inspired by the work of Martin and Rose and drawing on Systemic Functional Linguistics (www.readingtolearn. com.au); Pennycook's (2001) Critical Applied Linguistics; and moves towards a more inclusive curriculum design (Gouveia 2007). However, in keeping with the overall orientation of this chapter, I will focus here on a paper by Rogers and Mosley Wetzel (2013), as it is specifically oriented towards PDA and discusses methodological issues that are of particular relevance.

   In this paper Rogers and Mosley Wetzel present an individual case study of literary education aimed at marginalised groups in the Missouri State School System. Focusing on a workshop on "culturally relevant teaching", the authors draw on the tools of narrative analysis, critical discourse analysis and multi-modal analysis to "describe, interpret and explain the relationships between texts and social practices" with a particular emphasis on the construal of agency and the resources used by Leslie, the teacher presenting the workshop, "to construct a figured world of an educator, an educator of educators, and a change agent" (2013: 69). In this way the paper can be said to be "positive" in a double sense as it deals with the empowerment of both the student and teacher involved as the "workshop provides Leslie a vehicle to position herself not only as an educator, but an educator of other teachers and as an agent of social change" (2013: 78). As the authors argue (2013: 88), "[o]ver time, these discourse processes accumulate into narratives people tell themselves about what they can accomplish, propelling them toward future actions" while the dissemination of such discourses and practices and "productively gaining a foothold within institutionalized contexts is a long-term process that involves multiple opportunities to call on narratives and rhetorical strategies, depending on the audience, context, and purpose" (2013: 89).

As with my own work in Guyana, therefore, Rogers and Mosley Wertzel's case study relies on local contextualisation and a fine-grained analysis of discourse features and their relation to the specifics of the context described. However, their work goes beyond mine in involving the subjects as participants in the analysis and dissemination of good practice and as a result more directly works towards the Design of future practice.

In an earlier paper Rogers (2012) discusses how, as both a member of the elected school board of St. Louis public schools and a researcher in education, she worked with the Board to advocate for a return to elected governance following a period of state takeover. While this paper does not explicitly identify itself as within the framework of PDA, it provides a link between Rogers's work and other work on social activism while introducing Scollon's (2010) framework of *Public Consultative Discourse Analysis* (PCDA), which has clear links with PDA in that "PCDA is never just discourse analysis but is a form of discourse analysis which seeks to bring discourse analysis itself into the democratic and participatory negotiation of public policy" (Scollon 2010: 24). As Rogers (2012: 8–9) expands:

> Whereas other types of critical analyses often focus on social practices of the past, PCDA seeks to put the analysis to work in the policy-making process, making the results of the discourse analysis immediately relevant to the context. . . . PCDA is a reiterative process of critically analyzing discourses, reporting on findings, incorporating feedback into the deliberations, and conducting further analyses.

Rogers outlines in her case study how the elected Board she was working alongside drew on close analyses of "the textual devices that contribute to power and consent" (2012: 1) in a variety of data sources, such as minutes of meetings, media reports, transcripts of public hearings, and policy documents, not only to consider how "how school governance [is] constructed through public discourses during a period of re-evaluation" (2012: 2) but to use the analyses to influence public policy by "reframing the state's charge; foregrounding the 'public' in public education; and creating a counternarrative" (2012: 1). As Rogers (2012: 18) argues, such counternarratives not only question dominant knowledge, they also serve to "build community among those at the margins of society" and "teach that new stories, over time, can create new realities". In this particular case the process met with only limited success in terms of concrete changes to legislation: the final report recommended an extension of the appointed form of governance in the immediate term with an eventual return to an elected board, with diminished powers, as a permanent form of governance. However, the process of consultation and drafting of the response by the elected Board in itself was largely positive in that:

> A group of democratically elected people wrote the board's report. It was deliberated, written, revised, presented, and finalized in public. . . Drafts of the elected school board's report were widely circulated through video, executive summary, full report, and press releases. The elected board actively solicited feedback, criticism, and comments. Notices of the meetings were "pushed" to the public. . . . The writing and presentation of the transition report caused the elected board to cross boundaries with data, focus, and presentation style. . . .
>
> *Rogers 2012: 20*

In this way the aims of PCDA – consciousness raising and increased activism through the collective processes, culminating in the writing of the report – are combined with the critical gaze of CDA in "framing, historicizing, and disrupting textual silences" as a first stage in creating a counternarrative (2012: 20). As such, Rogers emphasises the complementary role of the activist and academic when she points out (2012: 9) that while the Board's own analyses "often did not include a formal linguistic analysis but, rather, sensitivity to the way in which discourse and power operate", this participatory analysis can be supported by a closer linguistic analysis. Rogers's use of PCDA therefore adds a further variable to what may be considered the "P" of PDA in the incorporation of the subject community themselves in every aspect of the analysis of discourses and their circulation and the formulation and promulgation of counter-discourse.

Social activism is also the focus of research by Humphreys (2013) who uses an SFL-based approach "to account for intertextual resources deployed by one adolescent activist across multiple texts in a complex network of social affiliations" and to show "how particular patterns of manifest intertextuality enable the young activist to build solidarity with his fellow young affiliates and to mobilise social action" (Humphreys 2013: 167). Building on Gee's (2000: 105) concept of social affiliation and affinity groups built around common endeavours or practices, Humphreys takes on board SFL work on "bonding icons" (Stenglin 2004) and Tann's (2010: 88) framework for examining the discursive resources which rally audiences "around communal ideas and dispositions" to explore the use of intertextuality by one particular blogger, Bonofan, in order to build up his own personal capital (cf. Bartlett above) while creating solidarity across a diverse readership (2013: 162) characterised not in terms of sociocultural grouping "but around (potential) commitment to social action" (2013: 164). As Humphreys (2013: 164) goes on to say, "[f]rom a PDA perspective these resources can be interpreted as strategies for broadening the Gemeinschaft and removing boundaries between adult and adolescent discursive politics". There is thus a connection with Macgilchrist's work and my own in the way Humphreys interprets the success of the blog in terms of the creation of intersecting but not overlapping commonalities of interest between different groups and the hybrid cultural capital accrued by the blogger as the dual-voiced expert.

As a necessary antidote to the perhaps overly rosy spectacles adopted in some PDA work – Martin's celebration of right-on texts, my own advancement of a utopian collaboration across cultures – I shall finish this section on social activism with a mention of Schröter's (2015) celebration of the dystopic through her examination of punk culture – P(unk)DA? – as a site that "nourishes a critical distance from and critical attitude towards hegemonic discourse" (Schröter 2015: 2). Specifically, Schröter analyses lyrics from post-Wall German punk and how they "undermine an exculpatory argumentation in hegemonic public and political discourse that failed to tackle racist ideology and racist violence" (2015: 2). In focusing on punk as a subculture, Schröter (2015: 3) argues that "more attention should be paid to a broader variety of voices in discourses, especially by looking at the continuum between hegemony and resistance", going beyond what she sees as the tendency in PDA to "look at 'healing' discourses that 'make the world a better place', archly commenting that "[t]here is reason to doubt that punk could be seen, or would like to be seen, in terms of 'positive discourse'". Rather, Schröter (2015: 5) sees punk lyrics as representing "a counter-discourse which is marked by disturbance, disagreement and distance" and, far from wishing to be accepted by the hegemonic forces of the day, "Punks usually have no problem with implying themselves as ugly, deprived, undesirable". However, such a stance also creates solidarity within the punk movement and helps to sustain it as an alternative movement, so suggesting the conditions of possibility for uptake of such counter-discourses that is missing from more celebratory PDA.

In this vein, Schröter (2015: 19–20) calls for further analysis of "niches of counter-discourse as sites of resistance and alternative thinking, framing and talking" and asks what we might learn from stigmatised or discriminated groups "regarding effective strategies to undermine the pervasive power of hegemonic discourse and to what extent we can or want to include examples of such strategies in teaching towards critical language awareness".

Conclusion

A week after the shootings at the Bardo Museum in Tunisia, in which 22 people, mostly European tourists, were killed by Islamic extremists, I flew to the country to attend the first conference of the Systemic Functional Linguistics Association of Tunisia (SYFLAT – http:// www.syflat.tn). One paper in particular (Farhat 2015) stood out: beginning with images of the slain terrorists and huddled tourists, Farhat, a Tunisian academic, asked what we as critical discourse analysts could do in the face of such immediate and real problems.[3] In a follow-up (pers. comm.) Farhat expanded on the motivation for her talk:

> The reason behind this urgent call for global research and for more collaborative inter-ventionist actions is that research in the human sciences is visibly *not* congruent with the pace of threats and ascending problems in different communities around the world. It is also hard to translate research findings to directly target social problems and cause change in societies. In academia, most studies are descriptive and critical; but rarely explicitly interventionist. Most researchers work individually; even research units and teams gather with view of distinguishing themselves from one another. . . . This paper is part of an ongoing project [see Farhat in progress] that aims at synthesising alternative studies in the humanities that have so far contributed in initiating this active perspec-tive in research. This project is going to be a heap of stones set up as a landmark for all researchers who believe in interventionist research. Ideally, we want to help creat-ing a cairn for researchers who believe in the role of humanities in directly serving communities.

Farhat calls for a "nexus of practice" (Scollon and Scollon 2004) linking researchers in dis-course and the social sciences to address questions such as how a consensus is reached that religious war is a duty or that torture of terrorist suspects is legitimate behaviour. Such a practice means not just looking at the texts that promote consensus but also a consideration of the contexts in which such texts have proven effective; it also calls for a consideration of what type of texts will help foster an alternative consensus in specific and particular social contexts.[4]

From the overview of PDA provided above, we can suggest how the different analytical approaches can all provide the individual stones that, once joined in a nexus of practice, will form a cairn for positive and interventionist orientations to discourse:

- critique of regressive practice (CDA);
- identification of alternative practice as model (Martin, Stibbe, Humphreys) or as existing effective critique (Schröter);
- design of alternative practices based on current social conditions and linguistic practices in a specific global (Macgilchrist) or local (Bartlett) context;

- involvement of subjects in critiques and design (Rogers);
- evaluation of short and long-term uptake and effect of Design.

Notes

1 My thanks to Rebecca Rogers for her comments on an earlier draft of this chapter.
2 www.asfla.org.au/isfc2005/home.html, accessed March 30, 2015
3 We must of course be aware of the limitations of what can we hope to achieve, recognising that different forms of oppression and marginalisation are not merely discursive and cannot be resolved by simply altering the discursive superstructure (see for example Ebert 1995).
4 See the following article, however, for an indication of the government response when we attempt to engage with such issues: www.timeshighereducation.com/news/researchers-have-no-right-to-study-terrorist-materials/402844.article

Further reading

Bartlett, T. (2012). *Hybrid voices and collaborative change: Contextualising positive discourse analysis*. London and New York: Routledge.
In this book-length case study of discourse between Amerindian villagers and international aid workers in Guyana, I offer a critique and development of Martin's approach to PDA and suggest that a deeper analysis of context is necessary if analysis is to contribute to the development of alternative discourses.
Kress, G. (2000). Design and transformation: New theories of meaning. In B. Cope and M. Kalantzis (eds.), *Multiliteracies: Literacy learning and the design of social futures,* 153–161. Abingdon: Routledge.
This paper is the precursor of Martin's work on PDA and establishes the need to go beyond the critique that characterises Critical Discourse Analysis and to consider the means of designing alternative and empowering discourses.
Macgilchrist, F. (2007). Positive discourse analysis: Contesting dominant discourses by reframing the issues. *Critical Approaches to Discourse Analysis Across Disciplines* 1(1): 74–94.
This paper considers the most successful means of publishing articles that challenge the accepted worldview of the newspaper in which they appear, developing a framework of analysis according to the means by which competing discourses are presented and discussed.
Martin, J. R. (2012 [2004]) Positive discourse analysis: Solidarity and change. In Wang Zhenhua (ed.), *CDA/PDA: Volume 6 in the collected works of J.R. Martin,* 278–298. Shanghai: Shanghai Jhao Tong University Press.
This paper is where the term Positive Discourse Analysis first appears and sets the frame for much of Martin and his colleagues' continuing work in applying linguistic analysis to areas of practical concern.

References

Alba-Juez, L. (2009). *Perspectives on discourse analysis: Theory and practice*. Newcastle: Cambridge Scholars Publishing.
Bartlett, T. (2012). *Hybrid voices and collaborative change: Contextualising positive discourse analysis*. London and New York: Routledge.
Benwell, B. and Stokoe, E. (2006). *Discourse and identity*. Edinburgh: Edinburgh University Press.
Blommaert, J. (2005). *Discourse: A critical introduction*. Cambridge: Cambridge University Press.
Bourdieu, P. (1991). *Language and symbolic power*. Cambridge, MA: Harvard University Press.
Cope, B. and Kalantzis, M. (2000). Designs for social futures. In Cope and Kalantzis (eds.).
Cope, B. and Kalantzis, M. (eds.) (2000). *Multiliteracies: Literacy learning and the design of social futures*. Abingdon: Routledge.
Ebert, T. (1995). (Untimely) critiques for a red feminism. www.marxists.org/reference/subject/philosophy/works/us/ebert.htm
Farhat, S. (2015). Research in the humanities: Implications for interventionist positive critical discourse analysis. SFL's got talent! Implications for critical discourse analysis. In *First Tunisian International Systemic Functional Linguistics Conference,* March 2015.

Fill, A. and Mühlhäusler, P. (eds.) (2001). *The ecolingusitics reader.* London and New York: Continuum.

Gee, J. P. (1999). *An introduction to discourse analysis: Theory and method.* London: Routledge.

Gee, J. P. (2000). Identity as an analytic lens for research in education. *Review of Research in Education* 25: 99–125.

Gouveia, C.A.M. (2007). The role of a common European framework in the elaboration of national language curricula and syllabuses. *Cadernos de Linguagem e Sociedade (Papers on Language and Society)* 8(2006/2007): 8–25.

Humphreys, S. (2013). Bonofan: The role of intertextuality in mobilising social action. In C.A.M. Gouveia and M. F. Alexandre (eds.), *Languages, metalanguages, modalities, cultures: Functional and socio-discursive approaches,* 155–176. Lisbon: BonD.

Kendall, G. (2007). What is critical discourse analysis? Ruth Wodak in conversation with Gavin Kendall. *Qualitative Social Research* 8(2): 29. http://nbn-resolving.de/urn:nbn:de:0114-fqs0702297

Kress, G. (1996). Representational resources and the production of subjectivity: Questions for the theoretical development of critical discourse analysis in a multicultural society. In C. R. Caldas-Coulthard and M. Coulthard (eds.), *Texts and practices: Readings in critical discourse analysis,* 15–31. London: Routledge.

Kress, G. (2000). Design and transformation: New theories of meaning. In Cope and Kalantzis (eds.), 153–161.

Luke, A. (2002). Beyond science and ideology critique: Developments in critical discourse analysis. *Annual Review of Applied Linguistics* 22: 96–110.

Macgilchrist, F. (2007). Positive discourse analysis: Contesting dominant discourses by reframing the issues. *Critical Approaches to Discourse Analysis Across Disciplines* 1(1): 74–94.

Martin, J. R. (2012a [2004]). Positive discourse analysis: Solidarity and change. In Wang Zhenhua (2012a ed.), The Collected Works of J. R. Martin. Shanghai: Shanghai Jiaotong University Press.

Martin, J. R. (2012b). The author's introduction. In Wang Zhenhua (2012a ed.).

Martin, J. R. (2012c [2007]). Towards a framework of peace sociolinguistics: Response. In Wang Zhenhua (2012a ed.), The Collected Works of J. R. Martin. Shanghai: Shanghai Jiaotong University Press.

Martin, J. R. (2012d [2006]). Vernacular deconstruction: Undermining spin. In Wang Zhenhua (2012a ed.), The Collected Works of J. R. Martin. Shanghai: Shanghai Jiaotong University Press.

Martin, J. R. (2012e [2000]). Close reading: Functional linguistics a tool for critical discourse analysis. In Wang Zhenhua (2012a ed.), The Collected Works of J. R. Martin. Shanghai: Shanghai Jiaotong University Press.

Martin, J. R. and White, P.R.R. (2005). *The language of evaluation: Appraisal in English.* Basingstoke: Palgrave Macmillan.

Maton, K. (2014). *Knowledge and knowers: Towards a realist sociology of education.* Abingdon, New York: Routledge.

O'Halloran, K. (2003). *Critical discourse analysis and language cognition.* Edinburgh: Edinburgh University Press.

Pennycook, A. (2001). *Critical applied linguistics: A critical introduction.* London and New York: Routledge.

Rogers, R. (2012). In the aftermath of a state takeover of a school district: A case study in public consultative discourse analysis. *Urban Education* 20(10): 1–29.

Rogers, R. and Melissa Mosley Wetzel, M. (2013). Studying agency in literacy teacher education: A layered approach to positive discourse analysis. *Critical Inquiry in Language Studies* 10(1): 62–92.

Scollon, R. (2010). *Analyzing public discourse: Discourse analysis in the making of public policy.* London: Routledge.

Scollon, R. and Scollon, S. W. (2004). *Nexus analysis: Discourse and the emerging Internet.* New York: Routledge.

Schröter, M. (2015). 80,000,000 Hooligans. *Critical Discourse Studies* 12(4). DOI: 10.1080/174059 04.2014.1002508

Stenglin, M. K. (2004). *Packaging curiosities: towards a grammar of three-dimensional space.* Unpublished PhD thesis, University of Sydney.

Stibbe, A. (2014). An ecolinguistic approach to critical discourse studies. *Critical Discourse Studies* 11(1): 117–128.

Tann, K. (2010). *Semogenesis of a nation: An iconography of Japanese Identity.* Unpublished PhD thesis, University of Sydney.

van Dijk, T. (ed.) (1997). *Discourse studies: A multidisciplinary introduction. Volume 2: Discourse as social interaction.* London: Sage.

Vygotsky, L. S. (1978). *Mind in society: The development of higher psychological processes.* Cambridge: Harvard University Press.

Wang, Z. (ed.) (2012a). *CDA/PDA. Volume 6 in the collected works of J. R. Martin.* Shanghai: Shanghai Jhao Tong University Press.

Wang, Z. (ed.) (2012b). *Forensic linguistics. Volume 8 in the collected works of J. R. Martin.* Shanghai: Shanghai Jhao Tong University Press.

Wodak, R. and Meyer, M. (2009). *Methods for critical discourse analysis.* Los Angeles, London, New Delhi, Singapore and Washington, DC: Sage.

Part II
Analytical methods

10

Systemic functional linguistics

Meriel Bloor and Thomas Bloor

1. Systemic functional linguistics: aims and applications

This chapter is concerned with the application of Systemic Functional Linguistics (henceforth SFL) to Critical Discourse Analysis (CDA). For those readers who are not familiar with SFL, it is important to realise that it developed as a branch of linguistics with specific theoretical principles and the aim of increasing our understanding of how human language works. Since this task involves describing and explaining language in use, SFL linguists have devised a complex set of analytic tools and techniques that have proved useful in applied studies such as education, communication studies and forensic linguistics as well as CDA. SFL then is not a type of critical discourse studies but rather an independent discipline with features that CDA practitioners have applied productively to understanding how discourse works. In this chapter we look at a few of the ways in which SFL has been applied with benefit to the critical analysis of language in use in social contexts, and we also consider some of its limitations.

The theoretical approach in SFL focuses on the meaning-making resources of language within specific social and cultural contexts. Since its earliest manifestations, SFL has been concerned with social action or 'what people do with language'. SFL uses the term lexicogrammar to encapsulate the idea that vocabulary (lexis) is inextricably linked to grammatical choices that are available in a language. These choices are contained in system networks which offer paradigmatic options that carry significant meaning, as, for example, the difference between negative and positive evaluation. These systems characterise the large body of options that are available to speakers to create meaning in context. Unlike purely formal models of linguistics, SFL claims that the semantic networks, which are social and cultural constructs, carry meaning potential, which is 'unfolded' within texts (spoken or written) in specific contexts of situation.

Meaning fulfils the three overarching components of the semantic system known as metafunctions: *ideational, interpersonal* and *textual,* each of which is reflected in instances of language use (Halliday and Matthiessen 2004: 29–31). Any clause embraces ideational, interpersonal and textual meanings.

It is also a tenet of SFL that "the study of discourse cannot be separated from the study of the grammar that lies behind it" (Halliday and Matthiessen 2013: 658). This latter point is clearly a controversial position in critical discourse studies, particularly as the word 'discourse' is open to many different interpretations (see, for example, Blommaert 2005: 2–4; Bloor and Bloor 2007: 6–7).

2. Relevance to CDA

Since the 1970s, starting with what was known as Critical Linguistics (e.g., Kress and Hodge 1979; Fowler et al. 1979), there has been a close relationship between SFL and CDA, and certain shared commonalities have frequently been noted, for example by Young and Harrison (2004: Introduction), who highlight the role of language as a social construct. This involves the constant effects of language events on social action and the influence of social action, in turn, on the development of language. The critical discourse analyst Fairclough (2003, 2004) supports transdisciplinary work in which, for example, linguists engaged in text analysis enter into dialogue with discourse analysts – and maybe with specialists from other relevant disciplines – in order to develop their own theories and research agendas. Elsewhere, he has drawn attention to the type of language analysis that could be considered appropriate for critical discourse work and listed ten questions concerning lexis, grammar and textual features, the grammar questions being closely drawn from systemic functional grammar (Fairclough 1989: 109–139, discussed in Bloor and Bloor 2013: 237–238).

One strength of SFL when compared with more formal schools of linguistics is that it is has always been concerned with more than clause and sentence grammar and has worked with instances of 'authentic' language (recorded or written) rather than with examples constructed by the linguist. A major early contribution to discourse analysis in general, including CDA, was *Cohesion in English,* an early work of Halliday and Hasan (1976). It drew attention to the many aspects of English that cannot be accounted for by those traditional grammars that merely describe and classify words, sentences and their constituent parts. Work on textual cohesion has been incorporated into further studies of spoken and written discourse, incorporating the information structure and the thematic structure of texts. Further work on meaning above the clause, usually referred to as discourse semantics, (for example, Martin 1992) has enriched the understanding of textual features. Martin and White's (2005) account of appraisal and evaluation has particular relevance to CDA. Appraisal is a word which covers the analysis of the way in which speakers or writers express their attitude or positively or negatively evaluate proposals in the discourse. The evaluation can relate to either interpersonal or ideational meaning.

3. Objections to SFL in CDA

As is clear from the variety of CDA projects described in the current volume, there are branches of critical discourse studies that have little to do with linguistics or any type of textual analysis. The original editors of the key journal *Critical Discourse Studies,* an international group (Fairclough, N., Graham, P., Lemke, J., Wodak, R. 2004: 1–7), welcomed, in their introduction to the new journal, submissions from 'a range of disciplines', and this seems to have become the norm, with input from sociology, anthropology, ecology and political science, among other fields. Although we have elsewhere supported this view (Bloor and Bloor 2014), it is arguable that critical discourse studies has become so diffuse that most practitioners can appreciate only a minority of the publications and there is little sign of the 'clarity and consensus' that was hoped for. Certainly the complexity of SFL lexicogrammar, with its many levels of analysis, can appear unnecessarily obscure for the common CDA goals of addressing power, gross inequalities and injustice. While acknowledging the earlier contribution of SFL to CDA, van Dijk (2008: 29–30) objects to SFL "as a framework for the study of discourse", in part because it involves "too much linguistic (lexicosyntactic) sentence grammar" and "too much esoteric vocabulary". We would not claim that all CDA practitioners need to be SFL linguists, but, as we attempt to demonstrate in Sections 4 and 5 of this chapter, some aspects of close lexicogrammatical analysis find a place in CDA.

van Dijk (2008: 28–55) also objects to what he sees as limitations in the SFL theory of context, specifically referring to early work of Halliday, which has since been considerably developed. SFL has embraced elaborations of the early accounts particularly with respect to discourse, and, as far as we can see, would welcome many of van Dijk's own contributions to the subject. More seriously, van Dijk is concerned about what he sees as the 'anti-mentalist' position of SFL (seemingly based on his reading of Halliday 1978). van Dijk takes a socio-cognitive approach to CDA and points to the distinction between his position and Halliday's with regard to 'psychological interpretation'. van Dijk is interested in individual 'mental models' (2008: 58–61; 120–123), evidenced in his analysis of a speech by Tony Blair. He provides a list of factors that he claims the speaker, at that time Prime Minister of the UK, consciously represents, including 'intentions, purposes and goals'. While this accords with what most people would see as 'common sense', the traditional SFL position would be that the job of the linguist is to account for how the language system provides the means for Blair's presentation of his identity, political action, social attitudes and so on to be realised linguistically, but that the analyst has no way of establishing the true nature of Blair's internal mental model, which may at some level be completely different from those attitudes given voice in a specific discourse event, particularly, as van Dijk admits, since these may be interpreted differently by different listeners.

In fact, some aspects of cognitive linguistics are in no way alien to SFL. Halliday (2001: 199) references Rosch's (1978) prototype theory in acknowledging the importance of 'core signification' in grammatical classification systems. Halliday and Matthiessen (2006: 72; 273; 424–429) compare SFL approaches with cognitive approaches to some linguistic issues, finding similarities, referring to the work of Lakoff and Johnson (1980) on metaphor theory and Fillmore's parallel system of transitivity. Halliday's model of lexicogrammar has always incorporated work on mutual knowledge (sometimes called 'common ground') as part of Information Structure, where the clause pattern is said to incorporate both Given and New information, the term Given indicating information that the speaker/writer assumes to be 'shared' with the listener/reader either because of previous mention or because it is considered to be contextually or culturally common knowledge (Halliday 1970 and elsewhere, discussed in Bloor and Bloor 2013: 65–83). Given or New can be designated by specific lexical signalling or by word order and, in the spoken language, by intonation. Halliday and Matthiessen (2006: 595–604) also consider the ways in which theories of cognition are construed.

Some writers have specifically condemned the influence of SFL and linguistics in general. Blommaert (2005: 34–35) refers to what he calls the problem of "*linguistic bias in CD*" (his italics), one reason being, he explains, that "linguists have no monopoly over theories of language". In particular he is concerned that SFL is the 'only' theory of language presented. His main objection to linguistics, however, seems to be that "the emphasis on linguistic analysis implies an emphasis on available discourse, discourse which is there". He explains this rather puzzling claim by arguing that "the bias restricts the space of analysis to textually organized and explicitly linguistically encoded discourse" rather than to the social conditions surrounding it: "where it comes from and goes to".

Others have argued that CDA may need a closer account of aspects of social context in combination with any linguistic analysis, a position we support. For example, Galasiński

(2011: 263) employs both SFL and ethnography in his investigations of doctor-patient inter-action in psychiatric hospitals, arguing that "a firm anchoring in a lexicogrammatical analysis of the data gives ethnography an empirical basis". Barkho (2011), whose work is discussed further in Section 5 below, also supports "moving beyond the analysis of textual output" by incorporating ethnographic techniques into his research.

Blommaert's position is that critical discourse studies, including his own work, does not need the analysis of recorded texts since it is focused on the socio-historical and ethno-graphic bases of power and identity and on "the global structures of inequality" (Blommaert 2005: 235), which are seen as necessarily mediated through language. Nevertheless, we would argue, power and inequality can be realised in language and are often institutionally enforced through texts. Where there exists linguistic evidence of injustice, exploitation, prejudice or deception, we would argue that SFL is the model of choice if only because of its concerns with social context, seen as central in functional theory.

4. SFL and context

The SFL theory of context appears deceptively simple and limited, being based on the notions of *field, tenor* and *mode*. However, each of these component parts covers multiple sub-sections, each relating to the social and cultural environments in which the discourse is constructed, allowing it to account for the many distinct forms of linguistic discourse from face-to-face interaction between a small child and a parent to the complexity of legal text. An analyst of political discourse, say, is likely to address the socio-cultural settings in which the discourse events take place, and SFL approaches to context can provide a focus for its investigation.

To give a little more detail, we can say that whereas *Field* is the term used for the subject matter of any texts involved in the discourse event, *Tenor* is the term used for social status of those involved in the discourse and the nature of the relationship between speaker and listener or writer and reader. These relationships may be socially distant as when an ill person accesses medical information online (Bloor, M. 2016), a situation in which the semantic space may be so great as to cause a breakdown in comprehension. *Mode* concerns channel, speech or writ-ing, online or film, but may include diagrams, emoticons or even toys (Gregory and Carroll 1976; Halliday and Hasan 1989: 3–14; van Leeuwen 2008). Less precisely, the term 'mode' has also been applied to the rhetorical role played by language users in a specific context: instructional, explanatory, persuasive, critical, apologetic and so on (Halliday and Matthiessen 2006: 320–327).

However, even as we cannot always fully understand a text out of context, the social setting of any text is rarely detectable in its entirety from the text alone, and, for this reason, critical discourse analysts often combine methodologies in their research, using, for example, ethno-graphic techniques or sociological and historical data, to support their research.

5. Lexicogrammatical tools for text analysis

We have already mentioned van Dijk's objections to the esoteric terminology and general complexity of SFL analysis. It is important to understand that the grammar is complex only because language is complex. SFL attempts to describe and explain multiple aspects of mean-ing and to show how they relate to each other. Each area of analysis has its own set of descrip-tive terms, which provide the 'toolbox' that can be used in critical commentaries on texts and on communicative interaction in specific social settings. In a recent publication on how meaning is construed in text, Halliday and Webster (2014) illustrate the analysis of texts using

- Analysis of the linguistic elements that express experience of the world and of our own consciousness (using *Process,* and *Participant* and *Circumstance* analysis, the main components of *the transitivity system*). These are the resources that enable us to organise, represent and understand our perceptions of the world. They form what is known as the *ideational component.*
- Analysis of the linguistic elements that express roles, attitudes, demands and social and personal relations (including mood, modality, appraisal, politeness). This *interpersonal component* is seen as 'acting out social relationships'.
- Analysis of the linguistic elements that serve to construct cohesive and coherent chunks of language in use (including means of reference, rhetorical structure theory and thematic structure). This is known as the *textual component.*

In the practice of critical analysis, the ideational component can raise awareness of how writers can represent reality in relatively negative or positive ways. The interpersonal component can point to the nature of the interactive relationship perceived by the speaker or writer. We illustrate how this works in examples of three newspaper headlines referring to the same event in the British economy. The textual component could be exemplified showing how the headlines refer to details in the subsequent news reports, but space constraints mean we cannot reproduce them here.

This analysis is slightly simplified:

(i)   UK falls into deflation
(ii) UK's period of deflation to recover within weeks
(iii) Will deflation affect your lifestyle?

In (i) we have a finite declarative clause purportedly representing a fact. The major Process *falls* is designated as a Material Process with the Actor *UK* falling *into deflation.* Since the process is metaphorical and clearly a negative act, deflation is seen as an undesirable place which is seen in the new information. This is expressed diagrammatically as:

(i)

UK	falls	into deflation
Subject	Finite/Predicator (verbal group)	Adjunct
Participant: Actor	Process: Material	Circumstance: Location
Given	New information	

In contrast to (i) above, Example (ii) below gives a positive message representing a speedy recovery (as from an illness). Grammatically, it uses what Halliday termed a 'grammatical metaphor'. The substance of the whole clause in (i) is condensed into a Nominal Group (*UK's period of deflation*). This enables it to become Subject of a clause and Actor of a Material Process (*recover*). Moreover, it is presented as 'Given' or presupposed, shared knowledge (section 3 above). The whole headline is a non-finite clause where the infinitive verb (*to recover*) carries a future meaning.

(ii)

UK's period of deflation	to recover	within weeks
Subject	Non-finite Predicator	Adjunct
Participant: Actor	Process: Material	Circumstance: Temporal
Given	New information	

The headline below, Example (iii), comes from the personal finance section of a newspaper and is a question addressed directly to the readers, presumably to attract them to an article relating deflation to their personal circumstances. It clearly illustrates the interpersonal function of the interrogative clause and differs grammatically from (i) and (ii) above in terms of Mood which are both declarative clauses.

(iii)

Will	deflation	affect	your lifestyle?
Finite	Subject	Predicator	Complement
	Participant: Actor	Process: Material	Participant: Goal

As well as these key lexicogrammatical tools, SFL tools include

- statistical comparison techniques
- comparisons of lexical density and frequency
- Rhetorical Structure Theory
- corpus linguistics

An additional current interest in SFL (Halliday and Matthiessen 2006: 231 and Halliday and Webster 2014: 18–20 and elsewhere), and one which may prove to be of particular relevance to CDA, is the question of *indeterminacy* in language.

In actual instances of language use, these analytic resources interact throughout.

5.1 Lexis and collocation

In CDA, it is perhaps the lexical component of the grammar that has been of major significance, especially in the critique of derogatory and discriminatory use of gendered language and abusive racial terminology. This has not necessarily utilised SFL tools (van Dijk 1998: 277–312, for instance) but much has. A connected concern has been the continued construction of the detailed racial, religious and ethnic categorization used in national censuses, education systems and on birth certificates at various times in the Republic of South Africa, the United States, Latin America and elsewhere and its subsequent use in institutional control. (Feagin 2000: 102–137; Bloor and Bloor 2007: 88–92). The complexity of systems used to categorise and control human beings is illustrated from a report by the US Census Bureau (Humes, Jones and Roberts 2011), which lists the categories and details the possible combinations of the six basic racial categories used, including six categories for those who report only one race, and 57 for those who report two or more races.

Lexis has also played an important part in critiques of environmental discourse and the ways in which 'actual and metaphorical space' are discursively constructed. (McElhinny 2006: 123). McElhinny's detailed study of the texts relating to a specific cultural landscape north of Toronto shows how environmental protestors develop the discourse needed to preserve the land for social use.

Other aspects of lexical study of interest have been collocation, connotation and usage in specific varieties and contexts. Collocation concerns the specific co-text of a word and the way the combination of words in a phrase can carry significant changes in meaning. Thus, for example, the word *family* takes on specific positive or negative values depending on the context of use and its collocates. Presented positively, we find *family values* (much loved by the British Prime Minister Thatcher) and *hard-working families* (a favourite of current politicians) while *Holy Family* retains its Christian religious associations. *Problem families, dysfunctional families* and even *single parent families* have been used by politicians and the media less favourably. Family members, such as *brother* and *sister,* take on different senses in political or Trades Union groups (and in some religious contexts) where they are used as terms of address to express solidarity with other members of an organisation or perceived groups.

Barkho's (2011) study of the news reporting of conflict in the Middle East uses both ethnographic techniques and SFL analysis of imposed lexical choices (see also Barkho and Richardson 2010). He interviewed editors and journalists in two news broadcasting institutions (BBC and Al-Jazeera English), and described how they exercised control over news reporting in English with the use of confidential internal guidelines. These 'guidelines' are themselves texts that, Barkho explains, "inevitably keep in place each radio station's own discursive and social interpretations" of conflict situations (2011: 307) He discusses various aspects of the language of the Guidelines, but here we focus on the lexis.

Barkho (2011: 300–303) considers the restrictions on the lexicon and how this sustains specific ideologies. The BBC, while requiring journalists to "avoid using terminology favoured by one side or another in any dispute", nevertheless make it obligatory to use the terms they specifically recommend. The collocation of the neutral word *territories* is a case in point. Lexically, journalists are told that Israel's preferred phrase to describe the West Bank and Gaza Strip is *disputed territories* and told to use this rather than *occupied territories,* thus contradicting its own requirement to avoid favouring either side in the conflict. Al-Jazeera, on the other hand, specifically says that they will not use the term '*disputed territories*'. Their guidelines read: "Israel prefers the term. We will not use".

5.2 Transitivity in SFL

A widely used tool of analysis in CDA is the SFL transitivity system, which should not be confused with the simpler transitive/intransitive dichotomy in traditional grammar.

In SFL transitivity analysis, three categories can be identified: *processes, participants* and (optionally) *circumstances*. Each category has a number of subcategories. As far as CDA is concerned, when realised in discourse, this is a focus of analysis in the critical evaluation of *content* and *ideology*.

Consider the following example (1) from a recent newspaper article, which is a reply to a rhetorical question given by the journalist: 'But can we trust Mr Cameron's promises?' The Process in the clause is italicised.

(1) His government (Actor) *has overseen* (Process: Material) dramatic increases in most forms of taxation.

This clause clearly presents Cameron's government as allowing increases in taxation, but does not emphasise the government's total responsibility for the increases as would be the case if the journalist had written (2):

(2) His government (Actor) *has* dramatically *increased* (Process: Material) most forms of taxation.

Moreover, the writer could have avoided presenting the government as Actor in this case and so deflected responsibility. 'Under his government' is here a Circumstance: Location (in time):

(3) Most forms of taxation (Actor) *have increased* (Process: Material) dramatically under his government.

Li (2011) uses SFL analysis of transitivity in contrasting newspaper headlines and news reports of the collision that took place on 1 April 2001 between a US surveillance plane and a Chinese fighter jet in the South China Sea. As a result, the Chinese plane crashed, the pilot was killed, and the US plane made an emergency landing on Hainan Island where the plane and the crew were held in custody. She contrasts reports in the *New York Times* with those in *China Daily,* an official English language newspaper published in China.

   She first argues that the concept of construal in cognitive linguistics is consistent with the SFL concept of transitivity, following the principle that meaning in text is "always representation for some ideological point of view, as managed through the inevitable structuring force of transitivity" (Fowler 1991: 214). She then seeks to support this view with an analysis of the transitivity structures in headlines and front page news articles using SFL tools to demonstrate how the papers differ in creating versions of reality and in apportioning blame for the incident. She contrasts the numbers of different types of processes in the two newspapers and points to the variation in choice of participants and processes. For example, the *New York Times* (NYT) stresses the role of the USA in attempting to reach a settlement to the dispute, by presenting US citizens as 'sayers' in verbal processes, in contrast to *China Daily* (CD), in which the Chinese have prominence as 'sayers':

• President Bush (Sayer) demanded (Verbal Process) the prompt and safe return of the crew. (NYT)
• White House officials (Sayer) said (Verbal Process) they wanted to lower the diplomatic temperature. (NYT)
• President Jang (Sayer) praised (Verbal Process) Wang and Zhao for their courage.
• The general (Sayer) pointed out (Verbal Process) that the US side should take full responsibility for the collision.

Li also makes use of many other aspects of SFL transitivity analysis, demonstrating, as she claims, that writers' choices of transitivity patterns are ideologically oriented rather than neutral choices.

5.3 Group and clause

Fairclough (2004: 106) discusses the language used by Prime Minister Blair to construct "a relationship between the global and the national". Fairclough's main concern is to see the text as a part of a much wider study of the 'new capitalism' and its "impact on politics, education, artistic production, and many other areas of social life" (2004: 103).

Having identified Blair's use of the nominal groups *the modern world, the new global economy, the new world* and *the new economic order,* he extends lexical analysis to demonstrate how these constructed nominal groups are used at clause level to shift the responsibility of political action away from himself or the government and onto supposed global forces. After Hay and Rosamund 2002, he sees this as a rhetorical strategy that can legitimise "national policy change in terms of inexorable and uncontrollable processes" (2004: 114). His analysis shows how such nominal groups are used as participants in clauses. For example, in the following examples from Blair's speech the italicised nominal groups represent the constructed abstract concept of some kind of unified economic reality. In Example (1) it is shown to be subjected to 'change', an abstract metaphor that is not attributed to any outside agent in the sense of a human participant. In linguistic terminology the abstract nominal group can take on a variety of grammatical roles, such as Subject of a clause fulfilling the role of Goal in (1) and of Actor in (2) and (3). This same abstract 'world' is itself presented as a powerful force that can influence not only the functioning of business but also, in (3), of government. Note also that 'challenge' is arguably a verbal process, representing a spoken act metaphorically. This, however, points to the questionable reality of the whole utterance.

(1) *The modern world* is swept by change.
(2) *This new world* challenges business to be innovative and creative, to improve performance continuously, to build new alliances and ventures.
(3) But *it* also challenges government to create and execute a new approach to industrial policy.

This construct forms the basis of the rest of the speech which goes on to present 'it' as the reason for 'a culture of enterprise' and 'commercial success' in everything from government and business to creativity, education and even knowledge.

Elsewhere, Fairclough (2001) points to linguistic characteristics that pervade neo-capitalist discourses. One of the foremost is that processes are presented without accountable human agents as in the examples above. Other characteristics are the use of a timeless historical present tense that implies a general truth and the unquestioning statement of controversial policies. These are major features of the political speech that we discuss in the next section of this chapter.

6. Case study: a political speech

In this section, we continue to investigate the linguistic features identified by Fairclough (2001, 2004) which are employed by certain politicians to construct ideas designed to effect social change. Fairclough (1993) was almost certainly the first CD analyst to address the significant fact that education in Britain has increasingly adopted a market-oriented discourse.

In related work, Mulderrig (2005), using SFL-influenced corpus analysis, investigated the grammar of government white papers on education, commenting on the use of managerial discourse. Mautner (2005) studied the discourse around the key words related to the idea of the *entrepreneurial* university, addressing the changing relationship between universities and business worldwide. In her article, she cites a short statement from a speech on higher education given by David Blunkett (2000), then Secretary of State for Education and Employment, in which he promotes major restructuring of the university sector. Here, we look in more detail at features of that speech to illustrate how the language used presents government's policy as an unavoidable consequence of the way the world is.

Contextually, the mode is a public speech, written-to-be-spoken. Blunkett was speaking as policy maker to an educated and informed audience. The speech was presented to a university audience rather than to the general public and differs in many respects from speeches of Prime Minister Tony Blair to the general public. Many of Blair's speeches were characterised by a markedly frequent use of interpersonal features: personal pronouns, interrogatives, appraisal (in this case explicit, positive stance), and simple and incomplete clauses.

Blunkett, on the other hand, is speaking more formally. Given the context, he must have expected his speech to be published, quoted in the press, and read critically by people in higher education. The lexis is often specialised and abstract. There are few instances of specific appraisal or evaluation. Grammatically, the sentences tend to be complex, and typically involve long nominal groups and the use of traditional and grammatical metaphor. The full speech has 26 pages, over a hundred numbered paragraphs and over 10,575 words, so it cannot be reproduced here in full, but typical features and selected paragraphs will be discussed.

Although the speech is said to be 'on higher education', it is essentially about finance. In the UK, we have traditionally looked to universities for teaching and research, but in Blunkett's discourse, their 'role' is changing to a focus on competition, business and the economy. Interestingly, the word *money* itself appears only once in the whole speech:

• Money now moves round the globe at the touch of a button, and the sums are huge.

The sentence is in a paragraph (8) that does not mention universities, but introduces the 'global market', the same global economy that Fairclough identified as responsible for 'challenging the government'.

A major feature of Blunkett's lexis is the use of metaphor to represent non-human concepts as Actors in processes normally undertaken by people. One example is the word *role,* not used for a human being but applied to higher education:

• The role of higher education in securing economic competitiveness
• The wider role of higher education in the knowledge economy
• Nor is this role limited to science and technology sectors; innovation in the arts is crucial to business competitiveness
• This critical role places a special responsibility on higher education institutions to forge links with business

Notice, however, that the expression *knowledge economy* appears ten times in the speech. Other indicative expressions from the speech include: *the global market for higher education, the growth of the learning markets, business-university partnerships, corporate universities, the University for Industry, links with business.*

Here are two typical paragraphs, with verbal groups italicised, and numbered as in the original:

(9) The powerhouses of the new global economy *are* innovation and ideas, skills and knowledge. These *are* now the tools for success and prosperity as much as natural resources and physical labour power *were* in the past century.

(10) Higher education *is* at the centre of these developments. Across the world, its shape, structure and purposes *are undergoing* transformation because of globalisation. At the same time, it *provides* research and innovation, scholarship and teaching which *equip* individuals and businesses *to respond* to global change. World class higher education *ensures* that countries *can grow* and *sustain* high-skill businesses, and *attract* and *retain* the most highly-skilled people. It *endows* people with creative and moral capacities, thinking skills and depth knowledge that *underpin* our economic competitiveness and our wider quality of life. It *is* therefore at the heart of the productive capacity of the new economy and the prosperity of our democracy.

The first four clauses have relational (identifying) processes, known as 'equatives'. This indicates that the two key participants are interchangeable in terms of the Subject and Complement functions if we ignore cohesive constraints. Thus, the Complement, '*innovation and ideas, skills and knowledge*' is presented as being equivalent to '*the powerhouses of the new global economy*'. The first sentence in (10) is also relational, but here the process is attributive, because being 'at the centre of these developments' (Attribute) is presented as a quality that higher education (Carrier) possesses. The final sentence has the same process and participant pattern: "It is at the heart of the productive capacity of the new economy and the prosperity of our democracy".

The further 11 verbal groups are material processes. Six have 'higher education' or its products (*research, innovation, scholarship, teaching*) as participants. The verbal groups are: *are undergoing, provides, equip, ensures, endows, underpins*. Of the other five, one (*respond*) has the Actor *individuals and businesses*). The other four (*can grow, sustain, attract, retain*) have *countries* as Actor. Thus higher education is presented as responsible not only for businesses responding to global change but also for countries growing and sustaining businesses.

With the exception of the final clause of (9) referring to 'the past century', the ideas in paragraphs (9) and (10) are presented in the present simple tense as indisputable facts, relating to processes that are existential (for example *is, are*) and material (*grow, sustain, equip*). They are not questioned and no arguments are offered to support them. This confident stance is seen throughout. Take the example:

- There is no doubt [[that globalisation and the arrival of the knowledge economy have intensified the competitive pressures on higher education institutions]].

This sentence has two clauses; the second is indicated with double square brackets. The sentence begins "There is no doubt", showing that the author believes the ensuing proposition [that etc.], but doesn't expressly state it as his belief but rather as an unchallengeable fact. It is an existential process rather than a relational (attributive) or mental process. Compare *I have no doubt,* which attributes the lack of doubt (i.e., the claim that the proposition is true) to the author; or *I do not doubt,* which by denying the mental process of doubting in the case of the author implies the mental process of believing. In both instances of these hypothetical alternatives, unlike the actual original, the responsibility for the embedded claim is explicitly with the author. It is a basic principle in SFL that meaning is fully understood only against the range of choices available to the speaker.

The sentence also contains an example of a grammatical metaphor, another frequent feature in Blunkett's technique. '*The knowledge economy*' is a condensation of various complicated claims into a nominal group (= a thing) which can '*arrive*' (material process), but this process is also nominalised as '*arrival*', which is in turn capable of conflating with the function of Actor in a material process '*have intensified*'. '*The competitive pressures on higher education institutions*' condenses the notions that some people compete and thereby press higher education institutions (to unspecified action). Human actions are presented as abstract entities (*pressures*), and the whole proposition resembles the statement of an axiom of physical science, seemingly irrefutable. This is a feature of the whole text: the inevitability of the marketization of universities that must become part of the for-profit sector of the economy, epitomised in the term '*the knowledge economy*'.

At the end of section 2 above, we mention appraisal analysis, a way in which we consciously or unconsciously express our stance or attitude to the topic under discussion. In Blunkett's speech he is clearly advocating and promoting a series of policies leading to closer links between the universities and business and the marketization of education, but it is surprising how few explicit examples of appraisal occur in the text. Where they do, they appear as positive evaluations of practices that Blunkett seeks to encourage. The word *important,* for example, is applied to the following, with the paragraph number in parentheses: *diversity* (30); *research funding* (42 and 43); *reforms* (being introduced by government) (62); *collaboration between universities* (82); *entrepreneurial universities* (which are said to be *as important* as *entrepreneurial businesses*) (87).

Most examples of positive appraisal come between paragraphs 38–55, when Blunkett evaluates *successful programmes* of partnerships between universities and business or industry. *Contract work for industry* and *industrial liaison* he refers to as *vital work* (paragraph 51 and 52), and *higher education-business links* are also evaluated as *vital* (54).

In contrast to *success,* in paragraph (55), he uses the word *need* (italicised) to make a negative evaluation. Here he is not expressing the view of the universities; it is not necessarily what the universities themselves 'need' or 'want'. Blunkett is expressing his own personal stance (or the government's position) that the universities should *open up to business, become more entrepreneurial and aggressive, become more responsive to new markets, and generate income from new sources.*

(55) Universities *need* to have incentives, particularly through the rationalised and better focused government support I have outlined, to open up to business. But they also *need* to become more entrepreneurial and aggressive in seeking new markets. For genuine diversity to flourish in higher education, universities and colleges *need* to become more responsive to new markets, and to generate income from new sources, as the most successful have done.

In SFL terminology, 'need' here is not a Mental Process expressing desire or emotion, but an Attributive: Possessive Process expressing the negative idea that, in the view of the speaker, universities lack attributes that they ought to have. From the point of view of appraisal, Blunkett is making a negative judgement in order to pursue his ideological aims of making "changes in the shape, structure, management and funding of the sector", (paragraph 79). That includes moving education funding away from the responsibility of the state and making it the responsibility of the institutions themselves to raise money from business and industry, from research-funding bodies, from the 'consumers' (British and international students) and from purchasers of specialist courses.

7. Conclusion

In this chapter we have attempted to indicate how systemic functional linguistics has been applied in critical discourse analysis. We have also discussed some of the objections to the use of linguistic analysis and argued for a blending of methods in appropriate studies. This has necessitated the use of some technical terminology, but space forbids, of course, anything like a complete account of the tools available.

For readers who would like a fuller account of the analytical potential of this branch of linguistics applied to the study of texts, we recommend Halliday and Webster (2014: 219), which, although not CDA, contains detailed analysis of long speeches from varied sources (Nixon, Obama and Steve Jobs among others) and shows how ideational, interpersonal and textual meaning 'are discoverable in text', and how some types of analysis (including statistical analysis) can help us gain new perspectives on meaning in discourse.

Further reading

Bartlett, T. (2014). *Analysing power in language: A practical guide*. London, New York: Routledge.
This textbook introduces the analysis of discourse using SFL tools, but always with a consideration of a critical dimension. To this end, Bartlett refers to social factors that are relevant to the text in question (such as speaker status and their cultural capital) and engages readers in discussion questions about such issues.
Martin, J. R. and White, P. R. (2005). *The language of evaluation: Appraisal in English*. Basingstoke, New York: Palgrave Macmillan.
This is the first account of the appraisal framework, an approach to linguistic analysis situated within SFL. Appraisal theory examines the way language users can negotiate position (such as status, power and values) and express attitudes (such as judgement, appreciation and attitude). It has been applied to the issue of subjectivity v. objectivity in journalism. See also: Peter White's website www.grammatics.com/appraisal
Halliday, M.A.K. and Webster, J.J. (eds.) (2009). *Continuum companion to systemic functional linguistics*. London, New York: Continuum.
This collection of articles by key SFL linguists addresses both the significant principles of functional linguistics and explains how they relate to contexts of application. It includes a useful chapter on resources and key words.
Bloor, T. and Bloor, M. (2013). *The functional analysis of English,* 3rd edn. London, New York: Routledge.
For readers with no background in SFL, this introduction provides the terminology and methods of analysis necessary for using the lexicogrammar. It includes a chapter on applications of Halliday's work and one on historical perspectives. It incorporates a detailed glossary and practice exercises with answers.

References

Barkho, J. (2011). The role of internal guidelines in shaping news narratives: Ethnographic insights into the discursive rhetoric of Middle East reporting by the BBC and Al-Jazeera English. *Critical Discourse Studies* 8(4): 297–309.
Barkho, J. and Richardson, J. (2010). A critique of BBC's Middle East news production strategy. *American Communication Journal* 12: 1–15.
Blommaert, J. (2005). *Discourse*. Cambridge: Cambridge University Press.
Bloor, M. (2016). The construal of terminal illness in online medical texts: Social distance and semantic space. In S. Gardner and S. Alsop (eds.), *Systemic functional linguistics in a digital age,* pp. 12–133. London: Equinox.
Bloor, M. and Bloor, T. (2007). *The practice of critical discourse analysis*. London and New York: Routledge. (Former publishers: Hodder Arnold).
Bloor, M. and Bloor, T. (2014). Critical discourse analysis. In K.P. Schneider and A.-M. Simon-Vanden-Bergen (eds.), *Pragmatics of discourse,* 189–214. Berlin: Mouton de Gruyter.
Bloor, T. and Bloor, M. (2013). *The functional analysis of English,* 3rd edn. London and New York: Routledge.
Blunkett, D. (2000). Speech on Higher Education. Given at Greenwich University, February 2000. Accessed April 2015, http://cmsl.gre.ac.uk/dfee
Fairclough, N. (1989). *Language and power*. London: Longman.

Meriel Bloor and Thomas Bloor

Fairclough, N. (1993). Critical discourse analysis and the marketization of public discourse: The universities. *Discourse and Society* 4(2): 133–163.

Fairclough, N. (2001). Critical discourse analysis as a method in social scientific research. In R. Wodak and M. Meyer (eds.), *Methods of critical discourse analysis,* 121–138. London: Sage.

Fairclough, N. (2003). *Analysing discourse: Textual analysis for social research.* London and New York: Routledge.

Fairclough, N. (2004). Critical discourse analysis in researching language in the new capitalism: Overdetermination, transdisciplinarity, and textual analysis. In L. Young and C. Harrison, (eds.), Systemic linguistics and critical discourse analysis. 103–122. London: Continuum.

Fairclough, N., Graham, P., Lemke, J., Wodak, R. (2004). Introduction to discourse studies. *Critical Discourse Studies* 1(1): 1–7.

Feagin, J. R. (2000). *Racist America.* New York and London: Routledge.

Fowler, R. (1991). *Language in the news: Discourse and ideology in the press.* London: Routledge.

Fowler, R., Hodge, B., Kress, G. and Trew, T. (1979). *Language and control.* London: Routledge and Kegan Paul.

Galasiński, D. (2011). The patient's world: Discourse analysis and ethnography. *Critical Discourse Studies* 8(4): 253–265.

Gregory, M. and Carroll, S. (1976). *Language and situation: Language varieties and their social contexts.* London: Routledge and Kegan Paul.

Halliday, M.A.K. (1970). Language structure and language function. In J. Lyons (ed.), *New horizons in linguistics,* 140–165. Harmondsworth: Penguin.

Halliday, M.A.K. (1973). *Explorations in the functions of language.* London: Edward Arnold.

Halliday, M.A.K. (1978). *Language as a social semiotic.* London: Edward Arnold.

Halliday, M.A.K. (2001). Is the grammar neutral? In J.J. Webster (ed.), *On language and linguistics,* 271–292. Volume 3 of Halliday's collected works. London/New York: Continuum.

Halliday, M.A.K. and Hasan, R. (1976). *Cohesion in English.* London: Longman.

Halliday, M.A.K. and Hasan, R. (1989). *Language context and text: Aspects of language in a social-semiotic perspective.* Oxford: Oxford University Press.

Halliday, M.A.K. and Matthiessen, C.M.I.M. (2006). *Construing experience through meaning: A language-based approach to cognition.* London and New York: Continuum. (Original Edition 1999).

Halliday, M.A.K. and Matthiessen, C.M.I.M. (2013 [2004]). *Introduction to functional grammar.* London and New York: Routledge.

Halliday, M.A.K. and Webster, J. J. (2014). *Text linguistics: The how and why of meaning.* Sheffield: Equinox.

Hay, C. and Rosamund, B. (2002). Globalization, European integration and the discursive construction of economic imperatives. *Journal of European Public Policy* 9(2): 147–167.

Hodge, B. (1979). Newspapers and communities. In R. Fowler, B. Hodge, G. Kress and T. Trew (eds.), *Language and control,* 157–174. London: Routledge and Kegan Paul.

Humes, K. R., Jones, N. A. and Roberts, R. (2011). Overview of race and Hispanic origin: 2010. United States Census Bureau, Accessed January 2016, www.census.gov

Kress, G. and Hodge, R. (1979). *Language as ideology.* London: Routledge.

Lakoff, G. and Johnson, M. (1980). *Metaphors we live by.* Chicago: University of Chicago Press.

Li, J. (2011). Collision of language in news discourse: A functional–cognitive perspective on transitivity. *Critical Discourse Studies* 8(3): 203–219.

McElhinny, B. (2006). Written in sand: Language and landscape in an environmental dispute in Southern Ontario. *Critical Discourse Studies* 3: 123–153.

Martin, J. (1992). *English text: System and structure.* Amsterdam: Benjamins.

Martin, J. R. and White, P.R.R. (2005). *The language of evaluation.* Basingstoke: Palgrave Macmillan.

Mautner, G. (2005). The entrepreneurial university. *Critical Discourse Studies* 2(2): 95–120.

Mulderrig, J. (2005). The grammar of governance. *Critical Discourse Studies* 8(1): 45–68.

Rosch, E. (1978). Principles of categorization. In E. Rosch and B.B. Lloyd (eds.), *Cognition and categorization,* 27–48. Hillsdale: Erlbaum.

van Dijk, T. (1998). *Ideology: A multidisciplinary approach.* London: Sage.

van Dijk, T. (2008). *Discourse and context,* Chapter 2. Cambridge: Cambridge University Press.

van Leeuwen, T. (2008). *Discourse and practice.* Oxford and New York: Oxford University Press.

Young, L. and Harrison, C. (eds.) (2004). *Systemic functional linguistics and critical discourse studies: Studies in social change.* London and New York: Continuum.

11

Critical discourse studies and context*

John Flowerdew

Introduction

Discourse Studies is concerned with the study of the interaction of text and context, and Critical Discourse Studies is concerned with a critical approach to such analysis. As Richardson writes (this volume) "CDA is, properly, the critical analysis of text in context". Furthermore CDS sees discourse as both socially constituted and constitutive; that is to say, there is a dialectical relation between social context and text. In actual practice, however, work in CDS has tended to place more emphasis on the structure and functions of text and talk than the context within which it occurs. Context often tends to be assumed as a given. As Martinez Guillem (this volume) states, "a definition of context is assumed to stem out of the ways in which this notion is deployed in particular analyses". This makes it difficult to write a typical handbook chapter on the topic of context in CDS, given that CDS studies focussing primarily on the topic are not available. And yet, Martinez Guillem continues, "as van Dijk (2008) emphasises, if the notion of context is so crucial in our studies, instead of taking it for granted we may benefit from devoting some time to the examination of context per se".

In the absence of books and articles specifically devoted to context in CDS, what I will do in this chapter, therefore, is, following some preliminary definitions and characterisations of context, review various approaches to context from different schools of discourse analysis which might be applicable and which may have been applied in CDS. CDS is, after all, an approach rather than a method, and therefore different conceptions of context may be relevant depending on the goals of the study. Following this, I will present a case study CDS analysis of my own which embodies a rich notion of context, focussing on the Hong Kong *Occupy* movement, in order to show a variety of approaches to context with regard to this event.

Definitions and characterisations of context

First, I should at least provide some possible definitions of context, even though, as Goodwin and Duranti (1992: 2) state, context is "notoriously hard to define". One rather general definition is that of Blommaert (2005: 251), who defines it as "the totality of conditions under which discourse is being produced, circulated and interpreted". Somewhat more specific is the definition provided by van Dijk (2005: 237) who defines context as "the cognitive, social, political, cultural and historical *environments* of discourse" (original emphasis). (See Flowerdew 2014 for further definitions). Early approaches used various metaphors to depict context. Thus Goodwin and Duranti (1992) adopt the metaphor of figure (the text) and ground (the context). Various others invoke the metaphor of the frame, where context is the frame within which the text is located (Bateson 1955; Goffman 1974; Tannen 1993). Other researchers prefer to focus on levels of context. Thus, Halliday and Hasan (1985) distinguish text, co-text, context of situation and context of culture. In addition to co-text, Wodak (2002) includes in her model of context the other texts and discourses that the text draws upon, the conditions of text production, distribution and reception, and the wider sociopolitical context.

Text and context are generally construed to be in a "mutually reflexive" relationship (Goodwin and Duranti 1992: 31; also van Dijk 2008), where text influences context and context influences text. Analysis, according to this view, involves a continual shunting between text and context (Fairclough, Mulderrig and Wodak 2011). The process by which text and context come together in the creation of meaning is referred to as contextualisation (by text, we nowadays mean any semiotic feature, including signs, symbols and physical embodiment). According to van Dijk (2008) (and other social-cognitivists), contextualisation is regulated by what he refers to as a 'K-device', which is the mutual knowledge shared by speaker and hearer. Knowledge – which may be personal, interpersonal, group, institutional, national or cultural – is stored as mental models, which are invoked in discourse processing (van Dijk 2005; see also Boyd and Filardo-Llamas this volume). Another factor that needs to be taken into account is that context is dynamic, changing as the discourse progresses (Goodwin and Duranti 1992; O'Halloran, Tan and E 2014). It is also negotiated between the participants in a discourse, depending upon their mental models. Where mental models do not match, there may be misunderstanding; either that, or power, which, as Foucault emphasises, is another important contextual feature (e.g., Rabinow 1991) may decide which interpretation is to prevail.

A particular type of contextual relation that has received a lot of attention in CDS is that of intertextuality (Bakhtin 1981; Kristeva 1980), the process whereby textual features of one text reappear in another. This means that an individual text may not be analysed without considering other prior texts with which it may relate. Intertextuality is often used to create presuppositions, to negate elements of prior text, and for the purposes of parody and irony. Fairclough (1992) breaks intertextuality down into *manifest* intertextuality and *constitutive* intertextuality: the former refers to overt uses of citation, quotation and paraphrase, while the latter refers to generic features that do not leave an obvious trace (Flowerdew 2013: 144). Constitutive intertextuality is sometimes referred to as *interdiscursivity* by other CDS practitioners. When an element from one text is decontextualized and inserted into another text, this process is referred to as recontextualisation (also resemiotisation); such a process inevitably involves the application of a new meaning to the recontextualised element, which, of course, makes the process amenable to manipulation. Identity, the image one has of oneself or is held by others and which can apply to individuals or to groups, although not usually mentioned as a feature of context, is also an important contextual factor, because the image one has of oneself or of others will affect one's interpretation of their actions and motivations.

Some early models of context

Malinowski, Firth, Halliday, Sapir and Whorf

Since de Saussure's (1977 [1916]) distinction between langue and parole and Chomsky's later (1965) separation of competence from performance, there has been a trend in linguistic theory to deny a role for context and to focus on the decontextualized sentence. At the same time, however, other, more socially oriented linguists emphasised the importance of context in the interpretation of utterances. As the anthropologist Malinowski famously stated:

> A word without linguistic context is a mere figment and stands for nothing by itself, so in the reality of a spoken living tongue, the utterance has no meaning except in the context of situation.
>
> *(1923: 307)*

Firth, a colleague of Malinowski, and Halliday, a student of Firth's, similarly emphasised the role of context, distinguishing between the context of situation (for text), and the broader context of culture (for situations) (Halliday 1999: 7). At the same time, Sapir and Whorf, more cognitive in orientation, developed the idea of a language representing the mental life of its speakers. Thus, the famous Sapir-Whorf hypothesis states that the culture underlying a language represents the context within which that language will be interpreted (e.g., Pinker 1994).

Hymes

Another influential model of context is represented by Hymes's (1962) SPEAKING mnemonic (Table 11.1), a set of features that can be used in interpreting any utterance:

Hymes's model was originally developed for his ethnography of communication, but has also been applied more widely.

Pragmatics

Pragmatics, and in particular Gricean pragmatics (Grice 1989 [1967]; Sperber and Wilson 1995), assigns an essential role in communication to context. The role of context is clear in Grice's (1989 [1967]) cooperative principle, according to which the interpretation of utterances is an inferential process, based on rational thought and context. As Polyzou (this volume), puts it, "Broadly speaking, cognitive pragmatics accounts provide the potential for accounting for the impact of context on discourse and of discourse on context, mediated by the cognitions of the participants in discursive and social action". Presupposition, indirect speech acts, irony, and face and politeness phenomena are other features dealt with in pragmatics which depend upon context for their interpretation. Analysis of such contextual features makes it possible to reveal the implicit assumptions that may lay behind a given utterance. One critique

Table 11.1 Hymes's speaking mnemonic

Setting	Physical or abstract setting (e.g., office or church service)
Participants	Speaker, hearer, overhearer
Ends	Purpose, goals and outcomes
Act Sequence	Form the event takes, ordering of speech acts
Key	Tone, manner, spirit of the speech acts
Instrumentalities	Channel or mode (e.g., telephone, spoken or written)
Norms	Norms of interaction and interpretation
Genre	Type of speech event (e.g., story, joke, lecture)

of pragmatic approaches to CDS is that, while pragmatics does involve inference and therefore context, it is too individualistic and takes an idealised view of communication and fails to take into account socio-contextual factors and power imbalances in interaction (Fairclough 2001: 7–8, as reported in Polyzou this volume). In spite of this critique on the part of Fairclough, he does employ pragmatic analysis in his own work (see also Wodak 2007 for a positive view of the role of pragmatics in CDS.)

More recent models

Since these early models of context, different schools of linguistics and discourse analysis have developed notions of context further. Given that CDS is an approach and not a (single) method, as already mentioned, different conceptions of context may be relevant, depending on the goals of the study. I will now mention some of these models and briefly outline how I see their potential strengths and weakness for CDS.

Conversation Analysis (CA)

CA views context as constructed moment by moment through conversational moves (Bhatia, Jones and Flowerdew 2008: 16). There are in fact two views here: a strong view and a weak view. Representing the strong view, Schegloff (e.g., 1987) emphasises what he refers to as *procedural consequentiality*, the idea that the evidence of context needs to be located in the sequence of speaker turns. The weaker view argues for going outside the immediate interactional context to the institutional context to arrive at a more grounded analysis (e.g., Drew and Heritage (1993).[1] In fact, there was an interesting debate between Billig (1996, 1999), Schegloff (1997, 1999) and Wetherell (1998) on whether or not to go outside the text.

As far as it might be applied in CDS, CA allows critical discourse analysts to do fine-grained analysis of naturally occurring data in real-life contexts. Given the critique of the strong view of not going outside the text, combining CA with other social research methodologies, such as ethnography, may help to counter these criticisms (Flowerdew 2012). Waring (2014), for example, takes into account both the institutional and the sequential contexts in a CA analysis of second language classroom interaction.

Systemic Functional Linguistics (SFL)

SFL is an approach to grammar and discourse that has a three-dimensional model of context: field of discourse (the subject matter of the text), tenor of discourse (the relations between the participants and their attitudes, as presented in the discourse), and mode of discourse (the channel (speech or writing) and rhetorical role (didactic, persuasive, aggressive, etc.) (see Bloor and Bloor, p. 154). Together these three dimensions work together to constitute different varieties of language, i.e., registers (Halliday, McIntosh and Strevens 1964). For example, a pedagogic register is characterised by Rose and Martin (2014) as sequences of learning activities (field), pedagogic relations between learners and teachers (tenor) and modalities of learning – spoken, written, visual and manual (mode).

A number of CDS practitioners have claimed allegiance to SFL (e.g., Fowler 1996; Fairclough 2003). SFL enables critical discourse analysts to identify form–function links and thereby to relate language form to context. Some criticise SFL for lacking enough attention to analysing context (van Dijk 2008), and that it may be difficult to decide which feature of the lexicogrammar corresponds to which contextual parameter. Proponents of SFL, on the other hand, argue that SFL is still the only school with a robust model to link text and context systematically.

Ethnographic approaches

Ethnographic approaches to discourse and context owe much to American anthropological linguistics (e.g., Hymes 1962) and regard social context as the central aspect of communication. Ethnographic approaches have had an important influence on CDS (e.g., Krzyżanowski 2011, this volume; Reisigl and Wodak 2001; Wodak 2014), encouraging analysts to rely relatively less on close analysis of linguistic data and more on text-external social and contextual factors. There is, thus, a danger in overlooking linguistic evidence, while at the same time the risk of not-in-depth-enough ethnographic analysis. However, as Krzyżanowski (2011) argues, there is no doubt that the use of ethnography, combined with more traditional (textual) data sources, allows CDS to better understand text-external social and contextual factors.

Cognitive Linguistics (CogLing)

The CogLing approach to discourse views contexts as mental models (e.g., van Dijk 2009; Hart this volume). Contexts are considered as ultimately constructed in the cognitive systems of interacting group members. Evidence for the mental conceptualisation of context can be found by tracking patterns in language use. For example, the study of conceptual metaphor (Lakoff and Johnson 1980) can reveal ideological functions (e.g., Charteris-Black 2004; Ng this volume). Or, in a rather different approach, grammatical patterning may also be related to ideological functions (e.g., Hart 2014, this volume). In this regard, the CogLing approach to context reveals its antecedents in the critical linguistics of Fowler, Hodge, Kress and Trew (1979), the precursor to CDS.

It is a claim of cognitive approaches to CDS that they include a cognitive interface between discourse and society, whereas most CDS studies only describe and explain discourse in terms of its social and political contexts. For example, O'Halloran (2003) revisits the interpretation stage of CDS from a cognitive point of view, and proposes an "idealized reader framework" which integrates various cognitive theories. Cognitive approaches thus offer an analysis of the interpretation stage of discourse. "Interpretation-stage analysis is necessary if one wants to account for the discursive construction of social and political contexts since contexts are ultimately construed in the cognitive systems of interacting group members" (Hart 2014: 163).

Corpus Linguistics (CorpLing)

CorpLing's potential for the study of the text/context interface in CDS lies in its ability to compare the use of language in a specific target corpus of text and a reference corpus, to show how language use in a specific context varies from that found more generally. For example, Baker's (2014) critical analysis of the discourse of homosexuality used corpus tools to show how the meaning of the word *always* in such discourse in the *Daily Mail* may be specific to the particular context of that newspaper. Pioneering work on corpus approaches to CDS are cited in Subtirelu and Baker this volume. CorpLing allows CDS to work with much larger data volumes, thus reducing researcher bias (Hardt-Mautner 1995). It also allows CDS to qualitatively and quantitatively examine a given language feature's collocational environments, semantic patterns and discourse functions (Hardt-Mautner 1995). In my 1997 corpus-based study of the discourse of the last Hong Kong governor, Chris Patten, I showed how the consistent use in positive environments of certain words and phrases (referred to as semantic prosody) like *rule of law, the individual, economy* and *democracy* contributed to the last British Hong Kong Governor's creation of a myth about the British legacy to Hong Kong. The following words, for example, collocated with the word *economy* or *economic: choice, freedom, fairness, cheerfulness, growth, good health, virtues, benefits, positive change, success, talent* and *initiative* (465). CorpLing has been criticised for decontextualizing data and for limiting the analysis to a bottom-up type of investigation (Widdowson 1998, 2000, 2004; Swales 2002). This may be alleviated, of course by integrating CorpLing with other context-oriented approaches to discourse (Flowerdew 2008; Baker et al. 2008).

Multi-Modal Discourse Analysis (MMDA)

If the view on context of corpus linguistics might be described as being at a micro-level, then that of multi-modal discourse analysis can be viewed at the opposite extreme, at a macro-level, because it involves all semiotic systems, not just language use, which is the focus of corpus linguistics (and which, until relatively recently, has traditionally been the main focus of all approaches to CDS). MMDA is influenced by the work of Halliday (1978) and was pioneered by Kress and van Leeuwen (1996) (both followers of Halliday and CDS practitioners) (Ledin and Machin this volume). This work opened up a whole new paradigm for the study of text and context. Text is now seen as one semiotic mode among others and, as I stated in my 2014 chapter, "context has become text" (Flowerdew 2014: 17). As Ledin and Machin (this volume) put it, MMDA focusses "specifically on how different semiotic resources are deployed in the re-contextualization of social practices for ideological purposes". An interesting example of critical MMDA is O'Halloran, Tan and E's (2014: 249) study on televised and online news in which discourse views language and semiotic resources as "sets of interrelated systems which construe discourse, context and culture". As Ledin and Machin (this volume) suggest, however, MMDA is still in its early stages as far as CDS is concerned.

Historical approaches

Many CDS practitioners emphasise the historical dimension of context (Blommaert 2005; Fairclough 1992; van Dijk 2005; Wodak 2006) (see Achugar this volume). Clearly, to understand any event, action or situation, one needs to know something about what led up to it. Wodak's Discourse-Historical Approach (Reisigl, this volume; Wodak 2009) puts particular emphasis on history, as does my own Historiographical Approach (Flowerdew 2012). The latter approach, as well as emphasising the important role of history in the interpretation of discourse, argues that a diachronic, historiographical approach can make a contribution to historiography, the writing of history, in so far as it can create first readings and interpretations of important events. I highlight the Historiographical Approach here, because I will apply this approach to the case study I present below.

Case study: Hong Kong *Occupy* and context

My case study will take the Hong Kong *Occupy* event as its focus. In 2014, for 79 days, thousands of protesters occupied major roads and paralysed traffic in three major political and commercial centres in Hong Kong, demanding what they labelled 'true' or 'real' or 'genuine' universal suffrage for the election of Hong Kong's leader. This contrasted with what they labelled the 'fake' universal suffrage being put forward by the government, a type of universal suffrage where everyone would have the right to vote, but where only two or three candidates carefully screened by the Hong Kong and Beijing governments would be allowed to stand for election. The full title of this movement was *Occupy Central[2] with Peace and Love*. The movement came to be known as the *Umbrella Movement* because (usually yellow) umbrellas were used by the *Occupiers* to shield themselves when, in the early days of the occupation, the police used pepper spray and batons to try to disperse them. The yellow umbrella became the symbol of the movement, just as the sunflower had become the symbol of an earlier social movement in Taiwan. Unlike many other social movements, the Hong Kong *Occupy* was for the most part peaceful. As with Gandhi's non-violent civil disobedience, *Occupy* claimed the moral high ground. Many journalists and other commentators remarked on how well-behaved the *Occupiers* were, not only being non-violent, but also taking care to make sure that no damage was done to property and that any detritus was removed in an orderly fashion. The *Occupy* event ended when bailiffs were brought in to disperse the *Occupiers*, acting on behalf of local businesses that claimed that their livelihoods were being negatively affected.

In line with my historiographical approach, a study of the *Occupy* event (and its context[s]) can be seen as a first historiographical draft concerning the event. Clearly, an event such as *Occupy* is by its very nature multi-modal. It is an event rather than a text or corpus of texts, which is the more traditional focus of CDS. But following Ricoeur's (1971) argument that meaningful actions can be considered as texts, more recent conceptions of CDS as the study of any form of semiotic entity, not just written or spoken language, and the Pragmatic view of language as social action, *Occupy* can be viewed as a political statement, as a (bodily) semiotic act (Butler 2011). Indeed, it occupied a number of semiotic, or discourse, spaces. The main centre was outside the Legislative Council building, the main political institution in Hong Kong; the second centre was the Mongkok area, a densely populated working class area; and the third area of occupation was Causeway Bay, a major commercial/shopping centre. Each of these venues thus had symbolic value, and its symbolic and physical identity was transformed by the new context it found itself to be in by *Occupy*. More broadly, the values expressed by *Occupy* can be viewed as an ideology, a discourse in the Foucauldian sense of the term, or a big D discourse in Gee's (1999) terminology. Finally, *Occupy* is an example of a social practice in CDS terms.

In line with my historiographical approach to political discourse analysis (Flowerdew 2012), the event needs to be seen in its historical context. My previous work on Hong Kong political discourse, since 1990 (Flowerdew 1998, 2012) has attempted to reveal how political discourse in Hong Kong has developed over time. A distinctive feature of this historiographical approach is the claim that "there is a role for discourse analysis in the writing of history" (2012: 17), to create critical readings of events over time as they unfold. In the space of this short case study, clearly, I am not able to provide an adequate account from that perspective here (but see Flowerdew 1998, 2014). Very briefly, however, *Occupy* can be seen as a result of a stage in a long line of political texts. These texts begin at least with the ambiguous language regarding democratic development of the Sino-British Joint Declaration of 1984 and the Hong Kong Basic Law of 1990 (the two documents that set out the terms of the exchange of sovereignty of Hong Kong from Britain to the People's Republic of China in 1997, as a Special Administrative Region [SAR] of that country, but exercising a high degree of autonomy, labelled by the Chinese leader Deng Xiao Ping, 'one-country, two-systems').[3] In 2007, the authorities in Beijing pledged to allow Hong Kong residents to elect their chief executive (political leader) for the first time in 2017. However, on August 31, 2014, the National People's Congress Standing Committee of the PRC set down strictures for the nomination of potential candidates that would allow the central government to continue to control who could stand for the chief executive election. Dissatisfaction with this ruling in Hong Kong was the immediate trigger for the *Occupy* event. Another historical contextual factor is the Chinese tradition of student-led movements. The revolution that overthrew the Qing dynasty in 1914 was instituted by students. And, of course, the 1989 Tiananmen movement was student-led. This contextual dimension no doubt made the authorities in Beijing and Hong Kong more wary.

Other contributory causes have also been attributed to the movement, involving increasing Mainland influence in Hong Kong's affairs, including, in addition to political interference, large numbers of property purchases by Mainland citizens, leading to inflated prices, and large numbers of Mainland tourists putting a strain on Hong Kong's infrastructure. Also, commentators have referred to similar reasons for disaffected youth as in other jurisdictions, such as lack of well-paid job opportunities and unaffordable property prices.

In addition to this local historical dimension, *Occupy* needs to be seen in the context of other social movements. One of the initiators of the movement was a Hong Kong academic, Benny Tai Yiu-ting, who was very knowledgeable about such events and the theory of social movements (Flowerdew 2016). His ideas had a lot to do with how *Occupy* panned out. In 2014, there was an exhibition at the Victoria and Albert Museum, in London: 'Disobedient Objects', which plotted the historical development of social movements through their objects. Such movements involving direct action were started by activists at the beginning of the 20th century, involving strikes and other forms of civil disobedience. The exhibition included the Women's Social and Political Union (WSPU) (Emmeline Pankhurst's suffragettes), Gandhi, the US civil rights and anti-Vietnam war movement, other *Occupy* movements in, e.g., New York and Los Angeles and, significantly for this paper, Hong Kong *Occupy*. So, clearly, this exhibition contextualised Hong Kong *Occupy* within this historical tradition of social movements and thereby helps us to understand it better. Furthermore, many of the practices on the part of the *Occupiers* were taken up from other similar movements. Some of the songs used had previously been used elsewhere; the 'Lennon Wall', where thousands of sticky notes of support were posted outside the Legislative Council, was previously used in 1989 in Prague. These phenomena can be seen as manifestations of the contextual factor of globalisation.

A further contextual factor concerns identity and the contrasting 'imagined communities' for Hong Kong of those who supported *Occupy* and the (sizeable) number of people who opposed it (Lee 2016). In Flowerdew (2016), I compared these contrasting positions to imagined conceptions of Hong Kong, as follows:

- Imagined community of *Occupiers*

  - Western conception of democracy
  - They cite the *International Covenant for Civil and Political Rights* as a standard for universal suffrage
  - They are against the claimed collusion of HK government and property developers and other tycoons
  - They consider civil disobedience as a valid form of protest

- Imagined community of Mainland and HK governments and Hong Kong anti-*Occupiers*

  - The importance of nation-building: emphasis on one country over two systems
  - They cite the Basic Law and rulings by the National People's Congress and its affiliates
  - They argue for "Gradual and orderly progress according to the actual situation" (Hong Kong Basic Law)

- They seek to construct a hegemonic patriotic discourse (legislators must 'love China and love HK')
- Hong Kong should be "an economic city" (not a political city)
- *Occupy* is 'illegal' and contrary to the 'rule of law'

As well as these more political contextual factors concerning identity, there were innumerable cultural markers (see Flowerdew 2016). On one level the *Occupy* sites can be interpreted as contexts created by the *Occupiers* to represent the sort of society they envisage living in. The sites were like small villages, with tents, kitchens, religious shrines, first-aid posts, study areas and even massage parlours. Rows of tents were given street names and numbers so that mail could be delivered. Everything was done on a cooperative, non-hierarchical basis (there was no *Occupy* leader). At the same time, the sites could be seen as indexing the autonomy that had been promised to Hong Kong, but was perceived to be being eroded. Many features emphasised the unique Hong Kong (Cantonese) identity (Hong Kong has Cantonese as its mother tongue, while the Mainland has standardised Mandarin Chinese; Hong Kong uses the traditional Chinese characters in its writing system, while the Mainland has moved over to simplified characters). Cantonese in speeches, songs and slogans and other message can therefore be seen as a contextual symbol of struggle and solidarity against Mainland influence. The use of English in many of the written messages can be seen as symbolic of an international, as opposed to a Mainland, outlook, as well as a marker of Hong Kong identity (English remains an official language in Hong Kong, along with Chinese).

This brings me to consider the intertextual and interdiscursive features of the *Occupy* event. From the interdiscursive point of view, the whole event was modelled on other *Occupies,* as already indicated. It can thus be seen in terms of a recontextualisation or resemiotisation of these events. Martín Rojo 2014: 585) alludes to the similarity of various *Occupies* in her introduction to her special edition of *Language and Politics,* writing as follows:

> There are striking similarities in the way public spaces were occupied and transformed into political arenas for debate and vindication, and in the role played by online social networks as places for intervention, communication and meeting. . . . Furthermore, a number of similarities connected to the ideologies, principles and aims have been also identified. These social movements are primarily being led and constituted by people demanding democracy and rejecting the economic system underlying the current financial crisis and their political regimes.

There are innumerable more micro interdiscursive features of *Occupy*, for example the various genres involved – slogans, placards, songs, etc. – or the creation of a village (not such a micro feature, in fact). In terms of intertextuality, as in life in general, it was everywhere, but a few salient examples can be referred to here. There were many references to the number 689 (for example on the back of tee shirts); this is a reference to the number of votes the current chief executive was elected by under the prevailing political system (the implicature is clearly that this is undemocratic). Another slogan (in English) I noted on a wall was "I want government of the people, by the people, and for the people", a reference to the Gettysburg address. Another slogan (this time in Chinese), "Hold on to the freedom in the rain", is from a Cantonese pop song. Similarly "Do You Hear the People Sing?" from *Les Miserables* sung in Cantonese and English and posted up in both English and Chinese was an ever-present refrain.

In studies of other *Occupy* movements (e.g., Martín Rojo 2014), much emphasis has been given to the contextual factor of space. Lefebvre's (1991) *Right to the City* is often quoted (e.g.,

Harvey 2008; Chun 2014). Lefebvre argued that social space is produced by the relationships it inhabits. In *Occupy,* new meanings were thus given to the spaces that were occupied. As noted by Chun (2014: 670), also, the use of various online platforms "enable[s] the uptakes and resemiotizing of the protest signs' discourses to continue beyond the immediate encampment site". This also references another contextual variable, that of the channel, or instrumentality, of production, the use of mobile platforms and various forms of social media.

Apart from space, however, time should not be neglected as an important contextual factor. One of the reasons the *Occupiers* were able to sustain the movement for so long was also through the use of mobile devices and social media. At times, the sites were nearly deserted, but if any action was initiated by the authorities, social media would immediately be used by those remaining to bring thousands of *Occupiers* down to the sites. Of course, as they were mostly students (many of them from high schools, not just universities), the *Occupiers* could afford to be patient and flexible with their time. They did not have jobs to go to, for the most part. On the other hand, after an initial aggressive response, where they used tear gas and pepper spray against the *Occupiers,* the authorities realised that this only encouraged more support, so they moved over to a waiting strategy. By the end of the 79 days of Occupation, the *Occupiers* were tired and dispirited, a lot of their support from the public had been lost, and winter was coming on, making sleeping in the streets less feasible. For this reason, some pro-*Occupy* commentators have argued that the movement should have retreated when its popularity was high and it could exert the threat of returning at any time. This again shows the importance of the temporal contextual feature.

Clearly, to fully understand *Occupy,* one needs to experience it personally, using ethnographic methods. In my case, I was, of course, exposed to the events as reported in the digital and print media on a daily basis. In addition, many of my students were active participants and were able to inform me of what was happening. Furthermore, I made repeated visits to the various sites at various times of the day and night to observe at first hand and interview participants (this is where I noted the slogans referred to above, for example).

What about the more micro approaches to context, such as theories of co-text, as in CA or CorpLing? As I am analysing the whole event, I have not focussed on any individual texts, but obviously studies could be made at this level (see, e.g., Flowerdew 2016, where I analyse in detail an interview involving a pro- and anti-*Occupy* person; see also Wong (2015) for a corpus-based study). To give just one finding from Wong's corpus analysis of *Occupy* newspaper reports, her data demonstrate how references to the police were made in a pro-Beijing newspaper in linguistic environments in which they are presented as vulnerable yet professional in their handling of violent protesters, while, in contrast, a liberal newspaper more often presented the police in environments in which they were aggressors.

An important macro (and micro) contextual feature which is important for understanding the *Occupy* movement, of course, is power. In the political field, power in Hong Kong ultimately lies in the hands of the Mainland government. This is exemplified by the constant possibility that, as in the Tiananmen incident of 1997, the PLA might intervene to break up the movement (although this did not happen). However, the *Occupiers* also had power in so far as they could threaten the government, especially in the early stages of the movement, when the authorities, arguably, panicked and used tear gas against the demonstrators. The *Occupiers* also had power insofar as they could create popular support for the movement and against the government.

Power relations are represented in the socio-cognitive context of *Occupy,* in the conceptual metaphors, for example. The government side employed metaphors relating to war/conflict/ violence and sickness/disease/physical or bodily harm, with the *Occupy* side represented as the aggressive force. They refer to the movement as an *outbreak,* as threatening the *well-being* of Hong Kong and as a *blow* to the economy. The *Occupy* side also used the war/conflict/violence metaphors, but represented itself as the side in the conflict exercising care and restraint and standing up for their rights. Thus they want to "*fight* for a democratic political system", and "the *struggle* for genuine democracy in Hong Kong goes on".[4]

Finally, I should address the issue of reflexivity and the position of the author, also referred to as self-disclosure (see Flowerdew 1999 where I discuss this issue). As a person socialised into the British way of life (although a permanent Hong Kong resident, having arrived in 1989), it is quite likely that my selection and interpretation of contextual features to consider in my analysis of *Occupy* would be different from, say that of a Hong Kong Chinese, or a Mainland Chinese person. There are limits to how much self-disclosure is appropriate, however; no two people are the same, after all, even ignoring any cultural differences. Nevertheless, my nationality and upbringing are quite likely to have affected my positioning, and this is an important feature of context that needs to be considered. (Although one way of reducing such possible bias is through the use of multiple methods [triangulation]).

Conclusion

From this review and case study, it is clear that there are many models of context. In my case study, I have tried to show how as many approaches as possible might be applied. This means that my analysis is necessarily superficial. I could have focused on fewer contextual features and done a deeper analysis. The model of context adopted very much depends on the analyst, the particular goals of the analysis and the context of the study. This raises the broader question as to whether CDS is more of a science or an art. Whichever is the answer, context remains a fascinating and highly important feature of any CDS study. One general trend in approaches to context is a move away from the notion of the text as the focus and the context that influences it. The text is now more often decentred in favour of a more multidimensional framework, as I hope I have shown in my case study. This is the way that the field is moving and it is one that is likely to continue.

Notes

* Part of the review part of this chapter is developed from my introductory chapter to Flowerdew, J. (2014). *Discourse in context.* London: Bloomsbury. The case study, however, is original.
1 See Waring (2014) for further discussion of this dichotomy.
2 Central refers to the central business district, where *Occupy* was originally planned to take place, although that in fact did not happen.
3 In fact, a truly historiographical approach needs to go back to the seizure of Hong Kong by Britain from China in 1842, as is the case in my earlier study (Flowerdew 1998).
4 I am indebted to Carl Ng for these examples.

Further reading

van Dijk, T. A. (2008). *Discourse and context: A sociocognitive approach.* Cambridge: Cambridge University Press.
van Dijk, T. A. (2009). *Society and discourse: How context controls text and talk.* Cambridge: Cambridge University Press.
These two theoretical volumes present van Dijk's socio-cognitive view of the role of context in discourse and cognition.
Duranti, A. and Goodwin, C. (1992). *Rethinking context: Language as an interactive phenomenon.* Cambridge: Cambridge University Press.

This is a seminal collection of papers considering the role of context in the study of discourse from various perspectives. The main thesis of the volume is that language and context should be considered interactively defined phenomena.

Fetzer, A. (2004). *Recontextualizing context: Grammaticality meets appropriateness*. Amsterdam: Benjamins.

This volume presents a model for understanding the relation between language and language use and the roles of cognitive context, linguistic context, social context and sociocultural context and their relationship to grammaticality, acceptability and appropriateness.

Flowerdew, J. (ed.) (2014). *Discourse in context*. London: Bloomsbury.

This volume presents a collection of analyses of spoken, written and multi-modal discourses in a range of situations and contextual domains. The contributors represent different approaches and methods in their analyses, including conversation analysis, corpus linguistics, critical discourse analysis, ethnographic discourse analysis, mediated discourse analysis, multi-modal discourse analysis and systemic functional linguistics. Each of the authors outlines the role of context in their approach to the study of discourse.

References

Baker, P. (2014). Considering context when analyzing representations of gender and sexuality: A case study. In J. Flowerdew (ed.), *Discourse in context,* 27–48. London: Bloomsbury.

Baker, P., Gabrielatos, C., KhosraviNik, M., Krzyżanowski, M., McEnery, A. M. and Wodak, R. (2008). A useful methodological synergy? Combining critical discourse analysis and corpus linguistics to examine discourses of refugees and asylum seekers in the UK press. *Discourse and Society* 19(3): 273–306.

Bakhtin, M. (1981). Discourse in the novel. In M. Holquist (ed.) and C. Emerson and M. Holquist (trans.) *The dialogic imagination: Four essays*, 259–422. Austin, TX: University of Texas Press.

Bateson, G. (1955). A theory of play and fantasy. *Psychiatric Research Reports* 2: 39–51.

Bhatia, V. K., Flowerdew, J. and Jones, R. H. (eds.) (2008). *Advances in discourse studies*. London, New York: Routledge.

Billig, M. (1996). *Arguing and thinking: A rhetorical view of social psychology*, 2nd edn. Cambridge: Cambridge University Press.

Billig, M. (1999). Whose terms? Whose ordinariness? Rhetoric and ideology in conversation analysis. *Discourse and Society* 10(4): 543–558.

Blommaert, J. (2005). *Discourse*. Cambridge: Cambridge University Press.

Butler, J. (2011). Bodies in alliance and the politics of the street [Online]. Accessed November 23, 2015, http://eipcp.net/transversal/1011/butler/en

Charteris-Black, J. (2004). *Corpus approaches to critical metaphor analysis*. London: Palgrave Macmillan.

Chomsky, N. (1965). *Aspects of the theory of syntax*. Cambridge, MA: MIT Press.

Chun, C.W. (2014). Mobilities of a linguistic landscape at Los Angeles City Hall Park. *Journal of Language and Politics* 13(4): 653–674.

De Saussure, F. (1916/1977). *Course in general linguistics*. C. Bally and A. Sechehaye (eds.) and R. Harris (trans.). Glasgow: Fontana/Collins.

Drew, P. and Heritage, J. (1993). *Talk at work: Interaction in institutional settings*. Cambridge, Cambridge University Press.

Duranti, A. and Goodwin, C. (1992). *Rethinking context: Language as an interactive phenomenon*. Cambridge: Cambridge University Press.

Fairclough, N. (1992). *Discourse and social change*. Cambridge: Polity.

Fairclough, N. (2001). *Language and power,* 2nd edn. London: Longman.

Fairclough, N., Mulderrig, J. and Wodak, R. (2011). Critical discourse analysis. In T.A. van Dijk (ed.), *Discourse studies: A multidisciplinary introduction,* 2nd edn, 357–378. London: Sage.

Fetzer, A. (2004). *Recontextualizing context: Grammaticality meets appropriateness*. Amsterdam: Benjamins.

Flowerdew, J. (1998). *The final years of British Hong Kong: The discourse of colonial withdrawal*. Basingstoke and New York: Macmillan and St. Martin's Press.

Flowerdew, J. (1999). Description and interpretation in critical discourse analysis. *Journal of Pragmatics* 31: 1089–1099; reprinted in Teubert, W. and Krishnamurthy, R. (2007) *Corpus linguistics: Critical concepts in linguistics,* 42–53. London: Routledge.

Flowerdew, J. (2012). *Critical discourse analysis in historiography: The case of Hong Kong's evolving political identity*. New York: Palgrave Macmillan.

Flowerdew, J. (2013). *Discourse in English language education*. London: Routledge.

Flowerdew, J. (ed.) (2014). *Discourse in context*. London: Bloomsbury.

Flowerdew, J. (2016). A historiographical approach to Hong Kong occupy: Focus on a critical moment. In J. Flowerdew and R. Jones (eds.), *Language and politics,* 15(5), 527–548. Special edn.

Flowerdew, L. (2008). Corpora and context in professional writing. In V. Bhatia, J. Flowerdew and R. Jones (eds.), *Advances in discourse studies,* 115–127. London: Routledge.

Fowler, R., Hodge, B., Kress, G. and Trew, T. (1979). *Language and control*. London: Routledge and Kegan Paul.

Gee, J. P. (1999). *An introduction to discourse analysis: Theory and method*. London: Routledge.

Goffman, E. (1974). *Frame analysis*. New York: Harper & Row.

Goodwin, C. and Duranti, A. (1992). Rethinking context: An introduction. In A. Duranti and C. Goodwin (eds.), *Rethinking context: Language as an interactive phenomenon,* 1–42. Cambridge: Cambridge University Press.

Grice, H. P. (1989/1967). Logic and conversation. In H.P. Grice (ed.), *Studies in the way of words,* 22–40. Cambridge, MA: Harvard University Press.

Halliday, M.A.K. (1978). *Language as social semiotic*. London: Longman.

Halliday, M.A.K. (1999). The notion of 'context' in language education. In M. Ghadessy (ed.), *Text and context in functional linguistics,* 1–24. Amsterdam, Philadelphia: Benjamins.

Halliday, M.A.K. and Hasan, R. (1985). *Language, context and text: Aspects of language in a socialsemiotic perspective*. Geelong: Deakin University Press.

Halliday, M.A.K., McIntosh, A. and Strevens, P. (1964). *The linguistic sciences and language teaching*. London: Longmans.

Hardt-Mautner, G. (1995). Only connect: critical discourse analysis and corpus linguistics. *UCREL Technical Paper 6,* Lancaster University, Lancaster. Accessed January 19, 2015, http://ucrel.lancs.ac.uk/papers/techpaper/vol6.pdf

Hart, C. (2014). *Discourse in contexts*. J. Flowerdew (ed.). London: Bloomsbury Academic.

Harvey, D. (2008). The right to the city. *The New Left Review,* Online. Accessed February 16, 2013, http://newleftreview.org/II/53/david-harvey-the-right-to-the-city

Hymes, D. (1962). The ethnography of speaking. In T. Gladwin and W.C. Sturtevant (eds.), *Anthropology and human behaviour,* 13–53. Washington, DC: The Anthropological Society of Washington.

Kress, G. and van Leeuwen, T. (1996). *Reading images*. London: Routledge.

Kristeva, J. (1980). Word, dialogue and the novel. In L. Roudiez (ed.) and T. Gora, A. Jardine and L. Roudiez (trans.), *Desire in language: A semiotic approach to literature and art,* 64–91. New York: Columbia University Press.

Krzyżanowski, M. (2011). Ethnography and critical discourse studies. Towards a problem-oriented research dialogue. *Special Issue of Critical Discourse Studies* 8(4): 231–238.

Lakoff, G. and Johnson, M. (1980). *Metaphors we live by*. Chicago: University of Chicago Press.

Lee, F. (2016). Opinion polling and construction of public opinion in newspaper discourses during the umbrella movement. In J. Flowerdew and R. Jones (eds.), *Special edition of language and politics* 15(5): 589–608.

Lefebvre, H. (1991). *The production of space*. Oxford: Blackwell.

Malinowski, B. (1923). The problem of meaning in primitive languages. In C.K. Ogden and I.A. Richards (eds.), *The meaning of meaning,* 296–336. London: Harcourt-Brace.

Martín Rojo, Luisa. (2014). Occupy: The spatial dynamics of discourse in global protest movements. Introduction to *Special Issue of Journal of Language and Politics* 13(4): 583–598.

O'Halloran, K. (2003). *Critical discourse analysis and cognitive linguistics*. Edinburgh: Edinburgh University Press.

O'Halloran, K. L., Tan, S. and E, M.K.L. (2014). A multimodal approach to discourse, context and culture. In J. Flowerdew (ed.), *Discourse in context,* 247–272. London: Bloomsbury.

Pinker, S. (1994). *The language instinct*. Harmondsworth: Penguin.

Rabinow, P. (ed.) (1991). *The Foucault reader: An introduction to Foucault's thought*. London: Penguin.

Reisigl, M. and Wodak, R. (2001). *Discourse and discrimination*. London: Routledge.

Ricoeur, P. (1971). The model of the text: Meaningful action considered as a text. *Social Research* 38: 529–562.

John Flowerdew

Rose, D. and Martin, J. (2014). Intervening in contexts of schooling. In J. Flowerdew (ed.), *Discourse in context*, 273–300. London: Bloomsbury Academic.

Schegloff, E. A. (1987). Between macro and micro: Contexts and other connections. In J. Alexander, B. Giessen, R. Munch and N. Smelser (eds.), *The micro-macro link*, 207–234. Berkeley: University of California Press.

Schegloff, E. A. (1997). Whose text? Whose context? *Discourse and Society* 8(2): 165–187.

Schegloff, E. A. (1999). Schegloff's Texts' as 'Billig's Data': A Critical Reply. *Discourse and Society* 10(4): 558–572.

Sperber, D. and Wilson, D. (1995). *Relevance: Communication and cognition,* 2nd edn. Oxford and Cambridge: Blackwell Publishers.

Swales, J. M. (2002). Integrated and fragmented worlds: EAP materials and corpus linguistics. In J. Flowerdew (ed.), *Academic discourse,* 150–164. London: Longman.

Tannen, D. (ed.) (1993). *Framing in discourse*. Oxford: Oxford University Press.

van Dijk, T. A. (2005). Contextual knowledge management in discourse production: A CDA perspective. In R. Wodak and P. Chilton (eds.), *A new agenda in (critical) discourse analysis,* 71–100. Amsterdam: Benjamins.

van Dijk, T. A. (2008). *Discourse and context: A sociocognitive approach*. Cambridge: Cambridge University Press.

van Dijk, T. A. (2009). *Society and discourse: How context controls text and talk*. Cambridge: Cambridge University Press.

Waring, H. Z. (2014). Turn allocation and context: Broadening participation in the second language classroom. In J. Flowerdew (ed.), *Discourse in context,* 301–320. London: Bloomsbury Publishing.

Wetherell, M. (1998). Positioning and interpretive repertoires: Conversation analysis and post-structuralism in dialogue. *Discourse and Society* 9: 387–412.

Widdowson, H. G. (1998). Context, community and authentic language. *TESOL Quarterly* 32: 705–716.

Widdowson, H. G. (2000). On the limitations of linguistics applied. *Applied Linguistics* 21(1): 3–25.

Widdowson, H. G. (2004). *Text, context, pretext: Critical issues in discourse analysis*. Oxford: Blackwell.

Wodak, R. (2002). The discourse historical approach. In R. Wodak and M. Meyer (eds.), *Methods in critical discourse analysis,* 63–94. London: Sage.

Wodak, R. (2006). History in the making/The making of history: The 'German *Wehrmacht*' in collective and individual memories in Austria. *Journal of Language and Politics* 5(1): 125–154.

Wodak, R. (2007). Pragmatics and critical discourse analysis: A cross-disciplinary inquiry. *Pragmatics and Cognition* 15(1): 203–225.

Wodak, R. (2014). Discourse and Politics. In J. Flowerdew (ed.), *Discourse in context,* 321–346. London: Bloomsbury.

Wong, M. (2015). Conflicting news discourse of political protests: a corpus-based cognitive approach to CDA. Poster presented at *Corpus linguistics 2015,* July 21–24, 2015, Lancaster University, UK.

12

Ethnography and critical discourse studies

Michał Krzyżanowski

Introduction

This chapter presents a problem-oriented merger of critical discourse analysis (CDA) and ethnography. It takes stock of a number of recent developments that significantly altered both critical-analytic and ethnographic research practice. Whilst ethnography and CDA have never formed first-hand associations, the recent years have seen a number of developments that significantly altered both of them as well as their orientation towards cross-disciplinary research dialogue. Those developments have not only changed ethnography and CDA internally but also opened up CDA to fieldwork and ethnography and vice versa.

Originally associated mainly with explorations of lexical and grammatical aspects of predominantly written texts, CDA has eventually developed into a broader field of research of Critical Discourse Studies or CDS. The latter, while still drawing on some of the CDA's original ideas (e.g., on the interplay of language/discourse and ideology as well as of their constitutive force in social relations), clearly reaches beyond the traditional 'schools' or 'trends' of the movement (Krzyżanowski and Forchtner 2016). Whilst, to be sure, some areas of CDA still remain devoted to the textually oriented analyses (especially Fairclough 2009), other areas of CDA/CDS have seen the movement towards more contextually focussed and actor-related types of analysis (for overview, see Krzyżanowski 2010).

As a result of moving towards exploring discourse from the point of view of its situatedness in respective contexts, some areas of CDA embarked on rethinking of some of its fundamental concepts such as, most notably, text and context. Having previously been treated in a rather limited way – mainly as a description of 'inanimate' social-political conditions or as a physical 'setting' of communicative practices – context was thus for a significant period of time approached in many areas of CDS as a certain addition to textual analyses and not as part of the actual analysis in CDA (cf. Krzyżanowski 2010; Blommaert et al. 2001; Flowerdew, this volume). This, however, has changed recently, and, in turn, allowed to scrutinise the key and traditional context-related analytical notions of CDA such as, e.g., recontextualisation (cf. Bernstein 1990, Wodak 2000; Krzyżanowski 2016) or interdiscursivity (cf. Fairclough 2001, Reisigl and Wodak 2009). It also re-emphasised the necessity to increase focus on contextual-to-textual macro-micro mediation (cf. Wodak 2006) in the analytical process.

CDS's move towards the more contextually-bound studies which relate fieldwork and ethnography to detailed analyses of 'situated' linguistic and other communicative practices has been matched by parallel developments in some other strands of research on language in/and society. We have seen, for example, a revival of the key proposals of 'ethnography of speaking' – originally initiated by Dell Hymes – and the development of the related 'linguistic ethnography' that combines "linguistic analysis with ethnography, in order to probe the interrelationship between language and social life in more depth" (Tusting and Maybin 2007: 576). The neo-Hymesian ideas have also been crucial in Scollon and Scollon's (2003, 2004, 2007) approach known as Mediated Discourse Analysis or 'nexus analysis' (see also Jones 2012). The latter has argued for in-depth (ethnography-based) exploration of loci in which discourses and practices are seen as intersecting within limits of the contextually conditioned 'affordances' and 'constraints' (Jones 2012).

On the other hand, ethnography has also recently acquired a significantly different and definitely a broader meaning which by now clearly exceeds its original denotation as just one of the key methods or techniques of anthropological research practice (cf., inter alia, Gobo 2008). This change has mainly taken place under the ever more pressing need to rethink the original remit of ethnography as initiated in, and strongly associated with, the social anthropology of Malinowski in the late 19th and early 20th century. In its classic sense, the social-anthropological ethnographic research was, namely, preoccupied with 'distant' cultures and societies, in what could often be seen as a post-colonial approach which looked at the 'other' cultures and societies as inherently 'exotic' and 'different' (especially if compared to forms of social, political and economic organisation in, e.g., Europe). The original meaning of ethnography also focused on exploration of cultures and societies – i.e., of 'them' – in a rather simplified way that treated the studied groups as closed and homogeneous. In line with such approaches, ethnography in the traditional sense encompassed just the 'on-site' research 'in the field', which, however, often remained insensitive to social, political and economic as well as historical conditions and wider contexts of development and change of the studied societies and social groups.

Recent years have brought a significant rethinking in ethnography and the broadening of its scope and its research philosophy. Ethnography has, namely, gradually "ceased to be associated with its objects of study (that is, with 'who' or 'what' is studied) and has become a designate of a certain research perspective (thus, related to a certain 'how')" (Oberhuber and Krzyżanowski 2008: 182; Krzyżanowski 2011b). Such a new perspective – often called 'reflexive ethnography' (Davies 1999) – has been aptly described by Brewer (2000: 11) who claimed that ethnography has now become "not one particular method of data-collection but a style of research that is distinguished by its objectives, which are to understand the social *meanings* and activities of people in a given 'field' or setting" (emphasis in the original). While still largely consisting of fieldwork and related techniques as key methods of context-sensitive explorations (cf. below), ethnography has now become a designate of a complex and ordered, though not necessarily linear, research process which informs the work of researchers throughout the duration of their work (for examples, see Heller 2001; Wodak, Krzyżanowski and Forchtner 2012). Ethnography is now linking context-sensitive explorations across various social contexts where it is crucial to highlight parallels and interplays of context-specific dynamics. Ethnography hence encompasses – often interchangeably or simultaneously – political (Kubik 2009; Aronoff and Kubik 2013), organisational (Yanow 2012; Ybema 2014, Ybema et al. 2009) and policy-making analysis (Yanow 2000) as well as ethnographies of such contexts as medical settings (Galasiński 2011) or education institutions (Rogers 2011).

A crucial development in ethnography of late is also its long-awaited endorsement of *power* as one of the central components of studied social contexts and as probably the key factor fuelling the dynamics of studied forms of social, political (including politico-economic) and organisational change. As argued by Agar in one of the recent editions of his classic *The Professional Stranger* (see Agar 2008), the endorsement of power in ethnography was probably one of those developments that allowed it to (finally) adjust its views to the dynamics of contemporary social contexts and to the critical trends of analysis. It helped ethnography to recognise the fluidity, complexity and inherent diversity of the explored social fields – until recently often treated as 'settings' rather than 'contexts'. It also allowed for the fact that processes and phenomena studied and observed in the course of ethnographic fieldwork (e.g., individual and/or collective identifications) may have their ontology both within and beyond the studied groups as well as may also be motivated by dynamism of social power structures.

Indeed, the inherent multiplicity of studied social milieus has become the central object of research in ethnography of late. While originally preoccupied with 'fixed' and usually isolated social groups, ethnographers have, namely, now come increasingly to study the fluidity and complexity of examined social contexts. They have, thereby, attempted to embrace the diversity of studied spaces and have increasingly become preoccupied with contexts in which representatives of different social groups interact and where their practices intersect. For example, in his excellent ethnographic study of urban regeneration Ocejo (2014) has argued that finding and ethnographically exploring spaces in which different people and groups interact – in his case night-bars and hang-out taverns of New York City – allows not only treating those as 'windows' to the studied social context/s but also as sites where traces of wider social and politico-economic processes (e.g., late-modern urban gentrification, rise of new inequalities, etc.) visibly come to the fore and cut across one another. In a similar vein, political and organisational ethnographers (see, inter alia, Bellier and Wilson 2000b; Krzyżanowski 2011a) have long conducted ethnographies of organisations while looking at them as specific 'microcosms' of social, political and organisational realities and therefore as the key objects of critical exploration.

Finally, whilst changing its general perspective and becoming a certain style of research, ethnography has also broadened the scope of its techniques and methods. Those methods, which now form the very broad idea of 'fieldwork' in ethnography, range from different kinds of observations (including what is also sometimes labelled 'ethnographic observations'; Krzyżanowski and Oberhuber 2007) yet often verge at the intersection of participant and non-participant immersion (Gobo 2008). The observations are now also documented by means of not only notes but also recordings and visual imagery and also include an array of observation-supporting and supplementing techniques such as individual and group interviewing of different types of participants who are deemed to play direct or indirect role in the observed practices.

The Discourse-Ethnographic Approach (DEA)

Discourse-Ethnographic Approach (DEA) highlighted here takes stock of the recent developments within ethnographic and critical-analytic research highlighted above. The key critical-analytic inspiration for the approach comes from the Discourse-Historical Approach in Critical Discourse Studies (see Krzyżanowski and Wodak 2009; Wodak 2001; Reisigl and Wodak 2009; Wodak and Krzyżanowski 2008) from which the DEA adopts a variety of principles. These include, inter alia, a *strong orientation towards problem-focused research* as well as a *devotion to analysing how discourses evolve and change over time as well as spatially,* i.e., across

181

multiple spaces and genres. Just like the DHA, the DEA is also interested in how discourses and their key elements are *recontextualised* in/across other discourses (see Bernstein 1990, for the original meaning of the term 'recontextualisation'; see also Krzyżanowski 2016) and how thus various interdiscursive connections are established.

As such, the DEA also profits from various discourse-oriented ethnographies conducted within the DHA. These range from seminal early studies of interactions in inter alia, medical and courtroom settings (see especially Wodak 1975; Wodak, Menz and Lalouschek 1990) to the discourse-ethnographic work performed by the DHA researchers in organisational and politico-organizational settings (for the most recent studies see, inter alia, Krzyżanowski and Oberhuber 2007; Wodak 2009; Krzyżanowski 2010; Wodak, Krzyżanowski and Forchtner 2012). So far, research deploying DEA revolves mainly around problem-oriented relationships between CDA/CDS and ethnography applied to political organisational contexts (see below for examples). The key ethnographic inspirations of the DEA therefore originate within various ways of conducting political and organisational ethnographies (for recent accounts see: Aronoff and Kubik 2013; Kubik 2009; Ybema 2014; Ybema et al. 2009) including as settings of policy-making and production of regulatory meanings (Wright 1994; Shore and Wright 1997; Yanow 2000).

Ethnography and CDS are analytically mobilised in the DEA as complementary general frameworks. However, their merger also penetrates deeper, i.e., into mezzo- and micro-levels of analysis where triangulating between a set of stages of analytical research allows for different aspects of the ethnographic and discursive analyses to be carefully balanced. In case of the analyses presented below, such a balance is especially achieved in three stages of research (only selected aspects of which can be presented below due to limitations of space). The DEA must hence be viewed as reaching beyond the micro understanding of its major constituent parts – ethnography and CDS – as well as drawing extensively on their larger epistemological premises.

The central definition of ethnography followed in the DEA goes beyond its frequent treatment as 'the fieldwork' itself or as just a 'method' or a 'data-collection technique' (for discussion, see Hammersley 1992). Instead, *ethnography is viewed by the DEA as a complex, situated and ordered though not necessarily linear research process* which informs exploratory work from the point of view of initial theorising and hypothesising, through collecting data and the actual fieldwork, up to the systematic analyses of discourses and interactions and interpretation of findings (Wodak, Krzyżanowski and Forchtner 2012). On the other hand, from the point of discourse analysis, the DEA's approach rests on CDS's approach to *discourse as a social practice* and the idea that there exists "a dialectical relationship between a particular discursive event and the situation(s), institution(s) and social structure(s), which frame it" (Fairclough and Wodak 1997: 258). By the same token, the DEA also follows the more strictly discourse-historical ideas of discourses as 'historical', whereby they are viewed as "always connected to other discourses which were produced earlier as well as to those which are produced synchronically or subsequently" (Wodak 1996: 19; see also Reisigl and Wodak 2009). Just like the DHA, the DEA also locates discourse and discourse theory below the middle-range level of theorisation. This means that, whereas the key concepts such as discourse, text or context are central for the DHA, they are the basis of discourse-oriented theory that underlies the analytical methodology. On the other hand, various social- and political-scientific theories which allow explaining and highlighting the nature of the studied social, political and organisational problems are treated as grand theories which also underpin the post-analytical interpretation of the findings of problem-oriented discourse-ethnographic research.

The DEA follows some of the key principles and concepts of the DHA. Among others, these include, in particular: problem-orientation, studying various spaces and genres as well as operating within a multilevel and highly differentiated definition of context (for details, see Krzyżanowski 2011a). However, the DEA also seeks to extend their meaning, especially while drawing on insights from other areas of CDS as well as from the wider social sciences. It recognises the fact that the key constituent elements of context require a more dynamic, agent-oriented view that would allow recognising not only the key constituent parts (levels) of the studied milieus but also their dynamic and socially constructive character (interactions, roles of participants, changes in practices and behaviour over time, etc.). The DEA hence adds to the DHA's definition of context (Wodak 2001) insights from the socio-cognitive approach in CDS which argues that contexts are "not some kind of objective condition or direct cause, but rather (inter) subjective constructs designed and ongoingly updated in interaction by participants as members of groups and communities" (van Dijk 2008: x).

On the other hand, the DEA also sees all social 'practices' as inherently linked and recognises discourse as the key locus of recontextualisation of those practices and the key site of reflection of their changing forms of articulation across social fields. Thereby, the DEA endorses the view that "all texts, all representations of the world and what is going on in it, however abstract, should be interpreted as representations of social practices" (van Leeuwen 2008: 5). Similarly, "as discourses are social cognitions, socially specific ways of knowing social practices, they can be, and are, used as resources for representing social practices" (van Leeuwen 2008: 6). Furthermore, DEA endorses the view that the way practices are structured is strongly dependent on the social fields in which they are prototypically nested (as elements of field specific-habitus; see Bourdieu 2005; Krzyżanowski 2014). Accordingly, local contexts such as organisations and institutions are often seen therein as defining for the ways in which practices are undertaken, often in a path-dependent way and, very often, in the course of reproduction of local customs, beliefs and norms.

DEA as a research process

Key elements of research design in DEA

Research design in DEA usually comprises three key elements/stages:

(A) *Problem-Definition, Theorisation and Pre-Contextualisation,*
(B) *Fieldwork including Contextualisation,* and
(C) *Discourse-Historical Analysis.*

In stage (A), i.e., *Problem-Definition, Theorisation and Pre-Contextualisation,* the central problem of research is crystallised (along with key, relevant research questions) and its social significance is highlighted. At this stage, one also undertakes identification of key theories (including of grand-theoretical nature) and concepts that will inform the general conceptualisation of the problem as well as the eventual, post-analytical interpretation of findings.

Stage (B) – *Fieldwork including Contextualisation* – encompasses research conducted 'in the field', i.e., ethnographic observations, interviews as well as a collection of textual and other data and information. As such, the fieldwork serves several functions, the main of which are: conducting research as such (in the course of observations), collecting data for analyses conducted later on (interviews, collection of textual data) and obtaining further information as the basis of field-based contextualisation (through observations, interviews, background information collection).

The final stage of DEA research – i.e., *Discourse-Historical Analysis* (C) – encompasses the process of final analyses of textual data (including from interviews and other forms of data collection and other genres encountered in the field) in line with key stages of DHA-driven examination (for details see Krzyżanowski 2010, see also Wodak this volume). The analyses start with the process of generic classification that helps ordering the materials according to various genres and practices as well as to provide initial lines of intertextual links between various sets of data. An entry-level (thematic) and in-depth (argumentation- or, if need be, interaction-oriented) analysis follows in order to discover further features of the analysed discourses as well as to distinguish between different textual and linguistic forms those discourses may take within various studied spaces and practices. The final aim of the analysis is to sketch interdiscursive relationships between various discourses and discovering patterns of recontextualisation across practices and genres.

Case study/application of DEA: discourse-ethnographic analysis of identities in the EU institutions

In order to present how various elements of DEA research design work in practice, an illustrative case study is presented below. In order to facilitate its readability, the case study follows the key stages (A, B, C) of the research design enumerated above.

A: problem-definition, theorisation and pre-contextualisation

A.1 Problem-definition and research questions

The research exemplified here deals with the problem of *how identities are formed and transformed in discourses and practices of various European Union (EU) institutions* and *how different forms of institutional bodies (especially the differences between short-lived and established institutions) influence the dynamism of identity construction within various spaces.*

A.2 Theorisation/conceptualisation

While many social-theoretical and social-scientific approaches to collective or organisational as well as European identities (see Krzyżanowski 2010 for extensive overview) have been selected as a grand-theoretical framing, the research presented here chooses to follow two central middle-range theoretical concepts, both of them originating in the field of anthropology of supranational institutions (see above). The first of them is that of *engrenage* (or *institutional/ organisational immersion*) while the other, and closely related one, is that of *organisational culture*.

'*Engrenage*' (in English: 'enmeshing' or 'immersion') is viewed by Abélès (2000: 35) as "an 'action trap' in which once the agents are set in a specific course of action, they find themselves obliged to take further actions which point them in a direction which they did not necessarily intend to follow". Thus, *engrenage* serves as a poignant description of how a peculiar linear culture of an institution/organisation – often including of its symbolic and discursive construction of that institution's 'constant progress' – can be (re) produced, in our case in the European Union's institutional practices.

The other driving concept – of *organisational culture* – has been proposed by Shore (2000) in his related approach to organisational anthropology in supranational political contexts (for related accounts see, e.g., Ybema, Yanow and Sabelis 2011). In Shore's view, the notion is based on, on the one hand, the critique of the concept of political and, on the other hand, of corporate culture. While the former is viewed by Shore as "a gloss to describe the sum of political attitudes, dispositions, practices and institutions created by a particular political system: the 'subjective orientation of people towards politics'" (Shore 2000: 130), the corporate culture designates "informal characteristics of a company or organisation (. . .) [MK: which] can be identified, isolated, abstracted and cultivated in order to promote 'organisational change'" (Shore 2000: 131). It is from combination of those two definitions that Shore develops his idea of institutionally-specific '*organisational culture*': as he argues a peculiar *modus vivendi* (Shore 2000: 132) of an institution located at the intersection of its formal and informal characteristics as well as of its objective rules and procedures and subjective attitudes and experiences of those involved in its processual development.

A.3 Pre-contextualisation

The main source here are previous ethnographic studies conducted in the EU-institutional contexts. These studies, which include anthropological work on such EU contexts as the European Parliament (see Abélès 1992, 1993) and, in a large number of cases, the practices at the EU's supranational administration, i.e., the European Commission (cf. Abélès 2000a, 2004; Abélès, Bellier and McDonald 1993; Bellier 2000; Shore 2000) have shown extensively that identities and agencies are negotiated in the EU across a variety of contexts, and that the patterns of those negotiations are in most cases institutionally specific. Within those studies, often based on long-term multi-layered ethnographies, the most prominent remain the works of Abélès (2000, 2004; see also Shore and Abélès 2004), who formulates his famous claim that, in fact, as embodied in its institutions, the EU in general is a constant social as well as institutional process and thereby remains a rather elusive and a virtual construct. Accordingly, many EU institutions construct their identities not only in a practice- but also discourse-based way that allows for the constant (re) definition of efficiency-driven progress yet, importantly, without a pronounced aim or goal or the clear awareness of the point of departure. As Abélès claims, in the EU institutions "everything happens as if Europe will be inventing itself every day, thereby reconfirming its permanence" (2000: 33).

Insights from the said anthropological research are supplemented by various discourse-ethnographic analyses conducted across EU institutions including in its short-lived institutional bodies (see especially. Muntigl, Weiss and Wodak 2000; Krzyżanowski 2010; Krzyżanowski and Oberhuber 2007) and in established institutions (Wodak 2009; Wodak, Krzyżanowski and Forchtner 2012). These studies have shown how to relate collection and analysis of textual data with observations of EU-institutional milieus. They have also pointed to the challenges of fieldwork in the context of immense internal complexity within, and diversity across, EU institutions as far as, inter alia, patterns of organisational behaviour, production and reproduction of meanings, or interactional behaviour in multilingual contexts are concerned. Those studies have also provided patterns of dealing with political meanings including in interviews with politicians or in policy texts often resting on various patterns of recontextualisation of wider political ideologies.

Of course, allowing for the context of research, a bulk of pre-contextualising knowledge has been obtained from a variety of studies on EU politics and institutions conducted on such topics as, e.g., complexity and reform of EU institutions (Egberg 2004, 2005; Kassim 2004, 2008), the EU's democracy and democratic deficit (e.g., Follesdal and Hix 2006; Pollak 2007; Majone 2005), EU's relationships with its member states in the context of Europeanisation

(Featherstone and Radaelli 2004) or communication and democracy in the EU (Michailidou 2008; Krzyżanowski 2012, 2013).

B: fieldwork and contextualisation

The bulk of fieldwork (including contextualising activities) was devoted to the *reconstruction of the processes and practices involved in everyday work of the studied institutional contexts,* and to *discovering patterns and forms of their (possibly distinct) local organisational cultures.*

Among the main findings of the fieldwork were the observed differences between the organisational behaviour of representatives of long-term established institutional bodies (in our case, the European Commission) on the one hand, and the short-lived institutional organisms (e.g., the 2002–2003 European Convention drafting the EU Constitution) on the other. As the fieldwork revealed, the long-term institutional bodies such as the European Commission based their works on long-established patterns of organisational behaviour. Those patterns are best displayed in a variety of meetings (see Figure 12.1) that are usually conducted in similar spaces and are undertaken in a highly patterned, hierarchical order (e.g., chair of the meeting is usually a director or head of unit that is taking part in the meeting). The meetings are often taking place by means of videoconferences (with participants present in Brussels and other in Luxembourg offices) that often constitutes an obstacle to direct responses and more spontaneous communication.

As has become evident from the study of one of European Commissions' Directorates General (i.e., its units dealing with specific policy remits or specific areas of services), observations of meetings undertaken throughout one week, (from the top-level meeting of Directors

Figure 12.1   'Regular' meeting of a unit at the European Commission (2009)

down to the lower-level meetings of various subordinate units), showed that meanings and topics defined at the top level effectively penetrated 'down' the hierarchy throughout the week. The observations of long-established EU institutions also show that, through strict and path-dependent patterning of communication, the individual agency of officials is often constrained. They thus submit to collective (organisational) patterns of behaviour, often those dependent on the institutions in question or the more local (e.g., Directorate-specific) patterns. Importantly, the observed patterns were very stable over time and hence they were not prone to change for any unexpected reasons.

On the other hand, fieldwork at the short-term institutional bodies of the EU – such as, e.g., the 2002–2003 European Convention (see Krzyżanowski 2010) – have shown that their practices are certainly not uniform in nature (see Figure 12.2) and depend on institutional practices in which their members originate. At the same time, the institutional processes in short-lived bodies are prone to change immensely over time. Therefore, a totally different fieldwork strategy needs to be selected with fieldwork occurring at different times/phases of Convention's work. Undertaking fieldwork at different moments of development of an institutional body such as the Convention helped observe its development and change but also an immense transformation of its members' behaviour. The latter was, in most cases, dictated by

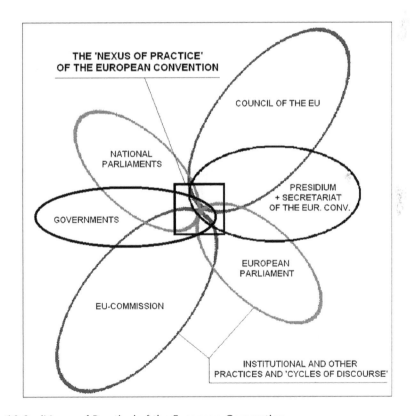

Figure 12.2 'Nexus of Practice' of the European Convention

Source: Oberhuber, F. and Krzyżanowski, M. (2008). *Discourse analysis and ethnography*. In: Wodak, R. and M. Krzyżanowski, Michał (eds.), *Qualitative discourse analysis in the social sciences,* 182–203. Basingstoke: Palgrave Macmillan.

Reproduced with permission of Palgrave Macmillan.

Michał Krzyżanowski

political motivations and was related to the fact that the bodies that 'sent' their representatives to the Convention (EU member states' national parliaments or governments, EU institutions) wanted to have their say on the final outcome of the Convention's works, i.e., the first EU constitution. Thus, the initially limited attention of Convention's members in its works and proceedings increased significantly over time with, e.g., the plenary sessions also becoming much more lively and filled with heated exchanges. Over time, the *politics of the couloir* (i.e., the process of political dealing on the backstage; cf. also Wodak 2009) clearly lost its value to be replaced by the more pronounced and clear assertions of positions and ideas held in the plenary. The observation of the short-lived bodies such as Convention also allows tracing certain origin-specific patterns of organisational behaviour. Hence, while some members (especially national parliamentarians) were much more prone to discuss things in plenary settings, other politicians skilful in either backstage diplomacy (especially representatives of national governments) or in internal workings of the EU (especially representatives of permanent EU institutions) were clearly more prone to undertake backstage negotiations, often away from the spotlight of the plenary sessions.

The final crucial issue resulting from fieldwork pertained to observing the ways in which communication and its channels were structured. As has become evident, the ways in which communication tends to be organised in short-lived bodies such as the Convention is rarely evident to the outsiders and hence it requires a thorough process of ethnographic observations and eventual reconstruction (Krzyżanowski and Oberhuber 2007; see Figure 12.3).

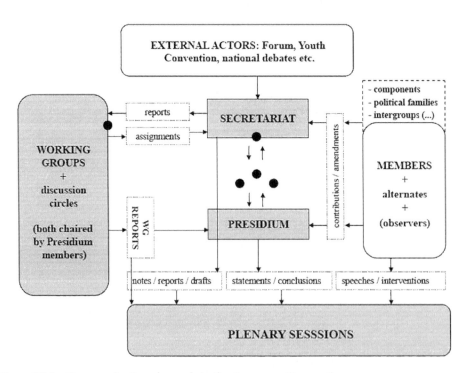

Figure 12.3 Communication channels in the European Convention

Source: Krzyżanowski, M. and Oberhuber, F. (2007). *(Un)doing Europe: Discourses and practices of negotiating the EU constitution*. Brussels: PIE-Peter Lang.

Reproduced with permission of Peter Lang.

Supplemented by a variety of additional data (gathered from members, assistants, observers, involved think tanks and analysts), the observations pointed to the fact that the communication was tightly controlled – by the so-called Convention's secretariat, obviously consisting mostly of skilful EU officials – that thus could also strongly influence the process of the Convention's overall deliberations. It hence allowed the Secretariat – and the Convention's powerful Presidium – to become the key axis controlling communication and thereby also the entire decision-making process.

C. discourse-historical analysis

C.1 Generic classification

The following text types (genres) have been used as sources of empirical data (NB: many of those texts were collected in the process of fieldwork described above):

The exemplary analysis of discourses about organisational practices in the EU follows the key DHA category of 'topoi' (for details and definitions, see Krzyżanowski 2010, Reisigl and

Table 12.1 C.2. Discourse-historical analysis – example: meta-discourses on practice and agency in the European Convention

	Established institutions (European Commission)	Short-lived institutions (European Convention)
Interviews	• Semi-structured interviews with key officials at the studied EC Directorates – including Directors, Heads of Units, Individual Officials	• Semi-structured interviews with Convention members, their auxiliary staff and assistants supporting Conventioneers in both EU and national contexts
Observations	• Participant observations of meetings at various levels of studied institutional hierarchies	• Non-participant observations of the plenary sessions • Participant observations of working groups
Documents	• Official documents related to policy and its implementation • Speeches of key officials • Legal texts regulating practices at the European Commission • Semi-official documents concerning internal procedures and codes of conduct	• Official documents including proposals and reports as well as speeches of EU and Convention officials, (during Convention) and final documents (e.g., Draft Constitutional Treaty) • Legal texts (e.g., EU treaties) • Semi-official and subversive documents (collected in the studied settings of Convention's works, e.g., posters, leaflets, unauthorised proposals)
External Sources	• Academic analyses of the European Commission, its multilingualism, etc. • Mass media discourse on European Institutions (especially European Commission), its multilingualism, etc.	• Video tapes of the plenary sessions • Speeches of national politicians • Academic and, e.g., think-tank analyses of EU constitutional process and institutional reform • Mass media coverage of works and proceedings of the European Convention

Wodak 2009) that focus on the key argumentation schemes deployed by the speakers in their discursive accounts and interpretations of practice.

The discourses of members of the European Convention concerning their experiences of organisational practices revolve around two *topoi:* those of *a positive assessment of the European Convention* and those of *its negative assessment.*

Examples 1 and 2 (below) show how the *topos of positive assessment* was realised, in both cases in discursive accounts of representatives of the EU institutions (in the highlighted cases, Members of the European Parliament). The discourse mainly boiled down to praising the ways in which the Convention was organised but also to displaying a set of some very positive views on, e.g., how diversity of voices was in fact coped with to the benefit of the Convention as an organisational process. Whereas in the first case (Example 1) the speaker points to the thoroughness of the Convention process, in the second case (Example 2) the speaker empha- sises (including in metaphorical ways – note the audibly emphasised economising metaphor 'to invest') that a Convention method 'proved' to be a perfect method for deliberation of views originating from as many contexts and milieus as those represented in the European Convention:

Example 1:

> I expected wh-what we have got (.) I think we've been able to analyse the problems of the existing s-system a lot more thoroughly than I had expected so that's good [AD, 13–19][1]

Example 2:

> It was a positive experience not only for me personally (↓) but I think it was an effort of people coming from (.) different aaa backgrounds (↑) national parliaments (↑) members of government (.) Commission (.) European Parliament (.) civil society the social partners (.) really trying to INVEST to build something in common (.) that was amazing (↑) it was not there from the start on (.) it it was built on (.) during the process and that that PROVES for to me that the process is is yy is a really really good idea to to try to build on (.) common approaches [AvL, 9–15]

Contrary to the above, the *topos of negative assessment* – practically omnipresent in discourses on practice of national parliamentarians taking part in the Convention – points to the ways in which the Convention was set up very strictly in accordance of wishes of powerful actors, in most cases the EU institutions. The realisation of the topos highlighted below (see Example 3) allowed the speaker to argue that the way the Convention was set up only strengthened the position of such power players as the European Commission or the European Parliament and thus allowed their views to become prominent. It also argues that the fact that national parlia- mentarians are not acculturated organizationally in the EU-institutional contexts proves detri- mental to their political position and fuels their inability to present, and defend, their opinions:

Example 3:

> I hoped that at least to start with it would the Convention would deal with ideas it would be free thinking (.) it would be creative (.) but instead it has yyy degenerated rather quickly into a process of institutional bargaining (.) and I noticed yyy that each of the existing institutions and vested interests are each bidding fore more influence and a good example of that is the Commission's paper today (.) which is clearly arguing for more power for the Commission simply (.) yyy as simple as

that (.) and the European Parliament also defends its interests (.) the only (.) group that doesn't do that very well is the national parliamentarians because we are (.) very varied we don't know each other we come from many different countries we are not an institution so we are in danger of losing out

[DHA, 17–26]

As the brief analysis shows, the discrepancy of views expressed in discourses – and encompassed by respective *topoi* – dovetails with the results of ethnographic analyses undertaken during fieldwork (see above). As the discourse shows, there existed namely a huge discrepancy between members of the European Convention, especially as far as their individual/collective agency was concerned. As has been shown before, the way the Convention was set up was – as explored in the observations and related ethnographic methods – crucial to strengthening voices and agency of some (especially those from EU institutions and powerful member states) and weakening the voices and agency of others (especially the dispersed national parliamentarians, usually with very limited experience in the EU contexts). This, in turn, is clearly reflected in *discourses on practice that show that the way power positions were strengthened by organisational cultures and engrenage* – especially of those skilful in EU organisational processes and deliberations – proved central to the observed organisational processes. It also shows that negotiation of power and agency, emphasised in the analysed discourses, was crucial in both discourses and practices and that their interrelated analysis is thus central to a thorough, context-specific discourse-ethnographic exploration of the studied organisational milieus.

Conclusions

This chapter has presented Discourse Ethnographic Approach, a combination of Critical Discourse Studies and Ethnography that takes stock of the recent developments in those research traditions. As the chapter shows, there exists an immense need for combining CDS and Ethnography in problem-oriented studies. This is particularly relevant in studies on complex social and political contexts in which power is central for the ways identities and agency are trans/formed and negotiated, often on an ongoing basis. By presenting examples of examinations driven by the proposed, integrative Discourse-Ethnographic Approach (DEA), the chapter has highlighted ways in which results of, on the one hand, extensive fieldwork and ethnography and, on the other hand, of the closely related critical analysis of discourses of (social) actors' shaping those spaces and acting therein, can be combined and closely interrelated.

Note

1 Transcription symbols used in all examples: (.) – short pause; (6.0), (8.0), (9.0), . . . – longer pause (six seconds, eight seconds, nine seconds duration, etc.); (unread. 6.0) – unreadable elements of speech; [– overlapping speech; Mhm. Eeeee – paraverbal elements; ((leans back)), ((laughs)) – non-verbal behaviour; [Heimat] – elements of original language (difficult to translate); I would not say so – regular speech; THIS – stressed/accentuated element of speech, (↑) – rising intonation (if significant); (↓) – falling intonation (if significant). Coding according to name/surname initials of the interviewees.

Further reading

Agar, M. (2008). *The professional stranger: An informal introduction to ethnography*, 2nd edn. London: Emerald. A classic introduction to ethnography which explains all of its key basics and now also highlights necessity of critical exploration of power in ethnographic research.

Gobo, G. (2008). *Doing ethnography*. London: Sage.
One of the most recent comprehensive introductions to ethnography showing its internal variety as well as diversity of methods in contemporary ethnographic research practice.

Krzyżanowski, M. (ed.)(2011b). *Ethnography and critical discourse analysis*. Special Issue of *Critical Discourse Studies* 8(4). London: Routledge.
This journal special issue highlights various possibilities of combining critical discourse studies and ethnography while researching different public and everyday contexts.

Ocejo, R. (2014). *Upscaling downtown: From bowery saloons to cocktail bars in New York City*. Princeton, NJ: Princeton University Press.
An interesting recent study which shows how a multi-sited ethnography can be deployed in a problem-oriented research.

Wodak, R., Krzyżanowski, M. and Forchtner, B. (2012). The interplay of language ideologies and contextual cues in multilingual interactions: Language choice and code-switching in European Union institutions. *Language in Society* 41(2): 157–186.
An interesting and systematic study which shows how ethnography and language analysis can be combined within research on multilingualism and linguistic diversity in political-institutional contexts.

References

Abélès, M. (1992). *La Vie Quotidienne au Parlement Européen*. Paris: Hachette.

Abélès, M. (1993). Political anthropology of a transnational institution: The European Parliament. *French Politics and Society* 11(1): 1–19.

Abélès, M. (2000). Virtual Europe. In I. Bellier and T.M. Wilson (eds.), *An anthropology of the European Union*, 31–53. Oxford: Berg.

Abélès, M. (2004). Identity and borders: And anthropological approach to EU Institutions. *Twenty first century papers no. 4*, University of Wisconsin-Milwaukee, Milwaukee, WI.

Abélès, M., Bellier, I. and McDonald, M. (1993). *An anthropological approach to the European Commission*. Brussels: The European Commission.

Agar, M. (2008). *The professional stranger: An informal introduction to ethnography*, 2nd edn. London: Emerald.

Aronoff, M. and Kubik, J. (2013). *Anthropology and political science: A convergent approach*. Oxford: Berghahn Books.

Bellier, I. (2000). A Europeanised elite? An anthropology of European Commission officials. *Yearbook of European Studies* 14: 135–156.

Bellier, I. (2002). European identity, institutions and languages in the context of the enlargement. *Journal of Language and Politics* 1(1): 85–114.

Bellier, I. and Wilson, T. M. (eds.) (2000a). *An anthropology of the European Union*. Oxford: Berg.

Bellier, I. and Wilson, T. M. (2000b). Building, imagining and experiencing Europe: Institutions and identities in the European Union. In I. Bellier and T.M. Wilson (eds.), *An anthropology of the European Union*, 1–27. Oxford: Berg.

Bernstein, B. (1990). *The structuring of pedagogic discourse*. London: Routledge.

Blommaert, J., Collins, J., Heller, M., Rampton, B., Slembrouck, S. and Verschueren, J. (2001). Discourse and critique: Part one. *Critique of Anthropology* 21(1): 5–12.

Bourdieu, P. (2005). The political field, the social science field, and the journalistic field. In R. Benson and E. Neveu (eds.), *Bourdieu and the journalistic field*, 29–47. Cambridge: Polity Press.

Brewer, J. D. (2000). *Ethnography*. Buckingham: Open University Press.

Davies, C. A. (1999). *Reflexive ethnography*. London: Routledge.

Egberg, C. (2004). An organisational approach to European integration: Outline of a complementary perspective. *European Journal of Political Research* 43: 199–219.

Fairclough, N. (2001). Critical discourse analysis as a method in social scientific research. In. R. Wodak and M. Meyer (eds.), *Methods of critical discourse analysis*, 121–138. London: Sage.

Fairclough, N. (2009). *Critical discourse analysis*, 2nd rev. edn. London: Pearson Education.

Fairclough, N. and Wodak, R. (1997). Critical discourse analysis. In T. A. van Dijk (ed.), *Discourse as social interaction*, 258–284. London: Sage.

Featherstone, K. and Radaelli, C. M. (eds.) (2004). *The politics of Europeanization*. Oxford: Oxford University Press.

Follesdal, A. and Hix, S. (2006). Why there is a democratic deficit in the EU: A response to Majone and Moravcsik. *Journal of Common Market Studies* 44(3): 533–562.

Galasiński, D. (2011). The patient's world: Discourse analysis and ethnography. *Critical Discourse Studies* 8(4): 253–265.

Gobo, G. (2008). *Doing ethnography*. London: Sage.

Hammersley, M. (1992). *What's wrong with Ethnography? Methodological explorations*. London: Routledge.

Heller, M. (2001). Critique and sociolinguistic analysis of discourse. *Critique of Anthropology* 21(2): 117–141.

Jones, R. (2012). *Discourse analysis*. London: Routledge.

Kassim, H. (2004). A historic accomplishment? The Prodi commission and administrative reform. In D.G. Dimitrakopoulos (ed.). *The changing European Commission*, 33–63. Manchester: Manchester University Press.

Kassim, H. (2008). 'Mission impossible', but mission accomplished: The Kinnock reforms and the European Commission. *Journal of European Public Policy* 15(5): 648–668.

Krzyżanowski, M. (2010). *The discursive construction of European identities: A multilevel approach to discourse and identity in the transforming European Union*. Frankfurt am Main: Peter Lang.

Krzyżanowski, M. (2011a). Political communication, institutional cultures, and linearities of organisational practice: A discourse-ethnographic approach to institutional change in the European Union. *Critical Discourse Studies* 8(4): 281–296.

Krzyżanowski, M. (ed.) (2011b). *Ethnography and critical discourse analysis*. (Special Issue of *Critical Discourse Studies* 8(4)). London: Routledge.

Krzyżanowski, M. (2012). (Mis)communicating Europe? On deficiencies and challenges in political and institutional communication in the European Union. In B. Kryk-Kastovsky (ed.), *Intercultural (mis) communication past and present*, 185–213. Frankfurt am Main: Peter Lang.

Krzyżanowski, M. (2013). Policy, policy communication and discursive shifts: Analyzing EU policy discourses on climate change. In P. Cap and U. Okulska (eds.), *Analyzing genres in political communication: Theory and practice*, 101–134. Amsterdam: Benjamins.

Krzyżanowski, M. (2014). Values, imaginaries and templates of journalistic practice: A critical discourse analysis. *Social Semiotics* 24(3): 345–365.

Krzyżanowski, M. (2015). International leadership re-/constructed? Ambivalence and heterogeneity of identity discourses in European Union's policy on climate change. *Journal of Language & Politics* 14(1): 110–133.

Krzyżanowski, M. (2016). Recontextualisations of neoliberalism and the increasingly conceptual nature of discourse: Challenges for critical discourse studies. *Discourse & Society* 27(3): 308–321.

Krzyżanowski, M. and Forchtner, B. (2016). Theories and concepts in critical discourse studies: Facing challenges, moving beyond foundations. *Discourse & Society* 27(3): 253–261.

Krzyżanowski, M. and Oberhuber, F. (2007). *(Un)doing Europe: Discourses and practices of negotiating the EU constitution*. Brussels: PIE-Peter Lang

Krzyżanowski, M. and Wodak, R. (2009). *The politics of exclusion: Debating migration in Austria*. New Brunswick: Transaction Publishers.

Kubik, J. (2009). Ethnography of politics: Foundations, applications, prospects. In E. Schatz (ed.), *Political ethnography: What immersion contributes to the study of power*, 25–52. Chicago: The University of Chicago Press.

Lazar, M. (2007). Feminist critical discourse analysis: Articulating a feminist discourse praxis. *Critical Discourse Studies* 4(2): 141–164.

Majone, G. (2005). *Dilemmas of European integration*. Oxford: Oxford University Press.

Michailidou, A. (2008). Democracy and new media in the European Union: Communication or participation deficit? *Journal of Contemporary European Research* 4(4): 346–368.

Muntigl, P., Weiss, G. and Wodak, R. (2000). *European Union discourses on unemployment*. Amsterdam: Benjamins.

Oberhuber, F. and Krzyżanowski, M. (2008). Discourse analysis and ethnography. In R. Wodak and M. Krzyżanowski (eds.), *Qualitative discourse analysis in the social sciences*, 182–203. Basingstoke: Palgrave Macmillan.

Ocejo, R. (2014). *Upscaling downtown: From bowery saloons to cocktail bars in New York City*. Princeton, NJ: Princeton University Press.

Pollak, J. (2007). *Repräsentation ohne Demokratie: Kollidierende Modi der Repräsentation in der Europäischen Union*. Vienna: Springer.

Reisigl, M. and Wodak, R. (2009). The discourse-historical approach (DHA). In R. Wodak and M. Meyer (eds.), *Methods of critical discourse analysis,* 2nd edn, 87–121. London: Sage.

Rogers, R. (2011). *An introduction to critical discourse analysis in education.* London: Routledge.

Scollon, R. and Scollon, S. W. (2003). *Discourses in place.* London: Routledge.

Scollon, R. and Scollon, S. W. (2004). *Nexus analysis.* London: Routledge.

Scollon, R. and Scollon, S. W. (2007). Nexus analysis: Refocusing ethnography on action. *Journal of Sociolinguistics* 11(5): 608–625.

Shore, C. (2000). *Building Europe: The cultural politics of European integration.* London: Routledge.

Shore, C. and Abélès, M. (2004). Debating the European Union. *Anthropology Today* 20(2): 10–14.

Shore, C. and Wright, S. (eds.) (1997). *Anthropology of policy: Critical perspectives on governance and power.* London: Routledge.

Tusting, K. and Maybin, J. (2007). Linguistic ethnography and interdisciplinarity: Opening the discussion. *Journal of Sociolinguistics* 11(5): 575–583.

van Dijk, T. A. (2008). *Discourse and context: A sociocognitive approach.* Cambridge: Cambridge University Press.

Van Leeuwen, T. (2008). *Discourse as practice.* Cambridge: Cambridge University Press.

Wodak, R. (1975). *Das Sprachverhalten von Angeklagten bei Gericht.* Kronberg/Ts: Scriptor.

Wodak, R. (1996). *Disorders of discourse.* London: Longman.

Wodak, R. (2000). Recontextualization and transformation of meanings: A critical discourse analysis of decision making in EU-meetings about employment. In S. Sarangi and M. Coulthard (eds.), *Discourse and social life,* 185–206. London: Pearson Education.

Wodak, R. (2001). The discourse-historical approach. In R. Wodak and M. Meyer (eds.), *Methods of critical discourse analysis,* 63–95. London: Sage.

Wodak, R. (2006). Mediation between discourse and society: Assessing cognitive approaches in CDA. *Discourse Studies* 8(1): 179–190.

Wodak, R. (2009). *The discourse of politics in action: Politics as usual.* Basingstoke: Palgrave Macmillan.

Wodak, R. and M. Krzyżanowski (eds.) (2008). *Qualitative discourse analysis in the social sciences.* Basingstoke: Palgrave Macmillan.

Wodak, R., Krzyżanowski, M. and Forchtner, B. (2012). The interplay of language ideologies and contextual cues in multilingual interactions: Language choice and code-switching in European Union institutions. *Language in Society* 41(2): 157–186.

Wodak, R., Menz, F. and Lalouschek, J. (1990). *Alltag auf der Ambulanz.* Tübingen: Narr.

Yanow, D. (2000). *Conducting interpretive policy analysis.* Newbury Park, CA: Sage.

Yanow, D. (2012). Organizational ethnography between toolbox and world-making. *Journal of Organizational Ethnography* 1(1): 31–42.

Ybema, S. (2014). The invention of transitions: History as a symbolic site for discursive struggles over organizational change. *Organization* 21(4): 495–513.

Ybema, S., Yanow, D. and Sabelis, I. (eds.) (2011). *Organizational culture.* Northampton, MA: Emerald Publishing.

Ybema, S., Yanow, D., Wels, H. and Kamsteeg, F. (eds.) (2009). *Organizational ethnography: Studying the complexities of everyday life.* London: Sage.

13

Pragmatics and critical discourse studies

Alexandra Polyzou

Introduction

From Morris's first definition of Pragmatics as the study of the relation between signs and their users (1938: 6–7), this is one aspect all approaches to pragmatics have in common, which has set it apart from previous approaches to linguistics looking at language as an abstract, idealised system. The shift from langue/competence to parole/performance is of course crucial for Discourse Analysis, and subsequently the critical study of discourse, which I will henceforth term Critical Discourse Studies or CDS, and I see it as including any critical approach to discourse such as Critical Linguistics, Feminist Linguistics, Critical Discourse Analysis, areas of Intercultural Communication, etc. Although much of the chapter focusses on aspects of and work within Critical Discourse Analysis (CDA), I also make reference to critical scholars who would not necessarily label themselves as CD Analysts. Therefore, I use the acronym CDA when referring to scholars specifically aligning themselves with the CDA field, and CDS to refer to any critical work on discourse, which may include but not be limited to CD Analysts. In this chapter I argue that despite criticisms that Pragmatics is individualistic and does not take context sufficiently into account (Fairclough 2001 [1989]: 7–8), it has been valuable both theoretically and methodologically for the critical analysis of discourse.

Furthermore, I discuss specifically cognitive approaches to Pragmatics (Relevance Theory and Cognitive Linguistics) as a helpful way to operationalise the examination of the discourse-society-cognition interface (van Dijk 1998, 2003, 2005, 2006, 2008). Broadly speaking, cognitive pragmatic accounts provide the potential for accounting for the impact of context on discourse and of discourse on context, mediated by the cognitions of the participants in discursive and social action ('members' resources', in Fairclough's terms, 2001: 8–9). Finally, I propose a socio-cognitive approach to presupposition aiming to account for ideological inferences and taken-for-granted assumptions in discourse which I illustrate with the analysis of a media text (from the Greek version of *Marie Claire,* Feb. 2006), focussing specifically on gender ideologies.

Background

During the early days of CDA, Fairclough (2001: 7–8) criticised Pragmatics, in particular the Anglo-Saxon tradition, primarily associated with the work of Austin (1962, 1975) on Speech

Acts and Grice (1975) on implicature. Fairclough's criticisms revolve around two significant points. First, he argues that Pragmatics does not take into account the conditions and power imbalances of the social world, and instead postulates an ideal, smooth communicative situation. Second, he finds problematic the theorisation of the participants of communicative events, which "understates the extent to which people are caught up in, constrained by, and indeed derive their individual identities from social conventions" (2001: 7–8). I will address these criticisms in turn.

Both Austin and Grice have been describing what they saw as norms of communication, in an attempt to begin explaining how 'ordinary communication' works as opposed to the formalised language philosophy prevalent at the time. This limited scope has led Fairclough to suggest that Pragmatics "often appears to describe discourse as it might be in a better world, rather than discourse as it is" (Fairclough 2001: 8). One might thus imagine that Pragmatics postulates a sort of Habermasian 'ideal situation' (Habermas 1970, 1979, 1981 – see Chilton 1987 on the analogy between Habermas and Grice in that sense). One could perhaps envisage Grice (1975) describing an 'ideal speech situation' where the Maxims of the Co-operative Principle always hold – and which is clearly not the 'default case' in communication.[1] But then Habermas, whose work has been very influential in CDS, has also been criticised for the fact that his 'ideal speech situation' does not exist (see Forchtner 2010, for a discussion). Importantly, however, neither Grice nor Habermas claim that this is normally the case.

There are two interpretations of Grice that help address Fairclough's criticism, which I will look at in turn. The first one is considering the Co-operative Principle and the Maxims as an ideal aim, and the second as a cognitive reality which influences discourse processing in specific ways (by generating implicatures).

In the former case, the Maxims are not a reality but rather a goal, not necessarily attainable, but rather a direction towards which communicators must aim to move, achieving more and more successful communication the closer they are to the goal. 'Successful communication' could be, in the minimalist sense (see Chilton 2004: 20), 'achieving (optimal) understanding' – in the narrow sense of simply making meaning out of strings of sounds or visual symbols. Neo-Gricean pragmatics and Relevance Theory also focus on this level quite extensively – see e.g., Sperber and Wilson (1986: 161). CDS would be more concerned with communication in a broader sense – we might consider communication successful for one participant only if that participant has met her goals regardless of or even at the expense of another. Or we might argue that communication is more successful the more equal the power dynamics surrounding it are, in that sense the closer it resembles Habermas's (or Grice's) 'ideal speech situation' (a 'maximalist' interpretation of the Co-operative Principle – Chilton 1987).

In the latter case, looking at pragmatic norms such as Austin's Felicity Conditions of Grice's Maxims as cognitive principles rather than prescriptive norms, we could argue that such Maxims are not necessarily meant to be followed – by flouting Maxims we generate humour, literary texts, politeness or simply save time by not spelling out every single detail. This interpretation is still too narrow for critical discourse analysts – we still need to enrich the analysis by looking at the broader context – is humour used at someone's expense? And if yes, why and how can the speaker get away with it? Why do certain speakers need to employ more, or more deferential, politeness strategies than others? Does poetic usage of language, in both fiction and non-fiction, convey underlying ideologies, taking certain ideological assumptions for granted while discrediting others?

The differences outlined so far between Pragmatics and Critical Discourse Analysis, or CDS in general, do not constitute irreconcilable differences in epistemological foundations, but rather differences in scope. We can still see pragmatological analysis as an essential first step, as arguably for any type of discourse to have any effect whatsoever it first needs to be understood on a very essential level by a number of people. In addition, and more interestingly, Pragmatics will also look at cases where things don't work – where Maxims are violated, or where Speech Acts are performed infelicitously. Pragmatics may then focus on what happens to the communication then, in the sense of understanding (will we take something as a joke? As a mistake? As nonsensical?). CDS, turning to context and thus expanding the initial analysis, can tell us *why* participants were led to communicate in this way (Fear? Lack of access to particular cognitive and/or discursive resources? Institutional constraints?), and look at the further effects such indirectness may have on the broader social context (such as rendering certain facts or voices invisible, or normalising ideological assumptions). Thus, Pragmatics would be able to deal with situational context, while Critical Discourse Studies would be able to link this to the broader socio-cultural and political context (Fairclough 1995a; Wodak 2004).

Acknowledging this difference in scope not as a shortcoming, but rather a useful methodological distinction, can also help counter Fairclough's second criticism – that of individualism. Both Pragmatics and CDS deal with 'the user' of language (or other forms of semiosis); CDS explicitly and systematically theorises 'the user' as a product and producer of this broader context in addition to the immediate interactional communicative goals and effects. This supplements, rather than opposes, pragmatological accounts of the discourse users. Indeed, Mey (1989), taking stock of the trajectory of pragmatics up to that point, and offering his vision for the future, argues that "there is a pragmatic aspect to all linguistic phenomena" (1989: 829; see also Verschueren 1987), and that pragmatics "should get itself involved in improving the human environment" (Mey 1989: 830). To the extent that this has been done, critical approaches to discourse have been crucial in providing this widening of scope. Historically, the fact that Pragmatics "has provided a space for investigating the interdependence of language and social context which was not available before its inception", albeit "a strictly constrained space" (Fairclough 2001: 8), has been a valuable first step, in that it acknowledges the crucial interdependence of language and context in discourse. The explicit theorisation of what is 'not said' in Pragmatics indeed points to context and helps counter more recent criticisms that critical linguists 'read into' texts ideologies that are not in fact there (Cameron 2005).

Bringing CDS and pragmatics together

The difference in scope, as well as the overlap, between Pragmatics and CDS is reflected in conferences and publications focussing primarily on Pragmatics or CDS. The former often happily include applications of pragmatics for critical analyses of discourse dealing with issues of ideology and power in media, political, medical, institutional and intercultural contexts (e.g., Borutti 1984; Harris 1995; Magalhães 1995; Sbisà 1999; Maillat and Oswald 2009; Cap 2014; Hansson 2015; Croom 2015), including the branch of 'emancipatory pragmatics', aiming to move away from Western-centeredness in pragmatics applications (Hanks 2014).

Likewise, publications focussing on the critical analysis of discourse include looking at parameters addressed in pragmatics (e.g., Fetzer and Bull 2012; Fetzer 2013; Polyzou 2015a; Murphy 2015; Efe and Forchtner 2015). However for the most part pragmatic concepts don't figure very prominently in titles or keywords in CDA work. This is perhaps not surprising given that CDA and CDS in general are eclectic and data driven. Although it is very unlikely that any given piece of discourse may not include speech acts, implicatures or presuppositions, and depending on the definition, indirectness, vagueness and resulting inferencing will be a feature of all discourse (see Sperber and Wilson 1995 [1986]; Channel 1994; O'Halloran 2003), these specific linguistic features may not be necessarily the most relevant for answering the research questions of the project.

It should be noted that uses of pragmatics tools for critical discourse analytical purposes may be more widespread than initially evident, because CDS eclecticism means that pragmatic parameters will form only part of the analysis rather than being the focus of a whole paper, chapter or article. The usefulness of Pragmatics for critical analysis has been explicitly acknowledged, for example in relation to ideological aspects of speech acts (Fairclough 2001: 131). Speech Act Theory has been further expanded in theorising genres as broad types of speech/communicative acts (Bhatia 1993: 13; Swales 1990: 58; van Leeuwen 2008: 348; Polyzou 2008; Tsiplakou and Floros 2013) and in the concept of performativity, namely the 'doing' of identities through semiosis (Butler 1990, 1993).

In relation to the study of indirectness and its various strategic uses in discourse, Chilton (2004) extensively applies the pragmatic concepts of implicature and presupposition to the analysis of political discourse. Wodak (2007) also makes a strong case for the application of Pragmatics for CDA by highlighting how extreme right-wing discourse has been indirectly communicating anti-Semitic beliefs through the use of allusion, presupposition and implicature. Sarazin (2009, 2015) looks extensively at unstated meanings arising through implicature and frames. Presupposition also contributes to non-obvious expression of ideological beliefs in discourse and has formed part of wider critical analyses, as in Magalhães (1995), Fairclough (2001: 127 ff.), Christie (2000: 24–25; 88 ff.), Bekalu (2006), Talbot (2010: Ch. 7), Kosetzi and Polyzou (2009), Polyzou (2013), KhosraviNik (2015) and Flowerdew (1997, 2012; Flowerdew and Leong 2010). In section 4, I discuss presupposition and ideology in more detail.

Thus, the difference of scope is not necessarily a weakness insofar as CDS utilises these tools with its usual eclecticism and supplements them with rigorous social analyses, while Pragmatics can provide valuable contributions to systematic and context-sensitive analysis of meaning. The realm of 'meaning', and in particular 'meaning in the real world' is crucial for the socio-cognitive representations that constitute, contribute to or challenge ideologies and guide social action. My position is that we need to understand how meaning works both in terms of abstract principles and in the implementation (or not) of these principles in context – indeed we might need to have an idea of the former before we proceed to the latter. Ultimately, following an emancipatory agenda, we may aim to interfere with the socio-cognitive meaning-making processes we study, both in campaigns against discriminatory language (which can be cynically seen as mere exercises in political correctness but can have very real positive impact on vulnerable social groups) but crucially in continuing to challenge and uncover 'taken-for-granted' and therefore socially acceptable inequalities which may be reproduced in discourse in a less obvious way exactly due to unstated premises, felicity conditions, connotations/associations – presupposed shared mental representations in general.

In the present chapter I have not focussed equally on all possible aspects of Pragmatics relevant to critical analysis. Following Mey's broad definition we could arguably include aspects such as modality, deixis and conversation analytical categories, in addition to categories I only touch upon here and below, such as politeness and metaphor. Not all pragmaticians though would include these in 'Pragmatics proper' (although undoubtedly they are important categories of discourse analysis); so I have chosen to focus on the less contestable prototypical Anglo-Saxon tradition. I would like to move on to advocate a cognitive pragmatic perspective as particularly suitable for CDS.

Reviewing the work currently done in bringing cognition into the critical study of discourse is beyond the scope of this chapter, as this is covered elsewhere in this handbook (see

Hart, this volume), but it is important to point out that adopting a cognitive linguistic perspective addresses the problem of selecting a theory of language. According to Fairclough "[t] extual analysis presupposes a theory of language and a grammatical theory, and one problem for [CDA] is to select from amongst those available" (1995b: 10). Fairclough, like many scholars in CDA and Critical Linguistics, often selects and applies Systemic Functional Linguistics for his analyses (Halliday 1985), to which cognitive linguistics bears affinities in terms of socio-functional orientation. However, there is a large body of work that does not explicitly follow either SFL or Cognitive Linguistics. O'Halloran (2003) points out that not making the choice of (socio-)linguistic theory explicit can lead to problematic analysis, while Chilton emphasises that, by ignoring cognition and its workings, CDA may appear to be making claims "in a theoretical vacuum" (2005: 34; see also van Dijk 1998: 43–46). Therefore, a critical discourse analyst must self-consciously and explicitly adopt a theory of language. I would further add that the selected theory must be compatible with the epistemological positions of CDS, and that Cognitive Linguistics is one of the most compatible available theories.

Presupposition and CDS: a socio-cognitive approach

From a cognitive perspective, presupposition constitutes the ground in figure-ground distinctions in discourse, which is necessary for understanding the discourse and not possible to question or negate unless said ground is explicitly foregrounded/drawn attention to (see Polyzou 2015a for a more detailed account of the framework). Thus, presuppositions can only be negated through what I would call 'metarepresentational negation', two types of which are 'cross-frame negation' (in Frame Semantics – Fillmore 1985; Marmaridou 2000) and 'metalinguistic negation' (in Horn 2004, as well as Relevance Theory).

Most often analysts consider presupposition on the noun-phrase level (existential presupposition – presupposing the existence of the referent) or on the clause-sentence level. I propose that presupposed material is ubiquitous in discourse and can be analysed on a number of (interconnected) levels including:

- Lexical level (presupposed frames): These are of interest to critical analysis as lexical choices (Fairclough 1992), referential and predicational strategies (Reisigl and Wodak 2001), and they figure as an important feature in the representation of social actors (van Leeuwen 1996), including metaphorical representations (see e.g., Fairclough 1992: 194–198).
- Clause/sentence level: prototypically in English these involve single clauses (I stopped smoking → I used to smoke, I regret arguing with her → I argued with her); however, in Greek the gerund would be realised as a telic subordinate clause. Thus this category would include single-clause as well as complex sentences. Co-ordinating conjunctions such as 'but' and 'or' also carry presupposed given assumptions (what Grice has termed conventional implications – see Grice 1975; Levinson 1983: 127), but this discussion is beyond the scope of this chapter.
- Discourse level: Previously I have defined this as background knowledge of broader discursive formations, which would inevitably include socio-cognitive ideological assumptions (Polyzou 2015a). Here I would like to propose dividing this category into sub-categories according to Fairclough's discourse types – discourse, genre and style (1992, 1993, 2003). In the following analysis I will focus on presupposed discourses and generic expectations, but I have briefly addressed style in earlier work (2008, 2015b – see also Flowerdew and Leong 2010).

I also propose an additional 'pragmatic competence' level, which is in fact a meta-level, in the sense that it includes presupposed assumptions about the way discourse operates in general, so it is a presupposition *about* presuppositions, such as 'Felicity's condition' discussed by Goffman (1983), or that referring expressions have referents (Frege 1948 [1892]: 221) – in short, that people have reasons for their behaviour, including communicative behaviour (Thomas 1995: 121–122). It is at this level that people's 'theories of mind' operate, i.e., assumptions about how to 'decode' and understand other people's feelings and thoughts.[2] Thus, while the above levels (lexical to discourse) are concerned with declarative knowledge (beliefs and assumptions), the pragmatic meta-level is about procedural knowledge (how to 'make sense' of discourse and the world) – see van Dijk (2003: 90) on types of knowledge.

Case study

I would like to demonstrate the application of the framework in relation specifically to gender-related ideological assumptions underlying a lifestyle magazine text. The text is from the Greek version of *Marie Claire* (Feb 2006), translated into English (see Appendix for both versions. Line numbers are the same in both versions. I have tried to keep as closely as possible to the original in terms of translation, but provide additional commentary as required in the following analysis).

The text is broadly an 'advice text' – specifically, it provides advice about how the (presumably female heterosexual) readers can increase the sexual desire of their (presumably male heterosexual) partner. Inevitably the analysis will not be exhaustive, but I am hoping to illustrate the different levels on which we can consider ideological presuppositions in the text.

Headline

The word-for-word translation of the headline would be 'Raise his libido to the heights!', which I have freely translated as follows:

(1)   Make his libido skyrocket! (l.7)

Analysing this from the narrowest text-bound perspective, the headline existentially presupposes that 'he' – i.e., a male being – exists, and that he has a libido (his libido exists). Much more is derived as readers draw on their background knowledge, 'contextual assumptions' (Sperber and Wilson 1995 [1986]) or 'member's resources' (Fairclough 2001 [1989]).

The headline is the very first element of the text we normally read, so 'his' is not anaphoric, and due to the genre and its distribution it cannot be deictic either. Such non-anaphoric third person pronouns, e.g., 'he/him/his' are very often found in magazine texts with no further elaboration. A Hornean analysis would look at this as triggering an implicature by flouting the Maxim of Quantity – we are not told who 'he' is, therefore we must work it out. We work out that the referent is a male sexual partner based on shared heteronormative assumptions about monogamous active heterosexuality.

Other background knowledge utilising processing here is the readers' familiarity with the genre 'lifestyle magazine'[3] which typically includes content on (heterosexual) relationships, as by now use of mere pronouns to refer to partners constitutes a generic convention. Presumed heterosexuality and knowledge of the genre also includes knowledge on whether the lifestyle magazine in question is 'men's' or 'women's', and makes it more likely to interpret 'he' in (1) as the male partner of a presumed female heterosexual reader rather than of a gay male reader.

Analysing the speech act, we recognise it as a prototypically directive one due to the imperative. Again, knowledge of the genre leads us to interpret this as suggestion or advice rather than a command or request. In line with the felicity conditions of advice speech acts, and politeness principles (Brown and Levinson 1987) the inferred (by the reader), presented as taken for granted (by the text producer) assumptions here are that making one's partner's libido skyrocket is desirable and beneficial – otherwise it would not constitute felicitous advice, or not advice at all – and in the latter case would require some facework to mitigate the command or request.

The existential presupposition about the male libido, as well as the frame semantics of the term, evoke associations with Freudian psychoanalysis, but also more broadly folk cultural understandings about the 'Male Sexual Drive' (Hollway 1984), namely that such a thing exists and that it can metaphorically go up and down, i.e., increase or decrease, and that it is desirable for any man to have a 'high' libido.

Therefore, broadening the scope from the more micro-linguistic elements of such a sentence, discursively/ideologically, the headline and the whole article are based on the assumptions that everyone is heterosexual (female readers and male partners) and in (or at least aspiring to be in) a monogamous relationship where sex (or at least the male partner's desire for sex) is a desirable feature. These assumptions are normative as they are both taken for granted (backgrounded and not questioned), and also positively evaluated in that the reader is given advice on how to increase this presupposed male sexual desire.

Sentence-level presupposition

Numerous ideological assumptions are also presented as 'given' through classical sentence-level presuppositions (the presupposed assumptions are underlined):

(2)   Did you know that *23% of men prefer watching television than having sex*? (l.9)
(3)   No matter how much *we believe that men have nothing else on their mind but. . . you-know-what* . . . (l.16–17)
(4)   . . . the latest research [survey] of *Durex* reveals that *23% of men prefer television and other sedentary sports to sex*. (l.17–18)
(5)   . . . stop *nagging about his performance (l.32)*

Example 2 constitutes informative presupposition, presenting information presumed to be new to the reader (and then repeated in Example 4). The 'presupposition triggers', i.e., the phrases introducing the presupposed assumptions, frame the proposition that "23% of men prefer TV to sex" as definitely true and incontestable. In that sense the information is only backgrounded in relation to the reader's ignorance of it up until that point. Namely, this is definitely the case, but it is only now that we know it (since the research by *Durex* has revealed it/since we have been reading the article).

This emphasis on ignorance has a further pragmatic function – this new information is not only incontestable and hitherto unknown, but also surprising, and potentially unsettling. This is because on the speech act level this serves to justify the necessity of the advice as a felicity condition. Giving someone advice to solve a non-existent problem is not felicitous, so here the lack of interest in sex on behalf of 23% of the male participants in a survey is set up as a problem that needs to be addressed.

The necessity of advice is also justified through example (3). Here it is taken for granted that 'we [presumably women] believe that men have nothing else on their mind' but sex.

Again it is necessary to presuppose this belief on behalf of the readers (including the author(s) for solidarity) in order to dismantle it by presenting the results of the survey. Clearly if the reader was never under the impression that men only think of sex, she wouldn't need to be told that they actually don't.

'Stop nagging' clearly presupposes (takes for granted) that the reader nags, i.e., is engaging in a type of talk carrying negative characteristics. On the discursive level this draws on very widespread and commonplace assumptions about women's talk – that women do talk – a lot – but also that they complain; they do so perhaps in a high-pitched voice; they do so persistently and inconsiderately, etc.

Existential presuppositions and framing

We need to distinguish between existential presuppositions, merely presupposing the existence of something, and lexical choices, which frame the said 'something', the referent, in particular ways. The two interact in conjunction to evoke ideological beliefs.

Throughout the text it is taken for granted, through existential presuppositions, that there is a male partner in the female reader's life, and that there is one partner (he, your partner, your lover). The lexis chosen to refer to this partner reflects more specifically the framing of both the person and the relationship of this person to the reader.

The masculine pronoun, as well as the grammatically masculine nouns 'partner' and 'lover', indicate that the partner is male. Importantly, there is no vocabulary indicating a marital relationship, such as 'spouse/husband' or 'marriage'. This indicates that in the context (Greece 2006) marriage is no longer such a strong normative assumption to the extent that it used to be – it is now acceptable to talk in public about extramarital sex and provide advice on it. Nevertheless, the use of the term 'partner' (the Greek term can also be translated as 'companion' or 'comrade'), and, pragmatically, the lack of need of disambiguation for the pronouns 'he/him' etc., evokes a relatively stable long-term relationship. Multiple and/or very short-term partners still constitute a social stigma for women, and consequently textually they are not treated as the default type of partner. On the other hand, 'partner' is a superordinate term which includes a marital partner, thus not excluding married readers.

The existential presupposition of a partner of course does not mean that the text authors naively assume that every reader has a partner. The same as the sex, number and sexual orientation of partners involved, the presupposition is normative – to paraphrase Sbisà (1999: 501), what ought to be true. The same as a lesbian or straight male reader, a single female heterosexual reader reading this will be receiving the message that she somehow departs from expectations – if she doesn't have a partner, she ought to have one.

Discourse level

The above illustrative analyses on the frame and sentence level have perhaps helped make more transparent the (types of) specific textual anchors evoking ideological assumptions in the text. At the same time it is clear that only looking at these levels does not fully account for the discourses underlying the text. For that we need to look both at what is not presupposed but rather asserted/presented as new, as well as widen the scope to look at the associations and implications of the narrow-scope presuppositions involved. For example, it has taken a widening of scope of the analysis to consider that the persistent existential presupposition of a male referent further evokes a specific type of male person – a sexual partner – presumably fulfilling the heteronormative requirements of the social context – monogamous, heterosexual, of the 'appropriate' age and other demographic characteristics, etc.

Likewise, the setting up of the 'problem' in the 'problem-solution' structure of this instance of an advice text has included not only (3) and (4), but also the existential 'the *45% of women who say that they would like more sex*' (l.19), the rhetorical 'Unbelievable?' (l.10) and exclamation marks indicating that these facts are indeed unbelievable, surprising and unpleasantly so (l.20, l.22). Thus lack of sexual desire on behalf of a man is constructed as a problem, evoking normative assumptions about both male and female sexuality.

On the discourse level thus we have a Male Sexual Drive discourse, which is also manifested through the framings/associations of the presupposed male 'libido', 'sexual drive', 'erotic mood' and 'testosterone levels'. On the other hand, we have a Passive Femininity discourse manifested on various levels. Two main features of the Passive Femininity are predominant in this text – manipulativeness and domesticity.

On the frame level, the way the reader is admonished to influence her partner's behaviour is not by persuading him, or arguing with him (rationally or otherwise) – that would be 'nagging'. Instead, she is supposed to do what I have translated (deliberately awkwardly) from Greek as 'drifting him' – i.e., making him drift. That is, he should be carried away, not making a conscious decision (or any decision at all). On the clause/sentence level, this is supposed to happen 'without him realising' (l.33–34) – thus, it is not *asserted* or even suggested that the male partner shouldn't realise he is being 'seduced' – it is taken for granted, needing no further explanation or elaboration. The focus is rather on *how* to achieve this, rather than on whether this should be the aim in the first place. Throughout the text, the reader is advised to expose her partner to various ways to increase his libido without telling him what they are for. Twice she is in fact advised to lie – once through the projected direct speech, with the assertion that a 'sex shrub' is 'nothing, darling, just a multivitamin' and once through being told to convince her partner to go for a walk through 'excuses'.

It is anyway taken for granted that the reader will lie when she does not want to have sex as well: 'if you don't feel like sex [. . .] remove the [cinnamon] stick from his pillow [. . .] so that you will not start with the lies again "darling, I have a headache"' (l.71–74). 'Again' is a typical clause level presupposition trigger – clearly it is taken for granted that the reader has been lying before. Discursively this, in conjunction with the direct speech, draws not only on stereotypical beliefs about the (lack of a) female sexual drive, but also about the way a woman would go about achieving her goals – through lying and excuses.

The domestic aspect of the Passive Femininity presupposed underlies the specifics of the speech acts related to advice, and specifically the content. The use of unmitigated imperatives is rather a matter of style, constructing the advice-giver as an authority and the content as beneficial to the recipient (therefore not an imposition). However, when someone is advised to do something unusual, some justification is needed for this course of action. For example, it takes some explanation as to why it has to be cinnamon or garlic that the reader has to give her partner. What does not require any explanation is that she will be taking care of the couple's nutrition anyway – making cookies, preparing the weekly menu, making her partner cups of tea and even giving him multivitamins. Any similar advice addressed to men, if it is given at all, would include suggestions that a man might want to make a meal to impress his partner (or, more likely, prospective partner) – here cooking is a given, the question rather is what to cook.

These assumptions draw on very persistent stereotypes about feminine behaviour, taking even the less desirable aspects (manipulation) for granted. Another non-obvious presupposed assumption of passivity emerges if we look more closely at why the 'problem' addressed in this advice text is a problem. The first reason given earlier in the text is that, while some men are not very interested in sex, 45% of the women in the survey "say that they would like more sex" – therefore, women not getting what they want out of their relationship. And women want more sex because they enjoy sex more, especially as they grow older (l.25–26), an assertion which is put as such because it may well be 'new information' for some of the readers. Soon afterwards, however, this is qualified with "we women translate differently the erotic game/game of love: it gives us a sense of affection and security from our partner, consequently if he is not in the mood, we get frustrated and feel that he is rejecting us" (l.26–27). Thus, while men's sexual desires are related to their libido and testosterone levels (a physical sexual drive), women's are related to emotional needs for affection, security and acceptance (if present at all). This is further elaborated on with the existential "the typical female insecurities" (l.29–30), presupposing that typically women will be insecure about their appearance and blame this for their partner's lack of sexual desire. Finally, the negative polarity question takes female passivity for granted: "Isn't it what you were after? Him acting and you reacting?" (l.97). In short, women are assumed to only want sex to fulfil their emotional needs, and most importantly to need to be desired rather than feeling desire and fulfilling it. Their passivity explains the need for manipulation and lack of initiative, perhaps due to fear of rejection – in terms of absences in the text, nowhere is the reader to either talk openly to her partner or initiate sexual activity (as opposed to similar texts in other magazines, such as *Cosmopolitan*, with a slightly different profile and target readership).

Concluding remarks

The analysis of a single text can only provide a snapshot of aspects of the social issue in question in any project, and it needs to be noted that not all discourse in the contemporary Greek context follows exactly the same assumptions as the ones identified here. Nevertheless these assumptions are by no means unusual or exceptional either – and the designation of 'old/ shared/given' vs. 'new' information in the text indicates as well as reinforces that. In the above analysis I hope to have indicated more or less clearly both the linguistic triggers (or 'cues') linking to these assumptions, as well as the breadth of scope of analysis leading to each finding. The broader the scope the more of the analysts' knowledge and interpretation is required – and this is where social theory and sociological research becomes more relevant – while the narrower scope analysis is more in line with more traditional pragmatic analyses. The model presented above is only one way we can employ for CDS, in addition to other work discussed here and in other chapters of this volume.

Conclusion

Pragmatics has been one of the earliest attempts to link language and context in linguistics, as well as consider language use as action rather than merely a reflection of states of affairs in the world, and as such at least in principle is in consonance with critical and social constructivist approaches to discourse. The discussion here has primarily focussed on the Anglo-Saxon Pragmatics tradition (with some mention of Habermas) and then moved on to cognitive approaches to Pragmatics (and CDS) aiming to demonstrate the epistemological and methodological compatibility of these approaches with CDS. Indeed there are a number of meeting points and overlaps, as demonstrated by the research already fruitfully combining CDS. Pragmatics concepts and/or Cognitive Linguistic theoretical and methodological considerations. Importantly, the narrower (micro) applications of Pragmatics combine well with broader (macro) discursive structures or types, which then correspond to narrower or broader socio-cognitive structures, from frames to ideologies.

Acknowledgements: I would like to thank Paul Chilton and the editors for their comments on earlier drafts of this chapter. Any remaining weaknesses are my own.

Further reading

Cameron, D. (2005). Relativity and its discontents: Language, gender and pragmatics. *Intercultural Pragmatics* 2–3: 321–334.

This article discusses how pragmatic theory accounts systematically for indirect ideological meanings in discourse. It includes an overview of main pragmatic concepts and illustrative examples.

Oswald, S. (2014). It is easy to miss something you are not looking for: A pragmatic account of covert communicative influence for (critical) discourse analysis. In C. Hart and P. Cap (eds.), *Contemporary studies in critical discourse analysis,* 97–120. London: Bloomsbury.

This chapter provides a relevance-theoretical definition of manipulation as covert communicative influence. It demonstrates how discourse can result in manipulation by exploiting the function of cognitive faculties.

Polyzou, A. (2015). Presupposition in discourse: Theoretical and methodological issues. *Critical Discourse Studies* 12(2): 123–138.

This article provides an overview of the main pragmatic approaches of presupposition, with a focus on how they have been used within critical discourse studies. It provides a critique of current approaches and an introduction to the presupposition model applied in this chapter.

van Dijk, T. A. (2005). Contextual knowledge management in discourse production: A CDA perspective. In R. Wodak and P. Chilton (eds.), *A new agenda in (critical) discourse analysis: Theory, methodology and interdisciplinarity,* 71–100. Amsterdam, Philadelphia: Benjamins.

This chapter highlights the role of social cognition – in particular, knowledge management – in discourse. It touches upon a range of parameters from a cognitive perspective and provides an illustrative textual analysis to show how background/contextual knowledge comes into play in (ideological) discourse.

References

Austin, J. L. (1962). *How to do things with words: The William James lectures delivered at Harvard University in 1955.* Oxford: Clarendon.

Austin, J. L. (1975). *How to do things with words,* 2nd edn. Oxford: Oxford University Press.

Bhatia, V. K. (1993). *Analysing genre: Language use in professional settings.* London, New York: Longman.

Bekalu, M. A. (2006). Presupposition in news discourse. *Discourse & Society* 17(2): 147–172.

Borutti, S. (1984). Pragmatics and its discontents. *Journal of Pragmatics* 8: 437–447.

Brown, P. and Levinson, S. (1987). *Politeness: Some universals in language use.* Cambridge: Cambridge University Press.

Butler, J. (1990). *Gender trouble: Feminism and the subversion of identity.* New York: Routledge.

Butler, J. (1993). *Bodies that matter: The discursive limits of "sex".* New York: Routledge.

Cameron, D. (2005). Relativity and its discontents: Language, gender and pragmatics. *Intercultural Pragmatics* 2–3: 321–334.

Cap, P. (2014). Applying cognitive pragmatics to critical discourse studies: A proximization analysis of three public space discourses. *Journal of Pragmatics* 70: 16–30.

Channel, J. (1994). *Vague language.* Oxford: Oxford University Press.

Chilton, P. (1987). Co-operation and non-co-operation: Ethical and political aspects of pragmatics. *Language and Communication* 7(3): 221–229.

Chilton, P. (2004). *Analysing political discourse: Theory and practice.* London, New York: Routledge.

Chilton, P. (2005). Missing links in mainstream CDA: Modules, blends and the critical instinct. In R. Wodak and P. Chilton (eds.), *A new agenda in (critical) discourse analysis,* 19–51. Amsterdam, Philadelphia: Benjamins.

Christie, C. (2000). *Gender and language: Towards a feminist pragmatics.* Edinburgh: Edinburgh University Press.

Croom, A. (2015). Slurs and stereotypes for Italian Americans: A context-sensitive account of derogation and appropriation. *Journal of Pragmatics* 81: 36–51.

Efe, I. and Forchtner, B. (2015). 'Saying sorry' in Turkey: The Dersim massacre of the 1930s in 2011. *Journal of Language and Politics* 14(2): 233–257.

Fairclough, N. (1989/2001). *Language and power*. London: Longman.

Fairclough, N. (1992). *Discourse and social change*. Cambridge: Polity Press.

Fairclough, N. (1993). Critical discourse analysis and the marketization of public discourse: The universities. *Discourse and Society* 4(1): 133–168.

Fairclough, N. (1995a). *Media discourse*. London: E. Arnold.

Fairclough, N. (1995b). *Critical discourse analysis: The critical study of language*. London: Longman.

Fairclough, N. (2003). *Analysing discourse: Textual analysis for social research*. London: Routledge.

Fetzer, A. (ed.) (2013). *The pragmatics of political discourse: Explorations across cultures*. Amsterdam, Philadelphia: Benjamins.

Fetzer, A. and Bull, P. (2012). Doing leadership in political speech: Semantic processes and pragmatic inferences. *Discourse & Society* 23(2): 127–144.

Fillmore, C. C. (1985). Frames and the semantics of understanding. *Quaderni di Semantica* VI: 222–254.

Flowerdew, J. (1997). The discourse of colonial withdrawal: A case study in the creation of mythic discourse. *Discourse and Society* 8(4): 493–517.

Flowerdew, J. (2012). *Critical discourse analysis in historiography: The case of Hong Kong's evolving political identity*. Basingstoke: Palgrave Macmillan.

Flowerdew, J. and Leong, S. (2010). Presumed meaning in the discursive construction of socio-political and cultural identity. *Journal of Pragmatics* 42(8): 2240–2252.

Forchtner, B. (2010). Jürgen Habermas' language-philosophy and the critical study of language. *Critical Approaches to Discourse Analysis Across Disciplines* 4(1): 18–37.

Frege, G. (1892/1948). Sense and reference. *The Philosophical Review* 57(3): 209–230.

Goffman, E. (1983). Felicity's condition. *American Journal of Sociology* 89(1): 1–53.

Grice, H. P. (1975). Logic and conversation. In P. Cole and J. Morgan (eds.), *Syntax and semantics: 3: Speech acts*, 41–58. New York: Academic Press.

Habermas, J. (1970). Towards a theory of communicative competence. In H.P. Dreitzel (ed.), *Recent sociology*, Vol. 2, 114–148. New York: Macmillan.

Habermas, J. (1979). *Communication and the evolution of society*. London: Heinemann.

Habermas, J. (1981). *Theorie des kommunikativen Handelns*. Frankfurt: Suhrkamp.

Halliday, M. (1985). *An introduction to functional grammar*. London: Edward Arnold.

Hanks, W. (2014). Editorial: Introduction to emancipatory pragmatics, Special issue Part 3: From practice theory to ba theory. *Journal of Pragmatics* 69: 1–3.

Hansson, S. (2015). Calculated overcommunication: Strategic uses of prolixity, irrelevance, and repetition in administrative language. *Journal of Pragmatics* 84: 172–188.

Harris, S. (1995). Pragmatics and power. *Journal of Pragmatics* 23: 117–135.

Hollway, W. (1984). Gender differences and the production of subjectivity. In J. Henriques, W. Hollway, C. Urwin, C. Venn and V. Walkerdine (eds.), *Changing the subject: Psychology, social regulation and subjectivity*, 227–263. London: Methuen.

Horn, L. (2004). Implicature. In L. Horn and G. Ward (eds.), *The handbook of pragmatics*, 3–28. Oxford: Blackwell.

KhosraviNik, M. (2015). *Discourse, identity and legitimacy: Self and other in representations of Iran's nuclear programme*. Amsterdam, Philadelphia: Benjamins.

Kosetzi, K. and Polyzou, A. (2009). Ο ΤΕΛΕΙΟΣ ΑΝΤΡΑΣ, Ο ΑΝΤΡΑΣ Ο ΣΩΣΤΟΣ – 'THE PERFECT MAN, THE PROPER MAN' – Construals of masculinities in Nitro, a Greek men's lifestyle magazine – an exploratory study. *Gender and Language* 3(2): 143–180.

Levinson, S. C. (1983). *Pragmatics*. Cambridge, New York: Cambridge University Press.

Magalhães, M.I.S. (1995). A critical discourse analysis of gender relations in Brazil. *Journal of Pragmatics* 23: 183–197.

Maillat, D. and Oswald, S. (2009). Defining manipulative discourse: The pragmatics of cognitive illusions. *International Review of Pragmatics* 1: 348–370.

Marmaridou, S. (2000). *Pragmatic meaning and cognition*. Amsterdam, Philadelphia: Benjamins.

Mey, J. (1989). The end of the copper age or pragmatics 12 ½ years after. *Journal of Pragmatics* 13: 825–832.

Morris, C. (1938). *Foundations of the theory of signs*. Chicago: University of Chicago Press.

Murphy, J. (2015). Revisiting the apology as a speech act: The case of parliamentary apologies. *Journal of Language and Politics* (2): 175–204.

O'Halloran, K. (2003). *Critical discourse analysis and language cognition*. Edinburgh: Edinburgh University Press.

Polyzou, A. (2008). Genre-based data selection and classification for critical discourse analysis. In M. KhosraviNik and A. Polyzou (eds.), *Papers from the Lancaster University Postgraduate Conference in Linguistics and Language Teaching (LAEL PG),* Vol. 2. www.ling.lancs.ac.uk/pgconference/v02/06-Polyzou.pdf

Polyzou, A. (2013). *Presupposition, (ideological) knowledge management and gender: A socio-cognitive discourse analytical approach*. Unpublished PhD thesis, Lancaster University, Lancaster, UK.

Polyzou, A. (2015a). Presupposition in discourse: Theoretical and methodological issues. *Critical Discourse Studies* 12(2): 123–138.

Polyzou, A. (2015b). Discourse, gender and power: Looking at lifestyle magazines. Paper presented at *Cutting Edges Research Conference 2015,* July 3, Canterbury Christ Church University, Canterbury, UK.

Reisigl, M. and Wodak, R. (2001). *Discourse and discrimination*. London: Routledge.

Sbisà, M. (1999). Ideology and the persuasive use of presupposition. In J. Verschueren (ed.), *Language and ideology: Selected papers from the 6th international pragmatics conference,* Vol. 1, 492–509. Antwerp: International Pragmatics Association.

Swales, J. M. (1990). *Genre analysis: English in academic and research settings*. Cambridge: Cambridge University Press.

Sarazin, P. (2009). Geschichte kurz gemacht: Implikaturen vom Sprecher und Inferenzen seitens des Hörers. Paper presented at the *37th Austrian Conference on Linguistics,* Saltzburg, Austria.

Sarazin, P. (2015). *The role of implicatures from framings in argumentation concerning trade agreements between the European Union and developing countries*. Unpublished PhD thesis, Lancaster University, Lancaster, UK.

Sperber, D. and Wilson, D. (1986/1995). *Relevance: Communication and cognition*. Oxford: Blackwell.

Talbot, M. (2010). *Language and gender*, 2nd edn. Cambridge: Polity Press.

Thomas, J. (1995). *Meaning in interaction: An introduction to pragmatics*. Harlow: Longman.

Tsiplakou, S. and Floros, G. (2013). Never mind the text types, here's textual force: Towards pragmatic reconceptualization of text type. *Journal of Pragmatics* 45(1): 119–130.

van Dijk, T. A. (1998). *Ideology: A multidisciplinary approach*. London, Thousand Oaks, CA, New Delhi: Sage.

van Dijk, T. A. (2003). The discourse-knowledge interface. In G. Weiss and R. Wodak (eds.), *Critical discourse analysis: Theory and interdisciplinarity,* 85–109. Houndmills, Basingstoke, Hampshire: Palgrave Macmillan.

van Dijk, T. A. (2005). Contextual knowledge management in discourse production: A CDA perspective. In R. Wodak and P. Chilton (eds.), *A new agenda in (critical) discourse analysis: Theory, methodology and interdisciplinarity,* 71–100. Amsterdam, Philadelphia: Benjamins.

van Dijk, T. A. (2006). Discourse, context and cognition. *Discourse Studies* 8(1): 159–177.

van Dijk, T. A. (2008). *Discourse and context: A socio-cognitive approach*. Cambridge: Cambridge University Press.

Van Leeuwen, T. (1996). The representation of social actors. In C.R. Caldas-Coulthard and M. Coulthard (eds.), *Texts and practices: Readings in critical discourse analysis*. London: Routledge.

Van Leeuwen, T. (2008). News genres. In R. Wodak and V. Koller (eds.), *Language and communication in the public sphere*. Berlin: de Gruyter.

Verschueren, J. (1987). Introduction. In J. Verschueren and M. Bertuccelli-Papi (eds.), *The pragmatic perspective: Selected papers from the 1985 international pragmatics conference,* 3–8. Amsterdam, Philadelphia: Benjamins.

Wodak, R. (2004). Critical discourse analysis. In G. Gobo, C. Seale and D. Silverman (eds.), *Qualitative research practice,* 197–213. London: Sage.

Wodak, R. (2007). Pragmatics and critical discourse analysis: A cross-disciplinary inquiry. *Pragmatics & Cognition* 15: 203–225.

Appendix I

Marie Claire, Feb 2006, pp 157–158

Only4YOU

Pg 157

SEX

ΑΝΕΒΑΣΕ ΤΗ ΛΙΜΠΙΝΤΟ ΤΟΥ ΣΤΑ ΥΨΗ!

Ήξερες ότι το 23% των ανδρών ηροτιμά να βλέπει τηλεόραση από το να κάνει σεξ; Απίστευτο; Η μήπως το ίδιο προτιμά και ο σύντροφός σου; Αν, λοιπόν, θέλεις να τον παρασύρεις σε κάτι πιο ευχάριστο από το να κάθεστε στον καναπέ, το παρακάτω κείμενο σε αφορά . . . ! Από την Ελένη Κιτσή.

Μερικοι Προτιμουν Την . . . TV

Όσο και να ηιστεύουμε ότι οι άνδρες δεν έχουν τίποτε άλλο στο μυαλό τους παρά μόνο το . . . ξέρεις ποιο, η τελευταία έρευνα της Durex αποκαλύπτει ότι το 23% των ανδρών προτιμά την τηλεόραση και άλλα καθιστικά σπορ από το σεξ. Αν συγκρίνουμε αυτό το ποσοστό με το 45% των γυναικών που λένε ότι θα επιθυμούσαν περισσότερο σεξ (και σε συχνότητα και σε ποσότητα!), καταλήγουμε στο συμπέρασμα ότι έχουμε περισσότερες πιθανότητες να ακούσουμε το περίφημο «όχι απόψε, αγάπη μου, έχω πονοκέφαλο» παρά να το πούμε εμείς! Και αυτό εξηγείται επιστημονικά: τα επίπεδα τεστοστερόνης αρχίζουν να πέφτουν μετά τα 30, επηρεάζοντας αρνητικά την ερωτική διάθεση των ανδρών. Με τις γυναίκες, πάλι, συμβαίνει το αντίθετο. Η σεξουαλικότητά μας ωριμάζει με τα χρόνια. Όσο μεγαλώνουμε απολαμβάνουμε περισσότερο το σεξ, ίσως επειδή εμείς οι γυναίκες μεταφράζουμε αλλιώς το ερωτικό παιχνίδι: μας δίνει μια αίσθηση στοργής και ασφάλειας από το σύντροφό μας, επομένως αν εκείνος δεν έχει διάθεση, απογοητευόμαστε και νιώθουμε ότι μας απορρίπτει. Πώς μπορούμε, λοιπόν, να αποφύγουμε τις κλασικές γυναικείες ανασφάλειες, του τύπου «Δεν θέλει να κάνουμε σεξ, άρα δεν με θέλει, άρα είμαι το τέρας της φύσης, άρα φταίει η κυτταρίτιδα, μπλα, μπλα, μπλα» και να ανεβάσουμε τη λίμπιντό του στα ... ύψη; Για αρχή σταμάτα την γκρίνια για τις επιδόσεις του, γιατί επιβαρύνεις την ήδη δύσκολη κατάσταση. Ξύπνησε την ερωτική του διάθεση χωρίς να το πάρει χαμπάρι, ακολουθώντας τα εφτά εύκολα tips που σου προτείνουμε.

Pg 158

Tip No 1:
ΦΤΙΑΞ'ΤΟΥ ΕΝΑ ΤΣΑΪ ...

... ή ένα οποιοδήποτε αφέψημα τέλος πάντων. Μήπως θέλεις κάτι πολύ πιο ισχυρό; Έχεις ακούσει ποτέ για την νταμιάνα; Είναι ένα καταπληκτικό βότανο από τη Νότια Αμερική, που έχει άμεση επίδραση στο πέος, προκαλώντας υπεραιμία και κατά συνέπεια διέγερση, σύμφωνα με τους σεξολόγους. Αν πάλι πιστεύεις ότι δεν θα τον πείσεις εύκολα να πιει το ... σεξοβότανο (μεταξύ μας, είναι αρκετά πικρό), η νταμιάνα κυκλοφορεί και σε συμπληρώματα διατροφής – «δεν είναι τίποτε, αγάπη μου, μια απλή πολυβιταμίνη». Αν δεν τη βρεις στα καταστήματα υγιεινών τροφών, μπορείς να παραγγείλεις νταμιάνα από το Ίντερνετ, στη διεύθυνση www.riohealth.co.uk.

Tip No 2:
ΓΙΝΕ ΒΡΑΖΙΛΙΑΝΑ ...

Αν ο σύντροφός σου έχει κάνει focus στα επαγγελματικά του, μάλλον το σεξ δεν είναι και το πιο δυνατό του σημείο – αυτή την εποχή τουλάχιστον. Μήπως, λοιπόν, του χρειάζεται κατουάμπα, το περίφημο βραζιλιάνικο βότανο; Είναι ένα διεγερτικό που προκαλεί φαντασιώσεις και βοηθά στην καταπολέμηση του στρες και της κόπωσης, που είναι και οι κυριότεροι κατασταλτικοί παράγοντες της λίμπιντο. Πρόσφατες έρευνες έδειξαν ότι αυξάνει κατακόρυφα την ερωτική διάθεση μέσα σε πέντε μόλις μέρες. Κυκλοφορεί και σε μορφή σκόνης. Μπορείς να τη βρεις στο site www.nohealth.co.uk.

Tip No 3:
ΚΑΙ ΣΤΗΝ ΚΟΡΦΗ ... ΚΑΝΕΛΑ!

Επιστήμονες από το Ίδρυμα Ερευνών Όσφρησης και Γεύσης του Σικάγο πειραματίστηκαν με περισσότερες από διακόσιες διαφορετικές μυρωδιές για να βρουν ποια ερεθίζει περισσότερο τους άνδρες και κατέληξαν στην κανέλα! Το άρωμα κανέλας αυξάνει τη ροή του αίματος στο πέος, βοηθώντας έτσι στη στύση. Φτιάξ'του, λοιπόν, κουλουράκια κανέλας ή, αν δε σε ενθουσιάζει η προοπτική να γίνεις ... ζαχαροπλάστης, βάλε ένα ξυλαράκι κανέλας κάτω από το μαξιλάρι του για να το μυρίζει την ώρα που υποτίθεται ότι ήθελε να κοιμηθεί. Συμβουλή: αν δεν έχεις όρεξη για σεξ, θέλεις απεγνωσμένα να κοιμηθείς ή βαριέσαι του θανατά, βγάλε το ξυλαράκι από το μαξιλάρι του. Προληπτικό μέτρο για να μην αρχίσεις πάλι τις ψευτιές «αγάπη μου, έχω πονοκέφαλο».

Tip No 4:
ΑΠΟ ΠΟΤΕ ΤΟ ΣΚΟΡΔΟ ΕΙΝΑΙ ΑΦΡΟΔΙΣΙΑΚΟ;

Κι όμως . . . Το σκόρδο μπορεί να μη σου ακούγεται (ούτε και να μυρίζει) καλά, αλλά μπορεί να διεγείρει τον εραστή σου, σύμφωνα πάντα με τους σεξολόγους. Όπως η κανέλα, το σκόρδο περιέχει αλλικίνη, που προκαλεί υπεραιμία στο πέος. Ετοίμασε, λοιπόν, ένα εβδομαδιαίο μενού με φαγητά που να περιέχουν άφθονο σκόρδο, όπως ζυμαρικά με σάλτσα, ψητά ή έναν παραδοσιακό μπακαλιάρο σκορδαλιά. Αν πάλι βρίσκεσαι στα όρια της απελπισίας, φτιάξ' του το περίφημο γαλλικό κοτόπουλο με 40 σκελίδες σκόρδο (θα βρεις τη συνταγή στο mardiweb.com/lowfat/poultry/htm).

Tip No 5:
ΕΝΑ ΘΡΙΛΕΡ ΘΑ ΑΝΕΒΑΣΕΙ . . . ΤΟ ΣΑΣΠΕΝΣ!

Ξέχνα το «Pretty Woman», το «Λογική και Ευαισθησία» και, γενικά, ό,τι σε ρομαντική κομεντί ή δακρύβρεχτο ρομάντσο. Αν θέλεις σεξ, προτίμησε το «Blair Witch Project». Οι ειδικοί υποστηρίζουν ότι οι ταινίες τρόμου αυξάνουν τα επίπεδα της ντοπαμίνης – η ορμόνη που προκαλεί ερωτική διέγερση –, τα οποία μειώνονται κατακόρυφα σε μια μακροχρόνια σχέση (βλ. «Ο έρωτας κρατάει τρία χρόνια», σελ. 66). Επιπλέον, ένα θρίλερ θα επιταχύνει τους σφυγμούς του και θα τον κρατήσει σε εγρήγορση, πράγμα που σημαίνει ότι με το παραμικρό άγγιγμα θα είναι έτοιμος να αναλάβει δράση. Αυτό δεν επιδίωκες; Να δράσει αυτός και να αντιδράσεις εσύ;

Tip No 6:
ΚΑΝΤΕ ΜΙΑ ΒΟΛΤΑ

Μία ώρα στον καθαρό αέρα μπορεί να αυξήσει τα επίπεδα της τεστοστερόνης μέχρι και 69%, σύμφωνα με πανεπιστημιακές έρευνες. Ο λόγος είναι ότι η ηλιακή ακτινοβολία διεγείρει την υπόφυση που, με τη σειρά της, ευθύνεται για την έκκριση τεστοστερόνης. Τι περιμένεις, λοιπόν; Βγείτε μια βόλτα μέχρι το κοντινότερο καφέ. Βρες χίλιες δυο δικαιολογίες για να περπατήσετε λίγο παραπάνω και να μην πάρει το αυτοκίνητο. Ή, ακόμα καλύτερα, πες του να πάρετε το αυτοκίνητο και να εξορμήσετε κάπου ερημικά. Όπως παλιά . . .

Tip No 7:
ΤΟ ΣΕΞ ΠΕΡΝΑ ΑΠΟ ΤΟ ΣΤΟΜΑΧΙ

Η παραγωγή τεστοστερόνης εξαρτάται από τα επίπεδα ψευδαργύρου στον οργανισμό. Η έλλειψή του μπορεί να προκαλέσει στρες και κατά συνέπεια μειωμένη ερωτική επιθυμία. Βοήθησέ τον, λοιπόν, να βρει τη χαμένη του όρεξη για σεξ μαγειρεύοντας φαγητά πλούσια σε ψευδάργυρο. Καλές πηγές ψευδαργύρου είναι τα στρείδια και τα θαλασσινά, το καστανό ρύζι, το τυρί, τα αυγά, οι φακές, το κοτόπουλο, η γαλοπούλα και τα δημητριακά ολικής αλέσεως. Να τι θέλει ο έρωτας . . . μενού και φαντασία.

Appendix II

Marie Claire, Feb 2006, pp 157–158

Only4YOU

Pg 157

SEX

MAKE HIS LIBIDO SKYROCKET![4]

Did you know that 23% of men prefer watching television than having sex? Unbelievable? Or does your partner [masc.] perhaps also prefer the same? If, then, you want to 'drift him' to something more pleasant than you [Plural] sitting on the couch, the below text concerns you. . .! By Eleni Kitsi.

SOME [MASC.] PREFER. . .TV![5]

No matter how much we believe that men have nothing else on their mind but. . . you-know-what, the latest research of *Durex* reveals that 23% of men prefer television and other sedentary sports to sex. If we compare this percentage with the 45% of women who say that they would like more sex (both in frequency and in quantity!), we end up with the conclusion that we have more chances to hear the proverbial "not tonight, darling, I have a headache" than to say it ourselves! And this is explained scientifically: the testosterone levels start falling after 30, influencing negatively the erotic mood of men. With women, again, the opposite happens. Our sexuality matures with the years. As we grow older we enjoy sex more, maybe because we women translate differently the erotic game: it gives us a sense of affection and security from our partner, consequently if he is not in the mood, we get frustrated and feel that

he is rejecting us. How can we, then, avoid the typical female insecurities,
of the type "He doesn't want [us] to have sex, therefore he doesn't want me, therefore I am
the monster of nature, therefore it's the fault of cellulite, blah, blah, blah" and raise his
libido to the. . . heights? For starters stop nagging about his performance, because
you aggravate the already difficult situation. Awaken his erotic mood without
him realising, following the seven easy tips we are suggesting to you.

Pg 158

Tip No 1:
MAKE HIM A TEA. . .

. . . or any decoction anyway. Do you want something more powerful, perhaps?
Have you ever heard about damiana? It is an amazing herb/shrub from South
America, which has immediate impact on the penis, causing hyperaemia and
consequently stimulation, according to the sexologists. If again you believe that you will not
convince him easily to drink the. . . sex shrub (between us, it is quite bitter), damiana
comes in nutrition supplements too – "it is nothing, darling, just a
multivitamin". If you don't find it in health nutrition stores, you can
order damiana from the Internet, at the address www.riohealth.co.uk.

Tip No 2:
BECOME A BRAZILIAN [fem] . . .

If your partner [masc] has been focussing on his professional [issues], probably sex is not
exactly his strongest point – at least not this period. Does he, then, maybe
need catuaba, the celebrated [famous?] brazilian shrub? It is a stimulant that
causes phantasies and helps combat stress and fatigue,
which are the main factors suppressing libido. Recent
research has shown that it increases dramatically the erotic mood in just five
days. It comes in form of powder too. You can find it on the site
www.nohealth.co.uk.

Tip No 3:
AND CINNAMON ON TOP! [intertextual reference to Greek idiom irrelevant to the topic]

Scientists from the Smell and Taste Treatment and Research Foundation of Chicago
have experimented with more than two hundred different smells to find
which stimulates men more and they ended up with cinnamon! The scent
of cinnamon increases the blood flow to the penis, thus helping with erection. Make him,
then, cinnamon cookies or, if you are not excited by the prospect of becoming. . .
a baker, put a cinnamon stick under his pillow so that he
smells it at the time when supposedly he wanted to sleep. Advice: if you don't feel like
sex, you desperately want to sleep or you can't be bothered to save your life, remove the stick
from his pillow. Precautionary measure so that you will not start with the lies again "darling,
I have a headache".

Tip No 4:
SINCE WHEN IS GARLIC APHRODISIAC?

And yet. . . Garlic may not sound (or smell) well to you, but
it can stimulate your lover, always according to sexologists. Like
cinnamon, garlic contains allicin, which causes hyperaemia to the penis. Prepare,
then, a weekly menu with foods that contain plenty of garlic, like
pasta with sauce, roasted [dishes] or a traditional cod skordalia.[6] If again
you are on the border of despair, make him the famous French chicken with 40
cloves of garlic (you will find the recipe on mardiweb.com/lowfat/poultry/htm).

Tip No 5:
A THRILLER WILL RAISE. . . THE SUSPENSE!

Forget about "Pretty Woman", "Sense and Sensitivity" [means *Sense and Sensibility*]
and, generally, anything in
romantic comedy or tearful romance. If you want sex, prefer the "Blair
Witch Project". Specialists support that horror movies increase the levels
of dopamine – the hormone which causes sexual stimulation – which plummet
in a long-term relationship (see 'Love lasts three years,' pg.
66). Moreover, a thriller will speed up his pulses and will keep him
alert, which means that with the slightest touch he will be ready to
undertake action. Isn't it what you were after? Him acting and you reacting?

Tip No 6:
TAKE [pl.] A WALK

One hour in the fresh air can increase testosterone levels up to
69%, according to University research. The reason is that sun
radiation stimulates the gland which, in turn, is responsible for the secretion
of testosterone. What are you waiting for, then? Go out [pl.] on a walk until
the nearest café.
Find a thousand and one excuses [for you] to walk a bit longer and [for him] not to take the
car. Or, even better, tell him [that you should] take the car and make an excursion
somewhere solitary. Like the old times. . . .

Tip No 7:
SEX GOES THROUGH THE STOMACH

Testosterone production depends on the levels of zinc in the organism.
Its lack can cause stress and consequently reduced sexual
desire. Help him, then, find his lost appetite for sex by cooking
foods rich in zinc. Good zinc sources are mussels and
seafood, brown rice, cheese, eggs, lentils, chicken, turkey
and wholemeal cereals. This is what love needs. . . menu[7] and imagination.

Notes

1 Grice's (1975) formulation of the Co-operative Principle is: make your contribution such as is required, at the stage at which it occurs, by the accepted purpose of direction of the talk on which you are engaged. The four Maxims are: *Maxim of Quantity:* Give the right quantity of information. Specifically, (a) make your contribution as informative as required, (b) do not make your contribution more informative then required; *Maxim of Quality:* Try to make your contribution one that is true. Specifically, (a) do not say that which you believe to be false, (b) do not say that for which you lack adequate evidence; *Maxim of Relation:* Be relevant; *Maxim of Manner:* Be perspicuous. Specifically, (a) avoid obscurity, (b) avoid ambiguity, (c) be brief, (d) be orderly.
2 For an elaboration of this level, see Polyzou (2015a: 148–150).
3 Or, to be more precise, 'super-genre' – cultural textual products like lifestyle magazines function as 'umbrella genres' containing texts of lower-level genres such as interviews, recipes, fashion pages, feature articles, etc. (see Polyzou 2008: 107–108).
4 Word-for-word 'RAISE HIS LIBIDO TO THE HEIGHTS!'
5 Intertextual reference to the film *Some Like it Hot,* translated in Greek as 'Some prefer it hot'
6 http://en.wikipedia.org/wiki/Skordalia
7 Wordplay of homophonous expressions. Μενού: menu, με νου: with mind/sense

14

Metaphor

Carl Jon Way Ng

Introduction: metaphor and critical research

Metaphor analysis has been gaining credence as a profitable tool in critical discourse studies (CDS). Cognitive approaches to metaphor, as the dominant paradigm in metaphor studies today, assert that metaphor is not merely about how we talk about something, but more significantly, how we may think about particular subjects in systematic ways (e.g., Lakoff and Johnson 1980; Kövecses 2002; Goatly 2007). Such authors argue that, because metaphor has a cognitive basis, examining its realisations in text and talk can help us discern dominant and structured ways with which people conceive of aspects of reality. In turn, particular metaphors can be strategically deployed to construct and perpetuate particular worldviews and versions of reality for addressees. Insofar as CDS is concerned with the exercise of power to influence perception and action in and through discourse, the analysis of metaphor can help probe ideological structures and foundations in text and talk, and discern the concepts and ideologies purveyed in discourse. In short, metaphor can no longer be seen as merely rhetorical or decorative, but also constitutive of reality, and acknowledged for its ideological character. It is this ideological potential that makes metaphor analysis an appropriate tool for critical research.

Following this, I provide an overview of the cognitive approach to the study of metaphor, before surveying a range of critical research that has given attention to metaphor in the analysis of discourse. In doing so, it will become apparent that the cognitive view of metaphor as a product of embodied experience needs to be complemented with a consideration of the context in which it is used, the latter an aspect that is sometimes only implicitly acknowledged in cognitively oriented accounts of metaphor. The chapter then analyses an instance of branding and promotional discourse, in the process also advocating greater analytical attention on metaphor beyond language, especially visual image, given the increasing salience of the latter in contemporary discourse and communication.

Metaphor and cognition

Metaphor has traditionally been viewed as belonging to the province of poetic and literary language. As a figure of speech, metaphor is employed when a word or phrase denoting a particular object or idea is used in place of another to suggest likeness. Used for rhetorical effect, metaphor is also common in persuasive communication to create vividness and impact. In this light, it is seen as a supplementary ornament to dress up the message, rather than having any real part in constructing meaning. This account of metaphor has however been found to be inadequate as the linguistic turn in metaphor studies gave way to the current cognitive emphasis.

The turn to a cognitive orientation in metaphor studies is most commonly associated with Lakoff and Johnson (1980; also Lakoff and Turner 1989; Lakoff 1993) with the seminal publication of *Metaphors We Live By*. Within this paradigm, which has come to be known as cognitive metaphor theory (CMT), metaphor is seen as a cognitive process that involves conceptualising one thing in terms of another. The metaphorical expressions found in language are therefore deemed to be the realisations of the kinds of concepts held at the cognitive level. Metaphor, in this regard, is at once a process of the mind and its signification in the form of linguistic/semiotic realisations. A related upshot of the cognitive turn is an acknowledgement of the ubiquity of metaphor. As Lakoff and Johnson (1980: 3) maintain, "[o]ur ordinary conceptual system, in terms of which we both think and act, is fundamentally metaphorical in nature". If this is the case, then metaphor will be pervasive in our thinking, and expressed ubiquitously in text and talk. Metaphor is thus stripped of its artistic aura, with the result that metaphor analysis is applicable to literary texts as it is to everyday discourses as well as the 'powerful' discourses in which CDS research is interested.

In classical CMT, metaphor encompasses a mental process where a target domain is conceptualised in terms of a source domain. The former is usually more abstract, complex and subjective, while the latter tends to be more concrete, physical and familiar. The better-delineated nature of the source and the rich knowledge that discourse participants have of it allows it to give structure and clarity to the target to make the latter more comprehensible. It is common, for example, to think of education as a journey. In this case, EDUCATION as the more abstract target is conceptualised in terms of the more concrete source JOURNEY (typographically rendered in small capital letters, i.e., EDUCATION IS JOURNEY). Linguistically, the metaphor can be realised when education is described as something students *embark* on, and when they are promised a *head start* by educational institutions so that they are not *left behind*. Other times, the focus may be on students *exploring new frontiers*.

CMT stresses that the mapping of elements between the target and source is not random, but involves systematic and structured correspondences between the two domains. In our example above, an understanding of what a journey involves provides us with a structure to organise our understanding of education. For instance, the participants involved, such as students, correspond to the travellers on the journey. The difficulties they face as part of their education are akin to obstacles they come across as they move forward on their path, and their goals can be conceived of as destinations. At the same time, these linguistic realisations can also define the details of this path-oriented forward movement and specify the kind of movement in which participants are supposedly engaged. For example, *head start* and *a step ahead* add a competitive quality, specifying the movement to be a kind of race where some participants have the advantage of starting before the others or of being ahead. EDUCATION becomes a competitive activity in its framing as RACE. Conversely, *exploring new frontiers* plays down the emphasis on a defined path and urgency to reach a particular destination, foregrounding the more exploratory and perhaps more self-paced nature of education.

What is equally significant is that the same subject can be conceptualised using metaphors that may be quite different. EDUCATION, for instance, can be seen in terms of a COMMODITY, encompassing learning experiences that are *valuable, rich, enriching* or *rewarding* (see, e.g., Goatly

2002). A framing like this positions the relationship between educational institutions and students as one between sellers and buyers, and reinforces the idea of education as accruing external rewards. In fact, given that institutions serve a variety of stakeholders including industry and prospective employers, students and graduates can also be conceived of as the 'products' on offer, and described as *assets* or as of *value* to employers. Because source domains help to give structure to conceptualizations of target domains, the relative prominence and currency of, say, forward movement- or wealth-based metaphors of education in particular contexts can give us an idea of how people think about education or how their ideas of education could take shape. For critical research, such insights relating to metaphor are important because they provide an indication of how particular topics are conceptualised, and how such thinking may condition participants to act in particular ways in relation to the topics at hand (Lakoff and Johnson 1980: 156).

A key insight of CMT is that conceptual metaphors have their origins in our embodied experiences, especially as infants (Lakoff and Johnson 1980). For instance, the experience of serious illness forcing us to physically lie down generates the orientational metaphor SICKNESS AND DEATH ARE DOWN (e.g., *fell ill*) and its converse HEALTH AND LIFE ARE UP (e.g., *rose from the dead*). Similarly, the nature of sight where our field of vision acts as a boundary delineating what we can see gives rise to the ontological metaphorical concept VISUAL FIELDS ARE CONTAINERS (e.g., *out of sight*). And from a young age, we learn to crawl and stumble towards objects we want, giving us our experience of the kind of purposeful path-oriented movement from which the JOURNEY metaphor is derived. Such embodied experiences are captured in basic knowledge structures known as image schemas. The PATH image schema, for instance, has its basis in our experience of (forward) motion, and encompasses a starting location and a destination, the path between these two points, and a directedness towards the endpoint. It is also possible for different elements of the schema to be stressed, which then gives emphases to different aspects of the metaphor, foregrounding different meanings. Where more attention is drawn to the components of directedness, a single path and a single endpoint, for example, the dimension of goal-orientedness is emphasised (Chilton 1996: 52).

In recent years, there has been some interest in the more dynamic, ad hoc and contingent cognitive operations related to metaphor during discourse. This had led to some critical scholars giving attention to what is known as conceptual blending theory (see Fauconnier and Turner 2002; also Koller 2004; Hart 2008; see Charteris-Black 2004, for another approach that integrates CMT, pragmatic theory and corpus analysis). It should be noted that blending theory is a theory of cognition rather than one of metaphor per se, though it applies to metaphor as a cognitive phenomenon. Nonetheless, while blending theory maintains the cognitive basis of metaphor, it conceives of metaphor as involving a multidirectional integration of material and structure from (at least) four mental spaces, unlike the unidirectional mapping across two domains posited by classical CMT. Among the four spaces, two are input spaces, roughly equivalent to CMT's two domains. There is also a generic space capturing structural characteristics that are common to the input spaces, which in turn maps these elements into the input spaces. Partial conceptual structure from these input spaces as well as from the generic space is projected into a fourth blended space to produce an emergent structure unique to the blend (Fauconnier and Turner 1996; Fauconnier and Turner 2002: 47–48). As further blending processes take place within the blended space, selected structure and material from background knowledge associated with elements in (but not necessarily from) the input spaces, especially those that are relevant to the addressor's intention, are also recruited for the blending operation (Hart 2010: 117). Consequently, the blended space contains structure that is a product of blending operations rather than that which is copied directly from the input spaces. In this regard, the conceptual blend is one that is unique and 'customised' for the discursive context, and is more than the sum of its parts (Koller 2004: 11). Blending theory, while still cognitive in nature, hence allows for greater creativity and strategy, as well as contextual and communicative specificity in metaphor production.

The variant conceptions of metaphor under CMT and blending theory are, however, not incompatible. Hart (2010: 122–123; see also Lakoff and Johnson 2003: 261–264) explains that the kind of metaphor generated by blending constitutes short-term mental representations while conceptual metaphors are part of knowledge structures in long-term memory. Which view of metaphor to lean towards would depend on whether the analyst is more interested in the broader ideological patterns and structures that imbue texts or the cognitive processes of meaning construction and metaphor production in specific discourse contexts and episodes (Hart 2014: 138–139). The two types of mental representations interact in that the more entrenched long-term mental structures of which conceptual metaphor is part form the basis on which blending takes place, providing resources for blends as well as constraints on what blends are possible (see also Grady, Oakley and Coulson 1999). In this regard, the kind of metaphors posited by classical CMT can be seen as providing the conceptual potential from which cognitive blending operations generate specific metaphors in discourse.

Metaphor, context and discourse

Lakoff and Johnson's (1980) seminal work has often been credited with invigorating a cognitive emphasis to the study of metaphor, and linking conceptual formation to bodily experiences. Notwithstanding the quasi-universality of embodied experience however, different metaphors for the same subject, or different aspects of the same or related metaphors, can enjoy different degrees of prominence in different societies and contexts. Indeed, Lakoff and Johnson (1980: 14) remind us that metaphors "have a basis in our physical and cultural experience" – a point that is sometimes overlooked in cognitively oriented accounts of metaphor. Analyses of metaphor choice and use would therefore need to consider specificities of the context, broadly conceived, and their interactions with embodied experience. As intimated earlier, moves to complement classical CMT with blending theory can be seen as one such endeavour, given that blending operations can draw on context-relevant material not directly copied from the input spaces, and blending theory assigns more attention to the discourse context by considering the contingency of online cognitive operations.

It is important to remember that the conceptual formation based on embodied experience does not take place in a vacuum to begin with; contextual factors like social organisation, architecture, national culture, political governance and myriad others, to varying degrees, shape our physical environment and our physical interaction with this environment (Chilton 1996: 49). Furthermore, even after childhood when embodied concepts have more fully developed, context affects what metaphorical concepts are actually drawn on as well as how they are specifically developed for use. While much metaphor use may not be particularly conscious, contextual dynamics may in fact cause metaphor use to be highly strategic; discourse participants may intentionally deploy particular metaphors to frame topics in self-advantageous ways in discursive contexts where objectives are reasonably fixed, like in a debate or promotional campaign. Considering the social context of metaphor use as part of discourse is in fact central to the practice of CDS, which sees discourse as both socially-constituted and -constitutive. Metaphor, even if partly based in embodied experience, is also a function of pragmatic choices and never independent of its context of use.

An understanding of the sociocultural dimensions of metaphor underlies Chilton's (1996: 251–291) explanation for why Gorbachev's idea of 'the European house', promulgated as part of Soviet reform policy, did not go down well in Europe. The house metaphor is derived from the CONTAINER schema (consisting of the elements of interior, boundary surface and exterior), which in turn has its basis in the experience of bodily interaction with the physical environment. Experiences of 'house' are, however, contextually mediated, with culturally specific experiences of size, shape, structure, surrounding space, use and function, barriers and so on. Unlike the typical Soviet experience with communal blocks, the Western 'house' is understood in terms of "a culture of private space and individualism" (p. 266). Hence, despite the experience of space and containment having some degree of universality, Chilton shows how cultural mediations of this experience led to divergent interpretations of the metaphor, and had real impact on how the European community responded to Gorbachev's overtures and Soviet foreign policy.

Contextual variables can also be located in historical experience and memory. Indeed, Musolff's (2014) study shows that these influence the way shared metaphorical concepts take hold and develop in semantically variant ways in the context of different national cultures, particularly for the case of body metaphors being applied to political entities (as instantiated in English by expressions like *body politic, head of state* and *long arm of the law*) in British, French and German public discourses. In mainstream German public discourse, for instance, the use of *Volkskörper* ('people's body') usually takes on a critical or problematic tenor not present in other national contexts. This can be attributed to "the historical resonance of *Volkskörper* in German with its echoes of Nazi jargon" (p. 54), where discourse-historical evidence of antecedent metaphor use shows how the metaphor was implicated in Nazi propaganda and used to justify genocidal practices. Certainly, the underlying STATE-BODY metaphor, derived from the experience of body, is constant across the national discourses, having been developed and translated from medieval Latin into European vernacular languages during the early modern period as a shared concept. However, divergent socio-historical experiences, national cultures and political ideologies going back decades if not centuries, such as in the case of Germany's experience with National Socialism, has caused the metaphor to branch out into variant but interconnected discourse traditions. It is of course debatable whether present-day users are able to articulate the metaphor's precise historical formulations and associations (though Musolff suggests that approximate knowledge of its discourse-historical status is present). Nonetheless, even if precise knowledge is absent, context-specific uses and development of metaphor can be entrenched and conventionalized over time to become part of the socio-cognitive models of members of a particular discourse community (see van Dijk 2008, for a socio-cognitively oriented multidisciplinary theory of context).

While Chilton and Musolff's insights might suggest a certain level of 'unconsciousness' and determinism regarding the use of metaphor, in that their users are in some ways 'products' of sociocultural embodiment, Goatly's (2007) wide-ranging account of the dominant metaphors in the contemporary lexicon of Western societies and economies makes the motivatedness of metaphor use more explicit. Significantly, he points to the element of ideological control, arguing that some metaphors have been appropriated and perpetuated in the service of particular social and economic ideologies, and have become implicated in hegemonic attempts for social domination (335–402). As a case in point, he explains how a late twentieth-century ascendancy of earlier economic philosophies associated with David Hume, Adam Smith and Thomas Malthus, among others, helped constitute an ideological consensus on capitalism. This is aided by the circulation of metaphors that privilege competition, industry and efficiency, constructing areas of our lives in terms of these values (e.g., COMPETITION IS RACE,

ACTIVITY IS FIGHTING and TIME IS MONEY/COMMODITY). The dominance of such metaphors not only reflects, but in turn reinforces and legitimates a particular tradition of capitalist thinking in Western society. Significant for CDS research, therefore, is the understanding that metaphors, especially in their ability to "define in significant part what one takes as reality" (Chilton and Lakoff 1995: 56), are as much ideological as their origin is at least partly physical. Particular metaphors can therefore be strategically deployed to construct and circulate particular ideological paradigms, helping to structure worldviews and condition subjectivities.

Such a property of metaphor can take on an especially pernicious quality when particular recurring patterns of metaphor come to normalise certain ways of thinking about groups of people, which, if negative, justify their discrimination. For example, the circulation of right-wing political discourses, which have systematically framed immigration/immigrants as invasions and natural disasters (see e.g., El Refaie 2001; Flowerdew, Li and Tran 2002; Charteris-Black 2006; Hart 2010: 144–157), seems to have naturalised the notion of immigrants as a threat. Charteris-Black (2006), for instance, found that natural disaster metaphors, especially relating to floods and tidal waves, are common in British right-wing discourse (i.e., IMMIGRATION IS NATURAL DISASTER), as instantiated by expressions like *flood of asylum seekers* and *massive and unnecessary wave of immigration*. Another dominant metaphor conceptualises the country as a container (i.e., NATION IS CONTAINER), where an unacceptable level of pressure can build up within it to cause perforation and where it can be penetrated from outside as a bounded area, hence generating expressions like *Britain is full up* and *secure our borders*. Charteris-Black argues that because the most dominant disaster metaphors relate to fluids, and containers also frequently contain fluids, there is a conceptual link between the two metaphorical concepts, which work together to provoke an emotional response of fear, serving to legitimate the anti-immigration/immigrant policies of the political right.

The motivated and strategic nature of metaphor in the discourse context is given explicit attention in Steen's (2008, 2011) three-dimensional model of metaphor consisting of the linguistic, conceptual and communicative dimensions, where each dimension is separate but related. The linguistic dimension pertains to the linguistic form taken by the metaphor, where it can be constructed, for example, in the form of an analogy or simile, a regular metaphor, or even indirectly, such as when the target is not directly realised in the text. The conceptual dimension of metaphor relates to the commonly invoked delineation of metaphors as novel or conventional. More significantly, at the communicative dimension, metaphors can be categorised as deliberate or non-deliberate. Deliberate metaphors, through the way they are communicated, are recognised as metaphors and "ineluctably shift the perspective of the addressee from the local topic of a message to another conceptual domain from which that local topic is to be re-viewed" (Steen 2008: 224). Taking a more moderate position, Ng and Koller (2013) suggest that rather than effecting radical conceptual change, deliberate metaphors can also serve to reinforce and elaborate existing conceptualizations, especially when the metaphors used are highly conventional in the discursive context. The notion of deliberate metaphor is obviously not without contention, the issue of how it can be identified in analysis being one. Nonetheless, in foregrounding the strategic intentionality of metaphor in communication, the model draws explicit attention to the ideological potential of metaphor, where it can be deployed to influence cognition (and not only that metaphorical concepts feed into realisation) – a point that is sometimes only implicit in accounts of cognitive metaphor.

The identification of deliberate metaphor is likely to be less problematic when we turn our attention to other semiotic modes, especially visual and multi-modal metaphor. Certainly, there has been substantial research on visual rhetoric, of which metaphor is seen as a part (e.g., Forceville 1996; Messaris 1997; McQuarrie and Mick 2003). Less forthcoming, however, is research on the visual instantiations of metaphor within a cognitive paradigm, especially in the context of critical research. One exception is Koller's (2005) study of visual metaphor in business magazines, where metaphors of WAR (e.g., *launching a marketing campaign*), SPORTS and GAMES (e.g., images of boxing and wrestling which mesh both metaphors) are found to recur across verbal and visual modes to constitute the dominant cognitive models underlying business media discourse, at the same time reflecting and reinforcing prevalent attitudes and the wider socioeconomic context of the discourse. That these metaphors share the semantic feature of 'competitiveness' indicates that their occurrence is not random or coincidental, but form a cohesive underlying conceptual cluster that characterises the social practice of business fields like marketing. While it is probably impossible to determine the deliberate use of metaphor with absolute certainty through textual analysis alone, metaphor clusters of the type detected in the study are a strong indicator of deliberateness (see also Beger 2011). Moreover, visual text, by dint of the way it is produced, is much more conscious and intentional in its design than verbal text, especially in highly crafted texts like advertisements, marketing material and texts used in branding; where metaphor is visually expressed here, it is highly likely to be a conscious effort to influence concepts held by addressees, especially if the same metaphor is reiterated in the verbal text. This is even more so for multi-modal metaphor, whose target and source are mapped across different modes (Forceville 2009), making it even less likely to be coincidental. Given the increasing salience of images in contemporary discourse and communication, the analysis of visual and multi-modal metaphors can provide insight into the kind of concepts that are actively constructed and circulated in particular discourses and contexts. Considering them alongside verbal metaphor would also give a more comprehensive picture of the concepts purveyed. If metaphor is truly a conceptual phenomenon that can be realised across semiotic modes (though in mode-specific ways), we would be remiss not to give attention to metaphor beyond the verbal mode in critical research. Considering visual and multi-modal metaphor would be a good start.

Metaphor in multi-modal texts: an example from branding and promotion

In this section, I give an example of how metaphor analysis can be employed in critical research by way of analysing an instance of branding and promotional discourse in the form of Singapore Management University's (SMU) 2013/14 annual report. The analysis, which looks at metaphor not only in language, but also visually and multi-modally (involving verbal-visual mapping), also seeks to venture a case for analytical attention on visual and multi-modal metaphor.

The analysis is situated within a context where branding and promotion are deemed to be important activities for universities. Much has been written about how the practices of the market, including discursive practices, have become entrenched in higher education (e.g., Mautner 2005; Lin 2009; Brown 2011). Universities, even if not profit-driven organisations in the conventional sense, have adopted practices intended to boost organisational efficiency and competitiveness, in order to succeed in a higher education quasi-market. Such developments have been spurred by neoliberal government policy characterised by deregulation, liberalisation, privatisation and marketization of the higher education sector (Steger 2005: ix; Birch and Mykhnenko 2010), designed to 'free' universities to be more nimble and responsive to market competition.

In this context, documents like annual reports have become key multi-modal branding and promotional texts directed at stakeholders. As highly designed texts that constitute an important part of these organisations' branding and promotional discourse, examining their use of metaphor would provide insight into how organisations represent themselves in an effort to engender favourable audience dispositions towards themselves. In the SMU annual report under analysis, metaphorical expressions that represent the organisation as a living organism (i.e., ORGANISATION IS LIVING ORGANISM) or more specifically, person (i.e., ORGANISATION IS PERSON), are among the most dominant and developed. Even though an organisation consists of animate as well as inanimate aspects, it is discursively ascribed traits, abilities and identities of living beings when conceptualised as a living organism. In the SMU report, the organisation's development and increasing success are represented in terms of a living being *evolving* and having *grown tremendously in size*. It is also *look[ing] forward to. . . the next exciting phase of. . . growth*, being no longer just the *new kid on the block*. While the last expression is highly idiomatic and rather clichéd, we are likely to see its use here as conscious and deliberate, representing the organisation as a person, but not the one it once was. Presumably, this person has grown to become more mature and now has a *growing reputation*.

Organisations can also be depicted as engaging in physical activity associated with living beings, with the most significant of these is in the form of (FORWARD) MOVEMENT, often used to frame an organisation's change and development. Hence, the organisation is described as being on a *journey,* having *moved beyond being a predominantly management university,* and capable of reaching *even greater heights*. Other times, the journey is specified to be a quest (e.g., *Advancing the Quest for Knowledge*), with a clear sense of purpose. Derived from the PATH schema, the notion of 'quest' foregrounds the path and especially destination components of the schema, where it is clear, in this case, that the endpoint is knowledge. The organisation also uses a *roadmap* to help *propel it[self] well into the next decade* and *make the leap to scale greater heights*. As we can see, the organisation is described as having developed and continuing development and success through metaphors that represent it as a dynamic actor engaged in purposeful self-propelled activity; in terms of orientation, the metaphorical expressions define this movement to be (a combination of) both forward and upward.

Significantly, such a verbal self-representation is visually reinforced by an image taking up about two-thirds of the cover page (Figure 14.1). In as far as the cover occupies a highly salient position, the representation encapsulated in the image is also prioritised, becoming a sort of organising idea for the whole document.

The organisation, as metonymically represented by the person in graduation attire, is depicted to be running on an ascending path. A visual metaphor – where both source and target are represented visually – is constructed here, where the organisation as target is shown to be engaged in the source activity of running, reinforcing the dynamic verbal representation of the organisation. The run itself appears to represent the organisation's process of fulfilling its 2025 vision, which, as the verbal text suggests, is to become *A GREAT UNIVERSITY.* This process entails a series of steps in the areas of *Transformative Education, Cutting Edge Research* and becoming a *Leading Asian City University,* each visually represented as a step up the ascending path, eventually reaching the goal of *A GREAT UNIVERSITY.* This is hence an instance of multi-modal metaphor, with the visual depiction of running on an ascending path representing the process of fulfilling the organisation's vision illuminated by the verbal text. That the image depicts the person as nearing the goal rather than at the start of the path emphasises the importance of reaching the endpoint; in this case, giving more attention to particular elements of the PATH schema from which the run metaphor is derived gives rise to an emphasis on goal-orientedness, an attribute ascribed to the organisation.

However, subsumed within the multi-modal metaphor is another verbal metaphor expressed by *Leading Asian City University,* which indexes a race or at least a journey where

Figure 14.1 SMU Annual Report

Verbal metaphor: THINKING IS RACING.
Visual metaphor: ORGANISATION IS RUNNER.
Multi-modal metaphor: FULFILLING VISION IS RUNNING.

being in the lead ahead of other competitors is important. The design of the image in fact draws attention to this by depicting *Leading Asian City University* as the specific step on which the runner is. The interaction of metaphors or, seen another way, the subsuming of the verbal metaphor within the multi-modal metaphor, represents the run to fulfil the organisational vision as entailing the race to become a leading university as a necessary step.

The competitive quality of these representations is also bolstered by the verbal text at the top left corner of the image (*THINKING A STEP AHEAD*). We are told in the Editor's Note later that this is the theme of the report. However, its proximity to the visual depiction of the run(ner) – notice how the verbal text extends into the 'shadow' framing the run – makes it seem a part of the image or at least a kind of verbal anchor for the visual representation, which, by virtue of its salient position on the cover, also makes it an anchor for the document as a whole. The verbal phrase conveys a competitive metaphor that associates THINKING with RACE, where one seeks to stay ahead of competitors. The metaphor is reiterated later in the document with discussions of what the organisation has done to achieve *THOUGHT LEAD-ERSHIP*, simultaneously representing the organisation as a leader in the race. The idea is reinforced and elaborated in the Chairman's Message, the first section following the Contents:

> *Fifteen years ago, these distinctive features [of SMU] set us apart from the tertiary education land-scape in Singapore. However, since then, they have become more widely accepted and adopted. It was*

from this realisation that we embarked more than a year ago on a radical re-think of our competitive advantage.

Not only does the use of *embarked* reinforce the representation of thinking as a forward–moving activity (specifically a journey), which in this case is also one associated with competition (i.e., *re-think of our competitive advantage*), the use of *set us apart* also suggests that the organisation has been trying to maintain its lead, putting distance between itself and its competitors.

Whether we see the overarching competitive verbal metaphor indexed by *THINKING A STEP AHEAD* as subsuming the multi-modal metaphor, or the two metaphors as mutually reinforcing, it is not difficult to see the consonance between them. The connection is further accentuated by the fact that the run in which the person is engaged involves taking physical steps (as visually depicted), with the visualisation therefore echoing the verbal expression (*STEP AHEAD*). However, while the process of (adopting and) fulfilling the vision (as represented multi-modally) is the result of or at least connected to the organisation thinking a step ahead, and both metaphors are based on the same PATH schema, it would be appropriate to see them as conceptually connected but separate with different target domains. Moreover, while fulfilling the organisational vision may entail competition with other organisations in some areas (particularly in the race to become a leading university), there is no evidence to suggest that the competitors are pursuing the same vision in its totality; after all, this is supposed to be SMU's vision (although being *A GREAT UNIVERSITY* is a vision general enough to apply to most universities). Notwithstanding this, the metaphors all derive from the same schema, and the organisation figures in all the target domains either fully or implicitly; this makes the metaphors complementary, where they work together as a cluster to provide a more elaborate and fuller representation of the organisation. Note that the competitiveness feature is also shared by the GAMES metaphor (*GAME CHANGER*), as well as what could be a WAR/FIGHT metaphor (*Cutting Edge Research* in the image, but also elsewhere in the document, *evolve to stay on the edge, retain its edge* and *Honing SMU'S Edge*).[1] As we can see, a consideration of the relationship between verbal and visual text and the interaction between verbal, visual and multi-modal metaphors can enrich our understanding of the concepts constructed and circulated in and though the text.

This short analysis has demonstrated the salience of anthropomorphic metaphors in an instance of corporate branding and promotional discourse. They are not likely to be unique to this specific text or organisation. The use of animate and anthropomorphic metaphors reflects a context of higher education quasi-market competition, within which organisations seek audience identification by presenting themselves as persons with desirable personalities and attributes (Koller 2009), consistent with contemporary trends in branding (Aaker 1997; Kapferer 2004; Csaba and Bengtsson 2006). As Lakoff and Johnson (2003: 34) assert, "[anthropomorphic metaphors] allow us to make sense of phenomena in the world in human terms – terms that we can understand on the basis of our own motivations, goals, actions, and characteristics". An explanation of metaphor in discourse would therefore need to consider sociocultural and discursive contexts, in this case characterised by a globalised neoliberal ideology influencing higher education practices, impelling organisations to foster addressor-addressee affinity by exploiting cognitive models of personhood. On this count, the salient representations of the organisation as dynamic and competitive also point to textual valorizations of a neoliberal worldview privileging competitive, self-steering subjectivities.

To be sure, such metaphors are not the only possibilities for universities. The STRUCTURE/ BUILDING metaphor, leveraged to show the organisation as *successfully built* on *strong foundations,* can be found in SMU's report. Expressions depicting the anthropomorphized organisation as a nurturing gardener are present as well (e.g., *we. . . nurture tomorrow's leaders* and *SMU. . . nurtures leaders of the future*) (though note the intended targets/products of this nurturing). Nonetheless, these alternatives lack the salience of the metaphors we have been discussing. This salience is especially bolstered by having the image positioned on the cover, as an indication of the kind of concepts prioritised. The use of both visual and multi-modal metaphor to construct and circulate these concepts reinforces them and makes the communication highly deliberate and the concepts less easily ignored, as does the form of the image as a schematic cartoon-type sketch deliberately designed to convey particular meanings and symbolise particular concepts. That the organisational metaphors favoured here are not particularly novel might not come as a surprise. The analysis of metaphor intimates how the use of metaphor has come to reflect as well as constitute concepts that are a part of the dominant ideological paradigm within a particular context. While discursive-conceptual choices, of which metaphor is part, are in principle open to discourse participants, the possibilities can in reality be circumscribed by hegemonic ideologies that have achieved naturalised status in these contexts.

Conclusion

That metaphor analysis is an appropriate tool for critical research should be apparent from the above review of relevant literature and case study. In as far as CDS is concerned with the ideological structures of discourse and its potential for contributing to social dominance, metaphor is implicated in this exercise of power. As a function of cognition, the analysis of metaphor provides a means for critical researchers to understand the concepts that people hold of reality as well as probe how particular structures of thought, especially as part of dominant ideological paradigms, are purveyed to addressees in discourse. However, given that metaphor also involves signification in text and talk and is therefore a function of situated use, it behoves the critical researcher to understand the context, broadly conceived, within which metaphor is developed and employed, and to discern the mediations of the sociocultural and discursive context on metaphor.

Since the identification and analysis of metaphor are primarily done through examining its realisations in text and talk, researchers need to venture beyond verbal metaphor to look at metaphor in other modes. In this chapter, I have sought to venture a case for the analysis of visual and multi-modal metaphor alongside verbal metaphor, especially given that visual image and multi-modality have become important features of contemporary discourse and communication, characterising many of the texts in which critical researchers are interested. If doing so yields more comprehensive insights and helps us to attain a fuller understanding of the kind of concepts constructed and circulated in and through discourse, then we should be the better for it.

Acknowledgements

The author thanks Singapore Management University for permission to reproduce Figure 14.1.

Note

1 A key meaning of 'edge' is something that is farthest out, which is consistent with the endeavour to maintain one's lead so as to be as far out in front as possible from competitors. But the use of *honing* and *cutting* also points to 'edge' as the sharp side of a blade, cutting instrument or weapon, indexing the seriousness of purpose involved in organisational competition.

Further reading

Charteris-Black, J. (2004). *Corpus approaches to critical metaphor analysis*. Basingstoke: Palgrave Macmillan.
Charteris-Black's Critical Metaphor Analysis approach integrates CMT, pragmatic theory and corpus analysis to explain why metaphor choices are not merely cognitive and ideological, but also governed by cultural and historical considerations within specific discourse contexts.
Semino, E. (2008). *Metaphor in discourse*. Cambridge: Cambridge University Press.
In firmly situating the study of metaphor in the context of discourse, Semino goes beyond metaphor as conceptualization to also consider metaphor as a way to achieve various socio-rhetorical goals such as explanation, persuasion, obfuscation, justification and evaluation in particular texts, genres and discourses.
Thibodeau, P. H. and Boroditsky, L. (2011). Metaphor we think with: The role of metaphor in reasoning. *PLOS ONE* 6(2): e16782. DOI: 10.1371/journal.pone.0016782.
While not discourse-analytic research in the conventional sense, the study offers experimental evidence of how the use of different metaphors can shape the way people reason about social issues like crime as well as ways of addressing them, and hence helps to buttress assumptions of metaphor's (often covert) cognition-influencing effects inherent in much CDS research.

References

Aaker, J. L. (1997). Dimensions of brand personality. *Journal of Marketing Research* 34(3): 347–356.
Beger, A. (2011). Deliberate metaphors? An exploration of the choice and functions of metaphors in US-American college lectures. *metaphorik.de* 20: 39–60.
Birch, K. and Mykhnenko, V. (2010). Introduction: A world turned right way up. In K. Birch and V. Mykhnenko (eds.), *The rise and fall of neoliberalism: The collapse of an economic order?*, 1–20. London: Zed Books.
Brown, R. (2011). The march of the market. In M. Molesworth, R. Scullion and E. Nixon (eds.), *The marketisation of higher education and the student as consumer*, 11–24. London: Routledge.
Charteris-Black, J. (2004). *Corpus approaches to critical metaphor analysis*. Basingstoke: Palgrave Macmillan.
Charteris-Black, J. (2006). Britain as a container: Immigration metaphors in the 2005 election campaign. *Discourse & Society* 17(6): 563–582.
Chilton, P. (1996). *Security metaphors: Cold war discourse from containment to common house*. New York: Peter Lang.
Chilton, P. and Lakoff, G. (1995). Foreign policy by metaphor. In C. Schäffner and A.L. Wenden (eds.), *Language and peace*, 37–59. Aldershot: Ashgate.
Csaba, F. F. and Bengtsson, A. (2006). Rethinking identity in brand management. In J.E. Schroeder and M. Salzer-Mörling (eds.), *Brand culture*, 106–121. Abingdon: Routledge.
El Refaie, E. (2001). Metaphors we discriminate by: Naturalized themes in Austrian newspaper articles about asylum seekers. *Journal of Sociolinguistics* 5(3): 352–371.
Fauconnier, G. and Turner, M. (1996). Blending as a central process of grammar. In A.E. Goldberg (ed.), *Conceptual structure, discourse and language*, 113–130. Stanford, CA: CSLI Publications.
Fauconnier, G. and Turner, M. (2002). *The way we think: Conceptual blending and the mind's hidden complexities*. New York: Basic Books.
Flowerdew, J., Li, D.C.S. and Tran, S. (2002). Discriminatory news discourse: Some Hong Kong data. *Discourse & Society* 13(3): 319–345.
Forceville, C. (1996). *Pictorial metaphor in advertising*. London: Routledge.
Forceville, C. (2009). Non-verbal and multimodal metaphor in a cognitivist framework: Agendas for research. In C. Forceville and E. Urios-Aparisi (eds.), *Multimodal metaphor*, 19–42. Berlin: Mouton de Gruyter.
Goatly, A. (2002). Conflicting metaphors in the Hong Kong Special Administrative Region education reform proposals. *Metaphor and Symbol* 17(4): 263–294.
Goatly, A. (2007). *Washing the brain: Metaphor and hidden ideology*. Amsterdam: Benjamins.
Grady, J. E., Oakley, T. and Coulson, S. (1999). Blending and metaphor. http://cogweb.ucla.edu/CogSci/Grady_99.html
Hart, C. (2008). Critical discourse analysis and metaphor: Toward a theoretical framework. *Critical Discourse Studies* 5(2): 91–106.

Hart, C. (2010). *Critical discourse and cognitive science: New perspectives on immigration discourse*. Basingstoke: Palgrave Macmillan.

Hart, C. (2014). *Discourse, grammar and ideology: Functional and cognitive perspectives*. London: Bloomsbury.

Kapferer, J.-N. (2004). *The new strategic brand management: Creating and sustaining brand equity long term*. London: Kogan Page.

Koller, V. (2004). *Metaphor and gender in business media discourse: A critical cognitive study*. Basingstoke: Palgrave Macmillan.

Koller, V. (2005). Designing cognition: Visual metaphor as a design feature in business magazines. *Information Design Journal + Document Design* 13(2): 136–150.

Koller, V. (2009). Brand images: Multimodal metaphor in corporate branding messages. In C. Forceville and E. Urios-Aparisi (eds.), *Multimodal metaphor*, 45–71. Berlin, Germany: Mouton de Gruyter.

Kövecses, Z. (2002). *Metaphor: A practical introduction*. Oxford: Oxford University Press.

Lakoff, G. (1993). The contemporary theory of metaphor. In A. Ortony (ed.), *Metaphor and thought*, 202–251. Cambridge: Cambridge University Press.

Lakoff, G. and Johnson, M. (1980). *Metaphors we live by*. Chicago: The University of Chicago Press.

Lakoff, G. and Johnson, M. (2003). *Metaphors we live by*, 2nd edn. Chicago: The University of Chicago Press.

Lakoff, G. and Turner, M. (1989). *More than cool reason: A field guide to poetic metaphor*. Chicago: University of Chicago Press.

Lin, A. (2009). Local interpretation of global management discourses in higher education in Hong Kong: Potential impact on academic culture. *Inter-Asia Cultural Studies* 10(2): 260–274.

McQuarrie, E. F. and Mick, D. G. (2003). Visual and verbal rhetorical figures under directed processing versus incidental exposure to advertising. *Journal of Consumer Research* 29(4): 579–587.

Mautner, G. (2005). The entrepreneurial university: A discursive profile of a higher education buzzword. *Critical Discourse Studies* 2(2): 95–120.

Messaris, P. (1997). *Visual persuasion: The role of images in advertising*. London: Sage.

Musolff, A. (2014). Metaphor in the discourse-historical approach. In C. Hart and P. Cap (eds.), *Contemporary critical discourse studies*, 45–66. London: Bloomsbury.

Ng, C.J.W. and Koller, V. (2013). Deliberate conventional metaphor in images: The case of corporate branding discourse. *Metaphor and Symbol* 28(3): 131–147.

Steen, G. (2008). The paradox of metaphor: Why we need a three-dimensional model of metaphor. *Metaphor and Symbol* 23(4): 213–241.

Steen, G. (2011). What does 'really deliberate' really mean? More thoughts on metaphor and consciousness. *Metaphor and the Social World* 1(1): 53–56.

Steger, M. B. (2005). *Globalism: Market ideology meets terrorism*, 2nd edn. Lanham: Rowman & Littlefield.

van Dijk, T. A. (2008). *Discourse and context: A sociocognitive approach*. Cambridge: Cambridge University Press.

15

Rhetoric and argumentation

Manfred Kienpointner

1. Introduction

In this contribution, I would like to begin with an overview of ancient and modern tradi-tions of rhetoric and argumentation. These traditions can be useful for Critical Discourse Studies because they provide important research tools for the critical analysis of spoken or written texts. This short overview will first deal with Classical Rhetoric (Aristotle, Cicero and Quintilian), then introduce the New Rhetoric developed by Chaim Perelman and Lucie Olbrechts-Tyteca and subsequently finish with a brief survey of contemporary theories of argumentation. After this short overview, I would like to select some especially important tools for the description and critical evaluation of argumentative texts. Firstly, argument schemes are described. Secondly, norms of rational argumentation, which can be used for the critical analysis of potentially fallacious arguments, are discussed. Thirdly, the techniques of verbal presentation are dealt with. A short case study will apply the insights of rhetoric and argumentation theory to the critical analysis of a specific argumentative text, taken from the genre of political rhetoric. The speeches I have chosen are M.K. Gandhi's *Quit India* speeches (August 7–8, 1942).

2. Research paradigms

2.1 Classical rhetoric

In Europe, rhetoric and argumentation were established as serious disciplines by Aristotle (384–322 BC), whose *Topics* and *Rhetoric* are still to be considered as milestones of human thought. Whereas rhetoric later focussed more narrowly on stylistics, Aristotle mainly con-ceived rhetoric as a theory of argumentation: Two of the three books of Aristotle's *Rhetoric* (cf. Aristotle 2002) are devoted to argumentation theory.

Aristotle (rhet. 1.1, 1354a) described rhetoric as the (monological) counterpart of dialectic. Both disciplines are not limited to any particular domain of subjects. Dialectic is described in Aristotle's *Topics* as the art of philosophical disputation, that is, the art of supporting a thesis in a dialogue without contradictions, on the basis of generally accepted opinions (*éndoxa*: those opinions which are held true by all persons or by the majority of them or by all experts or by the majority of experts or by the most distinguished experts; top. 1.1, 100a–b). More specifically, Aristotle defined rhetoric "as an ability, in each [particular] case, to see the available means of persuasion" (rhet. 1.2, 1355b; cf. Kennedy 2007: 37).

Aristotle distinguishes three types of proof: *lógos*, *éthos* and *páthos* (rhet. 1.2, 1356a). While he places a special emphasis on *logos* (proof by the arguments presented in the speech), he also extensively deals with proof through the credibility of the character of the speaker (*ethos*) and proof by the emotional disposition of the audience (*pathos*) (rhet. 2.1–17). None of these "proofs", not even "enthymemes" (rhetorical arguments), are comparable to logical proofs in the narrow sense, that is, the deductively valid syllogisms, which are for the first time described in Aristotle's *Analytics*. Logical proofs, in the narrow sense, start from true and explicitly stated premises and follow logically valid inference schemes in order to confirm their conclusions (e.g., *Modus Barbara*: "All A are B; all B are C; therefore, all A are C", e.g.: "All human beings are mortal; all Greeks are human beings; therefore, all Greeks are mortal").

The precise definition of "enthymeme" has been the focus of extensive scientific debate (cf. Sprute 1982: 131f.; Rapp 2002: 323ff.). This does not prevent enthymemes from being reconstructed as some type of formally valid inference scheme, that is, some sort of syllogism (rhet. 1.1, 1355a). However, the examples for enthymemes in Aristotle's *Rhetoric* show that enthymemes normally have to be reconstructed as instances of inference schemes of propositional logic (e.g., *Modus ponens:* "If p, then q; p; therefore: q") rather than as instances of inference schemes of Aristotelian syllogistics. For example, Aristotle mentions the claim *Dorieus won a crown* (rhet. 1.2, 1357a). This claim can be justified with the help of the argument *Dorieus won at the Olympic games.* There is no need to mention the further premise *If you win at the Olympic games, you win a crown*, which would make the *Modus ponens* fully explicit.

According to Aristotle, rhetorical arguments (enthymemes) are usually formulated briefly, without being totally explicit, for the convenience of the audience (rhet. 1.2, 1357a). Therefore, enthymemes have traditionally been interpreted as abbreviated syllogisms. This, however, does not follow from Aristotle's remarks, which only claim that enthymemes are often formulated shorter than a fully explicit proof (cf. Rapp 2002: 324; Kennedy 2007: 42, n. 55). Enthymemes normally start from merely probable assumptions, which are accepted by (almost) everybody in the audience. Furthermore, sometimes enthymemes are not even logically valid, as in the case of circumstantial evidence (e.g., arguments by non-necessary signs; rhet. 1.2, 1357b): For example, *Somebody breathes rapidly* can be evidence for the claim *Somebody has fever,* but this is not a necessary sign (as the addition of the implicit premise *If somebody has fever, this person breathes rapidly* results in the invalid "affirming the consequent-scheme": "If p, then q; q; therefore: p").

It is interesting to see that Aristotle, the founder of formal logic, did not see rhetorical arguments as intrinsically fallacious because he did not believe that questions of morality, justice and political action could be decided by logical proofs in the narrow sense:

> few of the premises from which rhetorical syllogisms are formed are necessarily true (most of the matters with which judgment and examination are concerned can be other than they are; for people deliberate and examine what they are doing, and [human] actions are all of this kind, and none of them [are], so to speak, necessary.
>
> *(Kennedy 2007: 42; rhet. 1.2, 1357a)*

Moreover, Aristotle was right to insist on the fact that in the case of important public issues it is always possible to argue plausibly for and against the same controversial thesis (rhet. 2.25, 1402a): "for the syllogisms are derived from commonly held opinions [*endoxa*] and many opinions are opposed to each other" (Kennedy 2007: 190). However, Aristotle also insisted that this possibility to argue for both sides of a controversial issue, which is unique to dialectic and rhetoric, should not be abused and that it is not acceptable to argue for "what is debased" (Kennedy 2007: 35; rhet. 1.1, 1355a). Furthermore, Aristotle optimistically assumes that ultimately truth will prevail in a controversy (rhet. 1.1, 1355a).

The main instrument for finding arguments is the *tópos/locus* ("place"). Unfortunately, Aristotle does not define *topos* sufficiently, not even in his *Topics,* where he provides a comprehensive list of more than 300 *topoi.* There is, however, a reconstruction of the Aristotelian concept of *topos,* which can explain at least the vast majority of Aristotle's uses of this term in his *Topics.* This reconstruction was established by de Pater (1965: 147ff.), who defines *topos* as a combination of a device to find arguments and a guarantee which grants the plausibility of the step from arguments to conclusion. In the latter function, the *topos* functions as a general, law-like statement, which is a (usually implicit) premise of the enthymeme and can be compared to Toulmin's inference warrant (cf. below, section 2.3). De Pater's reconstruction has been criticised because it cannot explain all passages in the *Rhetoric* where Aristotle uses the term *topos* (cf. Bornscheuer 1976: 42f.; Eggs 1984: 406ff.; Rubinelli 2010: 72ff.), but its main findings are widely accepted (cf. Sprute 1982: 160; Kienpointner 1992: 179; Rapp 2002: 335; van Eemeren et al. 2014: 69).

Here is one example for the illustration of the double function of the *topos* taken from Aristotle's list of 28 *topoi* in his *Rhetoric* (rhet. 2.23, 1399a): Aristotle recommends to look at the positive or negative effects/consequences of an action. The search formula could be reconstructed as follows: "Look at the good/bad consequences C1, C2. . ., Cn of an action A". This *topos* is then presupposed as an inference warrant of a causal argument: "If A has the good consequences C1, C2, . . ., Cn, A should be done"/"If A has the bad consequences C1, C2, . . ., Cn, A should not be done".

Aristotle illustrates this *topos* by presenting arguments both for and against the same controversial issue, namely, the decision to be educated or not (cf. Kennedy 2007: 179): "the wisdom [acquired] is a good thing [. . .] ; one should be educated; for one ought to be wise"; "being envied is an evil result of being educated, [. . .] therefore, [it may be argued,] one should not be educated; for one ought not be envied". Arguments based on good or bad consequences of actions are indispensable within everyday argumentation. Later on, these were called Pragmatic Arguments by Perelman/Olbrechts-Tyteca (cf. below, section 2.2).

After his list of 28 *topoi,* Aristotle presents a catalogue of fallacious enthymemes (rhet. 2.24, 1401aff.), in this way anticipating the insight that every plausible type of argument can be paralleled with a fallacious counterpart. This catalogue is similar to the list of 13 fallacies which Aristotle presented in his *Sophistical Refutations* (cf. Aristotle 1955). The central core of this list (e.g., the use of the invalid inference scheme "affirming the consequent", the fallacious representation of a chronological sequence of actions as a causal relationship (*post hoc ergo propter hoc*), circular reasoning (*petitio principii,* etc.) was later called by Hamblin (1970: 9ff.) the Standard Treatment of fallacies.

Aristotle mainly focussed on rhetoric as a theory of plausible argumentation. Therefore, he treated the other stages of speech production (arrangement, style, memorization and delivery) rather briefly in book 3 of his *Rhetoric.* As to formulation (style), he deals with the virtues of style, with a focus on clarity, but also with remarks on grammatical correctness, adequacy, brevity and embellishment (figures of speech such as metaphor, hyperbole, irony, parallelism etc.). Aristotle generally advises trying to find a middle course between simplicity and exaggerated artificialness. In his treatment of figures of speech, Aristotle gave prominent place to metaphor (rhet. 3.2, 1405a).

For a detailed definition of metaphor, Aristotle refers to a passage in his *Poetics* (21, 1457b), where he defines metaphor as the transfer of a noun from its proper species or genus to another one, or as an analogical transfer. Genus-species transfers today are rather classified as metonymies (cf. e.g., Plett 2000: 192), so Aristotle's definition of metaphor is a very broad one. Metaphors by analogy involve the equivalence of the relations between two pairs of concepts (e.g., *the wine cup : Dionysus = the shield : Ares*). Aristotle gives the example of the metaphors *the shield of Dionysus* and *the cup of Ares* as metaphors produced by analogy (rhet. 3.4, 1407a). He recommends using something beautiful as the source domain of the metaphor and gives the advice that metaphors should be neither ridiculous nor unclear.

Two further properties of Aristotle's concept of metaphor deserve to be mentioned: 1. Metaphor is said to create a kind of intellectual pleasure in the audience because it offers some cognitive surprise, which leads to a growth of knowledge in a relatively easy and hence pleasant way. Using *stubble* for *old age* creates a transfer, which is easily recognised because of the common genus "things that have lost their bloom" (rhet. 3.10, 1410b; Kennedy 2007: 218). Therefore, according to Aristotle, metaphor is not merely a kind of stylistic embellishment, but also has a cognitive dimension (cf. Ricœur 1975: 10; Rapp 2002: 369). 2. The competence of using metaphors efficiently cannot be learned from others and is a clear sign of a natural ability to recognise similarities (rhet. 3.2, 1405a; poet. 22, 1459a). In his *Topics*, Aristotle takes a more critical look at metaphors and criticises the fact that they are always obscure, but acknowledges that metaphors can make an unknown concept more understandable (top. 6.2, 139b-140a).

The most important contribution of later Greek and Roman rhetoric was not so much the development of fundamentally new theoretical insights, but the detailed elaboration of Aristotle's rhetorical concepts and the establishment of practical catalogues of arguments, styles and figures of speech. For example, Cicero (106–143 BC) managed to reduce the long lists of more than 300 *topoi* in Aristotle's *Topics* and to improve the rather incoherent list of 28 *topoi* in Aristotle's *Rhetoric*. In his early treatise *De inventione* (1.34ff.), Cicero establishes a more manageable catalogue of ca. 30 argumentative *loci* (= *topoi*), focussing on the search of arguments concerning persons, their acts and the causes, effects and circumstances of their acts. In his major treatise on rhetoric, *De oratore,* Cicero presented an even shorter catalogue of about 20 more abstract, Aristotelian *loci* (or. 2.163ff.). These catalogues proved to be enormously influential throughout antiquity, and even in medieval and early modern times. Moreover, in *De inventione* (inv. 1.35.61) Cicero also presents a general model of argumentation (*ratiocinatio*) with four premises and a conclusion, which in many respects resembles the famous Toulmin scheme (cf. section 2.3 below).

With his treatise *Institutio oratoria,* the Roman rhetorician Quintilian (40–96 AD) provided the finest and most comprehensive overview of ancient rhetoric. In this treatise, amongst many other things, he summarised and fused Aristotelian and Ciceronian catalogues of *topoi/loci*.

As far as style and figures of speech are concerned, a trichotomy of styles (grand or magnificent style, middle or moderate style, simple or humble style) was developed and the inventory of rhetorical figures was enlarged considerably (cf. Kienpointner 2011). In the *Ars rhetorica ad Herennium* (unknown authorship, 1st century BC), more than 60 figures of speech were integrated into three major classes, namely, tropes (e.g., metaphor, metonymy, hyperbole), figures of diction (e.g., anaphor, parallelism, climax) and figures of thought (e.g., definition, description, personification). This typology proved to be very influential throughout the Middle Ages and early modern times, and despite some modifications survives even into our times (cf. Corbett and Connors 1999: 379), although a clear distinction between the three major classes has never been established.

2.2 New rhetoric

In early modern times, the philosopher Petrus Ramus (1515–1572) suggested that rhetoric should be restricted to a theory of stylistic techniques which found many followers. Moreover, René Descartes's (1596–1650) verdict against all forms of merely probable reasoning deprived rhetorical argumentation theories of their status as a serious discipline. Thus, rhetoric was gradually reduced to a theory of style (cf. Genette 1970).

The most important revival of rhetoric was developed by the Belgian philosopher Chaim Perelman (1912–1984) and the Belgian sociologist Lucie Olbrechts-Tyteca (1899–1987) in their famous *Traité de l'argumentation* (1983 [1958]). In their influential "New Rhetoric" (cf. Golden and Pilotta 1986, Kopperschmidt 2006, Friedman and Meyer 2012), they re-established rhetoric as a theory of plausible argumentation in the Aristotelian tradition. Perelman/Olbrechts-Tyteca tried to show that outside of disciplines such as formal logic and mathematics, and especially in the fields of political and religious argumentation, there is no room for proofs *more geometrico*. Moreover, they claim that all arguments are directed towards an audience (Perelman and Olbrechts-Tyteca 1983: 18), and that their plausibility has to be judged in relation to that audience. However, in spite of this "dominant role of the audience" (van Eemeren et al. 2014: 262), the New Rhetoric avoids radical relativism by the introduction of the "universal audience" (Perelman and Olbrechts-Tyteca 1983: 39). Rational argumentation is an appeal to the universal audience, and goes beyond the acceptability for a specific audience. Although it is very difficult to define the universal audience (cf. the criticism of van Eemeren et al. 2014: 266), it can be approximately described as the totality of all normal adult human beings.

New Rhetoric's most attractive contribution to the study of argumentation is its monumental typology of argumentative schemes. On the one hand, this is a revival of Aristotelian rhetoric and dialectic, with approximately 30 argument schemes corresponding to most of the Aristotelian *topoi* (cf. Perelman and Olbrechts-Tyteca 1983: 255). On the other hand, empirically interesting new types of arguments are integrated in this classification.

The weaknesses of this typology, however, have also been shown by the subsequent literature. Perelman/Olbrechts-Tyteca do not establish a general model of argumentation and they do not present their argument schemes explicitly, nor do they sufficiently discuss the problems of the delimitation of their schemes and their critical evaluation. For the application of argumentation theory to the descriptive and evaluative purposes of Critical Discourse Studies, typologies of argument schemes must provide explicit versions of argument schemes, verbal indicators which allow the identification of argument schemes, and lists of critical questions designed for the critical evaluation of argument schemes (cf. section 3 below for the application of these analytical tools within Critical Discourse Studies).

2.3 Contemporary argumentation theories: Toulmin's model, Walton's new dialectic, van Eemeren/Grootendorst's pragma-dialectics

Perelman/Olbrechts-Tyteca did not try to develop a general, prototypical model of argumentation. This gap has been filled by the British philosopher Stephen Toulmin (1922–2009), who first presented his famous model of argumentation in his book *The Uses of Argument* (1958). Toulmin saw his model as more suitable for the description of reasonable procedures of everyday argumentation than the inference schemes of formal logic. Moreover, he assumes that the categories of his model are field-independent, whereas specific instances of argumentation belong to different fields of argumentation (e.g., law, business, politics). The six categories in Toulmin's model are functionally motivated and are here listed according to the slightly modified version in Toulmin, Rieke and Janik (1984: 98ff.): A controversial "claim" is justified by "grounds" (facts); the relevance of the grounds in relation to the claim is guaranteed by a "warrant" (an inference rule, that is, a rule of thumb, a principle, a law of nature, a value); the warrant itself is supported, if necessary, by "backings" (the body of (scientific) experience justifying the generalisation expressed by the warrant); a "qualifier" (e.g., adverbs such as *certainly, probably*) which makes the strength of the conclusion explicit; and, finally, a "rebuttal" (exceptional circumstances which undermine the force of the supporting arguments).

Toulmin, Rieke and Janik (1984: 97) give the following example: *Hannah Smith is presumably* (qualifier) *entitled to vote at town meetings* (claim) because *Hannah Smith is a local taxpayer* (grounds), and *all local taxpayers are normally entitled to vote at town meetings* (warrant), given the fact: *the relevant legal and constitutional provisions being what they are* (backing), with the exception of: *Hannah Smith is a noncitizen, a minor, a lunatic, or other disqualified person* (rebuttal).

Toulmin's model has been widely used for the analysis of the structure of everyday arguments and still is enormously influential in contemporary argumentation theory (cf. van Eemeren et al. 2014: 233ff.), but it has also been criticised because it is often difficult to distinguish and reconstruct its elements in an authentic argumentative text. Moreover, Toulmin has not adequately taken into account the developments in modern formal logic.

The Canadian philosopher Douglas Walton has revolutionised the study of fallacies. Influenced by Pragma-Dialectics and Aristotle's dialectic, Walton developed a "New Dialectic", which analyses and evaluates arguments according to their goals in different types of dialogues: Examples (cf. Walton 1998a: 31ff.) are the persuasion dialogue (a joint attempt to resolve a conflict of opinion with the help of reasonable arguments), negotiation (a joint effort to make a deal, that is, to maximise one's own benefits and to find a compromise), eristic dialogue (a verbal fight, where all participants try to win and release powerful emotions).

Walton also established a more realistic look at the traditional list of fallacies, that is, the Aristotelian list of fallacies, supplemented by some of the *argumentum ad-X*-fallacies (such as *argumentum ad hominem* (forms of personal attacks), *argumentum ad verecundiam* (appeals to authority), *argumentum ad baculum* (scare tactics). Walton suggests that these traditional fallacies are better viewed as weak, but not necessarily fallacious arguments, which, however, can shift the burden of proof in the absence of strong evidence and more conclusive arguments.

Walton considers such arguments as instances of "presumptive reasoning" (cf. Macagno and Walton 2014: 182). Furthermore, Walton published detailed studies on most of the traditional fallacies, for example, on *argumentum ad hominem* (Walton 1998b) and *argumentum ad verecundiam* (Walton 1997). Walton also co-authored more general books on emotional appeals in everyday argumentation (Macagno and Walton 2014) and on argument schemes (Walton, Reed and Macagno 2008).

From 1984 onwards, the Dutch linguists Frans H. van Eemeren and Rob Grootendorst (1944–2000) developed the framework of Pragma-Dialectics, which can be called the most comprehensive and most influential research programme within contemporary argumentation theory (cf. van Eemeren and Grootendorst 1984, 1992, 2004; for an overview cf. van Eemeren et al. 2014: 517ff.). Pragma-Dialectics combines the study of speech acts occurring in argumentative discussions ("pragmatics") with insights from normative dialectic ("dialectics"). A reconciliation of normative and empirical approaches to the study of argumentation has been its general goal from the very beginning. In order to achieve the multiple goals of argumentation studies, van Eemeren and Grootendorst (2004: 9ff.) suggest five "estates" of research:

1   In the philosophical estate, the concept of "reasonableness" has to be clarified, because it is fundamental to all argumentation theories and provides them with a philosophical basis. As far as Pragma-Dialectics is concerned, the basic view is a critical perspective (related to Karl Popper's critical rationalism).

2   In the theoretical estate, a theory is derived from the philosophical premises. In the case of Pragma-Dialectics, the theory regards each argumentation as a critical discussion, that is, "as part of an explicit or implicit discussion between parties who try to resolve a difference of opinion [. . .] by testing the acceptability of the standpoints concerned" (van Eemeren and Grootendorst 2004: 21). Fifteen norms for the rational resolution of a conflict of opinion have been established. These norms were also briefly reformulated as a code of conduct for rational discussants with "ten commandments", for example, Commandment 1 (the "freedom rule"): "Discussants may not prevent each other from advancing standpoints or from calling standpoints into question"(van Eemeren and Grootendorst 2004: 190ff.).

According to Pragma-Dialectics (cf. van Eemeren and Grootendorst 1992, 2004: 158ff.), all fallacies can be systematically treated as violations of the norms of reasonable argumentation.

3   In the analytical estate, the systematic application of "reconstruction transformations" (deletion, addition, substitution, permutation) helps to reconstruct the argumentative structure of a given text, by deleting speech acts which are not relevant for the resolution of a conflict of opinion (e.g., greetings), by adding relevant material that has been left implicit (e.g., premises), by substituting confusingly ambiguous expressions by un-equivocal formulations, for example, rhetorical questions by statements.

4   In the empirical estate, qualitative research is carried out in order to show how argumentative moves (e.g., the expression of standpoints, arguments and doubt) and argument structure (complex argumentation) can be reconstructed on the basis of different types of "argumentative indicators" (e.g., connectives, particles, adverbs, verbs) (van Eemeren, Houtlosser and Snoeck Henkemans 2007). A series of experiments conducted with differing groups of informants has shown that pragma-dialectical discussion rules are "generally speaking, to quite a high degree intersubjectively valid" (van Eemeren, Garssen and Meuffels 2009: 222ff.).

5   In the practical estate, Pragma-Dialecticians try to enhance argumentative competence by furthering reflection about argumentation by making its results accessible to a wider public.

Within the last few years, Pragma-Dialectics has been extended by van Eemeren and Peter Houtlosser (1956–2008), who introduced the important concept of "strategic maneuvering", that is, "the continual efforts made in all moves that are carried out in argumentative discourse to keep the balance between reasonableness and effectiveness" (van Eemeren 2010: 40).

More specifically, strategic manoeuvring tries to combine reasonableness and effectiveness by a suitable selection of arguments ("topical potential"), by an adaptation to the expectations of the audience ("audience demand") and by selecting the most persuasive verbal expressions ("presentational devices") (van Eemeren 2010: 93f.).

3. Tools for critical research

3.1 Argument schemes and critical questions

During the last few decades, catalogues of *topoi/loci* taken from Classical Rhetoric and the typology of argument schemes developed by Perelman/Olbrechts-Tyteca's New Rhetoric have been taken up and new typologies have been established. In these new typologies (cf., e.g., Kienpointner 1992; Garssen 1997; Walton, Reed and Macagno 2008), argument schemes are documented according to considerably enhanced standards. They are explicitly presented, taken from corpora of authentic empirical examples, more precisely delimited with the help of argumentative indicators and last, but not least, critically tested as to their reasonableness by lists of critical questions. In this way, interesting tools for the analysis and evaluation of argumentative discourse have been created. To give but one example: One of the most important means of political argumentation is the Pragmatic Argument. Pragmatic Arguments are a type of causal argumentation which evaluates political decisions, initiatives and activities by pointing out their positive or negative effects (cf. Perelman and Olbrechts-Tyteca 1983: 357ff.; Kienpointner 1992: 340; Walton, Reed and Macagno 2008: 100ff.). According to the effects of the respective actions, Pragmatic Arguments can be represented in both a positive and in a negative version; here I present only the positive version:

Pragmatic Argument (Positive version):

If act A has positive effects B, C, D [. . .] and has no, or fewer, or less important negative effects than an alternative act X, A should be done/should be evaluated positively.

Act A has positive effects B, C, D [. . .].

Act A has no, or fewer, or less important negative effects than an alternative act X.

Therefore: Act A should be done/should be evaluated positively.

Some critical questions concerning Pragmatic Arguments could be:

Does act A really have the effects B, C, D [. . .]?

Are B, C, D [. . .] really positive/negative?

Does A really have no/fewer/only less important positive/negative effects than alternative act X?

Does act A have further effects, and are these (mainly) positive or (mainly) negative?

Critical Discourse Studies have often taken up argument schemes such as the Pragmatic Argument as an analytical tool. Following the Topical tradition, argument schemes have been called *topoi*, and lists of more abstract, Aristotelian *topoi* (cf. Fairclough and Fairclough 2012), as well as catalogues of more context-specific *topoi* (cf. Reisigl and Wodak 2001; Wengeler 2003; Wodak 2011) have been applied to the description and critical evaluation of political discourse. Fairclough and Fairclough (see Chapter 1 and Chapter 16, this volume), for example, provide a detailed description of the structure of practical arguments, which are a central pattern of argumentation within political discourse. They outline their structure as a combination of arguments from goals and circumstances to claims for action, where also negative consequences of these actions are taken into account (cf. Fairclough and Fairclough 2012: 48 and 51). Fairclough and Fairclough (2012: 61ff.) follow Pragma-Dialectics and Douglas Walton as far as the evaluation of practical arguments by lists of critical questions is concerned.

Following a discourse-historical perspective, Ruth Wodak and Martin Reisigl show that certain aspects of political argumentation, such as thematic threads in discourse on war, immigration or environment can be profitably analysed with the help of context-specific "topoi" such as the "topos of threat", the "topos of imminent danger", the "topos of history", the "topos of economic usefulness" or the "topos of exploitation". Here the Discourse-Historical Approach (cf. Reisigl and Wodak 2001: 74f.; Wodak 2011: 44) or similar frameworks such as the one developed by Martin Wengeler (2003) can provide a useful overview of frequently employed content-specific types of argument.

3.2 Figures of speech and the verbal presentation of arguments

From Aristotle onwards, metaphor has received most attention as a rhetorical figure. In more recent theories of metaphor, its cognitive impact, which was already recognised by Aristotle (cf. above, section 2.1), has been underlined (cf. Ricœur 1975; Lakoff and Johnson 1980). As conventional metaphors shape our view of reality, and creative metaphors can even change our view of reality, they can no longer be seen as mere ornaments of speech, but have a clear argumentative value (cf. Ng, this volume; Perelman and Olbrechts-Tyteca 1983: 534ff.; Pielenz 1993). This view can be generalised for many of the traditional figures of speech (metonymy, hyperbole, irony, rhetorical question, etc.) and some of them have even been explicitly designed as techniques of argumentation, for example, *concessio* (to concede a point of minor importance, but to insist on the most important standpoint) or *praemunitio* (to anticipate counter arguments). Therefore, following Pragma-Dialectics, rhetorical figures can generally be seen as techniques of strategic manoeuvring (verbal presentation). The strategic use of figures of speech in (political) discourse is described in many contributions within Critical Discourse Studies; cf., e.g., Wodak 2011: 106ff.; Fairclough and Fairclough 2012: 92ff.

Combining central concepts of Critical Discourse Studies with historiography and corpus linguistics, John Flowerdew shows how the history of Hong Kong in the years before 1997 and afterwards can be described as a struggle for ideological hegemony through discursive means (cf. Flowerdew 2004: 1552, 2012: 6ff.). Using a broad variety of discourse genres such as political speeches, newspaper articles and museum expositions, Flowerdew demonstrates that rhetorical strategies, such as the use of indexicals or certain figures of speech (especially metaphor; cf. Flowerdew 2012: 153ff.), are important discursive devices, which are used by the various parties of this struggle in order to achieve the goal of discursive hegemony.

Finally, there have been interesting attempts to replace the old trichotomy of tropes, figures of diction and figures of thought by more consistent and explicit typologies based on linguistic units (e.g., phonemes, morphemes, phrases, clauses, sentences and texts) and four stylistic operations (addition, deletion, substitution, permutation) (cf. Plett 2000; Kienpointner 2011).

4. A case study: Gandhi's speech *Quit India*

Here I will first present a short overview of Gandhi's "rhetorical biography" and the historical context of his legendary speeches *Quit India* (August 7–8, 1942). Finally, I would like to apply some of the theoretical and analytical tools of Classical Rhetoric, New Rhetoric and modern argumentation theory in order to describe and critically evaluate some central passages of this speech.

Mohandas Karamchand Gandhi (1869–1948), called "Mahatma" by his followers, was born in Porbandar, a town in the west of India. Due to his relatively wealthy social background, he received a good education, including studying law in Great Britain. Nevertheless, he was one of those great orators of human history who were not natural born speakers, but in their early years had to overcome great physical and mental obstacles before developing a brilliant rhetorical competence (cf. Demosthenes [384–322 BC] and Winston Churchill [1874–1965], who had to compensate for speech disorders). Gandhi's major problem as a speaker was the fact that he was a very shy person when he was young.

After having studied law in Great Britain, Gandhi returned to India in 1891. During his first public appearance as a lawyer in Mumbai (in 1891 still called Bombay), he had to pass the word to a colleague because he failed to proceed due to his nervousness. And even five years later, when he had already become a successful lawyer in South Africa and had achieved a considerable reputation as a speaker for the rights of the Indian minority, Gandhi still had problems speaking in public. In the year 1896, when the famous lawyer Pherozeshah Mehta (1845–1915) organised a political meeting in Mumbai and encouraged Gandhi to speak over there, Gandhi felt intimidated by the big audience and could not finish his speech.

However, after having successfully fought for the rights of the Indian minority in British South Africa (1893–1915) by developing his method of non-violent disobedience (*satyagraha*: "insistence on truth", Gandhi 1993: 315; cf. R. Gandhi 2005), and shortly after his return to India in January 1915, he already was an accomplished public speaker, who did not hesitate to provoke the powerful elite. In the presence of the British Viceroy, Lord Charles Hardinge (1858–1944), and Annie Besant (1847–1933), the influential socialist, theosophist and co-founder of the Benares Hindu University, as well as many rich Indian maharajas and a crowd of young students, on the occasion of the inauguration ceremony of the Benares Hindu University (February 6, 1916), Gandhi delivered a legendary speech, exposing the extreme poverty and other social problems of colonial India. After having called himself an anarchist, although not a prototypical one (*I myself am an anarchist but of another type*; cf. Gandhi 1961 [vol. 15]: 153), Gandhi was not able to finish his speech because Mrs. Besant and others interrupted him forcing him to stop.

In the following decades, Gandhi held a great number of speeches, in many different situational and institutional contexts, most of the time with enormous success. For example, towards the end of his life, he delivered a remarkable speech at the Inter-Asian Relations Conference (New Delhi, April 2, 1947), before a huge audience of approximately 20,000 visitors, delegates and observers.

Among his most notable speeches were the three public addresses to the *All Indian Congress Committee* (A.I.C.C.) in Bombay, on August 7–8, 1942, when the *Quit India Resolution* of the Indian Congress was suggested by Gandhi and passed by the A.I.C.C. Two of these speeches were originally delivered in Hindi, only the third one in English. The following analysis relies on the English translation of the first two speeches and the English original of the third speech.

A first global look at Gandhi's *Quit India* speeches shows that an essential part of Gandhi's persuasive strength was his rhetorical *ethos*. He practised what he preached. Throughout his political career in India, he engaged in daily physical work, lived according to a very strict diet, wore self-spun, simple clothes (*khadi*), tried to ease poverty, fought for the rights of the "untouchables" (*Dalits,* called *Harijans* by Gandhi) and also tried to extend women's rights, and spent years in jail solely for propagating his ideas of the basic method of non-violence (*ahimsa*).

These facts notwithstanding, his political enemies of the time and his critics today accuse(d) him of maintaining implausible standpoints on some important issues. For example, in a public speech (Tinnevelly, January 24, 1934; cf. Gandhi 1961 [vol. 63]: 38) he controversially claimed that the devastating earthquake in Bihar in 1934 was *a divine chastisement,* that is, God's punishment of Hindus for their oppression of the Dalits. There is no doubt that this is a problematic (superstitious) *argumentum ad verecundiam*. Gandhi's rejection of modern technology (cf. Gandhi 1993: 397ff.) can also be criticised. His belief in "naturally" different roles and spheres of life for men and women can be criticised from a feminist point of view (cf. Gandhi 1961 [vol. 78]: 45). However, so far no one has been able to provide substantial evidence for hypocrisy or other kinds of discrepancies between Gandhi's words and his deeds, as Lal (2008) and Trivedi (2011) argue in favour of Gandhi. Moreover, his emphasis on living like his poor followers seems to constitute a universally characteristic property of the rhetoric of charismatic leaders. This has been shown by cross-cultural research which compared Gandhi's speeches to those of US presidents and other social leaders in the West (cf. Bligh and Robinson 2010).

As far as verbal presentation is concerned, Gandhi's speeches are of a rather simple style, with relatively short sentences and relatively few figures of speech. Classical rhetoric would assign the category of "humble style" to many of them, with relatively few attempts to arouse *pathos* in the audience. This way of strategic manoeuvring with verbal presentation, however, adds clarity and the impression of sincerity to Gandhi's rhetoric. This is not to say that Gandhi did not use figures of speech impressively. They could be used to even greater effect because they were not used frequently. For example, he portrays the horrible violence (*himsa*) during World War II with the metaphor WAR IS FIRE: [. . .] *the earth is being scorched by the flames of himsa* (Gandhi 1961 [vol. 83]: 371). Furthermore, Gandhi uses metaphor to vehemently criticise the political campaign of the Muslim League against himself: *To me, these abuses are like bullets* (VERBAL ATTACKS ARE BULLETS; Gandhi 1961 [vol. 83]: 192).

In the same way, Gandhi occasionally uses rhetorical questions to put more emphasis on a point of criticism against the Muslim League which was led by Muhammad Ali Jinnah (1876–1948): *The Prophet treated even enemies with kindness and tried to win them over by his fairness and generosity. Are you followers of that Islam or of any other?* (Gandhi 1961 [vol. 83]: 191); *How can we agree to the domination of one community over the others?* (Gandhi 1961 [vol. 83]: 194f.).

Moreover, brevity is a figure of speech in itself (*brevitas*; cf. Plett 2000: 144). For example, in the opening paragraph of the final section of his *Quit India* speeches, which was spoken in English, Gandhi uses relatively short sentences (average length of the five sentences quoted below: 12.8 words per sentence; many similarly short passages can be found throughout his *Quit India* speeches), mostly simple main sentences, either without any subordinate clauses or with only one subordinate clause. This makes his self-presentation as a *chief among equals,* not as a powerful political leader in the traditional sense, even more effective (Gandhi 1961 (vol. 83): 201):

> *I have been called their leader or, in the military language, their commander. But I do not look at my position in that light. I have no weapon but love to wield my authority over any one. I do sport a stick which you can break into bits without the slightest exertion. It is simply my staff with the help of which I walk.*

I would like to end with a short treatment of Gandhi's arguments (*logos*). Gandhi was well aware of the most important argument schemes which are useful in the political sphere. For example, he showed great skill in manoeuvring strategically with the "topical potential", by selecting contextually appropriate instances of specific argument schemes such as the Pragmatic Argument.

Gandhi skillfully uses the Pragmatic Argument, for example, to emphasise positive effects of the kind of democracy he would like to establish with the help of *satyagraha* (defined by Gandhi (1993: 315f.) as "insistence on truth, and force derivable from such insistence"): *In the democracy which I have envisaged, a democracy established by non-violence, there will be equal freedom for all. Everybody will be his own master* (Gandhi 1961 [vol. 83]: 371). On the other hand, the aggressive policy of the Muslim League against Gandhi is criticised as discrediting Islam (a negative effect). This criticism is formulated with the help of a self-answered rhetorical question (*subiectio;* cf. Plett 2000: 31f.): *But what of those who indulge in abusing? They bring discredit to Islam* (Gandhi 1961 [vol. 83]: 192). Moreover, and rightly so, we can say with the wisdom of hindsight that Gandhi points out that if the Muslim League refuses to find a joint policy with the Congress, Hindu nationalists such as Vinayak D. Savarkar (1883–1966) will gain the upper hand and this will lead to a civil war (another forceful application of the Pragmatic Argument): *If you distrust the Congress, you may rest assured that there is to be a perpetual war between the Hindus and the Mussalmans* (Gandhi 1961 [vol. 83]: 193).

Gandhi also uses the Argument from Alternatives (cf. Kienpointner 1993) as a central element of his argumentation in the *Quit India* speeches. He establishes a dilemma between freedom and death: *The mantra is: "Do or Die". We shall either free India or die in the attempt; we shall not live to see the perpetuation of our slavery* (Gandhi 1961 [vol. 83]: 197). Of course, the following critical question can be applied to this Argument from Alternatives: "Are there really only two alternatives of action?" In spite of the danger of becoming a Black and White Fallacy, Gandhi's *ethos* and his willingness to die for his ideals add considerable weight to this argument.

5. Conclusion

As I have tried to show, rhetoric and argumentation have a lot to offer for the purposes of Critical Discourse Analysis. The most important insights of Classical Rhetoric deal with the structure of everyday argumentation, with the Aristotelian enthymeme and *topos* as the key concepts. Moreover, Classical Rhetoric has established useful catalogues of argument schemes, fallacies and figures of speech. Modern theories of argumentation have taken up these concepts, and elaborated the existing typologies considerably as far as empirical documentation, standards of explicitness and delimitation are concerned. Moreover, detailed norms of rational argumentation have been established, especially within van Eemeren/Grootendorst's Pragma-Dialectics. This framework has also developed a more comprehensive view of the classical fallacies as violations of the norms of rational argumentation. Furthermore, Walton's New Dialectic has established a more realistic view of many traditional fallacies, considering them as instances of weak, but not necessarily fallacious, argumentation. The analysis of some passages of Gandhi's *Quit India* speeches (August 7–8, 1942) has served as a case study in order to demonstrate the applicability of rhetoric and argumentation theory in the analysis of political discourse.

Further reading

Aristotle. (2007). *On rhetoric: A theory of civic discourse.* George A. Kennedy (trans.), with Introduction, Notes and Appendices. New York: Oxford University Press. Aristotle's Rhetoric continues to be one of the most important theoretical approaches to rhetoric and argumentation.

Perelman, C. and Olbrechts-Tyteca, L. (1983 [1958]). *Traité de l'argumentation: La Nouvelle Rhétorique.* Bruxelles: Éditions de l'Université de Bruxelles. Perelman/Olbrechts-Tyteca's treatise on argumentation revived the Aristotelian theory of argumentation and contains a highly influential typology of argument schemes.

Toulmin, St. E., Rieke, R. and Janik, A. (1984). *An introduction to reasoning.* New York: Macmillan. This is a practical handbook in which the famous "Toulmin scheme" is applied to the analysis of a variety of argumentative texts from many different fields.

Eemeren, F. H. van and Grootendorst, R. (2004). *A systematic theory of argumentation*. Cambridge: Cambridge University Press. In this book van Eemeren and Grootendorst provide an updated version of the theory of Pragma-Dialectics, which is the single most influential contemporary theory of argumentation.

Walton, D. N., Reed, Chr. and Macagno, Fabrizio. (2008). *Argumentation schemes*. Cambridge: Cambridge University Press. This book presents the most comprehensive and sophisticated typology of argument schemes which is available today.

References

Source Texts and Literature on Gandhi's Rhetoric:

Arp, S. (2007). *Gandhi*. Reinbek: Rowohlt.

Bligh, M. C. and Robinson, J. L. (2010). Was Gandhi "charismatic"? Exploring the rhetorical leadership of Mahatma Gandhi. *The Leadership Quarterly* 21: 844–855.

Gandhi, M. K. (1961). *Collected Works,* Vol. 83. New Delhi: Ministry of Information and Broadcasting, 181–185, 189–200, 201–206. Downloaded from February 14, 2015, www.gandhiserve.org

Gandhi, M. K. (1993). *The essential writings of Mahatma Gandhi*. R. Iyer (ed.). New Delhi: Oxford University Press.

Gandhi, R. (2005). Mohandas Gandhi, Abdul Ghaffar Khan, and the Middle East today. *World Policy Journal* 22(1): 89–94.

Lal, V. (2008). The Gandhi everyone loves to hate. *Economic and Political Weekly* 43(40): 55–64.

Trivedi, H. (2011). Revolutionary non-violence. *Journal of Postcolonial Studies* 13(4): 521–549.

Literature on Rhetoric and Argumentation:

Aristoteles. (2002). *Rhetorik*. Chr. Rapp (trans.) with a commentary. 2 vols. Berlin: Akademie Verlag.

Aristoteles. (2004). *Topik*. T. Wagner and Chr. Rapp (trans.) with a commentary. Stuttgart: Reclam.

Aristotle. (1955). *On sophistical refutations: On coming-to-be and passing away: On the cosmos*. E.S. Forster and D.J. Furley (trans.). Harvard, MA: Harvard University Press.

Aristotle. (2007). *On rhetoric: A theory of civic discourse*. George A. Kennedy (trans.) with Introduction, Notes and Appendices. New York: Oxford University Press.

Bornscheuer, L. (1976). *Topik*. Frankfurt/M.: Suhrkamp.

Cicero. (1884). *De inventione*. W. Friedrich (ed.). Leipzig: Teubner.

Cicero. (1976). *De oratore*. H. Merklin (ed. and trans.). Stuttgart: Reclam.

Corbett, E.P.J. and Connors, R. J. (1999). *Classical rhetoric for the modern student*. Oxford: Oxford University Press.

Eggs, E. (1984). *Die Rhetorik des Aristoteles*. Frankfurt/M.: Lang.

Fairclough, I. and Fairclough, N. (2012). *Political discourse analysis*. Oxford: Routledge.

Flowerdew, J. (2004). Identity politics and Hong Kong's return to Chinese sovereignty: Analysing the discourse of Hong Kong's first chief executive. *Journal of Pragmatics* 36: 1551–1578.

Flowerdew, J. (2012). *Critical discourse analysis in historiography: The case of Hong Kong's evolving political identity*. London: Palgrave Macmillan.

Friedman, B. and Meyer, M. (eds.) (2012). *Chaïm Perelman (1912–2012)*. Paris: Presses Universitaires de France.

Garssen, B. (1997). *Argumentatieschema's in pragma-dialectisch perspectief*. Amsterdam: IFOTT.

Genette, G. (1970). La rhetorique restreinte. *Communications* 16: 158–171.

Golden, J. L. and Pilotta, J. J. (eds.) (1986). *Practical reasoning in human affairs*. Dordrecht: Reidel.

Hamblin, C. L. (1970). *Fallacies*. London: Methuen.

Kienpointner, M. (1992). *Alltagslogik*. Stuttgart: Frommann-Holzboog.

Kienpointner, M. (1993). The empirical relevance of Ch. Perelman's New Rhetoric. *Argumentation* 7(4): 419–437.

Kienpointner, M. (2011). Figures of speech. In J. Zienkowski, J.-O. Östman and J. Verschueren (eds.), *Discursive pragmatics*, 102–118. Amsterdam: Benjamins.

Kopperschmidt, J. (2006). *Die Neue Rhetorik*. München: Fink.

Lakoff, G. and Johnson, M. (1980). *Metaphors we live by*. Chicago: Chicago University Press.

Macagno, F. and Walton, D. N. (2014). *Emotive language in argumentation*. Cambridge: Cambridge University Press.

Perelman, Ch. and Olbrechts-Tyteca, L. (1983 [1958]). *Traité de l'argumentation: La Nouvelle Rhétorique*. Bruxelles: Éditions de l'Université de Bruxelles.

Pielenz, M. (1993). *Argumentation und metapher*. Tübingen: Narr.

Plett, H. F. (2000). *Systematische rhetorik*. München: Fink.

Quintilian. (1972/1975). *Institutio oratoria/Ausbildung des Redners*. H. Rahn (ed. And trans.). 2 vols. Darmstadt: Wissenschaftliche Buchgesellschaft.

Rapp, C. (2002). Einleitung. In Aristoteles (ed.), *Rhetorik*, trans. with a Commentary, Vol. 1, 169–451. Berlin: Akademie-Verlag.

Reisigl, M. and Wodak, R. (2001). *Discourse and discrimination*. London: Routledge.

Ricœur, P. (1975). *La métaphore vive*. Paris: Seuil.

Rubinelli, S. (2010). *Ars Topica*. Dordrecht: Cluwer.

Sprute, J. (1982). *Die Enthymemtheorie der aristotelischen Rhetorik*. Göttingen: Vandenhoeck & Ruprecht.

Toulmin, St. E. (1958). *The uses of argument*. Cambridge: Cambridge University Press.

Toulmin, St. E., Rieke, R. and Janik, A. (1984). *An introduction to reasoning*. New York: Macmillan.

Van Eemeren, F. H. (2010). *Strategic maneuvering in argumentative discourse*. Amsterdam: Benjamins.

Van Eemeren, F. H., Garssen, B. and Meuffels, B. (2009). *Fallacies and judgments of reasonableness*. Amsterdam: Benjamins.

Van Eemeren, F. H. and Grootendorst, R. (1984). *Speech acts in argumentative discussions*. Dordrecht: Foris.

Van Eemeren, F. H. and Grootendorst, R. (1992). *Argumentation, communication, and fallacies*. Hillsdale, NJ: Erlbaum.

Van Eemeren, F. H. and Grootendorst, R. (2004). *A systematic theory of argumentation*. Cambridge: Cambridge University Press.

Van Eemeren, F. H., Houtlosser, P. and Snoeck Henkemans, A. F. (2007). *Argumentative indicators in discourse*. Dordrecht: Springer.

Van Eemeren, F. H., et al. (2014). *Handbook of argumentation theory*. Dordrecht: Springer.

Walton, D. N. (1997). *Appeal to expert opinion*. University Park, PA: Penn State Press.

Walton, D. N. (1998a). *The new dialectic*. Toronto: Toronto University Press.

Walton, D. N. (1998b). *Ad Hominem arguments*. Tuscaloosa, AL: University of Alabama Press.

Walton, D. N., Reed, C. and Macagno, F. (2008). *Argumentation schemes*. Cambridge: Cambridge University Press.

Wengeler, M. (2003). *Topos und Diskurs*. Tübingen: Niemeyer.

Wodak, R. (2011). *The discourse of politics in action*. London: Palgrave Macmillan.

16

Deliberative discourse

Isabela Fairclough

Introduction

'Deliberation' is one of the most frequent keywords in political science journals. A search within the titles, keywords and abstracts of articles published in some of the most influential journals in the field over the last ten years typically yields dozens of results (e.g., 24 articles in *Political Theory*). An identical search within *Discourse & Society, Discourse Studies* and *Journal of Language and Politics* yields surprisingly few results: two, zero and six articles, respectively, featuring 'deliberation' or 'deliberative' in titles, keywords or abstracts. A full text search for these terms produces these results: 32 articles in *Journal of Language and Politics,* 41 in *Discourse & Society* and 15 in *Discourse Studies,* compared to 216 in *Political Theory* and 114 in *British Journal of Political Science* since 2005. While, judging by these statistics, discourse analysts appear to be less interested in the study of deliberation, political analysts seem to regard it as the "organizing principle of political communication research", its "central organizing theme" (Gastil and Black 2008). On this view, political communication research is a form of *deliberation critique,* where political and media practices are constantly measured against the deliberative ideal.[1]

However, neither political theorists nor discourse analysts seem to be aware of the way deliberation is theorised in argumentation theory, as an argumentative *genre,* nor of how deliberative practice can be systematically evaluated as *argumentative* activity. This chapter attempts to address this failure of communication across disciplinary divides and provide a framework for the analysis and evaluation of deliberative practice, usable by analysts of political discourse in various disciplines. I will suggest that deliberation fundamentally involves the critical testing of alternative proposals for action, followed by choice among those proposals that have withstood critical testing, as a basis for decision and action.

I will also integrate analysis and evaluation of argumentation with a CDA perspective (see Kienpointner, this volume, on argumentation theory in CDA), and indicate how a dialectical approach to argumentation can contribute to CDA concerns with ideology and power. For this purpose, I will develop an analysis included in Chapter 6 of Fairclough and Fairclough (2012), of the parliamentary debate on the proposal to increase higher education tuition fees in the UK. I will keep the primary focus on a dialectical approach to argument evaluation (i.e., one in which the acceptability practical proposals and arguments depends on their capacity for withstanding critical questioning), but I will redefine the argument scheme for deliberation and its associated set of critical questions. I will also reflect on how rhetorical concerns can be integrated into a basically dialectical view by examining how certain considerations were made selectively more salient in the tuition fees debate, including by metaphorical re-definition, so as to attack the opponents' standpoint more effectively and thus hopefully re-direct the deliberative outcome. I will discuss these aspects under the broad umbrella of 'framing theory' (Reese, Gandy and Grant 2001; D'Angelo and Kuypers 2010).

Deliberation from a dialectical and rhetorical perspective

In this chapter I analyse deliberative discourse in the political field, with a narrow focus on parliamentary discourse (arguably, the paradigmatic case of deliberative discourse). Not all deliberative situations are political: people deliberate, either by themselves or together with others, on all sorts of non-political, private issues. The political field, however, is inherently connected with argumentation and deliberation, though this is not to say that *all* political discourse is argumentative or deliberative. In politics, arguments coexist with narratives, descriptions and explanations (other macro speech acts), deliberation coexists with negotiation, adjudication and mediation (other genres) and (in Aristotelian terms) 'deliberative rhetoric' coexists with so-called 'epideictic (ceremonial) rhetoric'. Politics is inherently connected with argumentation and deliberation because it is oriented to decision-making, but also because the political is an *institutional* order whose very fabric gives people reasons for acting in particular ways. The rights and obligations that people have in virtue of being part of the political order will figure as premises in their reasoning. Searle (2010) calls such reasons "deontic reasons" (Fairclough and Fairclough 2012, 2013; Fairclough 2016).

Politics is about making choices and collective decisions about what action to take in response to a situation. Because of fundamental differences of interests, purposes and values, and different ways of interpreting the situation, making collective decisions is almost invariably an adversarial process in which participants will advocate conflicting lines of action. There is both unreasonable and reasonable disagreement in politics. While unreasonable disagreement can legitimately hold the prospect of disagreement resolution (one party can be expected to retract their standpoint), reasonable disagreement may persist without producing a convergence of views, with apparently 'good' arguments being put forward on all sides. This situation is typical of political parties that may advocate different policies in light of legitimate goals and values that are either different (reasonable value pluralism) or fairly similar, but differently weighted or prioritised.

According to Kock (2009, 2013), deliberation over what to do when several reasonable alternatives are possible was the proper domain of Aristotelian rhetoric. For Aristotle, he observes, rhetoric was relevant to those domains where *choice* among alternatives was involved – the moral, political and legal domains. The fact that in these domains there will almost always be divergent reasonable arguments on any issue opens up a legitimate space for rhetorical argumentation, aimed at changing an audience's priorities and persuading them to adopt a standpoint that is not the one and only reasonable standpoint they ought to choose. It also opens up a space for trying to make a weak argument, or a worse alternative, look better than it actually is. There is, in other words, a legitimate and an illegitimate use of rhetorical argumentation, underlying a commonly held positive or a negative view of rhetoric (Fairclough and Fairclough 2012: 56–61).

The framework presented here (as in previous work) integrates the rhetorical perspective *into* the dialectical one. To take a dialectical perspective on argumentation is to view a process of *critical questioning* as crucial in assessing the reasonableness of a (practical, epistemic or evaluative) standpoint. For example, a practical proposal is unreasonable if critical questioning uncovers *critical objections* against it, such as unacceptable potential consequences. Consequences, however, can be made to look more or less (un)acceptable by being rhetorically presented in a particular way (the same being true for any other premise or conclusion.) Critical questioning would also ask whether such ways of representing are acceptable. Are particular ways of 'framing' a 'problem' or a proposal's alleged consequences rationally acceptable or not?

Deliberation and debate in argumentation theory

Deliberation is an argumentative genre in which practical or pragmatic argumentation is the main argument scheme. Van Eemeren (2010: 138–143) distinguishes among *genres, activity types* and concrete *speech events*. A particular parliamentary debate (e.g., the debate that took place on 9 December 2010 in the British Parliament on the proposal to raise tuition fees) instantiates the more abstract category of parliamentary debate as *activity type* (i.e., a specific genre format), which in turn instantiates the abstract *genre* of deliberation. Deliberation and debate are thus placed at different levels of abstraction: 'deliberation' is an abstract genre, while 'debate' is an activity type, instantiated in particular concrete 'debates'.

The intended outcome of deliberative activity types is a normative-practical conclusion (judgement) that can ground decision and action. For any individual agent, this cognitive outcome can be followed by an *intention* to act, a *decision* to act and by the *action* itself, but does not need to be. Parliamentary debates require more than the minimal outcome of a normative-practical judgement. It is part of their underlying institutional point that they should lead to a decision for action, yet this decision may not be in agreement with the normative judgement arrived at by each and every participant who has been involved in deliberation. This is to say that disagreements among *all* participants are not necessarily resolved, and the outcome that can be reasonably expected is a collective decision, not a shared (unanimous) normative judgement. From an external perspective, the critic may look at such unresolved disagreement as a legitimate manifestation of reasonable pluralism in weighing and prioritising values. Interestingly, however, from the perspective of each individual engaged in the debate, disagreement may seem unreasonable to the end, as argumentative opponents will tend to be viewed as being wrong and in possession of unreasonable proposals (proposals leading to unacceptable consequences) (Fairclough and Fairclough 2012: 200–207).

Starting from Walton's (2006, 2007a) classification of *dialogue types* ('persuasion dialogues', 'information-seeking dialogues', 'inquiry dialogues', 'negotiation dialogues', 'deliberation dialogues' and 'eristic dialogues'), informal logicians have proposed a useful analytical framework for reconstructing 'deliberative dialogue', involving eight stages or moves (McBurney, Hitchcock and Parsons 2007). The starting point is said to be an *open question* that expresses a problem to be solved in a particular situation (the *Open* stage). The open question is followed by a discussion of what goals should be pursued, what constraints on action there might be and what perspectives might be used to evaluate proposals (*Inform*). Proposals are then made (*Propose*), jointly discussed and evaluated (*Consider*), then accepted, rejected or revised (*Revise*). Finally, an option is recommended (*Recommend*), accepted or rejected by each participant, and the deliberation dialogue is closed (*Confirm, Close*). Various activity types will diverge more or less significantly from this normative template. Parliamentary debates do not start from an open question, but seem to begin directly with the *Propose* stage at which only one proposal (a 'motion') is submitted and critically tested.

Analysing and evaluating deliberative practice: argument schemes and critical questions

The approach to political discourse developed in Fairclough and Fairclough (2012), drawing on both CDA and argumentation theory, and underlain by a critical rationalist philosophical perspective (Miller 1994, 2006), suggests a view of deliberation essentially consisting of the critical testing of alternative proposals for action. The most significant 'perspective' in light of which proposals are to be tested is a consequentialist one: would the consequences be acceptable or not? The term 'consequence' refers both to the goals (as intended consequences, generated by particular normative sources) and to other foreseeable consequences, intended or unintended (for example, risks). Unacceptable consequences include impacts on goals which should arguably not be undermined (e.g., other agents' legitimate goals), as well as impacts on arguably non-overridable 'deontic reasons' such as rights and obligations (Searle 2010), arising from institutional facts (e.g., moral norms, laws, rules, commitments), which should act as constraints on what agents can reasonably choose to do. This section defines some of the concepts involved in analysing deliberation and suggests a deliberation scheme and a set of critical questions for the evaluation of deliberative activity types (Fairclough 2015, 2016).[2]

Argumentation in deliberative activity types is succinctly represented in Figure 16.1, a restatement of the scheme proposed in Fairclough and Fairclough 2012, connecting two argument schemes, practical/pragmatic arguments from goals and from consequence. Deliberating agents put forward practical proposals that might help them resolve practical problems and achieve their goals (intended consequences). Deciding to adopt proposal A will be reasonable if the conjecture (hypothesis) that A is the right course of action has been subjected to thorough critical testing in light of all the knowledge available and has withstood all attempts to find critical objections against it. A critical objection is an overriding reason why the action should not be performed, i.e., a reason that has normative priority in the context (or is not overridden by another, stronger reason, in the process of 'weighing' reasons). If the proposal withstands critical questioning, then it can be provisionally accepted, subject to rebuttal by critical objections arising at a later stage, or by emerging negative feedback, as the action unfolds.

The centre and right-hand side of Figure 16.1 represent arguments from goals and positive consequence that can (allegedly) count in favour of the conclusion. The left-hand side represents the argument from negative consequence that can in principle rebut that conclusion, if the consequences are deemed unacceptable (if they are critical objections). However, predicted negative consequences need not constitute critical objections against a proposal. This could be because, should they arise, there is some 'Plan B', some 'mitigating' or 'insurance'

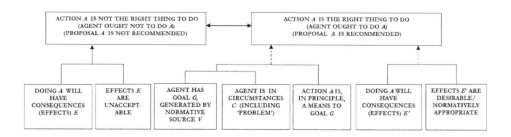

Figure 16.1 Proposal for the structure of practical reasoning in deliberative activity types

Table 16.1 Critical questions for the evaluation of practical proposals

---

Challenging the rational acceptability ('truth') of the premises

---

(CQ1) Is it true that, in principle, doing $A_1 \ldots A_n$ can lead to G?

(CQ2) Is it true that the Agent is in circumstances C (as stated or presupposed)?[4]

(CQ3) Is it true that the Agent actually has the stated/presupposed motives (goals and underlying normative sources)?

Challenging the reasonableness of the conclusion

(CQ4) Are the intended consequences of doing $A_1 \ldots A_n$ acceptable?[5]

(CQ5) Are the foreseeable unintended consequences (i.e., risks) of doing $A_1 \ldots A_n$ acceptable? [If not, is there a Plan B, mitigation or insurance strategy in place that can make it reasonable to undertake $A_1 \ldots A_n$?]

Challenging the inference

(CQ6) [Among reasonable alternatives,] is A_n comparatively better in the context?

(compensation) strategy in place, or because they can be traded off against the positive consequences. In such cases, the conclusion in favour of A may still stand, in spite of counter-considerations. In deliberative activity types, critical testing goes together with a weighing of reasons (as the etymology of the word suggests: *libra* means 'scale', *librare* means 'to weigh') and the final judgement will be made *on balance*.

There are three ways of challenging a practical argument: challenging the premises, the conclusion and the inference (Walton 2007b). In the set of questions I suggest in Table 16.1 questions CQ1–CQ3 attempt to undermine the premises of the argument from goals, questioning their 'truth' or rational acceptability. If it is the case that the acceptability of these premises can be taken for granted, questions CQ4 and CQ5 come in to test the practical proposal (conclusion) itself, and may indicate that it ought to be abandoned. The point of critical questioning is, therefore, first to eliminate the unreasonable proposals from a set of alternatives; secondly, if several reasonable alternatives have survived, to enable non-arbitrary choice amongst them, in light of whatever criteria are relevant in the context (CQ6). All of these critical challenges can themselves be challenged – this is the essence of the dialectical process as a process of open-ended critical dialogue. For example, while the critic may question the reasonableness of a proposal on the grounds of unacceptable consequences, the proponent may claim that the consequences are not unacceptable because they can be successfully mitigated; this claim can in turn be disputed.[3]

Critical questioning in this format integrates deliberation about means and deliberation about goals within a single recursive procedure. A successful challenge will redirect the deliberative process to some antecedent stage or to the starting point. If the goals or other consequences are unacceptable, then a new practical proposal has to be made and the testing procedure will start again.

The critical examination of the proposal to increase higher education tuition fees: arguments and counterarguments

The debate on tuition fees that took place in the House of Commons on December 9, 2010 was a critical examination of the proposal ('higher education motion') to increase fees to a maximum of £9,000 a year. (The transcript is publicly available in the Hansard Report[6] and is 45,167 words long). On behalf of the government, as proponent, the Business Secretary (Vince Cable) begins by making the following argument: tuition fees should be increased, in a context of lack of funds (cuts of 25% need to be made in the education budget to help reduce the deficit), in order to ensure a financially sustainable higher education system which maintains high-quality standards of performance and is based on a progressive system of graduate contributions. The proposal has been, he says, critically examined in government (where alternatives have also been examined) and has emerged as 'the only practical alternative'. The graduate repayment system is 'progressive': no up-front fees will be charged, repayment of loans will begin at a certain income threshold (£21,000) and any outstanding debt will be written off after 30 years. The argument in favour of increasing fees has implicitly withstood critical questioning in government, and is now being submitted to Parliament for debate and voting.

During the course of the debate, the opponents of the motion argue that tuition fees should not be increased, primarily on the grounds of unacceptable unintended consequences (CQ5): the proposal will have an unacceptable impact on social mobility. The individual premises which allegedly support it are also challenged. The stated goals and values are said not to be the 'real' ones (i.e., there are allegedly covert, ideological goals at stake), and the stated goals will not be achieved (no money will be saved) – the argument fails CQ3 and CQ1 respectively. There is also a strong argument against increasing fees invoking the promise not to increase fees made by the Liberal-Democrats before they were in government, as well as from a commitment to fairness. Commitments create obligations which act as deontic constraints on action; these are in principle non-overridable, which is why disregarding them would be unacceptable (the proposal would fail CQ5).

Having identified the main arguments and main lines of criticism, let us look more closely at how these arguments and critical challenges are formulated linguistically in various ways by the participants. Unacceptable potential consequences are predominantly expressed in terms of the 'risk that the increased debt will put off poorer people', or will 'deter people from poor backgrounds from going to university' (10 relevant concordance hits for 'put off', 19 for 'deter*', 49 hits for 'poor*' in combination with 'deter', 'put off', 'discourage' and similar contexts). There are other ways of expressing undesirable consequences: 23 hits for 'impact' – on budgets, universities, students, the poor; 16 for 'effect' – on access, social mobility, students. The supporters of the motion deny that such negative consequences will materialise, on the basis of evidence from the past. ('The evidence. . . since fees came in. . . shows that. . . fees supported by loans do not deter poor students from going to university'.)[7]

The values of 'fairness', 'progressivity' and 'social mobility' are used as reasons both in arguments for and against the motion. In arguments in favour, they are supposed to be the normative sources – here, legitimate values, institutional commitments and active concerns – underlying the goals. (Briefly, the government has an institutional commitment to fairness, as a collectively recognised value, *and* is actively motivated by a concern for fairness). In arguments against, they appear as non-overridable values and commitments that the proposal will allegedly affect adversely. (This is to say: the proposal will damage social mobility or will be unfair; this is unacceptable; therefore, the proposal should be rejected). There are 68 relevant occurrences of '*fair*' (including 'unfair', 'fairness') in arguments that challenge the proposal on the grounds of being unfair, or endorse it on the grounds of being fair. This means either that the proposal allegedly fails CQ5 (the foreseeable consequences will be the opposite of what is arguably intended, i.e., fairness will be negatively affected), or that it successfully withstands CQ5 (there will be no negative impact on fairness). The first passage below is part of an argument against the proposal, the second is part of an argument in favour, advanced respectively by David Blunkett (Labour) and Alok Sharma (Conservative):

> Introducing a £9,000 a year fee on top of cuts in youth and careers services across the country is a deliberate, consistent and unfair attack on young people in our country and their future. That is why it should be rejected. It is not fair to young people and their families, it is not fair to universities, and it is not fair to our country and the future of Britain...
>
> The coalition's proposed system is fair. The Institute for Fiscal Studies says that it is more progressive than the current system... It is fair to all taxpayers that students, who will on average earn significantly more than non-graduates in their lifetime, make a contribution to their education after they graduate; it is only fair to... students and their parents that they do not have to find any money up-front; and it is fair because graduates will pay less per month than they do under the current system.

'Social mobility' is another key expression (42 occurrences, in either argumentative or narrative passages, e.g., about how social mobility decreased during Labour governments). In arguments, 'social mobility' is used either to refute the proposal, by alleging that the impact on social mobility will be unacceptable (the proposal fails CQ5), or to support it, by alleging that the proposal is fully compatible with a concern for social mobility (it withstands CQ5): raising tuition fees will not deter students from applying. There are also 46 occurrences of 'access*' ('fair access', 'improving access'), 37 of 'participation' ('widening participation') and 42 of 'progressive'/'progressivity', mainly in arguments in favour of the proposal, which (thanks to the repayment scheme) is generally thought to be 'progressive'.

There are numerous attempts to challenge the proposal by arguing that it is not the only alternative, that there are other, more reasonable choices that are being disregarded. One intervention argues that, rather than cutting the budget for education, the government ought to make bankers contribute more to reducing the deficit. Another supports a business education tax, which would allegedly generate £3.9 billion and thus allow tuition fees to be scrapped altogether. A third focuses on taxing the wealthy and pursuing tax evasion: the £6 billion in uncollected tax from Vodafone is said to amount to more than a whole year's tuition fees. Labour's own alternative, it is said, would have been a moderate increase ('a few hundred pounds'), not a trebling of fees.

Overall, there are 21 relevant concordance hits for 'choice*' (i.e., referring to the government's choice of action), 29 for 'choose' ('chose', 'chosen'), 19 for 'option' ('opt*') and 20 for 'alternative*', in arguments that either present the increase in tuition fees as the only reasonable alternative, or deny that this is the case (as well as denying that the government 'had no choice'). According to a Labour MP,

> the Conservatives say that there is no choice: they have to raise fees to make up the funding shortfall. There is a choice, however. They could choose not to cut the funding budget by 80%, and they could choose not to privatise university teaching.

Suggesting that there are other reasonable options, while denying the reasonableness of the proposal that is being debated, means that a return to the starting point is desirable (though procedurally impossible in this debate), and other alternatives should be critically tested instead. There are many appeals for more time, asking the Government 'to row back a little bit, to think again, to delay this decision today and to give proper, grown-up, sensible consideration to all the possible alternatives'. As one Labour MP observes, 'policy made speedily and on the hoof is not good policy'. In other words, more extended debate is needed for a decision that is not only procedurally legitimate (the result of voting), but legitimate in a more substantive sense (the result of considered deliberation).

Decision-making, framing and rhetoric

'Framing' is an interesting analytical concept, but by all accounts a very confused and ill-defined one. Framing theorists are the first to acknowledge that their field is a "fractured paradigm", with a highly "scattered conceptualization" at its core (Entman 1993: 51). Loosely, framing is said to involve the selective emphasis of a particular *perspective* or *angle* on an issue, generating the highly vexing phenomenon of "framing effects", where "(often small) changes in the presentation of an issue or an event produce (sometimes large) changes of opinion" (Chong and Druckman 2007: 104).

I suggest that, whenever decision-making is at stake, framing can be best understood from an argumentative perspective, as a process whereby a particular *premise* is made more salient or emphasised by the arguer as an overriding consideration that the audience should reason from. A second mechanism is often at work, where the basic premises of the deliberation scheme (goals, consequences, circumstances) can themselves be supported by other premises in the form of rhetorically persuasive definitions, metaphors and analogies, which (via their inherent bias) will potentially shift the conclusion (decision) in favour of a proposal or against it. Figure 16.2 shows three of the possible locations of such 'X amounts to Y', or 'X is a kind of Y', or 'X is like Y' premises, within the deliberation scheme (see Fairclough and Mădroane 2015, for the analysis of an environmental policy debate in these terms, and Fairclough 2016 for the analysis of the debate on austerity policies in the UK).

The alleged consequences of the proposal to increase tuition fees are formulated in various ways by its critics, in order to make clearer to the audience what the proposal (allegedly) amounts to and thus increase the persuasiveness of the counterargument. The consequences are thereby made selectively more salient, as the allegedly overriding reasons on the basis of

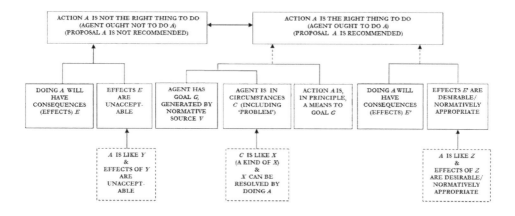

Figure 16.2 'Framing' decisions: the argumentative function of metaphors, analogies and definitions

which that the audience should decide. The proposal is said to unacceptably 'move', 'shift' or 'transfer' the entire cost of, and responsibility for, education onto the students and away from the state, and unacceptably 'replace' state funding by private funding (14 relevant expressions in total), impose 'crippling' lifelong debt burdens on students (6 occurrences of 'burden'), 'destroy the opportunities, hopes and life chances of a whole generation' (1), 'demoralise higher education' (1), and so on. Its consequences are also expressed metaphorically as 'breaking the partnership' between state, society and students (3 occurrences), with the state 'stepping out' of its obligations; similarly, as damaging the balance between what students, the state and employers ought to contribute to education (8 relevant occurrences of 'balance'). As one MP puts it, the 'government have thrown away the scales and are loading the whole cost – not a bigger part, but the whole cost – of a university education on to the graduate'. As the example below shows, such consequences (occasionally made even more salient by the use of metaphor) are intended to conclusively reject the proposal:

> The essential ingredient of this debate is that we are breaking the partnership between student, state and university. We are saying that the state can step out of the arrangement, and that the arrangement should be entirely between the student and the university. It is my contention that that is unacceptable.

The proposal is also redefined metaphorically six times as an 'attack' and once as an 'assault' ('an assault on the entire ethos of the British university'), and also as a case of 'pulling the drawbridge up' or 'pulling the ladder away from poorer students'. Such metaphors (in 'X = Y' premises) support the premise which says that the consequences are unacceptable, thus feeding into the argument against the proposal (left-hand side of diagram):

> Tonight, Opposition Members speak for ordinary working people. . . and for all those who are outraged by this attack on the ambitions and aspirations of the brightest and best of Britain's next generation. An abstention tonight is not enough. I urge the House to reject these proposals.

Positive consequences can also be made rhetorically more salient, hence potentially overriding. Increasing tuition fees is said to amount to 'putting power in the hands of students and universities'. On the right-hand side of the diagram, this way of re-framing the consequences (as *empowering* students) will support the argument in favour.

Challenging the 'terms of debate'

While most of the debate focuses on whether the proposal survives criticism in light of its impact on publicly recognised, legitimate goals and values, there is also some questioning of the stated premises of the argument from goals. There is one main intervention (by David Blunkett, Labour) which claims that the choice to increase fees is 'ideological', not 'economic', and two which say that it is 'political', not 'economic', i.e., it is not motivated by the need to reduce the deficit. According to Blunkett,

> The position is very clear: the scheme is designed to change the architecture of higher education in this country. It is ideologically based, not logically based (. . .) That is a simple fact, and that is why this is a value-laden, ideological issue, not one of rationality, not one of deficit reduction.

The government's alleged commitment to fairness is also challenged. In other words, the argument, as stated, is a rationalisation, or fails CQ3 (the overt reasons are not the real reasons):

> Does my hon. Friend agree that it is impossible to explain to students... that the proposals are fair, when the Government are rowing back on the bankers' levy? Does that not show what their priorities are for this country?

Beyond this, there is surprisingly little questioning of the stated premises of the proposal, and practically no significant critical engagement with the presuppositions and underlying assumptions of the debate. In some interventions, students are referred to as 'consumers' or 'customers' (3 times in total), while higher education is referred to as a 'market' (12 times), with student choice presented as a fundamental mechanism, yet such representations seem to be presupposed or taken for granted, and are not challenged:

> The proposed changes will be an important step in ensuring that the money follows the student and will go further towards making universities more accountable to students as customers.

There is an overwhelming presence of what we might call, in Fillmorian terms (see FrameNet n.d.) a 'commercial transaction frame'. This includes a concern for the quality of the 'student experience' (6 concordance hits) in terms of getting 'value for money', in a context where some universities are apparently delivering 'poor service' and 'simply pass[ing] the cost on to the consumer – in other words, the student'. It also includes Vince Cable's suggestion that universities should not 'defy the principle of operating on a competitive cost basis', i.e., should not choose to operate 'like a cartel', uniformly charging the maximum £9,000. On the whole, not surprisingly, the arguments are formulated to a large extent in financial terms, in terms of 'money' (54 hits), 'costs' (46), 'paying' (142 hits for '*pay*'), 'funding' (113), 'charging' (31), 'spending' (15), 'investment' (18), 'interest' (10 hits in the relevant sense) and 'debt' (42). There are only three interventions that refer to the undesirability of 'privatising' education, but this is understood only in terms of replacing public funding by self-funding.

The most interesting challenge to the premises of the argument, and to the very nature of the disagreement, appears in a handful of interventions (e.g., by John Denham, Labour, below) that try to redefine *what is really at stake* in the debate. What is at stake, allegedly, is the very principle of state-funded education, the balance between what the state and students should contribute:

> [T]oday's vote is on a narrow issue – the fee cap. Behind that, however, is the most profound change in university funding since the University Grants Committee was set up in the 1920s. It is the ending of funding for most university degrees. It is a huge burden of debt on graduates. (. . .) Fees are being trebled simply to reduce the 80% cut in the funding of university teaching, not to raise extra money. Most graduates will be asked not to pay something towards their university education, but to pay the entire cost of their university education. (. . .) That is what is at stake today.

As Denham goes on to suggest, potential agreement on the progressive nature of the repayment scheme should not obscure the fact that there is (or should be) significant disagreement on whether the state should withdraw so completely from supporting higher education, on whether the system should be altered so radically.

What seems to be suggested in such interventions is that the parliamentary debate is on the wrong issue, and that another, more fundamental debate ought to take place first, in preparation for voting, a debate that would challenge premises and assumptions that are here taken for granted. This debate would presumably challenge the 'problematization' of the situation and the stated goals, suggest other legitimate goals and explore alternative proposals. This would be a case of deliberation over the ends of political action as well as over political alternatives, which cannot technically occur here, yet whose need is suggested repeatedly. The general lines of Browne Review, commissioned by Labour in 2009 to 'prepare the way for an increase in tuition fees' (as Cable announces right from the beginning), are taken for granted in this debate, and not questioned. There are 41 references to the Browne Review, none of which takes issue with its recommendations.

To conclude, apart from a few tangential remarks (e.g., on the mistaken belief 'that subjects have no value unless they have a value in the marketplace'), there was no substantive critique of a number of assumptions: that students are rational consumers; that universities are businesses (commercial enterprises) selling services; that education is a market in which the only way to improve quality is to operate according to laws of supply and demand; that making students pay will create more choice, more accountability and drive up quality. The 'terms of debate' (see Norman Fairclough's chapter in this volume) were not questioned, while (sadly) a huge amount of time was spent on arguing from consequences which have, for the most part, not materialised (e.g., student numbers have not gone down). Some predicted consequences have materialised, though: practically all universities in England have rushed to charge the maximum amount,[8] and it is also likely that more debt than originally anticipated will never be paid off, which cancels out the financial benefits of increasing fees, as was predicted by those who argued that 'the policy does not make economic sense'. The benefit seems to be mainly on paper: from an accounting perspective, repayable loans are not categorised as state spending, which makes it possible to disguise the actual increase in government borrowing and public sector net debt (McGettigan 2013: 2).

A growing literature on these recent changes to higher education, including Collini (2012) and McGettigan (2013), challenges the (neoliberal) assumptions above and frames its critique in terms which are very different from those in which the parliamentary debate was cast. For Collini (2012, Chapter 7), the analogies between universities and businesses, students and consumers, are spurious. One shared premise of this critique is that austerity provided the pretext for a covert privatisation agenda, intended to open up higher education to private equity and commercial companies that will distribute profits to shareholders and owners. Another is that 'as we creep towards a corporatized marketplace', and as government funding for education disappears, so will public accountability, democratic governance and the protection of the public interest (McGettigan 2013: 2–3, 152–154). One cannot help feeling therefore that the December 2010 debate missed the main point of the proposed changes, in spite of those few interventions (Blunkett, Denham) that warned about the bigger agenda that was arguably involved. Nobody thought of exploring what 'privatisation' might involve, beyond the replacement of public funding by self-funding. For example, how it might open the way for profit-making private education providers (operating on the back of taxpayer-funded loans), or lead to alterations to the original terms of the loan (including the possible sale of the so-called student loan book). More significantly, nobody challenged the proposal in terms of the potential erosion of the public, democratic accountability of universities in the corporate management structures of the future, nor in terms of the fundamental adulteration of the education process that might result from putting a financial transaction at the heart of the lecturer-student relationship.

Conclusion

The approach to CDA I have presented above (and in Fairclough and Fairclough 2012) views analysis of action and genres as having primacy over analysis of 'representations' and 'discourses.' 'Representations' (e.g., of proposed reform as an 'attack' on young people) are critically significant insofar as they support particular lines of action, by entering (as constituents of premises) in agents' arguments about what to do. The *agency-structure dialectic* manifests itself in the way discourses provide agents with particular reasons for action (beliefs, goals, values).

The analysis has shown how a particular policy proposal was defended and challenged in a dialectical process of critical questioning designed to lead to decision and action. In particular, it has shown how various rhetorically effective representations of what the proposal would allegedly amount to were used in arguments designed to support or refute it, as part of the deliberating agents' plan of action. In so doing, the analysis has tried to illustrate how normative critique (both by participants and by analysts as critics) can proceed in a systematic manner, while also indicating that not all the possibilities for questioning that are in principle available were used effectively, at least not on this particular occasion.

Given the actual balance of political forces in Parliament, it is impossible to know whether the outcome would have been different, if deliberation had been more extended. It is a fact that MPs usually vote according to the party whip. However, this is not the result of some non-overridable institutional obligation: it is possible for MPs to 'rebel' or to 'defy the whip', without losing their MP status. In the tuition fees debate, 21 Liberal-Democrats and 6 Conservatives voted against the motion (with three resigning from ministerial positions in order to do so), which reduced the government's Commons majority from 83 to 21. There were finally 323 votes in favour and 302 against (BBC 2010). The increase in fees was therefore not a foregone conclusion, and the attempts to argumentatively direct the outcome in another direction were not by definition futile. In studying argumentation in institutional contexts, what agents may be disinclined or unwilling to do must not be confused with what is institutionally disallowed or impossible, in virtue of whatever (desire-independent, extrinsic) deontic constraints on decision-making might operate (i.e., obligations arising from regulative or constitutive rules).

The conclusions of normative critique can open the way for explanatory critique of why, in this case, the debate failed to properly address a number of relevant issues (e.g., why it failed to imagine the consequences of 'privatisation' beyond the impact on social mobility), or why the critical challenges were not more effective in changing the outcome or redirecting the debate to the 'real issues'. Some of these causes may be addressed in terms of ideology and power, for example in terms of the existence of a broad cross-party neoliberal consensus over the 'terms of debate' ('universities as businesses', 'students as customers') and of a government majority in Parliament, but also in terms of institutional, procedural constraints (e.g., on what can be subject for debate and what can't, given a specific 'motion'). It has also been suggested that the December 2010 'snap vote' was a "tactical means to curtail debate both inside and outside Parliament" (McGettigan 2013: 5–6), part of a deliberate and illegitimate strategy to prevent extensive discussion. Explanatory critique of why this particular debate was in many ways limited and inefficient would thus be articulated with normative critique of deliberation.

Notes

1 In spite of the scarcity of journal articles in CDA, there are several edited volumes and monograph chapters that focus on deliberative activity types: Chilton (2004), Reisigl and Wodak (2001), Wodak (2009), van Dijk and Wodak (2000). Outside CDA, Ilie (2003) has developed a pragma-rhetorical

approach to parliamentary discourse. A pragmatic perspective underlies a few edited volumes: Bayley (2004), Ilie (2010) and a special issue of *Journal of Pragmatics* (Ilie 2010) on parliamentary debate. Over the last decades, the main theoretical contributions to the linguistic study of deliberation have come from argumentation theory. Pragma-dialecticians have focused on the way in which argumentation in deliberative activity types is shaped by 'institutional preconditions' or 'extrinsic constraints' – see van Eemeren (2010), van Eemeren and Garssen (2010) and a special issue of the *Journal of Argumentation in Context,* edited by Lewinski and Mohammed (2013), including Garssen (2013) and Mohammed (2013). Several deliberative activity types have been investigated to date: Prime Minister's Question Time (Mohammed 2009), parliamentary debate (Ihnen Jory 2012), political interviews (Andone 2013).

2 Underlying this discussion is a (fallibilist) critical notion of reasonableness or rational acceptability. A standpoint is (tentatively) acceptable if it withstands the most testing criticism directed against it in light of all the knowledge available to the critics. Acceptability of potential consequences (e.g., risks) should be tested from the perspective of all those affected by a proposal.

3 Testing typically begins with CQ4, unless there are reasons to challenge the (presupposed) acceptability of the premises.

4 E.g., the 'problem' and any constraints are as stated, the agent is capable of performing the action, etc.

5 These include the goals and other intended (e.g., planned) impacts.

6 Hansard, 9 December 2010, Column 540–629, at www.publications.parliament.uk/pa/cm201011/cmhansrd/cm101209/debtext/101209-0002.htm

7 I have used Antconc (Anthony 2014), a corpus analysis toolkit for concordancing and text analysis.

8 According to the Complete University Guide, at www.thecompleteuniversityguide.co.uk/

Further reading

Fairclough, I. and Fairclough, N. (2012). *Political discourse analysis.* London: Routledge.
The book provides an analytical framework for the analysis and evaluation of practical reasoning in deliberative activity types and illustrates this framework by looking at various public debates, e.g., on austerity policies and bankers' bonuses in the wake of the 2008 financial crisis.
Fairclough, I. (2016). Evaluating policy as argument: The public debate over the first UK Austerity Budget. *Critical Discourse Studies* 13(1): 57–77.
This article provides a revised version of the framework introduced in Fairclough and Fairclough (2012). It also indicates how rhetorical concerns (e.g., concerns with 'framing' or the persuasive function of metaphors) can be integrated within a basically dialectical perspective on argument evaluation.
Van Eemeren, F. H. (2010). *Strategic maneuvering in argumentative discourse.* Amsterdam: Benjamins.
Frans H. van Eemeren brings together the dialectical and the rhetorical dimensions of argumentation by introducing the concept of strategic maneuvering. Chapter 5 deals with argumentation in conventionalized practices in various institutional contexts (in the political, legal and other fields).
Walton, D., Reed, C. and Macagno, F. (2008). *Argumentation schemes.* New York: Cambridge University Press.
Providing a compendium of nearly 100 argument schemes, each accompanied by a matching set of critical questions, this book is a valuable resource for learning how to identify, analyse and evaluate argumentation in everyday communicative practice.
Searle, J. R. (2010). *Making the social world: The structure of human civilization.* Oxford: Oxford University Press.
Philosopher John Searle explains how language creates and maintains the elaborate structures of human social institutions. Institutions create and distribute power relations ('deontic powers'), which in turn motivate human actions in a way that provides the 'glue' that holds human civilization together.

References

Andone, C. (2013). *Argumentation in political interviews.* Amsterdam: Benjamins.
Anthony, L. (2014). AntConc (Version 3.4.3w) [Computer software]. Tokyo, Japan: Waseda University. www.antlab.sci.waseda.ac.jp/
Bayley, P. (2004). *Cross-cultural perspectives on parliamentary discourse.* Amsterdam: Benjamins.

BBC. (2010). Tuition fees vote: Plans approved despite rebellion, December 9. www.bbc.co.uk/news/uk-politics-11952449

Chilton, P. (2004). *Analysing political discourse.* London: Routledge.

Chong, D. and Druckman, J. N. (2007). Framing theory. *Annual Review of Political Science* 10: 103–127. DOI: 10.1146/annurev.polsci.10.072805.103054

Collini, S. (2012). *What are universities for?* London: Penguin.

D'Angelo, P. and Kuypers, J. A. (eds.) (2010). *Doing news framing analysis: Empirical and theoretical perspectives.* New York: Routledge.

Entman, R. M. (1993). Framing: Toward clarification of a fractured paradigm. *Journal of Communication* 43(4): 51–58.

Fairclough, I. (2016). Evaluating policy as argument: The public debate over the first UK Austerity Budget. *Critical Discourse Studies* 13(1): 57–77. DOI: 10.1080/17405904.2015.1074595

Fairclough, I. (2015). A dialectical profile for the evaluation of practical arguments. In B. Garssen, D. Godden, G. Mitchell and A. F. Snoeck Henkemans (eds.), *Proceedings of the 8th conference of the international society for the study of argumentation.* Amsterdam: SicSat. http://rozenbergquarterly.com/issa-proceedings-2014-table-of-contents/

Fairclough, I. and Fairclough, N. (2012). *Political discourse analysis.* London: Routledge.

Fairclough, I. and Fairclough, N. (2013). Argument, deliberation, dialectic and the nature of the political: A CDA perspective. *Political Studies Review* 11(3): 336–344.

Fairclough, I. and Mădroane, I. D. (2015). An argumentative approach to policy "framing", competing "frames" and policy conflict in the Roşia Montană case. In B. Garssen, D. Godden, G. Mitchell and A. F. Snoeck Henkemans (eds.), *Proceedings of the 8th conference of the International Society for the Study of Argumentation.* Amsterdam: SicSat. http://rozenbergquarterly.com/issa-proceedings-2014-table-of-contents/

FrameNet Project (n.d.) International Computer Science Institute at Berkeley, CA. https://framenet.icsi.berkeley.edu/fndrupal/

Garssen, B. (2013). Strategic maneuvering in European parliamentary debate. *Journal of Argumentation in Context* 2(1): 33–46.

Gastil, J. and Black, L. (2008). Public deliberation as the organizing principle of political communication research. *Journal of Public Deliberation* 4(1), Article 3. www.publicdeliberation.net/jpd/vol4/iss1/art3

Ihnen Jory, C. (2012). *Pragmatic argumentation in law-making debates.* Amsterdam: Sic Sat.

Ilie, C. (2003). Discourse and metadiscourse in parliamentary debates. *Journal of Language and Politics* 1(2): 269–291.

Ilie, C. (ed.) (2010a). *European parliaments under scrutiny: Discourse strategies and interaction practices.* Amsterdam: Benjamins.

Ilie, C. (ed.) (2010b). *Pragmatic perspectives on parliamentary discourse.* Special Issue of *Journal of Pragmatics* 42(4): 879–1172.

Kock, C. (2009). Choice is not true or false: The domain of rhetorical argumentation. *Argumentation* 23(1): 61–80.

Kock, C. (2013). Defining rhetorical argumentation. *Philosophy and Rhetoric* 46(4): 437–464.

Lewiński, M. and Mohammed, D. (eds.) (2013). *Argumentation in political deliberation.* Special issue of *Journal of Argumentation in Context,* 2 (1). Amsterdam: Benjamins.

McBurney, P., Hitchcock, D. and Parsons, S. (2007). The eightfold way of deliberation dialogue. *International Journal of Intelligent Systems* 22(1): 95–132.

McGettigan, A. (2013). *The great university gamble.* London: Pluto Press.

Miller, D. (1994). *Critical rationalism: A restatement and defence.* Chicago: Open Court.

Miller, D. (2006). *Out of error: Further essays on critical rationalism.* London: Routledge.

Mohammed, D. (2009). *'The honourable gentleman should make up his mind.' Strategic manoeuvring with accusations of inconsistency in prime minister's question time.* Unpublished doctoral dissertation, University of Amsterdam.

Mohammed, D. (2013). Pursuing multiple goals in European Parliamentary debates: EU immigration policies as a case in point. *Journal of Argumentation in Context* 2(1): 47–74.

Reese, S. D., Gandy, O. H. and Grant, A. E. (eds.) (2001). *Framing public life: Perspectives on media and our understanding of the social world.* Mahwah, NJ: Erlbaum.

Reisigl, M. and Wodak, R. (2001). *Discourse and discrimination.* London: Routledge.

Searle, J. R. (2010). *Making the social world: The structure of human civilization.* Oxford: Oxford University Press.

Van Eemeren, F. H. (2010). *Strategic maneuvering in argumentative discourse*. Amsterdam: Benjamins.

Van Eemeren, F. H. and Garssen, B. (2010). In Varietate concordia – United in diversity. European parliamentary debate as an argumentative activity type. *Controversia* 7(1): 19–37.

Walton, D. (2006). *Fundamentals of critical argumentation*. New York: Cambridge University Press.

Walton, D. (2007a). *Media argumentation*. New York: Cambridge University Press.

Walton, D. (2007b). Evaluating practical reasoning. *Synthese* 157: 197–240.

Wodak, R. (2009). *The discourse of politics in action*. Basingstoke: Palgrave Macmillan.

Wodak, R. and van Dijk, T. A. (eds.) (2000). *Racism at the top: Parliamentary discourses on ethnic issues in six European states*. Klagenfurt: Drava Verlag.

Part III
Interdisciplinarity

17

Critical discourse studies and social theory[1]

Bernhard Forchtner

Introduction

While the diverse research programme called Critical Discourse Analysis (CDA) and, more recently, Critical Discourse Studies (CDS) emerged out of linguistics (Wodak and Meyer 2016), its success as a framework for doing research across the (critical) social sciences is due to its recognition of the relation between language use and contexts and structures. Intimately linked to this stance is the view that CDS is not interested in language use per se but the workings of and effects on power relations through meaning making (among many, see Wodak 1996: 17). Against this background, 'doing' CDS requires as much reflection on linguistic means as on understanding the social (Fairclough 1992: 1f). This chapter aims to offer an overview of how the social has been understood, that is, of social theory in CDS.

What do social theories offer? In short: they provide a "relatively systematic, abstract and general reflection on the workings of the social world" (Baert and Carreira da Silva 2010: 1) – and consequently concern the interplay of action, order and change. In so doing, theories offer conceptual frameworks through which particular discursive events can be understood as elements of the social in the first place. Looking at publications in relevant journals, edited volumes and monographs, it is evident that much has changed for the better since Chouliaraki and Fairclough (1999: 1) argued that CDS has not made systematically explicit the theories that it relies upon. At the same time, however, their attempt has remained rather unique. In writing that, I do not mean to belittle the significance of existing references to a diverse range of scholars such as Louis Althusser, Pierre Bourdieu, Judith Butler, Michel Foucault, Anthony Giddens, Antonio Gramsci, Jürgen Habermas, Ernesto Laclau and Chantal Mouffe, Claude Lefort, Jacques Rancière and others. These references fulfil their purpose in individual projects and might open up space for subsequent theoretical elaboration. However, what I am interested in here are comprehensive and detailed discussions of possible synergies and contradictions of social theories brought together in a CDS framework, of social theory and CDS 'as such'. The lack of relevant comprehensive investigations might simply testify to CDS's eclecticism, pluralism and celebration of inter-/transdisciplinary (Weiss and Wodak 2003: 6) – yet, it also indicates that Chouliaraki and Fairclough's observation still holds some truth.

Therefore, a series of questions has remained relevant and are approached differently by the various strands in CDS: for example, how is the relation between action and structure perceived (that is: are structures always already encompassing individuals and 'push' them in certain directions or do individuals act free and independently). What is the relation between the discursive and extra-discursive (or, as some might ask: is there any such a thing as 'the extra-discursive')? And subsequently: how do we understand central notions in CDS like critique and emancipation, demystification and ideology, power and hegemony?

In the following, I discuss these questions by engaging with so-called 'core' strands in CDS associated with Norman Fairclough, Teun van Dijk and Ruth Wodak; approaches which have shaped, and still exert a considerable influence on, the field. Broadly speaking, these strands approach these and related issues from two directions: on the one hand, Karl Marx and (neo-)Marxist approaches; on the other, Michel Foucault and other post-structuralists (see Titscher et al. 2000: 51; Wodak and Meyer 2009: 20). It is true that (these) social theories are not equally important to every strand in CDS, whether or not belonging to 'the core'. For example, van Dijk's orientation to social psychology leads him towards cognition instead of sociology. In turn, especially Fairclough's Dialectical-Relational Approach, but also Wodak's Discourse-Historical Approach (DHA), draw more extensively on social theories.

While I aim for an accessible introduction to the role social theories have played in 'core' strands in CDS, let me at least briefly indicate a couple of relevant, more recent developments in some areas of CDS. Corpus linguistics studies related more or less explicitly to CDS have usually defined themselves through reference to linguistic sources but have also pointed to social theories. For example, Baker (2014: 3f) adopts a Foucauldian notion of discourse and draws on Judith Butler's understand of gender. Due to its novelty and substantive discussion, O'Halloran's (2012) introduction of Gilles Deleuze and Félix Guattari to corpus linguistics is worth mentioning as well. Taking a post-foundational perspective, Macgilchrist (2016) discusses ontological and epistemological assumptions underlying research done in CDS, research which, she argues, focuses on the construction of social orders and stability instead of their fissures and dislocations. Drawing on theorists such as Laclau, Lefort and Rancière, she discusses key concepts – critique, rationality and validity – in CDS. The notable interest in Queer Theory within CDS (see, for example, Thurlow 2016; Milani 2015) should also be mentioned here. In addition to these developments, often rooted in rather recent debates, there are also more classic theories adopted in CDS which, however, neither belong to (neo-)Marxism nor post-structuralism. For example, the work of Goffman (1990) has been taken up by Wodak (for example Wodak 2009) in her analysis of interactions in a study on the working life of Members of the European Parliament. This enables her to take advantage of a toolkit for analysing performances in order to better understand the working of texts in particular material settings.

The structure of this article is as follows: I start by looking briefly at CDS's widely acknowledged predecessor, Critical Linguistics (CL). Subsequently, I turn to (neo-)Marxist elements in the aforementioned 'core' strands in CDS, ranging from Marx's writings to Gramsci, the Critical Theory of the Frankfurt School and Bourdieu. The next section addresses post-structural sources, in particular the work of Foucault as well as Laclau and Mouffe. I conclude my review with a brief note on the diverse, socio-theoretical foundations of CDS.

At the beginning. . .

In the ground-breaking work of critical linguists, emerging in the 1970s, there was a concern to make particular representations of reality and discrimination in and through language use visible – but rather little explicit discussion of social theories.[2] In carving out a space for their vision of linguistics, (not only) sociolinguistics was rejected for describing instead of criticising the role of language in and for social processes (for example Fowler and Kress 1979: 189ff). While sociolinguistics allegedly separated "the concepts of 'language' and 'society'", CL emphasised the integral role of language use in confirming and consolidating these structures. Social structures were seen as operating "in a deterministic fashion" towards "linguistic variety" (Fowler and Kress 1979: 194). This 'original source-centred' approach showed little awareness of reception or agency – something Fowler (1996: 7) later criticised by stressing dynamic processes of reception. Relatedly, CL emphasised the need for 'unveiling' and 'demystification' language use they regarded as 'dehumanizing' (Fowler and Kress 1979: 196) – but rejected the idea that an unmediated access to reality is possible. For them, ideology was ever-present as "a systematic body of ideas, organized from a particular point of view" and manifest in linguistic choices (Kress and Hodge 1979: 6).

In a similar vein, Trew (1979: 95) rejected the possibility of 'raw' or unmediated perception. Rather, perceptions are always mediated by 'theory or ideology' (1979: 95), adding that he found Foucault's and Althusser's notions of knowledge and ideology/ideological state apparatuses 'useful on this issue' (Fowler et al. 1979: 217n; while their ideas resemble that of other practitioners of CL, neither Foucault nor Althusser are mentioned in, e.g., the index to Kress and Hodge 1979). Indeed, Althusser favoured a broad notion of ideology and viewed subjects as largely determined by ideological state apparatuses (ISAs) and, ultimately, economic structures (which, in turn, depend on the state in order to reproduce the former) – although ISAs are later also described as sites of struggle (Althusser 2001: 126). ISAs, for example the education system (CL has largely investigated communications ISA), function '*by ideology*' and complement the repressive state apparatus which functions primarily by (physical) repression. The latter ensures the work of ISAs in the face of possible deviance, such as in the case of the police (Althusser 2001: 97). Going beyond classic notions of ideology as a false representation of 'reality', Althusser (2001: 109–115) defined ideology as "*represent[ing] the imaginary relationship of individuals to their real conditions of existence*" which "*has a material existence*". Ideology is thus a question of material existence and practices. While there is no life outside ideologies, *particular* ideologies constitute the sort of subjects required in a *particular* social formation (and can be criticised on the basis of what Althusser viewed as scientific knowledge, i.e., knowledge which has been cleansed of ideological notions such as in the case of Historical Materialism which emerged out of classical political economy). It is in this context that Althusser (2001: 115–124) famously speaks of the *interpellation* of individuals, the transformation of individuals into subjects, which implies their 'happy' submission to the respective commandments. This aspect would be taken up a few years later when others followed the route prepared by CL.

Marx and (neo-)Marxist influences

Being influenced by the social turmoil of the 1960s and 1970s, it is not surprising that many of those who would later write under the banner of CDA/CDS have been strongly influenced by Marx and neo-Marxists. Many authors are thus fundamentally sceptical concerning capitalism as a mode of organising social relations (besides Fairclough, see, for example, Richardson 2007). Their Marxism is, however, an anti-reductionist one which recognises the significance of language and culture in and for contemporary capitalist societies. At the same time, scholars situating themselves in this tradition – in particular Fairclough and, to a slightly lesser extent, Wodak – adopt a realist ontology by drawing on the critical realism of Roy

Bhaskar and his distinction between the real, the actual and the empirical (Fairclough, Jessop and Sayer 2002).

Although Marx has had a paramount influence by providing a framework for understanding social dynamics in capitalist societies in general, it has only been rather recently that his view on language has been elaborated on explicitly and in much detail. In an article entitled 'Marx as Critical Discourse Analyst', Fairclough and Graham (2002) not only repeat their long-held conviction that language has become ever more central in late capitalism but also argue that Marx was well aware of the link between language and other dimensions of the social – that is, the dialectics between the discursive and the material dimension of social life. Drawing on Marx's writing they (2002: 313) outline his view on ideological relations between language, consciousness, social life and civil society, thereby offering a model in order to understand the interplay between the discursive and the extra-discursive.

Returning briefly to the relation between ISAs and the economy in Althusser, the latter has been quite prominent in Fairclough's work (1989: 39, 1992: 86f; see also Chouliaraki and Fairclough 1999), especially his notions of ideology, interpellation and overdetermination. In addition, some strands in CDS (Wodak 1996: 11; Fairclough 2003: 160f) refer to Anthony Giddens's theory of structuration in order to make sense of the problem of order. Here, subjects are not simple bearers of structure but active players in the reproduction of society, able to reflexively monitor their doing (Giddens 1993: 128f).

More specifically, Althusser's structuralism has led (in particular) Fairclough to draw on Gramsci and his focus on struggle. In fact, Gramsci also had an elaborated take on language (Ives 2004), viewing language as historical and permitting all social relations. While there are gestures towards Gramsci in various strands of CDS (see for example Krzyżanowski and Wodak 2010 in their work on multilingualism), he features most extensively in Fairclough's approach (e.g., 1992: 91–96, 2014; Chouliaraki and Fairclough 1999). The notion of hegemony is the most relevant concept taken up in CDS and describes domination based on consent (though backed up by coercion), spreading through 'private' organisations such as the church, trade unions and schools, instead of domination through sheer coercion, violent revolution and the capturing of the state apparatus. Politics is thus viewed as a struggle for hegemony, something which has become important as (Western) societies moved from a war of movement (characterised by a situation in which revolutionary activism might succeed) to a war of position (a situation in which only civil society struggles over hegemony can lead to transformation; see Gramsci 2011: 168f).

Mentioned as another key influence is the Critical Theory of the Frankfurt School (among many, see Fairclough and Wodak 1997: 260f; Reisigl and Wodak 2001: 32). Indeed, there are a couple of reasons which make their members' ideas attractive to CDS: already the first generation, including authors such as Theodor W. Adorno, Walter Benjamin, Erich Fromm, Max Horkheimer, Siegfried Kracauer, Leo Löwenthal, Herbert Marcuse, Franz Neumann and Friedrich Pollock, showed a keen interest in modernity and new, emerging forms of capitalism. Proponents were furthermore conscious of the significance of culture and (consequences of) its commodification, clearly departed from Marxist orthodoxy, opposed 'real existing socialism' and, finally, argued for a dialectical method opposing positivism (Horkheimer 1975; Adorno et al. 1976). Yet, the influence of the first generation seems to be largely limited to the DHA in CDS and hardly exceeds the mentioning of the *Dialectic of Enlightenment* (for example Reisigl and Wodak 2001: 32) or *The Authoritarian Personality* (Reisigl and Wodak 2001: 13f; Wodak 2015: 154f).

Though this is partly justified given the increasingly abstract and contemplative orientation of especially Adorno, their work nevertheless provides inspiration. For example, Horkheimer's

(1993: 11) interdisciplinary programme, which called for theoretically informed, empirical investigations of the link between economy, psychology and culture (including areas such as fashion, law, public opinion, etc.), is clearly speaking to the interdisciplinary character of CDS. Indeed, their empirical programme, a rich mixture of detailed discussions of empirical data constantly related to theoretical arguments, remains a resource waiting to be fully explored. Let me just mention four of them in order to illustrate this: in *The Salaried Masses,* originally published in 1930, Kracauer (1998: 29) provided a beautiful ethnography, exploring the 'exoticism of a commonplace existence' of white-collar workers. Löwenthal and Norbert Guterman's (1949) *Prophets of Deceit,* a study of American agitators (nowadays, we would speak of radical right-wing activists), could almost be republished as a CDS study today. Far better known is Adorno et al.'s (1950), *The Authoritarian Personality,* which combines statistical analysis with detailed discussion of extracts from interviews. Finally, a study by the Frankfurters based on analysis of focus groups was published in 1955 and dealt with the legacies of National Socialism in post-war Germany (see, for example, Adorno 2010).

While the first generation of Critical Theory has, for better or worse, played a limited role in CDS, the social theory of Habermas, the main theorist of the second generation, has had substantial influence on various CDS practitioners.

Within CDS, the DHA has most fundamentally justified its aim "*for* emancipation, self-determination and social recognition" (Reisigl and Wodak 2001: 34) through reference to Habermas. Its topic-centred definition of discourse includes a reference to the exchange of validity claims (Reisigl and Wodak 2009: 89), a key Habermasian concept. And although differences remain (Reisigl 2011: 467), Habermas is thus (more or less) integrated into the conceptual core of this strand. Yet, the concept of validity claims (truth, rightness and truthfulness) and its implications could take up an even more fundamental position. The raising and discussion of validity claims is linked to Habermas's separation of social action into communicative and strategic. While strategic action is success-oriented, oriented towards achieving a goal, communicative action is oriented towards understanding and based on "idealizing performative presuppositions" (Habermas 2008: 28) which include

> the shared presupposition of a world of independently existing objects, the reciprocal presupposition of rationality or 'accountability,' the unconditionality of context-transcending validity claims such as truth and moral rightness, and the demanding presuppositions of argumentation that force participants to decenter their interpretive perspectives.

Besides a reference to a *realism after the linguistic turn* which thematises the relation between discursive and extra-discursive (Habermas 2003), the point here is that strategic action sits parasitically on top of these decentring presuppositions (inclusiveness, equal communicative rights, sincerity and freedom of repression/manipulation). For example, lying gains its force from the fact that it acts as if a sincere exchange of claims takes place. Habermas reconstructs these presuppositions as counterfactual assumptions of communication oriented towards understanding which are key when validity claims are not only exchanged (communicative action) but questioned/justified (Habermasian discourse).

Linked to this, and a more frequent point of reference in CDS, is the concept of an ideal-speech situation (ISS) which is characterised by the aforementioned, decentring presuppositions. The ISS has often been misunderstood as being idealistic and out of touch with factual conditions. However, Habermas (1997: 322) has long clarified that these aspects are not hypostatized but concern counterfactually anticipated presuppositions of action oriented towards understanding. That is, participants have to assume that they contribute quite freely and equally, that they are participating in a cooperative search for truth and/or rightness, and that the speaker is not manipulative but is raising claims which s/he considers to be true, right and truthful. We are thus talking about weak but pragmatically unavoidable presupposition of interaction oriented towards understanding (Forchtner 2011, Forchtner and Tominc 2012, Zhang et al. 2011: 98; see Chilton 2010 for another take on validity claims in CDS). These presuppositions are *pragmatically* held because the possibility for radical emancipation is not grounded in an ultimate, external foundation. They are nevertheless *unavoidable* because whenever we say what we mean in action oriented towards understanding, we necessarily raise validity claims which rest on idealised assumptions. Finally, these presuppositions are *weak:* although they are rooted in human interaction, nothing forces the speaker not to capitalise on the trust of her/his counterpart in order to deceive her/him. As such, the presuppositions are not *idealistic* but *idealising* (Habermas 2008: 26ff). Formal pragmatics demonstrates that we interact on the basis of weak idealisation, that egalitarian and inclusive interaction is inherent in our social practice. These presuppositions are fundamental in order to understand Habermas's emancipatory project and the notion of deliberative democracy which informs the DHA (Reisigl and Wodak 2001: 263–266).

Chouliaraki and Fairclough (1999: 83–89, 134–137) have offered a fruitful discussion of Haberman focusing on the notion of the public sphere and the distinction between system and lifeworld. Although they review criticism of Habermas and stress the importance of recognising difference in the search for consensus, they, also link Habermasian elements to a research agenda for CDS. These are (1999: 88) the rationalisation of the lifeworld (*'linguistic reflexivity'*: how does communicative interaction 'turns back on itself'), the colonisation of the lifeworld by systems (*'colonisation of discourse'*), the reaction of the lifeworld via social movements (*struggles over discursive practices'*) and the uncoupling of system and lifeworld and changing boundaries between language and other types of semiosis as well as semiosis and other types of social interaction (*'linguistification/delinguistification'*). Focusing on the system/lifeworld distinction (coordinating action based on an instrumental logic or mutual understanding) Fairclough (2003: 110–112) furthermore offers an operationalisation of Habermas's approach, pointing to materials which are written as if an exchange of knowledge takes place (as if exchange is based on communicative action) – although what actually takes place is an 'activity exchange' (offers, demands, selling, custom, soliciting).

Against this background, let me return to the issue of ideology. Most CDS-informed studies define discourses as ideological as far as they mystify structures of power, structures which need to be revealed (Wodak and Meyer 2009: 8–9). More specifically, Chouliaraki and Fairclough (1999: 26f) view ideologies as discursive constructions of relations between practices which sustain domination. Habermas abandons the theory of ideology in favor of the colonisation thesis and the concept of *systematically distorted communication,* an explicitly intersubjective condition in which an actor does not suspend the presuppositions of communicative action consciously ('manipulation') but in which at least one participant deceives himself 'about the fact that he is acting with an attitude oriented to success and is only keeping up the appearance of communicative action' ('unconscious deception', 1984: 332f). Whether or not this offers a way forward for CDS remains to be discussed (see Wodak 1996: 28). In contrast, not only post-structuralists view this differently (see below): van Dijk's (1998: 8) socio-cognitive approach, for example, works with a broad (or 'neutral') definition of ideology, viewing it as 'the *basis of the social representations shared by members of a group'*.

Linked to the issue of ideology is that of power. Traditional notions of power emphasise power as resting in individual or collective actors. The DHA, for example, draws on Max Weber's definition of power, that is, the ability to restrict the agency of others (Reisigl and

Wodak 2009: 88f) – though Wodak (2009: 34–37) has also referred to Lukes's (2005: 29) three-dimensional concept of power. The first dimension concerns the ability to make and impose decisions in blatantly observable situations and conflicts of interests, for example in a meeting. The second adds a focus on non-decision-making, potential issues and covert conflicts. Lukes's third dimension of power, finally, points to the ability to suppress latent conflicts based on subjective and real interests. Chouliaraki and Fairclough (1999: 24) complement a post-structuralist, productive notion of power (see below) with a view on power linked to domination, of power as systemically linking practices and positions in social fields. Habermas's concept of power has, however, not been taken up; that is, the juxtaposition of the various norm-free forms of strategic (instrumental) power with communicative power. The latter develops "only in undeformed public spheres; it can issue only from structures of undamaged intersubjectivity" (Habermas 1997: 148).

Let me close this section by turning to Pierre Bourdieu. The latter has caught the imagination of CDS practitioners first and foremost with his concept of the linguistic market (see Blommaert 2015 on the linguistic market in general and Unger 2013 on the linguistic market in relation to the Scots Language). Other studies have drawn on key categories such as habitus, the concept through which Bourdieu (1990: 52–65) claims to overcome the divide between structure and agency. For example, Wodak et al. (1999) utilise Bourdieu in their work on national identity and national habitus and Wodak (2011) draws on his conceptual framework in her analysis of the professional habitus of members of the European Parliament. More theoretical discussions include that of Chouliaraki and Fairclough (1999: 99–106, 112–118) who celebrate Bourdieu's rich toolkit (field, habitus, symbolic capital and power) but criticise his lack of theory of forms of mediation as fields with their specific logics and capitals, his lack of detailed analysis of actual interaction and, more generally, his tendency of viewing language use as a by-product of sociological categories which does not acknowledge the 'generative force' of discourse. Forchtner and Schneickert (2016) work towards an integration of Bourdieuan categories, especially habitus (see above), field (a space of objective relations between positions and with their own logics and rules) and strategy (objectively organised without necessarily being subjectively intended [Bourdieu 1990: 15, 62], that is: a result of how well an actor's habitus fits the requirements of a specific field, for example due to a particular upbringing), into the DHA, addressing in particular theoretical contradictions between Bourdieu and Habermas. Other relevant concepts Bourdieu elaborates on include the concept of ideology, being not simply about ideas and beliefs, but also habitual, non-conscious embodied reactions. This is an important point, as underlying, naturalised systems of classification too often serve the interests of those dominating the 'social cosmos' (Bourdieu and Wacquant 1992: 97). The notions of 'symbolic domination' and 'symbolic violence' (Bourdieu and Wacquant 1992: 167f), instead of ideology, address this 'complicity' of social actors affected by these classifications in sustaining existing inequalities. Closely related is the question of power. Although power, in Bourdieu's account, is diffusely spread across social fields (depending on the possession capital and its configuration), Bourdieu remains close to the above approaches in that there are centres which *hold* more power than others, which *exercise* power from above.

Post-structural influences

Turning now to post-structuralism, Foucault stands out as a point of reference for 'core' branches in CDS – accompanied sometimes by the discourse theory (DT) of Laclau and Mouffe.[3] Let me begin with reviewing the reception of Foucault before moving to DT.

265

Both the 'early' (archaeological) as well as 'later' (genealogical) Foucault are reviewed in much detail by Fairclough (among many, see Fairclough 1992: 37–61, 2003: 123f) and Chouliaraki and Fairclough (1999: 89f).[4] While the early Foucault (1989: 89) conceives discourse as not being related to a "primary ground of experience, nor to the *a priori* authority of knowledge; but that we seek the rules of its formation in discourse itself" – the late Foucault (1990) shows less interest in abstract rules than in discourse as joining power and knowledge. Not only is his notion of discourse constitutive (and replaces the notion of ideology); the same is true of his concept of power which has no centre (be it a class, a state or an individual), has no outside but is everywhere and is thus productive, as well as both intentional and nonsubjective (1990: 92–96). Elements Fairclough (1992: 55f and 68), and many other proponents of CDS, particularly embrace are Foucault's view of discourse as constitutive for subjects, social relationships, objects and conceptual frameworks; the insistence that discourse practices are interdependent (intertextuality); the discursive nature of power, the political nature of discourse and the discursive nature of social change; as well as the notion of 'order of discourse' which Fairclough defines as the order of ways of meaning making through particular combinations of genres, discourses and styles in particular social fields. Similarly, van Leeuwen (2008: vii) draws on Foucault's concept of discourse as 'constructions of specific aspects of reality', that is: knowledge, combining this with a notion of discourse as a social practice and legitimation. This does, however, not mean that there has been no criticism. Fairclough (1992: 56–61), for example, is critical of a too abstract notion of discourse (without analysing actual language use), an exaggerated understanding of power and a relativist outlook, criticism shared by many others in CDS (although Wodak has put far less emphasis on Foucault's work, she makes similar points, see Wodak 1996: 24–26; see also Montesano Montessori 2011 and the feminist CDA of Lazar 2007).[5]

Whilst Foucault has influenced many CDS practitioners, the influence of Laclau and Mouffe is not as extensive. Although there have been encounters between the DHA and DT (Sjölander and Payne 2011), it has been especially Chouliaraki and Fairclough (1999) who have undertaken an evaluation of DT against the background of CDS.

Laclau has shown little interest in particular methods (Torfing 1999: 25) but has provided a broad range of categories in order to understand the social. Key sources of DT are Gramsci's notion of hegemony (see above) and Jacques Derrida's notion of discourse, implying a necessary surplus of meaning and thus the inability to fix meaning once and for all. Based on anti-essentialist ontology and post-foundationalist epistemology, the fact that things have no pre-given meaning facilitates an idea of radical contingency. On a 'manifestly political' level, this leads them to reject, for example, class reductionism and economic determinism.

Social life, however, aims for closure and requires (some) certainty – something which emerges through discourse. Discourse provides a system of relations between elements – but as its elements cannot gain their meaning from anything extra-discursive, the separation (which we still find in Foucault) between the discursive and the non-discursive collapses (Laclau and Mouffe 2001: 107). This notion of discourse emerges through 'articulations', that is: the establishment of relations between radically contingent elements, of a meaningful complex of elements (Laclau and Mouffe 2001: 105). Systems of difference can be partly stabilised around nodal points (Laclau and Mouffe 2001: 112f), another central term. By being related to a central signifier, a relative stable arrangement is secured. For example, articulations by environmentalists might establish environmental protection as a nodal point around which previously central concepts such as the state circulate. This might have happened in the course of a disruptive moment, for example a reactor incident ('dislocation', see Laclau 1990: 39–43; see Stavrakakis 2000 for a DT-inspired analysis of Green politics). Moments of dislocation give rise to agency, requiring subjects to respond and engage in struggles over hegemony by establishing particular combinations of the logic of difference and the logic of equivalence. That is, the above environmentalists might establish a chain of equivalence which ultimately includes left- and right-leaning environmentalists, unified in their antagonism towards those endangering the environment. As an increasingly hegemonic discourse (resulting from these activists' articulations), they have expended the initial discourse but, in turn, the centre of gravitation will more and more turn into a 'feel-good' signifier, emptied of specific meaning. In such a framework, power, similar to Foucault's notion, is productive and not repressive. As articulation creates identities through exclusion of elements, all social relations are relations of power (Laclau and Mouffe 2001: 142). In turn, ideological aspects of discourse are characterised by the desire for closure while, simultaneously, disguising the contingent character of discourse and, thus, the impossibility of a full identity (Laclau 1997: 320). A study which has engaged with this conceptual framework in detail while, at the same time, drawing on concepts in CDS in order to conduct detailed, textual analysis is Macgilchrist's (2011) work on the news coverage of Russia.

Chouliaraki and Fairclough (1999: 121–126) draw on Laclau and Mouffe, viewing DT as a possibility to bring together Marxism and, in particular, the Gramscian concept of hegemony with post-structuralist theories of discourse. More specifically, they view the concept of articulation as valuable in order to understand the openness and continuous reconstitution of the social. While their discussion includes an overview of the aforementioned categories, it also gives room to criticism which takes up and extends earlier criticism of Foucault (see above). For example, they (1999: 120) claim that while postmodern theories provide a necessary critique of essentialist assumptions in many classical approaches by emphasising the discursive construction of what seems natural, they also "undermine the critical project – [and thus] critical theory needs to reassert itself against them through partly assimilating them". Their main criticism of Laclau and Mouffe in particular is that social structures need to be taken much more seriously than they tend to do. According to Chouliaraki and Fairclough (1999: 125), Laclau and Mouffe's focus on the unrestrained openness of the social ignores that contingency "depends upon how persons and practices are positioned within social structures". While both DT as well as this stream in CDS more or less agree that meaning of everything depends on discourse, Chouliaraki and Fairclough insist that the social arises out of dialectical relations between semiosis (discourse) and non-discursive aspects, that there are structural constraints to the contingency of meaning making.

Often inspired by post-structuralist theories, there is also a feminist current within CDS (see Wodak 1997, Lazar 2005, 2007). These writings do not 'only' analyse gender-related issues but also attempt to transfer and carve out parallels between feminism and CDS. As such – and this could be an interesting avenue for future research – feminist critical discourse analysis might benefit from drawing not only on post-structuralism but also feminist ethics of care (Tronto 1994, Held 2007) in order to understand and critique the social.

Conclusion

A strong link between CDS and social theory is a necessity if the former wants to live up to its own claims. Explicit and detailed elaborations on theoretical aspects are thus as important as detailed textual analysis given that texts are always also social objects embedded in and facilitating the reproduction of relations of power and domination.

While it was impossible to give more than a brief overview of links between the 'core' CDS and social theory, the above illustrates that CDS's position vis-à-vis social theory is a

Bernhard Forchtner

heterogeneous one. Some approaches draw almost exclusively on other disciplines, for example cognitive sciences while many younger practitioners have included more recent theoretical approaches. And even the work of Fairclough and Wodak shows differences in terms of the extent of social theory involved and use of particular theories.

Bringing together different theoretical approaches in one framework offers a flexible toolkit for problem-oriented research – yet, it can also lead to a situation in which theories contradict each other at various levels. Much more, the idea of problem-oriented research in which the choice of methods and theoretical concepts depend on the object of research is not without problems. While such pragmatism is undoubtedly crucial, with regard to the use of methods, it might overlook that it is only from within certain conceptual universes that we 'see' problems and are able to formulate questions.

This last point touches explicitly on the issue of critique which is differently conceived and justified, depending on the theoretical framework to which a researcher is committed. I do not mean to discuss different categories of critique – from Chouliaraki and Fairclough (1999: 32f) to Reisigl and Wodak (2001: 32–35) and Fairclough (2014) – but the grounds on which certain phenomena become problematic in the first place. On the one hand, primarily Marxist inspired scholars in CDS aim to make interconnections visible, including hidden resources of meaning creation and their role in the prolonging of human suffering. This project still attaches significance to a Kantian inspired idea of autonomy (and/or the condition of undamaged intersubjectivity) and Marx's critical method directed against alienation and reification. On the other hand, post-structuralists view openness and difference as paramount; and while there is little disagreement with neo-Marxists here, post-structuralists will insist on (inter)subjectivity not being in any way independent of the play of difference. In emphasising the significance of contingency, they view critique in terms of making "harder those acts which are now too easy" (Foucault 1981: 456). Whatever stance practitioners take vis-à-vis these issues, due to CDS's success as a framework for doing research across the (critical) social sciences, they will remain important points of reference, forcing practitioners to think about the role of other theories, possible contradictions in existing settings and even the lack of socio-theoretical thought.

Against the background of the above pages, the existent links between CDS and social theory are more than justified and should be deepened further. As it is unlikely, that CDS, as a diverse research programme, will manage to agree on the definition of basic concepts, each 'strand' – be it 'core' or beyond – faces the task to clarify its understanding of the social.

Notes

1 I thank Christian Schneickert, Felicitas Macgilchrist and the editors of this handbook for comments on an earlier version of this chapter. All mistakes remain of course my own. The research leading to these results has received funding from the People Programme (Marie Curie Action) of the European Union's Seventh Framework Programme (FP7/2007–2013) under REA grant agreement no. 327595.
2 John B. Thompson (1984: 126) too pointed to their innovative analysis of language before noting that socio-theoretical concepts are not "clearly defined and situated within a systematic social theory". However, see also writings such as *Social Semiotics* (Hodge and Kress 1988).
3 Outside CDA, discourse analysis almost exclusively draws on Foucault and other post-structuralists (for an approach comprehensively inspired by Foucault and which is sometimes included in the canon of CDS, see Jäger and Maier 2016).
4 This widely held periodization is at least problematic given that, despite a change in 'tactics', the overall focus on subject-constitution and knowledge has remained unchanged (Foucault 1982).
5 Criticism of Foucault's notion of power and domination (1990: 93, 1982: 795) is widespread (for example Fraser 1981; Taylor 1984; Habermas 1987: 266–293) and, along these lines, Stuart Hall (2000:

268

xv) notes concisely that since "power is everywhere [according to Foucault], resistance *is,* ultimately, a concept without a home".

Further reading

Chouliaraki, L. and Fairclough, N. (1999). *Discourse in late modernity: Rethinking critical discourse analysis.* Edinburgh: Edinburgh University Press.
This is still the most detailed discussion of the link between CDS and social theory, covering an extensive range of theorists.
McKenna, B. (2004). Critical discourse studies: Where to from here? *Critical Discourse Studies* 1(1): 9–39.
This classic statement argues for CDS's 'transformative radical teleology' in its discussion of the need for a strong social theory element in CDS.
Wodak, R. and Meyer, M. (eds.) (2016). *Methods of critical discourse studies.* London: Sage.
Now in its third edition, this volume offers both a general introduction to CDS (including a discussion of socio-theoretical concepts) and introductory chapters to various approaches in CDS.

References

Adorno, T.W. (2010). *Guilt and defense: On the legacies of national socialism in postwar Germany.* Cambridge, MA: Harvard University Press.
Adorno, T.W., Frenkel-Brunswik, E., Levinson, D.J. and Sanford, R.N. (1950). *The authoritarian personality.* New York: Harper & Brothers.
Adorno, T.W., Albert, H., Dahrendorf, R., Habermas, J., Pilot, H. and Popper, K.R. (1976). *The positivist dispute in German sociology.* New York: Harper & Row.
Althusser, L. (2001). Ideology and ideological state apparatus. Notes towards an investigation. In *Lenin and philosophy and other essays,* 85–126. New York: Monthly Review Press.
Baert, P. and Carreira da Silva, F. (2010). *Social theory in the twentieth century and beyond.* Cambridge: Polity.
Baker, P. (2014). *Using corpora to analyse gender.* London: Bloomsbury.
Blommaert, J. (2015). Pierre Bourdieu and language in society. Accessed February 17, 2016, www.til burguniversity.edu/upload/adc80ed2–01a6–48f2–996e-be527ba84092_TPCS_126_Blommaert.pdf
Bourdieu, P. (1990). *The logic of practice.* Stanford, CA and Cambridge: University Press and Polity.
Bourdieu, P. and Wacquant, L.J.D. (1992). *An invitation to reflexive sociology.* Cambridge: Polity.
Chilton, P. (2010). The language-ethics interface: Reflections on linguistics, discourse analysis and the legacy of Habermas. In R. de Cillia, H. Gruber, M. Krzyżanowski and F. Menz (eds.), *Discourse, politics, identity,* 33–43. Tübingen: Stauffenburg.
Chouliaraki, L. and Fairclough, N. (1999). *Discourse in late modernity: Rethinking critical discourse analysis.* Edinburgh: Edinburgh University Press.
Fairclough, N. (1989). *Language and power.* London: Longman.
Fairclough, N. (1992). *Discourse and social change.* Cambridge: Polity.
Fairclough, N. (2003). *Analysing discourse: Textual analysis for social research.* Oxon: Routledge.
Fairclough, N. (2014): What is CDA? Language and power twenty-five years on. Accessed February 17, 2016, www.academia.edu/8429277/What_is_CDA_Language_and_Power_twenty-five_years_on
Fairclough, N. and Graham, P. (2002). Marx as critical discourse analyst: The genesis of a critical method and its relevance to the critique of global capital. *Estudios de Sociolinguistica* 3(1): 185–229.
Fairclough, N., Jessop, B. and Sayer, A. (2002). Critical realism and semiosis. *Journal of Critical Realism* 5(1): 2–10.
Fairclough, N. and Wodak, R. (1997). Critical discourse analysis. In T. A. van Dijk (ed.), *Introduction to discourse studies: Discourse and interaction,* Vol. 2, 258–284. London: Sage.
Forchtner, B. (2011). Critique, the discourse-historical approach and the Frankfurt School. *Critical Discourse Studies* 8(1): 1–14.
Forchtner, B. and Schneickert, C. (2016). Collective learning in social fields: Bourdieu, Habermas and critical discourse analysis. *Discourse and Society* 27(3): 293–307.
Forchtner, B. and Tominc, A. (2012). Critique and argumentation: On the relation between the discourse-historical approach and pragma-dialectics. *Journal of Language and Politics* 11(1): 31–50.
Foucault, M. (1981). So it is important to think? In *Essential works of Foucault 1954–1984. Volume 1,* 454–464. London: Penguin.

Bernhard Forchtner

Foucault, M. (1982). The subject and power. *Critical Inquiry* 8(4): 777–795.

Foucault, M. (1989). *The archaeology of knowledge*. London: Routledge.

Foucault, M. (1990). *The history of sexuality. Volume I.* London: Vintage.

Fowler, R. (1996). On critical linguistics. In: C.R. Caldas-Coulthard and M. Coulthard (eds.), *Text and practices: Readings in critical discourse analysis*, 3–14. New York: Routledge.

Fowler, R., Hodge, R., Kress, G. and Trew, T. (1979). *Language and control*. London, Boston, Henley: Routledge & Kegan Paul.

Fowler, R. and Kress, G. (1979). Critical linguistics. In: R. Fowler, R. Hodge, G. Kress and T. Trew (eds.), *Language and control*, 185–213. London, Boston, Henley: Routledge & Kegan Paul.

Fraser, N. (1981). Foucault on modern power: Empirical insights and normative confusions. *PRAXIS International* 3: 272–287.

Giddens, A. (1993). *New rules of sociological method: A positive critique of interpretative sociologies.* Stanford, CA: Stanford University Press.

Goffman, E. (1990). *The presentation of self in everyday life*. London: Penguin.

Gramsci, A. (2011). *Prison notebooks, Volume 3*. New York: Columbia University Press.

Habermas, J. (1984). *The theory of communicative action. Volume I. Reason and the Rationalization of society.* Boston, MA: Beacon Press.

Habermas, J. (1987). *The philosophical discourse of modernity. Twelve lectures*. Cambridge: Polity.

Habermas, J. (1997). *Between facts and norms: Contributions to a discourse theory of law and democracy.* Cambridge: Polity.

Habermas, J. (2003). Introduction: Realism after the linguistic turn. In *Truth and justification*, 1–49. Cambridge, MA: MIT Press.

Habermas, J. (2008). Communicative action and the detranscendentalized "use of reason". In *Between naturalism and religion: Philosophical essays*, 24–76. Cambridge: Polity.

Hall, S. (2000). Foreword. In N. Poulantzas. *State, power, socialism*, vii–xviii. London: Verso.

Held, V. (2007). *The ethics of care: Personal, political, and global*. Oxford: Oxford University Press.

Hodge, R. and Kress, G. (1988). *Social semiotics*. Cambridge: Polity.

Horkheimer, M. (1975). Traditional and critical theory. In *Critical theory: Selected essays*, 188–252. London: Continuum.

Horkheimer, M. (1993). The present situation of social psychology and the tasks of an Institute for Social Research. In *Between philosophy and social science: Selected early writings*, 1–14. Cambridge, MA: MIT Press.

Ives, P. (2004). *Gramsci's politics of language: Engaging the Bakhtin circle and the Frankfurt School.* Toronto: Toronto University Press.

Jäger, S. and Maier, F. (2016). Analysing discourses and dispositives: A Foucauldian approach to theory and methodology. In R. Wodak and M. Meyer (eds.), *Methods of critical Discourse studies*, 109–136. London: Sage.

Kracauer, S. (1998). *The salaried masses: Duty and distraction in Weimar Germany.* London: Verso.

Kress, G.R and Hodge, R. (1979). *Language as Ideology*. London, Boston, MA, Henley: Routledge & Kegan Paul.

Krzyżanowski, M. and Wodak, R. (2010). Hegemonic multilingualism in/of the EU institutions: An inside-outside perspective on the European language policies and practices. In C. Hülmbauer, E. Vetter and H. Böhringer (eds.), *Mehrsprachigkeit aus der Perspektive zweier EU-Projekte: DYLAN Meets LINEE*, 115–135. Frankfurt: Peter Lang.

Laclau, E. (1990). *New reflections on the revolution of our time*. London: Verso.

Laclau, E. (1997). The death and resurrection of the theory of ideology. *MLN* 112(3): 297–321.

Laclau, E. and Mouffe, C. (2001). *Hegemony and socialist strategy: Towards a radical democratic politics.* London: Verso.

Lazar, M. (2007). Feminist critical discourse analysis: Articulating a feminist discourse praxis. *Critical Discourse Studies* 4(2): 141–164.

Lazar, M. (ed.) (2005). *Feminist critical discourse analysis: Studies in gender, power and ideology*. Basingstoke: Palgrave.

Löwenthal, L. and Guterman, N. (1949). *Prophets of deceit: A study of the techniques of the American agitator.* New York: Harper and Brothers.

Lukes, S. (2005). *Power: A radical view*. Basingstoke: Palgrave.

Macgilchrist, F. (2011). *Journalism and the political: Discursive tensions in news coverage of Russia.* Amsterdam: Benjamins.

270

Macgilchrist, F. (2016). Fissures in the discourse-scape: Critique, rationality and validity in post-foundational approaches to CDS. *Discourse and Society* 27(3): 262–277.

Milani, T. M. (2015). Sexual citizenship: Discourses, spaces and bodies at Joburg Pride. *Journal of Language and Politics* 14(3): 431–454.

Montesano Montessori, N. (2011). The design of a theoretical, methodological, analytical framework to analyses hegemony in discourse. *Critical Discourse Studies* 8(3): 169–181.

O'Halloran, K. (2012). Deleuze, Guattari and the use of web-based corpora for facilitating critical analysis of public sphere arguments. *Discourse, Context and Media* 2(1): 40–51.

Reisigl, M. (2011). Grundzüge der Wiener Kritischen Diskursanalyse. In R. Keller, A. Hirseland, W. Schneider and W. Viehöver (eds.), *Handbuch der Sozialwissenschaftlichen Diskursanalyse. Band 1,* 459–498. Wiesbaden: VS.

Reisigl, M. and Wodak, R. (2001). *Discourse and discrimination: Rhetorics of racism and anti-Semitism.* London: Routledge.

Reisigl, M. and Wodak, R. (2009). The discourse-historical approach. In R. Wodak and M. Meyer (eds.), *Methods of critical discourse analysis,* 2nd edn, 87–121. London: Sage.

Richardson, J. E. (2007). *Analysing newspapers: An approach from critical discourse analysis.* Basingstoke: Palgrave.

Sjölander, A. E. (2011). Introduction: Comparing critical discourse analysis and discourse theory. In A. E. Sjölander and J. Gunnarsson Payne (eds.), *Tracking discourses: Politics, identity and social change,* 13–48. Lund: Nordic Academic Press.

Stavrakakis, Y. (2000). On the emergence of Green ideology: The dislocation factor in Green politics. In D. Howarth, A. J. Norval and Y. Stavrakakis (eds.), *Discourse theory and political analysis: Identities, hegemonies and social change,* 100–118. Manchester: Manchester University Press.

Taylor, C. (1984). Foucault on freedom and truth. *Political Theory* 12(2): 152–183.

Thompson, J. B. (1984). *Studies in the theory of ideology.* Cambridge: Polity.

Thurlow, C. (2016). Queering critical discourse studies or/and Performing 'post-class' ideologies. *Critical Discourse Studies* 13(5): 485–514.

Titscher, S., Meyer, M., Wodak, R. and Vetter, E. (2000). *Methods of text and discourse analysis: In search of meaning.* London: Sage.

Trew, T. (1979). Theory and ideology at work. In R. Fowler, R. Hodge, G. Kress and T. Trew. *Language and Control,* 94–116. London: Routledge & Kegan Paul.

Torfing, J. (1999). *New theories of discourse. Laclau, Mouffe, Žižek.* Oxford: Blackwell.

Tronto, J. (1994). *Moral boundaries: A political argument for an ethic of care.* London: Routledge.

Unger, J. W. (2013). *The discursive construction of the Scots language: Education, politics and everyday life.* Amsterdam: Benjamins.

van Dijk, T. A. (1998). *Ideology: A multidisciplinary study.* London: Routledge.

Van Leeuwen, T. (2008). *Discourse and practice: New tools for critical discourse analysis.* Oxford: Oxford University Press.

Weiss, G. and Wodak, R. (2003). Introduction: Theory, interdisciplinary and critical discourse analysis. In G. Weiss and R. Wodak (eds.), *Critical discourse analysis: Theory and interdisciplinarity,* 1–32. London: Palgrave.

Wodak, R. (1996). *Disorders of discourse.* London/New York: Longman.

Wodak, R. (ed.) (1997). *Gender and discourse.* London: Sage.

Wodak, R. (2009). *The discourse of politics in action.* Basingstoke: Palgrave.

Wodak, R. (2015). *The politics of fear: What right-wing populist discourses mean.* London: Sage.

Wodak, R., de Cillia, R., Reisigl, M. and Liebhart, K. (1999). *The discursive construction of national identity.* Edinburgh: Edinburgh University Press.

Wodak, R. and Meyer, M. (2009). Critical discourse analysis: History, agenda, theory and methodology. In R. Wodak and M. Meyer (eds.), *Methods of critical discourse analysis,* 2nd edn, 1–33. London: Sage.

Wodak, R. and Meyer, M. (2016). Critical discourse studies: History, agenda, theory and methodology. In R. Wodak and M. Meyer (eds.), *Methods of critical discourse studies,* 3rd edition, 1–22. London: Sage.

Zhang, H., Chilton, P., He, Y. and Jing, W. (2011). Critique across cultures: Some questions for CDA. *Critical Discourse Studies* 8(2): 95–107.

18

Discourse-Theoretical Analysis (DTA)

Nico Carpentier

Introduction

As one of the many approaches in the field of discourse studies, discourse theory mostly builds on two strands: the theoretical work of Foucault on the one hand, and Laclau and Mouffe on the other. Although related, these two discourse-theoretical strands have a considerable number of differences, in their theoretical elaborations and in their interpretations. In this chapter, I will focus on the latter strand which found its main manifestation in the 1985 book *Hegemony and Socialist Strategy* (HSS) (Laclau and Mouffe 1985).

The chapter's first objective is to provide an overview of Laclau and Mouffe's discourse theory, which is particular because of its strong emphasis on discursive struggle and on contingency. This objective necessitates ample time and space to be spent on explaining their discourse-theoretical basics. Also one of the main problems that discourse theory (and, *in extenso,* discourse studies as a whole) faces – the invisibility of the material – is critically assessed in this chapter. The second objective is to show how Laclau and Mouffe's discourse theory can be deployed in actual research to make sense of particular social realities.

To further clarify the workings of Laclau and Mouffe's discourse theory, and its applicability, I analyse a case study using discourse-theoretical analysis (DTA – see Carpentier and De Cleen 2007). This case study deals with the broadcasts of three radio shows, and their audience reception, of the Cypriot community web radio station MYCYradio, which functions within a conflict-transformative and participatory-democratic remit. In this section, both the discursive and material aspects, as part of the MYCYradio assemblage, are scrutinised, to demonstrate the capacity of (Laclau and Mouffe's) discourse theory to make sense of a particular social reality.

Sketching discourse theory

Laclau and Mouffe's HSS is a highly valuable but complex and hermetic work, which – as has been argued elsewhere (Carpentier and De Cleen 2007; Carpentier and Spinoy 2008)[1] – can be read on three interrelated levels. The first level, which we can call discourse theory in the strict sense, refers to Laclau and Mouffe's social ontology (Howarth 2000: 17) and to the position they negotiate between materialism and idealism, between structure and agency. At this level, we can find the vocabulary and the mechanics of discourse theory. A second – and strongly related – level is what Smith (1999: 87) has called Laclau and Mouffe's political identity theory. Key concepts at this level are antagonism and hegemony. Here, (more) attention is given to how discourses, identities and their nodal points are constructed and obtain fixity through political processes. Laclau and Mouffe's post-Marxist approach becomes even more evident at the third level, where their plea for a radical democratic politics places them in the field of democratic theory (see Held 2006, for an overview of this field). While situating themselves within the "classic ideal of socialism", Laclau and Mouffe (1985: 190) at the same time plead for a "polyphony of voice" in which the different (radical) democratic political struggles – such as antiracism, antisexism and anticapitalism – are allotted an equally important role (Mouffe 1997: 18).

In this brief introduction to discourse theory, I will focus on the first two levels only, as the third level finds its main application within democratic theory. At the first (ontological) level of Laclau and Mouffe's discourse theory, their interpretation of the key concept of discourse is developed. Their theoretical starting point is that all social phenomena and objects obtain their meaning(s) through discourse, which is defined as "a structure in which meaning is constantly negotiated and constructed" (Laclau 1988: 254). The concept of discourse is also described as a structured entity which is the result of articulation (Laclau and Mouffe 1985: 105), which is in turn viewed as "any practice establishing a relation among elements[2] such that their identity is modified as a result of the articulatory practice". As these definitions indicate, the articulation of discursive elements plays a vital role in the construction of the identity of objects as well as of individual or collective agents. The articulation of these elements produces discourses that gain a certain (and very necessary) degree of stability. Discursive stability is enhanced by the role of privileged signifiers, or nodal points. Torfing (1999: 88–89) points out that these nodal points "sustain the identity of a certain discourse by constructing a knot of definite meanings". Or to use Laclau and Mouffe's (1985: 113) words:

> The practice of articulation consists in the construction of nodal points which partially fix meaning; and the partial character of this fixation proceeds from the openness of the social, a result, in its turn, of the constant overflowing of every discourse by the infinitude of the field of discursivity.

Discourses have to be partially fixed, since the abundance of meaning would otherwise make any meaning impossible: "a discourse incapable of generating any fixity of meaning is the discourse of the psychotic" (Laclau and Mouffe 1985: 112). But this fixity is only partial, and Laclau and Mouffe emphasise the contingency of discourses at several levels (see Carpentier and Van Brussel 2012). At the first level of their discourse theory, the notion of the field of discursivity (Laclau and Mouffe 1985: 112) plays an important role to theorize this contingency, as the field of discursivity contains an infinite number of elements which are not connected to a specific discourse at a given moment in time. Instability enters the equation through the idea that these unconnected elements can always be articulated within a specific discourse, sometimes replacing (or disarticulating) other elements, which affects the discourse's meaning. Due to the infinitude of the field of discursivity and the inability of a discourse to permanently fix its meaning and keep its elements stable, discourses are liable to disintegration and re-articulation. Another way that the overdetermination of discourses (and the impossibility to reach "a final closure" [Howarth 1998: 273]) is made explicit is through the concept of the floating signifier. This concept is defined as a signifier that is "overflowed with meaning"

(Torfing 1999: 301). Floating signifiers will in other words assume different meanings in different contexts/discourses, again enhancing contingency. Thirdly, and later on, (mainly) Laclau will refer to the Lacanian concept of lack to theorize this structural openness. For Laclau (1996: 92), the contingency of structures originates from "the structure [not being] fully reconciled with itself" and "inhabited by an original lack, by a radical undecidability that needs to be constantly superseded by acts of decision". This allows Laclau, in relation to the subject, to distinguish between subject and subjectivation, and between identity and identification. The impossibility of the multiplicity of identities to fill the constitutive lack of the subject prevents their full and complete constitution because of the inevitable distance between the obtained identity and the subject, and because of the (always possible) subversion of that identity by other identities. In Laclau's (1990: 60) own words: "the identification never reaches the point of full identity".

At the second level of discourse theory, we can find more emphasis on political processes and discursive struggles, for whose analysis two key notions are mobilised: hegemony and antagonism. For Laclau and Mouffe, hegemony refers to situations where particular discourses obtain social dominance. Originally, Gramsci (1999: 261) defined this notion in relation to the dominance that social actors obtained through the creation of alliances. For Gramsci, this dominance was based on the formation of consent, rather than on the (exclusive) domination of the other, without, however, excluding a certain form of pressure and repression. Howarth (1998: 279) describes Laclau and Mouffe's interpretation of Gramsci – an interpretation which focuses more on the discursive – as follows: "hegemonic practices are an exemplary form of political articulation which involves linking together different identities into a common project". The objective of hegemonic projects is to construct and stabilise nodal points that are the basis of a social order, the main aim being to become a social imaginary, or the horizon that "is not one among other objects but an absolute limit which structures a field of intelligibility and is thus the condition of possibility of the emergence of any object" (Laclau 1990: 64).

Hegemonic practices suppose an open system, which makes articulation possible. In a closed system there would only be repetition, and nothing could be hegemonized (Laclau and Mouffe 1985: 134). Mere articulation, however, is not sufficient to be able to speak of hegemony. According to Laclau and Mouffe (1985: 135–136), antagonistic practices linking elements in so-called chains of equivalence are a prerequisite: "in other words, that hegemony should emerge in a field criss-crossed by antagonisms and therefore suppose phenomena of equivalence and frontier effects. But, conversely, not every antagonism supposes hegemonic practices". Antagonisms have both negative and positive aspects, as they attempt to destabilise the "other" identity but desperately need that very "other" as a constitutive outside to stabilise the proper identity. When the question arises how antagonisms are discursively constructed, Laclau and Mouffe refer to the logic of equivalence and the creation of chains of equivalence. In such chains different identities are equated to each other – made equivalent – and opposed to another negative identity. To put this differently: In the logic of equivalence a number of identities are brought into one discourse, which unites them without dissolving their specificity. Howarth (2000: 107) uses as illustration the letters a, b and c for the equivalent identities (in which $a=b=c$) and the letter d for the negative identity. The logic of the equivalence results in the formula: $d = -(a,b,c)$, of which the final result is the coming into being of two antagonistic poles. Laclau (1988: 256) gives an example of a possible chain of equivalence:

> For instance, if I say that, from the point of view of the interests of the working class, liberals, conservatives, and radicals are all the same, I have transformed three elements that were different into substitutes within a chain of equivalence.

Laclau and Mouffe also discern logics of difference, in which existing chains of equivalence are broken and the elements are incorporated in another discursive order (Howarth 1998: 277). As opposed to the logic of the equivalence, the logic of difference weakens existing antagonisms and relegates them to the margins of a society. Applied to Howarth's play with the four letters this would mean that d = -(a, b, c) changes into (d, a, b) = -c in which the constitutive outside d has succeeded to disarticulate the two identities (a and b) from the chain of equivalence a=b=c and to incorporate them in the own discursive order.

Contingency plays an equally important role at the second level. In other words, contingency is not only intra-discursive, but also generated through inter-discursive political struggles. Laclau and Mouffe's discourse theory, in its indebtedness to conflict theory, sees discourses enter into struggles in attempts to attain hegemonic positions over other discourses and, thus, to stabilise and saturate the social. Through these struggles and through the attempts to create discursive alliances, or chains of equivalence (Howarth 1998: 279; Howarth and Stavrakakis 2000: 14), discourses are altered, which in turn produces contingency. In contrast, when a discourse eventually saturates the social as a result of a victorious discursive struggle, stability emerges. In this scenario, a social imaginary is created, which pushes other meanings beyond the horizon, threatening them with oblivion. But this stabilisation, or sedimentation, is temporal. As Sayyid and Zac (1998: 262) formulate it, "Hegemony is always possible but can never be total". There is always the possibility of resistance, of the resurfacing of a discursive struggle, and the re-politicization of sedimented discourses, combined with the permanent threat to every discourse of re-articulation. And, again, this generates contingency.

Discourse theory's relationship to materiality

Some authors have critiqued Laclau and Mouffe's position as idealist. As Joseph (2003: 112) wrote: "the idea that an object only acquires an identity through discourse is a clear example of the epistemic fallacy or the reduction of intrinsic being to transformative knowledge". He continued that Laclau and Mouffe's idealism "reduce[s] material things to the conceptions, not of an individual or a *geist,* but of a community". (Joseph 2003: 112 – emphasis in original) Others, in particular Geras (1987: 65), were harsher in their language, accusing Laclau and Mouffe of a "shamefaced idealism". This critique in turn provoked responses of disagreement with Geras's rather extreme position, but maintained the idealism thesis. For instance, Edward (2008) argued that it was appropriate "to label LacLau and Mouffe as idealist because their discourse analysis concentrates on how interpretations and meanings are given to the world from humans. This is their 'constructivist idealism' [. . .]".

In Laclau and Mouffe's (1985; see also Laclau 1990) work, we do find a rather clear acknowledgement of the materialist dimension of social reality, which is indeed combined with the position that discourses are necessary to generate meaning for the material. This – what Howarth (1998: 289) calls their – "radical materialism" opposes the "classical dichotomy between an objective field constituted outside of any discursive intervention, and a discourse consisting of the pure expression of thought" (Laclau and Mouffe 1985: 108). Pre-empting the idealism critique, their position is defended through a series of examples that refer to materiality:

> An earthquake or the falling of a brick is an event that certainly exists, in the sense that it occurs here and now, independently of my will. But whether their specificity as objects is constructed in terms of "natural phenomena" or "expressions of the wrath of God" depends upon the structuring of a discursive field. What is denied is not that such objects

exist externally to thought, but the rather different assertions that they could constitute themselves as objects outside any discursive condition of emergence.

(Laclau and Mouffe 1985: 108)

Several other authors have defended Laclau and Mouffe's claim on a non-idealist position (e.g., Glynos and Howarth 2007: 109). Also Torfing (1999: 45–48) argues that Laclau and Mouffe's model is materialist because it questions the symmetry between the "realist object" and the "object of thought". This – what Torfing calls a – non-idealist constructivism pre-supposes "the incompleteness of both the given world and the subject that undertakes the construction of the object" (Torfing 1999: 48). One more author who defends Laclau and Mouffe against the idealism critique is Hall (1997: 44–45) who constructs his own language game in order to make this point:

> Is Foucault saying [. . .] that "nothing exists outside of discourse?" In fact, Foucault does not deny that things can have a real, material existence in the world. What he does argue is that "nothing has any meaning outside of discourse". As Laclau and Mouffe put it: "we use [the term discourse] to emphasize the fact that every social configuration is meaningful".

But there are also more specific traces of the material in Laclau and Mouffe's discourse theory. A first trace can be found in Laclau's use of the notion of dislocation. Although this concept already featured in HSS, it took a more prominent role in *New Reflections on the Revolution of our Time*, where Laclau used it to further theorize the limits of discursive structures. In most cases, dislocation gains its meaning in relation to the discursive, for instance, when Laclau (1990: 39) claims that "every identity is dislocated insofar as it depends on an outside which denies that identity and provides its condition of possibility at the same time". In this mean-ing, dislocation supports the notion of contingency, but is also seen as the "very form of pos-sibility" (Laclau 1990: 42), as dislocations show that the structure (before the dislocation) is only one of the possible articulatory ensembles (Laclau 1990: 43). It thus becomes "the very form of temporality, possibility and freedom" (Laclau 1990: 41–43, summarised by Torfing 1999: 149).

At the same time; there is also a more material use of the dislocation, for instance, when Laclau (1990: 39) talks about the "dislocatory effects of emerging capitalism on the lives of workers": "They are well known: the destruction of traditional communities, the brutal and exhausting discipline of the factory, low wages and insecurity of work". This connec-tion between the dislocation and material events becomes even clearer in Torfing's (1999: 148 – my emphasis) description of the dislocation, which, according to him "refers to the emergence of *an event, or a set of events,* that cannot be represented, symbolized, or in other ways domesticated by the discursive structure – which is therefore disrupted". Despite the theoretical importance of the dislocation as a link to the material, its exclusive negative load necessitates an addition, which I would suggest to label the *invitation.* The invitation captures processes where the material –through its materiality – calls upon the discursive to attribute particular meanings. Contingency remains present, as the invitation can always be declined, and other discourses can be used to provide meaning to the material.

As Biglieri and Perelló (2011) have argued, it is particularly in Laclau's *On populist reason* (2005) that the material[3] is introduced, through the concept of social heterogeneity. Laclau defines this concept as a particular exteriority: "[. . .] the kind of exteriority we are referring to now presupposes not only an exteriority to something within a space of representation, but to the space of representation as such. I will call this type of exteriority social heterogeneity" (Laclau 2005: 140). Biglieri and Perelló (2011: 60) label it "a structure with a beyond". It is through the invocation of Lacan, for instance, when Laclau writes that "the field of representation is a broken and murky mirror, constantly interrupted by a heterogeneous 'Real' which it cannot symbolically master" (Laclau 2005: 140), that the material regains more prominence.

Even if there are traces of the material, (mainly) in Laclau's work, and despite Laclau and Mouffe's plea for a position that Howarth (1998: 289) termed "radical materialism" as a "tertium quid", their strong orientation towards the analysis of the discursive components of reality, and more specifically towards the analysis of signifiers such as democracy, socialism and populism, remains. Practically speaking, this means that in their specific analyses they will pay considerably less attention to material components of reality (as for example bodies, objects, organisations, technologies or human interactions). If we return to some of the critiques of Laclau and Mouffe's alleged idealism, we can find these types of arguments. For instance, Edward (2008) writes:

> Unlike Deleuze and Guattari, Laclau and Mouffe are more concerned with discourse than they are about geology (inorganic), biology (organic), and technology (alloplastic). [. . .] Their discourse analysis can only explain the construction of the world when there is discourses [sic] and articulation of meaning.

This type of critique can also be used to strengthen discourse theory, and to render the material more visible. For instance the Deleuzean notion of the assemblage (Deleuze: 2006: 177), with its capacity to incorporate both the material and the discursive, can be used to provide further theoretical support. The object, the technology, the landscape, the organisation, the body and the machine (to name but a few materialities) can then be seen to consist of an endless and restless combination of the material and the discursive that invites for particular discourses and materialities to become part of the assemblage, and that in turn assist in further discourses and materialities to be produced.

A Cypriot case study: MYCYradio

In order to illustrate the dynamical workings of the discursive and material, and in particular the role of the material within a discourse-theoretical context, this chapter contains a brief case study on the broadcasts and audience reception of a Cypriot web radio community station, named MYCYradio, which is based in Nicosia, the capital of Cyprus. However complex the history and politics of the island, it suffices here to explain that Cyprus has been geographically and ethnically divided since 1974, when Turkey invaded the north and occupied more than one third of the island, after decades of intercommunal tensions and violence. Since then, the two major communities, the Greek Cypriot and the Turkish Cypriot, have been living in two different parts of the country: the Republic of Cyprus in the south, which is officially recognised by the international community, and the Turkish-held auto-declared Turkish Republic of Northern Cyprus in the north, recognised only by Turkey.

During the past decades there have been ongoing negotiations for a peaceful reunification of the island. The last peace plan proposed by the United Nations in 2004, known as the "Annan Plan", in the form of a federation of two constituent states, was rejected by referendum in the Greek Cypriot community and accepted in the Turkish Cypriot community. As it had to be accepted by both communities in order to be applied, the island remains divided up today, although negotiations are still ongoing (see also Carpentier and Doudaki 2014; Carpentier 2014a).

Despite the lack of legal framework for community media, the first community media organisation was established in Cyprus in 2009, in the form of the Cyprus Community Media Centre (CCMC), located in the UN-guarded buffer zone, in Nicosia. Initially not a broadcasting organisation, it focussed on providing training, loaning equipment to member organisations (that are part of the Cypriot civil society), creating productions for other organisations, staging public events and offering media advice to members. Only in 2012, CCMC started a web radio station, MYCYradio.

Although we can sometimes find contestations and contingencies, CCMC and its web radio station MYCYradio identify themselves by reverting to a transformational discourse (CCMC 2009; MYCYradio 2012), which resists the still present social antagonism between north and south that continues to characterise Cypriot society. The aim of this discourse is to transform this social antagonism into what Mouffe (2005) called agonism. In an agonistic configuration, there is still a "we/they relation" but it consists of social relationships "where the conflicting parties, although acknowledging that there is no rational solution to their conflict, nevertheless recognize the legitimacy of their opponents" (Mouffe 2005: 20). Secondly, CCMC and MYCYradio also identify with a community media discourse (see Carpentier, Lie and Servaes 2003), which defines them as alternative to the Cypriot mainstream media, grounded in rhizomatic civil society networks and deploying participatory practices. With this discourse, CCMC and MYCYradio mostly resist the hegemonic position of Cypriot mainstream media in mediating social reality.

Methodologically, this case study uses a discourse-theoretical analysis (DTA – as elaborated in Carpentier and De Cleen 2007). DTA builds on the basic principles of qualitative research, but uses sensitising concepts that originate from discourse theory, in combination with research-specific sensitising concepts. Similar to poststructuralist discourse analysis (Angermuller 2014), this methodology applies a macro-textual (and macro-contextual – see Carpentier and De Cleen 2007: 276ff) definition of discourse, which sees "texts as material surfaces in which discursive practices were inscribed" (Pêcheux's DA3, as summarised by Angermuller 2014: 10). The first part of the case study is based on a (summary of a) discourse-theoretical analysis of the radio broadcasts of three MYCYradio shows: the Turkish Cypriot *One Percent*, the Greek Cypriot *Downtown Choris Bakira* and the mixed-community *Cyprus Oral History Project*. This analysis, which has already been published (Carpentier 2015), centred on ten episodes of each show, broadcast between September and November 2013. The second part of the case study reports on the reception analysis (Staiger 2005) of these three radio shows. Between 24 April and 22 May 2014, ten focus group discussions[4] were organised in collaboration with CCMC, in which 74 respondents took part, discussing a selection of fragments[5] from the three MYCYradio shows. Here, the discourse-theoretical analysis of the focus group discussions compliments and strengthens the results of the analysis of the radio show content. In the third and last part of the case study, the data of the reception analysis are revisited to look how the material features in the focus groups, and how it is seen to interact with the discursive component of the analysis. For the combination of these three parts the label of a discursive-material analysis is used.

The discursive strategies towards conflict transformation

A first analysis, purely focussed on the discourses of conflict transformation as they can be found in the broadcasts of the selected MYCYradio shows (that was published earlier in

Carpentier (2015)), pinpoints the presence of four main re-articulations, each of which contribute to a more agnostic articulation of the Cypriot conflict. A first re-articulation is the overcoming and decentralising of the divide, where the radio producers offer a wide variety of subtle narrations on how the separations and distinctions between Greek Cypriots and Turkish Cypriots – and sometimes between Greece and Turkey – are overcome, bypassed or decentred. Many of these narrations concern contemporary everyday life in Cyprus and its many spheres, such as educational, professional, linguistic, relational, culinary and identity-related spheres. Other accounts mention the ways that institutions overcome the divide, while yet others contain narrations that decentre the divide, questioning its centrality for Cypriot society. The second re-articulation is the deconstruction of the self, a process that is based on processes of anti-homogenization and pluralization. In discourses that are strongly antagonistic (such as war discourses), the self becomes glorified and homogenised – as the self is seen as united in its courageous battle against the enemy. Deconstructions of the self undermine this discursive positioning. In the MYCYradio broadcasts, these deconstructions firstly consist of critiques or rediculizations of particular components of the self (such as the 'own' political system, the army, the church, the media, . . .) or of the entire 'own' culture and ideology, where the passive and uncritical nature of Cypriot society, the "victim psychology" (*One Percent,* broadcast 20 November 2013) and its consumerist and intolerant characteristics are frequently mentioned. Thirdly, there is a reconfiguration of time, with a nostalgic return to the pre-conflict past, which becomes represented as an idyllic era of co-habitation and peace. Alternatively, the focus is placed on the future, which includes explicit discussions about the solutions for the Cyprus Problem, and the requirements for their implementation. This variation contributes to the agonist re-articulation through the communication of the implicit belief that solutions can be realised and that a future without the Cyprus Problem can be imagined. The fourth re-articulation consists of a straightforward narration of the cost of the conflict and the division. The narrations of the conflict, especially in the *Cyprus Oral History Project* programme, are very detailed memorializations of the fear, pain and destruction that characterised the intra-communal violence in the 1960s and the Turkish invasion in 1974. More than attributing blame, these memorializations demonstrate the suffering caused by war, which ironically unifies both Greek and Turkish Cypriots, without privileging one side's suffering.

In the reception of the three radio shows, these four re-articulations are also acknowledged (with many variations and contestations). For instance, in the discussions that are related to one particular re-articulation, namely the deconstruction of the homogeneous self, we find more emphasis on Cypriot diversity, the rejection of the juxtaposition of Greek Cypriot and Turkish Cypriot communities (which leads to their homogenization), and the acknowledgement of the existence of other communities (apart from the Greek Cypriot and Turkish Cypriot communities). Respondent FG5F_TL[6] formulates this as follows:

> I feel uncomfortable here. I don't think that the communities are homogeneous. When you talk about [. . .] the Turkish Cypriot community, I have a problem with that. Basically, I have an understanding of hybridity. I never felt a Turkish Cypriot. My language is Cypriot Turkish but I can't define myself as a Turkish Cypriot. At the same time, it's a mistake to perceive Cypriot Greeks and [Greeks] as wholes. From the moment that you put [these identities] into mould, the mistake starts.

In addition, a fifth re-articulation comes to the fore in the reception of the radio shows. This re-articulation is a celebration of ordinariness, where the everyday life experiences and common sense of ordinary people that are given a voice in the radio shows are seen as an important instrument to counter the nationalist ideologies of political and mainstream (elite) actors. For instance, in one of the Turkish Cypriot focus groups, respondent FG9C_TNL says: "[. . .] We are listening to the real people's personal experiences, maybe they generalise a bit but I think it's important to hear something alternative". Another example is the following brief exchange, about one of the fragments, which they compare to the one they have listened to before:

FG6E_TNL: It is much more from the community.

FG6D_TNL: More sincere. She told about real pains, real experiences. It was very sincere talk and not in political way.

FG6B_TNL: The main idea was the same on both conversations but this aligns much more with the individual experience. It covers it. It's much more effective.

As is often the case (Carpentier 2014b), ordinary people are defined as different from societal elites, as also the intervention of respondent FG8G_GNL, comparing mainstream media to community media, illustrates: "We listen to shady politicians, corrupted individuals, bullies, and we don't listen to people who have an opinion, who have intellectual richness and culture. . . . We don't listen to [such] people. Unfortunately, voices like that aren't heard".

The materiality of radio broadcasting and conflict transformation

The above-discussed analysis has an explicit focus on the discursive, which brings out relevant sense-making structures when it comes to the Cyprus Problem and its agonistic re-articulations. But at the same time, the analysis hardly highlights the material dimension. For this reason, another analytical layer should be added, resulting in a discursive-material analysis, which combines the analysis discussed earlier with an explicit analysis of the material dimension. I should immediately remark that this analysis of the material dimension(s) of MYCYradio's conflict transformative capacity is based on the reception data. This methodological and analytical choice implies an analysis of the representations (by audience members) of the representations generated by the radio producers, and the way that these representations contain traces of the material. Nevertheless, we can use these data to take notice of the traces of the material, discursified as always.

A first set of references to the material, in relation to conflict transformation, refers to the people that produce the radio shows and their guests. One dimension here is the material use of particular languages. Although the content of the narrations remains important, the mere use of Greek by Turkish Cypriots (or vice versa) is considered significant, as the citation illustrates below:

the fact that we have a Turkish Cypriot woman who speaks Greek, I'd say, putting myself in the position of a Greek Cypriot audience, the most interesting bit was that they spoke Greek. [. . .] because I believe that these people have gone through the trouble of learning the other [ethnic group's] language, and when the other person listens to them speaking his language, their contribution to the creation of a co-existence culture is huge.

(Respondent FG2C_GL)

Another dimension is the material interaction between humans, where the radio shows allow voices to cross the divide. As respondent FG1E_EL says: "[what is] interesting, was hearing, let's say if you're living in the Greek Cypriot community, hearing what a Turkish Cypriot thinks is important to Greek Cypriots". Also the interaction, in the radio programmes, of people from different ethnicities is considered significant for conflict transformation.

A second cluster of references deals with MYCYradio's web radio production and broadcasting technologies. The focus group respondents mainly discuss the advantages and disadvantages of webcasting, and the ways that internet technologies allow (and disallow) for material access to MYCYradio's voices. Simultaneously, we can find references to particular audience practices (e.g., listening in the car), as also illustrated by the reference to the socio-demographic category of age by this respondent:

> I think it's good to be a web radio but except this, I think it has to turn back to classical radio in terms of reaching all the parts of the community. For example, the older people are not used to the internet, at least people around me.
>
> *(Respondent FG6A_TL)*

But also the production facilities of MYCYradio are mentioned in the focus groups, as several of these meetings take place at the CCMC, and respondents find themselves in the militarised buffer zone at the Ledra Palace crossing between north and south Cyprus, with its assemblage of barb wire, flags, barricades, propaganda material, check points, police officers, UN peace keepers, destroyed buildings and strong NGO representation (in renovated buildings). Respondents also find themselves in close proximity to the MYCYradio studio, with its many technologies, which are (obviously) very necessary for the radio shows to be produced.

> I first came and saw the studio, it made an impression on me that you have a profess... I don't understand stuff like that, nor have I worked as a producer at some point, but what I see here seems quite professional [in English] to me, and it was a very good thing that there was a, so to speak, a nice establishment [in English] in which a nonprofessional may do something almost professional [...].
>
> *(Respondent FG2F_GL)*

The third cluster of references to the material is related to the role of the organisational structure of MYCYradio, and its participatory practices of power-sharing and decentralised decision-making. MYCYradio's role in conflict transformation is connected to its economic structure, and how it, as a non-for-profit organisation has gained a fairly high level of independence from market and state influences (and from the Cypriot political parties). One respondent, FG2F_GL, expresses this as follows: "Well, this is a strong point, the fact that it is done by a nonprofessional group without financial benefit from this whole situation". Also the organisation's participatory nature, with material collective ownership and decentralised decision-making structures, is seen to facilitate the radio station's agonism, as one of the respondents summarises: "it is more about not having a hierarchical structure in the radio, I guess" (Respondent FG6D_TL).

By way of conclusion – cross-fertilizations

Sometimes a conclusion should start with explaining what a text does not want to do. In this case, it is necessary to emphasise that both the theoretical exposé and the analysis of the MYCYradio broadcasts are not to be read as a critique of Laclau and Mouffe's key discourse-theoretical elaborations. On the contrary, this chapter should be read as a defence of this strand of discourse theory, which aims to show its theoretical elegance and analytical strength and to critically work with one of the weaknesses of this theoretical model. Discourse theory's strength lies in its in-depth analysis of the mechanics of discourses, their political nature and the struggles it generates, and their oscillations between fixity and contingency. Moreover, Laclau and Mouffe's ultimate starting point, that meaning resides in discourses, is deeply shared by me. At the same time, it is indispensible to discuss, without blind admiration for discourse theory, this model's weaknesses, and in particular, the absence of the material in the actual practise of discourse-theoretical work (and not such much the absence of the material in the core elaboration of the discourse-theoretical model).

This chapter does not propose to change the premises of discourse theory, but to look for ways to increase the visibility of the material within the discourse-theoretical framework, acknowledging that the material sometimes presents itself to us and that the "encounter with the material" (to paraphrase Lacan) can have a disruptive, dislocatory and traumatising impact on particular discursive orders. But, keeping Foucault's analytics of power (1978) in mind, I would like to argue that this impact can also be generative and productive, which returns us to the notion of the invitation. The encounters with the material are arguably one more level of contingency to be added to the discourse-theoretical equation, which also implies that these materialities cannot impose themselves on our discursive orders. Encounters with the material create invitations to be included in the already existing assemblages of discourses and materialities. Given the context of contingency, these invitations can still be completely ignored and go unnoticed, be rejected as oddity, or be accepted but re-articulated by applying discourses far outside the invitation.

The case study, however modest it is, illustrates these dynamics, where we can see how a series of broadcasts within a Cypriot community web radio station offers counter-hegemonic discourses that attempt to rearticulate the social antagonism that has characterised Cyprus for more than half of a century, by offering a more agonistic discourse on the other, aimed at transforming the Cyprus Problem. Also here, it would be easy to ignore the material, and focus on the world of words and ideas. But this would be unfair towards the complexity of this case study, as the materiality of the radio station's economics, politics, spatial orderings and human interactions cannot be placed outside these counter-hegemonic discourses, but interact with them on an equal footing, invite these discourses to give meaning to these materialities, and form discursive-material assemblages that allow for MYCYradio's conflict transformative, participatory-democratic and communicative roles to be played out.

Notes

1 Parts of this section have already been published in these two texts.
2 Elements are seen by Laclau and Mouffe as differential positions which are not (yet) discursively articulated. Moments are differential positions, which are articulated within a discourse.
3 To do justice to Biglieri and Perelló's (2011) work, they refer to the Lacanian Real.
4 As *Cyprus Oral History Project* contained both the voices of Greek Cypriots and Turkish Cypriots, two focus groups were in English, two in Greek and two in Turkish. *Downtown Choris Bakira* had two focus groups discussing it in Greek; *One Percent* has two in Turkish. For each pair of focus groups, one included people that had listened more than once to MYCYradio, and one included respondents that had not (and often did not know the radio station at all). In addition, a series of socio-demographic and ideological criteria were used to generate diversity.
All broadcasts and all focus group discussions were transcribed, and whenever necessary, translated in English. All respondents (and radio producers) granted permission for the material to be used in academic research.

5 For *One Percent* and *Cyprus Oral History Project,* there were five fragments, for *Downtown Choris Bakira* there were three. Because of time constraints, each focus group only discussed one radio show.
6 To protect the respondents' anonymity, their names have been replaced by a code. The first three digits refer to one of the ten focus groups (FG4), the fourth digit is respondent-specific. The first letter after the underscore refers to the language of the focus group (Turkish, Greek or English), and the second letter to their listener status (Listener, or Non-Listener). All citations are rendered in English.

Further reading

Carpentier, Nico and Spinoy, Erik (eds.) (2008). *Discourse theory and cultural analysis: Media, arts and literature.* Cresskill, NJ: Hampton Press.
This edited volume contains an introduction to discourse theory, combined with a series of chapters that deploy discourse theory for research in the fields of media, arts and literature.
Howarth, David. (2000). *Discourse.* Buckingham, Philadelphia: Open University Press.
Howarth's book provides an introduction to a series of structuralist and post-structuralist approaches in discourse studies, including discourse theory.
Laclau, Ernesto and Mouffe, Chantal. (1985). *Hegemony and socialist strategy: Towards a radical democratic politics.* London: Verso.
This book is the seminal publication where Laclau and Mouffe outline the basic principles of discourse theory.
Phelan, Sean and Dahlberg, Lincoln (eds.) (2011). *Discourse theory and critical media politics.* Houndmills: Palgrave Macmillan.
This edited volume combines discourse theory with a reflection on media and social theory.
Torfing, Jacob. (1999). *New theories of discourse: Laclau, Mouffe and Žižek.* Oxford: Blackwell.
New theories of discourse contains a detailed discussion of Laclau and Mouffe's discourse theory, and offers a good introduction for those interested in the basics of their discourse theory.

References

Angermuller, J. (2014). *Poststructuralist discourse analysis: Subjectivity in enunciative pragmatics.* Houndmills: Palgrave Macmillan.
Biglieri, P. and Perelló, G. (2011). The names of the real in Laclau's theory: Antagonism, dislocation, and heterogeneity. *Filozofski vestnik* XXXII (2): 47–64.
Carpentier, N. (2014a). The Cypriot web radio MYCYradio as a participatory mélange: Overcoming dichotomies in the era of web 2.0. *Sociologia e Politiche Sociali* 17(2): 91–108.
Carpentier, N. (2014b). Reality television's construction of ordinary people: Class-based and nonelitist articulations of ordinary people and their discursive affordances. In Laurie Ouellette (ed.), *A companion to reality television,* 345–366. Chichester: John Wiley and Sons.
Carpentier, N. (2015). Articulating participation and agonism. A case study on the agonistic re-articulations of the Cyprus problem in the broadcasts of the community broadcaster MYCYradio. *Cyprus Review* 27(1): 129–153.
Carpentier, N. and Van Brussel, L. (2012). On the contingency of death: A discourse-theoretical perspective on the construction of death. *Critical Discourse Studies* 9(2): 99–115.
Carpentier, N. and De Cleen, B. (2007). Bringing discourse theory into media studies. *Journal of Language and Politics* 6(2): 267–295.
Carpentier, N. and Doudaki, V. (2014). Community media for reconciliation: A Cypriot case study. *Communication, Culture and Critique* 7(4): 415–434.
Carpentier, N., Lie, R. and Servaes, J. (2003). Community media – muting the democratic media discourse? *Continuum* 17(1): 51–68.
Carpentier, N. and Spinoy, E. (eds.) (2008). *Discourse theory and cultural analysis: Media, arts and literature.* Cresskill, NJ: Hampton Press.
CCMC, Cyprus Community Media Centre. (2009). Foundation charter. Accessed May 1, 2014, www.cypruscommunitymedia.org/images/stories/CCMCFoundationCharter.pdf
Deleuze, G. (2006). Two regimes of madness: Texts and interviews 1975–1995. Ames Hodges and Mike Taormina (trans.) and David Lapoujade (ed.). New York: Semiotext(e).

Nico Carpentier

Edward, M. (2008). A (brief) critique of LacLau and Mouffe's discourse analysis. Struggleswith philosophy.wordpress. https://struggleswithphilosophy.wordpress.com/2008/09/11/a-brief-critique-of-laclau-and-mouffes-discourse-analysis/

Foucault, M. (1978). *History of sexuality, Part 1. An introduction.* New York: Pantheon.

Geras, N. (1987). Post-Marxism? *New Left Review* 163: 40–82.

Glynos, J. and Howarth, D. (2007). *Logics of critical explanation in social and political theory.* New York: Routledge.

Gramsci, A. (1999). *The Antonio Gramsci reader: Selected writings 1916–1935.* London: Lawrence and Wishart.

Hall, S. (1997). The work of representation. In Stuart Hall (ed.), *Representation, cultural representations and signifying practices,* 13–64. London: Sage.

Held, D. (2006). *Models of democracy,* 3rd edn. Cambridge: Polity.

Howarth, D. (1998). Discourse theory and political analysis. In E. Scarbrough and E. Tanenbaum (eds.), *Research strategies in the social sciences,* 268–293. Oxford: Oxford University Press.

Howarth, D. (2000). *Discourse.* Buckingham, Philadelphia: Open University Press.

Howarth, D. and Stavrakakis, Y. (2000). Introducing discourse theory and political analysis. In David Howarth, Aletta J. Norval and Yannis Stavrakakis (eds.), *Discourse theory and political analysis,* 1–23. Manchester: Manchester University Press.

Joseph, J. (2003). *Hegemony: A realist analysis.* London and New York: Routledge.

Laclau, E. (1988). Metaphor and social antagonisms. In C. Nelson and L. Grossberg (eds.), *Marxism and the interpretation of culture,* 249–257. Urbana: University of Illinois.

Laclau, E. (ed.) (1990). *New reflections on the revolution of our time.* London: Verso.

Laclau, E. (1996). *Emancipation(s).* London: Verso.

Laclau, E. and Mouffe, C. (1985). *Hegemony and socialist strategy: Towards a radical democratic politics.* London: Verso.

Latour, B. (2005). *Reassembling the social: An introduction to Actor-network-theory.* Oxford: Oxford University Press.

Mackenzie, A. (2002). *Transductions: Bodies and machines at speed.* London and New York: Continuum.

Mouffe, C. (1997). *The return of the political.* London: Verso.

Mouffe, C. (2005). *On the political.* London: Routledge.

MYCYradio. (2012). MYCYradio foundation charter. Accessed May 1, 2014, http://mycyradio.eu/the-charter/

Norman, D. A. (2002). *The design of everyday things.* New York: Basic Books.

Sayyid, B. and Zac, L. (1998). Political analysis in a world without foundations. In Elinor Scarbrough and Eric Tanenbaum (eds.), *Research strategies in the social sciences,* 249–267. Oxford: Oxford University Press.

Smith, A. M. (1999). *Laclau and Mouffe: The radical democratic imaginary.* London, New York: Routledge.

Staiger, J. (2005). *Media reception studies.* New York: New York University Press.

Torfing, J. (1999). *New theories of discourse: Laclau, Mouffe and Žižek.* Oxford: Blackwell.

19

Critical discourse analysis and media studies

Sean Phelan[1]

There are two ways to set up a discussion of critical discourse analysis and media studies. First, we would privilege something called Critical Discourse Analysis, the capitalised identity embodied in the acronym "CDA". This approach has some obvious advantages. It gives an immediate focus and coherence to the discussion. It suggests reflection on a particular research tradition now well known across the social sciences.

The second approach would be wary of an institutionalised CDA identity. This impulse is sometimes discernible in CDA scholarship itself – in looser descriptions of CDA as a research "network" (Fairclough cited in Rogers 2004), "movement" or "attitude" (van Dijk 2015), or, as this collection illustrates, in the embrace of Critical Discourse Studies (CDS) as an alternative master category that seeks to signify greater theoretical and methodological openness than the CDA label. Instead of positioning media studies and critical discourse analysis as discrete fields, this perspective highlights the importance of the concept of discourse to the emergence of media studies in the 1970s and 1980s. It encourages us to see interdisciplinary affinities in a genealogical way; reframed as a lower-case category, we might say media scholars were already doing a kind of critical discourse analysis before "CDA" became an established identity. It also invites consideration of other discourse analytical traditions that depart from the linguistic underpinnings of CDA. For all its genuine enthusiasm about interdisciplinarity, CDA is still primarily defined as *linguistic* analysis. Some would even suggest that discourse analysis which is not grounded in close linguistic analysis of texts is not really discourse analysis at all, but merely speculative theorising and commentary.

This chapter straddles a line between these two approaches. My own recent work is aligned with the second approach, because of its debt to Laclau/Laclau and Mouffe's discourse theory (see Carpentier, this volume; Dahlberg and Phelan 2011). Accordingly, I normally avoid using the label CDA, because of a concern that it can sound like a built-in "approach" that does things of its own accord, independently of its contextual application (Billig 2013). At the same time, it would be idiosyncratic to write this chapter and pretend that CDA did not exist as an institutionalised approach with its own particular histories and conventions, especially since it colours many media scholars' perceptions about what discourse analysis is. This chapter therefore focuses on CDA, but embeds the discussion in some general reflections on the place of the concept of discourse in media studies.

Preliminary caveats can also be attached to the category of media studies; for starters, depending on one's institutional location, it might come under the guise of mass communication, communications or communication studies. On the one hand, the field has an obvious referent: media studies examines the political, social, economic and cultural implications of individual mediums like newspapers, television and radio, and their combined power and authority as "the media". Yet, on the other hand, the boundaries and location of media studies is not so straightforward; consider, for instance, how different nominal entities – politics, economy, identity and so on – are increasingly conceptualised as "mediated" or "mediatized" objects (Livingstone 2008). The qualified definition raises questions about the ontological status of media and mediation that go beyond the focus of this chapter. The salient point here – one at the heart of the relationship between critical discourse analysis and media studies – is that we cannot understand the discursive constitution of society independently of the structural, and structuring, dynamics of large-scale and micro-scale media.

The rest of the chapter is organised into four sections. I first reflect on the emergence of CDA as a distinct approach in the 1980s and 1990s, especially as it resonated with the theoretical division between political economy and cultural studies in media studies.[2] I then consider how CDA has been applied and critiqued in media research. Section 3 considers possible future iterations of media discourse studies, in ways that go beyond the notion of a prescriptive CDA paradigm. I end with an empirical illustration that, informed by my own work on neoliberalism (Phelan 2014), explores how we might reimagine ideology critique of media discourses.

Media studies and the historical emergence of CDA

CDA – like its antecedent identity "critical linguistics" (Fowler 1991) – had its origins in the desire of linguists from different academic milieux to develop forms of textual analysis that could illuminate questions of power beyond the limitations of traditional linguistics (Fairclough 1989; Fairclough and Wodak 1997; van Dijk 1991). These scholars engaged with a wider body of critical theory, in which concepts like discourse, representation and ideology had become increasingly prominent in the 1970s and 1980s. The coupling of grounded linguistic analysis and social theory embodied an analytical ideal – an antidote to a theoreticism that, however suggestive, was inclined to invoke the concept of discourse in abstract, sometimes nebulous ways.

CDA represented an intervention in a theoretical debate where the status of discourse had energised polemical exchanges between poststructuralists, Marxists and others in different fields (see Laclau and Mouffe 1990). CDA scholars lamented how the constitutive role of discourse and language had been historically neglected in the social sciences. Yet, they simultaneously distanced themselves from the notion that social analysis was reducible to the category of discourse, by emphasising the "dialectical" relationship between discursive (i.e., meaning-making) practices and other social practices. On its own terms, therefore, CDA signalled the arrival of a theoretical middle ground – between stylized post-structuralist claims about the discursive nature of society and a Marxist analytic that stressed the materiality of the social independently of discourse.

This in-between identity was best captured by Norman Fairclough, who sought to bridge the gap between different critical theory traditions and linguistic analysis. Instead of reinscribing a division between the "Marxist" concept of ideology and the "Foucauldian" concept of discourse, he brought both concepts together (as others did) to highlight the ideological significance of discursive practices (Fairclough 1989; Fairclough 1992). This approach was refined in his 1999 book with Lilie Chouliaraki, which emphasised the importance of "critical realism" to CDA's social ontology (Chouliaraki and Fairclough 1999). Critical realists like Roy Bhaskar were likewise committed to forging a theoretical middle ground, between social constructivist theories that stressed the importance of human meaning and agency, and objectivist approaches that highlighted structural conditions beyond the immediate purview and control of human agents (see Glynos and Howarth 2007).

How might we situate the founding rationale of CDA, especially in Fairclough's work, when evaluated from the perspective of similar debates in media and communication studies? We might recast it as an attempt to bridge the division between Marxist political economy theories that emphasised the determining power of economic structures, and cultural studies approaches that stressed the importance of discourse and human subjectivity. Early CDA work on media recognised its debt to previous research, both inside and outside linguistics (Fairclough 1995; van Dijk 1991; see Kelsey, this volume). The Frankfurt School, Birmingham School of cultural studies and the Glasgow University media group were all cited as important antecedents. These reference points transcended any notional division between political economy and cultural studies, though the work of Stuart Hall (1988) – cultural studies' figurehead – was especially important in anticipating Fairclough's theoretical position. Both interrogated a Marxist theoretical reflex that regarded the analysis of ideology and discourse as relatively superficial matters. At the same time, both looked to different structuralist and poststructuralist sources to formulate approaches that remained embedded in a broadly Marxist analysis of capitalism.

Fairclough (1995) framed his approach to media discourse as a development of the semiotic methods of cultural studies scholars. The influence of cultural studies is discernible more generally in CDA research – in affirmations of the importance of critical media literacy, the politics of knowledge, and the concepts of hegemony and ideology, and in the desire to critically intervene beyond the academy.

Yet, with some exceptions (see, for example, Allan 1998), the links to cultural studies have not been especially prominent in CDA and, sociologically, "cultural studies" and "CDA" exist as quite separate scholarly universes. This divergence of traditions can, in one sense, be prosaically explained. CDA emerged through the work of linguists based at linguistics department, who, whatever their interdisciplinary ambitions, still needed to publish their work in journals with credibility among linguists. Their scholarly habitus was attuned primarily to the theoretical and analytical concerns of their home discipline.

However, the demarcation of CDA and cultural studies invites a more speculative explanation, especially if we privilege a media studies assessment of CDA. Fairclough's desire to combine poststructuralist and Marxist political economy insights necessitated constructing a theoretical identity that had to avoid seeming too close to either. In addition, CDA scholars might have had good reasons for wanting to distinguish themselves from cultural studies analyses of media, because of the periodic disparaging of the latter for making inflationary claims about discourse (Philo and Miller 2000). Another differentiating factor was CDA scholars' comparative attention to questions of method. The charge of methodological dilettantism sometimes made against cultural studies could not be made as easily against CDA. Indeed, one plausible reason for the popularity of CDA among media scholars in the 2000s was its currency as an "analytical toolkit" that promised neophytes (this author included) an immediate answer to the question of "what method or methodology are you using?".

Conversely, given the negative stereotypes associated with the concept of discourse, we might say CDA researchers needed to proactively establish credibility among political economy researchers. Cultural studies scholars would have needed little convincing about the importance of discourse. However, political economy scholars represented a more sceptical audience. Fairclough's valorization of the Marxist concept of "the dialectic" was therefore rhetorically significant, because it signalled a desire to avoid the charge of discursive reductionism. His subsequent embrace of the term "cultural political economy" (Fairclough 2006) was similarly telling. Those who avow the label in media studies tend to be political economy scholars and, in some cases, proponents of a "critical realist" approach (Deacon et al. 2007). The work of media researchers like Richardson (2007) (see also Berglez 2006; Graham 2002) was also important in giving Fairclough's (2002) "language of new capitalism" research programme a stronger "materialist" identity. By underscoring the dangers of an "idealist" analysis of media discourse, Richardson articulated a version of CDA more palatable to political economy scholars, because it anticipated their basic anxieties about discourse approaches and terminologies.

The point of the foregoing discussion has *not* been to reinscribe a theoretical division between cultural studies and political economy, a debate that sometimes did little to satisfactorily clarify the relationship between discourse and materiality. Rather, I am suggesting that we cannot properly understand CDA's founding rationale independently of its proponents' wish to formulate an analysis of language and social life that went beyond the controversies about the status of discourse in different fields. However, as we will now see, we also cannot clearly grasp how CDA has been critically interrogated in media studies independently of earlier antagonisms, and the suspicions that are still projected onto the concept of discourse.

Articulating CDA in media studies

We can identify two distinct kinds of researchers in the interdisciplinary space between CDA and media studies: linguists who analyse media and, of most interest here, media scholars who apply CDA theories and methods. These differ in their choice of concepts and methods; we are less likely to see a discussion of systemic functional linguistics in a media journal. But perhaps they differ more in the expectations that come from operating in different disciplinary universes. Scholars writing primarily for linguistic audiences will be expected to show a level of technical proficiency – as linguists – that will be less salient in media studies. Conversely, media researchers might be expected to discuss the general status and legitimacy of textual analysis. The cumulative effect is to normalise a situation where "doing CDA" can mean quite different things in different academic contexts.

CDA has usually been deployed to analyse discrete media texts and the intertextual relationship between thematically linked media content. Since the early media-based work of van Dijk (1991), Fairclough (1995) and others (see Bell 1991; Fowler 1991), CDA scholars have developed an extensive set of concepts for analysing media. We can identify at least three levels of analysis that often come together in the same research project. One strand of research – the one closest to linguistics – highlights the structural conventions of media texts and language (see, for example, Banda and Mawadza 2015; Teo 2000). Researchers explicate the semantic and grammatical properties of different media genres (reportage, editorials, interviews, etc.) and the ideological function of particular text types such as headlines and leads. A second strand concentrates on the interdiscursive and intertextual character of media discourses (see, for example, Craig 2013; Kelsey 2013). Scholars explore how certain ways of representing the world, performing identity and constructing social belonging are normalised in media spaces; questions of who gets to speak, what discourses are privileged and what discourses are absent are foregrounded. A third strand focuses on the sociological implications of media discourses (see, for example, Mendes 2012; Olausson 2014). Analysts examine how media representations inflect the discursive constitution of different social phenomena: for example, capitalism, neo-liberalism, racism, climate change and feminism.

While CDA has been used to analyse different media, the literature has primarily focused on written journalism. The bias towards news and current affairs media established in early CDA scholarship was later consolidated by work aligned with the emerging field of journalism studies (Richardson 2007; Carvalho 2008). The research appeal of journalistic texts has arguably increased in the digital ecology, because of easier access to newspapers' historical archives. The low financial and temporal costs of converting written journalism into research data enable a relatively easy uptake of CDA methods, especially for students and researchers without large research budgets. Digitization has also allowed scholars to integrate CDA into the analysis of large corpora of media texts (Gabrielatos and Baker 2008), as a supplement or alternative to analyses of small samples.

Some of the most innovative recent research has focused on the different modalities of media discourse (Machin 2013). Researchers have analysed semiotic forms that were relatively marginalised – if not invisible – in linguistically based analysis, such as the visual design and branding of texts (Machin and Niblock 2008), the interplay of audio and visual communication (Eriksson 2015) and the discursive relationships between human and non-human actors (Roderick 2013). Scholars have also examined the different forms of individual and collective identity enabled in internet-based media (Chiluwa 2012). As the mediums of print, radio and television become elements within a convergent digital ecology, the future vibrancy of CDA media research will partly depend on researchers' ability to get to grips with discursive universes where, as Bouvier (2015: 153) suggests, "algorithms themselves become realisers of discourse".

CDA researchers continually emphasise the dialectical relationship between text and social context; we might call it the governing theoretical assumption of the paradigm. Yet, media sociologists have criticised CDA for its narrow textual focus, in a fashion that recalls political economy critiques of cultural studies. For instance, Philo (2007: 185) suggests Fairclough and van Dijk produce "text only" analysis of media, without offering a satisfactory "account of the social and political structures which underpin the content of texts" (186). He unfavourably compares CDA approaches to the methods he and others developed at the Glasgow Media School, which examine how "meanings [are] circulated through the key dimensions of production, content and reception" (194).

Philo voices a criticism that, in its most benign form, is implicit in the media researcher's decision to combine CDA and political economy. The methodology suggests an obvious division of labour: CDA will be used to analyse media texts, while political economy will be used to explain their structural production and circulation. Philo's argument recalls Blommaert's (2005: 35) critique of CDA for its "linguistic bias". Blommaert argues CDA is oriented towards an excessive problematization of "discourse which is there" in the text to the neglect of a dynamic social account of the power struggles in which the text is embedded.

Philo and Blommaert's critiques seemingly converge. Yet, the differences between them are important because of how they illuminate some of the general confusion about the status of discourse and textual analysis in media studies (Fürsich 2009). Philo presupposes a relatively straightforward distinction between the discursivity and materiality of media practices. Textual analysis of media is useful, but it needs to be connected to contextual analysis of how media texts are materially produced and circulated. Philo effectively situates the analysis of media (re) presentations on a different analytical level to the analysis of media production and reception. Any distinction between "textual analysis" and "discourse analysis" is collapsed, since both are exclusively tied to an analysis of media content.

In contrast, Blommaert interrogates CDA's textualist bias from a perspective that emphasises the discursivity of *both* text and context. He therefore allows us to recast the other two dimensions of Philo's totality – media production and reception – as equally important analytical horizons to the discourse analyst. A decade on from Blommaert's critique, we can make the same point by highlighting how CDA is increasingly applied in ethnographic studies that transcend a narrow textual focus (see, for example, Krzyżanowski, this volume; Macgilchrist and van Hout 2011; Wodak 2009).

Read defensively, Blommaert (2005) merely restated points already recognised by CDA scholars. However, that he needed to make the argument at all is symptomatic of how CDA research has sometimes been formulaically applied. We know what such analysis looks like in media research. Some contextual discussion of social and media structures at the front end of the article, and maybe some more in the conclusion. And centring everything, as the privileged object of analysis, is a sample of media texts. Done well, such analysis produces rich insights, and illuminates the dynamic relationship between text and context. Done badly, it can seem tautologous, and amount to little more than an illustrative technical display – by non-linguists! – of different CDA concepts.

The next section explores how the relationship between (a lower case) critical discourse studies and media studies might develop in the future. The challenge invites a particular framing for media researchers: in an interdisciplinary space dominated by linguistic approaches, how might media scholars formulate ways of doing critical discourse studies that better address the concerns of our own field?

Future possibilities

I have four broad suggestions. Some of the ideas sketched below are already being done by researchers. Some have likely been done in work I am unfamiliar with. Taken together, they suggest ways of doing media-based discourse analysis that go beyond the notion of a prescriptive CDA method or paradigm.

First, critical discourse studies needs to clearly position itself as a field that addresses all four analytical tiers of the media studies totality of production, representation, distribution and reception, and extends its analysis to entertainment media and popular culture (see, for example, Edwards 2016; Eriksson 2015; Schröter 2015; Wodak 2009). One way of broadening the scope of the field would be through greater engagement with other discourse-theoretical traditions, including those based on a social ontology that would question CDA's founding distinction between discursive and extra-discursive practices (see Carpentier this volume; Dahlberg and Phelan 2011). For practical reasons, most research will still likely focus on analysing given media texts; it is simply easier to analyse ten news stories about the "refugee crisis" than interview the ten journalists who wrote them, never mind construct ethnographic studies of how the articles were produced. Nonetheless, even within the limits of conventional textual analysis, there is the potential for more studies that go beyond a one-dimensional focus on "the media", and which systematically compare journalists' source material (including press releases) with published media stories. For those with the resources to carry out ethnographic or interview-based studies of media production, the research possibilities are more open-ended. Such work would highlight what social and institutional agents *do* with texts and discourses (see, for example, Erjavec and Kovačič 2013), as a supplement or alternative to relatively static analyses of media texts. Conversely, it would also illuminate what discursive regimes do to social agents, in moulding the subjectivities and affective dispositions they bring to the production of media.

A similar argument can be extended to media audiences. Fairclough (1995) recognised the importance of audience interpretations in his book on media discourse. Yet, audience analysis has been relatively invisible in CDA research (an exception is Edwards 2016), no doubt partly for similar practical reasons that have hindered the analysis of media production. As a thought experiment, perhaps we can imagine the emergence of audience-based discourse studies where, instead of starting with given media texts, researchers begin with an analysis of how media audiences have been discursively constituted. This approach would displace the analytical centrality of the text, and call into question the residual behaviourism embedded in the image of individual media texts having "effects" on audiences. This work could build on insights in the existing audience/reception analysis literature, and reinvigorate the dialectical intuitions of Hall's (1980) encoding/decoding model. It could also develop a sharper sociological focus by highlighting the discursive affinities between the ways of acting, representing and being (Fairclough 2003) normalised in centring media (Couldry 2003) and the dispositional tendencies normalised and enabled elsewhere. Such work would be particularly well suited to illuminating the dynamics of digital media cultures, where audiences are simultaneously consumers, distributors and producers of texts.

Second, media discourse studies could challenge existing divisions between quantitative and qualitative methods, and trouble the default positioning of discourse analysis as a qualitative approach. The emergence of frameworks that apply CDA insights on a corpus-based scale offer one template for such work (Subtirelu and Baker, this volume; Gabrielato and Baker 2008); pragmatic combinations of CDA and content analysis offer another (Mendes 2012). Such hybrid methodologies mitigate the criticism that critical discourse research is based on "unrepresentative", "self-serving" samples. They also potentially enrich our understanding of media power, by enabling large-scale analyses of how media ways of naming the social world are disseminated and naturalised, and internalised or resisted by agents in other social fields (Couldry 2008). This work could develop the diachronic impulses of "discourse-historical" CDA (Wodak 2009), and exploit the research opportunities that come from the digitization of media archives. It could also address the increasing fixation with "big data"; indeed, the interpretative strengths of critical discourse studies offer an important analytical foil to tendencies that read large-scale data assemblages as objective representations of the social, without any critical evaluation of their conditions of possibility.

Third, media researchers need to develop forms of critical discourse studies that fret less about applying the codified protocol of linguistic analysis. This, I should hasten to add, is *not* to advocate for a dilettante approach that does not take discourse seriously. Rather, I am suggesting that a methodologically correct focus on linguistic detail can inculcate a kind of "aspect blindness" (Wittgenstein 1973: 213), which obscures how the most politically convincing and illuminating answers to our research questions are sometimes "not to be found in the text" (Molina 2009: 186; see also Carvalho 2008). Price's (2010) work offers one exemplar of such an approach. Different linguistic concepts are applied, but in a relatively unobtrusive way; what centres the analysis is a sophisticated study of the power dynamics and political motivations that shape what appears in the media. Another exemplar is the media research of Chouliaraki (2012), Fairclough's former collaborator. The phrases "critical discourse analysis" and "critical discourse studies" are noticeably absent from her most recent book, and the analysis is without the kind of methodological protocol prescribed in CDA handbooks. For all that, we should not conclude that Chouliaraki is no longer doing critical discourse analysis; on the contrary, her analysis of the role of mediated dynamics in the historical constitution of humanitarian discourses is clearly informed by the concerns of her nominally CDA work.

Fourth, media discourse researchers need to reinvigorate our commitment to ideology critique by reengaging with the concept of ideology in media studies (Phelan 2016) and the status of the "critical" in critical discourse studies (van Dijk 2015). CDA analyses of media have typically been governed by what Scannell (1998: 256), drawing on Ricoeur, calls a "hermeneutics of suspicion". Media discourses are regarded suspiciously because they ideologically misrepresent the social order and conceal structural inequalities. This perspective is, as we know from CDA research and elsewhere, often justified. Media universalize particular understandings of the social world that are contestable, but which conceal or belittle their contestability behind the impression of a naturalised, common-sense order. However, Scannell argues that a mode of default suspicion can foreclose interpretative engagement with the sedimented condition of the social world, and subordinate the phenomenological richness of mediated interactions (Scannell 2013) to the "being in the head" of ideology critique (Scannell 1998: 261). He does not suggest that media researchers should replace a "principled suspicion" with a default "hermeneutics of trust", because "to do so would be to replace one absurdity (the denial of world) by another (the denial of self-reflecting reason)" (267). Instead, he highlights the analytical limitations of ideology critiques that are too quick to juxtapose the falseness of media representations with a relatively unproblematized notion of "truth" directly accessible to the analyst (264).

Journalism, ideology and neoliberalism

I want to end this chapter with an empirical illustration that considers the practical implications of Scannell's argument as it informs my own work on neoliberalism and media (Phelan 2014). In a September 2013 opinion piece for *The Irish Times,* the paper's then economics editor, Dan O'Brien, criticised a speech given by Irish President Michael D. Higgins on the need for an ethical economy. O'Brien denounced the speech as "highly ideological and one-sided", because of what he saw as Higgins's exclusive citation of left-wing thinkers (among them Michel Foucault, David Harvey, Ruth Levitas, Philip Mirowski and Jamie Peck). Not only did Higgins's speech disparage the "non-leftists" it mentioned, "worst of all, it excluded the majority who occupy the middle ground and who carry little or no ideological baggage".

O'Brien argued that the speech contravened Higgins's role as Irish President, which has traditionally been regarded as a largely ceremonial office above politics. Higgins's "increasingly political and partisan" interventions threatened the constitutional convention that the presidency should not be used "as a platform to advance a political agenda". "The president is moving into dangerous territory", O'Brien warned, by usurping the neutral and apolitical comportment of the office with speeches that exalt "some quite extreme figures" on the intellectual left.

O'Brien's sharpest remarks were directed against Higgins's use of the word "neoliberal", the "favourite term of abuse" of "the reactionary left". The term "makes dialogue impossible", O'Brien suggested, "because nobody anywhere defines himself/herself as 'neoliberal'". The "conscious ideological project" attributed to neoliberals by Higgins and others is nothing other than a left-wing "conspiracy myth". Left polemics against neoliberalism are grounded in reductive binaries that bear no relation to current political realities in Ireland and elsewhere:

> The setting up of an us-versus-neoliberals contest is not only divisive, it is grossly reductionist. Most people support both competitive markets and state-organised redistribution. The choice is not binary. To the chagrin of hardline ideologues on both the left and free market right, Ireland and peer countries have a mix of market and state in economic life.

So, what to make of this text in light of my earlier reflections on ideology? First, we can see how it might be interrogated in terms already familiar to us from media and journalism studies. O'Brien offers a perfect illustration of the ideological work done by journalists when they invoke the notion of "balance" (Hall et al. 2013) as a kind of policing mechanism regulating what can and cannot be "reasonably" said in the public sphere. O'Brien reproaches Higgins not simply for commending left-wing thinkers, but because he primarily cited figures on the left to the detriment of a balanced discussion. O'Brien aligns his own position with that of "most people", in opposition to the "hardline ideologues on both the left and free market right". His stance exemplifies journalism's alignment with the imaginary of the "sensible centre" (Louw 2005: 76), because of the assumption that those on "the middle ground. . . carry little or no ideological baggage" (O'Brien 2013).

This critique illuminates some crucial features of our text. It shows how journalists often do their most important ideological work when they disavow ideology. As a supplement, we might also imagine a critical political economy analysis of O'Brien and *The Irish Times,* which highlights how the paper has internalised the logic of neoliberal capitalism and is structurally primed to interrogate Higgins's speech.

Nonetheless, I want to reformulate Scannell's (1998: 261) argument as a challenge: how might we develop a form of ideology critique attuned to an "ontology of being in the world", as a supplement to the traditional emphasis on ideological media representations that mask social reality?

Glynos and Howarth's (2007: 157) discussion of the role of self-interpretations in critical social analysis is a useful resource for sharpening a political reading of Scannell. They describe the "passage through self-interpretations [as. . .] a necessary starting point for any social science investigation". As with Scannell's critique of a default hermeneutics of suspicion, Glynos and Howarth's target is forms of theoretical explanation that appeal to causal structures over and above agents' own self-interpretations of their practices. For example, let's imagine a critique of O'Brien's journalism that reads it as symptomatic of neoliberalism, *irrespective* of anything he says about neoliberalism.

At the same time, Glynos and Howarth (2007: 157) argue that our "understanding and explanations" of social practices cannot simply stop at describing "contexualized self-interpretations", as if we have no other methodological option but to take agents at their word, and simply catalogue different representations of the world. Rather, they suggest we need to illuminate the (onto-political) conditions of possibility that enable such interpretations to "be" in the first place.

Glynos and Howarth capture a set of analytical intuitions broadly aligned with Scannell's (2013: 221) focus on sedimented social and media practices – what he calls, following Boltanski, the media's phenomenological entanglement in the "politics of the present". Both point to the importance of formulating a mode of critical analysis that passes through agents' own self-interpretations. And both capture a pragmatic impulse to understand discursive practices that, in a default suspicious mode, we might be inclined to dismiss as nothing other than self-serving ideology.

What are the practical implications of these reflections for our analysis of O'Brien's article? A mode of ideology critique attuned to an ontology of being in the world would focus on the political and discursive work done by O'Brien when he invokes the signifier "ideology" to censure Higgins. This simple shift in perspective reverses the normal comportment of ideology critique. Instead of treating ideology as a conceptual name for the "deep structure" that explains the distortions of the media "surface" (Scannell 1998), attention is focused on its use as a category for ridiculing political identities that talk of something called "neoliberalism".

This approach recasts O'Brien's text as an exemplar of some of the paradoxical features of "actually existing neoliberalism" (Brenner and Theodore 2002: 349) – namely, that despite the critical use of neoliberalism as the name for the dominant ideology, the term ideology is perhaps still most commonly attributed – in media discourse – to those who challenge neoliberal orthodoxies. Decades on from what critics would see as the institutionalisation of neoliberalism, it is neoliberalism's antagonists who are still represented as the ideological ones. Ideology is the exclusive property of those on the margins, against those who occupy the ideology-free "middle ground".

Yet, there is more going on in O'Brien's text, for in his schema, ideology is not simply the property of the "reactionary left". He also distances himself from "hardline ideologues. . . on the free market right". In effect, he both disparages the concept of neoliberalism, while also paradoxically othering a nominal "free market" identity that many would see as a shorthand *for* neoliberalism.

O'Brien's anti-ideology identity is not only animated by a journalistic habitus that is self-construed as objective and balanced. It is also mediated by a particular understanding of neo-liberalism. On the one hand, he questions the coherence of the concept. Yet, on the other, he implicitly attributes a particular definition of neoliberalism to left critics – of a "free market" project opposed to the state. His own attribution of a "free market" identity to the "hardline ideologues of the. . . right" therefore seeks to undercut left-wing claims about the universalism of neoliberalism, because of his assumption that mainstream political economy is governed by a pragmatic "mix of market and state".

O'Brien is certainly not the first to define neoliberalism as a "free-market" project. Yet, as many of the thinkers cited in Higgins's speech have argued, the notion that neoliberalism can be satisfactorily conceptualised through the image of a market/state dichotomy is itself deeply reductionist. Foucault (2008) could already see in 1978 that neoliberals were driven by a desire to reconstitute the state as an agent of market rationality, in contrast to a philosophy of laissez-faire liberalism. Peck (2010: 277) makes a similar point: "neoliberals too are statists (just different kinds of statists)". O'Brien rearticulates the same discursive logic that enabled an elite political and media construction of Celtic Tiger Ireland as a non-ideological formation, however incoherent that description might seem to critics of the Irish case (Phelan 2014).

The discursive logics underpinning O'Brien's stance are obviously contestable, and have been increasingly challenged in Ireland and elsewhere since the 2007–2008 global financial crisis. One manifestation of this – as the article itself illustrates – has been the increasing media visibility of the term "neoliberalism" as a name for the dominant ideology. Another has been an arguably growing popular recognition (on both left and right) of the ideologically com-plicit nature of media discourses, which has been partly enabled by the feedback mechanisms of social media. Both of these counter-hegemonic impulses were evident in how O'Brien's article was interrogated in the comments sections directly underneath (and also in letters to the editor, and alternative media). One commenter suggested – echoing my analysis here – that "the assumption that the majority who occupy the middle ground are not in the grip of an ideology is exactly what makes you yourself a 'reactionary' and an 'ideologue', Dan". A second observed it's "hilarious to read a neoliberal denying the existence of neoliberalism". And a third argued that O'Brien "should take a good hard look in the mirror" for obscuring "the crucial point" of Higgins's speech: "that what appears to us as mere pragmatism is in fact the product of a deep ideological commitment".

Unsurprisingly, some who commented on O'Brien's article affirmed its characterization of Higgins. However, the critical responses capture the bigger point: that contestation over what is and isn't "ideological", what is and isn't "neoliberal", and what is and isn't "political" are all part of a mediatized "politics of the present". Higgins's speech, O'Brien's critique and the criti-cisms of O'Brien evoke a wider political and discursive struggle between those who cannot see beyond the restoration of a social and economic order institutionalised in the 1970s and 1980s and those who want to disclose the conditions for a radically different kind of society.

Let me end by briefly clarifying the implications of the approach signposted here. I have suggested it might be productive for critical media discourse researchers to examine what social actors *do* with the term "ideology", and other signifiers of ideological commitment, in media spaces. Attention is focused on how popular subjectivities are discursively positioned through the mediatized naming and non-naming of identities as "ideological", "neoliberal", "political", and so on. In one sense, this approach is consistent with what researchers have been doing all along; CDA scholars are hardly indifferent to the ideological potency of labels. However, when mediated by an analytical perspective that is less concerned with documenting the semantic organisation of individual texts, it offers an empirical route into critically understanding the ideological and political comportment of neoliberalised regimes that are articulated as post-ideological. As with traditional ideology critique, this approach is attentive to the ideologically distorting effects of media representations. Yet, it also recasts ideology as "a property of politics, not a malfunction" (Finlayson 2012: 753). It questions its historical status as a pejorative category of critical analysis.

Our example is again illustrative, because, for all their differences, Higgins, O'Brien and O'Brien's critics agree on one fundamental point – that ideology is a bad thing. At the same time, their own discursive identities are made possible by how they attribute the term to others. Ideology can certainly be a bad thing and, contra O'Brien, we have lots of good reasons for critiquing the pernicious effects of neoliberal ideology. Nonetheless, as critical analysts of media discourse, perhaps we need to do more than simply reinforce a pejorative view of the concept. Perhaps we also need to illuminate its status as a discursive category of political life – one equally pertinent to the media politics of bringing a new social order into being as it is to critiquing the existing order.

Further reading

Bell, A. and Garrett, P. (1998). *Approaches to media discourse*. Oxford: Blackwell.
This anthology is still one of the best introductions to media discourse analysis. It includes chapters from Norman Fairclough, Teun van Dijk, Stuart Allan, Gunther Kress and Theo van Leeuwen, and Paddy Scannell's "two hermeneutics" essay referenced earlier.
Dahlberg, L. and Phelan, S. (2011). *Discourse theory and critical media politics*. Basingstoke: Palgrave Macmillan.
This edited volume examines the implications of Laclau and Mouffe's discourse theory for critical media and communication studies. Briefly comparing discourse theory to CDA in the introduction, the book offers a perspective on media and discourse that has been less prominent, if gaining traction, in the critical discourse studies literature.
Fairclough, N. (1995). *Media discourse*. London: Arnold.
This book offers a good introduction to Fairclough's work, and is grounded in analysis of different media genres, including currents affairs broadcasting, documentary and reportage.
Machin, D. and van Leeuwen, T. (2007). *Global media discourse: A critical introduction*. London: Routledge.
This book highlights the multi-modal character of media discourse, and includes illustrations from different national contexts and different lifestyle and entertainment media. It is also sensitive to wider media studies debates about the political economy of media globalization.
Richardson, J. E. (2007). *Analysing newspapers: An approach from critical discourse analysis*. Basingstoke: Palgrave Macmillan.
John Richardson's book offers a good introduction to the value of CDA approaches in journalism studies, while also interrogating the narrow textualist tendencies of some CDA research. It transcends its explicit focus on newspapers, and is an equally useful reference for students and researchers examining today's news ecology.

Sean Phelan

References

Allan, S. (1998). News from NowHere: Televisual news discourse and the construction of hegemony. In A. Bell and P. Garrett (eds.), *Approaches to media discourse,* 105–141. Oxford: Blackwell.

Banda and Mawadza A. (2015). "Foreigners are stealing our birth right": Moral panics and the discursive construction of Zimbabwean immigrants in South African media. *Discourse & Communication* 9(1): 47–64.

Bell, A. (1991). *The language of news media.* Blackwell: Oxford.

Berglez, P. (2006). *The materiality of media discourse.* Orebro: Orebro University Press.

Billig, M. (2013). *Learn to write badly: How to succeed in the social sciences.* Cambridge and New York: Cambridge University Press.

Blommaert, J. (2005). *Discourse: A critical introduction.* Cambridge: Cambridge University Press.

Bouvier, G. (2015). What is a discourse approach to Twitter, Facebook, YouTube and other social media: Connecting with other academic fields? *Journal of Multicultural Discourses* 10(2): 149–162.

Brenner, N. and Theodore, N. (2002). Cities and the geographies of "actually existing neoliberalism". *Antipode* 34: 349–379.

Carvalho, A. (2008). Media(ted) discourse and society. *Journalism Studies* 9(2): 161–177.

Chiluwa, I. (2012). Social media networks and the discourse of resistance: A sociolinguistic CDA of Biafra online discourses. *Discourse & Society* 23(3): 217–244.

Chouliaraki, L. (2012). *The ironic spectator: Solidarity in the age of post-humanitarianism.* Cambridge: Polity.

Chouliaraki, L. and Fairclough, N. (1999). *Discourse in late modernity: Rethinking critical discourse analysis.* Edinburgh: Edinburgh University Press.

Couldry, N. (2003). *Media rituals: A critical approach.* London: Routledge.

Couldry, N. (2008). Media discourse and the naturalisation of categories. In R. Wodak and V. Koller (eds.), *Handbook of communication in the public sphere,* Vol. 4, 67–88. Berlin: Mouton de Gruyter.

Craig, G. (2013). How does a prime minister speak? Kevin Rudd's discourse, habitus, and negotiation of the journalistic and political fields. *Journal of Language and Politics* 12(4): 485–507.

Dahlberg, L. and Phelan, S. (2011). *Discourse theory and critical media politics.* Basingstoke: Palgrave Macmillan.

Deacon, D., Pickering, M., Golding, P. and Murdock, G. (2007). *Researching communications: A practical guide to methods in media and cultural analysis.* London: Bloomsbury.

Edwards, E. B. (2016). "It's irrelevant to me!" Young Black women talk back to VH1's love and Hip Hop New York. *Journal of Black Studies.* DOI: 10.1177/0021934715627124

Eriksson, G. (2015). Ridicule as a strategy for the recontextualization of the working class: A multimodal analysis of class-making on Swedish reality television. *Critical Discourse Studies* 12(1): 20–38.

Erjavec, K. and Kovačič, M. P. (2013). Abuse of online participatory journalism in Slovenia: Offensive comments under news items. *Medij. istraž.* 19(2): 55–73.

Fairclough, N. (1989). *Language and power.* London: Longman.

Fairclough, N. (1992). *Discourse and social change.* Cambridge: Polity.

Fairclough, N. (1995). *Media discourse.* London: Arnold.

Fairclough, N. (2002). Language in new capitalism. *Discourse and Society* 13(2): 163–166.

Fairclough, N. (2003). *Analysing discourse: Textual analysis for social research.* London: Routledge.

Fairclough, N. (2006). *Language and globalization.* London: Routledge.

Fairclough, N. and Wodak. R. (1997). Critical discourse analysis. In T.A. van Dijk (ed.), *Discourse as social interaction: Discourse studies: A multidisciplinary introduction,* Vol. 2, 258–284. Thousand Oaks, CA: Sage.

Fenton, N. (2006). Bridging the mythical divide: Political economy and cultural studies approaches to the analysis of the media. In E. Devereux (ed.), *Media studies: Key issues and debates,* 7–27. London: Sage.

Finlayson, A. (2012). Rhetoric and the political theory of ideologies. *Political Studies* 60(4): 751–767.

Foucault, M. (2008). *The birth of biopolitics: Lectures at the Collège de France, 1978–1979.* Basingstoke: Palgrave Macmillan.

Fowler, R. (1991). *Language in the News: Discourse and Ideology in the Press.* London: Routledge.

Fürsich, E. (2009). In defense of textual analysis: Restoring a challenged method for journalism and media studies. *Journalism Studies* 10(2): 238–252.

Gabrielatos, C. and Baker, P. (2008). Fleeing, sneaking, flooding: A corpus analysis of discursive constructions of refugees and asylum seekers in the UK press, 1996–2005. *Journal of English Linguistics* 36(1): 5–38.

Glynos, J. and Howarth, D. (2007). *Logics of critical explanation in social and political theory*. London: Routledge.

Graham, P. (2002). Hypercapitalism: Language, new media and social perceptions of value. *Discourse & Society* 13(2): 227–249.

Hall, S. (1980). Encoding/decoding. In S. Hall, D. Hobson, A. Lowe and P. Willis (eds.), *Culture, media, language: Working papers in cultural studies, 1972–1979,* 128–138. London: Routledge.

Hall, S. (1988). *The hard road to renewal: Thatcherism and the crisis of the left*. London: Verso.

Hall, S., Critcher, C., Jefferson, T., Clarke, J. and Roberts, B. (2013). *Policing the crisis: Mugging, the state and law and order,* 35th anniversary edn. Basingstoke: Palgrave Macmillan.

Kelsey, D. (2013). The myth of the "Blitz spirit" in British newspaper responses to the July 7th bombings. *Social Semiotics* 23(1): 83–99.

Laclau, E. and Mouffe, C. (1990). Post-Marxism without apologies. In E. Laclau (ed.), *New reflections on the revolution of our time,* 97–132. London: Verso.

Louw, E. (2005). *The media and political process*. London: Sage.

Macgilchrist, F. and Van Hout, Tom. (2011). Ethnographic discourse analysis and social science. *Forum: Qualitative Social Research* 12(1). www.qualitative-research.net/index.php/fqs/article/view/1600

Machin, D. (2013). What is multimodal critical discourse studies? *Critical Discourse Studies* 10(4): 347–355.

Machin, D. and Niblock, S. (2008). Branding newspapers. *Journalism Studies* 9(2): 244–259.

Mendes, K. (2012). "Feminism rules! Now, where's my swimsuit?": Re-evaluating feminist discourse in print media 1968–2008. *Media, Culture & Society* 34(5): 554–570.

Molina, P. S. (2009). Critical analysis of discourse and of the media: Challenges and shortcomings. *Critical Discourse Studies* 6(3): 185–198.

O'Brien, D. (2013). Presidency ill-served by economic partnership. *The Irish Times,* September 20. www.irishtimes.com

Olausson, U. (2014). The diversified nature of "domesticated" news discourse: The case of climate change in national news media. *Journalism Studies* 15(6): 711–725.

Peck, J. (2010). *Constructions of neoliberal reason*. Oxford: Oxford University Press.

Phelan, S. (2014). *Neoliberalism, media and the political*. Basingstoke: Palgrave Macmillan.

Phelan, S. (2016). Reinvigorating ideology critique. *Media, Culture & Society* 38(2): 274–283.

Philo, G. (2007). Can discourse analysis successfully explain the content of media and journalistic practice? *Journalism Studies* 8(2): 175–196.

Philo, G. and Miller, D. (2000). Cultural compliance and critical media studies. *Media, Culture, & Society* 22(6): 831–839.

Price. S. (2010). *Brute reality: Power, discourse and the mediation of war*. London: Pluto.

Richardson, J. E. (2007). *Analysing newspapers: An approach from critical discourse analysis*. Basingstoke, Palgrave Macmillan.

Roderick, I. (2013). Representing robots as living labour in advertisements: The new discourse of worker – employer power relations. *Critical Discourse Studies* 10(4): 392–405.

Rogers, R. (2004, May). Interview with Norman Fairclough. In Companion Website to R. Rogers (ed.), *An introduction to critical discourse analysis in education*. New York: Routledge. http://cw.routledge.com/textbooks/9780415874298

Scannell, P. (1998). Media-language-world. In A. Bell and P. Garrett (eds.), *Approaches to media discourse*. Oxford: Blackwell.

Scannell, P. (2013). *Television and the meaning of "live": An enquiry into the human situation*. Cambridge: Polity.

Schröter, M. (2015). 80,000,000 Hooligans: Discourse of resistance to racism and xenophobia in German punk lyrics 1991–1994. *Critical Discourse Studies* 12(4): 398–425.

Teo, P. (2000). Racism in the news: A critical discourse analysis of news reporting in two Australian newspapers. *Discourse & Society* 11(1): 7–4.

van Dijk, T. A. (1991). *Racism and the press*. London: Routledge.

van Dijk, T. A. (2015). Critical discourse studies. In D. Tannen, H. E. Hamilton and D. Schriffin, D. (eds.), *The handbook of discourse analysis*. Wiley Blackwell: Oxford.

Wittgenstein, L. (1973). *Philosophical investigations*. Oxford: Blackwell.

Wodak, R. (2009). *The discourse of politics in action: Politics as usual*. Basingstoke: Palgrave Macmillan.

20

Critical discourse analysis and history

Mariana Achugar

[Our] task is to brush history against the grain.

Walter Benjamin

The past has become an area of focus for CDA. What does the past mean today? How is the past used to serve current political agendas? How do we use the past to give meaning to ourselves as individuals and members of groups? "A historiographical approach to (critical) discourse analysis will seek to reveal the hidden assumptions in received and naturalized historical accounts, with a particular emphasis on the language used in their elaboration" (Flowerdew 2012: 17). Investigating discourses about the past opens up a space to explore the dynamic nature of meaning-making practices. Exploring the construction of the meanings of the past involves focusing on representations and receptions of discourses. When making meaning, we give continuity to our experience beyond an instance connecting past, present and future. In every instance our actions make history impacting others, but at the same time we are affected by the actions of others with whom we coexist and who have come before. The discourses about our experience as historical beings foreground or background certain parts of this phenomenon. The discourses construct a narrative of heroes or victims. However, from a critical perspective our objective is to construct a past that is quotable in all of its moments (Benjamin 1968) making visible hegemonic and counter-hegemonic narratives that form part of larger power struggles.

The past is not there for us to collect as a pre-existing object; it has to be constructed through semiotic work. The practices connected to the construction of the past require social actors' work in identity-building processes that link us to social groups such as a family, a political group or a nation. Discourses about the past occur in social practices associated with everyday experiences like sharing anecdotes in a family, but also in more institutionalized practices such as the writing of history textbooks.

What discourses about the past are naturalized? How are discursive practices used to reproduce or challenge dominant representations of the past? What are the hegemonic discourses of the past in particular cases? How are counter-hegemonic views about the past dealt with in public discourses? How do young people who did not experience contested past events learn about them? How are discourses about the past used to construct national identities? These are some of the questions that CDA researchers have explored from a historiographical approach (Flowerdew 2012).

Historiographical CDA has explored the representations of the past as content and practice. This dual aspect of discourses about the past entails investigating how they are produced and received, but also exploring those discourses that deal with contested pasts. The exploration of discourses about situations that have contemporary political and moral impact has provided a critical lens to our understandings of the meaning and uses of the past.

The CDA historiographical approach aims to contribute to our understanding of the (re) production of inequality and discrimination in contemporary societies. Focusing on the uses of the past to (re)produce power differences, in the ways in which official history silences victims, or in how states and institutions erase their responsibility for violations of human rights; work in this area has shown the destructive use of history. But the critique has also been expanded to go beyond demystification to raising critical awareness to provide alternative readings of the past. Taking on these challenges researchers have responded as scholars and also citizens by brushing history against the grain.

Memory, history and historiography

How is history made? Historiography focuses on the construction of historical discourse. However, the study of the discourses of the past is not the monopoly of historians; several fields of study are devoted to this endeavor. Looking at some key issues in the interdisciplinary exploration of the past enables us to understand the contributions CDA can make to this area of investigation.

Work in historiography has identified *representation* as a key issue in the construction of discourse about the past. The discourse about the past is defined by an *aporia* of the presence of something that is absent marked by temporal distance (Ricoeur 2010). Discourses about the past (re)construct events that occurred in a different time and in that process make a distinction between past and present. This representation is not the past, so as a present construction of the meaning of that past event it is shaped by the circumstances in which it is produced "[. . .] the very problem of historiographical work: the relation between the 'meaning' which has become an object, and the 'meaning' which today allows it to be understood as such" (de Certeau 1988: 34). This dilemma has been explored through two constructs: memory and history.

The distinction between these different types of discourses about the past has pointed out different types of experiences with the past – memory more connected with the lived experience (testimony), and history more related with the reformulation of this experience into a scientific discourse. These two types of discourses about the past make different claims: memory attempts to be faithful to the past, while history aims to be truthful. At the representational level, there is also a difference in the space and time where these two types of discourse are produced. Memory represents lived time and space (*I was there*), while history represents the locus of enunciation of the historian (*someone somewhere did something*). Memory is focused on continuity while history foregrounds change and the reasons for change. However, both discourses serve to show the dialectics of understanding the present through the past and the past through the present. Our position as the one remembering or making history shapes the meaning of the past we construct. Memory and history are related in various ways.

First, memories constitute the raw material for the construction of historical discourse. The *testimony* becomes the *document* by indexing a past that is larger. History uses those reconfigurations of testimony as documents to extend the remembering process and correct it. Memories are fragments of the past that history brings together to explain their meaning. From this perspective the transformation that memories undergo in the historical operation combine documentation, explanation and representation. This process includes choices and interpretation throughout these operations that are determined by the location of the historian. Taking a critical perspective on historical discourse requires us to connect history to its place of production. These places of production produce silencing effects (Trouillot 1995). Historiographical research is produced from certain socioeconomic, political and cultural locations. So we not only need to consider what history says about a society, but also the function history serves in it (de Certeau 1988).

Memory and history are also different in terms of knowledge status and social legitimacy. Different contexts afford different value to these two forms of making meaning about the past. One gains its power from the closeness to the past, while the other from its distance. In different situations, arguments that are based on *having been there* or *documentary proof* produce different legitimacy. For example, in the court of law or in a Truth and Reconciliation commission witness testimony is a legitimate source of validation for an argument. On the other hand, in academic debates, documentary proof and checking alternative perspectives become more valid sources of authority. These are important problems to consider, because they represent knowledge construction spaces where critical approaches provide a lens to look at power issues and the reproduction of inequality in debates about the past. For example, debates about the veracity of witnesses accounts (e.g., Rigoberta Menchú's case)[3] or the questioning of the Holocaust based on *historical relativity* and the literary nature of historical discourse have pointed out the need to explore the processes of production of knowledge about the past.

Within historiography there have been several debates about what constitutes historical knowledge. The epistemological uniqueness of historical knowledge as different from fiction was being explicitly debated following Barthes's (1981[1967]) and White's (1973) foregrounding of history's use of narrative and rhetorical tropes to emplot events and construct the past. This debate brought up issues related to the access to the "real", and accuracy of representation, but also the problem of relativity. If historical discourse is only fabricated constructions of the past, then what happens with the traces and effects of those events on people? What is the moral consequence of saying that all narratives are equally possible? These debates resulted in arguments that brought up the importance of acknowledging the process of production and practices of historians, and not just the end product (i.e., narrative). It is important to differentiate between *what occurred* and *what has been said to occur,* even when the difference between the two is ambiguous and contingent (Trouillot 1995). To get to the narrative that presents history as a complete and closed story, historians analyze traces, engage in documentary production and evaluate different sources to come up with an interpretation and write up a history (de Certeau 1988; Ricoeur 2010). These debates about historical knowledge pointed to its uniqueness; it is indirect, indexical and conjectural (Ginzburg 1992). Historical knowledge is constructed through semiotic practices that allow the interpretation of traces as indexes of social meanings. But many of these traces are concrete (i.e., dead bodies, monuments, diaries) and they limit the variety and significance of historical narratives (Trouillot 1995).

Some historians' practices provide a systematic method that allows the identification of change, but also of lasting structures. For example, looking at the past at different time scales enables us to explore the dialectic nature of our historical experience. The principle of variation of scales allows historians to show how different scales provide various details and levels of complexity. The variation of scales allows a focus on microhistory and macrohistory as diverse perspectives that provide different information about the meaning of the past. Structure, moment and event as different scales become interdependent making historical interpretation more probabilistic (Ginzburg 1992; Ricoeur 2010). "History is only able to recognize what continually changes, and what is new, if it has access to the conventions within which lasting structures are concealed" (Koselleck 2004: 275). Thus, we need to incorporate different scalar perspectives when exploring the meanings of the past.

Scales operate as conceptual metaphors that integrate time and space in historical discourse/thinking. The understanding of historical time as a form of consciousness enables us to think of individuals as historical beings with agency and not only as conditioned by social structures. The recognition of human agency in the making of history makes visible the difficulty of constructing a global and totalizing history. This also means that our knowledge of the past is subject to historical time, thus it is always provisional and open to revision. Historical knowledge performs a political function distinguishing scholarly work from that of the common people. But it is also the product of particular contingencies and interests. "There is no history that can be constituted independently of the experiences and expectations of active human agents" (Koselleck 2004: 256).

The circulation and reception of discourse about the past has also been integral to the investigation of history. Passing on the experience of others or oneself, as well as understanding the experience of others, are inter-subjective processes (Halbwachs 1992; Welzer 2010; Wertsch 2002) mediated by semiotic resources. Remembering involves discursive practices by which social actors in interaction with subjects and objects through time and space give meaning to the past. These meaning-making processes involve power differences and collective symbolic practices that problematize the notion of discourse of the past as homogenous and constant. The duration and the permanence of certain discourses in particular groups or times makes visible the plurality and multiplicity of temporality in social phenomena. In anthropological terms, "any 'history' constitutes itself through oral and written communication between generations that live together and convey their own respective experiences to one another" (Koselleck 2002: 27). This means we need to explore not only representations of the past, but also the processes by which these representations circulate. These aspects open up a space to explore issues of appropriation and contestation of hegemonic discourses about the past.

From these transdisciplinary explorations, we can derive some principles that inform the investigation of discourses about the past. CDA from a historiographical approach needs to:

1   contextualize representations of the past in social practices
2   locate the context of production of historical discourse
3   investigate the context of reception of discourse about the past
4   explore varying scales and indexical meanings of discourses about the past
5   consider claims to legitimacy, valuing and social distribution of discourse about the past

CDA studies have considered these principles when exploring contested discourses about the past. The critical discursive approach provides a complementary perspective to the work of other disciplines by focusing on the semiotic aspects of history. CDA provides a detailed description and interpretation of the role of discursive practices, strategies and linguistic patterns that characterize the construction of hegemonic and counter-hegemonic discourses about the past. The main contributions of CDA are to show *what* semiotic resources are deployed to construct the past and *how* discourses of the past are used to serve particular present agendas. This type of analysis also provides detailed information about the types of meanings made in discourses about the past that can potentially serve as evidence or historical document data (also see Flowerdew 2012). In the following section, we will look at some emblematic examples of historiographical CDA that have focused on discourses about contested recent pasts.

Contested pasts and CDA

The interrelation between the actions and interpretations of a community produce the discourse about the past. The construction of contested pasts requires a semiotic mediation of experience that not only represents, but also orients and organizes meanings. These meanings are always tentative, and open to revision because historical knowledge is co-constructed and validated by a community. The construction of discourses about the past is an active process. The meanings of discourses are not found in a text, but in the processes by which complex semiotic relations between discourses and readers/authors are made. CDA has explored the ways in which people make history and shape their historical consciousness in contested contexts.

There is extensive work on the historical discourse that has identified the lexico-grammatical and discourse-semantic features that characterize this type of discourse (e.g., Coffin 2006; Martin 2003; Martin, Maton and Matruglio 2010; Unsworth 1999; Schleppe-grell 2004). They have identified a taxonomy of history genres, distinct lexico-semantic patterns that map onto different types of texts, and key linguistic features such as nominalization of social actors and periods, reasoning within the clause through verbs, as well as ambiguous use of conjunctions. This work offers a manner to theorize the way in which historical meanings and knowledge are constructed through language.

There is a growing scholarship in CDA that explores contested discourses about the past (e.g., Anthonissen and Blommaert 2007; Bietti 2014; Galasińska and Galasińska 2010; Heer et al. 2008; Oteíza and Pinto 2011; Richardson and Wodak 2009; Verdoolaege 2008; Wodak and Richardson 2013). In this section, I will review some emblematic examples of this scholarship. The examples have been selected because they represent a variety of cases from around the world and methodological contributions to our understanding of the role of discourse in the construction of the past. The focal studies are presented in chronological order.

Schiffrin (2001) focuses on the use of the term "concentration camp" in an exhibition about the Japanese internment camps in the US during the second world war and in particular to the reaction of the Jewish community to the use of that term. Using a comparative method and a corpus that includes catalogs, dictionaries, academic texts, memoirs, newspapers and handouts from the exhibition, the analysis centers on intertextuality, narrative, rhetorical figures, presuppositions and reference. The findings show that collective narratives about the events resolve the conflict negotiating the meaning of the term by diluting the agency and responsibility of those involved in the events. The analysis identifies the linguistic configurations used to attribute roles (i.e., victim vs. perpetrator; witness vs. observer), focalizes the events through the use of nominalizations (Nazi camps as places of torture), represents actors in functional terms through metonymy (i.e., perpetrators as countries) and elides responsibility through passive constructions. The interpretation of the debate shows the controversy is resolved by comparisons and definitions with different hierarchical co-occurrence patterns such that "concentration camp" implies "internment camp" but not the reverse. The meaning of "concentration camps" is a dispute over how to construct collective history.

Wodak (2006) deals with collective and individual memories in Austria in connection with an exhibition about the Wehrmacht. The study focuses on the argumentative patterns of justification and legitimation on narratives about the Wehrmacht. Using a corpus of interviews conducted by Ruth Beckerman to people who attended the exhibition, Wodak shows how intergenerational transmission occurs across three generations (the participants, their children and grandchildren). The analysis centers on interdiscursivity, intertextuality and recontextualization as discursive mechanisms for the transmission of memory. The findings show that there are a variety of strategies to construct positive self-presentation and positioning as victim to construct a positive image. The legitimation strategies and justification arguments vary across generations. There is avoidance of the topic, normalization of the situation, and relativization or trivialization of events. Family narratives are used directly or indirectly to authorize discourse by connecting speakers to the actual experience. There are also recurrent topoi used in the argumentation that problematize historical knowledge and dispute the concept of "war crimes".

Blommaert, Bock and McCormick (2007) focus on South Africa's Truth and Reconciliation Commission victim hearings as a site where pre-existing inequalities persisted and were expressed in the degree of "hearability" of the testimonies. The authors use the concept of *pretextuality* to explain the relative hearability of different stories in connection with the varying degrees of competence in language varieties, narrative skills and literacy. The analysis situates the testimonies and the TRC in the larger social, political and cultural contexts that provide a frame to the performances. They look at the historicity of the discourses, foregrounding the fact that all meaning in discourse is historical, pointing to the social meanings that go beyond those that are linguistically articulated. Focusing on intertextuality and the different legitimacy that specific forms of discourse have in a particular context they show how in the TRC, despite the favorable circumstances, the voices of the subalterns were not necessarily heard beyond the immediate context of the trials. Because the communicative resources used (e.g., dialect or slang use), expressing high emotion, using stylistic devices that were considered folkloric and failing to meet expectations of iconicity (e.g., not using emotion in a narrative of suffering) were seen as inappropriate; the discourses did not achieve "hearability". But this was a dialogic process, the interlocutors, those leading the proceedings, utilized discursive strategies that reshaped the witnesses' accounts by contextualizing them, extending the narrative, staging the performances and concluding the testimony for them. This process produced different effects from those that the speakers wanted to convey, making their stories not hearable because there was no uptake from the audience. The testimonies were not recognized in the intended way in the public sphere as they were read differently in the context of production and reception. Those testimonies closest to contemporary generic, moral, and political expectations were considered "memorable".

Martin (2008) explores how a children's book about the Kokoda campaign during the Pacific war between Australia and Japan constructs reconciliation in multi-modal ways. The story constructs the parallel story of two soldiers, a Japanese and an Australian one. The multimodal analysis relates images and text focusing on genre, thematic progression, agency and evaluation. The findings show that the flow of information provides a balanced amount of space and time to Australians and Japanese. However, agency is constructed through middle voice as being caused from the inside, and marking it as a feature of things more than people. The representation of the Japanese mitigates their role as aggressors in the region. However, the representation gives the Australian soldier more than double the agency than is given to the Japanese. The Japanese, on the other hand, are represented as directly attacking the Australian soldier. However, the Japanese soldier is humanized, encoding more affective evaluations in connection to them. Family pictures are used to align the reader with the protagonists. The soldiers look directly at the reader and establish contact with the audience. The use of monochrome and sepia colors creates distance in time. At the end, the images of the book represent reconciliation in literal terms through photographs of the real soldiers. There is also an analysis of *bondicons,* icons that invoke ideologies in condensed ways, such as the use of national flowers to convey nationalist ideologies or family pictures as a universal human experience everyone can connect to. The visual and narrative meanings complement each other and cooperate to construct the discourse of reconciliation.

Flowerdew (2012) examines how the past was created by politicians, museum curators, journalists and the general public in Hong Kong's transition from British colony to Special Administrative Region of China. It is a diachronic study from the period 1992–1999 intended to capture what stays the same and what changes. The data comes from a broad range of sources: participant observation, interviews, documents, public pronouncements, museum exhibition and branding materials. The analyses focus on conditions of production and of reception exploring the linguistic choices in the texts. The analytic tools used include: rhetorical tropes (metaphors, metonymy) as argumentative devices, footing and participation framework, genre and intertextuality as well as corpus linguistic techniques. The findings of the analyses are integrated to show how discursive formations are constructed through the interplay of discourses about the past coming from various social actors. A unique feature of this work is the exploration of intercultural and multilingual communication aspects in the process of constructing identities and national discourses that use the past. The study shows how official discourses changed during the period of transition, but remained the same in others. Political discourse became more in line with mainland China ideologies, but in connection to economic issues the official position has remained constant (international center of trade and finance). The historical approach of this study reveals how political discourse in Hong Kong developed over time and how identity is a site for power struggles and resistance. A distinctive feature of this historiographical approach is the claim that "there is a role for discourse analysis in the writing of history" (Flowerdew 2012: 17) to create critical readings of events over time.

Oteíza (2014) explores the semantic resources used in Chilean history textbooks to negotiate intertextuality in the discourse about the recent past. There is a particular focus on the way in which official discourses about violations of human rights (i.e., Rettig report and Valech Report) and the collective memories that circulate in society are recontextualized in historical explanations of pedagogical discourse. Using the concept of intertextuality, the author shows the link between evaluation of events and participants to create topological semantic regions of attitudes that flow one into another. The analysis demonstrates how history textbooks intertextually connected to the construction of explanations about the violations of human rights during the latest dictatorship in Chile (1973–1990). These intertextual links function as interpersonal negotiations of attitudes that originate in collective memories, individual opinions and official government documents.

Contributions of CDA to historiography

These emblematic studies demonstrate, how the exploration of discourses of the past has yielded interesting analytic resources developing and expanding notions of *intertextuality, recontextualization* and *resemiotization.* In addition, there is a diachronic perspective exploring a historical phenomenon or case throughout time. Thus, some of the actual research techniques used are transdisciplinary, borrowing from the practices of historians and historical sociologists. The object of study is also historical in the sense of exploring *change* and the dynamic nature of discourse in relation to the construction of orders of discourse (Foucault 1969; Fairclough 1992).

One of the most representative examples of the contributions of this line of work to CDA and historiography is the Discourse-Historical Method (e.g., Wodak et al. 1999). This method provides a clear description of how to integrate historical context to critical discourse analysis highlighting the importance of historicity to understand the continuities of discourses. The method highlights the importance of scales by modeling different levels of context to situate the discourse analysis. Triangulation of different types of data to make the corpus including ethnographic fieldwork is another distinctive feature. Among the conceptual apparatus of DHM, intertextuality is a key concept used in this method to trace the relation and development of constructions of the past across time and space. Discursive strategies such as legitimatition, argumentation and topoi are typically explored together with more lexico-grammatical features that realize agency. This method also requires an interdisciplinary group to provide depth of interpretation and various perspectives on the topic.

Another important contribution to historiography in CDA has come from work informed by linguistic anthropology (e.g., Blommaert 2003; Blommaert et al. 2007). These contributions have foregrounded the importance of situating discourse in its context of production and reception as well as in history. Historical layering is one of the ways in which this historicity has been addressed. This work attempts to capture the layered simultaneity and historicity in synchronic studies of discourses (Blommaert 2005), using concepts such as indexicality, recontextualization and re-entextualization (Silverstein and Urban 1996; Bauman and Briggs 1990). The importance of ethnography is also evident in the situated nature of this type of work. This approach also foregrounds the significance of place as a category used to create and recreate ways of connecting and belonging anchored in particular geographic or imagined spaces.

Analyzing the construction of the past: family conversations about the Uruguayan dictatorship

This illustration comes from a linguistic ethnography (Achugar 2016) that explored how young people learn about the most recent dictatorship in Uruguay (1973–1985)[4] in different contexts. These youths came into contact with discourses about the past that enabled them to engage in semiotic work connecting past and present. In this section, I analyze one family interview out of a collection of 20 conducted during 2010. The goal is to investigate the process through which representations and orientations to a recent traumatic past are constructed in situated forms of participation.

Why do family conversations matter in processes of intergenerational transmission? Family narratives provide a context to create and re-create individual and group identity. Families have different styles for reminiscing and these differences affect how individuals remember (Fivush 2008). Family conversations have been one of the practices studied to understand how youth are socialized into political discourse in the private sphere (e.g., George 2013; Gordon 2004; Ochs and Taylor 1992) and also to explore how the historical self develops (Wineburg et al. 2007).

The social purpose of anecdotes is to share an emotional reaction through a sequence of events that is out of the ordinary concluding with the protagonist's reaction. (Martin and Rose 2008: 56). This type of personal narrative can be defined by a number of discursive features: chronology, evaluation and a moral stance (Ochs and Capps 2001). The participation framework (Goffman 1981) arrangement includes a teller and an author (the one whose experience is being recounted). These roles can be distributed among several people depending on the community. The listeners can be involved in different ways including being an attentive audience, posing questions or supplying details.

This example belongs to a family with a left-leaning political ideology. In this section of the interviews, participants were invited to share what they talked about when they conversed about the dictatorship in their families. Many of the interviewees stated that the topic did not typically emerge as part of family conversations. However, several pointed out that current events and political discussions served as triggers to bring the past back to life. The following anecdote was retold in the interview and provides an illustration of one of the ways in which personal narratives are used to make sense of the past in the context of the family.

Diego's case

Diego was a 16-year-old who attended a public high school in an economically disadvantaged neighborhood. He was not a very good student, but he participated in several extra-curricular activities including private English lessons and soccer. His future plans involved becoming a professional soccer player. His father was in his early forties and was an active union member working in a specialized chemical factory. Diego had a younger brother. The conversation took place at their home.[5] Diego (DIE) and his father (FAT) recount a family anecdote about the dictatorship.

*FAT: <Ah (.) and> later on you have (.) you heard (.) don't you remember (.) I mean (.) the anecdotes of the [/] of your uncles when [/] when (.) well they went out and [/] they went out to[/] to [/] walk and the [/] the milicos [military] would bust you. &=laughs.

*DIE: Ah (.) yes (.) when *you told me that* (..) that you had to go around with a little book that [///] as if you were working (.) or else they would <arrest you>.

*FAT: <the certificate> of work.

*DIE: The certificate of work.

*INV: Because they would arrest you?

*DIE: They would arrest you. And well (.) *I remember that* (..) that grandma went to get you.

*FAT: Mhm.

*DIE: *Grandma went to get you in ja(jail)* [/] to prison [.] to the jailhouse.

*FAT: Yes.

*DIE: *You were with your cousin or: I don't know who.*

*FAT: With Gustavo who is now in Spain. =&laughs.

*DIE: It is Ela?

*DAT: Nah (.) later.

*FAT: *We were [/] we were [/] (.) well (.) we had gone (.) I mean (.) this (.) from work and [/] and (.) well (.) and (. . .) they took us.*&=laughs. well (.) at that. . . it wasn't so much the period of the dictatorship (.) I mean (.) because we already were. . . . But (.) well (.) I remember that they took us. Well (.) because there were still some [///] some (.) well (.) eh (.) regulations from <that time (.)> right?

*INV: <Sure 9.) that had not> changed.

*FAT: well (.) they had not changed. So (.) we were talking maybe about eighty four (. . .) <yes (.) eighty four (.) eighty five it was (.) around that time.

*INV: <and it was still (.) yes (.) yes (.)> yes.

*FAT: well (.) and (.) ok (.) eh (.) I didn't have that work permit and that day I told him (.) anyways even if I had shown the permit (.) the documents (.) all of it (.) we were [/] with the clothes from work (.) I mean (.) and anyway they brought us down. Good bye (.) they took us anyway. Well (.) and they had us for all of [/] a complete night there until the next day in the morning when they called my old lady and the mo (mother) [/] the mother of my [///] my [/] my aunt. And (.) well (.) ok (.) and there they [/] they set us free.

The exchange begins with the father offering an example of a potential anecdote to elaborate on the uncle's story (line 1–3). The father positions the son as knowing and encourages him to remember a particular event, "Don't you remember", "You heard" (line 1). However, the way he refers to it represents the anecdote as a general type of experience marked by the choice of indefinite past (imperfect), "*salían* a caminar y los milicos te *llevaban* en cana" [you went out for a walk and the milicos (military) would bust you] (lines 2–3). Diego accepts his father's request to continue with the narration of the family anecdote and here we see the shift in point of view, going from the uncle's experience (third person plural) to the father's experience (second person singular) (lines 4–5). However, the use of the second person singular continues providing the anecdote with an ambiguous status as both personal and impersonal. The second person singular impersonal construction that gives the anecdote a general meaning valid for the period beyond the family's experience is supported by the use of the imperfect, which also makes the events undefined in the past. The son's rendition paraphrases, through an indirect report, the gist of the story, but changes the source to the father (line 4). This anecdote includes the series of events evaluated negatively with a moral consequence that positions the military as irrational. Father and son then repeat the phrase, "the work permit" aligning themselves in the evaluation of the experience and its meaning by using the same label to refer to it (lines 6–7).

In the next turn, the son elaborates the anecdote, focusing on more details of a particular instance of this general anecdote (lines 9–16). His father's experience as protagonist of the anecdote brings in another voice as source, Diego himself. His recollection is then presented as legitimate and as valid as that of the direct participants in the events. He reconstructs the story and the father validates his narrative by offering minimal support ("Sí", laughing and providing some details in lines 13 and 15). The leading role as teller and author is that of the son, even though it is not his experience being reconstructed he is the one whose point of view is being animated. The son then opens up the space for the father to take on the leading role as teller by positioning himself as not knowing the details ("you were with your cousin or I don't know who", line 14). This allows the father to come in as a source that has more legitimacy for having been the direct protagonist of the events. The father's narration shifts the point of view to an inclusive third person plural that connects the first anecdote with this one, " we were (..) we had come out of work and they took us" (lines 18–19). This reformulation of the anecdote provides more details and a different point of view, but the same evaluation. The different versions of the anecdote provide a deeper understanding of what it was like to live at that time ("eighty four", "we had the work uniforms") (lines 24–32), and reinforce the negative evaluation of the dictatorship as a period where they would put you in jail for petty bureaucratic reasons like not having your paperwork despite being grimy and in work clothes.

Father and son co-construct the anecdote, in the process changing the teller role and the participation framework. The teller is first only an animator that revoices another's experience using indirect speech. Then there is a superposition of points of view by which they move into the teller and author being conflated using first person point of view and indirect discourse to project what has happened. There is alignment in terms of the evaluations and also an explicit identification of the voices that are brought to bear in the narrative. The direct appeal to the memories of the indirect witness (son hearing stories from direct sources) and the protagonist (the father) provide legitimacy to the story; however, there seems to be more weight given to the protagonists' perspective (as evidenced by the son deferring to the father for getting more details).

The transformation of the personal into public makes the anecdote an exemplary story from which we can learn about what life was like in the dictatorship, not just this particular family's life story. Throughout the conversation there is a negative evaluation of the dictatorship that highlights the random implementation of rules by those in power, which made individuals subject to illogical regulations. This is the moral teaching of the anecdote that provides an interpretative framework to make sense of the past linking individual experience and larger historical events.

The representations of the past constructed in these anecdotes serve as grounding to back the moral stance held by the participants. The anecdotes are told from different points of view that provide a variety of framings: witness, protagonist, indirect witness and impersonal voice. These points of view are realized through a variety of discursive resources including: direct and indirect discourse, past narrative voice, hypothetical past in the future (subjunctive and conditional). Even though the anecdotes are constructed using different discursive resources, their rhetorical function is similar: supporting the moral stance through evaluations that produce different levels of distance in interpersonal terms. These variations in interpersonal distance produce effects in terms of the power, affective involvement and familiarity of the participants with the past. These representations thus serve the speakers' interpersonal orientations to the past constructing axiological communities. As shown above, parents and children tend to share their evaluations and moral stance in relation to the dictatorship, even when they do not share the same level of detail in terms of information. In most cases, parents and youth co-construct the anecdotes to produce a unified representation and orientation to the past. However, youth sometimes bring in anecdotes from other spheres of experience to support or challenge the family's stance.

The most important function of these family conversations is their role in passing on a moral stance towards the dictatorship, more than an "accurate" or "historically based" representation of the past. The opportunities to construct meanings together and explore the different layers of semiotic meaning allow youth to expand their understanding of the past. On the other hand, cultural reproduction through the passing on of personal narratives like anecdotes becomes less important in terms of understanding the actual historical facts and more about aligning in terms of evaluations of that past.

In family conversations about the recent past, there is an attempt to "reanimate" or "re-perform" key cultural texts (Silverstein and Urban 1996) highlighting the fact that there are certain grand narratives about the dictatorship that occupy a special position in the social imaginary of the period. Anecdotes function as a tool for transduction, the process that makes the recent past transmittable across generations to serve present needs at different scales (i.e., family identity or socio-political positions).

Conclusions

Considering current historical processes that have produced political turmoil, transnational communities and migration, there is a continued need for historiographical CDA. To understand the uniqueness of historical moments, we need to situate them in larger landscapes of time and space. Future historiographical CDA needs to continue developing analytic methods and concepts that allow us to explore the socially distributed nature of discourses about the past. It is important that more work integrates not only the analysis of representations in particular texts or instances, but also the processes and social practices where the past is constructed. The exploration of intertextual positionings and dialogism appear to be fertile areas to expand our work. It will be also important to integrate the circulation and reception of meanings to the study of discourses of the past. This requires that we conduct more ethnographic work to be able to situate text and explore how they are used across time and space. In addition, multi-modal analyses will be important in capturing the multisemiotic meaning-making practices that are used to construct the past. Critical work in this area needs to focus also on comparing across cases to learn about the hegemonic and counter-hegemonic practices that enable uses of the past to serve present-day agendas. Collaborations in multidisciplinary groups organized around an area of interest will be key to exploring the complexity of these processes.

Acknowledgements

I would like to thank Miranda Carpenter-Achugar for her editing and suggestions. I also benefited from Brian Carpenter's comments; all the problems and mistakes left are my sole responsibility.

Notes

1 Thanks to the editors for feedback on an earlier draft and to Ian Goodwin for helping me clarify the argument.
2 Put simply, the political economy/cultural studies debate involved a disagreement about the relative role of economic processes, versus culture and discourse, in the constitution of social and media structures (see Berglez 2006; Fenton 2006). Political economy scholars affirmed the centrality of a Marxist analysis of capitalism, while cultural studies scholars embraced (then novel) post-structuralist and post-modernist theories.
3 Rigoberta Menchú's testimony written by Elizabeth Burgos provided a first-person account of the army's genocide of the indigenous population in Guatemala. The veracity and legitimacy of this testimony was later challenged by some academics questioning the "truth" and political investment of *testimonio* as a genre. See Arturo Arias (ed.) (2001) *The Rigoberta Menchú Controversy*.
4 At the political, public and educational level the period of the dictatorship is still a controversial topic in Uruguay. There are two narratives about the dictatorship that circulate in the public sphere: one that establishes that the events are the result of a confrontation between the guerrilla and the armed forces ("the theory of two demons", Demasi 2004); and the other, that explains the coup d'état as the result of a gradual deterioration of democratic institutions since the beginning of the 1960s caused by multiple causes (e.g., deep social and economic crisis, lack of strong political leadership, growing authoritarian practices and repression from the State, guerrilla movement activities, politization of the military and international influence). For more information about the Uruguayan case see Lessa (2013).
5 The participants provided informed consent to use parts of the interview when reporting the findings of this work.

Further reading

Flowerdew, J. (2012). *Critical discourse analysis in historiography: The case of Hong Kong's evolving political identity*. New York: Palgrave Macmillan. This book offers a variety of discourse analytic strategies to explore the changes in discourse practices used to reconstruct the past looking at the case of Hong Kong after British colonial rule.
Koselleck, R. (2004). *Futures past*. New York: Columbia University Press. This book provides a perspective on history as discourse. It is an introduction to the conceptual history approach where the historical dimensions of meaning and the complexities of historical concepts such as time and movement are explained.

Ricoeur, P. (2004). *Memory, history, forgetting*. Kathleen Blamey and David Pellauer (trans.). Chicago: University of Chicago Press. This book explores the rhetorical and hermeneutical traditions of thinking about discourses of the past.

Trouillot, M. (1995). *Silencing the past*. This book explores how history is written, how to account for silences in historiography as a form of discourse where erasure emerges as a commonly used strategy to construct the past.

Wodak, R. (2006). History in the making/The making of history: The 'German *Wehrmacht*' in collective and individual memories in Austria. *Journal of Language and Politics* 5(1): 125–154.

This article is an excellent example of the Discourse-Historical Approach. Methodologically the Discourse-Historical Approach places emphasis on the historical dimensions of meaning making. From a CDA perspective Wodak's work provides some of the more detailed and transdiciplinary approaches to understanding how Europeans have dealt with their Nazi past.

References

Achugar, M. (2016). *Discursive processes of intergenerational transmission of recent history: (Re)making our past*. New York: Palgrave MacMillan.

Anthonissen, C. and Blommaert, J. (eds.) (2007). *Critical linguistics perspectives on coping with traumatic pasts*, DAPSAC series. Amsterdam: Benjamins.

Arias, A. (ed.) (2001). *The Rigoberta Menchú controversy*. Minneapolis, MN: University of Minnesota Press.

Barthes, R. (1981). The discourse of history. *Comparative Criticism* 3: 7–20.

Bauman, R. and Briggs, C. (1990). Poetics and performance as critical perspectives on language and social life. *Annual Review of Anthropology* 19: 59–88.

Benjamin, W. (1968). Theses on the philosophy of history. In H. Arendt (ed.), *Illuminations: Walter Benjamin essays and reflections*, 253–264. New York: Schoken Books.

Bietti, L. (2014). *Discursive remembering: Individual and collective remembering as a discursive, cognitive and historical process*. Berlin: DeGruyter.

Blommaert, J. (2003). Orthopraxy, writing and identity. In J.R. Martin and R. Wodak (eds.), *Re/reading the past: Critical and functional perspectives on time and value*, 177–194. Amsterdam, Philadelphia: Benjamins.

Blommaert, J. (2005). *Discourse: A critical introduction*. Cambridge: Cambridge University Press.

Blommaert, J., Bock, M. and McCormick, K. (2007). Narrative inequality in the TRC hearings: on the hearability of hidden transcripts. In C. Anthonissen and Blommaert, J. (eds.), *Critical linguistics perspectives on coping with traumatic pasts*, 33–64. DAPSAC series. Amsterdam: Benjamins.

Certeau, M. de (1988). *The writing of history*. New York: Columbia University Press.

Coffin, C. (2006). *Historical discourse: The language of time, cause and evaluation*. London: Continuum.

Fairclough, N. (1992). *Language and power*. Harlow: Longman.

Fivush, R. (2008). Remembering and reminiscing: How individual lives are constructed in family narratives. *Memory Studies* 1(1): 49–58.

Flowerdew, J. (2012). *Critical discourse analysis in historiography: The case of Hong Kong's evolving political identity*. New York: Palgrave Macmillan.

Galasińska, A. and Galasiński, D. (eds.) (2010). *The post-communist condition: Public and private discourses of transformation*. Amsterdam: Benjamins.

George, R. (2013). 'What's a vendetta?' Political socialization in the everyday interactions of Los Angeles families. *Discourse & Society* 24(1): 46–65.

Ginzburg, C. (1992). *Clues, myths, and the historical method*. Baltimore, MD: John Hopkins University Press.

Goffman, E. (1981). *Forms of talk*. Philadelphia: University of Pennsylvania Press.

Gordon, C. (2004). 'Al Gore's our guy': Linguistically constructing a family political identity. *Discourse & Society* 15(5): 607–631.

Halbwachs, M. (1992). On collective memory. Lewis Coser (ed. and trans.). Chicago: University of Chicago Press.

Heer, H., Manoschek, W., Pollak, A. and Wodak, R. (eds.) (2008). *The discursive construction of history*. Steven Fligestone (trans.). New York: Palgrave Macmillan.

Koselleck, R. (2002). *The practice of conceptual history: Timing history, spacing concepts*. Stanford, CA: Stanford University Press.

Koselleck, R. (2004). *Futures past*. New York: Columbia University Press.

Lessa, F. (2013). *Memory and transitional justice in Argentina and Uruguay: Against impunity*. New York: Palgrave Macmillan.

Martin, J. R. (2003). Making history: Grammar for interpretation. In J.R. Martin and R. Wodak (eds.), *Re/reading the past: Critical perspectives on time and value*, 9–57. Amsterdam: Benjamins.

Martin, J. R. (2008). Intermodal reconciliation: Mates in arms. In L. Unsworth (ed.), *New literacies and the English curriculum: Perspectives*, 112–148. London: Continuum.

Martin, J. R., Maton, K. and Matruglio, E. (2010). Historical cosmologies. Epistemology and Axiology in Australian Secondary School History. *Revista Signos* 43(74): 433–463.

Martin, J. R. and Rose, D. (2008). *Genre relations: Mapping culture*. London: Equinox.

Martin, J. R. and Wodak. R. (eds.) (2003). *Re/reading the past: Critical perspectives on time and value*. Amsterdam: Benjamins.

Ochs, E. and Capps, L. (2001). *Living narrative: Creating lives in everyday storytelling*. Cambridge, MA: Harvard University Press.

Ochs, E. and Taylor, C. (1992). Family narrative as political activity. *Discourse & Society* 3(3): 301–340.

Oteíza, T. (2014). Intertextualidad en la recontextualización pedagógica del pasado reciente chileno. *Discurso & Sociedad* 8(1): 109–136.

Oteíza, T. and Pinto, D. (eds.) (2011). *En (re)construcción: discurso, nación e identidad en los manuales escolares*. Chile: Editorial Cuarto Propio.

Richardson, J. and Wodak, R. (eds.) (2009). Discourse, history, and memory. Special issue of *Critical Discourse Studies* 6(4): 231–321.

Ricoeur, P. (2010). *Memoria, Historia y Olvido*. México: Fondo de Cultura Económica.

Schiffrin, D. (2001). Language and public memorial: "America's concentration camps". *Discourse & Society* 12(4): 505–534.

Schleppegrell, M. (2004). *The language of schooling*. Mahwah: LEA.

Silverstein, M. and Urban, G. (1996). The natural history of discourse. In Silverstein, M. and G. Urban (eds.), *Natural histories of discourse*, 1–18. Chicago: University of Chicago Press.

Trouillot, M. (1995). *Silencing the past: Power and the production of history*. Boston, MA: Beacon Press.

Verdoolaege, A. (2008). *Reconciliation discourse*. Amsterdam, Philadelphia: Benjamins.

Welzer, H. (2010). Re-narrations: How pasts change in conversational remembering. *Memory Studies* 3(10): 5–17.

Wertsch, J. (2002). *Voices of collective remembering*. Cambridge: Cambridge University Press.

White, H. (1973). *Metahistory: The historical imagination in nineteenth-century Europe*. Baltimore, MD: Johns Hopkins University Press.

Wineburg, S., Mosborg, S., Porat, D. and Duncan, A. (2007). Common belief and the cultural curriculum: An intergeneracional study of historical consciousness. *American Educational Research Journal* 44(1): 40–76.

Wodak, R. (2006). History in the making/the making of history: The 'German *Wehrmacht*' in collective and individual memories in Austria. *Journal of Language and Politics* 5(1): 125–154.

Wodak, R., de Cillia, R., Reisigl, M. and Liebhart, K. (2009 [1999]). *The discursive construction of national identity*. Edinburgh: Edinburgh University Press (2nd revised edition).

Wodak, R. and Richardson, J. (eds.) (2013). *Analyzing Fascist discourse: Fascism in talk and text*. New York: Routledge.

21

Critical discourse analysis and politics[1]

Laura Filardo-Llamas and Michael S. Boyd

1. Political language

> *Because Selma shows us that America is not the project of any one person. Because the single-most powerful word in our democracy is the word 'we.' We the People. We shall overcome. Yes we can. That word is owned by no one. It belongs to everyone.*
>
> – President Barack Obama, 7 March 2015

The quote above can serve as a starting point for a discussion about language and politics. First of all, it is illustrative of the issues that CDA embraces when investigating political discourse (PD), i.e., "the semiotic dimensions of power, injustice, abuse, and political-economic or cultural change in society" (Fairclough, Mulderrig and Wodak 2011: 357). The dimension of power is clearly reflected in the dominant role of the speaker – the president of the United States. Yet, the same speaker, as a representative of the historically oppressed, and excluded, Black minority, has also been, seemingly, a victim of a power system and discourse dominance that perpetuated injustice and abuse against a minority group. The quote (and the entire speech) focuses on political and cultural change among African Americans in US society over the past 50 years. The speech, then, could be seen as an example of a discourse practice that aims to further transform social practices. At first glance, the quote might appear rather different from those in many CDA-inspired investigations in that the speaker is not producing or reproducing social inequalities, but rather he is extolling the virtues of the civil rights movement and the transformation of a formerly dominated minority group into a dominant one. However, the text is no less salient for our purposes, being an example of what van Dijk (1997: 11) calls "resistance and counter-power against such forms of discourse dominance." We cannot forget that Obama is exploiting his prominent and powerful position in order to spread the perception of a changed status quo among African Americans. We might also argue that Obama is reshaping social practice through discourse practice, and, more specifically, the commemorative speech genre.

As with most CDA investigations, we need to consider the immediate and wider contexts which define the text. This includes the co-text, situational context as well as socio-cultural and historical context, because such features, "particularly those such as socially defined *role, location, timing,* are pivotal in the definition of political discourse" (Chilton and Schäffner 2002: 16). The excerpt is taken from a 32-minute speech[2] given on 7 March 2015 to commemorate one of the pivotal moments in the US civil rights movement: when some 600 marchers who were attempting to leave Selma on their way to the Alabama State Capitol in Montgomery to demand equal voting rights for African Americans were attacked on a bridge by state and local police with clubs and tear gas. Both the location Obama chose for his speech, the Edmund Pettus Bridge in Selma, and the timing, the 50th anniversary of one of the central events in the civil rights movement, are crucial in defining the immediate and wider contexts. Furthermore, as part of the wider historical context we need to understand that these violent events sparked further protests, which culminated on 25 March 1965 in the final march of some 25,000 protesters, led by Martin Luther King, to the capitol. The events surrounding Selma led to the passage of the Voting Rights Act of 1965, which banned unfair practices in voter registration. As noted by Combs (2013: 6), the events that began on 7 March 1965 represent a watershed moment for the American civil rights movement.

If we return to the text, Obama refers to the events – metonymically and metaphorically – simply as "Selma," strategically recontextualising one part of a greater historical event as a turning point for African Americans. The metaphor is expanded to include all Americans, and specifically those who support – to cite another line from the speech – "the idea of a just America and a fair America, an inclusive America." In the short excerpt above the first person plural pronoun is used eight times and, for the most part, with a shifting meaning, from the inclusive "shows us," "glorious task we are given," and "this great nation of ours" to the historically recontextualised examples "We the people" from the preamble of the US Constitution, "We shall overcome" from the song widely used in the Civil Rights movement, and "Yes we can" from Obama's own PD. The general effect of the first-person plural pronoun is textual and pragmatic cohesion that reinforces group identity and unity (Boyd 2013; Filardo-Llamas 2015). Cohesion is further strengthened through the recontextualisation of various discourses: from Obama's own discourse and, on a more historical level, those drawn from the events at Selma and the civil rights movement. Such "relocation" of discourse (Chouliaraki and Fairclough 1999) can be a powerful tool in itself, allowing for the transformation of social or discursive practices and creating new ones (Busch 2006: 613).

While this short discussion has allowed us to introduce some of the most salient aspects of PD analysis, we have not yet addressed the important question of what exactly PD is. No one would doubt that the excerpt above is political because it is uttered by a politician in political circumstances, but we may still wonder where one needs to draw the line between political and non-political texts. First, we might consider the many other "official" participants in PD: "political institutions, governments, political media, and political supporters operating in political environments to achieve political goals" (Wilson 2001: 398). But what about citizens and voters who watch or listen to a political speech on YouTube, or those who read about politics in the media, namely, the recipients of political communication? The latter also need to be considered as active subjects who "reconstruct [. . .] the text as a system of means which may be more or less congruent with the ideology which informs the text" (Fowler 2009: 275). Such a view embraces all participants in the political process (van Dijk 1997: 13), who form a complementary relationship of production and reception. Thus, any (critical) analysis of PD needs to consider both "official" texts and speakers and the public that has to make sense of them, which occurs more and more through new media. Such media, as we shall see below, make political texts and actors more widely available to the public.

We may further ask if PD should be defined solely on the basis of its participants. In other words, how might we delimit the field of politics by relying on the nature of activities or practices accomplished by a political text? van Dijk (1997:16–18) discusses a number of issues that may determine whether a text is political or not, such as *whether it relates to political systems and/or shared values and ideologies typical of different political systems, whether it can be related to political institutions, organisations or groups, whether political relations are established,* or *whether it is part of the political process.* While it may not be possible to answer all of these questions when confronted with an ostensibly political text, they can help us to better categorise certain types, or genres, of political communication. Reisigl and Wodak (2009: 91) categorise political genres on the basis of eight different political functions: lawmaking procedure, formation of public attitudes, party-internal formation of attitudes, inter-party formation, organisation of international relations, political advertising, political executive, and administration and political control. One important aspect missing from all of these categorisations, however, is the notion of persuasion, which Chilton (2008: 226) sees as an integral part of PD, including "persuasive rhetoric, the use of implied meaning, the use of euphemisms, the exclusion of references to undesirable realities, the use of language to rouse political emotions, and the like." The double understanding of persuasion as an intention or as an effect determines the division of political genres we provide below, which is based on two overarching categories: political participants or possible political effect.

Taking the notions mentioned above as a point of departure, it is the objective of this chapter to provide an account of the different possibilities for doing critical analysis of PD. Through an analysis of several examples of PD, we intend to go through most of the aspects that have been covered in previous CDA studies while trying to show the wide array of methodological approaches that have been followed.

2. Literature review

PD analysis saw its boom in the late 20th century, even though its origins can be traced back to classical rhetoric and authors such as Aristotle or Cicero (Pujante 2003: 37). Making an analogy with Hart's (2014: 2) description of CDA, two main approaches to the study of PD can be found throughout history: PD Studies and PD Analysis.[3] Although both focus on the role that language has in shaping – and being shaped – by politics, the former takes philosophy, sociology, political science, and social-psychological approaches as their point of departure, whereas the latter is characterised by its use of applied linguistics.

Two significant aspects should be taken into account within the scope of PD Studies. First, Michel Foucault's (1981) description of discourse as a social practice performed through language and organised in terms of power relationships contributed to introducing the notion of "text" into the debates about PD. Second, social and psychological approaches have tried to achieve descriptive precision of the study of language in PD through the study of political myths and symbols and the use of quantifiable and empirical accounts of political utterances in their analysis (see the first section of chapters in Kaal, Maks and van Elfrinkhof 2014).

More interesting to the present discussion is PD Analysis, which in Europe can be traced back to Critical Linguistics, one of the first disciplines to focus on the relationship between language and ideology (Fowler et al. 1979). Highly influenced by generative-transformational grammar and informed by a strong belief in language as a tool through which behaviour could be changed, this body of work tried to uncover the persuasive power of specific syntactic forms. As such, Critical Linguists tried to reveal instances of misrepresentation and/or discrimination in public discourse through a process of "defamiliarization and conscious-raising" (Fowler 2009: 273).

With its strong interest in power and ideology, CDA naturally shares ground with politics and political actors, and a great deal of work in the field has been devoted to PD. Closely tied to this is the notion within CDA that language becomes more powerful when it is used by powerful people, who often make use of inclusionary and exclusionary strategies (Wodak and de Cillia 2006: 714). Different trends for the study of PD within CDA include Wodak et al.'s (2009; cf. Wodak 1989; Reisigl and Wodak 2009) Discourse-Historical Approach, Fairclough's (1989, 2010) Dialectical-Relational Approach, van Dijk's (1993, 1997) Sociocognitive Approach, Chilton's (2004) Cognitive-linguistic Approach, or Charteris-Black's (2005) Critical Metaphor Analysis.[4] The main distinguishing feature among all these representatives arguably lay in the aspects which acquire a mediating role between language and politics, which are, in sequential order, history, discourse practice, social cognition, cognitive processing, and conceptual metaphor theory.[5]

Acknowledging this mediating entity is of key significance if we wish to interpret and explain (Fairclough 1989) the relationship that is established between textual choices and their use – and effect – in political contexts. This is why a number of these elements, such as history (and intertextuality), the use of discourse practices (and expected PD genres), and the cognitive processing of discourse, are crucial for the analysis proposed in this chapter.

3. Methodological approaches

What follows has been organised as an attempt to convey the different perspectives that have been followed when doing PD analysis, particularly by taking into account their possible relation to the three-stage approach to CDA (Fairclough 1989). Chilton and Schäffner (2002: 25) argue that three main perspectives should be considered when analysing PD: textual features, interaction, and representation. These, in turn, are inextricably linked to Halliday's (2004) metafunctions of language: textual, interpersonal, and ideational. Likewise connections can be established with the notions of text and context (understood both as situational context and background knowledge), and the three stages in CDA: description, interpretation, and explanation. Below we will briefly discuss how each of these stages can be exploited for PD analysis.

3.1 Analysis of text-related features: genre

Linguistic choices reflect not only how a text is constructed, but they are also related to all the major social functions of language (Chouliaraki and Fairclough 1999: 50), transmitting the three metafunctions. Their analysis is essential not only for the study of textual construction but also for understanding how a text may disseminate ideological beliefs and the social effect this may have. In this stage, however, we are particularly concerned with the relationship that can be established between textual features and their role in helping a text to adjust to social expectations. In a broader understanding of Halliday's (2004) textual metafunction – usually concerned with explaining how texture is achieved through cohesion and coherence – we are, at this point, interested in the textual choices which help in making a text fulfil social expectations about what PD should be like. Thus, instead of adopting a purely descriptive view of the textual choices characterising different types, or genres, of political texts, we shall also try to explain the social role that those choices have in different social contexts.

Genres can be defined as "global linguistic patterns which have historically developed in a linguistic community for fulfilling specific communicative tasks in specific situations"

(Chilton and Schäffner 2002: 19). They are broadly determined by discourse communities, i.e., the groups of individuals whose membership is related to their social role and who inter-communicate with a text. According to Fairclough (1989: 29–37), each social domain has an associated "order of discourse" (Foucault 1981) – or a structured collection of discursive prac-tices connected with particular social domains (Fairclough 1989: 29–37). The socio-political struggle for power is reflected in changes in the order of discourse, which attest the dominat-ing ideology of the time. CDA is particularly interested in the role that certain genres play "in the exercise of power and influence [and. . .] in the very definition of politics and political institutions" (Chilton and Schäffner 2002: 21). It is this shifting nature of political genres that makes it necessary for them to be constantly adapted and redefined.

An example of the "fluid and shifting character" of (mediatised) political genres (Cap and Okulska 2013: 6) can be found in blogs. In her study of Polish and UK official political blogs, Kopytowska (2013: 381) sees such mediatised blogs as an emerging genre in PD that breaks down "the ontological divisions between the public and the private." Her analysis considers the importance of mediatisation and proximisation which combine to reduce the distance between (political) blogs and their audiences through the creation of a virtual community. This is similar to what happens when speeches (Boyd 2011) and other political genres, such as debates (Boyd 2013) and interviews, are broadcast on YouTube as short fragments or in their entirety (Reisigl 2008: 259), often leading to the reshaping of these genres (Boyd 2011, 2014a, 2014b; Cap and Okulska 2013: 8–9). Thanks to new media, political genres are now more widely accessible and, importantly, the reception factors have been altered significantly by new communication paradigms such as text and video commenting, sharing, or liking, which encourage different forms of user-mediated interaction (Boyd 2011, 2014b). Cap and Okulska (2013: 9) question the actual role of "authorship" (production) as a defining feature of political genres due to the "intensity of migration" into new media. All of this implies a "re-imagining" (Fairclough 2010) of the political genres, as their distinguishing features are arguably now less clear-cut, and their textual construction shall be analysed not only by looking at a unitary text, but also by considering the "genres and combinations" new media genres and texts draw upon (Fairclough 2006: 33). In Figure 21.1 we have tried to capture this distinction by proposing a non-exhaustive list of some possible political genres and divid-ing them according to van Dijk's (1997) dichotomy between political participants/possible political effect.

Intertextual relations between different types of genres are of key importance for under-standing how political genres can evolve, and how this can affect other socio-political prac-tices. Some examples can be seen in the recontextualisation of Barack Obama's "Yes, we can" speech into a song in the 2008 presidential election campaigns (Filardo-Llamas 2015), in the representation of political events in murals and commemoration plaques in the streets of the main Northern Irish cities (Filardo-Llamas and González-Cascos 2014; Filardo-Llamas 2012), or in the relation that can be established between the multiple political genres that can be part of one single political campaign. This may happen, for instance, as a consequence of the use of deliberate polysemy, as we can find with the use of the word "deal" by the Democratic Unionist Party in 1998 to imply both the political meaning of agreement and the metaphori-cal meaning of economic negotiation as a means to delegitimise the peace agreement that had been signed in Northern Ireland (Filardo-Llamas 2014). Even if the double political and metaphoric meaning was the most common use, the word was visually recontextualised, and a new type of "deal" was referred to in one of the political manifestos produced by the same party five years later, during the election campaign for Northern Ireland's Assembly (Figure 21.2).

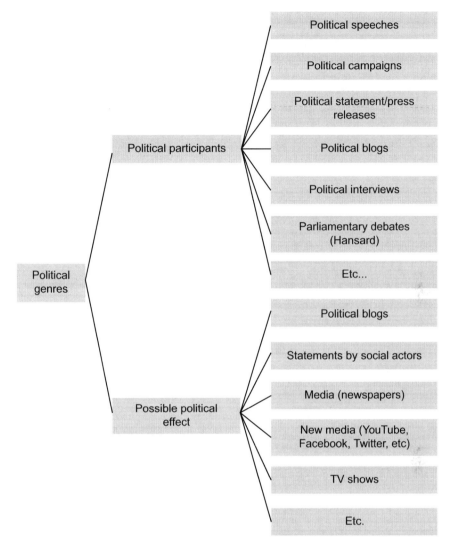

Figure 21.1   Sample of possible political genres

Figure 21.2   Cartoon distributed by the DUP at the 2003 Assembly elections

3.2 Analysis of representation: ideological beliefs

According to Chilton (2004: 46) "representation is one of the obvious functions of discourse," since through language we usually present a given view of reality. This resembles Halliday's (2004) ideational metafunction, which explains how we interact with the world surrounding us when we communicate. When politicians use language, they try to imbue their view of society with an objective veil by relying on evidence, authority, or truth (Chilton 2004: 23), but, as much as they try, we cannot neglect that their view of reality is quite frequently determined by ideological beliefs (van Dijk 1998).

The notion of representation – understood as the creation of a mental space stimulated by a text (Chilton 2004: 50) – advocates in favour of incorporating a cognitive dimension within the study of PD. As argued by Hart (2014: 9), it is by studying how discourse is cognitively processed that we may understand "the *effects* of ideological or perspectivized language use on hearers' mental representations and evaluations of reality." This is, in fact, what should be done in CDA's interpretation stage of the analysis.

Two notions are important to explain representation. First, perspective (Filardo-Llamas, Hart and Kaal 2015) – and its ideological implications – is vital for understanding how PD works, as it is the logical consequence of "bringing the viewer's body into particular alignments with elements in the scene depicted and prior universal embodied experiences" (Hart 2014: 83). To understand this, it is necessary to do an analysis of the discourse worlds that are spread in each instance of discourse and how these interact with the deictic centre. A discussion of all the linguistic categories that may result in a perspectivised text is well beyond the scope of this chapter, but further information can be found in Chilton (2004), Hart (2010, 2014), and Filardo-Llamas (2013, 2014, 2015).

Likewise context, defined as a construct of "socio-cultural conventions from which the online pragmatic processing of language takes its bearing" (Widdowson 2004: 54), is also important. As many as four levels of context have been identified in the CDA literature, including the co-textual context, the intertextual and discursive relation with other texts, the context of situation, and the broader socio-political context (Benke and Wodak 2003: 225). All of them have a bearing on how discourse is processed as they belong to what is known as the speaker's common ground, which is regulated by what van Dijk (2008: 54) calls the "K-device," i.e., the knowledge that both speaker and recipients share. Different types of knowledge may influence the construed mental representations, including personal, interpersonal, group, institutional, national, or cultural knowledge (van Dijk 2005: 77–90).

At the basis of this is lexical representation, as mental models lie at the core of lexical selection. Lexical items serve both for cohesion at the level of co-text and coherence with the wider context and, when taken together, can create "a common underlying metaphorical schema" (Chilton and Schäffner 2002: 29) as well as "emphasize or de-emphasize political attitudes and opinions, garner support, manipulate public opinion, manufacture political consent, or legitimate political power" (van Dijk 1997: 25). Yet how do we study such (lexical) phenomena within a wider context? Are lexical phenomena a manifestation of the speaker's recurring discourse? Some tools from Corpus Linguistics (CL) may indeed represent "a powerful heuristic tool helping clear pathways to discovery," allowing for the analyst to "look *beyond* the text proper in order to unearth socially meaningful interpretations that can then be enlisted to do socially transformative work" (Mautner 2009: 124; see also Baker et al. 2008; Baker, this volume). CL tools can also provide twofold quantitative and qualitative analytical methods for "direct empirical evidence about the connotation of words" (Stubbs 1996: 121), thereby demonstrating the link between textual-related features and representation. In our analysis, they will allow us to filter various discourse strands in a large amount of data to determine the relationship between a specific political speech and, on the one hand, other texts and, on the other, user-generated discourse based on the original text in the form of comments, ultimately demonstrating how genres are being "colonized" (Chouliaraki and Fairclough 1999) by new actors (new media users) and new discourse practices (text commenting).

3.3 Analysis of interaction: political stance

Chilton and Schäffner (2002: 32) explain the analysis of interaction as reflecting how the speaker – and the audience – are positioned in relation to the communicative situation and to their "interlocutors, their physical location, the point in time of the ongoing utterance and where they are in the ongoing discourse." If we adapt this definition to Halliday's interpersonal function, political stance is arguably equivalent to evaluation (Hart 2014: 7), or "the way that speakers code or implicitly convey various kinds of *subjective opinion* in discourse and in so doing attempt to achieve some *intersubjective consensus* of values with respect to what is represented" (Hart 2014: 43, our emphasis). These are, in our view, the two most significant elements of stance.

When looking at evaluation, CDA has traditionally focused on modality.[6] Consequently, it can be argued that the two elements of stance, epistemic and affective (Chilton and Schäffner 2002: 31), correspond to the traditional modal uses: epistemic and deontic. The former refers to the evaluation of the propositional content, reflecting the speaker's "commitment to the truth of a proposition" (Chilton 2004: 59). Even if this is implicitly evaluative, it can be argued that striving for epistemic control may serve in managing how beliefs and ideologies are spread discursively (Marín-Arrese 2015: 2), i.e., it influences how via PD reality is represented.

Deontic modality is linked to normativity, understood as a way of (de)emphasising the speaker's authority (Chilton 2004: 59). Applying a narrow definition of Halliday's interpersonal metafunction, the interaction dimension can be understood as the one explaining the relationship between speaker and audience. In institutional settings, such as those characterising PD, this interpersonal metafunction becomes a status function which carries "deontic powers" (Fairclough and Fairclough 2012: 72). This is a direct consequence of the human ability to impose functions on others and regulate what others do. The analysis of deontic modality becomes, thus, particularly important for study of PD, as it is through it that intersubjective consensus may be achieved: when the required political actions are based on a group of shared beliefs between speaker and audience, the social rightness of those actions is legitimised. This final effect of PD may be manifested in the audience's reaction, something that has often been neglected in CDA approaches to PD. Exceptions to this can be, however, found in studies about comments in new media (Boyd 2011, 2014a, 2014b; O'Halloran 2010, 2014).

4. Case study

In this section we will briefly apply selected aspects of the methodological overview in section 3 to the analysis of Obama's "A More Perfect Union" (2008),[7] delivered during the 2008 primary election in the United States. This speech attempted to address criticism of Obama's relationship with his controversial former pastor, Jeremiah Wright, and, more generally, the issues of race and racism that had hitherto been lacking in the campaign. As a campaign speech, however, it was also meant to promote Obama's own political position and help him to achieve power and influence among the other Democratic primary presidential candidates.

Both the genre and situational context of the speech influence the justification strategies Obama adopts for the discursive formation of the text. This is used especially "in the narrative creation of national history" and "to justify or relativise a societal *status quo ante* by emphasising the legitimacy of past acts of the 'own' national 'we'-group which have been put into question" (Wodak et al. 2009: 33).

The speech also tests the importance of new media, and its various YouTube versions, which generated a significant number of often lengthy and relatively positive[8] text comments (Boyd 2009, 2011, 2014b). Furthermore, the impact and effect of new media, together with its recontextualising capability, in the case of Obama has been demonstrated (Harfoush 2009; Castells 2009; Filardo-Llamas 2015). As we have already argued, new media have become an integral part of modern politics and political campaigns, and YouTube, in particular, has become an important means of (re)distributing PD and its various genres.

To understand people's reaction to this speech, we need to identify first the linguistic features salient to the text and the representation triggered by them. Closely related to the justification strategy is Obama's use of person deictics. Specifically, the first-person plural *we* is widespread, and its meaning depends on the speaker/hearer's "deictic positioning" (Chilton 2004: 204) in context. As we can see in the examples and Figure 21.3 below, "we" may have a shifting indexing scope, thus allowing the speaker to address, and create a bond with, an increasingly wider audience.

1   I am married to a black American who carries within her the blood of slaves and slave-owners – an inheritance we pass on to our two precious daughters.
2   This was one of the tasks we set forth at the beginning of the campaign – to continue the long march of those who came before us.
3   For the African-American community, that path means embracing the burdens of our past without becoming victims of our past.
4   This is where we are right now. It's a racial stalemate we've been stuck in for years. [. . .] I believe deeply that we cannot solve the challenges of our time unless we solve them together – unless we perfect our union by understanding that we may have different stories, but we hold common hopes; that we may not look the same and we may not have come from the same place, but we all want to move in the same direction – towards a better future for our children and our grandchildren.
5   We the people, in order to form a more perfect union. (Obama 2008)

A close analysis of the examples can help us to see how the high indexical value of the pronoun "we," and its possibility for acquiring meaning in context, include an increasingly widening audience within its referential scope. Particularly interesting are the inclusive uses of the pronoun, addressing both the African-American community and/or all Americans (examples 3 and 4). Two linguistic strategies can be identified. On the one hand, the indexed community may be made explicit through the use of noun phrases such as "African-American community" (3), or adjectives such as "all", "one," or (4) "together." On the other hand, ambiguity may be exploited through the co-textual lack of a referential expression to identify the indexed group, thus making the speech – and its content – appealing to both communities. This is particularly useful since Obama is trying to make a global appeal by dealing with the topic of race, which is generally divisive.

The main effect of these shifting pronominal uses is that Obama's speech – and implicitly his role as future president – becomes universalised. Through this, combined with intertextual uses of other socio-political texts such as the speeches by Martin Luther King or the US Constitution

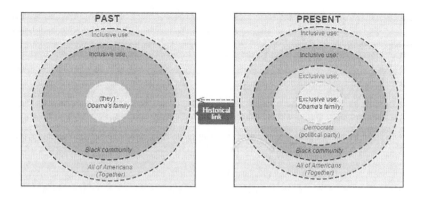

Figure 21.3 Shifting uses of Obama's first person plural pronoun

(example 5), he manages to associate the first person plural pronoun with a new meaning which reflects historical, social, and personal change (Boyd 2009; Filardo-Llamas 2015).

The idea of inclusiveness can be also seen in the increasingly widening scope of the spaces indexed throughout the speech: spaces occupied throughout Obama's personal narrative, or by other people related to him (such as Rev. Wright or his family), and spaces occupied by common people. The plethora of individuals' stories accounted for in the speech show that Obama relies on a strategy of individualisation combined with categorisation[9] (van Leeuwen 1996: 48–54), which is also seen in the references to "the barbershop," "the church," "the street," "rural communities," or "urban black neighborhoods." All of these places have a metonymic relation with the overarching term "this country." A pictorial representation similar to Figure 21.3 could be made, and parallel widening scopes could be established for the first person plural pronoun and space deictics.

Inclusiveness is further encouraged through metaphors, particularly those based on the conceptualisation of governing as creating, and politicians as builders (Charteris-Black 2005: 141), mainly triggered through the lexical items "build" and "rebuild."[10] Particularly interesting is the latter as the use of the prefix "re-" implies the need to change what is implicitly considered faulty. This idea permeated Obama's speeches during the 2008 election campaign, justifying his constant call for change, something that also emerges in our corpus-based analysis. This change is to be seen in the resulting building: "a powerful coalition of African Americans and white Americans."

A corpus-based analysis allows us to measure both recontextualisation of certain linguistic phenomena in Obama's discourse in general and interaction with the original speech by text receivers. First, it helps to determine general discourse practices (of Obama in the 2008 primary campaign) over a large set of data representing different texts, genres, and discourses, allowing us also to check some of the observations made in the qualitative analysis above. A comparison of eight of Obama's campaign speeches (OCSC, 26,701 words) to a 14 million-word reference corpus of political speeches (CORPS, Guerini, Strapparava and Stock 2008) pointed to a high incidence of pronominal use and nominalisation, indicators of the interpersonal metafunction,[11] as we can see in the simplified keyword[12] list provided in Table 21.1.

The pronoun "we" and the lexical items "dream" and "change" are interesting. The widespread use of the first-person plural is reconfirmed, providing empirical data for Obama's personal discourse style. Likewise, subsequent concordance analysis demonstrated that, for the most part, the selected terms were used as nouns (*dream* 96%, *change* 61%). Further analysis

Table 21.1 Keywords OCSC vs. CORPS

Keyword	Freq	%	Keyness
WE	905	3.46	440.4139709
DREAM	79	0.30	194.6068726
THEY	295	1.13	133.7588196
CHANGE	92	0.35	131.1374207
BLACK	47	0.18	126.1341858
COST	52	0.20	103.1677246
HE	164	0.63	78.46853638

indicates a high frequency of nominalisation also with *hope* and *struggle*. These findings not only confirm the representation evoked by this speech, but also stress the importance of the words "change" and "hope" in Obama's discourse (cf. Filardo-Llamas 2015). Thus, Obama's political stance is related to the demand for the audience(s) to react to the need and desire for change.

To examine the audience's reaction to this, we have studied discourse practices among text receivers on YouTube with tools taken from CL. Boyd (2014a) analysed some 11,000 comments (400,000+ tokens) to gauge the extent to which users adopt different forms of generally positive recontextualisation practices in their textual reactions to Obama's "A More Perfect Union." Even though at first sight most of the comments posted on YouTube may appear as antagonistic and overtly racist, a corpus-based analysis demonstrates that many are indeed positive in nature. A frequency list of the comments corpus was compared with the Open ANC (Ide and Suderman 2007) reference corpus to flesh out lexical items that might be indicative of positive and negative presentation and recontextualisation. The search was, thus, limited to items with a strong referential value, pronouns, examples of web-speak, and other terms related to Obama and his discourse practices. A simplified keyword list is provided in Table 21.2.

Table 21.2 Keywords comment corpus vs. Open ANC

Keyword	Freq	%	Keyness
HE	5470	1.25	8896.984375
AMERICA	1640	0.38	6849.742188
VOTE	1352	0.31	6020.510254
SPEECH	3289	0.75	5591.123535
PRESIDENT	1906	0.44	5403.819336
HOPE	1123	0.26	4529.97168
COUNTRY	1193	0.27	3311.304443
HIM	1616	0.37	3022.231689
RACE	683	0.16	2442.638916
SPEECHES	401	0.09	2273.41626
GREAT	1106	0.25	2268.198975
AMAZING	489	0.11	2174.72998
CHANGE	933	0.21	2092.111816

Interestingly, most of the terms appear to be positive in nature and two of them, "hope" and "change," might be seen as recontextualisation of Obama's own discourse. In contrast to the keywords in Table 21.1, the top item is the third-person singular pronoun "he," pointing to a high degree of referentiality to Obama and the speech, which is reconfirmed by the items "speech/speeches," or "president." The adjectives "great" and "amazing" generally collocate with "speech(es)" indicating even more positive recontextualisation, and a positive reaction to Obama's demand. While a full discussion of all of the items in Table 21.2 is beyond the scope of this study, we should also note the high frequency of the first-person singular pronoun, which Boyd (2014a: 260) sees as "personal participation and commitment on behalf of the commentators." In general, however, the striking thing about these data are that they are generally of a positive character and would appear to indicate a high degree of recontextualisation demonstrating that it takes places on multiple textual and contextual levels.

5. Conclusion

After a short review of different trends and methodological approaches for the study of PD throughout time, in this chapter we have presented a short sample of what could be considered PD Analysis: following a comprehensive, and linguistic, methodology for the study of PD. While we have necessarily limited our analysis to selected items and only a few specific genres have been mentioned, the approach proposed here is meant to be applicable to any political genre. Still, the analysis shows the importance of adopting interdisciplinary tools which can help us to explain the complex relation between language and PD. Thus, we have embraced aspects of Hallidayan Systemic Functional Linguistics, Cognitive Linguistics, and Corpus Linguistics when describing textual features. However, if the analysis of PD is to be made within the CDA paradigm, the notion of critique should be incorporated. This can be done by paying special attention to the interpretation – which types of knowledge are activated by the speech? – and explanation stages – what is the effect of the speech? Does it adjust to social expectations? Have these expectations changed throughout time?

The texts we have chosen for the introduction and the analysis prove another point: *any* political text is worthy of critical analysis. Indeed, CDA-inspired research of political texts need not be limited to texts that (re)produce social inequalities, rather any text uttered by a political actor or with political consequences beckons further study due to the very nature of politics itself. This leads us to another important aspect, that of text production and reception. In today's Internet-dominated world, in which political texts can reach the masses by means of the latest cutting-edge technology, text receivers not only have more immediate access to political texts but also more and more ways to react to them. All of this undoubtedly plays a defining role in politics and PD practices, and no critical account of PD should ignore the power of "technologically-mediated spaces" (Wodak and Wright 2006).

Notes

1 This research has been partly funded by the Spanish Ministry of Economy and Competitiveness (project FFI2013–40934-R: "Constructivist rhetoric: Discourses of identity" [RECDID]). The authors discussed and conceived of this chapter together. Parts 1, 3, and 5 were written by both authors in equal part; L. Filardo-Llamas was mainly responsible for section 2 and 3.2 and M.S. Boyd for 3, 3.1, 3.3. In Part 4, L. Filardo-Llamas dealt mainly with the parts focusing on qualitative analysis, while M.S. Boyd dealt mainly with the parts focusing on quantitative (corpus) analysis.

2 The transcript and commentary can be found at https://medium.com/@WhiteHouse/president-obama-s-speech-in-selma-8336cdedf37c, while the video is available on YouTube: www.youtube.com/watch?v=gvAIvauhQGQ

3 See Chilton and Schäffner (1997: 207–211), Wilson (2001: 399–400), and Blommaert (1997: 3–7) for a more comprehensive description of the different disciplines that have dealt with the study of PD.

4 This list is by no means exclusive, and more PD studies could be named. In this brief description we have only included those authors who either describe themselves or are generally grouped with CDA practitioners.

5 A wider and more comprehensive account of examples of PD analysis within CDA can be found in Wodak and de Cillia (2006).

6 More elements, such as appraisal theory, have been recently incorporated to the study of evaluation in CDA. See Hart (2014: 43–46; 59–65) for a more comprehensive account.

7 Obama, Barack. 2008. Sen. Barack Obama addresses race at the Constitution Center in Philadelphia. *The Washington Post,* March 18. Available at www.washingtonpost.com/wp-dyn/content/article/2008/03/18/AR2008031801081.html?sid=ST2008031801183

8 Boyd (2014a) reports an average of 38.4 words per comment in a 400,000+ word corpus of text comments of two different YouTube versions of the speech.

9 Although the participants described in the stories are apparently individualised, the everyday actions they do turns them into categories that can be used to describe society as a whole.

10 Other metaphorical uses include the conceptualization of politics as a journey or the use of religious language.

11 Both the qualitative and corpus analysis have also indicated a high incidence of modality which will not be discussed here due to space limitations.

12 Keywords are those words that exhibit a higher frequency when compared with a larger reference corpus (Scott 2006).

Further reading

Chilton, P. and Schäffner, C. (2002). Introduction: Themes and principles in the analysis of political discourse. In P. Chilton and C. Schäffner (eds.), *Politics as text and talk: Analytic approaches to political discourse,* 1–41. Amsterdam: Benjamins.
This chapter addresses the linguistic nature of political discourse. To do so, the authors review some of the linguistic principles governing the behaviour of discourse in politics, such as speech acts, the co-operative principle, politeness theory, or validity claims. Some instruments for the analysis of political discourse are also offered.

Fairclough, N. and Fairclough, I. (2012). *Political discourse analysis: A method for advanced students.* London: Routledge.
This book provides the authors' description of their approach to the study of political discourse. The authors establish a link between the analysis political discourse and CDA/CDS by relying mainly on the notion of argumentation. After presenting their rationale and methodological proposal, the authors apply it to the study of different types of political genres.

van Dijk, T. A. (1997). "What is Political Discourse Analysis?" In J. Blommaert and C. Bulcaen (eds.), *Political linguistics,* 11–52. Amsterdam: Benjamins.
In this chapter the author attempts to outline a definition and an explanation of what political discourse is. An overview of the different domains of politics and their relation to discourse is provided, and a proposal of the different discursive strategies that can be analysed in the study of political discourse is presented.

Wilson, J. (2001). Political discourse. In D. Schiffrin, D. Tannen and H.E. Hamilton (eds.), *Handbook of discourse analysis,* 398–415. Oxford: Blackwell.
In this chapter the author provides an overview of what political discourse is. Several approaches to the study of political discourse are collected in it, including aspects such as the study of syntax, the importance of relevance theory, or the study of phonological aspects in political discourse.

Wodak, R. and de Cillia, R. (2006). Politics and language: Overview. In K. Brown (ed.), *Encyclopedia of language and linguistics,* 706–719. Oxford: Elsevier.
In this chapter we find a historical overview of the different approaches that have been adopted in the study of political discourse. Aspects like the notion of language planning and language policies are also included in the review of the field presented. In the second section of the chapter, an overview of current approaches to the study of political discourse is presented.

References

Baker, P., Gabrielatos, C., KhosraviNik, M., Krzyżanowski, M., McEnery, T. and Wodak, R. (2008). The useful methodological synergy? Combining critical discourse analysis and corpus linguistics to examine discourses of refugees and asylum seekers in the UK Press. *Discourse & Society* 19(3): 273–306.

Benke, G. and Wodak, R. (2003). Remembering and forgetting. The discursive construction of generational memories. In M.N. Dédaic and D.N. Nelson (eds.), *At war with words,* 215–244. Berlin: Mouton de Gruyter.

Blommaert, J. (1997). Introduction: Language and politics, language politics and political linguistics. In J. Blommaert and C. Bulcaen (eds.), *Political linguistics,* 1–10. Amsterdam: John Benjamins.

Boyd, M. S. (2009). De-constructing race and identity in US presidential discourse: Barack Obama's Speech on Race, *Atlantis. Journal of the Spanish Association of Anglo-American Studies* 31: 75–94.

Boyd, M. S. (2011). (New) political genres for the masses? YouTube in the 2008 US Presidential Elections. In S. Sarangi, V. Polese and G. Caliendo, (eds.), *Genre(s) on the move: Hybridization and discourse change in specialized communication,* 27–44. Naples: Edizioni Scientifiche Italiane.

Boyd, M. S. (2013). Reframing the American dream: Conceptual metaphor and personal pronouns in the 2008 US presidential debates. In P. Cap and U. Okulska (eds.), *Analyzing genres in political communication,* 297–319. Amsterdam: Benjamins.

Boyd, M. S. (2014a) Participation and recontextualization in new media: Political discourse analysis and YouTube. In B. Kaal, I. Maks and A.M.E. van Elfrinkhof (eds.), *From text to political positions: Text analysis across disciplines,* 243–296. Amsterdam: Benjamins.

Boyd, M. S. (2014b) (New) participatory framework on YouTube? Commenter interaction in US political speeches. *Journal of Pragmatics* 72: 46–58.

Busch, B. (2006). Media, politics, and discourse: Interactions. In K. Brown (ed.), *Encyclopedia of language and linguistics,* 609–616. Oxford: Elsevier.

Cap, P. and Okulska, U. (2013). Analyzing genres in political communication: An introduction. In P. Cap and B. Okulska (eds.), *Analyzing genres in political communication,* 1–26. Amsterdam: Benjamins.

Castells, M. (2009). *Communication power.* Oxford: Oxford University Press.

Charteris-Black, J. (2005). *Politicians and rhetoric: The persuasive power of metaphor.* Basingstoke: Palgrave.

Chilton, P. (2004). *Analysing political discourse: Theory and practice.* London: Routledge.

Chilton, P. (2008). Political terminology. In R. Wodak and V. Koller (eds.), *Handbook of communication in the public sphere,* 223–242. Berlin: Mouton de Gruyter.

Chilton, P. and Schäffner, C. (1997). Discourse and politics. In T.A. van Dijk (ed.), *Discourse as social interaction,* 206–230. London: Sage.

Chilton, P. and Schäffner, C. (2002). Introduction: Themes and principles in the analysis of political discourse. In P. Chilton and C. Schäffner (eds.), *Politics as text and talk: Analytic approaches to political discourse,* 1–41. Amsterdam: Benjamins.

Chouliaraki, L. and Fairclough, N. (1999). *Discourse in late modernity: Rethinking critical discourse analysis.* Edinburgh: Edinburgh University Press.

Combs, B. H. (2013). *From Selma to Montgomery: The long march to freedom.* New York: Routledge.

Fairclough, N. (1989). *Language and power.* London: Longman.

Fairclough, N. (2006). Genres in political discourse. In K. Brown (ed.), *Encyclopedia of language and linguistics,* 32–38. Oxford: Elsevier.

Fairclough, N. (2010). *Critical discourse analysis: The critical study of language.* Harlow: Longman.

Fairclough, N. and Fairclough, I. (2012). *Political discourse analysis: A method for advanced students.* London: Routledge.

Fairclough, N., Mulderrig, J. and Wodak, R. (2011). Critical discourse analysis. In T.A. van Dijk (ed.), *Discourse studies: A multi-disciplinary approach,* 357–378. London: Sage.

Filardo-Llamas, L. (2012). To live in the heart (and mind) of others. The construction of memory in Northern Irish commemorative plaques, *CADAAD Journal* 5(2): 152–170.

Filardo-Llamas, L. (2013). 'Committed to the ideals of 1916': The language of paramilitary groups: The case of the Irish Republican Army. *Critical Discourse Studies* 10(1): 1–17.

Filardo-Llamas, L. (2014). Between the union and a United Ireland: Shifting positions in Northern Ireland's post-agreement political discourse. In B. Kaal, I. Maks and A.M.E. van Elfrinkhof (eds.), *From text to political positions: Text analysis across disciplines,* 207–224. Amsterdam: Benjamins.

Filardo-Llamas, L. (2015). Re-contextualizing political discourse: An analysis of shifting spaces in songs used as a political tool. *Critical Discourse Studies* 12(3): 279–296.

Filardo-Llamas, L. and González-Cascos, E. (2014). Memory and identity in the public sphere: Northern Irish murals. In Y. Kalyango, Jr. and M. Kopytowska (eds.) *Why discourse matters. Negotiating identity in the mediatized world*. New York: Peter Lang.

Filardo-Llamas, L., Hart, C. and Kaal, B. (2015). Introduction for the special issue on space, time and evaluation in ideological discourse. *Critical Discourse Studies* 12(3): 235–237.

Foucault, M. (1981). The order of discourse. In R. Young (ed.), *Untying the text: A post-structuralist Reader*, 48–78. London: Routledge.

Fowler, R. (2009). Notes on critical linguistics. In J.E. Joseph (ed.), *Language and politics: Major themes in English studies*, Vol. IV, 271–282. London: Routledge. (Reprinted from Steele, R. and Threadgold, T. (eds.) (1987). *Language topics: Essays in honour of Michael Halliday*, Vol. 2, 481–492. Amsterdam: Benjamins.).

Fowler, R., Hodge, R., Kress G. and Trew, T. (1979). *Language and control*. London: Routledge and Kegan Paul.

Guerini, M., Strapparava, C. and Stock, O. (2008). Corps: A corpus of tagged political speeches for persuasive communication processing. *Journal of Information Technology and Politics* 5(1): 19–32.

Halliday, M.A.K. and Matthiessen, C.M.I.M. (2004). *An introduction to functional grammar*, 3rd edn. London: Hodder Education.

Harfoush, R. (2009). *Yes we did. An inside look at how social media built the Obama brand*. Berkeley, CA: New Riders.

Hart, C. (2010). *Critical discourse analysis and cognitive science: New perspectives on immigration discourse*. Basingstoke: Palgrave Macmillan.

Hart, C. (2014). *Discourse, grammar and ideology: Functional and cognitive perspectives*. London: Bloomsbury.

Ide, N. and Suderman, K. (2007). The Open American National Corpus (OANC). www.AmericanNationalCorpus.org/OANC.

Kaal, B., Maks, I. and van Elfrinkhof, A. (eds.) (2014). *From text to political positions: Text analysis across disciplines*. Amsterdam: Benjamins.

Kopytowska, M. (2013). Blogging as the mediatization of politics and a new form of social interaction: A case study of 'proximization dynamics' in Polish and British political blogs. In P. Cap and U. Okulska (eds.), *Analyzing genres in political communication*, 379–421. Amsterdam: Benjamins.

Lister, M., Dovey, J., Giddings, S., Grant, I. and Kelly, K. (2009). *New media: A critical introduction*, 2nd edn. London: Routledge.

Marin-Arrese, J. (2015). Epistemic legitimisation and inter/subjectivity in the discourse of parliamentary and public inquiries. *Critical Discourse Studies* 12(3): 261–278.

Mautner, G. (2009). Checks and balances: How Corpus Linguistics can contribute to CDA. In R. Wodak and M. Meyer (eds.), *Methods of critical discourse analysis*, 2nd edn, 122–143. London: Sage.

Obama, Barack. (2008). Sen. Barack Obama addresses race at the Constitution Center in Philadelphia. *The Washington Post*, March 18. Available at www.washingtonpost.com/wp-dyn/content/article/2008/03/18/AR2008031801081.html?sid=ST2008031801183

O'Halloran, K. (2010). How to use corpus linguistics in the study of media discourse. In A. O'Keeffe and M. McCarthy (eds.), *The Routledge handbook of corpus linguistics*, 563–577. London: Routledge.

O'Halloran, K. (2014). Counter-discourse corpora, ethical subjectivity and critique of argument: An alternative critical discourse analysis pedagogy. *Journal of Language and Politics* 13(4): 781–813.

Pujante, D. (2003). *Manual de retórica*. Madrid: Castalia.

Reisigl, M. (2008). Rhetoric of political speeches. In R. Wodak and V. Koller (eds.), *Handbook of communication in the public sphere*, 243–269. Berlin: Mouton de Gruyter.

Reisigl, M. and Wodak, R. (2009). The discourse historical approach (DHA). In R. Wodak and M. Meyer (eds.), *Methods of critical discourse analysis*, 2nd edn, 87–121. London: Sage.

Scott, M. (2006). *Oxford Wordsmith tools version 4.0*. Oxford: Oxford University Press. www.lexically.net/wordsmith/

Stubbs, M. (1996). *Text and corpus linguistics*. Oxford: Blackwell.

van Dijk, T.A. (1993). Principles of critical discourse analysis. *Discourse and Society* 4(2): 249–283.

van Dijk, T.A. (1997). What is political discourse analysis? In J. Blommaert and C. Bulcaen (eds.), *Political linguistics*, 11–52. Amsterdam: Benjamins.

van Dijk, T.A. (1998). *Ideology. A multidisciplinary approach*. London: Sage.

van Dijk, T.A. (2005). Contextual knowledge management in discourse production: A CDA perspective. In Wodak and Chilton (eds.), *A new agenda in (critical) discourse analysis*, 71–100. Amsterdam: Benjamins.

van Dijk, T. A. (2008). *Discourse and context: A sogiocognitive approach.* Cambridge: Cambridge University Press.

Van Leeuwen, T. (1996). The representation of social actors. In C. Caldas-Coulthard and M. Coulthard (eds.), *Text and practices: Readings in critical discourse analysis,* 32–70. London: Routledge.

Widowson, H.G. (2004). *Text, context, pretext: Critical issues in discourse analysis.* Oxford: Blackwell.

Wilson, J. (2001). Political discourse. In D. Schiffrin, D. Tannen and H. Hamilton (eds.), *Handbook of discourse analysis,* 398–415. Oxford: Blackwell.

Wodak, R. (ed.) (1989). *Language, power and ideology. Studies in political discourse.* Amsterdam: Benjamins.

Wodak, R. and de Cillia, R. (2006). Politics and language: Overview. In K. Brown (ed.), *Encyclopedia of language and linguistics,* 706–719. Oxford: Elsevier.

Wodak, R., de Cillia, R., Reisigl, M. and Liebhart, K. (2009). *The discursive construction of national identity,* 2nd edn. Edinburgh: Edinburgh University Press.

Wodak, R. and Wright, S. (2006). The European Union in cyberspace. *Journal of Language and Politics* 5: 251–275.

22

Critical discourse studies in/of applied contexts

Crispin Thurlow

> Critical discourse analysts ought in our view to be aiming to function as "organic intellectuals" in a range of social struggles. . . , but ought at the same time to be aware that their work is constantly at risk of appropriation by the state and capital.
>
> (Fairclough and Wodak 2010: 110)

For a field that garnered its momentum and reputation by critiquing professional practices (e.g., news reporting à la van Dijk 1993), corporate ideologies (e.g., managerialism in higher education à la Fairclough 1993) and institutional sexism (e.g., female leadership in schools à la Wodak 1996), critical discourse studies is oddly deficient when it comes to the breadth and depth of its engagement with workplace settings. This is all the more surprising given its core commitment to action-oriented – which is to say, *applied* – research. The world of work is certainly a site of fruitful intervention, not least because it is the site where so many people's everyday social struggles take place. Furthermore, language nowadays sits powerfully at the heart of people's livelihoods, and we find more and more people doing work where language is not only an essential skill for securing work but is the very product of this work. This is a world where language is constantly and everywhere at work – something to be controlled and crafted, something to be bought and sold.

To be sure, there are critical discourse analysts who do address certain workplace settings and who devote their attention to the analysis of "workplace discourse". Following the lead of Luke (2002), a cursory review of back issues of a leading journal like *Discourse & Society* confirms this. But there are two striking oversights across this work. First, whole domains of work and explicit language work (or *wordsmithery?*) remain largely neglected, with scholarly attention locked on a handful of settings: education, the media, medicine and the law. Second, the literature of workplace discourse consistently treats workers and workplaces as objects of study rather than as self-reflexive sources of expertise or as sources of valid linguistic insight from which language scholars themselves might learn. With a few exceptions (see below), we find the language of the workplace being effectively detached from workers and re-presented, knowingly and expertly, on their behalf by discourse analysts. All of which seems to run contrary to the collaboration and social engagement ethos of critical discourse studies. It certainly seems at odds with the spirit of the Gramscian "organic intellectuals" invoked by foundational scholars Norman Fairclough and Ruth Wodak (see quote above) – in other words, engaged, sectarian scholars willing to get their hands "dirty" working with "the people".

Without doubt, scholarly engagements with the world of work are intellectually and ideologically risky, perhaps even more so than usual given the proximity of the marketplace, which is to say capitalism. Besides, there are workers and there are workers: some at the privileged, receiving ends of capital and others at the patently disadvantaged end of things. The situation is rendered all the more fraught at a time when scholars are being pressured for "public scholarship" and "community engagement" in ways that are visibly and measurably convenient to neoliberal imperatives (see Thurlow 2015). As Fairclough and Wodak note above, our scholarly interventions in the everyday lives of "real" people – however sincere and honourable – are easily co-opted by the oppressive (or, at least, problematic) systems we mean to critique and change. Partly for this very reason, critical discourse scholars have what Luke (2002: 98) describes as a "penchant. . . for radical scepticism towards system and structure". Nonetheless, if critical discourse studies is to fulfil its self-professed *raison d'être,* then we are surely compelled to take these risks and connect more directly, more collaboratively and productively with the world of work. We are obliged to extend the scope of our analytic/applied research and to listen more directly to the perspectives of workers, many of whom are language experts in their own right.

The current chapter is intended as a critical-cum-practical intervention. The chapter is organised into three parts: the first part summarises the applied principles of critical discourse studies (CDS) and its overlap with applied linguistics (AL); the second part reconsiders the missed opportunities in CDS and allied literatures on workplace, professional, institutional and organisational discourse; the third part of the chapter briefly presents some directions – and fraught possibilities – in workplace research. Perhaps a little unusually for a handbook chapter, I do not offer a blow-by-blow review of the literature, but rather a call for critical discourse scholars (and other *applied* language scholars) to revivify their core principles in the form of properly collaborative engagements with the world of work and, most especially, the work of contemporary language workers. And, to be clear, these engagements should be done not for the sake of "impact" – serving ourselves up to corporatist agendas – but rather for the sake of integrity and, maybe, intellectual reciprocity.

Part 1: The applied principles of CDS (and the critical ethos of AL)

The social theory that undergirds CDS is awash with terms seeking to pin down the nature of large-scale economic shifts in rich post-industrial countries over the last fifty years or more: "post-Fordism", "information society", "knowledge economy", "liquid modernity", "neoliberalism" and "network society" are well-recognized examples. Generally speaking, all of these terms are aligned with the idea that certain previously manufacture-based economies centred around the production of goods have been transformed into economies that are nowadays predominantly rooted in the provision of services and in the commoditization of knowledge. (To be clear: the kind of manufacturing and industrial labour that capitalism depends on has not been simply replaced, but rather displaced or located elsewhere; see Soja 1989; also Harvey 2006). These far-reaching economic changes have inevitably had a transformative impact on – and emerged in conjunction with – the reorganisation of cultural and social life. Specifically, and notably, much of this has centred around the rise of communication as a site of, and resource for, economic exchange in what has sometimes been characterised as the *semioticization* of contemporary life (e.g., Lash and Urry 1994; Baudrillard 1994) or what Fairclough (1999) characterises as the "textual mediation" of social reality.

It is in this broader context that we find more and more workers turning to – or being obliged into – language as part of what Iedema and Scheeres (2003: 318) refer to as the "new textualization of work":

> workers are expected to speak and write in ways not commonly or directly associated with their work in the here-and-now. These language and literacy tasks are new and different, because they do not accompany what happens *during* the work or occur just with those that people work with. . . . Rather they are *about* and *in addition to* the work, with people whom the workers do not necessarily and directly have work contact with.

Indeed, a number of critical language scholars like Norman Fairclough (e.g., also 1999), Deborah Cameron (2000a, 2000b, 2010) and Monika Heller (2003, 2010, 2011) are well known for tracking the ways language has been centred and affected as part of the broader post-industrial commodification of knowledge and communication. For many, like Heller and Cameron, the iconic example of these new forms of labouring – the poster children, if you will – are call-centre workers. Here we find an industry, an entire workforce, of deterritorialized, "disembodied" (i.e., on the other end of a phone) speakers wholly reliant on talk for a living. At the heart of Monica Heller's research – consistent with Iedema and Scheeres (2003: 318) – is an interest in understanding how so many different working contexts have come to depend on language as both a *process* or vehicle and a *product* or outcome of labouring, what she dubs the "wordforce". This is a world where factory workers and medical doctors alike are no longer simply doing their work – making things or fixing people – but must also be able to reflexively account for their labour. In other words, they must be able to write it up and talk about it and generally put it into words. This is also a world where a range of low-paid workers are additionally exploited (and typically unremunerated) for their linguistic/multilingual abilities (see Duchêne and Heller 2012; Roberts 2010). Against this backdrop and within this context, we might reasonably expect to find CDS's core engagement with applied contexts.

A founding ideal of CDS is, of course, the desire to improve people's lives and to effect social change by feeding our critiques and insights back into the "on the ground" sites of our investigations. Following the writing of Teun van Dijk and Ruth Wodak (e.g., van Dijk 2009; Reisigl and Wodak 2009), Lin (2014: 214) summarises the core commitments of CDS. Top of the list is the need for "socially committed research" that contributes to "the understanding and tackling of social problems", research that is "problem-oriented" and which offers "practical implications and applications". Speaking for themselves, and writing specifically for applied linguists, Fairclough and Wodak (2010: 101 and 109) top their own list of CDS's core principles with "addressing social problems" and round off their list with the need for "socially committed" research that treats the analysis of discourse as a mode of "social action". In many respects, CDS is a project of critical language awareness (cf. Fairclough 1999), drawing attention to the role of language and its power to shape the way people conduct their everyday and institutional business. And the idea is always to raise an awareness of the way texts and talk function in people's lives within the so called public sphere.[1]

Although the workplace is not singled out or named specifically, we see in CDS an underlying or implicit concern for the everyday life of language and for sites of power where the mechanisms of representation are controlled and exercised. One allied domain of scholarly activity that does profess a more direct engagement with workplace settings is applied linguistics. In many ways, the boundary between CDS and AL is nowadays quite blurred as scholars working on topics like language learning and teaching have become increasingly interested in issues of power, inequality and discrimination – most especially in the contexts of colonial and postcolonial critiques of English-language pedagogy and the political economies of language learning/instruction more generally (e.g., Canagarajah 1993, 1999; Pennycook 1990, 2001). There is no doubt that applied linguists have sought to engage CDS approaches in their research, particularly as applied linguists themselves turned to critical perspectives more generally. In her slightly idiosyncratic review of critical discourse analysis in applied linguistics, Lin (2014) singles out three areas where she see CDS being deployed in applied linguists: studies of textbooks and school curricula; school leadership and student identities; and public-media discourse. In their review of CDA and AL meanwhile, Mahboob and Paltridge (2013) consider how critical approaches have most notably been used in the study of language policy, language teaching and learning, and language testing. In these two reviews, we see how wedded AL is to the study of very particular workplace settings: most notably educational ones. This brings me to the second part of my chapter.

Part 2: The limits of CDS (and AL) – missed opportunities?

To be sure, the academic literature is awash with research on language in the workplace, and there are hundreds of studies that examine any number of institutional and professional contexts. With surprisingly few exceptions, however, discourse analysts (critical or otherwise), applied linguists and other language scholars tend to write about the same old domains. Examples of this are to be found in large anthologies and handbooks in these allied fields; for example, chapters falling under the rubric of "Institutional Settings" (Gee and Handford 2011), under "Political, Social, and Institutional Domains" (Schiffrin, Tannen and Hamilton 2001), under "Interaction" or "Application" (Wodak, Johnstone and Kerswill 2011), under "Applied Linguistics" (Aronoff and Rees-Miller 2001) or "Applied Sociolinguistics" (Mesthrie 2011) and chapters under "Applied Linguistics in Action" (Simpson 2013). There are critically minded scholars within sociolinguistics/discourse studies who are concerned with the "lower orders" of working life, with, for example, call centres and other poorly paid, highly regulated types of service work.[2] Across the board, however, language scholars seem to be especially enchanted with the "high" professions. Probably as a product of our own bourgeois sensibilities, priorities and networks, we therefore end up knowing a lot about medicine (health communication), the law (forensic linguistics), journalism (media discourse) and, of course, education (still the dominant preoccupation of applied linguistics). One of the more commonly cited criticisms of CDS is that it tends to reinscribe the belief that power is neatly or particularly located in the elite domains of society (e.g., Breeze 2011); indeed, a cursory review of *Discourse & Society* certainly shows a preponderance of studies of medical (top of the list), legal, media and corporate settings. With almost no exception.

CDS is certainly not alone with its restricted purview. In this regard, we might single out the 2011 handbook *Mapping Applied Linguistics: A Guide for Students and Practitioners* by Hall and his colleagues, which is endorsed by one famous discourse analyst (James Gee) as a "major contribution to the very definition and foundations of the field" and by a well-known applied linguist (Angel Lin) as a "comprehensive introduction to the field". Under the section heading "Language and expert uses" – and following a section dedicated to "Language, Learning and Education" – we find chapters on translation, lexicography, forensic linguistics and language pathology.[3] The field of applied linguistics continues, for the most part, to be dominated by its attention to educational workplaces. Following a 2004 special issue on forensic linguistics and a 2003 special issue on medical discourse (see below), it's been quite a while since the journal *Applied Linguistics* made substantial commitments to engaging workplace contexts beyond language learning and second-language pedagogy. (With just two or three isolated papers in the last decade.) Flowerdew and Wei (2013) is one slightly more recent volume that does expand the reach of applied linguistics; with four chapters grounded in educational/language-learning contexts, four on media/news discourse and one of courtroom/forensic discourse, we also find studies looking at healthcare, corporate, advertising and political texts and contexts. While the field does sometimes move into more diverse terrains, the heartland of AL continues to be education.

Beyond the narrow range of working domains that typically occupy discourse scholars, there are workplaces we leave almost completely unexplored. There are so many other worlds of contemporary language expertise beyond the iconic "easy target" world of call centres: places or domains where people's professional livelihoods depend – in explicit, direct and material ways – on the crafting, honing, manipulation, design and expression of words. One might call these people language engineers, although I prefer the slightly old-fashioned notion of wordsmiths. With one or two notable exceptions (e.g., Kuiper's 1996 studies of sportscasters and auctioneers), there seems to be very little research in/on some otherwise pretty obvious domains of wordsmithery like dialect coaches, voice-over artists, speech writers and campaigners, technical writers and copy-editors, public relations officers (cf. Sleurs and Jacobs 2005) and advertising copywriters, to name a few. This, I think, is a missed opportunity which should be rectified.

The boundaries of language work are, of course, not always easily drawn. To what extent, for example, are we to view the work of typographers as that of "designer" rather than "writer"? The language-specific tasks and skills of teachers, physicians and managers are undeniable, too. As Jaworski (2014) shows nicely in his work on the sociolinguistics of art, there are realms or domains where ostensibly non-linguistic work draws on language. Besides, as I noted from the outset, under post-industrial capitalism we find an increasingly diverse range of workers being obliged into language work. It would, of course, also be incorrect to suggest that language work is a distinctly contemporary or modern phenomenon. Throughout history, we find cultural figures and occupational roles marked by an attention to/dependence on wordsmithery: oracles, scribes, town criers, muezzins and story tellers are all obvious cases in point. By the same token, long-standing traditions of language workers such as actors, priests, teachers, politicians and poets all continue into the present day. On this point, it may well prove to be another limitation of applied approaches to workplace studies in CDS that they are seldom rooted historically; ours is a field which arises from and tends to focus on the cultural politics of contemporary post-industrial societies.

Most well-recognized scholars of workplace discourse like Koester (2006, 2010) and Holmes (2006; Holmes and Stubbe 2003), for example, all tend to follow the conventions established by Drew and Heritage (1992; see also Connor and Upton 2004, on corpus-analytic approaches). As with so many studies on workplace discourse, Koester and Holmes's research hinges on analyses of isolated (which is not to say invalid or non-representative) samples of everyday institutional/professional language use and social interactions. However richly contextualised and carefully detailed their studies are, language is invariably abstracted and recontextualized as a "text" (or, better yet, a transcript) for analysis and discussion. Typically, we find language being removed from workers and re-presented (knowingly and expertly) by academics on their behalf. There is certainly very little work within discourse studies that privileges the perspectives of workers themselves. For example, for all their research on (sic) translation and language teaching practices, applied linguists tend not to think about – not explicitly or directly anyway – the translators or language teachers as practitioners and as people. Addressing applied linguists in particular, Sarangi (2005) offers his own pointed summing up of the limitations of professional discourse studies over the last 30 years or more: the bottom line, he notes, is that workplaces and workers are treated as largely detached objects of analysis rather than sites of deeper engagement or collaboration.

On this last point – the matter of collaboration – it seems all the more surprising that neither applied linguists nor critical discourse analysts evidence much in the way of direct application and uptake. Rees-Miller (2001: 639–650) explains things in a way that surely resonates for CDS scholarship too:

> much work in applied linguistics has not reached a stage where specific solutions to problems can be suggested in particular settings. . . . This suggests a one-way street in which theory is at the starting point, and the applied linguist directs traffic from theory to practice.

Too infrequently, says Rees-Miller, do linguists (applied or otherwise) bother to see if or how the theory traffic they are directing arrives as its desired destination. It is what makes Sarangi and Candlin's (2003) special issue of *Applied Linguistics* exceptional and, it must be said, exemplary. With papers from practitioners, here we have an explicit discussion of the possibilities and pitfalls of collaborations between academics and non-academics (in this case, medical practitioners and healthcare workers). Perhaps not surprisingly, it is anthropologists and other ethnographically minded researchers who usually come closest to direct, concrete engagements between academia and other kinds of workplace (e.g., papers in Cefkin 2009). Even closer still are those scholar-practitioners like "design anthropologists" (see Wasson 2009) who work in businesses rather than universities using ethnographic methods for organisational and consumer research. For the most part, there is seldom anything closely resembling the explicit collaboration or the kind of "thick participation" of which Sarangi talks. In my cursory review of *Discourse & Society* articles published since the journal's founding in 1990, the study by Wagner and Wodak (2006) of professional women's biographical accounts of their own work stands alone as a project explicitly privileging the perspective of workers themselves.

In Cameron's (2000b, 2008) two sister publications about the discourse practices (and ideological ramifications) of call centre work (what she refers to as "communication factories"), she demonstrates the insights to be gained from turning CDS to/against the workplace, and against language work in particular. The first paper is an exemplary critical discourse analysis of the way language is standardised and the way worker's language use is disciplined, all of which points to the problematic and, specifically, gendered ways language is nowadays reified as a set of skills and commodified for the purposes of the global marketplace (see also Cameron 2000a, for a more extensive, multi-sited discussion of these processes). It is the second paper, however, that I orient to here. While still concerned with the language-ideological and lived experience of "top-down" talk, Cameron turns her attention to some of the on-the-ground ways call centre workers manage, negotiate and sometimes resist the regulatory, standardising practices of service manuals, training programmes, etc. In other words, and even though her paper is titled "Talk from the Top Down", Cameron invites us to think this time about bottom-up talk by attending to the ways locally managed, in-the-moment talk is structured by the institutional discourses of which it is a part. Her principal aim in this second paper is to show how micro-analytic approaches to institutional talk (e.g., by Conversation Analysts) are inherently flawed in not accounting properly for the ways workplace discourse is structured by normative systems of regulation and surveillance. Having said this, she also goes on to acknowledge and then conclude that: "Clearly, [workers] are not just 'cultural dopes' who mechanically follow the rules handed down to them" (152). And here's the rub.

While I am motivated by the inherent possibilities of combing the kind of bottom-up/top-down analysis that Cameron presents, I still find it lacking in one key way: evidence of the way speakers themselves speak about their institutionalised talk. We have elegantly – and convincingly – produced evidence that workers are managing language, but no clear evidence of the ways they themselves make sense of these moments. Are they, for example, aware of them? How do they feel about the top-down/bottom-up tension? What are their own priorities or concerns when it comes to working with language? It is these kinds of questions which bring me to the third part of my chapter.

Part 3: New (or not so new) directions for CDS – fraught possibilities?

> *To effect change, institutionalized critique needs to invoke discourses recognized within the social practice it critiques. . . . For [critical interventions] to be effective, discourses of value must be found that are recognized by the critic and the critiqued.*

(van Leeuwen 2014)

In sum, even a cursory review of the workplace literature within CDS and allied fields reveals a determined interest in institutional/professional domains, although with a breadth and depth of engagement that is somewhat limited. It is with these limitations in mind that the final part of the chapter turns to some new (or not so new) directions for CDS, all of which are inevitably fraught with methodological and epistemological risks.

In addition to its core objective of social critique, CDS is also principally committed to exposing gaps in academic orthodoxy and to exposing them as ideological/hegemonic (Billig 2003: 40). If, however, we are to move beyond what Billig (2003: 44) sees as a mere "rhetoric of critique" – a self-serving exercise in academic branding (e.g., "CDA") – the field needs to remain "open to new forms of writing and to beware of its own linguistic orthodoxies". And it is the last of Billig's points that I wish to end with here: the question of our linguistic orthodoxies. In addition to expanding the *breadth* of workplace research in CDS, there seems also be a need to *deepen* our research. And this could/should happen in ways which van Leeuwen pinpoints nicely in his observations quoted above, and which echo Rees-Miller's earlier comments about the disconnect or lack of reciprocity between language scholars and other (language) workers. And I want to illustrate this with a quick case-study demonstration.

Case study: advertising copywriters

Working hand-in-glove with branding agents and with art directors, copywriters are some of the key "word people" at the heart of any advertising campaign. Part of what draws me to advertising is that, like many other critical discourse analysts, my work often entails representing, interpreting and critiquing the products of these professional language workers. Reasonably or not, I have on more than one occasion been asked (and have asked myself) in response to otherwise trenchant, critical analyses, "So, how do you know the advertisers didn't already know this?". Well, I am beginning to recognise that the answer may not be absolutely necessary to my work, but it would certainly enhance my work.

It is clearly the case that advertisers/copywriters know their language; they also do language really well. And not simply in moments – as with the German-made examples in Figures 22.1 and 22.2 – where they are advertising language schools. But also when they frequently take up and play with the politics of language as an explicit subject matter, as with Figure 22.3 where South African advertisers for Nando's cleverly seized upon a high profile language ideological debate that ensued when a member of parliament said "fuck you" to the deputy speaker of the house. It is moments like these that probably prompted Cook (2008, n.p.) to state the following: "Advertising is one of the most prominent, powerful, and ubiquitous contemporary uses of language. . . . Advertising's creative use of language makes it a particularly rich site for language and discourse analysis." Indeed, Cook has himself been hugely influential in driving linguistic/discourse-analytic research on advertising. His 2008 four-volume the "language and advertising" research is a tour de force. At the risk of sounding churlish, however, it is striking to see the rather meagre attempt (in one relatively short, slightly negatively framed section in Volume 4) at making space for the voice of insiders. From within CDS, a rare – and perhaps unique – instance of a scholar attending to the voices/perspectives of advertisers is Kelly-Holmes's (1998) analysis of reports, interviews and speeches by marketers in Eastern Europe.

As is true of so much workplace discourse analysis, we end up knowing quite a lot about what linguists and discourse analysts think about advertising, but we know next to nothing about the way advertisers think about language themselves. How, for example, copywriters

Figures 22.1 and 22.2 The linguistic work of copywriters

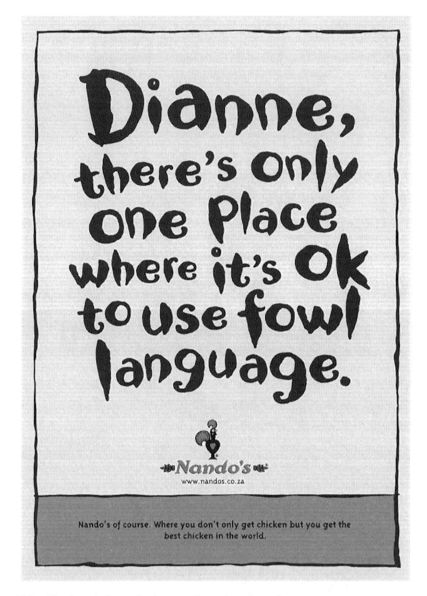

Figure 22.3 The linguistic work of copywriters (continued)

come to their wordsmithery; where and how they learn their skills and hone their craft; how they reflect on and theorise the nature of their language work. (Yes, we are not the only ones who theorise!). In the same presentation from which the quote above is taken, van Leeuwen also noted how institutional practices are often learned through osmosis and, as such, not always easy to pinpoint or to articulate – even for insiders. Of course, nowadays workplace practices are increasingly taught (and regulated) through "explicitly programmed protocols" (see also Cameron 2000b). In this regard, S. Candlin (2003) considers what she sees as some of the challenges faced by discourse analysts looking to collaborate with non-academics. As a starting point, she argues, academics should pay close attention to the kind of training professionals receive. This has certainly been my initial port of call as I prepare to understand where, as emblematic modern-day wordsmiths, copywriters learn their applied linguistics – even if this is not what they (or we) would call it. What points of contact, I wondered, might we find between our ways of knowing and doing language, and theirs? An initial survey of some of the leading US-American advertising textbooks demonstrates the disconnect between their ways of framing things and ours. The following are just three extracts lifted from the dozen or so textbooks I have looked at.

Extracts 1, 2 and 3: "Linguistics" for copywriters [4]

A successful copywriter is a savvy marketer and a literary master, sometimes described as a "killer poet". Copywriters love words. . . Copywriters get paid good money for playing very skilful word games. They are experts on words, or rather, students of them.

. . . an effective headline: usually no more than 10 words, should contain an action verb, contain an interest-provoking idea. . . the slogan should be short, clear and easy to remember.

Communication [is] the process of establishing a commonness or oneness of thought between a sender and a receiver. . . . Semiotics involves the study of the nature of meaning and asks how our reality – words, gestures, myths, products/services, theories – acquire meaning.

As the first book explains – the only one, I might add to attend explicitly to copywriting – the work of the copywriter is framed unequivocally as that of wordsmith – "literary master" or "killer poet" even. Not, it has to be said, with a background in linguistics per se but, so students are told, in literature. Beyond this, however, everything is rooted in a highly conventional, transactional "Sender-Message-Receiver" model of communication. Generally speaking, we find that language is elided from communication. In fact, there are no entries for "language" whatsoever in any of the indexes of the books I looked at. With just the one fleeting – and somewhat questionable – reference to "semiotics" (Extract 3), linguistic considerations are strikingly absent. References to grammar, syntax and style are rendered as bullet-pointed skill sets where students are taught, for example, that good headlines must not exceed 10 words and must have an "action verb". Nowhere did I find a discussion of metaphors, punning, language play, humour, etc. or any other complex pragmatic and semantic issues. Needless to say, the performative, constitutive nature of language is overshadowed completely by its supposedly neutral/reflective nature, and – just to be quite clear – questions of power and representational politics are non-existent.

It certainly seems that the disconnect between linguists and copywriters is a two-way street: linguists not listening to copywriters and copywriters not attending to linguists! What are we to make of this? A vast domain of language workers seemingly ignorant of and/or with no regard for academic language work? Do they really have nothing to learn from us, or we from them? The "problem" with our work as linguists – as self-appointed language experts – is that we just don't listen very much. (Or we only listen very selectively.) When it comes to language itself, we rather like to *tell* people but not *ask* people. Partly, I think, this is because we continue to be dogged by the fraught relationship between theory and practice, between academic knowledge and "real world" knowledge, and between descriptive research and applied research. Nonetheless, in his well-known statement in support of critical applied linguistics, Pennycook (1990: 25–26) argues that: "[we would] do well to be more humble in the world, listening to the many alternative views of language and learning, rather than preaching our views as the newest and best".

337

Nor is it just a matter of listening better. Another unfulfilled potential lies in the avoidance of sustained, collaborative engagements – in our practice and/or in our writing. Everywhere we find examples of academics getting very close to domains of work, but not close enough or, perhaps, not for long enough. This does not mean that "best practice" examples are completely non-existent. Janet Holmes and her colleagues have, for example, created an online workplace resource based on their research (http://worktalk.immigration.govt.nz/), and Jan Blommaert (2005) writes candidly about his "expert witness testimony" in sites of immigration.[5] There are even rare instances of CDS scholars writing more explicitly about their collaborative engagements in applied contexts (e.g., Koller, n.d; also papers in the Sarangi and Candlin 2003 special issue). Usually, however, we read about opportunities for direct intervention and concrete application and we hear reference to these "possibilities", but seldom do we hear about actual outcomes and uptake. Why do we not write more about these engagements? Why do we not create validated spaces in which to write about them? Are the politics of these engagements just too fraught to share?

Conclusion

Theo van Leeuwen (above) reminds us that, in order for our work to effect change, at whatever level, it needs to be recognised within the sites of our intervention, and this means our critiques must be valued by more than just ourselves. As awkward and fraught as this might be, we need, therefore, to find ways to make ourselves relevant and useful. And this may mean having to forego some of our "linguistic orthodoxies" (Billig 2003) and, perhaps, be willing to dislodge or rather decentre the linguist as the ultimate arbiter of language and, by extension, the critical discourse analyst as the authority on power and its uses (cf. Luke 2002). Standing from without a system or institution or workplace is ideal for the purposes of critique; it is only from within a system, however, that one is able to effect change. Throughout the literature on workplace discourse (within critical discourse studies as elsewhere), we find evidence of research that sits tantalisingly close to direct intervention and collaboration with non-linguists. Many ostensibly application- or action-oriented discourse studies end with recommendations for the potential uses of their "findings" back for the "real world" contexts of their research. And if scholars are indeed undertaking these kinds of collaborations and making concrete contributions, they tend to exclude this work from their publications such is the demand for theoretical over the practical. Or, at least, such is the tenacity of our theory-practice binary. In the way of a conclusion – since there really are no neat conclusions or solutions – I return to the principles that undergird the field of CDS and as they are articulated by kind of "big thinkers" we revere (Foucault and Deleuze in Bouchard 1977: 208):

Foucault: In this sense theory does not express, translate, or serve to apply practice: it is practice. . . . it is an activity conducted alongside those who struggle for power, and not their illumination from a safe distance. . . .

Deleuze: Precisely. A theory is exactly like a box of tools. . . . It must be useful. It must function. . . . If no one uses it, beginning with the theoretician himself (sic). . . , then the theory is worthless or the moment is inappropriate.

Acknowledgements

Material used in this chapter was first presented at the Finnish Association of Applied Linguistics (AFinLA) conference in Turku, November 2013, and then as part of an invited panel

I organised for the conference "Sociolinguistics of Globalization" in Hong Kong, June 2015; I'm grateful to participants/panellists at these events for their comments and suggestions. I'm also grateful to my research assistant, Eva Kuske, for her help in tracking down some of the literature used in the current iteration of this work. I thank Nando's, a South African flame-grilled peri-peri chicken restaurant, for permission to reproduce their advert. Every reasonable effort was made to seek permission for using the other two adverts.

Notes

1 As I have been arguing elsewhere (Thurlow 2015), so-called public or community engagement starts *de facto* with our students and the publics already in our classrooms which are no-less-important or influential sites of language awareness raising and/or conscientizing. Our students inevitably go into other applied spaces of work, and hopefully with the critiques/insights learned through their studies. This is not a disingenuous defence of our scholarly "impact", but an essential fact of our educational mission and, for many, our civic service.

2 As used in discourse studies, the term "service work" seems very loaded. Why, I wonder, is selling a burger or a holiday package any more obviously service than, say, the selling of health, justice or knowledge that is the business of medics, lawyers and teachers?

3 The "definitive", "comprehensive" volume by Hall, Smith and Wicaksono (2011) includes a single page on critical discourse analysis as one of three examples of "social approaches to discourse analysis"; the impact of CDS on AL may not be so great after all.

4 The three extracts are taken from the following textbooks, respectively: Wells, William, Burnett, John and Moriarty, Sandra E. (2003). *Advertising: Principles & practice*. Upper Saddle River: Prentice Hall./ Belch, George E. and Belch, Michael A. (1993). *Introduction to advertising and promotion*. Homewood: Irwin./ Russell, J. Thomas and Lane, W. Ronald. (1996). *Kleppner's advertising procedure*, 13th edn. Upper Saddle River, NJ: Prentice Hall.

5 As Flowerdew (2013) notes, Holmes and her colleagues have sometimes negotiated the goals of their research projects with non-academic participants who are treated as collaborators and consultants (see Holmes, Marra and Vine 2011).

Further reading

The central premise of this chapter is that our best work has yet to be done; nonetheless, the following recommendations are very good places to start.

Cameron, D. (2000). *Good to talk? Living and working in a communication culture*. London: Sage.

One of the world's leading critical discourse scholars, this well-known book makes an outstanding contribution to our understanding of the politics and practices of language at work.

Holmes, J., Marra, M. and Vine, D. (2011). *Leadership, discourse and ethnicity*. Oxford: Oxford University Press.

Janet Holmes is an internationally regarded figure in the field of workplace discourse studies. This co-authored book, in particular, is exemplary in its collaborative/consultative approach to their research participants.

Sarangi, S. and Candlin, C. N. (2003). Trading between reflexivity and relevance: New challenges for applied linguistics. *Applied Linguistics* 24(3): 271–285.

This is the introductory paper in a special issue of the journal *Applied Linguistics;* all the papers in this issue are worth reading, but especially the three response papers by Aaron Cicourel, Angus Clarke and Sally Candlin.

References

Aronoff, M. and Rees-Miller, J. (eds.) (2001). *The handbook of linguistics*. Malden, MA: Blackwell.

Baudrillard, J. (1994). *Simulacra and simulation* [English translation]. Ann Arbor, MI: University of Michigan Press.

Billig, M. (2003). Critical discourse analysis and the rhetoric of critique. In G. Weiss and R. Wodak (eds.), *Critical discourse analysis: Theory and interdisciplinarity*, 35–46. London: Palgrave Macmillan.

Blommaert, J. (2005). *Discourse: A critical introduction*. Cambridge: Cambridge University Press.

Bouchard, D. F. (1977). Intellectuals and power: A conversation between Michel Foucault and Gilles Deleuze. In D.F. Bouchard (ed.), *Language, counter-memory, practice: Selected essays and interviews by Michel Foucault,* 205–217. Ithaca, NY: Cornell University Press.

Breeze, R. (2011). *Critical discourse analysis and its critics*. Pragmatics, 21(4): 493–525.

Cameron, D. (2000a). *Good to talk? Living and working in a communication culture*. London: Sage.

Cameron, D. (2000b). Styling the worker: Gender and the commodification of language in the globalized service economy. *Journal of Sociolinguistics* 4(3): 323–347.

Cameron, D. (2008). Talk from the top down. *Language & Communication* 28: 143–155.

Cameron, D. (2012). The commodification of language: English as a global commodity. In T. Nevalainen and E. C. Traugott (eds.), *The Oxford handbook of the history of English,* 352–361. Oxford: Oxford University Press.

Canagarajah, A. S. (1993). Critical ethnography of a Sri Lankan classroom: Ambiguities in student opposition to reproduction through ESOL. *TESOL Quarterly* 27: 601–626.

Canagarajah, A. S. (1999). *Resisting linguistic imperialism in English teaching*. Oxford: Oxford University Press.

Candlin, S. (2003). Issues arising when the professional workplace is the site of applied linguistic research. *Applied Linguistics* 24(3): 386–394.

Cefkin, M. (2009). *Ethnography and the corporate encounter: Reflections on research in and of corporations*. New York: Berghahn Books.

Connor, U. and Upton, T. A. (eds.) (2004). *Discourse in the professions: Perspectives from corpus linguistics*. Amsterdam: Benjamins.

Cook, G. (ed.) (2008). *The language of advertising*. London: Routledge.

Drew, P. and Heritage, J. (eds.) (1992). *Talk at work: Interaction in institutional settings*. Cambridge: Cambridge University Press.

Fairclough, N. (1993). Critical discourse analysis and the marketization of public discourse: The universities. *Discourse & Society* 4(2): 133–168.

Fairclough, N. (1999). Global capitalism and critical awareness of language. *Language Awareness* 8(2): 71–83.

Fairclough, N. and Wodak, R. (2010). Critical discourse analysis in action. In C. Coffin, K. O'Halloran and T. Lillis (eds.), *Applied linguistics methods: A reader: Systemic functional linguistics, critical discourse analysis and ethnography,* 98–111. London: Routledge.

Flowerdew, J. (2013). Introduction: Discourse in context. In J. Flowerdew and L. Wei (eds.), *Discourse in context: Contemporary applied linguistics,* 1–26. London: Bloomsbury.

Flowerdew, J. and Wei, L. (2013). *Discourse in context: Contemporary applied linguistics*. London: Bloomsbury.

Gee, J. P. and Handford, M. (eds.) (2011). *The Routledge handbook of discourse analysis*. Hoboken, NJ: Taylor & Francis.

Hall, C. J., Smith, P. H. and Wicaksono, R. (2011). *Mapping applied linguistics: A guide for students and practitioners*. London & New York: Routledge.

Harvey, D. (2006). *Spaces of global capitalism: Towards a theory of uneven geographical development*. London: Verso.

Heller, M. (2010). The commodification of language. *Annual Review of Anthropology* 39: 101–114.

Holmes, J. (2006). *Gendered talk at work*. Malden, MA: Wiley-Blackwell.

Holmes, J., Marra, M. and Vine, D. (2011). *Leadership, discourse and ethnicity*. Oxford: Oxford University Press.

Holmes, J. and Stubbe, M. (2003). *Power and politeness in the workplace*. Harlow: Pearson Education.

Jaworski, A. (2014). Metrolingual art: Multilingualism and heteroglossia. *International Journal of Bilingualism* 18(2): 134–158.

Kelly-Holmes, H. (1998). The discourse of Western marketing professionals in Central and Eastern Europe: Their role in the creation of a context for marketing and advertising messages. *Discourse & Society* 9(3): 339–362.

Koester, A. (2006). *Investigating workplace discourse*. London: Routledge.

Koester, A. (2010). *Workplace discourse*. London: Continuum.

Koller, V. (n.d.). Applying critical discourse analysis: Research and intervention in health communication. PowerPoint presentation. Accessed August 26, 2015, www.academia.edu/4436103/Applying_critical_discourse_analysis_Research_and_intervention_in_health_communication

Kuiper, K. (1996). *Smooth talkers: The linguistic performance of auctioneers and sportscasters.* Mahwah, NJ: Erlbaum.

Lash, S. and Urry, J. (1994). *Economies of signs and spaces.* London: Sage.

Lin, A. (2014). Critical discourse analysis in applied linguistics: A methodological review. *Annual Review of Applied Linguistics* 34: 213–232.

Luke, A. (2002). Beyond science and ideological critique: Developments in critical discourse analysis. *Annual Review of Applied Linguistics* 22: 96–110.

Mahboob, A. and Paltridge, B. (2013). Critical discourse analysis and applied linguistics. In C. A. Chapelle (ed.), *The encyclopedia of applied linguistics.* Accessed August 14, 2015, www.academia.edu/2356788/ Critical_Discourse_Analysis_and_Critical_Applied_Linguistics

Maybin, J. and Swann, J. (eds.) (2010). *The Routledge companion to English language studies.* London: Routledge.

Mesthrie, R. (ed.) (2011). *The Cambridge handbook of sociolinguistics.* Cambridge: Cambridge University Press.

Pennycook, A. (1990). Towards a critical applied linguistics for the 1990s. *Issues in Applied Linguistics* 1: 8–28.

Pennycook, A. (2001). *Critical applied linguistics: A critical introduction.* Mahwah, NJ: Erlbaum.

Rees-Miller, J. (2001). Applied linguistics. In M. Aronoff and J. Rees-Miller (eds.), *The handbook of linguistics.* Malden, MA: Blackwell.

Roberts, C. (2010). Language socialization in the workplace. *Annual Review of Applied Linguistics* 30: 211–227.

Sarangi, S. (2005). The conditions and consequences of professional discourse studies. *Journal of Applied Linguistics* 2(3): 371–394.

Sarangi, S. and Candlin, C. N. (2003). Trading between reflexivity and relevance: New challenges for applied linguistics. *Applied Linguistics* 24(3): 271–285.

Sarangi, S. and Roberts, C. (eds.) (1999). *Talk, work, and institutional order: Discourse in medical, mediation, and management settings.* Berlin: Mouton de Gruyter.

Schiffrin, D., Tannen, D. and Hamilton, H. E. (eds.) (2001). *The handbook of discourse analysis.* Malden, MA: Blackwell.

Simpson, J. (ed.) (2013). *The Routledge handbook of applied linguistics.* London: Routledge.

Sleurs, K. and Jacobs, G. (2005). Beyond preformulation: An ethnographic perspective on press releases. *Journal of Pragmatics* 41: 1251–1273.

Soja, E. (1989). *Postmodern geographies: The reassertion of space in critical social theory.* London: Verso Press.

Thurlow, C. (2015). *Where did all the teachers go? The divisive implications of "impact" and "community engagement".* Paper presented at the 4th iMean conference, Warwick University, England, 09–11 April.

van Dijk, T. (1993). *Elite discourse and racism.* Newbury Park, CA: Sage.

van Leeuwen, T. (2014). Multimodal legitimation. In keynote address for the 5th *Critical Approaches to Discourse Analysis Across Disciplines Conference,* Budapest, September 1–3, 2014.

Wagner, I. and Wodak, R. (2006). Performing success: Identifying strategies of self-presentation in women's biographical narratives. *Discourse & Society* 17(3): 385–411.

Wasson, C. (2009). Linguistic anthropology. In F. Bargiela-Chiappini (ed.), *The handbook of business discourse,* 194–212. Edinburgh: Edinburgh University Press.

Wodak, R. (1996). Power, discourse, and styles of female leadership in school committee meetings. In D. Corson (ed.), *Discourse and power in educational organizations,* 31–54. Cresskill, NJ: Hampton Press.

Wodak, R., Johnstone, B. and Kerswill, P. (eds.) (2011). *The Sage handbook of sociolinguistics.* Los Angeles: Sage.

Part IV
Social divisions and power

23

Class and class warfare

David Block

Introduction

A radical view of CDA. . . emphasises the power behind discourse rather than just the power in discourse (how people with power shape the 'order of discourse' as well as the social order in general, versus how people with power control what happens in specific interactions such as interviews). It correspondingly emphasises ideology rather than (just) persuasion and manipulation. It views discourse as a stake in social struggle as well as a site of social struggle, and views social struggle as including class struggle. It sets as an objective for CDA raising people's consciousness of how language contributes to the domination of some people by others, as a step towards social emancipation. This is radical stuff, one might say! But isn't this just 1970s radicalism which is now terribly old-fashioned, out of date as well as out of fashion? I don't think, so let me explain why.

(Fairclough 2014: 2)

In this way, Norman Fairclough explains what he terms a "radical view" of Critical Discourse Analysis (CDA) in the introduction of the third edition of *Language and Power.*There is a kind of call to arms in this statement as Fairclough seems intent on reminding CDA researchers of the Marxist or quasi-Marxist roots of CDA – or, at least that corner of CDA that Fairclough has always inhabited (see Fairclough 2010, for an account of his trajectory over three decades). Definitions of CDA are not always easy to come by and when they are provided they are often oblique and indirect. This might be because, as Zotzmann and O'Regan (2016: 114) explain, CDA "is neither constituted by an homogeneous theoretical framework, nor by a set of fixed methodological tools. . . [as] each individual research project fine-tunes its theoretical and conceptual framework as well as its methodology to its object of investigation". Still, there is some common ground across different theoretical and methodological frameworks, and following Fairclough (2010: 4), CDA may be understood as "the [*transdisciplinary*] analysis of dialectal *relations between* discourse and other objects, elements or moments, as well as analysis of the 'internal relations' of discourse" (Fairclough 2010: 4). Elsewhere, Wodak (2014: 303) highlights how "CDA is characterized by the common interest in demystifying ideologies and power through the systematic and retroductable [comprehensible] . . . investigation of semiotic data (written, spoken, or visual)" (Wodak 2014: 303). The focus is thus not exclusively on discourse as language, but on *semiosis*, the processes through which multiple semiotic modes are deployed or simply emerge in "the inter-subjective making of meaning" (Fairclough, Jessop and Sayer 2010: 220). In addition, CDA always contains an "explicit commitment to a critique of problematic social practices with a view of transforming them for the better... [and a]nalyses conducted... usually contain a normative component" (Zotzmann and O'Regan 2016: 114). This normative component is important because it embodies a "conviction that there is no neutral and value-free social science and claims about the apolitical nature of linguistic analysis are regarded to be themselves ideological, i.e., they conceal their own political interests" (Zotzmann and O'Regan 2016: 114). As Wodak puts it, "CDA researchers... attempt to make their own positions and interests explicit while retaining their respective scientific methodologies and while remaining self-reflective of their own research process" (Wodak 2014: 303). In short, CDA aims not just to analyse discourse in different contexts but to propose alternative ways of organising society.

Over the past three decades CDA researchers have worked in varied ways while always incorporating in their work an interest in combatting injustices in contemporary societies. However, one thing that I note as a relative outsider to CDA is the way that the political economy angle, usually present in Fairclough's work, has become a minority strand in CDA – albeit, a still important one – and many researchers have tended to concentrate on *cultural* injustice in their work. Thus there has been a great deal published on nationalism, racism, xenophobia, gender bias, homophobia and environmentalism, and somewhat less which is inspired in political economy. Two special issues of *Critical Discourses Studies,* 'Class and discourse' (Machin and Richardson 2008) and 'Post-Marxist discourse theory and critical political economy' (Phelan and Dahlberg 2014), are something of an exception in this regard. My interests lie in Fairclough's camp of CDA as I have recently argued for a clear, explicit and unequivocal political economy angle on a range of language and society issues, focusing especially on class (Block 2014, 2015, 2016; Block, Gray and Holborow 2012). It is this perspective that I bring to CDA and the one which I will develop in this chapter.

From a realist perspective (Bhaskar 1989), CDA is situated in the discursive realm of human activity, as opposed to the material realm. And this means that where CDA can help in class analysis is in the analyses of class as culture, as meaning-making, as (re)presented reality and so on, somewhat in the tradition of Raymond Williams (1977). For example, CDA is useful as a way of understanding how working class interests and sensibilities intersect with the rise of right-wing populist parties in most European countries in recent years, from the *Front National* in France to *Chrysí Avgí* (Golden Dawn) in Greece. Marsdal (2013) observes that the rise of these parties is inflected by a shift in emphasis in the public sphere from traditional economic interests (public services, equitable tax regimes, workers' rights) to 'values-based' interests (immigration, incarceration policies, recognition issues such as LGBTQ rights and feminism). CDA also allows us to make sense of how 'anything goes' often characterises right-wing semiosis, via "discursive and rhetorical strategies which combine incompatible phenomena, make false claims sound innocent, allow denying the obvious, say the 'unsayable' and transcend the limits of the permissible" (Wodak 2013: 32–33). In the latter part of this chapter, I return to the notion of 'anything goes' in the discussion of how the political right in Spain demonise those who challenge their authority as they engage in class warfare against the popular classes. This will come at the end of a very selective discussion of some of the ways in which class has figured as a key construct in CDA research. First, however, I discuss class as a construct.

Class

In January 2011 the BBC launched the great British Class Survey (GBCS), which was based on ongoing empirical research and scholarship by Savage and several co-researchers (Bennett et al. 2013; Savage et al. 2014). The survey captured the attention of a part of the British population and the media, and over 160,000 people eventually responded. However, the results of the survey could not be said to be very reliable as the sample was self-selected: in effect it was the kind of people who would bother to complete a BBC survey on class (i.e., they were middle class, well-educated and used to having their voice heard). Thus 75% of the respondents ended up being situated in the upper part of the class scale which emerged from the survey. An additional survey, carried out by a professional survey company called GfK, and based on a considerably smaller sample of 1,026 respondents, produced results that were probably more reflective of the state of class relations in the UK. In this case 37% of respondents were situated in the upper part of the class scale. Still, as Mills (2014: 439) notes somewhat unforgivingly, the GfK sample constitutes "a flimsy source upon which to build... [an] inductive edifice" (Mills 2014: 439).

In both surveys, Britons were placed in one of seven categories which the designers of the survey deemed relevant for the 21st century class system in Britain. These categories were: Elite, Established middle class, Technical middle class, New affluent workers, Traditional working class, Emergent service works and the Precariat. Glosses of these categories, along with the results of the two surveys carried out, are reproduced in Table 23.1 below.

There are, no doubt, a fair few problems with an approach to class which categorises individuals as members of a broader society in this way. As authors such as Skeggs (2004), Jones (2011) and Tylor (2013) remind us, discussions about class are not just about people being classified, or even how they *do* class in their day-to-day lives; rather, there is also the issue of *who* decides how people are classified. In addition, much has been made of the 'new' class in such discussions – the 'precariat'. The precariat, as a concept, can be found in the work of Italian Marxist scholars such as Bologna (1987), but it has been spread around the Anglophone world and internationally in recent years by Standing (2011). Interestingly, and depending on how one looks at such matters, it is not really a class category along the same lines as the other six categories in Savage et al.'s (2013) model, given that the very notion and reality of precariousness clearly cuts across at least three of the other class positions. Thus, sales and retail assistants (New affluent workers), secretaries (Traditional working class) and bar staff (Emergent service works) are all subject today to the vicissitudes of the current labour market, as are many civil service workers across Europe, it should be added. And this means, among other things, that many people, assumed to be in stable employment, live their lives not knowing if they have a job from one week to the next (or even one day to the next).

In direct reference to Savage et al. (2013), Bradley (2014) cautions that a fixation on categories may cause us to lose sight of the fact that from Marx and Weber onwards, class has always been understood in relational terms: it is not about individually embodied traits and characteristics; rather, it is about how people are interconnected and articulated in broader economic, political, social and cultural webs. This articulation extends to different indexicals of identity, such as race, and how race and class intersect, an angle which, as Rollock (2014) notes, Savage et al.'s model cannot contemplate. Rollock makes the point that a comparison of the life experiences of middle-class white people and middle-class black people in contemporary Britain reveals how "blackness does not grant... an equivalent degree of privilege as... whiteness does ...." (Rollock 2014: 446). Finally, Mills (op. cit.) questions the entire purpose

David Block

Table 23.1 Classes, survey results, example occupations and descriptions

Class	% GBSC	% GfK	Example occupations (Savage et al. 2013: 231–232)	Description (Savage et al. 2013: 230)
Elite	22	6	high-level systems managers (financial, high-tech, personnel, organisational), lawyers, doctors, dentists	Very high economic capital (especially savings), high social capital, very high highbrow cultural capital
Established middle class	43	25	electrical engineers, occupational therapists, town planners, special education needs teachers	High economic capital, high status of mean contacts, high highbrow and emerging cultural capital
Technical middle class	10	6	pilots, pharmacists, higher education teachers, natural & social sciences professionals, physical scientists	High economic capital, very high mean score on social contacts, but relatively few contacts reported, moderate cultural capital
New affluent workers	6	15	Electricians, plumbers, sales and retail assistants, postal workers, kitchen and catering assistants	Moderately good economic capital, moderately poor mean score of social contacts, high range, moderate highbrow but good emerging cultural capital
Traditional working class	2	14	Secretaries, van drivers, cleaners, care workers	Moderately poor economic capital, though with reasonable house price, few social contacts, low highbrow and emerging cultural capital
Emergent service workers	17	19	Bar staff, nursing auxiliaries, assemblers and routine operatives, customer service workers	Moderately poor economic capital, though with reasonable household income, moderate social contacts, high emerging (but low highbrow) cultural capital
Precariat	<1	15	Cleaners, van drivers, care workers	Poor economic capital, and the lowest scores on every other criterion

of the exercise which Savage et al. have engaged in, wondering how one can develop what is seemingly a stand-alone model of class, disconnected from a specific context and specific research interests and questions. Context counts and Savage et al.'s model certainly is open to the kind of criticism that Mills develops to some extent.

The model of class developed by Savage et al. is clearly Bourdieusian in orientation and, as I have argued elsewhere (Block 2014), a kind of default Bourdieusian approach to class has taken over in sociology and, closer to home, in sociolinguistics. From the 1960s onwards, Bourdieu (1977, 1984) provided a range of useful terms for understanding class in late 20th century societies, and his constructs have been adapted to contexts around the world. In particular, researchers have found helpful his notions of *fields*, as arenas, of social practices constituted and shaped by particular ways of thinking and acting; *symbolic capitals*, in particular *cultural capital* (as legitimised knowledge and knowhow) and *social capital* (as social relations facilitating paths to success in individual life trajectories); and *habitus*, (as acquired dispositions in a constant state of renewal and revision in the light of ongoing experiences). All of these constructs, of course, are derived from the kind of scholarship which Bourdieu was exposed to during his formative years as an intellectual, from the late 1940s onwards, and importantly, there is much in his work which derives from Marx (1990) and Weber (1968).

Like Marx, Bourdieu sees capitalist societies as fundamentally and characteristically unequal and he sees inequality in class terms, as a matter of material conditions and processes (see his *economic capital*). However, like Weber, he sees inequality as emergent not only around and through control over the means of production, but also as intrinsic to sociocultural practices of individuals. These practices index different levels of prestige and status – or relative levels of 'distinction' and 'taste' in Bourdieusian terms (Bourdieu 1984) – and are dependent on the relative symbolic capital (cultural and social capital) which individuals are in possession of. However, the Bourdieusian view on class is by no means free of deficiencies (Block 2017a; Holborow 2015). Harvey (2014) has contested the use of 'capital' to refer to 'personal endowments', arguing that while "[c]apital undoubtedly uses... signs of distinction in its sales practices and pitches, . . . that does not mean that distinction is a form of capital" (Harvey 2014: 187). Rather, Harvey argues, distinction is about the symbolic orders emerging from and intertwined with the ongoing development of capitalism and the economic inequalities which come with this development. Another problem has to do with *habitus:* it is a 'structuring structure' internal to the individual, but it is also a *psychological* structure and therefore requires some consideration of the study of dispositions and attitudes in behavioural psychology. Yet Bourdieu, like so many anthropologists and sociologists preceding and succeeding him, seems to have something of an aversion to psychology, which only rivals the aversion to all that is social found among those working in psychology (see Lizardo 2004, for a thoughtful discussion).

Notwithstanding these and other reservations about aspects of Bourdieu's work, his view of class, as I note above, has become central to any discussion of the phenomenon. Bearing this in mind, I have in recent years attempted to frame class for my own purposes by drawing on the foundational work of Marx and Weber and the more recent contributions of Bourdieu, and a range of other scholars (e.g., Crompton 2008; Sayer 2005; Wright 2005). I have put together a *constellation of interrelated dimensions* model to capture the long list of dimensions that index class: in different ways in different contexts, cultures and societies. This model, in a constant state of revision, consists of five general categories which are then subdivided into dimensions as follows:

Economic resources

- Property: land and housing
- Property: other material possessions, such as electronic goods, clothing, books, art, etc.
- Income: salary and wages
- Accumulated wealth: savings and investments

Sociocultural resources

- Occupation: manual labour, unskilled service jobs, low-level information-based jobs, professional labour, etc.
- Education: level of formal education attained and the corresponding cultural capital acquired
- Technological knowhow: familiarity and ability to use evolving technologies

- Social contacts and networking: people regularly associated with as friends and acquaintances in class terms (the extent to which middle class people tend to socialise with middle class people, working class people with working class people, and so on)
- Societal and community status and prestige: embodied, achieved and ascribed

Behaviour

- Consumption patterns: choice of shops, buying brands or not, ecological/organic consumption, etc.
- Symbolic behaviour (e.g., how one moves one's body, the clothes one wears, the way one speaks, how one eats)
- Pastimes: golfing, skiing, cockfighting, watching television

Life conditions

- Political life: one's relative position in hierarchies of power in society
- Quality of life: in terms of physical and psychological comfort and health
- Type of neighbourhood: a working class neighbourhood, a middle class neighbourhood, an area in the process of gentrification

Spatial conditions

- Mobility: physical movement (from highly local to global)
- Proximity to other people during a range of day-to-day activities
- Dimensions and size of space occupied: layout of dwelling or place of work, size of bedroom, size of office, etc.
- Type of dwelling: trailer, house (detached/semidetached), flat (studio, small, large), etc.

Adopting this broad view of class is not without its problems and should be 'handled with care'. However, I see it as a working model, and a heuristic via which we can understand how class and class relations are constituted and indexed in different societies around the world. In particular, it is worth bearing in mind at all times the way in which class intersects with a range of identity dimensions, such as race, ethnicity, gender, sexuality, religion, nationality, age and dis/ability (Block and Corona 2014). In addition, just as contemporary capitalism (neo-liberalism) is 'variegated', that is, it develops and evolves in very different ways across different geographical locations (Peck 2010), so too are class and class relations: they may be said to exist in all societies with a minimally developed economy, but they will manifest themselves in very different ways from one context to the next.

Class in CDA research

Beyond a few notable exceptions (Machin and Richardson 2008), class has not been a central focus among CDA researchers, and this may be because of the way that class, understood in relational terms as outlined above, is about being in the world and is therefore taken up by those researchers (usually called 'sociolinguists'!) who wish to examine activity (especially communication) *in situ* (e.g., Rampton 2006). Still, in the past several years, there has been an emerging body of research around the analysis of how public policy talk, the media and public declarations by politicians – just to cite three domains of discourse – construct class and class relations. I will now cite and discuss one example examining each of these three domains, extending the discussion somewhat as regards public declarations by politicians, as this is a topic which I have explored in my own work.

Turgeon, Taylor and Niehaus (2014) provide a good example of how public policy talk can construct class and class relations, as they critically analyse how welfare-to-work programme managers in the United States talk about welfare recipients, using what they call 'classtalk'. The authors do not offer a concrete definition of the term 'classtalk', but they do state that it "invokes a 'culture of poverty' ideology and ignores structural conditions and causes of poverty" (Turgeon et al. 2014: 669). In other words, it is talk which positions individuals in terms of vague and superficial folk theories, focussing on the surface-level appearance of the class as opposed to the how and why of its existence. For Turgeon et al., classtalk "is reflective of US meritocracy and neoliberalism. . . [and] reflects broader welfare discourses of difference, dependency, personal responsibility, and the 'culture of poverty'" (Turgeon et al. 2014: 669). The consequences of these framings of the poor as responsible for their poverty and therefore as 'underserving' (Katz 2013) is not clear given that there is no discussion of a link between use of class talk and actions taken by managers against the interests of welfare claimants. Still, the authors do a good job of showing how, against the backdrop of a society inundated with neoliberal discourses of being and behaviour, class and class relations are talked into existence, especially as regards the sociocultural and symbolic resources of welfare claimants. The latter are positioned at the lower end of society in terms of education, technological knowhow, social contacts and status, all of which would help them to obtain employment, which would, in turn, lift them out of poverty and allow them to consume more and better, live in a nicer home in a nicer neighbourhood and overall have a better quality of life.

Elsewhere, in an article about how the media construct class and class relations, Eriksson (2015; this volume) examines how *Ullared,* a Swedish reality show which focuses primarily on working-class shoppers at a low-budget outlet store, demonises and ridicules the less successful in society. This kind of class-based phenomenon is not often associated with Sweden and other Nordic countries, which have ways been presented as paradigms of social democratic values, such as egalitarianism and the general fight against inequality, far more than most of their European neighbours. However, it seems that things are changing, as the aforementioned notion of the 'undeserving poor' and what Levitas (1998) calls "a moral underclass discourse" have crept into circulation and come to take hold in the public imaginary in ways similar to what has long been the case in the UK (Bennett 2013; Skeggs 2004; Wood and Skeggs 2011). It is worth noting that this discursive shift has occurred as a superstructural phenomenon, as the base of the Swedish economy has been (neo)liberalised over the past decade. For example, a more regressive tax regime has been introduced and public services funding has been cut, with the result that inequality has risen.

Eriksson adopts two key constructs to help him understand how *Ullared* positions working class people as unworthy. First, there is Skegg's notion of "inscription", as "the way value is transferred onto bodies and read off them, and the mechanisms by which it is retained, accumulated, lost or appropriated" (Skeggs 2004: 13). Second, there is Lyle's notion of the middle class gaze, as

> a mode of production (symbolic as well as material) which is underpinned by an anxiety about the working classes that has historically entailed the (mis)recognition of the working class as being of lesser value, as particularly suited to specific forms of labour, and as a pathological, abject other.
>
> *(Lyle 2008: 320)*

For Eriksson, this gaze is "organized around certain discourses of identity, fashion, actions and values, and [which] promotes a superior, more credible position, which appears to be the natural, normal and respectable way of seeing things" (Eriksson 2015: 24).

Bearing these concepts in mind, Eriksson shows how the class portrayals and performances occurring on *Ullared* are about the embodiment (in the subjects themselves) of those aspects of working- and lower-class values that the middle-class mainstream deem to be tasteless and the product of an inferior education. The characters appearing on the programme are examples of 'pathological' or 'flawed' consumers (Bauman 2005) in that while they do spend money and therefore behave as good citizens in a capitalist economy, they do not do so in the 'correct' way. In effect, their consumption patterns – where they shop, what they buy and how they consume (excessive eating and drinking) – along with their symbolic behaviour – how they talk, how they walk, how they dress and so on – come together to construct them (in the eyes of middle class viewers) as new-age villains, as surely one of the chief ills of contemporary Swedish society is the existence and permanence on Swedish soil of *Ullared* shoppers. In many ways, *Ullared* can be said to be engaged in a form of class warfare, a term which I have used elsewhere (Block 2017b, 2018a, 2018b) "to capture how the neoliberal policies adopted over the past four decades have constituted not only a point of conflict and struggle but an actual attack on the well-being and even survival of the popular classes in countries around the world". My concern in formulating this definition is twofold.

First, there is a material angle and the way in which neoliberal economic policies have had detrimental effects on the life chances of a large proportion of the general population in countries around the world. For example, Harvey (2010, 2014) suggests that many of the practices of governments and financial institutions in recent years have constituted what he calls "accumulation by dispossession", in simple terms the transfer of property and wealth from the less well-off to the wealthy. Examples of government policies include the privatisation of state-owned and -operated industries and services and the sale of state-owned assets: in both cases, what is (in theory) owned by the people is bought by the wealthiest individuals and collectives in society, or indeed, in the world at large. Financial sector examples of accumulation by dispossession include the recent *preferentes* (preferred clients) scandal in Spain, in which people with modest savings and incomes, who had entrusted their money to banks in investment funds, found that they were left with nothing when the same banks collapsed. Another example is banks reclaiming flats and houses upon eviction of the tenants when the latter default on their mortgages or rent.

Class warfare and public declarations by politicians

Class warfare may be pursued materially, as in the dispossession by accumulation examples just cited, but it can also be carried out through the media, as Eriksson (2015) makes clear, and it is a reality in the domain of political speeches and other communications. This is clearly the case in Spain where from the year 2013 onwards a very public discursive conflict, class-based to be sure, arose between the governing party (the conservative *Partido Popular;* herafter PP), a faithful backer of the banks and all banking activity, and the PAH (*Plataforma de Afectados por la Hipoteca;* 'Platform for those Affected by Mortgages').[1]

The PAH is a grass-roots organisation which campaigns on behalf of individuals and families who because of unemployment, personal tragedy (e.g., death of a breadwinner) or other events are unable to make mortgage or rent payments and therefore are either threatened with eviction from their homes or are actually evicted. On the organisation's website (PAH 2015), one finds a mission statement in which the class-based nature of the struggle facing evictees is made clear around a contrast between 'they' (in reference to representatives of the capitalist class) and 'we' (the general population and the PAH). As regards the former, there is reference to how 'they steal our homes and condemn us to continue paying for them'; how the 'banks. . . continue to display an antisocial attitude, evicting families and accumulating a huge stock of empty houses, disregarding the social function of housing'; and how [t]he government protects such actions, neither stopping them nor seeking solutions (author's translation). Meanwhile, the PAH is positioned in terms of its 'social project', whereby it campaigns for 'the recovery of the right to housing in response to a generalized state of housing emergency generated artificially and intentionally by banks and the government' (author's translation).

Evictions normally occur with little or no provision of alternative accommodation and they can be traumatic experiences, at times leading to evictee suicides. In addition, according to the draconian 1946 Spanish mortgage law, passed during the Franco regime, it is impossible for an evictee to waive the remainder of a mortgage after eviction has taken place.[2] In 2013, as it became clear that the government was not going to reform these and other egregious aspects of the 1946 law, the PAH decided to add a new form of protest to its repertoire. Until this time the organisation's activity had consisted of three primary modalities: (1) assemblies, which served to provide information as well as legal, practical and emotional support; (2) a webpage, which served as a means of disseminating information; and (3) a presence at home evictions, with a view to protesting against them and, where and when possible, preventing them. In 2013, they added a fourth activity, *escraches,* which were more focussed demonstrations in which groups of activists protested outside the homes and/or workplaces of politicians. The targets of *escraches* are individuals deemed to have decision-making capacity with regard to the regulation of banks and practices such as home evictions (e.g., members of the governing party), and the purpose is to publicly shame them. Protesters usually carry placards and signs with messages such as *sí se puede, pero no quieren* (yes, it can be done, but they don't want to), in clear reference to PP politicians and their unwillingness to make significant changes to the mortgage law. Protesters also chant, but these chants are never physically threatening (chanting 'Who paid for your house?' hardly constitutes an aggression). To date, no cases of protestor violence against the targets of *escraches* have been reported.

The PP and its right-wing media supporters were unhappy about this new form of protest from the start, but it was the *escrache* which occurred outside the home of the vice president (i.e., vice prime minister) Soraya Saenz de Santamaria on 5 April 2013 which raised the temperature and led to a series of declarations by prominent members of the PP. These statements seemed designed to change public understandings of the conflict from class warfare to something far more sinister. For example, on April 13, 2013, Maria Dolores de Cospedal, the General Secretary of the PP likened the PAH *escraches* to 'pure Nazism' and called them an attempt to 'violate the law' during a meeting of PP party members (Rachidi 2013). However, it was her colleague, Esperanza Aguirre, Head of the PP in the Autonomous Community of Madrid, who on April 14, 2013, went to the extreme of writing the following text about the PAH and *escraches* in a blog on her official webpage:

> Spanish society, its legitimate political representatives and, of course, the state's judicial and police forces must react to and stand up to the impudence, the cockiness and the impunity with which emulators of the worst forms of totalitarianism in history have decided to harass, insult and intimidate members of the Partido Popular who have been

elected by their fellow citizens. No one with even the slightest sense of democracy can or should show complacency when faced with the spectacle, which is becoming habitual, of fanatics who with total impunity disrupt the home life of some members of the Partido Popular. These violent stalkers set themselves up as models of all that is good but they are merely followers of the worst totalitarian tactics of the last century: the harassment with which the Hitler Youth or Castro's patrols tried and try to intimidate those who do not submit to their designs. And they are also imitators of the bullying tactics of the followers of ETA in the Basque Country, this bullying that has prevented the citizens of this part of Spain from living in freedom.

(Aguirre 2013; Author's translation from the original in Spanish)

This text is clearly designed to shift the focus of debate from government support for the interests and actions of banks, to a claim of victim status for members of the PP. Or, put another way, it aims to shift the debate away from class warfare perpetuated by the ruling class on the popular classes to a dubious debate about democratic principles. It is also highly intertextual – that is, it brings forward into the present genres, voices and other elements from texts produced in the past (Fairclough 2010), constituting a "topos of history as teacher" (Wodak et al. 1999). Thus, apart from mixing in references to ETA and Cuba, it draws on a recognisable discourse about the horrors of the Nazi era in Germany, making the case that we must learn from the errors of the past and condemn the 'totalitarian tactics' of the PAH in the present. According to this scenario, PP members, as the targets of *escraches,* are the persecuted Jews of our time, while PAH members (home evictees and those who help them) are Hitler's henchmen. The text is also a good example of Wodak's notion of 'anything goes' (Wodak 2013). First, when she says that home evictees are victimising the powerful (i.e., PP members), Aguirre adopts "discursive and rhetorical strategies which combine incompatible phenomena" (Wodak 2013: 32-33). She also "makes false claims sound innocent" (Wodak 2013: 33) when she states that PAH members "are merely followers of the worst totalitarian tactics of the last century". Third and finally, Aguirre "says the unsayable and transcends the limits of the permissible" (Wodak 2013: 33) when she likens PP members to the persecuted Jews of Nazi Germany, a rhetorical twist which is surely beyond the pale.

However, the text lacks coherence in the context in which it is produced, as beyond its shock value, crassness and insensitivity to the descendants of Holocaust victims, the intertextual twist that it incorporates and its appeal to history as teacher are rather shaky. I say this because Spain was occupied with the Spanish civil war from 1936 to 1939 and then officially neutral during the Second World War, despite Franco's public expressions of fascist solidarity with Nazi Germany. During the civil war and thereafter, there was no wholesale attack on Spanish Jews, who indeed would have numbered just a few thousand at the time. However, Franco did often rail against 'Jewish conspiracies' in public, and as a National-Catholic fascist, he would have had little sympathy for the plight of the Jews in Nazi Germany. Given this history (admittedly presented in an over-brief and partial way here), Spanish people do not respond to 'just like Hitler' claims in the same way as the citizens of countries which suffered the Nazi occupation (e.g., Poland, France, Holland). However, given Franco's lack of sympathy to the Jewish people, and the fact that the PP has clear and unequivocal historical links to the Franco regime (the party, in its earlier incarnation as *Alianza Popular* - the Popular Alliance - was founded in 1978 by a former Franco era minister, Manuel Fraga), one could argue that PP representatives arguably have far more links to the persecutors of Jews in 1930s Nazi Germany than the persecuted Jews themselves.

In the end, the PAH-as-Nazis intertextual turn comes across as a cynical rhetorical ploy. Quite possibly, polling showed that attempts to turn people who have lost their homes and their livelihood into victimizers of privileged politicians was not ever going to work. In any case, shortly after this type of rhetoric entered the public sphere, it receded and virtually disappeared, and the PP was thus not successful in its attempt to impose on the general public their portrayal of the working class and poor who protest under the banner of the PAH. However, where the media assault failed, a more material tool, in the form of law enforcement, continued to work: home evictions continued and a new public order law[3] was passed in parliament (the PP using its parliamentary majority against the opposition of every other party with representation). The law included fines for participation in public demonstrations and protests deemed 'illegal', measures clearly aimed at stopping the activities of organisations such as the PAH and stifling opposition in general. Nevertheless, in the midst of such police-state tactics on the part of the PP, the May 2015 municipal elections brought some hope. Across Spain, in most of the largest cities (including Madrid, Barcelona, Zaragoza and Valencia), left-wing coalition governments came to power, with one of the founders of the PAH, Ada Colau, becoming the mayor of Barcelona. These new mayors have not been as successful as they no doubt had hoped to be with regard to actually stopping home evictions. In effect, they have no authority to change laws which continue to favour the interests of banks over those of the population at large. However, they have been considerably better than their predecessors at providing support to evictees, especially after evictions have taken place.

There is surely much more that could be said about this case, but I will end my discussion here for space reasons with three key points about how all of this is related to class, class relations and class warfare. First, several of the dimensions of class outlined above are at play here: (1) economic resources, as the loss of a job leads to the loss of property; (2) life conditions, in terms of the relative positions of actors in hierarchies of power in society and their quality of life (their physical and psychological comfort and health); and (3) spatial resources, as regards the types of dwellings and social conditions which evictees will leave behind and end up living in. Second, as I note above, this is a good example of class warfare as there is an attack on the material well-being of citizens via the actions of the state apparatuses (Althusser 2008), with the political class, the banks, the legal system and the police all playing their respective parts. Third and finally, it is worth noting how, via processes of semiosis (meaning-making), we see a flow of events and phenomena in the realm of the economic base and the socio-political superstructure moving into the symbolic realm, where they are created and recreated, presented and represented. Thus a conflict in the material realm undergirds a conflict in the discursive realm.

Conclusion

In this chapter, I have attempted to make the case for a more class-centred CDA, or in any case for class to be brought to the fore in CDA research which is concerned with materially based inequalities in society. Such a move would mean a fuller embrace of Fairclough's 'radical view' of CDA, and a firmer base in political economy, as outlined in the quote which opens this chapter. I have discussed a few cases in which class has figured as part of the critical analysis of discourse, but my point is that there should be more of this kind of work than is currently the case. Of course, one big issue is whether or not CDA, given how it has been carried out to date, is actually appropriate to the exploration of constructs such as class, which are emergent in the flux and flow of ongoing social events and activity. In a discussion of the interface of

CDA with ethnography, Krzyżanowski (2011: 231) writes of a move towards CDS – critical discourse studies – stating that

> while still drawing on some of the CDA's original ideas (e.g., on the interplay of language/discourse and ideology as well as of their constitutive force in social relations), [CDS] clearly reaches beyond the traditional 'schools' or 'trends' of the movement. . . towards more contextually oriented and actor-related types of analysis.

A move in this direction seems consistent with Monica Heller's calls for a 'critical ethnographic' approach to the study of language and society issues (Heller 2011). Perhaps a fusion of Krzyżanowski and Heller is what is needed if we are to move towards a more political economy and class-based CDA (or CDS!).

Notes

1 The discussion that follows is an altered and shortened version of the discussion of the same events which appears in Block (2018a, 2018b).
2 It is indeed perhaps surprising that such a law should have remained on the books for so long given that when in power from 1982 to 1996 and from 2004 to 2011, the Spanish Socialist Party could have attempted to change it, but did not.
3 The *Ley Orgánica de Seguridad Ciudadana* (Organic Law of Public Security), known to many as the *Ley Mordaza* (the gag law).

Further reading

Block, D. (2014). *Social class in applied linguistics*. London: Routledge.
In this book, the case is made for the inclusion of class as a key construct in applied linguistics research in general (and especially as regards sociolinguistics research).
Block, D. (2018a). The materiality and *semiosis* of inequality and class struggle and warfare: The case of home evictions in Spain. In R. Wodak and B. Forchtner (eds.), *Routledge handbook of language and politics*. London: Routledge.
This chapter focuses on the same case of discourses in conflict between the Partido Popular and the PAH, but does so within the frame of inequality, class struggle and class warfare.
Fairclough, N. (2010). *Critical discourse analysis: The critical study of language*. London: Longman.
Something of a classic in presenting the evolution of Fairclough's thinking on CDA over the 1980s, 1990s and 2000s, and an inspiration for the approach to public discourses in this chapter.
Wodak, R. (2013). 'Anything goes' – the haiderization of Europe. In R. Wodak, M. KhosraviNik and B. Mral (eds.), *Right wing populism in Europe*, 23–38. London: Bloomsbury.
In this chapter, Ruth Wodak explains the notion of 'anything goes' in political discourses in Austria and beyond.
Wodak, R. (2014). Critical discourse analysis. In C. Leung and B. Street (eds.), *The Routledge companion to English studies*, 302–317. London: Routledge.
A recent account and discussion of the state of play in CDA which serves as a basis for the approach to public discourses in this chapter.

References

Aguirre, E. (2013). El acoso a los políticos del Partido Popular [The harassment of members of the Partido Popular], blog entry. Accessed March 14, 2013, http://esperanza.ppmadrid.es/el-acoso-a-politicos-del-partido-popular/
Althusser, L. (2008 [1971]). *On ideology*. London: Verso.
Bauman, Z. (2005). *Work, consumerism and the new poor*. Maidenhead: Open University Press.
Bennett, J. (2013). Chav-spotting in Britain: The representation of social class as private choice. *Social Semiotics* 23(1): 146–162.

Bennett, T., Savage, M., Silva, E., Warde, A., Gayo-Cal, M. and Wright, D. (2009). *Culture, class, distinction*. London: Routledge.

Bhaskar, R. (1989). *Reclaiming reality*. London: Verso.

Block, D. (2014). *Social class in applied linguistics*. London: Routledge.

Block, D. (2015). Identity and social class: Issues arising in applied linguistics research. *Annual Review of Applied Linguistics* 35: 1–19.

Block, D. (2016). Social class in language and identity research. In S. Preece (ed.), *The Routledge handbook of language and identity,* 241–254. London: Routledge.

Block, D. (2017a). Migration, language and social class. In S. Canagarajah (ed.), *Routledge handbook on migration and language,* 133–148. London: Routledge.

Block, D. (2017b). Discourses in conflict: resource inequality, class warfare and home repossessions. *Social Semiotics*, DOI: 10.1080/10350330.2017.1301790

Block, D. (2018a). The materiality and *semiosis* of inequality and class struggle and warfare: The case of home evictions in Spain. In R. Wodak and B. Forchtner (eds.), *Routledge handbook of language and politics,* TBP. London: Routledge.

Block, D. (2018b). *Political economy in sociolinguistics: Neoliberalism, inequality and social class*. London: Bloomsbury.

Block, D. and Corona, V. (2014). Exploring class-based intersectionality. *Language, Culture and Curriculum* 27(1): 27–42.

Block, D., Gray, J. and Holborow, M. (2012). *Neoliberalism and applied linguistics*. London: Routledge.

Bologna, S. (1987). The theory and history of the mass worker in Italy. *Common Sense*, 11/12. https://libcom.org/library/theory-history-mass-worker-italy-sergio-bologna

Bourdieu, P. (1977). *Outline of a theory of practice*. Cambridge: Cambridge University Press.

Bourdieu, P. (1984). *Distinction*. London: Routledge.

Bradley, H. (2014). Class descriptors or class relations? Thoughts towards a critique of Savage et al. *Sociology* 48(3): 429–436.

Crompton, R. (2008). *Class and stratification*, 3rd edn. Cambridge: Polity.

Eriksson, G. (2015). Ridicule as a strategy for the recontextualization of the working class. *Critical Discourse Studies* 12(1): 20–38.

Fairclough, N. (2010). *Critical discourse analysis: The critical study of language*. London: Longman.

Fairclough, N. (2014). *Language and power*, 3rd edn. London: Routledge.

Fairclough, N., Jessop, B. and Sayer, A. (2010 [2002]) Critical realism and semiosis. In N. Fairclough (ed.), *Critical discourse analysis: The critical study of language,* 202–222. London: Longman.

Harvey, D. (2010). *The enigma of capital*. London: Profile Books.

Harvey, D. (2014). *Seventeen contradictions and the end of capitalism*. London: Profile Books.

Heller, M. (2011). *Paths to post-nationalism: A critical ethnography of language and identity*. Oxford: Oxford University Press.

Holborow, M. (2015). *Language and neoliberalism*. London: Routledge.

Jones, O. (2011). *Chavs: The demonization of the working class*. London: Verso Books.

Katz, M. B. (2013). *The undeserving poor,* 2nd edn. Oxford: Oxford University Press.

Krzyżanowski, M. (2011). Ethnography and critical discourse analysis: Towards a problem-oriented research dialogue. *Critical Discourse Studies* 8(4): 231–238.

Levitas, R. (1998). *The inclusive society? Social exclusion and new labour*. London: Palgrave Macmillan.

Lizardo, O. (2004). The cognitive origins of Bourdieu's habitus. *Journal for the Theory of Social Behaviour* 34(4): 375–401.

Lyle, S. (2008). (Mis)recognition and the middle-class/bourgeois gaze: A case study of wife swap. *Critical Discourse Studies* 5(4): 319–330.

Machin, D. and Richardson, J. E. (eds.) (2008). Class and discourse. Special Issue of *Critical Discourse Studies* 5(4).

Marsdal, M. (2013). Loud values, muffled interests: Third way social democracy and right-wing populism. In R. Wodak, M. KhosraviNik and B. Mral (eds.), *Right wing populism in Europe,* 39–54. London: Bloomsbury.

Marx, K. (1990 [1867]). *Capital: A critique of political economy*, Vol. 1. Harmondsworth: Penguin.

Mills, C. (2014). The great British class fiasco: A comment on Savage et al. *Sociology* 48(3): 437–444.

PAH. (2015). Origin and justification [Online]. http://afectadosporlahipoteca.com/

Peck, J. (2010). *Constructions of neoliberal reason*. Oxford: Oxford University Press.

Phelan, S. and Dahlberg, L. (eds.) Post-Marxist discourse theory and critical political economy. Special issue of *Critical Discourse Studies* 11(3).

Rachidi, I. (2013). Cospedal tilda de "nazismo puro" los escraches de los ciudadanos contra políticos [Cospedal describes citizen *escraches* against politicians as "pure Nazism"]. *Cadena SER*. Accessed April 13, 2013, http://cadenaser.com/ser/2013/04/13/espana/1365810617_850215.html

Rampton, B. (2006). *Language in late modernity: Interaction in an Urban school*. Cambridge: Cambridge University Press.

Rollock, N. (2014). Race, class and 'the harmony of dispositions'. *Sociology* 48(3): 445–451.

Savage, M., Devine, F., Cunningham, N., Friedman, S., Laurison, D., Miles, A., Snee, H. and Taylor, M. (2014). On social class, Anno 2014. *Sociology,* pre-publication on line, July 2014, 20 pages.

Savage, M., Devine, F., Cunningham, N., Taylor, M., Li, Y., Hjellbrekke, J., Le Roux, B., Friedman, S. and Miles, A. (2013). A new model of social class? Findings from the BBC's Great British class survey experiment. *Sociology* 47: 219–250.

Sayer, A. (2005). *The moral significance of class*. Cambridge: Cambridge University Press.

Skeggs, B. (2004). *Class, self, culture*. London: Routledge.

Standing, G. (2011). *The precariat: The new dangerous class*. London: Bloomsbury.

Tylor, I. (2013). *Revolting subjects: Social abjection and resistance in neoliberal Britain*. London: Zed Books.

Weber, M. (1968 [1922]). *Economy and society,* Vols. 1 and 2. Berkeley, CA: University of California Press.

Williams, R. (1977). *Marxism and literature*. Cambridge: Cambridge University Press.

Wodak, R. (2013). 'Anything goes' – The haiderization of Europe. In R. Wodak, M. KhosraviNik and B. Mral (eds.), *Right wing populism in Europe,* 23–38. London: Bloomsbury.

Wodak, R. (2014). Critical discourse analysis. In C. Leung and B. Street (eds.), *The Routledge companion to English studies,* 302–317. London: Routledge.

Wodak, R., de Cillia, R., Reisigl, M. and Liebhart, K. (1999). *The discursive construction of national identities*. Edinburgh: Edinburgh University Press.

Wood, H. and Skeggs, B. (eds.) (2011). *Reality television and class*. London: Palgrave Macmillan.

Wright, E. O. (ed.) (2005). *Approaches to class analysis*. Cambridge: Cambridge University Press.

Zotzmann, K. and O'Regan, J. (2016). Critical discourse analysis and identity. In S. Preece (ed.), *The Routledge handbook of language and identity,* pp. TBP. London: Routledge.

24

Race/ethnicity

Susana Martínez Guillem

Introduction

This chapter discusses Critical Discourse Analysis (CDA) and race/ethnicity. Of course this is a general and ambitious title that cannot do justice to the breadth and depth of research on these topics that CDA/CDS scholars have engaged in and continue to produce throughout the globe. For this reason, and before diving into the discussion, I would like to make explicit here my own rationale for the selection of texts and contexts that follows.

My choices as author have two main effects: the first one is reductive, limiting most of the discussion to Western contexts, with the European Union, the United States, and Australia featuring most prominently, and in that order. The main reason for this is that, as Gramsci (1971) explained, intellectuals are organic to a particular social group, a system of relations that shapes their activities and from which they cannot be easily detached. This organicity thus sets the limits of my discussion.

Similarly, the shape of racial ideologies, as well as the ways they are reproduced and challenged in text and talk, are also historically, politically, and geographically constrained. In this sense, and even though "the West" is most definitely not a monolithic entity, there are, as my discussion will highlight, recognizable patterns throughout the contexts addressed in terms of what Omi and Winant call "racial formations" (1986) that are worth considering together.

The second consequence has a reverse, enlarging impulse, and it has to do with acknowledging and contributing to the transdisciplinary project that informs and grows with CDA (Threadgold 2003). To this end, and although I use the more recognizable label "CDA" throughout the chapter, both the review of research and the in-depth case study reflect and construct what I call a Critical Cultural Discourse Studies perspective, one that tries to capture the inevitable intersections and tensions among humanistic and social scientific traditions stemming from critical, discourse-oriented paradigms.

Race vs. ethnicity

The concepts of race and ethnicity, like all cultural keywords (Williams 1983) are relational, contested, and constantly evolving. In the realm of CDA, these terms have historically served similar analytical purposes, as in van Dijk's groundbreaking studies on "ethnic prejudice," where he showed how (privileged) speakers routinely engaged in discursive moves that normalized discrimination while at the same time denying individual prejudice (van Dijk 1984, 1987). However, the current ideological landscape in the West (on which I elaborate below) that constantly links racism to a shameful, now allegedly overcome past, and often proposes "ethnicity" or "ethnic relations" as a more adequate way to account for the contemporary nature of many conflicts (e.g., Hsu 2010), it has become imperative for CDA scholars to draw on terminology that allows for a vertical emphasis on systemic inequalities as opposed to horizontal identity differences.

In this context, race as a category of analysis, and racism as a dominant ideology, have come to inform most critical scrutiny of discursive practices that aims at exposing the systematic discrimination of particular, "othered" groups (Every and Augoustinos 2007; Teo 2000; van Dijk 1992, Wodak and Matouscheck 1993). The underlying assumption is that the term ethnicity does not seem to be fully equipped to account for how specific traits – even if they are referred to in discourse as "ethnic" – come to be treated as essential, thus constituting certain bodies and practices as inherently deficient in certain contexts.

The absence of a term such as "ethnicism" speaks to the preferred emphasis on (surmountable) differences rather than conflicts derived from power relations when examining patterns of inclusion and exclusion in many ethnicity-oriented studies (see Hervik 2004). For this reason, the rest of this chapter focuses on racism, together with whiteness and racialization, as the most productive conceptual lenses and areas of study developing the connections between critical discourse analysis and race.

Elite racism

An especially fruitful area of research for CDA scholars has been the study of racist ideologies as they manifest themselves, are produced and reproduced, through elite outlets. Even though "elite" is admittedly an imprecise and hard to isolate category, intrinsically related to the "non-elite," I use it here to highlight institutional discursive practices in the realms of politics, media, and schools. In these contexts, the main focus has been on how discourse (re)produces racist ideologies that contribute to marginalize and exploit those naturalized as "others."

The different elite spheres analyzed in this scholarship include media outlets (Harding 2006; Simmons and Lecouteur 2008), political settings (Blackledge 2006; LeCouteur, Rapley and Augoustinos 2001), organizations (Campbell and Roberts 2007; Tilbury and Colic-Peisker 2006), and schools (Bonilla-Silva and Forman 2000; Eriksson and Aronsson 2005).

A particularly relevant area in CDA studies on elite racism is the increasing articulation between race and immigrants, especially when looking at immigration policy – an argument that I develop in the case study below. A considerable amount of attention in this literature is being directed towards the discursive treatment of asylum seekers (e.g., Moore 2013; Every and Augoustinos 2007). Scholars see these kinds of links as intrinsically related to broader dynamics of inclusion and exclusion, and thus to other ideological constructs such as citizenship, nationality, or culture.

In this vein, a growing number of studies identify and critique discursive moves in media outlets that define citizenship in opposition to undesirable bodies (Erjavec 2009), the systematic incorporation of cultural elements in mediated discussions of immigration (Adeyanju and Neverson 2007), or the pervasiveness of prejudice and negative stereotypes about immigrants reproduced in the media (KhosraviNik 2009; Santa Ana 1999). Other analyses have tried to uncover these same dynamics in assumed-to-be neutral sites such as immigration laws or language policies (Gales 2009; Schmidt 2002) and in political discourse more generally (Charteris-Black 2006; Mehan 1997).

Everyday racism

A second, complementary area of CDA research concentrates on how in everyday, non-institutional contexts speakers often index widespread, stereotypical beliefs about others, thus building on and at the same time feeding broader ideologies such as racism, ethnocentrism, or xenophobia. As mentioned above, van Dijk's pioneering work on prejudice paved the way for the critique of everyday talk as a crucial site for normalizing and at the same time distancing speakers from racism, through routine practices such as storytelling, or the use of disclaimers (van Dijk 1993). More recent studies have continued this line of research, focusing on discursive moves used to avoid potential negative judgments, or the functions of disclaimers when engaging in explicitly prejudiced talk, both face-to-face, and in computer-mediated environments (Billig et al. 1988; Del-Teso-Craviotto 2009; Wetherell and Potter 1993).

Even though scholars often refer to these everyday contexts as "local" or "micro," as opposed to the "global," "macro" level of institutions (van Dijk 2002) it is important to highlight that this does not mean that they are considered less relevant for our understanding of racial formations. On the contrary, attention to everyday, local practices as a way to better account for power dynamics has become a priority for much research on discourse and racism. The assumption behind these initiatives is that speakers' "agency" is frequently part of the reproduction of inequalities, even when apparent good intentions inform our discursive practices (Martínez Guillem 2013a). These dynamics are much harder to identify, and therefore to deconstruct. It is in this context that the notion of micro-aggressions (Sue 2010) stands out as a way to capture the pervasive consequences of apparently equal everyday encounters, where representations and understandings of the "Other" are constantly negotiated.

Accounting for overt and covert racism

As seen in the brief overviews above, a common feature of both elite and everyday racism seems to be the increasingly covert ways in which it is reproduced. Especially in Western societies, where it has become culturally unacceptable to express this kind of prejudice directly (Chiang 2010; Lentin and Titley 2012), there is now a new crop of apparently inclusive keywords, such as multiculturalism, diversity, or integration, that are constantly (re)articulated to deviate direct attention from skin color as a relevant marker of difference, even though they tend to indirectly reinforce it.

A pressing issue for many CDA scholars in the first decades of the 21st century, then, is how to account for racism in a "post-racial" era. This is an era in which racism tends to be associated with individual prejudice, ignorance, and backwardness that result in direct manifestations of stereotypical beliefs about certain groups. Conversely, the indirect and pervasive ways in which speakers reproduce racism through less salient practices remain unchecked and are even defended as intrinsically tied to democratic values.

As Hill (2008: 46) puts it, covert forms of racism "do not precipitate the exchange of accusations and rationalizations and denials" that we see in other kinds of practices such as, for example, the use of slurs or generalizations when referring to particular groups. However, this indirect racism still draws on interest-serving legitimizations of what is normal, natural, or better in a particular context. Prevalent ideologies that favor monolingualism or the use of standard dialects, for example, consistently inform practices such as linguistic monitoring that reinforce privileged groups' attachment to the norm, and the construction of others as deficient or suspect (Mason Carris 2011).

In this context, many critical scholars find it useful to distinguish between race as a socially constructed category and *racialization* as a real process of social organization that systematically advances some (constructed as) racial groups over others. Racialization thus occurs, not when certain people are classified as black, or Muslim, but when, for example, "black" and "uneducated" or "Muslim" and "terrorist" become fixed synonyms. This process involves "ideological construction [. . .] as well as an apparatus of legal, political and social discrimination and oppression" (MacMaster 2001: 2). The processual notions of "racialization" or "racialized group" thus allow scholars to emphasize the need to account for the reality of racism without reifying "racial" categories, seeing "race" as ideological while still acknowledging its materiality, as well as to stress that "race is a product of racism, and not vice versa" (Solomos 2001: 199; see also Miles and Thranhardt 1995).

Racialization is thus a useful theoretical lens when pointing out the ways in which particular practices come to be stigmatized and at the same time associated to specific groups. Importantly, the linguistic marking of practices such as speaking a non-standard dialect, or engaging in certain religious rituals depends on and recreates unmarked categories that normalize the practices of the elites, as well as their privileged position in society. For this reason, many scholars see the notion of racialization as intrinsically intertwined with that of whiteness, highlighting their mutual dependency: racialization constructs whiteness, and whiteness constructs racialized individuals and groups.

When conceptualized *in situ* as a historically determined combination of different oppressive ideologies (see McLaren 1993), whiteness becomes an extremely useful theoretical place from which to engage with race as it intersects with other equally or even more important systems of social stratification such as nationality, linguistic ability, or social class. In short, whiteness allows scholars to address more indirect processes of racialization. To this end, it is important to engage these concepts through what Stuart Hall calls "radical historization," thus remembering that their meaning is not stable or durable across contexts, and analyzing how particular pasts affect their contemporary and possible future shapes. It is in this capacity that they become important heuristic tools to expose and critique prejudiced common sense.

Case study: white Europe, racialized immigrants: integration discourse in the European union

In the remainder of this chapter I would like to exemplify how the critical sociocultural lens provided by the notions of racialization and whiteness, together with close analysis of discursive practices, can aid scholars in the task of making visible covert forms of racism that inform different agenda-setting documents guiding past and current immigration policy in the European Union (EU). I thus put forward an understanding of CDA as a "broad, diverse, multidisciplinary and problem-oriented" approach that "will select its methods and areas of analysis on the basis of a theoretical analysis of social issues" (van Dijk 2001: 97).

My texts and the analysis presented here are part of a larger project examining immigration, multiculturalism, and inequality in the EU (Martínez Guillem 2013b, 2015). Specifically, I look at EU institutions as a fundamental site of reproduction of racial ideologies when it comes to certain immigrant groups, with especial attention to the interplay of cultural and economic aspects in these racialization processes.

In the analysis that follows, and drawing on Wodak (2007: 88), I engage in critique in three different but interrelated ways: a "Discourse-immanent critique" aimed at identifying internal contradictions, inconsistencies, or dilemmas within a practice; a "Socio-diagnostic critique" that draws on social theory and contextual knowledge in order to point out the "manipulative character" of some discursive practices; and a "prospective critique" that uses the insights gained through immanent and socio-diagnostic critique in order to "contribute to the improvement of communication."

EU and immigration: the fearful need of the other

As a first analytical step, I briefly address here the main developments regarding immigration law in the EU in the last 30 years and interpret them through the lenses of whiteness and racialization. Needless to say, the sphere of immigration cannot be understood as separate from other areas such as EU enlargement or social policy (Geddes 2008). Keeping this caveat in mind, I lay out here the historical legal background that paved the road for the EU's common immigration policy, highlighting the tensions, contradictions, and prejudices that have informed its development from the beginning. As I then show in my engagement with specific texts, these tensions are still very much present in contemporary initiatives to address human mobility into and within the EU.

Different authors have pointed to the early '70s as the historical moment when immigration controls in Western Europe became a generalized procedure (e.g., MacMaster 2001). Even though this region was then in the middle of an economic recession, the selective nature of the different immigration policies implemented – allowing, for example, "white" immigrants continuing access – suggests that they may have been "determined primarily by political considerations" and thus "economic recession served more as an excuse for illiberal measures rather than as a prime cause" (MacMaster 2001: 188). Immigration controls, from this perspective, had more to do with a perceived loss, across European states, of national identity and sovereignty, seen as under attack from "barbaric hordes" (MacMaster 2001: 189) after guest workers took advantage of family reunification policies and started to turn into permanent residents (Mynott 2002). In this scenario, immigrant became synonym with non-European – and more specifically, non-white – and what some authors refer to as "fortress Europe" came into existence (e.g., Gordon 1989; Cohen 1991).

Apart from – or maybe as a result of – clearly setting the ground with regards to (dis) preferred immigrants, the different policies aimed at regulating migration flows played a fundamental role in the different political advances towards so-called European integration. The Single European Act (SEA) of 1986/87 established the freedoms of movement for capital, services, and goods, but it also, and importantly, emphasized the need for free movement of labor. Later, the 1990 Schengen convention established the conditions that would lead to the abolition of internal border checks across some EU states – a definite turning point for the European project.

Usually presented as an unprecedented accomplishment for EU members, the materialization of the "Schengen area" also had direct consequences for non-European countries, and for the ways (im)migration would be approached from then on. From the beginning, it became clear that putting Schengen into practice would require implementing what member states saw as "compensatory measures" (Dell'Olio 2005). European immigration policy thus emerged as a way to compensate participants in the Schengen zone for the loss of direct control over their external – now internal – borders (Bia 2004).

The resulting "new vision" on immigration policy "created opportunities for new forms of restriction of control that were not possible at the domestic level" (Boswell 2003: 26). Schengen thus supplemented nationally based barriers for certain groups through, for example, the new category of "Third Country Nationals" (TCNs), which overwhelmingly comprises non-white immigrants (Garner 2007).

The most recent development in terms of EU legislation is the Treaty of Lisbon. Through this Treaty, the pillars of "Common Policy and Security Policy" and "Police and Judicial Cooperation in Criminal Matters," were grouped together in creating the merged area, envisioned since the Schengen agreement, of "Freedom, Security and Justice," aimed at simplifying the overall structural organization of the EU. This change in structure went hand in hand with significant discursive changes. Thus, for the first time, the language of this Treaty softened the previous emphasis on control measures when dealing with immigration, making an explicit reference to EU competence for migrant *integration* policy. Specifically, the different members acknowledged the EU's role in "promoting the integration of third-country nationals residing legally" (Art 79(4), Consolidated version of the TFEU [20081 OJCl 15/78). Importantly, this competence "is limited to incentive and supporting measures and excludes any harmonization of legislation" (Bell 2009: 149).

However, at the same time, this acknowledgment of the importance of integration as a fundamental component of immigration laws has been accompanied by the consolidation of a series of patterns increasing legal barriers for particular groups of potential immigrants in the different member states. Thus, the former favoring, when regulating migration, of "formal and/or informal links with specific countries," mostly derived from colonialism, has given way to "a common set of criteria for visas that ignore[s] preferential colonial ties and replace[s] them with mutual European obligations" (Levy 2005: 81). The obvious consequence of this shift has been "to make conditions of entry for developing-world nationals, and therefore access to labor markets, more difficult than those for other Europeans" (Levy 2005: 81; Garner 2007).

The incorporation of "integration" into the EU immigration vocabulary, therefore, has taken place in parallel to the consolidation of particular legislative measures establishing a new hierarchy of preferred and dispreferred immigrants. Next, I look in more detail at this inextricable link, showing how the notions and functions of integration put forward in different EU texts are a crucial regulating mechanism geared towards naturalizing a series of exclusionary practices with regards to particular immigrants.

Integration and/as control

In this section, I use the insights gained from an ideological understanding of legislative practices to inform my close analysis of integration discourse as both product and producer of those institutional frameworks. Specifically, I focus on the European Council's Common Basic Principles on Integration, adopted in 2004, its "conclusions on the strengthening of integration policies in the EU by promoting unity in diversity," adopted in 2007, as well as the official declarations of two different European Ministerial Conferences on Integration, held in Vichy, France (2009) and Zaragoza, Spain (2010).[1]

I propose to look closely at the ways in which these texts discuss the notion of integration as a way to dig deeper into the assumptions embedded in this concept, as well as how these assumptions relate to the particular actors and actions associated with integration practices. Even though, as my critique of immigration policy showed, recent EU policy developments clearly articulate the need for an integration component within immigration law, several questions still remain unanswered. For example, why are "integration measures" needed, what exactly will they consist of, who will be responsible for them, and what are the perceived consequences if they are not implemented?

In order to start digging into these questions, I focus on the ways the documents examined justify the need for integration through a series of disjunctive and prioritizing argumentative moves. My analysis reveals that, in their initial statements, all the documents present integration within a diunital framework that recognizes its dual nature. Thus, the different texts highlight the need to understand integration as a "two-way" phenomenon that involves immigrants and their host societies, carrying with it "obligations" as well as "rights" for all.

However, a closer examination reveals a strategy of disjunction aimed at solving several tensions by emphasizing, on the one hand, immigrants' responsibility for integrating, and on the other, host societies' right to marginalize those who don't. Specifically, the texts split the initial rights/duties unity in favor of a dichotomous and hierarchical framework where immigrants' economic rights are contingent upon their compliance with cultural obligations.

The first common basic principle adopted by the Council in 2004, for example, states that "integration is a dynamic, two-way process of mutual accommodation" (17) between immigrants and the host society. The Council's conclusions adopted in 2007 further specify that:

> The Council and the Representatives of the Governments of the Member States recognize that integration is a dynamic two-way process involving both immigrants and the host society, with responsibilities for both sides, which should be underpinned by an agreed value system. Involving the host society in this process is one of the major challenges to the achievement of successful integration policies and long-term social cohesion. All individuals must assume responsibility in this integration process – as well as state institutions, political parties, media, businesses and civil society. Migrants who aim to stay permanently or for the long term should make a deliberate effort to integrate, in particular learning the language of their host society, and understanding the basic values of the European Union.
>
> *(European Council 2007: 2)*

Echoing the EU's Common Basic Principles on integration, these "conclusions" first present integration in a seemingly balanced way, emphasizing its bidirectional nature as well as the existence of "responsibilities" for both immigrants and host societies. However, the "responsibilities" for "all individuals," as well as for "state institutions, political parties, media, businesses and civil society," remained unspecified beyond the use of term "involvement." When juxtaposed to the "deliberate effort to integrate" as an immigrant responsibility, "involvement" stands out as attached to voluntariness, and therefore not binding. Thus, even though the notion of "responsibilities" initially applies to the whole of societies, the range and degree of expected actions associated with these responsibilities varies greatly depending on the group discussed.

In the case of immigrants, the text attempts to quantify their expected "deliberate" efforts in terms of their ability to learn "the language of their host society," as well as understand "the basic values of the European Union." Once again, the initial, balanced suggestion of an "agreed value system" underpinning the "dynamic two-way" integration process becomes a one-way, upward path that only immigrants are expected to go through. As a result, rather than a shared responsibility towards a better, common goal, the "need to integrate" isolates particular groups, defined by their supposed lack of knowledge or embracement of a series of "values" that, according to the text, presents an obstacle in the road towards social inclusion.

The Vichy declaration of 2009 similarly builds on the Council's first common basic principle to specify as follows: "that principle also highlights the proactive character of integration policies and generates *rights and duties* for the migrant as well as the need for a *real effort* on

365

the part of the host society" (European Ministerial Conference on Immigration 2010). In the initial statements of this declaration, the signing ministers further state that:

> it is necessary to promote and explore the common basic principles in greater depth, around the following themes, among other important integration issues: promotion of the fundamental values of the European Union, the integration process, access to employment and the promotion of diversity in employment, the integration of women and the education of children, intercultural dialogue and principles of integration policy governance.
>
> *(European Ministerial Conference on Immigration 2008)*

Mirroring the documents produced by the Council, this declaration starts off with a seeming balanced approach to integration, identifying both immigrants and host societies, as well as economic and cultural "issues," as priorities when it comes to integrating practices. The order in which these different elements appear, however, already signals a preference for immigrants' role, and specifically their embracement of "fundamental" EU values, as the main driver of integration.

To further index this preference, the declaration specifically calls for an "effort" to "stress respect for the identities of the Member States and the European Union and for their fundamental values, such as human rights, freedom of opinion, democracy, tolerance, equality between men and women, and the compulsory schooling of children." Thus, the text constructs EU states' identities as both fixed and inevitably attached to a series of ideologies and practices that are presented as inherently positive *and* European. This "natural" attachment to the norm is, as I discussed above, a fundamental aspect of whiteness and its associated privileges. Immigrants, on the other hand, are urged to "respect" these identities, a move that antagonizes them as external to them, and therefore to the values that they represent.

By fixing the notion of a European (white) identity, the texts indirectly fix the notion of (racialized) immigrant as well, defining it in terms of the separate – if not oppositional – space that it occupies in relation to a set of "European fundamental values" that need to be "promoted" and "respected," thus implying a consistent lack of knowledge and/or unwillingness to abide by these values from the part of immigrants. As a result, the need for integration becomes a defining characteristic of immigrants, and "immigrant" emerges as a highly stigmatizing and rather immutable label, both of which are important conditions for racialization (Gilroy 1987; Lentin and Titley 2012).

In relation to this perceived need to preserve a unified EU identity, the declaration also stresses the importance, as part of the "integration process," of "the introductory phase," which would involve "primarily [. . .] learning the language, history and institutions of the host society," seen as "elementary knowledge and skills *conducive to* the immigrant's proper social, economic and cultural integration" (European Ministerial Conference on Immigration 2008, my emphasis). Through prioritizing EU identity-preservation practices, once again, the both/and initial approach to economic and cultural aspects of integration splits in favor of an understanding of integration as a fundamentally cultural route, and more specifically a process of cultural assimilation.

As we saw in the initial excerpt of the Vichy declaration, EU ministers do not completely dismiss economic factors affecting integration processes and practices. However, they separate them from and subordinate them to cultural ones. Thus, while the document presents access "to employment, housing, education and health and, more broadly, to all rights and public services" as a "major challenge for social cohesion," it also positions these immigrant rights as a second(ary) aspect of the "integration process," subject to the culturally-oriented duties discussed above.

As a result of this hierarchical division, the texts construct immigrants as always already located outside of the overall social formation – and thus subject to integration – but at the same time, as naturally lacking the specific qualities needed to be successfully integrated in it. In the overall metaphorical context of a "balance" between "rights" and "duties," this normalizes an *a priori* need for immigrants to earn their rights by, for example, learning the host society's "language, history and institutions." Paradoxically, it is through these essentializing exclusions that the EU reinforces its identity as endorsing "human rights," "democracy," or "tolerance;" conversely, it is the progressive trope of integration what facilitates the singling out of specific groups as deficient, and regulates their marginalization.

As a final example to illustrate how dividing and hierarchically arranging cultural and economic aspects of integration normalizes excluding dynamics, it is worth taking a close look at the different "policy areas of relevance for monitoring the outcome of integration policies" presented at the most recent ministerial conference on integration, held in Zaragoza in 2010. In this declaration, and following the general tone of the Vichy conference, integration is presented as "a driver for development and social cohesion." The text also establishes that the main aim of integration policies is "to ensure equal rights, obligations and opportunities for all." To this end, the document identifies "employment," "education," "social inclusion," and "active citizenship" as "priority areas" through which "the outcome of integration policies" can be monitored. The text justifies the relevance of these areas in the following terms:

> Employment is a vital part of the integration process, and efforts in education are essential in helping immigrants to become successful and more active participants in society. Not only access to the labour market is important but also entry into society more generally, which makes social inclusion an important area. The participation of immigrants in the democratic process as active citizens supports their integration and enhances their sense of belonging.

As a way to monitor the extent to which these integration goals are achieved, the declaration proposes a series of "core indicators" in relation to each "priority area," such as employment and unemployment rates, highest educational attainment, median net income, or citizenship status. Thus, when discussing ways to measure the degree of success of integration policies, the Zaragoza declaration highlights the importance of social and material outcomes. Through the different "core indicators" listed above, material, economic conditions are clearly presented here as the measurable consequence of successful or unsuccessful "practices." These data, in turn, are used to stress the need for specific policies geared towards facilitating the "integration process," thus reinforcing the notion that integration is a necessarily steps towards "social cohesion."

However, the ways in which those economic aspects are also a constraining, *preceding* factor when considering immigrants' suitableness for inclusion are not part of this formula. Similarly, (seen as) cultural factors such as degree of fluency in a particular language are not listed as possible *outcomes* of the (lack of) integration process. The text thus fails to acknowledge the co-constitutive relation among economic status and cultural marginalization when approaching integration. As Calavita (2005: 100) has persuasively argued, "if economic reality imposes on even xenophobes the need for immigration integration, economic realities also impede its full realization."

This emphasis on economic outcomes as succeeding and detached from cultural constrains thus reveals the contradictions embedded in what Horner and Weber (2011: 156) call a "statistical correlations model" of integration. According to these authors, this EU approach to integration, consolidated in the last decade, specifies an endpoint of the integration process while, at the same time, othering immigrants in the process. Thus, this model operates under the assumption that "a society can be seen as integrated if it offers equal rights and opportunities to all the different social groups living and working there, in such domains as education and the employment market."

In this context, economic "hard" indicators such as employment and unemployment rates, as well as social "soft" indicators such as feelings of belonging, are treated as evidence of (lack of) integration (Blommaert and Verschueren 1998). However, when considered solely as a *product* of other kinds of (seen as cultural) characteristics, these indicators have the potential to construct immigrants as inherently deficient and therefore not suitable for integration. Statistical "outcomes" end up working as an objective measure of the "integrative" potential of certain groups, thus justifying the need for policies such as "language and culture" tests for citizenship that place those same groups further away from integration (see Hogan-Brun, Mar-Molinero and Stevenson 2009; Extra, van Avermaet and Spotti 2009).

As the EU documents focusing specifically on integration show, the extent to which supposedly inclusive discourses and practices actually translate into inclusion is far from straightforward. Rather, as Horner and Weber (2011: 142) put it, "Integration is positioned as the process leading to the desirable goal of 'social cohesion' [. . .] but its effect tends to be that of strengthening an 'us' vs. 'them' discourse." It is thus important to pay close attention to the assumptions that inform integration discourses and practices, keeping in mind that "othering" and "deficit" are not just the causes of marginalization; they are also its results. Similarly, economic conditions cannot be considered pure outcomes of integration policies, but are also part of what constructs some groups as less integratable than others.

In this context, the different measures promoted in the texts analyzed, such as requiring immigrants to learn the state's official language(s), or to endorse a series of "core European values" are naturalized as the preconditions *sine qua non* social and economic equality cannot be granted. Integration thus becomes a racializing process of drawing attention to culturally salient characteristics perceived as incompatible with possible material benefits.

Conclusions

This chapter has focused on race and racism as important sites of theoretical and practical intervention for a critical project invested in highlighting how discursive practices (re)create social inequalities. Research on both institutional and everyday contexts reveals patterned ways in which speakers index and reproduce ideologies about different groups. Some of these include essentializing discursive moves, strategic use of narratives, or "us" versus "them" polarizations that go hand in hand with a systematic denial of racism through disclaimers. On the other hand, covert, "well-intentioned" forms of racial discrimination tend to escape this categorization and remain unscrutinized, thus normalizing the ideological frameworks that they necessarily rely on.

In this context, I offered an analysis and critique of this kind of seemingly progressive and harmless discourse as it permeates EU institutions. Specifically, I looked at recent immigration policy developments, as well as recommendations for integration practices, as manifestations of an indirect racialization that systematically excludes certain groups as it targets them for inclusion. In this process, the documents examined also recreate and secure a white European identity attached to a series of normalized and restricted values.

Overall, this chapter aimed to review and advance knowledge on the relationship between particular discursive practices and broader ideological systems with regards to race and racism – a relationship that is necessarily reciprocal, and constantly fueled with new tropes that serve naturalizing functions. In this sense, a critical cultural approach to discourse studies stands at an optimal position to perform a challenging, multilayered, and urgent task, grounded in four main goals: to identify the specific keywords and practices that matter at particular times and particular places; to analyze and interpret how they function as enablers and normalizers of broader ideological articulations; to explain the conditions of possibility for these dominant dynamics; and to document and propose ways in which they can be and are already being undone.

Note

1 The Council's "Common Basic Principles" on integration constitute the guiding basis for all EU initiatives related to integration. This document was "designed to promote a common European approach toward a framework for immigrant integration and to serve as a reference for the implementation and evaluation of current and future integration policies" (European Policy Centre 2005: 4). The Council's 2007 conclusions, on the other hand, are non-binding declarations including recommendations for EU states regarding future actions on different issues. The 2009 and 2010 conferences on integration were "informal meetings" bringing together the integration ministers in the different member states. As explained in the Council's Conclusions of June 2007, the general purpose of these conferences was "to review at a political level the scope for further action directed to strengthening the European framework for integration and the integration policies of the Member States, by promoting unity in diversity" (European Council 2007). The resulting official declarations were an attempt to summarize the main needs identified and compromises reached in terms of future actions. As with many EU official documents, these declarations are not legally binding.

Further reading

Flubacher, M. and Yeung, S. (2016). Discourses of integration: Language, skills, and the politics of difference. *Multilingua*. ISSN (Online) 1613–3684, ISSN (Print) 0167–8507, DOI: 10.1515/multi-2015–0076, August 2016.
This introduction to a special issue on integration and the politics of difference centers on "integration" as both policy practice and discursive regime, and its implications for migrants in the global north.
Martínez Guillem, S. (2016). The edges of praxis: Embracing constraints in (whiteness) theorizing. *Journal of Multicultural Discourses* 11(3): 262–268.
This commentary article reviews research in the field of Whiteness studies with an emphasis on nuance, context, and history in relation to the why, who, what, and how of whiteness theorizing.
Miles, R. (1989). *Racism*. London: Routledge.
This is a sociological approach to the study of racism that introduces the concept of racialization – as opposed to "race" – as a way to emphasize ideological processes and their relation to capitalism.

References

Adeyanju, C.T. and Neverson, N. (2007). "There will be a next time": Media discourse about an "apocalyptic" vision of immigration, racial diversity, and health risks. *Canadian Ethnic Studies* 39: 26.
Bell, M. (2009). *Racism and equality in the European Union*. Oxford: Oxford University Press.
Bia, M. T. (2004). Towards an EU immigration policy: Between emerging supranational principles and national concerns. *EDAP paper, 2/2004*, Working Paper.
Billig, M., Condor, S., Edwards, D., Gane, M., Middleton, D. and Radley, A. (1988). *Ideological dilemmas*. London: Sage.
Blackledge, A. (2006). The racialization of language in British political discourse. *Critical Discourse Studies* 3: 61–79.
Bonilla-Silva, E. and Forman, T. A. (2000). "I am not a racist but. . . ": Mapping white college students' racial ideology in the USA. *Discourse & Society* 11: 50–85.

Boswell, C. (2003). *European migration policies in flux: Changing patterns of inclusion and exclusion*. Oxford: Blackwell's and Chatham House.

Calavita, K. (2005). *Immigrants at the margins: Law, race, and exclusion in southern Europe*. Cambridge: Cambridge University Press.

Campbell, S. and Roberts, C. (2007). Migration, ethnicity and competing discourses in the job interview: Synthesizing the institutional and personal. *Discourse & Society* 13: 243–271.

Charteris-Black, J. (2006). Britain as a container: Immigration metaphors in the 2005 election campaign. *Discourse & Society* 17: 563–581.

Chiang, S. Y. (2010). "Well, I'm a lot of things, but I'm sure not a bigot": Positive self presentation in confrontational discourse on racism. *Discourse & Society* 21(3): 273–294.

Cohen, S. (1991). *Imagine there's no countries: 1992 and international immigration controls against migrants, immigrants, and refugees*. Manchester: Greater Manchester Immigration Aid Unit.

Dell'Olio, F. (2005). *The Europeanization of citizenship: Between the ideology of nationality, immigration, and European identity*. Burlington: Ashgate Publishing.

Del-Teso-Craviotto, M. (2008). Gender and sexual identity authentication in language use: The case of chat rooms. *Discourse Studies* 10: 251–270.

Eriksson, K. and Aronsson, K. (2005). "We're really lucky": Co-creating "us" and the "other" in school booktalk. *Discourse & Society* 16: 719–738.

Erjavec, K. (2009). The "Bosnian war on terrorism." *Journal of Language & Politics* 8: 5–27.

European Council. (2004). Common basic principles on integration, Luxemburg, November, 1–10.

European Council. (2007). Conclusions of the council and the representatives of the governments of the member states on the strengthening of integration policies in the European Union by promoting unity in diversity, Luxemburg, June 12 and 13, 1–4.

European Ministerial Conference on Immigration. (2008). Delaration approved by the representatives of the Member States. Vichy, November 3 and 4, 1–16.

European Ministerial Conference on Immigration. (2010). Draft declaration. Zaragoza, April 15 and 16, 1–16.

Every, D. and Augoustinos, M. (2007). Constructions of racism in the Australian parliamentary debates on asylum seekers. *Discourse & Society* 18: 411–436.

Gales, T. (2009). 'Diversity' as enacted in us immigration politics and law: A corpus based approach. *Discourse & Society* 20: 17.

Garner, S., (2007). The European Union and the racialization of immigration, 1985–2006. *Race/Ethnicity* 1: 61–87.

Geddes, A. (2008). *Immigration and European integration: Beyond fortress Europe?* 2nd edn. Manchester: Manchester University Press.

Gilroy, P. (1987). *There ain't no black in the union jack: The cultural politics of race and nation*. Chicago: University of Chicago Press.

Gordon, P. (1989). *Fortress Europe? The meaning of 1992*. London: Runnymede Trust.

Gramsci, A. (1971). *Selections from the prison notebooks*. New York: International Publishers.

Harding, R. (2006). Historical representations of aboriginal people in the Canadian news media. *Discourse & Society* 17: 205–235.

Hervik, P. (2004). Anthropological perspectives on the new racism in Europe. *Ethnos* 69: 149–155.

Hill, J. (2008). *The everyday language of white racism*. Oxford: Wiley-Blackwell.

Horner, K. and Weber, J. J. (2011). Not playing the game. Shifting patterns in the discourse of integration. *Journal of Language and Politics* 10: 139–159.

Hsu, R. (ed.) (2010). *Ethnic Europe: Mobility, identity and conflict in a globalized world*. Stanford, CA: Stanford University Press.

KhosraviNik, M. (2009). The representation of refugees, asylum seekers and immigrants in British newspapers during the Balkan conflict (1999) and the British general election (2005). *Discourse & Society* 20: 477–498.

LeCouteur Every, D. and Agoustinos, M. (2008). Constructions of Australia in pro- and anti-asylum seeker political discourse. *Nations & Nationalism* 14: 562–580.

Lentin, A. and Titley, G. (2012). The crisis of 'multiculturalism' in Europe: Mediated minarets, intolerable subjects. *European Journal of Cultural Studies* 15: 123–138.

Levy, C. (2005). The European Union after 9/11: The demise of a liberal democratic asylum regime? *Government and Opposition* 40: 26–59.

McLaren, P. (1993). Multiculturalism and the postmodern critique: Towards a pedagogy of resistance and transformation. *Cultural Studies* 7(1): 118–146.

MacMaster, N. (2001). *Racism in Europe*. New York: Palgrave.

Martínez Guillem, S. (2013a). Rethinking power relations in critical/cultural studies: A dialectical (re) proposal. *Review of Communication* 13(3): 184–204.

Martínez Guillem, S. (2013b). The dialectics of multiculturalism: Constructing "new citizens" in Spanish public broadcasting. *European Journal of Cultural Studies* 16(5): 620–639.

Martínez Guillem, S. (2015). Exclusive inclusion. *Critical Discourse Studies*. DOI: 10.1080/17405904.2015.1023327

Mason Carris, L. (2011). La voz gringa: Latino stylization of linguistic (in)authenticity as social critique. *Discourse & Society* 22: 474–490.

Mehan, H. (1997). The discourse of the illegal immigration debate. *Discourse & Society* 8: 249–270.

Miles, R. and Thranhardt, D. (eds.) (1995). *Migration and European integration: The dynamics of inclusion and exclusion*, 53–72. London: Pinter.

Moore, K. (2013). 'Asylum shopping' in the neoliberal social imaginary. *Media Culture Society* 35: 348–365.

Mynott, E. (2002). Nationalism, racism and immigration control. From anti-racism to anticapitalism. In S. Cohen, B. Humphries and E. Mynott (eds.), *From immigration controls to welfare controls*, 11–29. New York: Routledge.

Omi, M. and Winant, H. (1986). *Racial formation in the United States*. New York: Routledge.

Santa Ana, O. (1999). "Like an animal I was treated": Anti-immigrant metaphor in US public discourse. *Discourse & Society* 10: 191–224.

Schmidt, R. (2002). Racialization and language policy: The case of the USA. *Multilingua* 21: 141–161.

Simmons, K. and Lecouteur, A. (2008). Modern racism in the media: Constructions of 'the possibility of change' in accounts of two Australian 'riots'. *Discourse & Society* 19: 667–687.

Solomos, J. (2001). "Race," multiculturalism and difference. In N. Stevenson (ed.), *Culture and citizenship*, 198–212. London: Sage.

Sue, D. W. (2010). *Microaggressions in everyday life: Race, gender, and sexual orientation*. Hoboken, NJ: John Wiley & Sons.

Teo, P. (2000). Racism in the news: A critical discourse analysis of news reporting in two Australian newspapers. *Discourse & Society* 11(1): 7–49.

Tilbury, F. and Colic-Peisker, V. (2006). Deflecting responsibility in employer talk about race discrimination. *Discourse & Society* 17: 651–676.

van Dijk, T. A. (1984). *Prejudice in discourse*. Amsterdam: John Benjamins.

van Dijk, T. A. (1987). *Communicating racism: Ethnic prejudice in thought and talk*. Newbury Park: Sage.

van Dijk, T. A. (1992). Discourse and the denial of racism. *Discourse & Society* 3(1): 87–118.

van Dijk, T. A. (1993). *Elite discourse and racism*. Newbury Park, CA: Sage.

van Dijk, T. A. (2001). Principles of critical discourse analysis. In M. Wetherell et al. eds., *Discourse theory and practice: A reader*, 300–317. London.

van Dijk, T. A. (2002). Discourse and racism. In David Goldberg and John Solomos (eds.), *The Blackwell companion to racial and ethnic studies*, 145–159. Oxford: Blackwell, 2002.

Wetherell, M. and Potter, J. (1993). *Mapping the language of racism: Discourse and the legitimation of exploitation*. New York: Columbia University Press.

Williams, R. (1983). *Keywords. A vocabulary of culture and society*, rev. edn. New York: Oxford University Press.

Wodak, R. (2007). Discourses in European Union organizations: Aspects of access, participation, and exclusion. *Text & Talk* 27: 655–680.

Wodak, R. and Matouscheck, B. (1993). 'We are dealing with people whose origins one can clearly tell just by looking: Critical discourse analysis and the study of neo-racism in contemporary Austria. *Discourse & Society* 4(2): 225–248.

25

Feminist critical discourse analysis

Michelle M. Lazar

Introduction

Critical discourse analysis is a movement which seeks to raise critical consciousness about the discursive dimensions of social problems involving discrimination, disadvantage, and dominance with the aim of contributing to broader emancipatory projects. Among the many enduring social concerns investigated by CDA scholars, gender-based inequalities have constituted an important research focus. Belonging to the family of CDA scholarship, studies with a focus on gender share the main tenets of CDA (for example, van Dijk 1993; Fairclough, Mulderrig and Wodak 2011) and are enriched intellectually by other critical discourse research projects. At the same time, feminists' engagement with gender relations and ideologies has also contributed intellectually to wider CDA research. Notably, feminist studies had provided an impetus in the formative years of CDA scholarship in the 1980s (van Dijk 1991). Decades later, in a move to signal explicitly the ongoing contributions of feminist thought and politics in gender-related CDA studies, as well as the disciplinary hybridity which that has entailed, the term 'feminist critical discourse analysis' (or 'Feminist CDA'/'FCDA') was introduced (Lazar 2005; Walsh 2001).

Feminist CDA is a political perspective which investigates the complex and diverse ways by which gender ideologies that entrench power asymmetries become 'common sense' in particular communities and discourse contexts, and how they may be challenged. This includes discursively sustained assumptions and inequalities, ranging from overt to increasingly subtler forms of sexism. Focusing on social justice and transformation, the objective of FCDA is to demystify and challenge discourses that continue to buttress gendered social orders in various ways, which harm and foreclose socially progressive possibilities for individuals and groups.

The term 'feminist' in 'Feminist CDA' should clarify that beyond simply focusing on the category of 'gender' as an object of CDA research, FCDA is driven as much by current *feminist* epistemology and practice as it is by CDA principles. From the point of view of theory, this means that FCDA not only inherits, historically, its critical impetus from the Frankfurt School via CDA, but is informed by contemporary developments in critical feminist thought. The latter involves building on foundational feminist work of critiquing structural inequalities (associated with 'Second Wave' feminisms), while developing nuanced and contextualised understandings of gender politics, arising from feminists' current uptake of poststructural, transnational, queer, postcolonial and intersectional theories (associated with 'Third Wave' feminisms).[1] While keeping the critical focus, FCDA, then, shares the view that individuals negotiate between multiple social identities in any given context (Wodak 2003), and that the social categories of 'women'/'men', far from universal, fixed and binary are diverse, changing and plural.

In this chapter, six principles of FCDA are outlined, followed by a review of selected FCDA studies on a range of gendered social concerns in a variety of international contexts. The rest of the chapter focuses on a worked example involving a discourse on sexual violence – the objectives of which are to show the cultural particularities of the discourse, and at the same time, the discursive resonances of androcentric gender ideologies at play transnationally. Extending from the discussion of this case study, the chapter concludes by highlighting two directions for future research in FCDA.

Principles of feminist critical discourse analysis

Five interrelated principles of FCDA have been previously identified (Lazar 2005, 2014). The first is the ideological character of 'gender'. Taking a critical perspective on ideologies as group-based socio-cognitive representations of practices in the service of power (Fairclough 1992; van Dijk 1998), FCDA considers 'gender' as an ideological structure and practice, which divides people hierarchically into two blocs, based upon the presumed naturalness of sexual difference. Although contemporary theories have shown that gender-in-context is fluid and plural, a fixed binary with associated gendered stereotypes predominates in common sense understanding. This 'common sense' structure of gender gets (re)produced institutionally and renewed in everyday practice through the complicity of men and women generally, although the asymmetrical dualism can also be destabilised by those who refute its commonsensical premise. Gender, importantly, exists in a matrix of other socially stratified identities including sexuality, race/ethnicity, class, profession, age, culture and geopolitics. This means that the effects of gender structure are neither materially experienced nor discursively constructed in the same way for all women and men in every situation everywhere; yet, gender remains one of the important ideological structures in the intertwining and overlaying of these other identities.

Secondly, power is a central focus in critical investigations of gender identities and relations. Broadly, two conceptions of power have been valuable to FCDA. On the one hand, earlier feminist theories introduced the concept of 'patriarchy' to refer to a social system which privileges men at the expense of women (Mills 2008). Used as a critical concept, it points towards hegemonic masculinist dominance and systemic inequalities based on gender. While power cannot be said to be uniformly held or exercised by all men, simplistically, power does remain largely vested, materially as well as symbolically, in individual men and 'men' as a social group. Further, it is useful to view patriarchy not as a monolithic system, but as intersecting in complex ways with other systems of power such as heteronormativity, colonialism, capitalism and neoliberalism. On the other hand, Foucault's (1977) notion of power as widely dispersed and operating intimately and diffusely has been influential in feminists' understanding of modern relations of power. Foucault's ideas about the complex network of disciplinary systems and prescriptive technologies through which normalising power operates and produces self-regulating human subjects have been fruitfully adapted by feminists to explain "gender[ed] configurations of power" in contemporary societies (Diamond and Quinby 1988: xiv). Both kinds of power co-exist and intertwine in contemporary gender politics, which almost always involves dimensions of intimacy as well as crystallizations of larger patterns of social relations (Diamond and Quinby 1988). Both approaches to power also raise crucial questions of resistance and contestation, as well as counter-resistance and appropriation.

Thirdly, FCDA shares with CDA and feminist approaches a constitutive view of discourse. The relationship between discourse and the social is a dialectical one, in which discourse constitutes and is constituted by social practices (Fairclough 1992, passim). Every act of signification through language and other forms of semiosis contributes to the reproduction and maintenance of social identities, relations and orders as well as to contesting and transforming them. Feminist (and queer) scholars have emphasised the ongoing, iterative and active accomplishment of gender through discourse (West and Zimmerman 1987; Butler 1990). Rather than assume that gender categories are immanent, through their linguistic (and nonlinguistic) practices, people 'do' or 'perform' identities as 'women' and 'men' within particular social and historical constraints. As gender exists within 'sets of identities' (de Lauretis 1987), in the analysis of discourse, FCDA, then, aims to investigate how gender plays out in these identity matrices – as more or less relevant or salient – in given situations, as well as in the gendering of these other identities. The analysis of gender in discourse also includes examining the co-constructedness of gender relations in particular social situations and communities of practice. Ways of doing gender within and across the private and public spheres of life can show up ideological assumptions that entrench asymmetrical relations of power. These meanings expressed in discourse can be overt, subtle, unequivocal or ambivalent.

Fourthly, FCDA is interested in critical reflexivity as a practice. Critical awareness amongst people is seen as a generally pronounced feature of late modernity (Giddens 1991; Fairclough, Mulderrig and Wodak 2011), which is of interest to FCDA in the different ways that reflexivity gets harnessed by social actors in contemporary societies. One way is for critically aware persons and institutions to generate constructive dialogue and/or spearhead progressive social changes. Examples include speaking out against sexist commentary, instituting gender mainstreaming in organisations, or fostering environments that are inclusive of women, sexual minorities and transgender people. Another way that critical reflexivity gets harnessed is by persons and institutions that appropriate progressive feminist politics for non-feminist purposes. For example, advertisers are known to deploy feminist-sounding discourse strategically, for commercial gain – which beyond the intent to merely profiteer, can harm feminist politics in the process. Feminists are not exempt from turning a critical self-reflexive gaze upon ourselves, either. Whether in feminist theorisation or practice, the exercise of self-reflexivity is required continuously so that, in aiming for social justice, we ourselves do not inadvertently reconstitute patterns of privilege and exclusion, or bar progressive social change.

Fifthly, FCDA scholarship is considered analytical activism. Striving for a socially just society, in which gender does not predetermine one's sense of self and relationships with others, requires constantly imagining ways of 'doing' and 'becoming' that are socially inclusive and respectful of all persons. A way towards this goal, as hooks suggests, is by maintaining "an openness of conviction in voicing critique and in forming communities of resistance" (1984: 149). When viewed from a praxis perspective which dissolves boundaries between 'theory' and 'practice', academic feminists' work, like FCDA scholars', can be said to form communities of resistance and activism. In fact, in so far as the raising of critical consciousness through research and teaching are forms of feminist activism, the political critique of discourse can be viewed not only for action, but *as* action. This is rooted from a position of knowing that the discursive issues dealt with have material consequences for groups of women and men in specific communities and situations, and is driven by a conviction of contributing towards social change.

Further to the above, in this chapter, I highlight an added dimension of transnationalism as an important focus in FCDA research. Gender struggles are similar, yet different – and vice versa – across many parts of the world. Even though structured and experienced unevenly in many places, asymmetrical gender relations remain a persistent, intransigent concern globally (Acker 2006). Unlike politically debilitating effects of postmodern theories that eschew looking beyond the local and the individual, it is imperative for a vibrant feminist politics to engage with the transnational, in order to appreciate how gender ideologies operate in convergent as well as divergent ways, and how various kinds of discursive strategies are adopted in response to them. Such an approach calls for the importance of local, contextualised analyses of data combined with an awareness of wider social and discursive processes. This could offer greater insight into discourse strategies that are enacted in a local community of practice, yet which have wider global resonance as well. It also enables the investigation of discursive logics that are transnational in character (Lazar 2015a).

Studies in feminist CDA

Feminist CDA studies have investigated a range of gendered social concerns in a variety of domains internationally. Four key research foci are discussed in this section, which encompass traditional and ostensibly 'newer' gender ideologies. For each research focus, studies from two specific contexts are provided, indicative of how the investigated social concerns have resonances transnationally, yet manifested in very particular contextualised ways.

Gendered dichotomisation of public and private spheres

One research focus has centred on the entrenched gendering of the public and private spheres in many societies, where the public domain is associated traditionally with men and the domestic sphere with women. Even though a growing presence of women in the public realm is being witnessed in these societies, the acceptance of domestic labour by men continues to be lagging. Makoni's (2013) study attests to the powerful adherence to gendered dichotomization of public and domestic spheres in the discourse of Zimbabwean dual-career couples who had migrated to the UK. Linguistically analysing their responses to photographic 'triggers' depicting African men engaged in childcare and domestic chores, Makoni found the preservation of strong gendered norms that defined masculinity in terms of breadwinner roles and femininity in terms of household responsibilities. The gender identity of Zimbabwean men was perceived to have been threatened due to migration, which had sometimes necessitated their having to perform culturally feminine domestic tasks. Seen as assuming a new subordinate status as 'women', the men were perceived as having lost their social status as well as their masculine identity. The men's discourse constructed domesticity as a space of marginality and women-as-a-social-group as worthless. While some women had internalised these gendered norms and had accepted their subordinate position, Makoni observed that other women expressed non-conformist views. Significantly, the study showed how the dominant gendered norms upholding the public-private split intersected with racial, cultural and religious identity categories to safeguard the patriarchal traditions of the informants' place of origin, against perceived Western lifestyles of the host country.

In a study about contemporary gender ideologies in Vietnam, Nguyen (2011) shows that even where women are actively encouraged to participate in the public sphere, the private sphere remains primarily the domain of women. In analysing Vietnamese newspaper articles related to the national celebration of International Women's Day in 2010, Nguyen's findings revealed that Vietnamese women's public involvement received widespread coverage. Both their historical contributions in nationalist struggles as well as their contemporary achievements in conventionally masculine professions were amply acknowledged in the media. While this is indicative of gender equality, which is enshrined in the Vietnamese constitution and other legal provisions, Nguyen observes that Vietnamese women's participation in the public sphere is overtly linked to an agenda of national development and not associated with women's self-actualisation. Further, the recognition of women's public role does not translate into a redistribution of labour in the domestic front. The prevailing Confucian ideology, which supports a hierarchical gendered social order, emphasises a self-sacrificial domestic role for women as good mothers, obedient daughters-in-law and submissive wives. Nguyen argues that the assertion of Confucian principles reassures Vietnamese men of their culturally superior position, and keeps Vietnamese women in check at a time when they are increasingly proving themselves to be as capable as men in the public sphere.

Androcentricism in organisational structures

Even where women may be active in the public workforce, studies have documented the deep-seated androcentricism that underlies organisational practices and values in many cultural contexts. In this vein of studies, feminist CDA scholars have also investigated ostensibly more progressive organisational changes in order to understand whether and how this has affected women in employment, and especially women in leadership. For example, Wodak (2005) based her study on gender mainstreaming proposals in the European Union (EU) in the 1990s which, in principle, promoted comprehensive changes in gender roles and organisational practices. In analysing interview data of personnel employed in EU organisations, Wodak's initial findings indicated that indeed more women had been employed. The relatively open organisational structure also allowed women to negotiate their professional and personal identities in a range of different ways, from adhering to stereotypical masculine models to establishing distinctive, atypical ones. Nonetheless, she found that, on the one hand, women were still markedly underrepresented across particular member states, and especially at the highest levels of the EU organisations. On the other hand, her analysis revealed that even those women in positions of responsibility had to constantly justify their presence and achievements, and were still evaluated differently than their male counterparts. Wodak notes that although gender mainstreaming is a first step towards changing some structural inequalities, concomitant attitudinal changes must follow.

Writing specifically about the Spanish workplace culture, Martin-Rojo and Esteban (2005) noted the emergence of a new management model that was no longer legitimated solely by a hierarchical structure, but focused on relationships with peers and subordinates, and placed a premium on good communication skills. Although the new characteristics are associated traditionally with feminine qualities, Martin-Rojo and Esteban found that managerial women were negatively appraised by both male and female employees due to an entrenched prejudice of equating power and leadership with masculinity. From analysing the interviews and discussion groups held with employees, the scholars reported that unlike men, if women leaders adopted traditional masculine styles of management, they were perceived as overzealous and aggressive. However, if women managers followed the new relational model, they were perceived as lacking confidence and the authority to lead. As a result, it was found that Spanish women in positions of responsibility had to juggle to minimise their authority while exercising it. Furthermore, because the emergent model required that peers and subordinates accept those in authority, managerial women worried that they would offend them. Martin-Rojo and Esteban noted that the communicative behaviour of women managers was not only seen as inappropriate by employees, but that it contributed to their social isolation, making it difficult for them to gain recognition and promotion in the workplace.

Violence against women

Another important area of feminist discourse scholarship highlights the institutionally validated sexism at work in the discourse of violence against women. Using naming and transitivity analysis, Clark (1992) analysed news reports on physical and sexual violence of British women by strangers and intimate partners in a UK tabloid in the 1980s. Her findings revealed a pattern of blame (re)assignment, in which responsibility for an attack got transferred to the victim, or another woman, while excuses were found for the perpetrators, thus lessening their culpability. Victims in the reports were categorised as either 'genuine' or 'non-genuine' victims, based on notions of female respectability; 'genuine' victims were sexually 'unavailable' women like wives, mothers and girls, whereas 'non-genuine' victims were unmarried mothers, divorcees or blondes (drawing on particular stereotypes of Western white femininity). The distinction, as Clark noted, reflected a patriarchal viewpoint whereby women were categorised in terms of possible sexual encounters with men, rather than as autonomous individuals. Corresponding to the distinction of victim blameworthiness was the representation of perpetrators in either sub-human (as fiends or beasts) or human terms. 'Fiends' were men who were involved in stranger attacks of 'respectable' women, while 'non-fiends' were those who either attacked their spouses or women deemed 'available'. Clark observed that every permutation of blame entailed a patriarchal advantage accorded to British men. Husbands who attacked their wives were humanised and depicted sympathetically as victims of circumstances. Those named 'fiends' were excused for their crimes as they, too, were shown as acting out of past traumas.

Ehrlich (2001), too, reported on androcentric assumptions that undergirded the discourse of sexual assault adjudication processes involving a male defendant and two female complainants from a Canadian university. Her analysis revealed how these assumptions insidiously worked to legitimise male violence and reproduce gender inequalities. For example, through question–and–answer sequences during cross–examination, the complainants' credibility came under critical scrutiny, and they were, in fact, blamed for not resisting clearly and forcefully enough. Probable consent got inferred from what was institutionally deemed inadequate resistance, which minimised the defendant's culpability. Ehrlich noted that the adjudication processes failed to acknowledge the gendered power dynamics that had shaped and constrained the complainants' responses to the threat of sexual violence.

'New' postfeminist gender ideologies

FCDA studies have also investigated 'newer' gender ideologies and subjectivities that have become mainstreamed through popular discourses which have appropriated feminist signifiers. Talbot (2005) and Lazar (2006, 2009) have specifically examined 'commodity feminism' (Goldman 1992), which transforms a feminist politics into a lifestyle accessory for women consumers, premised upon popularised notions of freedom, choice and rights. Talbot (2005) discussed this in the discourse of the National Rifle Association (NRA), an influential gun lobby in the USA, which is supported by a profitable firearms business. She writes on how the NRA, hardly known for feminist activism, co-opted a range of progressive women-centric discourses in its promotional material, targeting American women since the 1990s. In a campaign called 'Refuse to be a Victim', the NRA explicitly drew upon feminist slogans of the 1970s, which had advocated an attitudinal change in women's traditional depictions as victims of violence. Together with this were threaded other women-oriented discourses, such as the discourse of reproductive rights, advocating American women's constitutional right to choose as well as the genre of personal safety advisory texts produced by US police departments and women's shelters, to protect women against battery and harassment. NRA's discourse, as a whole, constructed gun ownership as a personal matter and as women's ultimate self-empowerment. In promoting an unrestricted circulation of firearms as empowering, Talbot argues that the NRA preyed on women's legitimate fears, in order to recruit new female membership.

In a series of studies on contemporary advertising in Singapore, Lazar (2006, 2009) explored the constitution of a neoliberal postfeminist discourse, which addressed women consumers as empowered and entitled subjects. Through an analysis of a variety of postfeminist discursive themes, such as (personal and sexual) empowerment; confidence and agency through commodity consumption; a focus on self-indulgent pleasures; a reclamation of traditional feminine stereotypes; and a move specifically towards the 'girlification' of women, Lazar found that these 'new' modern subjectivities occupied a discursive space of ambivalence. At the same time as they appeared to celebrate feminism, they repudiated it, only to re-install updated versions of normative gender ideologies. The ambivalence, it is argued, contributes to fostering an insidious culture of post-critique, which numbs resistance and makes social criticism harder to articulate. For all its appearance to be pro-women, neoliberal postfeminist subjectivities offer limited and problematic visions of femininity and gender equality to a class of privileged women.

Doing FCDA: an example of the discourse of sexual violence

In this section, a feminist critical discourse analysis focusing on the discourse of sexual violence against women is presented as an illustrative case study. The example draws on commentary surrounding an internationally publicised attack, which came to be known as 'the Delhi rape'. On 16 December 2012, Jyoti Singh, a 23-year old physiotherapy student was returning home at about 8:30 P.M. after watching a movie in the city with a male friend, when she was brutally gang raped by six men on a moving bus. She died in a hospital two weeks later on 29 December 2012 from extensive injuries sustained from the attack. Three years on, based on this case, a documentary titled *India's Daughter* was produced by Assassin Films, and was scheduled to be televised in seven countries on International Women's Day on 8 March 2015. However, owing, partly, to a controversy surrounding the offensive statements made by one of the rapists interviewed in the documentary, the Indian courts banned its screening. The data for this section of the analysis includes the statements of Mukesh Singh, the interviewed rapist, and others in that documentary,[2] as well as statements by other public figures reported in news stories following the Delhi rape.

I have two aims in presenting the analysis of this material. Firstly, it is to unpack the dominant gender and sexual ideologies at work, as they intersect with notions of 'culture'. Secondly, in view of existing scholarship on the discourse of violence against women (e.g., Clark 1992; Ehrlich 2001), I aim to show that 'victim blaming' and 'perpetrator mitigation' function as wider *translocal/transcultural* discursive logics at work.

Victim blaming

Blaming the victim is associated with constructions of respectability, rooted in social and cultural mores (see Clark 1992). In the Delhi case, appropriate feminine conduct is signalled in adjectives and nominal phrases such as "dressed decently", "a decent girl", "a respected lady" and "a girl of respect", which, in fact, rehearse well-worn cross-cultural binary sexual stereotypes of women classified as either 'madonna' or 'whore'. The data reveals that Indian women's respectability is tied to regulated access to public spaces and viewed vis-à-vis traditional cultural norms. Transgression of either leads to victim blaming, suggesting that the victim brought the attack on herself – a familiar 'she had asked for it' trope.

Regulated access to public spaces takes the form of a curfew imposed tacitly upon Indian girls and women, which ranges from the evening to the early hours of the morning, as seen in the examples below:

(1) In our society we never allow our girls to come out from the house after 6:30 or 7:30 or 8:30 in the evening with any unknown person (M.L. Sharma, defence lawyer for the rapists).
(2) A decent girl won't roam at nine o'clock at night (Mukesh Singh, one of the convicted rapists).[3]
(3) All by herself till 3am at night in a city where people believe... you know... you should not be so adventurous (Sheila Dixit, former Delhi Chief Minister, quoted in relation to another assault case involving a woman returning home from work).

As evident from the use of the alternative conjunction "or" in example (1), the onset of the curfew period is quite indeterminate, which renders the public sphere virtually out of bounds to women from the entire span of the evening. In addition to the time regulation, access to public spaces for women is controlled by the requirement to be chaperoned. Out alone late, therefore, is construed as foolhardy (see example 3). Indeed, an Indian girl/woman may be accompanied only by 'suitable' others, namely, kin. The disapprobation found in example (1) concerning the accompaniment by unrecognised ("unknown") persons is further explicated below by the same defence lawyer, and echoed by a compatriot on his team.

(4) The moment she came out from her house with a boy who was neither her husband nor her brother, she left her morality and reputation as a doctor as well as girl's morality in the house and she came out just like a woman (M.L. Sharma, defence lawyer).
(5) That girl was with some unknown boy who took her on a date. [...] If very important, if very necessary, she should go outside. But she should go with their family members like uncle, father, mother, grandfather, grandmother, etc. etc. She should not go in night hours with her boyfriend (A.P. Singh, defence lawyer).

The lawyer's statement in example (5) makes clear that girls/women may be legitimately present in the public sphere only under extenuating circumstances (note the repeated emphasis of the intensifier "very" and the use of the conditional clauses "if ..."), and with family only (note the qualification presented by the adversative conjunction "but"). The two examples, with spatial references to "outside" ("came out", "go outside") based on an implied 'inside/outside' dichotomy, suggest a hierarchical gendering of space, in which women's presence in the public sphere is circumscribed (but not men's), and that women's 'natural' rightful space is in the domestic sphere. This is pointedly expressed in Mukesh Singh's extended statement (from example 2):

(6) Boy and girl are not equal. Housework and housekeeping is for girls, not roaming in discos and bars at night doing wrong things, wearing wrong clothes (Mukesh Singh).

The policing of public space is constantly enacted through expressions of prohibition, which strongly signal gender boundaries. In the examples above, this is manifest through modals of obligation ("you should not be so adventurous"; "she should not go in night hours with her boyfriend"), and through negative adverbials and polarity ("we never allow our girls to come out"; "a decent girl won't roam" / "not roaming"). The lexical choice 'to roam' also represents unrestricted mobility in public spaces, and carries connotations of censure for women.

The fact that Jyoti Singh had been 'outside' in the evening for leisure with a non-legitimate male companion is considered a morally transgressive act (see example 4), which makes the victim blameworthy and, in fact, punishable. In Mukesh Singh's recount of the rape, he explains the violence (the sexual assault on the victim and the physical assault of her male friend) as a form of discipline, using the metaphor of being taught a lesson. Morally errant behaviour apparently gives the perpetrators a right to intimidate – to question and attack – the transgressors and instill shame in them (see example 7). Interestingly, Mukesh Singh himself recognises the wrongful actions of the rapists (do "wrong things" with them); however, the rapists had relied on the stigma of shame of the victims, morally and culturally, to serve as a silencing strategy.

(7) [One of the rapists] asked the boy why he was out with a girl so late at night. [. . .] Those who raped, raped. They thought that if they do 'wrong things' with them, then they won't tell anyone. Out of shame. They'd learn a lesson (Mukesh Singh).

Respectability accrued from knowing 'a woman's place' is embedded within traditional Indian cultural norms, as seen in the following examples:

(8) They left our Indian culture. They were under the imagination of the film culture, in which they can do anything [. . .]. We have the best culture. In our culture, there is no place for a woman (M. L. Sharma, defence lawyer).
(9) Freedom has to be limited. These short clothes are Western influences. Our country's tradition asks girls to dress decently (Manohar Lal Khattar, top elected official of Haryana state, commenting about the case).
(10) [Mohan Bhagwat] said that rapes only occur in Indian cities, not its villages, because women there adopt Western lifestyles (Mohan Bhagwat, head of the pro-Hindu Rashtriya Swayamsevak Sangh, commenting about the case).

Indian culture is mentioned self-referentially in the first person plural pronoun ("our Indian culture"; "we have the best culture"; "our country's tradition"), and set up as an authentic self-identity against alien 'others' – "film culture" and "Western influences/lifestyles". References to westernisation, in particular, underscore a tension between the local in-group and the global out-group. In the case of example (10), this is played out even within the national urban-rural scale, in which the urban is unauthenticated by its association with westernisation, whereas the rural, by implication, is preserved as authentically Indian. The distancing of rape as an urban/Western-induced crime that occurs out 'there' in the Indian cities operates on an implied logic in which an unrestrained liberal culture is 'bad' and a restrained conservative culture is 'good'. Hence, the censure about film and Western culture in which one "can do anything" and the demand that "freedom has to be limited". Also, in the light of this operative logic, the deeply misogynistic comment – "In our culture, there is no place for a woman" – can be expressed unapologetically and, indeed, with a sense of cultural pride.

Victim blaming, in this case, is also extended to Jyoti Singh's unnamed male partner on that evening. In a news article, one of the defence lawyers reportedly said:

(11) "The man has broken the faith of the woman", Sharma said yesterday. "If a man fails to protect the woman, or she has a single doubt about his failure to protect her, the woman will never go with that man" (M.L. Sharma, quoted in MacAskill 2013).

The transitivity structures in which the man is positioned as Actor, coupled with the negative appraisal of his actions ("has broken", "fails"/ "failure") suggest that he was custodian of the woman and defaulted on his responsibility (never mind the fact that he should not have been out with her in the first place). This reveals a patriarchal logic of women requiring protection by men from other (predatory) men. In this case, his failure to safeguard her is an indictment on his masculinity ("the woman will never go with that man"), and which caused her to be raped.

Perpetrator mitigation

Even when the perpetrators' culpability is acknowledged, it gets mitigated in a number of ways, which is consistent with Clark's (1992) and Ehrlich's (2001) findings. For instance, the horrific crimes of rape and murder, in this case, get reframed as a "tragedy", an "error" (see example 15) or an "accident" ("I can't say why this incident – this accident – happened", Mukesh Singh) through the process of relexicalisation. In this way, the acts are recontextualised as something other than violent crimes and diminishes the perpetrators' accountability.

Sexualising rape is another way in which perpetrators' culpability is downplayed and which detracts from the (feminist) view of rape as an act of power.

(12) You are talking about man and woman as friends. Sorry, that doesn't have any place in our society. A woman means, I immediately put the sex in his eyes (M.L. Sharma, defence lawyer).

(13) If a girl is dressed decently, a boy will not look at her in the wrong way (Manohar Lal Khattar, top elected official of Haryana state, quoted in Naqvi, 2015).

Here, excuses are made for rapists through two interrelated sexual stereotypes: that women are primarily sexual objects, and the uncontrollable sexual desire of (heterosexual) men; the latter, based on a hegemonic 'male sex drive discourse' (Hollway 1984). The intrinsic definition of 'woman', in M.L. Sharma's terms, means 'for sex' ("I immediately put the sex in his eyes"), which discounts entirely the possibility of a platonic relationship between women and men. Women, therefore, are obliged to take responsibility to obviate male sexual interest through practices of self-surveillance ("dress[ed] decently").

Mitigating the culpability of a perpetrator is also achieved through a strategy of blame sharing, in which the assailant and victim are both responsible for the violence committed against the victim. In the next example, part of the blame is assigned to the victim for failure to respond gender-appropriately during the attack.

(14) When being raped, she shouldn't fight back. She should just be silent and allow the rape. Then they'd have dropped her off after 'doing her', and only hit the boy (Mukesh Singh).

(15) This tragedy would not have happened if she had chanted God's name and fallen at the feet of the attackers. The error was not committed by just one side (Asharam, a spiritual guru, reported in AFP News, 2013).

These comments draw upon androcentric cultural stereotypes of feminine passivity and submissiveness. In this instance, Indian women are expected to perform these stereotypical traits even when being attacked. The modal of obligation ("she *shouldn't* fight back. She *should* just be silent and allow the rape") and the conditional clause ("if she had chanted God's name and fallen at the feet of the attackers") suggest that Jyoti's death could have been averted had she compliantly endured the rape or begged for mercy.[4] The rape here is presupposed as inevitable, conveyed rather casually through the sexual expression "after 'doing her'", which also represents the prerogative of the male perpetrators to be active participants. The victim's failure to respond 'correctly' to the situation, then, makes her partly responsible for her own death: "The error was not committed by just one side".

Unlike the categorical statement expressed plainly above, blame sharing is also construed figuratively, yet no less unequivocally.

(16) You can't clap with one hand. It takes two hands to clap (Mukesh Singh).
(17) She should not be put on the streets just like food. The 'lady', [...] are more precious than a gem, than a diamond. It is up to you how you want to keep that diamond in your hand. If you put your diamond on the street, certainly the dog will take it out. You can't stop it (M.L. Sharma, defence lawyer).

Presented in example (16) is a common idiomatic expression, which accords equal and mutual responsibility to both parties. Example (17) offers two metaphors of women as objects; as food and as gems (or "more precious than gems", in fact). Although on one hand, it appears flattering for women to be conceptualised as precious, on the other hand, it also construes women as properties for close safekeeping. In this example, the mutuality of blame arises from negligence to safeguard, which results in the inevitable. Note the certitude in the adverbial and modality ("certainly the dog will take it out"), and in the expression of fatalism ("You can't stop it"). Although the perpetrators are represented derogatorily in reference to the dog metaphor, which is indicative of their culpability, the victim, too, is to be blamed for putting herself out there as fair game.

Finally, the perpetrators' culpability also becomes diminished, when they are portrayed as victims themselves and socially excusable. This is found mainly in the socio-psychological discourse of institutional experts such as psychiatrists and NGOs.

(18) They all [the convicts] actually came from a very deprived condition, where their surroundings are not a very good place, overcrowding. That's a very common scene, where women have been tortured, beaten or sexually abused by their male partners or husbands.... And that is what makes them again and again surprised, "Why me?"
I would say as a psychiatrist that they are actually normal human beings with anti-social traits in them, which actually manifested very badly at that time. They have been doing such crimes and easily getting away with that. [...] They say that's been happening and that it's a "man's right". They don't think of the other person as a human being. The negative cultural values about a woman are also very, very important in this type of act (Sandeep Goyal, jail psychiatrist for the convicts).
(19) This boy [the convicted juvenile] was like millions of Indian children, who are like street children, toiling to survive [...]. And then whatever happened after that in the company

of gang rape that took place and was party to it. This boy, in my opinion, did not have any serious aberrations. This boy had suffered endless misery in life. He was a child in need of care and protection, where the family couldn't even look after the child [. . .] (Amod Kanth, head of Prayas, non-governmental organisation for rape victims and juveniles).

A first thing to note is that the expert assessments – that "they are actually normal human beings but with anti-social traits" (18), and "[t]his boy, in my opinion, did not have any serious aberrations" (19)-construct the perpetrators in human terms, albeit flawed, rather than as monsters.[5] The depiction of the rapists as human beings is important, as demonisation would only unhelpfully distance 'them' from 'us'; if monsters are non-human and extra-societal, then they cannot be held responsible for their actions (Clark 1992). Indeed, demonization of rapists obscures the reality of women violated so ubiquitously by men who are known and close to them (Udwin, personal communication). Furthermore, in extracts (18) and (19), expressions of impoverishment such as "very deprived condition", "overcrowding", "toiling to survive", "suffered endless misery in life", in fact, create a semantic field which represents the perpetrators, sympathetically, as victims of unfortunate class-based circumstances. In fact, the description of one of the rapists (a juvenile who, reportedly, had been savage in the assault), as "a child in need of care and protection", repositions him as a vulnerable under-aged victim, whose culpability becomes blurred, if not erased. In other words, regardless of humanising, rather than demonising, perpetrators, responsibility for their actions is still – and, arguably, even more – diminished. Moreover, transgressive gender-based and other criminal acts ("That's a very common scene where women have been tortured, beaten or sexually abused by their male partners or husbands"; "[t]hey have been doing such crimes and easily getting away") are routinised, and offered as explanatory background to the perpetrators' acts of rape and murder.

On the one hand, such a representation is a chilling indictment of a society that normalises a 'rape culture', to such an extent that perpetrators disavow the humanity of women ("They don't think of the other person as a human being"), show no remorse and are stupefied by their conviction ("makes them again and again surprised 'Why me?'"). Sandeep Goyal, in (18), emphatically notes (see the duplicated adverbial intensifier) that "the negative cultural values about a woman are very, very important in this type of act". Goyal's appraisal of "negative" gendered Indian cultural values is poignantly germane in contrast to the proud pronouncement, "in our culture, there is no place for a woman", by a defence lawyer quoted earlier (see 8).

On the other hand, in the absence of expressing outrage at the crime and challenging established mindsets, systemically, such discourse inadvertently shifts the blame generally on to 'society' and justifies the continued violence, while deflecting agency and responsibility for perpetrators' actions individually and socially as a group.

Conclusion

In conclusion, two larger lessons from the particular case study can be drawn, which are relevant for FCDA studies. The first emphasises the importance of adopting a transnational lens in FCDA studies, if we are to recognise and contest patterns of discourse that sustain gender ideologies locally and globally. Although the 'Delhi rape', discussed in this chapter, had sparked intense national and international coverage, neither this instance of coercive power nor the discourse surrounding it was uniquely shocking; if anything, it was sadly routine, not exceptional (Roy 2013). The discourse of sexual violence in this case, however, presented a 'critical discourse moment' (Chilton 1987), allowing for the critical unpacking of power and ideologies involving gender, heterosexuality, social class, culture and tradition/ modernity. The analysis surfaced the particular ways the culturally framed heteronormative gender ideologies were configured and expressed in condoning the acts of violence in this case. At the same time, from a transnational perspective, the analysis also evidenced widespread discursive logics pertaining to sexual violence more broadly, as seen in the two-pronged discursive strategy of blaming the victim and deflecting full responsibility from the perpetrators (cf. Clark 1992, Ehrlich 2001). The discourse of sexual violence, in this case and beyond, is founded on an androcentric worldview which genders and polices the public sphere punitively through notions of feminine 'respectability'; prescribes 'appropriate' feminine dispositions while practising masculine exceptionalism; places responsibility upon women; privileges a hegemonic discourse of male sexuality (Ehrlich 2001); and highlights the perpetrators' suffering while overlooking that of the victims'. Even in well-intentioned, ostensibly more progressive public discourses about sexual violence against women, similarly pervasive discursive logics seem to be at play, via the operation of a neoliberal ethic of female personal agency and responsibility. Take a recent anti-molestation public education campaign in Singapore, for example (Lazar 2015b). Although the National Crime Prevention posters urge women to be proactive and not be "a silent victim" of sexual assault, the underlying discourse, nevertheless places the onus on women to take active and full responsibility, through either preventive or redressive action. Note the imperatives addressed to women: "Don't get rubbed the wrong way, protect yourself", "Have someone escort you home when it's late", "Avoid walking through dimly lit and secluded areas alone", and "Shout for help and call 999! Don't be a silent victim". The text is accompanied by an image of a woman whose rear is featured prominently and her face revealed, in contrast to a male perpetrator attempting to touch her derriere, whose face is partially hidden. The campaign implies that women have been duly cautioned, and would have to bear personal responsibility and blame. In contrast, the culpability of perpetrators nor the need to educate them to effect attitudinal change is de-emphasised. Although in this chapter, the discourse of sexual violence was chosen as a point of focus, other kinds of gendered social concerns could usefully benefit from building upon existing studies, in developing a contextually sensitive, yet transnational perspective as well (see also Lazar 2015a).

The second lesson extends from the analysis of dominance provided in this chapter to consider, more holistically, the constellation of power dynamics at work in any given situation. This might be theorised in terms of *orders of power* (cf. 'orders of discourse', Fairclough 1992). At one level, the discourse of the 'Delhi rape' could be described as 'pre-feminist' in the sense that it seemed oblivious of feminist principles of gender equality and justice. However, at another level, the discourse carried reactionary elements of a 'backlash' (Faludi 1991), resenting and resisting social changes in favour, to some extent, of liberalisation of gender relations. The fact that the victim had gone out openly with a male friend to watch a movie in the city attested to the fact that it was not a 'big deal' for her, her friend or her family. She was a young woman out in the city for leisure and relaxation. Yet, as seen, the discourse of sexual violence surrounding her actions served actively to reinscribe traditional cultural restrictions on female conduct and mobility. At the same time, the 'Delhi rape' incident was notable for the protests that ensued, on an unprecedented scale, in the aftermath. The protests, which rocked the capital, assumed a variety of modes, including street protests and reclaim-the-night marches as well as discursively on social networking sites, challenging the normalisation of sexual violence against women and girls, and seeking speedier legal redress for the crimes committed (Roy 2013). Particularly noteworthy in this regard was the mobilisation of young people in these discursive and non-discursive protests. As noted by Roy (2013), "At a time when globally young women are self-identifying as 'postfeminist' – uninterested in feminist politics for its apparent lack of relevance to their lives – the galvanising of masses of young women over rape should be viewed as nothing short of transformatory". From the point of view of feminist CDA research, then, oppressive as well as transformatory relations of power must constitute significant ways for understanding gender dynamics in the contemporary period.

Notes

1 In feminist studies the terms 'Second Wave' and 'Third Wave' tend to be used to distinguish between earlier (1970s and 1980s) and more recent (since 1990s) feminist scholarship. Sometimes the terms are used to suggest the two as distinctly marked generations or sets of theory, with the 'Third Wave' constituting a break from the 'outmoded' 'Second Wave'. I find it useful to see these 'waves' dialogically, as a historical and theoretical development in feminist thought, with the 'Third Wave' offering more refined perspectives in addressing feminist politics.
2 I am very grateful to Leslee Udwin, producer and director of *India's Daughter,* for permission to quote the material from her documentary film, and for her useful comments on a draft of this chapter. I also thank Nina Venkataraman for obtaining for me a copy of the banned documentary.
3 Written English translation of Mukesh Singh's words spoken in Hindi was provided in the documentary.
4 Viewed in relation to Ehrlich's (2001) study, the issue of active resistance versus compliance during an attack reveals a double-bind for women, more generally. Whereas in the Delhi example, the victim was castigated for fighting back, in Ehrlich's study, the complainants were blamed for not resisting strongly enough. In fact, British and US research has shown that victims sometimes remain physically passive because of their legitimate fears of the escalating severity of the attack (Dobash and Dobash 1992, in Ehrlich 1998), as was borne out in Jyoti Singh's case.
5 This both contrasts with as well as supports Clark's (1992) findings. The contrast, in the present case, is the humanising, rather than the demonising, of rapists in stranger attacks. Yet, the depiction of the rapists as non-fiends, is also consistent with Clark's argument regarding 'non-genuine' victims of questionable conduct – which is how Jyoti Singh, to some extent, has been represented.

Further reading

Lazar, M. M. (ed.) (2005). *Feminist critical discourse analysis: Gender, power and ideology in discourse.* Basingstoke: Palgrave.
This is the first book volume, comprising nine studies, on feminist CDA of gender and sexuality in a variety of institutional domains across international contexts.
Lazar, M. M. (2014). Feminist critical discourse analysis: Relevance for current gender and language research. In S. Ehrlich, M. Meyerhoff and J. Holmes (eds.), *Handbook of language, gender and sexuality,* 2nd edn, 180–200. London: Wiley-Blackwell.
This chapter provides an updated and expanded explanation of the key principles of feminist CDA, with current examples, to underscore the relevance of this type of analysis at a time when sexism and feminism are being disavowed. The chapter also addresses criticisms of feminist CDA.
Walsh, C. (2001). *Gender and discourse: Language and power in politics, the church and organisations.* Harlow: Longman Pearson.
Drawing on CDA and feminist linguistics, this book shows how British women negotiate masculinist ideologies in a number of public institutional contexts.
Wodak, R. (2008). Controversial issues in feminist critical discourse analysis. In K. Harrington, L. Litosseliti, H. Saunston and J. Sunderland (eds.), *Gender and language research methodologies,* 193–210. Basingstoke: Palgrave.
This chapter raises issues pertinent to the study of identities and contexts in feminist CDA, drawing on a case study which uses the discourse-historical approach to CDA.

Michelle M. Lazar

References

Acker, J. (2006). Introduction: The missing feminist revolution symposium. *Social Problems* 53: 444–447.

AFP News. (2013). Indian guru blames Delhi rape victim. https://sg.news.yahoo.com/indian-guru-blames-delhi-rape-victim-070001674.html

Butler, J. (1990). *Gender trouble: Feminism and the subversion of identity*. London: Routledge.

Clark, K. (1992). The linguistics of blame: Representations of women in The Sun's reporting of crimes of sexual violence. In M. Toolan (ed.), *Language, text and context,* 2018–226. London: Routledge.

De Lauretis, T. (1987). *Technologies of gender: Essays on theory, film and fiction*. Bloomington, IN: Indiana University Press.

Diamond, I. and Quinby, L. (eds.) (1988). *Feminism and Foucault: Reflections and resistance*. Boston, MA: Northeastern University Press.

Dijk, T. A. van (1991). Editorial: Discourse analysis with a cause. *The Semiotic Review of Books* 2(1): 1–2.

Dijk, T. A. van (1993). Principles of critical discourse analysis. *Discourse and Society* 4(2): 249–283.

Ehrlich, S. (1998). The discursive construction of sexual consent. In D. Cameron and D. Kulick (eds.), *The language and sexuality reader*, 196–214. London: Routledge.

Ehrlich, S. (2001). *Representing rape: Language and sexual consent*. London: Routledge.

Faludi, S. (1991). *Backlash: The undeclared war against women*. London: Vintage.

Fairclough, N. (1992). *Discourse and social change*. London: Polity.

Fairclough, N., Mulderrig, J. and Wodak, R. (2011). Critical discourse analysis. In T.A. van Dijk (ed.), *Discourse studies: A multidisciplinary introduction,* 357–378. London: Sage.

Giddens, A. (1991). *Modernity and self-identity*. Cambridge: Polity.

Goldman, R. (1992). *Reading ads socially*. London: Routledge.

Hollway, W. (1984). Gender differences and the production of subjectivity. In J. Henriques, W. Hollway, C. Venn and V. Walkerdine (eds.), *Changing the subject: Psychology, social regulation, and subjectivity,* 227–263. London: Methuen.

hooks, b. (1984). *Feminist theory: From margin to centre*. Boston, MA: South End Press.

Lazar, M. M. (ed.) (2005). *Feminist critical discourse analysis*. Basingstoke: Palgrave.

Lazar, M. M. (2006). Discover the power of femininity!: Analysing global power femininity in local advertising. *Feminist Media Studies* 6: 505–517.

Lazar, M. M. (2009). Entitled to consume: Postfeminist femininity and a culture of post-critique. *Discourse and Communication* 3(4): 371–400.

Lazar, M. M. (2014). Feminist critical discourse analysis: Relevance for current gender and language studies. In S. Ehrlich, M. Meyerhoff and J. Holmes (eds.), *The handbook of language, gender and sexuality*, 2nd edn., 180–200. Chichester: Wiley Blackwell.

Lazar, M. M. (2015a). Transnational engagements: Postfeminist articulations and critique. Plenary paper presented at *The Sociolinguistics of Globalisation Conference,* June 3–6, 2015, Hong Kong University.

Lazar, M. M. (2015b). The discourse of victim-blaming: gender, culture and sexual violence. Paper presented at the *Language and Society Workshop,* Department of English Language and Literature, National University of Singapore, December 12, 2015.

MacAskill, A. (2013). Delhi rape victims are to blame, defendants' lawyer says. *Bloomberg News.* Accessed January 10, 2013, www.bloomberg.com/news/articles/2013-2001-2009/delhi-rape-accused-to-plead-not-guilty-lawyer-says

Makoni, B. (2013). Women of the diaspora: A feminist critical discourse analysis of migration narratives of dual career Zimbabwean migrants. *Gender and Language* 7(2): 201–229.

Martin-Rojo, L. and Esteban, C. (2005). The gender of power: The female style in labour organisations. In M. M. Lazar (ed.), *Feminist critical discourse analysis,* 61–89. Basingstoke: Palgrave.

Mills, S. (2008). *Language and sexism*. Cambridge: Cambridge University Press.

Naqvi, M. (2015). *A murder and rapist's views reflect those of many in India*. Associate Press. http://sg.news.yahoo.com/murderer-rapists-views-reflects-those-many-india

Nguyen, T.T.H. (2011). Gender ideologies in the Vietnamese printed media. In Majstorovic and I. Lassen (eds.), *Living with patriarchy*, 195–216. Amsterdam: Benjamins

Roy, S. (2013). Routine, not exceptional. *Warscapes,* January 28, 2013.

Talbot, M. M. (2005). Choosing to refuse to be a victim: "power feminism" and the intertextuality of victimhood and choice. In M.M. Lazar (ed.), *Feminist critical discourse analysis,* 167–180. Basingstoke: Palgrave.

Walsh, C. (2001). *Gender and discourse: Language and power in politics, the Church and organisations.* Harlow: Longman Pearson.

West, C. and Zimmerman, D. (1987). Doing gender. *Gender & Society* 1(2): 125–151.

Wodak, R. (2003). Multiple identities: The role of female parliamentarians in the EU Parliament. in J. Holmes and M. Meyerhoff (eds.), *The handbook of language and gender,* 671–698. Oxford: Blackwell.

Wodak, R. (2005). Gender mainstreaming and the European Union: Interdisciplinarity, gender studies and CDA. In M. M. Lazar (ed.), *Feminist critical discourse analysis,* 90–113. Basingstoke: Palgrave.

26

Sexuality in critical discourse studies

Heiko Motschenbacher

Introduction

While Critical Discourse Studies (CDS) is today a widely applied approach to language and gender (e.g., Kosetzi 2008; Lazar 2014, this volume; Wodak 2008), researchers in language and sexuality have drawn relatively little on CDS as an analytical framework to date. This lack of attention to CDS is due to the historical development of language and sexuality studies, a field which has had a strong focus on non-heterosexual (non-normative) identities, maybe to complement earlier research in language and gender, which often concentrated on normative, heterosexual femininities and masculinities. The study of non-normative sexualities, as found in Queer Linguistics – the most vibrant strand within contemporary language and sexuality studies – has proven to be most fruitful at the local level of concrete interactional contexts. This explains why ethnographic, bottom-up (rather than discourse analytic) approaches, often taking an in-depth look at sexuality-related identity performances in specific communities of practice, have figured prominently within the field (e.g., Jones 2012; Sauntson and Morrish 2012; Schneider 2013).

However, the scarcity of CDS-influenced work in language and sexuality studies is also surprising, because these two fields show obvious affinities, which suggest that they can be combined in highly useful ways (cf. Leap 2011; Motschenbacher and Stegu 2013). Among the aspects that they share is a focus on issues of power, a critical look at dominant discourses that is ultimately meant to induce social change, and a tendency of researchers to overtly acknowledge the political motivations on which their work is based.

The present article aims to establish a more systematic connection between CDS and language and sexuality studies. It does so by presenting an overview of earlier CDS-related studies on the discursive construction of sexuality (Section 2), sketching out essential theoretical considerations concerning a normativity-based approach to CDS for language and sexuality studies (Section 3), elaborating on basic patterns of the discursive construction of sexual normativity (Section 4) and illustrating sexuality-related CDS by means of a sample analysis (Section 5).

Overview of earlier studies

Early sexuality-related CDS dealt with the most overt forms of dominance in relation to (hetero)sexuality, namely male sexual harassment of and violence against women (e.g., Clark

1992; Ehrlich 2001; Kissling 1991). Such studies can be seen as complementing conversation analytic research on sexual harassment and dominance in heterosexual relationships (e.g., de Francisco 1991; Fishman 1978; Tainio 2003) by reframing male dominance as a wider social discourse as opposed to a local communicative phenomenon. Another early sexuality-related strand of discourse analysis was concerned with identity constructions in dating advertisements (e.g., Coupland 1996; Jones 2000). This work largely pre-dates the formation of language and sexuality as a more coherent field of study in the early 2000s, with central publications such as Cameron and Kulick (2003) and Bucholtz and Hall (2004). Almost needless to say, this research did not take much issue with the discursive formation of sexuality as such, but rather focused on the analysis of specific types of sexuality-related linguistic behaviour.

More recent work in language and sexuality is still concerned with taking a critical look at power issues in relation to sexuality. However, contemporary research does not so much concentrate on the power and agency of individual (male) social actors vis-à-vis their (female) victims, but rather conceptualises power in a Foucauldian sense, i.e., as a discursive formation that is shaped overindividually. In other words, the focus of interest has shifted towards a critique of the power of dominant sexuality-related discourses that are deemed harmful (for example, heteronormativity) and a foregrounding of alternative, often marginalised or silenced sexuality-related discourses.

A central aim of sexuality-related CDS is the questioning of hegemonic, stereotypical or essentialising identity discourses, of gender binarism as the fundamental mechanism on which heteronormativity is based, and of other mechanisms that lead to certain sexual identities, desires and practices to be perceived as preferable or more legitimate in comparison to others. Accordingly, CDS has recently turned its critical focus on the discursive production of (hegemonic) heterosexualities (e.g., Coates 2013; Motschenbacher 2012) and their interface with masculinities and femininities (e.g., Conradie 2011; Gill 2009) or the gendered body (e.g., Attenborough 2013). But also non-heterosexual identities have been scrutinised by CDS scholars, often for purposes of de-essentialisation (e.g., Baker 2005; Koller 2011, 2013; Milani 2013; Motschenbacher 2013). Other highly visible sexuality-related discourses that have been analysed using CDS approaches include heterosexism (e.g., McLoughlin 2008), heteronormativity (e.g., Teo 2014), homophobia (e.g., Lillian 2005; Peterson 2011), ex-gay rhetoric (Stewart 2008), pornography (e.g., Marko 2008) or non-normative desires such as objectophilia (Motschenbacher 2014a, 2014b). As the references given here illustrate, CDS-based research on the discursive construction of sexuality mainly analyses language use in public media genres, which cannot just be seen as representing our social world in certain ways but also as perpetuating or changing sexuality-related discourses.

A normativity-based approach to critical discourse studies

Normativity is a key concept in language and sexuality studies and has proven a valuable tool for the description of sexuality discourses across cultures (cf. Baker 2013; Motschenbacher 2014a, forthcoming). The power struggle associated with the competition of dominant and marginalised discourses surfaces in the perception of sexual practices, desires and identities as (non-)normative and affects sexuality-related communication. Normativity is not a fixed, macro-level phenomenon. What counts as normative, less normative or non-normative and which (non-) normativities language users draw on depends significantly on the communicative context (see Burleson, Holmstrom and Gilstrap 2005 or Kiesling 2013). For example, a certain (linguistic) practice such as inverted appellation (Bunzl 2000, Johnsen 2008) may be considered a non-normative practice of sexual identity stylisation on the social macro-level, but may enjoy the status of a local, community-based norm in certain non-heterosexual communities of practice, where it is rather heteronormative practices that would be considered non-normative. Heteronormativity can therefore be viewed as a macro-level (dominant) discourse that may be challenged locally by various alternative normativities and non-normativities.

Besides heteronormativity, Queer Linguistics has recently also critically targeted homonormativity, that is, practices that sketch out certain gay male and lesbian sexualities as normal or preferable (Koller 2013; Motschenbacher and Stegu 2013). This is a logical consequence of the queer linguistic scepticism towards identity categories and their associated normativities. Today it is difficult to claim that gay male and lesbian identities in Western societies are completely non-normative, because they have reached various degrees of public recognition and social acceptance. Such widely recognised minority sexualities may develop normativities of their own, for example, notions of what it means to be a 'good' gay man or lesbian woman in a certain context.

Focusing on normativity is a way to overcome earlier theoretical discussions revolving around the question whether identity or desire constitutes a legitimate starting point for language and sexuality research (Cameron and Kulick 2003, 2005; Bucholtz and Hall 2004). These debates have induced a more sophisticated thinking about the discursive materialisation of sexuality as a socially produced (rather than natural or biological) phenomenon. At the same time, they have highlighted that a strict separation of identity and desire in relation to sexuality is in most contexts not feasible. Both sexual desires/practices and identities can be described in terms of their normativity status. Central research questions in this respect are: How do language users orient to sexual normativity in their communication? Which clashes between macro-level normativities and micro-level (non-) normativities can be observed? How does power play a role in what is perceived as normative or normal?

Normativity is not a binary matter of normative vs. non-normative, but rather a continual and negotiable concept, i.e., linguistic performances of sexuality can be more or less (non-) normative and are shaped by interactants' motivations to normalise or delegitimise certain practices. In this sense, normativity is clearly related to what Bucholtz and Hall (2004: 503–505) call 'authorisation' and 'illegitimation' within their tactics of intersubjectivity framework. Contrasts between macro- and micro-normativities need to be locally negotiated in communication. The two normativity levels do not operate independently of each other. Social macro-norms structure concrete interactions and locally negotiated normativities feed into the materialisation of norms at the social macro-level, causing shifts in normativity over time.

In the following section, central linguistic aspects that are involved in the discursive construction of (sexual) normativity are outlined. These linguistic features are prototypical of normative construction and do not represent an exhaustive list. As the sample analysis in Section 5.2 will show, other linguistic means of orienting to sexual (non-)normativity may be, and frequently are, employed.

The discursive construction of sexual normativity: Basic patterns

Theoretical approaches to norms often distinguish descriptive from prescriptive norms (Bicchieri 2006; Hall and LaFrance 2012; Hogg and Reid 2006). Descriptive norms are quantitatively based and linked to observations of what people commonly do (without degrading other behaviours as deviant). The regularities associated with descriptive norms may turn into prescriptive norms and are then taken as yardsticks for acceptable behaviour and enforced by society through a sanctioning of violations. Rather than being clear-cut categories, descriptive and prescriptive norms represent a continuum ranging from lower to higher normative force. There is a certain tension between these two types of normativity, because what people commonly do does not necessarily have to conform to prescriptively enforced social norms. For example, it can be assumed that the normative ideal of heterosexual relationships (monogamy, lifelong faithfulness, being married, bearing children, fixed expectations in terms of the age and socioeconomic status of wife and husband, etc.) forms the exception rather than the rule when one looks at the actual lived experience of heterosexual couples.

The discursive construction of (sexual) normativity involves three basic patterns that will be explicated and illustrated below: the linguistic construction of descriptive normativities, of prescriptive normativities and of shifting normativities. Prescriptive normativities can be oriented to, for example, by exploiting linguistic means of expressing deontic modality. With deontic modality the conditioning factors are external to the performing subject, hence its affinity with social norms. It involves linguistic means that express an obligation or permission to do something (Palmer 2001: 9–10), typically based on norms in operation in the wider community or society. Compare the following set of statements:

Women desire men.
Women must/ought to/should/may desire men.

As is illustrated in these examples, the use of modal auxiliaries is a central linguistic means of expressing what social actors are obliged, expected or permitted to do. Note that the use of the plain indicative mood (*Women desire men.*) can be argued to possess the highest normative force, as it is used to state universal truths or unquestionable facts that do not even allow for any negotiation or counterexamples. Otherwise, language users can draw on auxiliaries of various normative strengths, ranging from *must,* with the highest degree of normativity, down to *may,* associated with the lowest normative force.

Descriptive normativities can be expressed, for example, through the (vague) quantification of social actors practising a particular behaviour or through the specification how frequently a certain behaviour takes place. Compare the following sentences:

All/Most/Many/Some/Few women desire men.

These sentences represent a cline ranging from the highest degree of sexual normativity (desires affecting *all women*) down to the lowest degree (desires affecting *few women*). At the same time, they represent a continuum ranging from the discursive construction of normative sexual desires (*women, all women, most women*) to less or non-normative sexual desires (*some women, few women*). Similar effects can be achieved by the use of frequency-denoting adverbs (*Women invariably/frequently/sometimes/rarely desire men.*).

Finally, among the linguistic features that are involved in practices of shifting normativities are imperative sentences and other syntactic devices that may be used to voice directive speech acts (see Moessner 2010). These can be seen as interactants' explicit attempts to induce people to act in specific ways and thereby to cause sexual norms to change. In other words, positive directives ('do this') provide language users with a means to engage in normalising practices that are meant to increase the legitimacy of a certain sexuality-related behaviour. Negative directives ('don't do this'), by contrast, may serve as linguistic strategies of illegitimation.

Sample analysis: Salt-N-Pepa – 'Let's talk about sex'

As has been shown previously, people tend to orient to sexual normativities quite frequently in interactions in which they discuss non-normative sexualities (such as objectophilia, see

391

Motschenbacher 2014a, 2014b). However, this does not mean that an orientation to sexual norms does not surface when people talk about (more) normative sexualities. This will, in the following, be demonstrated by means of a short CDS-based case study of the discursive construction of sexuality and sexual normativity in commercial pop music. For this purpose, the lyrics of the famous song 'Let's talk about sex' by US-based hip-hop group *Salt-N-Pepa*[1] have been chosen as data – firstly because this song explicitly topicalises sexuality and secondly because it was a huge success in many Western countries and can therefore be assumed to have influenced sexuality discourses on a large scale.

The analysis proceeds in two, mutually informing steps: a description of the cultural context in which the lyrics have been produced (Section 5.1), and a description of the linguistic features that are used to orient to sexual normativity (including non-normativity and normalising practices) in the text (Section 5.2). By doing so, the present study complements earlier research in the CDS tradition that dealt with female hip-hop discourse mainly from a gender perspective (cf. Richardson 2007). The lyrics of the song are given below.

1   Salt: Yo, I don't think we should talk about this
2   Spin: Come on, why not?
3   Salt: People might misunderstand what we're tryin' to say, you know?
4   Spin: No, but that's a part of life

[Chorus:]
5   Come on
6   Let's talk about sex, baby
7   Let's talk about you and me
8   Let's talk about all the good things
9   And the bad things that may be
10–13   Let's talk about sex [sung four times]

[Verse 1:]
14   Salt: Let's talk about sex for now
15   To the people at home or in the crowd
16   It keeps coming up anyhow
17   Don't decoy, avoid, or make void the topic
18   Spin: Cause that ain't gonna stop it
19   Now we talk about sex on the radio and video shows
20   Spin: Many will know, anything goes
21   Salt: Let's tell it how it is, and how it could be
22   How it was, and of course, how it should be
23   Those who think it's dirty have a choice
24   Pick up the needle, press pause, or turn the radio off
25   Will that stop us, Pep? Pep: I doubt it
26   Salt: All right then, come on, Spin

[Chorus repeated]

[Verse 2:]
27   Salt: Hot to trot, make any man's eyes pop
28   She use what she got to get whatever she don't got

29 *Fellas drool like fools, but then again they're only human*
30 *The chick was a hit because her body was boomin'*
31 *Gold, pearls, rubies, crazy diamonds*
32 *Nothin' she ever wore was ever common*
33 *Her dates, heads of state, men of taste*
34 *Lawyers, doctors, no one was too great for her to get with*
35 *Or even mess with, the Prez she says was next on her list*
36 *And believe me, you, it's as good as true*
37 *There ain't a man alive that she couldn't get next to*
38 *She had it all in the bag so she should have been glad*
39 *But she was mad and sad and feelin' bad*
40 *Thinkin' about the things that she never had*
41 *No love, just sex, followed next with a check and a note*
42 *That last night was dope*

[Bridge 1:]
43 *Oh, hey, ooh, ooh, ooh, take it easy now*
44 *Uh, alright*

[Chorus repeated]

[Bridge 2, sung twice:]
45 *Ladies, all the ladies, louder now, help me out*
46 *Come on, all the ladies, let's talk about sex, all right*
47 *Spin: Yo, Pep, I don't think they're gonna play this on the radio*
48 *Pepa: And why not? Everybody has sex*
49 *Spin: I mean, everybody should be makin' love*
50 *Pepa: Come on, how many guys you know make love?*

[Chorus repeated]

[Verse 3:]
51 *Salt: What we have here is subject to controversy*
52 *A three-letter word some regard as a curse, see*
53 *He may fiend and have a wet dream*
54 *Because he seen a teen in tight jeans*
55 *What makes him react like that is biological*
56 *But scheme of gettin' in those jeans, is diabolical*
57 *But of course he does it, and she gives him rap*
58 *And before you even know it, they jump in the sack*
59 *As a matter of fact, sometimes it's like that*
60 *But anyway, ready or not, here he cums*
61 *And like a dumb son-of-a-gun, oops, he forgot the condoms*
62 *"Oh well," you say, "what the hell, it's chill*
63 *I won't get got, I'm on the pill"*
64 *Until the sores start to puff and spore*
65 *He gave it to you, and now it's yours*
    [Chorus repeated four times with fade out]

393

Macro-level analysis

The song 'Let's talk about sex' was released in 1991 and turned out a huge commercial success across Western societies, topping the charts in many countries. The lyrics are performed by *Salt-N-Pepa,* a black female hip-hop group consisting of the three artists *Salt, Pepa* and *Spinderella.* The trio has been described as 'the most successful all-female hip-hop group of all time' (Gisnash 2006: 4), and their work can be characterised as (moderately) feminist in the sense that they represent strong female hip-hop artists who overtly question the male-centeredness of traditional hip-hop. In addition to this, the group has become famous for supporting a range of political issues in their songs, for example, raising awareness for low-birth-weight babies, AIDS education and domestic and inner-city violence.

The period in which 'Let's talk about sex' was created and released coincides with 'a growing sense that the new hip-hop nation should work together to achieve social change and real justice' (Gisnash 2006: 25). This indicates that hip-hop, at least at that time, was a liminal context in which artists could venture to tread on new social ground without having to fear social sanctions. This is not just the case in relation to sexuality but also in terms of gender, as Richardson notes:

> Both the general American Judeo Christian and the traditional black church or traditions of spiritual groundedness in black culture would ascribe chastity, virtue, innocence, heterosexuality and marriage to the all-American young female and shun such displays.
>
> *(Richardson 2007: 793)*

Female hip-hop artists show a tendency to breach at least some of these norms, and it could be argued that the genre of hip-hop grants them the licence to do so and, at the same time, demands such deviations from traditional norms.

Throughout the lyrics of the song, one finds linguistic features that are reminiscent of hip-hop slang and/or African American Vernacular English (AAVE; cf. Green 2002). These serve as indexes of genre (hip-hop) and race (black artists), thereby locating the respective constructions of sexual normativity in a particular milieu. Among the salient features is the use of the negated auxiliary *ain't* (l.18, 37), lack of the third person singular inflection (*she use; she don't got* [both l.28]), the alveolar pronunciation of *-ing* (*tryin'* [l.3], *feelin'* [l.39], etc.), slang vocabulary and spellings (e.g., *yo* [l.1], *hot to trot* [l.27], *fellas* [l.29], *boomin'* [l.30], *Prez* instead of *president* [l.35], *dope* [l.42], *cums* instead of *comes* [l.60], *chill* [l.62], etc).

Of course, 'Let's talk about sex' cannot be seen in isolation but also has to be related to larger discursive trends in Western popular music. One development that is typical of this genre in the late 1980s and early 1990s is the increasing (explicit) sexualisation of pop lyrics – a trend that could be said to be epitomised by 'Let's talk about sex' as much as hardly any other internationally successful pop song. Singing explicitly about sex at that time still amounted to a break with conventional norms and, therefore, functioned as a powerful attention-getting device. It signalled a departure from more traditional pop music, which typically used to draw on the construction of romantic – as opposed to explicitly sexualised – love scenarios.

Repercussions of this development can probably be verified in most if not all Western societies. If one searches, for example, the German top 100 annual charts from 1930 onwards[2] for songs that contain the form *sex* in their title, one finds that the first instance of such a sexually explicit song is in 1985, namely the song 'Sexcrime' by the group *Eurythmics* (rank 53 in the 1985 German annual charts). As the collocation with *crime* suggests, this early reference to sex is a clearly negative one, which is markedly different from the sexual references found in the following years. More positive attitudes towards sex are expressed by *George Michael's* 'I want your sex' (ranking 14th in 1987) and another sexually explicit song that does not contain the form *sex* in its title: *Madonna's* 'Justify my love' (ranking 66th in 1991). Both of these songs are written in minor keys, which may be taken to indicate the construction of a relatively serious approach to sexuality. This changed with *Salt-N-Pepa's* 'Let's talk about sex' (ranking 19th in 1991 and 31st in 1992) and *Color Me Badd's* 'I wanna sex you up' (ranking 25th in 1991), which are written in major keys and, as a consequence, create a more cheerful atmosphere. On the German pop music market, this trend was later on driven to the maximum by the German project *E-Rotic,* which in 1995 started to release sexually explicit up-tempo dance tracks that clearly lacked the depth with which the topic of sex was treated in the earlier songs outlined above, with titles like 'Max don't have sex with your ex' (ranking 49th in 1995) or 'Sex on the phone' (ranking 66th in 1995). As the explicitness of sexual references could probably not have gone much further, the annual charts after 1995 show hardly any sexually explicit songs, the only ones containing *sex* in the title being *Tom Jones and Mousse T.'s* 'Sex bomb' (ranking 28th in 2000) and *Kings of Leon's* 'Sex on fire' (ranking 86th in 2009).

Accordingly, one could argue that a song title like 'Let's talk about sex' made a lot of sense in the early 1990s, when public references to sexuality in pop songs were still felt to break a taboo, while today a similar song title would probably seem anachronistic, because the discussion of sex has entered the public media landscape. The evidence suggests that 'Let's talk about sex' was at least part (if not even an incentive) of a development that resulted in the increasing visibility of sex as a topic of public debate.

Even though song lyrics do not constitute naturally occurring conversational exchanges, it is evident that the artists are engaged in the negotiation of sexual norms in 'Let's talk about sex.' They render a local performance of sexuality that is shaped by macro-level sexual normativities and to some extent clashes with these, which in turn necessitates negotiating processes that shift sexual normativities into certain directions. The artists do not refer to same-sex relationships or desires, or to other non-heterosexualities, which means that they are concerned with the negotiation of sexual norms as they relate to heterosexuality as a macro-social normative discourse.

Micro-level linguistic analysis

As will become evident in the micro-level analysis of the linguistics features of the text, the lyrics of the song show linguistic traces of the three normativity-related mechanisms outlined in Section 4: descriptive normativity, prescriptive normativity and shifting normativity. More specifically, they exhibit heteronormativity as a dominant discourse and, at the same time, partly challenge traditional norms.

Prescriptive normativity is expressed in the text, for example, by means of constructions involving modal auxiliaries. These are used in connection with negation to orient to the norm that talking about sex is traditionally prohibited (*I don't think we should talk about this* [l.1]; *I don't think they're gonna play this on the radio* [l.47]). A relatively strong degree of normativity is expressed by the auxiliary *should,* which is used to talk about states of affairs that are deemed positive and therefore desirable by the artists (*how it should be* [l.22]; *everybody should be makin' love* [l.49]). A weaker degree of prescriptive normativity is expressed by the auxiliary *could* in the clause *how it could be* (l.21), which suggests that one can envisage sex to be done in 'better' ways. Also note that the syntactic parallelism in the passage

> *Let's tell it how it is, and how it could be*
> *How it was, and of course, how it should be* (l.21–22)

explicitly orients to the gap between people's actual sexual experiences (*how it is/was*) and normative expectations about what sex should be like (*what it could/should be*).

Another aspect that contributes to the construction of prescriptive sexual normativity in the text is the fact that the artists refer to how society at large tends to view sex or talk about sex as something negative (namely as *dirty* [l.23] and as *a curse* [l.52]). The normatively induced silencing of talk about sex is also supported by the use of euphemisms throughout the song. Even though the word *sex* is repeatedly used, the lyrics also contain a number of relatively vague references to sex. Among these is the strategy of referring to sex or talk about sex by means of pronouns (*it* [l.18, 21–23, 65], *this* [l.1, 47]), which have little semantic content and function mainly as deictics, or by means of vague nouns (*things* [l.8, 9], *three-letter word* [l.52]).

Finally, the artists also voice explicit value judgements of certain people's sexual behaviour in their song. The phrase *no love, just sex* (l.41) suggests that having sex without love is viewed as less than ideal. Similarly, a man who does not use condoms when having sex is stigmatised as a *dumb son-of-a-gun* (l.61).

Descriptive sexual normativities surface in the text where sex and talk about sex are characterised as something that is natural, unavoidable and therefore affects all human beings (*that's a part of life* [l.4]; *it keeps coming up anyhow* [l.16]; *that ain't gonna stop it* [l.18]) or all men (*they're only human* [l.29]; *biological* [l.44]). Interestingly, sexual aspects that affect all women are not explicated in the text. This gives the text a certain male perspectivisation that will be further explored below.

Other all-inclusive referential strategies are the use of generic *we* (l.19) in the sense of 'humankind', together with a present tense verb form that suggests factuality (*now we talk about sex on the radio and video shows*) and the use of maximally inclusive indefinite pronouns (*everybody has sex* [l.48]). It is self-evident that these strong descriptively normative constructions are exaggerations and can therefore be questioned with respect to their literal meaning: not all human beings engage in sexual activities or sexual talk, sex is clearly not an omnipresent conversational topic and not all people are helpless victims of biology.

At some points, the text also orients to weaker descriptive sexual normativities. For example, the slogan 'Anything goes' is described as something that *many* (i.e., not *everybody*) *will know* (l.20). And the sexual scenario sketched out in Verse 3 is also not constructed as a general human experience but as something that may occur (*sometimes it's like that* [l.59]).

Shifting sexual normativities can be observed in the various directive speech acts that the artists use in their lyrics. The fact that with these directives the artists aim at making other people do something suggests that what is being demanded is something that people would not normally do. Salient in this respect are the hortative constructions starting with *let's* that are repeated throughout the chorus of the song (*let's talk about sex*) but also occur individually in Verse 1 (*let's talk about sex for now* [l.14]; *let's tell it how it is* [l.21]). Such constructions seek to shift social norms from silencing sex as a topic to openly discussing it, and this is indicated to be necessary both in public (*in the crowd* [l.15]; *on the radio and video shows* [l.19]) and in more private contexts (*let's talk about you and me* [l.7]; *to the people at home* [l.15]).

Other directives that are used to shift sexual normativities in the text include imperative sentences (*don't decoy, avoid or make void the topic* [l.17]; *take it easy now* [l.43]; *come on* [l.46]). Related strategies are the explicit questioning of traditional norms by means of interrogative sentences (*come on, why not?* [l.2]; *and why not?* [l.48]) or elliptic sentences that function as directives (*louder now* [l.45]).

In terms of the distribution of the linguistic features that express sexual normativity, it is apparent that one finds fewer such features in Verses 2 and 3. Although some orientations to descriptive and prescriptive normativities can be found in these verses, they show a total absence of devices that are used for shifting normativity. The reason for this is that these verses focus on the description of the behaviour of specific social actors and are therefore mainly narrative. Still it is evident that these passages are also indirectly normative in the sense that they stage heterosexual – and only heterosexual – behaviour, while non-heterosexual identities and desires are ignored. Heterosexuality and difference-oriented discourses of masculinity and femininity in heterosexual relationships are thus set as the normative default.

As far as the representation of social actors (cf. Machin and Mayr 2013: Chapter 4; van Leeuwen 2008: Chapter 2) in the other, non-narrative passages is concerned, one finds the construction of two social groups with contrasting attitudes. The artists construct themselves as an in-group that challenges traditional sexuality-related norms (cf. use of inclusive *we/us* when the artists talk to each other; l.1, 3, 25) and that is in opposition to society at large, which is constructed by means of fairly general noun phrases (*people* [l.3], *many* [l.20], *those who think. . .* [l.23], *they* [l.47]). However, in the service of shifting normativities the artists also make an effort to extend the validity of their progressive attitudes by using forms such as all-inclusive first person plural references (repetition of *let's* throughout the song; generic *we* [l.19]) and indefinite pronouns (*everybody* [l.48, 49]).

In Verse 2, the main protagonist of the narrative is a female person, referred to by means of lexically female pronouns (*she* [l.28, 32, 35, 37–40]; *her* [l.30, 33, 34]) and personal nouns (*chick* [l.30]). She is said to engage in sexual activities with male persons, who are mainly described by means of lexically male (*any man* [l.27], *fellas* [l.29], *men of taste* [l.33], *a man* [l.37]), socially male (*fools* [l.29], *heads of state* [l.33], *lawyers, doctors* [both l.34]) or referentially male personal noun phrases (*the Prez* [l.35]). Moreover, the female protagonist is constructed – in a highly stereotypical fashion – in terms of her physical beauty and outer appearance (*hot to trot* [l.27]; *her body was boomin'* [l.30]; *gold, pearls, rubies, crazy diamonds* [l.31]; *nothin' she ever wore was ever common* [l.32]). In other words, she is discursively constructed as the object of the male gaze, while the men involved are not described in terms of physical attractiveness or appearance at all. Men are also delineated in a stereotypical light in this passage, because they are constructed as victims of their sexual desires (*make any man's eyes pop* [l.27]; *fellas drool like fools* [l.29]). They are described in an almost animalistic (and therefore dehumanising) way, as being naturally and unavoidably attracted to women, while women are not said to be similarly sexually focused.

Despite the heteronormativity of this scenario, it also needs to be noted that there is one aspect in which it clashes with traditional heteronormative discourses, namely the agency of the female subject. Traditional heteronormative discourses would see the man as the active pursuer of the woman in heterosexual courtship. But in the present text, it is the female protagonist who generally occurs either in grammatical subject position (e.g., *she use what she got* [l.28]) or as possessor (*her dates* [l.33]; *her list* [l.35]), never as the grammatical object of a sentence. This draws a picture of a woman who is in a position of power, because in principle she can have all men (even the most powerful ones) and choose with which men she socialises (*there ain't a man alive that she couldn't get next to* [l.37]). At the same time, male social actors are not explicated as subjects of any activities that involve agency (the 'most active' thing they are said to do is *drool* [l.29]).

Furthermore, one can detect a certain contradiction between the fact that this hip-hop track is performed by strong female artists, who generally have a pro-women attitude, and some of the wording used in Verse 2, which constructs women from a male point of view by using the derogatory label *chick* (l.30) and providing an excuse for men's being fixated on sex (*but then again they're only human* [l.29]).[3] This effect is further strengthened by the discursive construction of the female protagonist as the object of the male gaze.

Another aspect that is more in tune with traditional heteronormative discourses is the distinction between sex (as merely physical) and love (as associated with a deeper, more spiritual form of relationship).This distinction is drawn along gender lines, with men being in favour of sex and women in search of love:

> But she was mad and sad and feelin' bad
> Thinkin' about the things that she never had
> No love, just sex, followed next with a check and a note (l.39–41)

The same issue is also echoed later on in the song, when one of the artists asks the question *Come on, how many guys you know make love?* (l.50), which indicates that she does not see men as being able to engage in more serious love relationships that go beyond sexual activities.

Bridge 2 also orients to traditional sexual norms in that it addresses women specifically (*all the ladies* [l.45, 46]), encouraging them to speak out publicly about sex (*louder now* [l.45]). Singling out female addressees is, of course, not an unmotivated choice.Traditional discourses of hegemonic femininity ('good girl' discourses) forbid women to talk explicitly about sexual matters (see also Richardson (2007: 793) on the specificities of these discourses in US culture). As a consequence, the shift towards a higher visibility of talk about sex seems to be something that is particularly relevant for women, and maybe not so much for men, whose sexually explicit verbal behaviour may even form part of certain hegemonic forms of (working-class) masculinity.The danger of women becoming stigmatised when they talk explicitly about sex is also oriented to at the beginning of the song (*people might misunderstand what we're tryin' to say* [l.3]).

Verse 3 is on the surface constructed as a counterpart of Verse 2, i.e., while in Verse 2 the story of a female protagonist is narrated,Verse 3 centres on a male protagonist.The latter is mainly referred to by lexically male pronouns (*he* [l.53, 54, 60, 61, 65], *him* [l.55, 57]) and nouns (*son-of-a-gun* [l.61]), while his object of desire is first referred to gender neutrally as *a teen* (l.54) and then with the lexically female pronoun *she* (l.57). However, there is a certain asymmetry involved if one compares the representation of social actors in the two verses. While Verse 2 largely draws on a heterosexual *she* + *men* discourse, the heterosexual scenario in Verse 3 does not show a parallel *he* + *women* discourse. It rather exhibits an initial staging of *he* + *she* (e.g., *he does it, and she gives him rap* [l.57]), which in the end shifts to a *he* + *you* discourse, in which the artists address women specifically (e.g., *he gave it to you, and now it's yours* [l.3]). In other words, while the first scenario describes the female protagonist as engaging in sexual activities with several men, the second scenario does not extend beyond a single couple (even though the fact that the transmission of sexual diseases is topicalised in the text may imply changing partners over time).

The male protagonist in Verse 3 mainly occurs as the grammatical subject within sentences (e.g., *he does it* [l.57]) and therefore has a clearly higher degree of agency than the men in Verse 2. He is constructed as the active seducer, with an excessive, 'natural' drive to pursue women (*he may fiend and have a wet dream* [l.53]; *what makes him react like that is biological* [l.55]). At the same time, the female protagonist partly occurs as direct (*he seen a teen* [l.54]) and indirect object (*he gave it to you* [l.65]) in sentences in which the male protagonist forms the subject. In terms of the linguistic construction of agency in relation to gender, therefore,Verse 3 represents a more traditional picture.

Conclusion

As the preceding analysis has shown, *Salt-N-Pepa's* 'Let's talk about sex' is an excellent example of a popular culture text that engages in the negotiation of the sexual normativities at the time of its release. The lyrics show traces of competing normative discourses in relation to sexuality. The artists even explicitly orient to this competition, saying that sex is *subject to controversy* (l.51). Some of the discourses are more traditional (sex as silenced or taboo topic; sex as dirty; sex as a natural/biological phenomenon; heteronormativity; polarised gender roles), and some have come to the fore more recently (sex as a topic of public debate; female sexual agency). The juxtaposition of traditional sexual norms and partly clashing social realities dovetails with the hip-hop ideology of 'keeping it real', which demands authentic hip-hop artists to speak from their lived experience (Richardson 2007: 797). This practice highlights clashes between the social micro- and macro-level and is thereby likely to induce changes in sexual normativities.

CDS constitutes a useful approach for language and sexuality studies that can complement the ethnographic approaches that have predominated in this field (see also Weatherall et al. 2010 for a similar argumentation in relation to language and gender research). It does not locate sexuality-related linguistic performances at the level of local co-construction alone (such as in conversation analytic studies of speed dating interactions; e.g., Hollander and Turowetz 2013; Korobov 2011) but also views such performances in relation to wider social discourses, i.e., it shifts the focus from individual linguistic interactions to sexual performativity and the materialisation of discourses across linguistic performances.

It is well known that CDS traditionally represents a top-down approach, which typically identifies traces of discourses that are deemed problematic in linguistic data. However, as the analyses above have shown, a purely top-down approach is not feasible for studies that seek to uncover the way that normativity shapes the discursive construction of sexuality. It is essential for such studies to relate micro-level (performance-related) to macro-level (performativity-related) normativities and to highlight contrasts between these two levels of normativity that are indexical of changes in social norms.

Notes

1 The video clip can be found here: www.youtube.com/watch?v=ydrtF45-y-g (last access: 28 September, 2015).
2 The German annual charts can be found here: http://ua.canna.to/canna/jahrescharts.php (last access: 28 September, 2015).
3 Note that the legitimisation of men's behaviour as *human* contradicts the simultaneous construction of men as "sexual beasts" that was noted before.

Further reading

Baker, P. (2005). *Public discourses of gay men*. London: Routledge.
This book illustrates sexuality-related CDS using a range of corpus linguistic case studies on the discursive representation of same-sex sexualities in British and US American contexts.
Bucholtz, M. and Hall, K. (2004). Theorizing identity in language and sexuality research. *Language in Society* 33(4): 469–515.
This article responds to the desire-related approach to language and sexuality by advancing the theorisation of language and sexual identity in sociocultural linguistics through the tactics of intersubjectivity framework.
Cameron, D. and Kulick, D. (2003). *Language and sexuality*. Cambridge: Cambridge University Press.
This book represents a seminal text for the field of language and sexuality studies more generally and for the desire-centered approach to language and sexuality more specifically.
Ehrlich, S. (2001). *Representing rape: Language and sexual consent*. London: Routledge.
This monograph exemplifies sexuality-related feminist CDS in relation to the discursive representation of rape, sexual harassment and sexual consent, with a focus on legal settings.

Motschenbacher, H. (2014a). Focusing on normativity in language and sexuality studies. Insights from conversations on objectophilia. *Critical Discourse Studies* 11(1): 49–70.

This research article illustrates the use of normativity as an analytical concept in sexuality-related CDS through a study of the discursive construction of objectophilia on a German TV phone-in show.

Motschenbacher, H. and Stegu, M. (eds.) (2013). *Queer linguistic approaches to discourse.* Special issue: *Discourse & Society* 24(5). London: Sage.

This collection of research articles provides an overview of the breadth of sexuality-related discourse analysis from a queer linguistic perspective, with case studies on various cultures and sexualities.

References

Attenborough, F.T. (2013). Discourse analysis and sexualisation: A study of scientists in the media. *Critical Discourse Studies* 10(2): 223–236.

Baker, P. (2005). *Public discourses of gay men.* London: Routledge.

Baker, P. (2013). From gay language to normative discourse: A diachronic corpus analysis of Lavender Linguistics Conference abstracts 1994–2012. *Journal of Language and Sexuality* 2(2): 179–205.

Bicchieri, C. (2006). *The grammar of society: The nature and dynamics of social norms.* Cambridge: Cambridge University Press.

Bucholtz, M. and Hall, K. (2004). Theorizing identity in language and sexuality research. *Language in Society* 33(4): 469–515.

Bunzl, M. (2000). Inverted appellation and discursive gender insubordination: An Austrian case study in gay male conversation. *Discourse & Society* 11(2): 207–236.

Burleson, B. R., Holmstrom, A. J. and Gilstrap, C. M. (2005). 'Guys can't say that to guys': Four experiments assessing the normative motivation account for deficiencies in the emotional support provided by men. *Communication Monographs* 72(4): 468–501.

Cameron, D. and Kulick, D. (2003). *Language and sexuality.* Cambridge: Cambridge University Press.

Cameron, D. and Kulick, D. (2005). Identity crisis? *Language & Communication* 25(2): 107–125.

Clark, K. (1992). The linguistics of blame: Representations of women in The Sun's reporting of crimes of sexual violence. In M. Toolan (ed.), *Language, text and context: Essays in stylistics,* 208–224. London: Routledge.

Coates, J. (2013). The discursive production of everyday heterosexualities. *Discourse & Society* 24(5): 536–552.

Conradie, M. (2011). Masculine sexuality. A critical discourse analysis of FHM. *Southern African Linguistics and Applied Language Studies* 29(2): 167–185.

Coupland, J. (1996). Dating advertisements: Discourses of the commodified self. *Discourse & Society* 7(2): 187–207.

de Francisco, V. L. (1991). The sounds of silence: How men silence women in marital relations. *Discourse & Society* 2(4): 413–423.

Ehrlich, S. (2001). *Representing rape: Language and sexual consent.* London: Routledge.

Fishman, P. M. (1978). Interaction: The work women do. *Social Problems* 25: 397–406.

Gill, R. (2009). Mediated intimacy and postfeminism: A discourse analytic examination of sex and relationships advice in a women's magazine. *Discourse & Communication* 3(4): 345–369.

Gisnash, S. (2006). *The library of hip-hop biographies: Salt-N-Pepa.* New York: Rosen Publishing Group.

Green, L. J. (2002). *African American English: A linguistic introduction.* Cambridge: Cambridge University Press.

Hall, J. and LaFrance, B. (2012). 'That's gay': Sexual prejudice, gender identity, norms, and homophobic communication. *Communication Quarterly* 60(1): 35–58.

Hogg, M. A. and Reid, S. A. (2006). Social identity, self-categorization, and the communication of group norms. *Communication Theory* 16(1): 7–30.

Hollander, M. M. and Turowetz, J. (2013). 'So, why did you decide to do this?': Soliciting and formulating motives for speed dating. *Discourse & Society* 24(6): 701–724.

Johnsen, O. R. (2008). 'He's a big old girl!': Negotiation by gender inversion in gay men's speech. *Journal of Homosexuality* 54(1/2): 150–168.

Jones, L. (2012). *Dyke/girl: Language and identities in a lesbian group.* Basingstoke: Palgrave Macmillan.

Jones, R. H. (2000). Potato seeking rice: Language, culture, and identity in gay personal ads in Hong Kong. *International Journal of the Sociology of Language* 143: 33–61.

Kiesling, S. F. (2013). Flirting and 'normative' sexualities. *Journal of Language and Sexuality* 2(1): 101–121.

Kissling, E. A. (1991). Street harassment. The language of sexual terrorism. *Discourse & Society* 2(4): 451–460.

Koller, V. (2011). Analysing lesbian identity in discourse: Combining discourse-historical and socio-cognitive approaches. In C. Hart (ed.), *Critical discourse studies in context and cognition,* 119–142. Amsterdam: John Benjamins.

Koller, V. (2013). Constructing (non-)normative identities in written lesbian discourse: A diachronic study. *Discourse & Society* 24(5): 572–589.

Korobov, N. (2011). Gendering desire in speed-dating interactions. *Discourse Studies* 13(4): 461–485.

Kosetzi, K. (2008). Harnessing a Critical Discourse Analysis of gender in television fiction. In K. Harrington, L. Litosseliti, H. Sauntson, J. Sunderland (eds.): *Gender and Language Research Methodologies.* Basingstoke: Palgrave Macmillan, 227–239.

Lazar, M. M. (2014). Feminist critical discourse analysis: Relevance for current gender and language research. In S. Ehrlich, M. Meyerhoff, J. Holmes (eds.): *The Handbook of Language, Gender, and Sexuality.* Chichester: Wiley-Blackwell, 180–199.

Leap, W. L. (2011). Queer Linguistics, sexuality, and discourse analysis. In J.P. Gee, M. Handford (eds.): *The Routledge Handbook of Discourse Analysis.* London: Routledge, 558–571.

Lillian, D. L. (2005). Homophobic discourse. A 'popular' Canadian example. *SKY Journal of Linguistics* 18: 119–144.

Machin, D. and Mayr, A. (2013). *How to do critical discourse analysis.* London: Sage.

McLoughlin, L. (2008). The construction of female sexuality in the 'sex special.' Transgression or containment? *Gender and Language* 2(2): 171–195.

Marko, G. (2008). *Penetrating language. A critical discourse analysis of pornography.* Tübingen: Gunter Narr.

Milani, T. M. (2013). Are 'queers' really 'queer'? Language, identity and same-sex desire in a South African online community. *Discourse & Society* 24(5): 615–633.

Moessner, L. (2010). Directive speech acts: A cross-generic diachronic study. *Journal of Historical Pragmatics* 11(2): 219–249.

Motschenbacher, H. (2012). 'I think Houston wants a kiss right?': Linguistic constructions of heterosexualities at Eurovision Song Contest press conferences. *Journal of Language and Sexuality* 1(2): 127–150.

Motschenbacher, H. (2013). 'Now everybody can wear a skirt': Linguistic constructions of non-heteronormativity at Eurovision Song Contest press conferences. *Discourse & Society* 24(5): 590–614.

Motschenbacher, H. (2014a). Focusing on normativity in language and sexuality studies: Insights from conversations on objectophilia. *Critical Discourse Studies* 11(1): 49–70.

Motschenbacher, H. (2014b). Language, normativity and power: The discursive construction of object-ophilia. In H. Pishwa and R. Schulze (eds.), *The expression of inequality in interaction: Power, dominance, and status,* 239–264. Amsterdam: John Benjamins.

Motschenbacher, H. (forthcoming). Language and sexual normativity. In R. Barrett and K. Hall (eds.), *The Oxford handbook of language and sexuality.* Oxford: Oxford University Press.

Motschenbacher, H. and Stegu, M. (2013). Queer linguistic approaches to discourse. *Discourse & Society* 24(5): 519–535.

Palmer, F. R. (2001). *Mood and modality,* 2nd edn. Cambridge: Cambridge University Press.

Peterson, D. (2011). Neoliberal homophobic discourse: Heteronormative human capital and the exclusion of queer citizens. *Journal of Homosexuality* 58(6/7): 742–757.

Richardson, E. (2007). 'She was workin like foreal': Critical literacy and discourse practices of African American females in the age of hip hop. *Discourse & Society* 18(6): 789–809.

Sauntson, H. and Morrish, L. (2012). How gay is football this year? Identity and intersubjectivity in a women's sports team. *Journal of Language and Sexuality* 1(2): 151–178.

Schneider, B. (2013). "In Salsa, it's okay to be a woman": Legitimating heteronormativity in a culturally 'other' environment. *Journal of Language and Sexuality* 2(2): 262–291.

Stewart, C. O. (2008). Social cognition and discourse processing goals in the analysis of 'ex-gay' rhetoric. *Discourse & Society* 19(1): 63–83.

Tainio, L. (2003). 'When shall we go for a ride?': A case of the sexual harassment of a young girl. *Discourse & Society* 14(2): 173–190.

Teo, C. S. L. (2014). 'Let's apply for a flat!': Indexing marriage with public housing purchase in Singapore. In International Gender and Language Association (IGALA) (ed.), *IGALA8 – International Gender & Language Association Conference: Book of proceedings,* 152–171. Vancouver: Simon Fraser University.

van Leeuwen, T. (2008). *Discourse and practice: New tools for critical discourse analysis.* Oxford: Oxford University Press.

Weatherall, A., Stubbe, M., Sunderland, J. and Baxter, J. (2010). Conversation analysis and critical discourse analysis in language and gender research: Approaches in dialogue. In J. Holmes and M. Marra (eds.), *Femininity, feminism and gendered discourse,* 213–243. Newcastle: Cambridge Scholars Publishing.

Wodak, R. (2008). Controversial issues in feminist critical discourse analysis. In K. Harrington, L. Litosseliti, H. Sauntson and J. Sunderland (eds.), *Gender and language research methodologies,* 193–210. Basingstoke: Palgrave Macmillan.

27

Discourses about nationalism

Ruth Wodak

Introduction

Nationalism, once declared an obsolete force, especially after World War II and the establishment of the European Union, has obviously returned with renewed vigour. We encounter passionate nationalist movements everywhere, in Africa, South America, the Middle East, Southern Europe, and in the successor states of the former Soviet Union. Frequently, new nationalisms emerge, tied to religious beliefs such as Islamic nationalism. Indeed, it seems that – in spite of an ever more connected and globalised world – more borders and walls are being constructed to define nation-states and protect them from dangers, both alleged and real.

In the following, I will first discuss salient concepts such as nationalism and, inasmuch as they relate to it, also transnationalism, post-nationalism and cosmopolitanism. This necessarily brief summary leads to an integrated critical framework for (national) *identity politics* embedded in a discourse-historical approach, currently imagined as "body-politics" in many national publics (Musolff 2010; Norocel 2013; Wodak 2015). Thus, we are confronted with, on the one hand, globalised tendencies to transcend the nation-state frequently promoted as post-nationalism; and, on the other hand, with strong and virulent tendencies proposing a return to the nation-state, defined via cultural and ethnic (as well as racist and racialised) criteria. Finally, some texts representing re-nationalizing identity politics and politics of the past drawn from Hungarian and Austrian right-wing populist parties' campaigns serve to illustrate ever new border and body-politics.

Defining the terms

Modern *nationalism* originated in Europe in the period following the French Revolution, as a result of the emergence of industrial society and the establishment of the nation-state as the primary principle of social organisation. Nationalism and nationhood are thus regarded as projects of modernity, related to the centralising tendency towards the homogenisation of populations, thus defining modern statehood. In the contemporary post-industrial world, however, global trends of cultural fragmentation (connected to growing economic interdependence, consumerism, mass migration and the diffusion of communication networks) increasingly override national boundaries (see Wodak et al. 2009: 7ff., Krzyżanowski 2010: 29ff.; Delanty and Kumar 2006: 2–3; Sicurella 2015 for detailed overviews of theories on nationalism as well as discourses about nationalism).

Gellner defines nationalism as "primarily a political principle that holds that the political and the national unit should be congruent" (Gellner 1983: 1). He maintains that national-ism should be regarded as the general imposition of a high culture on society, where previ-ously low cultures had dominated the lives of the majority, and in some cases the totality, of the population. This implies the general diffusion of a school-mediated, academy-supervised idiom, codified for the requirements of a reasonably precise bureaucratic and technological communication. Importantly, Gellner emphasises the relevance of "social entropy": a moni-toring of the polity, extensive bureaucracy, linguistic standardisation (linguistic nationalism), national identification (an abstract community), a focus on cultural similarity as a basis for political legitimacy, and single-stranded social relationships (between single-dimensional social identities).

Anderson (1995: 49) in a similar vein defines nation-states as "imagined communities" or "imagined political communities", "imagined as both inherently limited and sovereign". They are imagined "because the members of even the smallest nation will never know most of their fellow-members, meet them, or even hear of them, yet in the minds of each lives the image of their communion" (1995: 49). In fact, all communities larger than primordial villages of face-to-face contact (and perhaps even these) are imagined in this sense and "are to be distin-guished, not by their falsity/genuineness, but by the style in which they are imagined" (1995: 49). He argues that the nation is imagined as limited "because even the largest [. . .], encom-passing perhaps a billion living human beings, has finite, if elastic, boundaries, beyond which lie other nations. No nation imagines itself coterminous with mankind" (50). Consequently, nationalism always has an inclusionary as well as an exclusionary logic.

Busch and Krzyżanowski (2007) and Wodak (2007) have provided ample critique of Anderson's conception of national identities and the nation-state, indicating that Anderson's concept presupposes homogenous imagined communities, an imaginary which does not fit current multicultural nation-states constituted through citizenship and heterogeneity. Thus, *identity,* in the complex struggle over belonging to a nation-state, is never static and defined once and for all; all (national, collective and individual) identities are dynamic, fluid and frag-mented; they can always be renegotiated, according to socio-political and situative contexts as well as to more global social change and ideologically informed categories. This is why the German sociologist Theodor W. Adorno famously claimed, "[i]dentity is the prototype of ideology" (1966: 151). Along this line of argument, Delanty and Kumar (2006: 3) emphasise that "nationalism is present in almost every aspect of political community and social arrange-ments. It pervades the global and local dimensions and can even take cosmopolitan forms".

At this point, it is important to mention the debate about the alleged contradiction between *collective* and *individual (national, regional, local) identities.* Triandafyllidou and Wodak (2003: 210) view identity "as a process, as a condition of being or becoming, that is constantly renewed, confirmed or transformed, at the individual or collective level, regardless of whether it is more or less stable, more or less institutionalized" and reject any artificial boundaries which have long dominated many academic debates. It is important, the authors argue, to discuss *how* and *through what* these identities come into being and believe that the respective *social action in context* should be seen as the basic locus of identity formation and renegotiation. Accordingly, whether those identities are collective or individual identities that are constructed therein proves obsolete. Hence, "a rigid distinction between individual and collective identities risks reifying, taking identities as an essential quality that people 'have' or as something concrete to which they 'belong'" (Triandafyllidou and Wodak 2003: 210: 211; see also Krzyżanowski 2010: 30–32.). Thus, collective identity cannot exist over and above individuals just like individuality, with its physical and cognitive-psychological referents – the body and the soul/mind – cannot exist over and above society. Collective identities are constantly in a process of negotiation, affirmation or change in specific interactions in context through the individuals who identify with a given group or social category and act in their name. The two levels are intertwined and mutually constituted (Triandafyllidou and Wodak 2003: 211).

Transnationalism refers to the establishment of social, cultural, economic and political ties that operate beyond the nation-state (Schiller, Basch and Blanc-Szanton 1992: ix; Vertovec 1999). Significantly, they need to be understood as existing only in relation to existing definitions and practices that can be called national. Trans-national activities can be defined as

> [t]hose that take place on a recurrent basis across national borders and that require a regular and significant commitment of time by participants. Such activities may be conducted by relatively powerful actors, such as representatives of national governments and multinational corporations, or may be initiated by more modest individuals, such as immigrants and their home country kin and relations. These activities are not limited to economic enterprises, but include political, cultural and religious initiatives as well.
>
> *(Portes 1999: 464)*

The notion of a *trans-national community* puts the emphasis on human agency: Such groups are the result of cross-border activities which link individuals, families and local groups. In combination with globalising tendencies, the sharp increase of trans-national communities is seen as undermining the means of controlling *difference founded on territoriality*. Castells (2007) views trans-national communities as a powerful challenge to the traditional ideas of nation-state belonging: The idea of a person who belongs to just one nation-state or at most migrates from one state to just one other (whether temporarily or permanently) is undermined by increasing mobility; by temporary, cyclical and recurring migrations; by cheap and easy travel, etc. In the context of globalisation, trans-nationalism can thus transcend previous face-to-face communities based on kinship, neighbourhoods or workplaces and extend these into remote virtual communities, which communicate at a distance, in network societies (Castells 2007; Capstick 2015). Castells argues that:

> Power is the most fundamental process in society, since society is defined around values and institutions, and what is valued and institutionalized is defined by power relationships. Power is the relational capacity that enables a social actor to influence asymmetrically the decisions of other social actor(s) in ways that favor the empowered actor's will, interests and values.
>
> *(2007: 10)*

In fact, the examination of how migrants establish ties, whether familial, religious or economic, between multiple localities has been a major focus of migration research since the 1990s. Schiller, Basch and Blanc-Szanton (1992: 11–13), for example, pointed out that an immigrant in New York may be called to talk to the Mayor of New York about the development of "our city" and on the next day return to his home town to talk about the development of "our nation". Through internet and satellite channels, social ties are maintained, establishing "continuity in time and in terms of people's emotional and cultural attachment to an imagined community that spread beyond national boundaries" (Georgiou 2006: 143–149).

Clearly, migrants have always lived in more than one setting, maintaining links with a real or imagined community in the state of origin. What is new today is the context of globalisation and economic uncertainty that facilitates the construction of social relations transcending national borders. The increase in mobility and the development of communication have contributed to such relations, creating a transnational space of economic, cultural, religious and political participation (Kastoryano 2000). El Naggar (2015) emphasises the salient notion of "*umma*" for Muslims across the globe: Intrinsic to Islam is the imagination of an *umma* – a global Muslim community – that encompasses many cultures and ethnicities. For example, Mandaville (2001: 172, 2007) points out that Muslims "come face to face with. . . shapes and colors of global Islam, forcing their religion to hold a mirror up to its own diversity. These encounters often play an important role in processes of identity formation prompting Muslims to revitalize and compare their understandings of Islam".

The search for a European transnational identity is also the object of much critical social science and discourse-analytic research (Boukala 2013; Carta and Morin 2014; Krzyżanowski 2010; Weiss 2002; Wodak and Weiss 2004, 2007; Wodak and Boukala 2014, 2015).[1] In contrast to migrants' transnational identities, European hegemonic identity is frequently perceived as established top-down, by the elites. Kumar (2003), for example, emphasises the common cultural characteristics of Europeans and claims that European identity is synonymous with European culture (2003: 35–36). Supporters of the transnational approach to European identity assume that a European identity based on common cultural characteristics, such as religion, would be able to unify the people of Europe and simultaneously distinguish them from the "others". However, the concept of transnational identity does not comprise political and state mechanisms that are obviously also relevant to the establishment of a common identity.

In his famous essay *Why Europe needs a Constitution*, Jürgen Habermas states that the European Union created a new political form. It is neither a "federal state" nor a "federation" (2001). It is "an association of sovereign states which pool their sovereignty only in very restricted areas to varying degrees, an association which does not seek to have the coercive power to act directly on individuals in the fashion of nation states" (2001: 5). Thus, the European Union does not exercise political power in respect to its members. For this reason, a more encompassing political framework would be necessary for institutional and political reinforcement of the Union: a European Constitution could lead to a re-regulation of the financial, social and foreign policies of the European Union, and could also strengthen the Union. However, Habermas views European identity as exclusively political. He emphasises the role of the public sphere for the cultivation of solidarity "between strangers" and the establishment of a collective European identity – this conception has been severely criticised ever since (see Wodak and Boukala 2014; Triandafyllidou, Wodak and Krzyżanowski 2009). Nevertheless, the emphasis on the necessity of democratisation of the European Union remains salient.

These debates have led some scholars to envisage the end of the "age of nationalism", suggesting that humanity is about to enter a *post-national era* in which nations and nationhood will gradually but inevitably lose their significance for large segments of the world's population. Political power is partially transferred from national authorities to super-national entities (the United Nations, the European Union, NAFTA and NATO). In addition, media and entertainment industries are becoming increasingly global and facilitate the formation of trends and opinions on a supra-national scale. Migration of individuals or groups between countries contributes to the formation of post-national identities and beliefs, even though attachment to citizenship and national identities often remains important (Koopmans and Statham 1999).

This attitude is encapsulated in the following, much-quoted paragraph by Hobsbawm:

> It is not impossible that nationalism will decline with the decline of the nation-state [. . .]. It would be absurd to claim that this day is already near. However, I hope it can at least be envisaged. After all, the very fact that historians are at least beginning to make some progress in the study and analysis of nations and nationalism suggests that, as so often, the phenomenon is past its peak. The owl of Minerva which brings wisdom, said Hegel, flies out at dusk. It is a good sign that it is now circling round nations and nationalism.
>
> *(Hobsbawm 1990: 192)*

The assumption that nationalism and nation-states are becoming obsolete as a result of increasing cultural fragmentation is one of the central tenets of postmodernism. Appadurai (1996) maintains that transnational trends, especially connected with global financial capitalism, have "de-territorialised" the nation-state, making it necessary for people to rethink themselves and their identities outside and beyond the national frame. Whereas the loss of political sovereignty of nation-states in the face of global processes is rarely disputed, the postmodernist argument that national identities are becoming increasingly hybridised and therefore less salient as a consequence of mass migration and the influx of culturally diverse economic migrants into more affluent Western societies (Bhabha 1990) has been met with strong objections (Wodak 2015). The opponents of the "post-national" paradigm point out that processes linked to globalisation have in fact recently led to the resurgence of nationalism in various parts of the world (Boukala 2013; Wodak and Boukala 2014, 2015). Indeed, Sicurella (2015) provides ample proof for such re/nationalising tendencies and the role of public intellectuals therein in the post-Yugoslavian nation-states.

Beck (2011), however, argues against "equating modern society with society organized in territorially limited nation-states" and assumes that the mediation of risks that operate on a global scale, such as financial crisis, climate change and nuclear threats, have created imagined *cosmopolitan communities* of global risks:

> Cosmopolitanism means all nations, all religions, all ethnic groups; all classes are and see themselves compelled given the potential of civilization and its potential for self-destruction to constitute a community with a common destiny in the interests of survival.
>
> *(Beck ibid: 1353)*

Cosmopolitanism thus contends that all human beings belong to a single community, based on a shared morality, relationship, view or structure extending beyond national boundaries or limits. Definitions of cosmopolitanism usually begin with the Greek etymology of "citizen of the world". However, as Appiah points out, "world" in the original sense meant "cosmos" or "universe", not earth or globe as current use assumes (Appiah 2006: xiv). Nation-building is never only a historical stage or period now concluded; nations also cannot be constructed and established once and for all. On the contrary, they are continuously reproduced, narrated and "enhabited" (Billig 1995) in order to subsist, especially in an increasingly globalised world. As Balibar maintains, the fundamental challenge is "to make the people *produce itself* continually as a national community. Or again, it is to produce the effect of unity by which the people will appear, in anyone's eyes, 'as a people', that is, as the basis and origin of political power" (Balibar 1991: 93–94; Sicurella 2015).

The discursive construction of national identities

Billig's study (1995) of *banal nationalism* refers to everyday representations of the nation which build an imagined sense or "imaginary" of national solidarity and belonging. Examples of banal nationalism include the use of flags in everyday contexts, sporting events, national songs/anthems, symbols on money, popular expressions and turns of phrase, patriotic clubs and the use of implied togetherness in the national press:

> [t]he term "banal nationalism" is introduced to cover ideological habits which enable the established nations of the West to be reproduced. It is argued that these habits are not removed from everyday life, as some observers have supposed. Daily, the nation is indicated, or "flagged", in the lives of its citizenry. Nationalism, far from being an intermittent mood in establishing nations, is the endemic condition.
>
> *(Billig 1995: 6)*

Many of these symbols are most effective because of their constant repetition and indirect, vague nature and references. They are perceived as harmless and naturalised. Billig claims that, in the established nation-states, nationhood operates as an implicit background for a variety of social practices, political discourses and cultural products, which only needs to be hinted at – that is, "flagged" – in order to be effectively activated. Pronouns such as "we" and "our", rather than grand memorable narratives, that "offer constant, but barely conscious, reminders of the homeland, making 'our' national identity unforgettable" (Billig 1995: 93) become relevant (see section 5 below).

The study of the discursive construction of national identities in particular has emerged as a research programme within the Discourse-Historical Approach (DHA), following the research conducted by Wodak et al. (2009 [1999, 1998]) on the construction of Austrian national identity/identities in public, semi-public and quasi-private discursive contexts. The key assumptions are:

- that nations are primarily mental constructs, in the sense that they exist as discrete political communities in the imagination of their members;
- that national identity includes a set of dispositions, attitudes and conventions that are largely internalised through socialisation and create a "national habitus", drawing on Bourdieu's concepts of habitus, capital and field (1990);
- and, lastly, that nationhood as a form of social identity is *produced, transformed, maintained and dismantled* through discourse (Wodak et al. 2009: 3–4).

Wodak et al. (2009) developed a differentiated discourse-analytical methodology and toolkit for the analysis of the construction of identity and difference. This conceptual and methodological step was accomplished through an in-depth interdisciplinary analysis of multiple data related to Austrian identity (political speeches, newspapers, interviews, focus group discussions). Further research was conducted on political speeches between 1945 and 1996 (Reisigl 2007), on national rhetoric in commemorative speeches (de Cillia and Wodak 2009; Wodak and de Cillia 2007) and the development of attitudes and debates on Austrian neutrality in comparison to Hungary (Kovács and Wodak 2003). In due course, the theoretical framework first published in German (1998) was developed further.

The systematic qualitative and quantitative analysis of the discursive construction of national identities comprised three dimensions: content, strategies and realisations (linguistic and otherwise). Five content-related areas were investigated:

- the construction of the *Homo Austriacus,*
- the narration and construction of a shared political past,
- the discursive construction of a shared culture,
- the discursive construction of a shared political present and future,
- the discursive construction of a "national body" (Wodak et al. 2009: 30).

In this way, *constructive discursive strategies*[2] encompass those linguistic acts which serve to "build" and establish a particular national identity. These are primarily linguistic utterances which constitute a national "we-group" through specific acts of reference, for example by using the pronoun *we* in connection with the toponymical labeling "Austrians", i.e., "we Austrians", which, directly or indirectly, appeals to solidarity and union. Expressions such as "to take on something together" or "to co-operate and stick together" frequently occur in these contexts. *Strategies of perpetuation and justification* maintain, support and reproduce a national identity perceived to be under threat. Justification and legitimization frequently refer to events of the past, which may influence the narratives of national history by employing the *topos of history* (see section 5 below). Of course, political decisions concerning the present and future have to be justified and legitimised, for example, through individual or collective, public or private, national narratives.[3]

Strategies of transformation transform a relatively well-established national identity or parts of it into another. Since 1955 and the then internationally signed Austrian State Treaty, the meanings of Austrian neutrality was frequently redefined (see Kovács and Wodak 2003 for an extensive analysis and discussion). Finally, *destructive strategies* demolish existing national identities or elements of them. For example, after 1989 and the fall of the so-called Iron Curtain and the end of the Cold War, the former Eastern Communist countries all had to redefine and reimagine their national identities (Galasinska and Krzyżanowski 2009; Triandafyllidou, Wodak and Krzyżanowski 2009). The same is true for the aftermath of the Yugoslavian war 1992–1996. The former multi-ethnic and multilingual state was destroyed and five new nation-states emerged, after a bloody war between former neighbours (Sicurella 2015).

Hence, from a discourse-historical point of view, *national identities are constructed in and by discourse* and the above mentioned discursive strategies which encompass manifold sub-strategies (Wodak et al. 2009: 35ff.), all of which serve realising different stages and degrees of uniqueness, sameness, distinctions and difference. National identities are continuously negotiated, co-constructed and re-produced discursively. On the one hand, as imagined community, they are stable enough to allow identification and cohesion of social groups. On the other, they are flexible and dynamic enough to be articulated by various actors in various contexts and for various audiences. Diachronically, they are subject to change (political, social, economic, etc.). Institutional and material social structures influence the construction of national identity; however, institutional practices may also conflict with identity imaginaries. The *discourse of sameness,* for example, emphasises national uniqueness and inward sameness, ignoring differences within. The *discourse of difference,* by contrast, emphasises the strongest differences to other nations.

Numerous publications replicated this approach and developed it further, in respect to multilingualism, European and other national identities, as well as to Austrian German.[4] Today, international research on discursive constructions of national identities has diversified, but still draws on the above-mentioned studies. Recent studies on the discursive construction of national identities were conducted on the secular and religious movements in Palestine (Amer 2012), the tensions between national and European identity in Poland (Krzeminski 2001) and Central-Eastern-Europe (Brusis 2000), regional identity (Paasi 2013), sports and national identity in Finland (Laine 2006), the significance of legislation in Denmark (Kjaer and Palsbro 2008), historical imagination in teaching in Cyprus (Christou 2007), large sports events (Smith and Porter 2004, Hack 2013) and practices of remembrance in Uruguay (Achugar 2009) as well as the trajectory of Hong Kong's complex and multilayered development (Flowerdew 2012). In addition to such studies focusing on a particular state or region, others have taken a comparative view (e.g., comparing the role of shared values in the multinational states of the UK and Canada, Henderson and McEwen 2005, and of the role of religion, self-image and external image in 23 nations, Rusciano 2003).

Some of the above-mentioned studies have elaborated the approach, e.g., by integrating other genres or data and respective methods. Others have placed new emphases or pointed out new dimensions of national identity:

(1) The topics of *competence in state language, citizenship and naturalisation*, commonly subsumed under *citizenship*, have received growing interest in recent years (no longer only by legal professions, see http://eudo-citizenship.eu/, Davy, Davy and Leisering 2013, but also by discourse analysts). This is notable on a national and European level (Gray and Griffin 2013). This new focus necessitates the analysis of both public and legal discourses on naturalisation and citizenship as well as the testing methods and materials used in the naturalisation process.

(2) Among the elements of the *Kulturnation* that have gained significance within the discursive construction of national identity are religious symbols, apart from language. The Islamic headscarf as metonymic symbol for otherness is a cultural element that has moved to the centre of debates relevant to national identity and integration in many European countries (Rosenberger and Sauer 2013; Wodak 2015).

(3) Numerous studies over recent years have pointed to the significance of the relationship, tension or overlap between *regional, subnational and national identities* on the one hand (Bußjäger, Karhofer and Pallaver 2010) and between *national and supra-national identities* on the other (Painter 2008; Mühler and Opp 2006; Haller et al. 1996). Relevant studies in similar fields have described the phenomena of inclusive and exclusive nationalism (Citrin and Sides 2004; Bruter 2005). Research has also documented an increasingly frequent strategic distancing from the EU or individual member states in public or quasi-public discourses, e.g., in political discourse (Fuchs 2013; Lodgea and Wegrich 2011) and media discourses or visual metaphors (Bounegru and Forceville 2012).

(4) Recent research on political discourse has emphasised the importance of *Web 2.0 and Social Media* (El Naggar 2015). A linguistically informed discourse-analytical perspective on national identities requires that online communication be included, since such easily accessible, quasi-private and at the same time quasi-public communication platforms as Facebook and Twitter allow *participation in political discourse and deliberation* (Morley and Robins 2002; Dorostkar and Preisinger 2012).

Nationalism, body and border politics

"Border politics" are part of national identity politics and are now increasingly defined by the national language ("the mother tongue"), by ethnicity and culture, transcending the political

borders of the nation-state. Such language policies imply a return to national language policies which essentialise the nation-state, projecting a homogenous culture, language and territory. Instead of cosmopolitanism or post-nationalism, a European citizenship and the common
European language policies which promote multilingualism (Krzyżanowski and Wodak 2011,
2014), we are witnessing a re/inventing of traditional, parochial, closed nation-states. Griffin
(1999: 316) accordingly concludes that the radical right "takes on highly culture-specific forms,
largely because it draws on nationalist myth whose contents are by definition unique to each
cultural tradition". Obviously, the concept of "mother tongue" relates to nativist "body-politics"
of viewing and conceptualising the nation as a body with the mother tongue symbolising the
national language (Musolff 2010; Wodak 2015). Indeed, Musolff (2010: 137–138) argues that

> the *body-state* metaphor and its *illness* and *parasite* scenarios have been "declared dead",
> "moribund" or at least deserving to be extinct in several schools of conceptual history.
> Its anti-Semitic associations have made it suspect on account of the memory of its use
> by the Nazis. Its semantic coherence has been seen as weakened in the modern era due
> to the demise of the humoral source of knowledge system and its replacement by new
> mechanically orientated scientific paradigms. [. . .] In its use by the Nazis, the metaphor
> helped to advance a genocidal ideology in its most brutal form, which is still remem-
> bered. [. . .] But the "German case" is not unique.

A close look at election posters by the Hungarian *Jobbik* in 2010 reveals that body-politics
combined with the well-known racist discourse about parasites is experiencing a revival (see
Figure 27.1 below).

Figure 27.1   Jobbik election poster 2010, translated: "Put an end to parasitism. You can also
vote Jobbik!"[5]

This poster represents a mosquito embedded in a stop sign. The colours of the Hungarian flag (red, white, green) evoke nationalism and imply that Hungary, represented by the right-wing populist *Jobbik,* should not be bothered or damaged by such pests, which come in swarms and also cause pain or even severe illness in case they should transmit contagious disease. Hungary, in short, should get rid of mosquitoes. However, the abstract noun employed, "parasitism", implies that this is a notable phenomenon, not just trivial everyday mosquitoes. This is a serious condition that has befallen Hungary and one that *Jobbik* will stop. If this is a condition, then one necessarily poses the question: Who causes or has caused this condition? Who are the parasites, i.e., mosquitoes? In the context of the 2010 *Jobbik* campaign, the answer is not difficult to find: Roma and Jews living in Hungary. Accordingly, the report by the "Human Rights First" Group (2014: 30) states that

> [t]hese two parties [i.e. Golden Dawn and Jobbik] are arguably among the most extreme in the E.P. [European Parliament] in their rhetoric, which is designed to fan hatred and legitimise its expression, and in the violence they have fomented. Their stance goes far beyond the Euroscepticism that was seen the primary driver of the victory of many other European far-right parties in the E.P. elections. In fact they are so antisemitic and extreme that even Marine Le Pen, whose Front National won the French election with a record 24.86 per cent of the vote, and Geert Wilders of the Netherlands declined to form a coalition with them in the European Parliament – thereby forfeiting the extra money, speaking time and influence they could have received by forming a parliamentary group.

The report (2014: 43) further maintains that "Jobbik used the crisis to pursue its anti-Roma agenda while Golden Dawn seized on it as an excuse to drive out migrants who were 'taking Greek jobs' out of the country". *Jobbik* have revitalised hatred against Roma, homosexuals, and Jews, "all of whom were targeted by the Nazis, and added new targets of hatred – including Israel, Muslims, and Western-leaning socialists. [Furthermore, Jobbik] began to organize grass-roots activists willing to act on those hatreds" (2014: 45). Of course, when accused of hate incitement in the case of Figure 27.1, the text producers would deny any discriminatory intentions (intention-denial and goal-denial; see van Dijk 1992). In this way, the strategy of calculated ambivalence is employed – people can infer the intended meaning. The abstract noun serves as a further linguistic trace for the metaphorical reading – getting rid of minorities not considered pure Hungarians and thus not accepted as Hungarian citizens in a Hungarian state.

This poster (amongst many other examples from the Austrian Freedom Party [FPÖ], the Greek Golden Dawn and the French Front National) illustrates that renationalising tendencies can be observed across several EU member states and that therefore a nativist body-politics seems to be "celebrating" a revival. By extending the model of Norocel (2013: 94), it could be claimed that not only does the "family" as source domain imply the "nation" as target domain in right-wing nativist discourse, but that the original source domain actually consists of the human (male) "body" (the *Volk*), which spreads to a "family" (multiple bodies incorporated by the *Volk*) and then encapsulates the "nation".[6]

Thus, in contrast to discursive and social constructivist approaches to nationalism (Anderson 1995; Wodak et al. 2009; see section 2 above), "nation" as defined by right-wing populist parties is a limited and sovereign community that exists and persists through time and is tied to a specific territory (space), inherently and essentially constructed through an in/out (member/non-member) opposition and its out-groups. Access to national identity/membership is defined via heritage and ancestry, thus via "blood" (de Cleen 2012: 97).[7] Such a notion of

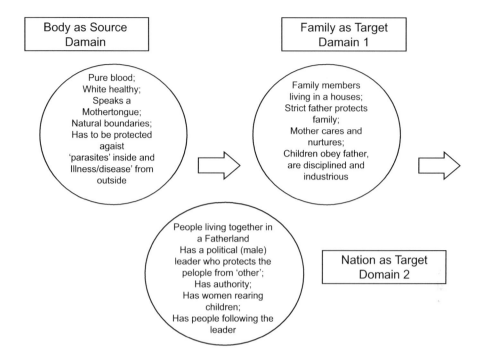

Figure 27.2 Body-politics and the "nation"

Source: adapted from (Wodak 2015: 76)

nation and nationalism is, of course, closely tied to concepts underlying racism; however, it is important to emphasise here that neither is racism necessarily nationalist, nor nationalism necessarily racist. For example, the connection to a territorial space must be perceived as a structural component of nationalism but not of racism. While racism as ideology and practice depends on the definition of groups and their fallaciously generalised negative characteristics, linked to biological categories, nationalism need not. Nevertheless, the conceptual boundaries are certainly blurred (Reisigl and Wodak 2001; de Cleen 2012).

Re/writing nationalist past/s

Nations and national identities as systems of cultural representation are based on (grand) historical narratives, which usually emphasise origins, continuity, tradition and timelessness (Hall 1996: 613–615). Sicurella (2015) proposes an eclectic framework based on categorisations first formulated by Kolakowski (1995), Smith (2007: 19), Hall (1996) and Wodak et al. (2009). The first element relates to myths of origins and ancestry, which may include tales of descent from heroic ancestors, associated with a foundational event. The second element is a teleological dimension, i.e., the belief that the national community has an intrinsic purpose or mission (a *telos*) entrusted to it by a specific deity. The third element is the fantasy of a pure, original and homogenous people and of pristine, ancestral homelands, which are perceived as the object of collective attachment and intimate devotion. The fourth and last element includes "myth-memories" of "golden ages" and glorious heroes, who are to be celebrated and commemorated. Thus, history and the *topos of history* are often mobilised in order to create national mythologies and *ad hoc* official narratives, which in turn serve to legitimate and reproduce national cultures and identities (see Forchtner 2014; Wodak 2015; Figure 27.3 below).

Identity politics form a core of *right-wing populist politics:* indeed, founding myths become revitalised to legitimise the myth of a "pure people" who belong to a clearly defined nation-state. Most right-wing populist parties thus reimagine and rewrite their national histories to legitimise their present agenda and future visions. They draw on the past to relive allegedly successful victories and/or previously grand empires. Many studies illustrate in detail that right-wing populist parties show a particular interest in debates over history and the ways in which politics and the public is and should be dealing with the past (Krzyżanowski and Wodak 2009; Engel and Wodak 2013; Wodak and Richardson 2013). At different moments in the 1990s and 2000s, they intervened in debates over the role that the respective European countries had played during the periods of fascism and communism as well as in the activities of remembrance of specific historical events related to these periods (Mudde 2007). For example, the then-leader of the Austrian FPÖ, Jörg Haider, infamously commemorated "decent" (*anständige*) victims of World War II while explicitly referring to former Austrian members of Nazi Waffen-SS units. Accordingly, history is rewritten to highlight foundation myths of a "pure people" in "homogenous" nation-states (Wodak and Forchtner 2014).

The Hungarian Jobbik, for example, yearns for the past of the Hungarian Empire; the Ukrainian Svoboda and related "groupuscules" of Neo-Nazis for their lost power they briefly held

Figure 27.3   The Hungarian Arrow Cross
Source: adapted from (Wodak 2015: 38)

during the Nazi era and the "Third Reich". Symbols of the past re-emerge, such as flags, logos, uniforms, hymns, slogans and so forth, and reinforce the revisionist ideologies of such right-wing populist and radical extremist parties. Flags and their related traditions "can be simultaneously present and absent, in actions [such as flag waving] which preserve collective memory without the conscious activity of individuals remembering" (Billig 1995: 42; McGlashan 2013). The emphasis of nationalist groups on intertextual references to national emblems, logos and flags as semiotic resources is a way of relating to the remembered (or imagined) present or past national, frequently imagined grand or grandiose cultures, communities and practices. Simultaneously, such symbols function as marketable brands which guarantee recognizability and – via indexicality – condense metonymically the agenda and programme of the respective party.

In Hungary, the official emblem of Jobbik members looks like the Árpád stripes, which date back to the 13th century and were reused in the 1930s and 1940s by the fascist and virulently antisemitic Party of the Arrow Cross (see Dettke 2014: 5; Figure 27.3).

The Jobbik poster slogan clearly presents the Árpád stripes and reads "radical change" (in this image the slogan has been covered with the oppositional slogans "Rotten Nazis", "the Gypsies should work", "The Arrow Cross should hang" and a Hitler moustache has been painted on the poster to indicate the proximity to Nazi ideology and insignia and functions as subversive resistance). As McGlashan suggests,

> [t]here is evidence here, through the lack of inclusion of the alternating horizontal red and white Arpád stripes, to suggest that Jobbik's logo is a form of calculated ambivalence. Earlier adopters of the Arpád stripes such as the nationalist Margyar Gárda and the Arrow Cross drew from the same coat of arms that Jobbik have in their symbolic behaviour, however, the Arpád stripes have strong connotations in modern Hungary with nationalist groups; as part of "*the Garda*" as a brand.
>
> *(McGlashan 2013: 306)*

Historical experiences and memories always also affect the present (Heer et al. 2008). Different historical experiences have also shaped the images of democracy and perceptions of fundamental values. The differences between perception and expectation, however, are particularly striking between old and new EU member states: Western Europe's dominant historical experience is National Socialism or Fascism (with the exception of the previously divided Germany: the former GDR has also experienced Communism). Central and Eastern European countries have experienced National Socialism, Fascism and Communism (Judt 2007; Wodak 2015).

The legacy of a totalitarian past and the associated difficulties of understanding and accepting heterogeneity as well as difficulties in coping with societal change have paved the way for current trends of right-wing populism as a means of preservation of some stable and conservative past and related values. Particularly, nationalist and xenophobic populism creates or rewrites its own concepts of history, charging them with nationalist ideas of homogeneity, and is able to fuel political conflicts between states and groups by using arguments (*topoi*) which appeal to past collective experiences or common-sense narratives. Of course, *topoi* are never per se right or fallacious – it always depends on the respective context. This is why appealing to and learning from the past could sometimes be a most useful, reasonable and sound argument; in other instances, such as the above, the *topos of history* is used in a misleading and simplistic, fallacious way. The related argumentation scheme, which claims that learning from the past is important for the present and that – such is implied – the past should be preserved, can be depicted as shown in Figure 27.4.

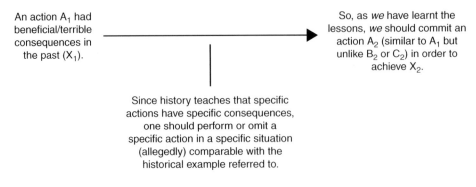

An action A₁ had beneficial/terrible consequences in the past (X₁).

So, as *we* have learnt the lessons, *we* should commit an action A₂ (similar to A₁ but unlike B₂ or C₂) in order to achieve X₂.

Since history teaches that specific actions have specific consequences, one should perform or omit a specific action in a specific situation (allegedly) comparable with the historical example referred to.

Figure 27.4 Topos of history

Source: adapted from (Wodak 2015: 40)

Revisionist narratives of the past are part and parcel of right-wing populist, nationalistic rhetoric and identity politics. Since the memory of the past shapes the conception of current collective identity, right-wing populist parties usually see their engagement in politics of the past as an integral part of their overall identity politics. In particular, some revisionist intellectuals and historians have been consistently involved in efforts to present their distinct versions of collective memory in academic and public discussions.

Notes

1 It is, of course, impossible to summarise the relevant approaches to European identity research here; see Boukala 2013 for an extensive discussion and overview.
2 See Wodak et al. (2009: 32ff.) for the definition of the various macro-strategies and sub-strategies which can be deconstructed when studying texts and talk about the discursive construction of national identities.
3 See Stone 2002; van Leeuwen 2007; Heer et al. 2008; Richardson and Wodak 2009a, b; de Cillia and Wodak 2009; Wodak and Auer-Boreo 2009; Wodak and Richardson 2013.
4 See Boukala 2013; de Cillia and Wodak 2006, 2009; Krzyżanowski 2010; Rheindorf and Wodak 2014; Reisigl 2007; Sicurella 2015; Wodak 2011, 2015.
5 "Human Rights First" Report 2014, "We are not Nazis, but". The rise of Hate Parties in Hungary and Greece and why America should care, New York; www.humanrightsfirst.org. Accessed August 5, 2014
6 Here, I will not dwell on other approaches to the conceptual metaphor of the NATION AS BODY/FAMILY as proposed by Musolff (2010) and Hart (2010). The latter also elaborates this metaphor by integrating the concept of *blending*, i.e., blending of two conceptual metaphors – metaphor of the HOUSE and metaphor of IMMIGRATION as threatening the house. In this chapter, I focus specifically on body and border politics – this diagram thus serves heuristic functions. In Wodak (2015), I also draw on body-politics when discussing antisemitism, Islamophobia and sexism, i.e., gendered body-politics in populist right-wing rhetoric.
7 Other scholars also use the terms 'ethno-nationalism' and 'ultra-nationalism' in this context (Rydgren 2005).

Further readings

Billig, M. (1995). *Banal nationalism*. London: Sage.
This is an exemplary book on everyday expressions of nationalism.
Wodak, R., de Cillia, R., Reisigl, M. and Liebhart, K. (2009). *The discursive construction of national identity*. Edinburgh: Edinburgh University Press.

The first study on manifestations of nationalism in various public spheres, while investigating the commemorative years 1995 and 2005 in Austria, as a case study.

Unger, Johann. (2013). *The discursive construction of Scots*. Amsterdam: Benjamins.

This book elaborates various approaches on the discursive construction of nationalism and integrates the discussion of language prestige (Bourdieu) with other manifestations of nationalism.

References

Achugar, M. (2009). Constructing the past and constructing themselves: The Uruguayan military's memory of the dictatorship. *Critical Discourse Studies* 6(4): 283–295.

Adorno, T. (1966). *Negative Dialektik*. Frankfurt/Main: Springer.

Amer, M. M. (2012). The discourse of homeland: The construction of Palestinian national identity in Palestinian secularist and Islamist discourses. *Critical Discourse Studies* 9(2): 117–131.

Anderson, B. ([1985] 1995). *Imagined communities: Reflections on the origin and spread of nationalism*. London: Verso.

Appadurai, A. (1996). *Modernity at large: Cultural dimensions of globalization*. Minneapolis, MN: University of Minnesota Press.

Appiah, K. A. (2006). *Cosmopolitanism: Ethics in a world of strangers*. New York: Norton & Company.

Balibar, É. (1991). *Race, nation, class. Ambiguous identities*. London: Verso.

Beck, U. (2011). 'We do not live in an age of cosmopolitanism but in an age of cosmopolitisation: The 'global order' in our midst'. *Irish Journal of Sociology* 19(1): 16–35.

Bhabha, H. K. (ed.) (1990). *Nation and narration*. London: Routledge.

Billig, M. (1995). *Banal nationalism*. London: Sage.

Boukala, S. (2013). *The Greek media discourse and the construction of European identity: Islam as radical otherness, collective identity and 'fortress Europe'*. Unpublished PhD Thesis, Lancaster University.

Bounegru, L. and Forceville, Ch. (2012). Metaphors in editorial cartoons representing the global financial crisis. *Visual Communication* 10(2): 209–229.

Bourdieu, P. (1990). *The logic of practice*. Cambridge: Polity Press.

Brusis, M. (2000). *European integration and national identity in East-Central Europe. Prospective member roles in an enlarged European Union* (Zentrum für angewandte Politikforschung). Munich, 1–8. Downloaded October 28, 2006, www.cap.uni-muenchen.de/download/2001/natident.doc

Bruter, M. (2005). *Citizens of Europe? The emergence of a mass European identity*. Basingstoke: Palgrave.

Busch, B. and Krzyżanowski, M. (2007). Outside/inside the EU: Enlargement, migration policies and security issues. In J. Anderson and A. Warwick (eds.), *Europe's borders and geopolitics: Expansion, exclusion and integration in the European Union*, 104–124. London: Routledge.

Bußjäger, P., Karhofer, F. and Pallaver, G. (eds.) (2010). *Föderalistisches Bewusstsein in Österreich: Regionale Identitätsbildung und Einstellung der Bevölkerung zum Föderalismus*. Vienna: Braumüller.

Capstick, A. (2015). *The multilingual literacy practices of Mirpuri migrants in Pakistan and the UK: Combining new literacy studies and critical discourse analysis*. Unpublished PhD thesis, Lancaster University.

Carta, C. and Morin, J. F. (eds.) (2014). *EU foreign policy through the lens of discourse analysis: Making sense of diversity*. Farnham: Ashgate.

Castells, M. (2007). Communication, power and counter-power in the network society. *International Journal of Communication* 1: 238–266.

Castells, M. (2009). *Communication power*. Oxford: Oxford University Press.

Christou, M. (2007). The language of patriotism: Sacred history and dangerous memories. *British Journal of Sociology of Education* 28(6): 709–722.

Cillia, R. de and Wodak, R. (2006). *Ist Österreich ein 'deutsches' Land? Sprachenpolitik und Identität in der Zweiten Republik*. Innsbruck: Studienverlag.

Cillia, R. de and Wodak, R. (eds.) (2009). *Gedenken im "Gedankenjahr": zur diskursiven Konstruktion österreichischer Identitäten im Jubiläumsjahr 2005*. Innsbruck: Studienverlag.

Citrin, J. and Sides, J. (2004). More than nationals: How identity choice matters in the new Europe. In R. K. Herrmann, T. Risse and M. Brewer (eds.), *Transnational identities: Becoming European in the EU*, 161–185. Lanham MD: Rowman & Littlefield.

Davy, U., Davy, B. and Leisering, L. (eds.) (2013). Exploring global social citizenship: Human rights perspectives. *International Journal of Social Welfare* 22 (Supplement 1).

De Cleen, B. (2012). *The rhetoric of the Flemish populist radical right party Vlaams Blok/Belang in a context of discursive struggle: A discourse-theoretical analysis*. Unpublished PhD Thesis, Vrije Universiteit, Brussels.

Delanty, G. and Kumar, K. (2006). Introduction. In G. Delanty and K. Kumar (eds.), *The Sage handbook of nations and nationalism*, 1–4. London: Sage.

Dettke, D. (2014). 'Hungary's Jobbik party, the challenge of European ethno-nationalism and the future of the European project' Centre for international relations, Wilson Center. *Reports and Analyses* 4/2014.

Dorostkar, N. and Preisinger, A. (2012). CDA 2.0 – Leserkommentarforen aus kritisch-diskursanalytischer Perspektive: Eine explorative Studie am Beispiel der Online-Zeitung derstandard.at. *Wiener Linguistische Gazette* 76: 1–47.

El Naggar, S. (2015). *The discursive construction of Muslim identities by contemporary Muslim televangelists in the West*, Unpublished PhD thesis, Lancaster University.

Engel, J. and Wodak, R. (2013). Calculated ambivalence and Holocaust denial in Austria. In R. Wodak and J.E. Richardson (eds.), *Analysing fascist discourse: European fascism in talk and text*, 73–96. London: Routledge.

Flowerdew, John. (2012). *Critical discourse analysis in historiography: The case of Hong Kong's evolving political identity*. Basingstoke: Palgrave.

Forchtner, B. (2014). Historia Magistra Vitae: The topos of history as a teacher in pubic struggles over self and other representation. In C. Hart and P. Cap (eds.), *Contemporary critical discourse studies*, 19–43. London: Bloomsbury.

Fuchs, D. (2013). What kind of community and how much community does the European Union require? In R. McMahon (ed.), *Post-identity? Culture and European integration*, 87–104. London: Routledge.

Galasinska, A. and Krzyżanowski, M. (eds.) (2009). *Discourse and transformation in Central and Eastern Europe*. Basingstoke: Palgrave.

Gellner, E. (1983). *Nations and nationalism*. Oxford: Blackwell.

Georgiou, M. (2006). *Diaspora, identity and the media: Diasporic transnationalism and mediated spatialities*. Cresskill, NJ: Hampton Press.

Gray, D. and Griffin, Ch. (2013). A journey to citizenship: Constructions of citizenship and identity in the British citizenship test. *British Journal of Social Psychology*, 53(2): 299–314.

Griffin, R. (1999). Afterword: Last rights? In S. Ramet (ed.), *The radical right in Central and Eastern Europe since 1989*, 297–321. Philadelphia: Pennsylvania State University Press.

Habermas, J. (2001). Why Europe needs a constitution. *New Left Review* 11: 5–26.

Hack, Ch. E. (2013). *Alpiner Skisport und die Erfindung der österreichischen Nation 1945–1964*. Unpublished PhD thesis, University Graz.

Hall, S. (ed.) (1996). *Questions of cultural identity*. London: Sage.

Haller, M. (ed.) (1996). *Identität und Nationalstolz der Österreicher : gesellschaftliche Ursachen und Funktionen, Herausbildung und Transformation seit 1945 : internationaler Vergleich*. Vienna: Böhlau.

Hart, C. (2010). *Critical discourse analysis and cognitive science: New perspectives on immigration discourse*. Basingstoke: Palgrave.

Heer, H., Manoschek, W., Pollak, A. and Wodak, R. (eds.) (2008). *The discursive construction of history: Remembering the Wehrmacht's war of annihilation*. Basingstoke: Palgrave.

Henderson, A. and McEwen, N. (2005). Do shared values underpin national identity? Examining the role of values in national identity in Canada and the United Kingdom. *National Identities* 7(2): 173–191.

Hobsbawm, E. J. (1990). *Nations and nationalism since 1780*. Cambridge: Cambridge University Press.

Human Rights First Report. (2014). "We are not Nazis, but": The rise of Hate Parties in Hungary and Greece and why America should care, New York. www.humanrightsfirst.org

Judt, T. (2007). *Postwar*. London: Penguin.

Kastoryano, R. (2000). Settlement, transnational communities and citizenship. *International Social Science Journal* 52(165): 307–312.

Kjaer, A. and Palsbro, L. (2008). National identity and law in the context of European integration: The case of Denmark. *Discourse and Society* 19(5): 599–628.

Kolakowski, L. (1995). Über kollektive Identität. In K. Michalski (ed.), *Identität im Wandel*, 47–60. Stuttgart: Klett-Cotta.

Koopmans, R. and Statham, P. (1999). Political claims analysis: Integrating protest event and political discourse approaches. *Mobilization: An International Quarterly* 4(2): 203–221.

Kovács, A. and Wodak, R. (eds.) (2003). *NATO or neutrality? The Austrian and Hungarian cases*. Vienna: Böhlau.

Krzeminski, I. (2001). The national identity and European consciousness of Poles. In P. Drulák (ed.), *National and European identities in EU enlargement*, 57–68. Prague: Institute of International Relations.

Krzyżanowski, M. (2010). *The discursive construction of European identities: A multi-level approach to discourse and identity in the transforming European Union.* Frankfurt/Main: Lang.

Krzyżanowski, M. and Wodak, R. (2009). *The politics of exclusion. Debating migration in Austria.* New Brunswick, NJ: Transaction Publishers.

Krzyżanowski, M. and Wodak, R. (2011). Political strategies and language policies: The 'rise and fall' of the EU Lisbon strategy and its implications for the union's multilingualism policy. *Language Policy* 10(2): 115–136.

Krzyżanowski, M. and Wodak, R. (2014). Dynamics of multilingualism in post-enlargement EU institutions: Perceptions, conceptions and practices of EU-ropean language diversity. In A.-C. Berthoud, F. Grin and G. Lüdi (eds.), *Exploring the dynamics of multilingualism,* 205–226. Amsterdam: Benjamins.

Kumar, K. (2003). *The making of English national identity.* Cambridge: Cambridge University Press.

Laine, T. (2006). Shame on us: Shame, national identity and the Finnish doping scandal. *International Journal of the History of Sport* 23(1): 67–81.

Lodgea, M. and Wegrich, K. (2011). Arguing about financial regulation: Comparing national discourses on the global financial crisis. *Political Science & Politics* 44(4): 726–730.

McGlashan, M. (2013). The branding of European nationalism: Perpetuation and novelty in racist symbolism. In R. Wodak and J.E. Richardson (eds.), *Analysing fascist discourse: European fascism in talk and text,* 297–314. London: Routledge.

Mandaville, P. (2001). Reimagining Islam in diaspora: The politics of mediated community. *International Communication Gazette* 63(2–3): 169–186.

Mandaville, P. (2007). *Global political Islam.* London: Routledge.

Martin, J. R. and Wodak, R. (eds.) (2003). *Re/reading the past.* Amsterdam: Benjamins.

Morley, D. and Robins, K. (2002). *Spaces of identity: Global media, electronic landscapes and cultural boundaries.* London: Routledge.

Mudde, C. (2007). *The populist radical right parties in Europe.* Cambridge: Cambridge University Press.

Mühler, K. and Opp, K.-D. (2006). *Region, nation, Europa: Die Dynamik regionaler und überregionaler Identifikation.* Wiesbaden: Verlag für Sozialwissenschaften.

Musolff, A. (2010). *Metaphor, nation, and the Holocaust.* London: Routledge.

Norocel, O. C. (2013). *Our people – a tight-knit family under the same protective roof.* Helsinki: Unigrafia.

Paasi, A. (2013). Regional planning and the mobilization of 'regional identity': From bounded spaces to relational complexity. *Regional Studies* 47(8): 1–14.

Painter, J. (2008). European citizenship and the regions. *European Urban and Regional Studies* 15: 5–19.

Portes, A. (1999). Conclusion: Towards a new world – the origins and effects of transnational activities. *Ethnic and Racial Studies* 22(2): 463–477.

Reisigl, M. and Wodak, R. (2001). *Discourse and discrimination: Rhetorics of racism and antisemitism.* London: Routledge.

Rheindorf, M. and Wodak, R. (2014). Der Wandel des österreichischen Deutsch: Eine textsortenbezogene Pilotstudie (1970–2010). *Zeitschrift für Deutsche Sprache* 42(2): 139–167.

Richardson, J. E. and Wodak, R. (2009a) The impact of visual racism – visual arguments in political leaflets of Austrian and British far-right parties. *Controversia* 2: 45–77.

Richardson, J. E. and Wodak, R. (2009b). Recontextualising fascist ideologies of the past: Rightwing discourses on employment and nativism in Austria and the United Kingdom. *Critical Discourse Studies* 4: 251–267.

Rosenberger, S. and Sauer, B. (eds.) (2013). *Politics, religion and gender: Framing and regulating the veil.* London: Routledge.

Rudling, P. A. (2013). The return of the Ukrainian far right: The case of VO Svoboda. In R. Wodak and J. E. Richardson (eds.), *Analysing fascist discourse: European fascism in talk and text,* 228–255. London: Routledge.

Rusciano, F. L. (2003). The construction of national identity – A 23-nation study. *Political Research Quarterly* 56(3): 361–366.

Rydgren, J. (ed.) (2005). *Movements of exclusion.* New York: Nova.

Schiller, N. G., Basch, L. and Blanc-Szanton, C. (eds.) (1992). *Towards a transnational perspective on migration: Race, class, ethnicity, and nationalism reconsidered.* New York: Academy of Sciences.

Sicurella, F. (2015). *Speaking for the nation: A critical discourse study of intellectuals and nationalism in the post-Yugoslav context.* Unpublished PhD Thesis, Lancaster University.

Smith, A. and Porter, D. (eds.) (2004). *Sport and national identity in the post-war world.* London: Routledge.

Smith, A. D. (2007 [1995]). *Nations and nationalism in a global era.* Cambridge: Polity Press.

Stone, D. (2002). *The policy paradox: The art of political decision making*, 2nd rev. edn. New York: W. Norton.

Triandafyllidou, A. and Wodak, R. (2003). Conceptual and methodological questions in the study of collective identities. *Journal of Language and Politics* 2(2): 205–223.

Triandafyllidou, A., Wodak, R. and Krzyżanowski, M. (eds.) (2009). *The European public sphere and the media: Europe in crisis*. London: Palgrave Macmillan.

van Dijk, T. A. (1992). Discourse and the denial of racism. *Discourse & Society* 3(1): 87–118.

Van Leeuwen, T. (2007). Legitimation in discourse and communication. *Discourse & Communication* 1(1): 91–112.

Vertovec, S. (1999). Conceiving and researching transnationalism. *Ethnic and Racial Studies* 22(2): 445–462.

Weiss, G. (2002). A.E.I.O.U. – Austrian Europe imaego, onus, unico. In af M. Malmborg and B. Stråth (eds.), *The meaning of Europe*, 263–283. New York: Berg.

Wodak, R. (2007). Discourses in European Union organizations: Aspects of access, participation, and exclusion. Special Issue *Text and Talk* 27(5–6): 655–680.

Wodak, R. (2011). *The discourse of politics in action: Politics as usual*, 2nd rev. edn. Basingstoke: Palgrave.

Wodak, R. (2015). *The politics of fear: What right-wing populist discourses mean*. London: Sage.

Wodak, R. and Auer-Boreo, G. (eds.) (2009). *Justice and memory – Confronting traumatic pasts: An international comparison*. Vienna: Passagen.

Wodak, R. and Boukala, S. (2014). Talking about solidarity and security in the age of crisis: The revival of nationalism and protectionism in the European Union – a discourse-historical approach. In C. Carta and J. F. Morin (eds.), *EU foreign policy through the lens of discourse analysis: Making sense of diversity*, 171–190. Farnham: Ashgate.

Wodak, R. and Boukala, S. (2015). European identities and the revival of nationalism in the European Union – a discourse-historical approach. Special Issue of *Journal of Language & Politics* 14(1): 87–109.

Wodak, R. and de Cillia, R. (2007). Commemorating the past: The discursive construction of official narratives about the 'rebirth of the second Austrian republic'. *Discourse & Communication* 1(3): 337–363.

Wodak, R., de Cillia, R., Reisigl, M. and Liebhart, K. (2009 [1999]). *The discursive construction of national identities*, 2nd rev. edn. Edinburgh: Edinburgh University Press.

Wodak, R., de Cillia, R., Reisigl, M., Liebhart, K., Kargl, M., and Hofstätter, K. (1998). *Zur diskursiven Konstruktion nationaler Identität*. Frankfurt/Main: Suhrkamp.

Wodak, R. and Forchtner, B. (2014). Embattled Vienna 1683/2010: Right wing populism, collective memory and the fictionalization of politics. *Visual Communication* 13(2): 231–255.

Wodak, R. and Richardson, J. E. (eds.) (2013). *Analysing fascist discourse: European fascism in talk and text*. London: Routledge.

Wodak, R. and Weiss, G. (2004). Visions, ideologies and utopias in the discursive construction of European identities: Organizing, representing and legitimizing Europe. In M. Pütz, A. van Neff, G. Aertsaeler and T.A. van Dijk (eds.), *Communication ideologies: Language, discourse and social practice*, 225–252. Frankfurt/Main: Lang.

Wodak, R. and Weiss, G. (2007). Analyzing European Union discourses: Theories and applications. In R. Wodak and P. Chilton (eds.), *New research agenda in critical discourse analysis: Theory and interdisciplinarity*, 121–137. Amsterdam: Benjamins.

28

Neoliberalism, globalization and critical discourse studies

Christian W. Chun

Introduction

The ongoing global economic crisis that began in 2007 has generated countless public discussions across multiple media platforms including traditional news outlets such as newspapers (both in print form and the increasingly preferred online mode for many readers), and the now seemingly ubiquitous social media. Throughout these discussions, people's accounts of the economy and the reasons for its current stagnation and/or slump appear to differ somewhat from the explanations offered by various economists and pundits in mainstream media publications in the US such as the *Washington Post* or the *New York Times*. In particular, many of these economists writing for the media tend to draw upon the dominant explanatory frames of the past four decades that have been characterized as "neoliberal" and/or "globalization" discourses. This chapter addresses hegemonic discourses that have now become an integral part of common-sense beliefs (Gramsci 1971; Hall 2011) and the accompanying counter-hegemonic discourses challenging these beliefs. These beliefs are enacted in the ways in which these discourses have been developed, disseminated, and mediated by powerful institutional agents and stakeholders such as media pundits writing influential opinion columns for the general public, and the readers themselves in their own responses and comments attempting to make sense of the economy and its crisis.

This chapter will first introduce the historical and theoretical constructs of neoliberalism and globalization narratives and policies as they have been implemented around the world beginning from the 1970s, and an accompanying overview of the varying contested views and interpretations of neoliberalism and globalization amongst researchers. It then traces how the discourses promoting neoliberalism and globalization and the interrelation between them have evolved and been adopted by government, corporate, and university stakeholders in the ensuing decades. Following this, the chapter will review how various scholars using critical discourse analytic approaches have addressed and analyzed these discourses. The chapter then introduces the theoretical notion of economic representations, i.e., the ways in which the economy is narrated and represented by mainstream economists as well as everyday people. Providing a brief sample case study, the chapter will examine the public's engagements with the mainstream representations of the economy in reader comments featured in a selected relevant opinion piece in the *New York Times*. This is done with the aim of contributing to a greater understanding of how people draw upon these mainstream economic discourses in their co-constructions of hegemonic "common sense" views of neoliberalism and globalization, the contradictions and anxieties stemming from the instabilities of these discourses, and the emergence of counter-hegemonic responses. In other words, how do people make sense of the economy, their relationship to it, and their own roles in it?

This chapter aims to contribute to our understanding of how people's discursive (inter) actions work to both maintain existing hegemonic institutions and their practices, and simultaneously provide avenues of thought, articulations, and actions to imagine and create economic alternatives. Thus, in analyzing how public everyday discourse operates in the co-constructions of neoliberalism and globalization discourses, the chapter explores how critical discourse analysis approaches may assist in the contestation of these hegemonic common-sense constructs and beliefs about the economy and society.

What is neoliberalism?

The development of neoliberal discourses

What is "neoliberalism" and why is this term used mainly by academics, and not by the general public? During the 25 year period following the end of World War Two that saw the emergence of the social welfare state in Western Europe, Canada, Australia, the UK, and the United States, neoliberalism was largely an "amalgam of free-market utopianism on the one hand, and a pointed, strategic critique of the prevailing Keynesian order on the other" (Peck, Theodore and Brenner 2009: 105). However, with the eruption of the OPEC oil crisis in the early 1970s and the ensuing major recessions in several Western countries including the UK and the US, this particular historical conjuncture proved to be neoliberalism's defining "crisis moment that it had long anticipated and which it was *designed* to exploit", and thus "in this sense, neoliberalism was both conceived and born as a crisis theory" (pp. 105–106). In contrast to the ideological and policy functions of the modern liberal state (exemplified in the US context with the advent of the 1930s–40s New Deal era of the Roosevelt Administration that vigorously ushered in social welfare programs and policies such as Social Security, and the corresponding government programs in the UK during Clement Attlee's tenure as prime minister), the "neo" in neoliberalism has been primarily about the "*remaking and redeployment of the state* as the core agency that actively fabricates the subjectivities, social relations and collective representations suited to making the fiction of markets real and consequential" (Wacquant 2012: 68, italics in original). In addition, this shift from the liberal to the neoliberal function of the state is reflected in the state's transfer of its social and communal well-being obligations traditionally associated with liberal governance (as practiced in the post-World War Two social welfare states) onto the individuals themselves, while at the same time increasing (or reengineering) its own regulatory and disciplinary functions in other areas such as the workforce and the prison system (Wacquant 2012). Thus, the institutional core of neoliberalism "consists of an *articulation of state, market, and citizenship* that harnesses the first to impose the stamp of the second onto the third" (Wacquant 2012: 71, italics in original).

The original proponent of neoliberalism was the Austrian economist Friedrich A. Hayek. In his book, *The Road to Serfdom*, published in 1944 at the height of World War Two, he argued that the most dangerous threat to individual freedom in the West was unwanted government interference through intrusive economic and social planning. His critique was aimed at what he saw was the totalitarian regime of Stalin's Soviet Union with its massive social planning, as well as the emerging social welfare state in the US with the New Deal. In claiming that the free market is the only capable and competent instrument for social management, Hayek argued against devising "further machinery for 'guiding' and 'directing'" individuals, and called for the creation of "conditions favorable to progress rather than to 'plan progress'" (240). Hayek's ideological framing that "a policy of freedom for the individual is the only truly progressive policy" (241) is a prominent and recurring motif in the last 35 years in the neoliberal discourse that champions the free market as the only viable social mechanism capable of providing any measure of freedom and "choice" to the public.

However, in contrast to this ideological stance of promoting the free market as the only path to freedom for everyday people, particularly as it has been implemented in countries such as the United States and the UK, neoliberalism at its core is fundamentally a political state project that seeks to subvert democratic governance by the general populace. This has been done in conjunction with interested corporate partners in attempting to monetize all aspects of the public domain in the pursuit of profits that have been declining elsewhere, namely in the traditional manufacturing sectors that sustained these countries for several decades following the post-1945 period. So although neoliberalism functions as a crisis theory, in fact it has come to embody the very boom and bust cyclical nature of capitalist-driven economies.

And although the general public is all-too cognizant of the neoliberal assaults on their livelihoods and the ensuing declining standards of living in the last three decades (at least in the US and UK), they are for the most part mainly unaware of the term itself, for as Peck, Theodore and Brenner (2009) pointed out, "neoliberalism" is "largely a critics' term" as it is primarily used "simultaneously, as an oppositional slogan, a zeitgeist signifier, and an analytical construct" (96). Thus, these writers argue, these contradictory usages and meanings have resulted in neoliberalism as a controversial keyword. The term itself has now functioned as a kind of "post-globalization keyword", which has "found wide currency since the late 1990s as a means of *denaturalizing* globalization processes, while calling attention to their associated ideological and political constructions" (97). Indeed, Peck, Theodore and Brenner (2009) argued that neoliberalism as a term has become quite globalized in its "ubiquitous applications and promiscuous affiliations" (97), so much so that Holborow (2012a) has been prompted to argue that if "applied linguistics is to make the links between language and society, if it is to embrace the realm of political economy and interdisciplinarity, it has to satisfactorily describe the contours of neoliberalism" (18).

However, this is easier said than done, for neoliberalism both as a concept and an ideology, as well as various institutional policies and instantiated practices labeled as neoliberal, are conflicted, contested, and contradictory in their discursive frames and material instantiations. For example, Ferguson (2010) stated that one prevailing and defining characteristic of neoliberal policies is the usual government cuts to social spending in the name of "austerity". However, he noted that several countries pursuing macroeconomic policies aligned with neoliberal tenets have in fact substantially increased their social spending, such as India, Brazil, and South Africa. In addition, the very contours themselves of neoliberalism are disputed among researchers. Indeed, Brenner, Peck and Theodore (2010) argued that the term has "become something of a *rascal concept* – promiscuously pervasive, yet inconsistently defined, empirically imprecise and frequently contested" (184). This is due to the fact that neoliberalism no longer refers "solely to the ideological 'creed' embraced by the evangelists of free markets", but rather it is also now "deployed as a basis for analyzing, or at least characterizing, a bewildering array of forms and pathways of market-led regulatory restructuring across places, territories and scales" (183). Consequently, Brenner, Peck, and Theodore have claimed that the concept of neoliberalism "has become, simultaneously, a terminological focal point for debates on the trajectory of post-1980s regulatory transformations *and* an expression of the deep disagreements and confusions that characterize those debates" (184). Peck, Theodore, and Brenner (2009) suggested instead that *neoliberalization* is a more apt term to encompass the complex dynamic processes and practices, and thus should be conceived as an "hegemonic *restructuring ethos,* as a dominant pattern of (incomplete and contradictory) regulatory transformation, and not as a fully coherent system or typological state form" (104, italics in original). In any event, in addition to all this, neoliberalism itself as a concept "refuses to go away" (Peck and Theodore 2012: 178).

What is globalization?

Unlike "neoliberalism", the term "globalization" has a much wider currency among the general public, so much so that "the term *globalization* is now such a key feature of our planetary lexicon. . . that the word itself has become nearly as inescapable as the very processes it is meant to describe" (Chun 2015: 68). And despite the fact that globalization is described by the many in the media as if it were "an entirely new phenomenon arising from the conditions of the immediate present" (Edwards and Usher 2000: 14), globalization can be rightfully viewed within a much longer time-frame going back to at least 500 years ago with the European invasion of the Americas, if not earlier in fact, with the trans-Eurasian trade with ancient China.

Because an in-depth discussion of the complex (and contested) dimensions of globalization are beyond the scope of this chapter, I briefly review here three key and overlapping conceptualizations, as usefully outlined by Kumaravadivelu (2008). One is the cultural imperialism thesis (e.g., Ritzer 1993) that regards globalization as culturally homogenizing processes in which the mainly American media and culture industries are the primary agents in imposing their culturally specific version of consumerist culture on the rest of the world through the selling of Hollywood blockbusters, fast food, and beverage chain outlets. The second line of thought (e.g., Giddens 2000) alternatively views globalization as complex heterogeneous processes operating locally in which the local cultural identities are reconfigured to resist in varying degrees. The third view (e.g., Appadurai 1996) sees globalization as both homogeneous and heterogeneous processes happening simultaneously. These result in what has been termed "glocalization" (Robertson, 1992, as cited by Kumaravadivelu 2008) in which "the global is brought in conjunction with the local, and the local is modified to accommodate the global" (Kumaravadivelu 2008: 44–45). However, what has been called "globalization" in these analyses and others (e.g., Bauman 1992; Chouliaraki and Fairclough 1999; Fairclough 2009) is viewed by others as "the international face of neoliberalism" (Saad-Fiho and Johnston 2005: 2). Inasmuch as the term "globalization" may serve as a cover concept for "accelerating capital expansion integrating (and in the process, destroying) local economies in the name of flexibility and adaptability of the 'free market'" (Chun 2015: 68), these debates about the nature of globalization are themselves ideological in the ways in which complex processes are named or ignored.

What does CDA have to say about neoliberalism and globalization?

Holborow (2012a: 14) has argued that "neoliberalism, as a social system and an ideology, is said to have invaded discourse; at the same time, discourse is deemed to reproduce and cement neoliberalism". Fairclough (2009: 340) observed that "all the highly complex and diverse contemporary processes of globalization inherently have a language dimension, because globalization and indeed social change in general are processes involving dialectical relations between diverse social elements or 'moments,' always including discourse". In addition to Fairclough's seminal work on critical discourse analysis of neoliberalism and globalization (e.g., Fairclough 2000, 2003, 2006, 2009, 2010), there have been several other critical approaches to the study of neoliberalism open to being viewed as part of critical discourse analytic work, in order to engage with the project of co-constructing the needed counter-hegemonic responses.

Jessop (2013) has outlined five such approaches examining neoliberalism:

- One approach is the examination of how its ideology emerged (covered in the afore-mentioned discussion of Hayek) during the 1940s that was dismissed by mainstream economists at the time as being on the fringe, only to achieve hegemonic status in the 1970s during the worldwide economic crisis.
- A second approach explores neoliberalism as a political project or even "a style of politics characterised by market-centrism, conviction politics and an authoritarian populism that can be moralising, polarising and especially. . . punitive" (Jessop 2013: 69).
- Closely interrelated is a third approach that views neoliberalism through the lens of an economic framework in its specifically economic policies purportedly designed to increase competition and spread market forces both locally and globally.
- A fourth approach interprets neoliberalism as "the form taken by a capitalist offensive against organised labour after the crisis of the post-war mode of growth in advanced capitalist economies, with neoliberal globalisation helping to shift the balance of power towards capitalist interests" (69–70), particularly those involving financial, industrial, and transnational forms of capital.
- A fifth approach situates neoliberalism and its specific hegemonic rise in its material practices and policies starting in the 1970s that is characterized by the "advance of globalisation based on free trade, transnational production, and the free movement of financial capital" (70).

These approaches are not mutually exclusive of course, as they all involve aspects of analytical examinations of the various economic policies and practices involving capitalism-driven market rules, corporate influence and governance, and national economic competitiveness. Some of these approaches, including the ideological approach, also are connected to the nature of neoliberal governmentality that is aimed at the disciplining of the self in the remaking of oneself to become an entrepreneur of oneself, all with the aim of releasing the state from its social support obligations (e.g, Foucault 1988, 2008).

All of these approaches highlight Holborow's (2012a: 14) argument that "perhaps due to its widespread presence, neoliberalism seemed to stand for a social representation and a social reality at the same time". Thus, in discussing Raymond Williams's use of ideology as "a theoretical category independent of language, a representational form which is driven by social interests and whose intention is to polemicise against other views" (Holborow 2012b: 39), Holborow claims that "neither language in its narrow sense nor discourse in even its broader social sense has any of this partisanship; their compass is too wide to be a predictable, combative instrument" (39). However, my understanding of discourse, which I aim to demonstrate later in the chapter, is that it serves as a narrative and framing vehicle in which one or more ideologies are presupposed, assumed, normalized, and reinforced through repeated variations of a theme; however, inasmuch as there can be multiple ideologies present in any discourse, there exists the potential for complex contradictoriness, or what Blommaert (2005: 130) referred to as discourse being "subject to layered simultaneity". This critical approach to discourse, according to Blommaert, entails examining the multilayered historicity running throughout people's discourses, some of which are "within (their) grasp. . . while others remain invisible but are nevertheless present" (130). The multiple layers of neoliberal and capital globalization discourses that the readers employ in addressing the economy will be explored later in the chapter.

One related approach that shares this critical approach to examining discourse in its layered historicity draws upon Raymond Williams's notion of keywords, which I have used in my own work (Chun 2015, 2017) in examining neoliberal discourses. Neoliberalism's ideologically invested meanings shifting and expanding over time in relation to the material social realities make the term one of the most important keywords of our era. Keywords, as Williams (1985: 15) explained, are "significant, binding. . . indicative words in certain forms of thought" reverberating throughout society. Keyword meanings, such as exemplified in the usages and understandings surrounding neoliberalism, are never fixed or settled, but instead are continually contested and challenged in and through multiple mediating sites such as the media, education, local and global networks, and political speeches. Keyword meanings are therefore "typically diverse and variable, within the structures of particular social orders and the processes of social and historical change" that embody "both continuity and discontinuity and also deep conflicts of value and belief" (22–23).

Not surprisingly, all these varying and interrelated conceptions of neoliberalism raise several questions. For example, how does neoliberalism actually reach into our everyday lives that impact it negatively, and if so, in what ways? How is neoliberalism differentiated from "capitalism"? What purposes does it serve to employ "neoliberalism" as a naming concept and signifier of complex phenomena rather than merely using the term "capitalism"? And, why has its use achieved a greater currency in academia in the past several decades, rather than the term it displaced, "capitalism"? In the brief sample case study that will follow, perhaps some of these questions can start to be addressed through what the everyday public has to say in their reader comments on the economy.

Economic representations: an overview

The ongoing global economic crisis has prompted numerous debates among economists, policymakers, politicians, and the public on its causes, and the accompanying unemployment, stagnant growth, and increasing inequality. Exploring the ways in which people think about their economy, construct their discursive representations of it, narrate its effects on their lives, and respond to dominant economic discourses (e.g., Chun 2012, 2013, 2015, 2017) is important to understanding how public understandings of the economy are enacted and disseminated across various forms of media. These at-times conflicting economic representations – the way the global, national, and local economies are perceived, conceived, and depicted (Ruccio 2008a) – between institutional stakeholders and the public raise a central issue of whose representations and voices count, and whose are heard, inasmuch as "understanding economic resources is also one way people organize how to make sense of their lives and estimate their powers of action as social agents" (Watkins 1998: 60).

Are the representations, narrations, discourses, and knowledge of the economy as constructed by people valid in their own right, or are these forms merely what has been called "ersatz economics" (McCloskey 1985b, as cited by Amariglio and Ruccio 1999: 20), and therefore can be dismissed out of hand? Indeed, "academic economists often consider such formulations to be. . . a mostly random set of irrational elocutions lacking both structure and consistency" (Ruccio 2008b: 2), and often "bemoan the low level of economic knowledge among the general citizenry" (3). Ruccio (2008b: 2) argues instead that, "the alternative is to recognize 'everyday' economic theories and statements as having their own discursive structure".

These discursive structures need to be explored in depth for the ways in which they reflect not only locally co-constructed knowledges but also the concerns of everyday people. In their literacy engagements with economic discourses and representations, they assume, create, and enact an identity that, following Klamer and Meehan (1999), I refer to here as "everyday economists" (Klamer and Meehan 1999). In Klamer and Meehan's (1999) framing, these everyday economists are people who are dealing with issues related to the economy in their daily lives. As such, they are "most likely to personalize the economy; they think in terms of people doing things, of right and wrong, of victories and defeats, of special interests, and of identities… these people, and we are all among them, think in dramatic terms, of winners, losers, and of power" (69). People engaging in their adopted roles as everyday economists offer us a window into how the general public perceives and views the economy from their different vantage points rooted in their experience, hopes, fears, and dreams. Although the construct of economic representations generated and produced outside of the academy in everyday life has been theorized, analytical investigations for the most part have been limited to the domain of films, music, poetry, novels, cartoons, advertising, and art (e.g., Ruccio 2008a; Ruccio and Amariglio 2003). In fact, there has been scant research on specifically the ways in which the general public has produced knowledge of the economy through intellectual engagement and debate in the media with economists, journalists, and pundits on pressing political and economic issues.

Case study: economic representations in a newspaper opinion column

This section addresses an opinion piece in the *New York Times* in its section, "The Opinion Pages" with the thematic subtitle, "The Great Divide", a series that focuses on the growing inequality in the United States. The title of the piece is "Rich people just care less", written by Daniel Goleman, a psychologist, and author of several best-selling books, most notably *Emotional Intelligence* and *Working with Emotional Intelligence*. I have already discussed his work on emotional intelligence in the workplace and its neoliberal ideological underpinnings elsewhere (Chun 2009). In his column, Goleman argues that the growing economic gap in the US may be impossible to reduce if the so-called empathy gap between the wealthy ("those with greater power") and the poor ("those with less") is also not addressed. Referring to the metaphors of "turning a blind eye", and "looking down on people", Goleman claimed that these indicate the social distance between the rich and the poor(er), a distance he contended that "goes beyond the realm of interpersonal interactions and may exacerbate the soaring inequality in the United States". Citing several studies, he observed that rich and higher-status people are less compassionate toward those who suffer hardships, and that this has "profound implications for societal behavior and government policy". In acknowledging that the income inequality in the US is at an all-time high in over a century, Goleman concluded that this gulf "troubles" him not because of the "obvious reasons" but because of the expansion of "an entirely different gap, caused by the inability to see oneself in a less advantaged person's shoes."

There are 954 comments from readers responding to Goleman's column. These are sorted in three categories: "All", "Readers' Picks", and "NYT Picks". In addressing how this newspaper's readership takes up this discourse of the economic and empathy gap, I selected the category of "Readers' Picks" to see which comments were looked upon favorably, or "recommended", by the *New York Times* readers. Argumentation, as defined by Richardson and Stanyer (2011: 986), is a "written or verbal exchange of views between parties with the aim of either justifying or refuting a standpoint in order to settle a difference of opinion". Following the methodology employed by Richardson and Stanyer (2011), the comments were examined regarding the argument schemes they adopted in engaging with Goleman's thesis that the empathy gap should be addressed as part of the attempt to reduce economic inequalities. The implication here is that this empathy gap is a significant obstacle to any redress of inequalities. An argument scheme is "the means by which an arguer defends his/her standpoint" (Richardson and Stanyer 2011: 986). Due to this being a brief sample study, I examined only the top 20 of these readers' picks, based on the number of the readers recommending the posted comment. These 20 reader comments were first coded according to whether they agreed with Goldman's premise or refuted it. In the agreement category, which totaled 16 out of 20 commenters, comments were further classified into six discursive and framing strategies they adopted in supporting Goleman's argument. These were personal stories and anecdotes, cultural attributions, psychological explanations and attributes, classical historical references, current day political observations, and the notion of choice. Some comments drew on more than one of the aforementioned framings. Among the four commenters who refuted Goleman's contention, they provided another explanation that I categorized as socioeconomic material practices. This was further subdivided into a historical or religious framing.

The comments that used a personal story approach drew upon several discourses. One commenter relates his experience working summer jobs in the 1960s as an adolescent from an affluent family, who discovered that working class people were "creative, highly intelligent, and as socially and politically aware as anyone from a more privileged background". While this indexes his own empathy toward the poor, he goes on to observe today's well-off youth have very little contact with the less well-off and this "will undermine the cohesion of our society". It is noteworthy here that this commenter attributes the imminent unraveling of society to the disconnection of the well-off with the rest of society rather than any economic systemic strains or possible imminent collapses.

Another comment, using a personal narrative, which garnered the most reader recommendations was written by "KC", who wrote that through "luck and hard work", s/he was able to make it into the "top 5% of wage earners in the US". However, KC related that s/he reminds people at cocktail parties that s/he was a recipient of government programs while growing up, and if this "uncomfortable" rejoinder "can make just a few people have more empathy towards the poor, it is worth it". KC then concluded, "empathy for the poor has definitely been lost". In positioning him/herself as an example of one who managed to overcome early socioeconomic disadvantages to join the upper ranks of wage earners yet still remembers his/her roots, KC partly attributes his/her personal success to government programs, which s/he argues are "either gone or severely reduced" and thus it is "unlikely" for someone like him/her "to get a similar result today". Thus, while KC agrees with Goleman that empathy has been lost, his/her highlighting the decline of government programs due to neoliberal austerity measures (without naming it as such), in a sense reveals the fissures in the hegemonic reframing Goleman employs in his focusing on the lack of empathy, rather than any material practices as being responsible for economic inequalities. By naming affective feelings as a major obstacle to be removed, Goleman in effect redirects the attention away from any focus on first re-instituting policies that would help people like KC in the future.

Three commenters addressed exactly this in their rebuttals to Goleman by citing historical practices that were ignored in Goleman's column. One commenter responded to Goleman's claim of "reducing the economic gap may be impossible without also addressing the gap in empathy" by arguing:

> Nonsense. Income inequality didn't decrease after 1929 because the very wealthy became more empathetic toward those less affluent than themselves. Rather, it decreased because we had a governing class, both Democrats and Republicans, who were willing to pass legislation benefiting the broad majority of American society in the face of opposition from moneyed interests. What's missing today is not so [much] empathy, which has probably always been in short supply among the wealthy, but rather political courage.

In rebutting Goleman by providing a historical reference to the New Deal's implementation by the Roosevelt Administration in the wake of the Great Depression ushering in the very programs KC mentioned aiding him/her, this reader provides an alternative reading to the causes of income inequality. Another commenter responded by asking, "Any idea how we might 'address' the gap in empathy? No?" by replying that "progressive income taxation" was the system the US had during the 1950s–1970s to compensate for this gap. A third commenter reframes Goleman's notion of the empathy gap by citing the practices of corporations that "cut tens of thousands of jobs, and renege on pensions, (and) the executives making those decisions refuse to take any responsibility for unemployment or for people needing government assistance". By calling attention to the specific practices of corporations and those who then choose to ignore the consequences of their actions, she recontextualizes Goleman's empathy gap in concrete materialities rather than abstract claims of affect. She further provides a historical reference in her admonition to these corporate executives to "study history and stop telling us to 'eat cake'".

The fourth commenter questioned Goleman's argument by asking, "How did the rich get rich in the first place? Not in a vacuum. On the backs of the poor". Interestingly, instead of supporting this with a historically based critique of an economic system designed to do this as the other three readers did, he uses a religious frame by referencing Buddhist philosophy, that observes we are all interconnected, and that "we are alive... because of the generosity of many, many invisible hands and hearts". Furthermore, he rebuts the neoliberal discourse insisting individuals are solely responsible for their own successes or failures (as in Thatcher's famous formulation, "there is no society") by citing the Buddhist philosophy that "everything arises in dependence upon multiple causes and conditions; nothing exists as a singular, independent entity". Indeed, this view is aligned with Marxist-based critiques of the ideology that attempts to present neoliberal capitalism as a singular stand-alone entity (e.g., Resnick and Wolff 2006).

Other commenters who agreed with Goleman used a variety of other discursive framings such as cultural values, as in one commenter's claim that "contempt for those less fortunate seems to be the American Way"; or psychological attributions in that "the capacity for empathy is determined in a large part by how much empathy we receive as babies and children". The former essentializes culture in such a way that ignores historical and social practices to the contrary, while the latter concentrates on explanatory micro-level behavior. Another commenter employed the notion of choice in his remark that "two of the world's richest men have set a great example of giving: it's WHAT YOU DO with the income that makes a difference". This comment effectively puts the onus on the individual in deciding how to spread the wealth, rather than any systemic checks and balances, which is the hallmark of neoliberal discourse and policies.

Interestingly, only one comment comes closest to explicitly referring to neoliberalism. This one draws on classical history in relating that the ancient Athenians and Republican Romans despised and "contemptuously dismissed" the "Ayn Rand type of 'philosophy'" in their advocacy of government serving "for the good of all". Here, the commenter drew upon several layers of historical discourses by citing classical philosophers such as Cicero in critiquing Ayn Rand, who has been linked to neoliberal philosophy in her 1950s writings such as *The Fountainhead,* a novel in which she presented the main character as heroic and admirable in his quest to achieve self-power by any means necessary as the true route to freedom and liberty. It is perhaps noteworthy that this commenter does not actually use the word "neoliberal" but rather employs the stand-in phrases, "the Ayn Rand type of 'philosophy'" and "Ayn Rand-like attitude", which actually might be more familiar to the *New York Times* readers than the term "neoliberalism". Nevertheless, the commenter, in making the case for classical values as they were favored by America's founders, situates the critique of neoliberal policies within this historical frame.

The commenters who draw upon a historicity of discourses – classical rhetorical, religious, and political-historical – in rebutting Goleman's insistence on an empathy factor as being a primary cause in the growing economic inequalities indicate in varying ways the presence of counter-hegemonic discourses to the neoliberal narrative that has achieved near-hegemonic dominance. These alternative economic representations by commenters enacting their role as everyday economists in their attempts to make sense of their situated lives provide important avenues for critical discourse analysts to explore in helping to develop discursive strategies and practices contesting hegemonic common-sense beliefs about empathy, the lack thereof, and the measurable widening economic gap that will be the actual cause for the undermining of societal cohesion.

Conclusion

One of the defining features of neoliberalism is the ideological displacement of agency from the government institutions implementing the post-World War Two social-welfare state settlement (e.g., healthcare, pensions, welfare) onto individuals themselves now deemed as being solely responsible for their own fortunes, and as it were, fate, in society. Correspondingly, neoliberal governance does not abandon any intervention at all; rather, it is the change of sites of government intervention and assistance that is the hallmark of actual neoliberal practices. These interventions are now not on behalf of the citizenry and populace in their struggle for relative prosperity or even minimal economic security and livelihoods. Instead neoliberal governing involves assisting major corporations that are "too big to fail" such as General Motors in their time of dire economic need.

Although the metaphor of the market is integral to neoliberal discourses inasmuch as it is argued to be the sole core component enabling liberty and freedom of choice (Couldry 2010), the discourses of neoliberalism and the accompanying interrelated ones of globalization somehow conveniently leave out the issues of which particular choices are offered, and to whom, the limits of the available choices, and just as importantly, who decides which choices are offered and/or available. By appealing to the strong desire for freedom and the emotions that this evokes in many people, neoliberal discourses propagate the idea a hyper, ultra-competitive market can offer the best option for freedom, however narrowly defined in the act of buying and selling. That any market has never been historically isolated from systemic and power-invested interests and constraints is conveniently never mentioned in neoliberal discourse.

Ferguson (2010: 166) provocatively points out that many critical researchers writing about neoliberalism all reach the same unsurprising conclusion: "neoliberalism is bad for poor and working people, therefore we must oppose it". If this conclusion is indeed unsurprising – and to whom, I might add – then for those of us who are using various critical discourse analytic approaches, we need to continue exploring the ways in which the general public recognizes that these policies (without being named as "neoliberal" as such) have not benefited them and have increasingly deserted them in the past 35 years, as several of the commenters that were highlighted above astutely noted. Moreover, it is also necessary to address how other people in their roles of everyday economists provide a variety of discursive framings, be they culture-based values, powerful personal stories, or the appeal of individual choice, in supporting the neoliberal underpinnings of Goleman's insistence on empathy rather than the lack of regulatory policies as being the barrier to economic inequalities. These framings are not to be discounted, for they are powerful resources in their perpetuating certain common-sense beliefs in maintaining the hegemony of neoliberal global capitalism.

Where do we go from here? Following the work of Boltanski and Chiapello (2005) and Fraser (2009), Bockman (2012: 312) argued that neoliberalism can be seen as "the result of elites integrating critiques of capitalism into capitalism itself as *sources of renewal*" (italics in original). Others have also offered a similar observation (e.g., Heath and Potter 2005; McGuigan 2009). However, I contend that with movements in the past few years such as Occupy Wall Street in the US, and the affiliated ones in the UK, Europe, South America, and Asia, with their powerful discourse naming the elite as the 1%, with the rest of us as the 99%, these critiques may not be so easily adapted as sources of renewal for neoliberal capitalism. As indicated by the high number of readers recommending the comments presented in this chapter, it appears that many people (at least those who read the *New York Times*) not only offer their own interesting critiques of neoliberal capitalism drawing upon various arguments, but also agree that something needs to be done. In this manner, critical discourse analysis can aid those challenging neoliberal common-sense beliefs in part by continuing to ask who benefits and who is left behind in our societies. In this manner, a primary aim of critical discourse analysis is to remake new common-sense beliefs based on our collective and communal agencies in solidarity among each other against the onslaught and ravages of neoliberalism.

Further reading

Chun, C. W. (2017). *The discourses of capitalism: Everyday economists and the production of common sense*. London: Routledge.
This book examines how people take up the discourses of several neoliberal keywords such as "the free market", "choice", and "freedom" in their everyday lives.
Ruccio, D. F. (ed.) (2008). *Economic representations: Academic and everyday*. New York: Routledge.
A seminal volume that examines how the capitalist economic system is discussed and mediated through various representations such as art, film, and advertisements, and disciplines outside the field of economics.
Saad-Fiho, A. and Johnston, D. (eds.) (2005). *Neoliberalism: A critical reader*. London: Pluto Press.
An excellent overview of neoliberal ideologies and the policy enactments in its various global contexts.

References

Amariglio, J. and Ruccio, D. F. (1999). The transgressive knowledge of "ersatz" economics. In R. F. Garnett (ed.), *What do economists know? New economics of knowledge,* 19–36. London: Routledge.
Appadurai, A. (1996). *Modernity at large: Cultural dimensions of globalization*. Minneapolis: University of Minnesota Press.

Bauman, Z. (1992). *Intimations of postmodernity*. London: Routledge.

Blommaert, J. (2005). *Discourse: A critical introduction*. Cambridge: Cambridge University Press.

Blommaert, J. (2008). Review of the book Language and globalization. *Discourse & Society* 19(2): 257–262.

Bockman, J. (2012). The political projects of neoliberalism. *Social Anthropology* 20(3): 310–317.

Boltanski, L. and Chiapello, E. (2005). *The new spirit of capitalism*. New York: Verso.

Brenner, N., Peck, J. and Theodore, N. (2010). Variegated neoliberalization: Geographies, modalities, pathways. *Global Networks* 10(2): 182–222.

Chouliaraki, L. and Fairclough, N. (1999). *Discourse in late modernity: Rethinking critical discourse analysis*. Edinburgh, Scotland: Edinburgh University Press.

Chun, C. W. (2009). Contesting neoliberal discourses in EAP: Critical praxis in an IEP classroom. *Journal of English for Academic Purposes* 8(2): 111–120.

Chun, C. W. (2012). The multimodalities of globalization: Teaching a YouTube video in an EAP classroom. *Research in the Teaching of English* 47(2): 145–170.

Chun, C. W. (2013). The 'neoliberal citizen': Resemiotizing globalized identities in EAP materials. In J. Gray (ed.), *Critical perspectives on language teaching materials*, 64–87. Hampshire: Palgrave Macmillan.

Chun, C. W. (2015). *Power and meaning making in an EAP classroom: Engaging with the everyday*. Bristol: Multilingual Matters.

Chun, C. W. (2017). *The discourses of capitalism: Everyday economists and the production of common sense*. London: Routledge.

Edwards, R. and Usher, R. (2000). *Globalisation and pedagogy: Space, place and identity*. London: Routledge.

Fairclough, N. (2000). *New labour, new language?* London: Routledge.

Fairclough, N. (2003). *Analysing discourse: Textual analysis for social research*. London: Routledge.

Fairclough, N. (2006). *Language and globalization*. London: Routledge.

Fairclough, N. (2009). Language and globalization. *Semiotica* 2009(173): 317–342.

Fairclough, N. (2010). *Critical discourse analysis: The critical study of language*, 2nd edn. London: Routledge.

Ferguson, J. (2010). The uses of neoliberalism. *Antipode* 41(S1): 166–184.

Foucault, M. (1988). Technologies of the self. In L.H. Martin, H. Gutman, and P.H. Hutton (eds.), *Technologies of the self: A seminar with Michel Foucault*, 16–49. Amherst, MA: The University of Massachusetts Press.

Foucault, M. (2008). *The birth of biopolitics: Lectures at the Collège de France, 1978–1979*. New York: Picador.

Fraser, N. (2009). Feminism, capitalism, and the cunning of history. *New Left Review* 56: 97–117.

Giddens, A. (2000). *Runaway world*. New York: Routledge.

Goleman, D. (2013). Rich people just care less. *The New York Times*, October 5, 2013. http://opinionator. blogs.nytimes.com/2013/10/05/rich-people-just-care-less/?_r=0

Gramsci, A. (1971). *Selections from the Prison notebooks*. Q. Hoare and G. Nowell-Smith (trans.). New York: International Publishers.

Hall, S. (2011). The neo-liberal revolution. *Cultural Studies* 25(6): 705–728.

Hayek, F. A. (1944). *The road to serfdom*. Chicago, IL: The University of Chicago Press.

Heath, J. and Potter, A. (2005). *The rebel sell: How the counterculture became consumer culture*. Hoboken, NJ: John Wiley.

Holborow, M. (2012a). What is neoliberalism? Discourse, ideology and the real world. In D. Block, J. Gray, and M. Holborow (eds.), *Neoliberalism and applied linguistics*, 14–32. London: Routledge.

Holborow, M. (2012b). Neoliberal keywords and the contradictions of an ideology. In D. Block, J. Gray, and M. Holborow (eds.), *Neoliberalism and applied linguistics*, 33–55. London: Routledge.

Holborow, M. (2013). Applied linguistics in the neoliberal university: Ideological keywords and social agency. *Applied Linguistics Review* 4(2): 229–257.

Jessop, B. (2013). Putting neoliberalism in its time and place: A response to the debate. *Social Anthropology* 21(1): 65–74.

Klamer, A. and Meehan, J. (1999). The crowding out of academic economics: The case of NAFTA. In R.F. Garnett (ed.), *What do economists know? New economics of knowledge*, 65–85. London: Routledge.

Kumaravadivelu, B. (2008). *Cultural globalization and language education*. New Haven, CT: Yale University Press.

McGuigan, J. (2009). *Cool capitalism*. New York: Pluto Press.

Peck, J. and Theodore, N. (2012). Reanimating neoliberalism: Process geographies of neoliberalisation. *Social Anthropology* 20(2): 177–185.

Peck, J., Theodore, N. and Brenner, N. (2009). Postneoliberalism and its malcontents. *Antipode* 41(S1): 94–116.

Resnick, S. A. and Wolff, R. D. (eds.) (2006). *New departures in Marxian theory*. New York: Routledge.

Richardson, J. E. and Stanyer, J. (2011). Reader opinion in the digital age: Tabloid and broadsheet newspaper websites and the exercise of political voice. *Journalism* 12(8): 983–1003.

Ritzer, G. (1993). *The McDonaldization of society*. Thousand Oaks, CA: Pine Forge Press.

Ruccio, D. F. (ed.) (2008a). *Economic representations: Academic and everyday*. New York: Routledge.

Ruccio, D. F. (2008b). Introduction: What are economic representations and what's at stake? In D.F. Ruccio (ed.), *Economic representations: Academic and everyday*, 1–31. New York: Routledge.

Ruccio, D. F. and Amariglio, J. (2003). *Postmodern moments in modern economics*. Princeton, NJ: Princeton University Press.

Saad-Fiho, A. and Johnston, D. (eds.) (2005). *Neoliberalism: A critical reader*. London: Pluto Press.

Wacquant, L. (2012). Three steps to a historical anthropology of actually existing neoliberalism. *Social Anthropology* 20(1): 66–79.

Watkins, E. (1998). *Everyday exchanges: Marketwork and capitalist common sense*. Stanford, CA: Stanford University Press.

Williams, R. (1985). *Keywords: A vocabulary of culture and society,* rev. edn. New York: Oxford University Press.

29

The discursive construction of terrorism and violence

Aditi Bhatia

Introduction

The fusion of politics and media over time has led to "political socialization" (Wilkins 2000), transforming politicians into media personalities, and often celebrities. This has increased academic interest in the study of political discourse, with the result that a variety of studies have been conducted undertaking the multifaceted nature of political discourse. Within the more general context of political discourse, the discourses of war, terrorism, and violence have also received a fair share of attention, particularly after the 9/11 terrorist attacks in America. More specific studies include: politics, war, and military discourse (Butt, Lukin and Matthiessen 2004; Graham, Keenan and Dowd 2004; Chouliaraki 2005; Graham and Luke 2005), terrorism and the media (Silberstein 2002; Norris, Kern and Just 2003; Achugar 2004), terrorism and categorisation (Oktar 2001; Edwards 2004; Leudar, Marsland and Nekvapil 2004), and terrorism more generally (Collins 2002; Llorente 2002; Elshtain 2003; Bhatia 2007, 2008, 2009, 2013, 2015).

Terrorism perceived as a socio-political construct is difficult to define objectively and universally; it is largely context-based. Terrorism cannot really be simplistically defined as the "systematic use of violence and intimidation to achieve some goal" (Collins English Dictionary and Thesaurus, 2001). This is a relatively superficial definition of a construct occurring "in a milieu of competing and conflicting religious, economic, cultural, psychological, and historical worldviews and ideologies" (Marsella 2004: 11). Often academics and political analysts find that terrorism as a word is "absurd and meaningless on its face except as a calculated element of propaganda" (Weinberg and Davis 1989: 4). The construct of terrorism, however, is a very effective tool in politics, the "word is [often] used by unscrupulous governments [and unofficially elected leaders] that want people to accept as their personal enemy someone the state [or group] has defined as its enemy" (Weinberg and Davis 1989: 4). It can often be a hypocritical and misleading term, which "we all righteously condemn. . . except where we ourselves or friends of ours are engaging in it. Then we ignore it. . . attach to it tags like 'liberation' or 'defense of the free world' or national honor . . ." (Taylor 1988: 3). Often it can also be difficult to pinpoint exactly who the authors or rather "voices" of such conceptualisations of terrorism really are, but the "faces" are always of prominent figures, whose expertise and authority earn them a following. It is easy to invoke here the complexities of Goffman's (1981) "speaker"-hood, what he refers to as principals and authors behind actors and animators. The fairly textured discourses of terrorism, thus, come to be regarded as "metaphorical-cocktails of political jargon" (Musolff 1997: 230), generating various categorisations attributable to different groups in society, rallying socio-political support, outcasting groups which breach the in-group's standards of normative behaviour, and eventually serving to sustain power structures and status quo. As such, much of the work that has been conducted on terrorism and political violence has occurred with the intention to illustrate how "emancipation, as well as domination, is achieved through discourse; [and how] . . . an analytical focus on hegemony must be balanced with a focus on discourses of empowerment-discourses designed to 'make peace not war', that successfully redistribute power without necessarily struggling against it" (Graham, Keenan and Dowd 2004: 216). The importance of discourse analysts in this scenario then is to be able to "influence discourse" (Graham, Keenan and Dowd 2004), helping shape a more macro narrative about political cause and effect.

Literature review

The 9/11 attacks in America brought with them a renewed interest in how political as well as unofficially elected gatekeepers of societies shaped the social reality of their, often unsuspecting, audiences. Although a plethora of work has been conducted on the construction of violence and terrorism from the standpoint of public policy, social studies, history, political science, economic studies, this chapter is interested specifically in the investigation of such discourses from a critical discourse analytical (CDA) perspective. What a review of much of the very valuable work on this topic finds is the emergence of a certain hegemonic, and largely American-centric, narrative that proceeds to divide the world into two narrowly defined and rigidly allocated parts, "us" and "them". Silberstein (2002), among the first to explore the development of such a "patriot rhetoric" in the creation of a post-9/11 identity, describes the rejuvenation of national beliefs in the build up to war, as the post-9/11 era saw the frantic remaking of the American identity. Collins and Glover (2002: 1–2) in their edited collection of essays illustrate particularly this point of Silberstein's, the creation of a rhetoric that justifies "America's New War", investigating the creation of categories such as evil, cowardice, civilisation, freedom, justice, and fundamentalism in order to illustrate "while language always shapes our lives, the effects of language during war are unique. Just as 'collateral damage' describes military damage in addition to the intended targets, 'collateral language' refers to the language war as a practice adds to our ongoing lexicon as well as to the additional meaning certain terms acquire during war time".

It has been the investigation of this very "collateral language" that has occupied much of the space on analytical boards. Graham, Keenan, and Dowd (2004: 199) use a discourse-historical approach to compare some key "calls to arms" speeches made in history, namely Hitler's, Pope Urban II's, and Queen Elizabeth I's, with George W. Bush's, in order to determine "the structure, function, and historical significance of such texts in western societies over the last millennium", finally identifying four rather generic features of such speeches which perform the function of announcing political war cries, features which have sustained over time, including a) creation of a legitimate and wholly good authority, b) appeal to the historical values of cultural values and traditions, c) construction of a wholly evil "other", and d) appeal for unity behind the wholly good, legitimate source of authority. Lazar and Lazar's (2004) research, similarly, with a specific focus on Bush, echoed the sentiment that post-9/11 a dominant, overarching narrative emerged, what they refer to as "discourses of New World Order", which established a new moral order, with particular reference to two faces of threat – Osama bin Laden and Saddam Hussein. Their analysis of Bush's speeches revealed similar findings to Graham, Keenan, and Dowd (2004), namely use of, what they define as, "outcasting strategies", including a) enemification, b) criminalization, c) (e)vilification, and d) orientalization, all of which serve to introduce into the discursive conceptualisations of violence and terrorism the "logic of binarism". Such "discursive bipolarity [then] perpetuates, in the post Cold-War international system, a blue print for heightened difference and conflict" (Lazar and Lazar 2004: 223). In the creation of a dominant, hegemonic narrative about a socio-political phenomena such as terrorism, binarism "establishes as a political fact the existence of clear and specific threats. . . [it] accommodates the fudging between these different kinds of degrees of threat, to constitute a largely undifferentiated enemy. . . [allowing the] 'them' and 'us' to be sketched in clear, simple and unidimensional lines, through strategic silences" (239).

Leudar, Marsland and Nekvapil (2004) arrive at similar conclusions through their study of Bush, Blair, and bin Laden's discourses employing Membership Categorisation Analysis (MCA), an offshoot of Conversational Analysis first proposed by Harvey Sacks (1992), but which as a method has more recently been appropriated to include a critical discourse analytical focus. They note in their analysis the occurrence of "double contrastive identity", whereby in a constantly evolving rhetoric on the War on Terror the categories of "us" and "them" are not only strongly present but also interchangeable. In other words, in extending the concept of dialogical networks, Leudar et al. find that people were often incumbents of the "us" and "them" categories, so while Bush and Blair categorised, attributed blame, and justified past violence on social, political, and moral grounds, bin Laden, in turn, cast them as the "others" on religious grounds. In both cases, "category-pairs are used in an opposition by the way in which the conflict is framed – as a religious war, on the one hand, and a war between civilization and barbarism, on the other" (262), and in which key figures attempt to more generally represent events and the relevant participants.

In his seminal work on the language of terrorism, Jackson (2005: 1), drawing on critical discourse analysis, explores how the language about the War on Terror has given birth to "a global campaign of counter-terrorism". Herein, "the public language of the American administration has been used to construct a whole new world for its citizens. . . [in which] terrorism threatens to destroy everything that ordinary people hold dear. . . ." (1). In the creation of this subjective reality, ordinary citizens are reminded of their cultural values, of their traditions of freedom and justice, and those public officials compiling such a narrative seek unity behind these very ideals of liberty and civilisation, ones they themselves epitomise, while those barbaric "others" fundamentally opposed to a life of goodness, are homogonenized as a singular, vilified entity, in militaristic terms as the "enemy". Jackson further points out that this narrative formula is not exclusively attributable to the American and British administrations, but rather the discursive strategies employed in the creation of the War on Terror narrative, echo the same tone employed by leaders of other conflicts around the world, including the internal conflicts in Rwanda, Bosnia, and the Balkans. What comes across then is that the discursive construction of violence and terrorism relies on a somewhat set script which includes "the creation of a sense of exceptional grievance and victimhood; the demonization and dehumanisation of an enemy other; the manufacture of a catastrophic threat and danger which demands immediate and forceful action; and the justification and legitimisation of pre-emptive (and preventive) counter-violence" (181).

It is this strengthening over-reaching narrative, what Chang and Mehan (2006) refer to as a "War on Terror script", which enforces a dominant definition of what is good or bad, who is "us" and "them" in the War on Terror in particular, and in the construction of violence more generally, that has been the focus of much of the subsequent research. Some key studies that have focused on how gatekeepers of society attribute coherent specific meaning to ambiguous, complex events and situations include Bhatia's (2007, 2008, 2009) studies which draw on a multidimensional analytical approach, using tools such as CDA, DHA, MCA, and Critical Metaphor Analysis (CMA) to investigate the language of contrasts in the understanding of the "terrorist". Her findings both further confirm the existence of a dichotomising discourse that has emerged especially post-9/11, but also more generally the nature of discourse which is drawn on constantly to shape and reshape what we understand as "objective reality", and laden with positive self-presentation and negative other-presentation. This is particularly evident in her study on the construction of metaphorical illusion in the rhetoric of Bush and bin Laden, especially the predominant use of religious imagery in both their speeches, thus resulting in the above mentioned "double contrastive identity".

This "War on Terror script" (Chang and Mehan 2006), as mentioned earlier, has also been applied to better understand the discursive construction of violence in other contexts around the world, again illustrating the rather ritualised nature and function of such discourses. Erjavec and Volcic (2007: 123), extending Bernstein's (1990) notion of recontextualisation to mean "relocation of a discourse from its context/practice to its appropriation within another context/practice", focus on how the American War on Terror rhetoric is recontextualised in the context of Bosnia, used to legitimise Serbian violence against Muslims, employing similar rules of ex/inclusion. Bartolucci (2010: 131) too points to the appropriation of the War on Terror discourse in the context of the Moroccan government's construction of terrorism through the redefinition of concepts such as "extremism" and "radicalism", concluding that

> Terrorism is a ubiquitous discursive construction with effects that impact greatly on several aspects of the public and private lives of individuals. Although loaded with assumptions, such a discourse, interlinked with other discourses such as on religion and identity, continues to be used uncritically.

Bartolucci (2010: 577) continues this thread of argument in her 2012 study of presidential discourses, drawing on a multidisciplinary CDA approach to analyse how a discourse of fear is so inherently intertwined with an understanding of terrorist/ism. As mentioned earlier, a key strategy used by public officials in their attempts to unite their audiences is to remind them that their very values are at risk, vulnerable to impending attacks at the hands of an enemy Other, resulting in, she rightly states, "a pervasive feeling of fear", which has led to an "*a priori* dismissal of non-violent alternatives to rather exhault a zero sum approach". What Silberstein (2002) earlier referred to as the proliferation of a "patriot rhetoric" in the build up to war, in which citizens are put in charge of their safety, and given the means to protect themselves.

What has emerged from some of the key studies on discursive constructions of terrorism and violence is the existence of a macro narrative, a bipolar discourse that splits the world in two clearly defined halves. There is the wholly good side, the nations, or people, or communities that form the "us" category metonymic of all the values attributed to this wholly positive side (eg., justice, freedom, democracy, civilisation, lawful) and legitimised because of these very values. The other half of this category-pair is the wholly evil "other", enemy of the good people who embody all those values that criminalise and vilify them, threatening the core of humanity. But what comes across even more clearly is that people cannot

> engage in war [and violence] without the mediating force of discourse. . . Warfare as an undertaking relies upon the organizational capacity of discourse to mobilize forces,

direct resources, and legitimize actions. The creation of enemies requires the discursive process of constructing an out-group and distancing that group from the humanity of the in-group.

(Hodges 2013: 3)

Most studies on the discursive construction of terrorism and violence have served to strongly emphasise the importance of discourse in the representation of thoughts and ideas, values and traditions, power, prejudice, and judgement, and ultimately the world we live in. The practice of discourse allows observation, interpretation, and evaluation of the social world, through tools such as metaphors, recontextualisation, and categorisation, which enable the constant reconceptualisation of our everyday reality. Considering the complex nature of such discourses and the purpose they serve in society, the need for a multi-perspective and multidimensional approach to critically account for the complexities of such discursive forms becomes even more apparent. A multidimensional approach can thus offer closer analysis of how the discursive construction of subjective realities is realised and exploited.

Multi-perspective approach: discursive illusions

There exist several distinct interpretations of CDA, but the basic tenets common to all address issues of power and ideology at play in society, focusing on language as social practice and particularly the way it is made possible through language use (Fairclough 1989; van Dijk 1993, 2001; Wodak 2001). It is in this regard that CDA is so unique, with its emphasis on investigation in a problem-orientated multidisciplinary manner; it is "not interested in investigating a linguistic unit per se but in studying social phenomena which are necessarily complex and thus require a multi-disciplinary and multi-methodical approach" (Wodak and Meyer 2009: 2).

It is in keeping this basic principle of CDA in mind that I propose the discourse of illusion as a multi-perspective and multi-methodological framework for the analysis of rich, complex public discourses. The discourse of illusion originates from our subjective representations of reality, but is often seen and presented as objective beliefs and perceptions. Our minds can be seen as being active participants in the construction of reality, influenced by a whole gamut of past experiences, sensations, cultural ideologies, and understandings. In this regard, an individual's conceptualisation of reality can be seen as a product of one's historical repository of experiences. One may say that people inhabit two realities: the subjective reality that we know and construct through our life experiences and ideological thinking, and the objective, physical reality of what is really out-there. It is safe to assume that we cannot access this objective reality directly, although our conceptual systems do enable us to create a *representation* of it, and *acting* (through various semiotic and linguistic means) on these subjective reconstructions can lead to the creation of discursive illusions.

To define it in simpler terms, the discourse of illusion is the product of a subjective conceptualisation of reality, emerging from a historical repository of experiences embodying various linguistic and semiotic actions, often leading to intended socio-political outcomes. The discourse of illusion is as such complex and multifaceted, requiring an appropriately integrated methodological approach to allow closer analysis of how it is realised, including intentions of the producer/actor, power struggles within social domains, in addition to the socio-political and historical contexts which influence the individual repositories of experience. A combined analysis that incorporates dimensions of historicity, linguistic, and semiotic action, further linked to an account of some of the social effects of these actions will, it is argued, permit the exploration of the dynamic discursive processes that give rise to those sociocultural and political tensions which imbue the discourse of illusion. The chapter analyses the data in term of the multidimensional framework of the discourse of illusion, drawing on three interrelated components (see Bhatia 2015 for a more comprehensive account of the theoretical framework Discourse of Illusion):

1   Historicity – habitus is key to the discourse of illusion, dealing as it does with the recontextualisation of past knowledge and experience into present day action. In order to analyse this, the framework draws on the concept of *structured immediacy* (Leudar and Nekvapil 2011), concentrating on "how participants enrich the here-and-now of action by connecting it to the past", and which I define as *the unconscious or conscious reconceptualisation of historical antecedents in an attempt to situate and present specific instances of current reality, often in relation to the future* (Bhatia 2015: 66).
2   Linguistic and semiotic action – subjective conceptualisations of the world give rise certain linguistic and semiotic actions, often through metaphorical rhetoric. To analyse this, the framework borrows elements of critical discourse analysis (CDA) focusing in particular on *critical metaphor analysis* (Charteris-Black 2004), which investigates the intention in the creation and diffusion of discursive metaphorical constructions.
3   Social impact – language and actions engender many categories and stereotypes, which can be analysed through Jayyusi's (1984: 183) concept of *categorisation* that explicates how people "organize their moral positions and commitments round certain category identities".

To enrich the investigation of the three interrelated components of history, linguistic and semiotic action, and social impact, which provide an account of the discourse of illusion, a range of lexico-syntactical and semantico-pragmatic tools, keeping the nature of the various discourse analytical models integrated in mind, are employed, including: temporal references, metaphor, topoi, insinuation, recontextualisation, positive/negative presentation, and identity construction (See Bhatia 2015 for a more detailed account of these linguistic tools in the context of the discourse of illusion).

Case study: discursive construction of terrorism

The Bush administration was perceived as the official sponsor of the War on Terror, enforcing a state of moral order through the "emotionalization of facts" (Menz 1989: 237). Analysis of President George W. Bush's speeches reveals the use of various rhetorical strategies drawing on a range of lexico-syntactical and semantico-pragmatic tools, in an attempt to build reality in favour of his administration's socio-political agendas, or what was previously discussed as an overarching hegemonic discourse that attempted to shape public understanding of terrorist violence. The aim here is not to condone or condemn any particular subjective conceptualisation of terrorism, but rather to explore how the discursive construction of terrorism is often a powerful tool of propaganda used to further specific socio-political goals.

The speeches, analysed chronologically, reveal three specific time periods within the speeches:

1   The pre-war period (i.e., from September 11, 2001, to the end of the year on December 11, 2001, exactly three months later) immediately after the 9/11 attacks and before the attack on Afghanistan, during which Bush's rhetoric was relatively aggressive while addressing an overwrought audience, reassuring them of "revenge" and justice.

2   The build-up to the war period (i.e., from the State of the Union Address given by Bush on January 29, 2002, till the end of major combat operations in Iraq on May 1, 2003) within which an explicit link was made between Iraq and terrorism, and continued to the end of major combat operations in Iraq. This "continuance" period generated discourses that offered a pretext for the war.

3   The post-war period (i.e., from July 23, 2003, to the State of the Union address given on January 31, 2006, considered the end of war due to ceasing of offensive military action) which revealed discourses that tried to justify a "faulty" war by focusing on the attainment of democracy.

Post-9/11 Attacks

After the 9/11 attacks on the World Trade Center, Bush capitalised on the constant influx of negative emotions, drawing on a morality metaphor within which evil and terrorism were personified in the image of Osama bin Laden (cf. Charteris-Black 2005): "Thousands of lives were suddenly ended by evil, despicable acts of terror" (Bush, 11/9/01). The "acts of terror" are hyperbolically labelled "evil", implicating terrorists themselves as evil men. Evil here opens up a range of religious imagery, invoking biblical concepts of good and evil. Phrases such as ". . . our nation saw evil, the very worst of human nature" (Bush 11/9/01) or "They don't represent an ideology. . . . They're flat evil" (Bush, 25/9/01) imply the rather categorical nature of "evil", which as a "type" categorisation denotes the kind of people that terrorists are, based on previous experiences with such people, drawing on the past to create data-structures (cf. Bednarek 2005) of our knowledge of the world built on our experience with it. The adverb "very" in conjunction with the superlative "worst" in the coordinated clause above portrays terrorists as the opposite of everything that the nation of "good folks" (Bush, 25/9/01) stand for. The "evil" of terrorists is amplified through their dissociation from any sort of organic ideology grown over time; evil thus becomes a part of the character of those "types" of people. The adjective "flat" further emphasises the extreme evil of terrorists without allowing them any grounds for explanation, they are evil by nature not consequence. The assignment of "evil" to one group automatically denotes its equal and opposite "verbal form – Good and *Bad*, Good and *Evil*, and Better and *Worse*" (Mackenzie 1929: 250). During the initial period after the 9/11 attacks, America became the "good" side in opposition to the "evil" terrorists who thought they could "diminish our soul" (Bush, 25/9/01).

Evil is further equated with barbarism, whereby barbarism is given the same intrinsic quality that is ascribed to evil – it is part of one's nature: "There are no rules. It's barbaric behaviour. . . that is beyond comprehension" (Bush, 17/9/01); "There is a great divide in our time. . . between civilization and barbarism" (Bush, 7/12/01). Barbarism is regarded in a contradictory manner here whereby it is seen as knowing no rules and being guided by no principles, it is determined to "achieve an objective that is beyond comprehension", but which also then attributes to the terrorists a sense of purpose and direction. Further emphasis on terrorism being hyperbolically conceptualised as barbarism is attained through the constant referral to civilisation and civilised society, which is aligned with the West: "The civilized world is rallying to America's side" (Bush, 20/9/01); "We wage a war to save civilization, itself. We did not seek it, but we must fight it" (Bush, 8/11/02). This here becomes a significant American political trope, the reticent cowboy who may not look for a fight, but who, when provoked, hits back harder. America is depicted as the leader of the civilised world, and by implication they are the country around which the civilised world is "rallying", the verb metaphorically conceptualising the War on Terror into a political campaign. This statement can be interpreted as implicit positive self-presentation, emphasising the goodness of America, while reinforcing further the illusive *us* vs. *them* divide between the civilised (or all those on the side of America) and the uncivilised. However, true to the nature of the discourse of illusion, participants often share "double contrastive identity" (Leudar, Marsland and Nekvapil 2004), whereby bin Laden, who is portrayed as barbaric by America, in turn accuses Americans of being "the worst civilization witnessed by the history of mankind" (24/11/02), the superlative "worst" depicting a powerful negative other-presentation of the opposite side, in a similar manner to Bush earlier. What the discourse of illusion can be seen as highlighting here is the conflict of contested versions of reality, the different but both subjective representations of realities put forward by elite individuals or groups in the pursuit of specific socio-political objectives. America is represented as the reluctant recipient of the role of leader of free world, they have waged a war to save civilisation, yet they "did not seek it". And despite the conjunction "but", there is a sense of shifting responsibility for waging the war, which will be fought and is on the agenda, but who put it there and specifically who is the "we" that is fighting the war is not made clear; instead the war is presented as something that just happens to be so crucial in saving "civilization itself" in the topos of external constraint (Wodak et al. 1999).

The discourses generated immediately after the 9/11 period represented disparate terrorist networks into a singular entity, which was wholly evil, yet fightable. A newly installed president who had not achieved any great feats was given a chance to become a strong, commanding leader. Bush's rhetoric went on to become boldly accusatory, laying blame on the "barbaric terrorists", catering to the core weaknesses of a distraught populace. Revenge was sworn but disguised as a cosmic struggle between two polar dualities – good and evil.

Pretext for war

Retributive justice and revenge did not prove legitimate enough reasons to take any kind of definitive action. While the international community condemned those who carried out the 9/11 attacks with no certain proof, future action was harder to plan. At this point terrorism donned a new face, indicating an "important shift in the would-be hegemonic discourse in the period since September 11. . . [which included] the constitution of a relation of equivalence between 'terrorism' and 'weapons of mass destruction' as co-members of the class of 'threats'" (Fairclough 2005: 48). In an apt example, Bush (7/10/02) declares, "Terror cells and outlaw regimes building weapons of mass destruction are different faces of the same evil", personifying evil and vilifying both "terror cells" and other "outlaw regimes" because they are building weapons of mass destruction. The labels of "outlaw" and "evil" "insinuate" (Huckin 2004) their equal and opposite category forms – lawful and good, and in this case these positive labels apply to the United States, reiterating the illusive *us* vs. *them* division. Further, Bush (17/3/03) declared "when evil men plot chemical, biological and nuclear terror, a policy of appeasement could bring destruction of a kind never before seen on this earth". Terrorism is conceptualised in this statement as "chemical, biological and nuclear", which if dealt with "appeasement" could in the disaster topos lead to "destruction of a kind never before seen". Time and date references ("this century", "never before") can be interpreted as both appeal to temporality as a higher form of authority and an invocation of history, past experiences, in an effort to exaggerate the threat posed by such "terror cells". Building a case for any kind of action, especially military, requires the guarantee that the threat is in fact "looming large", to put it simply. It is this justification that Bush seems to work towards in the months after 9/11.

In order to persuade audiences that immediate action is a matter of necessity, the topos of threat utilised by Bush generates the antonym *attack* vs. *self-defence* that engineers the required conditions: "They could attack our allies or attempt to blackmail the United States... indifference would be catastrophic" (Bush, 29/1/02). Repetition of the verb "attack" in conjunction with the hyperbolic adjective "catastrophic" works to arouse fear, immediacy of the impending threat, reiterating what Berrington (2002: 49) refers to as the "emotionalization" of events, whereby "sensationalism, dramatisation and exaggeration of events that were in themselves so horrific that they needed no embellishment" are drawn on to justifying present and future actions.

As part of the strategy of justification Bush again makes an appeal to history as a higher source of authority, declaring "History will judge harshly those who saw this coming danger but failed to act" (17/9/02); in this case history is personified to be a judge, almost reminiscent of the day of judgement. Contrasting the above statement with something Bush says a month later, "We know that Iraq and al Qaeda terrorist network share a common enemy – the United States of America" (7/10/02); we can see the use of "enemy" is reversed in meaning, whereby Iraq and al Qaeda (by this point the specific faces of terror) are still the evil, unlawful "other", but enemy in reference to America is in an effort to arouse fear and bring in a sense of vulnerability and victimisation. History is also invoked in the topos of illustrative example where Bush conjures memories of the nuclear bombing of Nagasaki and Hiroshima: "Knowing these realities, America must not ignore the threat gathering against us. Facing clear evidence of peril, we cannot wait for the final proof – the smoking gun – that could come in the form of a mushroom cloud" (7/10/02). The discourse of illusion takes effect here in the phrase "knowing these realities", where the subjective conceptualisation of reality presented by Bush is considered to be an objective fact. The threat, the hyperbolic "peril" of terrorism, is recontextualised into a quasi-nuclear war, shaping the course of the world in a particular direction. The use of emotionally charged vocabulary is an effort to gather support and allies as part of the strategy of perpetuation (Wodak et al. 1999).

The discourses produced during the build up to the Iraq invasion indicated that support would only be achieved if they were presented as a legitimate and progressive step in the metaphorical *War on Terror*. Evidence was provided in an attempt to persuade audiences that Iraq and Al Qaeda were an impending threat that needed to be dealt with as a matter of urgency. Any blame that America encountered for bombing Afghanistan, or for trying to create unfeasible correlations between Saddam Hussein and the 9/11 attacks, was deflected by the Bush administration through claims that the world was at risk, that Iraq illegally possessed WMDs, and that the United Nations was ineffective in containing Iraq, thus leaving America with no choice but to defend itself and its allies.

Justification for war

Terrorism was given yet another form when no weapons of mass destruction were found in Iraq: "With W.M.D. still elusive, President Bush has increasingly justified the invasion of Iraq as a bold effort to establish a beacon of democracy" (Kristof 2004). The invasion of Iraq was portrayed as a definitive step forward in the War on Terror, transforming terrorism into "a totalitarian empire that denies all political and religious freedom" (Bush, 28/10/05). Terrorism was conceptualised as "savage acts of violence" which strive to "stop the advance of freedom" (Bush, 28/6/05). As such terrorism came to represent the metaphorical divide between the "return of tyranny and the death of democracy" (Bush, 24/5/04). Over time the conceptualisation of terrorism evolved from its more specific, domestic-centric understanding as evil, to a more international yet specialised definition of terrorism as the possession of WMDs, to a very general yet powerfully dichotomising perception of terrorism as a lack of democracy: "triumph of democracy and tolerance in Iraq, in Afghanistan... would be a grave setback for international terrorism" (Bush, 7/9/03); "one of the victories in this battle against terror is going to be the spread of freedom" (Bush, 20/4/04); "The appeal of justice and liberty, in the end, is greater than the appeal of hatred and tyranny in any form" (Bush, 12/7/04). Democracy is portrayed as being "in this battle against terror" within which its "triumph" is equated with positive values such as "justice and liberty". Terrorism and tyranny are illustrated as unstable and subjective conceptualisations of socio-political reality, reiterated through terms such as "ideologies", "fanaticism", and "radicalism". The repeated use of the noun, both in plural and singular forms, emphasising the arbitrary nature of the practices and perceptions of the "other" group: "produce ideologies of hatred and produce recruits for terror" (Bush, 30/6/03); "terrorists are successors to the murderous ideologies of the 20th century" (Bush, 4/2/04); "a totalitarian political ideology, pursued with consuming zeal, and without conscience" (Bush, 24/5/04). The perceptions of reality put forward by terrorists, on the basis of which they act, is delegitimised by being hyperbolically depicted as "ideologies of hatred", "murderous", and "totalitarian", thus denying them any grounds for justification or explanation, as they are pursued with "zeal" but without "conscience". In this case, by distinguishing terrorist ideology from religion or at least a code of morality, Bush highlights the random and illogical nature of terrorist belief systems. An ironic danger in the proliferation of a Western-centric hegemonic discourse, such as the one being discussed, through gatekeepers of society, including public officials, political leaders, even the media, is the impact of it on smaller groups and individuals, such as Anders Breivik. His actions, while nothing short of terrorism themselves, are often explained as a consequence of how individuals often become involved in what can be understood as a

> global ideological battle [in which they can easily. . .] become quite actively involved [. . .] in a manner that is dangerous to the society in which they are living [. . .] Breivik's case shows the danger of the virulent anti-Muslim rhetoric that sometimes pollutes the political discourse in the West.
>
> *(Pantucci 2011)*

The objectification of the actions of America, the validation of their particular conceptualisation of reality, is achieved in part by discrediting the opponent's perception of reality for which Bush resorts not only to constant negative other-presentation but also, again, the appeal to history as a source of higher authority. History acts as a sponsor of legitimate actions since it is viewed by society as a record of past experiences and as a basis for future actions: "history will prove the decision we made to be the right decision" (Bush, 30/7/03); "we will finish the historic work of democracy in Afghanistan and Iraq" (Bush, 20/1/04); "we accept the call of history to deliver the oppressed and move this world toward peace" (Bush, 31/1/06). In these personifications, history is seen as carrying out actions such as proving, moving, and calling. Placing history in a position of power in the topos of appeal to authority as part of the strategy of legitimation (Wodak et al. 1999), America also aligns itself with history in order to come across as credible. Americans are shown as rising to the challenges history has set before them because they are a good and democratic nation. The invocation of history here is an explicit attempt to connect past frames of experiences with present ones to form new, possible meanings.

The discourses proceeding the end of combat operations in Iraq can be seen as monologues of justification attempting to minimise the blame of an illegal and unilateral war. From a pre-emptive strike, which was a method of defending the civilised world against dangerous attacks, the Iraq war became a strive for democracy, the solution to terrorism, and implementation of God's will that there should be freedom for all men, women, and children. The justification for the Iraq war was now the fight for all those who suffer oppression against tyrannous terrorism. It was no longer a step in the War on Terror but rather part of a global struggle against tyranny and ideologues of hatred.

Terrorism in the speeches by Bush is represented variously, depending on the socio-political context; it has been manipulated to further the political agendas of those in power. Terrorism has represented evil, barbarism, desire to possess weapons of mass destruction, and tyranny, and depending on its usage it has been possible to distinguish the motivations and intentions of those who put forward these conceptualisations of terrorism. This has also highlighted the rather illusive nature of the discourses of terrorism where the changing representations of the construct emphasise the subjective realities that we adhere to as legitimate and objective. It is important then to "recognize [that] 'terrorism' is simply a word, a subjective epithet, not an objective reality" (Whitbeck 2004).

Future directions

The analysis of this chapter revealed how the conceptualisations of terrorism were transformed over time in terms of their changing social and political contexts. The use of various rhetorical strategies and a range of lexico-syntactical and semantico-pragmatic tools in the construction of terrorism and political violence, and opposing realities, proceeded to give birth to discursive illusions. The evolvement of terrorism represents the pretext for war, the war in progress, and the blame negotiation and justification that followed the end of war. The generated discourses therefore illustrated not only subjective viewpoints but also provided some ground for under-standing the origins of such views. The discourse of illusion is thus grounded in a sociocultural mesh of beliefs and ideas about what the world is like and what it should be like. It illustrates how a particular group views the world, consistent with its culture and history, and what actions it then takes in order to change the world to be consistent with its perceptions of the world. The relationship between actions and what constitutes them, namely one's habitus and local as well as wider context, cannot be analysed in a simple, straightforward manner. Perhaps one could even say that by itself a single methodological approach may not be enough to analyse such historically and ideologically textured discourses. The social world is complex and symbolic, comprising "structure, agency and culture" (Sealey and Carter 2004: 184), the "stratified nature of the social world, then, as well as its complex and emergent features, make it impossible to apply a single approach to analysing it . . ." (202) (cf. Bhatia 2004). Although, it is possible to say that discourses and social structures are co-constitutive, it is individuals in society who determine which linguistic resources are essential to social mediation. In addition, Sealey and Carter (2004: 197) mention that the distinction between what the world really is and how it appears to us can be seen to be sourced by the individual histories and resources that people possess, how they are liberated and constrained by particular ideologies and trains of thought, and therefore, "what opportunities are afforded by virtue of their social location" (197). It is for this reason that within "the powers and properties of agency, structure and cul-ture, and consideration of agency in relation to motivation" (205) lies the intentionality behind created discourses that an integrated approach is necessary to study the discourse of illusion.

Further reading

Bhatia, A. (2015). *Discursive illusions in public discourse: Theory and practice.* New York, London: Routledge. This book, using a multi-perspective discourse analytical framework, explores various public discourses, including those of war and violence, in the contexts of the War on Terrorism and the Arab Spring.

Hodges, A. (ed.) (2013). *Discourses of war and peace*. Oxford, New York: Oxford University Press.

This edited volume drawing on research using various analytical methods, including critical discourse and narrative analysis, investigates how discourse is employed to create war and versions of peace in different global contexts.

Leudar, I., Marsland, V. and Nekvapil, J. (2004). On membership categorization: 'Us', 'them' and 'doing violence' in political discourse. *Discourse & Society* 15(2–3): 243–266.

This journal article employs Membership Categorization Analysis to establish how participants involved in contexts of conflict or crisis discursively construct notions of 'us' and 'them' to justify actions.

References

Achugar, M. (2004). The events and actors of 11 September 2001 as seen from uruguay: Analysis of daily newspaper editorials. *Discourse & Society* 15(2–3): 291–320.

Bartolucci, V. (2010). Analysing elite discourse on terrorism and its implications: The case of Morocco. *Critical Studies on Terrorism* 3(1): 119–135.

Bartolucci, V. (2012). Terrorism rhetoric under the Bush administration: Discourses and effects. *Journal of Language and Politics* 11(4): 562–582.

Bednarek, A. M. (2005). Frame revisited – the coherence-inducing function of frames. *Journal of Pragmatics* 37: 685–705.

Bernstein, B. (1990). *The structure of pedagogic discourse: Class, codes and control*, Vol. IV. London: Routledge.

Berrington, E. (2002). Representations of terror in the legitimation of war. In P. Scraton (ed.), *Beyond September 11: An anthology of dissent,* 47–54. London: Pluto Press.

Bhatia, A. (2007). Religious metaphor in the discourse of illusion: George W. Bush and Osama bin Laden. *World Englishes* 26(4): 507–524.

Bhatia, A. (2008). Discursive illusions in the American national strategy for combating terrorism. *Journal of Language and Politics* 7(2): 201–227.

Bhatia, A. (2009). Discourses of terrorism. *Journal of Pragmatics* 41(2): 279–289.

Bhatia, A. (2013). World of the impolitic: A critical study of the WMD Dossier. In A. Hodges (ed.), *Oxford series in sociolinguistics: The discourses of war and peace,* 95–116. Oxford: Oxford University Press.

Bhatia, A. (2015). *Discursive illusions in public discourse: Theory and practice*. New York: Routledge.

Bhatia, V. K. (2004). *Worlds of written discourse: A genre-based view*. London and New York: Continuum.

Butt, D. G., Lukin, A. and Matthiessen, C.M.I.M. (2004). Grammar- the first covert operation of war. *Discourse & Society* 15(2–3): 267–290.

Chang, C. G. and Mehan, H. B. (2006). Discourse in a religious mode: The Bush administration's discourse in the war on terrorism and its challenges. *International Pragmatics Association* 16: 1–23.

Charteris-Black, J. (2004). *Corpus approaches to critical metaphor analysis*. Hampshire: Palgrave Macmillan.

Charteris-Black, J. (2005). *Politicians and rhetoric: The persuasive power of metaphor*. New York: Palgrave Macmillan.

Chouliaraki, L. (2005). The soft power of war: Legitimacy and community in Iraq war discourses. *Journal of Language and Politics* 4(1): 1–10.

Collins, J. (2002). Terrorism. In J. Collins and R. Glover (eds.), *Collateral language: A user's guide to America's new war,* 155–173. New York: New York University Press.

Collins, J. and Glover, R. (eds.) (2002). *Collateral language: A user's guide to America's new war*. New York: New York University Press.

Edwards, J. (2004). After the fall. *Discourse & Society* 15(2–3): 155–184.

Elshtain, J. B. (2003). *Just war against terror: The burden of American power in a violent world*. New York: Basic Books.

Erjavec, K. and Volcic, Z. (2007). 'War on terrorism' as a discursive battleground: Serbian recontextualization of G.W. Bush's discourse. *Discourse & Society* 18(2): 123–137.

Fairclough, N. (1989). *Language and power*. New York: Longman.

Fairclough, N. (2005). Blair's contribution to elaborating a new "doctrine of international community". *Journal of Language and Politics* 4(1): 41–63.

Goffman, E. (1981). *Forms of talk*. Philadelphia: University of Pennsylvania Press.

Graham, P., Keenan, T. and Dowd, A. M. (2004). A call to arms at the end of history: A discourse – historical analysis of George W. Bush's declaration of war on terror. *Discourse & Society* 15(2–3): 199–221.

Graham, P. and Luke, A. (2005). The language of neofeudal corporatism and the war on Iraq. *Journal of Language and Politics* 4(1): 11–39.

Hodges, A. (2013). War, discourse, and peace. In A. Hodges (ed.), *Oxford series in sociolinguistics: The discourses of war and peace*, 3–19. Oxford: Oxford University Press.

Huckin, T. (2004). A non-Hallidayan approach to critical discourse analysis. Seminar presented at City University of Hong Kong, Department of English and Communication, Hong Kong, May 31.

Jackson, R. (2005). *Writing the war on terrorism: Language, politics and counter-terrorism*. Manchester: Manchester University Press.

Jayyusi, L. (1984). *Categorization and the moral order*. Boston, MA: Routledge & Kegan Paul.

Kristof, N. D. (2004). Sweet sound of dissent. *New York Times*, May 1. www.nytimes.com

Lazar, A. and Lazar, M. M. (2004). The discourse of the new world order: 'Out-casting' the double face of threat. *Discourse & Society* 15(2–3): 223–242.

Leudar, I., Marsland, V. and Nekvapil, J. (2004). On membership categorization: 'Us', 'them' and 'doing violence' in political discourse. *Discourse & Society* 15(2–3): 243–266

Leudar, I. and Nekvapil, J. (2011). Practical historians and adversaries: 9/11 revisited. *Discourse & Society* 22(1): 66–85.

Llorente, M. A. (2002). Civilization vs. Barbarism. In J. Collins and R. Glover (eds.), *Collateral language: A user's guide to America's new war*, 39–51. New York: New York University Press.

Mackenzie, J. S. (1929). The meaning of value. In D.S. Robinson (ed.), *An anthology of recent philosophy: Selections for beginners from the writings of the greatest 20th century philosophers*, 248–261. New York: Thomas Y. Crowell Company.

Marsella, A. J. (2004). Reflections on international terrorism: Issues, concepts, and directions. In F.M. Moghaddam and A.J. Marsella (eds.), *In understanding terrorism: Psychosocial roots, consequences, and interventions*, 11–47. Washington, DC: American Psychological Association.

Menz, F. (1989). Manipulation strategies in newspapers: A program for critical linguistics. In R. Wodak (ed.), *Language, power and ideology: Studies in political discourse*, 227–249. Amsterdam: John Benjamins.

Musolff, A. (1997). International metaphors: Bridges or walls in international communication? In B. Debatin, T.R. Jackson and D. Steuer (eds.), *Metaphor and rational discourse*, 229–237. Germany: Max Niemeyer.

Norris, P., Kern, M. and Just, M. (2003). Framing terrorism. In P. Norris, M. Kern, and M. Just (eds.), *Framing terrorism: The news media, the government, and the public*, 3–25. New York: Routledge.

Oktar, L. (2001). The ideological organization of representational processes in the presentation of us and them. *Discourse & Society* 12(3): 313–346.

Pantucci, R. (2011). What have we learned about Lone Wolves from Anders Behring Breivik? *Persepctives on Terrorism* 5(5–6). www.terrorismanalysts.com/pt/index.php/pot/article/view/what-we-have-learned/html

Sacks, H. (1992). *Lectures on conversation Volume I & II*. Oxford: Blackwell.

Sealey, A. and Carter, B. (2004). *Applied linguistics as social science*. London: Continuum.

Silberstein, S. (2002). *War of words: Language, politics and 9/11*. London: Routledge.

Taylor, M. (1988). *The terrorist*. London: Brassey's Defence Publishers.

van Dijk, T. A. (1993). Principles in critical discourse analysis. *Discourse & Society* 4(2): 249–283.

van Dijk, T. A. (2001). Multidisciplinary CDA: A plea for diversity. In R. Wodak and M. Meyer (eds.), *Methods of critical discourse analysis*, 1–13. London: Sage. Weinberg, L. B. and Davis, P. B. (1989). *Introduction to political terrorism*. New York: McGraw-Hill.

Whitbeck, J.V. (2004). A world ensnared by a word. *International Herald Tribune*, February 18, 6.

Wilkins, K. G. (2000). The role of media in public disengagement from political life.

Wodak, R. (2001). What CDA is about – a summary of its history, important concepts and its developments. In R. Wodak and M. Meyer (eds.), *Methods of critical discourse analysis*, 1–13. London: Sage.

Wodak, R., de Cillia, R., Reisigl, M. and Liebhart, K. (1999). *The discursive construction of national identity*. Edinburgh: Edinburgh University Press.

Wodak, R. and Meyer, M. (2009). *Methods of critical discourse analysis*. London: Sage.

30

Fascist discourse

John E. Richardson

Introduction

This chapter introduces and discusses critical approaches to the analysis of fascist discourse. Although in comparison with other topics – *inter alia,* newspaper reporting, race/racism, sex/gender – the examination of fascist discourse is thin, recently this has started to be remedied with notable contributions to the analytic and empirical literature. Whilst some may argue that this relative infrequency is reason to exclude a chapter on fascist discourse from a handbook on Critical Discourse Studies (CDS), I maintain that fascist discourse is vitally important to analyse, understand and oppose. Most obviously, fascist politics is inimical to the emancipatory agenda of CDS. CDS should be aimed at analysing and counteracting power abuse, and how this is variously represented, enacted, justified and achieved in and through discourse; fascist political projects (whether ideology, party or movement) epitomise power abuse *in extremis*. Studying such political outliers yields additional benefits in that it brings into better focus the dialectic between extremisms and the social and political mainstream. Consider, for example, the ways that mainstream UK parties censured the British National Party (BNP) whilst simultaneously aping their language in order to appear tough on immigration (Richardson 2008; see also Wodak 2011); or the way that the BNP adopt slogans and communication tactics of mainstream UK parties in order to appear more moderate (Copsey 2008; Richardson and Wodak 2009a).

The remainder of this chapter is structured as follows: first I briefly discuss the work of historians of fascism, focusing in particular on work defining the ideological core of fascism. I identify a problem with this work, and a solution in the form of the groundbreaking work of Michael Billig (1978). Following and building on this, I next discuss fascism and discourse, showing the ways that work has developed from early philology of Klemperer, through to more recent work in CDS.[1] Finally, I present a case study which applies my approach to the critical analysis of fascist discourse: a speech delivered by Nick Griffin, the then-leader of the BNP, at a party meeting in 2010.

Fascism and fascism studies

Since the end of the 1960s, a body of work has developed whose primary focus is on fascist ideology, and which aims to extract the ideological core of *"generic fascism* that may account for significant and unique similarities between the various permutations of fascism whilst convincingly accommodating deviations as either nationally or historically specific phenomena" (Kallis 2009: 4, emphasis added). This work on generic fascism has formulated lists of "significant and unique similarities", aiming to distil the "various permutations of fascism" down to a minimum number of necessary and sufficient characteristics: the so-called "fascist minimum" (c.f. Nolte 1968). Such work reaches its apotheosis in the work of Roger Griffin, whose one-sentence definition of fascism – "Fascism is a genus of political ideology whose mythic core in its various permutations is a palingenetic form of populist ultra-nationalism" (Griffin 1993a: 26), or "formulated in three words: 'palingenetic populist ultra-nationalism'" (1998: 13) – is, truly, a minimal fascist minimum. Indeed, the extreme brevity of his definition drew withering comment from Paxton (2005: 221), who suggests Griffin's "zeal to reduce fascism to one pithy sentence seems to me more likely to inhibit than to stimulate analysis of how and with whom it worked."

Fascism, Griffin argues, aims to rejuvenate, revitalise and reconstruct the nation following a period of perceived decadence, crisis and/or decline. Griffin uses the Victorian term "palingenesis", meaning "rebirth from the ashes", to characterise this central motivating spirit (*Geist*) of fascism, though it is only when combined with the other elements in the noun phrase, that his fascist minimum is given a sense of ideological form. Thus, in response to criticisms that "national rebirth" is not a uniquely fascist ideological commitment, Griffin argues: "I agree entirely [. . .] It is only when the two terms are combined ('palingenetic ultra-nationalism') that they form a compound definitional component" (Griffin 2006: 263–264). Detailing his noun phrase a little more, he uses

> 'populist' not to refer to a particular historical experience [. . .] but as a generic term for political forces which, even if led by small elite cadres or self-appointed 'vanguards', in practice or in principle (and not merely for show) depend on 'people power' as the basis of their legitimacy. I am using 'ultra-nationalism' [. . .] to refer to forms of nationalism which 'go beyond', and hence reject, anything compatible with liberal institutions or with the tradition of Enlightenment humanism which underpins them.
>
> *(Griffin 1993b: 36–37)*

Griffin's heuristic definition approaches fascism primarily as a set of ideological myths expounded by its leaders. As he has argued: "The premise of this approach is to take fascist ideology at its face value, and to recognize the central role played in it by the myth of national rebirth to be brought about by a finding a 'Third Way' between liberalism/capitalism and communism/socialism" (Griffin 1998: 238). There is no doubting the significant influence that Griffin's definition has had, particularly on American and British scholars. Some praise his scholarship and the heuristic value of his definition, and include themselves within his claimed 'new consensus' on fascism studies; others are far more circumspect about its politics and the degree of convergence that Griffin claims between his work and that of others. For example, Woodley (2010: 1) has argued that the "new consensus" in fascism studies developed by "revisionist historians" such as Griffin, "is founded less on scholarly agreement than a conscious rejection of historical materialism as a valid methodological framework". Mann (2004: 12) goes further, arguing:

> Griffin's idealism is nothing to be proud of. It is a major defect. How can a "myth" generate "internal cohesion" or "driving force"? A myth cannot be an agent driving or

integrating anything, since ideas are not free-floating. Without power organizations, ideas cannot actually *do* anything.

(Mann 2004: 12)

The three concepts Griffin identifies (palingenetic, populist, ultra-nationalist) may be necessary but, even combined, they are insufficient to properly define fascism or fascist discourse, since they are detached from material practices. In contrast, Billig's (1978, 1988a, 1988b, 1990) work offers a highly adaptable definition of fascism, both ideologically and as a political movement (for an extended discussion, see Richardson 2017). He argues that fascism is characterised by a shifting constellation of four general features. To be classified as "fascist", a party or movement needs to possess all four characteristics, the first three of which are ideological: (1) *strong-to-extreme nationalism;* (2) *anti-Marxism,* and indeed opposition to any mobilisation of the working class as a class for itself; and (3) *support for a capitalist political economy.*

Given its nationalism, fascist support for a capitalist political economy is usually of a protectionist, Statist or autarkic nature; at minimum it is opposed to finance or international capital, and aims for mercantilism protected within the borders of the nation-state. "In this respect it differs from traditional laissez-faire capitalism, which seeks to reduce the activity of the state to a minimum" (Billig 1978: 7). Whilst many fascist parties use populist, even pro-worker rhetoric, and oppose aspects of capitalism (particularly banking, "usury" and international capital), *no* variety of fascism whether as ideology, party or regime has been willing or able to replace capitalism. As Kitchen (1976: 85) argues, "the social function of fascism was to stabilise, strengthen and, to a certain degree, transform capitalist property relations", ensuring the continuation of capitalist political economy, the economic and social dominance of propertied and bourgeois classes, and thus the continued exploitation of the working classes. Accordingly, fascism should be regarded as "a specific form of post-liberal capitalism" (Woodley 2010: 133). Under fascism, "capitalism would be controlled but socialism destroyed" (Mann 2004: 19). Note that this does not mean that fascism is simply, and directly, the tool of capital*ists;* fascism is not a dictatorship of monopoly capitalists or any other "agents". Rather, a shared fear of the proletariat organising as a class for itself encourages an uneasy alliance between a mass fascist movement and the traditional elites of industry, politics and the military to protect capital*ism,* as a mode of political-economic accumulation and system of property relations.

Billig's (1978: 7) fourth feature is absolutely key, given that it distinguishes fascism from ideologies of both the political right and various political nationalisms: (4) *these ideological commitments are "advocated in such a way that fascism will pose a direct threat to democracy and personal freedom".* Fascists do not simply oppose Marxism, or left-wing politics more generally, they actively try to stamp them out – denying rights of political association, banning parties, and (ultimately) killing opponents. Fascism based itself "on a radical elitism, that is on the notion that certain human beings were intrinsically, genetically better than others, who consequently could be treated as if they did not have the right to exist" (Renton 2000b: 77). In Gabriele Turi's neat turn of phrase, fascism formulates "a mode of being and, above all, of not being" (Turi, 2002: 121, cited in de Grand 2006: 95).

Fascism exists as a mode of inegalitarian political action. And so, to capture this dimension of fascism, I propose an addition to Billig's definition: (5) *fascism is a political movement.* The mass, or 'popular', nature of fascism is vital, since it is the mass nature of fascism that distinguishes it from other forms of right-wing, authoritarian rule. The first three ideological components (nationalism, capitalism, anti-Marxism) are features common to many right-wing political ideologies, ranging from the traditional right-wing through radical and populist varieties;

it is the anti-democratic *weltanschauung* and violent methods which set fascism apart from parliamentary right-wing politics. However, non-fascist totalitarian or dictatorial regimes also use terror, violence and oppression; some of these oppressive regimes also advocate or orientate to the three ideological features Billig (1978) argues characterise fascism. The difference, therefore, is *the mass basis of fascism;* whether this mass base is invoked rhetorically (as often happens with post-WWII groupuscule movements), organised as a party or coalesced as a movement, fascism acts like "*an extra-parliamentary mass movement* which seeks the road to power through armed attacks on its opponents" (Sparks 1974: 16; emphasis added).

Fascism and discourse

As early as the 1940s, close links between general research on language and studies on political change were established, mainly in Germany. Linguistic research in the wake of National Socialism was conducted primarily by Klemperer (2013 [1957]) and Sternberger, Storz and Sußkind (1957). Klemperer and Sternberger sampled, categorised and described the words used during the Nazi regime: many words had acquired new meanings, other words were forbidden and neologisms were created. As Klemperer (2013: 15) explains:

> Nazism permeated the flesh and blood of the people through single words, idioms and sentence structures which were imposed on them in a million repetitions and taken on board mechanically and unconsciously. [Nazi discourse] increasingly dictates my feelings and governs my entire spiritual being the more unquestioningly and unconsciously I abandon myself to it.

Understandably, Nazi genocide has meant that, since 1945, there is little electoral cache in labelling a party or movement "fascist". However, as Billig (1978) points out, fascist movements during the inter-war period "encountered a qualitatively similar problem", resulting in concealment of the true intentions of the party. In the period between 1930 and 1933 (when Hindenburg appointed Hitler Chancellor of Germany), the Nazi party tried to appear more moderate in official discourse; they wanted to be perceived as a political party aimed at achieving power by constitutional means rather than violent direct action (Cohn 1967). Even during WWII, "Nazis used a euphemistic discourse [in official communiques] with which to conceal their crimes" (Griffin 2014: 39). Griffin (2014: 39–40), for example, quotes a letter written to the Chief of Himmler's personal staff in which the writer (SS-Major General Dr Harald Turner) shows "no qualms about stating that he and his subordinates had shot dead all the Jews they could lay their hands on. But when referring to industrialized mass murder, he then uses the phrase 'definitive clearing out' (*endgultiges Raumen*) of the camp [. . .] and places apostrophes around the expression 'Delousing Van' as an instrument of the extermination" (40).[2]

The contradictions between the pronouncements and actions of fascists are a direct reflection of the deceptions that they need to perform in order to appeal to a mass audience. Fascism is inherently and inescapably inegalitarian. This inegalitarianism is marked in two major ways: first, fascism seeks to deny and, in its regime form, reverse the small progressive victories that have helped ameliorate the structural violence that capitalism heaps onto the working classes (see Celli 2013; Kitchen 1976; Renton 1999). This entails that fascist discourse must conceal the ways it encodes the economic interests of the minority in order to entrench the exploitation of the majority. Even the liberal historian Roger Griffin acknowledges that Marxist approaches to the analysis of fascism have demonstrated "empirically how any apparent victory of [. . .] fascism can only be won at the cost of systematically deceiving the popular masses about the true nature of its rule" (1998: 5). This leads on to the second way that fascism enshrines and enacts inegalitarian politics: "fascist movements use ideology deliberately to manipulate and divert the frustrations and anxieties of the mass following away from their objective source [. . . whether through] an emphasis on essentially irrational concepts such as authority, obedience, honour, duty, the fatherland or race [. . . or] emphasis on the hidden enemies who have sinister designs on society and who threaten the longed-for sense of community" (Kitchen 1976: 86).

Contemporary politics presents two perpetually recurring discursive strategies for fascist parties: dissociating themselves from fascism or rehabilitating it. Parties taking the second route necessarily consign themselves to a position outside of democratic politics, leading the party down a pseudo-revolutionary path, trying to secure power through violence and "street politics" (Richardson 2011, 2013; Rudling 2013). Fascist parties seeking power through the ballot have universally adopted the first political strategy – explicit verbal dissociation from fascism, both in terms of political and ideological continuities. In Britain, this approach was initially exemplified by Oswald Mosley and the Union Movement (UM), wherein fascist euphemistic common-places used by the British Union of Fascists before the war were recoded for the UM re-launch after the war (Macklin 2007; Renton 2000a). Similar 'rebranding' has since taken place across Europe, wherein parties with fascist political predecessors – including the Austrian FPÖ and BZÖ (Engel and Wodak 2013), the French FN (Beauzamy 2013), the German REP and NPD (Posch et al. 2013), the Portuguese CDS/PP and PNR (Marinho and Billig 2013), the Romanian 'New Right' (Madroane 2013) and several others – both *orientate towards,* and simultaneously *deny,* any continuity with arguments and policies of previous movements. The result is an intriguing, and often contradictory, mix of implicit indexing of fascist ideological commitments accompanied by explicit denials of these same commitments. A successful discourse analysis of contemporary fascism should therefore

> recognise the possibility that different levels of ideological sophistication might be contained within the same piece of propaganda. An ambiguous symbolism might embrace both the simplified grammar of gut feelings and the more complex grammar of an ideology. The social scientist, like the successful propagandist, must understand the rules of both grammars.
>
> *(Billig 1978: 91)*

The increased success of the far- and extreme-right, from 2001 onwards, brought a concomitant increase in academic analysis of the discourse they produce and disseminate. In addition to important studies of single parties (Castriota and Feldman 2014; Richardson and Colombo 2013; Tilles 2014) or national traditions in fascism (see Copsey and Richardson 2015; Wodak and Richardson 2013), this work has contributed to Critical Discourse Studies in three principal ways. First, fascist discourse is analytically extremely rich, allowing us to explore many of key concepts in CDA. Analysing fascism certainly requires us to engage with questions of power, ideology and political discourse; however intertextuality and inter-discursivity are equally important, especially for examining how ideas, arguments and attitudes are transposed over time (Richardson and Wodak 2009a). The 'cultural Marxism' conspiracy theory is a case in point. This theory was developed "by American thinkers, most of them white nationalists, to explain the rise of political correctness and anti-racist beliefs as well as the advent of multiculturalism" (Beirich 2013: 96). Accordingly, political correctness developed directly from the work of the Frankfurt School, who "set out to translate Marxism from economic to cultural terms with the aim to destroy traditional Western values" (Cox 1999: 20). The theory did not stay put in America, but was adopted (and adapted) by extremists across Europe: since 2004, the Austrian Freedom Party (FPÖ) has been publishing conspiratorial assessments of the Frankfurt School and the Cultural Revolution through its educational institute, the Bildungsakademie; the BNP adopted the phrase and explanation after their poor showing in the 2014 European Parliament Elections; and the mass murderer Anders Behring Breivik referred to and discussed "cultural Marxism" in excess of 200 times in his so-called manifesto (Richardson 2015).

Recent work on multimodality and the affordances of genre are similarly valuable in demonstrating the ways that images (Colombo and Richardson 2013; Richardson and Colombo 2014; Richardson and Wodak 2009b; Richardson 2011; Wodak and Forchtner 2014), party logos (Engström 2014; McGlashan 2013), colour (Richardson 2008), music (Machin and Richardson 2012; Shekhovtsov 2013; Spracklen 2015) and the internet (Engström 2014; Turner-Graham 2014) are utilised as part of fascist political projects. Engström's (2014: 11) perceptive analysis of online visuals used by the BNP discusses the ways that the Union Flag is used to communicate "complex ideological messages consisting of conceptual structures from distant domain matrices, thus suggesting conceptual relations that are not necessarily obvious to an outsider."

Second, and building on this point, at the linguistic level, fascist discourse is typically ambiguous and disguised, and directed towards a seemingly contradictory set of ideological commitments (Billig 1978; Feldman and Jackson 2014; Richardson 2011; Wodak and Richardson 2013). Fascist discourse is especially complex at the semantic-pragmatic interface, given the ways that fascists use vagueness, euphemism, linguistic codes and falsehood as part of manipulative discursive strategies (Engel and Wodak 2013; Engström 2014). Nick Griffin's appearance on the BBC's flagship current affairs programme *Question Time* (22 October 2009) has been given significant attention, particularly for the way he put across "his political message through implicit meanings" (Bull and Simon-Vandenbergen 2014: 1; see also Cranfield 2012). Goodman and Johnson (2014) also analyse this programme, plus two radio appearances, focusing on the ways that Griffin attempted to present the BNP as moderate and, actually, the victim of an ill-defined "political elite" (see also Johnson and Goodman 2013). Fascists, like other racist political parties, use a strategy of calculated ambivalence (Engel and Wodak 2013) in order to "allow for multiple readings and denial of intended discriminatory messages" (Wodak and Forchtner 2014: 249) – and they are getting better at doing this (Wodak 2015). Edwards's comparative analysis of BNP Election manifestos, from 2005 and 2010, shows how their discourse changed, "growing more sophisticated in its knowledge of techniques of disguising racial prejudice" (2012: 256).

Given that vague noun phrases used to mark out in-groups and out-groups typically "have to be inferred from the context" (Engström 2014: 11), this points – third – to the vitally important role of context in critical analysis (Beauzamy 2013; Richardson 2013). CDA is, properly, the critical analysis of text in context, and it is only through contextualisation we can demonstrate that, when fascists use similar arguments or terms of reference to those in mainstream political discourse – e.g., Britain, British, democracy – they do not *mean* the same thing (Edwards 2012; Richardson and Wodak 2009a). The best of the recent research on fascist discourse addresses its complex levels of signification, viewing the semantic-pragmatic content of fascist discourse as a social semiotic accomplishment, in which cultural, political and historic contexts prove particularly salient. In short: fascists frequently do not say what they mean, or mean what they say, and knowledge of the complex intertextual, interdiscursive, sociolegal and organisational histories of fascism are required in order to fully make sense of fascist discourse.

Case study: Griffin speech at the BNP "Indigenous Family Weekend"

This chapter will now turn to a brief examination of a speech that Nick Griffin, the then-leader of the British National Party, gave in 2010, at an event called the BNP "Indigenous Family Weekend" (31 August 2010). My discussion draws on the discursive strategies proposed in the Discourse-Historical Approach to CDA (see Reisigl, this volume). Griffin's speech was essentially structured in two parts of unequal size. In the longer first section, Griffin details the degeneration of Britain and specifically argues that this political and cultural degeneration has an "ethnic" dimension. As part of this, he identifies four social groups that he regards as the enemies of the BNP (see quote below for details). In the second part of the speech he discusses the ways that party members can meet these challenges, predominantly through a form of cultural and civic entryism rather than explicit 'above the line' political campaigning as the BNP. Here I will concentrate on the first part of the speech, towards the end of which, Griffin provides the following summary of his argument thus far, and of the four different groups that oppose the party:

> these four groups: the Marxists, who encompass literally everybody who tells you the lie that all human beings are equal [. . .] together with the freaks, who just hate normality and decency. Together with those who profit from the destruction of cultures and identities, and together with those who want, consciously or perhaps subconsciously, our land, our wealth, our women [pause] because history is sexist, believe me. Those four groups, intertwined, have created this enormously powerful body which is waging a total war on our culture, our civilisation and our identity. We know it. Politically, they're waging a war on our party.

Thematically, this extract fits almost exactly with Billig's (1978) constellation definition of fascism, indexing the nationalist, anti-Marxist, anti-international capitalism and anti-egalitarian politics of the BNP. The extract also demonstrates the continued importance of what Byford (2011: 32) refers to as "the conspiratorial tradition of explanation" in fascist political ideology, and the ways that conspiracy is positioned as the (often *single*) motivating force in history.

Consider, first, the nominal and predicational strategies invoked in the ways that the four 'enemy groups' are named and described:

Nominal	Predicate
the Marxists	who encompass literally everybody who tells you the lie that all human beings are equal
the freaks	who just hate normality and decency
those	who profit from the destruction of cultures and identities
those	who want, consciously or perhaps subconsciously, our land, our wealth, our women

The party's opposition to these various 'enemy groups' is not only stated explicitly, but also signalled by the way that they are named and characterised: Marxists lie, the freaks hate and the nameless – whose basic humanity is even implicitly backgrounded by the way the noun phrase lacks a head noun (those [people/individuals/groups/etc.]) – profit from destruction and covet what properly belongs to Us. The perspectivisation is illuminating here, since it presupposes a male-centred discourse of (white) men talking to other (white) men, about protecting *their* (white) women. The tricolon "our land, our wealth, our women" simultaneously claims women as a possession of the men (those in the audience; in the party; the white men in the country?), and constructs these (our) women as a resource or asset, in the same way as "our" land and money. Griffin attempts to inoculate himself from the obvious sexism of this construction, by identifying this as the perspective of "history". However, the pause, and the hurriedness of this after thought (muttered almost *sotto voce*), marks it as an apparent or show concession to the audience.

Of course, it is insufficient to simply quote from this speech and presume that the nominals Griffin used accord with their conventional meanings: does Griffin really mean 'followers of Marx' when he refers to "Marxists", for example? In fact, he does not. Earlier in the speech, he elucidates 'Marxist', making it clear that he simultaneously means something more general and yet more specific. "Marxism", he explains, is less about Marx and "is far more about how you view people":

> the fundamentals of Marxism, is [sic] that everyone is essentially equal. And it is only our environment which changes us. That is the fundamental of it. Once you understand that, you understand that, the Marxist attack on our culture, because our culture is a symbol of our special identity and if we have a special identity we can't be equalled.

Griffin's general objections to Marxism, in this iteration at least, are therefore twofold: first, the political principle "everyone is essentially equal" cuts against the inegalitarianism of Griffin's fascist political project; and second, there is Marxism's apparent "attack on our [national] culture". Griffin's reasoning here is a little convoluted, but it can be reconstructed as follows: 'Marxism' is committed to equality; however, our culture is singular/distinct; our culture is therefore special, it is exceptional; as such, our culture has no equivalent; the existence of our special/exceptional culture therefore disproves the Marxist belief in equality; because of this, the Marxists "always wanted to destroy this country and our ideals more than anything else". Three characteristics of fascist ideology – nationalism, anti-Marxism, inegalitarianism – therefore play off and mutually reinforce each other in this account. The speech reveals: the continued central role of 'national culture' in fascist identity; the belief in the superiority of our national culture and the attendant implication of the inferiority of others; 'Marxism' is bad because it is anti-national, and should be opposed because it attempts to debase our culture on the basis of some wrongheaded egalitarianism.

However, for Griffin, 'Marxism' also means something far more specific due to its significant role in the conspiracy that "is waging a total war on our culture". Within the National Socialist ideological tradition, the struggle against Marxism is synonymous with the struggle against 'The Jew' (Kershaw 2008: 52). There is a definite sense of similarly coded language in Griffin's speech, in particular where he describes Marx*ists,* as opposed to Marx*ism:*

> to be a Marxist in modern Britain, in the modern West, isn't a matter of wearing a hammer and sickle armband on your sleeve, or wanting the workers to have the same wages as everybody else. Certainly not with the Marxists who are involved in high politics and high finance, where they've got far, far higher wages than the workers and they do not want to change that relationship.

Who, we should ask, are "the Marxists who are involved in high politics and high finance"? The incongruity of the statement needs to be resolved by the listener if it is to make any sense. The rather straightforward (and well known) opposition of Marxists to high finance suggests that Griffin is using "the Marxists" in a way other than its conventional meaning – that is, in a coded way. The extensive pedigree in fascist discourse of a direct association between both Jews and Marxism and Jews and capitalism – "Jewish Bolshevism" in Hitler's speeches and *Mein Kampf* (Kershaw 2008), "Jewish-German-Bolshevism" in the Protocols and its reception in Britain in the 1920s (Byford 2011) or "Cultural Marxism" in contemporary discourse (Richardson 2015) – pushes one towards parsing "the Marxists" in this formulation to mean "the Jews". However, Griffin remains ambivalent on this point.

The second group of people opposing the BNP are referred to in the extract above as "the freaks", who "just hate normality and decency". From an earlier point in the speech:

> the sad freaks who turn out on demonstrations against us, with the people of our blood [. . .]. People who are corrupt and rotten inside hate decency. It's about jealously. And so much of the attack on our culture, and on ours, and on this party, and on good people, is actually coming from people who simply can't begin to match it. And because they can't match it they want to tear it down and destroy it.

The predicational strategy in the first sentence of this extract offers an implicit racialization of the "freaks": Griffin states that they go to "demonstrations against us, *with* the people of our blood". This particular noun phrase ("the people of our blood") is used to denote (other) white people – they share 'the same blood' as members of the BNP and so, *sui sanguinis,* the same race. Griffin's construction logically distinguishes the "freaks" from "the people of our blood", and so constructs them as non-white. These "freaks" "hate decency" and so, in turn, can only produce degenerate culture. Again, though not spelled out in detail, this position indexes a significant and well-established rhetorical thread in British fascist discourse, associating Jews with debased culture in general and the conscious and intentional debasement of British culture in particular. For example, writing in the newspaper of the National Labour Party, the future leader of the National Front and BNP John Tyndall (1959: 4) argued: "The Jew [. . .] has created no true art. All he has, has been copied from others. [. . .] it is beyond the capacity of the Jew to create what is beautiful to the natural tastes of the European [. . .] By his systematic attack on all European culture the Jew is polluting and destroying the European soul". Griffin's vituperative attack, therefore, whilst not seeming explicitly anti-Semitic is nevertheless readable in such a way – thereby implicitly (but deniably) indexing a far more aggressive strain of political sentiment than its surface meanings suggest.

The third group of national enemies Griffin identifies are capitalists – though it is interesting and significant to note the particular agenda of capitalists that he criticises earlier in the speech:

> hugely important in terms of the destruction of Britain, there are those who profit from it [. . .] capitalism doesn't look at a tree and think "what a beautiful thing", capitalism looks at the tree and thinks "how much can I get if I cut it up? How much can I get if I sell it and what can I do with the piece of land on which it stands to make even more profit?" And that is why, they are hell-bent, these people, on destroying the culture and identity, not just of us, but of every single people on the planet.

The capitalism depicted here is international; in the interest of maximising profit, it is directed towards destroying national particularism; international capitalism stands outside all nations as the enemy of them all. It is the threat that (international or anti-national) capitalism poses to national "culture and identity" which marks it as beyond the pale in this account, not the exploitation of workers. Indeed, British *people* are curiously absent from Griffin's representation of British *culture* – an arboreal idyll categorised by capitalism as little more than a resource for their profit (not ours). However, the extract above also contains an interesting and subtle shift in referential strategy: the extract starts with a personification ("those who profit"), changes to an abstract noun ("capitalism"), albeit one possessed with the power to think and to look ("capitalism looks at the tree and thinks"), and ends by shifting back to a personification ("they are hell-bent, these people"). These referential transferences intimately associate a destructive system with the wishes and interests of a particular group of people, and so they simultaneously imply a solution: If the problem with capitalism is "these people", then capitalism can be salvaged with their removal from power and influence. Griffin is, again, strategically vague concerning the identity of "these people".

In his expanded description of the fourth and final enemy grouping, Griffin gets more explicit again regarding the 'ethnic' status of the conflict:

> those who would demolish Britain and Britishness, and England and Englishness, also encompass those who want to do so quite simply because they are consciously or subconsciously part of a rival ethnicity, culture, religion. This produces all sorts of interest groups, whose interest is in doing us down. Because if we, the people of these islands, who came from these islands and built these islands, if we are firmly in control of our own destiny, then it limits the capacity of other people to use our resources, our wealth, our people, our territory, for their own ends.

Griffin studiously avoids both the word race and racial markers (white, Black, etc.); instead the terms of distinction are "ethnicity, culture [and] religion". However, Griffin goes on to state that by "we" he is referring to "the people of these islands, who came from these islands and built these islands". In so doing, he constructs an exclusive definition of 'the people' as not only those who originated here (i.e., were born in Britain), but also those with a long-standing filial bond with Britain going back through time. His use of "came from", rather than 'come from' implies a citizenship based on heritage – a heritage of parentage or lineage. The alternative formulation – 'people who come from these islands' – whilst not a civic definition of citizenship would nevertheless allow, for example, children of immigrants to claim British nationality by virtue of being born and raised in the UK. Therefore, (national) *culture* is *inherited* in Griffin's speech and so acts as a homologue for race; resources, wealth and land are presumed a birthright of the 'ethnic British'; 'non-British others' are a threat to and a drain on our resources; and so, in a radical act which at minimum entails welfare chauvinism but could include repatriation (and everything else in between), They – i.e., all those that the BNP considers to be "consciously *or subconsciously* part of a rival ethnicity, culture, religion" – should be denied access to "our resources, our wealth, our people, our territory".

Conclusion

The study and analysis of fascism are contested territories. One justification for using the generic term 'fascism' is that it enables appreciation and comparison of tendencies common to more than one country and more than one period in time – and also that it helps draw out the interconnections between these different periods in time. Any appropriate theory of fascism can only begin with the idea that fascism must be interpreted critically; however, a critical approach does entail recourse to polemic. Instead it means that we need to take a step beyond the immediate, and take into account detailed analysis of the social, political and cultural factors as well as the significance of ideas and arguments (Iordachi 2010); to look at what fascists do as well as what they say; and to closely examine the dialectical relations between context and the text/talk of (assumedly/potentially fascist) political protagonists.

In the speech partially analysed here, Nick Griffin describes an international conspiracy between four overlapping and interlocking groups, whose aim is to "demolish Britain and Britishness, and England and Englishness". The BNP, as "the party of the ethnic British", oppose this destructive aim, and it is for this reason that the party also finds itself a target in this "war". Whilst the ideational content of the speech is, in one sense, well mapped out – the psychological, political and economic reasons 'why they hate us' are spoken about in detail – in another sense the speech remains extremely vague. Nominals like "the Marxists", "capitalists", "the freaks" and "non-British interest groups" are never tied to real world referents; the frequent use of anaphoric pronouns (they, those, these people, etc.) give a sense of firmness and assurance via repetition, but the noun phrases they refer back to are floating signifiers. These ambiguities are, of course, intentional – they are part of a *strategy of calculated ambivalence* (Engel and Wodak 2013) which allows Griffin, like all fascists, to speak on two simultaneous levels of meaning. At the denotative level, he presents the politics of the party as nationalist and enshrining the interests of "the ethnic British"; at the connotative level, he insinuates an elaborate anti-Semitic conspiracy theory. A conspiracy between (Jewish) Marxists and (Jewish) international capitalism is a standard feature of British fascist ideology and would be recognisable to a sizable portion of the BNP activists in the audience.[3] Similarly, cultural degeneracy and using multiculturalism to weaken 'the white race' are tropes strongly associated with Jews in fascist discourse. As Copsey (2007: 74) argues, for British fascists, "it has long been axiomatic that multiculturalism is a Jewish conspiracy". In this speech, Griffin treads a finely calculated line between *revealing* and *not revealing* such conspiracies, and the (Jewish) identities of the conspirators in particular.

Notes

1 Some of the authors cited below would not regard their work as CDA; however, I do think that they fit within the broader and more inclusive CDS.
2 At this stage in the war, civilians were being murdered on an almost unimaginable scale, by Einsatzgruppen and Einsatzkommandos, in countries to the East of occupied Poland. Over two days, 29–30 September 1941, Sonderkommando 4a murdered 33,771 Jews in Babi Yar ravine near Kiev, for example. The scale of murder – of men, women and children – was reported to exert "considerable psychological pressures" on some men, to the extent that some "were no longer capable of conducting executions and who thus had to be replaced by other men" (Gustave Fix, member of Sonderkommando 6, quoted in Klee, Dressen and Riess 1991: 60). Gassing Jewish civilians was offered as an alternative; vans were initially developed with an airtight compartment for victims, into which exhaust gas was piped while the engine was running. Wilhelm Findeisen (Einsatzgruppen C) explains how they operated: "The van was loaded at headquarters. About forty people were loaded in, men, women and children. I then had to tell the people they were being taken away for work detail. Some steps were put against the van and the people were pushed in. Then the door was bolted and the tube connected [. . .] I drove through town and then out to the anti-tank ditches where the vehicle was opened. This was done by prisoners. The bodies were then thrown into the anti-tank ditches" (quoted in Klee, Dressen and Riess 1991: 72). In December 1941, the Gas-Van Inspector August Becker was informed that "gas-van with drivers were already on their way to or had indeed reached the individual Einsatzgruppen" in the East (quoted in Klee, Dressen and Riess 1991: 69). The euphemism "delousing vans" draws on a typical Nazi biological metaphor, which characterises Jews as an infestation.
3 See YouGov (2009) 'European Elections', Fieldwork dates 29 May – 4 June 2009, available at www. channel4.com/news/media/2009/06/day08/yougovpoll_080609.pdf, Accessed August 19, 2014.

John E. Richardson

Further reading

Billig, M. (1978). *Fascists: A social psychological view of the National Front*. London: Harcourt Brace Jovanovitch.
The first monograph to take a discourse analytic approach to fascism. Billig skilfully dissects the surface and core of fascist ideology, showing the ways that contemporary fascism simultaneously conceals and signals its continued commitment to political extremism.
Feldman, D. and Jackson, P. (eds.) (2014). *Doublespeak: The rhetoric of the far right since 1945*. Stuttgart: ibidem-Verlag.
Though not completely discourse analytic, the chapters in this edited volume provide very useful critical examinations of the rhetoric of the extreme right in Europe and America.
Klemperer, V. (2013 [1947]). *The language of the Third Reich: LTI. Lingua Tertii Imperii*. London: Bloomsbury Academic.
Klemperer sampled, categorized and described the words used during the Nazi regime in order to present an indisputable case that the language of the Third Reich helped to create its culture.
Machin, D. and Richardson, J. E. (2012). Discourses of unity and purpose in the sounds of fascist music: A multimodal approach. *Critical Discourse Studies* 9(4): 329–346.
Fascists produce, circulate and recontextualise cultural texts. Taking a critical multimodal approach, Machin and Richardson analyse two related fascist songs and examine the ways that sound communicates political meaning.
Wodak, R. and Richardson. J. E. (eds.) (2013). *Analysing fascist discourse: European fascism in talk and text*. New York: Routledge.
This edited book focuses on continuities and discontinuities of fascist politics as manifested in discourses of post-war European countries. This collection shows that an interdisciplinary critical approach to fascist text and talk – subsuming all instances of meaning-making (oral, visual, written, sounds, etc.) – is necessary to deconstruct exclusionary meanings and to confront their inegalitarian political projects.

References

Beauzamy, B. (2013). Continuities of fascist discourses, discontinuities of extreme-right political actors? Overt and covert antisemitism in the contemporary French radical right. In R. Wodak and J.E. Richardson (eds.), *Analysing Fascist Discourse: European Fascism in Talk and Text,* 163–180. New York/London: Routledge.
Beirich, H. (2013). Hate across the waters: The role of American extremists in fostering an international white consciousness. In R. Wodak, B. Mral and M. KhosraviNik (eds.) *Right-wing populism in Europe: Politics and discourse,* 89–102. London: Bloomsbury Academic.
Billig, M. (1978). *Fascists: A social psychological view of the national front*. London: Harcourt Brace Jovanovitch.
Billig, M. (1988a). The notion of 'prejudice': Some rhetorical and ideological aspects. *Text* 8(1–2): 91–110.
Billig, M. (1988b). Rhetoric of the conspiracy theory: Arguments in national front propaganda. *Patterns of Prejudice* 22(2): 23–34.
Billig, M. (1990). Psychological aspects of fascism. *Patterns of Prejudice* 24(1): 19–31.
Bull, P. and Simon-Vandenbergen, A.-M. (2014). Equivocation and doublespeak in far right-wing discourse: an analysis of Nick Griffin's performance on BBC's Question Time. *Text & Talk* 34(1): 1–22.
Byford, J. (2011). *Conspiracy theories: A critical introduction*. Houndmills: Palgrave.
Castriota, A. and Feldman, D. (2014). 'Fascism for the third millennium': An overview of language and ideology in Italy's CasaPound movement. In Feldman and Jackson (eds.), *Doublespeak: The rhetoric of the far right since 1945,* 223–246. Stuttgart: ibidem-Verlag.
Celli, C. (2013). *Economic fascism: Primary sources on Mussolini's crony capitalism*. Edinburg, VA: Axios Press.
Cohn, N. (1967). *Warrant for Genocide: The myth of the Jewish world conspiracy and the Protocols of the Elders of Zion*. Chatto Heinemann: London.
Colombo, M. and Richardson, J. E. (2013). Continuity and change in populist anti-immigrant discourse in Italy: An analysis of Lega leaflets. *Journal of Language and Politics* 12(2): 180–202.
Copsey, N. (2007). Changing course or changing clothes? Reflections on the ideological evolution of the British National Party 1999–2006. *Patterns of Prejudice* 41(1): 61–82.
Copsey, N. (2008). *Contemporary British fascism: The British national party and the quest for legitimacy,* 2nd edn. Basingstoke: Palgrave-Macmillan.

Copsey, N. and Richardson, J. E. (eds.) (2015). *Cultures of post-war British fascism*. London: Routledge.

Cox, J. (1999). Cultural Communism at its roots. *Spotlight,* July 5, 1999.

Cranfield, J.L. (2012). Cultures of Aversion. *Wasafiri,* 27(4): 19–26.

De Grand, A. (2006). Griffin's new consensus: A bit too minimal? In R. Griffin, W. Loh and A. Umland (eds.), *Fascism past and present, east and west: An international debate on concepts and cases in the comparative study of the extreme right,* 94–98. Stuttgart: ibidem-Verlag.

Edwards, G. O. (2012). A comparative discourse analysis of the construction of 'in-groups' in the 2005 and 2010 manifestos of the British National Party. *Discourse & Society* 23(3): 245–258.

Engel, J. and Wodak, R. (2013). Calculated ambivalence and Holocaust denial in Austria. In R. Wodak and J.E. Richardson (eds.), *Analysing fascist discourse: European fascism in talk and text,* 73–96. New York: Routledge.

Engström, R. (2014). The online visual group formation of the far right: A cognitive-historical case study of the British national party. *Journal of Public Semiotics* 6(1): 1–21.

Feldman, D. and Jackson, P. (eds.) (2014). *Doublespeak: The rhetoric of the far right since 1945.* Stuttgart: ibidem-Verlag.

Goodman, S. and Johnson, A.J. (2013). Strategies used by the far right to counter accusations of racism. *Critical Approaches to Discourse Analysis across Disciplines,* 6(2): 97–113.

Griffin, R. (1993a). *The nature of fascism*. London: Routledge.

Griffin, R. (1993b [1998]). Fascism. In R. Griffin (ed.), *International fascism: Theories, causes and the new consensus,* 35–39. London: Arnold.

Griffin, R. (ed.) (1998). *International fascism: Theories, causes and the new consensus*. London: Arnold.

Griffin, R. (2006). Response: Da capo, con meno brio: Towards a more useful conceptualization of generic fascism. In R. Griffin, W. Loh and A. Umland (eds.), *Fascism past and present, east and west: An international debate on concepts and cases in the comparative study of the extreme right,* 243–283. Stuttgart: ibidem-Verlag.

Griffin, R. (2014). 'Lingua Quarti Imperii': The euphemistic tradition of the extreme right. In Feldman and Jackson (eds.), *Doublespeak: The rhetoric of the far right since 1945,* 39–60. Stuttgart: ibidem-Verlag.

Herf, J. (2006). *The Jewish enemy: Nazi propaganda during World War II and the Holocaust*. Cambridge, London: The Belknap Press of Harvard University Press.

Iordachi, C. (ed.) (2010). *Comparative fascist studies: New perspectives*. London/New York: Routledge.

Johnson, A. and Goodman, S. (2013). Reversing racism and the elite conspiracy: Strategies used by British national party leader in response to hostile media. *Discourse, Context & Media,* 2: 156–164.

Kallis, A. (2009). *Genocide and fascism: The eliminationist drive in fascist Europe*. London, New York: Routledge.

Kershaw, I. (2008). *Hitler, the Germans and the final solution*. New Haven, CT, London: Yale University Press.

Kitchen, M. (1976). *Fascism*. London: Macmillan.

Klee, E., Dressen, W. and Riess, V. (1991). *'Those were the days' the Holocaust as seen by the perpetrators and bystanders*. London: Hamish Hamilton.

Klemperer, V. (2013 [1957]). *The language of the Third Reich: LTI: Lingua Tertii Imperii*. London: Bloomsbury Academic.

Lipset, S. M. (1960). *Political man*. London: Heinemann.

Machin, D. and Richardson, J. E. (2012). Discourses of unity and purpose in the sounds of fascist music: A multimodal approach. *Critical Discourse Studies* 9(4): 329–346.

Macklin, G. (2007). *Very deeply dyed in black: Sir Oswald Mosley and the resurrection of British fascism after 1945*. London: I.B. Tauris.

Madroane, I. D. (2013). New times, old ideologies? Recontextualizations of radical right thought in postcommunist Romania. In Wodak and Richardson (eds.), *Analysing fascist discourse: European fascism in talk and text,* 256–276. New York: Routledge.

Mann, M. (2004). *Fascists*. Cambridge: Cambridge University Press.

Marinho, C. and Billig, M. (2013). The CDS-PP and the Portuguese parliament's annual celebration of the 1974 revolution: Ambivalence and avoidance in the construction of the fascist past. In Wodak and Richardson (eds.), *Analysing fascist discourse: European fascism in talk and text,* 146–162. New York: Routledge.

McGlashan, M. (2013). The branding of European nationalism: perpetuation and novelty in racist symbolism. In R. Wodak and J.E. Richardson (eds.), *Analysing fascist discourse: European fascism in talk and text,* 297–314. New York/London: Routledge.

Milza, P. and Bernstein, S. (1992). *Dictionnaire historique des fascismes et du nazisme*. Brussels: Editions Complexe.

Mosley, O. (n.d.) *European socialism* [self published].

Nolte, E. (1968). *Die Krise des liberalen Systems und die faschistischen Bewegungen*. Munich: R. Piper.

Paxton, R. O. (2005). *The anatomy of fascism*. London: Penguin.

Payne, S. G. (1995). *A history of fascism, 1914–1945*. London: Routledge.

Posch, C., Stopfner, M. and Kienpointner, M. (2013). German postwar discourse of the extreme and populist right, in R. Wodak, J.E. Richardson (eds.), *Analysing Fascist Discourse: European Fascism in Talk and Text*, 97–121. New York, London: Routledge.

Renton, D. (1999). *Fascism: Theory and practice*. London: Pluto Press.

Renton, D. (2000a). *Fascism, anti-fascism and britain in the 1940s*. Houndmills: Palgrave.

Renton, D. (2000b). Was fascism an ideology? British fascism reconsidered. *Race & Class* 41(3): 72–84.

Richardson, J. E. (2008). 'Our England': Discourses of 'race' and class in party election leaflets. *Social Semiotics* 18(3): 321–336.

Richardson, J. E. (2011). Race and racial difference: The surface and depth of BNP ideology. In N. Copsey and G. Macklin (eds.), *British national party: Contemporary perspectives*, 38–61. London: Routledge.

Richardson, J. E. (2013). Racial populism in British fascist discourse: The case of COMBAT and the British National Party (1960–1967). In Wodak and Richardson (eds.), *Analysing fascist discourse: European fascism in talk and text*, 181–202. New York: Routledge.

Richardson, J. E. (2015). Cultural-Marxism and the British National Party: A transnational discourse. In Copsey and Richardson (eds.), *Cultures of post-war British fascism*, 202–226. London: Routledge.

Richardson, J. E. (2017). *British fascism: A discourse historical analysis*. Stuttgart: ibidem Verlag.

Richardson, J. E. and Colombo, M. (2014). Race and immigration in far- and extreme-right European political leaflets. In C. Hart and P. Cap (eds.), *Contemporary Critical Discourse Studies*, 521–542. London: Bloomsbury Academic.

Richardson, J. E. and Wodak, R. (2009a). Recontextualising fascist ideologies of the past: Right-wing discourses on employment and nativism in Austria and the United Kingdom. *Critical Discourse Studies* 6(4): 251–267.

Richardson, J. E. and Wodak, R. (2009b). The impact of visual racism: Visual arguments in political leaflets of Austrian and British far-right parties. *Controversia* 6(2): 45–77.

Rudling, P. A. (2013). The return of the Ukranian far right: The case of VO Svoboda. In Wodak and Richardson (eds.), *Analysing fascist discourse: European fascism in talk and text*, 228–255. New York: Routledge.

Schmitz-Berning, C. (2000). *Vokabular des nationalsozialismus*. Berlin: Walter de Gruyter.

Shekhovtsov, A. (2013). European far-right music and its enemies. In R. Wodak and J.E. Richardson (eds.), *Analysing Fascist Discourse: European fascism in talk and text*, 277–296. New York/London: Routledge.

Skidelsky, R. (1981). *Oswald Mosley*. London: Macmillan.

Sparks, C. (1974). Fascism in Britain. *IS* 71: 13–28.

Spracklen, K. (2015). Nazi punks folk off: leisure, nationalism, cultural identity and the consumption of metal and folk music. In N. Copsey and J.E. Richardson (eds.), *Cultures of Post-War British Fascism*, 161–176. Oxon: Routledge.

Stackelberg, R. and Winkle, S. A. (eds.) (2002). *The Nazi Germany sourcebook: An anthology of texts*. London: Routledge.

Sternberger, David, Gerhard Storz and W. E. Süßkind. (1957). *Aus dem Worterbuch des Unmenschen*. Hamburg: Claassen.

Sternhell, Z. (1986). *Neither right nor left: Fascist ideology in France*. Berkeley: University of California Press.

Taylor, S. (1979). The National Front: Anatomy of a political movement. In R. Miles and A. Phizacklea (eds.), *Racism and political action*, 125–146. London: Routledge & Kegan Paul.

Tyndall, J. (1959). The Jew in art. *COMBAT* 3 April–June.

Tilles, D. (2014). *British fascist antisemitism and Jewish responses, 1932–1940*. London: Bloomsbury Academic.

Turner-Graham, E. (2014). "Breivik is my Hero": The dystopian world of extreme right youth on the Internet. *Australian Journal of Politics and History* 60(3): 416–430.

Weiss, J. (1967). *The fascist tradition: Radical right-wing extremism in modern Europe*. New York: Harper & Row.

Wodak, R. (2011). *The discourse of politics in action: politics as usual* (2nd edn.). Basingstoke: Palgrave Macmillan.

Wodak, R. (2015). *The politics of fear.* London: Sage.

Wodak, R. and Forchtner, B. (2014). Embattled Vienna 1683/2010: right-wing populism, collective memory and the fictionalisation of politics. *Visual Communication,* 13(2): 231–255.

Wodak, R. and Richardson, J. E. (eds.) (2013). *Analysing fascist discourse: European fascism in talk and text.* New York/London: Routledge.

Woodley, D. (2010). *Fascism and political theory: Critical perspectives on fascist ideology.* Oxon: Routledge.

Part V
Domains and media

Critical discourse analysis and educational discourses

Rebecca Rogers

Introduction

Critical Discourse Analysis is flourishing in educational research. Most remarkable is the accelerated publication rate of CDA-inspired educational research. Indeed, 46 articles were published between 1983 and 2003 (Rogers et al. 2005) versus 257 in the last eight years alone (Rogers and Schaenen 2014). This marks a six-fold increase in half the time. The popularity of the framework is also evidenced by conferences, well-attended pre-conference institutes at the American Educational Research Association, books, a wide range of publications in books and educational research using CDA published in 140 different journals around the world. CDA research in education is presented at the international conference *Critical Approaches to Discourse Analysis across the Disciplines* alongside of scholarship from political science, sociology and legal studies.

Indeed, educational researchers from Africa (e.g., Glaser and van Pletzen 2012), Asia (McCormick 2012), Australia (e.g., Kettle 2011), Europe (Martín Rojo 2010), Latin America (e.g., Costa and Saraiva 2012), the Middle East (e.g., Sheyholislami 2010), North America (e.g., Huckin Andrus and Clary-Lemon 2012) and the UK (e.g., Rocha-Schmid 2010) are turning to CDA to describe, interpret and explain the relationships between educational practices, institutional structures and societal narratives. Researchers are studying formal and informal classroom interactions, educational policies, textbooks and children's literature, and the representation of education in the media. Frequently referenced CDA frameworks are those associated with Gee (2005 [1999]), Fairclough (1992, 1995, 2003), Chouliaraki and Fairclough (1999), Luke (1995, 2002) and van Dijk (1993).

In this chapter, I draw on a literature review to point to the enormous amount of CDA research being conducted by education scholars (Rogers et al. 2005; Rogers and Schaenen 2014; Rogers et al. 2016). I show how the majority of CDA work in education in the past decade has focused on the bottom-up forces of teachers and learners across educational sites making room for transformational practices rather than on top-down forces associated with oppression and injustice. I share a schema toward inquiry orientation my colleagues and I developed to assess the reconstructive-deconstructive component of the research design and provide exemplar studies to represent variation in approaches across socio-political areas within educational research. Many of the studies discussed in this section foreshadow my focus on race, racism and anti-racism in educational practice, the subject of the case study to follow. Next, I provide an example of my own reconstructively oriented, school-embedded approach to CDA focused on racial justice. This case invites readers to consider how my analysis of an inter-racial alliance between teacher education students contributes to a broadened view of CDA, one in which critique is constructive and power is generative. The discussion reflects on the development of a sub-field of CDA that has been referred to as having a reconstructive orientation or Positive Discourse Analysis (Bartlett 2012; MacGilchrist 2007; Martin 2004; Rogers and Mosley 2013).

Deconstructive-reconstructive orientation toward CDA inquiry

Scholars of CDA have concerned themselves, by and large, with a critique of domination and oppression rather than the construction of liberation and freedom (Martin 2004). Understanding the ways in which more just social relations can be constructed through discourse is vitally important (Janks 1997; Kress 2003; Luke 2004; Martin 2004). Foucault (1980: 119) pointed out that power is everywhere and is neither inherently good nor bad. He believed that power "traverses and produces things, it induces pleasure, forms knowledge, produces discourse. It needs to be considered as a productive network which runs through the whole social body". Fairclough (1995) also understood power as operating *behind, through* and *within* discourses. Yet a large body of scholarship associated with the founding members of CDA focused on deconstructing how power was wielded over people (e.g., media, politics, neoliberal governments). Van Dijk's (2005: 352) conception of CDA is often cited as the foundational understanding of CDA. He defined CDA as a perspective that "primarily studies the way social power, abuse, dominance, and inequality are enacted, reproduced, and resisted by texts and talk in social and political context. With such dissident research, critical discourse analysts take explicit positions, and thus want to understand, expose, and ultimately resist social inequality".

Luke (1995: 12) emphasized the potential of CDA to operate both deconstructively and constructively. In their deconstructive turn, analysts illustrate how "systematic asymmetries of power and resources between speakers and listeners and between readers and writers can be linked to the production and reproduction of stratified political and economic interests". In its constructive turn, CDA sets out to "generate agency among students, teachers and others by giving them the tools to see how texts position them and generate the very relations of institutional power at work in classrooms, staff rooms and policy" (12–13). Similarly, Bloome and Talwalker (1997: 111) criticized the top-down understandings of power that predominated much of the early CDA work. They challenged analysts to broaden the conception of power without "diminishing a research and practice agenda that addresses inequitable power relations and the pain and suffering they cause".

By 2004, a number of scholars from around the globe were visibly calling for a reconstructive agenda. Martin (2004: 183) referred to this approach as "positive discourse analysis" which can provide a focus on "how people get together and make room for themselves in the world – in ways that redistribute power without necessarily struggling against it". The term positive discourse analysis (PDA) was used to signal a shift in analytic focus to the study of constructive forces. Bartlett (2012: 215; also this volume) wrote that PDA might be viewed as "a critical approach to discourse analysis that focuses on solutions rather than problems but which, rather than celebrating resistance *as resistance,* demonstrates how competing discourses can be effectively combined" (emphasis original). It is with this dialectic of the push-pull nature of power in mind to which I turn to examples from the field of educational research.

Reviewing CDA in educational research

Colleagues and I conducted a review of CDA in educational research from 2004–2012 to study patterns in the field over time (Rogers et al. 2016). We were following up on an earlier review, which taken together, synthesize almost 30 years of CDA research in education (Rogers et al. 2005). We searched five electronic databases from the years 2004–2012: ERIC (EBSCO), ArticleFirst (OCLC), PsycINFO (American Psychological Association), MLA International Bibliography (Modern Language Association) and Web of Science (Thompson Reuters). We searched each database separately so we would have a clear record of search results. Our search terms were "critical discourse analysis" and "education." We searched for peer-reviewed articles and identified 257 articles across all educational disciplines.

We entered information about each article into a spreadsheet for ease of access and counting. Next, we analyzed patterns in the scholarship including type of article, rate and location of publication, topics studied, educational levels and contexts, definitions of critical discourse analysis, depth of detail in analytic procedures and frequently cited scholars. We identified the range and frequency of socio-political topics in the field. We generated nine distinct socio-political areas of emphasis that captured educational researchers' attention: cultural and linguistic diversity (students' identities; cultural and linguistic diversity); teachers' identities; standards; race; sexuality/gender; disability; democracy; and cultural and linguistic diversity (global or local ideologies).

In light of deliberations in the field over issues of deconstructive/reconstructive aspects of CDA, we developed a schema to analyze these aspects of each study (Rogers and Schaenen 2014). The schema categorized how researchers attended to deconstructive-reconstructive orientation (highly reconstructive, a combination of structure and agency and deconstructive). We developed it based on the range of qualities we noticed in the data after reading a subset of the articles. We grouped each study into one of three categories (with a numerical value of 1, 2 or 3 assigned to each study) for each of the three qualities. This schema represented the author's critical orientation to the inquiry. Some researchers develop questions intentionally framed as "reconstructive"; other scholarship concentrates on discourses that sustain inequalities; still others mix and blend across these general tendencies. Thus we grouped studies according to the following criteria: If a researcher took up an oppressively written education policy to see how such a policy inscribed the harmful work happening by written mandate, that researcher was working in the 3-category, deconstructively oriented scholarship. If another analyst chose to engage with apparently liberational classroom talk that seemed to be empowering students, that analysis was likely to fall in the 1-category, reconstructive variety. There is always the possibility that the oppressive policy may, upon critical analysis, reveal some kind of unexpected opening for disruption; the apparently empowering classroom talk might, upon closer inspection, oppress in unexpected ways. We categorized these studies as 2s or referring to both structure and agency.

The interrelation of the schema and the spreadsheets allowed us to trace the correlations between and among qualities in our data. Creating this schema helped us see the various ways inquiry design decisions affect the epistemological and political qualities of the work. Due to the complexity of CDA and the interdisciplinary way in which it is enacted and studied, any review will be a cultural production.

Rebecca Rogers

Considering inquiry orientation in CDA research in education, 2004–2012

One of the striking findings was the tendency of educational researchers to take a reconstructive orientation in their CDA work. Indeed, 66 percent of the studies included some element of reconstruction or attention to discourses of learning or transformation. 34 percent of the 242 empirical studies ($N = 83$) focused their analysis on discourses that sustain inequalities, or took a deconstructive approach. These authors pull apart texts to show how inequity is reproduced. Authors of highly deconstructive studies were primarily working with written texts while those with a positive orientation tended to work with interactions.

Table 31.1 illustrates the trends in critical orientation of the inquiry, across socio-political foci. No socio-political area had more than 50% of studies with a deconstructive orientation. This shows the lean toward reconstructive that is apparent in educational research. We see that the socio-political areas that represented the highest levels of reconstructive activity (both 1s and 2s) were Cultural and Linguistic Diversity, Teachers' Identities (88%), Cultural and Linguistic Diversity, Students' Identities (76%) and Democracy (82%). The authors in these studies train their attention on the discursive contours of learning, transformation or emancipatory educational practices. Fifty-nine percent of the studies focused on race, racism and anti-racism were reconstructively oriented. Fifty percent of the studies in the socio-political area of gender and sexualities focused on discourses practices that sustained inequities, reflecting the highest amount of deconstructive framing across the socio-political areas.

Table 31.1 Socio-political area and orientation toward inquiry

Socio-Political Area	1s, Highly Reconstructive	2s, Structure and Agency	3s, Highly Deconstructive
Standards, Evaluation, Commercialization of Education, Neoliberalism (N = 62)	N = 0	N = 32	N = 30
Cultural/Linguistic Diversity & Teacher Identities (N = 42)	N = 3	N = 34	N = 5
Cultural/Linguistic Diversity & Student Identities (N = 38)	N = 1	N = 28	N = 9
Cultural/Linguistic Diversity & International, National, State, or Local Ideologies & Identities (N = 32)	N = 0	N = 18	N = 14
Race Racism/Anti-racism (N = 27)	N = 2	N = 14	N = 11
Democracy (N = 17)	N = 0	N = 14	N = 3
Disability (N = 12)	N = 0	N = 7	N = 5
Sexualities & Gender (N = 12)	N = 0	N = 6	N = 6
	Total = 6 (2. 5%)	Total = 153 (63.2%)	Total = 83 (34.3 %)

468

In the following sections, I offer examples of studies to illustrate the range of approaches to inquiry, including: highly reconstructive, attending to structure and agency and deconstructive. The studies chosen represent many of the socio-political foci shown in Table 31.1, and many emphasize race and identity, foreshadowing the case that follows.

Highly reconstructive

Studies with a reconstructive approach focused on learning, transformation or agency. Haddix (2010: 118) explicitly set out to study how Black and Latina preservice teachers exhibited agency through their linguistic hybridity. She drew on in-depth interviews and observations to understand the enactment of linguistic identities. Characteristic of highly reconstructive studies, she focused on how the teachers reconciled tensions in their teaching identities, not the tensions themselves. She chose two teachers who were meta-cognitively aware or exhibited "linguistic reflexivity" of differences across settings and also expressed tensions across these negotiations. Haddix's CDA framework drew on systemic functional linguistics and closely attended to language variety, identity and context. Her findings illustrate that the preservice teachers enact their own cultural identities most readily when they are in similar communities.

Young (2009: 2) examined a children's periodical created by W.E.B. Du Bois to provide positive and inspirational educational material for children and youth. Her approach to CDA merged insights from Foucault (1972), van Dijk (1993) and Huckin (1995) and examined the "counter-narratives or folk literacies that seek to educate within a cultural context". Her findings revealed how historical discourses of race, social class and politics were infused throughout the periodical in the words, images and layout of the text. She showed how counter-narratives within the text focus on the development of racial pride, authentic examples of African-American language, culture, and community, and the education of the whole person.

Studies finding both structure and agency

We identified 63% of the articles as illustrating both structure and agency in their CDA findings. This indicates that the authors deconstruct traditional power-knowledge binaries and recognize the tensions between structure and agency. The authors did not intentionally frame their article as a positive or reconstructive analysis but their use of critical social theory, data analysis and findings focus on learning, identity construction and social transformation. There were two clusters of studies within this category. The first represents those whose inquiry orientation leans more toward the bottom-up forces of agency, liberation and transformation. These studies focus primarily on what Martin (2004: 31) referred to as the power of "renovatory discourses". The second cluster of studies includes those that lean more toward a deconstructive inquiry orientation. Authors in this group attended to the top-down forces but also to how individuals create room for social change.

Martínez-Roldan (2005: 161) represents the first cluster of studies. She focused on a discussion of the book *Oliver Button is a Sissy* in a second grade, bilingual classroom and explored how "Latino/a children negotiate meanings around gender issues and gender identities within bilingual literature discussions". This focus on the negotiation of meanings and development of ideologies surrounding gender (or other socio-political issues) is at the heart of an approach that attends to both structure and agency. She merged Chicana feminist theory with Gee's (1999: 160) approach to CDA, emphasizing how language builds identities, relationships, politics and significance. Her findings showed that gendered ideologies are not static concepts but are constructed in moment-to-moment interactions. She represented the unfolding discussion and the way the children's initial comments demonstrated traditional gender polarization. However, as the conversation unfolded, they also crossed and resisted gender boundaries, as they developed an awareness of gender inequities. In this way, the children were "actively constructing gender".

Another cluster of studies was oriented more toward deconstruction, but the authors discovered that traditional power relations were not being entirely reproduced. Richardson's (2007: 791) research question identified both structure (stereotypical representations) and agency (negotiation). She asked, "How do young African American females negotiate stereotypical representations of African American culture, gender, labor and sexual values in rap music videos?". She engaged three African-American women in a "rap session" watching rap videos which lie at the intersection of black popular culture and mass media. New racism, Richardson argued, relies on global technologies to disseminate hegemonic identities. However, the African-American women in the "rap session" who examined music videos were not without agency. They recognized how they succumbed to racist stereotypes but also found language to empower themselves. About the women, Richardson wrote, they were "protesting sexist lyrics. . . [yet] still dance to some of the same songs" (799).

Strongly deconstructive

We identified approximately 34% of the articles as highly deconstructive. This research concentrates on the analysis of discourses that sustain inequalities and perpetuates inequities (e.g., neoliberalism, racism). The theorisation, analytic focus and findings all focus on the deconstruction of oppression and domination. The authors may suggest possibilities for disrupting oppressive practices but do so only in the conclusions or discussion.

Ayers (2005) studied the mission statements of 144 community colleges in the United States, searching for discursive traces of human capital theory and neoliberal ideology. His CDA was informed by SFL and Habermas's (1977) theory of dominance and ideology. The findings presented the linguistic realization and ideological effects of neoliberal discourses as represented in the mission statements. Ayers (2005: 545) wrote, "In effect, the representation of community college education through neoliberal discourse (a) subordinates workers/learners to employers, thereby constituting identities of servitude, and (b) displaces the community and faculty in planning educational programs, placing instead representatives of business and industry as the chief designers of curricula". In essence, the community college is a site for reproducing class inequalities that structure life in late capitalism. Like other studies with a deconstructive focus, Ayers demonstrated the discursive construction of domination.

Holyfield, Moltz and Bradley (2009: 518) examined focus group data from students at a predominantly white southern university in the United States to examine race talk and the construction of southern white identities. About CDA, the authors call on van Dijk (1993b) and argued that CDA can help to examine how the "interplay between knowledge and structure reveals how people make sense of race, how opinions and memory are biased, and how discourse reproduces domination and thus, white privilege". Findings revealed that whiteness remained largely an "unmarked" category as demonstrated via discursive strategies (downplaying and defensive diversions versus race competence).

A case study of reconstructively oriented, school-based CDA

In a yearlong teacher-research study, Melissa Mosley Wetzel and I examined our own teaching and our students' learning, using the theoretical and methodological tools of CDA (Rogers and Mosley Wetzel 2014). The elementary school was a neighborhood school, serving mainly African-American children. Our group of teacher-education students was mostly white, middle-upper class females (there were two white men and one African-American woman). Our teaching and research were framed by critical discourse studies (Rogers and Mosley Wetzel 2015). After obtaining informed consent, we collected and analyzed interviews, observations of classroom practice and written artifacts of learning. We pivoted between critical social theories related to neoliberalism, feminist pedagogy and critical race theory (CRT). My focus here is on an example of anti-racist pedagogy.

Institutionalized racism manifests itself through educational tracking, the school-to-prison-pipeline and racial profiling in the community. Racism operates at personal, institutional and societal levels and is upheld through the twin pillars of white privilege and internalized oppression. Thus, anti-racist efforts acknowledge the psychological, material and social realities of race for different groups of people. Throughout the course, we integrated readings, discussions, activities, mentor lesson plans and book club discussions on the topics of racism and anti-racism. Whereas critical race theory and whiteness studies examine racism within legal and institutional discourses (Bell 1992), racial literacy begins from the understanding that people discursively construct the racial worlds they inhabit, bringing them to life (Morrison 1992; Sealey-Ruiz 2011; Skerrett 2011).

For this particular analysis, I have focused my attention on a discussion amongst teacher education students that illustrated an inter-racial alliance. By inter-racial alliance, I mean people of color and white people working together for racial justice (Tochluk 2010). More specifically, I asked: what does the work of inter-racial allies look like and sound like? Guided by these questions, along with theoretical perspectives of CRT and a form of CDA that I have referred to as "positive discourse analysis" or "reconstructive discourse analysis". Procedurally, I drew on a tradition of CDA which relies on systemic functional linguistics (Bartlett 2012; Halliday 1978; Martin and Rose 2011) (see Bloor and Bloor, pages 133–147) to trace the interplay between the textual, ideational and interpersonal functions of language. My approach to CDA was rooted in an ethnographic tradition, which provided the context for me to attend to the accumulation and transformation of meanings and stances, across time and participants (Rogers 2011).

To model the practice of reading aloud to my teacher education students, I began class this day by reading aloud *Mr. Lincoln's Way* (Polacco 2001). This book features an inter-racial alliance between Mr. Lincoln, an African-American principal, and the grandfather of a young European-American boy referred to as "Mean Gene". In the book, Mean Gene exhibits racism at school toward his classmates. Together, the principal and grandfather intervene to help Gene think and act differently. The book portrays racism as an individual deviation rather than a structure of privilege and oppression, an issue I used to provoke discussion in class. When I finished the read aloud, I invited students' responses to the text.

Samantha asks: How do, you were saying about not, dismantling white privilege, how do you do that?

Rebecca: Great question. How do you not participate in white privilege? I'll throw that back to the group to talk about it for a minute.

Jonah, a white graduate student in class, has a history of working for social justice with regard to women's issues, worker's rights and anti-racism (Rogers, Mosley Wetzel and O'Daniels 2016). Jonah responded, talking to his group comprised of five other people.

Part of it,

I guess part of it is recognizing the habit.

part of it is that you,
by being white you are participating in it.
so, there are still ways to realize, as teachers,
we can find ways to alter, for instance,
how we teach history
so that we do not white wash history

Typical of his participation pattern in discussions of anti-racism, Jonah set a frame for the discussion by emphasizing the importance of white people recognizing their racial identity and the privilege that is inherently attached to it. His active and declarative statement "By being white you are participating in it" leaves little room for questioning the credibility of this position. Another part of his message was that white teachers can also act in ways that disrupt this privilege. This message was constructed through active/mental verbs ("recognize", "participate", "realize", "alter", "teach"). The effectiveness of this stance was achieved, in part, because he softened the epistemic privilege of his message in the first line "I guess". He also shifted the audience of his message from "you" to "we", perhaps in an effort to include himself in these efforts of anti-racism.

Tonya, the only African-American woman in class, also a graduate student, was in this group. Tonya was the first generation in her family to attend college. At the university, she double-majored in African-American studies and Education. She taught at an elementary school where she began a supplementary academic program for African-American students. She quickly expanded on Jonah's ideas and stated,

White privilege runs throughout society
and has to do with benefiting
from other people's misfortune. . . .
It also is rejecting white privilege. . .

Tonya built on Jonah's ideas about white privilege and provided examples that extended from the personal and the classroom to society. Using an imperative statement, she referenced the material impacts of white privilege on people of color, a point of view that Jonah had not addressed. Both Tonya and Jonah gave examples of how white people can intervene in systemic racism. They acted as inter-racial allies and educate their white colleagues through the messages they co-construct and the stances through which they communicate these messages.

The discussion continued for a few turns and Rex, another white man in the group, asked "What are all of the instances of white privilege? Where does it exist all of the places where white privilege exists?". Rex described growing up in a conservative family in a rural part of the state. He admitted having to unlearn stereotypes when he went away to college. He often took a colorblind approach in discussions, claiming it was better to not recognize racial differences. He was a member of Reserve Officers' Training Corps (ROTC) and planned on going into active military duty after college.

The transcript of this 13-second discussion can be found in Table 31.2. It represents the verbal transcript, a multimodal description of the interaction, an image that captures the modal density of the turn and a description of my analysis. I invite readers to read Table 31.2 alongside the analysis that follows.

If I were conducting the deconstructive variety of CDA, I might focus my analysis by pointing to the places where racism was being reproduced in this discussion. Certainly Tonya's efforts to explain white privilege to a group of white colleagues would be an example. Rex's

Table 31.2 Critical Discourse Analysis of inter-racial allies

Time	Image from Quicktime. From left to right: Melanie (white woman, back to the camera), Stephanie (white woman), Jonah (white male), Tonya (African-American woman), Rex (out of view, white male)	Verbal transcript	Multimodal description	CDA description
1:36		Rex: What are all of the instances of white privilege? Where does it exist all of the places where white privilege exists?	Leaning back in his chair. Hands folded in the air in front of him. Looks at Jonah and Tonya as he speaks.	**Textual:** Rapid succession of questions **Ideational:** Placing the burden of proof on others to identify white privilege **Interpersonal:** Defensive tone; passive stance
1:39		Jonah: Well, well, that's one of the big issues that you don't. . .	Jonah's hands outreached in a gesture that communicates sharing of knowledge. His gaze is on Rex. Tonya flips through her notebook and gaze is downward.	**Textual:** Immediacy of response **Ideational:** Acknowledges Rex's question about locating examples of white privilege **Interpersonal:** Challenges the assumption on which the question is built; beginning of direct confrontation
1:40		[Tonya: Let's deconstruct that, Rex.	Tonya has hand on hip, looks at Rex and is smiling. Jonah is in the process of reaching over to put his hand on her shoulder. Rex's gaze is on Tonya.	**Textual:** Overlapping talk with Jonah, poses a counter-question **Ideational:** Collective pronoun, invites a collaborative stance on deconstructing; topical silence: irony of a white man who holds privilege asking for examples of white privilege **Interpersonal:** Playful, direct

(Continued)

Table 31.2 (Continued)

Time	Verbal transcript	Multimodal description	CDA description
Image from Quicktime. From left to right: Melanie (white woman, back to the camera), Stephanie (white woman), Jonah (white male), Tonya (African-American woman), Rex (out of view, white male)			
1:40–1:49	Jonah: Tonya (laughter)	*Jonah reaches over and puts his hand on Tonya's shoulder while he is laughing. Tonya directs her attention from Rex to Jonah. Jonah is laughing. Samantha is laughing looking on. Tonya is smiling and her shoulders are facing Jonah and she is laughing.*	**Textual:** Overlapping talk, laughter **Ideational:** Saying Tonya's name; Recognizing Tonya's move to challenge Rex's lack of awareness **Interpersonal:** Empathy, negative judgment of Rex's request
	[Rex: Well do it. I'd like you to.	*Tone is confrontational, embarrassed. Gaze is straight at Tonya. Hands are raised by neck and folded.*	**Textual:** Micro-aggression, overlapping talk **Ideational:** Requests African-American woman to give examples of white privilege; ignores the examples previously given **Interpersonal:** Declarative statement, direct, confrontational, aggressive
	[Tonya: No, I think we should. I don't know either. I don't know either.	*Speaks to Jonah. . . Slight laughter in her voice. Jonah is chuckling and his head makes a beat gesture as Tonya talks.*	**Textual:** Overlapping talk, co-constructing humor with Jonah **Ideational:** Collective pronoun suggests joint activity of identifying white privilege **Interpersonal:** Uncertainty opens an invitation to others to co-construct examples
1:49	Jonah: I know, it's just. . .	*Jonah is laughing. His hand outstretched in air, leaning in, elbow over the table. Tonya's gaze is trained on her notebook.*	**Textual:** Co-constructing meaning with Tonya; trailing sentence **Ideational:** Acknowledges irony of an African-American woman explaining white privilege to a white man; incomplete thought **Interpersonal:** "Just" signals his negative judgment of the request which functions to build an alliance with Tonya.

micro-aggression is another example of hegemonic race relations. Jonah's laughter could be read as avoiding talk about racism. The placement of his hand on Tonya's shoulder might be interpreted as an attempt to silence her. When I shifted my lens to how the educators created space for the practices of anti-racism and the formation of inter-racial allies, I found another story to tell about this interaction.

The exchange was a sustained engagement with issues of race, racism and anti-racism which is often difficult for inter-racial groups to sustain (Tochluk 2010). Jonah and Tonya worked together as inter-racial allies to interrupt Rex's micro-aggression of asking others to name examples of white privilege and, at the same time, created a model for their white colleagues. Jonah positioned himself as an anti-racist ally with the immediacy of his response which both acknowledged and began to critique Rex's question. As Jonah spoke, his hands were outstretched, symbolizing an invitation to dialogue. Tonya interrupted Jonah with a more direct and confrontational statement, challenging Rex "let's deconstruct that, Rex". Her use of the collective pronoun invited a collaborative and collective stance toward engaging with anti-racism. Unspoken but signaled is the irony of a white man who benefits from white privilege asking for examples of its existence. She challenged Rex with a playful tone, perhaps hoping to engage Rex in a way that Jonah had not. Jonah, perhaps surprised by Tonya's direct questioning, put his hand on Tonya's shoulder, laughing and saying her name. This physical contact might be interpreted as a material reminder from Jonah to Tonya that she was not alone in the discussion. It might also be read as an artifact of sexist and racist discourses that attempt to silence "angry" African-American women.

Jonah's laughter was sustained for nine seconds, beneath this stretch of interactions. In this context, I argue that Jonah's laughter signaled his multiple locations in this discussion. On the one hand, his laughter negatively appraised the absurdity of Rex's request and signaled his solidarity with Tonya, a woman of color. It also functioned as a plea to Tonya that she did not need to respond (to which she responded "No, I think we should."). The laughter also may show his discomfort as a white man with privilege who identified as an anti-racist ally, confronting another white man.

Rex countered Tonya's confrontation with one of his own. "Well do it. I'd like to see you". This micro-aggression requested that Tonya, an African-American woman, deconstruct the way in which white privilege was embedded within his initial question.

Tonya, responding to both Jonah's laughter *and* Rex's request stated, "No, I think we should. I don't know either. I don't know either". Her use of the collective pronoun and admitted uncertainty invited inter-racial work. Jonah agreed but his trailing thought "just" signaled his continued negative judgment of Rex's request that Tonya identify examples of white privilege.

Indeed, there were imperfections in Jonah's efforts. He never directly confronted Rex, another white male. Instead, Tonya continued to explain white privilege to Rex. But what is also important to point out is that Tonya and Jonah created a lexical chain and stance that leaned toward the arc of anti-racism through the practice of an inter-racial alliance.

As a critical teacher educator who uses CDA to inform my practice, I am interested in how my students navigate the values, perspectives and resources associated with anti-racism. Anti-racism is both an individual and collective project; thus my analysis attempts to make sense out of how "ways of interacting", "ways of representing" and "ways of being" interact overtime as individual efforts and collective resources. As we saw, inter-racial allies are practiced through the moment-to-moment construal of ideas and stances and can be cultivated across time and context. If I want to foster discourses of anti-racism, I need to know more about the contexts in which they can emerge, how they are sustained and how awareness leads to action.

Discussion

In this chapter I have provided a snapshot of the intellectual life of CDA from the field of education. My focus has been on educational researchers' stance toward inquiry orientation, on a trajectory from deconstructive to reconstructive analysis. In the past 20 years alone, 242 articles have been published that use CDA to study education practices, policies and contexts. Of these, 66% are what I have referred to as reconstructively oriented, attending to learning, transformation and identity work. I would argue this surge of reconstructively oriented CDA scholarship of educational researchers invites the field of Critical Discourse Studies to attend more closely to the creative and diverse ways in which we engage with "critique", "discourse" and "analysis." Indeed, fields of study are shaped by the accumulation of scholarship over time. A similar archeology of scholarship in other fields might help make visible the boundaries of analysis and new conceptual possibilities.

While I have paid special attention to the reconstructive orientation, I do not want to suggest that there are better or worse approaches to CDA. Rather, these are different points in an analytic trajectory (depending on the time and point of gaze) and commitments to social theory. I propose we imagine this reconstructive-deconstructive orientation as a pivot point, allowing us to dissect discourses we like and situate these practices within a larger narrative of practice. Ultimately, what may be most important is researchers' awareness that their choice in inquiry orientation matters and there are distinctions amongst approaches. Where we rest our attention as a field may have consequences on the practices that might emerge.

CDA has been criticized for its written language bias and an over-emphasis on the artifact/text and an under-analysis on the historical and social conditions which give rise to the texts. These are questions related to discourses and also to analysis. Often, marginalized groups are using discourses in subversive and creative ways that require multimodal analysis. The approach I demonstrated in this chapter integrated multimodal analysis into the SFL framework. I analyzed how Jonah's laughter, for example, functioned to bolster the inter-racial alliance underway between he and Tonya. Also with regard to context, my analysis attended to the accumulation of meanings and stances, across time and participants. I argued that as people build their capacity to engage in inter-racial alliances they may become more consistent in working as an ally at personal, institutional and societal levels. We need to know more about the trajectory of practices leading up to moments of transformation (Blommaert 2005; Rogers and Labadie 2015). Likewise, deeper theorisation is in order of the dialectic of power, the reach of discourses and the variety of ways in which analytic frameworks can be used.

At this point a cautionary note may be necessary. With this swell of reconstructively oriented scholarship, there is the very real fear that conditions of structural inequity may be under-analyzed and under-theorised. As institutions of higher education are infiltrated with corporate led educational reform, it will be important for researchers to describe the hybridity of power across actors, institutions and networks. Educational researchers are learning to inquire with CDA into how meanings are made across educational sites in an increasingly digital world. There is a great deal of potential in studying how socio-political areas intersect – critical race theory and neoliberalism, for example. As global technologies continue to impact the face of public education from testing and publishing companies to interactions that occur in online learning spaces, CDA is amply prepared to handle the complex interplay between and among media, message, identity, learning and action in the social world. The tendency to deconstruct practices to show the stronghold of oppression will remain persistent over time. Whether analyses are conceived deconstructively or reconstructively, people who do CDA are predisposed to think about structure and agency (change-making, liberation, becoming, agency-improving through language practices).

In conclusion I would argue we need more and better examples of educators creating alternative, liberatory, renovatory discourses embedded within longitudinal studies that trace the dynamic nature of power and the materialist effects of transformative discourse practices. However, as this surge of reconstructive scholarship grows so, too, might distinctions across approaches that warrant further examination of whether a new variety of CDA has emerged.

Further reading

De Lissovoy, N. (2015). *Education and emancipation in the neoliberal era: Being, teaching, and power.* New York: Palgrave Macmillan.

De Lissovoy presents a critical analysis of the discursive and material processes that create racialized repression within schools in a neoliberal political economy. He moves on to argue that youth movements represent a knowledge project that fuse politics, theory and culture. He sets forward a theory of emancipation that foregrounds students' agency.

Hannah-Jones, N. (2015, July 31). *The problem we all live with* [Audio Podcast]. www.thisamericanlife.org/radio-archives/episode/562/the-problem-we-all-live-with

In this report, *New York Times Magazine* Reporter Nikole Hannah-Jones investigates how a little known state law in Missouri led to school integration across racial lines. Drawing on interviews with dozens of parents, teachers, administrators and community members, she thoughtfully integrates these narratives alongside a critical analysis of the history and political context of one of the most segregated cities in the United States. She re-centers attention not on the problem of the academic achievement gap between African Americans and white students but on the solution that educational reformers and parents know works but is rarely discussed: racial integration of public schools.

Mattheis, A. (2016). Political contestation and discourses of meaning: Revising Minnesota's school integration revenue statute. *Education Policy Analysis Archives* 24(107). http://dx.doi.org/10.14507/epaa.24.2314

The majority of school desegregation programs put into place in school districts were dismantled by the 1990s. Many states, including Minnesota, the case study state in this article, have budgets allocated specifically for desegregation. The author documents the convening, decision-making and ultimate recommendations of a legislatively mandated Integration Revenue Replacement Advisory Task Force in the state of Minnesota. Using Fairclough and Fairclough's (2012) political discourse analysis, the author identifies and examines how members of the Task Force represent two very different orientations – those who favor colorblind policies focused on academic achievement of all students and those in support of racial integration as a pathway to equitable educational outcomes. Focusing on moments of argumentation that resulted in compromise and majority agreement about the use of funds, the author shows how the Task Force's recommendation promoted racial integration *and* academic achievement. The article emphasizes the importance of focusing analytically on shared understanding in order to promote inclusive educational practices.

Sealey-Ruiz, Y. and Greene, P. (2015). Popular visual images and the (mis)reading of Black male youth: A case for racial literacy in urban preservice teacher education. *Teaching Education* 26(1): 55–76.

Race is a signifier that is discursively constructed and has material consequences. In this article, the authors illustrate how Black youth are mis-represented in the media as disinterested, uneducable and violent. These representations inform a collective narrative that informs day-to-day decisions, institutional practices, school funding and systemic policies. Together with their teacher education students, the authors engaged in re-reading and re-writing media images of Black youth. They argue that this practice of racial literacy can be a tool to bridge the divide between white teachers and their students of color.

References

Ayers, D. (2005). Neoliberal ideology in community college mission statements: A critical discourse analysis. *The Review of Higher Education* 28(4): 527–549.

Rebecca Rogers

Barrett, T. (2010). The problem-based learning process as finding and being in flow. *Innovations in Education and Teaching International* 47(2): 165–174.

Bartlett, T. (2012). *Hybrid voices and collaborative change: Contextualizing positive discourse analysis*. New York: Routledge.

Bell, D. (1992). *Faces at the bottom of the well: The permanence of racism*. New York: Basic Books.

Blommaert, J. (2005). *Discourse*. Cambridge: Cambridge University Press.

Bloome, D. and Talwalker, S. (1997). Critical discourse analysis and the study of reading and writing. *Reading Research Quarterly* 32(1): 104–112.

Costa, A. M. and Saraiva, L. A. (2012). Hegemonic discourses on entrepreneurship as an ideological mechanism for the reproduction of capital. *Organization* 19(5): 587–614.

Fairclough, N. (1992). *Discourse and social change*. Oxford: Blackwell.

Fairclough, N. (1995). *Media discourse*. London: East Arnold.

Fairclough, N. (2003). *Analysing discourse*. London: Routledge.

Foucault, M. (1972). *The archeology of knowledge and the discourse of language*. New York: Pantheon Books.

Foucault, M. (1980). *Power/knowledge: Selected interviews and other writings, 1972–1977*. New York: Pantheon.

Gee, J. (1999/2005). *An introduction to discourse analysis: Theory and method*. New York: Routledge.

Glaser, M. and van Pletzen, E. (2012). Inclusive education for deaf students: Literacy practices and South African sign language. *Southern African Linguistics and Applied Language Studies* 30(1): 25–37.

Haddix, M. (2010). No longer on the margins: Researching the hybrid literate identities of Black and Latina pre-service teachers. *Research in the Teaching of English* 45(2): 97–123.

Halliday, M.A.K. (1978). *Language as a social semiotic: The social interpretation of language and meaning*. Baltimore, MD: University Park Press.

Huckin, T. (1995). Critical discourse analysis. Functional approaches to written texts: Classroom applications. *TESOL-France Journal* 2(2): 95–111.

Huckin, T., Andrus, A. and Clary-Lemon, J. (2012). Critical discourse analysis and rhetoric and composition. *College Composition and Communication* 64(1): 107–129.

Holyfield, L., Moltz, M. and Bradley, M. (2009). Race discourse and the US confederate flag. *Race Ethnicity and Education* 12(4): 517–537.

Janks, H. (1997). Critical discourse analysis as a research tool. *Discourse: Studies in the Cultural Politics of Education* 18(3): 329–342.

Kettle, M. (2011). Academic practice as explanatory framework: Reconceptualising international student academic engagement and university teaching. *Discourse: Studies in the Cultural Politics of Education* 32(1): 1–14.

Kress, G. R. (2003). *Literacy in the new media age*. London: Routledge.

Luke, A. (1995). Text and discourse in education: An introduction to critical discourse analysis. *Review of Research in Education* 21(3): 1–48.

Luke, A. (1999). Critical discourse analysis. In J. Keeves and G. Lakomski (eds.), *Issues in educational research*, 161–173. Pergamon, Oxford.

Luke, A. (2002). Beyond science and ideology critique: Developments in critical discourse analysis. *Annual Review of Applied Linguistics* 22: 96–110.

Luke, A. (2004). Notes on the future of critical discourse studies. *Critical Discourse Studies* 38(1): 132–141.

McCormick, A. (2012). Whose education policies in aid-receiving countries? A critical discourse analysis of quality and normative transfer through Cambodia and Laos. *Comparative Education Review* 56(1): 18–47.

Macgilchrist, F. (2007). Positive discourse analysis: Contesting dominant discourses by reframing the issue. *Critical Approaches to Discourse Across the Disciplines* 1(1): 74–94.

Martin, J. (2004). Positive discourse analysis: Solidarity and change. *Revista Canaria de Estudios Ingleses* 49: 179–200.

Martin, J. and Rose, D. (2011). *Working with discourse: Meaning beyond the clause,* 2nd edn. London: Continuum.

Martín Rojo, L. (2010). *Constructing inequality in multilingual classrooms*. Berlin, Germany: De Gruyter Mouton.

Martínez-Roldan, C. (2005). Examining bilingual children's gender ideologies through critical discourse analysis. *Critical Inquiry in Language Studies* 2(3): 157–178.

Mosley, M. and Rogers, R. (2011). Inhabiting the tragic gap: Pre-service teachers practicing racial literacy. *Teaching Education* 22(3): 303–324.

Morrison, T. (1992). *Playing in the dark: Whiteness and the literary imagination*. New York: Vintage Books.

Polacco, P. (2001). *Mr. Lincoln's way*. New York: Philomel.

Richardson, E. (2007). 'She was workin like foreal': Critical literacy and discourse practices of African American females in the age of hip-hop. *Discourse and Society* 18(6): 789–809.

Rocha-Schmidt, E. (2010). Participatory pedagogy for empowerment: A critical discourse analysis of teacher-parents' interactions in a family literacy course in London. *International Journal of Lifelong Education* 29(3): 343–358.

Rogers, R. (2011). Tracking educational trajectories and life pathways: The longitudinal nexuses of critical discourse analysis and ethnography. *Critical Discourse Studies* 8(4): 239–252.

Rogers, R., Berkes, E., Mosley, M., Hui, D. and O-Garro, G. (2005). A critical review of critical discourse analysis. *Review of Research in Education* 75(3): 365–416.

Rogers, R. and Labadie, M. (2015). Critical literacy in a kindergarten classroom: An examination of social action. In B. Yoon and R. Sharif (eds.), *Critical literacy practice: Applications of critical theory in diverse settings*, 23–40. New York: Routledge.

Rogers, R. and Mosley Wetzel, M. (2013). Studying agency in teacher education: A layered approach to positive discourse analysis. *Critical Inquiry Into Language Studies* 10(1): 62–92.

Rogers, R., Mosley Wetzel, M. and O'Daniels, K. (2016). Learning to teach, learning to act: Becoming a critical literacy teacher. *Pedagogies: An International Journal* 11(4): 292–310, DOI: 10.1080/1554480X.2016.1229620

Rogers, R. and Schaenen, I. (2014). Critical discourse analysis in language and literacy research. *Reading Research Quarterly* 49(1): 121–143.

Rogers, R., Schaenen, I. Schott, C., O'Brien, K., Trigos-Carrillo, L., Starkey, K. and Chasteen, C. (2016). Critical discourse analysis in educational research: A review of the literature, 2004–2012. *Review of Educational Research* 86(4): 1192–1226.

Rogers, R. and Wetzel, M. (2015). Critical discourse analysis: A responsive tool for teacher researchers. *Annual Yearbook of the Literacy Research Association* 63: 256–267.

Sealey-Ruiz, Y. (2011). Dismantling the school-to-prison pipeline through racial literacy development in teacher education. *Journal of Curriculum and Pedagogy* 8(4): 116–120.

Skerrett, A. (2011). English teachers' racial literacy knowledge and practice. *Race, Ethnicity, and Education* 14(3): 313–330.

Sheyholislami, J. (2010). Identity, language, and new media: The Kurdish case. *Language Policy* 9: 289–312.

Tochluk, S. (2010). *Witnessing whiteness: The need to talk about race and how to do it*. Rowman & Littlefield Press.

van Dijk, T. (1993a). Principles of critical discourse analysis. *Discourse & Society* 4(2): 249–283.

van Dijk, T. (1993b). Analyzing racism through discourse: Some methodological reflections. In J.H. Stanfield and R.M. Dennis (eds.), *Race and ethnicity in research methods,* 92–134. Newbury Park: Sage.

van Dijk, T. (2001). Multidisciplinary CDA: A plea for diversity. In R. Wodak and M. Meyer (eds.), *Methods of critical discourse analysis,* 95–120. London: Sage.

van Dijk, T. (2005). Critical discourse analysis. In D. Schiffrin, D. Tannen and H.E. Hamilton (eds.), *The handbook of discourse analysis,* 352–371. Malden, MA: Blackwell Publishers Ltd.

32

Legal discourse

Jothie Rajah

Law is a form of discourse especially aligned to power in that the state is uniquely authorised to generate those forms of legal discourse conventionally recognised as law, such as legislation and judgments (Post 1991). This chapter considers CDS scholarship that enters questions and issues of law through state law's conventional sites and texts to demonstrate the inextricable enmeshments of law, language, and power. It also reviews scholarship that applies CDS to discourses of legitimacy that (arguably) appear in the place of conventional legal discourse in post-9/11 contexts.

The chapter traces these varieties of legal discourses to demonstrate some of the ways in which CDS, as an analytic approach, generates insights and analysis with an extensive inter-disciplinary reach.

A capacious conception of legal discourse

Law has, broadly speaking, been thought of in two ways: first, as autonomous and distinct from other spheres of existence, and second, as an inextricable and contingent part of all social life (Davies 2002, 4–5).[1] The first, which I will shorthand as positivist, dominates thinking in popular culture (e.g., Freeman 2005; Sherwin 2000), the legal profession, and legal education (Mertz 1994, 2007; Pether 1999a, 1999b, 2005). The second, which I will shorthand as critical, informs critical theory on law and much of the interdisciplinary scholarship on law.[2]

Approaching law through critical discourse studies (CDS) involves recognising legal discourse in both its positive and critical aspects, a concern particularly shared perhaps by the field of anthropological linguistics in its attention to language, culture, and social power (e.g., Conley and O'Barr 1998; Hirsch 1998; Mertz 2007; Richland 2008). CDS scholarship on positive law explicitly applies the literatures, approaches, and social justice ethos foundational to CDS (e.g., Fairclough 2002; van Dijk 1993; Wodak 2001) to engagements with texts such as judgments, legislation, and constitutions, and contexts such as trials, while repudiating the positivist tendency to render law abstract and disembedded.[3] Through CDS, legal discourse is situated within specific social contexts, and a heightened attention is paid to those questions foundational to critical studies, "democracy, equality, fairness, and justice" (McKenna 2004: 9).[4]

But the parameters of "legal discourse" might be read more capaciously as extending beyond the conventional texts and sites of positive law. A compound category, law's institutional manifestations and many meanings include the bureaucratic and regulatory, law as everyday conduct ("laws of social behaviour, laws of language, laws relating to what counts as knowledge and what doesn't" Davies 2002: 4), law as brute coercion, (the obvious examples are corporal and capital punishment), and a time and border transcending sense of law as justice and legitimacy.[5] Within these many meanings of law rests a tension: law is tied to the modernist structures of the (secular) state even as it precedes modernity (Fitzpatrick 2001) and exists at levels both below and above the state (Darian-Smith 2013).

In addition to applying the perspective of critical theory to detect law, well, quite simply everywhere and in everything, Heffer, Rock, and Conley's (2013) theorisation of "textual travel" in legal-lay communication holds the promise of revitalising and expanding the field of legal discourse. For Heffer, Rock, and Conley, textual travel involves attention to the shifting dynamics of form and meaning that emerge when texts generated in legal settings move through space and time to "those nodes of interaction when the legal world meets the everyday lifeworld... when people acting for the legal system from police call handlers to judges, interact with people encountering the legal process in a lay role" (Rock, Heffer and Conley 2013: 3).

While it is beyond the scope of this chapter to review legal discourse in all these aspects and processes, my hope is that by including literatures not immediately and typically thought of as "legal", scholars of CDS, already alert to the complexities of language and power, will explore many more manifestations and arenas of law than has hitherto been the case.

This chapter offers brief sections on legislation (II), international law (V), and law's categories (VI). The more extensive sections review literature relating to trials and legal professional actors (III), discourses of legitimacy (IV), and the extended case study drawn from my own work on rule of law discourse in Singapore (VII).

Legislation

As text, legislation has an oddly clean, ahistorical appearance. Judgments, that other primary source of positive law in a common law system, reveal argument and challenges to interpretation in a way that legislation does not. However, when legislation is scrutinised through CDS, the asymmetries of power inherent to legislative text can be made explicit. For example, the politics, oblique language, and overwhelming excess of text characterising the USA *PATRIOT Act* are shown to obstruct democratic accessibility and accountability (de Beaugrande 2004). More optimistically, a study of gay rights discourses in three ambits – legislative, institutional, and public – suggests "a progressive move towards a new 'hybrid' genre... which encapsulates the initial legislative and institutional message in a linguistic form that is both accessible and empathetic to the ultimate consumer: the LGBT community" (Hughes and Napolitano 2013: 228–229).

But perhaps because "[t]he most dramatic and most often dramatized stage for displaying and observing legal discourse is the courtroom" (Finegan 2012: 482) considerably more attention has been paid by CDS scholars to courtroom discourses than to legislation (although the extended case study in Part VII enters legal discourse through legislation).

Judges, trials, and the legal profession

Building on seminal work on courtroom discourses (e.g., Atkinson and Drew 1979; O'Barr 1982; Wodak 1985), an important body of CDS analysis of law attends to legal discourse in

courtrooms; demonstrating how this iconic and public legal arena functions as a site for the (re)
production of social identities and inequities. Two recent reviews of legal discourse (Ehrlich
2011; Finegan 2012), and a compendium of scholarship on language and law (Tiersma and
Solan 2012), are invaluable resources.

Finegan's (2012: 483) review of discourses in the language of the law focuses on "the
formal talk of lay litigants in small claims courts; the language of attorneys and witnesses in
cross-examination. . . and certain aspects of the discourse of appellate court opinions"; and
Ehrlich (2011: 361) focuses on "the interaction between lawyers and witnesses as well as how
this interaction constructs the various versions of events that emerge in trial contexts". In
this chapter's discussion of courtroom discourses, attention is drawn to some of the material
outside the scope of Ehrlich's and Finegan's reviews but there is also some overlap in noting
key contributions.

Thematic attention to courtroom discourses in trials relating to sexual violence is unsurprising given the CDS alertness to particularly vulnerable populations, alongside the extremely
high level of discursive power held by lawyers, especially when conducting cross-examination
(Conley and O'Barr 1998; Ehrlich 2011: 362). Of particularly significant influence here is
Matoesian's fine-grained analysis of the specifics of talk directed by counsel in rape trials,
evidencing discursive strategies designed to control witnesses and influence juries in the "war
of words, utterances, and ideas. . . in which the ability to perform knowledge through talk
represents the preeminent weapon of domination" (Matoesian 2001: 235. See also Matoesian
1993).

Related studies include: analysis of causal/psychologizing attributions relied upon by
judges in justifying verdicts and sentences in sexual assault trials, revealing a troubling judicial
tendency to conceal violence, mitigate perpetrators' responsibility, conceal victims' resistance,
and blame or pathologize victims (Coates and Wade 2004); lawyers' reformulations of witness
accounts through strategic management of cross-examination "so that the accused's responsibility for these acts of sexual aggression is obscured and/or that the events in question are
represented as consensual sex" (Ehrlich 2011: 364; Ehrlich 2007); and judgments in child
sexual abuse trials which demonstrate the highly problematic reasoning informing judicial
inferences of a child's consent to sexual contact (MacMartin 2002). On judicial constructions
of consent in a very different context of citizen-police encounters in the US, see Nadler and
Trout 2012.

Also of importance is Cotterill's well-known and comprehensive analysis of legal frameworks and linguistic consequences in the O.J. Simpson trial (2003). Cotterill's analysis draws
on court transcripts, police interviews, transcripts of grand jury and preliminary hearings,
pre-trial selection questionnaires, and video-recordings of publicly broadcast trial proceedings. She demonstrates the relationship between a range of legal frameworks (opening statements, the roles and relationships of participants and processes, direct and cross-examination,
witness testimony, closing arguments, jury deliberation, verdict), and the manner in which
these frameworks interact with linguistic processes relating to power, knowledge, storytelling,
strategic lexicalisation, question and answer format, reframing, and choices of metaphor.

Attention to the dynamics of neocolonialism informing language ideologies, legal processes, and the failure of justice marks an important contribution to studies of trials (Eades
2008, 2012, 2013). For example, Eades studies an Australian case known as the Pinkenba
case, precipitated by "six [armed] police officers approaching three young teenage Aboriginal
boys in a Brisbane street late one night, and telling them to get into three separate police
cars. Although never charged for any offence in relation to that night, the boys were then
driven 14 kms out of town to a dark industrial wasteland, where they were threatened and

abandoned" (Eades 2012: 479–480). In her analysis of the case, in which the boys testified in court against the police officers, Eades stresses the importance of attending to ideological continuities between the language of courtroom interactions and core language ideologies operative within society. She highlights the context of this trial: systemic oppression of Indigenous Australians through overpolicing and over-imprisonment. This context exposes as a legal fiction the construct of postcolonial citizen equality when "[a]s with other Indigenous minorities around the world, Australian Aboriginal people experience the legacies of colonial dispossession, with living conditions typical of people in third world countries" (Eades 2012: 472–473).

Through an analysis of the cross-examination, Eades demonstrates how language ideology, together with "constraints on ways of talking in court and adversarial manipulation. . . enabled the two defence counsel to reverse the boys' allegation of police abuse, and instead to construct the boys as liars" (Eades 2012: 481). Charges against the police were dropped. Courtroom discourse fed media portrayals of the boys as lying criminals, effectively legitimizing the actions of six armed policemen in their dealings with three young Aboriginal boys.

Additional layers and dynamics of courtroom discourse that have been disaggregated in a range of focused studies include: an argument about text and context through a scrutiny of the Anglo-American law of evidence and the "excited utterance" exception to the hearsay rule (Andrus 2011); a study of courtroom interpreting (Hales 2004); attention to the discourse of vulnerable witnesses, including children and those for whom standard English is not the primary language (Eades 2010); "impression management" in a closing statement designed to persuade jurors into affiliating with counsel's views, in part through the deployment of African American vernacular English (Hobbs 2003a); techniques of discursive control adopted by counsel in their questioning of medical experts (Hobbs 2003b); the construction and use of implicit categorizations in trial interactions between a lawyer and an expert witness, and the role of these categorizations in undermining that witness, both as individual and as expert (Winiecki 2008); "genre mixing between legal proceedings and theatrical performances", artfully deployed in the process of cross-examination so as to undermine the credibility of key witnesses (Bromwich 2013: 16); the deployment of interruption by judges and prosecutors, a discursive strategy indexing power relations in Chinese criminal trials (Liao 2013); a dispiriting assessment that, despite pro se rights, a criminal defendant who chooses to represent himself is deprecated and devalued by his audiences notwithstanding his "surprisingly well crafted" opening statement (Hobbs 2008: 231); and an analysis of civil judgments in China as responses to the project of judicial reform (Han 2011).

Also of interest is a cluster of studies examining discursive dynamics between the police and courts, including: analysis of the "wanderings" across space and time that occur in the creation of a text that commonly precedes the trial, the written police witness statement (Rock 2013: 78); a text known as the suspect's statement in Dutch criminal law, and the processes shaping this discourse, including those of police interrogation, and the trial (Komter 2013); the ways in which police interviews become embedded in the prosecution's case (Johnson 2013).

Pether's CDS reading of the jury instruction simplification project with reference to rape trials highlights a range of problematic effects and implications, including first, the tension between material realities of social inequity and "the legal fictions of democracy" inherent to "plain language" jury instructions; second, the "considerable oppositional mistrust" citizens experience vis-a-vis "this culture of the law and lawyers and of governmental authority in general"; third, the "obvious contradiction" between the simplified instructions to jurors, and the trials jurors actually experience, in which the law is more complex, technical, and specialized even as it is "often obviously less systematic and rational'"; and finally, the ways in which simplified jury instructions fail to register "the presence of discourses on gender and sexuality in operation in the law as in culture more generally" (Pether 1999a: 92–93).

Examination of the discourse generated by legal professional actors extends to their constructions of social identities, including: an analysis of the role of gender in shaping the professional identity construction of judges and lawyers (Bogoch 1999); a study of nationalistic discourse in the professional texts of Danish lawyers and legal academics (Kjaer and Palsbro 2008); the complex simultaneous construction of professional identity and status in tandem with "a constant bridge-building process with laypeople" in seeking to capture jurors' attention and interest (Anesa and Kastberg 2012: 15)

Keeping the focus on elite legal actors, but moving outside the processes of a courtroom trial, and the artefact of a judgment, CDS studies include: interviews with family court judges that reveal beliefs, values, and biases held by judges that distort law's capacity to protect already vulnerable populations – mothers and children – in cases of child custody when domestic violence is an issue (Naughton et al. 2015); analysis of the relatively recent arena of international commercial arbitration highlighting protectionism and elitism at work (Bhatia 2013; see also Bhatia, Candlin and Gotti 2012); the impact of corporate publicity management in transforming the genre of international commercial arbitration (Corona 2013); the dynamic between generic and rhetorical features of arbitral awards and the specific context of China (Han and Li 2011).

Discourses of legitimacy

If a critical conception of "law", coupled with a CDS approach, expands the borders of what we perceive as legal discourse, then discourses that engage with questions of legitimacy[6] might also be regarded as inherently legal in nature. Some examples are: a discourse of "unethical conduct", unfolding in the court-like space of a statutory authority that disciplines nurses (Dixon 2013); student self-positioning in disciplinary hearings relating to plagiarism (Nilsson, Eklof and Ottosson 2009); discursive legitimizations of leadership claims in the context of nuclear proliferation crisis (Schnurr et al. 2015); and the role of euphemistic language in impairing ethical decision-making in the notorious case of the Penn State University leadership's cover-up of the sexual abuse of children by the university's assistant football coach (Lucas and Fyke 2014).

A notable instance of CDS scholarship interrogating discourses of legitimacy is Richard Jackson's scrutiny of the public language of the so-called "war on terror" (2005). While conventional disciplinary classifications might situate Jackson's scholarship in fields other than Law (such as International Relations, Peace and Conflict Studies, or, more recently, Critical Terrorism Studies),[7] I see his 2005 monograph as "legal" because "legitimacy" and "justice" are central to humanist conceptions of "law"[8]

In disentangling the discursive fabric of the "war on terrorism", Jackson demonstrates how the strands of nationalism, political myth, xenophobic patriotism, racism, Islamophobia, imperialist ideologies, and a range of affective dynamics – principally, fear – have rescripted liberal democratic legal discourses. Notions of substantive and procedural justice, and the inalienability of human rights, have been displaced by

> all encompassing and smothering discourses [that] destabilise the moral community and replace non-violent political interaction with suspicion, fear, hatred, chauvinism and an impulse to defend violently the "imagined community".
>
> *(Jackson 2005, 182)*

Some other instances of CDS interrogations of post-9/11[9] discourses of legitimacy (some focusing on texts of positive law) are analysis attending to: continuities between the Cold War and the post-9/11 moments in US "national security" policy (Dunmire 2009, 2014); political myth in official legitimations of the "war on terror" (Esch 2010); the impact of 9/11 on immigration laws relating to "diversity" (Gales 2009); a comparative reading of "the political and corporate fields, where the tension between the leader and the law is replayed, and may be resolved in the crisis by the leader's suspension of the law" (Kerr 2008: 201); the effects of 9/11 on US constitutional discourses producing "a widespread and binary system of "justice", which replicates inside the nation's courts, practices of structural subordination based on race, and its frequent double, class" (Pether 2007: 156); Obama's statement on the killing of Osama bin Laden as a textual displacement of the substance and institutions associated with "law" by attributing to "justice" meanings drawn from US political myth (Rajah 2014a); post-9/11 terrorism detention practices and discourses, demonstrating the role of language choices in altering and legitimising state law and practice in the US, the UK, and Australia (Duffy 2012); and the "pragmalinguistic constructs... assertion, implicature and common ground variables" usefully explain the discursive strategies of legitimation in the "war on terror" (Cap 2006).

Sometimes, CDS speaks to questions of legitimacy in slightly backgrounded ways. For example, Kellner's analysis of how the two Bush administrations and "Islamic Jihadism" both deploy media spectacles of terror prompts his call to discount and distrust corporate media (2004). In pointing to the democratic deficit consequent upon ties between the US and media corporations, Kellner counters the received wisdom that constructs the US as a legal-political space emblematic of the protection of fundamental liberties, including freedom of the press.

Discourses of international law

International law doctrine rests on the legal fiction of sovereign parity and autonomy, a fiction that collapses in the face of persistent material inequalities and relations of dependence traceable to colonial and neo-colonial pasts and presents (Anghie 2005; Pahuja 2011). When CDS is applied to international law, ideological continuities between imperial pasts and neo-imperial presents have been made visible through a discourse analysis of categorisations and representations of the "foreigner" in Australian legislative, judicial, policy, and public texts (Lester 2014). A discursive unpacking of continuities and discontinuites between Eurocentric international law doctrine dating from the 16th century, alongside contemporary techniques for excluding the "foreigner", reveal how a masked racialised undercurrent in national and international law becomes instrumentalised by a state indifferent to human rights; undermining values and promises core to liberal legality and democracy (Lester 2014).

On related points, see Every and Augoustinos (2007) on constructions of racism in Australian parliamentary debates on asylum seekers, and Argren (2005) on constructions of international law in Sweden's major national newspapers.

Law's categories

When "law" is approached as "acts of language [that] are actions in the world" (White 1990, ix), legal categories become central to the manner in which law functions as a scheme of interpretation (Kelsen 1967: 4). Unsurprisingly, CDS's alertness to the (often concealed) power dimensions of language yields valuable critical insights into dynamics and contestations informing competing constructions of complex categories central to understandings of "law" on both national and transnational scales. Some examples of a CDS lens on analytic categories key to law are: "asylum-seeker", "asylum shopping", and "migrant" (Lester 2014; Moore 2013; Incelli 2013); "citizen" and "citizenship" (Amaya 2007; Anderson 2008; Bloch 2014; Gulliver and Herriot 2015; Thumin 2010; Hartley 2010; van Zoonen, Vis and Mihelj 2010); "contract" (Anderson 2008); "due process" (Lester 2014); "emergency" and "exception" (Kerr 2008); "evil" (Bhatia 2009); "human rights" (Yin 2007, Lester 2014); "informed consent" in the context of bio-medical research (Conley et al. 2013); "intellectual property" (Owen 2014); "justice" (Rajah 2014a); "law and order" and "crime" (de Gialdino 2007; Reyes-Foster 2014); "liberty" and "security" (Simone 2009); "national security" (Dunmire 2009, 2014); "preventative detention" (Duffy 2012); "rape victim" (Trinch 2013); "refugee" (Lester 2014); "rule of law" (Rajah 2012, 2015); "sovereignty" (Kerr 2008; Lester 2014); "terrorism" (Bhatia 2009; Duffy 2012; Jackson 2005; Kerr 2008).

Countering hegemony: a case study

Legal discourse in Singapore offers a potent illustration of Fairclough's point that "the relationship of language to power in national or local settings. . . [is] penetrated by processes and relations at an international level, and potentially contribute to shaping them" (2002, viii). For Singapore, a former British colony, legal discourse transcends the national in a range of ways. Perhaps the most significant of these arises from the Singapore state's celebration of English law as part of its "inheritance" (Chan 2009). In addition to the language of law being English – legislation and judgments are in English – English common law traditions, ideologies, and practices shape the field of law in cultural and behavioural ways (Rajah 2012, 2014b). For example, until 1993, judges wore "heavy red robes, full-bottomed wigs, and stiff collars" (*Straits Times*, January 10, 1993: 21). Robes are still worn by judges, and when appearing in open court, lawyers must wear a gown over their suits.

The discussion below is extracted from a larger project exploring the phenomenon of authoritarian rule of law (Rajah 2012). Briefly, applying the lens of CDS to legislation and discourses of legitimacy in Singapore, the project draws on theorising on the dual nature of British colonial law (Jayasuriya 1999) to map the manner in which an authoritarian polity has achieved the stature of rule of law nation despite rights-eroding laws and repressive politics. A CDS approach to legislation necessarily means attending to the orders of discourse (Fairclough 2002: 23–26) associated with the specific subjects of each enactment studied (vandalism, the press, lawyers, religion, public order) as well as intertextuality, sub-text, context, relevant state and non-state discourse, judgments, and the exclusion of a range of social actors, including the courts.

The discussion presented here is extracted from an analysis of legislation relating to the legal profession (Rajah 2012: 161–218). The language/power enmeshments of past and present, international and national (Fairclough 2002, viii) come to the fore in a particularly dynamic manner when it comes to lawyers because, arguably, Singapore lawyers embody a postcolonial paradox. As common law practitioners, Singapore lawyers access meanings of law derived from a wider common law discourse that exalts individual rights and the roles of law and lawyers in boldly advocating for and protecting rights. At the same time, lawyers socialised as Singaporeans are placed in a polity in which, despite the Westminster-model state structure and valorisation of basic legal freedoms via the Constitution, there is a low level of rights awareness, a recent history (and arguably ongoing climate) of intolerance of dissent, and a high level of state dominance of the public sphere. State discourse has constructed "citizenship" in terms of compliance: citizens are instructed to be dutiful and subordinate to the knowing and authoritative state. In the context of this paradox, despite the fundamental liberties of the

Constitution, citizens tend not to conduct themselves as empowered and rights-bearing.[10] In short, there is a clash between orders of legal discourse.

In *Authoritarian Rule of Law* (Rajah 2012), I use the terms "rule of law" and "rule by law" to capture these oppositional meanings of law. "Rule of law" is a shorthand signifying, as a fundamental attribute of legitimacy, law's capacity to scrutinise power and hold power accountable. "Rule *by* law" is a shorthand signifying the absence of law's capacity to be autonomous from power. If "rule of law" is, in general, held as exalted, representing an ideal "law" that operates as a bulwark against power, then "rule by law" is treated as an instrumentalist deployment of law by power; law in the service of power rather than in the service of "the people" or "justice".

Singapore's 1986 Legal Profession (Amendment) Act

In 1986, the paradoxes informing Singapore as (effectively) authoritarian on the one hand yet (apparently) common law, Westminster parliamentary democracy on the other, were made explicit through amendments to the *Legal Profession Act*. And consistent with a CDS alertness to context, the story of these amendments cannot be told without summarising events relating to Singapore's first opposition member of parliament.

In December 1981, a parliamentary seat was won, for the first time in Singapore's 16 years as an independent republic, by an opposition candidate, J.B. Jeyaretnam. With Jeyaretnam's electoral victory, and the first major recession to hit independent Singapore, a new political awareness revitalised the hitherto somewhat apathetic political sphere of unrelieved dominance of the ruling People's Action Party (PAP) (Chan 2000).

Jeyaretnam's entry into Parliament precipitated an onslaught of state regulatory, procedural, parliamentary, and legal processes, designed arguably to undermine this single opposition parliamentarian's political and legal career. Sections of the legal profession, the Catholic Church, performance artists, and the foreign press (for example, the *Asian Wall Street Journal* and the *Far Eastern Economic Review*), rallied directly or indirectly to the cause of Jeyaretnam and what he represented: an actualisation of the liberal law and politics promised by Singapore's formal legal-political structures.

When reporting on the state's mobilisation of its considerable legal-procedural apparatus against Jeyaretnam,[11] the domestic press did not suggest that these actions were disproportionate and politically motivated. However, off-shore publications did. The state responded by amending legislation governing what it categorised as "the foreign press", awarding the Singapore state extensive discretionary powers to restrict the circulation of "foreign press" found to be engaging in Singapore's domestic politics.

It is a reflection of the spirit of change moving through Singapore at the time that the Law Society did something it had not attempted since 1969: it issued a press statement questioning the terms of proposed legislation. Commenting on the *Press Bill,* the Law Society said,

There are ambiguities in the Bill. For example, the terms "engaging in" and "domestic politics" are not defined although these terms form the basis of the Bill. Since this Bill is aimed at foreign publications, which, – in the words which have been attributed to the Minister – "have been commenting frequently on local issues and distorting the truth", these terms should have been defined. The omission to define them will result in subjective interpretation and implementation of the Bill (Select Committee Report (hereafter "Report"), B 82–84).

This criticism is entirely consistent with rule of law principles about the need for law to be clear and accessible, and the common law expectation that legislation, in particular, should exhibit clarity by defining key terms (Tamanaha 2004: 63–70). The Law Society's press statement is informed by another rule of law assumption: that the operation of law should be predictable, objective, and transparent (Tamanaha 2004: 63–70).

Apart from being consonant with rule of law assumptions, the press statement was also in keeping with the *Legal Profession Act*. Under the *Legal Profession Act,* as it was then framed, the Council of the Law Society's functions included examining and reporting upon current or proposed legislation should it think fit, (section 39 (1)(c)) and protecting and assisting the public in all matters to do with law (section 39 (1)(f)). A rule of law scrutiny of power is implicit in this valourisation of lawyers as servants and protectors of the public. In short, when making the press statement, the Law Society was acting in accordance with its powers and duties, as framed by law at many levels: the *Legal Profession Act,* constitutional rights of freedom of speech and association (Article 14), and the conventions of trans-border common law discourse.

Despite these conceptual, discursive, and textual entitlements to question proposed legislation, the state insisted that the Law Society had, by making a public statement, violated the permissible in a range of ways. Legal discourse in Singapore has been profoundly shaped by the substance of this insistence and the manner in which it was delivered: Select Committee Hearings, ostensibly on the Legal Profession (Amendment) Bill, became the platform for a public excoriation of the Council of the Law Society.

Selective hearing: re-shaping legal discourse

The existence of Select Committees in Singapore is consistent with a parliamentary system modelled on Westminster. Select Committees have generally been constituted to examine draft legislation, often inviting submissions from the public and conducting hearings so as to take into account the responses of non-state actors.[12] The process increases the scope for informed and inclusive legislation. Select Committee Hearings are generally conducted in a courteous, collegiate manner. The Committee is generally appreciative of those invited to appear before the Committee as bearing certain expertise or representing certain views that need to be taken into account.

In general, Select Committee Hearings in Singapore have proceeded along the lines of the model I have described.[13] However, with the 1986 Legal Profession (Amendment) Bill, there were two significant departures. First, for the first time in Singapore's history, these Hearings were televised. They were, of course, widely covered in print media as well, but in televising these Hearings, the state made vividly, dramatically public its capacity to humiliate and diminish its critics.

Second, an especially adversarial framework was established by the state in three ways. First, it issued subpoenas to the Council requiring Council members to attend the Hearings (Report, B 110). In doing so, the state ignored the courteous readiness of the Council to appear before the Committee (Report A 3). Arguably, the strategy of subpoenaing the Council conveyed the Council's degraded status as hostile and untrustworthy individuals. Secondly, the state took evidence from the Council under oath (Report B 23), instead of engaging in a conversation with the Council, as is usually the case at Select Committee hearings.[14] Administering the oaths enabled the state to periodically remind Council members that they were under oath, thus punctuating the proceedings with the state questioning the veracity of Council members (SC Report B43–167). Third, with two exceptions, the manner in which the questions were put to the Council was akin to extremely accusatory and intimidating cross-examination.

In the process, it was often state actors who spoke more than the Council members, such that the narrative that was permitted to emerge was one managed and controlled by the state. Indeed, at one point, when the first Council member to be questioned attempted to resist the Prime Minister's re-formulation of his answers, the Prime Minister refused to allow that member to choose his own words. By insisting on certain words, the Prime Minister ensured his command of the very building blocks of discourse:

PM: You did not know of public disquiet, or you had no public disquiet?
Elias: Disquiet of the public is not the words I would choose. Let me use my own, if I may, Mr Prime Minister.
PM: No. My question to you was...
        (Report, B 36).

In the course of the Hearings, the state demarcated "law" as a narrow domain of knowledge and activity. In the state's formulation, "law" was sharply distinct from "politics", such that, in issuing a press statement on proposed legislation, the Law Society was challenging the government and violating the boundaries of the permissible (Report, B 88–90). Building on its imposition of a narrow, politically impotent domain of competence for law, the state denoted a range of issues as outside the expertise of the Law Society, including legislation relating to the press and issues of justiciability. In defining law this way, the Hearings enacted power's capacity "to impose and maintain a particular structuring of some domain or other – a particular way of dividing it into parts, of keeping the parts demarcated from each other, and a particular ordering of those parts in terms of hierarchical relations of domination and subordination" (Fairclough 2002: 10–11).

To demarcate a specific enactment as beyond the expertise of the legal profession is to discursively subordinate "law" to power; a move at the heart of "rule by law". In the state's discourse, "law" lacks the capacity to scrutinise and limit power.

The Hearings, beamed into homes, rendered watching citizens into a silent, passive audience. In tandem with the state's aggressive and frequent interruptions of the Council, the Council's capacity to respond or generate its own narrative was minimal. The result was that the already authoritative state's especially authoritative insistence on its own characterisations and interpretations dominated the event. For watching citizens, the Hearings became a lesson on first, how the state defined "law", and second, how the state may choose to respond to critics by publicly humiliating them, as it did the Council.

In the course of 18 months or so after the Hearings, three Council members of the Law Society were accused of being part of a Marxist conspiracy to overthrow the state, and were detained without trial. Francis Seow, who had been President of the Law Society at the time of the events I have described, was accused of collaborating with a US Embassy official to facilitate US interference in Singapore's domestic politics. Seow too was detained without trial. Collectively, the Select Committee Hearings and the subsequent detentions without trial of Council members scripted new and enduring meanings for Singapore's legal discourse.

Legal discourse in the 21st century

At this juncture, particularly with the death in March 2015 of Singapore's highly influential former prime minister, Lee Kuan Yew, and with the democratising potential of the internet, the question that arises is have state responses to critique softened since the events of 1986? In evaluating the impact of the internet on public discourse, I reviewed scholarship, prosecutions, and public chastisements of bloggers to argue that the entrenched political culture of citizen self-censorship, in tandem with state suspicion of media, and the periodic prosecutions of bloggers, have attenuated the potential of new forms of media to be potent players in public discourse (Rajah 2012: 156–160).

Two highly publicised recent prosecutions of bloggers, and a defamation suit against another blogger, suggest that chilled public discourse (George 2007; Kalathil and Boas 2003) is a feature of Singapore life that will not be easily dislodged. In November 2014, blogger Roy Ngerng was found to have defamed the Prime Minister. At the time of writing, Ngerng has been ordered to pay the Prime Minister's legal costs but damages have yet to be awarded. In March 2015, blogger Alex Au, characterised by the *South China Morning Post* as a "prominent dissident blogger" (5 March 2015), was fined S$8,000 for the criminal offense of scandalising the judiciary.[15] And in May 2015, 16-year-old blogger, Amos Yee, was "found guilty of uploading an obscene image and making remarks intending to hurt the feelings of Christians" (*Straits Times,* 12 May 2015).[16] In its report, CNN notes that Yee "published an expletive-laden YouTube video praising the death of Singapore's first Prime Minister, Lee Kuan Yew, calling him "totalitarian" and comparing him unfavourably to Jesus and Mao Zedong. Yee also posted an image showing two cartoon figures having sex, with the faces of Lee and the late British Prime Minister Margaret Thatcher digitally added" (McLaughlin, *CNN,* 6 July 2015).[17]

Yee was sentenced to four weeks imprisonment but because he had already been in remand for 55 days,[18] the court released him on the day of sentencing. All in all, the Singapore state's responses to bloggers, and in particular, its treatment of 16-year-old Yee, who was handcuffed and shackled at his trial (*Straits Times,* 7 May 2015),[19] point to profound continuities between the state's contemporary management of discourse and the practices established in the first 50 years of Singapore under the ruling People's Action Party.

Conclusion: collaborative bridging

Given the widespread applicability of CDS (can any field of discourse exempt itself from a CDS lens?), and the expansive understanding of the category "law" that might be adopted, it is baffling that more critical legal discourse scholarship does not exist. Surely, once law's positivist barriers are analytically dismantled, there is no sphere of the social that does not (also) implicate and involve law and legal discourse.

The (quantitatively) limited joint journeying of law and CDS might be attributed to law's positivist barriers, which may have intimidated and excluded scholars armed with CDS toolkits and convictions from exploring legal discourses. In looking to the future, a collegial solution offers itself: collaboration! Building on prior and important calls that have been made for greater interdisciplinarity in CDS (e.g., McKenna 2004; Luke 2002; Fairclough 2005), it is my hope that CDS scholars will collaborate across disciplinary and geographic spaces to scrutinise the language and power of law. For example, Peter Teo's already thorough and compelling CDS reading of racism in Australian newspapers (2000: 7), demonstrating the "asymmetrical power discourse between the (ethnic) law-breakers and the (white) law-enforcers" might be supplemented by a CDS reading of the legislative, judicial, and policy texts relevant to both violent crime and drug trafficking, but also law relating to racial discrimination. And with a study of newspaper editorials in Japan linked to the enactment of new legislation (Saft and Ohara 2006) which, again, is already thorough and compelling, it would be analytically significant to understand links between the language of the press editorials and the language of the legislative text.

In interrogating the conjunctions of text, power, and knowledge, and attending to law's particular actors, arenas, properties, practices, politics, economics, travels, and effects, CDS scrutiny of legal discourse contributes to the project of social justice that an elitist, positivist "law" might tend to disregard. There is much to hope for through increased interdisciplinary work linking law and CDS.

Notes

1 An enormous body of scholarship delves into the histories and philosophies informing this somewhat simplistic formulation of a divide in ways of understanding "law". For more detailed and nuanced analysis, in addition to Davies 2002, see Tomlins 2007 for a useful review of law as a relational concept and category, Mawani 2012 for a reconceptualisation of law as archive, Richland 2013 for a review of legal language scholarship through the concept of "jurisdiction", and Mertz 1994 for a review of the pragmatics, poetics, and social power of legal language.

2 Darian-Smith (2013) offers an invaluable review of the history and assumptions informing the interdisciplinary field of sociolegal studies. Sarat, Anderson and Frank (2010) offer a useful review of origins of, and prospects for, the field of law and the humanities.

3 One especially inspiring article has drawn together CDS, positive law, legal pedagogy, law reform, and self-reflexivity on interdisciplinarity: Pether 1999a.

4 Perhaps it is the pillar of social justice that distinguishes CLS approaches to legal discourse from the discourse analysis of law conducted by forensic linguistics, e.g., Shuy 2008.

5 Again, faced with the impossibility of reviewing and referencing a vast literature, I offer two highly influential formulations of law's inextricable connections to "justice": Derrida 1990 and Constable 2005.

6 Although not explicitly focused on legal discourse, also of interest is Phillips, Lawrence, and Hardy (2004), offering a useful review of the literature on the discursive constructions of legitimation in organizations.

7 See Bhatia, this volume, on the discourse of terrorism.

8 For a review drawing together sociolegal and humanist conceptions of law, see Mertz and Rajah (2014).

9 I use this shorthand, 9/11, with regret at its convenience and alert to the risk that the complex of meanings attaching to '9/11' may "erase the history and context of the events and turn their representation into a cultural political icon where the meaning of the date becomes both assumed and open to manipulation . . . a mythologising practice" (Jackson 2005, 7).

10 For detailed analysis of events that have shaped this tension in orders of legal discourse, see Rajah (2012: 117–180).

11 Jeyaretnam won his seat in November 1981. From January 1982, the state initiated a series of legal-administrative actions against Jeyaretnam through both court proceedings, and disciplinary hearings for breach of parliamentary privilege. For details, see Rajah 2012: 146–147.

12 Select Committees are constituted pursuant to Singapore's *Parliament (Privileges, Immunities and Powers) Act* (Cap. 217, 2000 Rev. Ed. Sing.) [*Parliament Act*] and parliamentary Standing Orders. Section 3 of *Parliament Act* states that the privileges, immunities, and powers of Parliament, the Speaker, Members, and committees shall be the same as those of the Commons House of Parliament of the United Kingdom at the establishment of Singapore.

13 I have reviewed the Select Committee Reports dating from 1965 to the present. Select Committees have generally conducted questioning in a courteous and collegiate manner. When questioning representatives of opposition political parties, the questioning has sometimes been rather aggressive (for example, the questioning of the Singapore National Front in Sing., "Report of the Select Committee on the Maintenance of Parents Bill", 8th Parliament, and the questioning of the Singapore Democratic Party in Sing., "Report of the Select Committee on Land Transportation Policy", 7th Parliament). I would evaluate the level of aggression and antagonism displayed toward the Law Society Council in 1986 as unmatched by the conduct of any Select Committee Hearings, either before or after the 1986 Hearing on the *LPA*.

14 None of the Select Committee Hearings conducted before or after these on the *LPA* appears to have administered oaths.

15 Singapore blogger Alex Au fined for 'scandalising' judiciary. www.scmp.com/news/asia/article/1730414/singapore-blogger-alex-au-fined-scandalising-judiciary
16 www.straitstimes.com/singapore/courts-crime/amos-yee-found-guilty-of-both-charges-sentencing-on-june-2-pending-probation
17 Singapore court frees 16-year-old blogger Amos Yee. www.cnn.com/2015/07/06/asia/singapore-teen-blogger-amos-yee-freed/
18 www.theonlinecitizen.com/2015/07/prosecution-of-amos-yee-group-of-citizens-and-parents-expresses-concern-to-pm-lee/
19 Amir, H. and Ho, Olivia. Teen blogger Amos Yee pleads not guilty to both charges at start of two-day trial. www.straitstimes.com/singapore/courts-crime/teen-blogger-amos-yee-pleads-not-guilty-to-both-charges-at-start-of-two-day

Further reading

Cotterril, J. (2003). *Language and power in court: A linguistic analysis of the O. J. Simpson Trial*. Basingstoke: Palgrave Macmillan.
Cotterill draws on court transcripts, police interviews, transcripts of grand jury and preliminary hearings, pre-trial selection questionnaires, and video-recordings of publicly broadcast trial proceedings to demonstrate the relationship between a range of legal frameworks and the manner in which these frameworks interact with linguistic processes relating to power, knowledge, storytelling, strategic lexicalisation, question and answer format, reframing, and choices of metaphor.
Eades, D. (2008). *Courtroom talk and neocolonial control*. New York: Mouton de Gruyter.
This monograph's focus on the cross-examination phase of a trial as a platform for neo-colonial ideologies and domination offers a compelling example of how each instance of language expresses histories and present practices articulating relations of power.
Ehrlich, S. (2011). Courtroom discourse. In R. Wodak, B. Johnstone and P. Kerswill (eds.), *The SAGE handbook of sociolinguistics* [Online]. Sage. (Accessed April 3, 2015).
This chapter, highlighting the constitutive nature of discursive practices, usefully reviews scholarship on interaction between lawyers and witnesses, and the manner in which this interaction shapes accounts that emerge in the contexts of trials.
Heffer, C., Rock, F. and Conley, J. (2013). *Legal-lay communication: Textual travels in the law*. New York: Oxford University Press.
This collection of essays makes an important contribution to dismantling received thinking about law as a separate and autonomous sphere of activity. By drawing attention to textual travel as relational, dynamic, and interactional, the book supplies a fresh analytic lens on the contingencies and fluidities informing law in relation to text and context.
Jackson, R. (2005). *Writing the war on terrorism: Language, politics, and counter-terrorism*. Manchester: Manchester University Press.
This monograph analyses the public language relating to the so called "war on terror", exposing the manner in which language has been used to construct public consent, legitimise state violence, and authorise departures from entrenched values and institutional practices relating to law in liberal democracies.

References

Amaya, H. (2007). Latino immigrants in the American discourses of citizenship and nationalism during the Iraqi war. *Critical Discourse Studies* 4(3): 237–256.
Anderson, A. N. (2008). The world as will and adaptation: The interdiscursive coupling of citizens' contracts. *Critical Discourse Studies* 5(1): 75–89.
Andrus, J. (2011). Beyond texts in context: Reconceptualization and the co-production of texts and contexts in the legal discourse, excited utterance exception to hearsay. *Discourse & Society* 22(2): 115–136.
Anesa, P. and Kastberg, P. (2012). On some communicatively salient complexities of knowledge asymmetries in a jury trial. *Text & Talk* 32(1): 1–19.
Anghie, A. (2005). *Imperialism, sovereignty and the making of international law*. New York: Cambridge University Press.

Argren, R. (2005). Reporting about Iraq: International law in the media during armed conflict. *Essex Human Rights Review* 2(1): 99–111.

Atkinson, J. M. and Drew, P. (1979). *Order in court: The organisation of verbal interaction in judicial settings*. Atlantic Highlands, NJ: Humanities Press.

Beaugrande, R. de (2004). Critical discourse analysis from the perspective of ecologism: The discourse of the "new patriotism" for the "new secrecy". *Critical Discourse Studies* 1(1): 113–145.

Bhatia, A. (2009). The discourses of terrorism. *Journal of Pragmatics* 41: 279–289.

Bhatia, V. K. (2013). International commercial arbitration: A protected practice. In C. Williams and G. Tessuto (eds.), *Language in the negotiation of justice: Contexts, texts, and applications*. Farnham and Burlington: Ashgate.

Bhatia, V. K., Candlin, C. N. and Gotti, M. (eds.) (2012). *Discourse and practice in international commercial arbitration: Issues, challenges and prospects*. Farnham and Burlington: Ashgate.

Bloch, K. R. (2014). 'Anyone can be an illegal': Color-blind ideology and maintaining Latino/citizen borders. *Critical Sociology* 40(1): 47–65.

Bogoch, B. (1999). Courtroom discourse and the gendered construction of professional identity. *Law & Social Inquiry* 24(2): 329–375.

Bromwich, W. (2013). 'Mrs Buckley, you're telling a pack of lies': Cross-examination in the High Court of Justiciary in Edinburgh. In C. Williams and G. Tessuto (eds.), *Language in the negotiation of justice: Contexts, texts, and applications*. Farnham and Burlington: Ashgate.

Cap, P. (2006). *Legitimation in political discourse: A cross-disciplinary perspective on modern US war rhetoric*. Newcastle: Cambridge Scholars Press.

Carcalho Figueiredo, D. de (2004). Representation of rape in the discourse of legal decisions. In L. Young and C. Harrison (eds.), *Systemic functional linguistics*. London, New York: Continuum.

Chan, H. C. (2000). Internal developments in Singapore. In V. Grover (ed.), *Singapore: Government and Politics*. New Delhi: Deep and Deep.

Chan, S. K. (2009). Keynote address by Chief Justice Chan Sek Keong, October 27, 2009 [Online]. www.supremecourt.gov.sg/data/doc/ManagePage/3021/CJ%20Keynote%20Address%20at%20 NYSBA%20International%20Seasonal%20Meeting_27%20Oct%202009.pdf

Coates, L. and Wade, A. (2004). Telling it like it isn't: Obscuring perpetrator responsibility for violent crime. *Discourse & Society* 15(5): 499–526.

Conley, J. and O'Barr, W. (1998). *Just words: Law, language, and power*. Chicago: Chicago University Press.

Conley, J. et al. (2013). The discourse of DNA: Giving informed consent to genetic research. In C. Heffer, F. Rock and J. Conley (eds.), *Legal-lay communication*. New York: Oxford University Press.

Constable, M. (2005). *Just silences: The limits and possibilities of modern law*. Princeton, NJ: Princeton University Press.

Corona, I. (2013). Arbitration across genres: From 'private resolution' to 'public war'. In C. Williams and G. Tessuto (eds.), *Language in the negotiation of justice: Contexts, texts, and applications*. Farnham and Burlington: Ashgate.

Cotterril, J. (2003). *Language and power in court: A linguistic analysis of the O.J. Simpson trial*. Basingstoke: Palgrave Macmillan.

Darian-Smith, E. (2013). *Law and societies in global contexts: Contemporary approaches*. New York: Cambridge University Press.

Davies, B. L. (2013). Travelling texts: The legal-lay interface in The Highway Code. In C. Heffer, F. Rock and J. Conley (eds.), *Legal-lay communication*. New York: Oxford University Press.

Davies, M. (2002). *Asking the law question: The dissolution of legal theory*, 2nd edn. Sydney: Lawbook Co.

Derrida, J. (1990). Force of law: The mystical foundations of authority. *Cardozo Law Review* 11: 920–1045.

Dixon, K. A. (2013). Unethical conduct by the nurse: A critical discourse analysis of Nurses Tribunal inquiries. *Nursing Ethics* 20(5): 578–588.

Duffy, M. (2012). *Turning the kaleidoscope: Fractured narrative and altered presumptions in anti-terrorism detention practices*. PhD thesis, McGill University in partial fulfilment of the requirements of the degree of Doctor of Civil Law.

Dunmire, P. (2009). '9/11 changed everything': An intertextual analysis of the Bush Doctrine. *Discourse & Society* 20(2): 195–222.

Dunmire, P. (2014). American ways of organizing the world: Designing the global future through U.S. National Security Policy. In C. Hart and P. Cap (eds.), *Contemporary critical discourse studies*. London, New York: Bloomsbury Academic.

Eades, D. (2008). *Courtroom talk and neocolonial control*. New York: Mouton de Gruyter.

Eades, D. (2010). *Sociolinguistics and the legal process*. Bristol: Multilingual Matters.

Eades, D. (2012). The social consequences of language ideologies in courtroom cross-examination. *Language in Society* 41: 471–497.

Ehrlich, S. (2007). Legal discourse and the cultural intelligibility of gendered meanings. *Journal of Sociolinguistics* 11(4): 452–477.

Ehrlich, S. (2011). Courtroom discourse. In R. Wodak, B. Johnstone and P. Kerswill (eds.), *The SAGE handbook of sociolinguistics*. SAGE Publications. Available from [Accessed: 3rd April, 2015].

Esch, J. (2010). Legitimising the "war on terror": Political myth in official-level rhetoric. *Political Psychology* 31(3): 357–391.

Every, D. and Augoustinos, M. (2007). Constructions of racism in the Australian parliamentary debates on asylum seekers. *Discourse & Society* 18(4): 411–436.

Fairclough, N. (2002). *Language and power*, 2nd edn. London: Longman.

Fairclough, N. (2005). Critical discourse analysis in transdisciplinary research. In R. Wodak and P. Chilton (eds.), *A new agenda in (critical) discourse analysis: Theory, methodology, and interdisciplinarity*. Amsterdam and Philadelphia: John Benjamins Publishing.

Farrelly, M. (2015). *Discourse and democracy: Critical analysis of the language of government*. New York: Routledge.

Finegan, E. (2012). Discourses in the language of the law. In J.P. Gee and M. Handford (eds.), *The Routledge handbook of discourse analysis*, 482. London and New York: Routledge.

Fitzpatrick, P. (2001). *Modernism and the grounds of law*. Cambridge: Cambridge University Press.

Freeman, M. (ed.) (2005). *Law and popular culture*. New York: Oxford University Press.

Gales, T. (2009). 'Diversity' as enacted in US immigration politics and law: A corpus-based approach. *Discourse & Society* 20(2): 223–240.

Gialdino, I.V. de (2007). Representations of young people associated with crime in El Salvador's written press. *Critical Discourse Studies* 4(1): 1–28.

Gulliver, T. and Herriot, L. (2015). 'Some liken it to the Arab Spring'. *Critical Discourse Studies* 12(2): 206–225.

Hales, S. B. (2004). *The discourse of court interpreting: Discourse practices of the law, the witness and the interpreter*. Amsterdam, Philadelphia: John Benjamins Publishing.

Han, Z. (2011). The discursive construction of civil judgments in Mainland China. *Discourse & Society* 22(6): 743–765.

Han, Z. and Li, X. (2011). Discourse of international commercial arbitration: The case of Mainland China. *Journal of Pragmatics* 43(5): 1380–1391.

Hartley, J. (2010). Silly citizenship. *Critical Discourse Studies* 7(4): 233–248.

Heffer, C., Rock, F. and Conley, J. (2013). *Legal-lay communication: Textual travels in the law*. New York: Oxford University Press.

Hirsch, S. (1998). *Pronouncing and perservering: Coast Kenyan courts*. Chicago: University of Chicago Press.

Hobbs, P. (2003a). 'Is that what we're here about?': A lawyer's use of impression management in a closing argument at trial. *Discourse & Society* 14(3): 273–290.

Hobbs, P. (2003b). 'You must say it for him': Reformulating a witness' testimony on cross-examination at trial. *Text* 23(4): 477–511.

Hobbs, P. (2008). It's not what you say but how you say it: The role of personality and identity in trial success. *Critical Discourse Studies* 5(3): 231–248.

Hughes, B. and Napolitano, A. (2013). From primary legislation to public presence: The language of gay rights: From legislation to lobbying. In C. Williams and G. Tessuto (eds.), *Language in the negotiation of justice: Contexts, texts, and applications*. Farnham and Burlington: Ashgate.

Incelli, E. (2013). Shaping reality through metaphorical patterns in legislative texts on immigration: A corpus-assisted approach. In C. Williams and G. Tessuto (eds.), *Language in the negotiation of justice: Contexts, texts, and applications*. Farnham and Burlington: Ashgate.

Jackson, R. (2005). *Writing the war on terrorism: Language, politics, and counter-terrorism*. Manchester: Manchester University Press.

Jayasuriya, K. (1999). *Law, capitalism and power in Asia: The rule of law and legal institutions*. London: Routledge.

Johnson, A. (2013). Embedding police interviews in the prosecution case in the Shipman trial. In C. Heffer, F. Rock, and J. Conley (eds.), *Legal-lay communication*. New York: Oxford University Press.

Kellner, D. (2004). 9/11, Spectacles of terror, and media manipulation: A critique of Jihadist and Bush media politics. *Critical Discourse Studies* 1(1): 41–64.

Kelsen, H. (1967). *Pure theory of law*. Berkeley: University of California Press.

Kerr, R. (2008). Discourse and leadership: Using the paradigm of the permanent state of emergency. *Critical Discourse Studies* 5(3): 201–216.

Kjaer, A. L. and Palsbro, L. (2008). National identity and law in the context of European integration: The case of Denmark. *Discourse & Society* 19(5): 599–627.

Komter, M. (2013). The interactional dynamics of eliciting a confession in a Dutch police interrogation. *Research on Language and Social Interaction* 36(4): 433–470.

Lester, E. (2014). *Making of migration law: The foreigner, sovereignty, and the case of Australia*. PhD thesis, Melbourne Law School.

Liao, M. (2013). Power in interruption in Chinese criminal courtroom discourse. In C. Williams and G. Tessuto (eds.), *Language in the negotiation of justice: Contexts, texts, and applications*. Farnham and Burlington: Ashgate.

Lucas, K. and Fyke, J. (2014). Euphemisms and ethics: A language-centered analysis of Penn state's sexual abuse scandal. *Journal of Business Ethics* 122: 551–569.

Luke, A. (2002). Beyond science and ideology critique: Developments in critical discourse analysis. *Annual Review of Applied Linguistics* 22: 96–110.

McKenna, B. (2004). Critical discourse studies: Where to from here? *Critical Discourse Studies* 1(1): 9–39.

MacMartin, C. (2002). (Un)reasonable doubt? The invocation of children's consent in sexual abuse trail judgments. *Discourse & Society* 13(1): 9–40.

Matoesian, G. (1993). *Reproducing rape: Domination through talk in the courtroom*. Chicago: University of Chicago Press.

Matoesian, G. (2001). *Law and the language of identity: Discourse in the William Kennedy Smith rape trial*. New York: Oxford University Press.

Mawani, R. (2012). Law's archive. *Annual Review of Law and Social Sciences* 8: 337–365.

Mertz, E. (1994). Legal language: Pragmatics, poetics and social power. *Annual Review of Anthropology* 23: 435–455.

Mertz, E. (2007). *The language of law school: Learning to "think like a lawyer"*. New York: Oxford University Press.

Mertz, E. and Rajah, J. (2014). Language-and-law scholarship: An interdisciplinary conversation and a post-9/11 example. *Annual Review of Law and Social Science* 10: 169–183.

Moore, K. (2013). Asylum shopping in the neoliberal social imaginary. *Media Culture Society* 35: 348–365.

Nadler, J. and Trout, J. D. (2012). The language of consent in police encounters. In P.A. Tiersma and L.M. Solan (eds.), *The Oxford handbook of language and law*, 326–339. Oxford: Oxford University Press.

Naughton, C. M., O'Donnell, A.T., Greenwood, R. M. and Muldoon, O.T. (2015). 'Ordinary decent domestic violence': A discursive analysis of family law judges' interviews. *Discourse & Society* 26(3): 349–365.

Nilsson, L., Eklof, A. and Ottosson, T. (2009). I'm entitled to make mistakes and get corrected: Students' self-positioning in inquiries into academic conduct. *Critical Discourse Studies* 6(2): 127–152.

O'Barr, W. M. (1982). *Linguistic evidence: Language, power, and strategy in the courtroom*. New York: Academic Press.

Owen, T. (2014). The 'access to medicines' campaign vs. Big Pharma. *Critical Discourse Studies* 11(3): 288–304.

Pahuja, S. (2011). *Decolonising international law: Development, economic growth and the politics of universality*. New York: Cambridge University Press.

Pether, P. (1999a). Critical discourse analysis, rape law and the jury instruction simplification project. *Southern Illinois University Law Journal* 24: 53–94.

Pether, P. (1999b). On foreign ground: Grand narratives, situated specificities, and the praxis of critical theory and law. *Law and Critique* 10: 211–236.

Pether, P. (2005). Is there anything outside the class? Law, literature, and pedagogy. *Cardozo Law Review* 26(6): 2415–2424.

Pether, P. (2007). Regarding the Miller girls: Daisy, Judith, and the seeming paradox of in Re Grand Jury Subpoena, Judith Miller. *Law and Literature* 19(2): 187–206.

Phillips, N., Lawrence, T. B. and Hardy, C. (2004). Discourse and institutions. *The Academy of Management Review* 29(4): 635–652.

Post, R. (2007) Introduction: The relatively autonomous discourse of law. In R. Post (ed.), *Law and the order of culture*, vii–xvi. Berkeley: University of California Press.

Rajah, J. (2012). *Authoritarian rule of law: Legislation, discourse and legitimacy in Singapore*. New York: Cambridge University Press.

Rajah, J. (2014a). Sinister translations: Law's authority in a post-9/11 world. *Indiana Journal of Global Legal Studies* 21(1): 107–143.

Rajah, J. (2014b). Flogging gum: Cultural imaginaries and postcoloniality in Singapore's rule of law. *Law Text Culture* 18: 135–165.

Rajah, J. (2015). 'Rule of law' as transnational legal order. In T.C. Halliday and G. Shaffer (eds.), *Transnational legal orders*. New York: Cambridge University Press.

Reyes-Foster, B. M. (2014). Creating order in the bureaucratic register. *Critical Discourse Studies* 11(4): 377–396.

Richland, J. B. (2008). *Arguing with tradition: The language of law in Hopi Tribal court*. Chicago: University of Chicago Press.

Richland, J. B. (2013). Jurisdiction: Grounding law in language. *Annual Review of Anthropology* 42: 209–226.

Rock, C., Heffer, F. and Conley, J. (2013). Textual travel in legal-lay communication. In C. Heffer, F. Rock and J. Conley (eds.), *Legal-lay communication*. New York: Oxford University Press.

Rock, F. (2013). "Every link in the chain": The police interview as textual intersection. In C. Heffer, F. Rock and J. Conley (eds.), *Legal-lay communication*. New York: Oxford University Press.

Saft, S. and Ohara, Y. (2006). The media and the pursuit of militarism in Japan: Newspaper editorials in the aftermath of 9/11. *Critical Discourse Studies* 3(1): 81–101.

Sarat, A., Anderson, M. and Frank, C. O. (2010). *Law and the humanities: An introduction*. New York: Cambridge University Press.

Schnurr, S., Homolar, A., MacDonald, M. N. and Rethel, L. (2015). Legitimizing claims for 'crisis' leadership in global governance. *Critical Discourse Studies* 12(2): 187–205.

Sherwin, R. K. (2000). *When law goes pop*. Chicago: University of Chicago Press.

Shuy, R. W. (2008). Discourse analysis in the legal context. In D. Schiffrin, D. Tannen and H.E. Hamilton (eds.), *The handbook of discourse analysis*. Blackwell. Accessed March 28, 2015, http://onlinelibrary. wiley.com/doi/10.1002/9780470753460.ch23/summary

Simone, M. A. (2009). Give me liberty and give me surveillance: A case study of the US Government's discourse of surveillance. *Critical Discourse Studies* 6(1): 1–14.

Strouhal, E. (1989). The case of W.: A critical journey to the border between psychiatry and justice. In R. Wodak (ed.), *Language, power, and ideology: Studies in political discourse*. Philadelphia and Amsterdam: John Benjamins Publishing.

Tamanaha, B. Z. (2004). *On the rule of law: History, politics, theory*. Cambridge: Cambridge University Press.

Teo, P. (2000). Racism in the news: A critical discourse analysis of news reporting in two Australian newspapers. *Discourse & Society* 11(1): 7–49.

Thumin, N. (2010). Self-representation in museums: Therapy or democracy? *Critical Discourse Studies* 7(4): 291–304.

Tiersma, P. M. and Solan, L. M. (2012). *The Oxford handbook of language and law*. Oxford: Oxford University Press.

Tomlins, C. (2007). How autonomous is law? *Annual Review of Law and Social Science* 3: 45–68.

Trinch, S. (2013). Recalling rape: Moving beyond what we know. In C. Heffer, F. Rock and J. Conley (eds.), *Legal-lay communication*. New York: Oxford University Press.

van Dijk, T. (1993). Principles of critical discourse analysis. *Discourse & Society* 4(2): 249–283.

White, J. B. (1990). *Justice as translation*. Chicago: University of Chicago Press.

Winiecki, D. (2008). The expert witnesses and courtroom discourse: Applying micro and macro forms of discourse analysis to study process and the 'doings of doings' for individuals and for society. *Discourse & Society* 19(6): 765–781.

Wodak, R. (1985). The interaction between judge and defendant. In T.A. van Dijk (ed.), *Handbook of discourse analysis Vol. 4 discourse analysis in society*. London: Academic Press.

Wodak, R. (2001). What CDA is about: A summary of its history, important concepts and its developments. In R. Wodak and M. Meyer (eds.), *Methods of critical discourse analysis*. London: Sage.

Wodak, R. (2013). Dis-citizenship and migration: A critical discourse-analytical perspective. *Journal of Language, Identity, and Education* 12: 173–178.

Yin, J. (2007). The clash of rights: A critical analysis of new discourse on human rights in the United States and China. *Critical Discourse Studies* 4(1): 74–94.

Zoonen, L. van, Vis, F. and Miheli, S. (2010). Performing citizenship on YouTube: Activism, satire and online debate around the anti-Islam video Fitna. *Critical Discourse Studies* 7(4): 249–262.

33

Critical discourse analysis and ecology

Arran Stibbe

Introduction

One of the criteria for working in Critical Discourse Analysis is, according to van Dijk (1993: 252), 'solidarity with those who need it most. Their problems are real problems, that is, the serious problems that threaten the lives or well-being of many'. Critical Discourse Analysts therefore tend to take the perspective of oppressed groups in society, working against exploitation and towards a more equitable society. Increasingly, however, the problems faced by oppressed groups are not just social but ecological, as climate change, biodiversity loss, resource depletion and chemical contamination make it difficult for them to achieve well-being or even meet their basic needs for survival. It is no longer enough to work towards an equitable society, since if that society consumes more than can be replaced by nature and produces more waste than can be absorbed by nature, then it will be unsustainable and on a pathway to collapse. Mary Midgley (2011: 111) claims that 'the Marxist account entirely ignored factors outside the human species... Marx was not concerned about the exploitation of natural resources... he saw capitalist imperialism simply as the oppression of one set of humans by another, not as a source of ecological disaster'. The same could be said for much work in Critical Discourse Studies in the past, although, as this chapter will describe, that has started to change.

The change arises from a general ecological turn with the humanities and social science, which has seen the rise of *ecopsychology, ecofeminism, ecosociology, ecocriticism, environmental communication* and *ecolinguistics*. All of these new disciplines recognise that the object of study, whether human minds, gender relations, society, literature, communication or language, has an influence on human behaviour and therefore on how humans treat the ecological systems that sustain life. Ecological humanities and social sciences are (in general) oriented towards helping to build not just fairer and more equitable societies, but also sustainable societies, which protect their ecological foundations. Glotfelty (2014), for instance, describes how 'Most ecocritical work shares a common motivation: the troubling awareness that we have reached the age of environmental limits, a time when the consequences of human actions are damaging the planet's basic life support systems'.

At the same time as linguists are moving towards fuller accounts of language which include consideration of ecological issues, there is an increasing focus on language among ecologists and environmental thinkers. Rather than treating ecological issues as technical problems to be solved by science, these thinkers see them as calling into question the fundamental stories that societies are built on – the stories we live by. This chapter uses the concept of 'story' in this sense as a lens for exploring the connection between language and ecology.

The chapter begins with the ecologists and environmental thinkers who expose and question the stories we live by. It then moves on to linguistic approaches which investigate how these stories are 'told' through discourse and cognitive structures. The linguistic approaches are illustrated through a critical analysis of the discourse of Native American sayings. Finally, the conclusion explores how the approaches described in the chapter can contribute to an engaged form of ecologically sensitive Critical Discourse Analysis.

Stories

Naomi Klein, in her book, *This Changes Everything: Capitalism vs. the Climate,* describes the impact that climate change will have on vulnerable populations around the world. She states that:

> There are ways of preventing this grim future, or at least making it a lot less dire. But the catch is that these also involve changing everything. For us high consumers, it involves changing how we live, how our economies function, even the stories we tell about our place on earth.
>
> *(Klein 2014: 4)*

Klein is among many commentators to suggest that dealing with ecological issues requires a fundamental reconsideration of 'the stories on which Western cultures are founded' (63). Dougald and Hine (2009), in *The Dark Mountain Manifesto,* write that the root of ecological crisis lies in 'the stories we have been telling ourselves', which include the 'story of human centrality, of our ever-expanding control over "nature", our right to perpetual economic growth, our ability to transcend all limits'. In *Change the Story, Change the Future: a Living Economy for a Living Earth,* Korten (2015: 1) writes 'When we get our story wrong, we get our future wrong. We are in a terminal crisis because we have our defining story badly wrong'. Korten urges a move away from stories that value money and markets above all else, towards ones which value life and the living earth. Charles Eisenstein (2013: 1–2) describes a prevailing 'Story of the People. . . in which humanity was destined to create a perfect world through science, reason and technology; to conquer nature, transcend our animal origins and engineer a rational society'. It is, according to Eisenstein, a story that has 'come to enslave us, that indeed is killing the planet' (8). Macy and Johnstone (2012: 15) criticise the 'business–as–usual story' which is 'told by most mainstream policy makers and corporate leaders. Their view is that economies can and must continue to grow'.

By the term 'story', Eisenstein means 'a matrix of narratives, agreements and symbolic systems that comprises the answers our culture offers to life's most basic questions' (2012: 4). A key aspect of this conception of 'story' is that people can forget that a certain perspective is just one possible perspective, and instead start to perceive it as just a transparent reflection of the way the world is. Macy and Johnstone (2012: 15) describe how 'When you're living in the middle of this [business–as–usual] story, it's easy to think of it as just the way things are'.

Kingsnorth and Hine (2009), similarly state that 'What makes this story [of human centrality] so dangerous is that, for the most part, we have forgotten that it is a story'.

In essence, these ecological thinkers are claiming that stories and myths which grew out of the Enlightenment have taken on new powerful forms within neoliberalism and transnational capitalism, to the extent that they are making the Earth less hospitable for human life. What these critics do not do, however, is analyse the detailed linguistic workings through which stories such as these are produced, reproduced and come to structure how we think about the world. That is a task that critical discourse analysis and cognitive linguistics are well suited for. In their own ways, these disciplines analyse linguistic features to reveal ideologies, metaphors, framings and other forms of story that we live by. If we combine linguistic approaches with the insights of environmental and ecological thinkers, then the result can be considered a form of *ecolinguistics*.

Stories and discourse

Ecolinguistics is a term which refers to a variety of different approaches with different methods and goals (Steffensen and Fill 2014). Early approaches tended to focus on how grammatical features and lexical items which are built into the language system prevent ecological thinking. Halliday (2001: 193) wrote that 'there is a syndrome of grammatical features which conspire... to construe reality in a certain way; and it is a way that is no longer good for our health as a species'. One example he gives is how human beings are represented in transitivity structures as the most animate of beings (thinking, doing and acting in the world), while inanimate objects are represented passively, as having things done to them (194). He points out that forests are not represented as actively doing things, even though they prevent flooding, provide oxygen, stabilise the soil and harbour wildlife. He concludes that 'The grammar does not present inanimate objects as doers... [which] makes it hard for us to take seriously the notion of inanimate nature as an active participant in events' (194). The problem with a language system approach is that it fails to consider how particular groups in society use language in particular ways to further their interests, and there is little prospect of changing the language system itself, a fact which Halliday himself concedes (196).

Later approaches have tended to focus on *discourse* rather than the language system. A discourse approach examines how particular groups in society select particular lexical items and grammatical structures from those available from the language system, and combine them in particular ways to tell stories about the world. Glenn (2004), Mitchell (2013) and Stibbe (2012), for instance, analyse the discourse of transnational agribusiness, showing how it represents animals in ways which promote exploitative and ecologically damaging farming. Glenn shows how a cluster of linguistic features within the discourse of agribusiness tells the story that FACTORY FARMING IS BENIGN:

> With the relatively recent advent of the factory farming industry... an assortment of corporate strategies have ensued that construct an image of a benevolently beneficial industry. Far from benign, however, factory farms are responsible for a tremendous amount of environmental damage.
>
> *(63)*

Mitchell (2013: 299) analyses farming magazines and discovers 'a strong discourse of production where the non-human animals are linguistically constructed as raw materials, production machines and product'. By representing the industry as beneficial to animals, or alternatively representing animals as objects who cannot feel, the discourse justifies and promotes industrial farming techniques. These techniques serve the financial interests of the agribusiness executives responsible for creating the discourse, but only through harming animals and imposing externalities (external costs) on local communities and future generations who suffer from the environmental damage caused.

The discourse approach is, of course, a form of Critical Discourse Analysis. A powerful group uses language in characteristic ways that convey a story (an ideology) that causes suffering and oppression to other groups. An ecolinguistic analysis simply considers a wider range of oppressed groups (including animals, current generations of humans who are suffering from pollution and resource depletion, and future generations of humans who will find it harder to meet their needs), and considers the impact of discourses on the wider systems that support life. Discourses such as transnational agribusiness can be considered *destructive* since they can encourage people to engage in ecologically destructive activities. Other discourses that could be considered as destructive are those of neoclassical economics or other dominant economic paradigms such as Keynesian economics, which either overlook the environment completely or contain a 'mechanistic conception of nature as devoid of significance except insofar as it could be moulded for human purposes and sold on the market' (Gare 1996: 143). Advertising, too, could be considered destructive, in encouraging people to purchase unnecessary and environmentally damaging products. Destructive discourses are addressed through *resistance,* e.g., raising critical language awareness that the stories that the discourse tells are not the only stories possible, that they potentially have a negative impact on the systems that support life, and that other stories are available.

As well as criticising the destructive impact of discourses such as advertising, economics and agribusiness, ecolinguistics also searches for new, positive stories to live by. Goatly (2014: 215), for instance, uses systemic functional grammar to analyse Wordsworth's *The Prelude*. Wordsworth's poetry, he finds, represents nature actively by placing animals, plants and rivers in the roles of *actors* in material processes and *sayers* in verbal processes. It encourages people to be more observant of the natural world by placing it as the *phenomenon* of mental processes. Goatly's conclusion is that 'to survive we had better take note of Wordsworth. . . rethink and respeak our participation in nature before it rethinks or rejects our participation in it'.

Goatly's analysis is just of one collection of poems, but these poems are manifestations of a wider discourse of romantic poetry which offers different perspectives on nature from those currently dominant in society. Discourses like this, which the analyst believes can be helpful in encouraging ecological thinking, can be considered *beneficial discourses*. Analysis of beneficial discourses is a form of Positive Discourse Analysis (Martin 2004, Bartlett 2012). The aim of PDA in this case is not to promote the works of Wordsworth or other Romantic poets, but rather to discover constellations of language features which tell a useful story. These language features could then be applied to a wide range of texts which shape how we think about nature, e.g., biology textbooks or ecology reports.

Many ecological studies of discourse are not of discourses which are clearly destructive, or ones which are beneficial, but ones which fall somewhere between the two, which can be called *ambivalent discourses*. Corporate greenwash, for example, is negative because it deceives customers into thinking that products are more ecologically beneficial than they actually are, but also positive in the sense that it conveys the story that the environmental performance of products matters. Sustainable development discourses are positive in emphasising that the environment needs to be protected as economies grow, but negative in failing to question whether the economies of countries that are already over-consuming actually do need to grow. There have been numerous studies of ambivalent discourses, including eco-tourism (Purnell 1997), sustainability (Kowalski 2013), greenwash (Alexander 2013), natural resources (Kurz et al. 2005), zoos (Milstein 2009), wildlife documentaries (Sealey and Oakley 2013) and environmentalism (Benton-Short 1999). Addressing ambivalent discourses may involve negotiating a common set of values between the analyst and those responsible for reproducing the discourse, and then working together to ensure that the discourse conveys those common values.

Stories in cognition

One of the most productive areas of ecolinguistic enquiry has focused on the cognitive level, and examined how particular frames and metaphors promote ecologically beneficial or destructive behaviour. Romaine (1996) and Nerlich and Jaspal (2012) take Lakoff and Johnson's (1980) expression 'metaphors we live by' and invert it to 'metaphors we die by'; that is, metaphors which encourage us to destroy the systems that we depend on for our survival.

Sometimes metaphors and framings are examined as part of particular discourses, but sometimes the cognitive structures cross large numbers of discourses and are of interest in their own right. For example, the framing CLIMATE CHANGE IS A PROBLEM TO BE SOLVED is shared across a great number of discourses and everyday ways of thinking about climate change. It tells a particular story about climate change – that once a solution is found the problem will disappear. Although widespread, it is not the only possible way to frame climate change. Greer (2013: 22) writes that 'many things we've conceptualised as problems are actually predicaments'. Framing climate change as a predicament leads to a different conceptual structure – although humanity can, and must, respond to a predicament, there is no response which can make a predicament simply disappear.

There have been studies of metaphor and frames in a wide range of areas, including climate change (Hulme 2009, Russill 2010), biodiversity issues (Christmas et al. 2013), conservation (Keulartz 2007, Larson 2011, Blackmore and Holmes 2013), development (Darnton and Kirk 2011), nature (Verhagen 2008), geoengineering (Nerlich and Jaspal 2012) and general environmental issues (Crompton 2010). While some of these studies are written for academic audiences, some are aimed at giving practical advice to NGOs and policymakers on how to frame environmental and development issues. What all the studies agree on is that how ecological issues are cognitively structured by framings and metaphors is important for how we think about the issues, and, importantly, how we act on them.

Blackmore and Holmes (2013: 42) propose a specific methodology to investigate frames, based on the following questions:

> What values does the frame embody?
> Is a response necessary?
> Can the frame be challenged? If so, how?
> Can (and should) a new frame be created?

A primary way that they evaluate frames is whether they trigger the *intrinsic* values (concern for others) that are associated with pro-environmental behaviour, or *extrinsic* values (i.e., profit, status and concern for self) that are associated with ecologically destructive behaviour. The examples they give of intrinsic frames are *discovery, working together, beauty in nature,* and *connection with nature,* which they contrast with the extrinsic frames of *commercial transaction* (which sees protecting nature as a business selling the product of conservation to a customer), or *ecosystems services* (which puts a price on nature).

A key issue for frames and metaphors is whether they tell a story of humans as part of the natural world, or separate from it. Cachelin, Norvell and Darling (2010: 671) write that 'if we humans consider ourselves apart from nature, we will not necessarily consider ourselves subject to nature's laws'. Verhagen (2008: 11) investigates the metaphor of NATURE IS A MACHINE, which 'justifies the exploitative and managerial character of Western civilisation' and clearly separates humans from nature. A variant of that metaphor is EARTH IS A SPACESHIP, which conveys the 'image of humans as managers and controllers' of nature (Mühlhäusler 2003: 180). Another metaphor, of 'ecological restoration', treats the Earth as a painting that needs caring for (Keulartz 2007: 31), but still separates the person doing the restoring from the painting (nature). Another metaphor which separates humans from nature is NATURE IS A BURNING LIBRARY (Väliverronen and Hellsten 2002: 236). In this metaphor, the extinction of species is viewed in terms of the loss of important (genetic) information that occurs when a library burns. It is a dramatic metaphor but still places humans outside the library trying to put the fire out, rather than inside the library burning along with the books.

In general, Russill (2010: 116) argues that it is essential to investigate frames and metaphors to discover how people make sense of ecological issues, since 'professional communicators have great power to shape public understanding, and build support for specific conclusions by accessing deeply shared metaphorical systems'.

An integrated framework for analysing stories

The recent book *Ecolinguistics: Language, Ecology and the Stories We Live By* (Stibbe 2015) proposes a cognitive framework that integrates the idea of 'stories we live by' from human ecology with critical discourse analysis, cognitive science, social psychology, identity theory and appraisal theory. In this framework, *stories* are underlying cognitive models that manifest themselves in text and exist in the minds of individuals or across the minds of multiple individuals in society. Stories that are common within a culture are the *stories we live by* and influence how people think, talk and act, with a consequent impact on how we treat the ecosystems that life depends on. There are eight forms that stories take, as follows:

- *Ideologies* are mental models shared by a group.
- *Framings* use a packet of knowledge about the world (a source frame) to tell a story about an area of life (a target domain).
- *Metaphors* are a form of framing where the source frame is concrete and distinctly different from the target domain.
- *Identities* are stories about what it means to be a particular kind of person.
- *Evaluations* are stories in people's minds about whether an area of life is good or bad.
- *Convictions* are stories in people's minds about whether a particular description of reality is true, uncertain or untrue.
- *Erasure* and *Salience* are stories in people's minds about whether an area of life is important and worthy of consideration.

All eight types of story exist at the cognitive level, as models in people's minds, but they manifest themselves in particular linguistic forms: discourses, trigger words for metaphors and framings, language that characterises people, appraisal patterns and erasure/salience patterns which disguise participants or represent them vividly. By analysing the linguistic features of texts (or discourses), it is possible to reveal the underlying story, which is then judged against an *ecosophy*.

Ecosophy is a term coined by Arne Naess (1995: 8) and is short for 'ecological philosophy'. It is 'a philosophy of ecological harmony. . . openly normative it contains norms, rules, postulates, value priority announcements and hypotheses concerning the state of affairs'. All Critical Discourse Analysis is (explicitly or implicitly) conducted against a vision of ideal human relations with other humans. Gavriely-Nuri (2012: 83) is explicit when she says that a Cultural Critical Discourse Analysis should be based on 'values, attitudes and behaviours based on the principles of freedom, justice and democracy, all human rights, tolerance and solidarity'. An ecosophy is a values framework for judging stories that includes consideration of relationships of humans not only with other humans, but also with the larger ecosystems they depend on for survival.

Ecosophies vary on a scale from anthropocentric (where the focus is only on human wellbeing), to ecocentric (where humans and other species are considered to have intrinsic worth). They can be optimistic (e.g., that changes in technology can solve environmental problems without any reduction in consumption or changes in social relationships), or pessimistic (e.g., that current civilisation is on an irredeemable trajectory towards collapse, and it is time to plan for a new kind of civilisation for after the collapse). And politically they can range from the far right, where market forces are seen as the solution to environmental problems, to socialist or anarchist responses which call for a new social order.

Stories are judged to be *destructive* (i.e., encouraging people to destroy the systems that life depends on) if they oppose the ecosophy, and are then resisted (e.g., through raising critical language awareness of the potential impact of the stories). They are *ambivalent* if they partially oppose but partially agree with the ecosophy, in which case it may be possible to work constructively with those who use the story to make adjustments. And stories are judged to be *beneficial* if they are seen as aligning with and agreeing with the ecosophy, and are then promoted. Promoting a 'story' means promoting the linguistic features which combine together to tell the story rather than specific texts that tell the story.

Stories and the discourse of Native American sayings

This section briefly puts the framework described above into practice by analysing a corpus of Native American sayings that are commonly used in environmental and ecological writing. One example is the following quotation attributed to Chief Seattle:

> Humankind has not woven the web of life. We are but one thread within it. Whatever we do to the web, we do to ourselves. All things are bound together. All things connect.

This quotation appears in Al Gore's book *Earth in the Balance,* in Molly Scott Cato's *Green Economics,* in Matlock and Morgan's *Ecological Engineering Design,* in Havercroft et al.'s *Carbon Capture and Storage,* in Makofske's *Technology, Development, and the Global Environment,* and in a vast range of other environmental books, reports and publications.

In Chief Seattle's metaphor, humans are very much part of the natural world, and the metaphor is useful in emphasising that concern for the environment is not just for the sake of exotic and beautiful species which are endangered, but for the survival of humans too. As Raymond et al. (2013) point out, 'In the web of life metaphor, humans are one part of a wider ecological system and have the responsibility to understand their impacts on. . . the broader system'. In general, the use of Native American sayings in ecological/environmental discourse is of interest to ecolinguistics because they are a device for presenting stories about the place of humans in the world that are very different from mainstream economic and environmental discourses.

The common quotations can be considered a discourse in their own right since they have characteristic linguistic features which encode a particular ideology. This is not a monolithic 'Native American Ideology', however, as if peoples across an entire continent all thought (and still do think) the same. The sayings have come from the past selectively, often at a considerable distance from the original. Furtwangler (1997), for instance, describes how Chief Seattle's speech was written down a significant time after it was given, based on notes written by someone who only heard it through an interpreter.

Instead of being a transparent and authentic representation of an ancient worldview, the discourse of Native American sayings could be considered a social construction of an ecological wise 'other' to express a story that speaks to contemporary environmental issues. As Greg Garrard (2012: 135) points out, there are dangers to essentialising an 'other' in this way. He writes that 'The Ecological Indian is clearly a stereotype of European origin', and 'at its cruellest, the Ecological Indian represents a homogenisation of. . . 600 or so distinct and culturally diverse societies' (136). The discourse can, however, be analysed in terms of the linguistic features it contains and how these features convey particular stories about the world, without treating it as an authentic record of a particular civilisation. While patronising stereotyping can certainly be dispensed with, there may be forms of language in the sayings that are useful in telling stories that align with the analyst's ecosophy.

This section is based on the ecosophy described in Stibbe (2015: 13), which is a) broadly ecocentric in valuing humans and other species, b) has a pragmatic focus on human wellbeing, since any solution that harms humans for the sake of other species is unlikely to be adopted, c) recognises environmental limits so calls for a reduction in global consumption, d) recognises social justice so calls for a redistribution of resources as total consumption declines and e) recognises that human survival (and existence) depends on continuous interaction with other species and the physical environment.

For the purposes of this analysis, 60 examples of Native American sayings were gathered into a corpus from a variety of online collections of quotes from various organisations, including *Californian Indian Education* (2015). This is not a representative sample, but the quotes are common ones, and therefore the corpus represents a significant usage of the discourse. The approach is a Positive Discourse Analysis one, which aims to discover beneficial stories (i.e., ones that that accord with the analyst's ecosophy), and determine what cluster of linguistic features give rise to those stories. If positive stories are found, then the language features which combine to tell these stories can be promoted as useful ways of communicating about the place of humans in the world. That is not to say that PDA is an uncritical approach – if there are negative aspects of a discourse then they need to be exposed to ensure they are not reproduced.

The discussion here is of the discourse of the quotes themselves, but as part of a larger study which analyses how the quotes are used in the context of environmental and ecological writing. Analysis of the context is beyond the scope of this chapter, but it is worth making three comments about how the quotations tend to be used. Firstly, the quotes are generally represented positively in environmental writing as a source of insight into ecological problems; secondly, the style of language of the quotes differs markedly from the surrounding text; and thirdly, the insights from the text are often re-described using the style of language of the surrounding text.

The discourse of Native American sayings constructs a power relationship between speaker and hearer that represents the Native American speaker as wise and knowledgeable, in relationship to a hearer who is either ignorant (in the case of a 'white' addressee) or innocent (when the addressee is a young Native American). The story behind this can be glossed as THE

NATIVE AMERICAN SPEAKER IS A WISE ADVISOR, and is an example of the most general form of story, an *ideology*. Linguistically, the ideology manifests itself in the use of the following features (with examples from the corpus):

- imperatives, e.g., '*Hold on* to what you believe'
- high modality, e.g., 'We *must* consider the impact of our decisions on the next seven generations' or 'We *need* to set an example of truth and action'
- second-person pronouns, e.g., '*You* will discover you cannot eat money'
- present tense 'zero conditionals', which represent the outcome of one state of affairs as necessarily leading to another state of affairs, e.g., '*When* you know who you are; *when* your mission is clear. . .You know that you are alive'.

These language features have a strong interpersonal function which, although it powerfully engages the reader, would be out of place and didactic in environmental/ecological writing if not in a quotation.

The story of the speaker as wise and hearer as ignorant is part of a larger *ideological square* (van Dijk) where positive aspects of an ingroup are emphasised, negative aspects downplayed and negative aspects of the outgroup are emphasised, with positive aspects downplayed. In this square, the Native Americans (or 'Red Nation', 'Indians', 'a red man', 'our people' or 'us') form the positive in-group while Europeans (or 'the white man', 'him', 'you', 'them') form the negative out-group. An example from the corpus of the ideological square is as follows:

> Only to the white man was nature a wilderness and only to him was the land 'infested' with 'wild' animals and 'savage' people. To us it was tame, Earth was bountiful. . . .

In context, however, the environmental/ecological writings are written by members of an industrial society for members of the same society, and appropriate the voice of the 'other' to reject the values of the society that both author and reader are part of. The discourse uses *appraisal patterns* to consistently represent the values of industrial civilisation negatively, and those of the Native Americans positively. In the quote above, 'infested' and 'savage' have negative semantic prosody (i.e., tend to be used in negative contexts such as 'infested with cockroaches') and are associated with the view of the 'white man', while 'bountiful' has positive connotations and is associated with the view of the ingroup (i.e., Native Americans). The pattern in general is to build up the positivity of the in-group values through a wide range of appraising items that have positive prosody or connotations, such as *peace, love, respect, truth, honesty, generosity, equity* and *brotherhood,* while associating the outgroup with negative appraising items, such as *sick, broken, selfish* or *separation*. The appraisal consists of not just lexical items but also antithesis, where a contrast is presented between something that is approved of and something that is condemned. For example in 'I do not think the measure of a civilisation is how tall its buildings of concrete are, but rather how well its people have learned to relate to their environment', the second clause is given positivity through aligning with the views of the speaker, who is already presented as wise, with the first part presented negatively.

When appraisal patterns are widespread within a culture they can become entrenched, i.e., become stories in people's minds about whether an area of life is good or bad. These cognitive stories are called *evaluations* (in Stibbe 2015: 83). A key aspect of the appraisal patterns in the Native American sayings is that they represent extrinsic (self-centred) values such as *wealth, power, money* and *fame* negatively, and intrinsic (other-centred) values such as *generosity, love,* and *respect* positively (e.g., *We do not want riches. We want peace and love.*). This is important since research shows that just reading about intrinsic values encourages people to express more care about the environment (Molinsky, Grant and Morgolis 2012, Blackmore and Holmes 2013). In this way the quotations are resisting widespread entrenched evaluations that represent extrinsic values positively and attempting to replace them with other evaluations.

An important issue in ecolinguistics is whether the natural world is represented saliently in texts through linguistic patterns which represent it prominently, or is erased through patterns which omit or distort it. As Leopold (1979: 214) notes 'We can be ethical only in relation to something we can see, feel, understand, love, or otherwise have faith in'. Often in mainstream environmental writing, plants and animals are represented abstractly as *flora* and *fauna,* or *stocks of biotic resources,* which erases them as individuals worthy of respect and care (Stibbe 2012). Cognitively, if the natural world is erased from widespread texts that people interact with daily it could set up stories in their minds that the natural world is not of importance or worthy of consideration.

In contrast to this, the discourse of Native American sayings has various ways to build up the salience of the natural world, including what can be called *sense images.* A sense image represents an aspect of nature as it appears to the senses of humans observing it, conveying a strong and vivid image to the hearer. Examples from the corpus are: *the cry of a loon, the flash of a salmon, the whisper of spruce needles, the fragrance of the grass* and *the flash of a firefly.* The focus on the names of specific species *loon, salmon, spruce* also builds salience since these are at the most concretely imaginable *basic level* (Lakoff and Wehling 2012: 41), as opposed to more abstract level of *bird, fish* or *tree,* or the even more abstract *organisms.* Metonymy too gives animals a salience by representing types of animals by specific, easily imaginable characteristics or actions 'Honour all with whom we share the Earth: Four-leggeds, two-leggeds, winged ones, swimmers, crawlers'. In this way the *salience patterns* in the text make the natural world more prominent in the minds of hearers, which, if repeated frequently enough, could build a story in their minds that nature is worthy of consideration.

There are many analogies in the sayings which compare humans with other aspects of nature:

- We live, we die, and like the grass and trees, renew ourselves.
- A frog does not drink up the pond in which it lives.
- The coyote is sly, so is the Indian.
- [Man must follow a vision] as the eagle seeks the deepest blue of the sky.

These also give salience to the natural world, and help build up the story that humans are comparable to the rest of life, which is important in not overlooking that, like all creatures, we depend on the natural world for our continued survival.

One of the framings used is EARTH IS A POSSESSION, for example in 'We do not inherit the earth from our ancestors, we borrow it from our children'. This framing is anthropocentric since humans are represented as owning the earth, but at least in this case it is the children who own the earth, which accords with intergenerational justice. More ecocentric metaphors are those of THE EARTH AS A MOTHER, THE SKY AS A FATHER and HUMANS AS CHILDREN (e.g., 'Honour the Earth, our Mother', 'Whatever befalls the earth befalls the children of the earth'). The entailment of this metaphor is that the earth should be respected, since the earth is (framed as) a parent, and a parent frame includes respect from children to parents.

This section has just commented on a few of the many framings, metaphors, evaluations, salience patterns and other stories in a corpus of Native American sayings. In general, while there are important caveats about the construction of the fictional 'ecological other', the sayings do provide a cluster of linguistic devices for telling stories about the world that differ markedly from the dominant stories of an unsustainable industrial civilisation. Some of these stories accord with the ecosophy used to judge them against in giving salience (and therefore moral consideration) to both human beings and other species, in bringing awareness of environmental limits and emphasising the dependence of humans on the more than human world. Further investigation of the discourse could help reveal clusters of linguistic features that could be applied in other areas of life beyond the quotes themselves to help tell stories that encourage people to protect the natural world.

Conclusion

This chapter has discussed three main approaches to the relationship between language and the ecosystems that life depends on. A discourse approach describes how powerful groups in society select clusters of linguistic features which tell particular stories, and aims to expose these stories and resist them if they are seen as encouraging behaviour that harms the ecosystems that life depends on. The cognitive approach is similar, but focuses on particular cognitive structures such as metaphors and framings, which may appear as part of a discourse or more widely across a range of discourses. The final approach combined the human ecology idea that the fundamental stories told in Western societies contribute to ecological destruction, with cognitive and discursive theories to expose and challenge those stories. The practical analysis showed how a discourse (Native American sayings) can be investigated in the search for positive stories that align with the analyst's ecosophy, while still keeping an eye open for negative aspects of the discourse which should not be reproduced.

A key conclusion is that linguists cannot do it on their own. The ecological issues that we face are not due to linguistic deficiencies in the language system which can be recognised and corrected through grammatical or semantic analysis alone. Instead, it is necessary for ecolinguists to analyse how linguistic features come together in particular discourses to tell stories about the world, and judge those stories according to an ecosophy. The quality of the analysis will depend entirely on the quality of the ecosophy. An ecosophy partly consists of value announcements (e.g., statements about whether only humans matter or whether other species matter too), but is also based on evidence (e.g., evidence of environmental limits and the degree to which society much change to live within them).

Ecolinguistic analysis, then, is highly interdisciplinary, bringing consideration of ethics, environment, ecology, economics and society to bear on the analysis of texts. It requires an expansion of focus of Critical Discourse Analysis from the oppression of some groups of humans by other groups of humans, to a wider view of the role of language in influencing how we treat the ecosystems that all life depends on.

Further reading

Fill, A. and Penz, H. (eds.) (2017). *Routledge handbook of ecolinguistics*. London: Routledge.
This book consists of chapters written by a large number of leading ecolinguistics, including those who take a Critical Discourse Analysis and Positive Discourse Analysis approach.
Steffensen, S. and Fill, A. (2014). Ecolinguistics: The state of the art and future horizons. *Language Sciences* 41: 6–25.
This journal article provides a useful overview of the broad range of research approaches which label themselves as 'ecolinguistics'.
Stibbe, A. (2012). *Animals erased: Discourse, ecology, and reconnection with the natural world*. Middletown, CT: Wesleyan University Press.

This book investigates how the forms of language used to describe animals can influence how they are treated, with consequences for both animal welfare and the environment.

Stibbe, A. (2015). *Ecolinguistics: Language, ecology and the stories we live by*. London: Routledge.

This book outlines a theoretical framework for ecolinguistics, combining Critical Discourse Analysis and cognitive science. It is based on analysis of the *stories we live by*, which are judged according to the ecosophy of the analyst, and applies the framework to a wide range of discourses from economics textbooks to Japanese haiku.

References

Alexander, R. (2013). Shaping and misrepresenting public perceptions of ecological catastrophes: The BP Gulf oil spill. *Critical Approaches to Discourse Analysis across Disciplines* 7(1): 1–18.

Bartlett, T. (2012). *Hybrid voices and collaborative change: Contextualising positive discourse analysis*. London: Routledge.

Benton-Short, L. (1999). *Environmental discourse and practice*. Oxford: Blackwell.

Blackmore, E. and Holmes, T. (eds.) (2013). *Common cause for nature: Values and frames in conservation*. Machynlleth, Wales: Public Interest Research Centre.

Cachelin, A., Norvell, R. and Darling, A. (2010). Language fouls in teaching ecology: Why traditional metaphors undermine conservation literacy. *Conservation Biology* 24(3): 669–674.

Californian Indian Education. (2015). Inspirational quotes: traditional knowledge and education [Online]. Californian Indian Education. www.californiaindianeducation.org/inspire/traditional/

Christmas, S., Wright, L., Morris, L., Watson, A. and Miskelly, C. (2013). *Engaging people in biodiversity issues: Final report of the biodiversity segmentation scoping study*. London: Simon Christmas Ltd.

Crompton, T. (2010). Common cause: The case for working with our cultural values [Online]. WWF-UK. http://assets.wwf.org.uk/downloads/common_cause_report.pdf

Darnton, A. and Kirk, M. (2011). Finding frames: new ways to engage the UK public in global poverty [Online]. Bond. Accessed January 24, 2014, http://bond3.brix.fatbeehive.com/data/files/finding_frames.pdf

Eisenstein, C. (2013). *The more beautiful world our hearts know is possible*. Berkeley, CA: North Atlantic Books.

Furtwangler, A. (1997). *Answering Chief Seattle*. Seattle: University of Washington Press.

Gare, A. (1996). *Nihilism inc.: Environmental destruction and the metaphysics of sustainability*. Como, NSW: Eco-Logical Press.

Garrard, G. (2012). *Ecocriticism,* 2nd edn. London: Routledge.

Gavriely-Nuri, D. (2012). Cultural approach to CDA. *Critical Discourse Studies* 9(1): 77–85.

Glenn, C. B. (2004). Constructing consumables and consent: A critical analysis of factory farm industry discourse. *Journal of Communication Inquiry* 28(1): 63–81.

Glotfelty, C. (2014). What is ecocriticism? [Online]. Association for the Study of Literature and Environment. Accessed June 23, 2014, www.asle.org/site/resources/ecocritical-library/intro/defining/glotfelty/

Goatly, A. (2014). Nature and grammar. In C. Coffin, A. Hewings, and K. O'Halloran (eds.), *Applying english grammar: Corpus and functional approaches,* 197–215. London: Routledge.

Greer, J. (2013). *The long descent: A user's guide to the end of the industrial age*. Gabriola Island, BC: New Society Publishers.

Halliday, M. (2001). New ways of meaning: The challenge to applied linguistics. In A. Fill and P. Mühlhäusler (eds.), *The ecolinguistics reader: Language, ecology, and environment,* 175–202. London: Continuum.

Hulme, M. (2009). *Why we disagree about climate change: Understanding controversy, inaction and opportunity*. Cambridge: Cambridge University Press.

Keulartz, J. (2007). Using metaphors in restoring nature. *Nature & Culture* 2(1): 27–48.

Kingsnorth, P. and Hine, D. (2009). The Dark Mountain project manifesto [Online]. Accessed May 31, 2014, http://dark-mountain.net/about/manifesto/

Klein, N. (2014). *This changes everything: Capitalism vs. the climate*. New York : Simon & Schuster.

Korten, D. C. (2015). *Change the story, change the future: A living economy for a living earth*. Oakland, CA: Berrett-Koehler.

Kowalski, R. (2013). Sense and sustainability: The paradoxes that sustain. *World Futures: The Journal of General Evolution* 69(2): 75–88.

Kurz, T., Donaghue, N., Rapley, M. and Walker, I. (2005). The ways that people talk about natural resources: Discursive strategies as barriers to environmentally sustainable practices. *British Journal of Social Psychology* 44(4): 603–620.

Lakoff, G. and Johnson, M. (1980). *Metaphors we live by*. Chicago: University of Chicago Press.

Lakoff, G. and Wehling, E. (2012). *The little blue book: The essential guide to thinking and talking Democratic*. New York: Free Press.

Larson, B. (2011). *Metaphors for environmental sustainability: Redefining our relationship with nature*. New Haven, CT: Yale University Press.

Leopold, A. (1979). *A Sand County almanac and sketches here and there*. Oxford: Oxford University Press.

Macy, J. and Johnstone, C. (2012). *Active hope: How to face the mess we're in without going crazy*. Novato, CA: New World Library.

Martin, J. (2004). Positive discourse analysis: Solidarity and change. *Revista Canaria de Estudios Ingleses* 49: 179–200.

Midgley, M. (2011). *The myths we live by*. New York: Routledge.

Milstein, T. (2009). 'Somethin' tells me it's all happening at the zoo': Discourse, power, and conservationism. *Environmental Communication: A Journal of Nature and Culture* 3(1): 25–48.

Mitchell, L. (2013). Farming: Animals or machines? *Southern African Linguistics and Applied Language Studies* 31(3): 299–309.

Molinsky, A., Grant, A. and Margolis, J. (2012). The bedside manner of homo economicus: How and why priming an economic schema reduces compassion. *Organizational Behavior & Human Decision Processes* 119(1): 27–37.

Mühlhäusler, P. (2003). *Language of environment, environment of language: A course in ecolinguistics*. London: Battlebridge.

Naess, A. (1995). The shallow and the long range, deep ecology movement. In A. Drengson and Y. Inoue (eds.), *The deep ecology movement: An introductory anthology*, 3–10. Berkeley: North Atlantic Books.

Nerlich, B. and Jaspal, R. (2012). Metaphors we die by? Geoengineering, metaphors, and the argument from catastrophe. *Metaphor and Symbol* 27(2): 131–147.

Purnell, A. (1997). *Representations of nature: An ecolinguistic analysis of South Australian nature-based tourism promotion*. Adelaide: University of Adelaide, Mawson Graduate Centre for Environmental Studies.

Raymond, C., Singh, G., Karina Benessaiah, Bernhardt, J., Jordan Levine, Harry Nelson, Turner, N., Bryan Norton, Jordan Tam and Chan, K. (2013). Ecosystem services and beyond: Using multiple metaphors to understand human – environment relationships. *BioScience* 63(7): 536.

Romaine, S. (1996). War and peace in the global greenhouse: Metaphors we die by. *Metaphor and Symbolic Activity* 11(3): 175–194.

Russill, C. (2010). Temporal metaphor in abrupt climate change communication: An initial effort at clarification. In W.L. Filho (ed.), *The economic, social and political elements of climate change*, 113–132. London: Springer.

Sealey, A. and Oakley, L. (2013). Anthropomorphic grammar? Some linguistic patterns in the wildlife documentary series 'Life'. *Text & Talk* 33(3): 399–420.

Steffensen, S. and Fill, A. (2014). Ecolinguistics: The state of the art and future horizons. *Language Sciences* 41: 6–25.

Stibbe, A. (2012). *Animals erased: Discourse, ecology, and reconnection with the natural world*. Middletown, CT: Wesleyan University Press.

Stibbe, A. (2015). *Ecolinguistics: Language, ecology and the stories we live by*. London: Routledge.

Väliverronen, E. and Hellsten, I. (2002). From 'burning library' to 'green medicine' the role of metaphors in communicating biodiversity. *Science Communication* 24(2): 229–245.

van Dijk, T. (1993). Principles of critical discourse analysis. *Discourse & Society* 4(2): 249–283.

Verhagen, F. (2008). Worldviews and metaphors in the human-nature relationship: An ecolinguistic exploration through the ages. *Language and Ecology* 2(3): 1–18.

34

Journalism and critical discourse studies

Darren Kelsey

Introduction

This chapter accounts for three developmental stages of qualitative approaches to CDA in journalism studies. It starts with approaches to Critical Linguistics (CL), which began to account for the social production of language in news texts (Fowler et al. 1979; Trew 1979; Kress 1983; Fowler 1991; Bell 1991; Hodge and Kress 1993). It then covers a second development where CL frameworks informed expansive models of Critical Discourse Analysis (CDA) that were designed to rigorously interrogate journalistic texts, discursive practices and social contexts (van Dijk 1988a, b, 1991; Richardson 2007; Kelsey 2015c). This second stage also accounts for the transnational developments that have occurred across the field of critical discourse studies. The third section accounts for more recent developments in CDA that have expanded beyond linguistic analysis through multimodal approaches (Machin and Mayr 2012; van Leeuven and Kress 2011) to news media and, more recently, online news (Kelsey 2015a; Bednarek and Caple 2012; Caple 2013; Knox 2007, 2010). There are many bodies of literature beyond the scope of this chapter – especially in the significant and highly respected quantitative (corpus) approaches that have been developed for large-scale studies on the language of journalistic content (Baker and McEnery 2015; Baker et al. 2008; Gabrielatos and Baker 2008). But this chapter shows readers how CDA and journalism studies have developed over time through a particular direction and design that is sensitive to the social production and ideological operations of news discourse. It demonstrates what CDA needs to do in order to continually progress and account for the rapid developments of multimedia platforms and online journalism.

Language, ideology and critical linguistics

CL provided the foundations of linguistic frameworks designed to critically interrogate journalistic material in relation to power and society (Fowler et al. 1979; Trew 1979; Kress 1983; Chilton 1985; Fowler 1979, 1991; Hodge and Kress 1993). With its connections to Halliday's (1978) Systemic Functional Linguistics, CL's focus on grammar and ideology provided an ideal framework for analysing language in political environments and critical contexts, such as newspapers. In *Language and Control* (1979) Fowler et al.'s seminal work developed CL through its micro analytical techniques in relation to more macro orientated contexts such a class structure and social power, which were significant to journalism studies. This work laid the foundations for expansive CL research on media texts that would provide the roots to CDA. Amongst various innovations, Trew's (1979) work on linguistic variation and ideology in newspaper discourse became a milestone text that paved the way for CL's introduction in critical media research. He showed how various linguistic mechanisms such as nominalization and passivisation, which later became familiar analytical traits in CDA, functioned in news stories. In doing so, Trew developed "systematic ways of isolating ideology in discourse to illustrate further aspects of the linguistic expression of the relations of newspapers and ideologies to social processes" (1979: 118). For example, Trew's work on press coverage of the 1977 Notting Hill Carnival (1979) showed how print news covered social violence through different language choices across texts that reflect the ideological interests of particular news sources, according to their accounts of social groups and their agency.

Most importantly, whilst this work showed how CL could be applied in journalism studies, this was only on the condition that the frameworks applied could understand the specific generic context and cultural landscape of the press. As a former journalist, Bell's (1991) work adopted this ethos. Bell was particularly astute in the insights he brought to CL: his ability to introduce practical and environmental analysis of news production shed light on how language is a product of explicit functional processes of the newsroom. Bell's work covered a range of practical journalistic factors such as the production of a news story that determined its structure and narrative. His experience meant he could account for the newsgathering processes of a newsroom and explain the values behind processes of news storytelling.

For media scholars adopting innovative but complex frameworks of CL theory in journalism studies, Fowler (1991) also provided an accessible approach. Fowler addressed the micro structures of language and power through to the macro ideological contexts of newspapers and their editorial values. He argued that the news media often reproduce the dominant order due to the ideological influence of those in positions of power. Powerful institutions "provide the newspapers with modes of discourse which already encode the attitudes of a powerful elite. Newspapers in part adopt this language for their own and... reproduce the attitudes of the powerful" (Fowler 1991: 23–24). Fowler provided a series of case studies including: linguistic formations in discriminatory discourses of gender and power between social groups; discursive constructions of public opinion and consensus in newspapers; and the argumentative generic conventions and forms of modality that newspaper editorials adopt in their style of "connecting" with readers. Fowler argued that language is always produced by sources with their own ideological interests: "Anything that is said or written about the world is articulated from a particular ideological position: language is not a clear window but a refracting, structuring medium" (1991: 10).

Fowler's approach was a welcome effort to explicitly address interdisciplinary nuances (through connections to media studies) that valued the work of critical media research (Philo et al. 1982), but was also committed to a more sophisticated understanding of *language* in media texts:

> The "standard position" of current students of the media is that news is a construct which is to be understood in social and semiotic terms; and everyone acknowledges the importance of language in this process of construction. But in practice, language gets

relatively meagre treatment, when it comes to analysis: the Glasgow Group, and Hartley, for example, are more interested in, and better equipped technically to analyse, visual techniques in television.

(1982: 8)

By Fowler's admission, there are multiple dimensions and discursive components in the construction of any newspaper text that are beyond the scope of CL. The layout, images, headlines, typography and other interactive elements of newspapers are not considered in his analysis. Particularly in the world of online news, stories are constructed through unique and complex textual and digitally interactive layouts that require multimodal frameworks to analyse them in their entirety (Bednarek and Caple 2012; Knox 2007, 2010). But Fowler was justifiably content in his focus on language from a CL perspective through a framework designed to do a specific job: interrogate the social and ideological role of language in the news. He acknowledged the importance of understanding contextual circumstances and processes of production behind news discourse, which his peers such as Bell (1991) had demonstrated the significance of. Subsequently, developments in CDA since CL have sought to further address the practical and contextual complexities of news content beyond exclusive analyses of language.

Critical discourse analysis and journalism studies

A significant development from CL to CDA came in the work of van Dijk (1988a, 1988b, 1991, 1998). This work presented a new, interdisciplinary approach to critical media analysis through a framework of discourse analysis and social cognition. van Dijk differentiated this approach from other critical media and communication research: "We. . . find that few approaches pay sufficient attention to the study of news as discourse in its own right. This is particularly true of the macrosociological approaches to news. We also believe that the cognitive dimension of news production and understanding has been neglected" (1988a: 2–3). From a discourse analytical grounding, van Dijk has always argued that news should be studied in its relevant context but still as a significant form of public discourse. He understood that mass communication research was already concerned with the economic, social and cultural contexts of news media, but he also stressed the importance of conducting structural analysis of news stories as a "qualitative alternative to traditional methods of content analysis" (1988a: vii). He claimed that news discourse was "explicitly linked to social practices and ideologies of newsmaking and, indirectly, to the institutional and macrosociological contexts of the news media" (1988: vii).

A useful example of this approach applied to journalistic material is his earlier work on racism in the press (1991). Following transnational research on the negative representations and stereotyping of racial minorities, van Dijk highlighted the institutional bias against ethnic minority leaders and workers, with minority journalists often discriminated against in professional environments (1991: X).

He addressed a range of theoretically informed discussions on key areas in his discourse analytic framework of the press: social cognition and the ideological processes and contexts of cognitive strategies; interrogations of structural and strategical processes in news production; the public reproduction of racism, beliefs and attitudes in the production and consumption of news; and the complexities of elite racism impacting upon journalistic practice and content. This socio-cognitive approach studied multiple dimensions of newspaper discourse and practice: headlines; subjects and topics; news schemata, argumentation and editorials; quotations and sources; meanings and ideologies; style and rhetoric; and the reproduction of news on ethnic affairs. This research was methodologically significant at the time due to the interdisciplinary theoretical scope and its synergy of quantitative (content analysis) and qualitative (CDA) approaches.

Another popular approach in critical media research, which again developed from its roots in CL, is Fairclough's (1995, 1998, 2001, 2003) three layered model of CDA. This framework transcended "the division between work inspired by social theory which tends not to analyse texts, and work which focuses upon the language of texts but tends not to engage with social theoretical issues" (2003: 2–3). Fairclough's approach includes "interdiscursive analysis, that is, seeing texts in terms of the different discourses, genres and styles they draw upon and articulate together" (Fairclough 2003: 3). This enables a critical outlook on "the relatively durable structuring of language which is itself one element of the relatively durable structuring and networking of social practices" (Fairclough 2003: 3).

The first layer of Fairclough's model is concerned with *textual analysis*. This is more than linguistic or grammatical analysis of texts; like CL it concerns the ideological role of language as a social product. As Paul Simpson explains, language is used by powerful groups to reinforce dominant ideologies and therefore needs to be studied as a site of ideological struggle (1993). Hence, the second layer of analysis is *discursive practice*. In terms of news discourse and journalism, textual features are all seen to occur through decision making processes in their cultural and professional contexts. Journalists and news organisations are wrapped up in cultural practices of time and place as well as their employers having their own editorial interests and socioeconomic agendas to fulfil. Attention to discursive practice means that processes of textual production and consumption are scrutinised. Discursive practices can account for the ways in which "authors of texts draw on already existing discourses and genres to create a text and. . . how receivers of texts also apply available discourses and genres in the consumption and interpretation of. . . texts" (Phillips and Jorgenson 2002: 69). This has been particularly important in Kelsey's work on journalism, mythology, memory and discourses of national narration (Kelsey 2015c). These elements reflect what Blommaert refers to in systems of reproduction, reception and remembering, which affect the way that texts are produced and consumed since socio-historical and cultural mechanisms form discourses and produce meaning (1999: 5–6).

In *Analysing Newspapers* (2007) Richardson provides a rigorous example of Fairclough's model applied in journalism studies. In terms of discursive practice, he argues that journalists are workers who are pressured and obliged to respond to editorial, professional and managerial pressures and constraints on their content. Richardson also discusses the issue of objectivity (2007: 86), where journalists reporting opinion must do so by reporting via sources and the views of people other than themselves. However, when sources are used to legitimise viewpoints and demonstrate objective reporting, issues regarding news access arise (Hall et al. 1978). Therefore, it is not the case that journalists are conspiratorially committed to elite sources or determined to reproduce dominant ideologies. Neither is it the case that a limited range of sources always dictates who speaks in the media. Rather, as Richardson points out, journalists need to use authoritative sources in order to protect themselves from criticism and appear to be objective.

Richardson (2007) continues to explore other levels of discursive practice at which processes of news production and consumption explain the dynamics of newspaper stories in relation to their readerships, editorial values and social context. In attempts to make sense of contradiction and ideological context in news stories, Kelsey has adopted aspects of this approach to CDA to examine the "paradoxical persuasions" of discourse (Kelsey 2015b; Kelsey 2015c). The "messiness" and inconsistencies of news demands a thorough cultural and political understanding of the social contexts in which the press operates. For example, Kelsey (2015b) analysed right-wing newspapers during the London riots to show how the *ideological consistencies* operating beyond the foreground and immediacy of individual news stories override the appearance of *discursive contradiction* across longitudinal contexts.

These micro-macro complexities of discursive practice take us to the third level of Fairclough's model. Fairclough's third level of analysis is concerned with *social practice*. This level expands beyond media texts and examines some of the wider social contexts of which the discourse is a product and/or responding to. This is often the level where CDA takes an explicit normative or political position in response to a problem, dominant ideology or exploitative social relations (Richardson 2007). It is here, in the overlapping ground between discursive and social practices, which supplement each other through the production and consumption of news texts, where CDA begins to oscillate between its linguistic roots and connections to social, cultural and critical theoretical analysis. This addresses broader questions regarding the social and political role of journalism; considering anything from what news says about the society in which it is produced to the impact it has on the (reproductive) social relations that it is a part of (Richardson 2007).

In Kelsey's research (2014, 2015c, 2015d, 2017) the analytical toolkits and insights of CDA covered so far have been synergised with cultural theory to analyse mythology and ideology in journalistic storytelling. Discourse Mythological Analysis (DMA) is a model that developed over time through two main objectives: to use the tools of CDA to analyse discursive constructions of mythology in news stories; and to show how myth theory can demonstrate cultural, semiotic, archetypal and ideological functions of news discourse and journalistic storytelling (Barthes 1993; Lule 2001; Kelsey 2015c). Analyses of news as a form of mythological storytelling are not uncommon in journalism studies (Lule 2001; O'Donnell 2003; Bird and Dardenne 2008). Lule argues that mythological storytelling justifies ideological standpoints: "Myth celebrates dominant beliefs and values. Myth degrades and demeans other beliefs that do not align with those of the storyteller" (2001: 184). This selective process is a highly politicised negotiation of discursive practices: "The diachronic and synchronic formations of mythology might articulate simple messages but they are complex processes that often provide sophisticated manipulations of popular stories, memories and identities" (Kelsey 2015c: 187). Journalists are storytellers (or mythmakers) in contemporary societies: "Like myth tellers from every age, journalists can draw from the rich treasure trove of archetypal stories and make sense of the world" (Lule 2001: 18). Equally, audiences often rely on the same archetypal conventions and familiar cultural mythologies to understand the stories they are told (Kelsey 2015c; Kelsey 2015d).

DMA combined Wodak's discourse-historical approach (Reisigl and Wodak 2009) and Fairclough's (1995) three-layered model to analyse the historical and social contexts of language, ideology and mythology. Wodak's approach examines the historical meanings, complexities, contradictions and ideological implications of words, phrases and stories in *diachronic* and *synchronic* contexts. In developing the DMA model Kelsey provided a detailed breakdown of differences between mythology, ideology and discourse, showing how discourse constructs myth, which carries ideology, yet ideology also informs discourse in the construction of mythology (Kelsey 2014, 2015c, 2015d). Since systematic frameworks for analysing the detailed discursive constructions of myth have been largely absent in myth theory (Flood 2002), DMA offers a systematic toolkit by drawing on CDA to apply cultural theories of mythology to news texts. It is important to understand how myth "arises from the intricate, highly variable relationship between claims to validity, discursive construction, ideological marking, and reception of the account by a particular audience in a particular historical context" (Flood 2002). DMA not only helps to fill this necessity that Flood points to, but it also provides a distinct synergy between journalism studies and discourse studies as research disciplines: "DMA [is] a systematic analytical framework that can be adopted to investigate discursive constructions and ideological operations of mythology in journalistic storytelling" (Kelsey 2015c: 3).

Through this summary of developments in CDA since CL we can see how this stage introduced significant expansions in critical media research. An impressive range of transnational and interdisciplinary approaches have seen CDA expand and develop into a cross-cultural field of research (Kuo and Nakamura 2005; Alvaro 2015; Flowerdew and Leong 2007, 2010; Hardt-Mautner 1995; Way 2015). These approaches have demonstrated how CDA can oscillate across cultures and contexts of power and language.

Transnational developments in CDA and journalism studies

The literature covered in this section shows how CDA has evolved transnationally to consider the discursive and journalistic dynamics that operate in processes of language translation, national and international environments, and other intercultural tensions of media and society. Kuo and Nakamura (2005) use CDA to analyse headlines, editorial choices (deletions and additions), linguistic variations, stylistic differences and thematic changes in translated Chinese versions of the same English language text. They argue that these translations are actually more *transformations* since the "differences found in the two Chinese texts are not arbitrary, but rather are ideologically motivated, that is, they reflect and construct the underlying opposed ideologies between the two [Chinese] newspapers" (2005: 393).

Alvaro also adopted a "sociolinguistic view of China's English language media and its attempted penetration of the global language community" (2015: 260). By adopting Kachru's Caliban dynamic as a metaphor, Alvaro examines how China disseminates ideological messages back to the "colonisers" through a Sinocentric from of English language (2015: 260). Alvaro's earlier work adopted CDA to examine Chinese media discourses "in which a dissident social actor is represented in China's state-run English-language press" (2013: 289). Alvaro shows how Chinese media discourses use *passive agent deletion, definition/re-definition, and the attribution of derogating qualities* to dissidents in news stories. He argues that this serves the purpose of similar dynamics to an ideological square (van Dijk 1998: 267), since this media introduces ideological bias through representations of positive-Self/negative-Other in the discourse on dissidents.

This international adoption of CDA applied to multiple journalistic genres is also reflected in Juuko's work on the Ugandan broadcast media's framing of environmental risk. Her analysis shows how media sources "reproduce the order of the hegemonic discourse, whereby, the wealthy elite are highly regarded while the poor ordinary people are marginalised" (Juuko 2015: 2). Whilst those marginalized voices occur in media coverage, "the situation is framed as a consequence of their activities, consequently 'blaming the victim', a strategy that usually serves to 'justify a perverse form of social action designed to change not society, but rather society's victim'" (Melkote and Steeves 2001: 331) (2015: 2). Way's work has also adapted CDA to analyse the ideological tensions of broadcast media in coverage of Turkish-Cypriot conflicts (2015). By examining radio news broadcasts in the Turkish Republic of Northern Cyprus, Way shows how media coverage aggravated relations with the Republic of Cyprus during a period when explicit efforts had been made to improve relations between the two regions. Way argues that whilst broadcasters appeared to be applauding the election of pro-federation politicians and diplomatic efforts to resolve the conflict, closer attention to the language of radio news did not reflect a pro-solution discourse. Instead, the lexical and grammatical construction of radio news perpetuated the conflict by communicating "uncertainty, suspicion and even threat, in each case slightly differently, to support each station's associated ideologies and interests which are consistently anti-unity" (2015: 2). This ideological context was a result of close relationships between "news media and politics where a plurality of stations offer a range of viewpoints but all are connected to political parties and interests whose concerns are mostly that of self-interest" (2015: 2).

The news media's role in constructions of national identity and its ideological significance in policy discourses were also examined by Flowerdew and Leong (2007) in their analysis of Hong Kong's reform debate. Their analysis examines "the role of metaphors in the discursive construction of the notion of patriotism in postcolonial Hong Kong" (2007: 273). By analysing news reports and opinion pieces from two local newspapers covering the issue of patriotism they provide an insight to "the role of language in constructing the identity of a patriotic Chinese" (2007: 273). Furthermore, this analysis helps to provide a better "understanding of the politics and tensions between the local and the national under the unprecedented 'one country two systems' arrangement of postcolonial Hong Kong" (2007: 273).

Issues of patriotism and national identity in news media have seen CDA adopted in European contexts to examine cultural constructions and ideological tensions in the European Union (Kelsey 2015d; Hardt-Mautner 1995). Hardt-Mautner (1995) examined how the British press represented and responded to the challenges of European integration and EU policy-making processes. Her analysis showed that national stereotyping features significantly in the news coverage of France and Germany, and data from the *Sun* newspaper was "used to illustrate strategies employed to make elite discourse more accessible to the lay reader" (1995: 177). Kelsey (2015d) has also shown how the British press and rhetoric of the UK Independence Party continue to play a significant role in media and public discourse around EU integration, membership and referendum debates.

The literature covered so far across two developmental stages of CDA has developed significantly since its initial foundations in CL and has become a transnational field of research. However, there are further cultural nuances and technological developments to account for, which are significant to CDA, in multimodal approaches to news discourse. Transnational scholarly efforts to introduce journalistic research to the field of CDA (and vice versa) have recently expanded through other frameworks concerned with the visual and technological developments of news media.

Multimodal CDA and online news

This section accounts for developments that have responded to the challenges of analysing multimodal discourse and, more recently, online news (Jones 2004; van Leeuven and Kress 2011; van Leeuwen 2004; Machin and Mayr 2012; Bednarek and Caple 2012; Caple 2013; Kelsey 2015a). The foundations of multimodal research are based on social semiotic theories (Barthes 1993; Thibault 1991) that have been commonly adopted in communication and language research (Halliday 1994; van Leeuwen 2004; van Leeuwen and Kress 2011). In this conceptual and analytical approach, no single component of a multimodal formation functions in isolation at any single moment. Van Leeuwen and Kress describe this as the study of "the material resources we use in multimodal communication, and the way we use these resources for purposes of communication and expression" (2011: 109). Similarly, Bednarek and Caple's (2012) approach considered discourse as an incorporation of both language and image in their semiotic modes that are simultaneously operating in their uses across different news sources (including print, broadcast and online), to show how various discourse analytical approaches can be applied to these formats.

Caple argues that "multisemiotic storytelling" has developed through online news environments (2013) and the images of online news provide multifunctional purposes in the construction of a story and its interactive dynamic with the reader. The traditional news"paper" story displays its familiar features online combined with other multimedia and interactive elements that are becoming increasingly relevant to developing forms of participatory communicative practice and multimodal analysis: "[Online news stories] represent the institutional news media in the sense that they are usually produced by media professionals. However, the more significant change is that they are published along with user-generated genres that have become popular through social media . . ." (Caple 2013: 83–84). Therefore, more expansive considerations of entire multisemiotic conventions provide the opportunity to see how stories stimulate particular readings, responses and debates that are significant to the communicative practices of news stories in their entirety. For example, Caple illustrates the significance of system networks and how to adopt metafunctional approaches to analysing news images (2013: 58). Caple's work is important because, amongst other innovations in this theoretical and analytical progress (Knox 2007, 2010), it shows how Halliday's framework of Systemic Functional Linguistics (SFL) can be adapted and applied through multisemiotic approaches to online news. Knox, for example, made significant advances in SFL for semiotic research by analysing the function of thumbnail images in newsbites and hard-news stories to show how they have become part of significant discursive practices in contemporary news production and consumption. Knox's work is important because he identifies newsbites (headline-plus-lead-hyperlink) on newspaper website homepages as complex signs containing hyper visual elements that attract and stimulate readers in different ways (also see Caple 2013; Bednarek and Caple 2012). Knox argues that newsbites operate as "independent texts in their own unique contextual environment to construe actors and events according to the institutional goals and ideologies of the newspaper" (2007: 26). This is particularly relevant to my case study below regarding the *Mail Online*.

Other adaptions of SFL have seen Halliday's work merged with Gestalt theories of perception psychology (Engebretsen 2012) to analyse the "cohesion/tension nexus in multimodal cohesive relations" (Caple 2013: 14). Whilst the move towards discursive-psychological frameworks can take this discussion of CDA into complex territory beyond the scope of this chapter, it is significant that recent work by Wetherell has also argued that approaches in discourse research are compatible with affect theory (Wetherell 2012; Kelsey 2017). This is important given that online news has become an increasingly interactive and participatory process between news stories and its readers with meanings and discursive contributions that complicate the traditional, more linear, process of news production and audience consumption. We can now access significant insights into what happens amongst groups and individuals when they come into contact with news stories.

Storytelling is highly emotive. As Wahl-Jorgensen argues, strategic rituals of emotionality in journalism manifest themselves "in the overwhelming use of anecdotal leads, personalised storytelling and expressions of affect. However, journalists never discuss their own emotions but instead 'outsource' emotional labour by describing the emotions of others, and drawing on sources to discuss their emotions" (2013: 129). It is also the case that ideologies influence emotions and emotions in turn influence ideologies (Kelsey 2015a), which inform discursive expressions, exchanges and events. Wetherell refers to these endless cycles as affective-discursive loops (2012: 53). As Wetherell argues, discourse often "makes affect powerful, makes it radical and provides the means to make affect travel" (2012: 19). In its entirety, human affect and emotion is "inextricably linked with meaning-making and with the semiotic (broadly defined) and the discursive" (Wetherell 2012: 20). The evolving dynamics of online news show us how discursive practices are intricately bound up in processes of *affecting* and *being affected* by social and technological changes in media cultures. Since Wetherell (2012) recently introduced the notion of *affective practice* to discourse analytical vocabulary, Kelsey (2015a) incorporated this through a multimodal framework of CDA for online news, which informs the case study below.

Multimodal case study: the *Mail Online*

Since current analyses of journalistic texts are so often embedded within the context of online media, CDA should continually find ways of understanding the media convergence factors and multimodal mechanisms involved in news production, consumption and participation. This analysis focuses on the commercial interests and discursive practices of the *Mail Online* through material from one news article: the embedded video of an assault that took place on a beach in Connecticut; the news text from the *Mail Online;* and the reader comments below the article, which provide insights to audience comprehension and responses that were less accessible for CDA research prior to online news.[1]

Embedded videos have become a significant feature of digital journalism. They provide a significant stylistic feature of the *Mail Online* that has a highly successful business model as the most popular newspaper website in the world. What is significant about the *Mail Online*'s success is the exacerbation of commercial and business interests that have increasingly impacted upon news content. As Richardson explains, "advertisers will not subsidise a news producer without an audience. And this pushes journalism towards increasing light, entertaining copy at the expense of more weighty examinations or more expensive long-term investigative reporting" (2007: 78–79). Online news that seeks to update its home page regularly across a 24-hour period seeks as much copy as possible to reproduce as quickly as possible. Hence, the *Mail Online* has been described by its editor, Martin Clarke, as "journalism crack". The *Guardian* followed up on this:

> "Journalism crack" is an apt metaphor for *Mail Online*'s user experience and the way rival news websites have adopted its reader retention methods – the much derided but utterly addictive "sidebar of shame", seemingly never-ending front page, and stories so stuffed with pictures and video they are more vertical gallery than text-based article.[2]

Mail Online content is often lifted from other social media platforms and reproduced for its own audience. This is a practice that Clarke has defended by claiming that the *Mail Online* improves stories with "new facts, graphics, pictures, or video", despite the fact that it has been accused of increasingly poor journalistic practice in a lack of attribution to sources of material it uses.[3]

Ironically, the *Mail Online* is not only competing with other newspapers for audiences to sell to advertisers, but it has to compete with the same social networks that it relies upon for its dissemination and sharing of content. *Mail Online* owner, Viscount Rothermere sees the likes of Twitter and Facebook as "frenemies", stating: "They are going to compete for advertising dollars, that's undoubtedly the truth, but they are a huge source of traffic for us. We are the most-shared site on Facebook in the UK and growing to become the same in the US" (2013).

Rothermere is quite frank about the blending of entrepreneurial and editorial interests that drive the *Mail Online*'s commercial success: "I'm very fortunate to come from a family where we believe in editorial and creativity – that's a major thing in our organisation. . . .And because our family are entrepreneurs, we sympathise and empathise with entrepreneurial spirit, and that has allowed us to diversify our business internationally" (2013).This blend of editorial and business interests delivered through its online format have turned the *Mail Online's* journalistic practice into a convergence exercise of multimedia platforms that can be used to constantly engage its readers with new content and sell its audiences to advertisers.The following multi-modal analysis sheds some light on the journalistic and user-generated content involved in the production, consumption and participatory features of an online news story.

Gender ideology and online news: the Connecticut beach fight

When 17-year-old Austin Haughwout used his drone to film aerial shots of Hammonasset Beach in Connecticut, 23-year-old Andrea Mears accused him of photographing people on the beach. Mears physically attacked Haughwout, called the police and accused him of assault. During the attack Haughwout used his phone to record the incident without Mears's knowl-edge.The video was used by the police who arrested Mears for assault. During the video of this attack we see Haughwout burdened with the voyeur stereotype, where he is accused of "perving" on people.The video shows Mears physically beating Haughwout whilst screaming threats and accusations at him for being a pervert. The recording was then featured in news stories online, where Mears was subjected to sexist abuse. From a critical perspective, despite Mears's guilt, we should still think about the ethical values of the news story and the video's circulation and reproduction: there is an argument to make regarding an invasion of Mears's privacy once the video had rightly served its purpose in proving the roles of victim and perpe-trator in this case. Nonetheless, the video was not just embedded in the story, it was the story.[4]

It is significant that this video is not journalistic – it is not even citizen journalism. It has appeared online in many contexts other than this news story. Even when the video is embed-ded in a news story it does not become a journalistic piece per se. However, it becomes a significant part of journalistic storytelling and it does influence how a story can (or cannot) be told; when an audience can see the events unfolding through this medium it does to some extent limit the creative or reproductive agency of the storyteller compared to a traditional print format. The video does not carry the same mystique as an "anonymous" source or "eyewitness" that we commonly see journalists using to legitimise an account of events in a story. Neither does it rely on the translation of a journalistic soundbite, nor is it used to infer the subjective interpretation of what a source supposedly said. Nonetheless, despite these factors, the storyteller is not left redundant or passive. As we see below, the discursive con-struction of the story in which the video is embedded can still influence its contextualisation and what the story is about. As we see below, its reproduction and convergence from one online media platform into a journalistic context, which stimulates responses from readers, is still an ideologically influenced practice.

The newsbite on the *Mail Online* video home page reads: "Crazed woman assaults man for flying drone on beach". The headline on the article page reads: "Moment angry woman assaulted a man for flying his drone on the beach and accused him of being a 'pervert'". "Crazed" implies madness and insanity, which lacks the same sense of agency that "angry" implies on Mears's part. We can only speculate about this editorial decision. But following Knox's (2007, 2010) point earlier, thumbnails and newsbites serve a purpose in attracting readers to click on stories, which in turn produces advertising revenue. Either way, the article is in no way sympathetic to Mears's position or how she was affected by Haughwout's agency. The problem here lies in the fact that this became a gendered communicative process; the user comments (below) make sexist remarks about Mears whilst expressing broader social commentary on perceptions of gender relations. Rather than contesting or condemning the mistake of Mears as an individual, some readers recontextualised this attack (ideologically) as an example of gender inequality, identifying men as the victims of common sexism, legal injustice and moral double standards.

Since the evidence in this video and the drone footage checked by the police demonstrate Haughwout's innocence, the article is able to tell a clear story that condemns the actions of Mears without leaving any remaining suspicion around Haughwout. Whilst it is not wrong to state Haughwout's innocence in this event, a broader contextual problem lies in the lack of attention or empathy given to concerns about privacy, intrusion and public anxieties around drone technologies. In another context, this could be a story about the growing social tensions and confusions caused by surveillance cultures and digital technologies (Kelsey 2015a: 16–17). But through the dichotomy of a "victim versus perpetrator" story, in which a "crazed" or "angry" woman attacks a young man, these other complexities and attention to social anxieties are interruptive details, which might compromise the spectacle that stimulates those responses in the user comments. Nonetheless, the suppression of empathy here is significant given the multiple public discourses and anxieties around surveillance technologies, privacy, crime, the internet and the affect that these concerns have on people's feelings, thoughts, perceptions and actions.

In the "best rated" comments under this article, we see the interdiscursive melee that this story stimulated, and the gender ideology that was central to that stimulation. Some of the "best rated" were brief, abusive and personal attacks on Mears's physical appearance: "She's lucky he didn't beat her fat ass on camera"; "She needs to get a mirror. Nobody would want to take pictures of her". But some of the most popular "best rated" comments speculated about the punishment Mears would (or would not) receive as a woman. C1 and C2 are the top rated comments (R1-R2 and R1-R6 are replies).[5]

C1: *Clever kid for filming it. Unfortunately, without the video, the police would undoubtedly have sided with her and he would have left in handcuffs. She'll probably get a slap on the wrist now and be on her merry way.*

    R1: True. Any woman that will beat a man like that will also lie and blame him if she can get away with it.

    R2: Imagine it the other way round. 26-year-old man attacks 16-year-old girl and rips off her shirt and unzips her pants. He's looking at serious jail time, she is looking at an inconvenient fine.

C2: *She belongs in jail. Equal punishment for women for equal crime.*

    R1: It is not an equal crime, if you had been paying attention in school you would know that a male body has a much greater muscle mass and therefore a great advantage physically over a female. This is no reason for women not to have equal rights however.

    R2: [R1], you are spot on. Not that we are excusing this behaviour at all from this "lady". Her behaviour is disgusting, and she should get punished. I hope that she grows up and changes from this incident. [R1], you are right though, if a man was to attack a woman this way she would be a lot worse off. Again, no excuse on the woman's behalf anyway. Oh, and R2. . . you're living in a fantasy world if you think most men even go to jail for assaulting women. They don't.

    R3: [R1], you're talking rubbish! Just because the female may be smaller does not make any difference at all. There are plenty of women bigger and more powerful than men.

    R5: Don't waste your time [R3], women only want equal rights when it suits them.

R6: He was doing what that woman accused him of. She jumped the gun without getting her facts straight and that's why she deserves to go to jail. I bet if it was the other way around you offer to burn him at the stake yourselves.

In this user-generated content we see feelings (stimulated by the story) of outrage and injustice expressed through discourses of (in)equality, double standards, hypocrisy, domestic violence, law and order, and morality. There are simultaneous dynamics operating between the dialogical contexts of readers interpreting this story, the affective practices that stimulate their emotive responses to the article, and the ideological tensions of the debate. There are interdiscursive practices in the argument under C2, which reflect the dialogical formation of gender ideologies that respondents are carrying, expressing and opposing through the dialogue of this exchange. Both sides of the argument attempt to empathise with their perceptions of how society and the legal system deal with gender violence. We also see Haughwout praised for filming ("smart kid"), on the assumption that he would have been charged with assault otherwise.

As Jones (2004: 22) points out, "what counts as context is not limited to the physical reality surrounding the text. Instead the focus is on the 'models' that people build up in their minds (and in their interaction) of the situation" (Jones 2004: 22). And as Wetherell argues: "Affective-discursive practices such as 'doing righteous indignation' or 'doing being the victim' are so salient and crucial in political life and yet are deeply methodical and mannered" (Wetherell and Beer 2014). This applies to multiple participants throughout this case, from Mears's actions in the video to the perceptions of those attacking her in the comments. They all follow the narratives they have constructed in their contextual interpretations of an article that plays on the divisive dichotomies of gender ideology.

What is interesting about the replies (challenging C2) that stimulated the debate is their effort to address some complexity beyond the assertions of those users who see this as a clear example of prejudice against men. This interruption to their understanding of the story is unwelcome, even though the respondents clearly state that they do not condone Mears's behaviour and they even agree that she should be punished. The way in which many users (in addition to those examples) responded expresses a deeper feeling of resentment and injustice that does not allow for any compromise. Haughwout's victimhood and the *Mail's* contextualisation of the story are used to justify their belief that men are subjected to injustice and unfair treatment in society.

Conclusion

This chapter has provided an overview of qualitative approaches to CDA in journalism studies. By recapping the relevance of CL in critical media research we can see how it has informed the theoretical and analytical roots of CDA since then. Furthermore, this chapter has accounted for multimodal approaches that are more applicable and dynamic in application to online news, which provides CDA with a new set of challenges compared to its focus on print and broadcast journalism in the past. A multimodal case study synergised approaches from across the chapter through a brief analysis that demonstrated the multimodal developments of CDA. The technological progressions of online news have exacerbated previous concerns about the commercial interests of news production and its impact upon journalistic content. The media convergence factors involved in the production, dissemination, consumption and participation processes of online news illustrate the multimodal dimensions that CDA needs to continually adapt and account for across transnational contexts. Researchers must continue to develop innovative approaches in CDA if the field is to keep up with these technological and cultural advances in journalism.

Notes

1 Gardner, J. (2012). Moment angry woman assaulted a man for flying his drone on the beach and accused him of being a 'pervert'. *Mail Online,* June 8. www.dailymail.co.uk/news/article-2652262/Thats-little-pervert-Bizarre-moment-crazed-woman-assaults-man-flying-drone-beach.html
2 www.theguardian.com/media/2013/sep/01/martin-clarke-mediaguardian-100-2013
3 Gardner, J. (2012). Moment angry woman assaulted a man for flying his drone on the beach and accused him of being a 'pervert'. *Mail Online,* June 8. www.dailymail.co.uk/news/article-2652262/Thats-little-pervert-Bizarre-moment-crazed-woman-assaults-man-flying-drone-beach.html
4 I have argued that surveillance cultures operate as affective practices since they regulate behaviour beyond merely human emotions; they influence our agency, actions and perceptions of spaces around us, through both semiotic processes and embodied meaning-making. For an extended analysis of this case beyond the journalistic focus in this chapter, and with further attention to surveillance theory in CDA, see Kelsey (2015a):
www.jdsjournal.net/uploads/2/3/6/4/23642404/darrenkelsey-jdsjournal-vol1-issue2.pdf
5 The comments selected for this analysis have been anonymised and corrected for grammatical errors. The rationale for this selection is explained through indicative data on the user rating system of the *Mail Online* (see Kelsey 2015a). Every effort has been made to contact the copyright-holders of website comments below. Please advise the publisher of any errors or omissions, and these will be corrected in subsequent editions.

Further reading

Caple, H. (2013). *Photojournalism: A social semiotic approach.* London: Palgrave.
Caple's work provides original and innovative approaches to analysing photojournalism in which she expands upon previous semiotic frameworks of analysis applied to online news and the multisemiotic.
Kelsey, D. (2015c). *Media, myth and terrorism: A discourse-mythological analysis of the 'Blitz Spirit' in British newspaper responses to the July 7th bombings.* London: Palgrave Macmillan.
Kelsey introduces the discourse-mythological framework that synergises myth theory with CDA to analyse ideological battlegrounds that operate through discourse, culture, memory, myth, politics and ideology.
Machin, D. and Mayr, A. (2012). *How to do critical discourse analysis: A multimodal introduction.* London: Sage.
Machin and Mayr's work on multimodality provides a comprehensive insight to the theoretical foundations and more recent developments in social semiotic frameworks that discourse analysts can adopt for multimodal research in journalism and news discourse.
Richardson, J. E. (2007). *Analysing newspapers: An approach from critical discourse analysis.* Basingstoke: Palgrave Macmillan.
By breaking down the key concepts and analytical frameworks of CDA, Richardson demonstrates how and why news discourse should be dealt with in its specific generic context through processes of production and consumption in news media.

References

Alvaro, J. (2015). Analysing China's English-language media. *World Englishes* 34: 260–277. DOI: 10.1111/weng.12137
Baker, P., Gabrielatos, C., KhosraviNik, M., Krzyżanowski, M., McEnery, T. and Wodak, R. (2008). A useful methodological synergy? Combining critical discourse analysis and corpus linguistics to examine discourses of refugees and asylum seekers in the UK press. *Discourse & Society* 19(3): 273–305.
Baker, P. and McEnery, T. (eds.) (2015). *Corpora and discourse: Integrating discourse and corpora.* London: Palgrave.
Barthes, R. (1993). *Mythologies.* London: Vintage.
Bednarek, M. and Caple, H. (2012). *News discourse.* London: Cintinuum.
Bell, A. (1991). *The language of news media.* Oxford: Blackwell.

Bird, S.E. and Dardenne, R.W. (2008). News as myth and storytelling: lessons and challenges. In K. Wahl-Jorgenson and T. Hanisch (eds.), *Handbook of journalism,* 205–217. London, Vancouver: Routledge.

Blommaert, J. (1999). The debate is open. In J. Blommaert (ed.), *Language ideological debates,* 1–38. New York: Mouton de Gruyter.

Caple, H. (2013). *Photojournalism: A social semiotic approach.* London: Palgrave.

Engebretsen, M. (2012). Balancing cohesion and tension in multimodal rhetoric: An interdisciplinary approach to the study of semiotic complexity. *Learning, Media and Technology* 37: 1–18.

Fairclough, N. (1995). *Critical discourse analysis: The critical study of language.* Essex: Longman.

Fairclough, N. (2003). *Analysing discourse: Textual analysis for social research.* London: Routledge.

Flowerdew, J. and Leong, S. (2007). Metaphors in the discursive construction of patriotism: The case of Hong Kong's constitutional reform debate. *Discourse & Society* 18(3): 273–294.

Flowerdew, J. and Leong, S. (2010). Presumed meaning in the discursive construction of socio-political and cultural identity. *Journal of Pragmatics* 42(8): 2240–2252.

Fowler, R. (1991). *Language in the news: Discourse and ideology in the press.* London: Routledge.

Fowler, R., Hodge, B., Kress, G. and Trew, T. (1979). *Language and control.* London: Routledge and Kegan Paul.

Gabrielatos, C. and Baker, P. (2008). Fleeing, sneaking, flooding: A corpus analysis of discursive constructions of refugees and asylum seekers in the UK Press 1996–2005. *Journal of English Linguistics* 36(1): 5–38.

Hall, S. et al. (1978). *Policing the crisis: Mugging, the state, and law and order.* London: Macmillan.

Halliday, M. (1978). *Language as a social semiotic: Social interpretation of language and meaning.* London: Hodder Arnold.

Hardt-Mautner, G. (1995). How does one become a good European? The British press and European integration. *Discourse & Society* 6(2): 177–205.

Hodge, R. and Kress, G. (1993). *Language as ideology,* 2nd edn. London: Routledge.

Jones, R. (2004). The problem of context in computer-mediated communication. In T. Levine and R. Scollon (eds.), *Discourse and technology: Multimodal discourse analysis,* 22–33. Washington, DC: Georgetown University Press.

Juuko, M. (2015). Framing environmental risk in the broadcast media in Uganda. *Journalism and Discourse Studies* 1(1): 1–17.

Kelsey, D. (2017). *Media and Affective Mythologies: Discourse, archetypes and ideology in contemporary politics.* London: Palgrave.

Kelsey, D. (2014). The myth of the city trickster: Storytelling, bankers and ideology in the *Mail Online*. *Political Ideologies* 19(3): 307–330. DOI: 10.1080/13569317.2014.951147

Kelsey, D. (2015a). Discourse, affect and surveillance: Gender conflict in the omniopticon. *Journalism and Discourse Studies* 1(2). www.jdsjournal.net/uploads/2/3/6/4/23642404/darrenkelsey-jdsjournal-vol1-issue2.pdf

Kelsey, D. (2015b). Defining the sick society: Discourses of class and morality in British, right wing newspapers during the 2011 England riots. *Journal of Capital & Class* 39(2): 243-264.

Kelsey, D. (2015c). *Media, myth and terrorism: A discourse-mythological analysis of the 'Blitz spirit' in British newspaper responses to the July 7th bombings.* London: Palgrave Macmillan.

Kelsey, D. (2015d). Hero mythology and right-wing populism. *Journalism Studies* 17(8): 971–988. DOI: 10.1080/1461670X.2015.1023571

Knox, J. (2007). Visual-verbal communication on online newspaper home pages. *Visual Communication* 6(1): 19–53.

Knox, J. (2010). Online newspapers: Evolving genres, evolving theory. In C. Coffin, T. Lillis, and K. O'Halloran (eds.), *Applied linguistics methods: A reader,* 33–51. London: Routledge.

Kress, G. (1983). Linguistic processes and the mediation of 'reality': The politics of newspaper language. *International Journal of the Sociology of Language* 40: 43–57.

Kuo, S. H. and Nakamura, M. (2005). Translation or transformation? A case study of language and ideology in the Taiwanese press. *Discourse & Society* 16(3): 393–417.

Lule, J. (2001). *Daily news, eternal stories: The mythological role of journalism.* New York: Guilford Press.

Machin, D. and Mayr, A. (2012). *How to do critical discourse analysis: A multimodal introduction.* London: Sage.

O'Donnell, M. (2003). Preposterous Trickster: Myth, news, the law and John Marsden. *Media Arts Law Review* 8(4): 282–305.

O'Halloran, K. (in press). Multimodal analysis and digital technology. In Anthony Baldry and Elena Montagna (eds.), *Interdisciplinary approaches to multimodality: Theory and practice: Readings in intersemiosis and multimedia.* Palladino: Campobas.

Philo, G., (1982). *Really bad news* (Vol. 3). Writers & Readers Publishing.

Philo, G. (2007). Can discourse analysis successfully explain the content of media and journalistic practice? *Journalism Studies* 8(2): 175–196.

Reisigl, M. and Wodak, R. (2009). The discourse-historical approach (DHA). In R. Wodak and M. Meyer (eds.), *Methods of critical discourse analysis,* 2nd rev. edn, 87–121. London, England: Sage.

Richardson, J. (2007). *Analysing newspapers: An approach from critical discourse analysis.* Basingstoke: Palgrave Macmillan.

Simpson, P. (1993). *Language, ideology and point of view.* London: Routledge.

Thibault, P. (1991). La langue enmouvement: Simplification, régularisation, restructuration. *LINX (Linguistique – Paris X, Nanterre)* 25: 79–92.

Trew, T. (1979). 'What the papers say': Linguistic variation and ideological difference. In R. Fowler, B. Hodge, G. Kress and T. Trew (eds.), *Language and control,* 117–156. London: Routledge and Kegan Paul.

van Dijk, T. (1988a). *News as discourse.* Hillsdale, NJ: Erlbaum.

van Dijk, T. (1988b). *News analysis.* Hillsdale, NJ: Erlbaum.

van Dijk, T. (1991). *Racism and the press.* London: Routledge.

van Dijk, T. (1998). *Ideology: A multidisciplinary approach.* London: Sage.

van Dijk, T. (2001). Critical discourse analysis. In D. Schiffrin, D. Tannen and H. Hamilton (eds.), *The handbook of discourse analysis,* 352–371. Oxford: Blackwell.

van Leeuwen, T. (2004). Ten reasons why linguists should pay attention to visual communication. In T. Levine and R. Scollon (eds.), *Discourse and technology: Multimodal discourse analysis,* 7–19. Washington, DC: Georgetown University Press.

van Leeuven, T. and Kress, G. (2011). Discourse semiotics. In T. van Dijk (ed.), *Discourse studies: A multidisciplinary introduction,* 107–125. London: Sage.

Way, L. (2015). A fly in the ointment: How Turkish cypriot radio news aggravates relations with the Republic of Cyprus. *Journalism and Discourse Studies* 1(1): 1–16.

Wetherell, M. (2012). *Affect and emotion: A new social science understanding.* London: Sage.

Wetherell, M. and Beer, D. (2014). The future of affect theory: An interview with Margaret Wetherell. Accessed March 27, 2017, www.theoryculturesociety.org/the-future-of-affect-theory-an-interview-with-margaret-wetherall/

35

Textbooks

Felicitas Macgilchrist

Introduction

Which knowledge, or whose knowledge, is of most worth in any given place and time? Researchers from a wide range of disciplines – and even the US State Department, which employs people to observe textbooks worldwide – consider school textbooks a unique resource to explore this question. Textbooks are one of the few media which are explicitly oriented to shaping the values, knowledges and subjectivities of the future generation. Textbooks result from a complex production process involving myriad institutions and individuals. Since this process involves multiple compromises among sometimes very different perspectives, textbooks reflect and co-constitute what is collectively accepted as sayable in a given time/space. At the same time, public debates have raged over which knowledges textbooks 'should' offer students.

Critical approaches to textbook discourse have helped reconceptualise textbooks as cultural and political practices (cf. Apple 2000; Provenzo, Shaver and Bello 2011). Within the broad interdisciplinary field of textbook studies, critical approaches foreground the cultural politics of education and of knowledge production. These studies do not approach textbooks as materials for facilitating learning. Instead textbooks are conceptualised as part of complex processes of addressing the young generation with an understanding of how the world works, what is important, and which ways of living/being are desirable, legible and unquestioned. Two signal strengths of *critical discourse analyses* of textbooks are, first, their insistence on a research aesthetic of 'smallness' and 'slowness' (cf. Silverman 1999). They pay close attention to how, inter alia, semantic, argumentation and lexicogrammatical patterns construct knowledges and address readers as particular student-subjects. Second, they draw on textbook discourse to trouble core conceptual issues such as the politics of visibility, the role of individual human agency in combating environmental destruction, or the apparent closure of (dominant) discourse.

In this chapter, I first give a brief overview of current concerns in textbook studies. Section 2 then focuses on critical approaches to textbook discourse. In Section 3, I present an illustrative example of a critical discourse studies approach to textbooks, exploring how a high school social studies textbook addresses its student-readers, and suggesting that critique may be returning to education through an unexpected back door: the economic rationality of competence-discourse.

Textbook studies

We are currently witnessing the consolidation of disparate approaches to textbooks into an emerging field of 'Textbook Studies' (Fuchs and Bock forthcoming). To sketch the field at the moment means accounting for a range of perspectives. Here, I will mention six (see Christophe 2014; Fuchs 2011).

First, the mainstay of textbook studies has long been content analyses, critiquing particular textbooks for inaccuracies and omissions, or more broadly critiquing the ideology of textbook narratives. Second, pedagogical research across the school subjects has investigated the extent to which textbook design helps or hinders teaching and learning processes. Third, a more practical orientation has been the work of revising textbooks in collaborative, often highly politically charged, contexts, e.g., the German-Israeli Textbook Commission which gives recommendations to Germany and Israel on appropriate textbook representations. Fourth, emerging work engages with the history and theory of the material artefact of the 'textbook', exploring the contours of this very specific and ever-changing 'medium'. Fifth, research is beginning to engage in depth with the uptake and use of textbooks and other educational media, be this in experimental settings or through ethnographic approaches. Finally – and this is where critical discourse studies comes in – a range of cultural and social theories, from postcolonial theory and queer theory to science and technology studies and neo-institutionalism, have focused their particular theoretical lens on textbooks, conceptualising textbooks as material-political-social-cultural artefacts and practices.

Critical discourse studies and textbook studies

While a number of scholars work from a specifically CDA perspective on textbooks, in this section I will operate from a broad understanding of the critical discourse analysis of textbooks. This includes, for instance, scholars working with systemic functional linguistics, with the traditions emerging from Fairclough's, Wodak's and van Dijk's work, and also analyses drawing on Foucault, Bourdieu, postcolonial thinking and other social theories. Each of these approaches is oriented to critical inquiry and to the role of discourse in constituting the (social) world. Overall, they share a motivation to show the contingency of particular discourse and practices, and "a sense that discourse, its contexts of production and reception, and the human subjects producing and consuming text/talk, could be, and can be, different, with significantly differing results" (Richardson et al. 2013: xviii).

There are many ways of mapping critical approaches to textbook discourse. I could orient to the critical issues which are analysed, pointing to the construction of gender (Barton and Sakwa 2012), racism (Marmer et al. 2010), nationalism (Philippou 2009), immigration (Höhne, Kunz and Radtke 2005) and other topics in textbooks. I could orient to theoretical interests, categorising studies according to those which draw prominently on systemic functional linguistics (SFL; Oteíza and Pinto 2008), Foucauldian thinking (Kaomea 2000), social semiotics (Bezemer and Kress 2010) or Critical Discourse Analysis (Rogers Stanton 2014). A further option is to delineate studies according to their field, with studies oriented to sociology (Barnard 2001), linguistics (Achugar and Schleppegrell 2005), history (Brown 2010), ELT (Taki 2008), environmental education (Xiong 2014) and other disciplines.

Instead, I have opted here to discuss a small – highly selective – range of studies according to how their findings speak to the *construction* of knowledge, the *theory* of knowledge and the *fragility* of knowledge constituted in and by textbooks. The first set of studies focuses on whether a particular (exclusionary/marginalising) discourse is being represented in textbooks and what sort of subject positions are being offered to readers. The second set tends to use more specifically linguistic or semiotic approaches to ask how a particular epistemology is being realised, e.g., what are the features of historical discourse and how do these features construe a particular worldview or address a particular kind of student-subject. The third set emphasises the non-closure of discourse, identifying ambivalences and tensions in textbooks. Often drawing more explicitly on Foucault or cultural studies, this third set explores the construction of hegemonic discourse and simultaneously the fissures or breaches which flag the fragility of this hegemony, i.e., the moments where 'progressive' or 'counter'-discourse is constructed. Given the inevitable overlaps among the three 'sets', my categorisation is itself quite a fragile construction.

Constructing textbook discourse

In keeping with the interests of critical inquiry, the core sociological categories of exclusion and marginalisation are the primary interests in the first set of studies. Textbook analyses identify gender inequality (Barton and Sakwa 2012), consumerist discourse (Taki 2008), nationalist discourse (Bolick et al. 2013) and the denial of racism (Binnenkade 2015). Historical discourse analyses highlight, e.g., authoritarian Fascist discourse in Franco's Spain (Pinto 2004), or a discourse of Australian loyalty to Great Britain in inter-war Australian textbooks (Sharp 2014). Generally, with their goal of presenting detailed empirical analyses, these publications generally explore individual case studies. On the issue of 'race' and 'ethnicity', for instance, a social studies textbook in Canada relegates racism to history and to explosive prejudices, rather than discussing systemic racist policies or structural divisions in society (Rezai-Rashti and McCarthy 2008: 531). In the USA, history textbooks frame indigenous peoples as passive (Rogers Stanton 2014). Chu (2015) analyses the representation of ethnic majority and minority groups in China, finding that the dominant Han group indeed also dominates primary level textbooks, with minority groups marginalised or portrayed in a stereotypical way. Similarly, in Spain, Muslims are largely invisible, and if they are present, the depiction is fairly simplistic, essentialising Muslims within the category of immigrant, in particular within the *history* of immigration (Arqué, Luque and Rasero 2012). In Germany, although studies identify changes in the discourse about immigrants over the years, they also highlight the consistent implicit understanding of Germans as white and monolingually German-speaking. People with migration backgrounds retain a marginalised status, with textbooks often still referring to German-born minority groups as 'foreigners' (Höhne, Kunz and Radtke 2005; Kotowski 2013). Taking these cases together, the critical discourse analysis of textbooks illustrates how in various contexts, the dominant societal group marginalises a minority group.

Other studies point to an array of intersecting marginalisations. Metro's (2011) analysis, for instance, highlights the potential of textbooks produced by different ethnic groups in Burma to fuel inter-ethnic animosity, since each group produces books which devalue the other ethnic groups. Agiro's (2012) analysis of leading American Literature textbooks used in Christian education points to discriminations along a range of categorisations: 'race, ethnicity, gender, social class, and physical and mental ability' (2012: 211). Also in the USA, Schwartz (2006) points to the intersection of class, Whiteness and language, as Anglo-Americans use a small textbook to learn Spanish in order to communicate with their Spanish-speaking house-keepers and gardeners. In Spain during Franco's regime, civics textbooks included sections on etiquette which realise gender, religious and class hierarchies (Pinto 2013). Anyon's (1979) classic analysis of economic and labour history in US textbooks also points to the intersection of class, gender, 'race' and migrant status with low wages and poor working conditions (1979: 368). Overall, these studies connect various aspects of social diversity, arguing that textbooks maintain the dominant social order, inviting readers to support the social, economic and political status quo.

Central to maintaining the social order is the way political participation is represented. Anyon (1979) also emphasises the backgrounding of radical, grass-roots political protest in US textbooks (1979: 370). In the field of environmental activism, Xiong's (2014) eco-critical discourse analysis of English language textbooks in China finds a prevailing 'shallow environ-mentalism'. While the books do address environmental topics to raise awareness of ecological destruction, they do not reflect on the underlying economic, cultural and political issues, nor do they encourage students to actively participate in transformative ecological practice. Writing against this, and drawing on Foucault's notion of pastoral power, Ideland and Malmberg (2015) trouble this very goal of individual actions and participation. Exploring how future 'eco-certified' citizens are addressed in education for sustainable development in Sweden, they note a faith in technological development and mathematical calculations which empha-sises the obligation of individuals to make free, conscious, rational choices in which they actively sacrifice personal pleasure for the benefit of the community and the planet. Again here, broader political, economic and systemic factors are underplayed in a neoliberal rational-ity which depoliticises environmental issues and focuses instead on individual actions.

Overall, this first set of studies focuses on the semantic content of textbooks, while often contextualising the content in curriculum and policy debates, and embedding the textbooks within broader cultural discourse or classroom practice. These critical analyses are motivated (at least in part) by the goal of finding out whether this kind of discourse is (still) being produced and offered to the young generation, and what kind of impact that could have on shaping society by, e.g., maintaining power hierarchies and supporting marginalising or dis-criminatory practices.

Theories of knowledge in textbook discourse

The second set of studies orients more explicitly to discourse as ways of knowing. While spe-cific issues are also the focus of these studies, I want here to foreground their fine-grained lin-guistic analyses of how writing in the disciplines construes particular epistemologies. A central point of departure for this approach to critical discourse analysis is systemic functional linguis-tics (SFL) and multimodal analysis. SFL has, for instance, highlighted the role of naturalisation, nominalisation, authorial voice and cause-and-effect relations in history textbooks (Achugar and Schleppegrell 2005; Gu 2015) and explored a range of genres in medicine (Macdon-ald 2002) and the sciences (Zhao 2012). Multimodal meaning-making practices have been explored in, for instance, history, math, the sciences and English as a Foreign Language (EFL) (Bezemer and Kress 2010; Derewianka and Coffin 2009; Guo 2004; Liu and Qu 2014).

Against this backdrop, explicitly critical analyses have taken particular issue with the lan-guage of history education. Drawing on a fine-grained analysis of grammatical metaphor and transitivity in a history textbook in Colombia, Moss (2010) argues that the textbook presents 'a deterministic view of history which precludes the possibility of change as a result of human intervention' (2010: 71). Martin, Maton and Matruglio (2010) explore the function of '-isms' (e.g., colonialism, nationalism, socialism) in history textbooks, arguing that when it comes to the mediation of '-isms' in educational settings, 'both epistemology (definitions and oppositions) and axiology (values and attitudes) matter' (2010: 450). Adopting the 'right' values is what measures one's legitimacy (or lack thereof) as a 'knower' in the field of history. Oteíza and Pinto (2008) focus on how contemporary textbooks engage with Allende's socialist government in Chile and the military coup in 1973 that led to Pinochet's dictatorship. She finds that, through their explicitly objective language, Chilean textbooks offer explicit and implicit evaluative judgements throughout the texts. By naturalizing history, for instance, and describing events as if 'things just happened', they imply that the coup was a necessary solution to the instability of Allende's government. Overall, the textbooks produce a 'conciliatory discourse', emphasising consensus and social stability.

These analyses foreground not only the content of how politics are represented, but also – and primarily – the epistemological issue of how disciplinary discourse constructs particular ways of knowing as legible and legitimate. For history, this includes ways of conceptualising time and causation, subtle forms of evaluation, the anthropomorphisation of countries, and attributions of agency and passivity.

Fragile textbook discourse

The first two sets of studies have in common an interest in the *dominant* modes of representation. The overarching goal is to unpack texts which reproduce knowledge formations and maintain socio-political hierarchies, pointing out that the story could always also be told differently. This third set of analyses looks more closely at the fragilities, ambivalences and tensions of textbook discourse.

Barnard (2001), for instance, analysing Japanese history textbooks, identifies the ambivalent role of Japanese people in the Rape of Nanking. He analyses the overwording in one extract, suggesting that the text is 'under ideological pressure' to dissociate Japanese individuals from the killing (as do the other Japanese textbooks), despite possible author interest in writing individual agency into the history book (2001: 524). Li (2009) finds three contradictory positions in Taiwanese history textbooks: A xenophilic discourse of self-deprecation and admiration for the West, a Taiwan-centric discourse of self-pride and contempt for the other, and also a Sinocentric discourse in which China is the subject and foreigners are the barbarians. Razmadze (2010) highlights ambivalences in the representation of Stalin in Georgian textbooks: In these books Stalin appears as both, on the one hand, fighting for the good of the nation as well as, on the other hand, a deep source of corruption. He both plays a part in the brutal Soviet domination as well as being a local advocate for peace. Macgilchrist and van Praet (2013) analyse the production of a history textbook and identify ambiguities and tensions in the way forms of political organisation and democratic practice are discussed.

Outwith history education, Brown (2010) examines how African-American scholars wrote textbooks for higher education curriculum studies in the early 20th century to counter dominant racial theories. Kaomea's (2000) Foucauldian deconstructive reading of Hawaiian studies textbooks focuses on how seemingly progressive indigenous educational policies can have paradoxical effects. She argues that the politics of visibility which some studies advocate, in which minority groups should become more visible in textbooks, has, in Hawai'i, been domesticated into a non-progressive politics which maintains dominant socio-economic practices. Curricular policies which aimed at making multicultural issues more visible through 'Hawaiian studies' have succeeded in bringing Native Hawaiians into the classroom. The course materials reproduce, however, the colonial dynamics of the past by presenting Native Hawaiians as attractive, kind, good-mannered people, addressing student-readers as docile Hawaiians, future cheap labour in the tourist industry and 'ambassadors of aloha' (2000: 324). What remains unsaid is the violent history of colonialism. In addition to highlighting this paradox, Kaomea also describes new grass-roots movements where highly committed and political teachers were writing a new textbook which reveals the dark side of colonisation, privileges Native Hawaiian voices and tells inspiring stories of local agency and resistance.

This third set of studies outlines a sense of the temporary, provisional matter of hegemonic constructions, which require a good deal of work to be maintained and reproduced. They attend not only to dominant discourse, with the assumption that discourse *could be* different, but also to how this 'different' discourse *is already being* enacted in moments of fracture which disrupt hegemonies. In this latter sense, these studies could also be seen as part of the project of 'positive discourse analysis' (PDA, cf. Bartlett, this volume), while always also maintaining a commitment to criticality.

Social studies and neoliberal/critical student-subjects

This final section draws on my own research on the production of textbooks.[1] Imagine a meeting, early in the process of producing a new textbook, which I will call *Politics I,* for a small federal state in Germany. Talking about social class and social inequality, one of the two authors says: 'these students don't know that and they don't live in their world like that, and then it ends up being about pity in the end and I want to avoid that' (author 'A2'). This was a 'rich point' for me (Agar 1996): a moment which surprised me, and made me ponder. What does it mean when textbook authors describe students at a *Gymnasium,* i.e., the elite type of secondary school, as not knowing about and not having experience of social class and social inequality?[2] It seems to imply that, firstly, none of these students is socially or economically disadvantaged; and, secondly, that their elite status in society is not considered part of social inequality.

Through two examples, I hope to show how *Politics I* offers students a vision of society in which hard work and achievement (*Leistung*) are what matters. In classic neoliberal terms and the logics of manageralism, competition and cost-benefit analysis: If you work hard, you can achieve anything; only those who pay into society deserve to get something out of it. This economic rationality is, however, simultaneously fissured by a set of tasks for the students which addresses them as critical student-subjects, and invites them to critique global social inequalities. The ironic thing is that it is precisely by addressing students as future elite managers that they are addressed as critical subjects.

Ethnographic discourse analysis

I understand ethnography as a 'way of seeing' (Wolcott 2008) as an onto-epistemological approach to the intricacies of human and more-than-human interaction, a set of methods for tracing the tangles and messiness of our daily doings, and also a way of constructing narratives which the ethnographer hopes will resonate with other situations. Since, however, I am primarily interested in adopting this way of seeing to explore specific discourse analytical questions, such as the construction and fissuring of hegemonic formations, I prefer to speak about 'ethnographic discourse analysis' (Macgilchrist and van Hout 2011).

The following draws on 18 months of fieldwork from 2009 to 2011 at one of the leading educational publishing houses in Germany, which is also one of the top 50 global book publishers. Fieldwork included interviews, informal chats, discourse-based interviews and participant observation in production meetings in which author teams discussed manuscripts for textbooks and other educational media. The latter led to over 200 hours of recorded meeting talk. *Politics I* was one of the textbooks which I followed from conception to publication.

Textbook production practices

As in every ethnographic case, this one has several specifics, including:

1) Curriculum: Each of the 16 federal states in Germany has its own education system, including its own curricula. Curricula in Germany are currently, as in much of the world, orienting away from required content and towards required competencies (outcomes orientation). For *Politics I,* the previous curricular guidelines (published in 1997) consisted of 51 pages, much of which specified the content with which students should engage. The current curriculum (2008), to which the authors oriented, was only 14 pages in total. Since the textbooks are the same size, this curricular slimming gives the publishing companies increasing power to select content.

2) Approval process: Most federal states in Germany require textbooks for politics to go through a formal approval process, including anonymised reviews from teachers and a final review from the federal state's Ministry of Education. This small state, however, is one of several states which have relinquished their right/duty to approve textbooks.

3) Previous books: The publishing house stipulated that 70% of *Politics I* was to be taken from previous versions which had been written for other federal states (an unusually high proportion). The authors' task was primarily to select content from other books and adapt it for their state curricular guidelines, i.e., to put the pages in a new order to meet the curriculum topics, reformulate tasks and headings, update out-of-date information, etc. For the remaining 30% they could write their own texts and select their own materials.

4) Outsourcing: The book's editor was self-employed. He was not paid for his hours, but received a fixed sum for finalising *Politics I.* Outsourcing editing goes hand in hand with other cost-cutting initiatives and expectations of increased efficiency.

5) Author meetings: The authors and editor met three times over 11 months from 2009 to 2010 during the production process, once to discuss their overall approach and to decide who would write each chapter, twice to discuss manuscript drafts. Each author read all chapters and gave feedback during production meetings, but each remained the primary author of their own chapters.

6) Party politics: The political opinions voiced by both authors could be described as liberal/conservative, matching the politics of the state government as the book was being produced.

Overall, this list highlights several entangled practices, giving the authors a certain amount of authorial freedom, and also tying them tightly to federal curricula, corporate economies and local politics.

Economic rationality

Transformations to the discourse of 'hard work and achievements' (*Leistung*) exemplify a shift in the status of a discourse of economic rationality. During the first production meeting, the team discuss how to present the required topic 'Changes and challenges in modern societies' as stipulated in the curricular guidelines. One author (A1) says:

> A1: [. . .] that every person in our society has the chance of upward mobility through hard work and achievements. [. . .] Because a kind of drive ehm it could be possible after all to document that, how for instance an early school-leaver eh learned a trade, started a company and then became a millionaire.
>
> (Audio: 20091010_Politik_03_00:38:54; my translation)

The textbook could document that upward social mobility is possible for anyone in this society who works hard and has personal drive. The author makes a classic element of the 'entrepreneurial self' relevant for passing on to the young generation: 'The myth of the self-made-man who rises from washing dishes to become a millionaire is alive and kicking' (Bröckling 2007: 52). The description overlaps with an economic rationality in which desirable subjects actively invest their time and energy in their futures, constantly aim to optimise themselves and their productivity and take responsibility (only) for themselves (Foucault 1982, Miller and Rose 2008).

A similar view is entextualised in the printed textbook. A German politician, Peer Steinbruck, is quoted as saying:

> Social equality must mean shaping a politics for those who do something for the future of our country: those who learn and acquire qualifications, who work, who have children and bring them up, who take the initiative and create jobs, basically: those who achieve something for themselves and for the society. These − and only these − are the people politics has to care about.[3]
>
> *(my translation)*

This statement explicitly foregrounds the responsibility of politics for those who take the initiative, work hard and achieve something for themselves and for society. In this extract, politics is *only* responsible for these achievers. This is a New Labour kind of 'entrepreneurial self', since the subject is no longer only responsible for itself, but also for society (Fairclough 2001).

A subtle change in the status of this discourse can be seen by comparing the co-text of Steinbruck's statement in the previous textbook and the new textbook *Politics I*. As noted above, much of the material in *Politics I* was taken and adapted from previous textbooks in the same series. Figure 35.1 shows the image which was positioned just below the statement in the previous book. The *Politics I* team decided to replace this photo with a new image (Figure 35.2).

The previous book includes an image of a man who looks like he is homeless or begging. The new book includes an image of a young ethnic minority woman at work. The caption describes her as a 'Turkish health care worker'. Placed below the verbal text, the former arguably resemiotises (i.e., translates from one semiotic mode to another, Iedema 2003) the categories of not working, not taking initiative and not creating jobs. The latter resemiotises the categories of doing something for the future of the country, of learning, acquiring qualifications and working hard.

This semiotic change marks a shift from a juxtaposition of potentially contradictory discourse (Figure 35.1) to a supporting relationship between words and image (Figure 35.2). Placing the utterance next to an image of a homeless person could invite students to discuss

Figure 35.1   Previous textbook page: 'Sozialstaat und Ungleichheit' ('Welfare state and inequality')

253.1 Die türkische
Pflegerin Zeliha Onurlu
vom Transkulturellen
Pflegedienst prüft
den Blutdruck bei einer
73-jährigen Frau, 2009.

Figure 35.2   New textbook page: 'Gesellschaft im Wandel' ('Changing society')

conflicting understandings of society or politics. The image shows something external to an economic rationality. It could invite students to criticise people who do not work, but the image also opens up the possibility of speaking about the socially unequal society in which they live and thus challenging Steinbruck's statement. The image of a health care worker, on the other hand, serves to illustrate the kind of person whom Steinbruck's understanding of politics should care about. It could invite a discussion on whether salaries are fair in the caring professions, or about gender roles in professional practice, but the image is unlikely to generate fundamental critique of an economic rationality.[4]

In this sense, and based on the very condensed analysis above, where the previous textbook resemiotised an economic rationality oriented to the good of the individual and the society, but also offered an image which interrupts this discourse, this extract from the new textbook (*Politics I*) only resemiotises the economic rationality. There were several examples of this type of transformation during the production of *Politics I*, in which a 'neoliberal' understanding of politics and economics was enacted by the authors and resemiotised in the final textbook. Given the brevity of this illustrative analysis, however, the following section will focus on moments which interrupt this kind of rationality.

Critically appraising an economic rationality

'It's very important to me to open up the debate, that's what it's all about, opening up debate', said one author (A2) in a production meeting. This author placed great emphasis on formulating chapter headings as questions. He wanted, he said, to invite students to argue over the materials. Also, when A2 took large chunks from previous textbooks as he was required to do, he reformulated most of the tasks for students. Some of these transformations, I suggest, make it easier for students to question the views offered in the textbook, and by doing so, to question the value of an economic rationality when it comes to social equality.

Table 35.1 illustrates the transformations to the title for a short journalistic article by Gabor Steingart about the global labour market (referred to as 'M3' and 'M4' in Table 35.1) and the three tasks accompanying the materials. The same article is printed in the previous and the new textbook. It includes statements such as: 'One of today's greatest delusions is the belief that the millions of migrant workers in China have nothing in common with the employees in Wolfsburg or Detroit.'

What is happening in these transformations? The title shifts from a neutral technical formulation to highly attitudinal lexis ('attack', 'world war'), implying that 'we', 'here' are being

Table 35.1 Transformations from previous to new textbook

	Previous textbook	New textbook (Politics I)
Article heading	The global labour market	Attack from the Far East – World war over prosperity
Task 1:	*Evaluate* the author's argument in M3 by *identifying and writing in a table* the characteristics and aspects of a "global labour market", the origins of and reasons for this global labour market, and its effects and consequences.	On the basis of your current knowledge and the materials, *discuss* the argument that "People are (only) objects whose actions are determined by the economy".
Task 2:	*Find out* what jobs your co-students want to have and allocate them to the appropriate sector. *Does* the argument about the increasing desirability of working in the tertiary sector (M1) fit your class?	Based on your current knowledge, *give your view on* Gabor Steingart's argument.
Task 3:	Drawing on the method on p. 210f., *explain* the information in the diagram on p. 58.	Drawing on your findings from Task 2, *critically appraise* the title of M4 ("World war over prosperity").

attacked. On the one hand, research on journalism suggests that this attitudinal title will operate as a frame for the article's argument, highlighting conflict among global workers and threat to local/domestic workers (van Dijk 1991). On the other hand, this specific contextualisation of a journalistic text in an educational medium means the title simultaneously operates as a prompt for critical discussion. A forceful title offers students more to grapple with than the calm descriptive specialist vocabulary of the previous title.

The processes of the tasks have also shifted. Where the previous textbook asked students to 'evaluate', 'find out' and 'explain', the new book invites them to 'discuss', 'give your view' and 'critically appraise'. Tracing these processes back to curricular guidelines shows how they map to different kinds of competencies. In Germany, lists are available which split competencies into three levels of increasing complexity, and suggest 'operators', verbal processes which should be used to formulate classroom tasks (see Table 35.2).

More broadly, the three levels in Table 35.2 can be related to the lower levels in the eight-level hierarchy of competencies described by the European Qualifications Framework (EQF). Higher levels in the EQF are designed for Bachelor, Master and PhD graduates. The EQF describes competence in terms of responsibility, autonomy, supervision and management skills. The competence related to *Gymnasium* school-leaving examinations, for instance, is described as:

> Exercise *self-management* within the guidelines of work or study contexts that are usually predictable, but are subject to change; *supervise* the routine work of others, taking some responsibility for the evaluation and improvement of work or study activities.
>
> *(European Commission; emphasis added)*

Overall, the higher the level, the more the student is addressed as a (future) manager or member of the decision-making elite. The operators in Table 35.2 participate in standardising the measurement of performance levels which enact social differentiation.

Although the previous textbook included a Level 3 operator in only one task, the current textbook uses operators from Level 3 in all three tasks. These tasks in *Politics I* thus address student-subjects as the future elite. Yet it is precisely these three tasks which invite students to 'critically appraise' the textbook texts. Task 3 in particular (Table 35.1) invites students to critique the attitudinal lexis of the title, and to see themselves as part of a globally entangled workforce which is by no means only interested in self-management and supervising routine work, or working hard to achieve something for themselves and their society. This task enacts an economic rationality through its Level 3 operator, yet simultaneously fissures the common sense of an entrepreneurial Level-3 self.

Critique is a word which has, since the 1970s, slowly lost its central pedagogical status as a radical critique of hegemonic knowledge or sedimented practices. It rarely appears in new curricula. But here it is, reappearing through the demands of an economically rationalised,

Table 35.2 Hierarchies of 'operators', the processes for formulating textbook tasks

Level	Operators
1 ('Reproduction')	'list', 'name', 'summarise', 'describe', etc.
2 ('Reorganisation and Transfer')	'analyse', explain', 'identify', 'list in a table', 'interpret', etc.
3 ('Reflection and Problem Solving')	to 'give reasons for', 'evaluate', 'discuss', 'give their views', 'critically appraise', etc.

output oriented curriculum. Just as Kruse (2010) notes that the EQF's competence orientation is (ironically) bringing critique back into higher education, so it seems that the new prominence of operators is bringing critique back into schools – at least in this case.

The objection may be raised here that this fissure is only tiny, and that it does not really disturb the overall subjectivation of students as self-optimising and self-managing individualist subjects. Negotiating the boundaries of an economic rationality is, in this view, always already part of this very rationality (Otto 2014). Even so, I would counter, these fissures at the edges of an overwhelmingly economic rationality in educational discourse do not disappear. An economic rationality, in this (hopeful) sense, sows the seeds of its own destruction. Perhaps indeed, one goal of discourse analysis is to find, describe and make more prominent those moments in which apparently coherent and smooth economic discourse is fissured in daily on-the-ground discursive practices, as for instance, Ball and Olmeido (2013) and Wrana (2006) have shown for educational discourse.

Concluding remarks

In this chapter, I have sketched current critical approaches to the discourse of textbooks. Drawing on a range of theories from SFL to Foucault, these studies ask how textbooks address the young generation with specific understandings of how the world works, of what is important, and what ways of living/being are desirable, legible and unquestioned. While the majority orients to dominant modes of representation, which maintain socio-political hierarchies, an increasing number of studies is orienting to fissures and ruptures in the discourse, asking where the dominant is disrupted, and what this means for the shaping of future socio-political orders.

One illustrative example traced transformations as a politics textbook was being produced. This example illustrates how a dominant economic rationality can be (multimodally) reproduced and strengthened in high school textbooks, but how at the same time, the very characteristics of an economic rationality (e.g., the aim of developing individual self-managerial competencies) open up a fissure in the economic rationality itself, by making room for a critique of dominant (economic) discourse. Whether these fissures enact what Williams (1977) has called 'residual' practices, remnants of the overtly critical orientation in the 1970s, or are signs of newly 'emerging' critical practices in the 'twilight' (Cox and Nilsen 2014) of neoliberalism, remains to be observed.

Notes

1 Some aspects of this analysis have been published in German (see Macgilchrist 2015).
2 *Gymnasium* has traditionally been an explicitly and exclusively academic school, oriented at pupils who plan to go to higher education. Pupils who received lower grades at primary level go to *Realschule* or *Hauptschule*. Parents in favour of comprehensive schooling can send children (with any grade) to a *Gesamtschule*. Changes are currently underway in Germany complicating this traditional division, but to date it remains largely intact.
3 To assure the relative anonymity of the publishing house where I conducted fieldwork, the publishing house has agreed that published materials can be included without formal citation.
4 This is not to say that students will not critique Steinbruck's statement. Classroom practice will inevitably exceed intentions of teachers or textbook authors. My interest here, however, lies in the affordances of the textbook's semiotic practices.

Further reading

Anyon, J. (1979). Ideology and United States history textbooks. *Harvard Education Review* 49: 361–386.

A classic study of history textbooks which, although using the term 'ideology', can also be read as a discourse analysis asking whose interests are served by the textbook constructions of labour and economic history.

Bezemer, J. and Kress, G. (2010). Changing text: A social semiotic analysis of textbooks. *Designs for Learning* 3: 10–29.

This paper draws on social semiotics to analyse how the use of modes (typography, image, writing and layout) has changed between the 1930s to the 2000s. It argues that these modes shape social relations between makers and users of textbooks, and it maps the multimodal textual changes to a shift from stable, vertical power structures to 'horizontal', more open, participatory knowledge production practices.

Ideland, M. and Malmberg, C. (2015). Governing 'eco-certified children' through pastoral power: Critical perspectives on education for sustainable development. *Environmental Education Research* 21: 173–182.

Drawing on Foucault's notions of governmentality and pastoral power, this article analyses how 'eco-certified children' are constructed as desirable subjects in textbooks, games and children's books. The discourse of education for sustainable development is characterized by scientific objectivity and a narrative of technological development. The eco-certified child emerges as knowing, conscious, rational, sacrificing and active, and is intimately woven into a broader neoliberal discourse.

Macgilchrist, F. (2017). *Textbook production: The entangled practices of developing textbooks and other educational media for schools.* edu.docs. http://repository.gei.de/handle/11428/73.

This collection draws on a long-term 'ethnographic discourse analysis' of the process of developing commercial textbooks to identify characteristics of how textbooks are produced. I may be biased but I do believe that analysis of textbook discourse (and media discourse more generally) is enriched by an understanding of the production process.

Oteíza, T. and Pinto, D. (2008). Agency, responsibility and silence in the construction of contemporary history in Chile and Spain. *Discourse & Society* 19: 333–358.

This CDA study draws on concepts from systemic functional linguistics to identify how participants and processes are represented and evaluated in textbooks from Spain and Chile. It shows how the texts give voice to some actors while silencing others, and analyses how this voicing/silencing constructs causality and historical explanations.

References

Achugar, M. and Schleppegrell, M. J. (2005). Beyond connectors: The construction of cause in history textbooks. *Linguistics and Education* 16: 298–318.

Agar, M. (1996). *Professional stranger: An informal introduction to ethnography.* New York: Academic Press.

Agiro, C. P. (2012). Comparative critical discourse analysis of student and teacher editions of secondary Christian American literature textbooks. *Journal of Research on Christian Education* 21: 211–234.

Anyon, J. (1979). Ideology and United States history textbooks. *Harvard Education Review* 49: 361–386.

Apple, M. W. (2000). *Official knowledge: Democratic education in a conservative age.* New York: Routledge.

Arqué, D. M., Luque, F. M. and Rasero, L. S. (2012). Islamophobia or no curriculum? The way in which Islam, Muslim culture and Muslim immigrants are treated in school textbooks in Catalonia. *Revista de Educación* 357: 257–279.

Ball, S. J. and Olmedo, A. (2013). Care of the self, resistance and subjectivity under neoliberal governmentalities. *Critical Studies in Education* 54: 85–96.

Barnard, C. (2001). Isolating knowledge of the unpleasant: The rape of Nanking in Japanese high-school textbooks. *British Journal of Sociology of Education* 22: 519–530.

Barton, A. and Sakwa, L. N. (2012). The representation of gender in English textbooks in Uganda. *Pedagogy, Culture & Society* 20: 173–190.

Bezemer, J. and Kress, G. (2010). Changing text: A social semiotic analysis of textbooks. *Designs for Learning* 3: 10–29.

Binnenkade, A. (2015). Voicing dissonance teaching the violence of the civil rights movement in the U.S. In C. van Boxtel, M. Grever and S. Klein (eds.), *Sensitive pasts. Questioning heritage education,* 261–279. New York: Berghahn Books.

Bolick, C. M., Lathan, J., Adcock, T. and Bartels, J. (2013). To be or not to be… digital: A critical rxamination of seven digital history textbooks for social studies educators. In W.B. Russell III (ed.), *Digital social studies,* 411–438. Charlotte, NC: Information Age Publishing.

Bröckling, U. (2007). *Das unternehmerische Selbst: Soziologie einer Subjektivierungsform*. Frankfurt a.M.: Suhrkamp.

Brown, A. L. (2010). Counter-memory and race: An examination of African American scholars' challenges to early twentieth century K-12 historical discourses. *Journal of Negro Education* 79: 54–65.Christophe, B. (2014). Kulturwissenschaftliche Schulbuchforschung – Trends, Ergebnisse und Potentiale. Eckert. Working Papers 2014/6. Accessed February 27, 2017, www.edumeres.net/urn/urn:nbn:de:0220-2014-00216

Chu, Y. (2015). The power of knowledge: A critical analysis of the depiction of ethnic minorities in China's elementary textbooks. *Race Ethnicity and Education* 18: 469–487.

Cox, L. and Nilsen, A. G. (2014). *We make our own history: Marxism and social movements in the twilight of neoliberalism*. London: Pluto Press.

Derewianka, B. M. and Coffin, C. (2009). Multimodal layout in school history books: The texturing of historical interpretation. In G. Forey and G. Thompson (eds.), *Text type and texture: In honour of Flo Davies,* 191–215. London: Equinox.

European Commission. (2015). Descriptors defining levels in the European qualifications Framework (EQF) [Online]. Accessed June 19, 2015, https://ec.europa.eu/ploteus/content/descriptors-page

Fairclough, N. (2001). The discourse analysis of new labour: Critical discourse analysis. In M. Wetherell, S. Taylor and S. J. Yates (eds.), *Discourse as data,* 229–266. London: Sage.

Foucault, M. (1982). The subject and power. In H.L. Dreyfus and P. Rabinow (eds.), *Michel Foucault: Beyond hermeneutics and structuralism,* 208–226. Brighton: Harvester.

Fuchs, E. (2011). Aktuelle Entwicklungen der schulbuchbezogenen Forschung in Europa. Bildung und Erziehung 64: 7–22.

Fuchs, E. and Bock, A. (2018/forthcoming). Palgrave handbook of textbook studies. London: Palgrave.

Gu, X. (2015). Evidentiality, subjectivity and ideology in the Japanese history textbook. *Discourse & Society* 26: 29–51.

Guo, L. (2004). Multimodality in a biology textbook. In K.L. O'Halloran (ed.), *Multimodal discourse analysis: Systemic-functional perspectives,* 196–219. London: Continuum.

Höhne, T., Kunz, T. and Radtke, F.-O. (2005). *Bilder von Fremden: Was unsere Kinder aus Schulbüchern über Migranten lernen sollen*. Frankfurt/M: Johann Wolfgang Goethe-Universität.

Ideland, M. and Malmberg, C. (2015). Governing 'eco-certified children' through pastoral power: Critical perspectives on education for sustainable development. *Environmental Education Research* 21: 173–182.

Iedema, R. (2003). Multimodality, resemiotization: Extending the analysis of discourse as multi-semiotic practice. *Visual Communication* 2: 29–58.

Kaomea, J. (2000). A Curriculum of Aloha? Colonialism and tourism in Hawai'i's elementary textbooks. *Curriculum Inquiry* 30: 319–344.

Kotowski, J. M. (2013). Narratives of immigration and national identity: Findings from a discourse analysis of German and U.S. Social studies textbooks. *Studies in Ethnicity and Nationalism* 13: 295–318.

Kruse, O. (2010). Kritisches Denken als Leitziel der Lehre: Auswege aus der Verschulungsmisere. *Die hochschule. Journal für wissenschaft und bildung* 1: 77–86.

Li, H.-Y. (2009). Critical analysis of discourse in one-guideline-one-version textbook policy. *Journal of Textbook Research Taiwan* 2: 1–32.

Liu, X. and Qu, D. (2014). Exploring the multimodality of EFL textbooks for Chinese college students: A comparative study. *RELC Journal: A Journal of Language Teaching and Research* 45: 135–150.

Macdonald, M. N. (2002). Pedagogy, pathology and ideology: The production, transmission and reproduction of medical discourse. *Discourse & Society* 13: 447–467.

Macgilchrist, F. (2015). Bildungsmedienverlage: Zur Ökonomisierung in der Schulbuchproduktion. *Die Deutsche Schule* 2015: 49–61.

Macgilchrist, F. and van Hout, T. (2011). Ethnographic discourse analysis and social science [51 paragraphs]. *Forum Qualitative Sozialforschung/Forum: Qualitative Social Research* 12. Accessed January 30, 2011, http://nbn-resolving.de/urn:nbn:de:0114-fqs1101183

Macgilchrist, F. and van Praet, E. (2013). Writing the history of the victors? Discourse, social change and (radical) democracy. *Journal of Language and Politics* 12: 626–651.

Marmer, E., Marmer, D., Hitomi, L. and Sow, P. (2010). Racism and the image of Africa in German schools and textbooks. *The International Journal of Diversity in Organisations, Communities and Nations* 10: 1–12.

Martin, J. R., Maton, K., and Matruglio, E. (2010). Historical cosmologies: Epistemology and axiology in Australian secondary school history discourse. *Revista Signos* 43: 433–463.

Metro, R. (2011). History curricula and the reconciliation of ethnic conflict: A collaborative project with Burmese migrants and refugees in Thailand, PhD thesis, Cornell University. Accessed February 28, 2017. www.researchgate.net/publication/277113440_History_Curricula_And_The_Reconciliation_Of_Ethnic_Conflict_A_Collaborative_Project_With_Burmese_Migrants_And_Refugees_In_Thailand.

Miller, P. and Rose, N. (2008). *Governing the present*. Cambridge: Polity Press.

Moss, G. (2010). Textbook language, ideology and citizenship: The case of a history textbook in Colombia. *Functions of Language* 17: 71–93.

Oteíza, T. and Pinto, D. (2008). Agency, responsibility and silence in the construction of contemporary history in Chile and Spain. *Discourse & Society* 19: 333–358.

Otto, M. (2014). *Der Wille zum Subjekt*. Bielefeld: transcript.

Pinto, D. (2004). Indoctrinating the youth of post-war Spain: A discourse analysis of a fascist civics textbook. *Discourse & Society* 15: 649–667.

Pinto, D. (2013). Education and etiquette: Behaviour formation in Fascist Spain. In R. Wodak and J.E. Richardson (eds.), *Analysing fascist discourse: European fascism in talk and text*. Amsterdam: Benjamins, 122–145.

Provenzo, E. F., Jr., Shaver, A. and Bello, M. (eds.) (2011). *The textbook as discourse: Sociocultural dimensions of American schoolbooks*. New York: Routledge.

Razmadze, M. (2010). Abgründe des Goldenen Zeitalters: Sowjetvergangenheit in Georgiens Schulbuch. *Osteuropa* 60: 91–103.

Rezai-Rashti, G. M. and McCarthy, C. (2008). Race, text, and the politics of official knowledge: A critical investigation of a social science textbook in Ontario. *Discourse: Studies in the Cultural Politics of Education* 29: 527–540.

Richardson, J. E., Krzyżanowski, M., Machin, D. and Wodak, R. (eds.) (2013). *Advances in critical discourse studies*. London: Routledge.

Rogers Stanton, C. (2014). The curricular Indian agent: Discursive colonization and indigenous (dys)agency in U.S. history textbooks. *Curriculum Inquiry* 44: 649–676.

Schwartz, A. (2006). The teaching and culture of household Spanish: Understanding racist reproduction in 'domestic' discourse. *Critical Discourse Studies* 3: 107–121.

Sharp, H. (2014). Representing Australia's involvement in the First World War: Discrepancies between public discourses and school history textbooks from 1916 to 1936. *Journal of Educational Media, Memory, and Society* 6: 1-23.

Silverman, D. (1999). Warriors or collaborators: Reworking methodological controversies in the study of institutional interaction. In S. Sarangi and C. Roberts (eds.), *Talk, work and institutional order: Discourse in medical, mediation and management settings*. Berlin: Mouton de Gruyter, 401-425.

Taki, S. (2008). International and local curricula: The question of ideology. *Language Teaching Research* 12: 127–142.

van Dijk, T. (1991). *Racism and the press*. London: Routledge.

Wolcott, H. F. (2008). *Ethnography: A way of seeing*. Plymouth: AltaMira.

Williams, R. (1977). *Marxism and literature*. Oxford: Oxford University Press.

Wrana, D. (2006). *Das Subjekt schreiben*. Hohengehren: Schneider.

Xiong, T. (2014). Shallow environmentalism: A preliminary eco-critical discourse analysis of secondary school English as a Foreign Language (EFL) texts in China. *The Journal of Environmental Education* 45: 232–242.

Zhao. (2012). *Knowledge building in physics textbooks in primary and secondary schools*, PhD, Xiamen University/University of Sydney.

36

Critical discourse studies and branding

Alon Lischinsky

Introduction

In a classic critique of advertising, Raymond Williams (1960) notes that modern marketing is far from being materialistically concerned with the functional usefulness of commodities. Rather than emphasising the practical benefits that can be reaped from consumption, marketing materials focus on associating the commodity with a certain kind of social experience. Beer, thus, is no longer promoted as a refreshing or nutritious drink, but becomes a symbol of friendship; the value of washing machines does not come from clean clothes, but from the envy their ownership can provoke in one's peers. Emphasis has shifted from the material product itself to what its consumption can express about the consumer's social identity, position and trajectory.

But, although the most salient and the best studied, advertising is far from the only genre employed to create and maintain such associations. In the half century since Williams's seminal analysis, the corporate sector has increasingly sought to standardise and harmonise the design of the myriad discursive forms in which it is encountered by both internal and external publics (Delin 2005: 6; Kärreman and Rylander 2008: 111): from product packaging and displays to brochures, websites, manuals and face-to-face or mediated interactions with company representatives, as well as genres whose textual properties are less obvious to the lay user, such as forms, bills or statements (Mautner 2008: 136), and even the physical layout and design of corporate offices, vehicles and points of sale or service. This complex ensemble of practices of semiotic design and integration, intended to manage the perceptions and dispositions of the audience towards the organisation and its products, conforms the discipline of *branding*.

The growing importance of such semiotic aspects is a distinctive characteristic of contemporary capitalism. While a comprehensive review of the relationship between branding and post-Fordism is beyond the remit of this chapter (for extended discussions, see Lury 1994; Mumby 2016), it is important to note the shift from the industrial economies of the 19th and early 20th century, in which business organisations focused on encouraging the newly affluent masses to consume new products; to the saturated post-Fordist markets, in which their primary concern is to create a distinctive brand identity that will differentiate their offering from functionally-equivalent alternatives, as well as anchoring consumer loyalty as products are quickly replaced by updated or redesigned models. Under these conditions, it is symbolic aspects that take priority; if consumption choices are made on the basis of the "emotional 'added values' which the product carries, over and above its inherent quality and obvious functional purpose" (McWilliam and de Chernatony 1989: 30), companies shift their strategic focus from the provision of goods and services to the management of the emotions, images and ideas associated with them (Flowerdew 2004: 579–580; Koller 2008c: 431; Thurlow and Aiello 2007: 309).

This primacy of the semiotic clearly suggests the usefulness of discourse-based approaches for branding scholarship (Thurlow and Aiello 2007: 310), even if branding – like other aspects of corporate communication (Koller 2008b: 155) – has received relatively little attention from critical discourse scholars, and no comprehensive theorisation of "the connection between a particular brand position and the multiplicity of visual and graphical resources that brand designers choose to express it" (Delin 2005: 5) is available. Mumby (2016) argues that only a focus on the discursive processes through which brands are constructed, disseminated and negotiated can bridge the gap between organisational studies oriented to the strategies organisations employ to achieve their desired market position and cultural studies that explore the meanings that commodities acquire in the lived experience of consumers. In the following sections, I first seek to conceptualise branding as a semiotic activity; I then provide an overview of critical-discursive approaches to the branding of products, places and politics; and, finally, illustrate these approaches through an analysis of the practices employed by the John Lewis retail chain to manage internal audiences' perception of the brand.

Marketing, management and meaning

It has become a commonplace in both critical and applied research to deplore the difficulty in giving an exact definition to the central concepts of *brand* and *branding*. Practitioner-oriented texts often define the former in terms similar to those of de Chernatony and Dall'Olmo Riley (1998: 419): a "name, term, sign, symbol or design, or a combination of them, intended to identify the goods or services of one seller or group of sellers and to differentiate them from those of competitors".

Visual identity may sometimes directly convey some of the key values associated with the brand; Thurlow and Aiello (2007: 320), for example, discuss how airline liveries connote their speed through the use of visual kinetic effects, and there is a small literature exploring the iconic potential of names, colour palettes and logos. Such direct expressions, however, are at best a minor part of the meaning of the brand. From a social semiotic point of view, visual identity serves primarily what Systemic Functional Linguistics calls a *textual* function (Halliday and Matthiessen 2014: 31). The presence of logos and the standardisation of texts and designs are intended to indicate that the multiple discourses in which they feature should be "read" together; they build intertextual links between the multiple occasions in which the audience interacts with the brand, tying them together as utterances that form a cohesive, overarching discourse. They are the condition of possibility of the brand's meaning rather than its meaning itself.

The ideational content of this discourse is partly drawn from lived experience: among the key sources of meaning for the brand are the identity of the social groups known to consume it and the environments in which they are encountered (Kärreman and Rylander 2008: 120; Koller 2007: 128). The mystique of rebellion surrounding Harley-Davidson motorcycles, for example, comes in part from its use by outlaw biker groups such as the Hell's Angels (Watson 1980). But these experiences only provide raw material that needs to be developed through

Alon Lischinsky

marketing communications that recontextualise and stabilise their significance. Branding *manages* the meanings attached to the brand, prioritising certain associations and evaluations while suppressing others in order to enforce one particular interpretation of the brand's identity and thus sustain the power of the corporate rhetoric within the discourse community that surrounds it (Flowerdew 2004: 585; Koller 2008a; Leitch and Motion 2007: 71; Machin and Thornborrow 2003: 462).

While the elements harnessed for this management of meaning may be partly motivated, the way in which they are assembled is ultimately open-ended. That is to say, the symbolic value that the brand acquires is arbitrary; there are no intrinsic limitations to the set of attributes with which it can be discursively imbued. Rather than having a stable, objective core, the brand acts as an "empty" or "floating" signifier that can be endlessly reformulated and recontextualised (Koller 2008b: 170; Mumby 2016). Branded communications are, in this sense, *performative* (Lowrie 2007: 992; Mautner 2008: 131): they do not simply express a pre-existing brand identity, but are the means through which brand identity is created, transforming a functional commodity into a socially meaningful entity and generating "economic capital through the exploitation and creation of symbolic capital" (Thurlow and Aiello 2007: 310).

In the same manner, it would be misleading to reduce this performance to an attempt to persuade audiences endowed with pre-existing tastes and preferences. Branding discourse has material, constitutive effects on the subjectivity of consumers and organisational members (Ng 2014: 206). One of the key mechanisms it employs in external communications is the careful crafting of a *brand user imagery* as an ideal that consumers are invited to pursue; internal branding practices, in turn, seek to shape organisational members into living embodiments of the brand values (Mautner 2008: 135). The brand thus mediates audiences' relationship to the social world by creating imagined brand communities that become symbolic and cultural resources employed by social actors to define themselves and their connections to others (Koller 2007: 127), alleviating the uncertainty and anxiety caused by the postmodern loss of more traditional forms of social belonging (Elliott and Wattanasuwan 1998: 139; Koller 2009: 63; Mumby 2016).

If the power of branding discourse lies in its usefulness for audiences' construction of their own identity, however, this also makes it precarious and provisional. In its appropriation by consumers' subjectivities the brand shifts outside the direct control of the marketer. While strategic views of branding tend to adopt a normative, functionalist perspective that assumes the meaning of the brand is determined by formal planned communications (Delin 2005: 6; Kärreman and Rylander 2008: 105; Vásquez, Sergi and Cordelier 2013: 136), a properly constructionist perspective must acknowledge its *semiotic pluralism:* the brand's meaning is continually renegotiated in social interaction, through the acts by which audiences signal that they recognise the brand and express their interpretation of it (Koller 2008a: 391; Leitch and Motion 2007: 73; O'Reilly 2005: 582). However closely integrated corporate messages may be, the organisation has no control over the order in which they are received, the varying attention that different customers pay to them, or the effect of other discourses on their interpretation. The standardisation and coordination of corporate discourses that is the basis of branding efforts seeks, but can never fully achieve, hegemonic control over audiences' perceptions of what the brand means.

The same properties that make brands flexible and adaptable to changing organisational strategies open them to contestation through accidental recontextualisation or deliberate resistance. Attempts to police the contexts in which a brand's distinctive symbols appear can backfire by generating opposition and critique; the exhaustive control of unauthorised uses of branded symbols and phrases during the 2012 London Olympics, for example, gave rise to media complaints of "trademark bullying" that had their own effects over audiences' perceptions and dispositions towards the Olympics brand (Parikka 2015). A complete understanding of the brand's meaning can thus only be achieved through an exploration of the "situated, heterogeneous and collective practices of representation" through which brands are reproduced, maintained and contested (Vásquez, Sergi and Cordelier 2013: 137). Nevertheless, discourse-oriented studies focused on audiences' responses to organisational branding efforts are rare (though see Crawford Camiciottoli, Ranfagni and Guercini 2014; Koller 2008b). In the remainder of this chapter, I focus primarily on explorations of the way in which corporations seek to manage the meaning that their stakeholders attach to brands.

Branding products, politics and places

The distance between the functional benefits that can be derived from consumption and the social meanings discursively constructed through branding can be clearly seen in that brands can exist without being materially embedded in any products. Branding practices are also employed by organisations providing intangible services, such as finance or tourism (Thurlow and Aiello 2007).

More generally, in any sector brands can be attached not only to specific goods and services, but to organisations themselves; *corporate branding* is the practice of managing the evaluations attached to the public image of an institution. These may not be necessarily identical to those of the products it markets (Koller 2008b: 390), and in fact are often managed with other organisational stakeholders in mind: the financial investors that a publicly-traded company such as Unilever seeks to secure, or the suppliers and partners with which it maintains ongoing relations, will be attracted by values quite different from those linked to Bovril, Dove or its other product brands.

As we will see in the case study concluding this chapter, corporate brands play an especially important role in shaping relations with current and prospective organisational members. The literature on organisational culture emphasises that a common and well-articulated set of values can secure staff loyalty and motivation, and encourage the workforce to enact the brand promise in all their interactions with customers (Kärreman and Rylander 2008: 106). Especially in light of the unequal power relations between the organisational officials in charge of determining brand identity and the employees that are asked to live it, branding techniques represent an important form of managerial control over members' emotional labour and self-perception (Vásquez, Sergi and Cordelier 2013).

The effects of these practices can be seen as well outside the commercial domain. As the example of the London Olympics mentioned above shows, branding and other organisational practices derived from the for-profit sector have been borrowed as the default form of public engagement in a growing range of activities, from education to public administration and sport (Mautner 2010). Attempts to stylise the projection of a public image and to manage its perception by audiences through the integrated design of communications are one of the key vehicles of the encroachment of managerial value systems and forms of relationship in an increasingly marketised society (Koller 2008b; Mautner 2012). The explicit adoption of branding in the political realm is closely associated with Tony Blair's New Labour, which not only employed research techniques devised for the consumer market and focused on the establishment of an emotional connection with potential voters, but also embraced the essential lability of commercial brands: the New Labour "brand" was redefined whenever it was necessary to provide differentiation from rivals (Scammell 2007). This "consumer model of political communication" erodes the boundaries between politics, entertainment and promotion, replacing the traditional focus on policies and issues with an emphasis on public spectacle and visibility (Aiello 2012; Ieţcu-Fairclough 2008; Mitsikopoulou 2008). Unger (2013), for example, discusses the use of PR techniques typical of the commercial sector to stage media debates about the renaming of the Scottish governing body.

A particularly extensive strand of research has addressed practices of place branding as a natural offshoot of commercial branding (de Michelis 2008): just like certain products can be loaded with specific qualities by the location in which they are produced – such as the prestige of Italian fashion design (Crawford Camiciottoli 2013) – cities, regions and countries can conversely gain from association with the products they market. Kaneva (2011) distinguishes three separate approaches to place branding: from the most explicitly instrumentalist, focused on enhancing the marketability of a nation's image for such purposes as tourism and financial investment; to political perspectives addressing the role of national reputation in international relations; to critical works that examine the implications of place branding practices for the definition of collective identities. The exploitation of stereotypes intended to satisfy the tourist gaze can result in forms of "commodity racism" (Kuehn 2009) that reify national cultures as inherently exotic and primitive. At a more local level, the redefinition of the purpose of city spaces according to a managerial logic of service provision shapes how community members relate to one another and to governing bodies, "depoliticising the polity" (Koller 2008c: 447). This may take the form of suppressing forms of civic expression that do not match these market-like dynamics (Flowerdew 2004), or exacerbating the oppression of minorities whose identities are seen as a liability for the promotion of the local brand (Kaneva and Popescu 2014).

The semiotics of branding

Given the breadth of practices, modes and genres that can be subject to centralised planning in the pursuit of a distinctive brand identity, it is hardly surprising that we lack a comprehensive description of how brand associations are discursively produced. In an extensive review article, Mick et al. (2004: 2) describe the field as "eclectic and fragmented", and such fragmentation is compounded by persistent disciplinary cleavages: scholars working under the banner of brand semiotics are largely unaware of current work in linguistics, and often operate from a structuralist point of view long since abandoned in the latter. A result of this is an unfortunate emphasis on static "codes" of denotation and association that unduly privilege the ideational function of branded communications to the expense of other aspects.

In fact, some of the most sophisticated treatments of branding discourse focus precisely on the interpersonal dimension: how the style and register they use indexes a certain "personality" (de Chernatony and Dall'Olmo Riley 1998: 422) for the brand. In one of the earliest applications of CDS to this subject, Flowerdew (2004: 583) discusses how the core values of the brand can be expressed in the voices it adopts, and the influential work of Delin (2005) develops this notion in terms of several systemic-functional parameters, most importantly that of tenor (Halliday and Matthiessen 2014: 33). Linguistic choices can project a specific social distance and hierarchy between brand and audience: brands that seek to maintain an image of authority and professionalism will adopt a detached and impersonal style, or index their credibility through strong epistemic modality and precise quantification (Flowerdew 2004: 589; de Michelis 2008). A deferential tenor may also be employed to create feelings of exclusivity in luxury products (Thurlow and Jaworski 2006).

On the other hand, brands wishing to be perceived as lively and spontaneous will tend to a more colloquial register. Machin and van Leeuwen (2005: 595ff; see also Machin and

Thornborrow 2003) show how the articulation of the *Cosmopolitan* brand involves borrowing features from youth speech and informal conversation: *Cosmo's* characteristic emphasis on pleasure is expressed not only in what it says, but also in the explicit playfulness of its linguistic style. In a different context, Iețcu-Fairclough (2008) discusses how the stylised use of disfluencies mimicking unscripted conversation can contribute to the development of a populist political brand. In the same manner, the choice of agentive roles can shape the relative positions of brand and customer: presenting products and services as means or enablements for everyday activities can help embed them in customers' envisioned life experience (Delin 2005: 21), while positioning the company as agent of mental or behavioural processes emphasises the human-like aspects of its personality (Murcia Bielsa 2012).

Conversely, the roles ascribed to customers will influence the way they conceive of themselves in relation to the brand – the brand user identity. Presenting consumers as agents will foster feelings of freedom, initiative and independence, especially when the events described in branding copy are focalised through the point of view of customers rather than the institution's (Delin 2005; Ng 2014: 400). Writing that animates the voice of the prospective consumer can also be used to persuasively embed presuppositions about their lifestyles, habits and aspirations, and the same purpose can be accomplished through definite descriptions headed by second-person possessive pronouns: readers who are told "don't shy away from your inner devil" (Machin and Thornborrow 2003: 468) are construed both as having "naughty" desires and as needing guidance to fulfil them. Second-person pronouns also contribute to an illusion of personalised involvement between the organisation and its customers, a phenomenon known as synthetic personalisation (Fairclough 1989: 62); together with direct addresses to the reader, this may be employed to suggest care for the desires and beliefs of customers (Koller 2008a; Machin and van Leeuwen 2005; Thurlow and Jaworski 2006).

Flowerdew (2004: 589) notes that these reader positioning mechanisms are not usually employed uniformly throughout the text. Rather, they are rather strategically deployed within specific rhetorical moves: direct address appears at the beginning of texts to draw readers in, but may be abandoned once their involvement is secure. In the same manner, nuances of pronominal reference can be employed to subtly but powerfully foster affiliation between the brand and its stakeholders. Inclusive uses of the first-person plural build solidarity by presupposing, without the need for explicit assertion, that writer and audience are part of a group with common interests and goals; texts that shift between this inclusive reference and a more restricted, institutional one further imply that the reader shares the organisations' ideals (Koller 2008a, 2008b, 2008c).

Research into ideational aspects of branding discourse has largely focused on what is predicated of or attributed to the brand.[1] Machin and van Leeuwen (2005: 590) discuss the strategic use of adjectives (such as "bold" or "warm") that can be taken both as a literal description of the product and as a reflection of the desired user identity. Corpus approaches have been used to identify specific lexical predicates and broader semantic fields that are unusually prevalent in branding copy, on the assumption that these will index the dominant values associated with the brand (Koller 2007, 2009); the repeated use of terms such as "contemporary" and "young", for example, show how fashion houses construct an image of freshness and modernity (Crawford Camiciottoli 2013). Unsurprisingly, a strong generic preference for positive appraisal has been noted (Murcia Bielsa 2012), especially through superlative forms (Koller 2008c; Osman 2008), although Iețcu-Fairclough (2008) shows that the absence of such strongly promotional predicates can be exploited to project honesty and down-to-earthness. Thurlow and Jaworski (2006: 110), in turn, note the use of comparative forms for creating hierarchies among products. This positive tone is often coupled with a marked vagueness; especially when values and not functional benefits are the issue, brand promises are strongly made but hard to define (Myers 1994). The abstracted nature of branded discourse has been explored particularly in its visual modality, showing that photographic elements serve as decontextualised symbols of brand values rather than documentary evidence of the product and its uses; the semiotic strategies identified include the elimination or stylisation of backgrounds, the use of highly artificial poses and generic models, and the over-rich artificial modality achieved through saturation, high detail and conspicuous colour coordination (Hansen and Machin 2008; Machin and Thornborrow 2003; Machin and van Leeuwen 2005; Ng 2014; Thurlow and Jaworski 2006). Koller (2007) discusses how brands present their global status through stylised representations of historical cultural artefact forms: modernity, for example, is conveyed by a standardised imagery of glass and steel. Brands can also convey an impression of luxury by elaborate product visuals that suggest delicacy while eliding any evidence of the human work these arrangements require (Jaworski and Thurlow 2011).

Discourse-oriented research directly addressing the iconography of brand identity, such as colour, design and logos, is relatively scarce, reflecting uncertainty about whether its connotative dimensions are in fact perceived by consumers who have little reason to attend to these aspects (Koller 2009: 51). Machin and Niblock (2008) explored the rebranding of the *Liverpool Daily Post*, in which the newspaper's intention to target a more sophisticated and fashionable audience was expressed in the choice of slimmer, more curved typography and a sparser and less regular layout; decluttering in general is associated with luxury branding (Jaworski and Thurlow 2011). Font case and style can also iconically express desired associations, such as the size and robustness of cars, especially when reinforced by logo shaps and composition: boxed containers suggest safety and protection, while vectorial shapes index speed and energy (Pérez Hernández 2013). Thurlow and Aiello (2007: 333) explore the highly stylised kinetic effects used by airlines for similar purposes, but also highlight that the striking regularities observed in branded liveries owe as much to institutional and cultural dynamics as to the nature of human perception: brands mark their distinctive identity, but at the same time need to draw from an existing pool of semiotic resources to remain recognisable. Similar pressures towards homogeneity can be observed in other industry sectors, such as the use of curved lines to signal dynamism or composite logos to express unity in diversity (Koller 2008c, 2009).

Case study: the John Lewis partnership

The following study focuses on the practices used by UK retail corporation John Lewis to manage its perception by internal audiences, looking at how the corporate brand is presented and promoted in the training materials given to new organisational members. My particular interest lies in the discursive construction of the identity category of "partner", as John Lewis employees are consistently referred to in branded communications, and what implications this identity may have for employees' relationship to the organisation and its stakeholders.

John Lewis is an upmarket retail and service chain; under the corporate name it holds 40 department stores and offers financial and insurance services, as well as operating 340 supermarkets under the separate Waitrose brand. Initially founded in London in the mid-1800s, it expanded throughout the 20th century through an extensive programme of acquisitions. In 2002 it undertook a comprehensive rebranding exercise, unifying the trade names of many of its stores and developing a standardised set of typographical, colour, design and tone-of-voice guidelines that harmonise the visual identity of its various brands.

The company is especially interesting for being co-owned by its employees. Publicly traded until the 1920s, the chain was settled in trust to its workers under its second Chairman, John

Spedan Lewis, as an "experiment in industrial democracy" (Lewis 1948, quoted in Cathcart 2013). Lewis described the founding principles of this experiment in a constitution written in 1928: shared power (in the form of an elected Partnership Council that oversees management and appoints members to the corporate board), gain (in the form of profit shares distributed to all members) and knowledge (in the form of open sharing of business information and figures through weekly meetings and internal communication materials). This co-ownership model has been widely lauded for both the economic and human effects of employee involvement and participation. As we shall see, this positive portrayal of John Lewis's organisational structure as essentially democratic and participative is an important part of the company's self-presentation towards new members.

At the same time, the real influence of this participation and involvement framework on corporate strategy has been questioned. Cathcart (2014) describes how a project conducted in 2005–2006 as a response to employees' negative perceptions of the organisation effectively removed the democratic functioning of Branch Councils, replacing them with forums that would give workers a voice but no vote over operational issues, such as opening hours or shift patterns. On the basis of interviews with members at all levels of the organisational structure, Cathcart noted differences in the interpretation of the organisation's principles between managerial and non-managerial staff. While the former viewed participation as necessary for ensuring management accountability and work-life balance, the latter understood it in terms of "good business practice" and linked satisfaction in employment to overall profit. As implementation was controlled by managers, the resulting arrangement promoted engagement but closely restricted its scope to aspects that would not raise contention about overall business strategy.

Methods

In this case study, I seek to examine how the role of the employee is constructed in the materials that articulate the nature of the John Lewis brand for new organisational members. Upon joining, these members are provided with a Partnership Pack that not only defines roles, rules and expectations, but also articulates the vision of the John Lewis Partnership, including the values and commitments attached to the corporate brand and Waitrose. The pack includes a *Welcome to the Partnership* brochure, an induction checklist, a guide to performance review practices and the *Partnership Handbook*.

These materials were scanned and converted to text format through OCR. The resulting documents contain approximately 29,000 tokens; documents were manually checked for conversion errors and uploaded to the Sketch Engine (Kilgarriff et al. 2014) for part-of-speech and grammatical relation tagging. Separately, the June 2015 version of the John Lewis constitution, comprising slightly more than 8,000 tokens, was converted to text format and uploaded for comparison.

My analysis explores the discursive construction of the relationship between employees and brand by focusing on the three key terms used to describe them in the corpus – PARTNER, PARTNERSHIP and the corporate name, as well as on the addressor/addressee relations established through the use of first- and second-person pronouns.

The discursive construction of partnership

The weight placed on this concept can be clearly seen in its pervasive presence in the documents; as Table 36.1 shows, PARTNER and PARTNERSHIP are the two top lexical lemmas, appearing

Table 36.1 Top lexical items by frequency

lemma (case insensitive)	f
PARTNERSHIP	254
PARTNER	261
WORK	199
PAY	177
MANAGER	144
BUSINESS	129
LEAVE	94
TIME	90
WEAR	85
USE	81

much more often than would be expected from their frequency in current general English. The notion also occupies a prominent place within the documents' structure: the opening sections of both introductory brochure and handbook focus on the reader's status as a partner and on the differences between this relationship and that of ordinary employment. The handbook explicitly focuses on explaining these differences in terms of shared purpose and identity: partners are defined by the legal commonality of their relation of co-ownership, but also by the assumption of a shared desire to put the corporate interest before any individual ones.

PARTNERSHIP is also the preferred term for organisational self-reference, and is conspicuously used in the documentation wherever the company name would normally be expected; the texts present it not only as owner of the material facilities (such as vehicles, premises or computers), but also as principal of the overall strategy and policy. This choice has a persuasive import; John Lewis is co-owned but not co-managed, but emphasising the former aspect in representations of managerial practices fosters an impression of democratic power and builds employee identification with corporate goals. Focusing on this shared identity through branding members as partners builds a tone of emotional belonging that would be absent in more detached terminology. The identification between employees and organisation is not simply presupposed, but explicitly stated in the definition of the corporate mission and of partners' duties and responsibilities.

The focus of these claims, however, lies on common responsibility for excellence in customer service and common financial benefit; the equality implied in the notion of partnering appears in the context of service and finance, but not authority or participation. Thus, the claimed mutuality is belied elsewhere in the documents. Although the opening section of the introductory brochure describes the position of the reader as a member in a community defined by joint ownership, the Handbook outlining roles and responsibilities repeatedly defines it as a relation of employment *by* the Partnership.

This inequality can also be seen in the strong association of the latter actor with verbs of permission and obligation, which constitute almost the entirety of the mental and behavioural processes in which the Partnership appears as agent. Partners, in turn, are represented as agents of material processes (such as driving or operating machinery) as well as behavioural ones related to the organisation's business (such as contributing to achieve branch objectives). Only rarely are they linked to mental or verbal processes in this manner; partners' connection with organisational policy is instead presented as mediated by bureaucratic structures, such as working parties or committees, whose input is then mediated by managerial ones.

In contrast, partners are the goal of a range of mental, behavioural and verbal processes focused on their performance and commitment to their duties. Significantly, the role of the organisation in these processes is largely downplayed; instead of being linked to specific actors, these processes appear almost invariably in the passive voice and without specification of agent, or are voiced by the undefined principal of the training documents, creating ambiguity about the source and motivation for these expectations. This underspecification contributes to naturalising expectations as simply part of the corporate culture, disconnecting them from decisions and regulations set by the organisations' management.

The tensions in the portrayal of the relationship between organisation and employees can also be seen in the ambiguous use of pronouns. There are 142 instances of the first-person plural (1PP) as subject, a number of which can only be construed as having inclusive reference – that is, encompassing both the principal of the document and its readers in the presupposition that the latter share the writers' intentions. This fosters an affiliative reading rather than one oriented to challenge or disinterestedly assess them: the uniqueness of the organisation, the principles of its code of conduct and the values attached to its brand are defined as a property of an imagined but rhetorically powerful "we".

This reading cannot be sustained in all cases, however; far more frequent are instances where the 1PP referent and the reader are explicitly contrasted, and the verb most strongly associated with this pronoun is in fact EXPECT, whose object is invariably the partner. Never-theless, voicing these expectations in 1PP makes it easier to suggest a distributive reading of these claims: not just management alone, but every individual member of the organisation is portrayed as bearing responsibility for these expectations and actively contributing to their preservation and satisfaction.

Direct address is also a pervasive feature of these documents; the second-person pronoun, putting together personal and possessive forms, is the most frequent term in the corpus. Especially in the opening sections of the document, this serves the purpose of synthetically establishing an interpersonal link on an individualised manner by making assertions that pre-suppose a detailed awareness of the addressee's beliefs, attitudes and needs.

However, possessive uses show that readers are principally addressed as part of a hierarchi-cal structure: the most frequent fixed phrases in which the term features identify the addressee by their position in the organisational chain of command or by their being subject to con-tractual rules and regulations whose violation would entail dismissal from the partnership. This subordination is also evident in the frequent use of strong deontic modality; the personal pronoun is closely associated with SHOULD, WILL, MUST and NEED TO, all of them expressing restrictions on the partners' agency regarding corporate goals.

The training materials seek to fix the meaning of the Partnership brand and of the partner status of organisational members in terms of emotional connections and financial rewards, claiming common ground and reciprocity in the relations between them and the organisation. The uniqueness of the corporate structure is explicitly and ostensibly presented, taking pride of place in the presentation of the training materials. At the same time, more subtle forms of positioning such as presuppositions downplay the inequalities in authority and participation attached to managerial control of corporate goals and strategy. It is noteworthy that the texts make repeated mention of "power" and "knowledge" as part of Principle 1, but the terms never appear in other contexts; while the constitution places great emphasis on discussing the participatory arrangements in the Partnership, the materials used to shape organisational members' understanding of their role discuss those notions only in a ritualised context, shying away from any further specifications.

Conclusion

In this chapter, I have sought to discuss the range of discursive features and strategies that can be used to manage the values and attributes that audiences associate with a brand. Alongside the nomination, predication and attribution strategies explored in most current work in brand semiotics, I have emphasised the importance of interpersonal features such as the tenor that characterises a brand's tone of voice and the way in which it creates acceptable reader positions. The above case study illustrates the subtlety with which such resources can be used to shape relationships not only with consumers, but also a range of other stakeholders. Nevertheless, even reliable descriptive scholarship in this topic is yet scarce, and a comprehensive critical theorisation of branding discourse is yet in the future.

Note

1 I exclude from this review work on the use of metaphor in branding discourse (but see Ng, this volume).

Further reading

Delin, J. (2005). Brand tone of voice. *Journal of Applied Linguistics* 2(1): 1–44.
This paper sets out the most explicit and systematic explanation of how the adoption of specific linguistic registers contributes to linking a brand with a certain social identity and constructing particular social relationships with customers and other audiences. It offers analytic tools designed not only for the scholar, but also the branding practitioner.
Koller, V. (2008b). Identity, image, impression: Corporate self-promotion and public reactions. In R. Wodak and V. Koller (eds.), *Handbook of communication in the public sphere,* 155–180. Berlin: Mouton de Gruyter.
Brand management seeks to maximise an organisation's control over the meaning of its brands, but can never fully determine it. In this chapter, Koller integrates the analysis of branding materials with an exploration of their processes of production and distribution (by authoring organisations) and reception and interpretation (by diverse audiences and communities of practice).
Mumby, D. K. (2016). Organizing beyond organization: Branding, discourse, and communicative capitalism. *Organization,* 23(6): 884–907. DOI: 10.1177/1350508416631164
Mumby argues that branding discourses do not just provide links between commercial organisations and their consumers, but function more broadly as key elements in processes of meaning construction and human identity formation. Brands are thus instrumental in producing and reproducing the characteristic social relations of "communicative capitalism".
Thurlow, C. and Aiello, G. (2007). National pride, global capital: A social semiotic analysis of transnational visual branding in the airline industry. *Visual Communication* 6(3): 305–344.
This paper shows how modes other than the linguistic can provide full resources for representation and communication in branding, by drawing both on perceptual associations derived from the human cognitive system and from strategically employed cultural symbolism. It also discusses how institutionalisation consolidates and anchors arbitrary symbolic connotations into a standardised set of stylistic contrasts.

References

Aiello, G. (2012). All together now: The recontextualization of branding and the stylization of diversity in EU public communication. *Social Semiotics* 22(4): 459–486.
Cathcart, A. (2013). Directing democracy: Competing interests and contested terrain in the John Lewis partnership. *Journal of Industrial Relations* 55(4): 601–620.
Cathcart, A. (2014). Paradoxes of participation: Non-union workplace partnership in John Lewis. *The International Journal of Human Resource Management* 25(6): 762–780.

Chernatony, L. de and Dall'Olmo Riley, F. (1998). Defining a "brand": Beyond the literature with experts' interpretations. *Journal of Marketing Management* 14(5): 417–443.

Crawford Camiciottoli, B. (2013). Crafting brand identity in the fashion industry: A linguistic analysis of web-based company communications. *Textus* XXVI: 81–90.

Crawford Camiciottoli, B., Ranfagni, S. and Guercini, S. (2014). Exploring brand associations: An innovative methodological approach. *European Journal of Marketing* 48(5/6): 1092–1112.

Delin, J. (2005). Brand tone of voice. *Journal of Applied Linguistics* 2(1): 1–44.

Elliott, R. and Wattanasuwan, K. (1998). Brands as symbolic resources for the construction of identity. *International Journal of Advertising* 17(2): 131–144.

Fairclough, I. (2008). Branding and strategic maneuvering in the Romanian presidential election of 2004: A critical discourse-analytical and pragma-dialectical perspective. *Journal of Language & Politics* 7(3): 372–390.

Fairclough, N. (1989). *Language and power*. London: Longman.

Flowerdew, J. (2004). The discursive construction of a world-class city. *Discourse & Society* 15(5): 579–605.

Hansen, A. and Machin, D. (2008). Visually branding the environment: Climate change as a marketing opportunity. *Discourse Studies* 10(6): 777–794.

Halliday, M.A.K. and Matthiessen, C. M. (2014). *An introduction to functional grammar*, 4th edn. London: Routledge.

Jaworski, A. and Thurlow, C. (2011). Silence is golden: The "anti-communicational" linguascaping of super-elite mobility. In A. Jaworski and C. Thurlow (eds.), *Semiotic landscapes: Language, image, space*, 187–218. London, New York: Continuum.

Kaneva, N. (2011). Nation branding: Toward an agenda for critical research. *International Journal of Communication* 5: 117–141.

Kaneva, N. and Popescu, D. (2014). "We are Romanian, not Roma": Nation branding and postsocialist discourses of alterity. *Communication, Culture & Critique* 7(4): 506–523.

Kärreman, D. and Rylander, A. (2008). Managing meaning through branding: The case of a consulting firm. *Organization Studies* 29(1): 103–125.

Kilgarriff, A., Baisa, V., Bušta, J., Jakubíček, M., Kovář, V., Michelfeit, J., Rychlý, P. and Suchomel, V. (2014). The Sketch engine: Ten years on. *Lexicography* 1(1): 7–36.

Koller, V. (2007). "The world's local bank": Glocalisation as a strategy in corporate branding discourse. *Social Semiotics* 17(1): 111–131.

Koller, V. (2008a). Corporate brands as socio-cognitive representations. In G. Kristiansen and R. Dirven (eds.), *Cognitive sociolinguistics*, 389–418. Berlin: De Gruyter.

Koller, V. (2008b). Identity, image, impression: Corporate self-promotion and public reactions. In R. Wodak and V. Koller (eds.), *Handbook of communication in the public sphere*, 155–180. Berlin: Mouton de Gruyter.

Koller, V. (2008c). "The world in one city": Semiotic and cognitive aspects of city branding. *Journal of Language and Politics* 7(3): 431–450.

Koller, V. (2009). Brand images: Multimodal metaphor in corporate branding messages. In C. Forceville and E. Urios-Aparisi (eds.), *Multimodal metaphor. Applications of cognitive linguistics*, 45–71. Berlin: De Gruyter.

Kuehn, K. M. (2009). Compassionate consumption: Branding africa through Product RED. *Democratic Communiqué* 23(2): 23–40.

Leitch, S. and Motion, J. (2007). Retooling the corporate brand: A Foucauldian perspective on normalisation and differentiation. *Journal of Brand Management* 15(1): 71–80.

Lowrie, A. (2007). Branding higher education: Equivalence and difference in developing identity. *Journal of Business Research* 60(9): 990–999.

Lury, C. (2004). *Brands: The logos of the global economy*. New York: Routledge.

Machin, D. and van Leeuwen, T. (2005). Language style and lifestyle: The case of a global magazine. *Media, Culture & Society* 27(4): 577–600.

Machin, D. and Niblock, S. (2008). Branding newspapers. *Journalism Studies* 9(2): 244–259.

Machin, D. and Thornborrow, J. (2003). Branding and discourse: The case of Cosmopolitan. *Discourse & Society* 14(4): 453–471.

McWilliam, G. and de Chernatony, L. (1989). Branding terminology – the real debate. *Marketing Intelligence and Planning* 7(7/8): 29–32.

Mautner, G. (2008). Language and communication design in the marketplace. In R. Wodak and V. Koller (eds.), *Handbook of communication in the public sphere*, 131–154. Berlin: Mouton de Gruyter.

Mautner, G. (2010). *Language and the market society: Critical reflections on discourse and dominance*. London: Routledge.

Mautner, G. (2012). The spread of corporate discourse to other domains. In H. Kelly-Holmes and G. Mautner (eds.), *Language and the market,* 215–225. London: Palgrave Macmillan.

Michelis, L. de (2008). Britain and "corporate" national identity. In R. Wodak and V. Koller (eds.), *Handbook of communication in the public sphere,* 203–222. Berlin: Mouton de Gruyter.

Mick, D. G., Burroughs, J. E., Hetzel, P. and Brannen, M. Y. (2004). Pursuing the meaning of meaning in the commercial world: An international review of marketing and consumer research founded on semiotics. *Semiotica* 152(1): 1–74.

Mitsikopoulou, B. (2008). Introduction: The branding of political entities as discursive practice. *Journal of Language and Politics* 7(3): 353–371.

Mumby, D. K. (2016). Organizing beyond organization: Branding, discourse, and communicative capitalism. *Organization,* 23(6): 884–907. DOI: 10.1177/1350508416663164

Murcia Bielsa, S. (2012). SFL and language branding. In J.S. Knox (ed.), *To boldly proceed: Papers from the 39th International Systemic Functional Congress,* 147–152. Sydney: 39th International Systemic Functional Congress.

Myers, G. (1994). *Words in ads*. London: Edward Arnold.

Ng, C.J.W. (2014). "We offer unparalleled flexibility": Purveying conceptual values in higher educational corporate branding. *Discourse & Communication* 8(4): 391–410.

O'Reilly, D. (2005). Cultural brands/branding cultures. *Journal of Marketing Management* 21(5/6): 573–588.

Osman, H. (2008). Re-branding academic institutions with corporate advertising: A genre perspective. *Discourse & Communication* 2(1): 57–77.

Parikka, J. (2015). The city and the City: London 2012 and the visual (un)commons. In D. M. Berry and M. Dieter (eds.), *Postdigital aesthetics: art, computation and design,* 203–217. Basingstoke: Palgrave Macmillan.

Pérez Hernández, L. (2013). Approaching the utopia of a global brand: The relevance of image schemas as multimodal resources for the branding industry. *Review of Cognitive Linguistics* 11(2): 285–302.

Scammell, M. (2007). Political brands and consumer citizens: The rebranding of Tony Blair. *The Annals of the American Academy of Political and Social Science* 611(1): 176–192.

Thurlow, C. and Aiello, G. (2007). National pride, global capital: A social semiotic analysis of transnational visual branding in the airline industry. *Visual Communication* 6(3): 305–344.

Thurlow, C. and Jaworski, A. (2006). The alchemy of the upwardly mobile: Symbolic capital and the stylization of elites in frequent-flyer programmes. *Discourse & Society* 17(1): 99–135.

Unger, J.W. (2013). Rebranding the Scottish executive: A discourse-historical analysis. *Journal of Language and Politics* 12(1): 59–79.

Vásquez, C., Sergi, V. and Cordelier, B. (2013). From being branded to doing branding: Studying representation practices from a communication-centered approach. *Scandinavian Journal of Management* 29(2): 135–146.

Watson, J. M. (1980). Outlaw motorcyclists: An outgrowth of lower-class cultural concerns. *Deviant behavior* 2(1): 31–48.

Williams, R. (1960). Advertising; the magic system. *New Left Review* 4(July/August): 27–32.

37

The critical analysis of musical discourse

Theo van Leeuwen

Introduction

Music is, and always has been, an integral part of public communication. It can create emotive allegiance to powerful nation states, religions, and today also brands, express the values these institutions stand for and rally people behind them. "Without music no State could survive", says the music master in Molière's *Le Bourgeois Gentilhomme,* and after the French revolution a National Institute of Music was created to "support and bestir, by its accents, the energy of the defenders of equality, and to prohibit the music which softens the soul of the French with effeminate sounds, in salons or temples given over to imposture" (quoted in Attali 1985: 55). Nestyev (961: 458) has described how Shostakovich was urged by the Soviet culture controllers to make his music "give enduring expression to the heroism of the people's lives in the period of the victory of socialism". Machin and Richardson (2012) have documented the "bestirring" role of music in Nazi Germany through a detailed analysis of the Horst Wessel song and the closely related Marching Song of the British Union of Fascists. In the workplace, Muzak is thought to increase productivity (van Leeuwen 1999: 38), in shops to enhance people's engagement with the "shopping experience" (Graakjær 2012). Everywhere, music plays a pivotal role in social, political and economic life. But music can also be subversive and challenge power. Massimo Leone (2012) has described how, in 1979, Khomeini tried to ban music altogether in Iran, declaring that it is "like a drug", and that "we must eliminate music because it means betraying our country and our youth". But he did not succeed: music instead strengthened and unified protest in Iran. In the West, popular music has often provided counter-hegemonic social commentaries (cf. e.g., Power, Dillane and Devereux 2012).

Yet, with few exceptions (e.g., Machin 2010; van Leeuwen 2012), critical discourse analysts have paid little attention to music, perhaps because music analysis is seen as too difficult, too specialist a domain for discourse analysts to enter, while most musicologists do not see music as discourse and refuse to deal with musical meaning. In this chapter I will argue that music can, and should, be analysed as discourse; I draw on the work of musicologists who *have* analysed music as discourse in proposing tools for the critical analysis of musical discourse that are accessible to non-musicologists, allowing the analysis of musical meaning to move beyond impressionistic description and adopt the same rigour critical discourse analysts apply when analysing language and speech. Derycke Cooke's *Language of Music* (1959), for instance, is an astounding compendium of musical motifs and convincingly brings out the quite constant meanings these motifs have had in Western music over the centuries. Alan Lomax's *Folk Song Style and Culture* (1968) is an equally impressive compendium of aspects of singing styles and their social meaning potentials. The work of the Canadian composer and theorist R. Murray Schafer (e.g., 1977, 1986) is replete with insights on almost all aspects of musical meaning. Susan McClary's feminist musicology (e.g., 1991) reveals the pervasiveness of gender discourses in music. The writings of John Shepherd (e.g., 1991) and Philip Tagg (e.g., 1982, 1984, 1990, 1994) on popular music are another rich source of ideas for studying how voice quality, tonality, musical time and many other aspects of music make meaning. Writers like these have shown that musical signifiers, aspects of melody, harmony, musical structure, rhythm and timbre, can be convincingly linked to social meaning potentials in ways that can help us to analyse both the hegemonic ideological work and the counter-hegemonic work of music in society, and to unlock the astounding potential of music to herald emergent, social, cultural, political and economic developments, often even before they become visible in other domains of social life (cf. Attali 1985).

Music as discourse

In his autobiography, Igor Stravinsky wrote (1936: 91):

> I consider that music is, by its very nature, powerless to express anything at all, whether a feeling, an attitude of mind, a psychological mood, or a phenomenon of nature. If, as is nearly always the case, music appears to express something, this is only an illusion and not a reality.

The music semiotician Jean-Jacques Nattiez echoed this: "Music, by itself, signifies nothing" (Nattiez 1971: 8), as have many other musicians, musicologists and music semioticians. Music was, and still is, widely viewed as autonomous and abstract, even if it can be aesthetically pleasing and emotively engaging. And the preferred form of listening to music is still widely held to be what Adorno (1976: 4) called "structural hearing" – focusing on the formal aspects of music in the way that can still be seen every day in classical music (and now also jazz) reviews.

In fact, Western music, especially in the context of 17th century Italian opera, quite deliberately set out to develop a "representative style", a set of resources that would allow music to tell stories, to evoke settings, characterise *dramatis personae* and signify actions. Susan McClary (1991: 35) has discussed this in her work on early Italian opera:

> One of the great accomplishments of seventeenth century culture was the development of a vocabulary by means of which dramatic characters and actions could be delineated in music (. . .). The achievements of the *stile rappresentativo* made possible most of the musical forms with which we still live today.

The musical forms that stem from this tradition have, in the 20th century, culminated in the global musical language of Hollywood film music, understood by anyone who has ever been exposed to Hollywood films.

Yet, there has been, from the early 19th century onwards, an increasing tension between the "descriptive" and the "melodious" aspects of music, between music as discourse and "pure" music. Schlegel, in 1798, could still see music as discourse, as "philosophy in sounds" (quoted in Dahlhaus 1985: 34):

> Must not pure instrumental music create its own text? And does not the theme undergo the same processes of development, confirmation, variation and contrast in music as the object of meditation in a train of musical thought?

But ever since the early 19th century, composers, musicologists and philosophers have begun to express a sense of embarrassment about "descriptive" music. Beethoven gave the movements of his *Pastoral Symphony* titles like "Scene by the Brook", "Happy Gathering of the Villagers" and "Thunderstorm", yet felt he had to defend the work as "more the expression of feeling than painting" (1985: 21). More than a century later, Honegger's *Pacific 231* "described" the sound of a steam locomotive. The whistle was played by strings abruptly sliding up. Brass, strings and timpani played the chugging of the engine, first low and slow, then gradually faster and higher. But on the sleeve notes (Erato 2292–45242–2), Honegger is quoted as downplaying the representational aspects of the piece: "What I was looking for in 'Pacific' was not so much to imitate the sounds of the locomotive, but to translate visual impressions and physical enjoyment with a musical construction".

In looking at music as discourse, however, we should pay attention to the "descriptive", and link it to discourse, in the case of Honegger, for instance, to the discourses of technology of the period – Russian constructivism, the work of Léger, Fritz Lang's *Metropolis,* and so on, all of which used machine motifs either to celebrate or to critique the new power of technology in society. Music can engage listeners emotively with such discourses, making them feel the majestic power of the machine and its promise of progress, or dread its mechanical monotony and de-humanizing effects.

McClary has written extensively about discourses of gender and sexuality in music, arguing that the "putting into discourse of sex" which, as Michel Foucault (1981) noted, started in the 17th century, coincided with the musical construction of gender in opera. It was there, said McClary (1991: 50) that men began to stifle their feelings while women were expected to indulge in emotional expression, so that men who *did* express emotions, e.g., Orfeo in Monteverdi's opera of the same name, were regarded as effeminate. It was there that extensive soliloquies by abandoned women and musically realised feminine seduction tactics offered the public insights into the female mind "revealing, without mediation, *what women are really like:* not docile, but insubordinate or threatening, unless they can be reconciled with a strong male authority" (1991: 52). McClary related the popularity of such discourses to the patriarchic backlash of the period (1989: 223):

> In the name of "entertainment", many contradictory models of power slipped by a guileless representation of the world itself (. . .). If we are to make sense of early opera – its achievements and its discontents – we must begin to unravel that tangle of gender, rhetoric and power that first found its voice in the musical convention of the *stile rappresentativo.*

Similar models informed instrumental music, for instance in the first parts of sonatas and symphonies. They can be reconstructed by paying close attention to key musical signifiers, as well, as, of course, the social context in which these signifiers were used.

• *Ascending and descending melodies*

555

Theo van Leeuwen

According to Cooke (1959: 102ff) ascending melodies, melodies rising in pitch, are "active" and "dynamic". This, Cooke argues, is because in singing pitch relates to vocal effort. The higher the notes, the greater the effort required from the singer. This is why songs that seek to energise people, to rally people behind a cause (for instance national anthems), have melodies characterised by rising pitch. Descending in pitch, by contrast, allows singers to decrease vocal effort, and is therefore more "passive", "inward-looking", and so on.

- *Large intervals/small intervals*

The same applies to the size of the intervals between the notes. Large energetic steps upwards are typical for "heroic", masculine music, small steps downwards for "sentimental" music and "ballads". Chromatism, which uses the smallest steps possible in Western tonality, is a standard device of "sentimentality" in music (cf. Marothy 1974).

- *Dotted rhythms and suspension*

Dynamic, energetic melodies may have "dotted rhythms" in which each note is anticipated by a short note (DAA-de- DAA- de- DAA-de-DAA), giving a sense of exact, precisely disciplined timing. In the case of "suspension", on the other hand, notes languidly linger and stretch, delaying the next note, and this, too, is a standard device of "sentimentality" in music.

As McClary, explains, the musical structure of two key genres in classical music, the sonata and the first part of symphonies, opens with a "masculine theme" that typically uses active, assertive musical signifiers such as ascending melodies, large intervals and dotted rhythms, and is usually also loud, and played by loud instruments such as brass and timpani. Then follows a "feminine" theme, typically more passive and sentimental, using descending melodies, small intervals and suspension, and played more softly and by gentler instruments such as woodwind or strings. Not all of these characteristics will of course always be present in every "masculine" or "feminine" theme, and variations can outline different kinds of "masculinity" and "femininity", as McClary (1991: 69–79) shows in a fascinating analysis of the first movement of Tchaikovsky's 4th symphony. After the two themes have been established, they begin to engage in interaction, travelling, during the "development" of the movement, through different tonal territories until, in the "resolution", the feminine theme is subjugated, transposed into the key of the masculine theme. With this schema, McClary says, many stories can be told – the violent stories of Beethoven, which "often exhibit considerable anxiety with respect to feminine moments and respond to them with extraordinary violence" or the gentler stories of Mozart and Schubert who "tend to invest their second themes with extraordinary sympathy" so that "one regrets the inevitable return to the tonic and the original materials" as the feminine theme is "brutally, tragically quashed in accordance with the destiny predetermined by the 'disinterested' conventions of the form" (McClary 1991).

Music as social interaction

The act of making music, and listening to music, is by nature a form of social interaction, and the relations of power and solidarity that are created by musical interaction are a primary source of musical meaning. In contrast to conversation, which is sequential (although various writers have pointed at the frequency of simultaneous speaking, e.g., Feld 1982; Tannen 1992), musical interaction is usually simultaneous, and this is of course at the heart of music's great power to unite people and create group feelings. Three broad kinds of simultaneous interaction can be discerned:

- *Social unison*

Social unison (or "monophony", as it is called in music theory) is a form of interaction in which all participants sing and/or play the same notes. Positively, this can create or represent solidarity, a positive sense of belonging to a group. Negatively, it can create or represent conformity, strict disciplining and a lack of individuality. Alan Lomax (1968: 157), in his ethnomusicological survey of song styles across the world, notes that social unison is the dominant form in "leaderless" societies in which there is an emphasis on consensus and conformity. But it occurs also in more complex societies such as ours, for instance in the pub, the sports stadium, the church, the school or the army.

The unison voices can fully blend, so that no individual voices stand out, or be "heterophonic", with individual voices standing out to a greater or lesser extent, so that both group solidarity and individual difference are signified. "Rough" choirs of this kind are common in advertising music, where they can signify that the product appeals to men as well as women, the young as well as the old and so on.

- *Social pluralism*

In "polyphony" *different* melodies are simultaneously played or sung by different instruments or singers. Each could stand on its own and still have musical interest, yet they all fit harmoniously together. It is therefore a form of interaction, in which the interacting parties are "equal but different". Lomax (1968: 165) found that two-voiced polyphony, in many of the smaller societies in which it is used, symbolises gender roles with a clear division of labour between men and women, but without the one being valued more highly than the other.

In the history of European music, polyphony began to develop from the 9th century, first in the form of "parallel organum", what we would now call "harmony lines", then in the form of counterpoint, where melodies are the inverse of one another (for example, if one goes up by two steps, the other simultaneously goes down by two steps), and finally into full musical pluralism, with melodies that are melodically and rhythmically independent yet fit well together.

- *Social domination*

In "homophonic" music, one voice (the melody) becomes dominant and the other voices subordinate, accompanying and supporting the dominant voice. On their own these subordinate voices would not have musical interest. They are meaningful only in relation to the whole. Their role is "harmonic" – they must "harmonise" with the dominant voice. Homophonic music therefore celebrates relations of inequality and domination, although these relations can of course be inflected or even subverted: with harmony comes disharmony – muffled tension and dissonance behind, or even overt clashes with, the melody, the hegemonic voice. The music must then seek to resolve this dissonance if it is to progress towards a harmonic resolution.

In European music homophony started in the age of the industrial revolution, and culminated in the symphony orchestra. Many writers, including Max Weber (1958 [1911]), have commented on the similarity between the organisation of the symphony orchestra and the factory, seeing in the symphony orchestra the same division of labour into in themselves meaningless functions, and the same importance of the supervisors who must bring all these functions together in an impressive whole. The symphony orchestra thus enacts and celebrates the values of the industrial age, and it is significant that countries like Japan and China, as soon as they began to industrialise on a large scale, also began to play Western symphonic music. In a documentary called *From Mao to Mozart: Isaac Stern in China* (Lerner 1981), the conductor of the Beijing Symphony Orchestra tells Stern of his interest in Mozart, whose music, he says, so clearly evokes the transition from feudalism to the industrial age – a view which Stern categorically rejects: music has nothing to do with politics.

But there are also sequential forms of musical interaction. "Call-response" patterns are common in many forms of music, and always involve the interaction between a real or symbolic leader and his or her followers, whether it is a priest and a congregation, a male singer and a group of female back-up vocalists, or an advertising jingle in which a male voice sings the praises of a washing powder and is responded to by a choir of housewives. Much can be learned from a close study of the relationships this can create (cf. van Leeuwen 1999: 71–77). There can, for instance, be a respectful distance between the part of the leader and the part of the choir, or the two can overlap, or even, in the end join forces. Lomax (1968: 158) has described how this happens in African performances:

Frequently the performance begins with the two parts just touching and, as the excitement of the performance grows, the chorus will encroach more and more upon the leader's time, until at last both are singing without letup in exciting rhythmic relationship to each other.

The same frequently occurs in contemporary advertising jingles (1968: 75):

Leader: So listen to me baby, Got a new plan, Why don't we
Leader + Chorus Take a shot of Comfort

And responses can be a full response which adds new information, as in the example above, or a simple affirmation, whether the congregation's "Amen" or "Halleluiah" or the female vocalists' rapturous "Aaah" (1968: 74), as in the example below:

Leader: *Take me to the stars And shoot me into space now Move. . .*
Chorus: *Aaaah. . .*

In an analysis of the aria "Bess You Are My Woman Now" from Gershwin's opera *Porgy and Bess* (1968: 86–90) I have shown that the same relationships can also inform vocal duets, and that lyrics and music can, at times, tell different stories – in this case, as I have analysed it, the lyrics celebrate newfound love while the music already foretells the inevitable end of the relationship.

Musical time

Musical time enacts and celebrates the timings of social interaction. Some forms of music adhere strictly to a regular, metronomic beat, just as some social institutions require strict adherence to the mechanical time of the clock. Other forms of music are polyrhythmic, allowing each player to keep his or her own time without endangering the cohesion of the whole. Musical choices of this kind may either characterise particular kinds of music or be used representationally, as in the example of the "masculine" and "feminine" themes of the sonata form.

- *Measured versus unmeasured time*

Unmeasured time does not have a regular beat, but a slow and ongoing drone that may fluctuate slightly and irregularly. It cannot normally be produced by the human voice, and for this reason tends to signify the 'non-human' – eternity and divinity, the grandeur of nature, the wide expanse of the cosmos. Special techniques such as circular breathing, and special technologies such as the church organ or the synthesiser are developed to produce them. In a historical documentary series about the impact of colonisation on Australian Aborigines (Perkins 2008), a drone sound, suggesting timelessness, is joined by a descending melody at the very moment the image cuts to a still of a large ship entering Sydney Harbour, as if to say, after 10,000s of years of unchanging Aboriginal culture, now the measurable time of history begins. But the melody descends – for the Aboriginal inhabitants of Australia this was not to be a story of progress, but a story of slow decline.

- *Metronomic and non-metronomic time*

Even measured time does not always have a strictly clock-like, metronomic beat. As already discussed, "suspension" stretches time, and in Afro-American music the beat is often anticipated or delayed. Music can thus either align itself with the time of the clock, or rebel against it. Philip Tagg has described the timing of rock music as an attempt to "gain some control over time through musical expression" in a context where such control is lacking and where mechanical time remains dominant "at work and in other official realms of power" (1990: 112). Disco, on the other hand, does not have "the same extent of subversion of clock time, not the same human appropriation of the mechanical pulse" (Tagg 1984: 31–32)

Major/minor

The major scale became the norm in Western music in the late Middle Ages. The hegemonic music of the time, the music of the Church, used, as its basic tonal material, a number of different modes, but shunned the Ionian mode, which corresponds to today's major scale, although that mode was widely used in secular music. Pope John XXI, in the middle of the 14th century, tried to ban the major scale (quoted in Harman and Mellers 1962: 123):

> Certain disciplines of the new school (. . .) display their method in notes which are new to us (. . .) they stuff our melodies with upper parts made out of secular songs (. . .) their voices are incessantly running to and fro, intoxicating the ear (. . .) We now hasten therefore to banish these methods (. . .) and to put them to flight more effectually than heretofore, far from the house of God (. . .) let nothing in the authoritative music be changed.

The ascendance of the major scale, the secular scale, was therefore subversive. It indicated a shift of cultural hegemony from the religious to the secular, and from the Church to the rising merchant class, and it came to be associated with the positive values of that class: belief in progress through human achievement science, industry, and so on. Minor, by contrast, literally depresses the major scale, by lowering the third, the sixth and the seventh note, and so became associated with everything that stands in the way of progress. For a long time pieces in a minor key had to have a "happy ending" (the "tierce de Picardie") – and happy endings of this kind are still common today in many Broadway songs.

These meanings have remained remarkably stable. As mentioned, Stalin urged Shostako-vich to make greater use of the major triad, to celebrate "the victory of socialism" (Nestyev 1961: 458), and wherever the ethos of industrial progress gained a foothold, the major triad soon followed. Cooke (1959: 55) notes that, after Independence, Indian sitar players began to add major thirds to the bass drone of *ragas,* which, until then, had always been a "bare fifth".

In the West we have of course "privatised" the discourse of music, and speak of major and minor in terms of "mood", with major as "happy" and minor as "sad", but in fact music fuses ideological meaning and emotion, and is precisely therein that its power lies.

Voice quality and timbre

Values and identities can also be expressed by voice qualities and instrumental timbres. Take vocal tension for example. We can recognise the sound of a tense voice, as it is higher, sharper and brighter than a lax voice. We know where such tension comes from – from excitement for instance, or apprehension. We can use it to express tension even when we do not actually feel tense. And we can recognise the quality also in the way musical instruments are played, or in other sounds. Just what tension will mean in a given context will of course depend on the other musical and non-musical signifiers it combines with, and on the social context in which the tense sounds are produced. Lomax (1968: 193) described how tensing of the voice in female singing is customary in societies where there is a good deal of sexual repression of women:

> It is as if one of the assignments of the favoured singer is to act out the level of sexual tension which the customs of the society establish as normal. The content of this message may be painful and anxiety-producing, but the effect upon the culture member may be stimulating, erotic and pleasurable since the song reminds him of familiar sexual emotions and experiences.

Other aspects of voice quality can be related to physical, bodily experiences and social experiences in similar ways.

- *Soft/loud*

Soft and loud are most crucially associated with distance, and therefore also with *social* distance (Hall 1966: 184–185). At "intimate" range we whisper, at "close personal" range we speak softly, and so on, and only at "public" range do we fully project our voices. The microphone and amplification have of course made it possible to disengage loudness as a signifying system from real social distance, so that we can now, for instance, whisper intimately to an audience of thousands, and mix up the "private" and the "public" in ways that were hitherto impossible.

- *High/low*

Because men's voices are on average lower than those of women and children, the mean-ings of pitch relate to gender and age in complex ways. Men use the higher regions of their range to assert themselves (in operas the tenors are the heroes), women the lower regions. In combination with, for instance, loudness, this has led to iconic models of female identity such as the low soft voice of Lauren Bacall in *To Have and Have Not,* for instance, at once asservive and seductive, or the higher, breathy of voice of Marilyn Monroe, at once childlike and vulnerable and seductive.

- *Vibrato/plain*

Like other aspects of voice quality, vibrato "means what it is". We can recognise trembling or wavering in the sound of a voice or instrument, and we know what causes it – emotion, whether it be love or fear. Vibrato is therefore equally good at pulling the heartstrings in a love song as creating a sense of fear and foreboding in the music of a horror film.

- *Breathiness*

In breathiness the sounds of voices and instruments mix with the sound of breathing. Again, we know where that comes from – exertion, or excitement. Soft, breathy voices can suggest intimacy and sensuality. Advertisers use it to give their message erotic appeal, and singers and instrumentalists use it for the same reason.

- *Roughness*

A rough voice is one in which we can hear other things beside the tone of the voice itself – friction, hoarseness, harshness, rasp. A smooth voice is a voice from which all noisiness is eliminated. Again, roughness means what it is: rough. We know it may come from the wear and tear of a hard life, or from the unvarnished, "hand-made", "lived in" qualities of the "authentic". Lomax (1968: 192) mentions that it is common in male speech and singing in hunting societies and strongly correlated with the assertiveness and resourcefulness a good hunter requires.

All these qualities are simultaneously present in every timbre, though in different proportions, and they can characterise the habitual style of a singer or instrumentalist or the preferred sound of a musical genre. The voice of the legendary jazz singer Billie Holiday, for instance, was tense and relatively loud, rather high, compared to other women jazz singers of the same period, and with just a touch of vibrato. These features combined to express Billie Holiday's identity as a singer: tense and tough, struggling to have her message heard, yet also vulnerable, and betraying suppressed emotion in the long notes.

Perspective

Music can use relative loudness to position the listener close to some parts of complex musical events and distance them from others. The closest part or parts will form the musical foreground or "figure", the part on which the listener is meant to focus most closely. The middle ground, or "ground", forms a kind of social setting for the "figure" and will be "heard but not listened to", and the background, or "field", is an even more distant, physical setting.

Musical perspective can be used representationally. In Charles Ives's *Housatonic at Stockbridge,* the music represents an early morning walk along the river Housatonic. The river is represented by soft, hazy, atonal chords, played by strings, and drifting along irregularly and seemingly haphazardly, with a piano adding twinkles of light. After a while we hear a hymn melody coming from a church on the other side of the river, played on horn and lower strings, very softly at first. Gradually this melody gets louder as we "walk towards it", until it clashes with the sounds of the river in a conflict between the unpredictable and ever-shifting rhythms of nature and the world of order and communal values expressed by the hymn – a conflict also expressed in many other American cultural products, e.g., in Westerns. But musical perspective can also characterise social relations, for instance the gender relations between a male solo singer and female "back-up vocalists". In contemporary "drum 'n bass" music, rhythm, the steady stabs of the bass and the complex and shifting rhythms of the drums are in the foreground, and fragments of other sounds, including, in one track, a voice singing "Give me some love", are soft, very distant, completely backgrounded by the insistent rhythm – melody, music speaking to you, makes place for rhythm, music to move on.

Case study: the marketization of musical discourse

I will end by showing how these various elements can come together in an integrated analysis, returning first to an example I have discussed earlier (van Leeuwen 1999: 60–64), the news signature tunes of the ABC, Australia's national, state-subsidized radio and television broadcaster, and then moving to an analysis of sonic logos, the signature tunes of contemporary companies.

For 32 years the ABC had used a news signature theme called "Majestic Fanfare". It had a simple call and response structure in which the "call" was played by unison trumpets, and the response a homophonic melody played by the whole orchestra, with harp glissandos particularly noticeable. The tune set up a relation between the news and its audience in which the news called the nation to attention, and in which the nation responded, in all its variety (as represented by the different instruments used), but at the same time harmoniously, without dissonance.

The trumpet theme was a typical masculine theme – a rising melody using large intervals and dotted rhythms, and set in a major key. Thus the voice of the news was (a) that of a leader ("call and response"), (b) active, "masculine" and nationalistic (the anthem-like melody) with militaristic connotations (the "bugle call" instrumentation), (c) disciplined (the dotted rhythm), (d) optimistic and confident (the major key) and (e) unified (social unison). The audience was characterised as (a) diverse, including even artistic, lyrical elements (the varied instrumentation and the harp glissandos), but nevertheless (b) harmoniously united with the main melody (social domination). In short, the news was characterised as assertive, vested with authority, emanating from a centre of power and obediently followed by a mass audience.

In the late 80s this theme was replaced with a new theme. It had three parts. The first part began with a synthesiser drone which continued throughout the whole part. Soon a call and response came in, just as in the old tune, but the call was now played by a single piccolo trumpet (the trumpet had shrunk, so to speak), and the response by a muted brass ensemble. Then the call and response were repeated. The middle section had a fast ostinato rhythmic pattern that could be taken as a musical imitation of, say, a teletypewriter. On top of this the voice of a newsreader read the headlines, punctuated by very short melodic phrases, which alternated between a rather harsh sounding motif, played by brass, and a softer, more lyrical one, played by a synthesiser. The final part repeated the call and response repeated one more time.

This new tune characterised the news in a different way. The synthesiser drone, which, on television, was shown with an image of a revolving satellite, suggested the news coming in via satellite (unmeasured synthesiser sound). The imperial self-assurance of the unison trumpets with their militaristically disciplined timing made place for a single piccolo trumpet, playing a minor and for the most part descending melody with jazz-like syncopation. Authority was played down, the former self-assurance much diminished, and an element of entertainment had entered (the syncopation, the "sentimental" rather than militaristic melodies). The news was also portrayed as *urgent* and *immediate* (the relentless ostinato pattern), and as *varied,* containing both "hard" and "soft" news (the alternation between the two kinds of melody in the middle section).

When I asked the composer why he had made these changes, many of the things he said tallied with my initial analysis, for instance the emphasis on the urgency, immediacy and variety of the news. But when I asked him why the tune was now in a minor key, he hesitated and wanted to confer with the arranger before answering. In the end he said "It's because the news is more dramatic today". I begged to differ. I felt that the composer, who was also a broadcaster, disagreed with recent changes in style of presentation, inspired by commercial television, and with changes in programming that did away with the ABC's previously well-patrolled boundary between news and current affairs, and that he had, perhaps subconsciously, expressed this by musically diminishing the former assertiveness and glory of the "Majestic Fanfare".

I am not the only one who has noticed. Chris May commented that a "persistent underlying beat is very voguish with news themes ate the moment and tends, on the BBC, for instance, to accompany a standing host in a trendy open-plan studio. The constant pulse musically denotes a heartbeat; the impression is not that the news is a staunch fixture, but rather an unsleeping hive of activity. It is a response to an increasing cynicism towards public broadcasting authorities – a popular resistance to trust, to be told what to think. Instead of claiming respect by harnessing the gravitas of the official, is there now a drive to establish an alternative credibility through remorseless business?" (May 2014)

But in corporate music the "heroic" characteristics of the old ABC tune are alive and well. Sung brand names have long been used in radio and television commercials, and many have ascending melodies with relatively large intervals, signalling energy and excitement (cf. Helms 1981) – the contour of the exclamation! Choirs then represent the harmonious unity of the happy consumers. Sonic company logos also tend to have rising melodies, positioning the corporations as aspirational and growing, and, at the same time creating audience anticipation.

Commissioned, in 1995, to compose a start-up musical tune for the 1995 Windows Operating System, Brian Eno was told it had to be "universal, optimistic, futuristic, sentimental, emotional" – and 3.8 seconds long.[1] The logo he came up with has a low note that ascends glissando-like to four identical high notes, a static "melody" that remains open, unresolved, a mood-setting intro to the computer user's activities. Towards the end a drone is coming in, perhaps suggesting space (the accompanying image shows an expansive blue sky). The soft, chime-like timbre, on the other hand, is very different from that of the ABC news tune, suggesting a calm, new age mood, as if sitting on a veranda, listening to the tinkling of the chime and contemplating the blue sky. Yet it also has an electronic edge, suggesting technological perfection.

Other IT company logos are not dissimilar. The Intel logo starts with a high impact "audio sparkle", an electronic sound laced with instrumental timbres, which first becomes louder, then softer again, then louder again, as if describing an orbit – the sonic equivalent of the dynamic circle that surrounds the company's name in the visual logo. This is followed by a four-note ascending "staccato" melody that spells "Intel Inside" and blends electronic sounds with bells, sound effects (hammering) and the sound of a marimba. Again, the optimism and forcefulness of the ascending melody is married to a timbre that combines the sounds of technological perfection with sounds aiming to evoke affective resonance. To discuss one more example, the AT&T logo also begins with a four-note ascending melody that remains unresolved, and its timbre mixes and old piano, a glockenspiel and a Wurlitzer, blending sounds that evoke technological perfection with the human touch of less than perfect or historic instruments.

Compared to the "Majestic Fanfare", there is therefore both continuity and change. The assertive optimism of the rising melody continues. But the timbre has changed. Instead of the militaristic bugle call, we now have timbres that blend technological perfection and human appeal, the former through electronic sounds, the latter through a variety of approaches that allows the differentiation necessary for branding – from the gentle, wind-driven sound of chimes to the nostalgia of old pianos and the sweet retro sound of the Wurlitzer.

Quite similar sounds can also be found on collections of the ring tones that provide for the expression of personal rather than corporate identity. While ring tone collections offer many identity choices, for instance through tunes with ethnic, mass media and musical style references, they also include tunes called "iPhone", "Google", "Apple", etc. which have much in common with the sonic logos of IT companies: simple ascending melodies and timbres that blend electronics with a human touch in a musical realisation of what Fairclough called "synthetic personalization" (1992: 140). The message Brian Eno was given, be "optimistic and futuristic" as well as "emotional" must also be "universal", entering the private as well as the public domain and being heard everywhere.

In short, and by way of conclusion, musical discourse analysis can reveal the musical expression of power, and of the values that support and legitimise it, just as assuredly as linguistic discourse analysis, provided close attention is paid to musical signifiers of the kind I have discussed in this paper. This does not require specialist musical knowledge and can be done by anyone who is willing to take the trouble to listen closely and with concentration.

However, despite the importance of music in the media, in entertainment and in the ceremonies of public life, the analysis of musical discourse has lagged behind the analysis of linguistically expressed discourse. I hope this chapter will encourage more critical discourse analysts to pay attention to music – especially to those forms of music, usually embedded in multimodal texts and public events that play a key role in the emotive legitimation of power, whether in the field of gender relations, politics or corporate power – or in its contestation.

Further readings

Leppert, R. and McClary, S. (eds.) (1987). *Music and society – The politics of composition, performance and reception*. Cambridge: Cambridge University Press.
An excellent series of papers on the ideological functions and meanings of popular as well as classical music in contemporary Western society.
Machin, D. (2010). *Analysing popular music – image, sound, text*. London: Sage.
An accessible guide to the critical analysis of popular music.
Tagg, P. (1994). From refrain to rave: The decline of figure and the rise of the ground. *Popular Music* 13(2): 209–222.
Philip Tagg's work should be an inspiration for anyone engaging in critical musical discourse analysis. This paper is just one example. Many others can be found on Tagg's website, www.tagg.org/articles
Van Leeuwen, T. (1999). *Speech, music, sound*. London: Macmillan.
This book explains and exemplifies the approaches to critical musical discourse analysis introduced in this chapter in greater detail.

References

Adorno, T. W. (1976). *Introduction to the sociology of music*. New York: Seabury Press.
Attali, J. (1985). *Noise – The political economy of music*. Manchester: Manchester University Press.
Cooke, D. (1959). *Language of music*. Oxford: Clarendon.
Dahlhaus, C, (1985). *Realism in nineteenth century music*. Cambridge: Cambridge University Press.

Fairclough, N. (1992). Critical discourse analysis and the marketization of public discourse: The universities. *Discourse & Society* 4(2): 133–168.

Feld, S. (1982). *Sound and sentiment – birds, weeping, poetics and song in Kaluli expression*. Philadelphia: University of Pennsylvania Press.

Foucault, M. (1981). *The history of sexuality*. Harmondsworth: Penguin.

Graakjær, N. (2012). Dance in the store: On the use and production of music in Abercrombie & Fitch. *Critical Discourse Studies* 9(4): 393–406.

Hall, E. T. (1966). *The hidden dimension*. New York: Doubleday.

Harman, A. and Mellers, W. (1962). *Man and his music*. London: Barrie and Jenkins.

Helms, S. (1981). *Musik in der Werbung*. Wiesbaden: Breitkopf und Hartel.

Leone, M. (2012). My schoolmate: Protest music in present-day Iran. *Critical Discourse Studies* 9(4): 347–362.

Lerner, M. (1981). *From Mao to Mozart: Isaac Stern in China* (documentary film, USA).

Lomax, A. (1968). *Folksong style and culture*. New Brunswick, NJ: Transaction Books.

Machin, D. (2010). *Analysing popular music*. London: Routledge.

Machin, D. and Richardson, J. E. (2012). Discourses of unity and purpose in he sounds of fascist music: A multimodal approach. *Critical Discourse Studies* 9(4): 329–345.

Marothy, J. (1974). *Music and the bourgeois, music and the proletarian*. Budapest: Akademiai Kiado.

McClary, S. (1989). Construction of gender in Monteverdi's dramatic music. *Cambridge Opera Journal* 1(3): 203–223.

McClary, S. (1991). *Feminine endings – music, gender and sexuality*. Minneapolis, MN: University of Minnesota Press.

May, C. (2014). What the ABC News theme says about you. *Limelight Magazine*. Accessed August 30, 2015, www.limelightmagazine.com.au

Nattiez, J-J. (1971). Situation de la sémiologie musicale. *Musique en jeu* 56: 3–18.

Nestyev, I. V., (1961). *Prokoviev*. Oxford: Oxford University Press.

Perkins, R. (2008). *The first australians* (documentary series produced by Film Australia).

Power, M. J., Dillane, A. and Devereux, E. R. (2012). A push and a shove and the land is ours: Morrissey's counter-hegemonic stance(s) on social class. *Critical Discourse Studies* 9(4): 375–392.

Schafer, R. M. (1977). *The tuning of the world*. Toronto: McClelland and Stewart.

Schafer, R. M. (1986). *The thinking ear*. Toronto: Arcana Editions.

Shepherd, J. (1991). *Music as social text*. Cambridge: Polity.

Stravinsky, I. (1936). *Chronicle of my life*. London: Gollancz.

Tagg, P. (1982). *Nature as a musical mood category*, 820. Göteborg: IASPM International Publications.

Tagg, P. (1984). Understanding Musical 'Time Sense': Concepts, Sketches and Consequences. In *Tvarspel – Festskrift for Jan Ling – 50 År* 9: 11–43. Göteborg: Skrifter fran Musikvetenskapliga Institutionen.

Tagg, P. (1990). Music in mass media studies – reading sounds for example. In K. Roe and U. Carlsson (eds.), *Popular Music Research*, Göteborg: Nordicom-Sweden (2): 103–115.

Tagg, P. (1994). From refrain to rave: The decline of the figure and the rise of the ground. *Popular Music* 13(2): 209–222.

Tannen, D. (1992). *You just don't understand – women and men in conversation*. London: Virago.

Van Leeuwen, T. (1999). *Speech, music, sound*. London: Macmillan.

Van Leeuwen, T. (ed.) (2012). Special issue: The critical analysis of musical discourse. *Critical Discourse Studies* 9(4): 319–328.

Weber, M. (1958 [1911]). *The rational and social foundation of music*. Carbondale and Edwardsville, IL: Illinois University Press.

38

The power of semiotic software
A critical multimodal perspective

Emilia Djonov and Theo van Leeuwen

Introduction

In a paper that played an important role in setting the agenda for critical discourse analysis, Norman Fairclough drew attention to what he called the "marketization of discourse", the "colonization of discourse by promotion" (1993: 142) in diverse social institutions and practices. Powered by neoliberal ideas blurring the boundaries between public and private life, shared and individual responsibility, forms of discourse associated with advertising have infiltrated professional, political and public service institutions, and gradually become the common sense of their everyday world, mixing fact and opinion, information and persuasion, and steering clear of anything that might be regarded as negative or critical. This process, as Fairclough (1993) argued, is reflected in and continues to advance three defining aspects of contemporary communication: (1) "technologization" – the building and imposition, typically top-down, of knowledge and norms about what constitutes effective discourse within a given institution; (2) "conversationalization", or "synthetic personalization", the appropriation of communication principles such as those used in informal, personal conversations, for the marketing goals of formerly self-effacing and impersonal official and professional discourse and (3) increased reliance on the promotional power of semiotic modes other than language (e.g., visual, aural and kinetic resources) and their multimodal interaction, and an associated "significant shift from what one might call signification-with-reference to signification-without-reference" (1993: 142), witnessed in the rise of "discourse aesthetics" (van Leeuwen 2015).

Digital technologies play a fundamental role in facilitating and disseminating promotional discourse in ever more domains of public and private life, as software "structures and makes possible much of the contemporary world" (Fuller 2008: 1). Software for making meaning, or semiotic software, is a major force in spreading new forms of writing and communication, in which words become elements of visual configurations such as word clouds and Microsoft SmartArt diagrams, and templates pre-structure, aestheticise and homogenise communication, overriding differences in its content and social context.

Ubiquitous semiotic software – be it office or social media applications – exercises enormous power. It is an inescapable, effectively mandatory tool for making meaning in education systems and public as well as private-sector organisations in the post-industrial world.

Proficiency in software use is a measure of success across a steadily widening range of academic and professional fields around the globe. This is echoed even in the learning outcomes that children are expected to work towards from a very young age.

Semiotic software – in contrast to earlier technologies such as the pen or the typewriter – enables users to select from a range of different semiotic resources, and incorporates and represents knowledge about what constitutes effective use of these resources in particular contexts. This artificial intelligence serves and reveals the interests of certain social groups (their communicative goals, norms and aesthetics). As the development of most ubiquitous semiotic software is unilaterally determined by the powerful (mostly American) companies that design and market it, its design reflects and promotes the neoliberal values that underpin global corporate culture. This is reflected in the mismatch between the influence of many software products well beyond the social practices they were originally designed for and the inability of their updates to address such expansions in their use, even when the arsenal of semiotic resources available in these products keeps growing. PowerPoint, for instance, was originally designed for pitching project ideas to management (Gaskins 1984), and, notwithstanding its widespread deployment in academic presentations, bullet lists persist as the default choice for presenting text in the body of a slide – succinctly and persuasively, in line with the affordances of "the grammar of little texts" (Halliday 1994 [1985]) that dominates advertising discourse. These affordances of bullet lists, however, are inadequate for constructing the complex arguments or narratives that different academic disciplines rely on. This creates tensions in the interaction between a software product's design and its use, which can lead users to either routinely and blindly conform to the communicative norms built into such products, potentially against their own interests, or rebel against these norms and use the resources software provides critically and creatively, against the grain of its design. For this reason it is crucial for critical discourse analysts to examine not just the texts and interactions produced with software but also software itself: the semiotic resources and choices it makes available, which among them are prioritised, how and why.

In this chapter, we argue that to understand the power of semiotic software we need to adopt a holistic perspective, one that is multimodal and critical, and pays attention to the interaction between software design and use and its relation to broader semiotic and social practices – past, present and emergent. Of the numerous computer features that, unlike hardware, cannot be physically manipulated, our focus here is on software for making meaning, that is, on software as a semiotic technology. This excludes the source code or algorithms designed by programmers, which are invisible to most computer users, and operating systems such as Windows, Linux and Mac OS, which serve as platforms for many different software tools. After reviewing existing approaches to the study of software, we present principles for studying semiotic software from a critical multimodal perspective and finally consider how PowerPoint, as a case study, incorporates the characteristics of marketised discourse outlined above.

(Critical) studies of semiotic software: a literature review

The idea that not only semiotic practices and artefacts (e.g., a written text, a painting or an architectural design) but also the technologies behind them warrant critical attention is not new. After buying his first typewriter in 1882, Nietzsche famously declared: "our writing tools are also working on our thought" (Nietzsche 2003: 172).

Nowadays, analogous sentiments pervade the strongly polarised public debate about the virtues and vices of ubiquitous software such as PowerPoint and social media tools such as Facebook, Twitter and Instagram. While some have praised PowerPoint, for instance for increasing presenters' confidence and eloquence (cf. Gold 2002), many have condemned it. One of its first and most ardent opponents, information design guru Edward Tufte (2003), has decried the over-simplification and misrepresentation of technical data resulting from the use of bullet lists, linear slide-by-slide presentation and illegible graphics, which in his view makes PowerPoint unsuitable for representing knowledge in engineering and its cognate fields. Massachusetts Institute of Technology psychologist and leading figure in the social studies of computers and technology, Sherry Turkle (2004), has criticised it for introducing persuasive corporate rhetoric into educational practices. With a broader focus on computers and human relationships, Turkle (2011: x) has argued since the 1980s that technologies are not "just tools": "We are shaped by our tools. And now, the computer, a machine on the border of becoming a mind, [is] changing and shaping us". Turkle's book *Alone Together* (2011), in particular, has captured, and informed, both sides of the debate surrounding social media and mobile technologies: namely, that as they tremendously increase our capacity to stay connected with others online, they diminish and devalue the much stronger potential for authenticity and intimacy afforded by face-to-face communication and real-life relationships. Public debate on the relationship between computer technologies, social life and communication can stimulate critical studies of semiotic software. Such studies, however, need to avoid the heavy reliance on anecdotal evidence characteristic of public debate, and pay systematic attention to the relationship between the design of software (its interface and the resources it makes available) and its role in diverse meaning-making practices.

Initial steps in that direction have been made in composition, cultural and media studies. In "Politics of the interface", composition scholars Selfe and Selfe (1994: 482) describe computer interfaces as reflecting and perpetuating highly asymmetrical relations of power such as colonialism and "the values of rationality, hierarchy and logocentrism characteristic of Western patriarchal cultures" (491). They contrast the default status of Standard American English with the complete lack of support that computer interfaces provide for non-standard dialects in any language, and view computer technology as reinforcing capitalist labour division principles. Yet, they see interfaces as "sites within which the ideological and material legacies of racism, sexism, and colonialism are continuously written and re-written along with more positive cultural legacies" (484). To mobilise this potential for positive social change, according to Selfe and Selfe (1994), composition students should learn both to use and to critique technology, and beware of the power that discourses promoting computer technology as a democratising force have to delegitimise critique.

Composition scholars have also critiqued specific software tools and the communication modes they support. Arola (2010) posits that the decline of the homepage (where authors had more control over design decisions) and the rise of social networking (where such control is increasingly limited) warrant critical attention to the rhetoric of visual design. In support of this position, Arola presents a case study of the ways in which built-in templates prescribe the identities individuals can construct with Web 2.0 tools such as MySpace (where identity is self-determined, as comments by others appear below and are much less salient than the content a user has uploaded, and where users with programming skills could modify the templates) vs. Facebook (where identity is constructed and more actively (re) negotiated with others, as Facebook "friends" can post both comments and content on one's Facebook timeline and their actions are announced through the visually and dynamically salient News Feed, and where built-in design templates cannot be modified). An earlier study, Sorapure (2006) shows how by supporting the use of typography, images, programming code and comments accompanying that code, the commercial animation and web design software Adobe Flash transforms traditional notions of writing. By enabling letters and words to be easily animated, Flash allows "text to convey information not only by how it looks but also by how it moves and morphs" (418), placing new multimodal literacy demands on its users. Sorapure's study also highlights a key difference between Flash, where Help functions encourage users to access and modify as well as comment on and share their understanding of programming code, and "software programs (e.g., Photoshop, iMovie, PowerPoint) that don't allow access to the underlying code [and therefore] are more restrictive and position writers more narrowly in line with what corporate planners and programmers intend" (422–423). Sorapure's analysis of Flash and its use in selected new media art works demonstrates that:

> Looking closely at a particular program makes one more likely to question its inevitability, to analyze particular features and functions of the tool, and to avoid seeing it as *merely* a tool or neutral instrument [and understand] the ways in which the program guides the hand of the writer.
>
> *(427–428)*

The field of composition studies has thus built a strong case for the critical study of software. Yet, it has not offered principles for exploring how software enables and constrains people's ability to achieve particular communicative goals in different social and cultural practices.

To investigate "how software is shaping our culture, and how it is shaped by culture in its turn" (Manovich 2013: 20) is the unifying goal of the newly established field of "software studies". First proposed by leading media theorist Lev Manovich (2001), the field unites media, cultural and art and design studies researchers interested in the interaction among advances in computing, cultural trends and creative practices. Within it, "platform studies" focus on the philosophy of programming code, algorithms and the open-source movement; this is acknowledged as "difficult due to [the] ephemeral nature [of code], the high technical skills required of the researcher and the lack of analytical or methodological tools available" (Berry 2011: 5).

Other software studies explore the user interfaces of commercial software products. *Software Takes Command* (Manovich 2013: 4), for example, is concerned with media authoring and editing applications such as Photoshop and After Effects, their use and implications for stakeholders in the creative industries (e.g., illustrators, [motion] graphic designers, animators, film and video editors, and media or architectural design companies), and is motivated by the question *"What is 'media' after software?"* (italics in original). Manovich (2013) argues that software is the engine of our contemporary, global information society (just as the combustion engine and electricity are the backbone of industrial society), and that to study software requires a shift in the object of research – from static documents, messages or works to "software performances", the experiences through which software re-configures social and cultural practices over time. Manovich (2013) demonstrates that as media authoring software enables design methods from previously distinct disciplines (animation, graphic design, special effects) to be easily combined within the same design space and workflow, and to be shared among software products, a new type of visual aesthetics has gained prevalence in contemporary culture – the aesthetics of media hybridity. As a mostly celebratory account of media authoring software, however, *Software Takes Command* (Manovich 2013) does not discuss the social values that such aesthetic trends promote. This is a departure from the more critical orientation of earlier software studies, such as Matthew Fuller's (2003) essay on the market economy microsphere in Microsoft Word's interface. Critical insights from software studies, in any case, have limited explanatory power, as they are not grounded in systematic analyses of software use and focus mainly on software in the creative industries.

Discourse analysis and related fields such as applied linguistics are well positioned to extend our knowledge of the ways software design and use reflect and shape social values and power relations across different semiotic practices and contexts. Yet, despite advances in critical and multimodal discourse analysis, this line of enquiry has until recently been ignored. Discourse studies have instead been concerned predominantly with specific (types of) texts and interactions, or the discourses mediated through particular technologies, rather than directly with these technologies themselves. Studies of PowerPoint discourse, for instance, have examined the use of language, images and visual design in slideshows (Campagna 2009; Finn 2010; Yates and Orlikowski 2007), their interaction with speech and gesture in the presentation of slideshows (Knoblauch 2008; Schnettler 2006; Stark and Paravel 2008), and the impact of this interaction on the reception of presentations (Bucher and Niemann 2012). These studies have shed light on the influence that academic disciplines and earlier as well as contemporary organisational genres and practices exercise over PowerPoint's use. They also readily acknowledge that PowerPoint's design itself both enables and constrains the meaning-making practices in which the software is embedded. Such acknowledgements, however, are typically relegated to descriptions of the context of the analysed slideshows and their presentations; the software itself is not analysed.

Applied linguists and discourse analysts have embraced software as a tool for language teaching and learning (e.g., Beatty 2013; Thomas, Reinders and Warschauer 2013) and for building, annotating and analysing linguistic and multimodal corpora (e.g., Bateman 2014; Coccetta 2011). Extending this *pragmatic* orientation to software, a recent collaboration involving social semioticians, mathematicians and computer scientists has not only produced software tools for multimodal transcription and analysis (O'Halloran et al. 2011), but employed these to address the central challenge of *critical* multimodal discourse analysis. The challenge consists in mapping patterns of low-level, expression features in complex multimodal events, and interpreting these in relation to high-level socio-cultural trends and values (e.g., temporal distribution of different semiotic choices in the debate between a climate activist and a climate denialist in O'Halloran, Podlasov and Tan 2013). Positioned at the cutting edge of research in digital humanities, multimodal and critical discourse analysis, and grounded in social semiotic theory, this work holds much promise for extending our understanding not only of the role different semiotic resources and their multimodal interaction play in reinforcing or redefining social relations and values but also of software as a technology for studying that role.

In sum, research in composition, cultural, media and design studies has raised awareness of the need to move beyond views of software as a neutral tool, culminating in the establishment of the field of software studies. Critical discourse analysis and its cognate fields, by contrast, have until recently ignored software as an object of study. In the following section, we note key reasons for this, as we introduce the dimensions of a critical multimodal approach to software, drawing on the framework we have developed for analysing semiotic software technologies and practices (Djonov and van Leeuwen 2012, 2013; Zhao, Djonov and van Leeuwen 2014; Zhao and van Leeuwen 2014).

Dimensions of the critical multimodal study of semiotic software

A holistic approach to the critical multimodal study of software would include three dimensions: software's design, its use, and their relationship to broader semiotic and cultural practices.

Software design: software as semiotic resource and semiotic regime

An important first step towards developing a critical approach to software is acknowledging its power as a resource for making meaning in society. Linguists like Whorf (1956) and Halliday (1978) and sociologists like Berger and Luckman (1966) have pointed out that languages, through their very lexicons and grammatical systems, structure the experiences and values of the societies they belong to, and thus shape the way members of these societies understand the world they live in. In Halliday's (1978: 16) words, "We try to explain the nature of language, its internal organization and patterning, in terms of the functions it has evolved to serve". Like language, software provides resources for acting in, and understanding, the world we live in, offering a range of choices, organised into menus and submenus that we can select from when making meaning (e.g., changing font size in Microsoft Word using the format > font > size menu). And just as languages have evolved to serve the needs and interests of the societies whose languages they are, so software products are designed to serve the needs and interests of the global corporations that develop them.

Software also differs from resources such as language or visual design because it is not a "dynamic open system" (Lemke 1984). It does not evolve in response to changing patterns in its use in different social contexts, which may be one reason why linguists and semioticians have generally not treated software as a worthwhile object of study in its own right. A software product's meaning-making potential is determined and periodically updated by software developers, whose decisions prioritise some semiotic choices and associated practices over others. Semiotic resources such as software are thus best defined as "semiotic artefacts" (Kress and van Leeuwen 2001; van Leeuwen 2005). As such, software is a kind of material semiotic resource that relies on and makes available certain modes (layout, font and colour) and media (visual, print, aural, electronic), and embodies developers' ideas about where and how these should be (co)deployed.

Every software product thus comes with a built-in "semiotic regime". This highlights another difference from language, visual design and other semiotic systems. Conventions for language use gradually become internalised, forming part of the repertoires of language users. Depending on the status such conventions enjoy (consider, for example, rules of spelling, grammar and punctuation) and a society's commitment to supporting equity in and through education, they may be more or less explicitly taught and more or less strictly and universally imposed by teachers, (sub)editors, textbooks, style guides and templates. By contrast, rules for using the semiotic resources available within a software product are externalised in and tacitly imposed by its design.

In fact, the influence of semiotic software design on contemporary meaning-making practices has been boosted by rising expectations for proficiency in software use and concomitant usability discourses promoting "universal" and "intuitive" design, which have almost eliminated the once all-pervasive training courses on everyday software such as email or office applications. Although an application's help menu may feature advice on how or when to employ certain choices, activating the help function is nowadays almost entirely at the discretion of individual users. Microsoft Word's animated paperclip character, for example, no longer pops up to offer unsolicited, written advice on formatting or other options that a writer should consider (cf. Fuller 2003). The more concealed in software interfaces communication norms become, the harder they are to flout. Ever more routinely, people's semiotic repertoire is restricted to the resources available within the software environments they navigate; for example, software recontextualises tactile resources as visual ones (Djonov and van Leeuwen

2011). The actualisation of this repertoire is also subject to digital interfaces making some options default or easier to access and activate than others. To expose the semiotic regime built into a software product, therefore, critical studies must examine it (1) as a system of choices, a paradigm offering various resources (e.g., font, colour, layout, animation) organised into menus and submenus, and (2) as a syntagm that assigns these choices different spatial and temporal values (see further Djonov and van Leeuwen 2012).

Notably, although a software interface presents selected semiotic resources organised in a particular spatio-temporal structure (i.e., a syntagm), it is not a text, not an act of communication that is internally cohesive and coherent (i.e., able to make sense in a particular external, situational and cultural, context) (Halliday and Hasan 1985). It does not fit even a broader definition of text as "a structure of messages or message traces which has a socially ascribed unity" (Hodge and Kress 1988: 6). This may have contributed to software remaining outside the scope, not only of linguistics and semiotics, the study of language and other communication modes as resources, but also of discourse analysis, the study of texts and interactions, of language and other communication modes in use.

Software use as semiotic practice

Critical studies of software must also consider software use and the discourses that surround it – i.e., the ways people justify why and how they use particular software tools. This entails examining how the products (i.e., the texts and interactions enabled through software) and practices of software use are shaped by both software design and its use in specific historical, cultural and institutional contexts.

The relationship between software design and use may be conceptualised as one of "instantiation", in analogy to that between the system of language and instances of its use (Halliday 2003). Any instance of software use actualises only some of the meaning-making potential built into a given application, as users select from options available in the application based on particular communicative goals and the norms about how these goals can be achieved in certain contexts. For example, Microsoft Excel allows users to complete a range of tasks such as: entering data in a spreadsheet (a table with a seemingly unlimited number of rows and columns), sorting and filtering such data, creating or applying built-in mathematical formulas, and visualising data through various kinds of charts or SmartArt diagrams. When Excel is used to take minutes in a business meeting (e.g., entering notes against meeting agenda items on key discussion points and conclusions, items to be actioned and who carries responsibility for each, and so on), only the first of these functions is activated, instantiating only some of Excel's meaning-making potential. Comparing how the same application is used for different communicative purposes and/or in different social contexts is a promising avenue for understanding the role software plays in communication and how its use reflects norms and power relations that may be at play beyond those built into its design.

While the same software tool can help fulfil different communication goals in different contexts, that is, construct texts and interactions that represent different genres, these texts and interactions are all multimodal – they make meaning through the interaction of choices that software users make from various communication modes or semiotic resources, such as colour, language, typography, layout, sound and so on. Exploring software use then involves analysing multimodal meaning-making. Research in multimodality has prepared the ground for such explorations, by mapping the meaning-making potential of individual modes such as visual design (Kress and van Leeuwen 2006 [1996]) and sound (van Leeuwen 1999), and by developing tools for analysing multimodal interaction—for example, extending the notion of "genre" beyond linearly structured verbal texts, and uncovering principles (e.g., framing, salience, rhythm) that apply across modes (yet in accordance with each mode's unique characteristics) and support multimodal communication (Kress and van Leeuwen 2001; van Leeuwen 2005). Recent years have also seen the emergence of frameworks for the critical analysis of multimodal discourse (Machin and Mayr 2012) and studies of the role particular semiotic resources and their interaction play in establishing and perpetuating or drawing attention to and subverting social divisions (cf. Djonov and Zhao 2014).

Understanding software use as a semiotic practice requires complementing the analysis of its resources and products with approaches for data collection and analysis, such as ethnographic observations and interviews, that can uncover the processes involved in it too. Interviews may to some extent compensate for the difficulties associated with recording and analysing processes of software use, and afford insights into the reasons people use particular software tools in particular ways. An interview may reveal, as discussed in Djonov and van Leeuwen (2012), that a poster was composed in Microsoft Word due to lack of access to or confidence in using graphic design software; that time constraints and productivity requirements led one to rely on default options, rather than diverge from them and, say, design new paragraph styles in Word or modify a referencing style in Endnote; that one's use of a particular application follows established institutional conventions or emulates a role model.

Software as part of the broader semiotic landscape

Critical studies of software need to examine software as part of the broader semiotic landscape, and develop accounts of the ways software design and use alike are shaped by people's knowledge and experiences of semiotic resources, norms and practices in the culture in general – from both across and outside software environments, and across diverse socio-historical and institutional contexts. Such accounts would consider how a software application contracts or expands the meaning-making potential of particular semiotic resources, reflects the communication practices it recontextualises and serves, and broader social and cultural discourses; this would help avoid the risk of attributing semiotic and social changes to software technology alone. To illustrate, Photoshop recontextualises photography and visual arts practices, while ProTools supports sound design practices by allowing users to digitally record, edit and produce audio compositions. In contrast, PowerPoint transforms earlier business presentation practices (Yates and Orlikowski 2007), and offers a very limited range of image editing options and sound effects; the latter, moreover, cannot be activated independently of visual elements, are rarely used, and have become even harder to find, still part of the animation menu but since PowerPoint XP (2002) no longer bundled with any animation effects. The addition of visual texture options such as "recycled paper", "water droplets" and "paper bag" in PowerPoint 1997, on the other hand, echoed the rise of environmentalism and the "new age" lifestyle (Djonov and van Leeuwen 2011).

In software use, too, meaning-makers employ their understanding of the potential of various semiotic resources (e.g., language, sound, mathematical symbols) and may incorporate semiotic artefacts (e.g., a photograph, video, clip art) created outside a given software environment. Kvåle (2016), for instance, exposes a gap between the expectations for minimalist, abstract visual representations that linguistics students brought to the task of drawing morphological tree diagrams, and the affordances of Microsoft Word's SmartArt tool. Kvåle argues that the tool is unable to meet such expectations but has the potential, boosted by Word's ubiquity in higher education, to colonise conventions for representing knowledge in various academic disciplines by promoting – through easy-to-use templates (e.g., the organisational chart) – the practices and values of office management, including the field's predilection for a more decorative ("artistic") visual style where words rather than non-verbal resources convey the main content.

Case study: PowerPoint and the marketisation of public discourse

This section illustrates how critical multimodal studies can use the principles outlined above to reveal the role software plays in the marketisation of public discourse – its technologisation, conversationalisation or synthetic personalisation, and aestheticisation. The examples come from a study of the interaction between PowerPoint's design and its use in corporate and higher education settings, in which we analysed:

1) all versions of PowerPoint for Windows released when the project commenced in 2009 (PowerPoint 3.0, 4.0, 1995, 1997, 2000, 2002/XP, 2003 and 2007)
2) 34 video-recorded presentations (24 university lectures and 10 business presentations) and the slideshow files used in them
3) follow-up individual interviews with the presenters.

PowerPoint imposes norms about what constitutes an effective presentation through both the semiotic resources it makes available and the way they are presented in its interface. For example, in contrast to graphic design software such as Adobe InDesign, where a project starts with building a grid, PowerPoint offers templates in its "Layout" menu, and options for viewing and changing the underlying grid are difficult to find. The templates are endorsed by Microsoft Office's online help, too: "Templates are files that help you design interesting, compelling, and professional-looking documents. All the formatting is complete; you add what you want to them". PowerPoint's help menu also advises users wanting to create their own templates to do that by modifying the pre-designed ones through "Slide Master", for efficiency – a value central to neoliberal discourses of productivity – and visual consistency, a must for successful branding.

Whereas earlier versions of PowerPoint offer over two dozen layout templates organised into four categories and labelled according to the position/function (e.g., "Title") and types of objects that can occupy (e.g., "Text", "Media Clip") the placeholders in a template (Figure 38.1 and Table 38.1 present PowerPoint 2003's layout templates), since PowerPoint 2007 these templates are less than a dozen, and have labels that emphasise not formal features (e.g., types of objects and their position) but the semantic potential of slide layout (see Figure 38.2). "Picture with Caption", for instance, suggests that verbal labels should anchor pictorial meanings, "Section Header" that a presentation can be organised into clearly demarcated sections, and "Comparison" that showing two pieces of content side by side is ideal for this particular rhetorical relation and vice versa. This change obscures alternative ways in which various objects can be distributed on a slide, and discourages users from changing the built-in templates. The software's temporal structure imposes norms about the effective use of layout in presentations, too: a "Title Slide" template automatically appears when one opens a blank presentation file; selecting "new slide" after that by default inserts a "Title and Content" slide; and bullet points appear as soon as one starts typing in the body of a content slide.

Diverging from choices privileged through the software's interface (e.g., not starting a slideshow with "Title Slide", or removing the bullets from a slide's body text) requires additional effort, and familiarity with design principles, which the design of ubiquitous software rarely makes explicit, even when it enforces them. Not surprisingly, all but two presentations

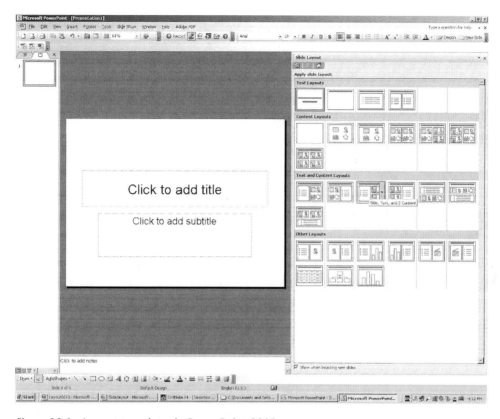

Figure 38.1 Layout templates in PowerPoint 2003

Table 38.1 Layout template labels and categories in PowerPoint 2003

Category	Templates (read from left to right in Figure 38.1)
Text	Title Slide; Title Only; Title and Text; Title and 2-Column Text
Content	Blank; Content; Title and Content; Title and 2 Content; Title, Content and 2 Content; Title, 2 Content and Content; Title and 4 Content
Text and Content	Title, Text and Content; Title, Content and Text; Title, Text and 2 Content; Title, 2 Content and Text; Title and Text over Content; Title and Content over Text; Title and 2 Content over Text
Other	Title, Text and Clip Art; Title, Clip Art and Text; Title, Text and Chart; Title, Chart and Text; Title, Text and Media Clip; Title, Media Clip and Text; Title and Table; Title and Diagram or Organization Chart; Title and Chart

in our data started with a "Title Slide", 88% of content slides had a title, and almost 60% of those with text in the body used bullet lists (see further Djonov and van Leeuwen 2013). Slides not using the default templates included "Thank you" slides and those presenting credits or (in the lectures) reference lists; such instances reflect users' ability to draw on norms other than, and potentially resist, those a software tool technologises.

PowerPoint also promotes another feature of promotional discourse – conversationalisation, or synthetic personalisation. It achieves this by facilitating what van Leeuwen (2006: 11)

Emilia Djonov and Theo van Leeuwen

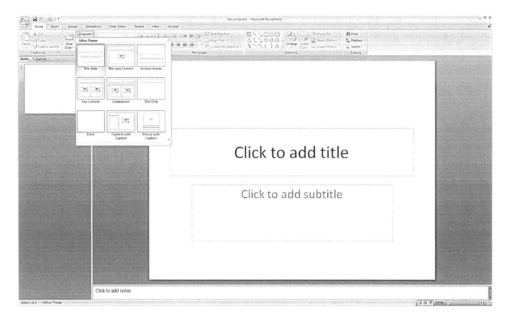

Figure 38.2 Layout templates in PowerPoint 2007

terms "new writing" and defines as "the writing of the information age", which employs visual resources (and their spatial logic) for establishing cohesion and coherence, and "privileges morsels of fact that can stand alone and mean what they mean without needing to be included into a larger web of meaning". Commodifying information limits the potential of this semiotic practice to represent coherently organised ideas and construct knowledge. Bullet lists, which epitomise new writing, for example, can be perceived at a glance, yet can convey only one kind of logical relation between items aligned with each other – co-hyponymy, where these items present ideas that are all at the same level of abstraction and subordinate to the same superordinate idea. Bullet list items, as mentioned earlier, typically employ what Halliday (1994 [1985]) has called "the grammar of little texts" (e.g., isolated nominal groups, prepositional phrases and non-finite or minor clauses). Such language is open to interpretation yet cannot be challenged, as it makes no statements; these qualities render it a valuable tool for appealing to wider audiences in advertising. Due to its reliance on spatial rather than temporal logic, and resulting inability to be read aloud, new writing can also stimulate a more active and dialogic engagement with the content it presents, encouraging, for example, a presentation's audience to draw on their own knowledge and experiences in interpreting the information on a slide and the presenter to explain that information to them.

These same affordances of new writing obscure not only the clarity of the information it presents but also the power relations between producers and consumers of information and knowledge at the heart of knowledge-based economies. This is evident in the interaction between the content presented on university lecture slides and the embodied communication that accompanies their presentation.

The speech accompanying the slide presented in Figure 38.3, from a cultural studies lecture on the Eastern vs. Western Europe divide, for instance, reveals that the top three bullets are questions raised by the fall of the Berlin Wall in 1989 and the bottom three are responses to

576

Since 1989...

- Disappearance of the East-West divide?
- End of Eastern Europe?
- Reunited Europe? One Europe?

- No common history
- Fears of an invasion by barbarians
- "Yes, you are European, but only of mixed blood" (Giuliano Amato, Italian PM, 2000)

Figure 38.3   A slide from a cultural studies lecture

these questions. It also establishes connections to concepts introduced earlier in the lecture and emphasises its central thesis that "the concept of an Eastern versus a Western Europe has existed throughout history", as well as explicitly refers students to their "mandatory" and "additional readings". As in all lectures in our data, the slides present educational content/ knowledge, while the lecturer's speech both clarifies that content and carries primary, if not exclusive, responsibility for construing the pedagogic relationship between lecturer and students and the goals, pacing and sequencing of the lecture. This tendency and the practice of uploading slideshows as stand-alone documents on online learning management systems reflect "the dominant view of universities today as providers of knowledge with students as customers" and background lecturers' expertise as curriculum designers and knowledge producers (Djonov and van Leeuwen 2014: 240).

PowerPoint presentations, like all public discourse, should also look good. A key resource for achieving this – which technologises and synthetically personalises discourse too – is the plethora of themes available across the Microsoft Office Suite, packaged into its products and online. Promoting new writing (specifically, multimodal cohesion) that is aesthetically pleasing and visually consistent, Microsoft Office support advises: "Use themes to simplify the process of creating professional designer-looking presentations. Theme colors, fonts, and effects not only work in PowerPoint, but they are also available in Excel, Word, and Outlook so your presentations, documents, worksheets, and emails can have a cohesive look".

As van Leeuwen (2015) argues, aesthetics has traditionally been defined in contradistinction to functionality, as pleasurable deviation from the norm that can create a sense of style and identify and at the same time draw attention to itself; this allows it to fulfil important functions in promotional discourse and corporate branding. Because aesthetics is not employed for representing specific ideas, it infuses discourse with meaning in covert ways, through vague reference to cultural values nowadays symbolised primarily by non-verbal elements. Microsoft Office themes each consist of a colour scheme, one or two font types and bullet symbols, and decorative graphics, and can suggest various identities and values, for example, through the energy and passion associated with red, the cool calm of pale blue, the rigid geometries of modernism, the flowery motifs and copperplate typography of yesterday, and so on. Through slide design themes, the values of office management and global corporate culture have gradually outnumbered if not completely replaced other values, as themes that featured concrete representations such as "Black Board", "Party" and "Habitat" have given way to more abstract ones with labels such as "Office" (the default theme), "Venture", "Executive", "Genesis", "Revolution", "Inspiration", "Adjacency", "Advantage" and "Apex".

Only one of the presentations in our data employed a theme chosen to suit its content – a cultural studies lecture on skin and touch (see Figure 38.4). Corporate presentations tended to use the company theme, and the rest either employed built-in themes that their authors found aesthetically pleasing, that is, in agreement with their personal style, or defaulted to the "Office" theme, with only four modifying it in some way (e.g., adding a colour background or changing the bullet symbols).

This evidences the ability of PowerPoint's themes to: technologise discourse, as selecting a theme automatically applies it across all slides in a presentation; synthetically personalise discourse as users select themes based on their personal or institutional styles and values; and aestheticise it by divorcing content and function from style. The overall effect is to homogenise discourse as design themes enable seemingly different styles to be applied to the same limited set of basic functional elements (a slide's title, written text, bullet points and so on) and promote the neoliberal values of global corporate culture.

Conclusion

For some time now, social theorists have pointed out that power resides not only in individuals and groups, but also in social institutions (Foucault 1977) and the administrative intervention into everyday practices such as health and family planning (Habermas 1976: 71–72). To a large degree such administrative intervention, whether in education, the workplace or the private sphere, is now redesigned by software companies and digitally implemented.

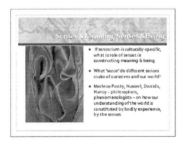

Figure 38.4   Slides from a cultural studies lecture on skin and touch with content-relevant theme design

In this chapter we have focused on the power of software to intervene in the ways people use language and other semiotic resources. This power rests, first of all, on the ever increasing necessity to use software in all spheres of post-industrial life. Limited or no ability to use software amounts to a form of illiteracy and a serious handicap. Software's power is also witnessed in its capacity to impose models of meaning-making on a wide range of contexts and genres. PowerPoint's "sales pitch" model of meaning making, we argued, has permeated higher education: rather than PowerPoint adapting to education, education has to adapt to it. And finally, software's ubiquity allows it to homogenise the use of language and other semiotic resources across the globe. It may be argued that software offers a multitude of choices, yet these are no more than different means to the same end; for instance, PowerPoint offers different theme designs for the same basic layout template options.

Our account has been critical, but is not a rear-guard action by academics who see their expertise, role and status threatened by the software industry. Rather, it makes the case for critical software literacy, aligned with Selfe and Selfe's (1994) argument that students should learn to use as well as critique new technologies. Such an attitude can raise awareness and even subvert the pervasive patterns and structures of semiotic software, as David Byrne (2003) demonstrated in an exhibition of art works created with PowerPoint titled *Envisioning Emotional Epistemological Information* (*EEEI*), which was subsequently published as a book-plus-DVD album. *EEEI* employs PowerPoint's animation options to explore a multimodal form of creative writing with kinetic typography at its centre (see further van Leeuwen, Djonov and O'Halloran 2013). In one of the exhibits, *Architectures of Comparison,* arrows do not point at something, or connect the parts of a flowchart, as is expected, but meander meaninglessly across the screen, accompanied by slow, dreamy music. In this way Byrne (2003) both extends the uses of PowerPoint and critiques the values that underlie it, as he explains in a statement accompanying this work: "Goal oriented behaviour is like sleepwalking. It is easy and purposeful, but what is its purpose? Its purpose is itself."

Further readings

Djonov, E. and Van Leeuwen, T. (2012). Normativity and software: A multimodal social semiotic approach. In S. Norris (ed.), *Multimodality and practice: Investigating theory-in-practice-through-method,* 119–137. New York: Routledge.

This chapter explores the role of normativity in the interaction between software design and use by adapting Roman Jakobson's notion of "markedness", Jan Mukarovski's "foregrounding" and Theo Van Leeuwen's "semiotic rules" to the critical multimodal study of software.

Leeuwen, T. van (2005). *Introducing social semiotics.* London, New York: Routledge.

Through a wide range of examples from diverse communication contexts, this book presents social semiotics as the necessarily critical and multimodal study of the ever-changing meaning-making potential of semiotic resources and its actualisation in social practices.

Zhao, S., Djonov, E. and Van Leeuwen, T. (2014). Semiotic technology and practice: A multimodal social semiotic approach to PowerPoint. *Text & Talk* 34(3): 349–375. DOI: 10.1515/text-2014–0005

This article introduces a social semiotic model for studying PowerPoint as a semiotic practice comprising three dimensions – the software's design, the multimodal composition of slideshows, and their presentation – and two semiotic artefacts, the software and the slideshow.

References

Arola, K. (2010). The design of Web 2.0: The rise of the template, the fall of design. *Computers and Composition* 27: 4–14.

Bateman, J. (2014). Using multimodal corpora for empirical research. In C. Jewitt (ed.), *The Routledge handbook of multimodal analysis,* 2nd edn, 238–252. Oxon, New York: Routledge.

Beatty, K. (2013). *Teaching and researching computer-assisted language learning,* 2nd edn. Oxon, New York: Routledge.

Berger, P. and Luckman, T. (1966). *The social construction of reality.* Harmondsworth: Penguin.

Berry, D. M. (2011). *The philosophy of software: Code and mediation in the digital age.* London: Palgrave.

Bucher, H.-J. and Niemann, P. (2012). Visualizing science: The reception of powerpoint presentations. *Visual Communication* 11(3): 283–306. DOI: 10.1177/1470357212446409

Byrne, D. (2003). *Envisioning Emotional Epistemological Information.* Print album and DVD. Todomundo.

Campagna, S. (2009). Projecting visual reasoning in research conference presentations. In M. Gotti (ed.), *Commonality and individuality in academic discourse,* 371–391. Bern: Peter Lang AG.

Coccetta, F. (2011). Multimodal functional-notional concordancing. In A. Frankenberg-Garcia, L. Flowerdew and G. Aston (eds.), *New trends in corpora and language learning,* 121–138. London, New York: Continuum.

Djonov, E. and van Leeuwen, T. (2011). The semiotics of texture: From tactile to visual. *Visual Communication* 10(4): 541–564. DOI: 10.1177/1470357211415786

Djonov, E. and van Leeuwen, T. (2012). Normativity and software: A multimodal social semiotic approach. In S. Norris (ed.), *Multimodality and practice: Investigating theory-in-practice-through-method,* 119–137. New York: Routledge.

Djonov, E. and van Leeuwen, T. (2013). Between the grid and composition: Layout in PowerPoint's design and use. *Semiotica* 2013(197): 1–34. DOI: 10.1515/sem-2013-0078

Djonov, E. and van Leeuwen, T. (2014). Bullet points, new writing, and the marketization of public discourse: A critical multimodal perspective. In E. Djonov and S. Zhao (eds.), *Critical multimodal studies of popular discourse,* 232–250. London, New York: Routledge: Routledge.

Djonov, E. and Zhao, S. (eds.) (2014). *Critical multimodal studies of popular discourse.* London, New York: Routledge.

Fairclough, N. (1993). Critical discourse analysis and the marketization of public discourse: The universities. *Discourse and Society* 4(2): 133–169.

Finn, J. (2010). Powell's point: 'denial and deception' at the UN. *Visual Communication* 9(1): 25–49.

Foucault, M. (1977). *Discipline and punish – the birth of the prison.* London: Allen Lane.

Fuller, M. (2003). *Behind the blip: Essays on the culture of software.* New York: Autonomedia.

Fuller, M. (2008). Introduction. In M. Fuller (ed.), *Software studies: A lexicon,* 1–13. Cambridge, MA, London: MIT Press.

Gaskins, R. (1984). Sample product proposal: Presentation graphics for overhead projection. www.robertgaskins.com/powerpoint-history/documents/gaskins-powerpoint-original-proposal-1984-aug-14.pdf

Gold, R. (2002). Reading PowerPoint. In N. J. Allen (ed.), *Working with words and images: New steps in an old dance,* 256–270. Westport, CT: Ablex.

Habermas, J. (1976). *Legitimation crisis.* London: Heineman.

Halliday, M.A.K. (1978). *Language as social semiotic.* London: Arnold.

Halliday, M.A.K. (1994 [1985]). *An introduction to functional grammar* (2nd ed.). London: Arnold.

Halliday, M.A.K. (2003). Introduction: On the "architecture" of human language. In J. Webster (ed.), *On language and linguistics: Volume 3 in the collected works of M.A.K. Halliday,* 1–29. London, New York: Continuum.

Halliday, M.A.K. and Hasan, R. (1985). *Language, context, and text: Aspects of language in a social-semiotic perspective.* Geelong, Victoria: Deakin University Press.

Hodge, R. and Kress, G. (1988). *Social semiotics.* Cambridge: Polity Press.

Knoblauch, H. (2008). The performance of knowledge: Pointing and knowledge in powerpoint presentations. *Cultural Sociology* 2(1): 75–97.

Kress, G. and van Leeuwen, T. (2001). *Multimodal discourse: The modes and media of contemporary communication.* London: Arnold.

Kress, G. and van Leeuwen, T. (2006 [1996]). *Reading images: The grammar of visual design,* 2nd edn. London: Routledge.

Kvåle, G. (2016). Software as ideology: A multimodal critical discourse analysis of Microsoft Word and SmartArt. *Journal of Language and Politics (Special Issue: Multimodality, Politics and Ideology)* 15(3): 259–273. DOI: 10.1075/jlp.15.3.02kva

Lemke, J. L. (1984). *Semiotics and education.* Toronto: Victoria College, Toronto Semiotic Circle Monographs.

Machin, D. and Mayr, A. (2012). *How to do critical discourse analysis: A multimodal introduction*. London, Thousand Oaks, New Delhi, Singapore: Sage.

Manovich, L. (2001). *The language of new media*. Cambridge, MA: MIT Press.

Manovich, L. (2013). *Software takes command*. London: Bloomsbury.

Nietzsche, F. (2003). *Kritische Gesamtausgabe: Briefwechsel (1880–1884)*. Berlin: De Gruyter.

O'Halloran, K. L., L, E.M.K., Podlasov, A. and Tan, S. (2013). Multimodal digital semiotics: The interaction of language with other resources. *Text & Talk* 33(4–5): 665. DOI: 10.1515/text-2013–0030

O'Halloran, K. L., Tan, S., Smith, B. A. and Podlasov, A. (2011). Multimodal analysis within an interactive software environment: Critical discourse perspectives. *Critical Discourse Studies* 8(2): 109–125. DOI: 10.1080/17405904.2011.558687

Schnettler, B. (2006). Orchestrating bullet lists and commentaries: A video performance analysis of computer supported presentations. In H. Knoblauch, B. Schnettler, J. Raab and H.-G. Soeffner (eds.), *Video-analysis: Methodology and methods of qualitative audiovisual data analysis in sociology*, 155–169. Frankfurt am Main: Lang.

Selfe, C. L. and Selfe, R. J., Jr. (1994). The politics of the interface: Power and its exercise in electronic contact zones. *College Composition and Communication* 45(4): 480–504.

Sorapure, M. (2006). Text, image, code, comment: Writing in Flash. *Computers and Composition* 23(4): 412–429.

Stark, D. and Paravel, V. (2008). PowerPoint in public: Digital technologies and the new morphology of demonstration. *Theory, Culture and Society* 25(5): 30–55.

Thomas, M., Reinders, H. and Warschauer, M. (eds.) (2013). *Contemporary computer-assisted language learning*. London, New York: Bloomsbury.

Tufte, E. R. (2003). *The cognitive style of PowerPoint*, 2nd edn. Cheshire, CT: Graphics Press.

Turkle, S. (2004). The fellowship of the microchip: Global technologies as evocative objects. In M. Suárez-Orozco and D.B. Qin-Hilliard (eds.), *Globalization: Culture and education in the new millennium*, 97–113. Berkeley: University of California Press.

Turkle, S. (2011). *Alone together: Why we expect more from technology and less from each other*. New York: Basic Books.

Van Leeuwen, T. (1999). *Speech, music, sound*. London: Macmillan Press Ltd.

Van Leeuwen, T. (2005). *Introducing social semiotics*. London, New York: Routledge.

Van Leeuwen, T. (2006). The new writing. *Wordrobe: A journal about the future of language* (August 2006, Free Launch Issue), 10–12.

Van Leeuwen, T. (2015). Looking good: Aesthetics, multimodality and literacy studies. In J. Rowsell and K. Pahl (eds.), *The Routledge handbook of literacy studies*, 426–439. New York: Routledge.

Van Leeuwen, T., Djonov, E. and O'Halloran, K. L. (2013). "David Byrne really does love PowerPoint": Art as research on semiotics and semiotic technology. *Social Semiotics* 23(3): 409–423. DOI: 10.1080/10350330.2012.738998

Whorf, B. (1956). *Language, thought and reality: Selected writings of Benjamin Lee Whorf*. Cambridge, MA: MIT Press.

Yates, J. and Orlikowski, W. (2007). The PowerPoint presentation and its corollaries: How genres shape communicative action in organizations. In M. Zachry and C. Thralls (eds.), *Communicative practices in workplaces and the professions: Cultural perspectives on the regulation of discourse and organizations*, 67–91. Amityville, New York: Baywood Publishing Company.

Zhao, S., Djonov, E. and van Leeuwen, T. (2014). Semiotic technology and practice: A multimodal social semiotic approach to PowerPoint. *Text & Talk* 34(3): 349–375. DOI: 10.1515/text-2014–0005

Zhao, S. and van Leeuwen, T. (2014). Understanding semiotic technology in university classrooms: A social semiotic approach to PowerPoint-assisted cultural studies lectures. *Classroom Discourse* 5(1): 71–90. DOI: 10.1080/19463014.2013.859848

39

Social media critical discourse studies (SM-CDS)

Majid KhosraviNik

Social media as communicative paradigm

The nature, location, and dynamic of discursive power in Social Media, or broadly speaking the participatory web, is fluid, changeable, and non-static (KhosraviNik 2014, KhosraviNik and Unger 2016). Social Media provides all forms of offline communication and beyond through mediation of electronic devices. I view and define Social Media by the communicative affordance they provide at the intersection of mass and interpersonal communication, i.e., as a new paradigm of communication. Social Media Communication is viewed as electronically mediated communication across any platforms, spaces, sites, and technologies in which users can: (a.) *work together in producing and compiling content;* (b.) *perform interpersonal communication and mass communication simultaneously or separately – sometimes mass performance of interpersonal communication and;* (c.) *have access to see and respond to institutionally (e.g., newspaper articles) and user-generated content/texts.*

This would then include obvious Social Networking Sites (SNSs) such as Facebook and Instagram; websites which are focused on crowd sourcing content, e.g., Wikipedia, electronic forums, etc.; link sharing/management sites, e.g., Digg or Balatarin; micro/blogging sites, e.g., tumblr and Twitter; and Instant Messaging Apps with the possibility of creating group communication such as WhatsApp and Telegram. The essence of Social Media therefore is their focus on facilitating 'participation and interaction, with the result that the content of what is developed and shared on the internet is as much a product of participation as it is of traditional creative and publishing/broadcasting processes' (Seargeant and Tagg 2014: 4).

The new communication protocol breaks away from the traditional clear-cut separation between producers and consumers of texts. The traditional unidirectional, one-to-many interface of mass media is replaced with what appears to be a (potential for) many-to-many dynamic of discursive practice. Amidst some exhilaration for the potential impact of Social Media on political communication, it is argued that mass media's concentrated power to push content onto audience is being replaced by a new form of participatory communication, which *could* lead to a fully decentralised and democratised access to discursive power. Although the utopian promises of the participatory web has not materialised (Morris and Ogan 2002: 137–138), e.g., reconnection with politics among the youth in the West, the changes in dynamic of discursive power cannot be ignored. As far as a Social Media Critical Discourse Studies (SM-CDS) approach is concerned, both macro/political/industrial and local communicative notions of power are still at play, even though the local communication dynamic of Social Media appears to have eroded the power of/behind discourse (see KhosraviNik 2014 for a detailed discussion).

Social media and critique

Even with the assumption that the dynamic of communicative power has changed for the benefit of ordinary text/content producers, macro critique of Web 2.0 practices at the industry level casts doubts on the postulation that Social Media would facilitate a democratised bottom-up discourse formation. For example Ritzer and Jurgenson (2010) view Social Media/Web 2.0 technologies as a similar but subtler form of *prosumption* processes – putting consumers to work – whereby the distinctions between producers and consumers erodes, e.g., self-service techniques in fast food or retail industries. From a Marxist perspective, such practices are based on 'exploitation of users' unpaid labour' (Fuchs and Sevignani 2013: 237, Fuchs 2014). Through this process, not only is value for profit created through the content production (including sharing of personal information) but also in that the prosumers fill the labour for distribution processes. In addition to that users' engagement on SNSs platforms brings about valorisation for the platform owner both because of the value of the content produced/distributed as well as increasing the ratio of online presence of users during which targeted adverts are presented to them.

In the meantime, the fact on the ground is that there is no absolute control over Web 2.0 resources at the service of and by corporations, i.e., capitalism faces resistance in harnessing all the prosumption processes. A variety of Social Media spaces and affordances are occupied by anti-capitalist and liberal movements or serve a non-profit purpose (Ritzer and Jurgenson 2010). In the same vein, it would be hard to argue for a Marxist notion of exploitation in the way that was possible for traditional modes of production/consumption with the fact that 'prosumers seem to enjoy, even love, what they are doing and are willing to devote long hours to it for no pay' (Ritzer and Jurgenson 2010: 22); a phenomenon Fuchs (2014) calls playbour.

On the one hand, the overall critique holds that spaces of democratic civil engagement are in one way or another influenced by vices of 'old' corporatisation processes (Street 2011, Holly 2008). For example, a vast majority of the virtual spaces follow commercial media funding models where audiences (consumers/users/prosumers) are *sold* to advertisers albeit in a more complicated, consensual, and participatory manner. Trading users' information for advertising purposes is the most common practice which has helped the rise of individually targeted advertising strategies through mechanisms such as Google Adsense, Adwords, and Facebook targeted advertising. To optimise this aim, Social Media architecture constantly works to increase the *degree* (in terms of amount of time, space, and types of activities) and *intensity* (more details, more multimodal, more releases of personal information) of ordinary users' engagement with the platforms. This leads to creation of: (a.) more audience for various advertising strategies – users as consumers and (b.) higher potential for, and precision of, targeted personalised advertising and algorithms – users as text co-producers; hence the more (potential for) accumulation of wealth for the corporations.

On the other hand, Social Media communicative paradigm has indeed challenged the traditional static understanding of media power. Social Media can and *have* provided new spaces of power for citizenry engagement, grass-root access, and use of symbolic resources – albeit differently in different socio-political contexts (Kelsey and Bennett 2014, KhosraviNik and

Zia 2014). Within digital discursive environments, 'the loci of power are much more diffuse and instruments of ideological control and discipline are more subtle and complex' (Jones, Chik, and Hafner 2015: 1).

Social Media Critical Discourse Studies (SM-CDS)

Participatory web has now created its native genres and forms of interaction, which may or may not resemble the traditional, non-electronically mediated communicative practices. Such digitally mediated communication forms combine various channels and modalities of communication as well as integrating synchronous and asynchronous modes of communication. This would pose a challenge in terms of genre definitions, which, in turn, impacts on issues of adopting/adapting linguistic methods and approaches in the analysis of such materials. For example, initially, Computer Mediated Communication (CMC), e.g., emails and Instant Messaging protocols, was largely ignored by mass media scholars as it resembled interpersonal communication (Morris and Ogan 2002: 136), while linguists took an interest in analysing such data by bringing in their traditions of analysing interactions (as discussed in detail by Herring 2010). It is not a surprise that many studies on CMC have tried to adopt and adapt research methods of Conversation Analysis and interactional sociolinguistics. Interaction in a broad sense, however, is a key aspect in Social Media Communication. Gee (2015: 1) defines interactions 'as a field which is focused on meaning making' and as such, as he claims, it is the essence of discourse analysis. At a more specific level, communicative forms have been classified as turn-taking modes, e.g., conversations and static texts, e.g., books and films. The argument here is that the current digital mode of practice is now turning even the latter static texts into interactive content, i.e., ultimately making them a product of 'us' rather than 'I' (2015: 7).

From another angle there is an emerging literature which foregrounds discursive *practice* as the central focus of discourse analysis in Social Media (Jones, Chik, and Hafner 2015, Barton and Lee 2013, Norris and Jones 2005) following from the discourse-in-action approach of Scollon (2001) and Scollon and Scollon (2004). The approach distinguishes the notion of discursive practice from a Faircloughian understanding of the term, which includes scrutiny of processes of production and consumption of discourses in terms of its genre and distribution (Fairclough 1992: 71). Practice in this approach, Jones et al. (2015: 2) argue, is seen 'more as a matter of the concrete, situated actions people perform with particular mediational means (such as written texts, computers, mobile phones) in order to enact membership in particular social groups'. Here, the 'basic unit of analysis is the mediated action, which is effectively the practice where the text is used' (Barton and Lee 2013: 14). In accord with Androutsopoulos's (2008) approach which emphasises locating the most relevant foci of data for analysis, the approach (largely used in Literacy Studies) starts from observation of practices to arrive at texts, while classic discourse analytical approaches (e.g., Herring 2004), including the main trends in CDS, start from the texts followed by layers of media and socio-political contextualisation (KhosraviNik 2010, 2015a). Although, in one way or another a CDS understanding of meaning making process would have to account for the context of data, the argument here is that an observational/communicative practice-based approach would fit more efficiently for discourse analysis on Social Media. Away from an assumption of mass-ness for audience in traditional media, we now deal with co-consumers and co-producers in their potentially endless diversification and in order to provide an explanation of dynamic of language online, as Barton and Lee (2013: 167) argue, 'we need to both closely look at the texts and to observe "users" lives and beliefs about what they do with their online writing'.

At the opposite side of the spectrum of foregrounding users, there is a body of studies in CMC which focuses on media technology as the entry point of analysis and explication. An emerging trend of research in CMC has started to move away from this mainstream calling for a shift of focus to *the social* as the point of explication, i.e., foregrounding society over technology in explications. Such socially oriented approach to Social Media discourse analysis would elaborate on 'characteristics and circumstances of society in the way that new affordances such as online public spheres are used and contextualised within different societies, communities, and demographic fractions' (KhosraviNik 2014: 294). Amidst a surge in linguistic studies on various kinds of web materials with the exhilaration for the newfound archives of logged data, this approach attempts to focus on users as members of pre-existing society rather than being merely part of virtual communities of practice shaped by technological affordances.

Susan Herring and Jannis Androutsopoulos have made substantial contributions in the shift towards a social and contextual analysis of language on Social Media. Speaking from traditions of Linguistics and Ethnography of Communication respectively, Herring (2004) and Androutsopoulos (2008) proposed models of Computer Mediated Discourse Analysis (CMDA) and Discourse-Centred Online Ethnography (DCOE). They contribute to clarification and categorisation of online linguistic genres and practices; call for a user-centred contextual approach to CMC analysis, and problem orientedness as the guideline for analysis. While decisively staying within Linguistics traditions, Herring (2004) postulates a (possible) progression from data to context (as one of her suggested trends in CMDA). Androutsopoulos argues for entry level of context for data collection with an emphasis on online context. From the SM-CDS angle, the main point is to note that *discourse is independent of the medium* although the magnitude, penetrability, and formal aspects of its realised forms may be heavily influenced by the medium.

Despite the fact that reactions against technology-oriented research in CMC are a valid endeavour for SM-CDS, these debates are not current tensions in CDS. Viewing discourse as language-in-use has always been a defining characteristic in the development of Critical Discourse Analysis (or CDS in general) – be it on traditional mass media texts or interpersonal communication. As such a SM-CDS model would be unapologetically comfortable in following a context dependent, critical analysis of communicative practices/content with a socio-political critique level. On the other hand, Androutsopoulos's approach can arguably be taken to speak to another concern in SM-CDS, i.e., how to arrive at a model for media level contextualisation (KhosraviNik 2015a: 6, KhosraviNik and Unger 2016) or the discursive practice level in Faircloughian sense (Fairclough 1992: 71). Nevertheless, the proposed horizontal contextualisation of discourse practice (accounting for: norms of production, consumption, and distribution of texts on different platforms), including the patterns of users' textual/semiotic/etc. practices in their online worlds, would need to be complemented by a vertical contextualisation level which embeds both the text and the medium (KhosraviNik 2015a: 6). That is, the discursive practices are to be vertically linked to the material socio-political contexts of society. In other words, as a conceptually crucial aspect of a viable SM-CDS, the study would need: (a.) a horizontal context substantiation which deals with the intertextuality among textual practices on (potentially) multi-sites and interconnectedness of Social Media users through observation and by linking the available textual platforms and practices horizontally across the sites, platforms, and genres and (b.) a vertical context substantiation which links both the micro-features of textual analysis and horizontal context to socio-political context of users in society, i.e., links to the societal discourses-in-place – the 'thick' context, to use Couldry's term (Couldry 2012).

SM-CDS demarcations

CDS cannot afford to shy away from the current and increasing discursive concentrations on digitally facilitated spaces – obviously. There is discursive power where there is communication concentration. The perception of inertia for SM-CDS is mainly due to a hiccup in scholarship, which is affecting social sciences across the board. While the theoretical challenges may be shouldered by adjacent (inter)disciplinary theorisations, there are several micro or meso level issues in methods and application of SM-CDS which need to be addressed. The bottom line in all this is that CDS should be defined as *a socially committed, problem-oriented, textually based, critical analysis of discourse* (manifested in communicative content/practices). Every word in this definition stands in relation to a specific debate in the field with the aim to carve out a fitting model for SM-CDS.

A crucial point is that critical theoretical conceptualisations on the role of media in society are still relevant in a general sense (Couldry 2012) including critical engagement with issues of media power in society and corporatisation trends in virtual spaces (Unger, Wodak, and KhosraviNik 2016). This is partly explained in that SM-CDS deals with discourse, not technology, as its central object of analysis. We are not only interested in what happens in media per se but in how it may shape and influence social and political sphere of our life worlds. Similarly by considering discourse as an independent unit of analysis, we go where discourse concentration goes. In doing that we are not postulating that there is an essential distinction between online and offline worlds but that there are intertextual and interdiscursive relations between these two levels of discursive practice. Discourses stretch across media industries and communication practices rather than being specific to an outlet or form. Even though we may decide to analyse texts and communication practices in a single outlet, SM-CDS needs to view the findings within a wider context. It has, in fact, *always* been the case that discourse formations and perceptions occur within a mix of mediatised and social practices.

In doing that the media-specific (horizontal) context of participatory web should not be taken as an equivalent of the vertical social context. In line with issues such as digital divide and in spite of difficulties in demographic and geographic accounting of online communities, sociological factors of class, agency, access, identity, gender, etc. should not be 'distilled into a bland cybernetic metaphor' (Couldry 2012: 117). Sweeping overstatement regarding the social and political power of Social Media stems from this very dilution of society into what goes on online in such a way that the availability of technological affordance per se is assumed to be the ultimate sufficient context *and* force for actual social, political, and cultural change in society. All media practices/content should be interpreted within a wider socio-political context of a given society. This is where a social, historical, cultural, psychological, or political account is provided for explication of the discourse under investigation (see KhosraviNik and Unger 2016, Unger, Wodak, and KhosraviNik 2016, Wodak and KhosraviNik 2013).

Having said that, there is a clear need for substantial engagement with literature on CMC and studies from Science and Technology approach to equip SM-CDS with the required insights into the workings of the new communication technologies. In the meantime, the engagement with such research with their predominately quantitative and 'scientific' epistemology should not (a.) cause an epistemological overhaul for social orientation of CDS, e.g., shades of media determinism and dilution of critique and (b.) force CDS into substantial tired defensive debates on old issues, e.g., why the descriptive level of analysis needs a critical explication. SM-CDS does not need to revisit and re-engage with its critical and epistemological roots, as a general approach – although there is considerable room for critical theorisation on nuances within a Social Media communication paradigm.

As a general orientation, observational approaches (Hine 2000) are now pushed more to the fore for SM-CDS, beyond the obvious function of locating relevant data and sampling justifications. It is now more difficult and less (than before) justified to separate texts from their immediate contexts of use. Consequently, integrative approaches in analysing discourse in action (Scollon and Scollon 2004, Jones et al. 2015, Barton and Lee 2013) could bring important insights for SM-CDS. On the other hand, this does not necessarily mean that there is a need for an overhaul of text/content-focused characteristic of CDS in favour of a full-fledged ethnographical turn. As such, conducting interviews and focus groups as classic audience studies methods can be incorporated in SM-CDS (as they have in the past, e.g., Krzyżanowski 2011) but application of such methods should only be justified within the specific scope and aims of every study rather than be deemed as an essential part and parcel of the research design. Questions about people's motivations, the meanings they attach to the resources they use, and relationship between participants (Androutsopoulos 2008: 2) could be very insightful, but in the meantime, the focus can be maintained on the form, processes, and projected meanings of the content itself and their calculated impacts in society. Audience methods, however, could enrich and be part of social contextualisation for the analysis of communicative content in SM-CDS.

Multimodality is also pushed more to the centre for SM-CDS. Multimodality has also *always* been the everyday experience of members of society in their exposures to discourses but (verbal) language has been considered as the core communication modality in (classic) CDA literature – for CDA's strong roots in Linguistics. The analysis of other modalities of communication has traditionally been bundled together as multimodal discourse analysis (Kress and van Leeuwen 2006, Machin and Mayr 2012) or as an *additional* level of analysis to discourse analysis (Herring 2004, Page et al. 2014). Interestingly in all the recent publications on analysis of language of participatory web there is an acknowledgement and/or a separate section on multimodal discourse analysis. If we take multimodal discourse analysis as an approach to account for all channels of communication other than verbal language, then the approach is also facing challenges in terms of describing communicative genres beyond the usual modalities of audio and visual channels. There are now meaning bearing forms (communicative resources), which are indigenous to participatory web such as tagging, likes, annotation, sharing, hyperlinks, etc. that need to be accounted for. Above all, at the higher level, there is the function of algorithms (Gillespie 2014) as one of the macro-level controllers of discourse/topics or new gate-keeping tool.

As arguable point as it may be, the power behind (media) discourse seems to have been compromised in participatory web which would indicate a potential for more proactive dynamism in interactions between media and society. Nonetheless, this does not necessarily or automatically mean that the boundaries of social constructs of identity and communities around Self and Other have dissolved accordingly in the society – or in the same way as the availability of technology affordances makes it appear. Neutralising (problematic) social structures and histories by drawing on (arguable) digital access to representations is undoubtedly reducing life worlds in unproductive ways. This is sometimes pursued with the intention of neutralising emancipatory interventions within a neoliberal exhilaration for what is assumed to be a 'post-ideological' era. On the other hand, even if we put aside all the macro-structural issues of power control and concentration and management of participatory web, despite the change in one-way flow of mass media discourses, power is still a central aspect in terms of the Habermasian notion of public sphere and management of power *in* discourse, i.e., bottom–up language in use (KhosraviNik 2014). This understanding can have bearing in both theorisation of critique in CDS (Forchtner 2011) as well as genre classifications of data at hand.

While a Foucauldian understanding of discourse is associated with analysis of the underlying structural/social conventions that give meanings to interactions, the Habermasian concept of communicative action relates to the quality of communicative action, and to the procedures and social settings that lead to the formulation and re-formulation of these social conventions (Farfan and Holzcheiter 2011: 141).

Macro-contextual issues of a given society should continue to be accounted for in explication of SM-CDS. This is where social and cultural power asymmetries as well as qualities, viability, and availability of public spheres are critically evaluated. One of the current disciplinary tensions in CDS across various disciplines is whether the research should progress from context to texts or the other way around. Either way, the central point remains that meanings are negotiated and that meanings reside within the society and social context, rather than the language or any other communicative content per se (KhosraviNik 2009). Therefore, there is a crucial point of caution in avoiding an unhelpful assumption of universality in qualities of societies in terms of their relations with Social Media affordances and political engagements. The obvious caveat here is not to fall in the Orientalist trap of understanding the difference in naïve essentialist ways. In accord with Couldry's (2012) critique of Castell's Network Society notion, it must be recognised that factors such as qualities and degrees of availability of free platforms of interaction in traditional media play a key role in CDS. As such, a SM-CDS approach would be interested both in the ways 'micro-level interactional and textual practices constitute our social worlds and the way that our everyday communicative/ representational practices are structured by the social order, larger systems of beliefs, and by hierarchies of knowledge' (Thurlow and Mroczek 2011: xxvii). Current popular topics in CDS such as various forms of identity, nationalism, racism, and Right-wing populism (Wodak and KhosraviNik 2013) are still relevant within the communicative dynamic of participatory web. Similarly the impact of such new affordances in disseminating problematic, e.g., discourses of exclusionary nationalism (Copsey 2003, KhosraviNik and Zia 2014) and positive impacts on public discourse and representation can also be subjects of research.

Persian nationalism on Facebook

While texts from official/institutional sources such as newspapers, TV news, magazines, speeches, and manifestos have been accessible (and necessary) targets of CDA, research on attitudes in society (for example, nationalism in grass-roots discourses) have always required a well-invested research apparatus or they have been difficult to access in some contexts. With the argument that Social Media could provide convenient access to such bottom-up discourses (KhosraviNik 2014, Unger, Wodak, and KhosraviNik 2016), I discuss the case of Persian national(ist) identity on Facebook.

Among other affordances for participatory communication, a Facebook feature, which is often utilised for political/social debates, is the Page function. Members can create their own themed groups on any topic and invite other users to join. In groups, members can post to message boards, add pictures, and post news and links. On paper, Facebook seems to combine 'the best features of local bulletin boards, newspapers, and town hall meetings and places them in one location that is available at any time in practically any location' (Westling 2007: 4).

As for the qualities of public sphere, post-revolutionary Iran has gone through various phases (see KhosraviNik 2015a for a comprehensive recap). Within early years of the new millennium, due to a number of factors, e.g., the state policy of containment of reformist press and development of digital spaces, which facilitated content production for common users, there came about a sharp surge in usage and distribution of content via blogging. Giacobino et al. (2014: 3) reports that 'between 2002 and 2010 the Persian blogosphere – or what is referred to as 'Blogistan' (Srebnerny and Khiabany 2010) – exploded in size and became the topic of numerous, essays, videos and books'. Yet by 2008 and afterwards, there was a visible decline in blogging dynamic in Iran. Although the state intervention in curbing the flow of blog texts, such as systematic filtering in 2004–2005 and onwards, played an undeniable role in the decline, from a technological point of view the crucial impact came from the emergence of Social Networking Sites, particularly Facebook. Apart from the fundamental impacts of draining a considerable online time of users from reading/writing blogs, on a more nuanced level, Facebook forced the commentary communication to move to Facebook posts from underneath the blog posts despite the continued issues of il/legality of and access to Facebook inside Iran. Similarly Facebook became an access host for a multimodal array of texts including reading materials as well as videos, music, and photos.

Discourse of Persian identity has long been present in the social fabrics of the Iranian society. With the popularity of Facebook, the discourse of Persian identity found a venue to consolidate itself on this semi-public virtual space. As a concentrated *discursive event,* KhosraviNik and Zia (2014) examine the content, discursive strategies, and consequences of this form of Iranian nationalist identity by focusing on a highly contentious debate about the naming of 'Persian' Gulf as a universal name. It is assumed that within such a focal point, predominate array of features, content, and strategies of Self (Persian) and Other (Arabs) constructions are communicated and/or perpetuated. Following on the Discourse-Historical Approach to CDA (Reisigl and Wodak 2016, KhosraviNik 2010, Reisigl, this volume), at the micro-level, the case study focuses on analysing commentaries, posts, and updates on or related to campaigns for preserving the name Persian for the gulf. It looks at the linguistic content, visual communication as well as the issues of typeface and orthographic mixtures. The study is based on analysis of the content and practices on one of the most popular Facebook Pages dedicated to this debate entitled Persian Gulf. The Page is said to be dedicated to 'Persian Gulf, its name, geography, history, culture and arts'. Membership is granted by clicking the 'like' icon on the Page. By doing this, members get a news feed on their Facebook home page; can comment on the statuses; and can view and comment on notes and pictures that are shared on the Page's wall.

On the analysis of the content of this nationalist discourse, it is evident that the nodal point of the discourse is on construction of similarity and difference in terms of Self and Other along the lines of Persians vs. Arabs. This manifests itself at all levels of referential, predicational, and argumentation levels (Wodak and Reisigl 2016) – although there is little visible argumentative content. A substantial amount of these references have racial (ised) nature, i.e., Self/Persians as Aryans and Other/Arabs as non-Aryans. Other referential categories in promotion of Self include references to Our glorified past, e.g., 'the largest empire in history' combined with frequent references to power, dominance, and courage, e.g., 'the land of lions'. All these are perceived and interpreted within a favourable historical narrative as the group's shared repertoire of assumed knowledge. Referentials denoting to permanency, endurance, uniqueness, and aesthetics are among the most frequent categories in references to 'our' Persian Gulf. At the predicational level the Self-identity is strongly associated to themes of continuity, passion for the country, and belonging, e.g., 'Persian Gulf is our birth certificate', 'has always been/will always remain Persian'. In terms of construction of Other identity within a dehumanisation agenda, an array of racial and culturally derogatory references, e.g., 'savage Bedouins', etc. are used. Predicational themes include attribution of perceived negative cultural practices and responsibility for negative impacts on Iran via Islamisation of Iran, e.g., 'they have brought slavery to Iran' (see KhosraviNik and Zia 2014 for detailed summary results).

Majid KhosraviNik

با اجازه شاعر: به رغم مدعیان، روز شب نخواهد شد
فروغ مهر به شب منتسب نخواهد شد
اگر تمامی دنیا به فتنه برخیزد
...
خلیج فارس خلیج ع*ر*ب نخواهد شد.
July 5 at 8:13pm · Like · ☐ 4

Figure 39.1 Orthographic communication of stance in discourse of Persian nationalism

Apart from the expected nodal point of Persian vs. Arabs where the Arabs are constructed as the external Other, there seems to be an Other-from-within construct which speaks to the way this Persian nationalist discourse views its relations to the official state identity. As the discourse views itself as a secular alternative to the official religious identity in Iran, it constructs the Iranian officials as the enemy from within at referential and predicational level and associates them to the constructed external-Other. The Iranian officials are referred to as 'Arab lovers', or 'the traitors and unpatriotic elements in Iran'. Predicationally this group is associated with 'being proud of their Arabic ancestors', 'being obsessed with religion', 'smirking at (real) Iranians', etc. Interestingly, the Persian nationalist discourse views an array of enemies from outside in a way that they are all anchored to the constructed Arab identity directly or by association. Consequently the Other identity seems to extend from Arab worshipers within Iran to the West and America, who are perceived to be in collusion against Iran. Negative predications against the West and specifically America include, 'having called Iranians savage and terrorists', 'having sold chemical weapons to Saddam to kill Iranians', and 'having funded terrorist groups against Iran'. This speaks to the fact that while this discourse has strong roots in what is perceived to be a cultural/historical narrative of national identity based on promotion of a pre-Islamic history of Iran, it is in fact very influenced by the contemporary geopolitics of the region and the post-revolutionary events in Iran, e.g., Iran-Iraq war (1980–1988).

Expected orthographic features of online language, e.g., initialism (LOL) word reductions (gd for good), letter/number homophones (U for you, 2 for two), etc. (Barton and Lee 2013) are used in this case with a creative practice of code-switching between Persian, English, and 'pinglish' (KhosraviNik and Zia 2014 for detail). One of the most common and strategic stylised forms of using language in this case is the way representation of the terms Arabs and Arabic are manipulated. An example of such manipulation is the use of the word Arab as a set of initials along with asterisks (ع*ر*ب) or examples of using A.R.A.B.I.A.N. Gulf in English. This is directly in line with one of the announced aims of the Page to avoid promoting the name Arabian Gulf and in fact, fight against it. As an effective backgrounding strategy in the digital space, the users avoid adding to the online content which could be recognised by Google algorithms as evidence of rightful association of the two words of Arabian and Gulf (see also the 'Google bomb' campaign against the use of the term by manipulating the Google search engine). This is very adamantly pursued both in the Persian and English references.

Multimodal rendering of the discourse

There is a popular trend in postcard and poster imageries in Iran in presenting the dramatic and nostalgic glories of the pre-Islamic history of Iran. The visualisation usually comprises a symbolic collage of various historical and political elements, which are rich in their significations in the Iranian cultural understanding. Posting, sharing, liking, and distribution of visuals is also a very common practice among ordinary users. As a parallel semiotic resource for such

590

discourse of Persian national identity, this kind of visual aids are often shared, promoted, and discussed in this case study as well. Interesting enough, very similar referential and predicational themes feature in visual representations. As part of such trend, an example of these posters – which functions as summary arguments for superiority and legitimacy of the proposed Persian identity—is analysed here.

Figure 39.2 is an example of visual representation of such identity with clear references to the Persian Gulf. The picture gives centrality and spatial foregrounding to the contentious body of water by placing it in the centre, followed by the name printed in a relatively contrasting colour of shining green in a large font in English and the equivalent in Persian. The top section of the image along with all the area considered to belong to Iran (including the sea areas of the Persian Gulf and the Oman Sea) are filled with symbolic and iconic representations of aspects of projected Persian identity, whereas the lower section of the image (Arabian territory) is basically represented as a barren land, except for the accentuated presence of a Persian Achaemenid soldier wrapped in Iran's flag. Although the appearance of the solider is manipulated with the addition of a modern Iranian flag, his otherwise historically accurate iconic look and the ostentatious large presence in the Arabian land denotes the projected ideals of dominance and control in this discourse which of course accords with the narrated history of the Persians in the region. There are four other low definition depictions of Persian iconic ancient prowess signs, i.e., Achaemenid soldiers copied from Persepolis sculptures and the image of Arash, the Archer: the mythical Persian hero who changed the fate of the war in favour of the Iranians vs. what has been referred to as the 'non-Iranians' of the time.

In terms of symbolism and in line with the representation of power and dominance, there is the metaphoric presence of a lion denoting the aggressively protective and domineering imputes of this Us-identity, while there is also an additional peace-loving character in the

Figure 39.2 Visual representation of Iranian Persian national(ist) identity

mix, symbolised through the two white pigeons. The 'mother' land is denoted via a female wrapped in a modern Iranian flag (though not with the Islamic Republic emblem), who is otherwise naked, and lying at the foot of the Achaemenid construction of the Cube of Zoroaster, which is the epicentre of *Naqsh-e Rustam,* the Necropolis of the 'great' Persian kings, Darius I and Xerxes I amongst others. The Cube of Zoroaster has come to be one of the most popularly praised icons of a historical glorious Persian identity in contemporary Iran. The feminine representation of the land is not an unprecedented phenomenon for Iran or nationalist discourses in general. In combination with heavily masculine Achaemenid soldiers, it invokes traditional patriarchal perception of females as dependent and powerless and in need of protection and patronage by men. This is intensified by the posture of the female and males presented. The main depicted female is presented in an unstable pose; lying down, not facing the audience, naked and in a vulnerable lower consciousness status (perhaps sleeping/ ill while being dangerously distracted from imminent dangers of the represented conflict side), whereas the males are in mostly visibly vertical postures, in full armour, and with serious expression of intent. In line with the unfavourable representation of the officials in Iran, the visual representation of this Persian identity discourse also includes, as part of Self-identity, an iconic image denoting the student riot of July 1999 in the middle of the right hand side of the poster, though represented very vaguely.

The last aspect – and perhaps an aberration of both historical authenticity and the findings of the textual analysis section – is the presence of six snapshots of female characters in lower degrees of resolution. As much as it can be seen, the projected females are all in traditional or what is assumed to be ancient attire. It is important to note that while a couple of these could be traced back to women's attires of more contemporary Iranian dress codes, in most cases they are what is believed (or discursively promoted) to be representative of ancient Iranian women and their attires. The projected presence of females in the poster (even though they are all in passive and/or vulnerable referential position) is an attempt at the claim to gender inclusivity (regardless of historic authenticity) for Self-identity. That is, to present a Self-identity which is modern and inclusive in addition to being powerful, dominant, and glorious in contrast to the 'retrograde' nature of the Arab/Other identity. It is noteworthy to mention that except for the issue of (lack of) gender inclusivity, all the other aspects of the visual and textual data show striking similarities in representations of Self and Other.

The approach employed in this research reveals the nature and qualities of exclusionary nationalism discourses, similarly found in several other countries and contexts (Wodak, KhosraviNik and Mral 2013). It is important to note that the aim of the research has not been to engage with the debate on the naming but to see how this topical point is used to express, construct, and disseminate this notion of Persian identity. The overall macro discursive/ideological outlook of the data indicates that this online community emphatically seeks to propagate a glorious Persian identity as lawful owners of the 'Persian' Gulf in opposition to construction of an extremely unanimous 'Arab' identity. It is evident that this debate stems from various perceived grievances, which have contributed to a crisis of identity in Iran. In an inarticulate and highly problematic manner, the discourse attempts to carve out a form of identity, which distinguishes itself from the supposed Arab identity as well as the perceived official identity. Interestingly, there are important similarities between the propagated Persian identity and the Islamic Republic's conservative discourse as they both assign a central value to power, defiance, and confrontation in their discursive bifurcation of Us and Them and emphasis on the nodal point of conflict (KhosraviNik 2015b; see KhosraviNik and Sarkhoh forthcoming for an account of Arabist discourses in the region). In its desire for rightful recognition and respect, there seems to be a strong current of infatuation with expression of power and a cultural tendency of slipping into a Manichean Us/Them bifurcation in some layers of the Iranian society.

Although this Social Media platform has afforded a space for consolidation, expression, and representation of this form of identity in what can (very arguably) be considered as the Iranian public sphere, the bias, aims, and orientations of this online community inhibit the formation of real deliberation on matters of national identity. Despite the fact that the members of this virtual community may see coherence in their expression of identity, the discourse is nothing short of an inarticulate racist outburst. 'Whatever the justification may be, such turn to extreme (and racist) nationalism in social discourses would render (or add to) the fertile ground for the rise of populist, exclusionary and authoritarian discourses which would seek presuppositions of superiority and exceptionalism in one way or another' (KhosraviNik and Zia 2014: 777).

Conclusion

This chapter has set out to discuss some of the issues that CDS is facing in its application to content arising from a Social Media Communication paradigm. The chapter has tried to show how central issues of power and methodological understandings could be envisaged for a SM-CDS approach. These debates aim to accommodate the new technological and epistemological challenges as well as argue for viability of a continued CDS approach for these new spaces of participatory communication. The chapter has also attempted to provide some sharply tuned considerations and suggestions along the lines of the call for new forms of interdisciplinarity towards future directions in theory and application of CDS in digital participatory spaces. The fact is that we need to continue true interdisciplinary reading and writing to be able to incorporate the new developments in communication technologies.

Apart from the more structural changes in the norms of communication, Social Media technologies continue to provide exciting communication and content on various topics which are obviously of interest for CDS on various topics. It is high time for CDS scholars to substantially venture into SM-CDS without losing the sight of the main principles of CDS. This venture would be much more multifaceted than considering Social Media as merely a data source.

An important note is that, despite (very serious and valid) macro-structural and industrial obstacles, which have been criticised deservedly, there is still a real sense of potentials and unpredictability about the way these new spaces of power could be taken up and used. This is the very reason why communication technologies continue to give jitters to industrial, corporate, or political controllers of symbolic resources. Putting aside the highly problematic nature of the Persian nationalist discourse discussed earlier, from the media and society point of view, this case can stand as an example of appropriation of these new spaces of communication to consolidate a discourse. The emphatic and popularity of the users' attempts to take up this afforded space only speaks to the excitement of newfound (perception) of power to influence the society. This is within the circumstance that the traditional venues of the public sphere in Iran are predominantly dedicated to propagating the official representations. In other words, characteristics of the 'thick' context of Iranian society determine the shape, popularity, and macro meanings of the contents in these digital spaces of interactions. This takes us back again to the issue of context in CDS and the fact that CDS should remain a *socially* oriented, critical analysis of discourse.

Further reading

KhosraviNik, M. (2014). Critical discourse analysis, power and new media discourse. In Y. Kalyango and M. Kopytowska (eds.), *Why discourse matters: Negotiating identity in the mediatized world,* 287–306.
This chapter concentrates on the notion of discursive power in Social Media communication as compared to mass media. It attends to the new interactive nature of Social Media and argues that the common assumptions about media (discursive) power may not apply to the new dynamic of text production and consumption in participatory web.

KhosraviNik, M. and Unger, J. (2016). Critical discourse studies and social media: Power, resistance and critique in changing media ecologies. In R. Wodak and M. Meyer (eds.), *Methods of critical discourse analysis,* 3rd edn. London: Sage.
This chapter attends to some of the macro-structural characterisations of discursive practice on Social Media and contextualises the CDS approach to Social Media within the traditions of Critical Discourse Studies as well as discussing two case study examples.

KhosraviNik, M. and Zia, M. (2014). Persian nationalism, identity and anti-Arab sentiments in Iranian Facebook discourses: Critical discourse analysis and social media communication. *Journal of Language and Politics* 13(4): 755–780.
This research paper reports on the results of a large case study within the framework of Social Media Critical Discourse Studies. It attends to some of the theoretical concerns, operationalises a data selection procedure, and carries out a critical analysis of a form of exclusionary nationalistic discourse, i.e., Persian nationalism among Iranians users on Facebook.

Unger, J., Wodak, R. and KhosraviNik, M. (2016). Critical discourse studies and social media data. In David Silverman (ed.), *Qualitative research,* 4th edn, 277–293. London: Sage.
This textbook chapter is set out to present Social Media CDS as an emerging critical approach within the larger scale of qualitative methodologies in Social Sciences. In an accessible style, the chapter seeks to introduce a procedure for conducting such research while attending to some of the conceptual, analytical, and ethical concerns.

Page, R., Barton, D., Unger, J.W. and Zappavigna, M. (2014). *Researching language in social media.* London: Routledge.
In this textbook, Page et al. outline some of the key issues in researching language in social media contexts. There are chapters on ethics, research design, and qualitative and ethnographic research, alongside more quantitative approaches.

References

Androutsopoulos, J. (2008). Potentials and limitations of discourse-centred online ethnography. *Language@ Internet* 5(8).

Barton, D. and Lee, C. (2013). *Language online: Investigating digital texts and practices.* Abingdon: Routledge.

Copsey, N. (2003). Extremism on the net: The extreme right and the value of the internet. In R. Gibson, P. Nixon, and S. Ward (eds.), *Political parties and the Internet: Net gain?* 218–233. London: Routledge.

Couldry, N. (2012). *Media, society, world: Social theory and digital media.* Cambridge: Polity Press.

Fairclough, N. (1992). *Discourse and social change.* Oxford: Blackwell Publishers.

Farfan, J.A.F. and Holzcheiter. (2011). The power of discourse and the discourse of power. In R. Wodak, B. Johnstone and P. Kerswill (eds.), *The Sage handbook of sociolinguistics,* 139–152.

Forchtner, B. (2011). Critique, the discourse-historical approach and the Frankfurt School. *Critical Discourse Studies* 8(1): 1–14.

Fuchs, C. (2014). *Social media: A critical introduction.* London: Sage.

Fuchs, C. and Sevignani, S. (2013). What is digital labour? What is digital work? What is their difference? And why do these questions matter for understanding social media. Triple C (Communication, Capitalism & Critique), Vol. 11 (2).

Gee, J.P. (2015). *Unified discourse analysis: Language, reality, virtual worlds, and video games.* London: Routledge.

Giacobino, L., Abadpour, A., Anderson, C., Petrossian, F. and Nellemann, C. (2014). *Whither Blogestan: Evaluating shifts in persian cyberspace.* Iran Media Program Center for Global Communication Studies, Annenberg School for Communication, University of Pennsylvania.

Gillespie, T. (2014). The relevance of algorithms. In T. Gillespie, P. Boczkowski, and K. Foot (eds.), *Media technologies: Essays on communication, materiality, and society.* Cambridge, MA: MIT Press.

Hay, C. (2002). *Political analysis: A critical introduction.* Basingstoke: Palgrave.

Herring, S. C. (2004). Computer-mediated discourse analysis: An approach to researching online behavior. In S. Barab, R. Kling, and J. Gray (eds.), *Designing for virtual communities in the service of learning,* 338–376. Cambridge: Cambridge University Press.

Herring, S. C. (2010). Computer-mediated conversation: Introduction and overview. *Language@Internet* 7, article 2.

Hine, C. (2000). *Virtual ethnography.* Sage.

Holly, W. (2008). Tablodisation of political communication in the public sphere. In R. Wodak and V. Koller (eds.), *Handbook of communication in the public sphere,* 292–316. Belin: Mouton de Gruyter.

Jones, R. H., Chik, A. and Hafner, C. (eds.) (2015). *Discourse and digital practices: Doing discourse analysis in the Digital Age.* London: Routledge

Kelsey, D. and Bennett, L. (2014). Discipline and resistance on social media: Discourse, power and context in the Paul Chambers 'Twitter Joke Trial'. *Discourse, Context & Media* 3: 37–45.

KhosraviNik, M. (2009). The representation of refugees, asylum seekers and immigrants in British newspapers during the Balkan conflict (1999) and the British general election (2005). *Discourse and Society* 20(4): 477–498.

KhosraviNik, M. (2010). Actor descriptions, action attributions, and argumentation: Towards a systematization of CDA analytical categories in the representation of social groups. *Critical Discourse Studies* 7(1): 55–72.

KhosraviNik, M. (2014). Critical discourse analysis, power and New media discourse. In Y. Kalyango and M. Kopytowska (eds.), *Why discourse matters: Negotiating identity in the mediatized world,* 287–306.

KhosraviNik, M. (2015a). *Discourse, identity and legitimacy: Self other representation in discourses on Iran's nuclear programme.* Amsterdam, Philadelphia: John Benjamins.

KhosraviNik, M. (2015b). Macro and micro legitimation in discourse on Iran's nuclear programme: The case of Iranian national newspaper Kayhan. *Discourse & Society* 21(1): 52–73.

KhosraviNik, M. and Sarkhoh, N. (forthcoming). Arabism and anti-Persian sentiments on participatory web: A social media critical discourse study (SM-CDS). *International Journal of Communication.*

KhosraviNik, M. and Unger, J. (2016). Critical discourse studies and social media: Power, resistance and critique in changing media ecologies. In R. Wodak and M. Meyer (eds.), *Methods of critical discourse analysis,* 3rd edn, 205–234. London: Sage.

KhosraviNik, M. and Zia, M. (2014). Persian nationalism, identity and anti-Arab sentiments in Iranian Facebook discourses: Critical discourse analysis and social media communication. *Journal of Language and Politics* 13(4): 755–780.

Kress, G. and van Leeuwen, T. (2006). *Reading images: The grammar of visual design.* London: Routledge.

Krzyżanowski, M. (2011). Ethnography and critical discourse analysis: Towards a problem-oriented research dialogue. *Critical Discourse Studies.* Special Issue: *Ethnography and Critical Discourse Analysis* 8(4): 231–238.

Machin, D. and Mayr, A. (2012). *How to do critical discourse analysis: A multimodal introduction.* London: Sage.

Morris, M. and Ogan, C. (2002). Internet as mass medium. In D. McQuail (eds.), *McQuail's reader in mass communication theory,* 134–145. London: Sage.

Norris, S. and Jones, R. H. (2005). *Discourse in action: Introducing mediated discourse analysis.* London: Routledge.

Page, R., Barton, D., Unger, J.W. and Zappavigna, M. (2014). *Researching language in social media.* London: Routledge.

Reisigl, M. and Wodak, R. (2016). The discourse-historical approach (DHA). In R. Wodak and M. Meyer (eds.), *Methods of critical discourse analysis,* 3rd edn. London: Sage.

Ritzer and Jurgenson. (2010). Production, consumption, prosumption: The nature of capitalism in the age of the digital 'prosumer'. *Journal of Consumer Culture* 10(1): 13–36.

Scollon, R. (2001). *Mediated discourse: The nexus of practice.* London: Routledge.

Scollon, R. and Scollon, S.W. (2004). *Nexus analysis: Discourse and the emerging internet.* London: Routledge.

Seargeant, P. and Tagg, C. (eds.) (2014). *The language of social media: Identity and community on the internet.* London: Palgrave Macmillan.

Srebnerny, A. and Khiabany, G. (2010). *Blogistan: The Internet and politics in Iran.* New York: I.B. Tauris.

Steet, J. (2011). *Mass media, politics and democracy.* (2nd ed). London: Palgrave Macmillan.

Thurlow, C. and Mroczek, K. (2011). *Digital discourse: Language in the new media.* Oxford University Press.

Unger, J., Wodak, R. and KhosraviNik, M. (2016). Critical discourse studies and social media data. In David Silverman (ed.), *Qualitative research,* 4th edn, 277–293. London: Sage.

Westling, M. (2007). Expanding the public sphere: the impact of Facebook on political communication [Online]. www.thenewvernacular.com/projects/facebook_and_political_communication.pdf

Wodak, R. and KhosraviNik, M. (2013). *Dynamics of discourse and politics in right-wing populism in Europe and beyond: An introduction,* xvii–xxviii. London: Bloomsbury.

Wodak, R., KhosraviNik, M. and Mral, B. (eds.) (2013). *Right-wing populism in Europe: politics and discourse.* London and New York: Bloomsbury Academics.

Wodak, R. and Mayer, M. (2009). *Methods of critical discourse analysis,* 2nd edn. London: Sage.

40

Critical discourse analysis of reality television

Göran Eriksson

Introduction

Reality TV, as Turner (2010: 32) states, is 'the most exorbitantly "noticed" form of programming in television history'. This form of programming has been widely discussed in the
media, where it has faced massive criticism from media commentators who associate reality
TV with humiliation and bullying and who see it as morally degrading. Reality TV has been
discussed as low-culture, a form of cheap, trivial and more or less empty entertainment. It
has also been immensely discussed by scholars. A rich variety of reality programming has
been critically explored from numerous theoretical and methodological perspectives (see,
e.g., Hill 2005; Kavka 2008; Ouellette and Hey 2008; Skeggs and Wood 2011, 2012). Despite
all the criticism (or perhaps due to it) reality TV has attracted huge audiences and become a
natural part of today's television schedules, often with a prominent position in prime time. It
has somehow become a taken-for-granted phenomenon and a natural part of many people's
everyday lives (Hill 2015).

Although reality TV is difficult to define, a key characteristic is its link to ordinariness. It
often involves what are conceived of as 'ordinary' people (cf. Bonner 2003; Turner 2010), i.e.,
participants who appear to be themselves and not to be following a script. Reality shows are
generally structured around mundane matters or domestic life, and do not hesitate to expose
more private and intimate aspects of participants' lives. Another, and closely related, key feature of reality TV is its capacity to provoke emotions (Kavka 2008; Skeggs and Wood 2012).
Emotions may appear banal but, as Sayer (2005) points out, they should be viewed as 'evaluative judgements'. Emotions suggest an understanding of one's own position or identity in
relation to the object provoking the feelings; they seem to be crucial to processes of otherness
because they can create and preserve distinctions between groups of people. So, even if the
genre appears to be a playful, rather trivial form of entertainment, it involves ideas about how
to value and understand participants and the activities they involve; reality TV can legitimate
or de-legitimate social practices and their participants and thereby do ideological work.

In the next section I describe the emergence of reality TV. This is followed by a section
introducing the reader to previous research with a specific focus on two prominent critical
approaches. Thereafter I present an approach useful for critically examining reality TV and

how it can provoke feelings. This methodology is based on the collections of methods called Multimodal Critical Discourse Analysis (MCDA) (see Machin and Mayr 2012, 2013; Machin and Ledin, this volume) and van Leeuwen's (2005, 2008) theorising on discourse as recontextualized social practice. These ideas are here adapted to the analysis of television. A basic assumption is to view actions and artefacts used in communication as *semiotic resources*. The presented approach suggests that in order to identify how reality TV can reproduce ideologies detailed analyses of how all the involved semiotic resources (talk, music, audio effects, graphics, camera work, editing, etc.) are combined to portray participants and their actions is necessary.

The examples I work with in this chapter concern the construction of social class. For a long time, especially during the 1980s and 1990s, it was not particularly fashionable to study such structural inequalities, but for some time now there has been a growing interest in exploring class relations (cf. Machin and Richardson 2008), not least to analyse the role played by reality TV in the reproduction of these conditions (Lyle 2008; Tyler 2008; Skeggs and Wood 2011, 2012). The examples I use is from a Swedish reality show – *A Mighty Journey with Morgan and Ola-Conny* – in which two working-class men travel to famous cities and tourist resorts. Issues of class are not explicitly raised in the programme; instead they are implied through how identities, actions and values are treated in discourse. In this case the participants are ridiculed. Through complex mixes of semiotic resources, they are constructed as making fools of themselves and thus become objects of mirth. It is these strategies of ridicule that I suggest can be revealed by the approach presented here.

The emergence of reality television

Reality TV appeared on a large scale in prime time in the USA and the UK during the 1990s, in a time of deregulation and fiscal scarcity (Hill 2005). For the media industry, reality TV provided a way to produce cheap and potentially profitable programming (Curnutt 2011), and it quickly became immensely popular. For many years now, and in many countries around the world, reality TV has had a prominent position on peak-time television.

The generic background of reality TV is certainly complex. It has, as Hill (2005) shows, links to the human-interest stories of tabloid journalism, to documentary television and magazine-like programming, and to infotainment. It also has links to popular entertainment in the form of talk shows, game shows, sports, leisure programming and comedy shows like 'Candid Camera'. The first form of (what came to be known as) reality TV to gain popularity was a factual entertainment format based on recontextualizations of crimes and the work of emergency services. Examples of such programming are *Crimewatch UK* (which started in 1984), *America's Most Wanted, Rescue 911* and *999 Lifesavers*. These programmes were soon accompanied by so called docu-soaps, presented as fly-on-the-wall productions following events and people at, for instance, airports and hospitals; lifestyle-oriented makeover shows; and reality game shows like *Survivor* and *Big Brother* (Hill 2005).

Today, a large variety of subgenres or formats are covered by the concept of reality TV. In addition to the above-mentioned programmes, this includes dating programmes, talent shows and a 'do-good' trend with numerous charity programmes (Murray and Ouellette 2009; Ouellette and Hay 2008). There is, however, a constant flow of new formats that combine established elements from older formats in new ways, making clear-cut categorization more or less unfeasible. There is no common aesthetic rule or convention that can be said to be a defining characteristic of the genre. Reality TV, as Hill (2005: 14) unerringly describes it, is 'an example of how television cannibalises itself in order to survive, drawing on existing genres to create successful hybrid programmes, which in turn generate a "new" television genre'.

Reality TV has also evolved into a genuinely cross-platform phenomenon. Programmes are available on websites where users can see all the episodes and access additional information, outtakes not shown in the programmes, blogs, information about the participants, etc. Some programmes also have their own Facebook pages and Twitter hashtags where viewers post comments and interact about particular episodes and events. Programme participants often have their own accounts on Twitter or Instagram where they communicate with followers. To a large extent, reality TV lives its life on the web today (Hill 2015).

Approaches to reality television

Reality TV has attracted massive research interest. For instance, scholars have focused on the industrial and commercial contexts of its advent (Raphael 2009) and discussed the changing business strategies connected to reality TV (Magder 2009); researchers have studied how audiences deal with the factuality of reality TV, how they evaluate the truth claims of different programmes and what they think they learn from them (Hill 2007), while others, like Andrejevic (2004), have discussed the exploitative dimension of reality TV and how value can be extracted from the commodification of surveillance. An immense number of studies focusing on particular programmes have been published in journals and edited volumes. (For the latter see, e.g., Holmes and Jermyn 2004; Heller 2007; Murray and Ouellette 2009; Lorenzo-Dus and Garcés-Conejos Blitvich 2013). Journals have also dedicated special issues to particular programmes such as *Big Brother* (Hill and Palmer 2002), genres like makeover programmes (Lewis 2008b) and themes like race and reality TV (Orbe 2008) and gender and reality TV (Negra, Pike and Radley 2013).

There are, however, two more distinctive perspectives that take a more critical interest in reality TV and discuss it in relation to its societal and political consequences and the spread of neoliberal ideology. Below I will present these two in more detail. With a starting point in Foucault's theorising on governmentality (often via Rose's [1989] reading), the first sees reality TV as a cultural technology which aims at fostering people to be good citizens. The other is based on post-Marxist theories and focuses on reality TV and how it can legitimate class differences.

Reality TV as a cultural technology

The research within this tradition has above all studied makeover television and explored the ways these programmes foster 'good' self-enterprising citizens (see, e.g., Parker 2003; Heller 2007; Ouellette and Hay 2008; Murray and Ouellette 2009). In general, makeover television makes interventions in people's lives with the aim of transforming them into better and happier versions of themselves. Studies of makeover television (mainly in the UK, USA and Australia) have convincingly shown that the participants are expected to adapt to middle-class values and tastes, which are constructed as normative and universally valid (see, e.g., Lewis 2008a; Ouellette and Hay 2008; Palmer 2003). Makeover programmes often start from the assumption that individuals should work on themselves in order to overcome problems and obstacles in their lives, and the changes often involve learning how to be more open-minded, flexible and prepared to collaborate with others. These always successful changes are understood as means for supporting discourses in line with neoliberal policies, i.e., as mechanisms for individualization to prepare oneself for such things as the dismantling of welfare systems.

A good example of such research is Ouellette and Hay's (2008) work on the 'do-good trend' of reality TV in the US. This trend emerged in times when welfare services were being reconfigured and the private sector was expanding in this area. The participants appearing in the show are (as in many other makeover shows) represented as somehow dysfunctional, not self-governing persons. They appear unable or unwilling to manage vital aspects of their everyday lives and are therefore in need of a change that can turn them into better and more self-governing human beings. Through these transformations the programmes promote behaviours and forms of conduct such as home ownership, self-sufficiency, entrepreneurialism and volunteerism, which are intimately linked to a neoliberal political rationality (Ouellette and Hay 2008). A programme like *Home Edition* does not just, as Ouellette and Hay (2008: 44) state, '"encode" these activities ideologically; it demonstrates them, enacts them, and directs TV viewers to a range of resources for accomplishing them on their own'. This approach reveals crucial aspects of reality TV's ideological power, but it has faced criticism for being overly deterministic, as the researchers tend to explain all kind of activities by the governmentality framework (see Skeggs and Wood 2012). This approach also involves, as Morley (2009: 489) points out, a functionalistic tendency that 'presumes the automatic success of a particular form of governmentality in producing a particular mode of subjectivity (the "entrepreneurial self")' and leaves no space for critical audience responses.

Reality TV and social class

Starting from a post-Marxist perspective, another strand of research in the last decade has begun to more explicitly address the question of reality TV and social class (see, e.g., Eriksson 2015; Skeggs and Wood 2012; Wood and Skeggs 2011; Skeggs 2009; Morley 2009; Tyler 2008; Lyle 2008). These scholars see reality TV as a form for exploitation which is 'generated through different forms of exchange, where the moral and the economic work through each other to produce new forms of value' (Skeggs and Wood 2011: 18). These approaches relate to Bourdieu's thoughts about diverse forms of capital, and see class as an effect of legitimations operating so as to make one class gain superiority over another. This is done through institutionalised processes of inclusion/exclusion, particularly through education and the formation of taste. Such processes delegitimise the excluded and tend to see them as responsible for their own exclusion. They are a form of 'symbolic violence' through which the middle classes create boundaries that exclude others and enable them to preserve their own advantages. Ascribing negative values to working-class behaviours, deeming them to be dysfunctional or tasteless, and sometimes more or less offensive, is, as Skeggs (2005: 977) states, 'a mechanism for attributing value to the middle-class self'. The middle-class selves are thus shaped in opposition to what are perceived to be working-class identities, and the excluded identities are understood as clearly separated from one's own.

The studies focusing on reality TV and social class have shown that reality TV has an inherent capacity to provoke feelings crucial for such boundary-forming processes (see, e.g., Skeggs and Wood 2012; Wood and Skeggs 2011; Lyle 2008; Tyler 2008). Historically, emotions like disgust or contempt towards the working class have been fundamental mechanisms in the making of middle-class identities, as part of what distinguishes the middle class from what it is not (Lawler 2005; Skeggs 2005). Sayer's (2005) idea is that emotions suggest an understanding of one's own social position or identity in relation to the object eliciting the feelings. For instance, looking at other people's behaviours with contempt suggests that they are seen as less worthwhile, while feeling envy implies that such behaviours are seen as valuable and might be something to strive for. Sentiments thus appear as crucial to processes of otherness, as they can create and preserve distinctions between groups of people (Miller 1997).

Skeggs and Wood (2012) pursue this post-Marxist perspective in their book-length study of female reality TV audiences. Both methodologically and theoretically innovative, this study explores in particular how ideology works through affective encounters between viewers and television. Affect is, according to this view, 'the missing link in the analysis of ideology' (2012: 184). The study explores this link in relation to four clusters of programmes, all of which somehow involve transforming the involved participants, who then appear to lack certain values. Of particular importance are these programmes' 'melodramatic moments' where intimate emotions are played out in public. As affect is always linked to ideas, the melodramatic moments become moments when social inequalities can be (and are) reinforced. The programme participants can demonstrate their abhorrence of other participants or the expert involved in the show, or they can show their joy or excitement over the transformations they have undergone. A crucial element of this creation of drama is what Skeggs and Wood (2012: 95–97) term the 'judgement shot' in which the participants are put in situations where they speak directly to the camera and evaluate their own or others' actions or emotive responses. These are moments when moral positions are exposed and reality TV invites viewer reactions to the participants' behaviours or lifestyles.

In order to understand these reactions, Skeggs and Wood (2012) used a particular method for viewing sessions called 'text-in-action', which could actually capture spontaneous reactions to reality TV, and combined it with interviews, both individual and in focus groups. The study demonstrates that viewers' reactions were related to the values linked to their social positions. For instance, working-class women reacted with contempt to a participant who saw paid work as the way to gain self-worth, as she thereby devalued the lives of the working-class respondents who were full-time mothers and above all defined their self-worth through sociality and maternity. Through their reactions the working-class respondents thus defended their human worth, while the middle-class respondents were less eager to do so. Instead the latter demonstrated it by displaying their knowledge and cultural taste. Skeggs and Wood's study also shows that the governmentality thesis is questionable. While the middle-class groups did not see the programmes' advice as advice, the working-class respondents could react to advice with anger. The makeover programmes seem to lack the ability to control viewers' reactions in this sense.

The study convincingly demonstrates the need to explore the affective dimensions of reality TV in relation to the making of social class. A key conclusion is that reality TV 'has become a sustainable form of intervention into the public evaluation of people' (Skeggs and Wood 2012: 233) and they therefore suggest that more research needs to be done on how reality TV works to evaluate personhood more generally. In the next section I put forward an approach that aims to be a response to this suggestion. Its purpose is to specify how the producers combine a range of semiotic resources to construct a position from which particular emotive responses become the 'preferred reading'. To understand such elements as meaning potentials means, as Skeggs and Wood show, that there is no 'automatic success' of such constructions; there is always space for reflective and oppositional readings. Viewers can always challenge the normative assumptions behind such constructions.

Approaching reality television with critical discourse analysis: a case study

The core idea of the methodology I suggest here is to treat actions and artefacts used in communication as *semiotic resources*. It is essentially based on the MCDA-approach, developed by Machin and Mayr (2012, 2013), and van Leeuwen's (2008) approach to Critical Discourse

Analysis (see also Kress and van Leeuwen 1996, 2001; van Leeuwen 2005). What I propose can be seen as a form of social actor analysis, implying a focus on the representational strategies used to depict participants and their actions.

A crucial premise is to see discourse as *recontextualization of social practice* (van Leeuwen 2008). This means that this approach concentrates on how 'social practices (including discursive practices) are turned into discourse (into representations of social practices) in the context of specific discursive practices' (van Leeuwen and Wodak 1999: 93). A particular programme represents what can be identified as specific social practices, but like all forms of recontextualization, the production process necessarily entails making choices about how to represent the practice in question. In such processes fundamental transformations take place. Van Leeuwen (2008) conceptualises these as follows: *substitutions* (some semiotic elements are replaced by others); *deletions* (some elements are deleted); *rearrangements* (the order of elements is changed); *additions* (new elements are added); *reactions* (participants' subjective reactions to activities are represented); and *purposes* (which are added to activities). Van Leeuwen (2008) also points out that recontextualizations involve *legitimations* and *evaluations* of social practices. Besides representing social practices, texts explain and legitimate (or de-legitimate and critique) these practices. They can also involve evaluations of these practices.

The choices made in the recontextualization process can be described as the 'doing of discourses'. These discourses constitute a form of knowledge or 'script' about what goes on in the social practice being represented and involve ideas about how to value and understand these activities (Machin and Mayr 2013: 359). When analysing a multimodal medium like television, it is important to keep in mind that such scripts consist of complex combinations of semiotic resources: spoken discourse (voice-overs, interactions between participants), audio (music, sound effects), visuals (camera work), graphics (written texts, other figures) and editing (cuts, how sequences are ordered).

I devote the rest of this chapter to providing examples of how this approach can be used. These examples come from the analysis of a docu-soap titled *A Mighty Journey with Morgan and Ola Conny* (Hereafter: *A Mighty Journey*; Sw: 'En stark resa med Morgan och Ola-Conny'), airing on Swedish television (Channel 5) since 2012. The programme is structured around the international travels of two working-class characters, storekeeper Morgan Carlsson and shop assistant Ola-Conny Wallgren. The two visit famous cities and tourist resorts, and the programme recontextualizes diverse social practices associated with travelling and tourism, like checking in and out of hotels, dining, going on guided tours, etc. *A Mighty Journey* is a spin-off from another show, *Ullared*, a docu-soap following events around a popular, low-cost rural shopping outlet. The programme zooms in on customers' consumption of cheap products, but a key element is that members of the outlet's staff also appear in the episodes. Some of them, like Morgan and Ola-Conny, appear regularly, and this exposure has made them well-known figures in Sweden.

Both shows are part of a wider trend of reality TV using representational strategies that ridicule working-class participants' behaviours, ideas and lifestyles (Eriksson 2015). In *A Mighty Journey* Morgan and Ola-Conny are represented as uneducated, insular and lacking the cultural and social resources necessary to handle the situations they face while travelling. They are generally constructed as making blunders and getting involved in circumstances characterised by confusion and misunderstandings, situations that easily come across as both comical for the viewer and embarrassing for the two participants.

The recontextualizations I will discuss in this section are thus characterised by what I see as the use of *ridiculing strategies*, i.e., the producers use various semiotic resources to make fun of the main characters' actions. The choices made to achieve comic effects – 'the doing of discourse' – are what the following analysis aims to reveal. A basic assumption is that laughter and ridicule are crucial to processes of boundary-formation and can play a role for how class differences are reproduced (Tyler 2008: 23). In what follows I focus especially on the construction of the participants' mental processes, i.e., processes that can be divided into three classes: cognition (thinking, knowing, understanding), affect (liking, disliking or fearing) and perception (seeing, hearing, perceiving). In spoken or written language, participants' mental processes are signalled by verbs, but in reality TV they are mainly signalled by other semiotic resources (e.g., music, images, sound effects and editing) and how they are combined.

Ridiculing strategies

An indispensable semiotic resource in *A Mighty Journey* consists of interactions between the main characters and other persons like waitresses, reception clerks, people in the street, shop assistants, etc. These interactions can be considered standard social practices while travelling. They are, of course, arranged for the purposes of the programme, and are somehow initiated by the production team, but they appear spontaneous and in that sense to be real situations. Other persons taking part in these sequences may have been instructed in advance about what will happen – after all the camera and production team are present – but judging by what is shown on screen, the talk that takes place in these situations appears to be unplanned and authentic (unscripted). How these sequences unfold seems to be highly unpredictable.

Despite this spontaneity, what the viewers ultimately receive are recontextualizations of the interactions, characterised by a number of choices made during the production process. An interaction is (most probably) chosen for a humorous potential that can be exploited in the editing process. By adding certain elements (e.g., sound, music, images) and deleting or rearranging parts of the interactions the main characters' mental processes, and especially their cognitive and perceptual abilities, are depicted in ways that help the viewer to see the humour in the situations. As there are no voice-overs in the show (except those voice-overs done by the main characters themselves), the visuals and the added effects (music, images, sounds), as well as how they are combined, are central to the construction of Morgan's and Ola-Conny's mental processes.

The interplay of talk and music

In the first example I will show how music is added and edited to interact with the participants' talk so as to create laughable situations. In this particular scene Morgan and Ola-Conny visit Venice Beach in Los Angeles and decide to buy ice-cream. It begins with Ola-Conny asking Morgan if they should have an ice-cream, and at this moment music is added (Figure 40.1A). Film scholars have pointed to the role of music in creating narratives and indicating mental states. Gorbman (1987) shows that music can, for instance, follow actions very closely or suggest the tempo of actions or moments of confusion. Music also has the capacity to set the mood of films, or particular scenes, and provides insights into characters' inner feelings (fear, joy, disillusionment, etc.) (see Wingstedt, Brändström and Berg 2010). In this case the music begins with a deep clarinet tone which very slowly bounces around a bit, a sound that in classical music often indicates something humorous. Semiotically it is soft, rounded, and a bit clumsy sounding, suggesting a childish domain, but also anticipating that something funny is about to happen. It could accompany the entrance of a circus clown wearing big red shoes and with a painted sad-face, or it could be part of a cartoon where the tempo is slow

Figure 40.1   Original episode aired April 15, 2013 by © Kanal 5, produced by *Bada Bing*

but something exciting is 'lurking around the corner'. A harsher, sharper, more agile sound that moved with greater precision would certainly create another atmosphere and elicit different viewer expectations.

The music fades when Morgan and Ola-Conny step inside the little shop, suggesting that this is the event the music has signalled will occur. Morgan orders two milkshakes with a heavy Swedish accent and the clerk behind the counter does not understand his order (Figure 40.1B). Morgan repeats 'milkshake' but it does not help. At this moment Ola-Conny joins in and repeats the word, which helps, as the clerk responds 'ah milkshake'. When the clerk asks what flavour they would like, Ola-Conny obviously does not understand the question and repeats 'milkshake', leading the clerk to rephrase the question. Ola-Conny provides the same answer as previously, demonstrating his limited knowledge of English.

This cuts to a shot from a side angle at the counter, and the two choose chocolate and raspberry. Morgan orders a small one in his a heavy Swedish accent, pronouncing 'little' *leet-lay*. This cuts to a medium shot focusing on the mixer while the clerk pours milk into it with his back to the camera. Here the next musical clip starts. It is a xylophone-type instrument combined with strings (probably violin) played pizzicato. With its quicker tempo and a sharper sound, it contrasts with the former musical clip. Nevertheless it leads one's thoughts to the same childish domain. It is a light, hollow sort of sound, lively and energetic, indicating that something simple and playful is going on.

While the clerk prepares the milkshakes Ola-Conny asks him what his favourite flavour is. The clerk says 'pistachio'. The camera follows his movement towards the counter and zooms in on a tub of light-green ice-cream, which he points to. When the clerk reaches the counter, the music rises in pitch, and then stops at the moment when he points out the ice-cream. Right when the music goes silent, Ola-Conny grunts understandingly and then says the Swedish word for pear (*päron*). The music is clearly fitted in with the ongoing talk; it goes quiet just before Ola-Conny's response, and the silence serves to accentuate this statement. To the clerk he says in Swedish 'we say pear in Sweden' (*vi säger päron i Sverige*) which reveals his lack of knowledge in this area. The Swedish word for pistachio ('*pistage*') has a very similar pronunciation to the English word 'pistachio', so for a Swedish audience it doesn't make any sense to interpret it as pear.

This is followed by a rather long and convoluted dialogue about how to translate the word raspberry. This discussion is provoked by a question from an invisible member of the production team who asks Ola-Conny about his choice, and he seems to be unsure what raspberry is. Morgan suggests that it is rhubarb, and as he does so the violin rises in pitch and then stops. There is then a direct cut to Ola-Conny who agrees that it must mean rhubarb. He repeats the Swedish word '*rabarber*' in a loud and clear voice, as if the salesperson would understand it if he articulated it clearly enough. Attempting to explain what rhubarb is he says 'big leaves' (Sw: *stora löv*) to the clerk, but as rhubarb is not a very common ice-cream flavour this appears as a rather odd suggestion. This leads the clerk to try to clarify what raspberry is, saying that it is a berry smaller than strawberries. Morgan and Ola-Conny continue discussing this issue, and Morgan then actually suggests '*hallon*', the Swedish word for raspberry, but Ola-Conny doubts this, and continues thinking aloud about what kind of berry it could be. This rather absurd discussion continues outside the shop with Ola-Conny trying to figure out the English word for '*jordgubbar*' (strawberries) (Figure 40.1C). He goes through the names of different berries and returns to the English term 'strawberry' trying to figure out what it means. He then clearly demonstrates his lack of knowledge when, in Swedish, he poses the question 'what the hell's the word for strawberries' (Sw: *vad fan heter jordgubbar*). This again demonstrates their limited cognitive capabilities and language skills.

So, in this brief sequence (1 min 54 sec), several more general representational strategies of ridicule are used to represent Morgan's and Ola-Conny's actions. The basis for this is to choose recorded interaction-sequences containing misunderstandings between participants. These misunderstandings are generally due to difficulties in reaching a joint understanding of the situation. A crucial element of these interactions is the off-screen but clearly audible interviewer who elicits comments or reflections about what is taking place. It is notable that he never tries to help the two to manage the situation, even if it seems obvious that he could. During editing, the producers delete parts of the original conversation (processes which I do not have access to) and add others, thereby directing attention to certain aspects of the original conversation. The addition of music is a crucial technique to establish a mental frame for these interactions and highlight particular utterances as especially entertaining (or silly), making them into jokes or punch lines. Together, these techniques form a scene in which the two main characters' ability to perceive and understand their surroundings is belittled and diminished.

The actions taking place in this scene easily come across as laughable, and it all stems from Morgan and Ola-Conny's apparently limited cognitive and perceptual abilities. It is more than obvious that their knowledge of the English language is limited. The well-educated Swedish middle class would know the right English terms for these berries (as would many children), and they would certainly know how to order a milkshake at Venice Beach. So, the two appear uneducated as well as incapable of logical thinking. These scripts fit well into a discourse of devaluing working-class people.

Zooming in on, and out from, details in the setting

Another semiotic resource, also related to the editing techniques and visual dimensions, that is used to stress Morgan's and Ola-Conny's mental states is to include images that help form scripts about their (mis-)perceptions of the situations they are in. Such images focus on particular details of the setting, and function as cues demonstrating their lack of attention to what appear to be crucial aspects of the situation.

A good example of this strategy is from the first season when Morgan and Ola-Conny are checking into their hotel in London. At the counter, the clerk gives them directions to their room and stresses that when they use the lift they must insert the key card into the slot to get to their floor (the 11th). Ola-Conny responds that he understands, but while walking towards the lift he admits to Morgan that he understood it in broad terms, but not completely. They soon get out of the lift but realise they are on the wrong floor. Back in the lift we see a thumb pushing the correct right button (Figure 40.2A), but it does not light up. This cuts to an image of the sign saying: 'Please insert your key card into the slot to access floors 3–14' (Figure 40.2B), suggesting that this text is hard to miss. When the door opens they are back on the ground floor (Figure 40.2C). They step out of the lift and inform the clerk that they are 'coming no up'. By integrating the image of the sign into the scene and linking it to the pair's failure to reach their floor, this sequence underlines their inability to comprehend even rather simple and common information about checking into hotels.

The opposite technique also occurs in the programme: the camera zooming out and bringing into view aspects of the setting of relevance for the ongoing interaction. This nevertheless seems to have a similar function. By zooming out the camera reveals elements of the setting that the participants seem to be unaware of, thereby demonstrating their narrow perceptual capacity. In these moments, the role of the camera shifts from that of a passive 'fly-on-the-wall', to being a more active participant in the ongoing events and noticing elements outside the main characters' reach.

Figure 40.2   Original episode aired April 2, 2012 by © Kanal 5, produced by *Bada Bing*

While in Las Vegas, Ola-Conny says several times that he associates this city with a giant neon cowboy who lifts his hat, and he expresses a desire to see it. One evening when Morgan surprises him by renting a limousine, Ola-Conny asks the chauffeur to take them there. According to the chauffeur they will find this sign near what seems to be a huge shopping mall, but they will have to get out of the car and walk to it. While they are walking through the mall, the chauffeur points in what he thinks is the right direction (Figure 40.3A). Here a musical soundtrack is turned up and the dialogue is turned down. We hear a monotonous synthesiser occasionally interspersed with the cheerful sound of bell-chimes. The talk continues, though more quietly and with a light echo effect indicating a dreamlike state of mind. This happens as the camera becomes a more active participant in the action, zooming out and changing perspective from a medium shot to a low-angle viewpoint. Behind Ola-Conny and the chauffeur, Morgan is turning towards a neon cowboy that is becoming visible in the background (Figure 40.3B). The music and sound effects reinforce what Morgan could be experiencing. They convey the kind of moment of powerful emotion when one becomes very focused on a particular object and everything else recedes into the background. The talk disappears and the visual experience becomes the main event. Morgan takes a step towards the others, points at the neon cowboy and draws Ola-Conny's attention to it. When Morgan says this, the echo effect is gone. The musical bit can still be heard, but is softer. When Ola-Conny discovers the sign, an image of a (probably different) neon cowboy sign is cut into the picture together with a yee-ha-sound, played while the cowboy lifts his hat (Figure 40.3C). The two soon discover that the cowboy in front of them is not lifting his hat, and Ola-Conny expresses his disappointment. At this moment we hear what must be the original background noise from the mall, which indicates that they are leaving the 'dream world' and returning to reality.

As these examples show, the visual work is certainly crucial to forming scripts that represent the participants as uneducated, silly or inattentive. Images that zoom in on details in the setting or certain facial expressions, and an active camera that can shift its role while events are unfolding, are dimensions of the visual work that help to establish such meanings. This also shows that the ridiculing strategy permeates the production team's work, from filming the two in diverse situations to the final editing where the programme gets its definite outline.

Discussion and conclusion

The above analysis reveals that two particular forms of de-legitimation play prominent roles, what van Leeuwen (2008: Ch. 6) terms *mythopoesis* and *moral evaluations*. The former refers to de-legitimation through storytelling. By using two already well-known characters with pre-established working-class identities, and setting them up in situations related to tourism, humorous stories about working-class behaviours can be constructed. The basic feature of this storytelling is what appears to be the two protagonists' lack of knowledge (especially language skills) and experience of the ways of the world, but these are formed and reinforced through the editing process and the use of multimodal semiotic resources. These recontextualizations contain moral evaluations. By repeatedly constructing Morgan and Ola-Conny as uneducated, silly and severely inexperienced in the ways of the world, the programme implies a viewpoint from which their actions easily can be seen as laughable or embarrassing (on their behalf). And it is their representation as working-class characters, and thus as part of working-class culture, that makes them laughable or embarrassing. It is notable that much of this evaluation, as well as the realisation of delegitimizing discourses, is carried out visually by making deletions and rearrangements, zooming in and out, and adding music and other sound effects.

Figure 40.3 Original episode aired April 22, 2013 by © Kanal 5, produced by *Bada Bing*

I read this ongoing delegitimation of the working class in entertainment media as part of a wider discursive and societal shift now taking place in Sweden. The ridiculing of working-class people belongs to a wider discourse that has gained particular importance within the neoliberal thinking that infuses today's political agenda and public debates. Increasingly we find the working class being represented as something problematic, with their behaviours and lifestyles depicted as inappropriate and less valuable than those of the middle class. What we are witnessing is the spread of 'a moral underclass discourse' which tends to see the working class's problems as an effect of their own culture, and not as structurally caused (cf. Levitas 1998). In the end such a discourse serves political purposes, as it facilitates political decisions that reduce social benefits like unemployment insurance and sick-leave benefits, thereby enabling tax reductions mainly benefitting people with higher incomes.

Further reading

Eriksson, G. and Machin, D. (2017). The role of music in ridiculing the working classes in reality television. In L. Way and S. MCKerrell (eds.), *Music as multimodal discourse: Semiotics, power and protest*, 21–45. London: Bloomsbury.
This paper looks at the precise deployment of music in reality TV. It argues that music can operate in a way that language and images cannot, providing ideas about, and evaluation of, characters, actions, setting and activities.
Sayer, A. (2005). *The moral significance of class*. Cambridge: Cambridge University Press.
This book discusses the moral experiences of people's experiences of class inequalities. Among other things it argues the importance of involving people's sentiments when discussing social class.
Wood, H. and Skeggs, B. (eds.) (2011). *Reality television class*. London: Palgrave Macmillan.
This edited volume contains a collection of papers concerned with how social class is reproduced in reality TV. It provides very useful theoretical insights and discussions in this area.

References

Andrejevic, M. (2004). *Reality TV: The work of being watched*. New York: Rowman and Littlefield Publishers.
Bonner, F. (2003). *Ordinary television: Analyzing popular TV*. London: Sage.
Curnutt, H. (2011). Durable participants: A generational approach to reality TV's 'ordinary' labor pool. *Media, Culture & Society* 33(/): 1061–1076.
Eriksson, Göran. (2015). Ridicule as a strategy for the recontextualization of the working class: A multimodal analysis of class-making on Swedish reality television. *Critical Discourse Studies* 12(1):, 20–38.
Gorbman, C. (1987). *Unheard melodies: Narrative film music*. London: BFI.
Heller D. (2007). *Makeover television: Realities remodelled*. London: I.B. Tauris.
Hill, A. (2005). *Reality TV: Audiences and popular factual television*. Abingdon: Routledge.
Hill, A. (2007). *Restyling factual TV: Audiences and news, documentary and reality genres*. London: Routledge.
Hill, A. (2015). *Reality TV*. London: Routledge.
Hill, A. and Palmer, G. (eds.) (2002). Big brother [Special Issue]. *Television and New Media*, 3, 3.
Holmes, S. and Jermyn, D. (2004). *Understanding reality television*. Abingdon: Routledge.
Kavka, M. (2008). *Reality television, affect and intimacy: Reality matters*. London: Palgrave Macmillan.
Kress, G. and van Leeuwen, T. (1996). *Reading images: The grammar of visual design*. London: Routledge.
Kress, G. and van Leeuwen, T. (2001). *Multimodal discourse: The modes and the media of contemporary communication*. London: Arnold.
Lawler, S. (2005). Disgusted subjects: The making of middle-class identities. *Sociological Review* 53: 429–446.
Levitas, R. (1998). *The inclusive society? Social exclusion and new labour*. London: Palgrave Macmillan.
Lewis, T. (2008a). *Smart living : Lifestyle media and popular expertise*. New York: Peter Lang.
Lewis, T. (ed.) (2008b). Television transformations: Revealing the makeover show [Special Issue]. *Continuum* 22(4): 441–446.
Lorenzo-Dus, N. and Garcés-Conejos Blitvich, P. (2013). *Real talk: Reality television and discourse analysis in action*. London. Palgrave Macmillan.

Lyle, S. (2008). (Mis)recognition and the middle-class/bourgeois gaze: A case study of Wife Swap. *Critical Discourse Studies* 5(4): 319–330.

Machin, D. (2013). What is multimodal critical discourse studies? *Critical Discourse Studies* 10(4): 347–355.

Machin, D. and Mayr, A. (2012). *How to do critical discourse analysis*. London: Sage.

Machin, D. and Mayr, A. (2013). Personalising crime and crime-fighting in factual television: An analysis of social actors and transitivity in language and images. *Critical Discourse Studies*. http://dx.doi.org/10.1080/17405904.2013.813771

Machin, D. and Richardson, J. E. (2008). Renewing an academic interest in structural inequalities. *Critical Discourse Studies* 5(4): 281–287.

Magder, T. (2009). Television 2.0: The business of American television in transition. In S. Murray and L. Ouellette (eds.), *Reality television: Remaking television culture,* 141–164. New York: New York University Press.

Miller, W. I. (1997). *The anatomy of disgust*. London: Harvard University Press.

Morley, D. (2009). Mediated class-ifications: Representations of class and culture in contemporary British Television. *European Journal of Cultural Studies* 12(4): 487–508.

Murray, S. and Ouellette, L. (2009). *Reality television: Remaking television culture*. New York: New York University Press.

Negra, D., Pike, K. and Radley, E. (eds.) (2013). Gender and reality TV [Special Issue]. *Television and New Media* 14(3).

Orbe, M. (ed.) (2008). Race and reality TV [Special Issue]. *Critical Studies in Media and Communication* 25(4).

Ouellette, L. and Hay, J. (2008). *Better living through reality TV*. Oxford: Blackwell Publishing.

Palmer, G. (2003). *Discipline and liberty: Television and governance*. Manchester: Manchester University Press.

Raphael, C. (2009). The political economic origins of reali-TV. In S. Murray and L. Ouelette (eds.), *Reality television: Remaking television culture,* 123–140. New York: New York University Press.

Rose, N. 1989). *Inventing ourselves: Psychology, power and personhood*. Cambridge: Cambridge University Press.

Sayer, A. (2005). *The moral significance of class*. Cambridge: Cambridge University Press.

Skeggs, B. (2005). The making of class and gender through visualizing moral subject formation. *Sociology* 39: 965–982.

Skeggs, B. (2009). The moral economy of person production: The class relations of self-performance on 'reality television'. *Sociological Review* 57(4): 626–644.

Skeggs, B. and Wood, H. (2011). Introduction: Real class. In H. Wood and B. Skeggs (eds.), *Reality television and class,* 1–29. London: Palgrave Macmillan.

Skeggs, B. and Wood, H. (2012). *Reacting to reality television: Performance, audience and value*. London: Routledge.

Turner, G. (2010). *Ordinary people and the media: The demotic turn*. London: Sage.

Tyler, I. (2008). "Chav mum chav scum": Class disgust in contemporary Britain. *Feminist Media Studies* 8: 17–34.

Van Leeuwen, T. (2005). *Introducing social semiotics*. London: Routledge.

Van Leeuwen, T. (2008). *Discourse and practice: New tools for critical discourse analysis*. Oxford: Oxford University Press.

Van Leeuwen, T. and Wodak, R. (1999). Legitimizing immigration control: A discourse-historical analysis. *Discourse Studies* 1(1): 83–118.

Wingstedt, J., Brändström, S. and Berg, J. (2010). Narrative music, visuals and meaning in film. *Visual Communication* 9(2): 192–210.

Wood, H. and Skeggs, B. (eds.) (2011). *Reality television and class*. London: Palgrave Macmillan.

41

Critical discourse analysis and film

John A. Bateman

Introduction: setting the scene

Although the original concerns of work in and around CDA were with 'verbal' or 'textual' forms of expression, calls for the inclusion of other communicative forms are now common. In their introduction to their extensive survey of CDA research, for example, Wodak and Meyer (2015: 2) explicitly signpost 'non-verbal (semiotic, multimodal, visual) aspects of inter-action and communication: gesture, images, film, the internet and multimedia' as appropriate targets. In this chapter, we pursue this with respect to film, setting out some of the issues that such an extension involves. These issues concern not only the object and practice of CDA but also raise interesting questions of where (and if!) 'boundaries' between CDA and other forms of analysis can usefully be drawn.

The reasons for engaging with film from a CDA perspective are many, largely overlapping with the equally diverse reasons for engaging with text and verbal language shown in other chapters of this handbook. Moreover, since both written and spoken language are common-place in film, techniques or hypotheses derived for language are also relevant for film analysis. Even apparently spontaneous spoken language, with all its 'paraverbal' dimensions of perfor-mance and social, regional and ethnic variation, becomes in the context of film just another representational resource. Such language choices can then naturally be seen as targets of CDA. The attribution of regional or ethnic dialects to certain characters rather than others (particu-larly where this choice is relatively free, as in animation), the employment of code-switching in films depicting ethnically diverse situations and several similar phenomena have all received critical consideration; Androutsopoulos (2012) offers useful discussion and examples.

Going beyond the strictly language-related components of film, many of the concerns raised for language also have natural correlates among other areas of a film's complete multi-modal ensemble. For example, where certain topics or groups may in verbal texts be rendered invisible by suppression, in film certain kinds of characters, actions or locations may similarly be effaced by not showing them or by showing them in a particular light. Equally, indications of social and ethnic positions can be given visually in terms of depicted attributes, gestures and actions rather than in language behaviour. Indeed, many communicative strategies appear shared across verbal discourse and audiovisual discourses more generally and have already received attention in critical media studies (e.g., Mack and Ott 2014; Holtzman, Sharpe and Gardner 2014). The 'filmic' construction of a broad range of social groups has been addressed, for example, extending significantly beyond the more traditional sociological variables of race, class and gender. Thus, depictions of mental instability (Fleming and Manvell 1986), of alcoholism (Denzin 2004), of terrorists (Vanhala 2010), of school teachers (Paietta 2007), of politicians (Gianos 1998), of old age (Cohen-Shavev and Marcus 2007) and countless others already constitute staples of film research (cf. Helsby 2005). Very few of these adopt methods from CDA, however, although Gatling, Mills and Lindsay's (2014) joint consideration of aspects of language, action and depicted objects in order to address the multimodal construction of 'middle age' in comedy films is one exception.

Most critical analyses of film have origins located in media studies and visual communication. The ideological and sociocultural import of images, even static images, has a considerable tradition of study of its own pre-dating CDA. For film, the potentially misleading or misdirecting role of (audio-)visual representations has received particularly close attention in work on documentaries, since in documentaries there are always (by definition) 'truth claims' of various kinds being made – even though the precise scope of such claims may not always be clear (cf. Rosenthal 1999; Nichols 2001; Kahana 2015). Issues of ideological construction are by no means limited to the documentary, however. Canonised in the literature, for example, is the extreme controversy that arose around David Wark Griffith's *Birth of a Nation* (1915).[1] This film is widely considered an aesthetic and production landmark in the development of cinema *tout court*, while simultaneously being condemned for what have been equally broadly considered as blatantly racist and white supremacist depictions (cf. Taylor 1996).

In important respects, the link drawn here to media studies exhibits many parallels to the development of CDA. Concerns with potential distortions in journalism and the mass media became a significant area of study in the 1940s and 1950s as questions of the political and ideological effect of media messages came under increasing scrutiny. Important techniques of qualitative and quantitative analysis were established, subsequently drawing on theoretical positions on the interrelationships between power, ideology and media founded on Foucault and Frankfurt School criticism, equally well known in the context of CDA. Moreover, just as concern with the analysis of verbal media messages subsequently combined with emerging linguistic techniques for textual analysis to give rise to traditional CDA, similar developments occurred with respect to visual analysis in media studies. It is therefore now not uncommon to hear of the need for *critical* visual analysis (e.g., Rose 2012). Nevertheless, although there is some work within CDA overlapping with these concerns – as in Richardson and Wodak's (2009) study of political argumentation and ideologically oriented visual representation – research in critical visual studies and CDA show few interactions. Texts promoting critical visual studies traditionally make no reference to CDA approaches and methods.

It is then broadly accepted both that films and their depictions of society are appropriate targets of critical analysis and that, sometimes, films may attempt to be actively critical themselves. This raises many opportunities for beneficial combinations of CDA questions and methods and the sociocultural analysis of film, even though this potential has hardly been tapped to date. To take this further, it is important that the long and varied traditions of critical analysis within film studies be sufficiently respected. We begin the discussion of the present chapter, therefore, by setting out in more detail something of this diversity of approaches within film studies that may usefully be considered in relation to the issues raised by CDA. We then address the question of whether CDA has its own distinctive contributions to make to critical film analysis and to what extent it is possible to differentiate a CDA of film from other critical stances that have been adopted. This in turn prepares the ground for a brief case study suggesting how discourse methods might be applied when critically analysing film. Finally, we conclude the chapter with a brief outlook for future potential directions for a film-oriented CDA and raise in particular the question of whether film offers a further medium in which CDA analyses can be undertaken.

Critical film analysis within film studies

Approaching film from a CDA orientation needs to be seen within the context of 'multi-modal CDA', in which methods explicitly targeting ensembles of diverse semiotic expressive resources are developed. CDA work of this kind is now becoming a major research direction in its own right; Ledin and Machin (this volume) provide more details. The extent to which this extension has been made for film is, however, still very limited. Moreover, a potential weak spot for such a development can be identified in Machin and Mayr's (2012: 209) observation that much of the work on multimodality emerging from linguistics over the past 10 years has tended to act as if it emerged independently both of other semiotic approaches and of work in other fields. This would be a disastrous strategy to pursue when attempting to establish a CDA of film, however. In many respects film studies became 'politicised' as a field far earlier than was the case with linguistics and CDA. Appropriate awareness of this long established tradition is therefore a prerequisite for any explicitly film-oriented CDA. Consequently, in this section, we briefly characterise some of the more important or influential of these film studies approaches from the perspective of their potential relevance for CDA.

Apparatus theory

Apparatus theory (Baudry 1974) is probably the most far reaching of associations between film and ideology to have been drawn and, as a consequence, is nowadays considered by the majority of researchers to have seriously overshot its target: we raise it here, therefore, both for completeness and as a point of comparison with other approaches we describe below. The essential idea of apparatus theory is that the very facts of the technological production and manner of consumption of film are already inescapably ideologically inscribed. The manner of technological production of showing images produced by a camera places the viewer in the position of that camera and so constructs the spectator as an 'all knowing' subject of a very particular 'externally controlled' kind. Moreover, since the production of film aims to create a seamless experience very different from the fragments from which films are actually built, the apparatus obscures its manner of construction, further positioning spectators in ways that hide film's ideologically conditioned, socioeconomic (i.e., generally capitalist) and gendered (i.e., generally male) conditions of production. The situation of consumption of films whereby subjects are placed unmoving in dark spaces is also seen in apparatus theory as a form of sub-jugation: spectators are then doubly bound, delivered over to the ideological workings of the apparatus itself.

Critiques made of this approach generally involve its disregard of the agentive role of spectators. As now well known from many forms of media research, films do not act 'automatically' on spectators as passive consumers; individual spectators are active interpreters, making sense of what they see and hear and bringing their own experiences and socio-cultural positions to bear. In addition, it would appear from apparatus theory that the use of film for diverse ideological purposes would be ruled out: simply using film as such would already have positioned recipients adversely, which again seems overly strong. Nevertheless, concern with an ideological pre-structured production industry is in many respects quite justified. Studies focusing on the appearance and roles of certain groups in both film production and the resulting films show considerable bias. Eschholz, Bufkin and Long (2002) document both the depiction and participation of women and racial/ethnic groups in film and TV, for example, revealing a state of affairs in considerable need of critique and action. Despite occasional claims that the situation has improved, current statistics on the number of woman directors, screenplay writers and major female characters in films paint a very different picture. The consequences of this continuing bias on film production should not therefore be underestimated.

Gender

More nuanced characterisations of intrinsic ideological placements of spectators are explored in feminist film theory, where it is the portrayal of women and gender relations that receives central attention. Here it is argued that certain decisions regularly taken in film production systematically construct restricted or imbalanced gender roles and, moreover, impose these on spectators. This aspect of film therefore needs to be problematized in order to perform much needed social critique. In this respect, much feminist film analysis may be characterised as pursuing aims entirely consonant with similar concerns voiced within CDA.

The starting point for feminist film theory is the seminal work of Mulvey (1975) and her application of certain aspects of Freudian psychoanalytic theory. The basic dimensions of Mulvey's model are the following. First, film is seen as essentially voyeuristic, inducing *scopophilia*. Second, that view is gendered in that gender distinctions are constructed as integral components of film design at all levels. Thus, in the traditional films on which Mulvey largely based her original analyses, it is the male characters who act and who drive the narrative forward. The function of female characters is 'to be looked at' – i.e., they support scopophilia and hold the action up rather than letting it unfold. This can be constructed employing the full gamut of technical devices available to film, including camera angles, camera distances, movement, durations of shots, lighting effects and many more. Well-known gendered motifs of technical device deployment include different lighting schemes for male and female characters, different degrees of focus (e.g., soft-focus for women characters) and so on.

Thus, following Mulvey's line of argument, it is far more likely that the introduction of a female character will be managed in a relatively passive fashion, allowing the camera to dwell on her, often from what might be assumed to be the perspective of others (in all likelihood male) in the film rather than in her own right. The camera is thereby seen to perform the 'male gaze': that is, the camera looks as a male figure in the narrative would be expected to look. Then, in a manner reminiscent of apparatus theory, this construction is taken to be imposed on *all* spectators, not just men. The camera and its positioning of spectators is consequently taken as intrinsically gendered.

Mulvey also draws conclusions for the larger narrative sweep of films drawing on the psychoanalytic model. Freudian notions of women constituting 'threats' for men – particularly as a source of 'castration anxiety' (in Freud's technical psychoanalytic sense) – are seen as leading to the emergence of particular kinds of roles for women, such as that of the femme fatale common in film noir. Such anxieties are also considered to be operative in both 'fetishism', in the form of star worship and, via voyeurism and control, narrative arcs involving punishment – as when, for example, the femme fatale is captured, imprisoned or reformed. A further case of a reoccurring narrative arc is that of the 'Oedipal trajectory', several illustrations of which are discussed in Mulvey's (1989) 'Afterthoughts' on her original proposals. The ease with which many films allow such descriptions may well speak to the fundamental nature of these narrative structures regardless of any claimed psychoanalytic foundations.

The films of Alfred Hitchcock have been found to be particularly rich in providing material for analyses of this kind (cf. Doane 1988; Modleski 1988), although he was probably himself equally familiar with these patterns and so may have deployed them deliberately. Regardless of this, however, the analyses offered remain highly illuminating and present valuable interpretative hypotheses, again regardless of whether one subscribes to the psychoanalytic model or not.

Although it is often straightforward to find examples where gender appears to be constructed in the manner feminist film analysts suggest, it is considerably more difficult to assess such cases' generality and actual effect. For example, one of Mulvey's earlier discussions involves the filmic depiction of women using close-ups and camera angles to construct the 'fragmented body' taken as typical for the male gaze; this is assumed to work against the development or depiction of full characters and to objectify the person shown. However, the extent to which such phenomena are present in films more broadly or are actually attended to by spectators as differentiating genders is not yet known. This might then be an area where a more explicit CDA-style treatment could be of benefit.

Genres

Although not an unproblematic construct in film theory (cf. Altman 1999), 'genres' often appear to be readily recognisable for film audiences and also contribute significantly to viewing choices. Consequently, Tudor (1974: 180) argues that it would be 'almost perverse' not to consider the sociocultural consequences of the prevalence and organisation of genres. The potential for ideological construction and misconstrual within particular genres has therefore also received critical attention, offering further opportunities for contributions from a CDA perspective.

In film studies, the genres most frequently addressed are the usual suspects of Westerns, gangster films and horror films, all of which combine highly conventionalised story arcs and stylistic choices. Common readings of these genres include statements expressed in terms of oppositions: Westerns raise issues of civilisation/wilderness, of freedom/law. Gangster films often involve mystification and the mechanistic operation of unseen forces, reducing individual choice and the possibility of morality; and horror films involve oppositions such as natural/supernatural and employ cumulative shock as a narrative strategy. Tudor suggests further that all three genres in fact exhibit a deeper, reoccurring pattern in which the use of violence is constructed as the ultimate and necessary solution to any problems raised (Tudor 1974: 213). Such genres may then both reflect and constitute social configurations that may be considered coercive, male-dominated and exploitative.

Other 'genres' have also been explored with respect to their ideological import. Particularly well known in this regard are science fiction films and war films. Science fiction, especially in the 1950s and early 1960s, has often been read as commenting on social issues as well as drawing more or less explicit connections to the Cold War then holding between the Soviet Union and the US. War films have also been picked out as offering sensitive indicators of broader social movements and attitudes. Kellner (2010), for example, draws out detailed resonances between the approach to war films taken in Hollywood and political positions in the 'Bush-Cheney Era'.

There are also genres that adopt ideological and political themes and criticism quite explicitly – indeed, social problems have always belonged to the repertoire of films, either in their own right or as part of the background web of presuppositions that a film constructs. The usual dimensions around which selections of problematic issues are organised include social problems, gender, race, nation, class and politics (cf., e.g., Benshoff and Griffin 2009;

Holtzman, Sharpe and Gardner 2014) – although any theme can be employed for probing social issues as these overviews provide ample examples for.

The documentary/fiction cline and social commentary

Broadly cross-cutting genres, issues concerning the 'authenticity' of filmic representations also raise significant challenges. Although one of the potential functions of film has always been to convey information about the real world rather than operating as a medium of storytelling, both the nature of truth in filmic depictions and the nature of fiction conspire to make such distinctions less than clear-cut. As Kuehl (1999) sets out, 'dramatized' documentaries are as old as cinema itself. In 1907, the Paris film company Films D'Art produced *L'Assassinat du Duc de Guise,* which was meant to portray a 'real event' from French history, complete with musical accompaniment and the theatrical style performances then conventional for the medium. Similarly, Georges *Méliès' Le Couronnement du roi Édouard VII* (1902) filmed not the coronation itself (due to technological production constraints such as lighting) but a 'construction' or 're-creation' of the supposedly real events. Subsequently, classic documentaries have regularly blurred the distinction between 'simply' documenting and re-creating – probably the most well-known case being Robert J. Flaherty's *Nanook of the North* (1922), which quite explicitly took the position that 'real events' need to be appropriately 'arranged' in order to function effectively as documentary. Also relevant here are Nichols's (2001: 99, 138) distinct documentary *modes of representation.*

Since there is then no clear divide between fiction and documentary films with respect to their expressive forms, it is generally more productive to see films as situated within a diversified space of possibilities for the filmic construction of the 'real'. Films then relate to situations and circumstances outside of film in various ways. For example, even completely fictional, narrative films may place their story against 'realistic' portrayals of the societal contexts for those stories, readily including (depictions of) real characters and historical events. Conversely, even presentations of 'factual' material can adopt more or less of the standard machinery of storytelling.

Well-known cases exist between the extreme points on this spectrum. Oliver Stone's *JFK* (1991), for example, explicitly sets out to problematize certain aspects of the treatment of the assassination of President Kennedy, taking issue with the 'official' record (Burgoyne 1996). Some criticise this film for its mixing of documentary and fictional material; others consider it more positively for its critical stance on government and the questions it raises concerning "possibilities and standards of history when it is represented in the visual media" (Rosenstone 1999: 334). Rather different, but still very much playing with notions of history and its relationship with the individual, is Robert Zemeckis's *Forrest Gump* (1994). In this purely fictional narrative, the main character is placed seamlessly within media depictions of a variety of actual historical events, thereby inviting viewers to address the boundary between the individual and history anew (cf. Sobchack 1996). Even straightforwardly fictional films can then include, or be considered from the perspective of, social critique.

Social situations are always being construed in films regardless of those films' intent and this makes them potentially relevant for critical readings. A particularly insightful treatment of the interlinking and mutual conditioning of aesthetics, politics and realism can be found in Kappelhoff (2015).

Thematic configurations

Analyses within film studies have also considered quite explicitly the points in the 'life' of a film where there are opportunities for incorporating 'messages' of a socio-political or other ideological nature. For example, drawing extensively on Gianos (1998) and analogous to discussions in CDA concerning the contexts relevant for analysis, Haas, Christensen and Haas (2015) delineate a range of such points: beginning with the original conception, where particular perspectives or themes might be selected; passing through the often economically driven (and hence ideologically shaped) processes of production, where the generally conservative nature of (increasingly large) investment necessary for film-making can exert a range of forces on what gets shown and how; and moving on to design decisions during the making of the film itself – music, sound and dialogue, editing and montage, composition, lighting, camera angles and special effects. Moreover, issues such as the casting of particular actors, the choice of locations and settings, as well as 'product placements', all constitute opportunities where meanings of various kinds can be included or excluded. There are even issues of distribution to be explicitly considered – as in who gets to see a film in what distribution formats. At each point, it may be possible to identify structural distortions or misrepresentations worthy of critical analysis.

This makes it important also to read thematic configurations and the approaches taken to these in film for their socio-historical and ideological import. Particularly impressive readings of this kind are offered by Ryan and Kellner (1988) and Haas, Christensen and Haas (2015), both of which address chronologically selected clusters of US films in order to map out the social issues being 'worked through' at the times of the considered films' production. Thus, the 1950s produced many films as responses to the Cold War and anti-communism, often, as remarked above, recoded as science fiction. The 1960s then see manifestations of both counterculture (*Bonnie and Clyde, Medium Cool, Easy Rider*) and reassertions of right-wing values of authority (*Dirty Harry, The French Connection*), while the 1970s show several highly conservative constructions (*Rocky, Star Wars, Close Encounters of the Third Kind, Superman*), as well as moving on to a more 'paranoid' construction of power relations depicting government and business as sources of evil, as in liberal conspiracy films (*The Parallax View, All the President's Men*). Since the 2000s and post-9/11, themes of security have understandably become particularly common (*White House Down, London Has Fallen* and many more).

Analyses of these kinds take the form of showing how a collection of films from some period reflect some constellation of social configurations by evaluating the role of individuals, of politics, of organisations and so on in ways differing from previous periods. This often allows broad changes in societal circumstances to be tracked with striking clarity. The links that Kellner, Haas and colleagues draw reveal films to be very sensitive barometers of the socio-political issues of their times. Their analyses also go well beyond critical discussions of individual films, showing how particular configurations of themes and their style of presentation reoccur. In all respects, therefore, this constitutes an important source of information for any further CDA-inflected film analysis.

What makes an analysis of film a CDA analysis?

The rapid growth and acceptance of the study of visual material – sometimes characterised as the 'visual' or 'iconic' turn (cf., e.g., Moxey 2008) – make it difficult for any field – including CDA – to continue marginalising the meaning contributions of the non-verbal. However, since film has already long been an object of critical analysis within film and media studies, the question arises as to whether CDA has anything distinctive of its own to add to this. The discussions by Kellner, Haas and others of quite broad and varied collections of films drawn from different historical periods certainly constitute detailed critical appraisals building on fine-grained descriptions. One might then also ask whether the broad range of critical analyses undertaken in film studies might already be considered a CDA of film.

We can take this issue further by considering more explicitly some of the advances that distinguish CDA from 'informed' commentaries or other kinds of critical discussions. Methodologically, issues of reliability and reproducibility have been addressed by drawing on results from linguistics, cognition, ethnography and other areas described in this handbook that together provide powerful techniques for textual analysis. Patterns revealed in this way go beyond what might be straightforwardly 'read off' of any document or performance analysed. Linguistic examples are well substantiated. This provides tools for textual analysis that construct compelling bridges between instantial texts and those texts' (sociocultural) interpretations. We need then to ask whether a similar development might be possible for film.

Ledin and Machin (this volume) begin setting out how this might look for multimodal analyses in general, and so it may be hoped that similar analytic and methodological refinements might be made for film. But in many respects these descriptive moves remain in their infancy and studies are generally limited to small-scale case studies. As a consequence, many multimodal CDA analyses presented still overlap with the kinds of details offered by critiques found in cultural studies. To talk of a genuine CDA of film, filmic discourse analysis will need to become substantially more robust. Few proposals capable of unravelling in detail the fine-grained interaction of 'filmic text' – seen as the distinctions and patterns drawn in the material artefact – and the take-up and use of those patterns by recipients in processes of guided interpretation are available.

Approaches that consider film as discourse by importing analytic techniques from discourse linguistics are now beginning to emerge, however; examples include van Leeuwen (1991), Iedema (2001), Bateman and Schmidt (2012), Tseng (2013) and Wildfeuer (2014). Analyses of this kind need to be seen as engaging with the artefacts analysed prior to any particular discussion of recipient interpretations since they characterise the patterns and regularities that a film makes available for interpretations as such. A further aim of much of this work is to support the application of corpus methods in order to improve the reliability and representativeness of analyses. As mentioned for verbal texts in the context of CDA by, for example, Subtirelu and Baker (this volume) and Mautner (2015), corpus linguistic methods can provide a useful check on proposed CDA interpretations. Corpus linguistic methods are now also being suggested for multimodal analyses and so it is logical to consider this for the purposes of multimodal CDA, including the analysis of film; Bateman (2014) offers an overview of approaches of this kind.

Until such frameworks are in place, multimodal interpretations of film and work drawing more on the analytic tools of film studies will necessarily overlap in reach. Both may serve as starting points for critical *filmic* discourse analyses. On the one hand, multimodal descriptions may be able to reveal mechanisms of meaning-construction employed in film in more detail, both with respect to potentially more quantitative investigations and in terms of more reliable statements of effects and take-up by viewers. On the other hand, film studies, particularly when connected with the detailed historical, political and social knowledge of the situations of production and reception exhibited in work such as that of Kellner, Haas and others, will continue to provide essential contextual information. Contributions from film studies will therefore remain crucial for any discourse analyses pursued.

An example analysis

In this section, we illustrate how some of the multimodal extensions to discourse analysis just mentioned may provide for an increased connection between film analysis and the concerns and methods of CDA. Verbal aspects will be included but will not play any central role, since these already fall within established CDA methods. The focus will instead be on specifically filmic mechanisms that call equally for critical analysis. The case study will of necessity be very brief, picking out only a selection of relevant phenomena; more extensive examples of how to perform such analyses can be found in, for example, Bateman and Schmidt (2012). Analysis is generally fine-grained and proceeds shot-by-shot (in the technical film sense), pulling out particular properties of the shot that have been found to contribute to filmic discourse organisation. These properties – including repetitions of audiovisual motifs constructing cohesion and spatio-temporal relationships signalled verbally, audially or visually – are placed in an unfolding multilayer filmic discourse structure. This is entirely analogous to the process of verbal text discourse analysis, but draws on a broadened repertoire of 'text'-building devices.

The specific analyses discussed build on such discourse descriptions for two extracts from Ron Howard's *Frost/Nixon* (2008). This offers a convenient illustration of filmic critical analysis because of the existence of two readily accessible media products: first, the original TV interviews conducted between David Frost and former US president Richard Nixon in 1977, post-Watergate and Nixon's resignation from office, and second, Howard's filming of Peter Morgan's play based around those same interviews. Depicting as it does a particularly troublesome series of events in US politics, it is natural that the film has already come under critical scrutiny within film studies (cf., e.g., Denham 2010). The principal question has been the extent to which the film's construction of issues of 'blame' and 'legality' can be seen as trustworthy.

The film opens with what is commonly described as a 'montage sequence' drawing on authentic TV footage from 1972 and beginning with the arrests within the Watergate Hotel. Although it is often suggested that such material lends authenticity, close analysis takes this further. The seven-minute opening sequence has three structural segments. The first segment (2'39", 48 shots) sets up the theme of the film: here the old TV material is intercut visually (but not audially) with fragmentary, often blurred but nevertheless high visual production value shots of Nixon preparing to give his televised resignation speech. The depiction of Nixon preparing for and opening his resignation speech is thereby placed within the authentic historical context of the news stories. The second structural segment (1'10", 11 shots) takes this mixing of worlds further, intercutting Nixon giving his speech with several first-person interviews with people reminiscing about the resignation. These interviews are shot with an 'in-between' visual quality of slightly washed out, side-lit daylight colours and reduced tonal variation and could, at first glance, also have been authentic. The third structural segment (2'48", 29 shots) then introduces Frost, showing him as a TV personality who gets the idea of interviewing Nixon while watching the 'live' TV broadcast of the resignation speech. The mixture between actual events and the film's depictions continues here. A further 'authentically staged' interview with Jack Brennan, the former Nixon Chief of Staff (played by Kevin Bacon) is intercut among the shots showing Frost, where we find usual high film production values *apart* from those images from the TV programme that he is watching. These exhibit the same degraded visual effects seen earlier in the opening sequence for genuine footage but show Frank Langella, the actor playing Nixon.

The fact-fiction line is thus placed in doubt during this opening sequence at multiple levels, and the consequences of such positioning for viewers remain seriously under-researched. Regardless of whether a viewer can 'rationally' work out what is original footage and what is re-enactment, the constant blurring of status between authentic material and narrative depictions may offer a powerful mechanism for weakening critical distance. This possibility needs to be considered in more detail when we address particular points made within the film – i.e., the hypothesis needs to be entertained that any position taken within the film will gain weight due, at least in part, to the weakening of the boundaries between documentary and fiction achieved in the opening.

Our second segment is the portion of the interview where Frost has the opportunity, portrayed as unforeseen in both the film and TV interviews, to ask Nixon directly whether there were more than 'mistakes' and whether he was ready to apologise to the people of the United States. In the original TV interview Nixon provides lengthy responses, is generally calm and collected, and often smiles. While it is usual that such 'text-heavy' material be reconfigured for film, this can be done in many ways, and the particular choices made in Howard's version use filmic techniques that significantly repoint meanings. Several broad differences between the two versions concerning the length and number of shots, and more diverse camera angles and shot scales can naturally be found. There are, however, in addition to this, particular differences that provide very different constructions of the interview. One prominent case that will have to suffice for illustrative purposes here is the use of 'silence', or unfilled pauses.

In the segment of the TV interview under discussion here, there is only one such pause (4s) as Frost gathers his thoughts to ask what many considered the central question of the interviews as a whole, that concerning Nixon's culpability. During this pause we see an over-the-shoulder shot of Nixon followed by a short (2.7s) medium shot of Frost (looking down, hand-on-face, thinking). The film version lingers on this moment, with 7 seconds of silence showing Frost in a closer medium shot while several expressions cross his face prior to him resolutely asking his pointed question in close-up. During this long question, Nixon is intercut, also in close-up, looking ill at ease. The contrast between TV and film versions can be seen well in Figure 41.1, both over-the-shoulder shots taken as Frost is posing his question. Nixon's evident strain, and perhaps even remorse, in the film version is taken considerably further in a second period of silence later in the sequence. Frost asks as a prompt ' . . . and the American people?', to which the response is a full 19 seconds of silence showing a deeply affected, almost distraught looking Nixon in close-up, who then provides statements that are not only considerably nearer to an 'apology' than any statements in the original TV sequence but also far more likely to exert an emotional appeal on viewers.

A close, analytic approach of this kind may, therefore, pinpoint areas and combinations of techniques in need of critical consideration. Nevertheless, as emphasised above with respect

Figure 41.1 Screenshots contrasting two over-the-shoulder views of Richard Nixon taken from corresponding points of the interview (left: original TV interview from *David Frost Interviews Richard Nixon*, directed by Jorn H. Winther, ©David Paradine Productions, 1977; right: Frank Langella from Ron Howard's *Frost/Nixon*, ©Universal Pictures, 2008). In the TV interview, Nixon begins answering the question immediately; in the film version, the character hesitates for 19 seconds.

to the necessary connections to be drawn between any potential CDA of film and established film scholarship, we also need to see such analyses against the background of what is regularly achieved within film studies.

Heller-Nicholas (2011), for example, comes to many similar conclusions using traditional film analysis methods. Where the closer, more analytic approach differs and possibly contributes more, however, is in the targeted reliability of the results: the points of difference between the TV and film versions of the interviews used structural properties of the artefacts themselves to identify where divergent meanings were being constructed. Moreover, the close connection drawn between the filmic mechanisms set out and postulated effect provides the basis necessary for empirical work – concretely, for example, the suggestion that the particular style of linking documentary material with fictional material loosens viewers' critical distinctions can then be subjected to detailed analysis by varying material (either in the original or by finding other film examples that can be cleanly differentiated along this dimension of description) and evaluating experimentally whether differing degrees of belief are exhibited. This kind of exploration cannot be done without first setting out in the kind of detail suggested here just what filmic devices are assumed to be responsible.

Conclusion and discussion: film as CDA?

As a final point, we return to the question briefly raised above concerning whether film itself can serve as CDA. The question is somewhat easier to address with regard to documentary films since these often in any case have the intention of pursuing argument. If the object of analysis of some documentary film was then to reveal systematic misconstruals in some other representations, then that might be considered CDA as much as any textual performance of CDA. In certain respects, however, such cases can be considered akin to 'illustrated' analysis texts. Rather more challenging is the question of whether more intrinsically 'filmic' examples of CDA might be produced – for example, the extent to which film essays, such as Chris Marker's *Sans Soleil* (1962), Godfrey Reggio's *Koyaanisqatsi* (1982) or Jean-Luc Godard's *Adieu au Langage* (2014), might carry arguments of a kind compatible with CDA is an interesting issue. Relations need to be drawn here with ongoing debates on the relation between film and philosophy (Wartenberg 2006): can a film 'do' philosophy, or can it only depict themes or situations that invite subsequent philosophical considerations among spectators so inclined? This overlaps with considerations within argumentation theory, where the issue of whether or not 'visual argument' is even possible has been hotly debated (cf., e.g., Alcolea-Banegas 2009; Groarke 2015). These are relevant concerns for any visual CDA.

Films performing social critique potentially relevant as pieces of CDA would need to draw attention to problematic discourse practices just as is the case with textual CDA. Well attested and popular areas of this kind for narrative film include journalism and the use of corporate or political power to suppress information. Such films, although fictional, nevertheless seek more or less explicitly to raise awareness so that the problematic practices may be challenged. Haas, Christensen and Haas (2015: 176–180) describe as examples of this both Alan J. Pakula's *All the President's Men* (1976), which led to changes in how campaign funds can be managed in the US, and James Bridges's *The China Syndrome* (1979), which similarly raised considerable discussion and awareness concerning nuclear power and safety issues. Films explicitly addressing media practices and the legal process also range from Oliver Stone's *JFK* (1991), mentioned above, to Tom McCarthy's *Spotlight* (2015).

In addition to these films of explicitly political intent, more veiled critiques can be found embedded in many otherwise 'purely' fictional films. Anthony and Joe Russo's *Captain America:*

the Winter Solder (2014) and *Captain America: Civil War* (2016), for example, can both be read as at least problematising the much criticised trade-off between security and surveillance that arose in the wake of the US Patriot Act. Films of this kind are perhaps less likely candidates for being considered as explicitly performed CDA-as-film, although their messages are far from hidden. Nevertheless, to accept them as performing CDA would bring further repercussions for demarcation: if such fictional films are accepted as examples of CDA, then perhaps pieces of literature exhibiting social critique need to be accepted as well? Is political satire then also CDA – particularly perhaps when it considers the use of discourse as a political weapon as in George Orwell's *1984*?

One final difference that this raises between traditional CDA and potential cases of filmic CDA involves media literacy. Again largely due to the long history of socio-political critiques of film we have seen summarised above, there is considerable awareness of the strategies that films can deploy for expressing criticism of social practices. This extends beyond subject matter and plot to include stylistic choices and the technical construction of film. To an extent that may well exceed the current situation in verbal literacy, there is considerable awareness of when films make ideologically slanted choices. It is increasingly difficult, for example, for explicit uses of Mulvey's hypothesised 'male gaze' to pass unnoticed in film, regardless of whether any particular viewer sees this as politically anachronistic or just another strategy of film style. Overly overt cases of 'Freudian' symbolism in films are similarly more likely nowadays to be met with amusement than to exhibit control. An increased literacy of this kind extends across all aspects of film. For example, returning once more to Stone's *JFK*, White (1996) suggests (as a historian) that the film employs novel techniques that deconstruct notions of historical fact with its mixture of documentary and fictional footage. But, as Staiger (1996) argues in opposition to White's claims, these techniques were by no means novel and, moreover, were well known to film audiences. Any deconstruction the film achieves needs then to be anchored with respect to audiences' reception practices as well as in the ways the film is constructed, as also pointed out in our example analysis above.

This actually offers considerable potential for film as a form of CDA. Films may reconstrue and misrepresent and, moreover, show that they are reconstruing and misrepresenting in ways that modern film viewers are well able to read. Thus, whereas many may still need to be convinced that linguistic patterns submerged beneath the surface of verbal texts have potential ideological import, this style of active reading and construal is already very much a part of how we engage with audiovisual media. Films depict, make visual and remake realities and, moreover, often rely crucially on the awareness of the audience that this is being done for their effect. It may then be that, in a certain sense, today's 'average film viewer' is *already* performing practical CDA on what they see to a far greater extent than that generally found in their interactions with verbal texts.

Note

1 Note that only abbreviated film references will be given throughout this chapter; for full production details, readers are referred to the invaluable IMDB website.

Further reading

Bateman, John A. (2014). Looking for what counts in film analysis: A programme of empirical research. In David Machin (ed.), *Visual communication,* 301–330. Berlin: Mouton de Gruyter.
This chapter introduces approaches to the empirical analysis of film and the use of discourse analysis for the audiovisual medium.

John A. Bateman

Benshoff, Harry M. and Griffin, Sean. (2009). *America on film: Representing race, class, gender and sexuality at the movies,* 2nd edn. Chicester, Sussex: Wiley.

This book provides a broad introduction suitable for those beginning with film of the depiction of social issues and of how such depictions can be analysed from a cultural perspective.

Haas, Elizabeth, Christensen, Terry and Peter J. Haas. (2015). *Projecting politics: Political messages in American films,* 2nd edn. New York and London: Routledge.

Kellner, Douglas. (2010). *Cinema wars: Hollywood film and politics in the Bush-Cheney era.* Chicester: Wiley-Blackwell.

These two books together provide a deeper, more politically-oriented discussion of films, drawing together the state of the art and previous literature into a detailed overview of the relationship of film and politics over several decades in the US.

References

Alcolea-Banegas, J. (2009). Visual arguments in film. *Argumentation* 23(2): 259–275.

Altman, R. (1999). *Film/genre.* London: British Film Institute.

Androutsopoulos, J. (2012). Introduction: Language and society in cinematic discourse. *Multilingua* 31: 139–154.

Bateman, J. A. (2014). Using multimodal corpora for empirical research. In Carey Jewitt (ed.), *The Routledge handbook of multimodal analysis,* 2nd edn, 238–252. London: Routledge.

Bateman, J. A. and Schmidt, K-H. (2012). *Multimodal film analysis: How films mean.* Routledge Studies in Multimodality. London: Routledge.

Baudry, J-L. (1974). Ideological effects of the basic cinematographic apparatus. *Film Quarterly* 28(2): 39–47. Translated by Alan Williams.

Benshoff, H. M. and Griffin, S. (2009). *America on film: Representing race, class, gender and sexuality at the movies,* 2nd edn. Chicester, Sussex: Wiley.

Burgoyne, R. (1996). Modernism and the narration of nation in JFK. In Vivian Sobchack (ed.), *The persistence of history: Cinema, television and the modern event,* 113–126. London, New York: Routledge.

Cohen-Shavev, A. and Marcus, E-L. (2007). Golden years and silver screens: Cinematic representations of old age. *Journal of Aging, Humanities, and the Arts* 1(1): 85–96.

Denham, B. E. (2010). Frost/Nixon: Historical accuracy and press/government relations. *Media Ethics* 21(2).

Denzin, N. K. (2004). *Hollywood shot by shot: Alcoholism in American cinema.* Piscataway: Aldine Transaction.

Doane, M. A. (1988). *Caught* and *Rebecca*: The inscription of femininity as absence. In Constance Penley (ed.), *Feminism and film theory,* chap. 12, 196–215. London: Routledge and British Film Institute Publishing.

Eschholz, S., Bufkin, J. and Long, J. (2002). Symbolic reality bites: Women and racial/ethnic minorities in modern film. *Sociological Spectrum* 22(3): 299–334.

Fleming, M. and Manvell, R. (1986). *Images of madness: The portrayal of insanity in the feature film.* Madison, NJ: Fairleigh Dickinson University Press.

Gatling, M., Mills, J. and Lindsay, D. (2014). Representations of middle age in comedy film: A critical discourse analysis. *The Qualitative Report* 19(23): 1–15.

Gianos, P. L. (1998). *Politics and politicians in American film.* Westport, CT: Praeger.

Groarke, L. (2015). Going multimodal: What is a mode of arguing and why does it matter? *Argumentation* 29(2): 133–155.

Haas, E., Christensen, T. and Haas, P. J. (2015). *Projecting politics: Political messages in American films,* 2nd edn. New York and London: Routledge.

Heller-Nicholas, A. (2011). David Frost vs. Goliath: History and entertainment in *Frost/Nixon*. *Screen Education* 62: 129–132.

Helsby, W. (ed.) (2005). *Understanding representation.* London: bfi Publishing.

Holtzman, L., Sharpe, L. and Gardner, J. F. (2014). *Media messages: What film, television, and popular music teach us about race, class, gender, and sexual orientation,* 2nd edn. Armonk, NY: Sharpe.

Iedema, R. (2001). Analysing film and television: A social semiotic account of *hospital: An unhealthy business*. In Theo van Leeuwen and Carey Jewitt (eds.), *Handbook of visual analysis,* chap. 9, 183–206. London: Sage.

Kahana, J. (2015). *The documentary film reader: History, theory, criticism.* Oxford: Oxford University Press.

Kappelhoff, H. (2015). *The politics and poetics of cinematic realism.* New York: Columbia University Press.

Kellner, D. (2010). *Cinema wars: Hollywood film and politics in the Bush-Cheney era.* Chicester: Wiley-Blackwell.

Kuehl, J. (1999). Lies about real people. In Alan Rosenthal (ed.), *Why Docudrama? Fact-Fiction on Film and TV,* 119–124. Carbondale and Edwardsville: Southern Illinois University Press.

Machin, D. and Mayr, A. (2012). *How to do critical discourse analysis: A multimodal introduction.* London: Sage Publications.

Mack, R. L. and Ott, B. L. (2014). *Critical media studies,* 2nd edn. Chicester, Sussex: Wiley-Blackwell.

Mautner, G. (2015). Checks and balances: How corpus linguistics can contribute to CDA. In Ruth Wodak and Michael Meyer (eds.), *Methods of critical discourse analysis,* 3rd edn, 122–143. London: Sage Publishers.

Modleski, T. (1988). *The women who knew too much: Hitchcock and feminist theory.* London: Routledge.

Moxey, K. (2008). Visual studies and the iconic turn. *Journal of Visual Culture* 7: 131–146.

Mulvey, L. (1975). Visual pleasure and narrative cinema. *Screen* 16(3): 6–18.

Mulvey, L. (1989). Afterthoughts on 'visual pleasure and narrative cinema' inspired by King Vidor's *Duel in the Sun* (1946). In L. Mulvey, (ed.) *Visual and other pleasures,* chap. 4, 29–38. London: Macmillan.

Nichols, B. (2001). *Introduction to documentary.* Bloomington, IN: Indiana University Press.

Paietta, A. C. (2007). *Teachers in the movies: A filmography of depictions of grade school, preschool and day care educators, 1890s to the present.* Jefferson, NC: McFarland & Co. Inc.

Richardson, J. E. and Wodak, R. (2009). The impact of visual racism: Visual arguments in political leaflets in Austrian and British far-right parties. *Controversia* 6(2): 45–67.

Rose, G. (2012). *Visual methodologies. An introduction to researching with visual materials* chap. 2. Towards a critical visual methodology, 3rd edn, 19–40. London, Thousand Oaks, CA, New Delhi: Sage.

Rosenstone, R. A. (1999). *JFK:* Historical fact/historical film. In Alan Rosenthal (ed.), *Why Docudrama? Fact-Fiction on Film and TV,* 333–339. Carbondale and Edwardsville, IL: Southern Illinois University Press. Originally published 1993.

Rosenthal, A. (ed.) (1999). *Why Docudrama? Fact-Fiction on Film and TV.* Carbondale and Edwardsville, IL: Southern Illinois University Press.

Ryan, M. and Kellner, D. (1988). *Camera Politica: The poetics and ideology of contemporary Hollywood film.* Bloomington: Indiana University Press.

Sobchack, V. (1996). Introduction: History happens. In Vivian Sobchack (ed.), *The persistence of history: Cinema, television and the modern event,* 1–16. London and New York: Routledge.

Staiger, J. (1996). Cinematic shots: The narration of violence. In Vivian Sobchack (ed.), *The persistence of history: Cinema, television and the modern event,* 39–54. London and New York: Routledge.

Taylor, C. (1996). The re-birth of the aesthetic in cinema. In Daniel Bernardi (ed.), *The birth of Whiteness: Race and the emergence of US cinema,* 15–37. New Brunswick, NJ: Rutgers University Press.

Tseng, C-I. (2013). *Cohesion in film: Tracking film elements.* Basingstoke: Palgrave Macmillan.

Tudor, A. (1974). *Image and influence: Studies of sociology of film.* London: George Allen & Unwin Ltd.

Vanhala, H. (2010). *The depiction of terrorists in blockbuster Hollywood films, 1980–2001: An analytical study.* Jefferson, NC: McFarland & Co. Inc.

van Leeuwen, T. (1991). Conjunctive structure in documentary film and television. *Continuum: Journal of Media and Cultural Studies* 5(1): 76–114.

Wartenberg, T. E. (2006). Beyond *mere* illustration: How films can be philosophy. *The Journal of Aesthetics and Art Criticism* 64(1): 19–32.

White, H. (1996). The modernist event. In Vivian Sobchack (ed.), *The persistence of history: Cinema, television and the modern event,* 17–38. London, New York: Routledge.

Wildfeuer, J. (2014). *Film discourse interpretation: Towards a new paradigm for multimodal film analysis.* Routledge Studies in Multimodality. London, New York: Routledge.

Wodak, R. and Meyer, M. (2015). Critical discourse analysis: History, agenda, theory and methodology. In Ruth Wodak and Michael Meyer (eds.), *Methods of critical discourse studies,* 3rd edn, 1–33. London: Sage Publishers.

Index

Note: Italicized page numbers indicate a figure on the corresponding page. Page numbers in bold indicate a table on the corresponding page.

abstract genre of deliberation 244
abstraction strategies 127
abstract knowledge structures 79
action schemas 86
activity types 17
additions in social practices 602
Adobe Flash 569
Adorno, Theodor W. 262–3
advertising copywriters 334–8, *335–6*
affective-discursive practices 521
affirmative character of discourse 140–1
affordances 63–4, 72–3
African Americans: racial theories in textbooks 529; rights of 312–13, 320–1; stereotypical depictions 470; white privilege and 471–2, 475
African American Vernacular English (AAVE) 394
agency and educational discourse 469–70
agribusiness discourse 499–500
Aguirre, Esperanza 353–4
All Indian Congress Committee (AICC) 237
Alone Together (Turkle) 568
alternative practice as model 144–5
ambivalence discourse 500, 529
American Educational Research Association 465
American Enterprise Institute 100, 102
America's New War 435
Analysing Newspapers (Richardson) 513–14
analytical activism 24, 374
analytics of power 265–6, 282
androcentricism in organisational structures 376–7
Androutsopoulos, Jannis 585
anecdote case study 306–8
Anglo-American law of evidence 483
Anglo-Saxon Pragmatics tradition 204
antagonistic practices 274
anti-Marxism 449
anti-Semitic prejudice 45, 415
apparatus theory in film discourse 614–15

applied linguistics (AL): advertising copywriters 334–8, *335–6*; discourse analysis in 570; introduction to 328–9; limits of CDS 331–4; principles of CDS 329–31; summary of 338
Applied Linguistics journal 331–3
appraisal analysis 136, 162
approval process in textbook production 531
argumentation theory: contemporary argumentation theories 232–4; deliberative discourse 242, 244, *245*, 245–6, **246**; elements of 24; political argumentation 18–19, 236, 243; practical argumentation 16, 19; Pragmatic Argument 235–6, 238–9; *see also* rhetoric and argumentation
arguments *(topoi)* 415
Aristotle (Aristotelian rhetoric) 228–31, 243
ArticleFirst (OCLC) database 467
aspect blindness 291
asserted continuities/discontinuities 54
Atlee, Clement 422
attack *vs.* self-defence 441–2
attribution of derogating qualities 515
Austin's Felicity Conditions of Grice's Maxims 196
Austrian Freedom Party (FPO) 452
authenticity of filmic representations 617
Authoritarian Personality (Adorno) 263
authoritarian rule of law 486–7
Authoritarian Rule of Law (Rajah) 487
author meetings in textbook production 531
axiological proximization 102–3, 104n9

banal nationalism 408
Bardo Museum shootings 144
Bartlett, T. 139–40
BBC survey on class 347
Beckerman, Ruth 303
behaviourism 291
behaviour patterns 350

beneficial discourses 500
bin Laden, Osama 436, 440, 485
Blair, Tony 153, 158–9
blending concept 139
Blunkett, David 160
body politics 410–13, *411*, *413*
Boehner, John 111–12
bondicons, defined 304
border politics 410–13
Bourdieu, Pierre 48, 265, 348–9
branding discourse: defined 541–3; introduction
    540–1; John Lewis partnership case study
    546–9, **548**; metaphor analysis 221–5, *223*;
    products, politics and places 543–4; semiotics
    of 544–6; summary of 550
break out concept 82–3
Bringing them Home (Martin) 136
British Class Survey (GBCS) 347
British National Party (BNP) 447, 453–6
Brown Corpus 106
Bush, George W. 100, 102, 130, 439–44
By God Mother, I Hate the War (Lev) 126

call-response patterns in music 558
Cameron, David 26–7, 35, 38, 40
capitalism/capitalist economies: contemporary
    capitalism 540; dislocatory effects of 276;
    free market path 423; imperialism and 497;
    introduction to 15; neoliberalism *vs.* 423;
    political economy and 449
Chilean history textbooks 304
China Daily 158
Chinese criminal trials 483
Churchill, Winston 237
circumstance analysis 19, 155, 157
citizenship competence 410
civil rights movement 312–13
class/class warfare: behaviour patterns 350; CDA
    research and 350–2; class model 347–9, **348**;
    economic resources 349; introduction to
    345–6; life conditions 350; public declarations
    by politicians 352–5; sociocultural resources
    349–50; spatial conditions 350; summary of
    355–6
classical rhetoric 228–31, 235
class model 347–9, **348**
clause/sentence level 199
Clinton, Bill 94, 96
CNN corpus 112–17, **114**
cognition: ecology discourse 501–2; mental
    models of 30–1, 34, 36; metaphor analysis
    215–18; personal cognition 30–1; processes
    in 29; social cognition 31–3; *see also* spatial
    cognition
cognitive commitment 79
cognitive interface: fundamental role of
    knowledge 34–5; introduction to 28–9; mind

and memory processing 29–33;
    personal cognition 30–1; social cognition
    31–3
cognitive linguistics (CogLing) 169
cognitive metaphor theory (CMT): cognition
    and 215–18; context and discourse 218–21;
    critical research and 215; in multi-modal texts
    221–5, *223*
cognitive psychology of discourse 30
coherence relations 33
collaborative bridging of legal discourse 490–1
collateral language 435
collective identities 404–5
collective narratives 302–3
collocation 156–7, 169
colonisation of discourse 264
Common Ground 28, 32, 34
common-sense beliefs *see* hegemonic discourses
communication: channels of European Union
    188; direct communicative intention 30;
    performative communications 542; public
    declarations by politicians 352–5; semiotic
    resources in 601–2; Sender-Message-Receive
    model 337
complexification 138
composition studies field 569
Computer Mediated Communication (CMC)
    584–5
Computer Mediated Discourse Analysis
    (CMDA) 585
Conceptual Blending Theory 78
conceptual 'contiguity' in geopolitical frame 96
Conceptual Metaphor Theory 78
conflict transformation strategies 278–80
Confucian ideology 376
conservative governments 27, 40–1
constellation of interrelated dimensions model
    349–50
constitutive view of discourse 374
construal, in language usages 79
constructive discursive strategies 409
contemporary argumentation theories 232–4
contemporary capitalism 540
content evaluation 157
contested pasts 302–4
context discourse 31, 53–4
contextural diversity 113
contradictory discourse 532
Control System 30
conversation analysis (CA) 168, 436, 584
Cooke, Derycke 554, 556
corporate branding 43
Corpus-Assisted Discourse Studies (CADS):
    collective/individual narratives 302–3; fiscal
    cliff negotiations *110*, 110–18, *112*, **113–14**,
    115, **116**, *117*; introduction 106–7; useful
    synergy 107–9

corpus linguistics (CorpLing) 169–70, 174, 236, 260, 318
Corpus of Contemporary American English (COCA) 109, 115–16, *116*
Corpus of Historical American English 109
cosmopolitanism 407
Cospedal, Maria Dolores de 353
counter-discourses 135
counter-hegemonic discourses 301
counternarratives 142
covert racism 361–2
critical analysis 155
Critical Applied Linguistics 141
Critical Cultural Discourse Studies perspective 359
critical discourse analysis (CDA): class/class warfare 347–9, **348**, 350–2; corpus techniques 107–9; discourse approach 500; Discourse-Ethnographic Approach 181–91; Discourse-Historical Approach and 49–50; educational discourse 467; emergence of 286–8; film discourse 618–19; inquiry orientation **468**, 468–70; introduction to 1–2, 5; keywords discourse **113**, 113–14, **114**; media studies 285–6; neoliberalism and globalization 424–6; objections to SFL in 152–4; Positive Discourse Analysis 133–4; radical view of 345–6; reality TV 601–3; school-based 470–5, **473**–4; semiotic software 570; SFL relevance to 152; social theory 259–60; spatial cognition 92–3, 96; of textbooks 525–6; Whorfian-style effect 78; *see also* feminist critical discourse analysis; film discourse; historiographical discourse; media studies; multi-modal critical discourse analysis; political discourse; pragmatics discourse; race/ethnicity discourse
critical discourse studies (CDS): approach to 14–16; context concept 53–4; definitions and characterizations 165–6; dialectical reasoning 13, 16–19; early models of context 166–8; educative function of politics 22–4; fascism discourse 447, 451; historical approaches 170; international law discourses 485; introduction to 1–7, 13–14, 165; journalism discourse 512–15; Kilburn Manifesto 19–24; legal discourse 480–1, 490–1; legitimacy discourse 484–5; media studies 285–6; overview of 7–9; pragmatics **167**, 167–8, 235–6; recent models of context 168–70; semiotic software 567–70; social theory 259–60, 268; summary of 24–5, 175; of textbooks 526–30; *see also* applied linguistics; Social Media Critical Discourse Studies
Critical Discourse Studies journal 152
critical ethnographic approach 356
Critical Linguistic CDS (CL-CDS): aims and commitments 77–9; formative models *93*,

93–7, *95*; introduction to 77; methodological frameworks 79–82, **81**; spatial cognition 92–3
Critical Linguistics (CL): Critical Applied Linguistics 141; defined 27–8; introduction to 1; journalism discourse 510; language and ideology 510–12; in public discourse 314; social theory 260
Critical Metaphor Analysis (CMA) 437
Critical Narrative Analysis (CNA) 120–1, 124
critical questioning process 244
critical race theory 476
critical realism 261–2, 287
critical reflexivity 374
critical research tools 235–6
critical social analysis 13
Critical Theory of the Frankfurt School 262
critique concept 50–1
Cultural Approach to Critical Discourse Analysis (CCDA): abstraction strategies 127; as branch of CDA 121–3; Critical Narrative Analysis 120–1, 124; estrangement strategies 126–8; general principles 123–4; hyper-causality strategies 129; impersonalization strategies 128; introduction to 120–1; summary of 129–30; war and peace in Israel 125–9
cultural codes 123–4
Cultural Discourse Studies (CDS) 122–3
cultural marginalization 367
cultural script approach 122
curiosity gap 139
curriculum in textbook production 531
Cypriot web radio community 272, 277–81
Cyprus Community Media Centre (CCMC) 278

Davies, Mark 109
decision-making and deliberative discourse *249*, 249–50
deconstruction 134
deconstructive-reconstructive orientation 466–7
definition/re-definition discourses 515
deictic expressions 33
deixis conception *93*, 97
deletions in social practices 602
Delhi rape case study 378–84
deliberation-decision-action-change 22
deliberative discourse: argumentation theory 242, 244; challenging debate terms 250–2; decision-making, framing and rhetoric *249*, 249–50; dialectical and rhetorical perspective 243–4; evaluation of *245*, 245–6, **246**; introduction to 242–3; summary of 253; tuition fees 246–9
democratic theory 273
Democratic Unionist Party 316
denaturalizing globalization processes 423
Derrida, Jacques 266
design anthropologists 333

destructive strategies 409
dialectical deliberation 16, 18, 243–4
dialectical reasoning 13, 16–19
dialogue types 244
diasporic voices 140
digital discursive environments 584
digital technologies 566
direct communicative intention 30
Discourse, Politics, Identity (DPI) 46
Discourse-Centred Online Ethnography
    (DCOE) 585
discourse concept: analysis in applied linguistics
    570; defined 2–3; discursive contradictions
    514; discursive hegemony 4; discursive practice
    journalism discourse 513; genre/style 31; in
    Kilburn Manifesto 20–1; overview of 51–3,
    52; production/comprehension processes 29;
    research on 546; world analysis 80–2, **81**
Discourse-Ethnographic Approach (DEA):
    critical discourse analysis 181–91; European
    Union institutions case study 184–91, *186–8*,
    189; fieldwork and contextualisation *186*,
    186–9, *187–8*; introduction to 179–83;
    overview of 169; as research process 183–4;
    summary of 191
Discourse-Historical Approach (DHA) 6;
    construction of national identities 408; context
    concept 53–4; corpus analyses of discourse
    108; critique concept 50–1; discourse concept
    51–3, **52**; Discourse-Ethnographic Approach
    from 181–2; general characteristics 48–54,
    52; history of 44–7; introduction to 44;
    journalism discourse and 514; positioning of
    49; Pragmatic Argument 236; research practice
    54–5; social theory 260; summary of 55
discourse-immanent critique 50–1, 362–3
discourse level 199, 202–4
Discourse Mythological Analysis (DMA) 514
discourse of difference 409
Discourse & Society journal 331–3
discourse-theoretical analysis (DTA): conflict
    transformation strategies 278–80; discourse
    theory and materiality 274–7; discourse
    theory overview 272–4; introduction to
    272; materiality of radio broadcasting 280–1;
    MYCYradio case study 272, 277–81; summary
    of 281–2
discourse theory (DT) 265–7, 272–7
discursive contradictions 514
discursive hegemony 4
discursive practice journalism discourse 513
Discursive Psychology 28
disputed territories 157
doctor-patient interaction 46
Du Bois, W.E.B. 469
dynamic adaptation of context model 31
dynamism in images 67

Eban, Abba 126–7
ecolinguistics 137–8, 499, 506
The Ecolinguistics Reader (Fill, Muhlhausler) 137
ecological disciplines 497
ecological thinkers 498–9
ecology discourse: cognition and 501–2;
    integrated framework 502–3; introduction
    497–8; overview of 499–501; stories about
    498–9; summary of 507
economic discourses 21
economic rationality 531–6, *533*, **534–5**
economic representations 349, 426–30
editorial discourse 35–9
Educating Rita film 136
educational discourse: critical discourse
    analysis 467; deconstructive approach 470;
    deconstructive-reconstructive orientation
    466–7; discussion on 476–7; inquiry
    orientation **468**, 468–70; introduction 465–6;
    of politics 22–4; Positive Discourse Analysis
    141–4; reconstructive approach 469–5, **473–4**;
    structure and agency 469–70
Eemeren, Frans H. van 233–4
Eisenstein, Charles 498–9
elite racism 360–1
embodied experience 218
emergent discourses of hybrid identity 141
Emotional Intelligence (Goleman) 427
emotion words 33
empathy discourse 428–9
encyclopaedic thesis 78–9
energy in images 67
engrenage, defined 184
entrepreneurial university idea 159
environmental discourse 157, 528
environments of discourse 166
episodic (autobiographical) memory (EM) 30
Epistemic Community 34
epistemic strategy of discourse 34–5
epistemological relations 14
ERIC (EBSCO) database 467
estrangement strategies 126–8
ethical decision-making 484
ethnicity discourse *see* race/ethnicity discourse
ethnographic approaches to discourse *see*
    Discourse-Ethnographic Approach (DEA)
ethnographic sociolinguistics 48
éthos proof 229
euphemization strategy 125
European Qualifications Framework (EQF)
    535–6
European transnational identity 406
European Union institutions case study:
    discourse-historical analysis **189**, 189–91;
    fieldwork and contextualisation 186–9,
    186–8; pre-contextualisation and 185–6;
    theorisation and 184–5

European Union (EU) racism case study 362–8
evaluations of social practices 602
everyday racism 361
evidentials in language 33
evil discourse 440
existential presupposition and framing 202
experientialist thesis 78
explanatory critique of discourse 14, 16
extremism 54, 437, 447
extrinsic values 501

Facebook 568, 582, 588–90, *590*
Fairclough, Norman 286–8
fairness values 247
false ideas 3
false tables and writing 72–4, **73**
Farage, Nigel 27
fascist discourse: conclusion 456–7; defined
    447–50; introduction 447; overview of 450–2;
    speech by Griffin, Nick 453–6
feeling-passion of common sense 22–3
feminist critical discourse analysis (FCDA):
    androcentricism in organisational structures
    376–7; gendered dichotomisation 375–6;
    introduction 372–3; perpetrator mitigation
    381–3; postfeminist gender ideologies 377–8;
    principles of 373–5; sexual violence discourse
    378–83; studies in 46, 375–8; summary of
    383–5; victim blaming 378–81; violence
    against women 377
feminist film theory 615–16
field, defined 154
fieldwork and contextualisation 186–9,
    186–8
figures of speech 236
film discourse: apparatus theory 614–15;
    authenticity of filmic representations 617;
    critical discourse analysis 618–19; critical film
    analysis 614–18; example analysis 619–22, *621*;
    feminist film theory 615–16; genre studies
    616–17; introduction to 612–14; summary of
    622–3; thematic configurations 617–18
fiscal cliff negotiations: background of 111; case
    study of 110, *110*; corpus-based approaches
    114–17, *115*, **116**, *117*; corpus collection and
    representativeness 111–12, *112*; discussions on
    117–18; extracting keywords **113**, 113–14, **114**
floating signifiers 273–4
Folk Song Style and Culture (Lomax) 554
Force-Dynamics 78
Foucault, Michel 265–6, 282, 314, 373, 555
Fox News corpus 112–17, **113**, *115*
framing: defined 81; deliberative discourse and
    249, 249–50; existential presupposition and
    202; partial reframing 139; radical reframing
    139; reframing strategy 139
"free market" identity 294

free motion 85
Fuller, Matthew 569
Functional Pragmatics 49
fundamental categories of groups 32
fundamental role of knowledge 34–5

Gandhi, Mohandas Karamchand 236–9
gendered dichotomisation 375–6
gender ideology 519–21
gender relations 374–5
generic fascism 447–8
generic knowledge 32, 34
genre studies in film discourse 616–17
The German Ideology (Marx) 262
German public discourse 219
German Wehrmacht 46
Gestalt theories of perception psychology 517
Glasgow Media School 289
Glasgow University media group 287
globalization: critical discourse analysis 424–6;
    defined 424; denaturalizing processes 423;
    hegemonic discourses 424–6
global linguistic patterns 315–16
global topics/themes 33
Goal premises 19
Goleman, Daniel 427–9
Gore, Al 503
grammatical metaphor 155, 161–2
Gramsci, Antonio 4
Gramscian political approach 20, 24
GraphColl tool 109
Great Depression 429
Green economic discourse 21
Griffin, Nick 453–7
Griffin, Roger 450–1
Grootendorst, Rob 233–4
Guy Fawkes masks 82, 85

Habermas, Jürgen 50, 263–5, 406
habitus 348–9
Hall, Stuart 20, 287
Halliday, Michael 61, 63
Hayek, Friedrich A. 422
hegemonic discourses: economic representations
    426–30; globalization 424–6; introduction to
    4, 421–2; legal discourse 486–90; neoliberalism
    422–6; overview of 274–5; social theory and
    267; summary of 430–1
Hegemony and Socialist Strategy (Laclau,
    Mouffe) 272
Heller, Monica 330
Herring, Susan 585
heteronormative practices 390
Higgins, Michael D. 292–5
higher level processing 30
historical comparison of language 37
historical knowledge 34

historical materialism 261
historiographical discourse: contested pasts
302–4; contributions to 304–8; introduction
298–9; memory and 299–302; summary of
308–9; Uruguayan dictatorship 305–8
Holocaust memory 300
homophonic music 557–8
homosexuality discourse 169
Hong Kong *Occupy* event 170–5
horizontal motion 85
humanitarian discourses 291
Hussein, Saddam 100–1, 436
hybrid identity discourses 141
hyper-causality strategies 129
hypodermic approach to ideology 138

idealism 272, 277
ideal-speech situation (ISS) 263
ideational component 155
identification, defined 81
identity discourse 4
identity politics 414
ideological alignment 38
ideological consistencies 514
ideological discourse: CDS-informed studies
264–5; introduction to 3–4; journalism
discourse and 292; neoliberalism and media
studies 292–5; political discourse and 318–19
ideological groups 32
ideological polarisation 33, 39
ideological square 3, 505
ideological state apparatuses (ISAs) 261
ideology evaluation 157
idiosyncratic local uptakes 141
image schema analysis 80
immigration discourse 26–7, 362–8, 405–6
impeded motion 85
imperialism 424, 497
impersonalization strategies 128
indeterminacy in language 156
indexical expressions 33
India's Daughter film 378
individual narratives 302–3, 404
inequitable distribution of power 4–5
in-groups 3, 452
inquiry orientation **468**, 468–70
inside-deictic-center (IDC) 98–9, 101
Institute for Fiscal Studies 248
Institute for Social Research in Hamburg 46
institutionalisation of neoliberalism 293
institutionalised racism 471–5, **473–4**
Institutio oratoria (Quintilian) 231
integrated framework of ecology discourse
502–3
Interactional Analysis 62
interdiscursivity 15, 166
intergenerational transmission 305–6

international development discourses 140
international law discourses 485
International Systemic Functional Linguistics
Congress 133
intersubjective consensus 319
intertextuality: defined 166; historiography
304–5; introduction to 6, 15; political
discourse 316
intrinsic values 501
intuitive design in semiotic software 571
Islamic discourse 144, 406
Israel, war and peace cultural studies 125–9
Iwokrama International Rainforest Conservation
and Development Programme 139

Jobbik campaign *411*, 411–12, *414*, 414–15
John Lewis partnership case study 546–9, **548**
journalism discourse: crack metaphor 518–19;
critical discourse studies 512–15; gender
ideology 519–21; introduction 510;
language and ideology 510–12; *Mail
Online* case study 518–19; online news
516–18; summary of 521–2; transnational
developments in 515–16
Journal of Multicultural Discourses 122
judges and legal discourse 481–4
justification strategies 125, 409, 443

keywords discourse 107–8, **113**, 113–14, **114**
Kilburn Manifesto (KM) 19–24
King, Martin Luther 313, 320
Klein, Naomi 498
knowledge discourse: abstract knowledge
structures 79; fundamental role 34–5; generic
knowledge 32, 34; historical knowledge 34;
language and 31; textbook studies discourse
528–9; theoretical knowledge 54; world
knowledge 31–2
Kokoda campaign in literature 303–4
Koselleck, Reinhart 48
Kulturnation 410

laissez-faire capitalism 449
Language and Control (Fowler) 511
language discourse: collateral language 435;
competence 410; components of film 612–13;
construal, in language usages 79; evidentials in
language 33; historical comparison of language
37; ideology and 510–12; indeterminacy in
language 156; knowledge discourse 31; lists
and bullet points 69–72, *70–1*; metaphorical
expression/meaning 33, 37–8; new capitalism
288; plain language jury instructions 483
The Language of Displayed Art (O'Toole) 61–2
Language of Music (Cooke) 554
Leading Asian City University 222–5, *223*
Lee Kuan Yew 490

legal discourse: capacious conception of 480–1; categories of law 485–6; collaborative bridging 490–1; countering hegemony 486–90; international law discourses 485; introduction 480; judges and trials 481–4; Legal Profession Act 487–8; legislation and 481; legitimacy discourse 484–5; reshaping of 488–9; in 21st century 489–90
Legal Profession Act (1986) 487–8
legitimacy discourse 100–3, 484–5, 602
Legitimation Code Theory (Maton) 137
Leone, Massimo 553
"Let's talk about sex" (song) 391–8
Lev, Yigal 126
lexical level 199
lexicogrammar model: axiological proximization 103; collocation and 156–7; historical discourse and 302; political discourse 318; spatial proximization framework and 100; systematic account of 96, 151, 153; tools for text analysis 154–9
lexis and collocation 156–7
life conditions 350
lifelong learning 107
linguistic analysis 15
linguistic bias 136, 153
literature review in political discourse 314–15
literature review of terrorism and violence 435–8
lived continuities/discontinuities 54
local discourse practices 140
logical inversion 138
lógos proof 229
Lomax, Alan 554, 557
longitudinal case study 139–40
long term memory (LTM) 29

Macgilchrist, Felicitas 138–9
madonna stereotype 379
Mail Online case study 518–19
major scales in music 559–60
Makushi Amerindian population case study 139–40
Male Sexual Drive discourse 200–4, 211–13
Manovich, Lev 569
Mapping Applied Linguistics: A Guide for Students and Practitioners (Hall) 331
marginalisations in textbook studies 527
marketization discourse: introduction to 16–17; musical discourse 562–4; public discourse 574–8, **575**, *575–7*; semiotic software 566
market-oriented buzzwords 74
Martin, Jim 136–7
Marxism: critical method 23; fascism and 449, 451–2; influences of 261–5, 287; speech by Griffin, Nick 453–6
materialism 261, 272, 275
materiality of radio broadcasting 280–1

May, Chris 563
McClary, Susan 554–6
meaningful discourse 30
meaning-making culture 346
meanings of words 33
measured time in music 559
mechanical process of conflict 127–8
media studies: articulating CDA in 288–90; emergence of CDA 286–8; future of 290–2; ideology and neoliberalism 292–5; introduction 35, 285–6
mediatisation 316
Meir, Golda 126
Membership Categorisation Analysis (MCA) 436
memory and critical discourse analysis 299–302
memory structures/organizations 32
mental models of cognition 30–1, 34, 36
Mental Process 162
Mental Spaces Theory 78
metaphor/metaphorical discourse: abstract knowledge structures 79; approaches to political discourse 315–19, *317*; in images 67; in language 33, 37–8; metaphor analysis 80; Million Mask March 82–7, *83–7*; summary of 87–8; *see also* cognitive metaphor theory
Metaphors We Live By (Lakoff, Johnson) 216
methodological frameworks 79–82, **81**
Methods of Critical Discourse Studies (Wodak, Meyers) 2
metronomic time in music 559
micropolitical strategies 141
Million Mask March 82–7, *83–7*
mind and memory processing 29–33
minority groups 135, 140, 312, 529
minor scales in music 559–60
MLA International Bibliography database 467
mode, defined 154
models of experience 31
moral evaluations in reality TV 608
Mosley, Oswald 451
mother tongue concept 411
multilingualism 48, 262, 409–11
multi-modal critical discourse analysis (MCDA): cognitive metaphor theory 221–5, *223*; criticisms of 62–4; introduction to 60–1; Kokoda campaign in literature 303–4; language, lists and bullet points 69–72, *70–1*; *Mail Online* case study 518–19; online news 516–18; origins of 61–2; photographs and layouts 65–7, *66*; photographs and writing 67–70, *69*; reality TV discourse 598; re-contextualisation of social practice 64; re-contextualisation of work practice 65; semiotic software 570–3; Social Media Critical Discourse Studies 587, 590–3, *591*; summary of 74–5, 225; writing and false tables 72–4, **73**
multi-modal discourse analysis (MMDA) 170

multisemiotic storytelling 517–18
musical discourse: introduction 553–4; major and minor scales 559–60; marketization in 562–4; musical time 558–9; overview of 554–6; perspective in 561–2; social interaction and 556–8; voice quality attributes 560–1
musical time 558–9
Muslim discourse 406
mutually reflexive relationship 166
MYCYradio case study 272, 277–81
mythopoesis in reality TV 608
myths of origins and ancestry 413–16

National Crime Prevention 384
national identities 408–10
National Institute of Music 553
nationalism, defined 404–7
nationalism discourses: body and border politics 410–13, *411*, *413*; construction of national identities 408–10; defining terms of 403–7; introduction to 403; re/writing past/s 413–16, *414*, *416*; strong-to-extreme nationalism 449
National Rifle Association (NRA) 377–8
National Socialism 45, 263, 450
nation-states, defined 404–7
Native American Sayings 503–6
Native Hawaiians 529–30
Nattiez, Jean-Jacques 554
naturalisation discourse 125, 410
Nazi Germany 45, 354–5, 450
neocolonialism 482
Neo-Gricean pragmatics 196
neoliberalism: critical discourse analysis 424–6; critical race theory and 476; defined 422–4; development of 422–4; economic policies 352; introduction to 21–2; media studies 292–5; textbook studies discourse 530–6
Neo-Marxist influences 261–5
Network Society notion 588
new capitalism 288
New Deal 429
New Labour 532, 543–4
New Reflections on the Revolution of Our Time (Laclau) 276
new rhetoric 232
New York Times 158, 421–2, 427
Nexus of Practice of European Union *187*
Nicomachean Ethics (Aristotle) 17
nominalisations 70–3, 125–6, 302
non-idealist constructivism 276
non-linguistic work 332
non-metronomic time in music 559
non-normative sexualities 388, 391–8
non-violent civil disobedience 171
normative critique of discourse 14, 16, 50, 389–91

North Rupununi District Development Board (NRDDB) 139–40
North Rupununi population case study 139–40
notion of power 373

Obama, Barack: case study of speech 313, 316, 319–23, *321*, **322**, 485; fiscal cliff negotiations 111–12
O'Brien, Dan 292–5
obstacles on path to motion 85
occupied territories 157
Oedipal trajectory of films 615
On Populist Reason (Laclau) 276
ontological dialectics 22
ontological existence 82
operationalised discourse 16
opinion words 33
order of discourse 15
orders of power 384
organisational culture 184–5
out-groups 3, 452
outside-deictic-center (ODC) 98–9, 101, 104n9
outsourcing in textbook production 531
overt racism 361–2

PAH *(Plataforma de Afectados por la Hipoteca)* 352–5
paradoxical persuasions of discourse 513–14
parasitism *411*, 412
parliamentary debate 244
parody 138
partial reframing 139
participant analysis 155, 157
partnership discourse 546–9, **548**
party politics in textbook production 531
passive agent deletion 515
path image schema 217, 222
páthos proof 229
patriarchal viewpoint 377
Peirce, Charles Sanders 48
People's Action Party (PAP) 487
perceptions and theory 261
performance management 67–8
performative communications 542
perpetrator mitigation 381–3
perpetuation strategies 409
Persian nationalism on Facebook 588–90, *590*
personal cognition 30–1
personification strategies 128
perspective in musical discourse 561–2
Pew Research Center 112
photographic theorists 63–4
photographs and layouts 65–7, *66*
photographs and writing 67–70, *69*
plain language jury instructions 483
polarisation between groups 32
political argumentation 18–19, 236, 243

political commemoration 46
political discourse: analysis of interaction 319; argumentation in 18–19, 236, 243; body politics 410–13, *411*, *413*; border politics 410–13; branding discourse 543–4; capitalism/capitalist economies 449; case study of Obama speech 319–23, *321*, **322**; class/class warfare 352–5; communication 352–5; conceptual 'contiguity' in geopolitical frame 96; critique of 50; educational discourse 22–4; educative function of 22–4; Gramscian political approach 20, 24; identity politics 414; ideological beliefs 318–19; intertextuality 316; introduction to 17, 312–14; lexicogrammar model 318; literature review 314–15; metaphor/metaphorical discourse 315–19, *317*; methodological approaches 315–19, *317*; micropolitical strategies 141; protests 82–7; Proximization Theory and 316; revolutionary political discourse 21; science journals 242; socio-political discourse 40–1, 434; speech case study 159–62; state political discourse 97; summary of 323; in textbook production 531; text-related features 315–16, *317*
political elite 452
popular philosophy 22
populism 36, 54
positive appraisal terms 36
Positive Discourse Analysis (PDA): appraisal by Martin, Jim 136–7; case study by Bartlett 139–40; ecolinguistics 137–8; educational discourse 466; in education and social activism 141–4; introduction 5, 133–4; investigative strategies of Macgilchrist 138–9; Native American Sayings 504; origins and orientations 134–5; summary of 144–5
Possessive Process 162
postfeminist gender ideologies 377–8
post-Marxist discourse 273, 346
post-structural influences 265–7
power behind/in discourse 14–15
PowerPoint software 67, 567–9, **575**, *575–6*
power relations 3–5
practical argumentation 16, 19
practical dialectics 22
practice-based research 46
Pragma-Dialectics theory 233–4
Pragmatic Argument 235–6, 238–9
pragmatics discourse: background 195–7; case study on 200–4; combination of 197–9; discourse level 199, 202–4; existential presupposition and framing 202; headline translation 200–1; introduction of 34, 195; Male Sexual Drive discourse 200–4, 211–13; overview of **167**, 167–8; sentence-level presupposition 201–2; socio-cognitive approach 199–200; summary of 204–5

pre-contextualisation 184–6
presuppositions and opinion 36, 38–9
pre-textuality concept 303
problematisation 17–18, 21
problem-definition 184–6
process analysis 155, 157
progressivity values 247
promotional brochure example 65–7, *66*
promotion and metaphor analysis 221–5, *223*
prospective critique 51
Proximization Theory: case study of 100–3; importance of 316; political discourse and 316; spatial cognition 93, 97–103, **99**; summary of 103–4
psychoanalytic model in film discourse 615
psycholinguistics 30
psychological theories of mental representations 28
PsycINFO database 467
Public Consultative Discourse Analysis (PCDA) 133, 142–3
public declarations by politicians 352–5
punk lyrics discourse 143–4

Qing dynasty 172
quasi-private discursive contexts 408
Queer Linguistics 388
Quit India speech 236–9

race/ethnicity discourse: elite racism 360–1; European Union case study 362–8; everyday racism 361; institutionalized racism 471–5, **473–4**; integration and/as control 364–8; introduction 359; overt *vs.* covert racism 361–2; race *vs.* ethnicity 359–60; summary of 368–9; violence and 143
racialization process 362
radical historization 362
radical materialism 275
radical reframing 139
radical view of CDA 345–6
Ramus, Petrus 232
Rand, Ayn 430
rascal concept 423
reactions in social practices 602
Reading Images (Kress, Van Leewen) 61–2
reality TV: approaches to 599–601; critical discourse analysis 601–3; as cultural technology 599–600; emergence of 598–9; introduction to 597–8; ridiculing strategies 602–8, *604*, *607*; social class and 600–1; summary of 608–10, *609*; talk and music interplay 603–6, *604*; zooming in/out on details 606–8, *607*
rearrangements in social practices 602
reasonableness concept 234
recontextualisation: discourse-historical analysis 53; historiography 304; introduction to 6;

market discourse 16; relexicalisation process 381; social practice 64, 602; work practice 65
reframing strategy 139
regressive practice critique 144
reification process 82
Reisigl, Martin 236
Relevance Theory 196
relevant categories of discourse 31
relexicalisation process 381
remembering discourse 30
representation analysis 318–19
research practice 54–5
restructuring ethos 424
retributive justice 441–2
revisionist narratives 416
revolutionary political discourse 21
rhetoric and argumentation: classical rhetoric 228–31, 235; contemporary argumentation theories 232–4; critical discourse and history 303; critical research tools 235–6; deliberative discourse 242–4, 249, 249–50; figures of speech and 236; introduction 228; new rhetoric 232; Pragmatic Argument 235–6, 238–9; *Quit India* speech 236–9; research paradigms 228–34; summary of 239
ridiculing strategies in reality TV 602–8, 604, 607
right-on texts 143
The Road to Serfdom (Hayek) 422
Russian constructivism 555

Sacks, Harvey 436
Salt-N-Pepa (hip-hop group) 391–8
scalar perspectives 301
schematisation strategy 31, 84
school-based critical discourse analysis 470–5, **473–4**
Chief Seattle 503–4
self-depreciation discourse 529
self-identity discourse 589
self-interpretations in critical social analysis 293
self-pride discourse 529
semantics in discourse 27, 31, 304
semiosis process 346
semiotic resources in communication 601–2
semiotics discourse: branding 540–1, 544–6; contemporary life 329; discourse-historical approach 51; introduction to 2–3; multi-modal critical discourse 63–4; pluralism 542
semiotic software: in broader semiotic landscape 573–4; critical studies of 567–70; design of 571–2; introduction 566–7; marketization of public discourse 574–8, **575**, 575–7; multimodal study of 570–4; software use 572–3; summary of 578, 578–9
semi-public discursive contexts 408

Sender-Message-Receive model of communication 337
sentence-level presupposition 201–2
sentences and Common Ground 32
sexuality in critical discourse studies: introduction to 388; macro-level analysis 394–5; micro-level analysis 395–8; non-normative sexualities 388, 391–8; normative-based approach 389–90; overview of 388–9; sexual normativity patterns 390–1; summary of 398–9
sexual normativity patterns 390–1
sexual violence discourse 378–83
shamefaced idealism 275
Shepard, John 554
short term memory (STM) 29
Singapore, legal discourse 486–90
Single European Act (SEA) 363
Sinocentric discourse 529
social activism 31–2, 141–4
social capital 348
social cognition 31–3
social constructivism 28
Social Media Critical Discourse Studies (SM-CDS): critique of 583–4; demarcations in 586–8; introduction 582–3; multi-modal rendering of 587, 590–3, *591*; summary of 593
social memory 31–2
social mobility values 247–8
Social Networking Sites (SNSs) 582
social pluralism 557
social practices 3–4, 64, 514
social reality 2, 13–17, 23, 272, 278, 329, 425, 435
social theory: beginnings of 260–1; introduction 259–60; Marxist and Neo-Marxist influences 261–5; post-structural influences 265–7; summary of 267–8
social unison 557
Socio-Cognitive Discourse Studies (SCDS): cognitive interface 28–35; editorial discourse 35–9; Hong Kong *Occupy* event 174–5; introduction to 6, 26–8; journalism discourse 512–13; media discourse 35; pragmatics and critical discourse studies 199–200; sociopolitical analysis 40–1; summary of 39–40, 88n2; *Telegraph* editorial, cognitive basis 35–40
sociocultural discourse 31, 318, 349–50
socio-diagnostic critique 51
socioeconomic discourse 20, 529
sociolinguistics 261, 332
socio-political discourse 40–1, 434
Software Takes Command (Manovich) 569
Sophistical Refutations (Aristotle) 230
Soviet Union totalitarian regime 219, 422–3
spatial cognition: critical discourse analysis 92–3, 96; formative models *93*, 93–7, *95*;

introduction to 92–3; Proximization Theory 93, 97–103, **99**; role of 79
spatial conditions 350
spatial proximization framework 100
Spatial-Temporal-Axiological (STA) 98
speaking mnemonic **167**
Speech Act Theory 33, 198
standard schematic structure 30
state-body metaphor 219
state political discourse 97
statistical correlations model of integration 368
Steinbruck, Peer 532
strong-to-extreme nationalism 449
structural configuration 81
structure and educational discourse 469–70
subjective opinion 319
substitutions in social practices 602
Sunday Bloody Sunday performance 136
symbolic capital 348
symbolic thesis 78
systematic collection of data 54
systematic discourse analysis 27
Systemic Functional Linguistics (SFL): aims and applications 151–2; context of 154; discourse-historical approach 48; group and clause 158–9; journalism discourse 510–11; lexicogrammar model 96, 151, 153; lexicogrammar tools for text analysis 154–9; lexis and collocation 156–7; multi-modality 61; multisemiotic storytelling 517–18; objections to, in CDA 152–4; overview of 168–9; political speech case study 159–62; positive discourse analysis 136, 141, 143; relevance to CDA 152; summary of 162–3; textbook studies discourse 528; textual function 541; transitivity in 157–8
Systemic Functional Linguistics Association of Tunisia (SYFLAT) 144

Tagg, Philip 554
Taiwan-centric discourse 529
taken-for-granteds 20–1
Telegraph editorial, cognitive basis 35–40
temporal adverb usage 36
tenor, defined 154
terrorism and violence discourse: discursive construction of 439–40; future directions 444; introduction 434–5; justification for war 442–4; literature review 435–8; multi-perspective approach 438–9; pretext for war 441–2
textbook studies discourse: construction of 527–8; critical discourse studies 526–30; economic rationality 531–6, *533*, **534**–5; fragility of 529–30; introduction 525–6; neoliberal/critical student-subjects 530–6;

overview of 526; production practices 531; summary of 536; theories of knowledge 528–9
textural analysis discourse: function of 541; immanent critique of 50–1; in journalism discourse 513; political discourse 315–16, *317*
Text World Theory 78
thematic configurations in film discourse 617–18
theoretical knowledge 54
Third Country Nationals (TCNs) 364
This Changes Everything: Capitalism vs. the Climate (Klein) 498
three-dimensional model of metaphor 220
three-layered model in journalism discourse 514
time-relatedness perspective 54
top-down discourse 14, 333
tópos/locus instrument 230
totalitarian regimes 422–3, 490
Toulmin, Stephen 232–3
trademark bullying 543
transdisciplinary analysis 14, 345
transformation strategies 409
transitivity in Systemic Functional Linguistics 157–8
transnationalism 405
trials and legal discourse 481–4
trickle-down economics 15
tuition fees discourse 246–9
Turkle, Sherry 568
two-way learning process 22

Ullared (Swedish reality show) 351–2
Umbrella Movement *see* Hong Kong *Occupy* event
understanding discourse 32
Union Movement (UM) 451
universal design in semiotic software 571
unmeasured time in music 559
untested concepts 63
Uruguayan dictatorship 305–8
useful synergy 107–9

Vichy declaration (2009) 365–7
victim blaming 378–81
Viennese Critical Discourse Analysis 44–5
Vietnam, gender identities 375–6
violence against women 377
violence discourse *see* terrorism and violence discourse
vision for research *(forskning)* 68, *69–70*
voice quality attributes 560–1
Voting Rights Act (1965) 313

Waldheim, Kurt 45
Walton, Douglas 233, 235
War on Terror 436–7, 484–5
weapons of mass destruction (WMD) 100–2, 442

Weber, Max 557–8
Web of Science database 467
White, Hayden 48
white privilege 471–2, 475
whore stereotype 379
Whorfian-style effect 78
Why Europe Needs a Constitution (Habermas)
    406
Wierzbicka, Anna 122
Williams, Raymond 425–6, 540
Wodak, Ruth 121, 236
Women's Social and Political Union
    (WSPU) 172
word-for-word headline translation 200–1
word meanings 33
working memory (WM) 29

Working with Emotional Intelligence (Goleman) 427
workplace discourse 328, 332
work practice, re-contextualisation 65
world knowledge 31–2
Wright, Jeremiah 319
writing and false tables 72–4, **73**
writing and photographs 67–70, *69*

xenophilic discourse 529

yin/yang perspective 138
Youth Justice Conferencing 137

Zaragoza declaration (2010) 367
Zimbabwean men, gender identities 375
Zone of Proximal Development (ZPD) 141